Mrs. H. Green

The University of Chicago School Mathematics Project

Advanced Algebra

Texas Teacher's Edition

Authors

Sharon L. Senk
Assistant Professor of Mathematics Education
Syracuse University
Syracuse, New York

Denisse R. Thompson
Assistant Professor
Department of Mathematics
Manatee Community College
Bradenton, Florida

Steven S. Viktora
Chairman, Mathematics Department
Kenwood Academy
Chicago Public Schools
Chicago, Illinois

Contributing Authors

Rheta Rubenstein
Mathematics Department Head
Renaissance High School
Detroit, Michigan

Judy Halvorson
Mathematics Teacher
John F. Kennedy High School
Bloomington, Minnesota

About the Cover
A stroboscopic photograph shows the regularity in the movement of
a rotating gyroscope. While the pivot remains stationary, the axis itself revolves,
outlining a cone.

Scott, Foresman and Company
Editorial Offices: Glenview, Illinois Regional Offices: Sunnyvale, California •
Tucker, Georgia • Glenview, Illinois • Oakland, New Jersey • Dallas, Texas

Acknowledgments

UCSMP Editorial Staff
Series Directors: Zalman Usiskin, Sharon L. Senk
Managing Editor: Natalie Jakucyn
Editors: James Flanders, Jerry Pillsbury
Technical Coordinator: Susan Chang

Editorial Development and Design
Scott, Foresman staff, Colophon Publishing Services, Kristin Nelson Design, Shawn Biner Design

We wish to acknowledge the generous support of the **Amoco Foundation** and the **Carnegie Corporation of New York** in helping to make it possible for these materials to be developed and tested.

Director of Evaluations: Sandra Mathison,
                               State University of New York, Albany

Assistant to the Director: Catherine Sarther
                               The University of Chicago

A list of schools that participated in the research and development of this text may be found on page *iii*.

ISBN: 0-673-45277-8

CONTENTS   Teacher's Edition

UCSMP Goals Meet Texas Needs.

As reports from national commissions have shown, students currently are not learning enough mathematics, and the curriculum has not kept pace with changes in mathematics and its applications.

In response to these problems, UCSMP has developed a complete program for grades 7–12 that upgrades the school mathematics experience for the *average* student. The usual four-year high-school mathematics content—*and much more*—is spread out over six years. The result is that **students learn *more* mathematics** and **students are better prepared for the *variety* of mathematics** they will encounter in their future mathematics courses and in life.

In addition, UCSMP helps students view their study of mathematics as worthwhile, as full of interesting information, as related to almost every endeavor. With applications as a hallmark of all UCSMP materials, students no longer ask, "How does this topic apply to the world I know?"

For a more complete description of the series, see pages T19–T50 at the back of the Teacher's Edition.

In short, UCSMP. . .

- Prepares students to use mathematics effectively in today's world.

- Promotes independent thinking and learning.

- Helps all students improve their performance.

- Provides the practical support you need.

Years of field-testing and perfecting have brought impressive results!

Imagine using a text that has been developed as part of a coherent 7–12 curriculum design, one that has been tested on a large scale *before* publication, and most important, has bolstered students' mathematical abilities, which is reflected in test scores. Read on to find out how UCSMP has done that, and more.

For a detailed discussion of the development and testing of Advanced Algebra, *see pages T46–T48.*

UNIQUE DEVELOPMENT

This book was developed at the University of Chicago with funds provided by the Amoco Foundation and the Carnegie Corporation of New York.

PLANNING

Initial planning was done with input from professors, classroom teachers, school administrators, and district and state supervisors of mathematics, along with the recommendations by national commissions and international studies. In particular, the **UCSMP secondary curriculum is the first full mathematics curriculum to implement the recommendations of the NCTM Standards committees.**

AUTHORSHIP

Authors were chosen for expertise in the relevant areas of school mathematics and for classroom experience. *Algebra* and *Advanced Algebra* writing teams were selected from a nationwide competition.

FIELD-TESTING AND EVALUATION

Pilot testing began with teaching and revising based on **firsthand experience** by the initial team of authors. Then, evaluation was made from **local studies,** and the materials were revised again. Further evaluation and revisions were based on **national studies.** And finally, the **Scott, Foresman input** includes enhancements, such as color photography and nearly 600 blackline masters, to better meet the needs of teachers and students.

Offers a Variety of Content and Applications

Advanced Algebra is designed to attract and keep students in mathematics—not to weed them out. It emphasizes facility with quadratic forms, powers, and roots, and the functions based on these concepts. Students study logarithmic, polynomial, and other special functions as tools for modeling real-world situations.

Consistent organization leads to mastery.

*The following features are **built into every lesson**, providing a consistent path for learning:*

Lesson Introduction

gets students reading mathematics on a daily basis. Provided are key concepts, relevant vocabulary, and meaningful examples for students to read and discuss. Topics are placed in real-world settings so students know why they are studying them.

LESSON 9-2

Exponential Decay

1988 Trans Am Firebird

In Lesson 9-1, the populations studied were increasing, so the constant growth factor is greater than one. Sometimes a growth factor is less than one. When this is true, the value of the function decreases over time. These situations are sometimes called **exponential decay** or **depreciation**.

Example 1 A Trans Am Firebird cost $6490 new in 1978. Suppose its value decreased exponentially and that the car depreciated 44% during its first 7 years.
a. What equation models its value?
b. Find the car's value in 1988.

Solution **a.** Because the car is depreciating in value by a constant factor, the situation can be modeled by an exponential function with equation $y = ab^x$. Here y is the value of the car; a is the original value, 6490; $b = 0.56$ (depreciating by 44% means the growth factor is $1 - .44 = 0.56$); and x is the number of 7-year intervals after 1978. Thus an equation modeling the value is

$$y = 6490(0.56)^x.$$

b. The year 1988 is 10 years after 1978. This is $\frac{10}{7}$ of a 7-year interval.

$$x = \frac{10}{7}.$$
$$y = 6490(0.56)^x$$
$$y = 6490(0.56)^{10/7}$$
$$y \approx 2835.$$

In 1988 the Trans Am was worth approximately $2835.

T6

Four Kinds of Questions

provide a variety of contexts, requiring students to really think about each problem.

Questions

Covering the Reading

In 1–3, match the line with a description of its slope.
1. horizontal line   (a) 0 slope
2. vertical line   (b) non-zero slope
3. oblique line   (c) slope undefined

4. The line whose equation is of the form $y = mx + b$ is oblique when m _?_ 0.

5. How many intercepts does an oblique line have?

Applying the Mathematics

In 13–15, (a) tell whether each line is vertical, horizontal, or oblique; (b) give all intercepts for each line; (c) graph each equation.
13. $y = 4$ 14. $2x - 3y = 18$ 15. $2x = 16$

16. Meg combines N oz of a solution that is 10% alcohol with Y oz of a solution that is 20% alcohol. She ends up with a mixture that contains 1.2 oz of alcohol.
    a. Write an equation relating N, Y, and the amount of alcohol in the mixture.
    b. Graph the equation you obtained in part (a) by finding the N- and Y- intercepts. Consider N the independent variable.
    c. Use your graph to find out how many ounces of the 20% solution must be added to 8 oz of the 10% solution to get the final mixture.

Review

18. A 3-line classified advertisement in a local paper costs $10.20 for five weekdays and $12.35 for a weekend edition. What is the cost of x ads during the week and y ads on the weekend? *(Lesson 3-3)*

19. You have some money saved from your job. You invest S of it in a savings account that pays 8% interest and the rest R in a checking account that pays 6%. You earn $84 interest in one year. *(Lesson 3-3)*
    a. Write an equation relating S, R, and the total amount of interest.
    b. Give three possible pairs of values for R and S.

20. The city police department pays police officers $1500 per month and pays their supervisors $2400 per month. The total payroll for the month is $60,000. *(Lesson 3-3)*
    a. Write an equation relating the number of police officers P, the

Exploration

23. Suppose you can get as many 22¢ stamps and 3¢ stamps as you want. You could make 24¢ using eight 3¢ stamps, but you cannot make 23¢ postage exactly. What is the largest value that *cannot* be made with these stamps?

24. a. Find the x- and y-intercepts of $\frac{x}{2} + \frac{y}{7} = 1$.
    b. Find the x- and y-intercepts of $\frac{x}{-5} + \frac{y}{6} = 1$.
    c. Based on parts a and b above, make a conjecture about the x- and y-intercepts of $\frac{x}{a} + \frac{y}{b} = 1$. Either prove your conjecture or give a counterexample to it.

1 COVERING THE READING

offers a variety of types of questions that allow students to try out what they've learned in the lesson introduction.

2 APPLYING THE MATHEMATICS

offers real-world and other applications of the lesson concepts.

3 REVIEW

keyed to past lessons, helps students maintain and improve performance on important skills and concepts, and previews ideas to prepare students for topics that will be studied later.

4 EXPLORATION

extends the lesson content, offering an interesting variety of applications, generalizations, and extensions, including open-ended experiments, research, and much more.

Prepares Students to Use Mathematics Effectively in Today's World

■ Real-world Applications

Lesson Integrating the History of Mathematics

Students study each mathematical idea in depth through applications and practical problems, providing opportunities to develop skills and to understand the importance of mathematics in everyday life.

In 19 and 20, refer to the population of Manhattan given on the opening page of the chapter. *(Lesson 2-4)*

19. Find the rate of change in population per year for the period 1890 to 1910.

20. What was the average yearly change in population between 1950 and 1970

Exploration

21. What did the keeper say to the parrot who needed to go on a diet?

22. Use the Manhattan Island population function given on page 605.
  a. Graph P using a function plotter.
  b. Use the graph to estimate the population in 1900, 1920, 1940, and 1960.
  c. Find the actual population of Manhattan Island in 1900, 1920, 1940, and 1960.
  d. How close are the estimates in part b to the actual values?
  e. According to the function P, when did Manhattan's population peak?
  f. How good is $P(x)$ in approximating the population of Manhattan for other dates?

LESSON

6-7

Analyzing Solutions to a Quadratic

Even as early as 1700 B.C., ancient mathematicians considered geometry problems that today we would solve using quadratic equations. However, the ancients did not have our modern notation. Euclid, who lived around 300 B.C., would have phrased the problem $x^2 - 5x = 20$ geometrically:

"If a certain straight line be diminished by five, the rectangle of the whole and the diminished segment equals twenty."

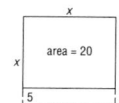

Five hundred years after Euclid, in about 250 A.D., the Greek mathematician Diophantus was the first to use symbols. Diophantus had no single symbol for an unknown: x is ζ and x^2 is $\Lambda\gamma$. He would have written the equation $x^2 - 5x = 20$ as follows:

■ Wider Scope

Advanced Algebra presents the history of major ideas and recent developments in mathematics and applications. In addition, it includes a substantial amount of geometry, which is used to develop and apply the algebraic concepts and to ensure skills maintenance.

Lesson on Fractals—a recent development in mathematics

LESSON

14-8

Fractals

Below is a curve called the Mandelbrot set, named after Benoit Mandelbrot, a French-born American mathematician who works for IBM. It was brought to the attention of the world in the 1970s, and is created using ideas related to powers of complex numbers beyond the scope of this book.

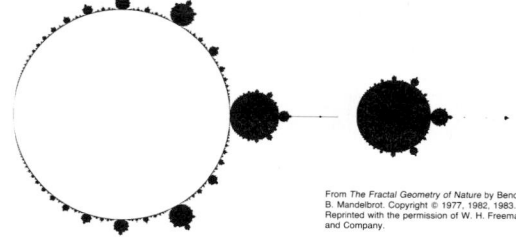

From *The Fractal Geometry of Nature* by Benoit B. Mandelbrot. Copyright © 1977, 1982, 1983. Reprinted with the permission of W. H. Freeman and Company.

The Mandelbrot set is an example of a *fractal.* Fractal objects are *self-similar,* that is, they do not change their appearance significantly when viewed under a microscope of arbitrary magnifying power. The word fractal is derived from the Latin word *fractus,* which means fragmented, broken, or irregular. Fractals often have very irregular, infinitely long boundaries.

Fractals may be abstract mathematical objects such as the Mandelbrot set or the pyramid shown below; or they may occur naturally as in the bark of a tree or the irregular coastline of Great Britain shown on the first page of the chapter.

Solution 1 Use the following key sequence:

$$2 \; \boxed{\sqrt[x]{y}} \; 3 \; \boxed{=}$$

Our calculator displays 1.2599211, which is about 1.26. The Delians had to make an altar with an edge about 1.26 times as long as the edge of the original altar.

Solution 2 Key in $2 \; \boxed{INV} \; \boxed{y^x} \; 3 \; \boxed{=}$. You should get 1.259911, the same answer as in Solution 1.

Check Key in $1.2599211 \; \boxed{y^x} \; 3 \; \boxed{=}$ to see whether $(1.2599211)^3 \approx 2$. It is.

The Delians did not have calculators, of course. They also did not have decimals, which were invented only in 1585. They could work with fractions, but no simple fraction cubed equals 2; that is, $\sqrt[3]{2}$ is irrational. The Delians did not have the mathematical tools to follow the oracle's advice.

Since $\sqrt[n]{x} = x^{1/n}$, the nth powers of these numbers are equal; that is, $(\sqrt[n]{x})^m = (x^{1/n})^m$, $x^{m/n}$. Also, if x is replaced by x^m in the definition, the result is $\sqrt[n]{x^m} = (x^m)^{1/n}$, which also equals $x^{m/n}$. Thus there are two radical expressions equal to $x^{m/n}$.

Root of a Power Theorem:

When $x > 0$, m and n are integers and $n \geq 2$, $\sqrt[n]{x^m} = (\sqrt[n]{x})^m = x^{mn}$.

Example 3 Simplify $\sqrt[3]{x^{12}}$.

Solution 1 Use the definition of $\sqrt[3]{\;}$: $\sqrt[3]{x^{12}} = (x^{12})^{1/3} = x^4$.

Solution 2 Use the Root of a Power Theorem: $\sqrt[3]{x^{12}} = x^{12/3} = x^4$.

■ Technology

Students learn how to use calculators and computers—tools they'll need in the real world. The evidence shows that the appropriate use of technology enhances student mathematical understanding and improves problem-solving skills.

c. $(2, 4)$ and $(3, 9)$
d. $(3, 9)$ and $(4, 16)$
e. Use your results from parts a to d to make a conjecture about the rate of change between the points (n, n^2) and $(n + 1, (n + 1)^2)$.
f. Prove your conjecture by calculating the rate of change for the points in part e.

11. You do not need a computer for this question. Here is a computer program in BASIC that takes a value of k and prints a list of solutions to $y = kx^2$.

```
10 PRINT "WHAT IS K?"
20 INPUT K
30 PRINT "SOLUTIONS TO Y = K * X ^ 2"
40 PRINT "X", "Y"
50 FOR X = -5 TO 5
60    LET Y = K * X ^ 2
70    PRINT X,Y
80 NEXT X
90 END
```

a. How many ordered pairs of solutions will be printed?
b. What is the first pair to be printed?
c. What is the last pair to be printed?
d. Describe the output that would result from changing line 50 to
    ■ FOR X = -5 TO 5 STEP .5.

Review

12. The Fahrenheit and Celsius scales indicate temperature. Temperature can also be measured in kelvins. This measurement is sometimes called measuring on the Kelvin scale, in degrees Kelvin. At a given altitude, the volume V of a fixed amount of air varies directly with its Kelvin temperature t. The lowest possible temperature occurs when t is zero, about -273° C. Suppose that a balloon contains 7.5 liters of air at 300 kelvins (about room temperature). *(Lesson 2-1)*
a. Write a specific variation formula for V in terms of t.
b. Use this formula to predict the volume of air in the balloon at temperatures of 400, 500, 600, and 1000 kelvins.

13. Architects designing auditoriums use the fact that sound intensity I is inversely proportional to the square of the distance d from the sound source. *(Lessons 2-2, 2-3)*
a. Write the variation equation that represents this situation.
b. A person moves to a seat 4 times farther from the source

LESSON

2-6

Using an Automatic Grapher

Graphs of equations are so helpful to have that there exist calculators and programs for personal computers that will automatically display graphs. Because computer screens are larger than calculator screens they can more clearly show more of a graph; but graphing calculators are less expensive, more portable and sometimes are easier to use.

Graphing calculators and computer graphing-programs work in much the same way; so we call them **automatic graphers** and do not distinguish between them. Of course, no grapher is completely automatic. Each has particular keys to press that you must learn from a manual. Here we discuss what you need to know in order to use any automatic grapher. Consult your calculator owner's manual or your **function grapher's** documentation for specific information about your grapher.

The part of the coordinate grid that is shown is called a **window**. The screen at the right displays a window in which

$$-2 \leq x \leq 12$$
$$\text{and} \quad -3 \leq y \leq 7.$$

On calculators, the intervals for x and y may be left unmarked. Usually you need to pick the x-values at either end of the window. Some graphers automatically adjust and choose y-values so that your graph will fit, but often you also need to choose the y-values. If you do not do this, the grapher will usually make use of a **default window**, that is, a window that is used whenever you do not specify the intervals on which to plot x and y.

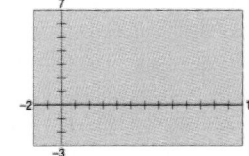

On almost all graphers, the equation to be graphed must be a formula for y in terms of x.

$$y = 3x^2 \text{ and } y = \tfrac{5}{9}(x - 32) \quad \text{can be handled.}$$
$$x = 4y \text{ and } x + y = 17 \quad \text{cannot be handled.}$$

On many graphers you enter equations by using the keys * / and ^

Develops Independent Thinking and Learning!

■ Reading

Great for Students:
Well-written explanations and examples enable students to successfully **apply** what they've read and also serve as a great reference tool, encouraging students to look for answers on their own. The reading also helps to **motivate** students by connecting mathematics to their world, which makes it more interesting to them.

Great for Teachers:
Because students can read and understand the text, you have the freedom to teach in a variety of ways. Instead of merely explaining every day what the text says, you can concentrate on developing further examples and explanations tailored to your students' needs.

■ Problem Solving

Every lesson contains a variety of problem-solving questions applying the mathematics. Students learn about the selection of problem-solving strategies to encourage efficient methods. In addition, requiring students to read helps develop thinkers who are more critical and aware.

T10

LESSON 2-8
Fitting a Model to Data I

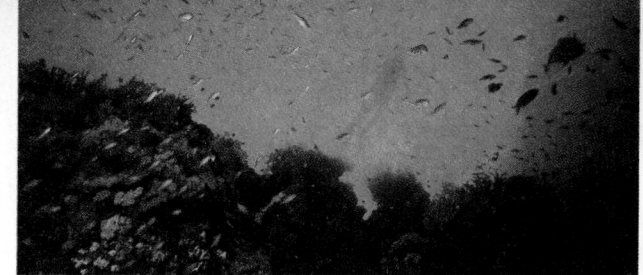

You may know that the water pressure on a deep sea diver increases as the diver goes deeper. How is the pressure related to the depth?

The following table gives the water pressure (in pounds per square inch, or psi) exerted on a diver at various depths (in ft).

Depth of diver (ft)	10	25	40	55	75
Pressure of diver (psi)	4.3	10.8	17.2	23.7	32.3

This information is graphed below. Because the pressure on the diver depends on the diver's depth, pressure is the dependent variable and is placed on the vertical axis. Depth is the independent variable and is graphed on the horizontal axis. The points seem to lie on a line through the origin. It makes sense that the origin is on this line because on the surface—that is, 0 feet under water—there is 0 pounds per square inch of water pressure. Therefore, it seems appropriate to describe the relation between the variables by saying the pressure varies directly as the depth.

Multiplying both numerator and denominator by $(n - r)!$, the theorem results.

Here are several applications.

Example 1 Five points are labeled in a plane, with no three collinear. How many triangles have these points as vertices?

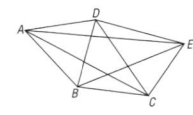

Solution 1 Draw a picture. Label the points A, B, C, D, and E. Form triangles with the points as vertices.
The possible triangles are (in alphabetical order) ABC, ABD, ABE, ACD, ACE, ADE, BCD, BCE, BDE, and CDE. So 10 triangles can be formed.

777

LESSON 1-6
Reasoning in Algebra

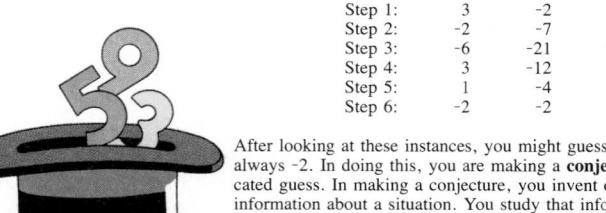

Consider this number trick.

Step 1: Pick a number.
Step 2: Subtract 5.
Step 3: Multiply the result by 3.
Step 4: Add 9 to the result.
Step 5: Divide the result by 3.
Step 6: Subtract the original number.

If you follow these steps with four arbitrary numbers, such as 3, -2, 1.4, and 10, the computations can be summarized as below.

Step 1:	3	-2	1.4	10
Step 2:	-2	-7	-3.6	5
Step 3:	-6	-21	-10.8	15
Step 4:	3	-12	-1.8	24
Step 5:	1	-4	-0.6	8
Step 6:	-2	-2	-2	-2

After looking at these instances, you might guess that the result is always -2. In doing this, you are making a **conjecture**, or an educated guess. In making a conjecture, you invent or are given some information about a situation. You study that information. Then you state something *not* given that you believe is true whenever the given is true. For instance, in this number trick it is not given that the final result is always -2. However, you have some evidence that the final result will always be -2.

After a conjecture is made, it is natural to ask whether it is always true. To do this, it is first necessary to do the trick in general. So we begin with a variable.

Chapter Review

The main objectives for the chapter are organized into sections corresponding to the four main types of understanding this book promotes: *Skills, Properties, Uses,* and *Representations.* Thus, the Chapter Review extends the multi-dimensional approach to understanding, offering a broader perspective that helps students put everything in place.

❝I feel that it is very important for students to read math, not to be intimidated by what appears to be a difficult problem, to feel comfortable with the symbolism in math, and know that they can read math.❞

Rita Belluomini, teacher, Rich South High School, Richton Park, IL

Skills include simple and complicated procedures for getting answers. The emphasis is on *how* to carry out algorithms.

Properties cover the mathematical justifications for procedures and other theory. To fully understand ideas, students must answer the common question, "But *why* does it work that way?"

Uses include real-world applications of the mathematics. To effectively apply what they learn, students must know *when* different models or techniques are relevant.

Representations provide concrete ways to conceptualize what it is that is being studied. Visual images, such as graphs and diagrams, are included here.

All these views have validity, and together they contribute to the deep understanding of mathematics that students need to have, in order to be independent thinkers and learners.

SKILLS deal with the procedures used to get answers.

Objective A: *Find the value of a function. (Lessons 7-1, 7-4, 7-5)*

1. If $f(x) = 2x - 3$, what is f(4)? 5
2. Suppose t: $n \to 5 - 4n^2$. Then t(-2) = __?__. -11
3. Let h: $a \to a^5$. Find h(-3). -243
4. If $g(x) = 4x^2$, find g(x + 2). $4x^2 + 16x + 16$
5. If $h(x) = 8x - 20$, find h(x + 5) - h(x). 40
6. If M: $x \to 3x^2 + 4x$, then M(2k) = __?__. $12k^2 + 8k$
7. [-2.5] = __?__ -3
8. Find f(x) for $-2 \le x < -1$, if f(x) = [x]. -2
9. |-5 - 9| = __?__ 14

Objective C: *Read simple BASIC programs with special functions. (Lessons 7-4, 7-5)*

In 17–20, use this program where N > 0.

```
10 INPUT N
20 PRINT 1000 * INT((N + 500)/1000)
30 END
```

17. **a.** What will line 20 print if you run the program and input 25,962? 26,000
    b. If $N = 1.2 \cdot 10^3$, what will line 20 print when the program is run? 1000
18. Describe what this program does when run. It rounds a number to the nearest thousand.

PROPERTIES deal with the principles behind the mathematics.

Objective E: *Determine whether a given relation is a function. (Lessons 7-1, 7-2, 7-4, 7-5)*

25. Is the relation described by the table below a function? If not, why not?

x	-1	-1	-4	0	-16
y	1	-1	2	0	-4

No, because -1 is mapped to both 1 and -1.

In 26–31, tell whether the set or rule describes a function.

26. {(1, 2), (2, 3), (3, 4), (4, 1)} function
27. $x = y^2$ not a function

In 34–39, give the domain and range of the function described. See margin.

34. $\{(2, -2), (3, -3), (-9, 9), (-\frac{1}{2}, \frac{1}{2})\}$
35. $y = x^4$
36. $f(x) = \sqrt{x}$
37. $f(x) = [x]$
38. $y = x^2 + 1$
39. $y + 5 = 3(x - 4)^2$

Objective G: *Determine relationships between a function and its inverse. (Lessons 7-6, 7-7)*

USES deal with applications of mathematics in real situations.

Objective H: *Find values of functions involving real data. (Lessons 7-1, 7-4, 7-5)*

In 45–47, let P(x) and B(x) be the populations of Philadelphia and Baltimore in year x.

	1900	1950	1980
Philadelphia	1,290,000	2,070,000	1,690,000
Baltimore	509,000	950,000	787,000

45. What does B(1950) represent? the population of Baltimore in 1950
46. **a.** Calculate P(1980) − B(1980). 903,000
    b. What does part a represent? See below.
    P(1950) − P(1900)

48. The famous scientist Galileo found a relationship between the distance d(t) a dropped object falls (in feet) in the time t (in seconds). $d(t) = 32t^2$. (Of course, he used different units.) What was the approximate distance fallen when $t = 1.5$? 72 feet

49. *Multiple choice* You earn $5 per hour. The time you work is rounded down to the nearest hour. What is a rule for the function that relates time t in hours to wages w in dollars? c
    (a) $w = 5t$ (b) $w = 5|t|$
    (c) $w = 5[t]$ (d) $w = 5(t - \frac{1}{4})$

REPRESENTATIONS deal with pictures, graphs, or objects that illustrate concepts.

Objective I: *Graph a function, given its rule. (Lessons 7-2, 7-4, 7-5)*

51. Graph f, where $f(x) = x^2 + 6x + 9$. See margin.
52. Graph g, if g: $x \to \frac{10}{x}$. See margin.
53. Graph $y = [x] + 4$. See margin.
54. If $h(x) = |x - 1|$, graph h. See margin.
55. Let $y = -2x^3$. Graph this function. See margin.
56. Refer to Question 50 above. Graph the relation between time t in minutes and cost c in dollars for the domain $0 \le t \le 10$. See margin.

In 63 and 64, use the graphs below.

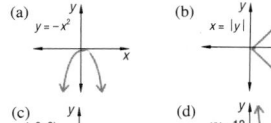
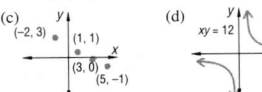

63. *Multiple choice* Which of the above is not a

T11

Helps Students Improve Their Performance

Strategies for increasing skill are combined in a unique fashion—and there is evidence that the result is a remarkable improvement in student achievement.

DAILY REVIEW reinforces skills learned in the chapter and combines and maintains skills from earlier chapters.

At least one **QUIZ** per chapter (in the Teacher's Resource File) offers further help to assess mastery.

The **SUMMARY** gives an overview of the entire chapter and helps students consider the material as a whole.

The **VOCABULARY** section provides a checklist of terms, symbols, and properties students must know. Students can refer to the lesson or to the Glossary for additional help.

Review

In 27 and 28, consider a closed rectangular box with dimensions h, $h + 2$, and $h + 5$. Write a polynomial in standard form for

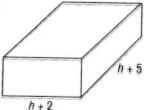

27. $S(h)$, the surface area of the box;

28. $V(h)$, the volume of the box. *(Lesson 11-2)*

29. A graphic designer works with sheets of paper 11 in. by 17 in. Suppose the designer lays out a rectangular design in the center of the sheet with a border of x in. on each side. *(Lesson 11-2)*
    a. Find the area of the design in the center if $x = 3$.
    b. Write an expression for $A(x)$, the area of the design in the center.

30. a. Let $f(x) = x^3 - x^2 - 12x$. Construct a table using integer values of x on the domain $-5 \leq x \leq 5$.
    b. Plot the eleven points in part a. Estimate what the graph of $y = f(x)$ looks like by drawing a smooth curve through the points.
    c. Check your work in part a by using a function grapher. *(Lesson 11-1)*

31. A function $P(x)$ is graphed at the right. *(Lessons 6-3, 6-4, 6-8)*
    a. Which word best describes the function: constant, linear, quadratic, or exponential? Explain how you know.
    b. For what value(s) of x does $P(x) = 0$?

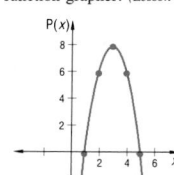

CHAPTER 7

Summary

A function is a correspondence that maps elements from one set (its domain) onto elements of the same or another set (its range). Functions are often named by the single letter f. The mapping notation f: $x \rightarrow 3x^2$, Euler's notation $f(x) = 3x^2$ and $y = 3x^2$ all describe the same quadratic function.

Some important functions have their own names.

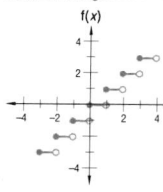

Greatest-integer function $f(x)$

INT: $x \rightarrow [x]$

Absolute-value function $f(x)$

ABS: $x \rightarrow |x|$

Identity function $f(x)$

I: $x \rightarrow x$

Squaring function

nth-Powering function, n even

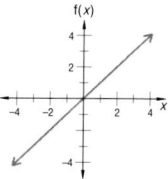

nth-Powering function, n odd

Vocabulary

Below are the most important terms and phrases for this chapter. You should be able to give a definition for those terms marked with *. For all other terms you should be able to give a general description and a specific example.

Lesson 7-1
*relation
*function
value of a function
Euler's f(x) notation
arrow or mapping notation

Lesson 7-2
*domain of a function
*range of a function
Vertical-Line Test for Functions

Lesson 7-3
composition of functions
composite of f and g, g ∘ f

Lesson 7-4
step function
*greatest-integer function, rounding-down function
[x], INT (X)
rounding-up function

Lesson 7-5
*absolute-value function
*identity function
*squaring, cubing, nth-powering function
*square-root function

Lesson 7-6
*inverse of a function f, f⁻¹
one-to-one correspondence, 1-1 correspondence
Horizontal-Line Test for Inverses

Lesson 7-7
Inverse-Function Theorem
*cube-root function

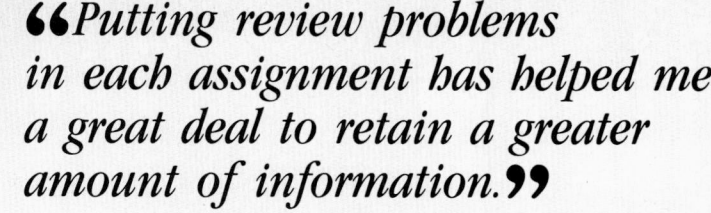

> **"Putting review problems in each assignment has helped me a great deal to retain a greater amount of information."**
>
> *Advanced Algebra* **student, Lake Park High School, Roselle, IL**

PROGRESS SELF-TEST provides the opportunity for feedback and correction—before students are tested formally. The Student Edition contains full solutions to questions on this test to enhance accurate self-evaluation.

CHAPTER REVIEW arranges questions according to the four dimensions of understanding—Skills, Properties, Uses, and Representations —to help students master those concepts that have not yet been mastered. Questions are keyed to objectives and lessons for easy reference.

CHAPTER TESTS in the Teacher's Resource File give you a choice of formats. The regular chapter test comes in parallel Forms A and B and corresponds closely to the Chapter Review. An alternative format is a chapter test in Cumulative Form. You decide which format best suits your needs!

CHAPTER 5

Chapter Review

Questions on **SPUR** Objectives

SPUR stands for **S**kills, **P**roperties, **U**ses, and **R**epresentations. The Chapter Review questions are grouped according to the SPUR Objectives for this chapter.

SKILLS deal with the procedures used to get answers.

...: Solve systems using the linear-
...on or substitution method. (Lessons

...le choice The system $\begin{cases} 2x + 3y = 19 \\ 4x - y = 17 \end{cases}$

...es $-7y = -21$ if you:

...ltiply the first equation by -2 and

...ltiply the second equation by 3 and

...ltiply the first equation by 2, the sec-
...quation by -1 and add.

...ltiply the second equation by 3 and
...ct.

...h choice in Question 1 does not help
...ve the system?

...lve and check.

... $4b = 18$
... $b = 22$
... $10n = 16$
... $-6n$
...$x - 4$
... $y = -2.5$
... $6y = -3$
... $8y + 22 = 0$
... $15t = 6$
... $3s$
... $\frac{2}{5}s$
... $3b - 2$
... $4c + 5$
... $5a + 1$

9. Consider the system $\begin{cases} y = 5x \\ -3x + 2y = -28 \end{cases}$.
  a. Name three methods you can use to solve this system.
  b. Solve and check the system.

■ **Objective B:** *Find the inverse and determinant of a 2 × 2 matrix. (Lesson 5-5)*

In 10–15, give: (a) the determinant; (b) the inverse, if it exists.

10. $\begin{bmatrix} 1 & 9 \\ -7 & 6 \end{bmatrix}$ **11.** $\begin{bmatrix} 2 & 0 \\ 0 & 1 \end{bmatrix}$

12. $\begin{bmatrix} 6 & 4 \\ -3 & 2 \end{bmatrix}$ **13.** $\begin{bmatrix} 1 & 4 \\ -3 & 6 \end{bmatrix}$

14. $\begin{bmatrix} 2 & -4 \\ 5 & -10 \end{bmatrix}$ **15.** $\begin{bmatrix} a & b \\ c & d \end{bmatrix}$

■ **Objective C:** *Use matrices to solve systems of equations. (Lesson 5-6)*

In 16–18, solve each system using matrices.

16. $\begin{cases} 2x - 9y = 14 \\ 6x - y = 42 \end{cases}$

17. $\begin{cases} 4a - 5b = -19 \\ 3a + 7b = 18 \end{cases}$

18. $\begin{cases} 3m = 4n + 5 \\ 2m = 3n - 6 \end{cases}$

19. $\begin{cases} \frac{1}{2} = 3x - 4y \\ \frac{2}{3} = x + 8y \end{cases}$

CHAPTER 5

Progress Self-Test

Take this test as you would take a test in class. Use graph paper and a calculator. Then check your work with the solutions in the Selected Answers section in the back of the book.

1. On a number line, graph $\{x: x \geq -5\} \cap \{x: x \geq 7\}$.

2. A graph of the system $\begin{cases} y = .5x - 2 \\ y = -x^2 \end{cases}$ is shown below. Approximate the solutions to the system.

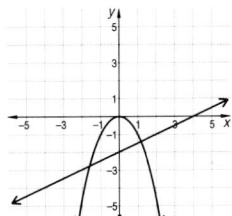

3. Consider the system $\begin{cases} 2x - 9y = 8 \\ 2x - 9y = -7 \end{cases}$.
  a. Is this system inconsistent?
  b. Why or why not?

In 4 and 5, solve each system.

4. $\begin{cases} s = 4t \\ r = t + 11 \\ 3r - 8s = 4 \end{cases}$ **5.** $\begin{cases} -3x + 3y = 2 \\ -4x - 2y = 3 \end{cases}$

6. At Eggs-N-Links Restaurant you can get a Double Duo Breakfast of 2 eggs with 2 sausage links for $2.78 and a Triple Quad Breakfast of 3 eggs with 4 sausage links for $4.99. From this information, what might Eggs-N-Links charge for 1 egg?

In 7 and 8, consider the system $\begin{cases} 8x + 3y = 41 \\ 6x + 5y = 39 \end{cases}$

9. *Multiple choice* The graph below shows the feasible set for which system?
(a) $\begin{cases} y \leq x \\ x \geq 2) \end{cases}$ (b) $\begin{cases} y > x \\ x \leq 2 \end{cases}$
(c) $\begin{cases} y \leq x \\ x < 2 \end{cases}$ (d) $\begin{cases} y < x \\ x < 2 \end{cases}$

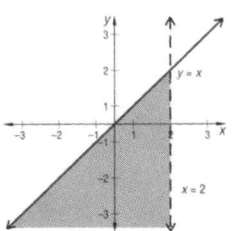

In 10–12, a furniture manufacturer makes upholstered chairs and sofas. On the average it takes carpenters 7 hours to build a chair and 4 hours to build a sofa. There are enough carpenters for no more than 133 worker-hours per day. Upholsterers average 2 hours per chair and 6 hours per sofa. There are enough upholsterers for no more than 72 worker-hours per day. The profit per chair is $80 and the profit per sofa is $70. How many sofas and chairs should be made per day to maximize the profit?

10. Translate the constraints into a system of linear inequalities.

11. Graph the system of inequalities and find the vertices of the feasible set.

12. Apply the Linear-Programming Theorem and interpret the results.

13. Which boundary is included in the solution set of $\begin{cases} y \leq 7 \\ y > x + 2 \end{cases}$?

Provides the Practical Support You Need

Continual involvement of teachers and instructional supervisors —in planning, writing, rewriting, and evaluating—has made this program **convenient** and **adaptable** to your needs.

Before each chapter you'll find the following:

Daily Pacing Chart
shows you at a glance two alternate ways to pace the chapter.

Testing Options
list the chapter quizzes and tests for ease of planning.

Objectives are letter-coded and keyed to Progress Self-Test, Chapter Review, and Lesson Masters, showing a **direct correspondence between what is taught and what is tested.**

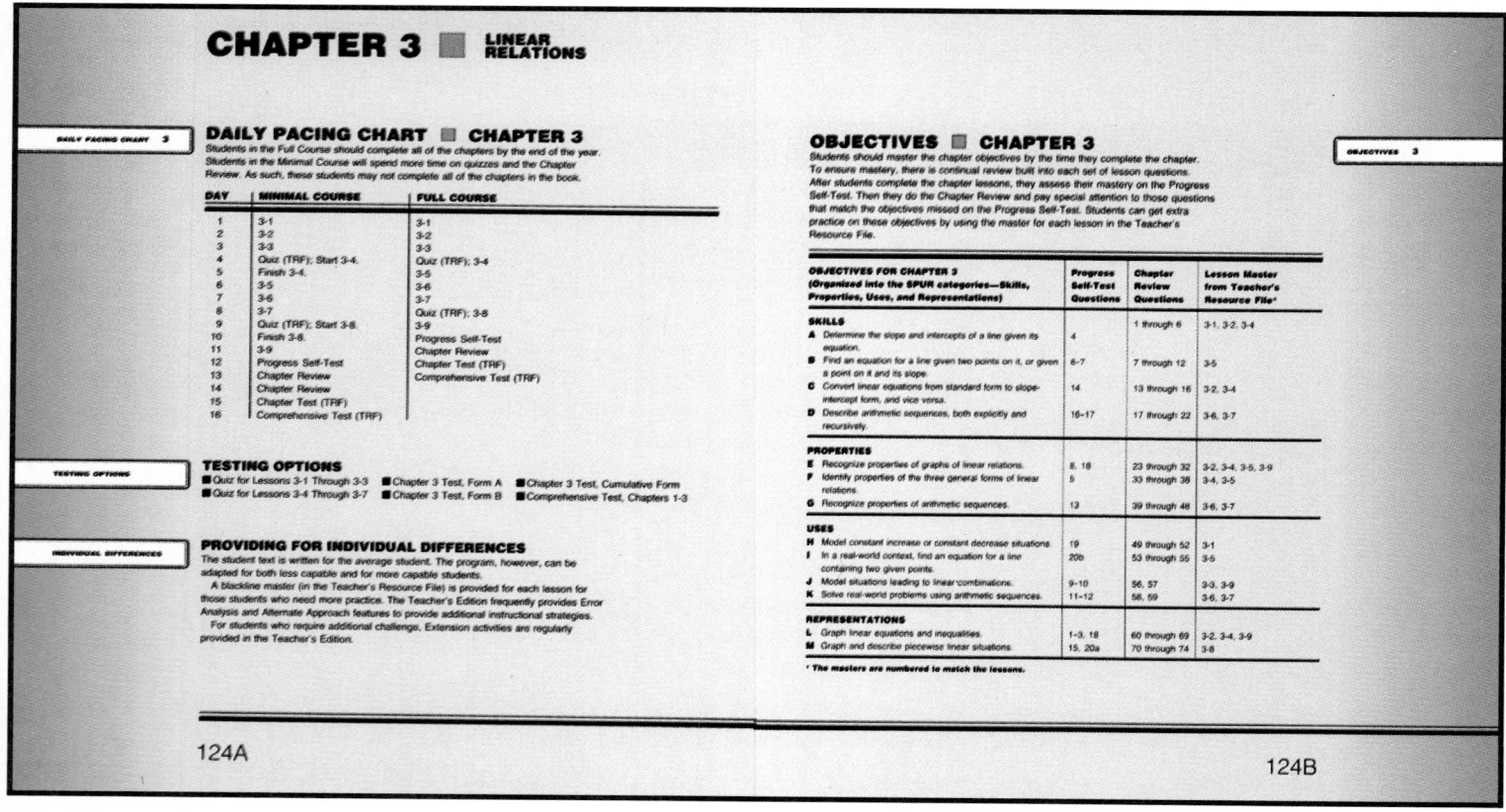

CHAPTER 3 ■ LINEAR RELATIONS

DAILY PACING CHART ■ CHAPTER 3

Students in the Full Course should complete all of the chapters by the end of the year. Students in the Minimal Course will spend more time on quizzes and the Chapter Review. As such, these students may not complete all of the chapters in the book.

DAY	MINIMAL COURSE	FULL COURSE
1	3-1	3-1
2	3-2	3-2
3	3-3	3-3
4	Quiz (TRF); Start 3-4.	Quiz (TRF); 3-4
5	Finish 3-4.	3-5
6	3-5	3-6
7	3-6	3-7
8	3-7	Quiz (TRF); 3-8
9	Quiz (TRF); Start 3-8.	3-9
10	Finish 3-8.	Progress Self-Test
11	3-9	Chapter Review
12	Progress Self-Test	Chapter Test (TRF)
13	Chapter Review	Comprehensive Test (TRF)
14	Chapter Review	
15	Chapter Test (TRF)	
16	Comprehensive Test (TRF)	

TESTING OPTIONS

■ Quiz for Lessons 3-1 Through 3-3   ■ Chapter 3 Test, Form A   ■ Chapter 3 Test, Cumulative Form
■ Quiz for Lessons 3-4 Through 3-7   ■ Chapter 3 Test, Form B   ■ Comprehensive Test, Chapters 1-3

PROVIDING FOR INDIVIDUAL DIFFERENCES

The student text is written for the average student. The program, however, can be adapted for both less capable and for more capable students.

A blackline master (in the Teacher's Resource File) is provided for each lesson for those students who need more practice. The Teacher's Edition frequently provides Error Analysis and Alternate Approach features to provide additional instructional strategies.

For students who require additional challenge, Extension activities are regularly provided in the Teacher's Edition.

OBJECTIVES ■ CHAPTER 3

Students should master the chapter objectives by the time they complete the chapter. To ensure mastery, there is continual review built into each set of lesson questions. After students complete the chapter lessons, they assess their mastery on the Progress Self-Test. Then they do the Chapter Review and pay special attention to those questions that match the objectives missed on the Progress Self-Test. Students can get extra practice on these objectives by using the master for each lesson in the Teacher's Resource File.

OBJECTIVES FOR CHAPTER 3 (Organized into the SPUR categories—Skills, Properties, Uses, and Representations)	Progress Self-Test Questions	Chapter Review Questions	Lesson Master from Teacher's Resource File*
SKILLS			
A Determine the slope and intercepts of a line given its equation.	4	1 through 6	3-1, 3-2, 3-4
B Find an equation for a line given two points on it, or given a point on it and its slope.	6-7	7 through 12	3-5
C Convert linear equations from standard form to slope-intercept form, and vice versa.	14	13 through 16	3-2, 3-4
D Describe arithmetic sequences, both explicitly and recursively.	16-17	17 through 22	3-6, 3-7
PROPERTIES			
E Recognize properties of graphs of linear relations.	8, 18	23 through 32	3-2, 3-4, 3-5, 3-9
F Identify properties of the three general forms of linear relations.	5	33 through 38	3-4, 3-5
G Recognize properties of arithmetic sequences.	13	39 through 48	3-6, 3-7
USES			
H Model constant increase or constant decrease situations.	19	49 through 52	3-1
I In a real-world context, find an equation for a line containing two given points.	20b	53 through 55	3-5
J Model situations leading to linear combinations.	9-10	56, 57	3-3, 3-9
K Solve real-world problems using arithmetic sequences.	11-12	58, 59	3-6, 3-7
REPRESENTATIONS			
L Graph linear equations and inequalities.	1-3, 18	60 through 69	3-2, 3-4, 3-9
M Graph and describe piecewise linear situations.	15, 20a	70 through 74	3-8

* The masters are numbered to match the lessons.

124A

124B

Overview anticipates and addresses your needs for the upcoming chapter.

Perspectives, a unique feature, provides the rationale for the inclusion of topics or approaches, provides mathematical background, and makes connections within UCSMP materials. This is interesting information you'll really use!

**Professional
Sourcebook for UCSMP**
Also at your fingertips is a **wealth of information** that includes valuable background material on topics ranging from research to review. See pages T19–T50 at the back of the Teacher's Edition.

$Ax + By = C$, the x-intercepts, the graphs of $x = a$ and $y = b$, and the method of graphing using both intercepts. Students should be able to graph from standard form as well as from slope-intercept form.

3-5
FINDING AN EQUATION OF A LINE
Many students will be familiar with finding an equation for a line through two points, either from their first course in algebra or from their geometry course. For most students this review will be helpful.

In geometry, students learn that there is one line (a) through two points (usually a postulate); (b) through a point parallel to a given line (often a postulate, Playfair's Parallel Postulate); and (c) through a point perpendicular to a given line (usually a theorem). This lesson shows students how to determine the equations for (a) and (b) algebraically.

We do not discuss (c) until Chapter 4 for two reasons: at that time, a simple way to determine the slopes of perpendicular lines will be given; and a second look at this lesson will provide a convenient review.

3-6
**ARITHMETIC SEQUENCES:
EXPLICIT FORMULAS**
A generation ago, this section would have been called *arithmetic progressions*. A progression is a special kind of sequence. The advantage of using the phrase *arithmetic sequence* is the connection between sequences and functions, namely that a sequence is a function whose domain is the set of positive integers (or sometimes some other set of integers).

Even the phrase "arithmetic sequence" disguises what is going on, and so the phrase *linear sequence* is introduced. The idea is simple: everything learned for lines

has analogues with linear sequences. For instance, just as one can find the equation of a line through two points, one can find a formula for a linear sequence given any two of its terms. Just as one can find the equation of a line given one point and its slope, one can find a formula for a linear sequence given one term and its constant difference. Thus, Lesson 3-6 provides a chance to review Lesson 3-5 by applying the slope-intercept and point-slope forms to discrete situations.

Specifically, by restricting the domain to natural numbers, the equations $y = mx + b$ and $y - y_1 = m(x - x_1)$ can generate arithmetic sequences. To show that the domains have been restricted, we use n for x and a_n for y and call the slope, m, the constant difference or rate of change, d. Thus, the equations become $a_n = dn + b$ and $a_n - a_1 = d(n - 1)$. These substitutions are usually understood by most students.

3-7
**ARITHMETIC SEQUENCES:
RECURSIVE FORMULAS**
This lesson discusses in detail a specific example of a recursive formula for sequences—namely, the recursive formula for sequences. The formula given by the theorem on page 160 is one of the simplest recursive formulas. In many respects, recursive formulas for arithmetic sequences are more natural than explicit ones. Indeed, the name *arithmetic progression* suggests that each term is found from the preceding ones.

When given an explicit formula for an arithmetic sequence, the recursive formula can be determined, and vice versa. However, if the sequence is not arithmetic, it may not be possible to determine one formula from the other. In fact, either the recursive or explicit formula may not be known.

Recursive formulas for sequences are used in computer

programming more often than explicit formulas. This concept also underlies the idea of proof by mathematical induction.

3-8
PIECEWISE LINEAR GRAPHS
Piecewise linear graphs model situations in which the rate of change is constant for intervals but not for the entire situation. These graphs are exceedingly common in applications. They provide a new and interesting way to provide practice in interpreting information about independent and dependent variables and rates of change from graphs.

As shown in Example 1, often there is a particular constant unit cost if you buy small amounts of a product and then a lower unit cost if you purchase larger amounts. Income taxes can often be represented with a piecewise linear graph.

The piecewise linear graph most familiar to students may be that of the absolute value function. This function and its graph are studied in Lesson 7-5.

3-9
LINEAR INEQUALITIES
This lesson expands the idea of graphing inequalities on a number line (discussed in Lesson 1-9) to graphing inequalities in the coordinate plane. The graphing of half-planes may be a review for some students. The idea is usually quite easy for students.

The boundary for a linear inequality separates the coordinate plane into three disjoint sets of points: the points on either side of the boundary and the points on the boundary line itself. One goal of this lesson is that students can identify which of these sets of points belong to the graph of an inequality.

124D

OVERVIEW ■ CHAPTER 3

Chapter 3 introduces situations that lead to the various forms of linear relations and connects these forms to Chapter 2 as generalizations of $y = kx$. Most students will remember some of these concepts from their earlier studies of algebra and geometry, but the emphasis on the usefulness of the forms should make this review interesting.

Chapter 3 is critical to the strong graphing theme carried throughout the other chapters. In later chapters, students will be expected to extend the work done in Chapter 3 to graphing nonlinear equations and to finding the equations of curves.

The chapter opens with two pairs of lessons. Lessons 3-1 and 3-2 explain how constant increase and decrease situations lead to the slope-intercept form of a line and its graph. Lessons 3-3 and 3-4 explain how linear-combination situations lead to equations in standard form and their graphs. The equations for horizontal and vertical lines are also introduced at this time.

Lesson 3-5 explains how to go from a graph, or two points, to an equation of a line and presents the point-slope theorem.

Lessons 3-6 and 3-7 build on the ideas about sequences presented in Chapter 1. These two lessons

describe arithmetic sequences as discrete instances of linear equations. In Lesson 3-7, students are shown how to interchange recursive formulas and explicit formulas.

Lesson 3-8 presents piecewise linear graphs, ideas which most students have not seen before. Piecewise linear graphs are useful in many real-world contexts.

Finally, the graphs of linear inequalities are introduced in Lesson 3-9. These are used extensively in Chapter 5 on *Systems*.

PERSPECTIVES ■ CHAPTER 3
The Perspectives provide the rationale for the inclusion of topics or approaches, provide mathematical background, and make connections within UCSMP.

3-1
CONSTANT INCREASE OR DECREASE
In this book, we do not classify situations by context. That is, we do not classify them as age, or distance-rate-time, or work, or digit, and so on. The classifications used in this book are conceptual, that is, by ideas that connect the mathematics with the situation. For lines, the ideas we want students to know are constant increase, constant decrease, and linear combination. This lesson is about constant increase or decrease. Linear combinations are discussed in Lesson 3-3.

Constant increase and constant decrease situations lead to equations of the form $y = mx + b$. Furthermore, m and b have simple interpretations: m is the amount of increase or decrease per unit change of x, and b is the initial value.

3-2
THE GRAPH OF $y = mx + b$
Lesson 3-1 identified applications of slope and y-intercept; this lesson relates them directly to graphing. It is important for students to be able to graph a linear equation quickly, and the techniques discussed in this lesson will allow them to do so.

Many students encountered slope in their first study of algebra, but some students may not understand the idea fully. Applications help to make slope a natural descriptor of lines. Students who have taken UCSMP *Algebra* and *Geometry* will have studied slope twice; UCSMP *Algebra* concentrates on applications of slope, and both books mention that parallel lines have equal slopes.

3-3
LINEAR COMBINATIONS
Just as constant increase or constant decrease situations lead into linear equations in slope-intercept form, linear combinations lead into

equations in the standard form $Ax + By = C$.

Equations in standard form are often necessary for solving linear systems, which will be discussed in Chapter 5. Thus, the kinds of situations given in this lesson will be quite useful when developing examples in Chapter 5.

It is possible, and quite common, to have linear combination of more than two variables, as in Example 1. The graph of $Ax + By + Cz = D$, an equation with three variables, is a plane. Such equations have more than three variables, the graph is called a *hyperplane*.

3-4
THE GRAPH OF $Ax + By = C$
In this lesson, students study graphs of situations in which a linear combination $Ax + By$ equals a constant. Several important concepts are reviewed: the graph of

124C

T15

Super Teaching Support
continued

1. TAILOR-MADE FOR TEXAS! The Texas Essential Elements covered in the lesson will be listed for you right on the Teacher's Edition page.

2. RESOURCES save you time by coordinating all of the ancillaries to the lesson.

3. OBJECTIVES are letter-coded for easy reference.

4. TEACHING NOTES provide everything you need, including reading tips, suggestions for discussing the examples, strategies for alternate approaches, calculator tips, estimation suggestions, dialogue to generate higher-order thinking, and more.

5. MAKING CONNECTIONS helps you connect present content and ideas to material covered in an earlier or later lesson, chapter, or text.

6. ERROR ANALYSIS pinpoints typical student errors and includes remediation strategies for correcting the errors.

7. ADDITIONAL EXAMPLES provide parallel examples to those in the text for added flexibility.

8. NOTES ON QUESTIONS highlight important aspects of questions and provide helpful suggestions to enhance learning.

9. MORE PRACTICE lists the Lesson Master for additional practice of the lesson skills and concepts.

10. EXTENSION offers high-interest activities for all students as well as enrichment activities for students needing additional challenge. These well-liked activities provide ideas for technology, estimation, mental math, careers, and additional applications.

11. EVALUATION tells what you need to know about the quizzes and tests. It also provides **Alternative Assessment** suggestions to encourage different evaluation formats, such as oral presentation and cooperative learning.

12. The **LESSON MASTERS** are pictured where you need them for your convenience.

1

TEXAS ESSENTIAL ELEMENT / 5A

LESSON 3-2

RESOURCES
■ Lesson Master 3-2
▱ Visual for Teaching Aid 10 provides the graph that is used to prove the theorem that two lines with the same slope are parallel.
▣ Computer Master 3

2

3-

LESSON

The Gra
$y = mx$

OBJECTIVES **3**

C Convert linear equations to slope-intercept form.
E Recognize that two lines are parallel if and only if they have the same slope.
F Identify the properties of the slope-intercept form of a linear relation.
L Graph linear equations using slope and y-intercept.

TEACHING NOTES **4**

Reading Proofs for the two theorems concerning parallel lines may be difficult for some students. Encourage them to read this material slowly, locating in the diagram each line, angle, and triangle as it is referenced.

Making Connections **5**
You may wish to go through the proof that equal slopes imply parallel lines as it uses SAS Congruence. Students appreciate seeing that an idea they learned in one mathematics course is useful in another course. The proof of the converse of the statement that equal slopes imply parallel lines, namely that parallel lines imply equal slopes, uses ASA Congruence.

132

6 **Error Analysis** Horizontal lines and their equations are discussed in **Example 3**; however, vertical lines are not discussed until Lesson 3-4. Anticipate the problem that students may have difficulty distinguishing a slope of 0 (a property of horizontal lines) from an undefined slope (a property of vertical lines) by avoiding the phrase "no slope."

T16

132

7

ADDITIONAL EXAMPLES
1. Graph lines (a) $y = 2x - 3$ and (b) $y = -\frac{2}{3}x + 1$ using slope and y-intercept. For (a), begin at -3 on the y-axis and go up 2 units for every unit to the right. For (b), begin at 1 on the y-axis and go down 2 units for every 3 units to the right.

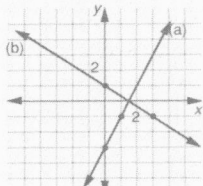

2. Solve for y and find the slope and y-intercept.
a. $x + y = 6$
b. $3x - 4y = 12$
c. $\frac{y}{6} + \frac{x}{3} = 1$

	Slope	y-intercept
a. $y = -x + 6$	-1	6
b. $y = \frac{3}{4}x - 3$	$\frac{3}{4}$	-3
c. $y = -2x + 6$	-2	6

3. Graph the equation $3y = 12x - 1800$. The slope-intercept form is $y = 4x - 600$. Since the y-intercept is -600, the y-axis should be numbered in units of 100 or 200. Since the slope is 4, it is easy to keep the axes to the same scale by numbering both of them by one hundreds. You could also graph the equation $y = 4x - 600$ on an automatic grapher and discuss scaling issues.

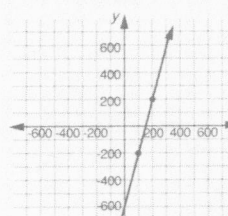

134

8

NOTES ON QUESTIONS
Question 14: The two equations are confused by some students. Point out that in the equation $y = 2x$, one can see that as the value of x changes, so does the value of y. The y-value can not be determined until the x-value is known. In the equation $y = 2$, however, the y-value is always 2, regardless of the value of x. It is helpful to write the equation $y = 2$ as $y = 0 \cdot x + 2$ to illustrate the independence of the value of y as the value of x changes.

Question 16: Some students may avoid this question because of the magnitude of the coordinates. These students think the problem is more difficult than it is. Point out that the properties of lines hold regardless of the values of the numbers and, with calculators, working with large or small numbers is not difficult.

Question 22: At first, it may seem that the question does not exemplify a constant decrease situation for the same reason as the tire-leak example used in the Extension for Lesson 3-1. However, water tanks are usually constructed to keep pressure constant at any water level.

Question 26: This question anticipates **Example 2** of the next lesson and should be discussed.

ADDITIONAL ANSWERS
4.b. Does $15 = 4 \cdot 2 + 7$? Yes.

5. Does $2(-1) = -3(4) + 10$? Yes, $-2 = -12 + 10$.

135

MORE PRACTICE
For more questions on SPUR Objectives, use *Lesson Master 3-2*, shown on page 137.

9

EXTENSION
Ask students if they think the slope can help determine the scales on the axes when graphing by hand. (yes) Use an example to illustrate this idea. The slope of the equation $25x + y = 75$ is -25. Numbering the y-axis by tens, twenties, or twenty-fives would be appropriate. The y-intercept is 75 and would be located easily on any one of these scales. Ask students if numbering by fives or fifties would be appropriate. (No; numbering by fives would make the graph too large and numbering by fifties, too small.)

10

EVALUATION
Alternative Assessment
In order to evaluate students' understanding of the relationship between the orientation of a line in a plane and its slope, use the following activity. Identify a horizontal and vertical edge of the chalkboard as the x- and y-axis of a coordinate plane. Then draw a line on the chalkboard and have students state whether the slope is positive, negative, or zero. After repeating this activity for five or six lines, call upon students to explain how to find the slope of any line.

11

Applying

ADDITIONAL ANSWERS
10.c.

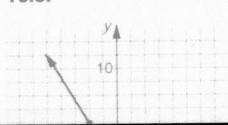

12

T17

Components Designed for Ease of Teaching

A TEXAS MANUAL provides complete correlations to the Texas Essential Elements, record forms, and more!

STUDENT EDITION,
full color

TEACHER'S RESOURCE FILE
About 600 blackline masters
to cover your every classroom need!

Quiz and Test Masters

Quizzes (at least one per chapter)

Chapter Tests, Forms A and B (parallel forms)

Chapter Tests, Cumulative Form

Comprehensive Tests (four per text,
including Final Exam, primarily multiple choice)

Lesson Masters
(one or two per lesson)

Computer Masters

Answer Masters
(provide answers for questions in student text;
oversized type to enable display in class,
allowing students to grade their own work)

Teaching Aid Masters
(patterns for manipulatives;
masters for overhead transparencies;
forms, charts, and graphs from the PE;
coordinate grids; and more)

TEACHER'S EDITION,
annotated and with margin notes

ADDITIONAL ANCILLARIES . . .

Solutions Manual

Computer Software

Visual Aids

"This approach makes the learning of advanced algebra more fun and beneficial."

***Advanced Algebra* student, Renaissance High School, Detroit, MI**

UCSMP
SCOTT, FORESMAN

The University of Chicago School Mathematics Project
Advanced Algebra

Authors

Sharon L. Senk
Assistant Professor of Mathematics Education
Syracuse University
Syracuse, New York

Denisse R. Thompson
Assistant Professor
Department of Mathematics
Manatee Community College
Bradenton, Florida

Steven S. Viktora
Chairman, Mathematics Department
Kenwood Academy
Chicago Public Schools
Chicago, Illinois

Contributing Authors

Rheta Rubenstein
Mathematics Department Head
Renaissance High School
Detroit, Michigan

Judy Halvorson
Mathematics Teacher
John F. Kennedy High School
Bloomington, Minnesota

About the Cover
A stroboscopic photograph shows the regularity in the movement of
a rotating gyroscope. While the pivot remains stationary, the axis itself revolves,
outlining a cone.

Scott, Foresman and Company
Editorial Offices: Glenview, Illinois Regional Offices: Sunnyvale, California •
Tucker, Georgia • Glenview, Illinois • Oakland, New Jersey • Dallas, Texas

UCSMP Editorial Staff
Series Directors: Zalman Usiskin, Sharon L. Senk
Managing Editor: Natalie Jakucyn
Editors: James Flanders, Jerry Pillsbury
Technical Coordinator: Susan Chang

Editorial Development and Design
Scott, Foresman staff, Kristin Nelson Design, Shawn Biner Design

We wish to acknowledge the generous support of the **Amoco Foundation** and the **Carnegie Corporation of New York** in helping to make it possible for these materials to be developed and tested.

Director of Evaluations: Sandra Mathison,
State University of New York, Albany

Assistant to the Director: Catherine Sarther
The University of Chicago

It takes many people to put together a project of this kind and we cannot thank them all by name. We wish particularly to acknowledge Carol Siegel, who coordinated the use of these materials in schools, and Peter Bryant, Dan Caplinger, Janine Crawley, Kurt Hackemer, Michael Herzog, Maryann Kannappan, Mary Lappan, Teresa Manst, and Victoria Ritter of our technical staff.

We appreciate the assistance of the following teachers who taught preliminary versions of this text, participated in the field-test research, and contributed ideas to help improve the text.

Rita Belluomini
Rich South High School
Richton Park, Illinois

Timothy Craine
Renaissance High School
Detroit, Michigan

Mary Crisanti
Lake Park West High School
Roselle, Illinois

Joe DeBlois
West Genessee High School
Camillus, New York

Cynthia Harris
Taft High School
Chicago Public Schools

Marilyn Hourston
Whitney Young High School
Chicago Public Schools

Marvin Koffman
Kenwood Academy
Chicago Public Schools

Sharon Llewellyn
Renaissance High School
Detroit, Michigan

Kenneth Lucas
Glenbrook South High School
Glenview, Illinois

Donald Thompson
Hernando High School
Brooksville, Florida

Jill Weitz
Brentwood School
Los Angeles, California

We wish to express our thanks and appreciation to the many other schools and students who have used earlier versions of these materials.

We also acknowledge the contribution of the text *Advanced Algebra with Transformations and Applications*, by Zalman Usiskin (Laidlaw, 1975), to some of the conceptualizations and problems used in this book.

UCSMP Advanced Algebra

The University of Chicago School Mathematics Project (UCSMP) is a long-term project designed to improve school mathematics in grades K-12. UCSMP began in 1983 with a 6-year grant from the Amoco Foundation. Additional funding has come from the Ford Motor Company, the Carnegie Corporation of New York, the National Science Foundation, the General Electric Foundation, GTE, and Citicorp.

The project is centered in the Departments of Education and Mathematics of the University of Chicago, and has the following components and directors:

Resources	Izaak Wirszup, Professor Emeritus of Mathematics
Primary Materials	Max Bell, Professor of Education
Elementary Teacher Development	Sheila Sconiers, Research Associate in Education
Secondary	Sharon L. Senk, Assistant Professor of Mathematics and Education, Syracuse University (on leave) Zalman Usiskin, Professor of Education
Evaluation	Larry Hedges, Professor of Education Susan Stodolsky, Professor of Education

From 1983-1987, the director of UCSMP was Paul Sally, Professor of Mathematics. Since 1987, the director has been Zalman Usiskin.

The text *Advanced Algebra* was developed by the Secondary Component (grades 7-12) of the project, and constitutes the fourth year in a six-year mathematics curriculum devised by that component. As texts in this curriculum complete their multi-stage testing cycle, they are being published by Scott, Foresman and Company. The schedule for first publication of the texts follows. Titles for the last two books are tentative.

Transition Mathematics	spring, 1989
Algebra	spring, 1989
Geometry	spring, 1990
Advanced Algebra	spring, 1989
Functions, Statistics, and Trigonometry, with Computers	spring, 1991
Precalculus and Discrete Mathematics	spring, 1991

A first draft of *Advanced Algebra* was written and piloted during the 1985-86 school year. After a major revision, a field trial edition was used in six schools in 1986-87. A second revision was tested during 1987-88. Results are available by writing UCSMP. The Scott, Foresman and Company edition is based on improvements suggested by the authors, editors, and some of the many teacher and student users of earlier editions.

Comments about these materials are welcomed. Address queries to Mathematics Product Manager, Scott, Foresman and Company, 1900 East Lake Avenue, Glenview, Illinois 60025, or to UCSMP, The University of Chicago, 5835 S. Kimbark, Chicago, IL 60637.

UCSMP *Advanced Algebra* is designed for a second-year course in algebra. It differs from other books for this course in six major ways. First, it has **wider scope** including substantial amounts of geometry integrated with the algebra. This is to correct the present situation in which many students who finish a second course in algebra forget what they learned in geometry. Also, we want to take advantage of all the mathematics students have had.

Second, **reading and problem solving** are emphasized throughout. Students can and should be expected to read this book. The explanations were written for students and tested with them. The first set of questions in each lesson is called "Covering the Reading." The exercises guide students through the reading and check their coverage of critical words, rules, explanations, and examples. The second set of questions is called "Applying the Mathematics." These questions extend student understanding of the principles and applications of the lesson. To further widen student horizons, "Exploration" questions are provided in every lesson.

Third, there is a **reality orientation** towards both the selection of content and the methods taught the student in working out problems. Algebra is rich in applications and problem solving. Being able to do algebra is of little ultimate use to individuals unless they can apply that content. Each elementary function is studied in detail for its applications to real-world problems. Real-life situations motivate algebraic ideas and provide the settings for practice of algebra skills. The variety of content of this book permits lessons on problem-solving strategies to be embedded in application settings.

Fourth, fitting the reality orientation, students are expected to use current **technology**. Calculators are assumed throughout this book because virtually all individuals who use mathematics today find it helpful to have them. Scientific calculators are recommended because they use an order of operations closer to that found in algebra and have numerous keys that are helpful in understanding concepts at this level. Computer activities are used to enhance algebraic concepts, and students are taught how to use a calculator or computer to graph and analyze functions.

Fifth, **four dimensions of understanding** are emphasized: skill in carrying out various algorithms; developing and using mathematical properties and relationships; applying mathematics in realistic situations; and representing or picturing mathematical concepts. We call this the SPUR approach: **S**kills, **P**roperties, **U**ses, **R**epresentations.

Sixth, the **instructional format** is designed to maximize the development of understanding. The book is organized around lessons meant to take one day to cover. Ideas introduced in a lesson are reinforced through "Review" questions in the immediately succeeding lessons; this gives students several nights to learn and practice each idea. The lessons themselves are sequenced into carefully constructed chapters. At the end of each chapter, a carefully focused Progress Self-Test and a Chapter Review, each keyed to objectives in all the dimensions of understanding, are then used to solidify performance of skills and concepts from the chapter so that they may be applied later with confidence. Finally, to increase retention, important ideas are reviewed in questions in later chapters.

CONTENTS

You have studied algebra. *Advanced Algebra* sounds as if this class will be like algebra was, but more difficult. That is half true. The content of this book is similar to that in first-year algebra. You will study more about variables, equations, and graphs. However, this book is not necessarily more difficult. Some questions are harder, but you know a lot more now than you did then. In particular, you know much more geometry and you have had a year's more practice with algebra.

Advanced Algebra studies a variety of topics, from lines to logarithms, from quadratic equations to conic sections, from systems to statistics, from matrices to trigonometry. It might be best described as "what every high school graduate should know about mathematics." It contains the mathematics that educated people around the world use in conversation and that colleges want or expect you to have studied. But it is not a hodge-podge of topics. The properties of numbers, graphs, expressions, equations, inequalities, and functions are ideas which run throughout the book.

In this course, you will learn the meaning of many of the keys on a scientific calculator that you may never have used before. We recommend a solar-powered calculator so that you do not have to worry about batteries, though some calculators have batteries which can last for many years and work in dim light. Yo also need to have a *ruler* and *graph paper*.

If you plan to buy a calculator, consider buying a *graphing calculator*. Throughout this book there are questions which are made easier with such a calculator, and you will find such a calculator particularly useful in your future mathematics courses. If you plan to go to college, a graphing calculator will be useful in many courses in business, the sciences, and statistics.

An important goal of this book is to assist you to become able to learn mathematics on your own, so that you will be able to deal with the mathematics that you see in newspapers, magazines, on television, on any job, and in school. The authors, who are all experienced teachers, offer the following advice.

1. You cannot learn much mathematics just by watching other people do it. You must work problems and participate in class. Some teachers have a slogan:

    Mathematics is not a spectator sport.

2. You are expected to read each lesson. Read slowly, and keep a pencil with you as you check the mathematics that is done in the book. Use the Glossary or a dictionary to find the meaning of a word you do not understand.

3. You are expected to do homework every day while studying from this book, so put aside time for it. Do not wait until the day before a test if you do not understand something. Try to resolve the difficulty right away and ask questions of your classmates or teacher. You are expected to learn many things by reading, but school is designed so that you do not have to learn everything by yourself.

4. If you cannot answer a question immediately, don't give up! Read the lesson again; read the question again. Look for examples. If you can, go away from the problem and come back to it a little later.

We hope you join the many students who have enjoyed this book. We wish you much success.

DAILY PACING CHART ■ CHAPTER 1

Students in the Full Course should complete all but one of the chapters by the end of the year. Students in the Minimal Course will spend more time on quizzes and the Chapter Review. As such, these students should complete about ten or eleven chapters.

For more information on pacing, see *General Teaching Suggestions: Pace* on page T35 of the Teacher's Edition. Quizzes and tests are provided in the Teacher's Resource File (TRF).

DAY	MINIMAL COURSE	FULL COURSE
1	1-1	1-1
2	1-2	1-2
3	1-3	1-3
4	1-4	1-4
5	1-5	1-5
6	Quiz (TRF); Start 1-6.	Quiz (TRF); 1-6
7	Finish 1-6.	1-7
8	1-7	1-8
9	1-8	1-9
10	1-9	Progress Self-Test
11	Progress Self-Test	Chapter Review
12	Chapter Review	Chapter Test (TRF)
13	Chapter Review	
14	Chapter Test (TRF)	

TESTING OPTIONS
■ Quiz for Lessons 1-1 Through 1-5   ■ Chapter 1 Test, Form A
■ Chapter 1 Test, Form B

PROVIDING FOR INDIVIDUAL DIFFERENCES
The student text is written for the *average* student. The program, however, can be adapted for both less capable and for more capable students.

A blackline master (in the Teacher's Resource File) is provided for each lesson for those students who need more practice. The Teacher's Edition frequently provides Error Analysis and Alternate Approach features to provide additional instructional strategies.

For students who require additional challenge, Extension activities are regularly provided in the Teacher's Edition.

OBJECTIVES ■ CHAPTER 1

Students should master the chapter objectives by the time they complete the chapter. To ensure mastery, there is continual review built into each set of lesson questions. After students complete the chapter lessons, they assess their mastery on the Progress Self-Test. Then they do the Chapter Review and pay special attention to those questions that match the objectives missed on the Progress Self-Test. Students can get extra practice on these objectives by using the master for each lesson in the Teacher's Resource File.

OBJECTIVES FOR CHAPTER 1 (Organized into the SPUR categories—Skills, Properties, Uses, and Representations)	Progress Self-Test Questions	Chapter Review Questions	Lesson Master from Teacher's Resource File*
SKILLS			
A Evaluate formulas.	1–4, 9, 20	1 through 6	1-2, 1-3, 1-4
B Use computer programs to obtain terms of sequences.	6	7 through 9	1-3, 1-4
C Simplify expressions by using field properties, definitions, or theorems derived from the Distributive Property.	7, 8	10 through 16	1-5
D Solve and check linear equations and linear inequalities.	10–12	17 through 23	1-7, 1-9
E Rewrite formulas.	5, 15	24 through 28	1-8
PROPERTIES			
F Use counterexamples to show errors in reasoning.	16	29 through 32	1-6
G Identify justifications in mathematical arguments.	17–19	33 through 37	1-5, 1-6
H State the domain for a variable n in a given situation.	21, 25	38 through 40	1-2
USES			
I Use sequences in real-world situations.	24	41, 42	1-3, 1-4
J Use the models for the four fundamental operations to describe situations.	22, 23	43 through 48	1-1, 1-7, 1-9
REPRESENTATIONS			
K Graph solutions to inequalities on a number line.	13	49, 50	1-9

* The masters are numbered to match the lessons.

2B

OVERVIEW ■ CHAPTER 1

Chapter 1 reviews concepts of elementary algebra within the context of new material. Language and important notation are introduced and reviewed using formulas and sequences. The formal study of sequences in Chapter 1 is probably new to most students. These general ideas are applied to arithmetic sequences in Chapter 3, and to geometric sequences in Chapter 8.

The strong geometric flavor in Chapter 1 continues throughout the book, serving three purposes. First, many students profit greatly from a visual representation of concepts they are learning. Second, blending geometry with algebra shows the interrelationships between these two branches of mathematics. And third, students' knowledge of geometry is reviewed and enhanced.

The computer work with BASIC that was begun in earlier UCSMP courses is reviewed in Chapter 1. Students and teachers who are unfamiliar with BASIC should refer to the BASIC Appendix at the end of the book. The language and programs are fairly elementary. The most sophisticated concept is the FOR . . . NEXT instruction. If possible, during Lesson 1-3 or 1-4, use a computer for demonstration or laboratory work.

The first lesson deals with describing situations using algebra. While Lesson 1-2 deals with formulas in general, Lessons 1-3 and 1-4 deal with explicit and recursive formulas for sequences. The different types of formulas are discussed to emphasize the need for flexibility in approach.

Lessons 1-5 through 1-9 provide instruction on the properties which justify the rewriting of expressions, formulas, and inequalities. Students are expected to follow mathematical arguments and, when proofs are within their reach, to do them.

The end-of-chapter material, optional in many books, is an integral part of this chapter and should not be skipped.

Before beginning this chapter, make certain your students have read the section entitled TO THE STUDENT so they know what materials they are expected to have.

It is assumed throughout this book that students have access to a scientific calculator. Beginning in Chapter 2, it is helpful for students to have access to either a graphing calculator or a computer with function graphing software.

Students are expected to read this book. Students who have used previous books in this series will be accustomed to reading mathematics. Others may not be and will need to adjust to this expectation. Specific suggestions are given throughout this chapter to assist you in teaching students to read mathematics.

PERSPECTIVES ■ CHAPTER 1

The Perspectives provide the rationale for the inclusion of topics or approaches, provide mathematical background, and make connections within UCSMP.

1-1

DESCRIBING SITUATIONS WITH ALGEBRA

There are three basic ways to translate a statement from English into algebra: word-for-word direct translation, patterning, and using models. Each example in this lesson illustrates one of these ways.

Many students are familiar only with direct translation. Students who have been through previous UCSMP courses should recognize the other ways. In particular, using a *model for an operation* will be new to some students. You may wish to explain that a model for an operation is a generalization of the uses of that operation. It helps students conceptualize when to use each individual operation. Tell students to use Appendix A for reference. We never expect students to state names for models, but we expect them to be able to choose the appropriate operation in a given situation.

1-2

FORMULAS

This lesson should not be difficult for students as it is mostly review. Students should be familiar with the names for the different number sets. Some books define the natural numbers to include 0; the choice really is arbitrary. Zero might even be called a counting number, for it is the count of a set with no elements (for example, the number of living dinosaurs). Other familiar concepts in this lesson are evaluating an expression and the rules for order of operations. The idea of the domain of a variable may be new to students; this concept, however, is quite important and will arise repeatedly during problem-solving activities.

This lesson introduces questions that review earlier lessons. We cannot stress enough how vital they are to this course. A large part of the practice students will have on a topic is distributed throughout Reviews in many lessons, some in the current chapter, some later in the book. Encourage students to use the section references at the end of each question to locate material for which they need help. We not only want to teach them to read a textbook, but also how to use it as a resource.

1-3

EXPLICIT FORMULAS FOR SEQUENCES

Sequences appear early in this book because (1) they provide a good vehicle for reviewing subscripts, which are needed; (2) they involve formulas; (3) they are examples of functions (although functions are not mentioned in Lesson 1-3); (4) they are important in *developing and identifying patterns,* which is an effective problem-solving strategy; and (5) they are interesting to students. Also, we feel it important to introduce some material early in the book that is new to students yet not too difficult.

An algebraic description of sequences will be new to most students. However, given a sequence, most students will be able to find the next term in the pattern. Most students probably have seen subscripted variables, such as x_1, y_1, x_2, y_2, as coordinates of points or in the formula for the slope of a line. However, they may not be familiar with the concept of a subscript as a counter or as a way to identify a particular item.

1-4

RECURSIVE FORMULAS FOR SEQUENCES

Lesson 1-4 provides a second day of work with sequences and subscripted variables. It also illustrates how the same idea can be described in more than one way.

Some sequences, such as the sequence of squares 1, 4, 9, 16, 25, . . . , are more easily described with explicit formulas for the nth term ($s_n = n^2$). Some, such as the Fibonacci sequence noted in the lesson, are more easily described using recursive formulas.

When an early term in a sequence is desired, it is usually easier to use a recursive pattern. When looking for a later term in a sequence, the explicit formula is usually quicker. Computers generally use recursive formulas when they generate sequences.

1-5

ALGEBRA AS A MATHEMATICAL SYSTEM

The formal treatment of mathematical reasoning introduced in this lesson is continued in the next few lessons of Chapter 1 and also as a theme throughout the book. Students are expected to follow mathematical arguments and to explain the processes undertaken from one step to the next. However, we do not expect students to memorize the names of postulates; thus, you might consider letting students have access to the names of the postulates during tests.

1-6

REASONING IN ALGEBRA

Students must be able to distinguish between a conjecture and a proof in order to appreciate the latter. Also, students must know how to *disprove* something by means of a counterexample.

This lesson connects two important themes from students' earlier work in algebra and geometry: the solving of equations and the notion of if-then statements. Students may be surprised to see them together. The idea is to stress the essential unity of mathematics by illustrating that the same logic is found in all branches of the subject.

1-7

SOLVING EQUATIONS

Earlier texts of this series stressed the solving of linear equations, and mastery was expected at that time. However, some students still need more practice. We try to distribute the practice in order to provide a

continual review and introduce other important concepts.

This lesson is designed to show continual use of the properties and applications associated with solving linear equations. In particular, the examples and exercises show that these properties work as well with fractions and decimals (numbers that often appear in applications) as they do with the integers students more commonly see.

1-8

REWRITING FORMULAS

This lesson emphasizes the importance of solving a formula for a variable other than the original isolated variable. Students need to understand that such manipulations make subsequent evaluations of the formula much easier.

The lesson also provides another day to work on solving open sentences. The additional practice enables students to feel more at ease with this type of problem.

1-9

SOLVING INEQUALITIES

In this book, inequalities are often discussed along with equations. We do this for two major reasons. First, there are analogies between equation-solving and inequality-solving which help students to understand them both. Second, the application situations which lead to equations can almost always lead in the same way to inequalities. For instance, in Example 3, if we ask when the man's weight will be 200 lb, an equation arises. If we ask when the weight will be 200 lb *or less,* an inequality arises.

The content of this lesson should not be new to students. Solving and graphing the solutions of inequalities are topics that most students have seen in a previous algebra course. Translating application problems into inequalities, however, may be new to students who have not had previous courses in this series.

CHAPTER 1

We recommend 12 to 14 days for this chapter: 9 to 10 on the lessons; 1 for the Progress Self-Test; 1 or 2 for the Chapter Review; and 1 for a Chapter test. (See the Daily Pacing Chart on page 2A.) If you spend more than 14 days on this chapter, you are moving too slowly. Keep in mind that each lesson includes Review questions to help students firm up content studied previously.

USING PAGES 2–3
Select a few students to read the text on page 2. Point out that the development of an algebraic notation was essential to the development of the subject itself.

Help students to understand that algebra has a long history, and that it is still being studied and developed today by research mathematicians working in universities and elsewhere. Point out the list of lesson headings so that students have an idea of what they will be studying in Chapter 1.

The Language of Algebra

*René Descartes
(seventeenth century)*

Pythagoras (sixth century B.C.)

Pierre de Fermat (seventeenth century)

2

*Babylonian stone tablet
with cuneiform writing
(ninth century B.C.)*

Problems that today we solve using algebra were considered by the Babylonians as long ago as 1700 B.C. But neither they nor the Greeks of classical times possessed a language of algebra. To the Greeks, an unknown quantity was imagined as a length. They thought of an unknown quantity multiplied by another as the area of a rectangle. So when today we write

$$x(x + 4),$$

they would write "the rectangle contained by a line segment and the segment increased by 4."

Slowly over the years the writing was shortened and shortened. By A.D. 850 the Arabs were putting problems in numerical terms. The word "algebra" is derived from the Arabic "al jabr" which means, literally, "the bone setting" or "putting back in place." This described the way the Arabs solved problems. For instance, to find

> the number, which when it is
> multiplied by 15, gives 180,

they would divide by 15 (put the multiplication back in place).

In the years 1200–1600, Arabic manuscripts were discovered by Europeans and, in the last half of that time period, a rebirth (the French word is "renaissance") of learning occurred in Europe. In 1591, the French mathematician François Viète (1540–1603) wrote a book, *Introduction to the Analytic Art,* in which he established the symbols and principles of what we call algebra.

Over the next 200 years, others refined algebra. By 1607, René Descartes and Pierre Fermat had graphed solutions to equations. In 1770, Leonhard Euler wrote his book *Elements of Algebra*, which became the standard textbook for many years for Europeans wishing to learn algebra. Many symbols Euler used in his book, like π and $\sin x$, became the standard symbols of algebra.

Today algebra is truly a universal language. Even in China, Japan, and the Soviet Union, large countries where written alphabets differ from English, algebra is taught using Latin letters like a and b and x and y and the same operation signs we use. In fact, a Soviet mathematics textbook for 8-year-olds, introducing letters for variables, states, "In mathematics, we use Latin letters, for example x, to denote unknown numbers. Memorize four other letters: *Aa, Bb, Cc, Dd.*"

This chapter reviews some of the basic ideas of algebra you have studied in previous years. It discusses sequences, one idea that may be new to you, in quite a bit more detail.

RESOURCES
■ Lesson Master 1-1

TEACHING NOTES

Reading Reading mathematics will be a new expectation for many students. To read well, a student must read carefully, watching for important terms and symbols. If you are concerned about your students' abilities to read, you could begin by having students read this lesson aloud. You may want to go around the class having students read one short paragraph each.

We strongly recommend *not* discussing this lesson until students have had an opportunity to read it in class and try the questions on their own. Point out that there are questions referring to the opening pages of the chapter (pages 2–3).

For more information on reading skills, see *General Teaching Suggestions: Reading* on page T37 of the Teacher's Edition.

LESSON

1-1

Describing Situations with Algebra

The language of algebra is based on numbers and variables. A **variable** is a symbol that can be replaced by any one of a set of numbers or other objects. When numbers and variables are combined, the result is called an **algebraic expression,** or simply an **expression.**

An expression using the variable r and the numbers π and 2 is πr^2.

In order to apply algebra, a person must be able to write algebraic expressions to describe situations.

One way to describe situations by algebra is by direct translation. For instance, you know that "the sum of m and n" is translated as "$m + n$," and "twice x" is translated as "$2x$."

You must be careful when translating directly. For instance, the phrase "less than" sometimes means the operation of subtraction, and sometimes it means the inequality symbol "$<$." It can be confused also with the single word "less." Here are examples.

Verbal Expression	Mathematical Expression
5 is less than 8	$5 < 8$
5 less than 8	$8 - 5$
5 less 8	$5 - 8$

Note how multiplication, subtraction, and an inequality are used to translate the following situation.

Example 1 Translate this sentence into algebra.
12 less than twice a number is less than five times the number.

Solution Let $n =$ the number.
Translate the sentence part by part.

12 less than   twice a number   is less than   five times the number

$$2n - 12 \qquad\qquad < \qquad\qquad 5n$$

An algebraic sentence (such as $2n - 12 < 5n$) consists of expressions related with a verb. The most common verbs in algebra are $=$ (is equal to), $<$ (is less than), $>$ (is greater than), $\leq$ (is less than or equal to), $\geq$ (is greater than or equal to), $\neq$ (is not equal to), and $\approx$ (is approximately equal to). In the sentence in Example 1, the two expressions $2n - 12$ and $5n$ are related by the verb $<$.

A second way to describe situations with algebra is to find a pattern.

4

Error Analysis If students have difficulty with the symbolic translations of *is less than, less than,* and *less,* discuss some of the following clues: *Is less than* is a verb expression and requires a mathematical verb, $<$. *Less than* translates numbers or variables in the opposite of their order of appearance; we translate *6 less than 8* as $8 - 6$. *Less* is another way to say *minus;* thus, 6 *less* 8 could also be read *6 minus 8* and translated $6 - 8$. Here are some additional examples.

Verbal expression	Mathematical expression
12 less *n*	$12 - n$
9 is less than *n*.	$9 < n$
8 less than *n*	$n - 8$
15 less 26	$15 - 26$
15 less than 26	$26 - 15$
15 is less than 26.	$15 < 26$

ADDITIONAL EXAMPLES
1. Translate each sentence into algebra.
a. Three less than two times a number is 10 more than the same number.
$2n - 3 = n + 10$
b. Six more than a number is less than 5 times that number.
$6 + n < 5n$

2. Allen has $75 in the bank. If each month he saves $25, how much money will he have after *m* months (neglecting interest)?
$75 + m \cdot 25$

3. Express the cost of *w* pencils at *b* cents per pencil.
bw

Example 2 Kim has a tape collection now containing 40 tapes. If Kim adds 2 tapes each week, how many tapes will she have after *w* weeks?

Solution Make a table. Notice in this table that the arithmetic is not carried out. That would hide the pattern.

Weeks from now	Tapes
1	$40 + 1 \cdot 2$
2	$40 + 2 \cdot 2$
3	$40 + 3 \cdot 2$
4	$40 + 4 \cdot 2$

The number in the left column, which gives the number of weeks, is always in a particular slot in the expressions at right. That shows a pattern:

w	$40 + w \cdot 2$

Kim will have $40 + w \cdot 2$, or $40 + 2w$ tapes after *w* weeks.

Check: To check the expression $40 + 2w$, pick a value for *w* not in the table. We pick $w = 10$, indicating 10 weeks from now. Then $40 + 2w = 40 + 2 \cdot 10 = 60$. This is correct. After 10 weeks there would be the 40 Kim started with and 20 more tapes, for a total of 60.

A third way to describe situations by algebra is to recognize common uses of the operations of arithmetic. These uses are summarized by models. A **model for an operation** is a pattern that describes many of the uses of that operation. For instance, one model for subtraction is "take-away." You learned these models starting in first grade, but you may not have given them names. A list of models is given in Appendix A. You do not need to know the names, but you need to be able to choose the correct operation.

Questions 18–26: En-
courage students who are
having difficulty with these
questions to substitute
number values for the
variables. For example,
Question 19 could read:
Mrs. Bell is 37 years old. A
friend is 4 years older.
Clearly, then, the friend is
37 + 4, or 41 years old, and
the operation is addition.

**Making Connections for
Questions 28–32:** These
questions deal with topics
from geometry. At appro-
priate times, geometric
concepts, examples, and
applications are used
throughout the text. The
names for the various polygons will be helpful in
reading Lesson 1-2. Students
usually enjoy learning how
algebra and geometry are
connected. Those students
who have not completed a
geometry course will need
additional help with the geometric content of this book.

Remind students that se-
lected answers to odd-
numbered questions are
provided in the back of the
book.

Example 3 Express the cost of y cans of orange juice at x cents per can.

Solution 1 Use a special case. 5 cans at 40¢ per can would cost
$2.00. That suggests multiplication. So y cans at x cents per can will
cost xy cents.

Solution 2 Recognize the model. The unit "cents per can," which can
be written as $\frac{\text{cents}}{\text{can}}$, signals a *rate*. The pattern of the *rate-factor
model* for multiplication is y cans at $x\frac{\text{cents}}{\text{can}}$. The result is xy cents.

Check Working with the units gives you a way to check your work.
The unit of y is cans. So the unit of xy is the "product" of the units.

$$x\frac{\text{cents}}{\cancel{\text{can}}} \cdot y \ \cancel{\text{cans}} = xy \text{ cents}$$

The units work out.

As Example 3 shows, there is often more than one way to translate
situations into algebra. You should strive to learn a variety of ways.
The expression you get a second way can be used to check the
expression you got the first way.

Questions

Covering the Reading

These questions check your understanding of the reading. If you cannot
answer a question, you should go back to the reading to help you find an
answer.

1. Who established the principles of what today we call algebra, and
   when? **Francois Viète; 1591**

2. The word "algebra" comes from the __?__ language and means __?__.
   Arabic; the bone setting

3. $2\pi r$ is an example of an __?__. **expression**

4. Name any variables in $2\pi r$. **r**

5. *True or false* Algebraic expressions in Japanese books use letters of
   the Latin alphabet. **True**

In 6–8, translate into an algebraic expression or sentence.

6. p less than y **y − p**

7. p is less than y. **p < y**

8. 7 less than three times a number is less than the number. **3x − 7 < x**

9. A person now owns 25 tapes and is buying 3 tapes a week. How many will there be after w weeks?   **25 + 3w**

10. Answer Question 9 if the person now owns N tapes.   **N + 3W**

11. A pattern that describes many of the uses of an operation is called a(n) __?__ .   **model**

12. Give an example of a rate unit.   **cents per can**

13. **a.** What is the cost of 10 cans of orange juice costing c cents per can?   **10c¢**
    b. What is the cost of m cans of orange juice costing c cents each?   **mc¢**

In 14–16, translate into words.   **See margin.**

14. $\leq$ 15. $\neq$ 16. $\approx$

17. Give an example of an algebraic sentence.   **See margin.**

Applying the Mathematics

These questions extend the content of the lesson. You should take your time, study the examples and explanations, try a variety of methods and check your answers with the ones in the back of the book.

In 18–22, tell whether the answer is $x + y$, $x - y$, xy, $\frac{x}{y}$, or $\frac{y}{x}$.

18. You give a friend y dollars. You had x dollars. How much do you have left?   **x − y**

19. Mrs. Bell is y years old. A friend is x years older. How old is the friend?   **x + y**

20. You drove x miles in y hours. What was your rate?   **x/y**

21. You buy x granola bars at y cents per bar. What is the total cost?   **xy¢**

22. A picture of a building is x times actual size. The height of the building is y. What is the height of the building in the picture?   **xy**

In 23–26, write an expression to describe each situation.

23. T liters of a fluid are taken away from a solution that has S liters in it. How much is left?   **S − T liters**

24. Barb is B years old. Her younger sister Yvette is Y years old. How many times as old as Yvette is Barb?   **B/Y**

25. Liz has E eggs and buys F eggs. How many eggs does she have altogether?   **E + F eggs**

26. Ben has been in office Y years. Bess has been in office $Y + 5$ years. How much longer than Ben has Bess been in office?   **5 years**

7

EXTENSION
Students can be encouraged
to find other examples of the
models for operations (see
Question 33). You might
consider using **small
groups** for this activity.
Divide the class into four
groups, each of which is assigned the task of finding
situations leading to each
operation. Then have the
groups present their examples to their classmates. In
this way, students get a
broad picture of situations
described by the models,
they see that the idea is not
difficult, and they are introduced to their classmates.

ADDITIONAL ANSWERS
29. quadrilateral

30. pentagon

31. hexagon

32. octagon

33.a. sample: You count x
boys and then count y girls
in a class. How many are
there in all?
b. sample: You have x
dollars and spend y dollars.
How much do you have
left?
c. sample: You read a
newspaper at x minutes
per page, and you have y
pages left to read. How
long will it take you?
d. sample: If there are x
girls and y boys in a class,
what is the ratio of girls to
boys?

34. sample: Descartes
invented analytic
geometry, wrote
philosophy, wrote
equations that defined
curves, and so on.

---

27. Dennis needs to fence the rectangular pasture shown in the figure below. One side borders a river and needs no fencing. He has 1150 ft of fence.

a. Let x be the width as labeled. Write an expression for the length, in terms of x. $1150 - 2x$ 27b) $(1150 - 2x)x$
b. Write an expression for the area of the pasture in terms of x.
c. Suppose the pasture must enclose at least 60,000 square feet. Write a sentence relating the area expression in part b to the area the pasture must enclose. $x(1150 - 2) \geq 60,000$

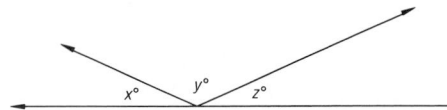
Review

Every lesson contains review questions to practice ideas you have studied earlier. If the idea is from an earlier course, the question is designated as being from a previous course.

28. *Multiple choice* Which sentence correctly relates the angle measures in the figure below? *(Previous Course)*   a
  (a) $x + y + z = 180$ (b) $x + y = 180 + z$
  (c) $y + z = x + y$ (d) none of these

In 29–32, give the name for the polygon with the indicated number of sides. *(Previous Course)*   See margin.
29. 4   **30.** 5   **31.** 6   **32.** 8

Exploration

33. Make up one example of a situation different from those in this lesson that can lead to each expression: See margin.
  a. $x + y$ **b.** $x - y$ **c.** xy **d.** $\dfrac{x}{y}$

34. In an encyclopedia, look up one of the mathematicians named on page 3. Find out some of the accomplishments of that person.   See margin.

8

LESSON 1-2

Formulas

Here is a sentence from the language of algebra:

$$d = \frac{n(n - 3)}{2}$$

This sentence tells you the number of diagonals d in a polygon having n sides. Some instances of this general relationship are drawn below.

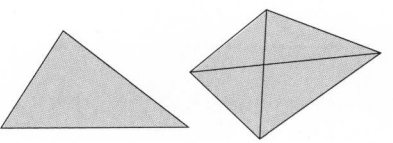 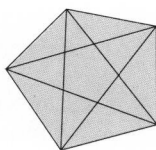 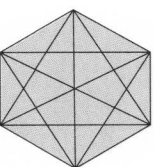

$n = 3, d = 0$ $n = 4, d = 2$ $n = 5, d = 5$ $n = 6, d = 9$

Before using a variable, you need to know what values it can have. The set of meaningful numbers or things that can be substituted for a variable is called the **replacement set** or **domain** for the variable. The replacement set for n in the formula above is the set of all possible numbers of sides a polygon can have. It would *not* make sense to substitute $n = 2$ into the formula, because there are no 2-sided polygons! Likewise $n = 4.7$ would be ridiculous, since you cannot have part of a side. So, possible values for n in the sentence

$$d = \frac{n(n - 3)}{2}$$

are natural numbers greater than 2. That is, $n = 3, 4, 5, \ldots$.
Here are some domains that have their own names:

the set of **natural numbers** or **counting numbers** $\{1, 2, 3, 4, 5, \ldots\}$;
the set of **whole numbers** $\{0, 1, 2, 3, 4, 5, \ldots\}$;
the set of **integers** $\{0, 1, -1, 2, -2, 3, -3, \ldots\}$;
the set of **rational numbers** (those numbers that can be represented by fractions) $\{\frac{2}{3}, 1\frac{9}{11}, -\frac{34}{10}, 239.6, 0.0004, $ and so on$\}$;
the set of **real numbers** (those numbers that can be represented by decimals) $\{1, 35$ million$, 2.34, \pi, 0, -7, \sqrt{5}, $ and so on$\}$;
the set of **positive real numbers** (those real numbers greater than zero).

Substituting for the variables and calculating a result is called **evaluating an expression.** In order to evaluate expressions you must use the rules for grammar and punctuation of the language of algebra. The following rules for order of operations are used to evaluate expressions worldwide.

LESSON 1-2

RESOURCES
■ Lesson Master 1–2

OBJECTIVES

Letter codes refer to the SPUR Objectives on page 2B.
A Evaluate formulas.
H State the domain for a variable in a given situation.

TEACHING NOTES

All students at this level have seen formulas. You might begin a discussion by asking students what formulas they remember from geometry. Area and/or volume formulas for common figures are usually mentioned first. This is a good time to acquaint students with the Geometry Appendix at the end of the book.

This is a good time to discuss the fact that the algebraic order of operations is built into many scientific calculators. It may be necessary to teach students how to use the power function and parentheses buttons on their calculators. Explicit mention of calculators is made in the next lesson.

Reading When reading a hierarchical list such as the number domains, students should stop their reading to ask: Is there a natural number that is not a whole number? (no) Is there a real number that is not positive? (yes, zero or any negative number) Encourage students to continue asking questions of this type as they read the lesson.

Rules for Order of Operations:

1. Perform operations within parentheses ( ), brackets [ ], or other grouping symbols like square root symbols or fraction bars, from the inner set of symbols to the outer set. Use the order given in Rules 2, 3, and 4.
2. Take powers.
3. Multiply and divide in order from left to right.
4. Add and subtract in order from left to right.

An **equation** is a sentence stating that two expressions are equal. A **formula** is a sentence stating that a single variable is equal to an expression with one or more different variables on the other side. Thus,

$$d = \frac{n(n-3)}{2}$$

is both an equation and a formula. But $a + b = b + a$ is an equation that is not a formula. Formulas are useful because they express important ideas with very few symbols and because they can be applied easily to many situations.

Example 1 Below is a dodecagon (12-sided polygon). How many diagonals does it have?

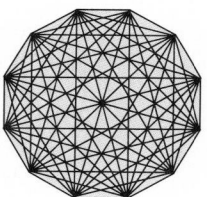

Solution Substitute $n = 12$ into the diagonal formula (given at the beginning of the lesson) every place n appears.

$$d = \frac{n(n-3)}{2}$$

Work in parentheses first.　$= \frac{12(12-3)}{2}$

$$= \frac{12(9)}{2}$$

$$d = 54$$

A dodecagon has 54 diagonals.

Using a formula is certainly quicker than trying to answer the question in Example 1 by counting the diagonals.

Here is an example using a science formula with more than one variable in the expression. It illustrates how to handle units in formulas.

■ ■ ■ ■ ■ ■ ■■ ■

Example 2 The formula $d = \frac{1}{2}gt^2$ tells how to find d, the distance an object has fallen during time t, when it is dropped in free fall from near Earth's surface. The variable g represents the acceleration due to gravity.

Near Earth's surface, $g = 32\dfrac{\text{ft}}{\text{sec}^2}$. About how far will a rock fall in 5 seconds if dropped close to Earth's surface?

Solution Substitute $g = 32\dfrac{\text{ft}}{\text{sec}^2}$ and $t = 5$ sec into the formula.

$$d = \tfrac{1}{2}gt^2$$

$$= \tfrac{1}{2}\left(32\,\dfrac{\text{ft}}{\text{sec}^2}\right)(5\text{ sec})^2$$

$$= \tfrac{1}{2}\left(32\,\dfrac{\text{ft}}{\text{sec}^2}\right)(5^2\text{ sec}^2)$$

$$= \left(16\,\dfrac{\text{ft}}{\text{sec}^2}\right)(25\ \cancel{\text{sec}^2})$$

$$d = 400\text{ ft}$$

In 5 seconds a rock dropped from near Earth's surface will fall about 400 feet.

Check The time units cancel out and you are left with feet. This is an appropriate measure for distance, so the unit checks. Does the distance seem reasonable to you?

Questions

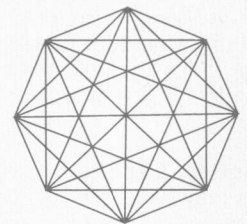

Covering the Reading

In 1–3, use the formula $d = \dfrac{n(n-3)}{2}$ for diagonals of polygons.

1. What do the variables n and d represent?
   n: number of sides; d: number of diagonals
2. What is a reasonable replacement set for n? $n = 3, 4, 5, \dots$

3. Find d when $n = 8$. Check your answer with a drawing. See margin.

4. Another name for replacement set is __?__. domain

5. **a.** Name a real number that is not an integer. samples: π, 5.8, $3\frac{1}{2}$
   b. Name a real number that is not a rational number.
      samples: π, $\sqrt{2}$, 0.10100100010000100000…

LESSON 1-2 Formulas 11

11

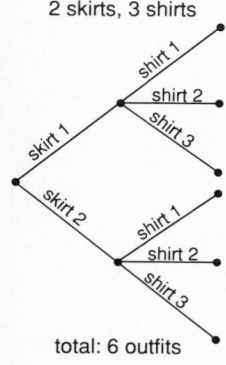

6. Which integers are not natural numbers?   integers ≤ 0

7. To evaluate $3 \cdot 5^{(4-2)}$, you must do these steps. Put them in order.
   a. Multiply.
   b. Take the power.
   c. Do the subtraction.   c, b, a

In 8 and 9, refer to Example 2. How far will a rock fall in four seconds:

8. if it is dropped from near Earth's surface?   256 ft

9. if it is dropped from near the surface of the moon, where
$g = 5.3\dfrac{\text{ft}}{\text{sec}^2}$?   42.4 ft

In 10–12, (a) Is the sentence an equation? (b) Is the sentence a formula?

10. $A = \pi r^2$ **11.** $6s^2 > 0$ **12.** $2(L + W) = 2L + 2W$
   a) yes b) yes   a) no b) no   a) yes b) no

Applying the Mathematics

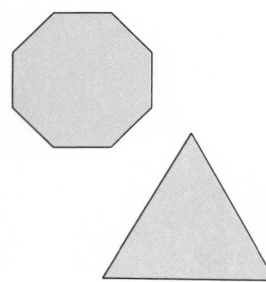

In 13 and 14, use the formula $T = 180(n - 2)$. Here T is the total number of degrees in the interior angles of a polygon with n sides. (Note: Formulas from geometry are summarized in Appendix B.)

13. What is the domain of n? $n = 3, 4, 5, \ldots$

14. Find the total number of degrees in the interior angles of an octagon.
   1080°

15. The area A of an equilateral triangle with length of side s is given by the formula $A = \dfrac{s^2}{4}\sqrt{3}$.
   a. State the domain for s. $s > 0$
   b. Use your calculator to find the area of an equilateral triangle with sides of 10 cm. Round to the nearest tenth.   43.3 cm²

12

16. Young's formula, $C = \left(\dfrac{g}{g+12}\right)A$, has been used to decide how much medicine C to give to a child under age 13 when the adult dosage A is known. Here g is the child's age measured in years. Suppose an adult dosage for a medicine is 600 milligrams. What is the dosage for a 3-year-old according to this formula? (Caution! Do not apply this formula yourself. Medicines should be taken only under the supervision of a physician or pharmacist.)   **120 mg**

In 17–19, evaluate each expression with $x = 15$, $y = -3$, and $z = 2$.

17. $\dfrac{x}{y} - z^3$ **-13**   **18.** $\dfrac{x}{(y-z)^3}$ $-\dfrac{3}{25}$ **19.** $\dfrac{x}{y-z^3}$ $-\dfrac{15}{11}$

20. Evaluate $2x^{y-1}$ when $x = 3$ and $y = 4$.   **54**

Review
A lesson number following a review question indicates a place where the idea of the question is discussed.

In 21–25, tell whether the answer is $a + b$, $a - b$, $b - a$, ab, $\dfrac{a}{b}$, or $\dfrac{b}{a}$. *(Lesson 1-1)*

21. A football player gains a yards on one play and gains b yards on the next. What is the total gain? $a + b$

22. A football player gains a yards on one play and loses b yards on the next. What is the total gain? $a - b$

23. How many outfits can be made from b skirts and a shirts? ab

24. Spend b dollars to buy a grams of perfume. What is the cost per gram? $\dfrac{b}{a}$

25. There are a juniors and b sophomores. How many more sophomores than juniors are there? $b - a$

In 26 and 27, let n be the number. *(Lesson 1-1)*

26. A number is doubled. The product is decreased by 7. The difference is divided by 2. What is the final value? $\dfrac{(2n-7)}{2}$

27. Translate into algebra: six greater than a number is less than sixty. $n + 6 < 60$

Exploration
28. Using the digits 1, 9, 8, and 7 *in the given order*, along with the operations of addition, subtraction, multiplication, division and powering, and any parentheses you wish, and taking the opposite of any number or quantity, find a way to calculate every integer from 1 to 10. Two examples are:

$$1 = 1^{987} \text{ and } 2 = 1^9 + 8 - 7.$$

[Hint: Taking a square root is raising to the $\frac{1}{2}$ power.]   **See margin.**

LESSON 1-2   *Formulas*   **13**

FOLLOW-UP

MORE PRACTICE
For more questions on SPUR Objectives, use *Lesson Master 1-2,* shown below.

EXTENSION
The following formulas estimate the height h (in centimeters) of an adult human in terms of the length F of the femur (thigh) bone (in centimeters).
   male: $h = 69.089 + 2.238F$
   female: $h = 61.412 + 2.37F$
Such equations are used in detective work by forensic (police) scientists and archaeologists to estimate height based on bone size. You and your students might examine a femur or skeleton from a biology teacher to test the accuracy of these formulas. Another activity would be to have students measure the distance from a knee to their hip joint to see how accurately the formulas measure their own heights.

NAME _____

LESSON **MASTER   1–2**
QUESTIONS ON **SPUR** OBJECTIVES

■ **SKILLS** *Objective A (See pages 53–56 for objectives.)*

1. In the formula $d = \dfrac{n(n-3)}{2}$, find d when $n = 15$.   **90**

2. In the formula $d = \dfrac{n(n-2)}{2}$, find d when $n = -7$.   **31.5**

3. If $h = \frac{1}{2}gt^2$, find h when $g = -9.8$ and $t = 4.5$.   **-99.225**

4. If $T = kPV$, find T when $k = 0.68$, $P = 2.5$, and $V = 200$.   **340**

5. If $x = \dfrac{2b}{a}$, find x if $a = -6.3$ and $b = 1.05$. $\dfrac{1}{3}$

6. Near the surface of the moon, the distance d that a rock falls in t seconds is $d = \frac{1}{2}gt^2$. If $g = 5.3 \frac{\text{ft}}{\text{sec}^2}$, find how far a rock falls in 5 seconds.   **66.25 ft**

■ **PROPERTIES** *Objective H*

7. For a polygon with n sides, $T = 180(n-2)$, where T is the total number of degrees in the polygon's interior angles. What is the domain of n?
   the set of integers greater than or equal to 3

8. P pieces of gold are placed in a treasure chest. State the domain of P.
   the set of positive integers

9. **a.** A cone of radius r and height h has volume $V = \frac{1}{3}\pi r^2 h$. State the domain of r and h.
   r and h are real numbers > 0.

   b. Find V to the nearest tenth if $r = 1.5$ in. and $h = 3.2$ in.
   7.5 cubic in.

2

RESOURCES
■ Lesson Master 1-3
▨ Visual for Teaching Aid 1:
   Pascal's Triangle. Use with
   Question 27.
▰ Computer Master 1
The Teaching Aids are available both as blackline masters and as overhead visuals.

OBJECTIVES

Letter codes refer to the SPUR Objectives on page 2B.
A Evaluate explicit formulas.
B Use computer programs to obtain terms of sequences given explicit formulas for them.
I Use sequences in real-world situations.

TEACHING NOTES

To help students learn the concepts of this lesson, you can use the following activities for the sequence 2, 4, 6, 8, 10, . . . , $2n$; $t_n = 2n$.
(a) Have students identify the third term (6) and then write it symbolically. ($t_3 = 6$) Do similar exercises with other terms.
(b) Ask students to provide the symbolic translation of "the fifth term of the sequence is 10." ($t_5 = 10$) Point out that the symbolic description is much more compact than words.
(c) Give students a statement such as $t_5 = 10$ and have them read it aloud. (*t* sub 5 equals 10, or the value of the fifth term is 10.)
(d) Indicate that t_n represents the general or nth term of the sequence. By giving n a value, a specific term of the sequence is indicated.

Explicit Formulas for Sequences

In mathematics, a **sequence** is an ordered list. Each item on the list is called a **term.** Many formulas come from observing the pattern of terms in a sequence.

Here are the first five terms of a sequence of figures, staircases made of unit squares

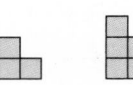 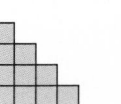 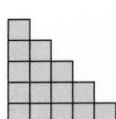 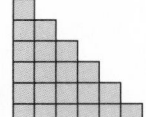

The number of unit squares in each staircase is a sequence of numbers:

$$3, 6, 10, 15, 21$$

There is a pattern, not so easy to see. Notice how the left and right columns are related.

Term	Number of squares
1st	$3 = \frac{2}{2} \cdot 3 = \frac{2 \cdot 3}{2}$
2nd	$6 = \frac{3}{2} \cdot 4 = \frac{3 \cdot 4}{2}$
3rd	$10 = \frac{4}{2} \cdot 5 = \frac{4 \cdot 5}{2}$
4th	$15 = \frac{5}{2} \cdot 6 = \frac{5 \cdot 6}{2}$
5th	$21 = \frac{6}{2} \cdot 7 = \frac{6 \cdot 7}{2}$

The general term is called the **nth term.** The number of squares can be given using n.

$$n\text{th} \qquad \frac{n + 1}{2} \cdot (n + 2) = \frac{(n + 1)(n + 2)}{2}$$

For instance, to find the 10th term in the sequence, let $n = 10$.

$$10\text{th} \qquad \frac{11 \cdot 12}{2}$$

There are 66 squares in the 10th staircase.

To represent the terms of a sequence, variables with subscripts are often used. A **subscript** is a number or variable written below and to the right of a variable. For instance, t_1, which is read "*t* sub 1," and t_n, which is read "*t* sub *n*," are **subscripted variables**. The subscript of t_1 is 1, and the subscript of t_n is n.

14

The subscript is often called an **index** because it *indicates* the position of the term in the sequence. In general, if t_n represents the nth term of the sequence, then the sentence "$t_1 = 3$" means that the first term of the sequence is 3. In the staircase sequence, $t_2 = 6$, $t_3 = 10$, $t_4 = 15$, $t_5 = 21$, and $t_n = \frac{(n + 1)(n + 2)}{2}$.

The sentence $t_n = \frac{(n + 1)(n + 2)}{2}$ is called an **explicit formula for the nth term** of the sequence 3, 6, 10, 15, 21, ... The domain for an explicit formula for the nth term of any sequence is the set of counting numbers. Explicit formulas are important because they can be used to calculate any term in the sequence by substituting a particular value of n.

■ ■ ■ ■ ■ ■ ■ ■■

Example 1   Consider the sequence of cubes of natural numbers:

$$1, 8, 27, 64, 125, ...$$

Suppose the subscripted variable t_n represents the nth term in this sequence.
a. What is the value of t_3?
b. Give an explicit formula for t_n.
c. Find the 30th term of this sequence.

Solution
a. The third term is t_3 Since the third term is known to be 27, $t_3 = 27$.
b. The cube of n is n^3, so $t_n = n^3$.
c. Substitute 30 for n on both sides of the explicit formula:

$$t_{30} = 30^3 = 27{,}000$$

The 30th term is 27,000.

When you substitute into a formula, as in part c of Example 1, you are calculating an *instance* of that formula.

Sequences arise naturally in many situations in science, business, finance, and other areas. The next example looks at a sequence in biology.

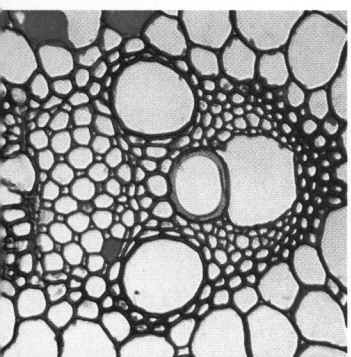

Reading   You may wish to pick phrases and sentences from this lesson and ask students to read them. For example, $t_n = \frac{(n + 1)(n + 2)}{2}$ is read "t sub n equals the quantity n plus one times the quantity n plus two all divided by 2." $t_n = n^3$ is read "t sub n equals n cubed" or "t sub n equals n to the third power." $P_n = 500(2)^{n-1}$ is read "P sub n equals 500 times 2 to the n minus 1 power."

Computer   Students may need some further discussion with the FOR . . . NEXT loop in the program of **Example 3**. This would be an excellent time to use a computer to demonstrate the BASIC programs. If this is not possible, you might want to run through the program of **Example 3** the way a computer would. Remind the students of the BASIC Appendix.
    For more information on computer skills, see *General Teaching Suggestions: Computers* on pages T42–T43 of the Teacher's Edition.

Example 2 A microbe reproduces by splitting to make 2 cells. Each of these cells then splits in half to make a total of 4 cells. Each of these splits to make a total of 8, and so on. Each splitting is called a *generation*. If a colony begins with 500 microbes, the equation

$$P_n = 500(2)^{n-1}$$

gives the number of microbes in the nth generation (assuming no microbes die).
Write:
a. the first term;
b. the fifth term of the sequence of populations of microbes given by this formula.

Solution Notice that the variable is in the exponent.
a. For the population in the first generation, substitute 1 for n in the formula.

$$P_1 = 500(2)^{1-1} = 500(2)^0 = 500(1) = 500$$

This checks with the given information: there are 500 microbes in the first generation.
b. For the population in the fifth generation, use $n = 5$ in the formula.

$$P_5 = 500(2)^{5-1} = 500(2)^4 = 500(16) = 8000$$

There are 8000 microbes in the fifth generation. You can check this by doubling the first population of 500 four times: $P_1 = 500$, $P_2 = 1000$, $P_3 = 2000$, $P_4 = 4000$, $P_5 = 8000$.

When you know an explicit formula for the nth term of a sequence, you can use a computer program to generate many terms of the sequence very quickly. Appendix C summarizes important features of the BASIC language. Below is a program using a FOR ... NEXT ... loop that prints the first ten perfect cubes. That is, it prints the terms generated by the formula

$$t_n = n^3$$

for integer values of n from 1 to 10. In line 20, the symbol ^ means "to the power." The semicolon at the end of line 20 (;) causes the terms to be printed in a row with only one space between successive terms.

```
10 FOR N = 1 TO 10
20    PRINT N ^ 3;
30 NEXT N
40 END
```

The computer will print:
■ 1 8 27 64 125 216 343 512 729 1000

16

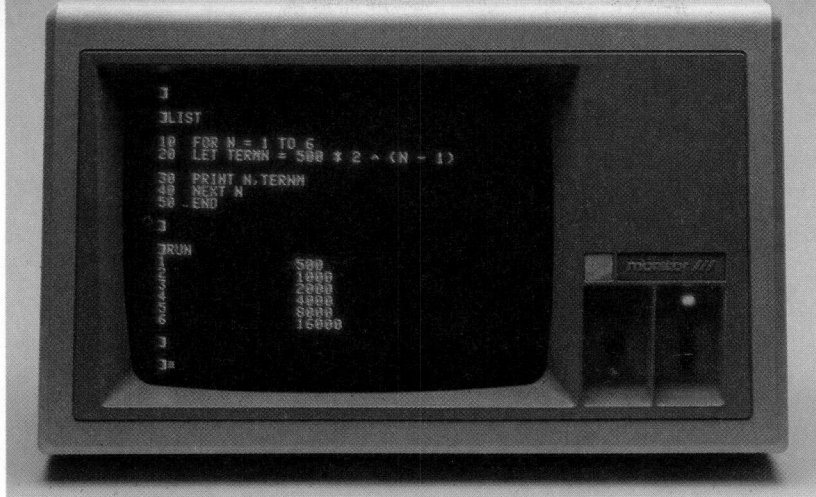

The above program can be modified to produce a given number of terms for any sequence when an explicit formula for the nth term is known. With a slight change, as shown in the following example, a computer can print out a table with both the index and the term of a sequence. Notice that variables in computer programs need not be single letters.

Example 3   What will this BASIC program print when run?

```
10 FOR N = 1 TO 6
20    LET TERMN = 500 * 2 ^ (N - 1)
30    PRINT N, TERMN
40 NEXT N
50 END
```

Solution   The FOR ... NEXT ... loop (lines 10–40) tells you that lines 20 and 30 are repeated for each integer from 1 to 6. Lines 20 and 30 tell you that the computer evaluates the formula $t_n = 500(2)^{n-1}$ and prints out the values of n and t_n each time it goes through the loop. The comma between N and TERMN in line 30 tells the computer to align the numbers in a table of two columns. Thus the computer prints the following.

1	500
2	1000
3	2000
4	4000
5	8000
6	16000

NOTES ON QUESTIONS
Questions 16–18: Students might be interested in deriving an explicit formula for each of these questions. The following pattern can be used: Martin's total salary for each year after the first year is his old salary plus a 5% raise, or 105% of his previous salary.

year	salary
1	18,000
2	18,000(1.05)
3	18,000(1.05)(1.05)
4	$18,000(1.05)^3$
.	
.	
.	
n	$18,000(1.05)^{n-1}$

Questions 24 and 25: Remind students that although algebraic order of operations is built into their calculators, they must still be careful of the format of their input. The key sequence

20 $\times$ 30 $\div$ 88 $-$

30 $=$ is quite different

from the key sequence 20

$\times$ 30 $\div$ (88

$-$ 30) $=$.

ADDITIONAL ANSWERS
3.

13.a.

. . . . .
. . . . .
. . . . .
. . . . .
. . . . .

21. sample:
```
10 FOR N = 1 TO 200
20    PRINT N * N
30 NEXT N
40 END
```

25. S is undefined for $N = 88$; S is negative for $N > 88$.

Questions

Covering the Reading

1. An ordered list of items is called a __?__. **sequence**

2. Each item in a sequence is called a __?__. **term**

In 3–5, refer to the sequence of staircases at the beginning of this lesson.

3. Draw the 6th term of the sequence. **See margin.**

4. Use the explicit formula for t_n to find the number of squares in the 6th staircase. **28**

5. List what will be printed when this program is run.

```
10 FOR N = 1 TO 8
20    PRINT (N+1)*(N+2)/2;
30 NEXT N
40 END    3, 6, 10, 15, 21, 28, 36, 45
```

6. The sentence $a_3 = 10$ is read __?__. **a sub 3 is 10.**

7. The general term of a sequence is called the __?__ term. **nth**

8. **a.** In the sentence $a_4 = 15$, 4 is called a __?__ or an __?__. **subscript, index**
   b. $a_4 = 15$ means that 15 is the __?__ term of the sequence.
   fourth

In 9–11, refer to Example 1.

9. Describe the sequence using words.
   the sequence of cubes of natural numbers

10. Give the explicit formula for the nth term. $t_n = n^3$

11. **a.** Which term of the sequence is 64? **fourth**
    b. What is the 64th term of the sequence? **262,144**

12. Refer to Example 2.
    a. Evaluate $P_n = 500(2)^{n-1}$ when $n = 7$. $P_7 = 32,000$
    b. How many microbes are in the 10th generation? **256,000**

Applying the Mathematics

13. **a.** Draw the next term in the sequence. **See margin.**

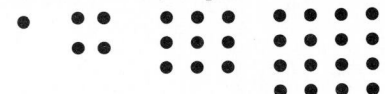

   b. Give a formula for S_n, the number of dots in the nth term.
   $S_n = n^2$

In 14 and 15, write the first four terms of the sequence with the given explicit formula.

14. $a_n = 5n - 3$ **2, 7, 12, 17**   15. $S_n = \dfrac{n(3n - 1)}{2}$ **1, 5, 12, 22**

In 16–18, Martin started with a company at an annual salary of $18,000. He gets an increase of 5% at the end of each year. Then the formula $s_n = 18,000(1.05)^{n-1}$ gives Martin's salary in his nth year.

16. Calculate the first three terms of the sequence. (Use your calculator.)
$18,000; $18,900; $19,845

17. At this growth rate, what would Martin's salary be in his 30th year with this company? $74,090.44

18. Complete this program so that it will print the first 30 terms of the sequence describing Martin's salary.

```
10 FOR N = 1 TO  ?
20    PRINT  ?
30 NEXT N
40 END    a) 30   b) 18000 * 1.05 ^ (N − 1)
```

Multiple choice In 19 and 20, which is a formula for the nth term of the sequence?

19. 2, 4, 8, 16, 32, ...   **c**
   (a) $t_n = 2n$ (b) $t_n = n^2$ (c) $t_n = 2^n$

20. 2, 9, 28, 65, 126, ...   **c**
   (a) $t_n = 7n - 5$ (b) $t_n = 7n^2 - 2$ (c) $t_n = n^3 + 1$

21. Write a BASIC program that prints the first 200 perfect squares.
   See margin.

Review

In 22 and 23, evaluate with $z = 0.5$, $x = -2$, $y = -6$. *(Lesson 1-2)*

22. $x + 3yz^2$ -6.5   **23.** $x + (9yz)^2$ 727

In 24 and 25, use the formula $S = \dfrac{20N}{88 - N}$. In this formula, N is the number of cars that pass an observation point in one minute, and S represents the average speed for heavy traffic (in mph).

24. Find the average speed of traffic if 30 cars pass the observation point per minute. *(Lesson 1-2)*   about 10 mph

25. Why are numbers greater than or equal to 88 not part of the domain of N? *(Lesson 1-2)*   See margin.

26. What percent of 80 is 56? *(Previous Course)*   70%

LESSON 1-3 Explicit Formulas for Sequences   19

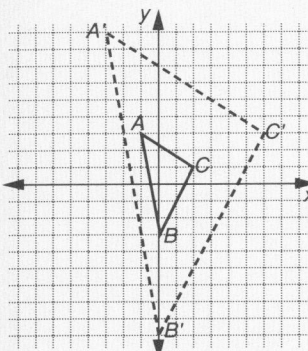
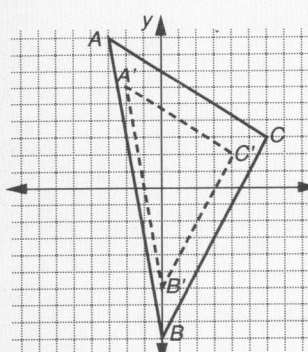
27. Graph the image of $\triangle ABC$ under a size change of magnitude 3. *(Previous Course)* **See margin.**

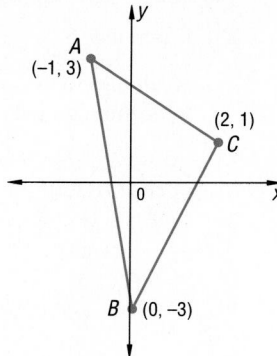

28. Graph the image of $\triangle ABC$ under a size change of magnitude $\frac{2}{3}$. *(Previous Course)* **See margin.**

Exploration

29. The array below is part of an infinite pattern called Pascal's Triangle. The first and last terms of each row are 1. Each other term, from the third row on, is the sum of the two diagonally above it.

```
              1
            1   1
          1   2   1
        1   3   3   1
      1   4   6   4   1
    1   5  10  10   5   1
    _   _   _   _   _   _   _
```

1, 6, 15, 20, 15, 6, 1 – – – – – – – –
1, 7, 21, 35, 35, 21, 7, 1
a. Write the next two rows in the array.
b. On what diagonals (oblique lines in the array) can you find the sequence of natural numbers? **2nd**
c. On what diagonals can you find the number sequence that comes from the staircase pattern at the start of this lesson? **3rd**

LESSON

1-4

Recursive Formulas for Sequences

Like computers, calculators can also be used to produce terms of a sequence quickly. For instance, to generate the sequence

$$2, 7, 12, 17, 22, \ldots,$$

you can begin with 2 and keep adding 5. Enter the following **key sequence** on your calculator and check that your **display** matches the one below.

Key Sequence   2 $\boxed{+}\, 5 \,\boxed{=}$ $\boxed{+}\, 5 \,\boxed{=}$ $\boxed{+}\, 5 \,\boxed{=}$ $\boxed{+}\, 5 \,\boxed{=}$

Sequence Displayed 2 7 12 17 22

When a sequence is generated by adding, subtracting, multiplying, or dividing by a constant, you should be able to write a key sequence for the numerical sequence.

■ ■ ■ ■ ■ ■ ■ ■

Example 1   Write a key sequence that generates the sequence

$$40, 20, 10, 5, 2.5, \ldots .$$

Solution   Notice that one way to construct this sequence is to start with 40 and divide by 2 to get the next term. One possible key sequence is

$$40 \ \boxed{\div}\, 2 \,\boxed{=} \ \boxed{\div}\, 2 \,\boxed{=} \ \boxed{\div}\, 2 \,\boxed{=} \ \boxed{\div}\, 2 \,\boxed{=}.$$

Check   Use your calculator. Verify that as the key sequence is entered, the calculator displays the sequence 40, 20, 10, 5, 2.5. Note that because dividing by 2 gives the same result as multiplying by 0.5, there is at least one more key sequence that could be used to generate this sequence.

LESSON 1-4

RESOURCES
■ Lesson Master 1-4
▣ Computer Master 1

OBJECTIVES

Letter codes refer to the SPUR Objectives on page 2B.
A Evaluate recursive formulas.
B Use computer programs to obtain terms of sequences given recursive formulas for them.

TEACHING NOTES

Although the vocabulary and symbolism for recursion will be new to most students, the concept is not. Students naturally describe sequences recursively, saying, for example, that "the sequence grows by adding 5."

Emphasize that recursive formulas have two parts: a starting point, and a rule for finding the nth term from one or more previous terms.

Reading   Some students may have difficulty with the notation for recursive formulas, because they have never seen an expression like $n-1$ in a subscript. Students need to be reminded that the subscript gives the position of the term. Stress that t_{n-1} is read "t sub n minus 1" and means the value of the term before t_n, and that t_{n-2} means the value of the term before t_{n-1}.

Notice that no explicit formula is given for the sequence of Example 1. Instead, you are told how to find each term of a sequence in terms of the preceding one. For instance, to find the 12th term of the sequence

$$40, 20, 10, 5, 2.5, \ldots,$$

you would divide the preceding term, the 11th term, by 2. This sequence is said to be formed *recursively*.

A **recursive formula** or **recursive definition** for a sequence is a set of statements that
a. indicates the first term (or first few terms) and
b. gives a rule for how the *n*th term is related to one or more of the previous terms.

A recursive definition for the sequence 40, 20, 10, 5, 2.5, ... is

$$\begin{cases} t_1 = 40 \\ t_n = \dfrac{t_{n-1}}{2}, \text{ for integers } n \geq 2. \end{cases}$$

The first line tells you that the first term of the sequence is 40. The second line tells you that the new term, t_n, is calculated by dividing the previous term, t_{n-1}, by 2. The brace at the left, {, indicates that both lines are needed for the recursive definition.

■ ■ ■ ■ ■ ■ ■■

Example 2 Evaluate the first four terms of the sequence defined by the recursive formula

$$\begin{cases} t_1 = 25 \\ t_n = t_{n-1} - 4 \text{ for } n \geq 2. \end{cases}$$

Solution The first term is given: $t_1 = 25$. The other terms are evaluated by applying the formula for t_n. That formula says that the *n*th term is found by subtracting 4 from the previous term. First we calculate t_2 from t_1. Let $n = 2$ in the formula for t_n.

$$t_2 = t_{2-1} - 4 = t_1 - 4 = 25 - 4 = 21$$

Then use t_2 to get t_3.

$$t_3 = t_{3-1} - 4 = t_2 - 4 = 21 - 4 = 17$$

Finally, use t_3 to find t_4.

$$t_4 = t_{4-1} - 4 = t_3 - 4 = 17 - 4 = 13$$

Thus the first four terms are 25, 21, 17, 13.

Recursive definitions are often used to generate terms of sequences on computers. However, in BASIC the subscripts for t_n and t_{n-1} are not necessary because of the way the LET statement works. For instance, the program below generates the first ten terms of the sequence defined recursively in Example 2.

```
10 LET T = 25
20 FOR N = 1 TO 10
30     PRINT T;
40     LET T = T - 4
50 NEXT N
60 END
```

Line 40 tells the computer to assign a new value of T that is 4 less than the old value of T. The computer will print this sequence:

■ 25 21 17 13 9 5 1 -3 -7 -11

Recursive and explicit formulas for sequences are useful at different times. An explicit formula lets you calculate a specific term in a sequence without having to know all the previous terms. For instance, when you evaluate the formula

$$t_n = \frac{(n + 1)(n + 2)}{2} \text{ for } n = 99, \text{ you find}$$

$$t_{99} = \frac{(99 + 1)(99 + 2)}{2} = \frac{100 \cdot 101}{2} = 5050.$$

That is, you can calculate that the 99th term in the staircase pattern at the start of Lesson 1-3 is 5050 without having to draw the pattern or write out all the previous terms.

A recursive formula is useful when the explicit formula is not known or is more difficult to use. For instance, an explicit formula for the **Fibonacci sequence,**

$$1, 1, 2, 3, 5, 8, 13, \ldots,$$

is quite complicated. However, by observing that each term from the third term on is the sum of the two previous terms, you can quickly calculate as many terms of the Fibonacci sequence as needed. A recursive definition for the Fibonacci sequence is

$$\begin{cases} t_1 = 1 \\ t_2 = 1 \\ t_n = t_{n-1} + t_{n-2}, \text{ for } n \geq 3. \end{cases}$$

Later in this course you will learn how to convert certain recursive formulas into explicit formulas for t_n, and vice versa. But for now you only need to be able to evaluate both types of formulas and find simple recursive formulas.

5. Write the sequence generated by the following BASIC program:

```
10 LET T = -7
20 FOR N = 1 TO 6
30     PRINT T;
40     LET T = 3 * T
50 NEXT N
60 END
```
-7, -21, -63, -189, -567, -1701

NOTES ON QUESTIONS
Questions 7 and 8: You may want to have students reverse the form of each question. After they have answered **Question 7**, ask them to give a mathematical statement of the formula; for **Question 8**, ask them to give a verbal statement.

Question 12a: Students may need to be reminded to use the correct order of operations when answering this question.

Question 14: The question gives the actual problem which in the 13th century led Leonardo of Pisa, known as Fibonacci, to study the sequence which now has his name.

Question 15: You may want to use this question as the basis for a discussion. Unless stated otherwise, the domain of *n* in a formula for a sequence is normally the set of natural numbers, because *n* corresponds to the ordinal numbers 1st, 2nd, 3rd, and so on. However, there are situations in which a sequence uses a different domain. For example, interest on an investment after *n* years can begin with $n = 0$. The zeroth term is the principal.

Question 18: This question reviews the distance and midpoint formulas which students should have had before this course. Since these formulas are used frequently in later lessons, it is worthwhile to spend some time using them now. Point out that the midpoint formula does nothing more than average the coordinates of the endpoints of a segment. It is often easier for students to recall the concept of averaging to find the coordinates of a midpoint than to remember a formula. In a similar fashion, it is helpful to stress the Pythagorean nature of the distance formula. This can be done by deriving the distance formula, using the Pythagorean Theorem.

Covering the Reading

In 1 and 2, write the first four terms of the sequence generated by the instructions.

1. Begin with 24; repeatedly press $\boxed{\times}$ 1.5 $\boxed{=}$. **24, 36, 54, 81, 121.5**

2. Begin with 4; repeatedly press $\boxed{-}$ 9 $\boxed{=}$. **4, -5, -14, -23, -32**

In 3–5, use the sequence 40, 20, 10, 5, ...

3. Write calculator instructions as in Questions 1 and 2, using multiplication to generate the first four terms. **40 $\boxed{\times}$ .5 $\boxed{=}$ $\boxed{\times}$ .5 $\boxed{=}$ $\boxed{\times}$ .5 $\boxed{=}$**

4. The 10th term of this sequence is .078125. What is the 11th term?
.0390625

5. Complete this program in BASIC so it will print the first 11 terms when run.

```
10 LET T = 40
20 FOR N = 1 TO a. __?__    11
30    PRINT T;
40    LET T = b. __?__    T/2 or T *.5
50 NEXT N
60 END
```

6. Suppose t_n is a term in a sequence. What symbol is used to represent the previous term? **t_{n-1}**

In 7 and 8, write the first five terms of the sequence defined by the recursive formula.

7. The first term is 7; each term after the first is 10 more than the previous term. **7, 17, 27, 37, 47**

8. $\begin{cases} t_1 = 5 \\ t_n = 3t_{n-1}, \text{ for } n \geq 2. \end{cases}$ **5, 15, 45, 135, 405**

9. Write the next two terms in the Fibonacci sequence after 13.
21, 34

10. *Multiple choice* Which recursive formula states that the *n*th term is four less than the previous term? **c**
    (a) $t_n = 4 - t_n$ (b) $t_n = 4 - t_{n-1}$
    (c) $t_n = t_{n-1} - 4$ (d) $t_n = t_{n+1} - 4$

Applying the Mathematics

11. Consider the sequence that begins 100, 94, 88, 82, 76, ... **See margin.**
    a. The first term is __?__.
    b. From the second term on, each term is __?__ the previous term.
    c. Write a recursive formula for the sequence.
    d. Write a BASIC program that will print the first 20 terms.
    See margin.

12. a. Write the first four terms of the sequence defined by $x_n = 3(4)^{n-1}$.
   b. Write the first four terms of the sequence defined by
$$\begin{cases} y_1 = 3 \\ y_n = 4y_{n-1}, \; n \ge 2. \end{cases}$$ **3, 12, 48, 192**
   c. *True or false* The sequences defined in parts a and b have the same terms. **true**

13. What will be printed when this program is run?

```
10 LET T = 1
20 FOR N = 1 TO 12
30    PRINT T;
40    LET T = T + (2 * N + 1)
50 NEXT N
60 END    1 4 9 16 25 36 49 64 81 100 121 144
```

14. Suppose that a pair of rabbits one month old cannot produce baby rabbits, but every month later they produce a new pair of rabbits. Suppose that each new pair of rabbits behaves in the same way, and that none of the rabbits dies. Let r_n represent the number of pairs of rabbits at the start of the nth month. At the beginning of the first month, there is one pair of rabbits, i.e., $r_1 = 1$. Similarly, $r_2 = 1$. But $r_3 = 2$ because the original pair of rabbits produces a new pair of rabbits. Find the following:
   a. r_4 **3** **b.** r_5 **5** **c.** r_6 **8** **d.** a recursive formula for r_n
$$r_1 = 1, r_2 = 1, r_n = r_{n-1} + r_{n-2}, n > 3$$

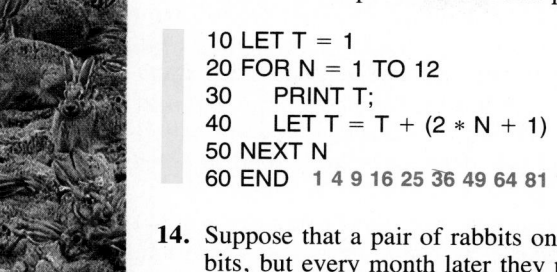

Review

15. What is the domain for n in a formula that finds the nth term in a sequence? *(Lesson 1-3)* {1, 2, 3, ...}

16. *True or false* When a computer reads a FOR statement it immediately jumps to the NEXT statement, skipping intermediate lines. *(Lesson 1-3)* **false**

17. Solve: $3 = 5p - 11$. *(Previous course)* **2.8**

18. Recall that the distance between two points with coordinates (x_1, y_1) and (x_2, y_2) is $\sqrt{(x_1 - x_2)^2 + (y_1 - y_2)^2}$, and the midpoint of the line segment joining them has coordinates $\left(\dfrac{x_1 + x_2}{2}, \dfrac{y_1 + y_2}{2}\right)$. *(Previous course)*
   a. Find the distance between (-4, -7) and (8, -2). **13**
   b. Find the coordinates of the midpoint of the line segment with endpoints at (-4, -7) and (8, -2). **(2, -4.5)**

Exploration

19. a. Give the first five terms of the sequence with the formula
$$t_n = n^4 - 10n^3 + 35n^2 - 49n + 24.$$ **1, 2, 3, 4, 29**
   b. What lesson should you learn from the answer to part a?
   Never assume the next term in a sequence. Even the simplest pattern may not continue.

LESSON 1-4 Recursive Formulas for Sequences **25**

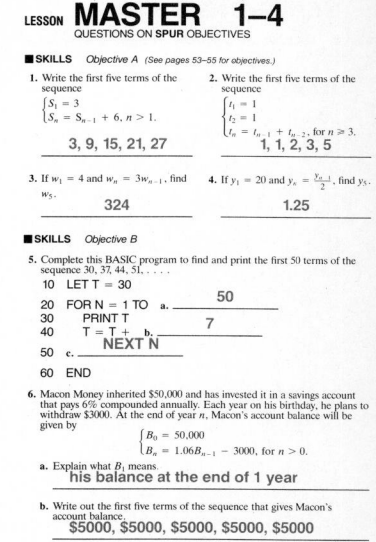

NAME _____

LESSON **MASTER 1–4**
QUESTIONS ON **SPUR** OBJECTIVES

■ **SKILLS** *Objective A (See pages 53–55 for objectives.)*

1. Write the first five terms of the sequence
$\begin{cases} S_1 = 3 \\ S_n = S_{n-1} + 6, n > 1. \end{cases}$
3, 9, 15, 21, 27

2. Write the first five terms of the sequence
$\begin{cases} t_1 = 1 \\ t_2 = 1 \\ t_n = t_{n-1} + t_{n-2}, \text{ for } n \ge 3. \end{cases}$
1, 1, 2, 3, 5

3. If $w_1 = 4$ and $w_n = 3w_{n-1}$, find w_5. **324**

4. If $y_1 = 20$ and $y_n = \frac{y_{n-1}}{2}$, find y_5. **1.25**

■ **SKILLS** *Objective B*

5. Complete this BASIC program to find and print the first 50 terms of the sequence 30, 37, 44, 51, ...
```
10 LET T = 30
20 FOR N = 1 TO  a. ___50___
30    PRINT T
40    T = T +  b. ___7___
       NEXT N
50 c. ___
60 END
```

6. Macon Money inherited $50,000 and has invested it in a savings account that pays 6% compounded annually. Each year on his birthday, he plans to withdraw $3000. At the end of year n, Macon's account balance will be given by
$\begin{cases} B_0 = 50,000 \\ B_n = 1.06B_{n-1} - 3000, \text{ for } n > 0. \end{cases}$
   a. Explain what B_1 means. **his balance at the end of 1 year**
   b. Write out the first five terms of the sequence that gives Macon's account balance. **$5000, $5000, $5000, $5000, $5000**
   c. After 5 years, how much has his inheritance appreciated? **$0**

4   Advanced Algebra © Scott, Foresman and Company

RESOURCES
- Lesson Master 1-5
- Quiz for Lessons 1-1 Through 1-5
- Visual for Teaching Aid 2 can be used for an initial discussion of the field properties of addition and multiplication of real numbers.

The Teaching Aids are available both as blackline masters and as overhead visuals.

OBJECTIVES

Letter codes refer to the SPUR Objectives on pages 2B.

C Simplify expressions using field properties, definitions, or theorems derived from the Distributive Property.

G Identify justifications in mathematical arguments.

TEACHING NOTES

Reading Stress that when reading a property that begins "For all *a*, *b*, and *c* . . . ," students should substitute particular values for *a*, *b*, and *c* in the statement of the property to help them understand the meaning of the property. For example, in the definition of subtraction, a student might first let $a = 2$ and $b = 3$. The definition would yield $2 - 3 = 2 + -3$. Then, a student might let $a = -3.8$ and $b = -2.1$, in which case the instance is $-3.8 - (-2.1) = -3.8 + (-(-2.1))$, which can be simplified (using the Opposite of an Opposite Property) to $-3.8 + 2.1$. Only by doing this can some students attain the reading comprehension needed.

LESSON 1-5

Algebra as a Mathematical System

Algebra is a language. It has expressions and verbs. The rules for order of operations are rules for writing and speaking; you can think of them as part of the grammar of algebra. Like other languages, algebra has *synonyms,* expressions that mean the same thing. For instance, for any numbers *a* and *b*, $5a + b = b + 5a$.

But algebra is different from other languages in that, like geometry, it is part of a mathematical system following strict rules of *logic*. Statements in a mathematical system are either assumed true or proved true. If they are assumed, they must be either **definitions** of terms, or **postulates,** or part of the given of a particular situation or problem. If they are proved, they are called **theorems.** Postulates, theorems, and definitions are called **properties.**

You are familiar with the postulates of addition and multiplication of real numbers. You may have seen them many times. We list them here for reference. Notice that each postulate for addition corresponds to one for multiplication, except for the distributive property, which relates the two. These properties are customarily called the **field properties.**

Postulate 1: Field Properties of Addition and Multiplication of Real Numbers

For any real numbers *a*, *b*, and *c*:

	Addition	**Multiplication**
Closure:	$a + b$ is a real number.	ab is a real number.
Commutative:	$a + b = b + a$	$ab = ba$
Associative:	$a + (b + c) = (a + b) + c$	$a(bc) = (ab)c$
Identity:	There is a number 0 with $a + 0 = 0 + a = a.$	There is a number 1 with $a \cdot 1 = 1 \cdot a = a.$
Inverse:	There is a number -a with $a + -a = -a + a = 0.$	If $a \neq 0$, there is a number $\frac{1}{a}$ with $a \cdot \frac{1}{a} = \frac{1}{a} \cdot a = 1.$
Distributive:	$a(b + c) = ab + ac$	

The most important definitions in algebra are those of subtraction and division. Subtraction of real numbers is defined in terms of addition.

Definition:

For any real numbers *a* and *b*,
$$a - b = a + -b.$$

You use this definition when you subtract positive and negative numbers:

$$3 - {-4} = 3 + 4 = 7$$

Division of real numbers is defined in terms of multiplication.

Definition:

For real numbers a and b, with $b \neq 0$,

$$a \div b = a \cdot \frac{1}{b}.$$

You use this definition when you divide fractions:

$$\frac{2}{3} \div \frac{4}{5} = \frac{2}{3} \cdot \frac{5}{4} = \frac{10}{12}$$

As for theorems, you know many of them, though when you learned them it is likely they were not proved. Here are a few of the more often used theorems.

Some Theorems of Algebra

Multiplication Property of 0:	For all a, $a \cdot 0 = 0$.
Multiplication Property of -1:	For all a, $a \cdot {-1} = {-a}$.
Opposite-of-an-Opposite Property: (Op-Op Property)	For all a, $-(-a) = a$.

Many theorems are based on the distributive property. Here is a list of some of the more important ones. Each can be called the Distributive Property, but we give it a special name.

Some Theorems Derived from the Distributive Property

Opposite of a Sum:	For all b, and c:	$-(b + c) = {-b} + {-c}$.
Distributive Property of Multiplication over Subtraction:	For all a, b, and c:	$a(b - c) = ab - ac$.
Addition of Like Terms:	For all a, b, and c:	$ac + bc = (a + b)c$.
Addition of Fractions:	For all a, b, and $c \neq 0$:	$\frac{a}{c} + \frac{b}{c} = \frac{a + b}{c}$.

A **proof** is an argument showing that a statement is true. As in geometry, reasons or justifications in a proof must be postulates, definitions, or theorems. It would take too much space and time to prove all the theorems you have already learned in your study of algebra. But you should be able to supply reasons in a proof from among the properties listed above. Supplying reasons is called *justifying* the steps.

Students may be wary of the proofs in **Example 1** and in **Question 11**. Reassure them that at this point they are not expected to create an original algebraic proof, but they should be able to follow the reasoning of a proof and supply logical reasons for its statements.

ADDITIONAL EXAMPLES

1. Supply justifications in this proof of the Opposite of a Sum Theorem.

$$-(b + c) = -1(b + c) \quad \text{(i)}$$
$$= -1 \cdot b + -1 \cdot c \text{(ii)}$$
$$= -b + -c \quad \text{(iii)}$$

(i) Multiplication Property of –1
(ii) Distributive Property of Multiplication over Addition
(iii) Multiplication Property of –1

2. In two years, the value of a house worth N increased by 28%. Write an expression for the value of the house after two years.
$N + .28N = 1.28N$

Example 1 Supply justifications in this proof of the Addition-of-Fractions Theorem.

$$\frac{a}{c} + \frac{b}{c} = a \cdot \frac{1}{c} + b \cdot \frac{1}{c} \qquad \text{a.} \underline{\hspace{2cm}}$$

$$= \frac{1}{c} \cdot a + \frac{1}{c} \cdot b \qquad \text{b.} \underline{\hspace{2cm}}$$

$$= \frac{1}{c}(a + b) \qquad \text{c.} \underline{\hspace{2cm}}$$

$$= (a + b) \cdot \frac{1}{c} \qquad \text{d.} \underline{\hspace{2cm}}$$

$$= \frac{a + b}{c} \qquad \text{e.} \underline{\hspace{2cm}}$$

Solution

a. The left side has division of a and b by c. The right side converts the division to multiplication. This can be done because of the definition of division.

b. The factors in the multiplication are reversed. This is justified by the Commutative Property of Multiplication.

c. The factor $\frac{1}{c}$ is distributed over the other two. This is justified by the Distributive Property.

d. Again the order of factors is switched, another use of the Commutative Property of Multiplication.

e. Here multiplication by $\frac{1}{c}$ is converted to division by c, the definition of division.

You see the phrase "for any" or "for all" preceding the properties mentioned above. This phrase means that any number or *expression* may be substituted for a, b, or c. So even complicated looking expressions may be instances of these simple properties.

$$-(4x^2 - 14) = -4x^2 + 14 \qquad \text{instance of Opposite-of-a-Sum-Theorem and definition of subtraction}$$

$$\sqrt{6y} + -\sqrt{6y} = 0 \qquad \text{instance of Inverse Property of Addition}$$

$$\frac{a}{y - 4} + \frac{7 - b}{y - 4} = \frac{a + (7 - b)}{y - 4} \qquad \text{instance of Addition-of-Fractions Theorem}$$

The major use of these properties is to enable you to write expressions in simpler forms.

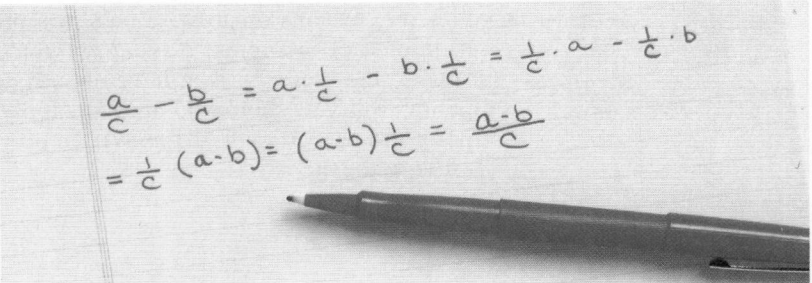

28

Example 2

Diane bought a ring for $P. After one year the ring increased in value 15%. Find an expression for the value of the ring after one year.

Solution The value of the ring increases 15% of the original price, or .15P. Add the increase in value to the original price; the value is then $P + .15P$. This expression can be simplified.

$$
\begin{aligned}
P + .15P &= 1P + .15P && \text{Multiplicative Identity} \\
&= (1 + .15)P && \text{Distributive Property} \\
&= 1.15p && 1 + .15 = 1.15
\end{aligned}
$$

The answer is 1.15P, or 1.15 times the original price. This is a simpler expression than $P + .15P$. It also shows that an increase of 15% is equivalent to multiplying by 1.15.

The purpose of a proof is to give a convincing argument. If you wish to be careful, put in all steps when simplifying. However, we encourage you to do steps in your head. The expert would go from $P + .15P$ to $1.15P$ in one step.

NOTES ON QUESTIONS
Questions 12 and 13:
Most students will remember the FOIL Theorem (though not necessarily this name) from their previous study of algebra. When discussing these questions, be sure to note that the FOIL theorem is really no more than a double application of the Distributive Property.

Questions

Covering the Reading

1. A postulate is a statement that is __?__ to be true, and a __?__ is a statement which can be proved. **assumed; theorem**

2. Sara N. Dippity now earns $W per year. She will receive a 5% raise next year. Find an expression for the amount of money she will earn next year. **1.05w**

In 3–5, give an instance of the theorem.

3. Distributive property of Multiplication over Subtraction
   sample: 6(5 − 4) = 6(5) − 6(4)
4. Op-Op Property
   sample: -(-5) = 5
5. Multiplication Property of -1
   sample: -10 · -1 = 10

In 6–8, an instance of what property is given?

6. $3 + -2y = 3 - 2y$ **definition of subtraction**

7. $4(x + 5) = 4x + 20$ **Distributive Property**

8. $463a + 281a = 744a$ **Distributive Property**

9. Supply justifications in this proof that the formula for the area of a trapezoid.

$$A = \tfrac{1}{2}h(b_1 + b_2),$$

can be rewritten as

$$A = \frac{h(b_1 + b_2)}{2}.$$

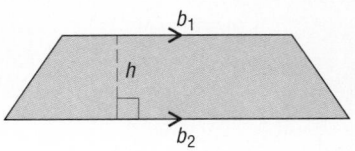

a. $\tfrac{1}{2}h(b_1 + b_2) = \tfrac{1}{2}[h(b_1 + b_2)]$ __?__ Assoc. Prop. of Mult.

b. $\qquad\qquad = [h(b_1 + b_2)] \cdot \tfrac{1}{2}$ __?__ Comm. Prop. of Mult.

c. $\qquad\qquad = \dfrac{h(b_1 + b_2)}{2}$ __?__ def. of division

10. **a.** What number is the additive identity? 0
    b. What number is the multiplicative identity? 1

11. The distributive property can be used to prove the FOIL Theorem: for all a, b, c, and d, $(a + b)(c + d) = ac + ad + bc + bd$.

    Supply all reasons in this proof.   See margin.

$$
\begin{aligned}
(a + b)(c + d) &= (a + b)c + (a + b)d & \text{(i)} \;\; \underline{\;?\;}\\
&= (ac + bc) + (ad + bd) & \text{(ii)} \;\; \underline{\;?\;}\\
&= ac + (bc + ad) + bd & \text{(iii)} \;\; \underline{\;?\;}\\
&= ac + (ad + bc) + bd & \text{(iv)} \;\; \underline{\;?\;}\\
&= ac + ad + bc + bd & \text{(v)} \;\; \underline{\;?\;}
\end{aligned}
$$

In 12 and 13, use the FOIL Theorem to rewrite the product as a sum.

12. $(x + 3)(y - 2)$
$xy - 2x + 3y - 6$

13. $(8x - 4)(3x + 9)$ $24x^2 + 60x - 36$

14. Show that the expression $\dfrac{180(n - 2)}{n}$ for the number of degrees in each angle of a regular n-gon can be written as $180 - \dfrac{360}{n}$.
See margin.

In 15 and 16, use the distributive property to rewrite the formulas.

15. $P = 2L + 2W$
$P = 2(L + W)$

16. $S = 2\pi rh + \pi r^2$ $S = \pi r(2h + r)$

In 17 and 18, use the distributive property to simplify each sequence formula.

17. $a_n = -1.2 + 2.4(n - 3)$ $a_n = 2.4n - 8.4$

18. $t_n = 4(3 - n) - 2(n - 8)$ $t_n = 28 - 6n$

In 19–21, simplify each expression.

19. $\dfrac{3x}{2y} + \dfrac{x}{2y}$ $\dfrac{2x}{y}$

20. $\tfrac{1}{3}(2y + 4y)$ $2y$

21. $(8x - 4) - (3x + 9)$
$5x - 13$

In 22–24, use the definition of division to simplify the complex fraction. *(Previous Course)*

22. $\dfrac{\frac{3}{4}}{\frac{4}{9}}$ $\frac{27}{16}$

23. $\dfrac{\frac{c}{5}}{\frac{c}{3}}$ $\frac{3}{5}$

24. $\dfrac{\frac{2a}{b}}{6a}$ $\frac{1}{36}$

25. What is the reciprocal of $\dfrac{1}{a}$? *a*

26. Solve. $5x - 8 = \frac{x}{2} + 7$ *(Previous Course)* $x = \frac{10}{3}$

27. Simplify. $\left(\dfrac{5}{x}\right)^0$, $x \neq 0$ *(Previous Course)* 1

28. A full-grown tree is y meters tall. A newly planted tree is only x meters tall. How many times as tall as the newly planted tree is the full-grown tree? *(Lesson 1-1)* $\frac{y}{x}$

29. Joe put d dollars into an account at 5.5% interest. How much interest will Joe earn in a year? *(Lesson 1-1)* .055d dollars

30. Describe the sequences printed by these two computer programs. *(Lesson 1-3)*

Program A
10 FOR N = 1 TO 100
20   PRINT N + 100
30 NEXT N
the whole numbers from 101 to 200, inclusive

Program B
10 FOR N = 100 TO 200
20   PRINT N
30 NEXT N
the whole numbers from 100 to 200, inclusive

31. The field properties hold with other operations and sets. Here is a set, with two operations, * and @. The results are found in the tables. For instance, $1 * 2 = 0$ and $1 @ 2 = 2$. **See margin.**

*	0	1	2
0	0	1	2
1	1	2	0
2	2	0	1

@	0	1	2
0	0	0	0
1	0	1	2
2	0	2	1

a. Calculate $1 * 0$ and $1 @ 0$.

b. Which operation seems more like addition; which more like multiplication?

c. What feature of the table indicates that * is commutative?

d. Verify that $1 @ (2 @ 2) = (1 @ 2) @ 2$. What property have you verified?

e. Verify that $1 @ (2 * 2) = (1 @ 2) * (1 @ 2)$. What property have you verified?

f. Make new tables for the two operations * and @ and the set $\{0, 1, 2, 3, 4\}$ that would satisfy the field properties.

LESSON 1-5 Algebra as a Mathematical System   31

FOLLOW-UP

MORE PRACTICE
For more questions on SPUR Objectives, use *Lesson Master 1-5*, shown below.

EVALUATION
A quiz covering Lessons 1-1 through 1-5 is provided in the Teacher's Resource File.

f.

*	0	1	2	3	4
0	0	1	2	3	4
1	1	2	3	4	0
2	2	3	4	0	1
3	3	4	0	1	2
4	4	0	1	2	3;

@	0	1	2	3	4
0	0	0	0	0	0
1	0	1	2	3	4
2	0	2	4	1	3
3	0	3	1	4	2
4	0	4	3	2	1

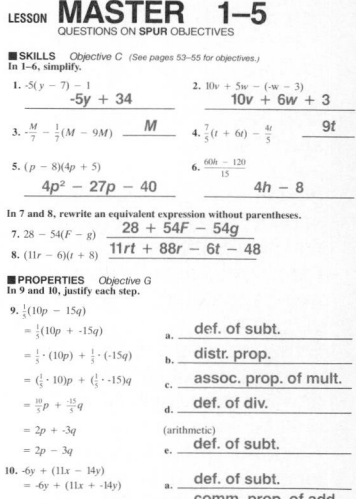

NAME _____

LESSON **MASTER** **1–5**
QUESTIONS ON **SPUR** OBJECTIVES

■ **SKILLS** *Objective C (See pages 53–55 for objectives.)*
In 1–6, simplify.

1. $-5(y - 7) - 1$ $-5y + 34$

2. $10v + 5w - (-w - 3)$ $10v + 6w + 3$

3. $\frac{M}{7} - \frac{1}{7}(M - 9M)$ M

4. $\frac{7}{5}(t + 6t) - \frac{4t}{5}$ $9t$

5. $(p - 8)(4p + 5)$ $4p^2 - 27p - 40$

6. $\frac{60h - 120}{15}$ $4h - 8$

In 7 and 8, rewrite an equivalent expression without parentheses.

7. $28 - 54(F - g)$ $28 + 54F - 54g$

8. $(11r - 6)(t + 8)$ $11rt + 88r - 6t - 48$

■ **PROPERTIES** *Objective G*
In 9 and 10, justify each step.

9. $\frac{1}{5}(10p - 15q)$
$= \frac{1}{5}(10p + -15q)$ a. __def. of subt.__
$= \frac{1}{5} \cdot (10p) + \frac{1}{5} \cdot (-15q)$ b. __distr. prop.__
$= (\frac{1}{5} \cdot 10)p + (\frac{1}{5} \cdot -15)q$ c. __assoc. prop. of mult.__
$= \frac{10}{5}p + \frac{-15}{5}q$ d. __def. of div.__
$= 2p + -3q$ (arithmetic)
$= 2p - 3q$ e. __def. of subt.__

10. $-6y + (11x - 14y)$
$= -6y + (11x + -14y)$ a. __def. of subt.__
$= -6y + (-14y + 11x)$ b. __comm. prop. of add.__
$= (-6y + -14y) + 11x$ c. __assoc. prop. of add.__
$= (-6 + -14)y + 11x$ d. __distr. prop.__
$= -20y + 11x$ (arithmetic)

Advanced Algebra © Scott, Foresman and Company   5

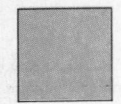

RESOURCES
■ Lesson Master 1-6
▯ Visual for Teaching Aid 3
displays the two number
tricks used in Additional
Example 1.
*The Teaching Aids are
available both as blackline
masters and as overhead
visuals.*

OBJECTIVES

*Letter codes refer to the
SPUR Objectives on page
2B.*
D Solve and check linear
equations.
F Use counterexamples to
show errors in reasoning.

TEACHING NOTES

Reading On the first page
of this lesson, the student
must read both down and
across. This is not uncommon in mathematics. When
reading material that has two
or more columns, suggest to
students that they ask themselves whether there is a
pattern going across or down
or both. For instance, in the
second listing of steps on the
first page of this lesson,
there is no pattern going
across, only one going down.

Stress to students that the
process of solving an equation involves the writing of
simpler equivalent sentences.
Students often will ask
whether they are required to
"show all steps." At this point
in algebra, most students
should start to do simple additions and multiplications in
their head. Encourage them
to do some steps mentally.
Accuracy, however, should
not be sacrificed for mental
computation.

LESSON

1-6

Reasoning in Algebra

Consider this number trick.

Step 1: Pick a number.
Step 2: Subtract 5.
Step 3: Multiply the result by 3.
Step 4: Add 9 to the result.
Step 5: Divide the result by 3.
Step 6: Subtract the original number.

If you follow these steps with four arbitrary numbers, such as 3, -2, 1.4, and 10, the computations can be summarized as below.

Step 1:	3	-2	1.4	10
Step 2:	-2	-7	-3.6	5
Step 3:	-6	-21	-10.8	15
Step 4:	3	-12	-1.8	24
Step 5:	1	-4	-0.6	8
Step 6:	-2	-2	-2	-2

After looking at these instances, you might guess that the result is always -2. In doing this, you are making a **conjecture**, or an edu-cated guess. In making a conjecture, you invent or are given some information about a situation. You study that information. Then you state something *not* given that you believe is true whenever the given is true. For instance, in this number trick it is not given that the final result is always -2. However, you have some evidence that the final result will always be -2.

After a conjecture is made, it is natural to ask whether it is always true. To do this, it is first necessary to do the trick in general. So we begin with a variable.

Step 1:	Pick a number.	n
Step 2:	Subtract 5.	$n - 5$
Step 3:	Multiply by 3.	$3(n - 5)$
Step 4:	Add 9.	$3(n - 5) + 9$
Step 5:	Divide by 3.	$\dfrac{3(n - 5) + 9}{3}$
Step 6:	Subtract the original number.	$\dfrac{3(n - 5) + 9}{3} - n$

Now the question is: Does this last expression always equal -2? For this, properties are needed. You are asked to supply the proof in the questions.

If you can prove a conjecture, then it is true. But not all conjectures are true. If you can find one **counterexample** to a conjecture, then it is false.

32

Example 1 Show by counterexample that

$$t_n = 2^{n-1}$$

is not an explicit formula for the sequence

$$1, 2, 4, 8, 15, \ldots .$$

Solution Only one counterexample is needed to show that the formula is wrong. The formula works for $n = 1, 2, 3,$ or 4. The fifth term gives the counterexample, for when $n = 5$, $t_n = 2^{5-1} = 16$. In the given sequence, $t_5 = 15$.

Recall that an **open sentence** is a sentence that may be true or false depending on what values are substituted for the variables. For example, the open sentence $x = 5$ is false when 7 is substituted for x and true when 5 is substituted for x. When you find values of one or more variables that make an open sentence true, you are *solving the sentence*. The values that make the sentence true are called the **solutions** of the sentence.

Notice that the following are all true when $x = 5$.

$$x = 5$$
$$2x = 10$$
$$2x + 7 = 17$$

The above equations are examples of **equivalent sentences**. Equivalent sentences are sentences with the same solutions. Usually, when you solve equations you try to find progressively simpler equivalent sentences until you find one, like $x = 5$, that has 5 as its obvious solution.

Below are the two postulates that are often applied to find equivalent equations.

Postulate 2: Properties of Equality

For all real numbers a, b, and c:
Addition Property of Equality: If $a = b$, then $a + c = b + c$.
Multiplication Property of Equality: If $a = b$, then $ac = bc$.

It may surprise you that when you solve an equation, you are constructing the statements of a proof.

For many students, proofs have an aura of difficulty. **Example 2** is designed to calm students' fears of proof by showing them that they already have done hundreds of proofs in algebra. All that was missing in their earlier work were the justifications.

ADDITIONAL EXAMPLES
1. Here are two number tricks. First do the trick with some specific numbers and make a conjecture about the result. Then prove the conjecture.
a. Pick a number.
  Multiply by 3.
  Subtract 6.
  Divide by 3.
  Add 2.
Conjecture: The result is always the number you started with.
Proof: n
  $3n$
  $3n - 6$
  $\dfrac{3n - 6}{3}$
  $\dfrac{3n - 6}{3} + 2$
Use the Distributive Property to simplify:
$n - \frac{6}{3} + 2 = n$

b. Pick a number.
  Add 4.
  Multiply by 6.
  Divide by 2.
  Subtract three times the original number.
Conjecture: the result is always 12.
Proof: n
  $n + 4$
  $6(n + 4)$
  $\dfrac{6(n + 4)}{2}$
  $\dfrac{6(n + 4)}{2} - 3n$

2. Solve and check.
a. $1.7y = 0.9 + 0.5y$
$y = .75$
b. $4(x + 6) = 2x - 1$
$x = \frac{-25}{2}$

33

Example 2   Solve $12 = 20 - 3t$.

Solution   We put in the statements and justifications. Solvers normally omit the justifications.

$12 = 20 + -3t$	definition of subtraction
$-8 = -3t$	Addition Property of Equality (Add -20 to each side.)
$-\frac{1}{3} \cdot -8 = -\frac{1}{3} \cdot -3t$	Multiplication Property of Equality
$\frac{8}{3} = t$	definition of division (left side) Inverse Property of Multiplication (right side)

We have proved: If $12 = 20 - 3t$, then $t = \frac{8}{3}$.

Check   Substitute $\frac{8}{3}$ for t in the original sentence. Use correct order of operations.
Does $12 = 20 - 3(\frac{8}{3})$?   Yes, because $12 = 20 - 8$.

Recall from geometry that a **conditional statement if p then q** (sometimes written $p \Rightarrow q$) has a related statement called its **converse**. The converse of "if p then q" is "if q then p."

In Example 2, the converse of "if $12 = 20 - 3t$, then $t = \frac{8}{3}$" is "if $t = \frac{8}{3}$, then $12 = 20 - 3t$."

In Example 2, the check of the solution is the proof of the converse. You need to prove both the statement and its converse to be certain you have solved an equation.

Questions

Covering the Reading

1. Define: conjecture.   an educated guess

2. What must be done to determine whether a conjecture is true?
It must be proved.

3. What can be done to determine if a conjecture is false?
Find a counterexample.

4. In Example 1, verify that the formula is true for $n = 1$ and $n = 4$.
$t_1 = 2^0 = 1$; $t_4 = 2^3 = 8$

5. What is an open sentence?   See margin.

6. What is a solution to an open sentence?
values that make the sentence true

Questions 18 and 19:
Finding one counterexample
for each question is sufficient
to disprove the statement.
Stress that a *single* false instance renders a statement
untrue.

Question 27: This ques-
tion is a historically famous
example of a conjecture that
is true for a fairly large
number of integers, but is not
true for all integers. The Distributive Property can be
used to show the conjecture
is not true when $n = 41$.
$t_{41} = 41^2 - 41 + 41 =$
$41(41 - 1 + 1)$
Thus, t_{41} has two integer factors greater than 1, so it is
not prime.

7. Which of the following sentences are equivalent to $3x = 12$?　a, c
　a. $3x - 1 = 11$　　　**b.** $3x + 1 = 11$　　　**c.** $x = 4$

8. *True or false* Equivalent sentences have the same solution(s).　true

9. What two postulates are often used to find equivalent equations?
addition and multiplication properties of equality

10. Give the converse of "If I am in Beijing, then I am in China."
If I am in China, then I am in Beijing.

11. What two statements must be proved in order to prove $12 = 20 - 3t$
if and only if $t = \frac{8}{3}$?　**See margin.**

12. Prove: $7 + 4x = -13$ if and only if $x = -5$.　**See margin.**

In 13 and 14, solve.

13. $200 - 3z = 300$　$z = -33\frac{1}{3}$　**14.** $128 = 12n - 4$　$n = 11$

Applying the Mathematics

In 15 and 16, which property was applied to derive the second equation
from the first?

15. $3a + 17 = 5a$　　　　　　**16.** $16 = .01c$
　$17 = 2a$　　　　　　　　　　　$1600 = c$
　Add. Prop. of Equality　　　　**Mult. Prop. of Equality**

17. Prove that $2.6(3a - 4) = 9.1$ if and only if $a = 2.5$.　**See margin.**

18. Show by counterexample that
　　$t_n = n^2 - n + 2$
　is *not* a formula that generates the sequence
　$2, 4, 8, 15, 26, \ldots$.　**$n = 4$ gives a counterexample, $t_4 = 14$.**

35

MORE PRACTICE
For more questions on SPUR
Objectives, use *Lesson Master 1-6*, shown on page 35.

ADDITIONAL ANSWERS
20.a. Add. of Fractions
b. Def. of Division;
Arithmetic
c. Comm. Prop. of
Multiplication
d. Multiplicative Inverse
Prop.
e. Multiplicative Identity
Prop.
f. Def. of Subtraction
g. Comm. and Assoc. Prop.
of Add.
h. Additive Inverse Prop.
i. Closure Prop.

21.a. -3; 2; 5.7
b. Your result in step 6 is
your number from step 1.
c. step 1: n
  step 2: $n - 4$
  step 3: $3(n - 4) = 3n - 12$
  step 4: $3n - 12 + 9 = 3n - 3$
  step 5: $\frac{3n - 3}{3} = n - 1$
  step 6: $n - 1 + 1 = n$

27.a.
```
10 FOR N = 1 TO 50
20    LET T = N * N - N +
        41
30    PRINT T;
40 NEXT N
50 END
```
b. sample: For $n = 41$, $t_n = 1681$, which is not prime.

---

19. Find a counterexample to this statement: For all a, b, and x,
$(a + b)^x = a^x + b^x$.
sample: $(3 + 2)^2 \neq 3^2 + 2^2$

20. Supply reasons in this proof of the number trick conjecture from this lesson.   **See margin.**

$$\frac{3(n - 5) + 9}{3} - n = \frac{3(n - 5)}{3} + \frac{9}{3} - n \qquad \textbf{a.} \ \underline{?}$$
$$= 3(n - 5) \cdot \tfrac{1}{3} + 3 - n \qquad \textbf{b.} \ \underline{?}$$
$$= (n - 5) \cdot 3 \cdot \tfrac{1}{3} + 3 - n \qquad \textbf{c.} \ \underline{?}$$
$$= (n - 5) \cdot 1 + 3 - n \qquad \textbf{d.} \ \underline{?}$$
$$= n - 5 + 3 - n \qquad \textbf{e.} \ \underline{?}$$
$$= n + \text{-}5 + 3 + \text{-}n \qquad \textbf{f.} \ \underline{?}$$
$$= n + \text{-}n + \text{-}5 + 3 \qquad \textbf{g.} \ \underline{?}$$
$$= 0 + \text{-}5 + 3 \qquad \textbf{h.} \ \underline{?}$$
$$= \text{-}2 \qquad \textbf{i.} \ \underline{?}$$

21. Consider the following number trick.   **See margin.**
Step 1: Choose a number.
Step 2: Subtract 4.
Step 3: Multiply by 3.
Step 4: Add 9.
Step 5: Divide by 3.
Step 6: Add 1.
a. Try this trick with -3, 2, and 5.7.
b. Make a conjecture about this trick.
c. Show statements that prove your conjecture. (You need not put in reasons.)

Review

22. Simplify. $2(3x - 5) - \frac{1}{4}(20 - 8x)$ *(Lesson 1-5)* $8x - 15$

23. Write the first five terms of the sequence generated by this recursive formula: $\begin{cases} t_1 = 3 \\ t_n = 4 - t_{n-1} \end{cases}$ *(Lesson 1-4)*   3, 1, 3, 1, 3

In 24–26, simplify. *(Previous course, Lesson 1-5)*

24. $\dfrac{2}{\frac{5}{9}}$ $\frac{18}{5}$

25. $\dfrac{\frac{a}{b}}{c}$ $\frac{ac}{b}$

26. $\dfrac{\frac{xy}{x}}{y}$ y^2

Exploration

27. Consider the sequence generated by the formula
$t_n = n^2 - n + 41$.   **See margin.**
a. Write a program in BASIC to print t_n for $n = 1$ to $n = 50$.
b. If you print the terms of the sequence, you will see that most of them are prime. Find a counterexample to the conjecture that all the terms are prime.

36

1-7

Solving Equations

In this lesson you will examine several situations in which the Distributive Property or related theorems are used to solve equations.

When an equation must be solved for a variable in the denominator of a fraction, as illustrated in Example 1, the Multiplication Property of Equality is applied twice.

Example 1

The *grade* of a highway measures its steepness as a ratio of the vertical rise over the horizontal run. A highway has an average grade of 2%. Over what horizontal distance does a car travel when it rises 150 meters on this road?

Solution   Write a sentence representing this situation. Use the definition of grade:

$$\text{grade} = \frac{\text{rise}}{\text{run}}.$$

Let x represent the run (horizontal distance). Then, since 2% = .02, we have:

$$.02 = \frac{150}{x}$$

Multiply by x. $.02x = 150$

Divide by .02 (This is equivalent $x = \dfrac{150}{.02}$
to multiplying by $\frac{1}{.02}$.)

$\qquad\qquad\qquad\qquad\qquad\qquad = 7500$ meters

Check   We need to know: If a car travels 7500 meters and rises 150 meters, is the grade 2%?
Is $\frac{150}{7500}$ = 2%? Yes, $\frac{150}{7500}$ = .02 = 2%.
So the car travels 7500 m to rise 150 m.

OBJECTIVE

Letter code refers to the SPUR Objectives on page 2B.
D Solve and check linear equations.

TEACHING NOTES

Reading   When justifications are given for the steps in solving an equation, one must read both across and down—across to see the justification, down to see how each step follows from the previous one. In equation solving, it is important to examine how each step follows from the previous one. Thus, reading the solution to an equation requires reading down only, while reading a proof requires reading both down and across.

Error Analysis   A frequent problem students have when "clearing fractions" from an equation containing fractions on one side only is to use multiplication only on that side of the equation. Use **Example 2** to illustrate that each side of an equation can be thought of as having implicit parentheses. Thus, the equation to be solved is really $(\frac{1}{4}E + \frac{1}{5}E + \frac{1}{6}E + 46) = (E)$. Stress that the Multiplication Property of Equality is applied to both sides, which are multiplied by 60.

You can solve equations involving more than one fraction by multiplying each side of the equation by the least common denominator of the fractions. This process eliminates the fractions from the equation.

Example 2 Stuart Dent works part time to earn spending money and to save for college. He spends $\frac{1}{4}$ of his monthly earnings on clothes, $\frac{1}{5}$ of his earnings on entertainment, and $\frac{1}{6}$ on transportation. He finds he has $46 left each month for savings. What are his monthly earnings?

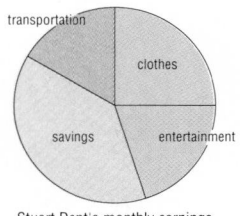

Stuart Dent's monthly earnings

Solution First write a sentence to represent the situation. Let E represent Stu's monthly earnings. The total of all Stu's expenditures and his savings equals his earnings.

$$\tfrac{1}{4}E + \tfrac{1}{5}E + \tfrac{1}{6}E + 46 = E$$

To eliminate or "clear" the fractions, multiply both sides of the equation by 60, which is the least common denominator of $\frac{1}{4}$, $\frac{1}{5}$, and $\frac{1}{6}$.

$$60(\tfrac{1}{4}E + \tfrac{1}{5}E + \tfrac{1}{6}E + 46) = 60E$$

$15E + 12E + 10E + 2760 = 60E$	Distributive Property
$37E + 2760 = 60E$	Addition of Like Terms

You want the variable terms on just one side of the equation, so add $-37E$ to both sides of the equation.

$2760 = 23E$	Addition Property of Equality
$120 = E$	Multiplication Property of Equality (Multiply by $\frac{1}{23}$.)

Stu earns $120 per month.

Check $\frac{1}{4}$ ($120) = $30 is spent on clothes.

$\frac{1}{5}$ ($120) = $24 is for entertainment.

$\frac{1}{6}$ ($120) = $20 is for transportation.

And $30 + $24 + $20 + $46 = $120.

When an equation contains decimals, you can find an equivalent equation with whole-number coefficients by multiplying each side by a sufficiently large power of 10.

38

Example 3 Suppose $20,000 is to be invested in two accounts, one of which pays 6% and one of which pays 8%. If an annual income of $1500 is needed and s dollars are invested at 6%, then

$$.06s + .08(20,000 - s) = 1500.$$

Solve this equation for s.

Solution Multiplying both sides by 100 will clear decimals.

$$100[.06s + .08(20,000 - s)] = 100 \cdot 1500$$

Distribute the 100. $6s + 8(20,000 - s) = 150,000$
Distribute the 8. $6s + 160,000 - 8s = 150,000$
Add like terms. $160,000 - 2s = 150,000$
Add $2s - 150,000$ to $2s = 10,000$
each side; reverse order.
Multiply both sides by $\frac{1}{2}$. $s = 5,000$

Check First, check the equation.
Does $.06 \cdot 5000 + .08(20,000 - 5000) = 1500$? Yes.
Now, check the situation.
If $5000 is invested at 6% and $15,000 at 8%, is the interest $1500?
Yes, the first interest is $300, the second $1200.

In Example 3, it might seem silly to invest some funds at a lower rate. However, often a higher interest rate means a higher risk. So it is wise not to put all the money in one place.

The theorem from Lesson 1-5 about the opposite of a sum is often applied in solving equations.

Example 4 Solve $6m - (5 - 9m) = 12$.

Solution

$6m + -(5 + -9m) = 12$ definition of subtraction (used twice)
$6m - 5 + 9m = 12$ Opposite-of-a-Sum Theorem
$15m - 5 = 12$ Addition of Like Terms
$15m = 17$ Addition Property of Equality (Add 5.)
$m = \frac{17}{15}$ Multiplication Property of Equality (Multiply by $\frac{1}{15}$.)

Check Substitute $\frac{17}{15}$ for m and follow order of operations.

Does $6(\frac{17}{15}) - (5 - 9 \cdot \frac{17}{15}) = 12$?

Does $\frac{102}{15} - (5 - \frac{153}{15}) = 12$?

Does $\frac{102}{15} - (-\frac{78}{15}) = 12$?

Does $\frac{180}{15} = 12$? Yes.

Question 16: This question reverses a problem that students have done in earlier lessons. The given information is the *value* of a term and the question asks for the position of the term.

Question 18: Many students, even after completing a full year of geometry, are woefully weak in their ability to answer questions about surface area and volume. Yet in the real world, objects are 3-dimensional, and the ideas of volume and surface area are important in calculus.

Question 23: Point out to students that the Pythagorean triples found in **Question 19** are solutions to the Diophantine equation $a^2 + b^2 = c^2$. A Diophantine equation, named after Diophantus, is one in which the solver is only interested in whole-number solutions.

ADDITIONAL ANSWERS
5. $.06s + 1600 - .08s = 1500$
$-.02s + 1600 = 1500$
$-0.2s = -100$
$s = 5000$

15.b. sample: A computer salesperson earns a 7% commission on sales up to a certain level and 5% on sales above that level but less than $100,000. If the salesperson's commission were $6500 in one month, find the dollar amount of sales that paid the 7% commission.

19.a.

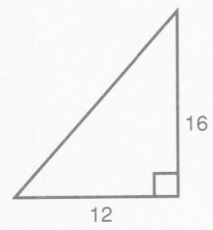

Questions

| Covering the Reading |

1. Refer to Example 1. Suppose the grade of the highway is 1.5%. Over what distance must a car travel to rise 0.5 m on this road?   **33.3 m**

In 2–4, refer to Example 2.

2. *True or false* The equations
$$\tfrac{1}{4}E + \tfrac{1}{5}E + \tfrac{1}{6}E + 46 = E$$
and $60(\tfrac{1}{4}E + \tfrac{1}{5}E + \tfrac{1}{6}E + 46) = 60E$
are equivalent.   **true**

3. Why was each side of the original equation multiplied by 60?
to clear fractions

4. Suppose that Stu gets a better paying job. Now he spends $\tfrac{1}{2}$ of his earnings on clothes. All the other fractions stay the same and he still saves $46 per month. What is his new salary?   **$345**

5. Solve the equation in Example 3 by following these steps in order, and write the result after each step.   **See margin.**
   a. Distribute .08.
   b. Add like terms.
   c. Subtract 1600 from each side.
   d. Divide each side by the coefficient of s.

6. Why is it often wise to invest money at different interest rates?
to protect against loss on a high-risk investment

7. a. According to the Opposite-of-a-Sum Theorem, $-(-2x + 9) =$ __?__.   **2x –**
   b. Solve the equation $12x - (-2x + 9) = 26$. $x = \tfrac{5}{2}$

In 8–11, solve each equation.

8. $\dfrac{12}{y} = 5$ $y = \tfrac{12}{5}$

9. $\dfrac{m}{3} + \dfrac{m}{7} = 1$ $m = \tfrac{21}{10}$

10. $4x - (x - 1) = 7$ $x = 2$

11. $0.05x + 0.1(2x) + 0.25(100 - 3x) = 20$ $x = 10$

| Applying the Mathematics |

In 12 and 13, solve.

12. $3y + 60 = 5y + 42$ $y = 9$ 13. $2z + 2 = 2 - 2z$ $z = 0$

14. A farmer grows three crops: wheat, corn, and alfalfa. He farms all the land he owns. On his farm $\tfrac{1}{3}$ of the land is planted with wheat, $\tfrac{2}{5}$ is planted with corn, and 60 acres are planted with alfalfa.
   a. How many acres of crops are on this farm?   **225 acres**
   b. How many acres of wheat are there?   **75 acres**
   c. How many acres of corn are there?   **90 acres**

15. Given $.07x + .05(100,000 - x) = 6500$.
   a. Solve the equation and check your solution. $x = 75,000$
   b. Make up a question that could be answered by solving the equation.   **See margin.**

16. The nth term of the sequence 1000, 997, 994, 991, ... is given by the formula $t_n = 1000 - 3(n - 1)$.
   a. Find n when $t_n = 850$.   n = 51
   b. Which term of the sequence is 850?   the 51st

17. The nth term of the sequence $\frac{1}{3}, \frac{1}{4}, \frac{1}{5}, \frac{1}{6}$, ... is given by the formula

$$a_n = \frac{1}{n + 2}$$

Which term of the sequence is $\frac{1}{99}$?   the 97th

Review

18. A cylindrical column of a building has a lateral area of 32.2 ft². If its radius is .5 ft, what is its height? *(Previous course)* (Refer to the Appendix of Geometry Formulas if necessary.)   about 10.2 ft

19. Use the sequence of right triangles below. *(Previous course, Lessons 1-2, 1-3, 1-4)*

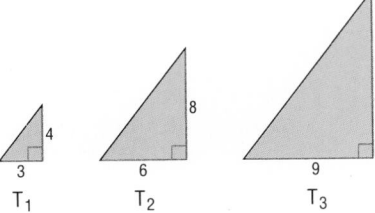

T_1 T_2 T_3

   a. Draw T_4 and label the lengths of the legs.   See margin.
   b. Find the length of each of the four hypotenuses. (Use the Pythagorean Theorem if necessary.) Write your answers in a sequence.   5, 10, 15, 20
   c. *Multiple choice* Which recursive formula below gives the sequence of the lengths of the four hypotenuses? (In all cases, $n \geq 2$.)   iv

   (i) $\begin{cases} t_1 = 1 \\ t_n = t_n + 1 \end{cases}$ (iii) $\begin{cases} t_1 = 5 \\ t_n = n + 5 \end{cases}$

   (ii) $\begin{cases} t_1 = 25 \\ t_n = 5(t_{n-1}) \end{cases}$ (iv) $\begin{cases} t_1 = 5 \\ t_n = t_{n-1} + 5 \end{cases}$

20. Simplify: $\dfrac{x + 2}{3y} + \dfrac{2x + 7}{3y}$. *(Lesson 1-5)* $\dfrac{x + 3}{y}$

21. Which of the following sentences is (are) equivalent to $20(x + 5) = 55$? *(Lesson 1-6)*   a, b
   a. $4(x + 5) = 11$ **b.** $x + 5 = \frac{11}{4}$ **c.** $4(x + 1) = 11$

22. Explain in one or two sentences the difference between a conjecture and a theorem. *(Lessons 1-5, 1-6)*   See margin.

Exploration

23. The Greek mathematician Diophantus, who lived in the second century A.D., was the first person to replace unknowns by single letters. There is a famous problem by which you can calculate how long he lived. The *Greek Authority* states: "Diophantus passed one sixth of his life in childhood, one twelfth in youth, and one seventh more as a bachelor. Five years after his marriage was born a son who died four years before his father, at half his father's final age." How long did Diophantus live?   84 yr

---

FOLLOW-UP

MORE PRACTICE
For more questions on SPUR Objectives, use *Lesson Master 1-7*, shown below.

EVALUATION
Alternative Assessment
To assess informally students' skills in rewriting formulas, have small groups of students work at the chalkboard on the same formula. Ask a student who has done the work correctly to explain his or her solution.

22. A conjecture is believed to be true based on instances; a theorem has been proved to be true for all cases.

NAME _____

LESSON **MASTER   1–7**
QUESTIONS ON **SPUR** OBJECTIVES

■ **SKILLS**   *Objective D (See pages 53–55 for objectives.)*
In 1–10, solve and check.

1. $\frac{1}{3}x = 9$ $x = 18$ 2. $\frac{3}{4}a - 1 = 76$ $a = \frac{308}{3}$

3. $\frac{5}{7}(m - 14) = -\frac{10}{21}$ $m = \frac{40}{3}$ 4. $\frac{9}{D} = 27$ $D = \frac{1}{3}$

5. $\frac{7}{10B} = 35$ $B = \frac{1}{50}$ 6. $8y - 217 = -25$ $y = 24$

7. $-6 - (r - 5) = 0.8$ $r = -1.8$ 8. $\frac{1}{12}(60x + 24) = -x$ $x = -\frac{1}{3}$

9. $.3(10 - z) - .5z = 70$ $z = -83.75$ 10. $1.7y = 0.9 + 0.5y$ $y = .75$

■ **USES**   *Objective J*

11. A bag of mixed nuts contains peanuts, cashews, and pecans: $\frac{1}{3}$ of the mixture is peanuts, $\frac{1}{5}$ is cashews, and 17 ounces of the mixture are pecans.

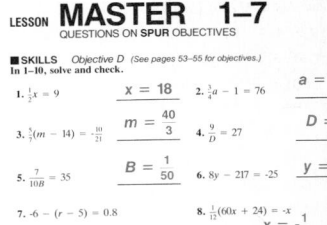

   a. How much does the bag of nuts weigh?
   $\frac{255}{7}$ oz ≈ 36 oz
   b. How much do the peanuts weigh?
   $\frac{85}{7}$ oz ≈ 12 oz
   c. How much do the cashews weigh?
   $\frac{51}{7}$ oz ≈ 7 oz

Advanced Algebra © Scott, Foresman and Company   7

41

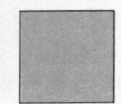
LESSON

1-8

Rewriting Formulas

You have studied how to use properties of algebra to simplify expressions and to solve equations. Algebraic properties also allow you to rewrite formulas in equivalent forms. Many times a formula is more useful if written in another form.

Consider the formula

$$d = rt,$$

where d is the distance an object travels, r is the rate at which it travels, and t is the time the object travels. If you want to calculate the distance traveled on an airplane going at a rate of $650 \frac{\text{miles}}{\text{hour}}$ for 2.5 hours, this formula is immediately useful. It gives d in terms of the variables for which you have values.

$$d = rt = (650 \tfrac{\text{miles}}{\text{hour}})(2.5 \text{ hr}) = 1625 \text{ mi}$$

But suppose you wanted to know how much time you would need to travel 380 miles if you drive $50 \frac{\text{miles}}{\text{hour}}$. It might be helpful to have a formula that gives t in terms of d and r. The properties allow you to rewrite $d = rt$ as follows.

$$d = rt$$

Divide both sides by r. $\dfrac{d}{r} = \dfrac{rt}{r}$

Simplify. $\dfrac{d}{r} = t$

Because you now have a formula for t, it is easy to answer the question asked earlier. Substitute $d = 380$ mi and $r = 50 \frac{\text{miles}}{\text{hour}}$ to get

$$t = \frac{d}{r} = \frac{380 \text{ mi}}{50 \frac{\text{miles}}{\text{hour}}} = 7.6 \text{ hr.}$$

You would need 7.6 hours to travel 380 miles.

42

The formulas $d = rt$ and $t = \dfrac{d}{r}$ are equivalent. The first is solved for d; the second is solved for t. Notice that when a **formula is solved for a variable,** that variable has coefficient and exponent equal to one.

Example 1 illustrates that the most useful version of a formula might depend on your background and location.

Example 1   Pierre grew up in New Orleans, where he learned to tell temperature using the Fahrenheit scale. When he visited his cousin Rae in Montreal, Canada, he found that temperature was reported in degrees Celsius. Because Celsius temperature readings did not mean much to him, Pierre converted Celsius C to Fahrenheit F using this formula:

$$F = 32 + 1.8C$$

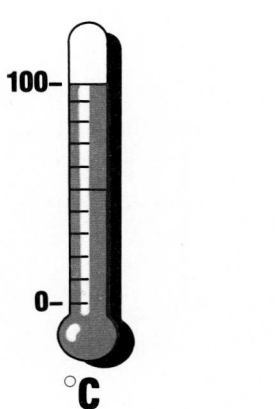

Rae visited Pierre the following summer. Rewrite the formula so she can use it to convert Fahrenheit to Celsius.

Solution   Given $F = 32 + 1.8C$

Subtract 32 from both sides. $F - 32 = 1.8C$

Divide both sides by 1.8. $\dfrac{F - 32}{1.8} = C$

So $C = \dfrac{F - 32}{1.8}$ is an equivalent formula that is suitable for Rae.

Check   Evaluate the formula for a pair of temperatures you know are equivalent. The boiling point of water is 212° F or 100° C.

Does $100 = \dfrac{212 - 32}{1.8}$?   Yes.

ADDITIONAL EXAMPLES

1. For an object that is accelerated at a uniform rate, $v = v_0 + at$ gives the final velocity v for an object with initial velocity v_0 at acceleration a for t seconds. Solve this formula for a; then solve for t.

$$a = \frac{v - v_0}{t};$$

$$t = \frac{v - v_0}{a}$$

2. $K = C + 273$ relates degrees Kelvin to degrees Celsius. Solve for C.
$$C = K - 273$$

3. Consider the formula $t_n = 4n + 11$.
a. Solve the formula for n.
$$n = \frac{t_n - 11}{4}$$
b. Find n when $t_n = 303$.
$$n = 73$$

4. $E = mc^2$ is Einstein's law relating energy and mass. The ratio of E to m is always equal to what quantity?
$$\frac{E}{m} = c^2$$

5. In a right triangle, the product of the legs is equal to what quantity?
$A = \frac{1}{2}l_1 l_2$, so $l_1 l_2 = 2A$. **The product of the legs is twice the area.**

Example 2 shows that you need to be careful when working with formulas that contain subscripted variables.

■ ■ ■ ■ ■ ■ ■ ■

Example 2   Consider the sequence formula $t_n = 4n + 11$.
a. Solve the formula for n.
b. Find n when $t_n = 103$.

Solution

a. $t_n = 4n + 11$ Given

$t_n - 11 = 4n$ Addition Property of Equality (Add -11.)

$\dfrac{t_n - 11}{4} = n$ Multiplication Property of Equality (Multiply by $\frac{1}{4}$.)

Observe that t_n is a single variable. You cannot remove the subscript n from the t.

b. Substitute 103 for t_n and evaluate.

$$n = \frac{t_n - 11}{4} = \frac{103 - 11}{4} = \frac{92}{4} = 23$$

Thus 103 is the 23rd term.
Notice that to find a value of n for a given value of t_n, it is much quicker to use $n = \dfrac{t_n - 11}{4}$ than to use $t_n = 4n + 11$.

Sometimes you may want to rewrite a sentence without solving for a particular variable. Consider the next example.

■ ■ ■ ■ ■ ■ ■ ■

Example 3   The formula

$$A = \tfrac{1}{2}d_1 d_2$$

gives the area of a rhombus in terms of the lengths of the diagonals d_1 and d_2. What is always true about the product of the diagonal lengths?

Solution   The product of the diagonal lengths is $d_1 d_2$. Multiplying both sides of $A = \tfrac{1}{2}d_1 d_2$ by 2 solves the equation for this expression. So

$$2A = d_1 d_2.$$

Thus, in a rhombus, the product of its diagonal lengths is twice its area.

44

Questions

Covering the Reading

In 1–3, refer to the formula $d = rt$ at the beginning of the lesson.

1. How far can a race car traveling 190 mph go in 1.4 hr? **266 mi**

2. The formula $t = \dfrac{d}{r}$ is solved for ___?___. **time t**

3. Find an equivalent formula that is solved for r. $r = \dfrac{d}{t}$

4. Refer to Example 1. Find the Celsius temperature equivalent to 86° F.
   30 degrees

5. Refer to Example 3. If the area of a rhombus is 24 cm², find the product of its diagonal lengths. **48 cm**

Applying the Mathematics

6. *Multiple choice* Which formula is easiest to use if you want to find N and you are given L and h? **a**

   (a) $N = 7Lh$ (b) $L = \dfrac{N}{7h}$ (c) $h = \dfrac{N}{7L}$

7. *Multiple choice* Which formula is easiest to use if you want to find T given L? **b**
   (a) $L = 100 + .04T$ (b) $T = 25(L - 100)$ (c) $.04T = L - 100$

8. Refer to the diagram below. Two angles with measures x and y are supplementary. To find y in terms of x, the following steps are written. Justify each step. **See margin.**

   $$x + y = 180°$$
   $$x + y + {-x} = 180° + {-x} \quad \textbf{a.} \ \underline{\ ?\ }$$
   $$x + {-x} + y = 180° + {-x} \quad \textbf{b.} \ \underline{\ ?\ }$$
   $$0 + y = 180° + {-x} \quad \textbf{c.} \ \underline{\ ?\ }$$
   $$y = 180° + {-x} \quad \textbf{d.} \ \underline{\ ?\ }$$
   $$y = 180° - x \quad \textbf{e.} \ \underline{\ ?\ }$$

   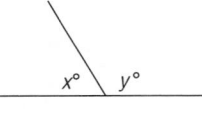

9. The formula $C = 2\pi r$ gives the circumference of a circle in terms of its radius r. Find the ratio of C to r. $\dfrac{C}{r} = 2\pi$

10. **a.** Solve the sequence formula $t_n = 4n^2$ for n. $n = \dfrac{\sqrt{t_n}}{2}$
    b. What term of the sequence is 196? **7th**

11. The *pitch P* of a roof is a measure of the steepness of the slant of the roof. Pitch is defined as the ratio of the vertical rise R to the span S as shown in the sketch below.

    That is, $P = \dfrac{R}{S}$.

    a. Solve this formula for S. $S = \dfrac{R}{P}$
    b. If a builder wants a roof to have a pitch of $\frac{1}{6}$ and a rise of 5 feet, what must be the span of the building? **30 ft**

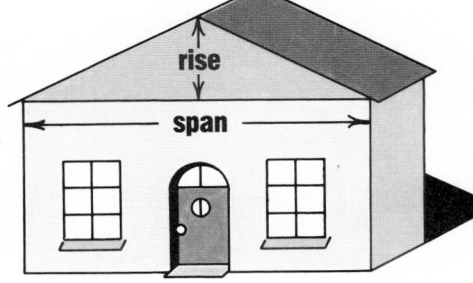

NOTES ON QUESTIONS

Question 7: Any of the three equations may be used to find T when given L; choice (b), however, is the easiest.

Question 12: Students may have some difficulty solving for m_1. Remind them to clear fractions as a first step and to think of m_1 as a single variable.

Question 14: The words *Skill Sequence* indicate that the parts of the question are related. Each succeeding part encompasses the skill needed to work the preceding part.

Question 18: A counterexample for this problem is a value for x, which is a solution to the equation $\dfrac{6 + x}{8 + x} = 2$. Thus, answering the question may require solving an equation.

ADDITIONAL ANSWERS
16. If $x = 6$, then $3x - 7 = 11$.

19. Each triangle with vertex *V* has area
$$\frac{\frac{1}{2}d_1 \cdot \frac{1}{2}d_2}{2}$$, so the total area of the four triangles is
$$\left(\frac{4\frac{1}{2}d_1 \cdot \frac{1}{2}d_2}{2}\right) =$$
$$2\left(\frac{1}{2}d_1 \cdot \frac{1}{2}d_2\right) = \frac{1}{2}d_1d_2.$$
Alternately, the area of the rhombus is half that of the rectangle. The area of the rectangle is d_1d_2. So the area of the rhombus is $\frac{1}{2}d_1d_2$.

20.a. since the 18th century in some scientific fields
b.

	°F	°C	Réaumur
Boiling	212	100	80°C
Freezing	32	0	0°C

12. In the late 1660s, Isaac Newton formulated the law of universal gravitation described by the formula
$$F = \frac{km_1m_2}{d^2},$$
where F is the force between two bodies with masses m_1 and m_2, k is the gravitational constant, and d is the distance between the bodies.
   a. Solve for m_1. $m_1 = \frac{Fd^2}{km_2}$
   b. Solve the formula for the product of the masses. $m_1m_2 = \frac{Fd^2}{k}$

13. Solve the sequence formula $a_n = a_1 + (n - 1)d$ for n.
$$\frac{a_n - a_1}{d} + 1 = n$$

Review

14. *Skill sequence* Solve each equation. *(Lesson 1-7)*
   a. $\frac{1}{3}n = 60$ 180
   b. $\frac{1}{3}n + 15 = 60$ 135
   c. $\frac{1}{3}n + \frac{1}{2}n + 15 = 60$ 54

15. Solve. $5 - 2(x - 7) - (3 - x) = 4$ *(Lessons 1-5, 1-7)*   12

16. Give the converse of: if $3x - 7 = 11$, then $x = 6$. *(Lesson 1-6)*   See margin.

17. A car is priced at d dollars. You can get it at 6% off this price. Write an expression in terms of d to describe:
   a. the amount saved   .06d   **b.** the new price *(Lessons 1-1, 1-5)*   .94d

18. Find a counterexample. For all x, $\frac{6 + x}{8 + x}$ is never equal to 2. *(Lesson 1-6)* $x = -10$

19. Let d_1 and d_2 be the lengths of the diagonals of rhombus *RHOM*. Use the diagram at the right to explain why the area A of the rhombus equals $\frac{1}{2}d_1d_2$. *(Previous course)*   See margin.

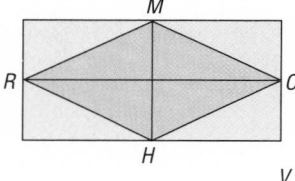

Exploration

20. In this lesson you have seen temperature measured on Celsius and Fahrenheit scales. In *War and Peace*, Leo Tolstoy describes a calm frost measured in "degrees Réaumur."   See margin.
   a. Find out when and where the Réaumur scale was used.
   b. Compare the freezing and boiling points of water on each of the three scales.

1-9

Solving Inequalities

Suppose that in order to qualify to compete in the long jump, you must jump at least 5 meters. Then, if J is the length of your jump, to qualify you must have $J \geq 5$. This open sentence is called an **inequality** because it contains one of the symbols $<$, $>$, $\leq$, or $\geq$. There are infinitely many solutions to the sentence $J \geq 5$, so they cannot all be listed. One way to describe all possible solutions is on a number line. The graph of the solutions to $J \geq 5$ is shown below.

The shaded circle means that 5 is included in the solution set. It is used in the graphs of inequalities of the form $\leq$ or $\geq$. An open circle at the endpoint indicates that the endpoint is not included in the solution set and is used for inequalities involving $<$ or $>$. The graph below shows all solutions of $m < -0.2$.

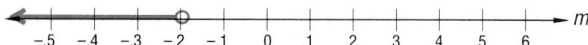

In each case the solution is an **interval.** The inequalities $J \geq 5$ and $m < -0.2$ describe the intervals symbolically. The graphs describe them visually.

The Postulates of Inequality ensure that solving an inequality is very much like solving an equation.

Postulate 3: Properties of Inequality

For all real numbers a, b, and c:
Addition Property of Inequality:
   If $a < b$, then $a + c < b + c$.
Multiplication Properties of Inequality:
   If $a < b$ and $c > 0$, then $ac < bc$.
   If $a < b$ and $c < 0$, then $ac > bc$.

OBJECTIVES

Letter codes refer to the SPUR Objectives on page 2B.
D Solve and check linear inequalities.
K Graph solutions to inequalities on a number line.

TEACHING NOTES

The open-circle, shaded-circle distinction seems to bother some students when graphing. Stress that any time a sentence is being graphed, only those points belonging to the solution set are to be graphed (or shaded). The open circle is an efficient way to mark a nonincluded endpoint of a ray or segment.

Throughout the books in this series, we emphasize that there are two parts to the check of an inequality's solution: (a) the substitution of the endpoint in the original sentence should give an equality; and (b) the substitution of a particular value in the solution set should give a correct inequality. These two parts are shown in the checks for **Examples 1 and 2.**

LESSON 1-9 Solving Inequalities   47

■ ■ ■ ■ ■ ■ ■■

Example 1 Solve and graph all solutions to $2m + 57 > 113$.

Solution $2m + 57 > 113$
$\qquad 2m > 56$ Addition Property of Inequality (Add -57.)
$\qquad m > 28$ Multiplication Property of Inequality (Multiply by $\frac{1}{2}$.)

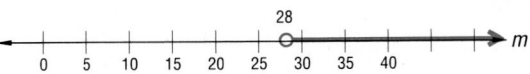

The inequality $m > 28$ is the simplest sentence equivalent to $2m + 57 > 113$. It shows there is a *set* of solutions. This set of solutions is written

$$\{m: m > 28\}$$

and is read "the set of all m such that m is greater than 28."

Check First check the endpoint. Substitute 28 for m in the original sentence. This checks the endpoint. The two sides should be equal. Does $2 \cdot 28 + 57 = 113$? Yes.
Now check the direction of the inequality. Pick a value of m in the solution set. We pick $m = 40$. Does it work? Is $2 \cdot 40 + 57 > 113$? Yes.

Notice that there are two Multiplication Properties of Inequalities in Postulate 3. Solving inequalities is different from solving equations only when you multiply or divide both sides of an inequality by a negative number. Then you must *reverse* the inequality sign.

■ ■ ■ ■ ■ ■ ■■

Example 2 Solve and graph all solutions to $-\frac{1}{3}R \ge 2$.

Solution Be careful! Multiply both sides by -3 and *reverse* the inequality.

$$-3(-\tfrac{1}{3}R) \le -3(2)$$

Now simplify. $\qquad\qquad\qquad R \le -6$

So the solution set is $\{R: R \le -6\}$.
Here is a graph of the solution set:
-12 -10 -8 -6 -4 -2 0 2

Check First substitute -6 for R to check the endpoint.
Is $-\frac{1}{3}(-6) = 2$? Yes.
Next pick a different value of R in $\{R: R \le -6\}$. We pick -12.
Is $-\frac{1}{3}(-12) \ge 2$? Yes, $4 \ge 2$, so the solution checks.

There are many applications for inequalities. The words "or less" might clue you to set up the inequality of Example 3.

48

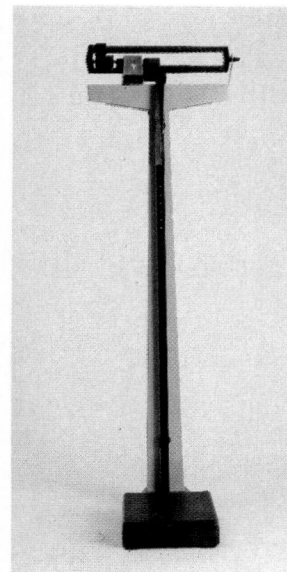

Example 3 A man weighing 275 lb is starting a diet that allows him to lose 2 lb per week. This means after w weeks, his weight will be $275 - 2w$ pounds. If he is able to stick to the diet, when will his weight be 200 lb or less?

Solution 1 His weight will be 200 lb or less when w satisfies $275 - 2w \leq 200$.

Subtract 275 from both sides. $\quad -2w \leq -75$

Divide both sides by -2 and reverse the inequality. $\quad \dfrac{-2w}{-2} \geq \dfrac{-75}{-2}$

$$w \geq 37.5.$$

Solution 2 To avoid multiplying by a negative number, add $2w$ to both sides of the inequality.

$$275 \leq 200 + 2w$$
$$75 \leq 2w$$
$$37.5 \leq w$$

Either way, the solution set to the inequality is $\{w: w \geq 37.5\}$. Now you must interpret the solution in the context of the problem. The shortest time needed to bring his weight to 200 pounds is 37.5 weeks. If he continues longer on the diet, his weight will drop below 200 pounds.

Questions

Covering the Reading

1. *Multiple choice* Which inequality is a translation of "x is greater than or equal to 5"? **d**
   (a) $x \leq 5$ (b) $5 \leq x$ (c) $5 \geq x$ (d) $x \geq 5$

2. Write an inequality for the set of numbers graphed below. $x < -15$

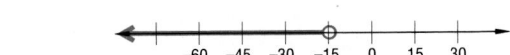

   $$-60 \quad -45 \quad -30 \quad -15 \quad 0 \quad 15 \quad 30$$

3. When you multiply or divide both sides of an inequality by a negative number, you must __?__ the inequality sign. **reverse**

4. Graph all solutions to $m < 42$. **See margin.**

5. Translate into words: $\{x: x < -3\}$. **the set of all x less than -3**

6. To check that $b \geq 9$ is the simplest sentence equivalent to $5 - \dfrac{b}{3} \leq 2$, what two values would you pick for b? Why must you pick two values? **See margin.**

7. Solve and graph all solutions to $.2m < 1.4$. **See margin.**

8. A woman weighing 190 lb plans to lose 2 lb per week. How long will it take her to bring her weight down to 135 lb or less? **27.5 weeks**

LESSON 1-9 Solving Inequalities **49**

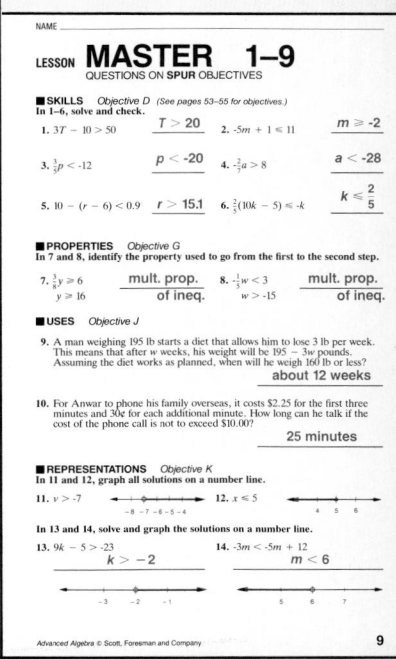

ADDITIONAL ANSWERS
9.a. If *C* is the
circumference, then
$0 < C \le 28$.
b.

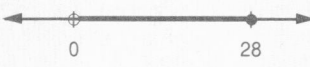

10.a. If *g* is the speed of
the gusts, then $g > 80$.
b.

11.a. Distributive Prop.
b. Add. of Like Terms
c. Add. Prop. of Inequality
d. Add. Prop. of Inequality
e. Multiplication Prop. of
Inequality

12. $n < -\frac{3}{2}$;

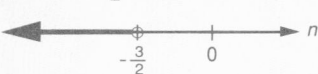

13. $x \ge \frac{1}{14}$;

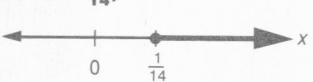

19. $-\frac{7}{3}$; Does $15 - \left(\frac{7}{-\frac{7}{3}}\right)$
$= 18$? Yes, $15 + 3 = 18$.

20. 10; Does $4 - 3(10 - 2)$
$= 5(6 - 10)$? Yes, $-20 =$
-20.

21. (left to right) 62°, 20.5°,
20.5°, 20.5°, 20.5°, 20.5°,
15.5°

22.a. $-6 < -3$, but $36 \not< 9$.
b. If $|r| \ge |s|$.

In 9 and 10, (a) translate the English into an algebraic inequality; (b) graph
all solutions to the inequality.   See margin.

9. A soccer rulebook says the circumference of the ball shall not be more
than 28 inches.

10. Gusts of over 80 kilometers per hour are expected.

11. Justify each step of the solution to $7(w + 1) \le 4(w - 2) + 3$.

$7w + 7 \le 4w - 8 + 3$	**a.** ___?___ See margin.
$7w + 7 \le 4w - 5$	**b.** ___?___
$3w + 7 \le -5$	**c.** ___?___
$3w \le -12$	**d.** ___?___
$w \le -4$	**e.** ___?___

In 12 and 13, solve and graph all solutions to each inequality.   See margin.

12. $-4n - 5 > 1$ **13.** $2(x + 1) \ge 3(1 - 4x)$

14. Given $a_n = 3 - 5n$. Find the first *n* for which $a_n \le -102$.   21

15. A truck weighs 5000 kg when empty. It is used for carrying 50 kg
sacks of pistachio nuts.
   a. Write a sentence for the total weight *T* of the truck loaded with
s sacks of pistachios. $T = 5000 + 50s$
   b. How many sacks of pistachios can the truck carry over a bridge
with a weight limit of 8000 kg? [Hint: *T* must be less than or equal
to the weight limit.]   60 sacks or fewer

16. Cheap Rentals rents cars at $10 per day plus 12¢ per mile. Ruby
needs a car for four days. How many miles can she drive if the total
cost of renting the car is not to exceed $100?   500 mi or less

17. A formula for the area of a triangle is $A = \frac{1}{2}bh$. Solve for *b*.
(Lesson 1-8) $b = \frac{2A}{h}$

18. Solve for *y*. $4x + y = 8 - y$ *(Lesson 1-8)* $y = 4 - 2x$

In 19 and 20, solve and check. *(Lesson 1-7)*   See margin.

19. $18 = 15 - \dfrac{7}{a}$ **20.** $4 - 3(x - 2) = 5(6 - x)$

21. Find the degree measure
of each angle in
the figure at the right.
(Previous course, Lesson 1-7)
See margin.

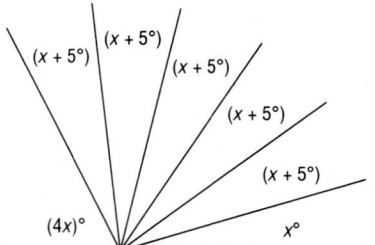

22. a. Find a counterexample to this statement:
If *r* and *s* are real numbers and $r < s$, then $r^2 < s^2$.   See margin.
   b. Under what conditions is $r^2 \ge s^2$?   See margin.

Summary

The language of algebra is based on numbers and variables. These are put together in expressions, and two expressions connected with a verb make up a sentence.

The order of operations and postulates are like a grammar; they tell what is allowed and what is not. Algebra also has its synonyms, in the form of equal expressions that take on the same values and equivalent equations that have the same solutions.

To use the language of algebra, you must be able to translate situations into it. This can be done by direct translation of words, by looking for patterns, or by using models for operations.

Algebra is a mathematical system, like geometry. It has definitions, postulates, and theorems. It also has conjectures and proofs.

Three kinds of postulates are discussed in this chapter. The postulates of addition and multiplication of real numbers help in obtaining equal expressions. The postulates of equality help in solving equations. Since formulas are equations, these postulates also help to solve formulas. The postulates of inequality help in solving inequalities. Subtraction is defined in terms of addition and division in terms of multiplication, so other postulates are not needed for these operations.

The formulas you have learned in previous years have been explicit formulas; one variable is given in terms of other variables. For sequences, there are also recursive formulas, in which terms of the sequence are determined by using the immediately preceding terms instead of being calculated directly. Computers can be programmed to work with either explicit or recursive formulas.

Vocabulary

Below are the most important terms and phrases for this chapter. You should be able to give a general description and a specific example of each and a precise definition for those marked with an asterisk (*).

Lesson 1-1
*variable, algebraic expression,
expression, model for an operation

Lesson 1-2
formula, equation, *domain, replacement set for a variable, evaluating an expression, *natural numbers, *counting numbers, *whole numbers, *integers, rational numbers, real numbers, order of operations

Lesson 1-3
sequence, term of sequence, subscript, index subscripted variable, explicit formula, nth term

Lesson 1-4
calculator key sequence, recursive formula, Fibonacci sequence

Lesson 1-5
definition, postulate, theorem, property field properties of addition and multiplication of real numbers, proof

Lesson 1-6
conjecture, counterexample, open sentence solution to a sentence, equivalent sentences conditional statement; if p, then q, *converse Addition Property of Equality, Multiplication Property of Equality

Lesson 1-8
solving a formula for a specific variable

Lesson 1-9
inequality, interval, Addition Property of Inequality, Multiplication Properties of Inequality

Progress Self-Test

For the development of mathematical competence, feedback and correction, along with the opportunity to practice, are necessary. The Progress Self-Test provides the opportunity for feedback and correction; the Chapter Review provides additional opportunities for practice.

We cannot overemphasize the importance of these end-of-chapter materials. It is at this point that the material "gels" for many students, allowing them to solidify skills and understanding. In general, student performance should be markedly improved after these pages.

USING THE PROGRESS SELF-TEST
Assign the Progress Self-Test as a one-night assignment. Worked-out *solutions* for all questions are in the Selected Answers section of the student book. Encourage students to take the Progress Self-Test honestly, grade themselves, and then be prepared to discuss the test in class.

Advise students to pay special attention to those Chapter Review questions (pages 53–55) which correspond to questions missed on the Progress Self-Test. A chart provided with the Selected Answers keys the Progress Self-Test questions to the lettered SPUR Objectives in the Chapter Review or to the Vocabulary. It also keys the questions to the corresponding lessons where the material is covered.

Take this test as you would take a test in class. Use a calculator. Then check your work with the solutions in the Selected Answers section in the back of the book.

In 1–5, use the two formulas below.

Sequence A   *Sequence B*
$t_n = 5 + 7n$ $\begin{cases} S_1 = 5 \\ S_n = S_{n-1} + 7, n > 1 \end{cases}$

1. Write the first four terms of sequence *A*.

2. Write the first four terms of sequence *B*.

3. Find t_8.   **61**   **See below for answers for 1, 2, and 7.**

4. Calculate S_8.   **54**

5. Solve the explicit formula for *n*. $n = \dfrac{t_n - 5}{7}$

6. What sequence will this program print when run?

```
10 FOR N = 1 TO 4
20     LET NTERM = 3*N + 40
30     PRINT NTERM
40 NEXT N
50 END   43, 46, 49, 52
```

7. Multiply and simplify. $(2x - 3)(6x - 5)$

8. Simplify: $3(4 + a) - (25 - a)$.   **4a – 13**

9. If $d = \frac{1}{2}gt^2$, find *d* when $g = 32$ and $t = 3$.
   144

In 10–12, solve.

10. $1.7y = 0.9 + 0.5y$ **.75**

11. $\dfrac{.7}{x} = 3$ **.23**

12. $.12x + .08(15{,}000 - x) = 1480$ **7000**

13. Solve and graph the solution set.   **See margin.**
    $\frac{1}{2}p \geq 1 + p$

14. *Multiple choice* Which of the following are *not* formulas?   **b, c**
    (a) $x = 3a + y$ (b) $3E = E + 1$
    (c) $\dfrac{a + 5}{2}$ (d) $w = \dfrac{r + 5}{n}$

1) 12, 19, 26, 33   2) 5, 12, 19, 26   7) $12x^2 - 28x + 15$

15. *Multiple choice* Which formula below is solved for *d*?   **b**
    (a) $2A = d_1 d_2$ (b) $d = rt$
    (c) $d^2 = (x_1 - x_2)^2 + (y_1 - y_2)^2$

16. Prove that this statement is not true by finding a counterexample. If $t^2 = 9$, then $t = 3$.
    t = -3

In 17–19, give a justification for each statement.

17. $3 + \sqrt{2} = \sqrt{2} + 3$ **See margin.**

18. If $4(3x - 8) = 11$, then $12x - 32 = 11$.

19. $\dfrac{a}{b} = a \cdot \dfrac{1}{b}$

In 20 and 21, use the formula $V = \frac{1}{3}\pi r^2 h$ for the volume of a cone.

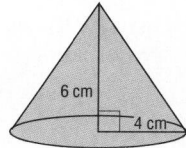

20. Find the volume of the cone above to the nearest cubic centimeter.   **101 cm³**

21. What is a reasonable domain for *r*?   **positive reals**

22. Express your rate if you travel 12 miles in *t* hours. $\dfrac{12}{t}$

23. John is 3 years older than Jane. If John is *J* years old, how old is Jane?   **J – 3**

24. Write a recursive formula for the following situation. Cherlyn's grandparents gave her $20 on her first birthday, $30 on her second, $40 on her third, and so on.   **See margin.**

25. If the length of a rectangle is 8.3 m, what values of the width *w* will make the perimeter less than 21.7 m?   **w < 2.55 m**

26. Name a real number that is not an integer.   **sample: π**

Chapter Review

Questions on **SPUR** Objectives

SPUR stands for **S**kills, **P**roperties, **U**ses, and **R**epresentations.
The Chapter Review questions are grouped according to the
SPUR Objectives for this chapter.

SKILLS deal with the procedures used to get answers.

■ **Objective A** *Evaluate formulas. (Lessons 1-2, 1-3, 1-4)*

1. In the formula $d = \dfrac{n(n-3)}{2}$, find d when $n = 17$.   **119**

2. If $d = \frac{1}{2}gt^2$, find d when $g = 32$ and $t = 2.5$.   **100**

3. In the formula $a_n = 20{,}000(.9)^n$, find a_{10} to the nearest hundredth.   **6973.57**

4. If $b_n = 2^{n-1}$, find b_4.   **8**

5. Write the first five terms in the sequence
$\begin{cases} t_1 = 10 \\ t_n = t_{n-1} - 7\ , \ n > 1. \end{cases}$ **10, 3, -4, -11, -18**

6. If $S_1 = 3$ and $S_n = 2S_{n-1}$ for $n > 1$, find S_5.   **48**

■ **Objective B** *Use computer programs to obtain terms of sequences. (Lessons 1-3, 1-4)*

7. What sequence will this program print when run?

```
10 FOR N = 1 TO 5
20    LET F = 3 * .1 ^ N
30    PRINT F
40 NEXT N
50 END        .3, .03, .003, .0003, .00003
```

8. Complete this BASIC program to find and print the first ten perfect squares.

```
10 FOR N = 1 TO  a. _?_   10
20    PRINT  b. _?_   N ^ 2
30 NEXT N
40 END
```

9. Complete this BASIC program to find and print the first 100 terms of the sequence:
$$20, 50, 80, 110 \ldots$$

```
10 LET T = 20
20 FOR N = 1 TO  a. _?_   100
30    PRINT T
40    T = T +  b. _?_   30
50 c. _?_   NEXT N
60 END
```

■ **Objective C** *Simplify expressions by using field properties, definitions, or theorems derived from the Distributive Property. (Lesson 1-5)*

In 10–16, simplify.

10. $-7 + 3(x - 4)$ **3x − 19**

11. $2y + x - (y - 11)$ **y + x + 11**

12. $\frac{2}{3}(c + 4c) - \dfrac{c}{3}$ **3c**

13. $20 - 5(a + b)$ **20 − 5a − 5b**

14. $(2m + 3)(m - 3)$ **2m² − 3m − 9**

15. $(a + c)(b + d)$ **ab + ad + bc + cd**

16. $\dfrac{3x + 6}{3}$ **x + 2**

■ **Objective D** *Solve and check linear equations and linear inequalities. (Lessons 1-7, 1-9)*

In 17–23, solve and check.

17. $\frac{3}{2}x = 9$ **6**

18. $\frac{3}{10}(t - 20) = \frac{6}{5}$ **24**

19. $\dfrac{6}{U} = 8$ **$\frac{3}{4}$**

20. $2V + 17 \le 23$ **V ≤ 3**

21. $8 - (w + 7) \le 0.5$ **w ≥ .5**

22. $\frac{2}{3}(6r - 3) > -r$ **r > $\frac{2}{5}$**

23. $.05(4500 - x) + .08x = 1200$ **32,500**

CHAPTER 1   Chapter Review   **53**

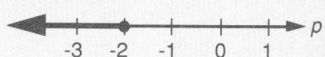
CHAPTER REVIEW

The main objectives for the chapter are organized here into sections corresponding to the four main types of understanding this book promotes: Skills, Properties, Uses, and Representations.

Skills include simple and complicated procedures for getting answers; at higher levels they include the study of algorithms.

Properties cover the mathematical justifications for procedures and other theory; at higher levels they include proofs.

Uses include real-world applications of the mathematics; at higher levels they include modeling.

Representations include graphs and diagrams; at higher levels they include the invention of new objects or metaphors to discuss the mathematics.

Notice that the groupings are not in increasing order of difficulty—there may be hard skills and easy representations; some uses may be easier than anything else, and so on.

■ **Objective E** *Rewrite formulas.* *(Lesson 1-8)* $n = \dfrac{4 - t_n}{5}$

24. Solve for n in the formula $t_n = 4 - 5n$.

25. The measure of an exterior angle of a regular polygon, θ, is given by

$$\theta = \frac{360}{n}$$

where n is the number of sides. Solve for n. $n = \dfrac{360}{\theta}$

26. Recall the formula $d = \frac{1}{2}gt^2$. What is the ratio of d to t^2? $\dfrac{g}{2}$

27. If $x = 3y$, then $\dfrac{x}{y} = \underline{\ ?\ }$. **3**

28. Which equation(s) is (are) solved for t? **a, d**

(a) $t = \dfrac{D}{R}$ (b) $10t - 5t^2 = h$

(c) $A_t = \frac{1}{2}h(b_1 + b_2)$ (d) $180(n - 2) = t$

PROPERTIES deal with the principles behind the mathematics.

■ **Objective F** *Use counterexamples to show errors in reasoning.* *(Lesson 1-6)*

In 29–32, find a counterexample to disprove the conjecture. **29) sample $(12 \div 6) \div 2 \neq 12 \div (6 \div 2)$**

29. Division is associative, that is, for all a, b, and c: $(a \div b) \div c = a \div (b \div c)$.

30. For all x, $x^2 \geq 1$. **$x = .5$**

31. If $m^4 = 16$, then $m = 2$. **$m = -2$**

32. The terms of the sequence with formula $t_n = n^2 - n + 11$ are all prime. **$n = 11$**

■ **Objective G** *Identify justifications in mathematical arguments.* *(Lessons 1-5, 1-6, 1-9)*

In 33–36, identify the property used to get from the first step to the second.

33. $5x + 17 = 85$
$5x = 68$ **Add. Prop. of Eq.**

34. $S = 2\pi r^2 + 2\pi rh$
$S = 2\pi r(r + h)$ **Dist. Prop.**

35. $\frac{1}{2}d < 9$
$d < 18$ **Mult. Prop. of Ineq.**

36. $h^2 - 3h + 4h + 5 = 0$
$h^2 + h + 5 = 0$ **Add. of Like Terms**

37. Justify each step in this rewriting of $-(y - x)$.
a. $-(y - x) = -(y + -x)$ **def. of subt.**
b. $= -y + -(-x)$ **Opp. of a Sum**
c. $= -y + x$ **Op-Op**
d. $= x + -y$ **Comm. Prop. of Add.**
e. $= x - y$ **def. of subt.**

■ **Objective H:** *State the domain for a variable in a given situation.* *(Lessons 1-2, 1-3)*

In 38–40, what is an appropriate domain for n in the following?

38. the formula for the number of diagonals $d = \dfrac{n(n - 3)}{2}$, where n is the number of sides in the polygon **$n \geq 3$; n an integer**

39. an explicit formula for t_n in a sequence **$n > 0$; n an integer**

40. $C = 1.30n$, the cost of a piece of beef weighing n pounds **$n > 0$; n real**

SES deal with applications of mathematics in real situations.

Objective I *Use sequences in real-world situations. (Lessons 1-3, 1-4)*

41. Sandra's annual salary is $26,000. She gets an increase of 6% at the end of each year. The sentence $a_n = 26{,}000(1.06)^{n-1}$ gives Sandra's salary at the end of n years.
    a. Write Sandra's salary for the first five years.   *See below.*
    b. At this growth rate, what would Sandra's salary be after 20 years with this company?   **$78,665.59**

42. Devin opened a savings account with $50. Each month he adds $15 to his account.
    a. Write the amounts in this account for the first six months.   *See below.*
    b. Write a recursive formula that generates the sequence giving his savings account balance. $S_1 = 50; S_n = S_{n-1} + 15, n > 1$

Objective J *Use models for the four fundamental operations to describe situations. (Lessons 1-1, 1-7, 1-9)*

43. The number of irrigated acres is I and the total number of acres is T. How many acres are not irrigated? $T - I$

44. The dimensions of a building are 100 times as large as the dimensions of its model. If a floor on the model is x cm long, how long is the floor on the building?   **100x**

45. There are s students per bus and b buses. How many students are there in all?   **sb**

46. Carol takes M minutes to walk B blocks. What is her walking speed? $\dfrac{B}{M}$

47. A baby blue whale weighs 4000 lb at birth and gains 200 lb a day while nursing. Then a formula that gives its weight W after d days of nursing is
    $$W = 4000 + 200d.$$
    a. Write an inequality that can be used to find the number of days a young blue whale has been nursing if it weighs at least 14,000 lb. (Baby blue whales nurse for 5 to 7 months.) $4000 + 200d \geq 14{,}000$
    b. Solve this inequality. $d \geq 50$

48. At Central High School all students are in grades 10, 11, or 12. This year $\frac{2}{5}$ of the students are in grade 10, $\frac{1}{3}$ are in grade 11, and 320 are in grade 12. How many students are at Central High this year?   **1200**

REPRESENTATIONS deal with pictures, graphs, or objects that illustrate concepts.

Objective K *Graph solutions to inequalities on a number line. (Lesson 1-9)*

49. Graph all solutions to $y \leq -6$.   *See margin.*

50. Solve and graph the solutions:
    $4x + 12 > 22$.   *See margin.*

41a) $26,000; $27,560; $29,213.60; $30,966.42; 32,824.40

42a) $50; $65; $80; $95; $110; $125

50.

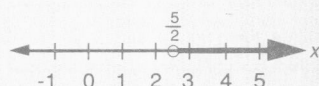

DAILY PACING CHART   2

DAILY PACING CHART ■ CHAPTER 2

Students in the Full Course should complete all but one of the chapters by the end of the year. Students in the Minimal Course will spend more time on quizzes and the Chapter Review. As such, these students should complete about ten or eleven chapters.

DAY	MINIMAL COURSE	FULL COURSE
1	2-1	2-1
2	2-2	2-2
3	2-3	2-3
4	Quiz (TRF); Start 2-4.	Quiz (TRF); 2-4
5	Finish 2-4.	2-5
6	2-5	2-6
7	2-6	2-7
8	2-7	Quiz (TRF); 2-8
9	Quiz (TRF); Start 2-8.	2-9
10	Finish 2-8.	2-10
11	2-9	Progress Self-Test
12	2-10	Chapter Review
13	Progress Self-Test	Chapter Test (TRF)
14	Chapter Review	
15	Chapter Review	
16	Chapter Test (TRF)	

TESTING OPTIONS

TESTING OPTIONS

■ Quiz for Lessons 2-1 Through 2-3   ■ Chapter 2 Test, Form A   ■ Chapter 2 Test, Cumulative Form
■ Quiz for Lessons 2-4 Through 2-7   ■ Chapter 2 Test, Form B

INDIVIDUAL DIFFERENCES

PROVIDING FOR INDIVIDUAL DIFFERENCES

The student text is written for the *average* student. The program, however, can be adapted for both less capable and for more capable students.

A blackline master (in the Teacher's Resource File) is provided for each lesson for those students who need more practice. The Teacher's Edition frequently provides Error Analysis and Alternate Approach features to provide additional instructional strategies.

For students who require additional challenge, Extension activities are regularly provided in the Teacher's Edition.

OBJECTIVES ■ CHAPTER 2

Students should master the chapter objectives by the time they complete the chapter.
To ensure mastery, there is continual review built into each set of lesson questions.
After students complete the chapter lessons, they assess their mastery on the Progress
Self-Test. Then they do the Chapter Review and pay special attention to those questions
that match the objectives missed on the Progress Self-Test. Students can get extra
practice on these objectives by using the master for each lesson in the Teacher's
Resource File.

OBJECTIVES FOR CHAPTER 2 (Organized into the SPUR categories—Skills, Properties, Uses, and Representations)	Progress Self-Test Questions	Chapter Review Questions	Lesson Master from Teacher's Resource File*
SKILLS			
A Translate variation language into formulas.	1–3	1 through 10	2-1, 2-2, 2-10
B Solve variation problems.	4	11 through 14	2-1, 2-2, 2-10
C Find slopes (rates of change).	7	15 through 20	2-4, 2-5, 2-7
PROPERTIES			
D Determine the effects of changes in the values of variables in a variation formula.	5–6	21 through 27	2-3, 2-10
E Identify the properties of variation graphs.	8–10	28 through 33	2-4, 2-5, 2-7
USES			
F Recognize variation situations.	11	34 through 38	2-2
G Fit an appropriate model to data.	16–17	39 through 42	2-8, 2-9
H Solve problems using joint and combined variation models.	18	43 through 48	2-1, 2-2, 2-10
REPRESENTATIONS			
I Graph variation equations and identify equations from graphs.	12–13	49 through 58	2-4, 2-5, 2-7
J Recognize the effects of a change in scale or viewing window on a graph of a variation equation.	15	59 through 62	2-6
K Read and interpret graphs of joint and combined variation.	14	63 through 66	2-9

* The masters are numbered to match the lessons.

OVERVIEW ■ CHAPTER 2

Chapter 2 has three interrelated ideas. The first is equations of variation. The second is a graphical representation of equations of variation. The third is modeling data using variation equations.

Lessons 2-1 through 2-3 and 2-10 introduce the basic language of variation. Lesson 2-3 concentrates on the important notion of how a change in one variable in a variation equation affects the other variable. We do not use proportions to solve variation problems, partly because we are trying to set up functions. In fact, we tell the students in Chapter 7 that they studied functions of variation in Chapter 2.

Lessons 2-4 through 2-7 concentrate on graphing equations of variation. In Lesson 2-6, students explore graphs of equations with an automatic grapher. Some of this material, namely the graph of $y = kx$ and possibly the graph of $y = kx^2$, will be review for your students. We emphasize that slope is a measure of the rate of change between points on a graph. The idea of slope is extended to nonlinear graphs. Students are expected to identify graphs of variation.

Lessons 2-8 and 2-9 introduce the idea of mathematical modeling from data. The emphasis is on situations that can be modeled by equations of variation. These lessons strengthen the work done on graphing earlier in the chapter, and set-up modeling as a major theme of this book. Lesson 2-10 presents the topic of combined and joint variation. When direct and inverse variations occur together, the situation is one of combined variation. In a joint variation, one quantity varies directly as the product of two or more independent variables, but not inversely as any variable.

PERSPECTIVES ■ CHAPTER 2

The Perspectives provide the rationale for the inclusion of topics or approaches, provide mathematical background, and make connections within UCSMP.

2-1

DIRECT VARIATION

The terms *dependent variable* and *independent variable* are used frequently in the book; therefore, it is important for students to know the meanings of these terms. Of course, the choice of the independent variable is often arbitrary, and this choice determines the dependent variable.

When students are given a formula, they usually understand that the variables are related, so that as one variable changes, so do the others. However, in Lesson 2-1, we are looking for a particular way in which the dependent variable changes. In Lesson 2-2, we think of dividing to get inverse variation.

The first three lessons of this chapter culminate in the Fundamental Theorem of Variation: If $y = kx^n$, and x is multiplied by c, then y is multiplied by c^n. Although it is not stated in Lesson 2-1, if n is positive, then $y = kx^n$ is a direct variation, and if n is negative, then $y = kx^n$ is an inverse variation.

2-2

INVERSE VARIATION

Of all the variation relationships in the physical world, the inverse square laws are among the most important since they occur so frequently. It is primarily because of them that inverse variation is taught at all.

The reason inverse square relationships are associated with light and sound intensity is that the set of points at a given distance from a given point is a sphere. If a sound S leaves a source at a given time, that sound will be dispersed on the surface of a sphere. Thus, the given amount of sound S is dispersed over an area $(4\pi r^2)$ proportional to the square of the radius. Therefore, at a given point on the sphere, the original amount of sound is divided by the square of the radius, which is why the intensity is proportional to the inverse square.

2-3

THE FUNDAMENTAL THEOREM OF VARIATION

Students may have some notion of the ideas of this lesson, but probably in the case of linear direct variation only. For instance, they know that if a person buys three times the number of onions than originally planned, then he or she will pay three times as much money for them.

Students typically have trouble with nonlinear variation situations. However, you should be able to exploit what students have learned in geometry about areas and volumes of similar figures. Point out that if $F \sim F'$ and x is the ratio of similitude, then the area of F' varies directly as the square of x (where the area F is the constant of variation), and the volume of F' varies directly as the cube of x (where the volume of F is the constant of variation).

For instance, suppose a rectangular box F with dimensions 3, 4, and 7 is similar to a rectangular box F'. Let $S_{F'}$ be the surface area of F', S_F be the surface area of F, $V_{F'}$ be the volume of F', and V_F be the volume of F. If the ratio of similitude is 5, then $S_{F'} = 5^2 \cdot S_F = 25 \cdot 122 = 3050$, and $V_{F'} = 5^3 \cdot V_F = 125 \cdot 84 = 10,500$.

2-4

THE GRAPH OF $y = kx$

Most of this lesson will be review for students. Those who have had previous UCSMP courses will have encountered slope twice before, in *Algebra* and in *Geometry*.

There are two important ideas to stress. First is the idea of slope as a rate of change. This idea is extended to nonlinear curves in the next lesson. Second is the idea that there are common features in the graphs of all equations of the form $y = kx$. We expect that students will recognize quickly what the graphs of important functions should look like. We also expect the reverse: students should be able to look at a graph and determine whether a simple equation could produce that graph. This latter idea is emphasized in Lessons 2-8 and 2-9.

2-5

THE GRAPH OF $y = kx^2$

This lesson extends the idea of slope to nonlinear graphs. An important idea is that constant slope is a characteristic of linear relations, and that nonconstant slope is a characteristic of non-linear relations.

This lesson introduces some of the properties of parabolas; additional properties are introduced later in the textbook. In this lesson, students should understand how the graph $y = kx^2$ is affected by the sign and value of k. They should be able to use this information to sketch the graph quickly.

2-6

USING AN AUTOMATIC GRAPHER

The automatic grapher is to graphing functions as the hand calculator is to arithmetic. In order to use one, you must know something about what to expect as an answer. You also must know the capabilities of the machine. In return, you get the advantage of more accurate and quicker performance than you could achieve by hand.

If fact, automatic graphers are far more important to graphing conceptually than calculators are to arithmetic. In arithmetic, a person can get answers to most questions by hand. But few people can graph a parabola as well as an automatic grapher can do. Thus, they provide for many students (and teachers) the first good graphs of equations that they have ever created.

The purpose of this lesson is to give students enough information so they can use automatic graphers throughout the rest of the course.

2-7

GRAPHS OF $y = \frac{k}{x}$ AND $y = \frac{k}{x^2}$

The hyperbola is introduced in this lesson as the graph of the equation $y = \frac{k}{x}$ rather than the more common equation $xy = k$. The form $y = \frac{k}{x}$ is used because it most clearly expresses the concept of simple inverse variation. This form also facilitates introducing the important concept of inverse square variation later in the lesson.

The notion of slope as rate of change is used again; this time exploring the idea that negative slope implies the curve is falling. Students who later take calculus will see this idea developed more thoroughly.

In this lesson, we ask students to determine the graph of a given equation. Starting in Lesson 2-8, we will ask the reverse question: Given a graph, what is its equation?

2-8

FITTING A MODEL TO DATA I

Each time students translate a real situation into an algebraic equation or numerical calculation, they are forming a mathematical model.

Students who have studied UCSMP *Algebra* (and perhaps other texts) have tried to find a line of good fit through a scatterplot. These students were describing a set of data with a linear mathematical model.

The mathematical models presented in this lesson are of a similar kind. Instead of looking for a linear relationship, we look for a variation relationship between two or more variables. We try to identify the kind of relationship and, if possible, the specific equation.

2-9

FITTING A MODEL TO DATA II

Students often get discouraged when they realize that some problems in mathematics are quite long. You can mention two facts about the use of mathematics in the real world. First, some people make their living doing mathematics. In so doing, they may spend days, weeks, or months working on the same problem. Second, computers have taken much of the tedium out of mathematical work. In certain situations, someone may have to determine the kind of variation represented in a graph, but a computer can then be used to determine an equation for the best fitting line or curve.

2-10

COMBINED AND JOINT VARIATION

This lesson continues the content of Lesson 2-9. Students now learn how to find the constant of variation. The study of combined and joint variation provides an opportunity to review the method of solving variation problems presented earlier in the chapter.

CHAPTER 2

Variations and Graphs

A construction worker walking on a board of a scaffold knows that too much weight will break the board. The largest weight that can be safely supported by a board depends on its width w, thickness t, and on the distance d between the board's supports.

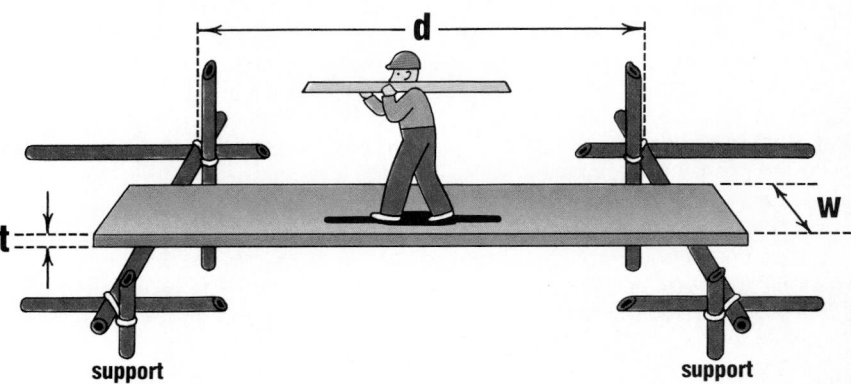

Using wider or thicker boards makes the scaffold stronger. Increasing the distance between the supports weakens the scaffold. Thus the strength varies as the distance is increased or as the dimensions of the board change. But how does it vary—a lot or a little? In this chapter, you will study variation, which examines how one quantity changes as others are changed.

The chapter begins with a simple relationship called direct variation.

56

OBJECTIVES

A Translate direct variation language into formulas.
B Solve direct variation problems.
F Recognize direct variation situations.

TEACHING NOTES

Motivate the learning of direct variation, both the definitions and uses of the terms, by using familiar examples such as those suggested by your students or given below.
(1) The cost of gas for a car varies directly as the amount of gas purchased.
(2) The price for cereal varies directly as the number of boxes purchased.
(3) The amount of sales tax varies directly as the total price of the goods purchased.
(4) The volume of a sphere varies directly as the cube of its radius.

Reading You may wish to have student volunteers read this lesson aloud in class. Point out to students that the language *varies directly as* and *varies directly with* are both acceptable expressions.

Stress the method for solving variation problems given in **Example 1**: Write the general variation formula, and use it to find *k*; then write the formula with the value of *k* in it, and use that formula to answer the question. This method is efficient for solving

LESSON

2-1

Direct Variation

In many places, you can get refunds for returning aluminum cans. For example, in New York, starting in 1987, you would get 5¢ per can returned. Thus, if r is the refund in cents and a the number of cans you returned, then

$$r = 5a.$$

Doubling the number of cans returned doubles your refund. Tripling the number of cans returned triples your refund. We say that r **varies directly as** a.

In Michigan you would get 10¢ per can returned, so $r = 10a$. Again, doubling the number of cans would double the refund; again r varies directly as a.

With the formula $A = \pi r^2$ for the area of a circle, as the radius r increases, the area A also increases. But if the radius is doubled, the area is quadrupled. Tripling the radius multiplies the area by 9.

In the formula $A = \pi r^2$, A varies directly as r^2. Often this wording is used: The area A varies directly as the *square* of r.

$A = \pi r^2$ $A = 9\pi r^2$

The formulas $r = 5a$, $r = 10a$, and $A = \pi r^2$ are all of the form $y = kx^n$, where k is a nonzero constant, called the **constant of variation,** and n is a positive number. They are all **direct-variation formulas.**

58

Definition:

A direct-variation formula is of the form $y = kx^n$, with $k \neq 0$ and $n > 0$

When y varies directly as x^n we also say y **is directly proportional to** x^n. For instance, the formula $A = \pi r^2$ can be read "the area of a circle is directly proportional to the square of its radius." Here $n = 2$ and $k = \pi$, so π is the constant of variation. In the formulas $r = 5a$ and $r = 10a$, $n = 1$ and the constant of variation is 5 for New York and 10 for Michigan.

Direct variation formulas occur often. For instance, after applying the brakes, the braking distance d needed to stop a car is directly proportional to the square of its speed s.

$$d = ks^2$$

The value of k depends on the type of car, the condition of the brakes, and the condition of the road.

Example 1 A certain car needs 25 ft to come to a stop if the brakes are applied at 20 mph. Assume that braking distance d and speed s satisfy the equation $d = ks^2$.
  a. Find k, and write the specific direct variation formula relating s and d.
  b. Find the distance needed to stop this car after the brakes are applied at 60 mph.

Solution
  a. You are given that $d = 25$ ft when $s = 20$ mph. To find k, substitute these values into the given equation $d = ks^2$.

$$25 = k \cdot 20^2$$
$$25 = 400k$$
$$k = \tfrac{1}{16}$$

Substituting $k = \tfrac{1}{16}$ into $d = ks^2$ gives

$$d = \tfrac{1}{16}s^2$$

as a formula relating speed and braking distance for this situation.

these types of problems—you might even call it an algorithm. Other algorithms are identified in later chapters.

ADDITIONAL EXAMPLES
1. Suppose that a pizza 12 inches in diameter costs $7.00. What should a pizza 15 inches in diameter cost? **Let P be the price of a pizza and d be its diameter. Then $P = kd^2$, and $k = \tfrac{7}{144}$. A 15-inch pizza will cost about $10.94.**

When discussing this example, point out that the quantity of ingredients for the crust and toppings, and hence the price, is proportional to the area, not to the linear dimensions.

2. Find the constant of variation if y varies directly as x, and $y = 32$ when $x = 0.2$. Find y when $x = 5$. **$k = 160$, so $y = 160x$. When $x = 5$, $y = 800$.**

3. The area of a circle varies directly as the square of the length of the diameter. Find the constant of variation. **$A = kd^2$. When $d = 1$, $r = \tfrac{1}{2}$ and $A = \pi r^2 = \tfrac{\pi}{4}$. Thus, $\tfrac{\pi}{4} = k \cdot 1 = k$, and the constant of variation is $\tfrac{\pi}{4}$.**

59

Question 1: This question provides an opportunity to review a large number of formulas for area and volume. In general, if all the figures covered by a formula are similar (in the geometric sense of the word), such as squares or spheres, then there exists a direct variation formula for their perimeter, area, or volume. Spheres have a surface area formula of the form $y = kx^2$, and a volume formula of the form $y = kx^3$. In the former case, $k = 4\pi$. In the volume formula, $k = \frac{4\pi}{3}$. Since all rectangular solids are not similar, their surface area and volume formulas are not simple direct variations. (The volume formula for a rectangular solid is a joint variation.)

Questions 12–15: Review the algorithm for solving variation problems. Students will use the algorithm frequently in Lessons 2-2, 2-3, and 2-10.

Error Analysis for Question 24b: Some students may multiply 0.206 mile per second by 4 miles. These students need to think of the units for the answer. The question asks for an answer in *time*; therefore, 0.206 mile per second must be divided into 4 miles, which "cancels" the mile units.

Question 25: It is important to note that not all braking distance formulas are direct variations. Some formulas consider the reaction time of the driver when computing braking distance. The formula $d = 1.1s + 0.05s^2$ gives stopping time in feet for a car traveling s miles per hour. $1.1s$ represents the distance traveled during the driver's reaction time, and $0.05s^2$ represents the distance traveled while braking.

b. Evaluate the formula when $s = 60$ mph.

$$d = \tfrac{1}{16}(60)^2$$
$$d = \tfrac{1}{16}(3600)$$
$$d = 225$$

Note that according to this formula, this car will need 225 ft to come to a stop after the brakes are applied at 60 mph.

Check The speed 60 mph is 3 times faster than 20 mph. The braking distance is 3^2 or 9 times farther. That is what you would expect for a direct variation in which d varies directly as the square of s.

Notice that to use variation to predict values, you carry out three steps.

1. Find the constant of variation.
2. Rewrite the variation formula using the constant.
3. Evaluate the formula.

In the variation formula $y = kx^n$, the value of y always depends on the value of x. For this reason, y is called the **dependent variable** and x the **independent variable**. In Example 1, the braking distance d depends on the speed s. In that situation, d is the dependent variable and s is the independent variable.

▪ ▪ ▪ ▪ ▪ ▪ ▪ ▪

Example 2 The weight w of an adult animal of a given species is known to vary directly with the cube of its height h.
a. Write an equation relating w and h.
b. Which is the dependent variable and which is the independent variable?

Solution
a. An equation for the direct variation is $w = kh^3$.
b. The dependent variable is w and the independent variable is h.

Questions

Covering the Reading

1. State an example from geometry of a direct variation formula. See margin.
2. In the formula $y = 3x^5$, __?__ varies directly as __?__ and __?__ is the constant of variation. y, x^5, 3

In 3 and 4, assume that y is directly proportional to the square of x.

3. *Multiple choice* Which equation represents this situation? b
   (a) $y = 2x$ (b) $y = kx^2$
   (c) $x = ky^2$ (d) $y = 2x^k$

60

4. Which is the dependent variable? *y*

5. Describe a situation in which the variation formula $r = .05n$ could be used. **See margin.**

In 6 and 7, suppose $y = -10x$.

6. Is this an example of direct variation? **Yes**

7. Find *y* when $x = 12$. **-120**

8. What three steps can be followed to predict values using variation? **See margin.**

In 9 and 10, refer to Example 1.

9. Find the distance needed to stop the car if its brakes are applied at 40 mph. **100 ft**

10. Suppose that some other car needs 30 ft to stop if its brakes are applied at 20 mph. What distance would it need to stop if its brakes are applied at 60 mph? **270 ft**

Applying the Mathematics

11. Suppose *W* varies directly as the fifth power of *z* and $W = 96$ when $z = 2$.
    a. Find the constant of variation. **3**
    b. Find *W* when $z = 10$. **300,000**

12. The power *P* generated by a windmill is directly proportional to the cube of the wind speed *w*.
    a. Write an equation relating *P* and *w*. Which of these is the dependent and which the independent variable? **See margin.**
    b. If a 10 mph wind generates 150 watts of power, how many watts will a 6 mph wind generate? **32.4 watts**

In 13 and 14, recall that when lightning strikes in the distance you do not see the flash and hear the thunder at the same time. You first see the lightning. Then you hear the thunder.

13. Write an equation to express this situation: "The distance *d* from the observer to the flash varies directly as the time *t* between seeing the lightning and hearing the thunder." $d = kt$

14. Suppose that lightning strikes a known point 4 miles away, and that you hear the thunder 20 seconds later. Then, how far away has lightning struck if 30 seconds pass between seeing the flash and hearing the thunder? **6 miles**

15. Refer to the formula $d = \frac{1}{16}s^2$ from Example 1. **See margin.**
    a. Pick a value for *s* and calculate the braking distance for that speed.
    b. Calculate the braking distance for twice that speed. **25 ft**
    c. According to your answers to parts a and b, when a car doubles it speed, it needs __?__ times the braking distance to stop. **See margin.**

ADDITIONAL ANSWERS
1. sample: $P = 4s$, where *P* is the perimeter of a square with sides of length *s*.

5. sample: Let *n* = the number of cans and *r* = the refund on *n* cans at 5¢ per can.

8. (1) Find the constant of variation; (2) Rewrite the variation formula using the constant; (3) Evaluate the formula.

12.a. $P = kw^3$; *P* is the dependent variable, *w* is the independent variable.

15.a. sample: If *s* = 10 mph, then *d* = 6.25 ft.
c. 4 (no matter what values were chosen in parts (a) and (b).

61

MORE PRACTICE
For more questions on SPUR
Objectives, use *Lesson Mas-
ter 2-1*, shown on page 61.

EXTENSION
It will help students to relate
direct variation to experiences they have had. Ask
each student to list three situations involving direct
variation which he or she is
familiar. Have students read
their examples to the class
and list on the chalkboard
any that you think may be
used for further discussion.

**ADDITIONAL ANSWERS
19. and 20.**

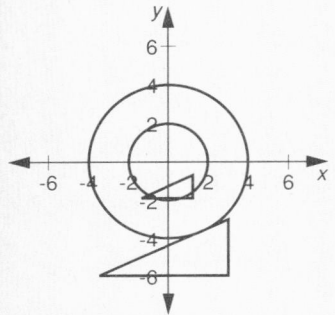

**24.b. about 19.4 sec;
Question 14 used 20
seconds for sound to travel
4 mi. They agree, given
that figures were rounded.
c. sample: humidity, air
pressure, pollution**

Review

In 16–18, refer to the graph below of the profits of the Acme Gadget Company. *(Previous courses)*

Profits (in $100,000)

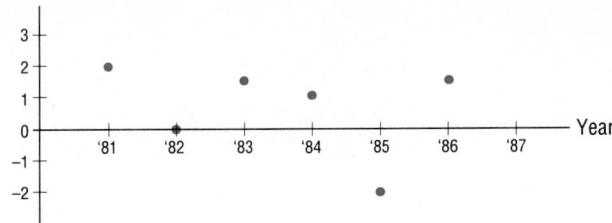

16. About how much profit did the company make in 1981?   **$200,000**

17. In what year(s) did the company lose money?   **1985**

18. During what time periods did the profits decline?   **1981–82, 1983–85**

In 19 and 20, copy the graph
below. Recall that a size change of
magnitude k means that coordinates are multiplied
by k. Graph the image of the given figure
under a size change of the given magnitude. *(Previous courses)*

19. magnitude 2 to the circle   **See margin.**

20. magnitude $\frac{1}{3}$ to the triangle   **See margin.**

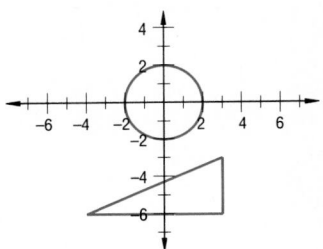

In 21–23, write as a power of 3. *(Previous course)*

21. $3^2 \cdot 3^4$ 3^6 **22.** $\dfrac{3^9}{3^2}$ 3^7 **23.** $(3^3)^5$ 3^{15}

Exploration

24. The speed of sound in air is about 1088 ft per second and the speed of light is about 186,000 miles per second.
   a. Convert the speed of sound to miles per second.   **0.206 mi/sec**
   b. Use your answer from part a to find the time it takes sound to travel four miles. Compare this answer to the values in Question 14.   **See margin.**
   c. What environmental conditions affect the speed of sound?
   See margin.
25. Find a manual for learning how to drive. Often these manuals contain charts of stopping and braking distances. Do the braking distances given there vary directly as the square of the speed?   **Yes**

62

Inverse Variation

In direct variation, as one variable increases in absolute value, so does the other. In another type of variation, as one variable increases in absolute value, the other decreases in a specific way. Here is an example.

Metro Car Sales hires students to wash cars in their display lots. The manager knows from experience that 36 students can wash all the cars in one hour. When fewer students work, each student needs to work more hours. If s equals the number of students who work and t equals the time (in hours) each student needs to work, then by the rate-factor model of multiplication,

$$st = 36 \text{ or } t = \frac{36}{s}.$$

Some combinations of s and t that might be used to finish the job are given in the chart below.

s	4	8	9	12	16
t	9	$4\frac{1}{2}$	4	3	$2\frac{1}{4}$

Notice that as s is doubled (say from 4 to 8), t is halved (from 9 to $4\frac{1}{2}$). This formula is of the form $y = \frac{k}{x^n}$ and is one instance of **inverse variation.** We say t **varies inversely as** s. In this example, the constant of variation k is 36.

Definition:

An inverse-variation formula is of the form $y = \frac{k}{x^n}$, with $k \neq 0$ and $n > 0$.

When y varies inversely as x^n, we also say y **is inversely proportional to** x^n. As with direct variation, inverse variation occurs in many kinds of situations.

Law of the lever: To balance a seesaw, the distance d a person is from the pivot is inversely proportional to his or her weight w.

$$d = \frac{k}{w}$$

Newton's Law of Universal Gravitation: The weight W of a body varies inversely with the square of its distance r from the center of Earth.

$$W = \frac{k}{r^2}$$

LESSON 2-2 Inverse Variation **63**

LESSON 2-2

RESOURCES
■ Lesson Master 2-2

OBJECTIVES

A Translate inverse variation language into formulas.
B Solve inverse variation problems.
F Recognize inverse variation situations.

TEACHING NOTES

It will help to relate inverse variation to experiences your students have had. The car wash example at the start of the lesson was chosen for this reason; it is used again in Lesson 2-7. It is an instance of the following generalization: The time required to do a job varies inversely as the number of people working on the job. Other examples are given below.
(1) The intensity of light varies inversely as the square of the distance from the light source.
(2) The volume of gas in a container varies inversely as the amount of pressure put on the gas.

In all of these situations, the product of the quantities in an inverse variation is constant. As the absolute value of the independent variables gets larger, the absolute value of the dependent variable gets smaller.

In **Example 2**, some students may not realize how the two values of r, 4000 and 22,000, were determined. Explain that r is the distance from the *center* of Earth to the astronaut, not from the surface of Earth to the astronaut.

The number n of oranges you can pack in a box varies inversely with the cube of an orange's diameter d.

$$n = \frac{k}{d^3}$$

In the picture below Nancy and Sam are trying to balance on a seesaw.

■ ■ ■ ■ ■ ■ ■ ■

Example 1 Sam, who weighs 40 pounds, is sitting 6 feet from the pivot.
a. Use the law of the lever to find the constant of variation for this situation.
b. Nancy weighs 45 pounds. How far away from the pivot must she sit to balance Sam?

Solution
a. Let $d =$ a person's distance in feet from the pivot.
Let $w =$ the person's weight in pounds.

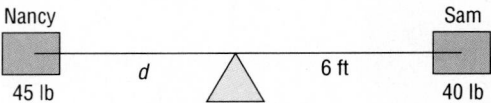

The law of the lever states that on a seesaw, the distance varies inversely as the weight, or

$$d = \frac{k}{w}.$$

To find k, substitute Sam's weight and distance into this equation.

$$6 = \frac{k}{40}$$
$$6 \cdot 40 = k$$
$$240 = k \quad \text{(The unit for } k \text{ is "foot-pounds.")}$$

b. You must find d when w equals 45 pounds. The work in part a tells you that the variation formula for this situation is

$$d = \frac{240}{w}.$$

Evaluate this formula when $w = 45$ lb.

$$d = \frac{240}{45}$$
$$d = 5\frac{1}{3}$$

Nancy must sit $5\frac{1}{3}$ feet away from the pivot to balance Sam.

Check Does 6 ft $\cdot$ 40 lb $= 5\frac{1}{3}$ ft $\cdot$ 45 lb? Yes.

64

You have probably seen pictures of astronauts floating almost weightless in space. Newton's Law of Universal Gravitation, which is an example of an **inverse-square variation,** can be used to calculate an astronaut's weight.

Example 2   If an astronaut weighs 135 pounds on Earth's surface, what will the astronaut weigh 18,000 miles above Earth's surface? (The radius of Earth is approximately 4000 miles.)

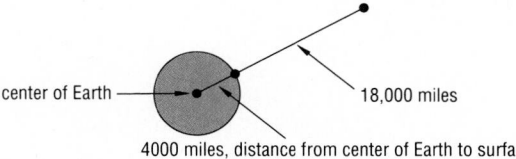

center of Earth

18,000 miles

4000 miles, distance from center of Earth to surface

Solution   Let W = the weight of the astronaut in pounds. Let r = the distance from the center of Earth to the astronaut. Since W varies inversely as the square of the distance,

$$W = \frac{k}{r^2}.$$

An astronaut 18,000 miles above Earth's surface is 22,000 miles from the center of the earth. You need to find W when $r = 22,000$.

First find k, the constant of variation, by substituting the values $W = 135$ lb and $r = 4000$ mi.

$$W = \frac{k}{r^2}$$

$$135 = \frac{k}{(4000)^2}$$

$$135 \cdot 4000^2 = k$$

$$135 \cdot 16,000,000 = k$$

For k so large, a calculator may use scientific notation. We can write

$$k = 2.16 \cdot 10^9.$$

Then $W = \dfrac{2.16 \cdot 10^9}{r^2}.$

Substitute $r = 22,000$ into the inverse-square formula and solve for W.

$$W = \frac{2.16 \cdot 10^9}{(22,000)^2}$$

$$\approx 4.4628 \text{ lb}$$

At 18,000 miles above Earth's surface, the astronaut weighs only about 4.5 pounds.

LESSON 2-2   Inverse Variation   **65**

NOTES ON QUESTIONS
Question 17:   The answer may surprise some students. Very tall basketball players should weigh quite a bit; a 7-footer should not weigh 7/6 as much as a 6-footer, but $(7/6)^3$ times as much. This is related to the Fundamental Theorem of Similarity, which students may have encountered in geometry: If two figures are similar, then the ratio of their volumes (areas) equals the cube (square) of the ratio of similitude.

MORE PRACTICE
For more questions on SPUR
Objectives, use *Lesson Mas-
ter 2-2,* shown on page 67.

EXTENSION
Small Group Work You
might wish to have students
work this problem in small
groups: The time needed to
travel a fixed distance varies
inversely with the average
rate. Tell students to select
an arbitrary distance, such as
100 or 500 miles, and then to
make a table of values of
rate and time. After each
group has completed its
table, discuss how changing
one variable affects the other
variable.

ADDITIONAL ANSWERS
**1. number of students who
work**

**7. The weight *W* of a body
varies inversely with the
square of its distance *r*
from the center of Earth, or
$W = \frac{k}{r^2}$.**

**23. sample: Newton
developed the differential
and integral calculus, a
theory of colors in optics,
and a law of cooling.**

Covering the Reading

In 1 and 2, refer to the Metro Car Sales problem.

1. The time to finish the job varies inversely as the __?__.   **See margin.**

2. Only 12 students are found to work. How long will it take them to complete the job?   **3 hours**

3. Which equation does *not* represent an inverse variation? (*k* is a constant.)   **a**

    a. $y = kx$ **b.** $y = \frac{k}{x}$ **c.** $xy = k$ **d.** $y = \frac{k}{x^2}$

4. The equation $y = \frac{k}{x^3}$ means *y* varies inversely as __?__.   **x^3**

In 5 and 6, refer to Example 1.

5. If Sam sits 5 feet from the pivot, how far away from the pivot must Nancy sit to balance him?   **$\frac{40}{9}$ ft ≈ 4.4 ft**

6. Find the distance needed to balance the seesaw below.   **$\frac{35}{18}$ m ≈ 1.94 m**

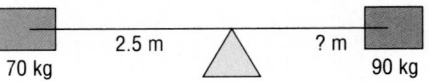

70 kg   2.5 m   ? m   90 kg

In 7 and 8, refer to Example 2.

7. State Newton's Law of Universal Gravitation.   **See margin.**

8. Find the weight of an astronaut in a space lab 300 miles above Earth if the astronaut weighs 150 lb on Earth.   **about 130 lb**

Applying the Mathematics

9. Suppose that *y* varies inversely as x^3 and that $y = 10$ when $x = 4$. Find the value of *y* when $x = 2$.   **80**

In 10 and 11, translate each statement into a variation equation.

10. The time *t* an appliance can be run on 1 kilowatt hour of electricity is inversely proportional to the wattage rating *w* of the appliance.   **$t = \frac{k}{w}$**

11. The intensity *I* of light varies inversely as the square of the observer's distance *D* from the light source.   **$I = \frac{k}{D^2}$**

12. Suppose in Question 11 that the light intensity is 30 lumens when the observer is 6.7 meters from the light.
    a. Find the constant of variation.   **1346.7**
    b. Find the light intensity when the distance between the observer and the light is 20 meters.   **about 3.37 lumens**

66

In 13–15, complete the sentence with the word "directly" or "inversely."

13. The volume of a sphere varies __?__ as the cube of its radius.   **directly**

14. At a given time of day, the height of a tree varies __?__ as the length of its shadow.   **directly**

15. The number of tiles needed to tile a floor varies __?__ as the square of the length of a side of the tile.   **inversely**

Review

16. At some restaurants, the price of a pizza varies directly with the square of its diameter. If you pay \$5.95 for a cheese pizza with a 10-inch diameter, how much should a 14-inch-diameter cheese pizza cost? *(Lesson 2-1)*   **\$11.66**

17. In 1985, the basketball player Manute Bol was 7'6" tall, and he weighed only about 200 pounds. Recall that a person's weight varies directly as the cube of his or her height. How much would you expect a man 5'10" tall with Manute's shape to weigh? *(Lessson 2-1)*   **94 lb**

18. Line *l* is parallel to line *m* in the figure below. The expressions represent angle measures. Find *y*. *(Previous courses, Lesson 1-6)*   **80°**

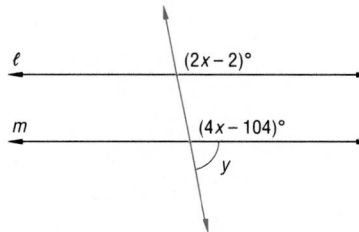

19. Solve: $7y + 2(4y + 1) \leq 10y$ *(Lesson 1-9)* $y \leq -\frac{2}{5}$

In 20–22, simplify *(Previous course)*

20. $x^{10} \cdot x^3$ x^{13} **21.** $\dfrac{x^{12}}{x^4}$ x^8 **22.** $(2x)^3$ $8x^3$

Exploration

23. Besides the Law of Gravitation, Isaac Newton discovered several other laws of classical physics. He was also very influential in the world of mathematics. Write a report about at least one other contribution of this remarkable person.   **See margin.**

NAME _____

■**SKILLS**   *Objective A (See pages 119–123 for objectives.)*
In 1–5, translate into a variation formula.

1. *A* varies inversely with *r*. $A = \dfrac{k}{r}$

2. *m* is inversely proportional to the square of *t*. $m = \dfrac{k}{t^2}$

3. *y* varies inversely with the cube of *x*. $y = \dfrac{k}{x^3}$

4. The number *n* of grapefruits that can fit into a box is inversely proportional to the cube of the diameter *d* of each grapefruit. $n = \dfrac{k}{d^3}$

5. The time required for a car to travel a given distance varies inversely with the speed at which the car is driven. $t = \dfrac{k}{s}$

■**SKILLS**   *Objective B*

6. *y* varies inversely as the square of *x*. If *x* = 3 when $y = -\frac{2}{3}$, find *y* when $x = \frac{1}{2}$.   **-8**

7. *y* varies inversely as the cube of *x*. If *x* = -5 when *y* = -2, find *y* when *x* = -2.5.   **-16**

■**USES**   *Objective F*
In 8–12, choose "directly" or "inversely" to complete each sentence.

8. The weight of a newspaper varies __directly__ as the number of pages it contains.

9. The speed of a runner varies __inversely__ as the time it takes her to travel a given distance.

10. The number of desks that can fit into a classroom varies __inversely__ as the size of the desks.

11. The area of a circle varies __directly__ as the square of its radius.

12. The perceived loudness of a radio varies __inversely__ as the square of the listener's distance from the speakers.

Continued   **11**

NAME _____
Lesson MASTER 2–2 (page 2)

■**USES**   *Objective H*

13. The number *N* of street-sweeping machines used to clean the streets of Gotham City is inversely proportional to the time *T* needed to do the job. If 125 machines take 10 days to finish a job, how many days would 200 street sweepers need? $6\frac{1}{4}$ **days**

14. The number of families that a truckload of grain can feed is inversely proportional to the amount of grain given to each family. If 35 families were given 8 kg each, how much grain would 50 families receive?   **5.6 kg each**

15. If you stand *d* meters away from a lightbulb, the intensity *I* of light reaching you is given by $I = \frac{k}{d^2}$. At 4 meters, the intensity is 67.5 units. What is the intensity at 8 meters?   **about 16.9 units**

16. The number of trees that can be planted per acre varies inversely as the square of the distance between each pair of trees. If planting 150 trees requires a distance of 8.5 feet between each pair, what is the necessary separation for 200 trees?   **about 7.4 feet**

12

RESOURCES
■ Lesson Master 2-3
■ Quiz for Lessons 2-1
Through 2-3

OBJECTIVE

D Determine the effects of changes in the values of variables in a variation formula.

TEACHING NOTES

When you discuss part (a) of the Fundamental Theorem of Variation in class, have students provide a justification for each line in the proof. Assume values are defined as in the proof.

1. $y_1 = kx^n$ Definition of direct variation

2. $y_2 = k(cx)^n$ Definition of direct variation; given

3. $y_2 = k(c^n x^n)$ Powers-of-a-Product Property

4. $= c^n(kx^n)$ Associative and Commutative Properties of Multiplication

5. $= c^n y_1$ substitution (step 1 into step 4)

In **Example 2,** it may help some students to see the equation rewritten as $dw = k$. Thus, if w is doubled, d must be halved to ensure the same product k.

68

LESSON

2-3

The Fundamental Theorem of Variation

In Lesson 2-1 you learned that after applying brakes, the distance d needed to stop a car is directly proportional to the square of its speed s. The braking distance d (in feet) and the speed s (in miles per hour) for a certain car were related by the equation $d = \frac{1}{16}s^2$. Some values of d and s are given in the following table.

s	10	20	30	40	50	60	80
d	6.25	25	56.25	100	156.25	225	400

What happens to the braking distance when the speed is tripled? One way to answer this question is to compare values from the table when the speed is tripled. For example,

if you go 20 mph, you need 25 feet to stop;

and

if you go 60 mph, you need 225 feet to stop.

Notice that when s is tripled, d is multiplied by nine. This pattern also holds if you compare the ordered pairs (10, 6.25) and (30, 56.25) from the above table:

$$30 = 3 \cdot 10$$

and

$$56.25 = 9 \cdot 6.25$$

Based on the two instances above, it seems reasonable to **conjecture** that if you triple a car's speed the braking distance needed to brake to a stop is multiplied by nine. The following example shows how to **prove** this conjecture.

■ ■ ■ ■ ■ ■ ■ ■

Example 1   Given the direct variation formula $d = \frac{1}{16}s^2$. Prove that if s is tripled, d is multiplied by nine.

68

Solution Let d_1 be the original distance (before tripling the speed) and let d_2 be the distance after tripling. To find d_2, s must be tripled. So replace s by $3s$. Here a proof is given in two-column form.

1.	$d_1 = \frac{1}{16}s^2$	given
2.	$d_2 = \frac{1}{16}(3s)^2$	substitution
3.	$= \frac{1}{16} \cdot 9s^2$	Power-of-a-Product Property
4.	$= 9 \cdot \frac{1}{16}s^2$	Associative and Commutative Properties of Multiplication
5.	$= 9 \cdot d_1$	substitution (step 1 into step 4)

Example 1 illustrates the following general theorem.

The Fundamental Theorem of Variation:

a. If y varies *directly* as x^n and x is multiplied by c, then y is multiplied by c^n.

b. If y varies *inversely* as x^n and x is multiplied by a nonzero constant c, then y is divided by c^n.

Proof:

We give the proof in paragraph form.
a. If y varies directly as x^n and y_1 is the original value of y, then

$$y_1 = kx^n.$$

When x is multiplied by c, a new value y_2 is generated and

$$y_2 = k(cx)^n.$$

Applying the Power-of-a-Product and the Associative and Commutative Properties gives

$$y_2 = k(c^n x^n)$$
$$= c^n(kx^n)$$
$$= c^n y_1.$$

b. If y varies inversely as x^n, then

$$y_1 = \frac{k}{x^n}.$$

When x is multiplied by c, a new value y_2 is generated. By an argument similar to the one above, you can show that

$$y_2 = \frac{y_1}{c^n}.$$

You are asked to supply the necessary steps in Question 15 at the end of the lesson.

ADDITIONAL EXAMPLES

1. Given the direct variation formula $d = \frac{s^2}{10}$, prove that if s is quadrupled, d is multiplied by 16.

Let d_1 be the original distance before quadrupling. To find d_2, s must be quadrupled. Replace s by $4s$:

1.	$d_1 = \frac{1}{10}s^2$	given
2.	$d_2 = \frac{1}{10}(4s)^2$	replace s with $4s$
3.	$= \frac{1}{10} \cdot 16s^2$	Power-of-a-Product Property
4.	$= 16\left(\frac{1}{10}s^2\right)$	Associative and Commutative Properties of Multiplication
5.	$= 16d_1$	substitution (step 1 into step 4)

2. In Jonathan Swift's *Gulliver's Travels*, the Brobdingnagians are similar to us but 12 times as tall. Since volume varies directly as the cube of height, the Brobdingnagians have 1728 times the volume we do. And since surface area varies directly as the square of height, they have 144 times the surface area. Compare the volume and surface area if:
a. they were only six times as tall.
$6^3 = 216$ times the volume, and $6^2 = 36$ times the surface area.
b. they were only twice as tall.
$2^3 = 8$ times the volume, and $2^2 = 4$ times the surface area.

3. Suppose y varies inversely as x^2 and x is tripled. What is the effect on y?
y becomes 1/9 as large.

NOTES ON QUESTIONS
Questions 6–13: These questions may be difficult for some students. Suggest that they substitute numbers for the variables in order to examine specific examples before reaching conclusions to the questions asked. *Examining specific cases* before forming a general conclusion is a good problem-solving strategy that students should know.

Alternate Approach for Questions 6–13: You can help develop students' intuition by using algebra to arrive at the answers. This more general approach may be discussed after students have worked through specific examples with numbers. Here are the algebraic solutions to **Questions 10 and 12.**

10. $y = \dfrac{10}{x}$

Replace x with $\frac{1}{2}x$ and we have

$y = \dfrac{10}{\frac{1}{2}x} = \dfrac{10}{\frac{x}{2}} = 2 \cdot \dfrac{10}{x}$

Thus, y is doubled when x is halved.

12. Original radius: r
Original circumference: $2\pi r$
Doubled radius: $2r$
Doubled circumference: $2\pi(2r) = 4\pi r$
Ratio of the larger circumference to the smaller one: $\dfrac{4\pi r}{2\pi r} = \dfrac{2}{1}$

Error Analysis for Question 15: Students may make the following error:

$\dfrac{k}{c^n x^n} = \dfrac{k}{c^n} \cdot \dfrac{k}{x^n}$

If this happens, remind students that they can multiply the fractions on the right side of the equation to check whether the product is equal to the left side. The product of the numerators here would be k^2, which indicates the error.

The Fundamental Theorem of Variation can be applied in many situations.

■ ■ ■ ■ ■ ■ ■ ■■

Example 2 In Lesson 2-2 you were given $d = \dfrac{k}{w}$ as the law of the lever. Nathan weighs twice as much as his daughter Stephie. Compare their distances from the pivot when they are balanced on a seesaw.

Solution Apply the Fundamental Theorem of Variation. Because Nathan weighs twice as much as Stephie, you are asked to find the effect of replacing w with $2w$ in the variation formula $d = \dfrac{k}{w}$. This is an inverse-variation equation with $n = 1$.

So when w is multiplied by 2, d is divided by 2. Thus Nathan's distance from the pivot is half that of Stephie's.

Questions

Covering the Reading

In 1 and 2, refer to the formula $d = \frac{1}{16}s^2$ and the table on speeds and braking distances at the start of this lesson.

1. The pairs (20, 25) and (40, 100) illustrate the pattern that if the car's speed is doubled, the braking distance is multiplied by __?__   4

2. Find two pairs of numbers that illustrate this result: if the car's speed is multiplied by four, then its braking distance is multiplied by 16. **See margin.**

3. If $y = kx^n$ and x is multiplied by c, then y is __?__   **multiplied by c^n**

4. If $y = \dfrac{k}{x^n}$ and x is multiplied by c ($c \neq 0$), then y is __?__.   **divided by c^n**

5. Refer to Example 2. Suppose Nathan weighs three times as much as his niece Oprah. Compare Nathan's and Oprah's distances from the pivot when they are balanced.
Nathan is $\frac{1}{3}$ as far from the pivot as Oprah.

Applying the Mathematics

In 6 and 7, $y = 5x^4$.

6. Describe the change in y when x is tripled.   **y is multiplied by 81.**

7. What happens to y when x is divided by three?   **y is divided by 81.**

In 8–10, state the effect that halving the x-values (multiplying them by $\frac{1}{2}$) would have on the y-values. **See margin.**

8. $y = 10x$ **9.** $y = 10x^2$ **10.** $y = \dfrac{10}{x}$

11. In a sentence or two, explain the difference in the effects on y-values of doubling the x-value in a direct variation and doubling the x-value in an inverse variation. **See margin.**

In 12 and 13, refer to the logos at the right. The radius of the larger logo is twice the radius of the smaller one.

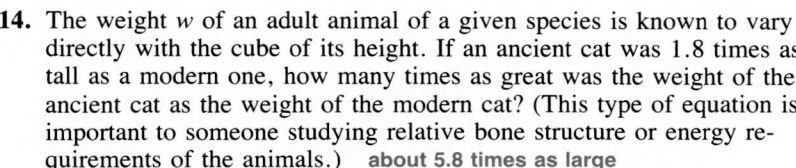

12. What is the ratio of the larger circumference to the smaller? $\frac{2}{1}$

13. What is the ratio of the larger area to the smaller? $\frac{4}{1}$

14. The weight w of an adult animal of a given species is known to vary directly with the cube of its height. If an ancient cat was 1.8 times as tall as a modern one, how many times as great was the weight of the ancient cat as the weight of the modern cat? (This type of equation is important to someone studying relative bone structure or energy requirements of the animals.)   **about 5.8 times as large**

15. Complete the proof of part b of the Fundamental Theorem of Variation. **See margin.**

Review

16. *Multiple choice* Most of the power of a boat motor goes into generating the wake (the track left in the water). The engine power P used to generate the wake is directly proportional to the seventh power of the boat's speed s. How can you express this relationship? *(Lesson 2-1)*
(a) $P = 7s$ (b) $s = kP^7$ (c) $P = ks^7$ (d) $P = k^7 s$ **c**

17. Suppose r varies directly as the 3rd power of s. If $r = 24$ when $s = 8$, find r when $s = 5$. *(Lesson 2-1)*   **about 5.86**

EVALUATION
A quiz covering Lessons 2-1
through 2-3 is provided in the
Teacher's Resource File.

ADDITIONAL ANSWERS
19.a. $x = 7, -7$

b. $x = \dfrac{7}{\sqrt{3}}, \dfrac{-7}{\sqrt{3}}$

c. $x = \dfrac{7}{2}, -\dfrac{7}{2}$

21.b. y is multiplied by 4,
8, and 16, respectively.

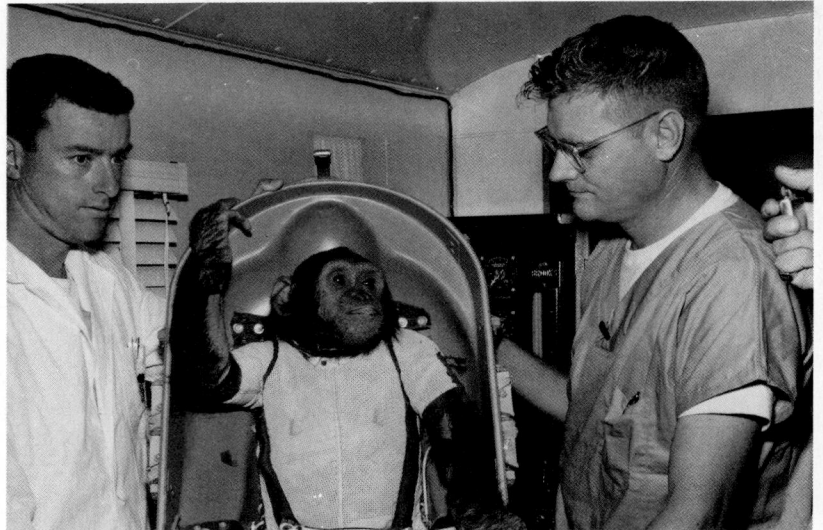

18. Use Newton's Law of Universal Gravitation, $W = \dfrac{k}{r^2}$, where $W =$ weight of a body and $r =$ distance from the center of the earth. Suppose a chimpanzee weighs 85 lb on the surface of the earth. How much will it weigh when orbiting in space 1,000 miles above the earth's surface? (Remember, the radius of the earth is about 4,000 mi.) *(Lesson 2-2)* **54.4 lb**

19. *Skill sequence* Solve. Remember to find two values for x. *(Previous course)*

    a. $x^2 = 49$ **b.** $3x^2 = 49$ **c.** $2x = \dfrac{49}{2x}$ **See margin.**

20. Use $a_n = 30 - (n - 1)$. Find the first value of n which makes $a_n < {}^-12$. *(Lessons 1-8, 1-9)* **44**

Exploration

21. Type the following BASIC program on your computer. This program finds values for the direct variation $y = x^n$ $(n > 0)$.

```
10 INPUT "A POSITIVE INTEGER"; N
20 PRINT "VALUES OF Y = X ^ N WHEN N = "; N
30 PRINT "X", "Y"
40 FOR X = -10 TO 10 STEP .5
50 LET Y = X ^ N
60 PRINT X, Y
70 NEXT X
80 END
```

    a. Run the program using $N = 1$. Notice that as x increases, y increases. When x doubles, what happens to y? **y doubles**
    b. Run the program for $N = 2, 3$, and 4. For each value of N, what happens to y when x doubles? **See margin.**

72

2-4

The Graph of $y = kx$

RESOURCES
- Lesson Master 2-4
- Visual for Teaching Aid 4 provides direct variation equations of the form $y = kx$.

OBJECTIVES

C Find the slope (rate of change) of the line through two points.
E Identify the properties of the graph of $y = kx$.
I Graph equations of the form $y = kx$ and identify an equation of the form $y = kx$ from its graph.

The purpose of this lesson is to study the properties of the graph of the direct variation formula $y = kx$.

Recall from the Questions in Lesson 2-1 that the length of time between seeing a flash of lightning and hearing thunder varies directly with the distance from the lightning. The formula $d = \frac{1}{5}t$ describes this situation for the values given in that lesson. This direct variation can also be represented graphically. Below is a table of some values that satisfy the equation $d = \frac{1}{5}t$.

t = time (in seconds)	0	5	10	15	20	25	30
d = distance (in miles)	0	1	2	3	4	5	6

Because the equation $d = \frac{1}{5}t$ is solved for d, we consider d the dependent variable and t the independent variable. When making graphs the independent variable is always plotted along the horizontal axis (x-axis) and the dependent variable along the vertical axis (y-axis).

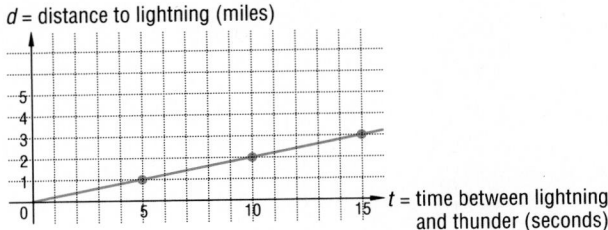

d = distance to lightning (miles)

t = time between lightning and thunder (seconds)

When *all* real-world solutions to the equation $d = \frac{1}{5}t$ are plotted in the coordinate plane, the graph is a ray starting at the origin and passing through the first quadrant. Note that neither distance nor time can be negative in this situation, so there are no points on the graph of $d = \frac{1}{5}t$ in any other quadrants.

LESSON 2-4   The Graph of $y = kx$ **73**

TEACHING NOTES

If students have not had much experience with slope, give some numerical examples and include the units. For instance, in the lesson's **Example**, calculate the slope as

$$\frac{5 \text{ miles} - 2 \text{ miles}}{25 \text{ seconds} - 10 \text{ seconds}}'$$

which gives 1/5 mile per second as the answer. Explain that the slope has *meaning*; it is a rate. In this case, the slope is the speed at which thunder travels, namely the speed of sound in air.

Stress to students that the slope of a line *does not* depend on the points chosen for calculating it.

Error Analysis An error students make when calculating slope is inverting the ratio. A mnemonic definition of slope is $\frac{\text{rise}}{\text{run}}$, or better yet $\frac{\text{"ryse"}}{\text{run}}$, which can help students remember that the change in vertical distance (y) is the first member of the ratio.

In general, the graph of $y = kx$ is a line through the origin. Recall that the steepness of a line is measured by a number called the **slope.** The slope of a line is the **rate of change** between any two points on the line. Let (x_1, y_1) and (x_2, y_2) be the two points. Then as pictured below, the expression $y_2 - y_1$ is the vertical change and $x_2 - x_1$ is the horizontal change.

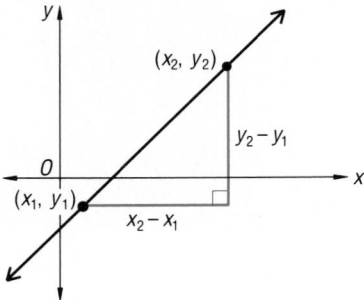

$$\text{slope} = \frac{\text{change in vertical distance}}{\text{change in horizontal distance}}$$

Definition:

The slope of the line through two points (x_1, y_1) and (x_2, y_2) equals

$$\frac{y_2 - y_1}{x_2 - x_1}.$$

Example Find the slope of the line with equation $d = \frac{1}{5}t$, where t is the independent variable and d the dependent variable.

Solution Find two points on the line. Then use the definition of slope. Either point may be considered (x_1, y_1).
Here we use $(x_1, y_1) = (10, 2)$ and $(x_2, y_2) = (25, 5)$.

$$\text{slope} = \frac{y_2 - y_1}{x_2 - x_1} = \frac{5 - 2}{25 - 10} = \frac{3}{15} = \frac{1}{5}$$

Regardless of the points chosen, the slope of the line $d = \frac{1}{5}t$ will be $\frac{1}{5}$. Check the visual pattern. For every change of 5 horizontal units there is a change of 1 vertical unit. An equivalent way to say this is that for every change of 1 horizontal unit, there is a change of $\frac{1}{5}$ of a vertical unit.

slope $= \frac{1}{5}$

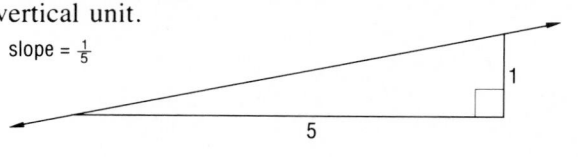
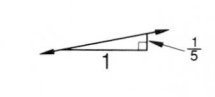

$$\frac{1}{5} = \frac{\frac{1}{5}}{1}$$

74

Notice the constant of variation in the equation $d = \frac{1}{5}t$ from Example 1 equals the slope of the line. Each value is $\frac{1}{5}$.

Below are graphs of four direct-variation equations of the form $y = kx$.

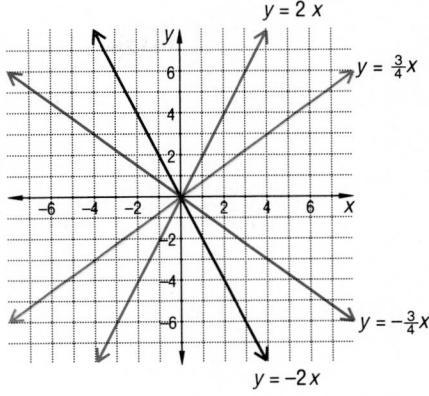

Observe that in each case the graph is a line through the origin with slope k. As examples, the slope of $y = 2x$ is 2 and the slope of $y = -\frac{3}{4}x$ is $-\frac{3}{4}$. This is true for all values of k.

Theorem:

The graph of the direct-variation equation $y = kx$ has constant slope k.

Proof:

Let (x_1, y_1) and (x_2, y_2) be two distinct points on $y = kx$, with $k \neq 0$. Then, substitute in the equations

$$y_1 = kx_1$$

and
$$y_2 = kx_2.$$

Subtract the equations:

$$y_2 - y_1 = kx_2 - kx_1$$

Use the distributive property:

$$y_2 - y_1 = k(x_2 - x_1)$$

Solve for k:

$$\frac{y_2 - y_1}{x_2 - x_1} = k$$

So k is the slope.

LESSON 2-4   The Graph of $y = kx$ **75**

NOTES ON QUESTIONS
Questions 7-9: The numbers in these items were purposely chosen to prevent students from calculating the slope solely by counting squares on a grid where each tick mark represents one unit.

Question 10: Students are required to draw a graph. Stress that c and g both represent quantities greater than or equal to 0; thus, as in the lesson's **Example**, the graph lies entirely in the first quadrant. Some students may have trouble scaling the axes. Remind them that the horizontal and vertical axes need not be drawn to the same scale and, for this reason, scales used when graphing should be clearly indicated.

6.a.

x	y = 3x	y = ½x
4	12	2
3	9	3/2
2	6	1
1	3	1/2
0	0	0
-1	-3	-1/2
-2	-6	-1
-3	-9	-3/2
-4	-12	-2

b.

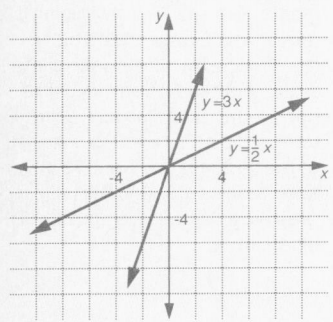

10.b. sample:

g	c
4	3.6
6	5.4
9	8.1

c.

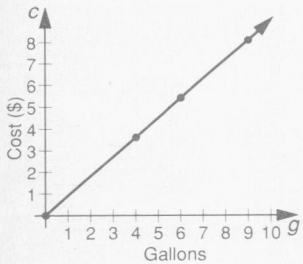

Cost ($) / Gallons

Questions

Covering the Reading

1. The slope of a line is found by dividing the change in __?__ distance by the change in __?__ distance between any two points on the line. **vertical; horizontal**

2. By definition, $\frac{y_2 - y_1}{x_2 - x_1}$ is the slope of the line through the two points __?__ and __?__. **$(x_1, y_1); (x_2, y_2)$**

3. What is the slope of the line $d = \frac{1}{5}t$? **$\frac{1}{5}$**

4. A slope of $-\frac{3}{4}$ means that for every change of 4 units to the right there is a change of __?__ units __?__; it also means that for every change of 1 unit to the right there is a change of __?__ units __?__. **3, down; $\frac{3}{4}$, down**

5. The graph of every direct variation equation $y = kx$ is a __?__, with slope __?__ and passing through the point __?__. **a line; k; (0, 0)**

6. Use the equations $y = 3x$ and $y = \frac{1}{2}x$.
   a. Complete the following table. **See margin.**

x	y = 3x	y = ½x
4		
3		
2		
⋮		
-4		

   b. On a single set of axes, graph both lines using the values from the table above. **See margin.**
   c. The slope of the line with equation $y = 3x$ is __?__. **3**
   d. The slope of the line with equation $y = \frac{1}{2}x$ is __?__. **$\frac{1}{2}$**

Applying the Mathematics

In 7–9, find the slope of:

7. a mountain road that rises 3.6 vertical meters for each 60 horizontal meters. **0.06**

8. the line through the points (6, 42) and (0, 0). **7**

9. a submarine dive if the submarine drops 2000 feet while moving forward 8000 feet. **$-\frac{1}{4}$**

10. The cost c of gasoline varies directly with the number of gallons g bought.
    a. If 15 gallons cost $13.50, find a formula for c in terms of g. **c = 0.9g**
    b. Make a table of three pairs of solutions to the equation in part a. **See mar**
    c. Graph these solutions. They should lie on a ray. **See margin.**
    d. What is the slope of the ray in part c? **0.9**

76

11. Graphs that slant up as you read from left to right have __?__ slope; graphs that slant down as you read from left to right have __?__ slope.
positive, negative

12. Match each graph with its equation. On each graph the *x*-axis and the *y*-axis have the same scale.

I. $y = 3x$ d

II. $y = -3x$ b

III. $y = \frac{1}{3}x$ a

IV. $y = -\frac{1}{3}x$ c

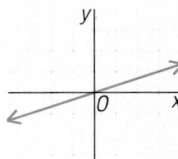 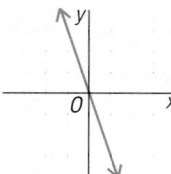

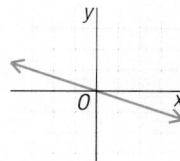 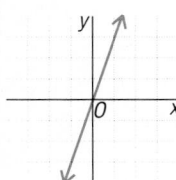

13. Refer to the drawing below.

a. Use the definition of slope to calculate the slope of the line. Simplify your answer.   **k**

b. What have you proved?   **See margin.**

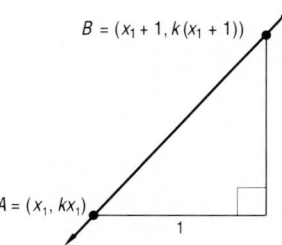

$B = (x_1 + 1, k(x_1 + 1))$

$A = (x_1, kx_1)$

1

Review

14. State whether the formula is a direct variation, an inverse variation or neither. *(Lessons 2-1, 2-2)*

a. $y = -\dfrac{8}{x}$ **inverse variation**

b. $y = -\dfrac{x}{8}$ **direct variation**

c. $y = x - 11$ **neither**

d. the law of the lever   **inverse variation**

e. the volume of a regular pyramid related to its base area if the height is held constant (You may want to refer to the Appendix of Geometry Formulas.)   **direct variation**

LESSON 2-4   The Graph of $y = kx$ 77

13.b. The slope of a line whose equation is of the form **y = kx** is **k**.

NAME _____

LESSON **MASTER 2–4**
QUESTIONS ON **SPUR** OBJECTIVES

■ **SKILLS**   *Objective C (See pages 119–123 for objectives.)*
In 1–3, find the slope of the line through the two given points.

1. (8, 14), (12, 21) $\dfrac{7}{4}$

2. (-16, 20), (12, -15) $\dfrac{5}{4}$ / 8

3. (2.5, -3.1), (-6.8, 4.9)   9.3

4. Find the slope of the graph at the right. $-\dfrac{3}{2}$

■ **PROPERTIES**   *Objective E*

5. The graph of the equation $y = -3x$ is a line having slope _____.

6. The graph of the equation $y = 0.07x$ is a line having slope _____.

-3
0.07

■ **REPRESENTATIONS**   *Objective I*
In 7–10, graph each equation.

7. $y = \frac{1}{3}x$

8. $y = \frac{1}{2}x$

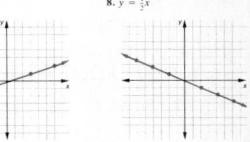

14   *Continued*   *Advanced Algebra © Scott, Foresman and Company*

NAME _____
Lesson MASTER 2–4 (page 2)

9. $y = 2x$

10. $y = -3x$

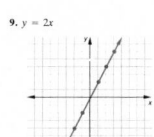 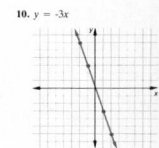

■ **REPRESENTATIONS**   *Objective J*

11. Match each graph with its equation. On each graph, the *x*- and *y*-axis have the same scale.

I. $y = 4x$ II. $y = -4x$
III. $y = \frac{1}{4}x$ IV. $y = -\frac{1}{4}x$

a. II   b. IV

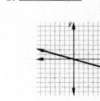

c. III   d. I

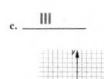

Advanced Algebra © Scott, Foresman and Company   15

77

MORE PRACTICE
For more questions on SPUR
Objectives, use *Lesson Master 2-4,* shown on page 77.

EXTENSION
To extend **Question 19**, have students find out how the terms are used. Have them talk to: (a) an accountant, an investment banker or an economist; (b) a roofer or some other person involved in construction; (c) a road construction worker, a driver of large trucks, or a commercial or amateur pilot.

EVALUATION
Alternative Assessment
Call upon three or four students to explain what they have learned in this lesson. Provide feedback on any incorrect statements students may make; that is, incorrect statements should be corrected. After all students have responded, give a brief summary of their responses.

ADDITIONAL ANSWERS
19.a. sample: economist
b. sample: mechanical engineer
c. sample: civil engineer

15. In the variation equation $W = \dfrac{k}{d}$, what is the effect on W if:

    a. d is tripled?   **W is divided by 3**

    b. d is halved? *(Lesson 2-3)*   **W is multiplied by 2**

16. Assume the cost of a spherical ball bearing varies directly as the cube of its diameter. What is the ratio of the cost of a ball bearing 6 mm in diameter to the cost of a ball bearing 3 mm in diameter? *(Lesson 2-3)* **8**

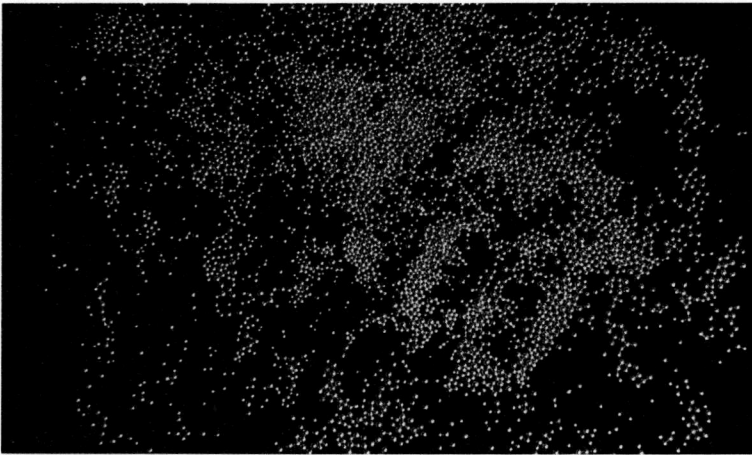

17. *Skill sequence*   Solve for x. *(Lessons 1-7, 1-8)*

    a. $3x = 2$ $x = \frac{2}{3}$ **b.** $3x = 2y$ $x = \frac{2y}{3}$

    c. $3x = 2y + 6$ $x = \frac{2y}{3} + 2$ **d.** $3(x + 5) = 2(y + 6)$ $x = \frac{2}{3}y - 1$

18. Find a counterexample to disprove the conjecture: If $a > b$ and $c > d$, then $ac > bd$. *(Lesson 1-6)* **sample:** $a = -7, b = -10, c = -1, d = -5$

Exploration

19. Each of the following terms is a synonym for "slope." Find out who might use each term. **See margin.**

    a. marginal cost   **b.** pitch   **c.** grade

LESSON
2-5

The Graph of $y = kx^2$

In Lesson 2-1 you learned that the distance needed to stop a car after applying the brakes varies directly with the square of the car's speed. The formula $d = \frac{1}{16}s^2$ describes this relation between braking distance and speed for a certain car. A table of some solutions to this equation is given below.

s	0	10	20	30	40	50	60	70
d	0	6.25	25	56.25	100	156.25	225	306.25

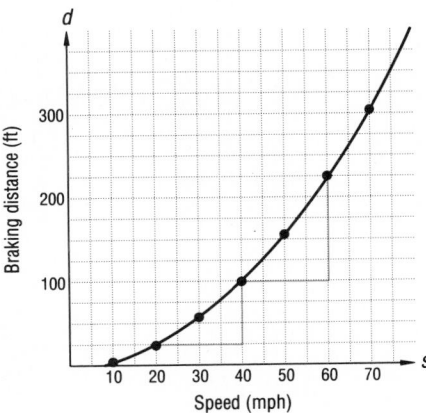

The points do not all lie on a straight line. This can be verified by calculating the rate of change between different pairs of points on the graph.

LESSON 2-5 The Graph of $y = kx^2$ 79

LESSON 2-5

RESOURCES
- Lesson Master 2-5
- Visual for Teaching Aid 5 provides the graph for the braking distance versus speed formula, which is used with **Example 1**.
- Visual for Teaching Aid 6 displays the graphs of $y = kx^2$ used in **Examples 2 and 3**.

OBJECTIVES

E Identify the properties of the graph of $y = kx^2$.

I Graph equations of the form $y = kx^2$ and identify an equation of the form $y = kx^2$ from its graph.

TEACHING NOTES

When discussing the graph on page 79, point out that the scale on each axis is different, which makes it difficult to estimate the slopes from the picture. Use this example to stress to students the importance of considering the scales on the axes before making assumptions about slope. Remind them that they should, in fact, always consider the scales when reading any graph.

Be sure students understand that the rate of change between points on a parabola *does* depend on the points chosen for calculating it.

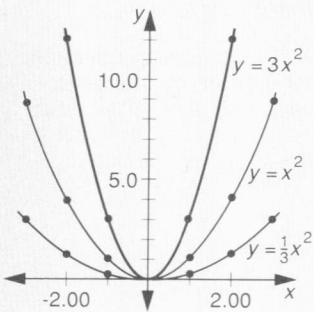
Example 1 Find the rate of change
a. r_1 between (20, 25) and (40, 100);
b. r_2 between (40, 100) and (60, 225).

Solution
a. Use the definition of slope:

$$r_1 = \frac{100\ \text{ft} - 25\ \text{ft}}{40\ \text{mph} - 20\ \text{mph}} = \frac{75\ \text{ft}}{20\ \text{mph}} = 3.75\ \text{ft/mph}$$

This means that on the average when driving between 20 mph and 40 mph, for every increase of 1 mph in speed, you need 3.75 more feet of braking distance.

b. Similarly, $r_2 = \dfrac{225\ \text{ft} - 100\ \text{ft}}{60\ \text{mph} - 40\ \text{mph}} = \dfrac{125\ \text{ft}}{20\ \text{mph}} = 6.25\ \text{ft/mph}$.

So on the average, between $s = 40$ and $s = 60$ for every change of 1 mph (the horizontal unit), there is a change of 6.25 feet of braking distance (the vertical unit).

Check Look at the graph. Is segment BC with slope 6.25 steeper than segment AB with slope 3.75?

Yes, it is.

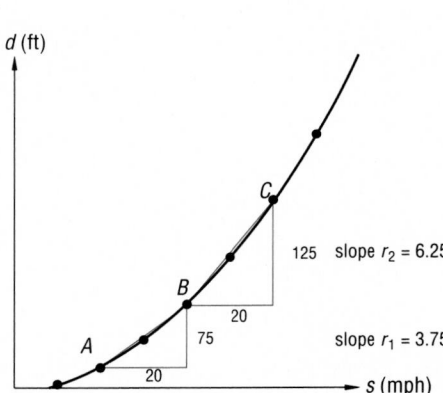

Because the rate of change between different pairs of points on the graph of $y = \dfrac{s^2}{16}$ is not constant, two conclusions can be drawn:
1. The graph of $y = \tfrac{1}{16}s^2$ is not a line.
2. The steepness of the graph cannot be described by a single number.
The equation $d = \tfrac{1}{16}s^2$ is a direct-variation formula of the form $y = kx^2$. In order to draw conclusions about the graphs of equations of this form, you must examine additional cases.

80

Example 2 Graph solutions to the following three equations:

$$y = x^2$$
$$y = 2x^2$$
$$y = \tfrac{1}{4}x^2$$

Solution Make a table of solutions. To save space, the value of the independent variable is written only once.

x	$y = x^2$	$y = 2x^2$	$y = \tfrac{1}{4}x^2$
0	0	0	0
1	1	2	$\tfrac{1}{4}$
2	4	8	1
3	9	18	$\tfrac{9}{4}$
-1	1	2	$\tfrac{1}{4}$
-2	4	8	1
-3	9	18	$\tfrac{9}{4}$

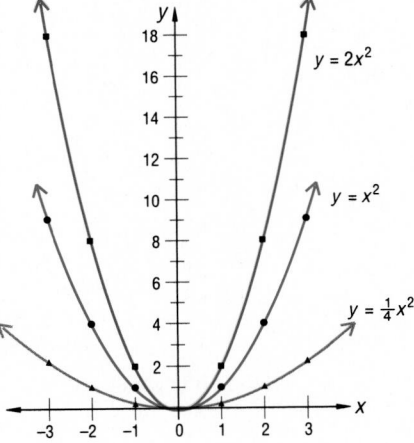

Observe that the graphs of $y = x^2$, $y = 2x^2$, and $y = \tfrac{1}{4}x^2$ are curves. These curves are called **parabolas**. Because each of these parabolas coincides with its reflection image over the y-axis, each is **reflection-symmetric**. The y-axis is the **line of symmetry**. Also, each parabola passes through the point (0, 0). The graph of $y = 2x^2$ goes up faster than the graph of $y = x^2$; the graph of $y = \tfrac{1}{4}x^2$ goes up more slowly.

The graph of $d = \tfrac{1}{16}s^2$ plotted at the beginning of this lesson goes up more slowly than any of the parabolas of Example 2. It is half a parabola because speed cannot be negative. There are no points in the second quadrant.

LESSON 2-5   The Graph of $y = kx^2$ 81

b. Graph solutions to the following:

$$y = -x^2$$
$$y = -3x^2$$
$$y = -\tfrac{1}{3}x^2$$

x	$y=-x^2$	$y=-3x^2$	$y=-\tfrac{1}{3}x^2$
0	0	0	0
±1	-1	-3	$-\tfrac{1}{3}$
±2	-4	-12	$-\tfrac{4}{3}$
±3	-9	-27	-3

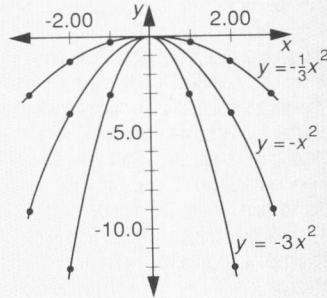

3. The force exerted by the wind on a sail of fixed area is modeled by the formula $F = 3w^2$, where force is measured in pounds and wind is measured in miles per hour. Graph this relationship for $0 \leq w \leq 10$. Using the graph, approximate the force on the sail from a 9-mph wind.

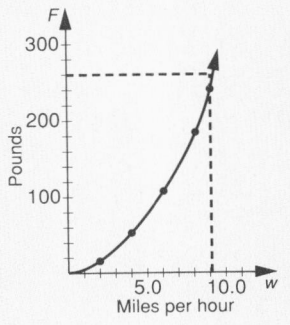

Estimated answer: 260 lb
Formula answer: 243 lb

Questions 8c and d:
Some students may find a
discrepancy between their
answers. If this is the case,
discuss the consequences of
estimation. If the number of
houses that can be served
by the water main is based
on overestimation, the
owners will have water supply problems. If the number
of houses is based on under-
estimation, it will not affect
the owners' water supply.

**Computer for Question
11:** If possible, demon-
strate use of this program in
class by first letting $k = 1$.
Use the output to review the
Fundamental Theorem of
Variation. Repeat for $k = 2$,
3, or any real number of your
choice. Regardless of the
choice of k, as x is multiplied
by c, y is multiplied by c^2.

Example 3 shows graphs of $y = kx^2$ for two negative values of k.

■ ■ ■ ■ ■ ■ ■ ■

Example 3 Graph solutions to the following two equations:

$$y = -x^2$$
$$y = -\tfrac{1}{4}x^2$$

Solution Make a table, using integer values of x from 4 to -4. Recall that $-x^2$ means "the opposite of x^2" or $-1 \cdot x^2$. Plot the ordered pairs.

x	$y = -x^2$	$y = -\tfrac{1}{4}x^2$
4	-16	-4
3	-9	-2.25
2	-4	-1
1	-1	-0.25
0	0	0
-1	-1	-0.25
-2	-4	-1
-3	-9	-2.25
-4	-16	-4

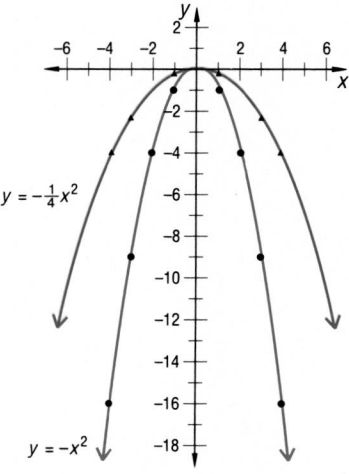

The graphs in Example 3 have shapes similar to those in Example 2. Again, each curve passes through the origin and is symmetric to the y-axis. However, we say that the curves in Example 3 "open down," while those in Example 2 "open up." In general, for $y = kx^2$, when $k > 0$ the parabola opens up and when $k < 0$ the parabola opens down.

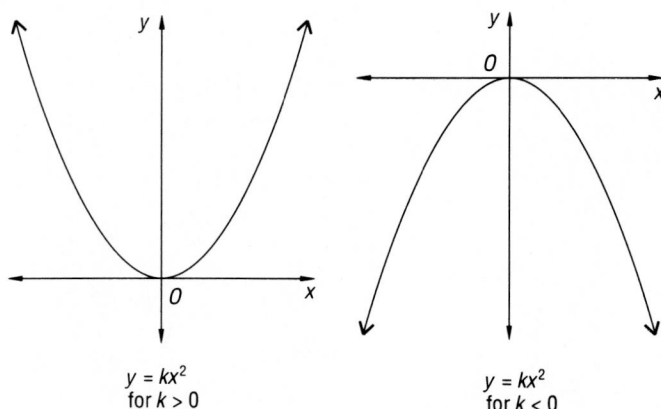

$y = kx^2$
for $k > 0$

$y = kx^2$
for $k < 0$

82

Questions

Covering the Reading

In 1–3, refer to the formula $d = \frac{1}{16}s^2$ relating speed and braking distance. *True or false*

1. The graph is a straight line. **False**

2. The rate of change on the graph is constant, regardless of the points used. **False**

3. The replacement set for *s* is the set of all real numbers. **False**

4. Name the type of curve that results from graphing $y = kx^2$ ($k \neq 0$). **parabola**

5. What does it mean to say that the graph of $y = kx^2$ is symmetric to the *y*-axis? **See margin.**

6. In general, for what values of *k* does the graph of $y = kx^2$
   a. open up? **when $k > 0$**   **b.** open down? **when $k < 0$**

7. **a.** Make a table of solutions for $x = -2, -1, 0, 1,$ and 2 for the following three equations. **See margin.**
   b. Graph the solutions on one set of axes. Use as the domain the set of real numbers between -2 and 2 inclusive. **See margin.**
   $$y = x^2 \qquad y = 3x^2 \qquad y = -3x^2$$

Applying the Mathematics

8. Let *N* represent the number of houses that can be served by a water main of diameter *d* centimeters. Suppose $N = \frac{1}{2}d^2$.
   a. Make a table of solutions for this equation. For values of *d* use 0, 10, 20, 30, 40. **See margin.**
   b. Graph these solutions. **See margin.**
   c. Estimate from your *graph* the number of homes that can be served by a main of diameter 35 cm. **about 600 homes**
   d. According to the *variation equation*, how many homes can be served by a main of diameter 35 cm? **612.5 homes**

9. Match each graph with the proper equation. Each graph has the same scale.
   $$y = \frac{1}{2}x^2 \quad y = -2x \quad y = -x^2 \quad y = 3x^2 \quad \text{See margin.}$$

   a.   **b.**   **c.**   **d.**

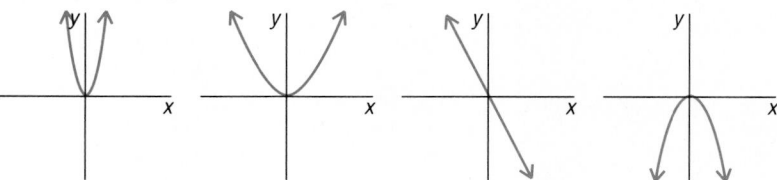

LESSON 2-5   The Graph of $y = kx^2$ **83**

ADDITIONAL ANSWERS
5. If the parabola is folded about the *y*-axis, the halves of the parabola coincide.

7.a.

x	y = x²	y = 3x²	y = -3x²
2	4	12	-12
1	1	3	-3
0	0	0	0
-1	1	3	-3
-2	4	12	-12

b.

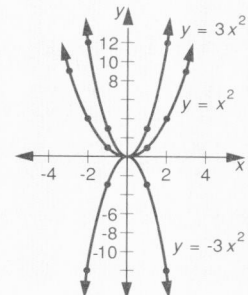

8.a.

d	N = ½d²
0	0
10	50
20	200
30	450
40	800

b.

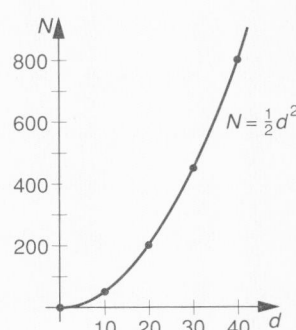

9.a. $y = 3x^2$ **b.** $y = \frac{1}{2}x^2$
c. $y = -2x$ **d.** $y = -x^2$

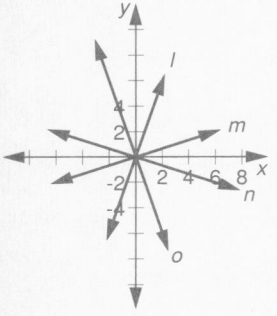
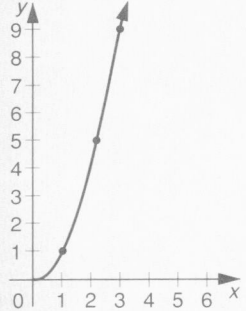
10. Refer to the table and graph of $y = x^2$ in Example 2. Find the rate of change between the points.
   a. (0, 0) and (1, 1) 1
   b. (1, 1) and (2, 4) 3
   c. (2, 4) and (3, 9) 5
   d. (3, 9) and (4, 16) 7
   e. Use your results from parts a to d to make a conjecture about the rate of change between the points (n, n^2) and $(n + 1, (n + 1)^2)$.
   f. Prove your conjecture by calculating the rate of change for the points in part e.   See margin.

11. You do not need a computer for this question. Here is a computer program in BASIC that takes a value of k and prints a list of solutions to $y = kx^2$.

```
10 PRINT "WHAT IS K?"
20 INPUT K
30 PRINT "SOLUTIONS TO Y = K * X ^ 2"
40 PRINT "X", "Y"
50 FOR X = -5 TO 5
60    LET Y = K * X ^ 2
70    PRINT X,Y
80 NEXT X
90 END
```

   a. How many ordered pairs of solutions will be printed?   11
   b. What is the first pair to be printed?   -5, 25k
   c. What is the last pair to be printed?   5, 25k
   d. Describe the output that would result from changing line 50 to

   ▨ FOR X = -5 TO 5 STEP .5.   See margin.

Review

12. The Fahrenheit and Celsius scales indicate temperature. Temperature can also be measured in kelvins. This measurement is sometimes called measuring on the Kelvin scale, in degrees Kelvin. At a given altitude, the volume V of a fixed amount of air varies directly with its Kelvin temperature t. The lowest possible temperature occurs when t is zero, about -273° C. Suppose that a balloon contains 7.5 liters of air at 300 kelvins (about room temperature). *(Lesson 2-1)*
   a. Write a specific variation formula for V in terms of t. $V = 0.025t$
   b. Use this formula to predict the volume of air in the balloon at temperatures of 400, 500, 600, and 1000 kelvins.   See margin.

13. Architects designing auditoriums use the fact that sound intensity I is inversely proportional to the square of the distance d from the sound source. *(Lessons 2-2, 2-3)*
   a. Write the variation equation that represents this situation. $I = k/d^2$
   b. A person moves to a seat 4 times farther from the source. The sound will be heard __?__ as intensely. $\frac{1}{16}$th

The graph of an inverse-square variation does not have a special name, so we shall just call it an **inverse-square graph**. The inverse-square graph is symmetric to the y-axis. Notice that the inverse-square graph, like a hyperbola, has two distinct branches. However, the two branches do *not* form a hyperbola because the shape of each branch, as well as the relative location of the branches, differs from a hyperbola.

Neither the hyperbola with equation $y = \dfrac{k}{x}$ ($k \neq 0$) nor the inverse-square curve $y = \dfrac{k}{x^2}$ intersects the coordinate axes. You can verify these results by zooming or rescaling to look more closely at the graphs near $x = 0$ or for very large or very small values of x. For instance, below you see three views of $y = \dfrac{16}{x}$ for different windows with large x values. Note that for all positive numbers x, $\dfrac{16}{x} > 0$.

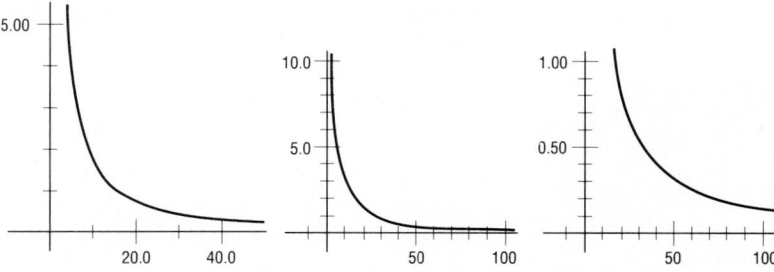

In general, when $x = 0$, $y = \dfrac{k}{x}$ and $y = \dfrac{k}{x^2}$ are undefined. So neither curve crosses the y-axis. Also, when $k \neq 0$ neither $\dfrac{k}{x}$ nor $\dfrac{k}{x^2}$ can ever equal 0. Thus neither curve crosses the x-axis.

Questions

Covering the Reading

1. A __?__ graph is made up of unconnected points.   **discrete**

2. A __?__ graph cannot be drawn without picking up the pencil.
   discontinuous

3. Refer to the graph of $t = \dfrac{36}{s}$ in this lesson.

   a. What is the rate of change between (4, 9) and (12, 3)? $-\frac{3}{4}$
   b. What is the rate of change between (12, 3) and (4, 9)? $-\frac{3}{4}$

4. What is the graph of $y = \dfrac{k}{x}$ called?   **a hyperbola**

FOLLOW-UP

MORE PRACTICE
For more questions on SPUR Objectives, use *Lesson Master 2-5*, shown below.

NAME _____

LESSON **MASTER   2–5**
QUESTIONS ON **SPUR** OBJECTIVES

■ **SKILLS**   *Objective C   (See pages 119–123 for objectives.)*
In 1 and 2, $y = 6x^2$.

1. Find the rate of change between $x = -2$ and $x = -1$.   -18

2. Find the rate of change between $x = -3$ and $x = -2$.   -30

In 3 and 4, $y = -3x^2$.

3. Find the rate of change between $x = 4$ and $x = 5$.   -27

4. Find the rate of change between $x = 5$ and $x = 6$.   -33

■ **PROPERTIES**   *Objective E*
In 5 and 6, consider $y = -8x^2$ and $y = \frac{1}{2}x$.

5. Which graph is symmetric to the y-axis? $y = -8x^2$

6. Which graph is a straight line? $y = \frac{1}{2}x$

■ **REPRESENTATIONS**   *Objective I*
in 7–10, graph each equation.

7. $y = \frac{1}{4}x^2$ 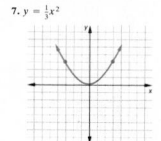   8. $y = -\frac{1}{4}x^2$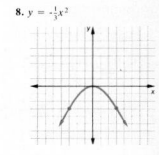

16   *Continued*   *Advanced Algebra © Scott, Foresman and Company*

NAME _____
Lesson MASTER 2–5 (page 2)

9. $y = 3x^2$ 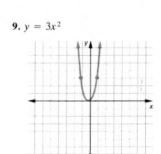   10. $y = -3x^2$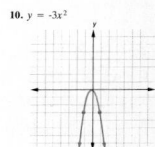

■ **REPRESENTATION**   *Objective J*

11. Match each graph with its equation. Each graph has the same scale.

   I. $y = \frac{1}{4}x^2$ II. $y = 4x^2$
   III. $y = -3x^2$ IV. $y = 4x$

   a. III   b. II
   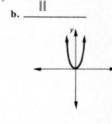

   c. I   d. IV
   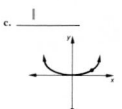   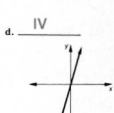

Advanced Algebra © Scott, Foresman and Company   **17**

RESOURCES
■ Lesson Master 2-6

OBJECTIVE

J Recognize the effects of a change in scale or viewing window on a graph of a variation equation.

TEACHING NOTES

When discussing this lesson, you should have either a classroom set of graphing calculators or a computer with a function graphing program for demonstration.

Some students may know how to use a calculator or computer for graphing. If so, they can help others. Do **Example 1** in class, changing the window for the different parts. Then, graph $y = 2x^2$ from **Example 2**. Have students graph the other parts.

As you do **Examples 1 and 2,** emphasize two things: (1) the specific technical requirements of your automatic grapher, and (2) the fact that no matter how the appearance of a graph may change from window to window, its mathematical properties do not change.

Even if students do not have access to an automatic grapher, this lesson should not be skipped. Students should be able to do the following questions: 1, 2a, 3–8, 13a, 14a, 15–18.

LESSON

2-6

Using an Automatic Grapher

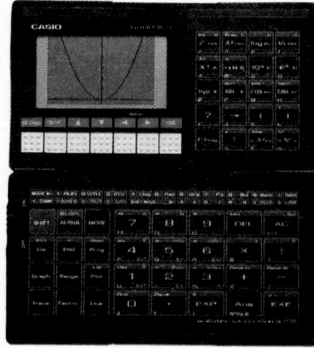

Graphs of equations are so helpful to have that there exist calculators and programs for personal computers that will automatically display graphs. Because computer screens are larger than calculator screens they can more clearly show more of a graph; but graphing calculators are less expensive, more portable and sometimes are easier to use.

Graphing calculators and computer graphing-programs work in much the same way; so we call them **automatic graphers** and do not distinguish between them. Of course, no grapher is completely automatic. Each has particular keys to press that you must learn from a manual. Here we discuss what you need to know in order to use any automatic grapher. Consult your calculator owner's manual or your **function grapher's** documentation for specific information about your grapher.

The part of the coordinate grid that is shown is called a **window**. The screen at the right displays a window in which

$$-2 \le x \le 12$$
$$\text{and} \quad -3 \le y \le 7.$$

On calculators, the intervals for x and y may be left unmarked. Usually you need to pick the x-values at either end of the window. Some graphers automatically adjust and choose y-values so that your graph will fit, but often you also need to choose the y-values. If you do not do this, the grapher will usually make use of a **default window**, that is, a window that is used whenever you do not specify the intervals on which to plot x and y.

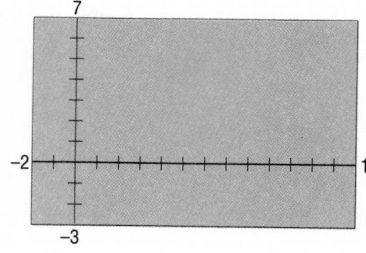

On almost all graphers, the equation to be graphed must be a formula for y in terms of x.

$$y = 3x^2 \text{ and } y = \tfrac{5}{9}(x - 32) \quad \text{can be handled.}$$
$$x = 4y \text{ and } x + y = 17 \quad \text{cannot be handled.}$$

On many graphers you enter equations by using the keys *, /, and ^ to indicate multiplication, division, and powering, respectively. For instance, to graph $y = 3x^2$ or $y = \tfrac{5}{9}(x - 32)$ you may need to enter

$$y = 3 * x \char`^ 2 \text{ or } y = (5/9) * (x - 32).$$

86

Automatic graphers generally follow the standard rules for order of operations stated in Lesson 1-2. The steps needed to graph an equation with an automatic grapher are:
1. Solve the equation you wish to graph for *y*, and enter it into your grapher.
2. Determine a window and key it in.
3. Give instructions to graph.

Example 1   Use an automatic grapher to sketch solutions to $\frac{y}{x} = 10$ in the following windows:

a. $-15 \leq x \leq 15$, $-10 \leq y \leq 10$
b. $-3 \leq x \leq 3$, $-30 \leq y \leq 30$
c. $-1.5 \leq x \leq 3.5$, $-40 \leq y \leq 40$

Solution   Rewrite the equation as $y = 10x$. How you enter it will vary from one machine to another. Typically, you might type $y = 10 * x$. Follow the instructions for your grapher to input the size of the window. Typical output is shown below.

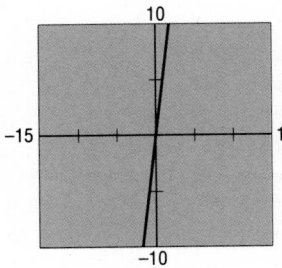 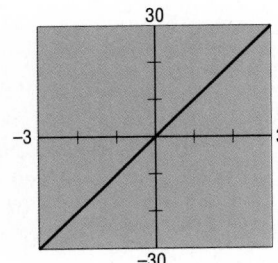

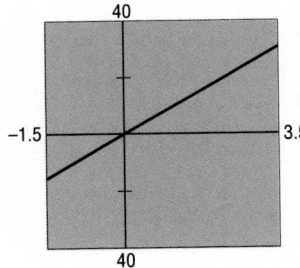

Notice that although the graphs appear to have different steepness, each is a line with a slope of 10. For every horizontal change of 1 unit, there is a vertical change of 10 units. The size of the viewing window on an automatic grapher may change your impression of the shape of a graph, but it does not change the mathematical properties of the graph.

Most automatic graphers can plot solutions to more than one equation at a time. Some allow you to plot many graphs simultaneously.

LESSON 2-6   Using an Automatic Grapher   **87**

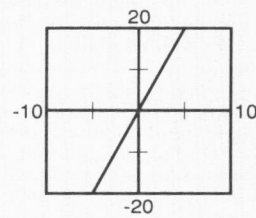
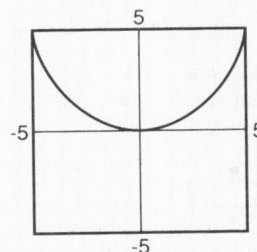

■ ■ ■ ■ ■ ■ ■■

Example 2   **a.** Graph $y = ax^2$ when $a = \frac{1}{2}$, 1, 2, and 3.
   b. What happens to the graph as a gets larger?

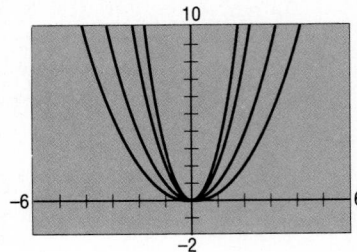

Solution

a. The question asks you to graph

$y = \frac{1}{2}x^2$
$y = x^2$
$y = 2x^2$
$y = 3x^2$

Each equation is already solved for y.
Enter one at a time, following the
instructions on your grapher. We use
the window $-6 \leq x \leq 6$, knowing that these parabolas are symmetric to the y-axis. The interval $-2 \leq y \leq 10$ is reasonable for comparing the parabolas.

b. As the value of a increases, the parabola looks thinner and thinner. The thinnest parabola is $y = 3x^2$. The parabola that looks widest is $y = \frac{1}{2}x^2$.

Some graphers have a **zoom** feature like those found on cameras. This feature enables you to change the window of a graph without retyping intervals for x and y. In general, there is no "best window." Usually a good window for a graph is one in which you can estimate the coordinates of the x- and y-intercepts (if any), and any other points you need in the problem. For instance in Example 2 above if you want to study the behavior of the four parabolas near the vertex, you may want to zoom by a factor of 10. (Typically, graphers zoom around the origin.) This means that the viewing rectangle now is determined by $-0.6 \leq x \leq 0.6$ and $-0.2 \leq y \leq 1$. The result is shown below.

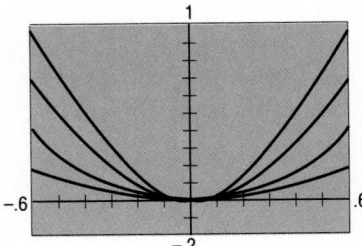

88

Again the thinnest parabola is the graph of $y = 3x^2$, and the widest is the graph of $y = \frac{1}{2}x^2$. To some people the two lowest graphs do not "look like" parabolas. However this is an illusion created by the window used. Each graph is a parabola; each has exactly the same mathematical properties— namely, vertex, symmetry line, rate of change between points—as it has when pictured in Example 2.

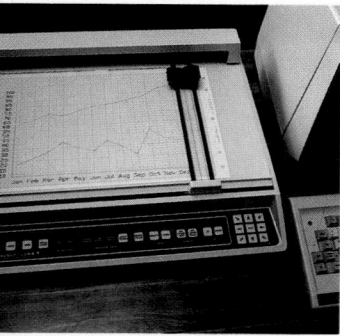

Many function graphers on computers will print **hard copy**, that is, a paper copy of a graph shown on the screen or stored on disk. If that is the case with your automatic grapher your teacher will probably accept such graphs in answer to homework questions. If hard copy is unavailable or unacceptable in your class, you must copy graphs from the grapher's screen to paper. When copying graphs always show:
1. the size of the window and the scales on the axes;
2. key features of the graph such as x- or y-intercepts or vertices;
3. its approximate shape.

Questions

Covering the Reading

1. On an automatic grapher, to what does the *window* refer?
   the part of the coordinate grid shown
2. **a.** What is a default window?   See margin.
   b. Does your automatic grapher have a default window? If so, describe it.   Many answers are possible.

3. Describe the window pictured at the right.
   the graph in the interval -50 ≤ x ≤ 30 and -10 ≤ y ≤ 4

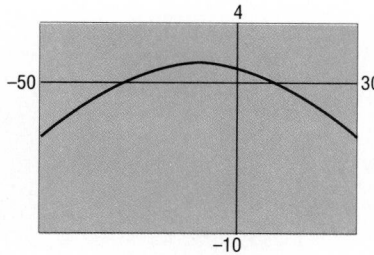

In 4–6, suppose that a grapher works only if an equation is input as a formula for y in terms of x. Decide whether the equation is in a form in which it can be graphed with that grapher.

4. $x = 3y$ No   5. $y = 1.3x^2$ Yes   6. $y = (4 - x)/2$ Yes

Question 7: This is a critical question. Some students may have become so accustomed to estimating slope by sight that they may have forgotten that slope is calculated from coordinates of points. Explain that if the axes have different scales, then sight can only tell you if the slope is positive or negative. Again, emphasize that a change in scale or viewing rectangle may change the appearance of a graph, but it does not change its mathematical properties.

Question 11a: Some students may not realize that the graphs are the same. They may think that something is wrong with the calculator or computer since they see only one graph.

Question 19: This question illustrates how much our perception of infinite curves is based on the window. With paper and pencil and a window such as -10 ≤ x ≤ 10, -10 ≤ y ≤ 10, a parabola then has a characteristic curved shape. However, change the window and the curve may look much like a ray (part a) or a line (part b).

ADDITIONAL ANSWERS
2.a. a window that is used whenever you do not specify the intervals on which to plot x and y.

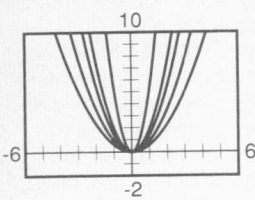
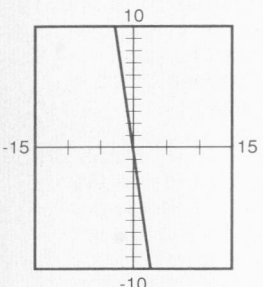
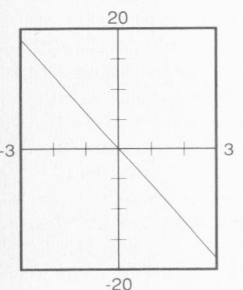
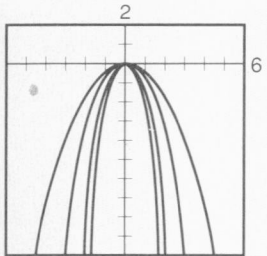
7. In Example 1, which window
   a. appears to have the steepest line? **the first**
   b. appears to show the line with the greatest slope? **the first**

In 8, refer to Example 2.

8. a. Which value of a gives the widest parabola? $\frac{1}{2}$
   b. Which value of a gives the thinnest parabola? **3**
   c. Make a copy of the graphs, and add a sketch of the graph of $y = 4x^2$ to it. **See margin.**

Applying the Mathematics

In 9–12, use an automatic grapher.

9. a. Graph $y = -6x$ using the following windows.
   (i) your default window, if any. **See margin.**
   (ii) $-15 \leq x \leq 15$, $-10 \leq y \leq 10$
   (iii) $-3 \leq x \leq 3$, $-20 \leq y \leq 20$
   b. What is the slope of each line drawn? **-6**

10. a. Graph on one set of axes $y = ax^2$ when $a = -\frac{1}{2}$, -1, -2, and -3. Use the window $-6 \leq x \leq 6$, $-10 \leq y \leq 2$. **See margin.**
    b. What happens to the graph as a gets smaller? **The graph gets thinner.**
    c. Compare and contrast these graphs to those in Example 2.
       See margin.

11. a. Use any convenient window. Graph on one set of axes:
       $$y = 100x$$
       and $y = 75x + 25x$. **See margin.**
    b. Sketch what appears. **See margin.**
    c. Predict what the graph of $y = (113x + 87x)/2$ will look like. Then use this formula in your automatic grapher to test your prediction.
       See margin.

12. The cost c of an above-ground swimming pool 6-ft deep varies directly as the square of its diameter d. Suppose a pool with diameter 12 ft costs $720.
    a. Write an equation for the relation between c and d. $c = 5d^2$
    b. Plot solutions to part a over a reasonable domain for d. **See margin.**
    c. Use your graph to estimate the cost of a pool with an 18-ft diameter. **See margin.**
    d. Check your estimate in part c by using the equation in part a. **See marg**

90

In 13 and 14, the graph below was drawn using the equations
$$y = 4.9x^2$$
and $y = -4.9x^2$
and the window $-1 \le x \le 1$ and $-7 \le y \le 7$.
Suppose the window was changed as given below.

a. Sketch what you think the screen would show.
b. Check your work by using an automatic grapher. **See margin.**

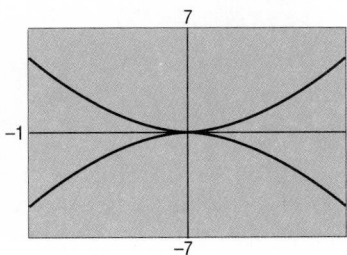

13. $-5 \le x \le 5$ and $-100 \le y \le 100$

14. $-0.1 \le x \le 0.1$ and $-1 \le y \le 1$

Review

15. *Skill sequence* Solve and check. *(Lessons 1-6, 1-7)*

   a. $12n = 18$ **1.5**

   b. $\frac{n}{12} = 18$ **216**

   c. $\frac{18}{n} = 12$ **1.5**

   d. $\frac{n}{12} + 3 = \frac{n}{18}$ **-108**

16. A tortoise is walking at a rate of $3\frac{ft}{minute}$. Assume this rate continues.
   a. How long will it take the tortoise to travel 60 feet? **20 min**
   b. How long will it take the tortoise to travel f feet? *(Lesson 1-1)* $\frac{f}{3}$ **min**

17. Simplify.
   a. $(2x + 3) + (4x + 5)$ **6x + 8**
   b. $(2x + 3) - (4x + 5)$ **-2x − 2**
   c. $(2x + 3)(4x + 5)$ *(Previous course, Lesson 1-5)* **8x² + 22x + 15**

18. If y varies directly as the cube of x, and y is 24 when x is 2, what is the average rate of change of y from $x = 2$ to $x = 3$? *(Lessons 2-1, 2-5)*
   57

Exploration

19. Consider graphing $y = x^2$ with an automatic grapher using the window $-a \le x \le a$, $-b \le y \le b$. **See margin.**
   a. Let $a = 3$ and $b = 10$ and graph.
   b. Select a large enough value of a so that the graph will seem to coincide with the y-axis. What value of a will do this on your grapher?
   c. What value of b is so large that the graph seems to coincide with the x-axis?

LESSON 2-6 Using an Automatic Grapher **91**

FOLLOW-UP

MORE PRACTICE
For more questions on SPUR Objectives, use *Lesson Master 2-6,* shown below.

11.a. and b.

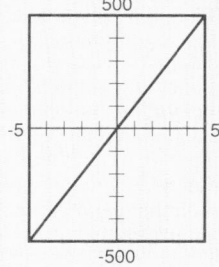

c.

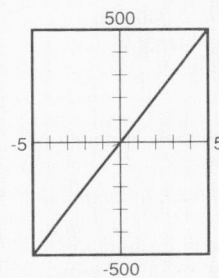

12.b., c., d., 13., 14., 19.a., b., c. See Additional Answers in the back of this book.

NAME _____

LESSON **MASTER 2–6**
QUESTIONS ON SPUR OBJECTIVES

■ REPRESENTATIONS *Objectives I and J*
(See pages 119–123 for objectives.)
In 1 and 2, write each equation as a formula for y in terms of x.

1. $y - 2x^3 = 3$ 2. $4xy = 1$

   $y = 2x^3 + 3$ $y = \frac{1}{4}x$

In 3–5, use the equation $y = \frac{1}{2}x^2$ and a graphing calculator.

3. What is the smallest window for y that will show all the points on the graph for $-2 \le x \le 2$? $0 \le y \le 2$

4. What point on the graph would be most interesting to zoom in on? $(0, 0)$

5. Sketch the graph of the function as it should appear on a graphing calculator using the condition of Question 3.

In 6 and 7, a ball rolls down a hill starting from rest. At time t, its distance d from the top of the hill varies directly with the square of the time.

6. Write an equation that describes the above. $d = kt^2$

7. If $k = 0.5$, graph distance against time using the window $0 \le t \le 2$ and $0 \le d \le 2$.

8. Graph $y = 3x$ over the domain $-5 \le x \le 5$.

18   *Advanced Algebra © Scott, Foresman and Company*

2-7

The Graphs of $y = k/x$ and $y = k/x^2$

The Metro Car Sales example of Lesson 2-2 is one instance of inverse variation. Recall that the number of students s hired to wash cars and the number of hours t each will need to work are related by the equation $t = \frac{36}{s}$. A graph of this relation is shown here.

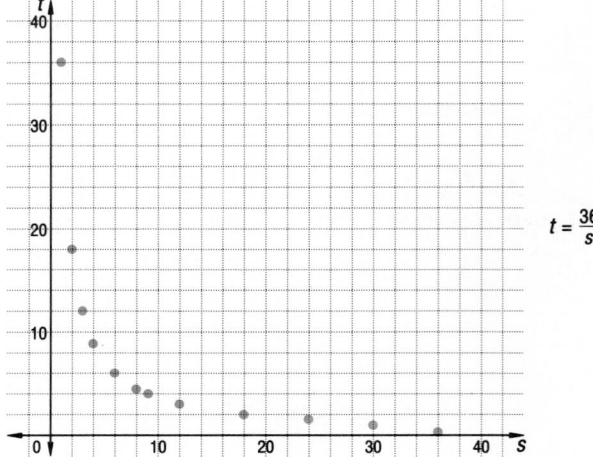

$t = \frac{36}{s}$

This graph has several properties. One is that it is made up of unconnected points. Such graphs are called **discrete** graphs. It would not make sense to connect the points of this graph because s, the number of students, can only be a whole number. A discrete graph is one type of **discontinuous** graph. A discontinuous graph cannot be drawn without picking up your pencil. In contrast, the graphs in Lessons 2-4 and 2-5, which can be drawn without picking up your pencil, are called **continuous** graphs.

A second property is that the graph never crosses the t-axis. If $s = 0$, then $\frac{36}{s}$ is undefined.

92

A third property is that the rate of change between any two points is always negative. For instance, between $(4, 9)$ and $(8, 4\frac{1}{2})$, the rate of change is

$$\frac{4\frac{1}{2} - 9}{8 - 4} = -1.125.$$

Between $(8, 4\frac{1}{2})$ and $(12, 3)$, the rate of change is
$$\frac{3 - 4\frac{1}{2}}{12 - 8} = -.375.$$

That these rates of change are different implies that the points do not lie on a line. The rate of change between any two points on the graph is negative, so each point on this discrete graph is lower on the graph as you read from left to right. This is similar to the idea that when the slope of the line $y = kx$ is negative, the line is falling.

Other properties of the graph of $y = \dfrac{k}{x}$ can be seen if x is assigned negative values.

■ ■ ■ ■ ■ ■ ■ ■

Example 1   Draw the graphs of $y = \dfrac{16}{x}$ and $y = \dfrac{-16}{x}$ for $x \neq 0$.

Solution   At the left below is a table of solutions. To save space, the independent variable x is written only once. The graphs are at the right.

x	$y = \dfrac{16}{x}$	$y = \dfrac{-16}{x}$
1	16	-16
2	8	-8
3	$5\frac{1}{3}$	$-5\frac{1}{3}$
4	4	-4
6	$2\frac{2}{3}$	$-2\frac{2}{3}$
8	2	-2
12	$1\frac{1}{3}$	$-1\frac{1}{3}$
16	1	-1
-1	-16	16
-2	-8	8
-3	$-5\frac{1}{3}$	$5\frac{1}{3}$
-4	-4	4
-6	$-2\frac{2}{3}$	$2\frac{2}{3}$
-8	-2	2
-12	$-1\frac{1}{3}$	$1\frac{1}{3}$
-16	-1	1

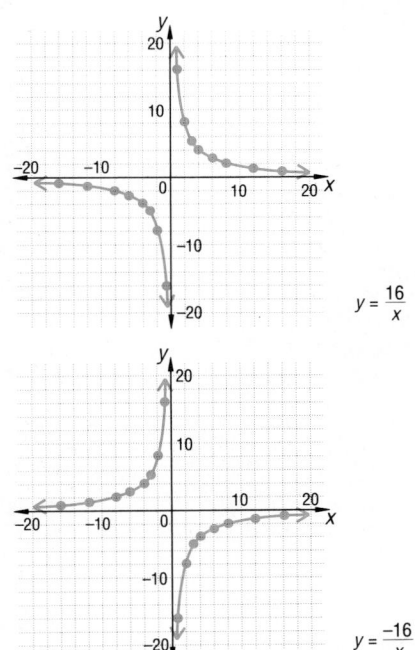

$y = \dfrac{16}{x}$

$y = \dfrac{-16}{x}$

LESSON 2-7   The Graphs of $y = kx$ and $y = kx^2$ **93**

1.a. Draw the graph of $y = \dfrac{12}{x}$.

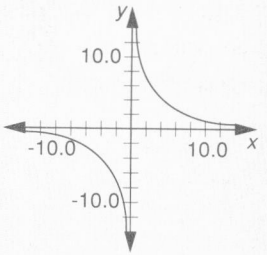

b. Find the rate of change between $x = 2$ and $x = 4$.
$-\frac{3}{2}$

2.a. Draw the graph of $y = \dfrac{36}{x^2}$.

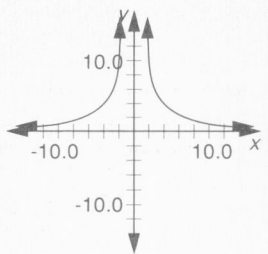

b. Draw the graph of $y = -\dfrac{36}{x^2}$.

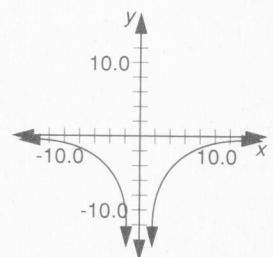

3. The illumination provided by a source of light varies inversely as the square of the distance from the source. For a certain source of illumination, the formula is $I = \frac{8000}{d^2}$.

Graph this relationship.

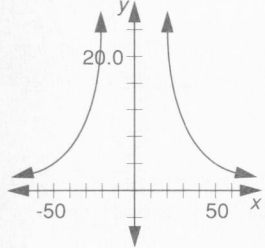

Note that if the source is in the middle of an area, then the illumination decreases on both directions, so the situation can be described using both branches of the inverse square curve.

The type of curve graphed in Example 1 is called a **hyperbola**. A hyperbola is not continuous, because you must pick up your pencil to draw the two separate parts, or **branches**. Also, a hyperbola is not discrete because all the points are connected to some other points.

You also have studied inverse-square variation. What does the graph of $y = \frac{k}{x^2}$ look like?

■ ■ ■ ■ ■ ■ ■ ■ ■ ■

Example 2 Graph $y = \frac{16}{x^2}$ and $y = \frac{-16}{x^2}$.

Solution Again a table of solutions is below at the left and the graphs are at the right. The values in the table were produced by an automatic grapher.

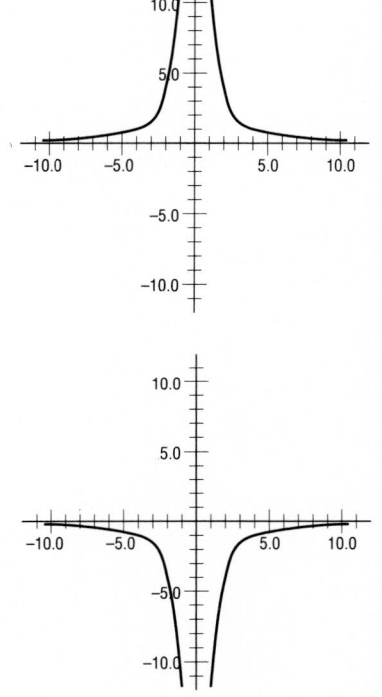

x	$y = \frac{16}{x^2}$	$y = \frac{-16}{x^2}$
-8	.25	-.25
-7	.326531	-.326531
-6	.444444	-.444444
-5	.64	-.64
-4	1	-1
-3	1.77778	-1.77778
-2	4	-4
-1	16	-16
0	***	***
1	16	-16
2	4	-4
3	1.77778	-1.77778
4	1	-1
5	.64	-.64
6	.444444	-.444444
7	.326531	-.326531
8	.25	-.25

(Note that for $x = 0$, no value of y is given. Instead *** is printed in the table. Our automatic grapher uses this symbol to indicate that 0 is not an element of the domain of x. That is, $\frac{16}{0^2}$ and $-\frac{16}{0^2}$ are not defined. Some function graphers state ERROR or some other message to indicate that a number is not part of the domain for the independent variable.)

94

The graph of an inverse-square variation does not have a special name, so we shall just call it an **inverse-square graph**. The inverse-square graph is symmetric to the y-axis. Notice that the inverse-square graph, like a hyperbola, has two distinct branches. However, the two branches do *not* form a hyperbola because the shape of each branch, as well as the relative location of the branches, differs from a hyperbola.

Neither the hyperbola with equation $y = \frac{k}{x}$ ($k \neq 0$) nor the inverse-square curve $y = \frac{k}{x^2}$ intersects the coordinate axes. You can verify these results by zooming or rescaling to look more closely at the graphs near $x = 0$ or for very large or very small values of x. For instance, below you see three views of $y = \frac{16}{x}$ for different windows with large x values. Note that for all positive numbers x, $\frac{16}{x} > 0$.

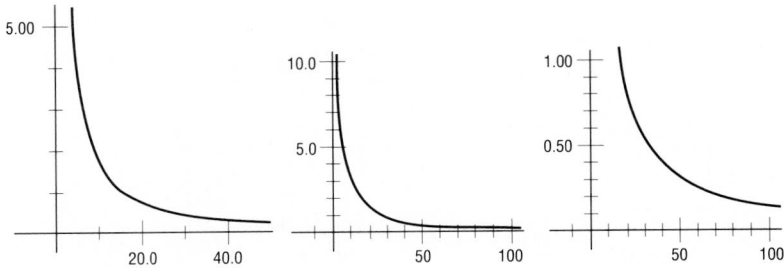

In general, when $x = 0$, $y = \frac{k}{x}$ and $y = \frac{k}{x^2}$ are undefined. So neither curve crosses the y-axis. Also, when $k \neq 0$ neither $\frac{k}{x}$ nor $\frac{k}{x^2}$ can ever equal 0. Thus neither curve crosses the x-axis.

Questions

1. A __?__ graph is made up of unconnected points. **discrete**

2. A __?__ graph cannot be drawn without picking up the pencil.
discontinuous

3. Refer to the graph of $t = \frac{36}{s}$ in this lesson.
   a. What is the rate of change between (4, 9) and (12, 3)? $-\frac{3}{4}$
   b. What is the rate of change between (12, 3) and (4, 9)? $-\frac{3}{4}$

4. What is the graph of $y = \frac{k}{x}$ called? **a hyperbola**

NOTES ON QUESTIONS
Question 11: Point out to students that the drop-off from $x = 2$ to $x = 6$ is much greater for the inverse square variation. Explain that this effect is due to the fact that a square term increases faster than a linear term. In cases of direct variation, the increase is greater for square variation than for linear variation.

Question 12: Note that the domain for d is $0 < d < \frac{l}{2}$, where l is the length of the seesaw. A typical seesaw board might be between 8 and 16 ft long.

Error Analysis for Question 18: Students may forget to multiply the 9 by the common denominator 12. To avoid this kind of error, advise them to subtract 9 from each side of the equation *before* multiplying by 12.

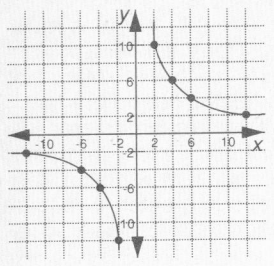
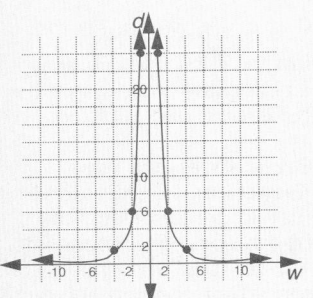
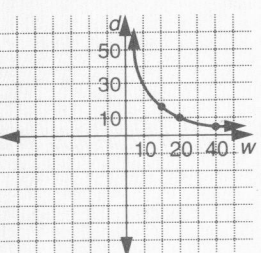
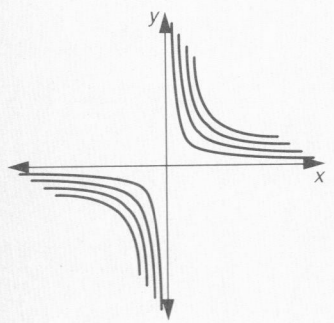
5. Find the rate of change between the points on the graph of $y = \dfrac{-16}{x^2}$ for which $x = 4$ and $x = 8$. $\frac{3}{16}$

6. *Multiple choice* Which equation has a graph that is symmetric to the y-axis ? $(k \neq 0)$ b

   (a) $y = \dfrac{k}{x}$ (b) $y = \dfrac{k}{x^2}$ (c) $y = kx$

7. In which quadrants are the branches of $y = \dfrac{-16}{x}$?   II and IV

8. In which quadrants are the branches of $y = \dfrac{k}{x^2}$:

   a. if k is positive?   I and II   b. if k is negative?   III and IV

Applying the Mathematics

In 9 and 10, which of the following words describe the graph?
a. continuous   b. discontinuous   c. discrete

9.   10.

   9) b   10) b, c

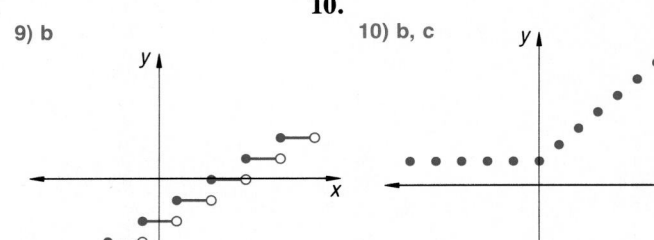

11. a. Draw a graph of $y = \dfrac{24}{x}$.   See margin.

   b. Find the rate of change from $x = 2$ to $x = 6$ for $y = \dfrac{24}{x}$.   -2

   c. Draw a graph of $y = \dfrac{24}{x^2}$.   See margin.

   d. Find the rate of change from $x = 2$ to $x = 6$ for $y = \dfrac{24}{x^2}$. $-\frac{4}{3}$

   e. Which of the two graphs is falling faster from $x = 2$ to $x = 6$?

12. Sam is once again on a seesaw. He weighs 40 pounds and is sitting 5 feet from the pivot. (Remember the law of the lever is $d = \dfrac{k}{w}$.)

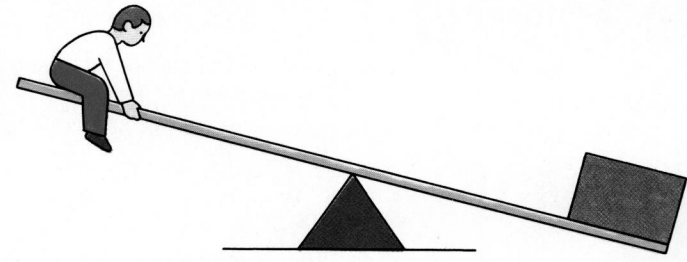

   a. Find k and then write the formula for the variation in this situation.
   b. Draw a graph of weights and distances from the pivot that would balance Sam.   See margin.

96

13. Examine the graph of $y = \dfrac{16}{x}$ on page 93.

  a. How many symmetry lines does the graph have? **2**

  b. Write an equation for each symmetry line. **y = x, y = -x**

  c. Does the graph of $y = \dfrac{-16}{x}$ have the same symmetry lines? If not, what are equations for its symmetry line(s)? **Yes**

14. a. Use an automatic grapher to graph on one set of axes the four curves $y = \dfrac{k}{x}$, where $k = 1, 2, 5,$ and 10. Use a window $-5 \le x \le 5,\ -10 \le y \le 10$. **See margin.**

  b. What happens to the graph of $y = \dfrac{k}{x}$ as k gets larger? **See margin.**

Review

15. In the figure at the left below, parabolas a and b are congruent. If parabola a has equation $y = 6x^2$, what is an equation for parabola b? *(Lesson 2-5)* **y = -6x²**

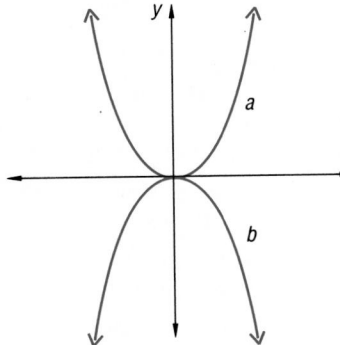

16. Why is the line graphed below *not* an example of a direct variation? *(Lesson 2-4)* **The line does not go through the origin.**

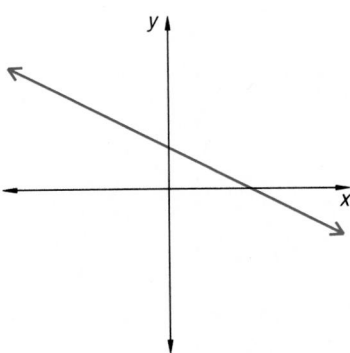

17. When trying to solve the equation $\frac{1}{2}x + \frac{1}{3}x + 5 = 10$, Mikki's first step was $3x + 2x + 30 = 60$. What two properties did she apply? *(Lessons 1-5, 1-6)* **Multiplication Property of Equality, Distributive Property**

LESSON 2-7   The Graphs of $y = kx$ and $y = kx^2$ **97**

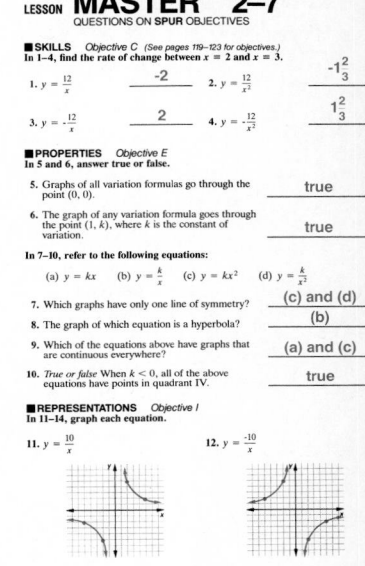
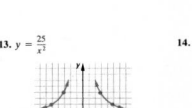
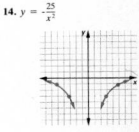
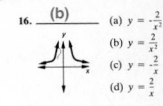
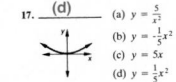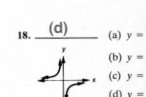

MORE PRACTICE
For more questions on SPUR Objectives, use *Lesson Master 2-7*, shown on page 97.

EVALUATION
A quiz covering Lesson 2-4 through 2-7 is provided in the Teacher's Resource File.

ADDITIONAL ANSWERS
19.b. by SAS or SSS (use the Pythagorean Theorem to show $\overline{EC} \cong \overline{CA}$)

20.a.

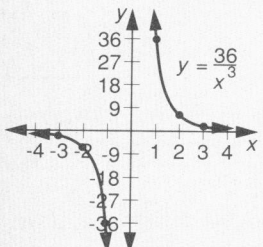

b.

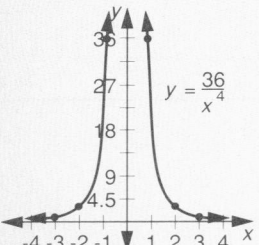

d.

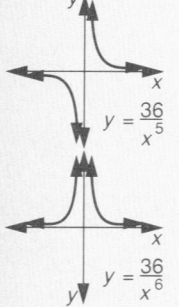

If the exponent of x is even, the graph is symmetric with respect to the y-axis.

---

18. Solve for x:
$\frac{1}{4}x + \frac{2}{3}x + 9 = 10$ *(Lesson 1-7)* $\frac{12}{11}$

19. In the graph below, the grid lines are 1 unit apart. Each labeled point is at an intersection of grid lines.
    a. Are triangles *ABC* and *EDC* congruent?   **Yes**
    b. If so, why? If not, why not?
    (Previous course)
    See margin.

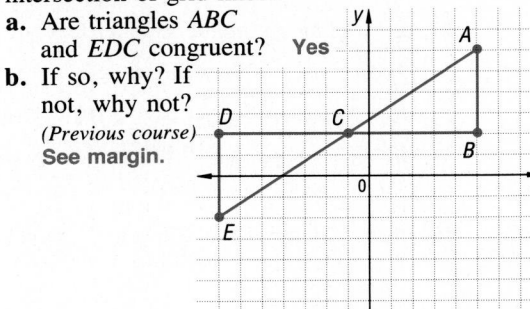

> **Exploration**

20. **a.** Draw the graph of $y = \dfrac{36}{x^3}$.   **See margin.**

    b. Draw the graph of $y = \dfrac{36}{x^4}$.   **See margin.**

    c. Use your answer to parts a and b to predict which one of the following equations will have a graph symmetric to the *y*-axis.   **(ii)**
    (i) $y = \dfrac{36}{x^5}$ (ii) $y = \dfrac{36}{x^6}$

    d. Use an automatic grapher to graph the equations in part C to test your prediction. What property of exponents justifies the result you observed?   **See margin.**

Fitting a Model to Data I

OBJECTIVE

G Find a direct or inverse variation model that approximates a relationship between two variables.

You may know that the water pressure on a deep sea diver increases as the diver goes deeper. How is the pressure related to the depth?

The following table gives the water pressure (in pounds per square inch, or psi) exerted on a diver at various depths (in ft).

Depth of diver (ft)	10	25	40	55	75
Pressure of diver (psi)	4.3	10.8	17.2	23.7	32.3

This information is graphed below. Because the pressure on the diver depends on the diver's depth, pressure is the dependent variable and is placed on the vertical axis. Depth is the independent variable and is graphed on the horizontal axis. The points seem to lie on a line through the origin. It makes sense that the origin is on this line because on the surface—that is, 0 feet under water—there is 0 pounds per square inch of water pressure. Therefore, it seems appropriate to describe the relation between the variables by saying the pressure varies directly as the depth.

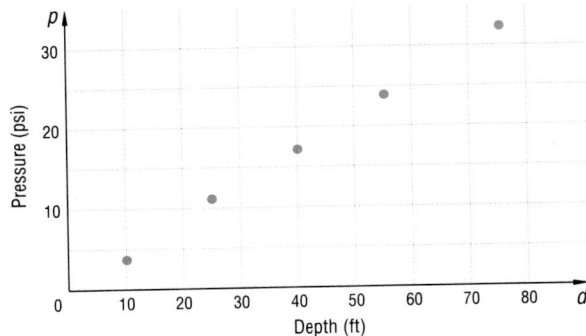

TEACHING NOTES

You may wish to begin the class by showing graphs of variation functions and asking for possible equations. For instance, here are some graphs you can show on the chalkboard or on an overhead projector.

(a)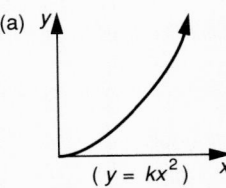

$(y = kx^2)$

(b)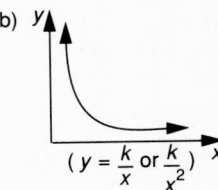

$(y = \frac{k}{x} \text{ or } \frac{k}{x^2})$

(c)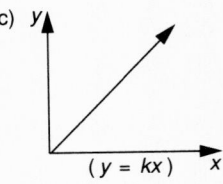

$(y = kx)$

At times, students have trouble identifying variables as being dependent or independent. Tell students that in many cases it is quite evident which is the dependent variable and which is the independent variable.

Explain that in some cases, the independent variable may be a matter of choice. In the equation $ab = 12$, unless there is some distinction made between the variables, it is just as credible to refer to b as the dependent variable as it is to refer to it as the independent variable.

ADDITIONAL EXAMPLES

1. Susan measured how far a marble rolled down a ramp in a given period of time. She obtained the following data:

Time (sec)	1	2	3	4	5
Distance (in.)	.3	1.2	2.6	4.9	7.6

Find an equation relating time t and distance D.
A graph suggests $D = kt^2$.
Calculation from the first point gives $k \approx .3$ in./sec^2.
So, $D \approx .3t^2$. This checks closely with the other points.

2. Rhoda and Ron measured the intensity of light from a lamp at various distances from the lamp and obtained the following data:

Dist. (m)	2	2.5	3	3.5	4
Inten. (watts/ m²)	560	360	250	185	140

Find an equation relating distance d to intensity I.
A graph suggests

$$I = \frac{k}{d} \text{ or } I = \frac{k}{d^2}.$$

The data are consistent with the second model. Calculation from the first point gives $k \approx 2240$ watts.

So, $I = \dfrac{2240}{d^2}$.

If p represents the pressure and d represents the depth, the formula for this variation is $p = kd$. The constant k can be determined from one of the data points. For instance, substitute $p = 4.3$ psi and $d = 10$ ft into the equation to get

$$4.3 = k \cdot 10$$
$$k = 0.43. \quad \text{(The unit is } \tfrac{\text{psi}}{\text{ft}}.\text{)}$$

This relation between p and d can be expressed as

$$p = 0.43d.$$

It is important to check that this formula holds for all the data in the table. You should see whether each data point satisfies the equation. For instance, if $d = 25$ ft, then

$$p = (0.43)(25)$$
$$= 10.75$$

which is close to the value of 10.8 psi in the table.

The equation $p = 0.43d$ is a mathematical model of the real-life relation between pressure and depth. A **mathematical model** is a graph or a sentence that describes data or a relation between variables. The formula $p = 0.43d$ holds true for all the values in the table. A good model is one that holds true for all the given information. In this book there are many examples of mathematical models.

The model $p = 0.43d$ makes it possible to predict the pressure on a diver at depths other than those given in the table. At a depth of 125 ft, for instance, the model predicts that the pressure on a diver would be

$$p = (0.43)(125)$$
$$= 53.75$$
$$\approx 53.8 \text{ psi.}$$

Here is another situation whose mathematical model involves variation.

▪ ▪ ▪ ▪ ▪ ▪ ▪▪

Example Perri Menter was investigating the relation between the volume and pressure of a gas in her laboratory. While she held the temperature in the laboratory constant, she varied the pressure (the independent variable) and measured the volume (the dependent variable) to obtain the following data.

Pressure (psi)	20	30	40	50	60	70	80
Volume (ft³)	83	55	42	33	28	24	21

100

The laboratory results are graphed below. The shape of the graph suggests two possible models: V varies inversely as P or inversely as the square of P.

a. Does $V = \dfrac{k}{P^2}$ model the data?

b. Does $V = \dfrac{k}{P}$ model the data?

c. Predict the volume of gas if the pressure is 45 psi.

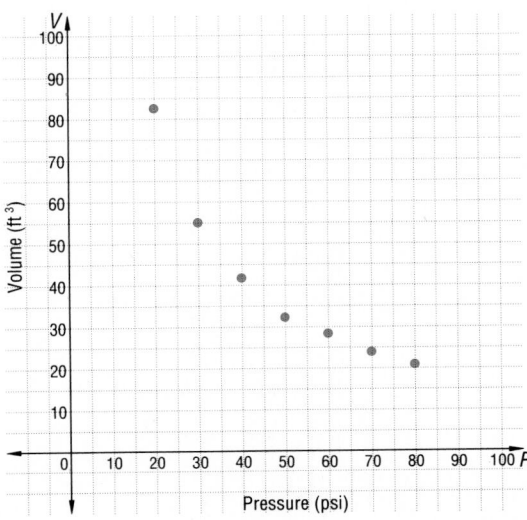

Solution

a. To test $V = \dfrac{k}{P^2}$, first substitute the coordinates of one data point to find k. For instance, if $P = 20$ psi, then $V = 83$ ft^3; so

$$83 = \frac{k}{(20)^2}$$
$$k = 33{,}200.$$

Next, decide whether the equation

$$V = \frac{33{,}200}{P^2}$$

is valid by substituting the coordinates of another data point. For instance, substitute $P = 30$ psi into this equation.

$$V = \frac{33{,}200}{(30)^2} \approx 37$$

This is not close to the value of 55 ft^3 found in the table. This counterexample shows that $V = \dfrac{k}{P^2}$ is not a correct model for the data.

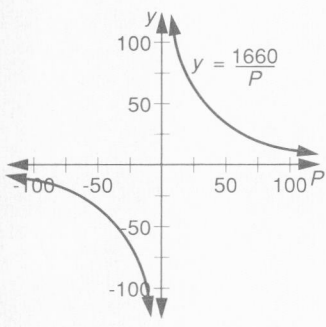
b. To test if $V = \dfrac{k}{P}$ is a correct model, again substitute 20 psi for P and 83 ft³ for V. For these values, $k = 1660$ ft³-psi and the model is

$$V = \frac{1660}{P}.$$

Now check whether this equation is valid for all the data of the experiment. For instance, if $P = 30$ psi, then

$$V = \frac{1660 \text{ ft}^3 \cancel{\text{psi}}}{30 \cancel{\text{psi}}} \approx 55 \text{ ft}^3.$$

This is the value in the table. It can likewise be shown that all the data satisfy the equation. Thus $V = \dfrac{1660}{P}$ is a good model for Perri Menter's data.

c. Substitute $P = 45$ psi into the model $V = \dfrac{1660}{P}$. Then $V = \dfrac{1660}{45} = 36.\overline{8}$, or about 37. So the model predicts a volume of 37 ft³ at 45 psi.

Check Use the graph. The point (45, 37) is on the hyperbola.

Questions

In 1 and 2, refer to the example about deep-sea diving.
1. Describe in English the variation between the pressure and the depth.
   Pressure varies directly with depth.
2. Use the model to predict the pressure on a diver who is 130 ft below the surface. 55.9 psi

3. Define: mathematical model. See margin.

In 4–7, refer to the example.
4. *True or false* As the pressure on the gas is increased, the volume of the gas is increased. False

5. Use the point (40, 42) to show that $V = \dfrac{33,200}{P^2}$ is not a good model for the volume and pressure data. See margin.

6. Verify that the point (40, 42) satisfies the formula $V = \dfrac{1660}{P}$.
   See margin.
7. Use the good model to predict the volume of the gas under a pressure of 18 psi. 92 psi

8. Which of the following words describe the graph of depths and pressures at the beginning of this lesson? a, c
   a. discrete   **b.** continuous   **c.** discontinuous

102

9. **a.** Graph all solutions to $y = \dfrac{1660}{P}$. **See margin.**

   b. How does this graph compare with that of $V = \dfrac{1660}{P}$ in the example? **See margin.**

10. Refer to the graph at the right.
   a. Which of the following equations could be a model for this graph? **II**

   I: $y = kx$
   II: $y = kx^2$
   III: $y = \dfrac{k}{x}$
   IV: $y = \dfrac{k}{x^2}$

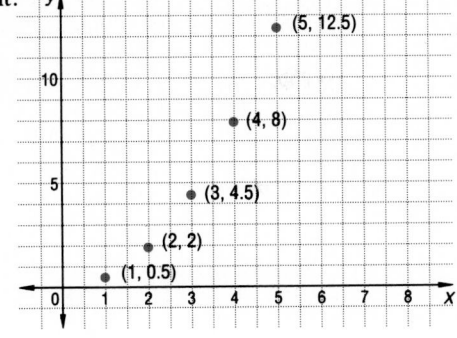

   b. Find the constant k for your model. $\frac{1}{2}$

   c. Test your model to see if y is 8 when x is 4. $\frac{1}{2} \cdot 4^2 = 8$

11. *Multiple choice* Which formula best models the graph at the right? **d**
   (a) $P = kh$ (b) $P = kh^2$
   (c) $P = \dfrac{k}{h}$ (d) $P = \dfrac{k}{h^2}$

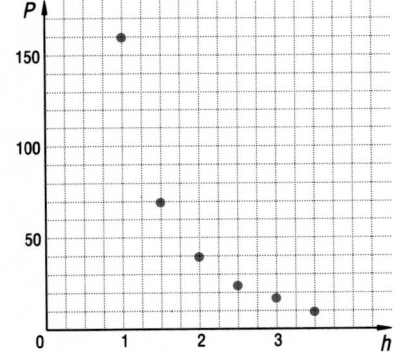

12. A scientist dropped a ball from a cliff and used a slow motion film to determine the distance it fell over different periods of time. The data are summarized below.

Time (sec)	1	2	3	4	5
Distance (m)	4.9	19.6	44.1	78.4	122.5

   a. Draw a graph to represent these data. Let t be the independent variable and d be the dependent variable. (Use a large enough scale on the d-axis to handle 122.5.) **See margin.**
   b. Pick the variation equation from those of Question 10a that best models this situation. Use one data point to calculate k and check the model with the other data points. $d = 4.9t^2$
   c. Predict how far the ball would fall in 4.5 sec. **99.2 m**

LESSON 2-8   Fitting a Model to Data I   **103**

NOTES ON QUESTIONS
Questions 9-12: Indicate to the students which graphs are discrete and which are continuous.

12.a.

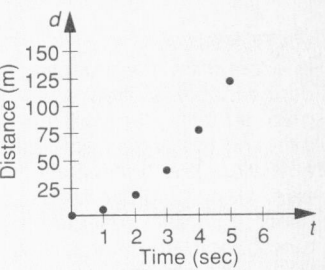

NAME

LESSON MASTER 2-8
QUESTIONS ON SPUR OBJECTIVES

■USES   *Objective G (See pages 119–123 for objectives.)*
In 1 and 2, do steps (a) through (d).
a. Draw a graph to represent the situation.
b. Find a general variation equation to represent the situation.
c. Find the value of the constant of variation and rewrite the variation equation.
d. Answer the question stated in the problem.

1. Ima Dippin used the water displacement method to measure the volume of cylinders with the same height but different radii. She collected the following data.

radius (cm)	1	2	3	4	5
water displaced (cm³)	8	32	72	128	200

What is the volume of a cylinder with radius 10″ and height like the others?
a.
b. $y = kx^2$
c. $y = 8x^2$
d. 800

2. As part of her bid, a contractor listed the number of different-sized ceramic tiles needed to cover the floor of a room.

Length of edge of one tile	1″	2″	3″	4″	5″
Number of tiles needed	7200	1800	800	450	288

How many 6″ tiles would she need?
a.
b. $y = \dfrac{k}{x^2}$
c. $y = \dfrac{7200}{x^2}$
d. 200

Advanced Algebra © Scott, Foresman and Company

21

EXTENSION
In economics, the independent variable is often graphed along the vertical axis and the dependent variable along the horizontal axis. Many graphs of economic data are presented in newspapers and magazines. Have students bring some examples of economic graphs to class and look for any that reverse the axes for graphing the independent and dependent variables. Then, point this fact out to students.

ADDITIONAL ANSWERS
14.a. *y* is halved.
b. *y* is divided by 4.
c. *y* is divided by 16.

Review

13. Find the rate of change between the points on $y = \frac{15}{x}$ where $x = 1$ and $x = 11$. *(Lesson 2-4)*   -1.36

14. Suppose that the value of x is halved. Find how the value of y is changed if y is directly proportional to   See margin.
   a. x.   **b.** x^2.   **c.** x^4 *(Lesson 2-1)*

In 15–18, match the graph to the most likely equation. *(Lessons 2-4, 2-5, 2-7)*

a. $y = 3x$ **b.** $y = -\frac{3}{x}$ **c.** $y = \frac{3}{x^2}$ 15. c   16. e   17. a
                                                                                  18. none of the equation

d. $y = -\frac{x}{3}$ **e.** $y = -\frac{1}{3}x^2$

15. 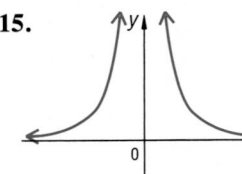   **16.**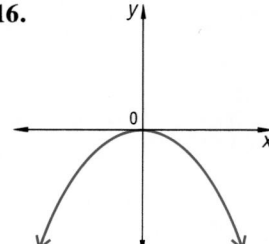

17. 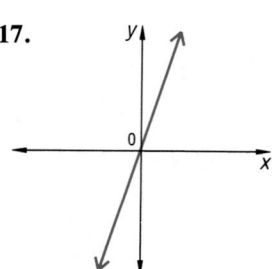   **18.**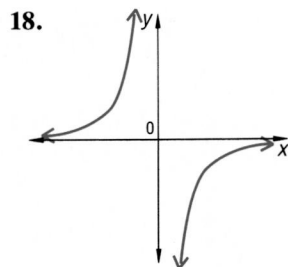

19. How long does it take to travel k kilometers at a rate of r kilometers per hour? *(Lesson 1-1)* $\frac{k}{r}$

Exploration

20. The maximum pressure that a deep-sea diver can withstand without using special equipment is about 65 psi.
   a. Find how deep a diver can go below the surface without special equipment.   151.2 ft
   b. How can divers go beneath the depth found in part a?
      in a bathysphere

104

LESSON

2-9

Fitting a Model to Data II

All through this chapter you have seen situations in which two quantities vary. In many real life situations there are more than two variables. Consider, for instance, the situation presented on the very first page of the chapter, where the problem is to determine how much weight can be supported by a board. Three quantities which influence this are the width w (front to back), the thickness t of the board, and the distance d between supports. What model describes the maximum weight MAXWT that can be supported in terms of the other three variables? The model cannot be described by a single graph in two dimensions because there are four variables to be considered. The goal is to find an equation relating w, t, d, and the dependent variable *MAXWT*.

One way to find a model is to investigate separately the relationship between the dependent variable, the weight, and each independent variable. This is done by keeping constant *all but one* independent variable.

We show this with a story. The data are made up, but the idea is not. Our heroine is again Perri Menter. She found the model as follows. First, she held two independent variables constant: d and t. She did this by choosing boards 2 in. thick and setting the supports 10 ft apart. Then she varied the widths of these boards and measured how much weight could be supported before the boards broke. Perri obtained the following data.

Width of board (in.)	w	1	2	3	4	5	6
Maximum Weight (lb)	MAXWT	27	53	80	107	133	160

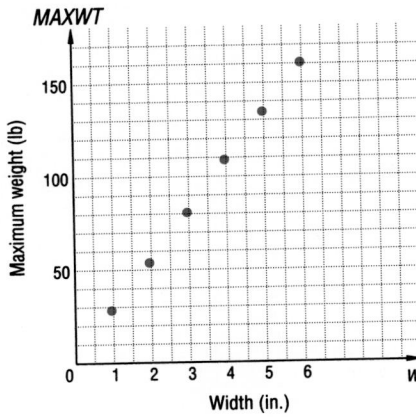

LESSON 2-9 Fitting a Model to Data II   105

RESOURCES
■ Lesson Master 2-9

OBJECTIVES

G Find a joint or combined variation model that approximates a relationship between variables.
K Read and interpret graphs of joint or combined variation.

TEACHING NOTES

Reading We suggest going through the reading with the class and then reviewing the questions in order. The reading is especially important because the sample problem is carried over into Lesson 2-10.

Students may need to be reminded that they are already familiar with situations involving more than one independent variable. For example:
(1) The volume of a square pyramid depends on both the height of the pyramid and an edge of the base.
(2) The distance an airplane travels in a straight path depends on the speed of the airplane and the time in flight.

Work through the Additional Example below with students. Have them decide on the appropriate coordinates for the graph. Students should readily see the relationships between P and D and between P and d.

Do not attempt to find constants of variation in this lesson. This is done in the next lesson.

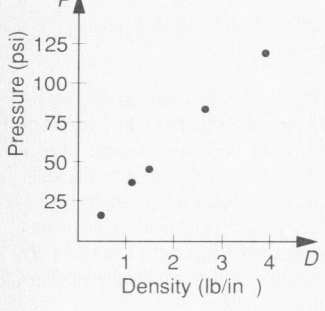
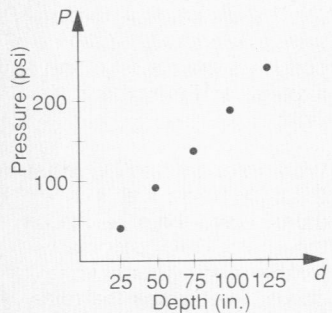
The graph above shows how the maximum weight $MAXWT$ depends on the width w. Because the points seem to lie on a line through the origin she concluded that $MAXWT$ varies directly as w.

Perri then investigated the relationship between $MAXWT$ and the thickness t. She held the distance d between supports constant at 10 ft and the width w constant at 3 in. She varied the thicknesses of the boards and measured the maximum weight that could be supported. The following table presents her findings.

Thickness (in.)	t	1	2	3	4	5	6
Maximum weight (lb)	$MAXWT$	20	80	180	320	500	720

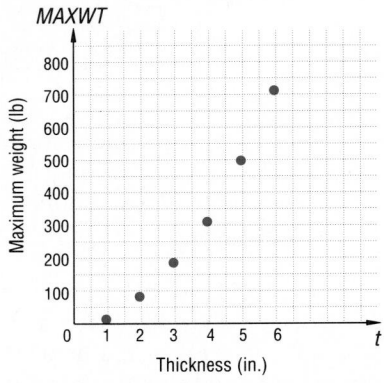

The graph above shows how $MAXWT$ depends on t. The points seem to lie on a parabola through the origin. This implies that $MAXWT$ varies directly as the square of t.

She investigated the relationship between $MAXWT$ and d by holding t and w constant. She chose boards for which t was 2 in. and w was 3 in. Perri obtained the following data.

Distance (ft)	d	1	2	3	4	5	6
Maximum weight (lb)	$MAXWT$	800	400	267	200	160	133

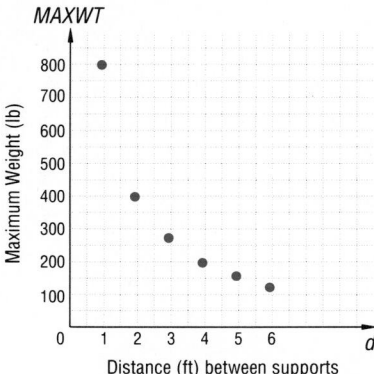

The graph shows how *MAXWT* depends on *d*. It is not immediately clear whether *MAXWT* varies inversely as *d* or inversely as d^2. However, it can be shown by the method of the last section that *MAXWT* varies inversely as *d*.

Ms. Menter summarized her findings as follows:

> *MAXWT* varies directly as *w* and the square of *t*;
> *MAXWT* varies inversely as *d*.

These relations can be expressed in a single formula as

$$MAXWT = \frac{kwt^2}{d}, \text{ where } k \text{ is a constant.}$$

Notice that each independent variable that varies directly as *MAXWT* is in the numerator, and the independent variable that varies inversely as *MAXWT* is in the denominator. The formula tells you that the greater the width and depth and the shorter the distance between supports, the stronger the board will be.

In the next lesson you will calculate the constant of variation *k* in this type of relationship.

Questions

Covering the Reading

1. *True or false* The variables *MAXWT*, *d*, *t*, and *w* can all be graphed on one set of axes.   False

2. How can one investigate the relationship between a dependent variable and more than one independent variable?   See margin.

3. How did Perri Menter determine that *MAXWT* varies directly as *w*?
   See margin.

4. What was the maximum weight supported by a board 10 ft long, 3 in. wide, and 5 in. thick?   500 lb

5. What is the shape of the graph of the relationship between *MAXWT* and *d*?   a hyperbola

6. In the formula $MAXWT = \frac{kwt^2}{d}$, any variable which varies directly as *MAXWT* is in the __?__ of the expression.   numerator

Applying the Mathematics

7. Use the method of Lesson 2-7 to show that *MAXWT* varies inversely as *d* and not d^2.   See margin.

Question 16b: This question asks students to rank the strength of different woods with respect to the amount of weight that a board can support. Due to their different strengths, these woods are used for different purposes. You might discuss some of these purposes.

ADDITIONAL ANSWERS
2. Hold all but one independent variable constant.

3. The points appeared to lie on a line through the origin.

7. Using $MAXWT = \frac{K}{d^2}$, with $K = 800$. Using this value of *K* when $d = 4$, $\frac{K}{d^2} = 800/16 = 50$. Yet $MAXWT = 200$ when $d = 4$. So this is not a good model. Using $MAXWT = \frac{K}{d}$, with $K = 800$. When $d = 4$, this model predicts $MAXWT = \frac{800}{4} = 200$, which is correct.

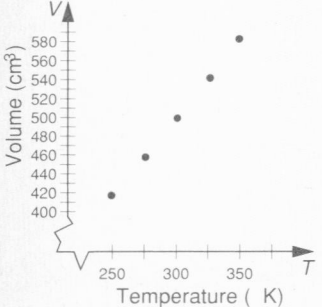
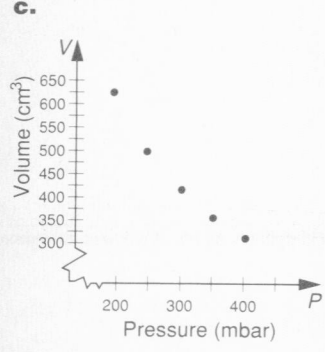
8. *Multiple choice* The two graphs below show the relationships between a dependent variable y and two independent variables x and z. Which equation best models this situation? c

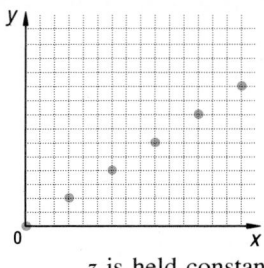 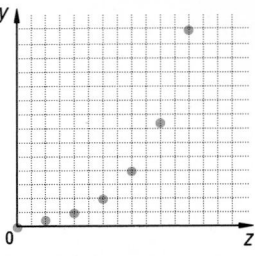

z is held constant   x is held constant

(a) $y = kx$ (b) $y = \dfrac{kx}{z}$ (c) $y = kxz^2$ (d) $y = kx^2z$

9. Cyrus Nathan Tist attempted to find how the volume of a gas (the dependent variable) depends on the temperature and pressure of the gas (the independent variables).
   a. When he held the pressure fixed at 250 millibars (abbreviated mbar), he obtained the following results. (The temperature is in degrees Kelvin, where Kelvin temperature = 273° + Celsius temperature.)

Temperature (°K)	250	275	300	325	350
Volume (cm³)	417	458	500	542	583

   Graph these data points. On the *V*-axis, start at 400 and increase the scale by 20s; that is, make marks at 400, 420, ..., 600. **See margin**
   b. How does *V* vary with *T*?   directly
   c. When Cy held the temperature fixed at 300°K, he obtained the following results.

Pressure (mbar)	200	250	300	350	400
Volume (cm³)	625	500	417	357	313

   Graph these data points. On the *V*-axis start at 300 and increase the scale by 50's.   See margin.
   d. How does *V* vary with *P*?   inversely
   e. Write an equation of variation to show how *V* depends on *T* and *P*. Do not solve for *k*. $V = \dfrac{kT}{P}$

10. Cy was trying to determine how the pressure exerted on the floor by the heel of a shoe depends on the width of the heel and the weight of the person wearing the shoe. He started by measuring the pressure (in psi) exerted by several people wearing a shoe with a heel width of 3.5 in. The data are summarized below:

Weight (lb)	62	85	100	128	154	180
Pressure (psi)	5.7	7.8	9.1	11.7	14.1	16.5

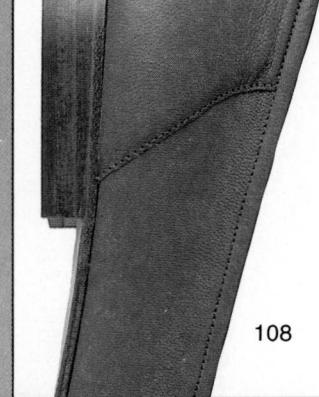

108

He then had his niece Ego, who weighs 142 lb, wear shoes with different heel widths, and he measured the pressure exerted. The data are summarized below:

Heel width (in.)	1	1.5	2	2.5	3	3.5
Pressure (psi)	159.0	70.7	39.8	25.4	17.7	13.0

Assuming that *PRESS* (the pressure), *w* (the weight), and *h* (the heel width) are related by a variation model, find an equation to describe that relationship. Do not solve for *k*. $Press = \dfrac{kw}{h^2}$

Review

11. Use $y = \dfrac{-20}{x^2}$.
   a. What real number is excluded from the domain of *x*?   0
   b. *Multiple choice* Which could be the graph of the equation? *(Lesson 2-7)*   iii

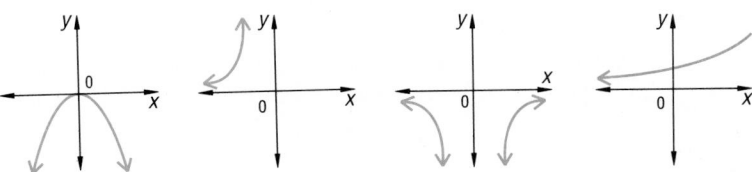

12. Which of the following equations have graphs that are continuous? *(Lessons 2-4, 2-5, 2-7)*   a, b
   a. $y = \dfrac{4x}{7}$ b. $y = .08x^2$ c. $y = \dfrac{-10}{x}$ d. $y = \dfrac{\frac{1}{3}}{x^2}$

13. The braking distance needed to stop a car is directly proportional to the square of the car's speed. *(Lessons 2-1, 2-5)*
   a. If it takes 50 meters to brake a car that was traveling 88 kph, how many meters will it take to brake a car traveling 100 kph?   64.6 m
   b. Find the rate of change for the braking distance between 88 kph and 100 kph.   1.22

14. The graph of the equation $y = \dfrac{3x}{4}$ is a ___?___ with slope ___?___. *(Lesson 2-4)*   line; $\frac{3}{4}$

15. The perimeter of a rectangle is to be less than 12.4 meters. Its length is 3.2 meters. What are the possible values of the width? *(Lessons 1-1, 1-9)* $0 \le w < 3.0$ m

Exploration

16. The ability of a board to support a weight also depends on the type of wood. In other words, the constant of variation *k* in the formula

$$MAXWT = \frac{kwt^2}{d}$$

depends on the type of wood.
   a. For a stronger kind of wood, is *k* larger or is *k* smaller?   larger
   b. Which is strongest: oak, birch, or pine?   birch

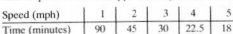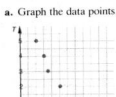
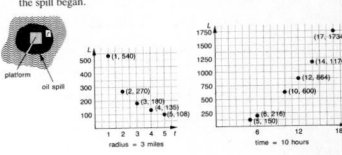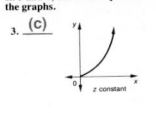
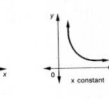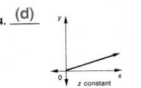
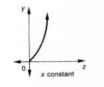

RESOURCES
■ Lesson Master 2-10

OBJECTIVES

D Determine the effects of changes in the values of variables in a combined or joint variation formula.
H Solve problems using joint and combined variation models.

TEACHING NOTES

Explain that in the real world, data are often inconsistent. If this is the case, then the use of judgment is required to get the most appropriate value. This idea is familiar to students. Point out that the grade they receive on a test is a simple mathematical model of their knowledge of the content of the test. Students realize that a test taken on a different day might yield different results. When results are inconsistent, a teacher has to use judgment to decide what grade to assign.

In the case of **Example 1**, different pieces of data from Lesson 2-9 can be used to calculate k. Remind students that if the values are inconsistent, then the model used may be incorrect.

In this book the discussion of the formula for the volume of a cone is helpful in developing the concept of joint variation, since most students are familiar with the formula from their geometry course.

LESSON

2-10

Combined and Joint Variation

In this chapter you have seen several situations where a dependent variable varies directly with some variables and inversely with others. When direct and inverse variations occur together, the situation is one of **combined variation**. Perhaps the simplest equation of combined variation is

$$y = \frac{kx}{z}$$

where k is the constant of variation. The equation can be translated as "y varies directly as x and inversely as z."

A combined-variation situation can have more than two variables, and the independent variables can have any positive exponent. You saw an instance of this in Lesson 2-9:

$$MAXWT = \frac{kwt^2}{d}.$$

This formula gives the maximum weight in pounds $MAXWT$ that can be supported by a board of width w in., thickness t in., and distance between supports of d ft. But it does not give an explicit value for the constant k. As you know, mathematical models can be used to make predictions, but this model cannot be used until the constant k is determined.

You can find k the same way you found the constant for direct and inverse variation. You need to find one instance that relates all the variables simultaneously. In Lesson 2-9 there are eighteen possible instances which can be used to find k. (Each of the three graphs used in deriving the formula for $MAXWT$ has six instances. For example, the first graph relating $MAXWT$ and w gives six possible pairs of numbers for w and $MAXWT$. For each of these pairs, $t = 2$ in. and $d = 10$ ft.) One instance you can use is $MAXWT = 27$ lb, $w = 1$ in., $t = 2$ in., and $d = 10$ ft. When you substitute into the formula, you get

$$27 \text{ lb} = \frac{k(1 \text{ in.})(2 \text{ in.})^2}{10 \text{ ft}}.$$

Solve this for k to get

$$67.5 \frac{\text{ft-lb}}{\text{in.}^3} = k.$$

This value for k should be checked by using other data points; you will do this in the questions at the end of the lesson. Thus, the formula becomes

$$MAXWT = \frac{67.5 \ wt^2}{d} \quad \text{or} \quad MAXWT = 67.5 \frac{wt^2}{d}.$$

Now it is possible to use this model to make predictions.

110

Example 1 Find the maximum weight that can be supported by a board 1.5 in. wide and 11.5 in. deep, with supports 20 ft apart.

Solution Use the preceding formula with $d = 20$ ft, $w = 1.5$ in., and $t = 11.5$ in. Then

$$MAXWT = \frac{(67.5)(1.5)(11.5)^2}{20} \approx 669.5.$$

The board can support about 670 lb.

Often a situation involving combined variation is expressed in English and must be translated into a mathematical statement.

Example 2 The time T that it takes a parade to pass a reviewing stand varies directly as the length L of the parade and inversely as the speed s of the parade.

Write a general equation to model this situation.

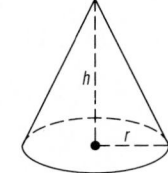

Solution Because T is described in terms of L and s, T is the dependent variable. Because T varies directly as L, L will be in the numerator. Because T varies inversely as s, s will be in the denominator. The equation is

$$T = \frac{kL}{s}.$$

Sometimes one quantity varies directly as the product of two or more independent variables, but not inversely as any variable. This is called **joint variation**. Perhaps the simplest equation of joint variation is

$$y = kxz,$$

where k is the constant of variation. The equation can be translated as "y varies jointly as x and z" or "y varies directly as the product of x and z."

As in combined variation, a joint variation situation can have more than two independent variables, and the independent variables can have any positive exponent. Recall from geometry the formula for the volume of a cone:

$$V = \tfrac{1}{3}\pi r^2 h.$$

LESSON 2-10   Combined and Joint Variation   **111**

1. The volume of a certain species of tree varies jointly as the height of the tree and the square of its girth. A tree 8.1 m tall with girth 1.5 m has a volume of 58.3 m³. Find the volume of a tree 23 meters tall with girth 2.4 m.
Let **V = volume of tree, h = height of tree, and g = girth. Then V = khg² and k ≈ 3.2. Thus, the volume of the 23-meter tree is approximately 424 m³.**

2. The power in an electrical circuit varies jointly as the current and the square of the resistance. The power in a circuit is 1500 watts when the current is 15 amps and the resistance is 10 ohms. Find the power in a circuit when the current is 20 amps and the resistance is 25 ohms.
Let **P = power, C = current, and R = resistance. Then P = kCR² and k = 1. The power in the second circuit is 12,500 watts.**

3. A baseball pitcher's earned run average (ERA) varies directly as the number of earned runs allowed and inversely as the number of innings pitched. In a recent year, a pitcher had an ERA of 2.56. He gave up 72 earned runs in 253 innings. How many earned runs would he have given up if he had pitched 300 innings, assuming that his ERA remained the same?
Let **E = earned run average, R = number of runs allowed, and I = number of innings pitched. The $E = \frac{kR}{I}$, which gives k ≈ 9. He would have given up about 85 earned runs.**

Question 12: Stress the four-step algorithm used to solve the problem. It is applicable to all variation problems in the text.

Question 15: This question is excellent for reviewing the concept of domain introduced in Lesson 1-2. Students may ask if the graph in part (a) is continuous, since each graph identified as continuous in the book has had an unbounded domain. Stress that the graph is continuous on the bounded interval $-3 \le x \le 3$.

Question 23: Almost any physics book is a good reference.

This can be expressed as "the volume varies jointly with the height and the square of the radius of the base." The constant of variation is $\frac{\pi}{3}$.

Example 3 The amount of heat H lost through a single pane window varies jointly as the area A of the pane and the difference $T_I - T_O$ in temperatures on either side of the window. Suppose when the indoor temperature is $T_I = 70°$ F and the outdoor temperature is $T_O = 0°$ F, the heat lost through a 12 ft^2 window is 950 BTUs (British thermal units). Find the amount of heat lost through a 16 ft^2 window if the indoor temperature is 75° F and the outdoor temperature is -5° F.

Solution First, write the general equation: H, A, and T are related by

$$H = kA(\underline{T_I} - T_O).$$

Now find k.
When $A = 12$ and $H = 950$, $T_I = 70°$ and $T_O = 0$.
Substitute. $950 = k \cdot 12(70 - 0)$
Solve for k. $k \approx 1.13$

Now rewrite the formula with the calculated value of k.

$$H \approx 1.13\, A(T_I - T_O)$$

Finally, substitute $A = 16$, $T_I = 75°$ and $T_O = -5°$.

$$H \approx (1.13)\,(16)\,(75 - {-5})$$
$$\approx 1446.4$$

The heat lost is about 1450 BTU, which is about as much heat as a small space heater provides.

Questions

Covering the Reading

1. *True or false* Combined variation involves both direct and inverse variations together.   **True**

In 2–4, refer to the example about the maximum weight that can be supported by a board.

2. *MAXWT* varies directly as _?_ and _?_ and inversely as _?_.
   width; square of thickness; distance between supports
3. Find k by using this data point from Lesson 2-9: *MAXWT* = 80 lb, $w = 3$ in., $d = 2$ in., and $L = 10$ ft. This checks that the value for k found in the text is reasonable.   **66.7 ft-lb/in^3**

112

4. Find the maximum weight that can be supported by a board with supports 16 ft apart, 11.5 in. wide, and 1.5 in. deep. (Use $k = 67.5$, as found in the text.)   about 109 ft apart

5. Translate into a single formula: R varies directly as L and inversely as d^2. $R = \dfrac{kL}{d^2}$

6. Translate the formula $V = \frac{1}{3}\pi r^2 h$ into English, using the language of variation.   See margin.

7. Refer to Example 3. Find how much heat is lost through a 10-ft^2 window when the indoor temperature is 72°F and the outdoor temperature is 34°F.   About 430 BTU

Applying the Mathematics

8. Translate into a single formula: The time t it takes to finish algebra homework varies directly as the number of questions assigned a and inversely as the number d that can be solved with the aid of a calculator. $t = \dfrac{ka}{d}$

9. One general equation for a combined variation is
$$y = k\frac{xz}{w}.$$
Solve for k in terms of the other variables. $k = \dfrac{wy}{xz}$

10. Use the formula for *MAXWT*. Suppose that the maximum load that can be supported by a board is 2250 lb, and that the constant of variation is $67.5\dfrac{\text{ft-lb}}{\text{in}^3}$. If the board is 10 in. deep and the supports are 12 ft apart, how wide is it?   4 in

11. Refer to Example 2. A parade 600 ft long walking at 2.5 mph needs 90 min to pass the reviewing stand. How long would it take a parade 500 ft long walking at 3 mph to pass the reviewing stand?   about 63 min

12. The wind force F on a vertical surface varies jointly as the area A of the surface and the square of the wind speed S. The force is 75 lb on a vertical surface of area 10 ft^2 when the wind blows at 40 mph.
    a. Using the given variables, translate the first statement into an equation of variation. $F = kAS^2$
    b. Find the constant of variation.   .00469 lb/mph^2 ft^2
    c. Rewrite the equation of variation using the constant found in part b. $F = .0047AS^2$
    d. Find the force exerted by a wind of 80 mph on a vertical surface of area 25 ft^2.   about 750 lb

13. y varies directly as x and inversely as z. Find how y changes when x and z are both doubled.   It stays the same.

NAME _____

MORE PRACTICE
For more questions on SPUR
Objectives, use *Lesson Master 2-10*, shown on page 113.

ADDITIONAL ANSWERS
14.a.

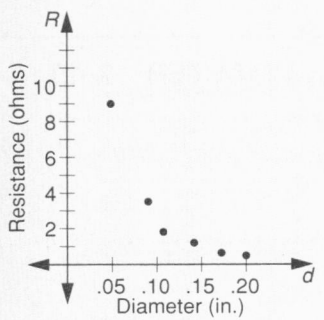

c.

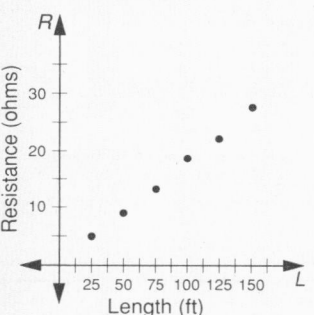

15.a.

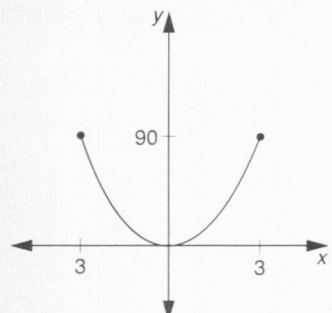

Review

14. The resistance R in an electrical circuit is related to the diameter d of the wire and the length L of the wire. *(Lessons 2-7, 2-8)*
   a. In an experiment, Perri Menter obtained the following data with a 50 ft wire.

Diameter (in.)	.05	.08	.11	.14	.17	.20
Resistance (ohms)	9.0	3.5	1.9	1.1	0.8	0.6

   Graph these data points.   **See margin.**
   b. How does R vary with d?   **inversely**
   c. With a wire of diameter .05 in. she obtained the following data.

Length (ft)	25	50	75	100	125	150
Resistance (ohms)	4.5	9	13.5	18	22.5	27

   Graph these data points.   **See margin.**
   d. How does R vary with L?   **directly**
   e. Write an equation that relates R, d, and L. You do not need to find the constant of variation. $R = \dfrac{kL}{d^2}$

15. Use the equation $y = 10x^2$. *(Lesson 2-5)*
   a. Graph the solution for $-3 \le x \le 3$.   **See margin.**
   b. What is the name of this curve ?   **parabola**
   c. Find the rate of change between $x = 1$ and $x = 2$.   **30**
   d. Should you expect that the answer to part c would be the same for any two points on the graph?   **No**

In 16 and 17, use the graph of $y = \dfrac{20}{x^2}$ at the right. *(Lessons 2-6, 2-7)*   **See margin.**

16. Sketch a graph of this equation on the window $-10 \le x \le 10$, $-10 \le y \le 10$.

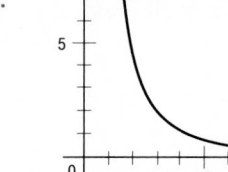

17. *True or false*   The graph of $y = \dfrac{20}{x^2}$ is a hyperbola.   **False**

In 18–20, an instance of a general property is given. Write the general property. *(Lessons 1-5, 1-6, 1-9)*   **See margin.**

18. $40y - y = 39y$

19. If $2 < 3 - z$, then $2 + z < 3$.

20. $\dfrac{2}{3} + \dfrac{x}{3} = \dfrac{2 + x}{3}$

In 21–22, solve. *(Lesson 1-9)*

21. $5 - 3x \le 86$ $x \ge -27$

22. $.05(y - 3) - (.2y - 5) > y + 1$ $y < 3.35$

Exploration

23. a. Find out what unit is used for heat in the metric system.   **Joules**
   b. How is this unit related to the BTU?   **1 BTU is about 1055 Joules.**

Summary

In a formula where y is given in terms of x, it is natural to ask how changing x (the independent variable) affects the value of y (the dependent variable). The rate of change $\frac{y_2 - y_1}{x_2 - x_1}$ between the two points (x_1, y_1) and (x_2, y_2) is the slope of the line connecting them.

Two types of formulas studied in this chapter are direct variation and inverse variation. When $k \neq 0$ and $n > 0$, formulas of the form $y = kx^n$ represent direct variation, and those of the form $y = \frac{k}{x^n}$ represent inverse variation.

In direct or inverse variation, simple changes occur in y when x is multiplied by a constant. When x is multiplied by c: if y varies directly as x^n, then y is multiplied by c^n, and if y varies inversely as x^n, then y is divided by c^n. Four special cases commonly occur, and their graphs have special names.

Direct-variation formulas

$$y = kx$$
y varies directly as x.
$$k > 0 \qquad k < 0$$

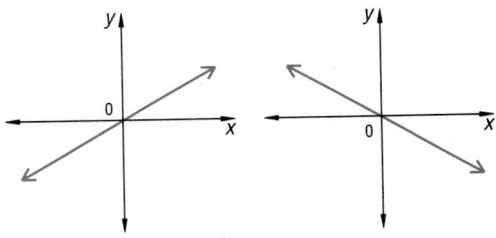

line

$$y = kx^2$$
y varies directly as the square of x.
$$k > 0 \qquad k < 0$$

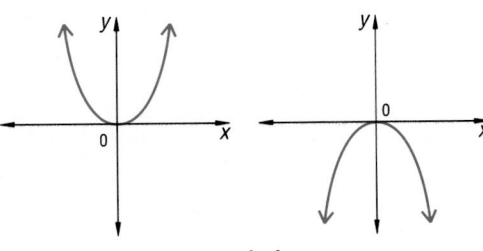

parabola

Inverse-variation formulas

$$y = \frac{k}{x}$$
y varies inversely as x.
$$k > 0 \qquad k < 0$$

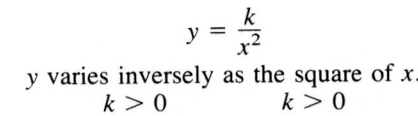

hyperbola

$$y = \frac{k}{x^2}$$
y varies inversely as the square of x.
$$k > 0 \qquad k > 0$$

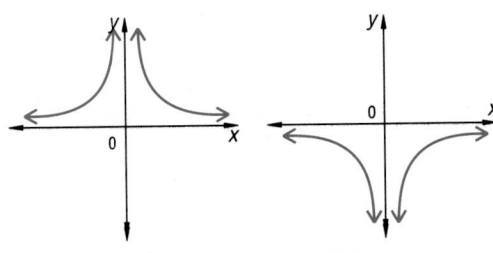

inverse-square curve

16.

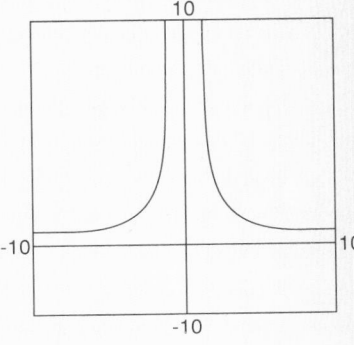

18. $ac - bc = (a - b)c$

19. If $a < b$, then $a + c < b + c$.

20. $ab + ac = a(b + c)$

Terms, symbols, and properties are listed by lesson to provide a checklist of things a student must know. Emphasize to students that they should read the vocabulary list carefully before starting the Progress Self-Test. If students do not understand the meaning of a term, they should refer back to the indicated lesson.

Definitions or descriptions of all terms in the vocabulary list may be found in the Glossary.

Formulas may involve three or more variables. If all the independent variables are multiplied, then joint variation occurs. If they are not all multiplied, the situation is one of combined variation. Variation formulas can be derived from real data by examining two variables at a time and comparing their graphs with those given above. We call this idea modeling, or forming a mathematical model of the data. Automatic graphers, such as graphing calculators or computers with graphing programs, are useful tools to help in graphing and in comparing graphs.

The applications of slope, variation, and modeling are numerous. They include many perimeter, area, and volume formulas; the inverse square laws of sound and gravity; and a variety of relationships among physical quantities such as distance, time, force, and pressure.

Vocabulary

Below are the most important terms and phrases for this chapter.
You should be able to state each in words and give a specific example.
For the starred (*) terms, you should be able to supply a good definition.

Lesson 2-1
direct variation*, directly proportional to, varies directly as, constant of variation, dependent variable, independent variable

Lesson 2-2
inverse variation*, is inversely proportional to, varies inversely as, inverse-square variation

Lesson 2-3
Fundamental Theorem of Variation

Lesson 2-4
*rate of change, *slope

Lesson 2-5
parabola, reflection-symmetric
line of symmetry

Lesson 2-6
automatic grapher, function grapher, window, default window, zoom feature
hard copy

Lesson 2-7
discrete, discontinuous, continuous
hyperbola, branches of a hyperbola
inverse-square curve

Lesson 2-8
mathematical model

Lesson 2-10
combined variation
joint variation

Progress Self-Test

Take this test as you would take a test in class. Use graph paper and a ruler. Then check your work with the solutions in the Selected Answers section in the back of the book.

In 1–3, translate into a variation formula.

1. y varies inversely as x. $\quad y = \frac{k}{x}$

2. The number n of trees that can be planted per acre varies inversely as the square of their distance d apart. $\quad n = \frac{k}{d^2}$

3. The weight w that a column of a bridge can support varies directly as the fourth power of its diameter d and inversely as the square of its length L. $\quad w = \frac{kd^4}{L^2}$

4. If S varies directly as the square of p and $S = 10$ when $p = 3$, find S when $p = 8$. $\quad S \approx 71.1$

5. For the variation equation $y = 3x^2$, what is the change in the y-value when an x-value is doubled? **See margin.**

6. For the variation equation $y = \frac{6}{x}$, what is the change in the y-value when an x-value is multiplied by c $(c \neq 0)$? **y values are divided by c**

7. Find the rate of change of the line through the points $(12, 18)$ and $(20, 30)$. $\quad \frac{3}{2}$

8. *True or false* All graphs of variation pass through the origin. **False**

9. The graph of $y = kx^2$ is called a __?__ and opens up if __?__. **parabola, $k > 0$**

10. Which word or phrase does not describe the graph below? **a**
a. continuous **b.** discrete
c. symmetric about the y-axis

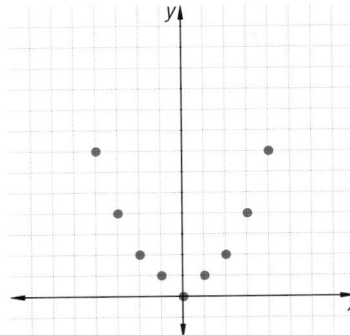

11. Fill in the blank with the word "inversely," "directly," or "neither inversely nor directly."
a. The surface area of a sphere varies __?__ as the cube of its radius. **directly**
b. The number of different shares you can buy varies __?__ as the cost of each share, if you invest exactly $10,000. **inversely**

In 12 and 13, graph on a coordinate plane. **See margin.**

12. $y = -5x$ **13.** $y = \frac{5}{x}$

In 14 and 15, *multiple choice*

14. Find the equation whose graph looks the most like the graph shown below. **c**
(a) $y = -3x$
(b) $y = -\frac{3}{x}$
(c) $y = -\frac{3}{x^2}$
(d) $y = -\frac{x}{3}$

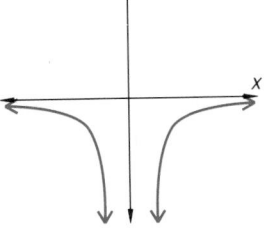

The Progress Self-Test continues on page 118.

PROGRESS SELF-TEST

We cannot overemphasize the importance of these end-of-chapter materials. It is at this point that the material "gels" for many students, allowing them to solidify skills and understanding. In general, student performance should be markedly improved after these pages.

USING THE PROGRESS SELF-TEST
Assign the Progress Self-Test as a one-night assignment. Worked-out *solutions* for all questions are in the Selected Answers section of the student book. Encourage students to take the Progress Self-Test honestly, grade themselves, and then be prepared to discuss the test in class.

Advise students to pay special attention to those Chapter Review questions (pages 119–123) which correspond to questions missed on the Progress Self-Test. A chart provided in the Selected Answers section in the student text keys the Progress Self-Test questions to the lettered SPUR Objectives in the Chapter Review or to the Vocabulary. It also keys the questions to the corresponding lessons where the material is covered.

ADDITIONAL ANSWERS
5. by the Fundamental Theorem of Variation in $y = kx^2$; if x is multiplied by 2, y is multiplied by 2^2. So, y-values are quadrupled.

12. and 13. See Additional Answers on page 118.

117

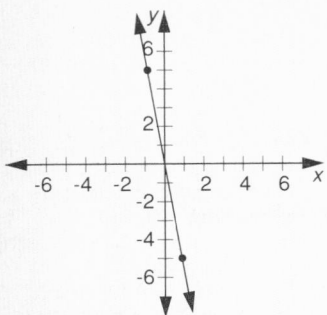
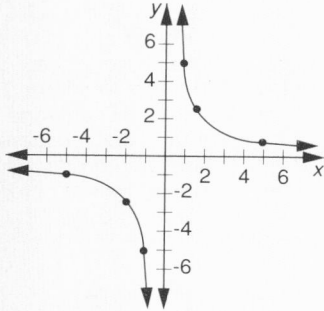
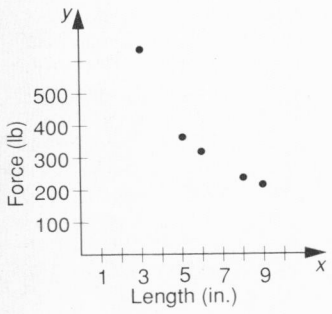
15. Below is a graph of $y = x^2$ on the window $-4 \le x \le 4$, $0 \le y \le 10$. Which cannot be a graph of this equation on some other window?
d

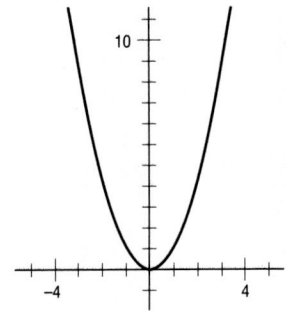

(a)   (b)

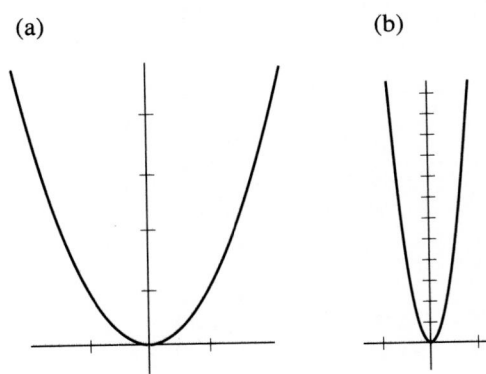

(c)   (d)

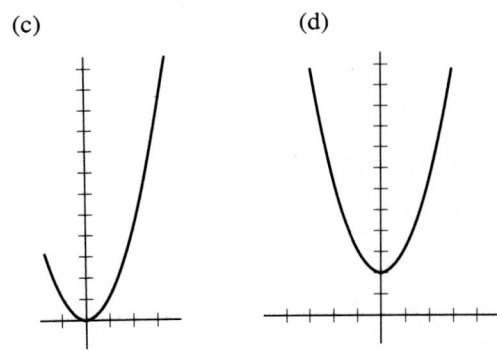

16. A worker removing the bolts from the back of a large cabinet knew that it was easier to turn a bolt with a long wrench than with a short one. He decided to investigate the force required with various wrenches. He obtained the following data.

Length of wrench (in.)	3	5	6	8	9
Force (lb)	620	372	310	233	207

a. Graph these data points. See margin.

b. Which variation equation is a better model for this situation, $F = \dfrac{k}{L}$ or $F = \dfrac{k}{L^2}$? $F = \dfrac{k}{L}$

c. How much force would be required to turn one of these bolts with a 12-in. wrench? 155 lb

17. Suppose that variables V, h, and g are related as illustrated in the graphs below. The points on the graph at the left lie on or near a parabola. The points on the graph at the right lie on a line through the origin.

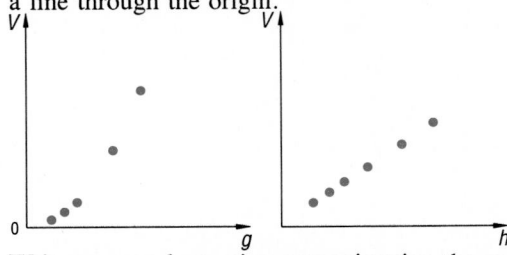

Write a general equation approximating the relationship among V, h, and g. $V = khg^2$

18. Poiseuille's Law states that the speed S at which blood flows through arteries and veins varies directly with the blood pressure P and the fourth power of the radius r of the blood vessel. Suppose that blood flows at a rate of .09604 cm^3/sec through an artery of diameter .14 cm when the blood pressure is a normal 100 units. What would be the blood pressure if cholesterol reduced the artery to .1 cm in diameter, and the speed stayed the same?
About 384 units

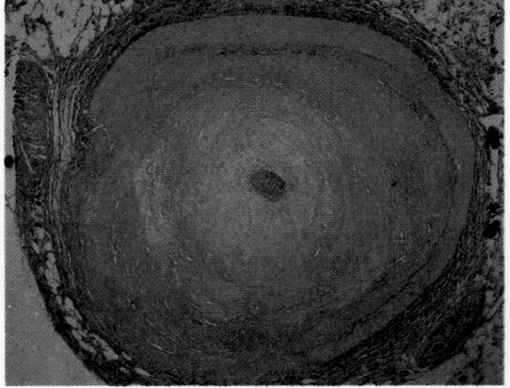

118

Chapter Review

Questions on **SPUR** Objectives

SPUR stands for **S**kills, **P**roperties, **U**ses, and **R**epresentations.
The Chapter Review questions are grouped according to the
SPUR Objectives for this chapter.

SKILLS deal with the procedures used to get answers.

■ **Objective A:** *Translate variation language into formulas. (Lessons 2-1, 2-2, 2-10)*

In 1–8, translate into a variation equation.

1. y varies directly as the square of x. $y = kx^2$

2. s varies inversely with p. $s = \dfrac{k}{p}$

3. The number n of congruent marbles that fit into a box is inversely proportional to the cube of the radius r of each marble. $n = \dfrac{k}{r^3}$

4. The area A of an image on a movie screen is directly proportional to the square of the distance d from the projector to the screen. $A = kd^2$

5. The rate of vibration U of a stretched string varies directly with the square root of the tension T and inversely with the product of its length L and diameter D. $U = \dfrac{k\sqrt{T}}{Ld}$

6. z varies jointly as x and t. $z = kxt$

7. The gravitational pull P of a star on a mass m varies directly as the mass and inversely as the square of the distance d from the star. $P = \dfrac{km}{d^2}$

8. At a given speed, the distance traveled is directly proportional to the time travelled. $a = kt$

9. In the formula $r = kstu$, r varies __?__ with __?__.   **jointly; s, t, and u**

10. If $V = k\pi r^2$, then V varies __?__ as __?__.   **directly; the square of r**

■ **Objective B:** *Solve variation problems. (Lessons 2-1, 2-2, 2-10)*

11. y varies directly as x. If $x = 4$, then $y = -12$. Find y when $x = -7$.   **21**

12. y varies directly as the square of x. When $x = -5$, $y = 75$. Find y when $x = 8$.   **192**

13. y varies inversely as the cube of x. If $x = 4$, $y = -\frac{1}{16}$. Find y when $x = \frac{1}{2}$.   **-32**

14. z varies directly as the square of x and inversely as y. When $x = 3$ and $y = 5$, $z = 4.5$. Find z when $x = -2$ and $y = -1.5$. $-\frac{20}{3}$ or $\approx$-6.7

■ **Objective C:** *Find slopes (rates of change). (Lessons 2-4, 2-5, 2-7)*

15. Find the slope of the line through the points $(15, 27)$ and $(20, 36)$.   **1.8**

In 16 and 17, $y = 5x^2$.

16. Find the rate of change between $x = -2$ and $x = -1$.   **-15**

17. Find the rate of change between $x = -3$ and $x = -2$.   **-25**

In 18 and 19, find the rate of change between $x = 3$ and $x = 4$.   **See margin.**

18. $y = \dfrac{9}{x}$ **-.75**

19. $y = \dfrac{9}{x^2}$ $-\frac{7}{16}$ = -.4375

20. What is the slope of the line below? $-\frac{1}{3}$

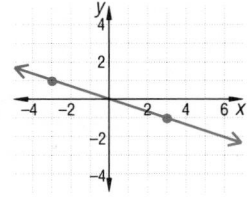

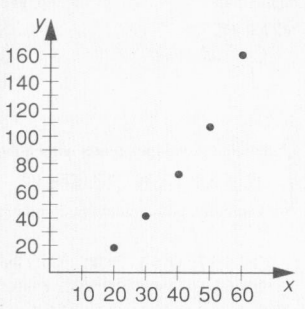

b. $L = ks^2$
c. $k = .045$; $L = .045s^2$
d. 220.5 ft

PROPERTIES deal with the principles behind the mathematics.

■ **Objective D:** *Determine the effects of changes in the values of variables in a variation formula.* *(Lessons 2-3, 2-10)*

In 21 and 22, suppose that in a variation problem the value of x is tripled. Tell how the value of y changed for each type of variation.

21. y varies directly as x. y is tripled

22. y varies directly as x^3. y is multiplied by 27.

In 23–24, suppose that p varies inversely as the square of q. How does the value of p change if q is

23. doubled? p is divided by 4

24. multiplied by ten? p is divided by 100

25. If $y = \dfrac{k}{x^n}$ and x is multiplied by any nonzero constant c, then y is __?__. divided by c^n

26. If $y = kx^n$ and x is divided by any nonzero constant c, then y is __?__. divided by c^n

27. If $y = \dfrac{kx^n}{z^n}$ and both x and z are multiplied by any nonzero constant c, then y is __?__. not

■ **Objective E:** *Identify the properties of variation graphs. (Lessons 2-4, 2-5, 2-7)*

28. The graph of the equation $y = kx$ is a __?__ having slope __?__. line, k

29. Graphs of all direct variation formulas go through the point __?__. (0, 0)

In 30–33, refer to these four equations:

(a) $y = kx$ (b) $y = kx^2$ (c) $y = \dfrac{k}{x}$ (d) $y = \dfrac{k}{x^2}$.

30. Which equations have graphs that are symmetric to the y- axis? b, d

31. The graph of which equation is a parabola? b

32. *True or false* All four equations have graphs which are continuous everywhere. False

33. *True or false* When $k > 0$, all four equations have points in quadrant I. True

USES deal with applications of mathematics in real situations.

■ **Objective F:** *Recognize variation situations. (Lessons 2-1, 2-2)*

In 34–38, complete with "directly," "inversely," or "neither directly nor inversely."

34. The number of adults invited to dinner varies __?__ as the number of pieces of silverware used. directly

35. The number of people invited to dinner varies __?__ as the amount of space each guest has at the table. inversely

36. The temperature in a house varies __?__ as the number of hours the air-conditioner has been on. neither

37. The volume of a cylinder of height 10 cm varies __?__ as the square of its radius. directly

38. Your height on a ferris wheel varies __?__ as the number minutes you have been on it.
neither

■ **Objective G:** *Fit an appropriate model to data. (Lessons 2-8, 2-9)*

In 39 and 40, do steps a to d.
  a. Draw a graph to represent the situation.
  b. Find a general variation equation to represent the situation.
  c. Find the value of the constant of variation and rewrite the variation equation.
  d. Answer the question stated in the problem.

39. Officer Friendly measured the length of car skid marks when the brakes were applied at different speeds. He obtained the following data.

Speed (mph)	20	30	40	50	60
Length of skid (ft)	18	41	72	113	162

How far would a car skid if the brakes are applied at 70 mph? See margin.

120

40. A man weighs 200 lb on the surface of Earth. The following table gives his weight at various distances from the center of Earth. (Remember: the radius of Earth is approximately 4000 mi.)

Distance (miles)	4000	4500	5000	5500	6000
Weight (lb)	200	158	128	106	89

How much would the man weigh on the top of Mt. Everest, which is about 4005.5 miles from Earth's center?   *See margin.*

41. Cyrus N. Tist tried to discover how the power in an electric circuit is related to the strength of the current and the resistance of the wire. When he held the current constant at 5 amps, he obtained the following data relating power P and resistance R.

Resistance (ohms)	5	10	15	20	25	30
Power (watts)	125	500	1125	2000	3125	4500

a. Graph these data points.   *See margin.*
b. How does P vary with R? *P varies directly as R^2*

Then Cy held the resistance constant at 10 ohms. He obtained the following data relating power P and current C.

Current (amps)	5	10	15	20	25	30
Power (watts)	500	1000	1500	2000	2500	3000

c. Graph these data points.   *See margin.*
d. How does P vary with C? *P varies directly as C*
e. Write an equation of variation relating P, R, and C. Do not find the constant of variation.   *P = kR²C*

42. Perri Menter performed an experiment to determine how the pressure P of a liquid on an object is related to the depth d of the object and the density D of the liquid. She obtained the graph on the left by keeping the depth constant and measuring the pressure on an object in solutions with different densities. She obtained the graph on the right by keeping the density constant and measuring the pressure on an object in a solution at various depths.

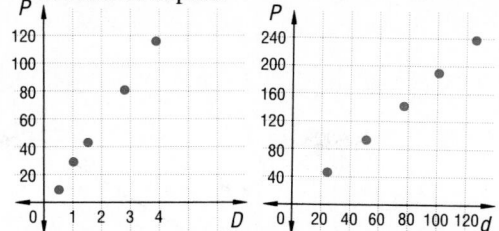

Write a general equation relating P, d, and D. Do not find the constant of variation. *P = kDd*

■ **Objective H:** *Solve problems using joint and combined variation models. (Lessons 2-1, 2-2, 2-10)*

43. Suppose the price of a pizza varies directly with the square of its diameter. At Vic Yee's pizza parlour an 8″ pizza costs $6.00. How much would a 12″ pizza cost?   *$13.50*

44. The refund r you get varies directly with the number n of cans you recycle. If you get a $7.50 refund for 150 cans, how much should you get for 400 cans?   *$20.00*

45. One of Murphy's Laws is that the time t a committee spends debating a budget item is inversely proportional to d, the number of dollars involved. If a committee spends 10 minutes debating a $300 item, how much time is spent debating a $1000 item?   *3 minutes*

46. Recall that Newton's Law of Universal Gravitation is $W = \dfrac{k}{r^2}$. If Ms. Smith's son Ian weighs 75 lb on the surface of Earth. How much will he weigh in space 50,000 miles from Earth's surface. (The radius of Earth is approximately 4000 miles.)   *41 lb*

47. The force needed to keep a car from skidding on a curve varies directly as the weight of the car and the square of the speed and inversely as the radius of the curve. Suppose 3960 lb of force is required to keep a 2200-lb car, traveling at 30 mph, from skidding on a curve of radius 500 ft. How much force is required to keep a 3000-lb car, traveling at 45 mph, from skidding on a curve of radius 400 ft?   *about 15,188 lb*

40.a.

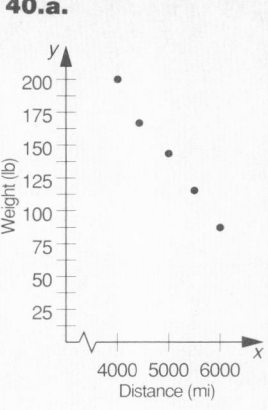

b. $w = \dfrac{k}{D^2}$

c. $k = 3.2 \times 10^9$;

$w = 3.2 \times \dfrac{10^9}{D^2}$

d. 199 lb

41.a.

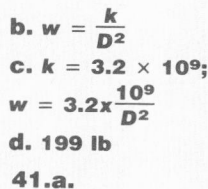

c.

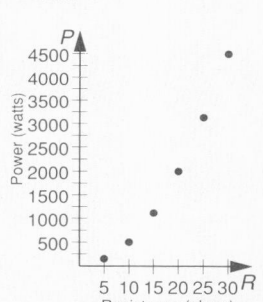

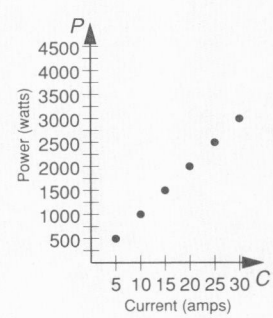

49.

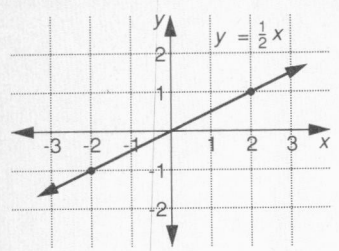

50.

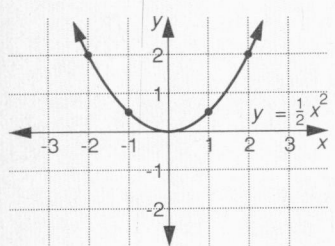

51.

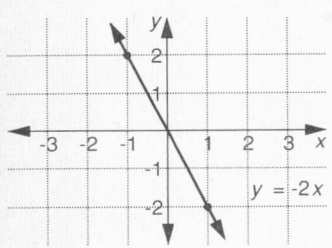

52.

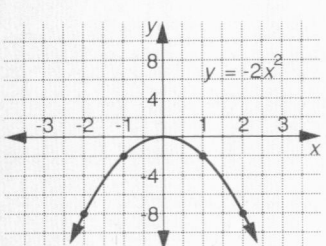

53.

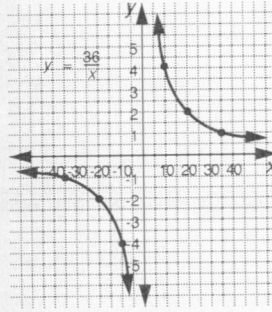

48. An object is tied to a string and then twirled in a circular motion. The tension in the string varies directly as the square of the speed and inversely as the radius. When the radius is 5 ft and the speed is 4 ft/sec, then tension in the string is 90 lb. If the radius is 3.5 ft and the speed is 4.4 ft/sec, find the tension in the string. **about 155.6 lb**

REPRESENTATIONS deal with pictures, graphs, or objects that illustrate concepts.

■ **Objective I.** *Graph variation equations and identify equations from graphs. (Lessons 2-4, 2-5, 2-6, 2-7)*

In 49–54, graph each equation. **See margin.**

49. $y = \frac{1}{2}x$ **50.** $y = \frac{1}{2}x^2$.

51. $y = -2x$ **52.** $y = -2x^2$

53. $y = \frac{36}{x}$ **54.** $y = \frac{36}{x^2}$

Multiple choice In 55–58, select the equation whose graph is most like that shown below. Assume the scales on the axes are equal.

55. (a) $y = 4x$ (c) $y = -\frac{1}{4}x$
c (b) $y = -4x^2$ (d) $y = -\frac{1}{4}$

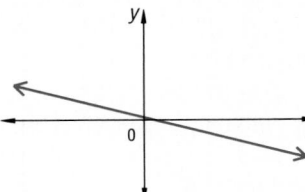

56. (a) $y = 10x^2$ (c) $y = -10x$
b (b) $y = -x^2$ (d) $y = -\frac{10}{x^2}$

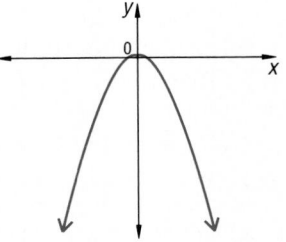

57. (a) $y = \frac{x^2}{6}$ (c) $y = \frac{-6}{x}$
b (b) $y = \frac{6}{x}$ (d) $y = \frac{-6}{x^2}$

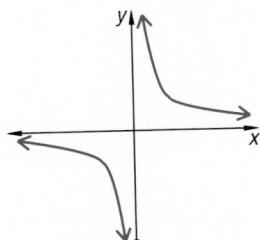

58. (a) $y = \frac{x^2}{6}$ (c) $y = \frac{-6}{x}$
d (b) $y = \frac{6}{x}$ (d) $y = \frac{-6}{x^2}$

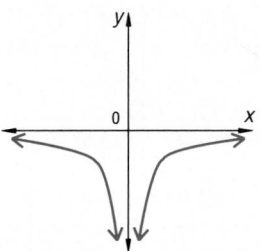

Objective J. *Recognize the effects of a change in scale or viewing window on a graph of a variation equation.* (*Lesson 2-6*)

In 59 and 60, a graph of $y = 4x$ is drawn below at left using the window $-5 \le x \le 5$, $-25 \le y \le 25$.

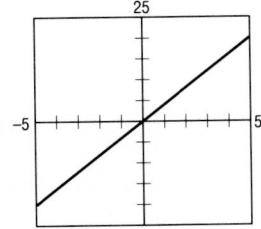 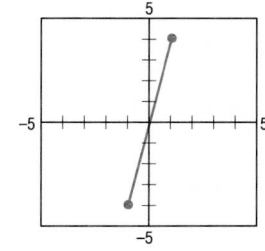

59. Sketch a graph of this equation on the window shown above at the right. **See above.**

60. Does the slope of the line $y = 4x$ change when the viewing window is changed? If so, how? **See margin.**

61. In the graph of $y = kx^2$ shown below, which cannot be the value of k? **d**
(a) 2   (b) 1
(c) 0.1   (d) -1

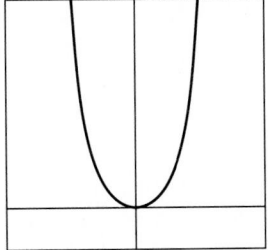

Objective K: *Read and interpret graphs of joint and combined variation.* (*Lessons 2-8, 2-9, 2-10*)

Multiple choice

62. Which of the following equations could model the relationship graphed in Question 59? **a**
(a) $y = kx$ (b) $y = \dfrac{k}{x}$
(c) $y = kx^2$ (d) $y = \dfrac{k}{x^2}$

63. Which of the following equations could model the relationship shown by the *two* equations $y = k_1x^2$ and $y = k_2z^2$? **d**
(a) $y = kx$ (b) $y = kxz^2$
(c) $y = kx^2z$ (d) $y = kx^2z^2$

64. Which of the following equations could model the relationship shown by the three equations $P = k_1Q$, $P = k_2R^2$, and $P = k_3S^2$? **a**
(a) $P = kQR^2S^2$ (b) $P = kQ^2R^2S^2$
(c) $P = \dfrac{kRS^2}{Q}$ (d) $P = \dfrac{k}{R^2S^2Q}$

EVALUATION
Three tests are provided for this chapter in the Teacher's Resource File. Chapter 2 Test, Forms A and B cover just Chapter 2. The third test is Chapter 2 Test, Cumulative Form. About two-thirds of this test covers Chapter 2 and one-third covers Chapter 1. For information on grading, see *General Teaching Suggestions: Grading* on page T44 in the Teacher's Edition.

ASSIGNMENT RECOMMENDATION
We strongly recommend that you assign Lesson 3-1, both reading and some questions, for homework the evening of the test. It gives students work to do after they have completed the test and keeps the class moving. If you do not do this, you may cover one less *chapter* over the course of the year.

54.

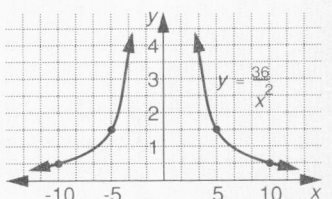

60. The slope appears to become smaller, but it is 4 in both cases.

CHAPTER 3 ■ LINEAR RELATIONS

DAILY PACING CHART ■ CHAPTER 3

Students in the Full Course should complete all of the chapters by the end of the year. Students in the Minimal Course will spend more time on quizzes and the Chapter Review. As such, these students may not complete all of the chapters in the book.

DAY	MINIMAL COURSE	FULL COURSE
1	3-1	3-1
2	3-2	3-2
3	3-3	3-3
4	Quiz (TRF); Start 3-4.	Quiz (TRF); 3-4
5	Finish 3-4.	3-5
6	3-5	3-6
7	3-6	3-7
8	3-7	Quiz (TRF); 3-8
9	Quiz (TRF); Start 3-8.	3-9
10	Finish 3-8.	Progress Self-Test
11	3-9	Chapter Review
12	Progress Self-Test	Chapter Test (TRF)
13	Chapter Review	Comprehensive Test (TRF)
14	Chapter Review	
15	Chapter Test (TRF)	
16	Comprehensive Test (TRF)	

TESTING OPTIONS

■ Quiz for Lessons 3-1 Through 3-3   ■ Chapter 3 Test, Form A   ■ Chapter 3 Test, Cumulative Form
■ Quiz for Lessons 3-4 Through 3-7   ■ Chapter 3 Test, Form B   ■ Comprehensive Test, Chapters 1-3

PROVIDING FOR INDIVIDUAL DIFFERENCES

The student text is written for the *average* student. The program, however, can be adapted for both less capable and for more capable students.

A blackline master (in the Teacher's Resource File) is provided for each lesson for those students who need more practice. The Teacher's Edition frequently provides Error Analysis and Alternate Approach features to provide additional instructional strategies.

For students who require additional challenge, Extension activities are regularly provided in the Teacher's Edition.

OBJECTIVES ■ CHAPTER 3

Students should master the chapter objectives by the time they complete the chapter.
To ensure mastery, there is continual review built into each set of lesson questions.
After students complete the chapter lessons, they assess their mastery on the Progress
Self-Test. Then they do the Chapter Review and pay special attention to those questions
that match the objectives missed on the Progress Self-Test. Students can get extra
practice on these objectives by using the master for each lesson in the Teacher's
Resource File.

OBJECTIVES FOR CHAPTER 3 (Organized into the SPUR categories—Skills, Properties, Uses, and Representations)	Progress Self-Test Questions	Chapter Review Questions	Lesson Master from Teacher's Resource File*
SKILLS		1 through 6	3-1, 3-2, 3-4
A Determine the slope and intercepts of a line given its equation.	4		
B Find an equation for a line given two points on it, or given a point on it and its slope.	6–7	7 through 12	3-5
C Convert linear equations from standard form to slope-intercept form, and vice versa.	14	13 through 16	3-2, 3-4
D Describe arithmetic sequences, both explicitly and recursively.	16–17	17 through 22	3-6, 3-7
PROPERTIES			
E Recognize properties of graphs of linear relations.	8, 18	23 through 32	3-2, 3-4, 3-5, 3-9
F Identify properties of the three general forms of linear relations.	5	33 through 38	3-4, 3-5
G Recognize properties of arithmetic sequences.	13	39 through 48	3-6, 3-7
USES			
H Model constant increase or constant decrease situations.	19	49 through 52	3-1
I In a real-world context, find an equation for a line containing two given points.	20b	53 through 55	3-5
J Model situations leading to linear combinations.	9–10	56, 57	3-3, 3-9
K Solve real-world problems using arithmetic sequences.	11–12	58, 59	3-6, 3-7
REPRESENTATIONS			
L Graph linear equations and inequalities.	1–3, 18	60 through 69	3-2, 3-4, 3-9
M Graph and describe piecewise linear situations.	15, 20a	70 through 74	3-8

* The masters are numbered to match the lessons.

OVERVIEW ■ CHAPTER 3

Chapter 3 introduces situations that lead to the various forms of linear relations and connects these forms to Chapter 2 as generalizations of $y = kx$. Most students will remember some of these concepts from their earlier studies of algebra and geometry, but the emphasis on the usefulness of the forms should make this review interesting.

Chapter 3 is critical to the strong graphing theme carried throughout the other chapters. In later chapters, students will be expected to extend the work done in Chapter 3 to graphing nonlinear equations and to finding the equations of curves.

The chapter opens with two pairs of lessons. Lessons 3-1 and 3-2 explain how constant increase and decrease situations lead to the slope-intercept form of a line and its graph. Lessons 3-3 and 3-4 explain how linear-combination situations lead to equations in standard form and their graphs. The equations for horizontal and vertical lines are also introduced at this time.

Lesson 3-5 explains how to go from a graph, or two points, to an equation of a line and presents the point-slope theorem.

Lessons 3-6 and 3-7 build on the ideas about sequences presented in Chapter 1. These two lessons describe arithmetic sequences as discrete instances of linear equations. In Lesson 3-7, students are shown how to interchange recursive formulas and explicit formulas.

Lesson 3-8 presents piecewise linear graphs, ideas which most students have not seen before. Piecewise linear graphs are useful in many real-world contexts.

Finally, the graphs of linear inequalities are introduced in Lesson 3-9. These are used extensively in Chapter 5 on *Systems*.

PERSPECTIVES ■ CHAPTER 3

The Perspectives provide the rationale for the inclusion of topics or approaches, provide mathematical background, and make connections within UCSMP.

3-1

CONSTANT INCREASE OR DECREASE

In this book, we do not classify situations by context. That is, we do not classify them as age, or distance-rate-time, or work, or digit, and so on. The classifications used in this book are conceptual, that is, by ideas that connect the mathematics with the situation. For lines, the ideas we want students to know are constant increase, constant decrease, and linear combination. This lesson is about constant increase or decrease. Linear combinations are discussed in Lesson 3-3.

Constant increase and constant decrease situations lead to equations of the form $y = mx + b$. Furthermore, m and b have simple interpretations: m is the amount of increase or decrease per unit change of x, and b is the initial value.

3-2

THE GRAPH OF $y = mx + b$

Lesson 3-1 identified applications of slope and y-intercept; this lesson relates them directly to graphing. It is important for students to be able to graph a linear equation quickly, and the techniques discussed in this lesson will allow them to do so.

Many students encountered slope in their first study of algebra, but some students may not understand the idea fully. Applications help to make slope a natural descriptor of lines. Students who have taken UCSMP *Algebra* and *Geometry* will have studied slope twice; UCSMP *Algebra* concentrates on applications of slope, and both books mention that parallel lines have equal slopes.

3-3

LINEAR COMBINATIONS

Just as constant increase or constant decrease situations lead into linear equations in slope-intercept form, linear combinations lead into equations in the standard form $Ax + By = C$.

Equations in standard form are often necessary for solving linear systems, which will be discussed in Chapter 5. Thus, the kinds of situations given in this lesson will be quite useful when developing examples in Chapter 5.

It is possible, and quite common, to have linear combinations of more than two variables, as in Example 1. The graph of $Ax + By + Cz = D$, an equation with three variables, is a plane. Such equations are studied in Chapter 14. If there are more than three variables, the graph is called a *hyperplane*.

3-4

THE GRAPH OF $Ax + By = C$

In this lesson, students study graphs of situations in which a linear combination $Ax + By$ equals a constant. Several important concepts are reviewed: the graph of

$Ax + By = C$, the x-intercepts, the graphs of $x = a$ and $y = b$, and the method of graphing using both intercepts. Students should be able to graph from standard form as well as from slope-intercept form.

3-5
FINDING AN EQUATION OF A LINE

Many students will be familiar with finding an equation for a line through two points, either from their first course in algebra or from their geometry course. For most students this review will be helpful.

In geometry, students learn that there is one line (a) through two points (usually a postulate); (b) through a point parallel to a given line (often a postulate, Playfair's Parallel Postulate); and (c) through a point perpendicular to a given line (usually a theorem). This lesson shows students how to determine the equations for (a) and (b) algebraically.

We do not discuss (c) until Chapter 4 for two reasons: at that time, a simple way to determine the slopes of perpendicular lines will be given; and a second look at this idea will provide a convenient review.

3-6
ARITHMETIC SEQUENCES: EXPLICIT FORMULAS

A generation ago, this section would have been called *arithmetic progressions*. A progression is a special kind of sequence. The advantage of using the phrase *arithmetic sequence* is the connection between sequences and functions, namely that a sequence is a function whose domain is the set of positive integers (or sometimes some other set of integers).

Even the phrase "arithmetic sequence" disguises what is going on, and so the phrase *linear sequence* is introduced. The idea is simple: everything learned for lines has analogues with linear sequences. For instance, just as one can find the equation of a line through two points, one can find a formula for a linear sequence given any two of its terms. Just as one can find the equation of a line given one point and its slope, one can find a formula for a linear sequence given one term and its constant difference. Thus, Lesson 3-6 provides a chance to review Lesson 3-5 by applying the slope-intercept and point-slope forms to discrete situations.

Specifically, by restricting the domain to natural numbers, the equations $y = mx + b$ and $y - y_1 = m(x - x_1)$ can generate arithmetic sequences. To show that the domains have been restricted, we use n for x and a_n for y and call the slope, m, the constant difference or rate of change, d. Thus, the equations become $a_n = dn + b$ and $a_n - a_1 = d(n - 1)$. These substitutions are usually understood by most students.

3-7
ARITHMETIC SEQUENCES: RECURSIVE FORMULAS

This lesson discusses in detail a specific example of a recursive formula for sequences—namely, the recursive formula for arithmetic sequences. The formula given by the theorem on page 160 is one of the simplest recursive formulas. In many respects, recursive formulas for arithmetic sequences are more natural than explicit ones. Indeed, the name *arithmetic progression* suggests that each term is found from the preceding ones.

When given an explicit formula for an arithmetic sequence, the recursive formula can be determined, and vice versa. However, if the sequence is not arithmetic, it may not be possible to determine one formula from the other. In fact, either the recursive or explicit formula may not be known.

Recursive formulas for sequences are used in computer programming more often than explicit formulas. This concept also underlies the idea of proof by mathematical induction.

3-8
PIECEWISE LINEAR GRAPHS

Piecewise linear graphs model situations in which the rate of change is constant for intervals but not for the entire situation. These graphs are exceedingly common in applications. They provide a new and interesting way to provide practice in interpreting information about independent and dependent variables and rates of change from graphs.

As shown in Example 1, often there is a particular constant unit cost if you buy small amounts of a product and then a lower unit cost if you purchase larger amounts. Income taxes can often be represented with a piecewise linear graph.

The piecewise linear graph most familiar to students may be that of the absolute value function. This function and its graph are studied in Lesson 7-5.

3-9
LINEAR INEQUALITIES

This lesson expands the idea of graphing inequalities on a number line (discussed in Lesson 1-9) to graphing inequalities in the coordinate plane. The graphing of half-planes may be a review for some students. The idea is usually quite easy for students.

The boundary for a linear inequality separates the coordinate plane into three disjoint sets of points: the points on either side of the boundary and the points on the boundary line itself. One goal of this lesson is that students can identify which of these sets of points belong to the graph of an inequality.

CHAPTER 3

Linear Relations

124

In Chapter 2 you studied direct variation which was modeled by equations of the form $y = kx$. The graph of $y = kx$ is a line, so $y = kx$ is called a *linear equation*. Many other situations can be modeled by linear equations. Here are three types.

Constant Increase

A crate weighs 30 kilograms when empty. It is filled with oranges weighing 0.2 kilogram each. Find the weight W of a crate containing n oranges.
Answer: $W = 30 + .2n$

Linear Combination

A group bought A adult tickets at $7 each and S student tickets at $3 each. The group spent $42. What equation relates A, S, and the total amount spent?
Answer: $7A + 3S = 42$

Point–Slope

Stuart Dent is conducting an experiment with a spring and a weight. The spring is 15 centimeters long when a 10-gram weight is attached, and its length increases 0.8 centimeter with each additional gram weight. Write an equation relating spring length L and weight W.
Answer: $L - 15 = .8(W - 10)$

In this chapter you will learn how to determine linear equations and inequalities used to model situations similar to these. You will also discover some efficient and powerful techniques for graphing lines and linear relations.

LESSON 3-1

OBJECTIVES

A Determine the slope and *y*-intercept of a line given its equation.
H Model constant increase or constant decrease situations.

TEACHING NOTES

Discuss situations A through D and **Examples 1 and 2** with students to identify the characteristics of a constant increase or decrease situation. Here are some other situations for class discussion.
(a) A salesperson gets a base salary of $2000 per month plus 3% of the sales.
(b) A student buys a used car for $900. Each year the student spends $250 on repair bills.
(c) The rental fee on an intermediate-size car is $39 per day and $.25 per mile.
(d) Myron has $2,500,000 under his mattress. He spends it at the rate of $35,000 per year.
    Note that virtually all models are accurate only over a limited domain. Ask students to explain why substitutions for *x* greater than 75 in **Example 2** are not reasonable. (The birdseed supply lasts only 75 days.) Ask students why the initial value of the constant increase or constant decrease is important. (It is the point from which the particular increase or decrease is computed.) Explain that this value is the *y*-intercept when the equation

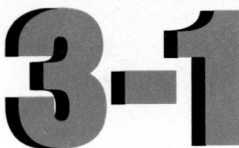

LESSON

3-1

Constant Increase or Decrease

Consider these situations:

    A. The temperature at 8:00 A.M. is 5° Celsius and increases 2° per hour over a five-hour period;
    B. A medical laboratory charges each patient an initial fee of $30 for consultation and an additional $10 per test;
    C. A 150-kg man goes on a diet and loses 1 kg per week;
    D. At the beginning of the month, Katie buys a 50-pound sack of wild-bird feed. She puts $\frac{2}{3}$ of a pound in the bird feeder each morning.

In each of the above situations there is a constant change applied to an initial condition. In A and B that change is a **constant increase**. In C and D the change is a **constant decrease.** These situations can all be modeled by linear equations. The following examples show how.

Example 1   The temperature is 5° Celsius and is increasing 2° an hour. What is the temperature after *h* hours?

    Solution   Write the temperature for several hours to find a general pattern.

Hours	Temperature (°C)
0	$5 + 0 \cdot 2 = 5$
1	$5 + 1 \cdot 2 = 7$
2	$5 + 2 \cdot 2 = 9$
3	$5 + 3 \cdot 2 = 11$
4	$5 + 4 \cdot 2 = 13$
5	$5 + 5 \cdot 2 = 15$

If *T* is temperature and *h* is the number of hours, then the equation relating *T* and *h* is

$$5 + h \cdot 2 = T$$
    or $$T = 2h + 5.$$

126

Because T is expressed in terms of h, T is the dependent variable and h is the independent variable. Recall that the independent variable is plotted along the horizontal axis and the dependent variable is plotted along the vertical axis. Thus solutions to the equation $T = 2h + 5$ are all the ordered pairs (h, T) whose values satisfy the equation. These pairs are shown on the graph below.

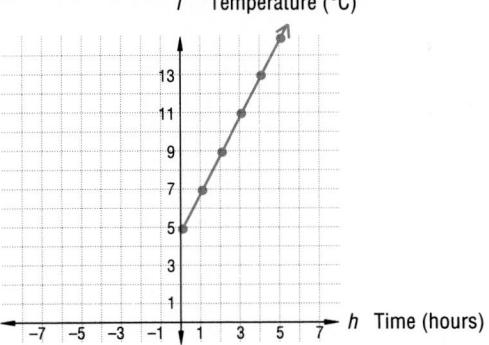

For hours starting with the initial reading, the graph is a ray. Points farther along the ray represent times and temperatures farther in the future. If you think of negative values of h as "hours ago," then the graph of $T = 2h + 5$ is a line including points to the left of the vertical axis and below the horizontal axis.

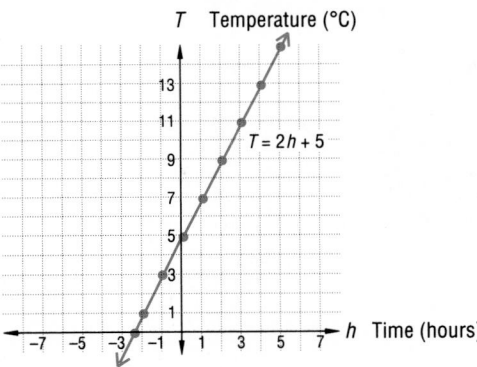

Recall that an intercept of a graph is the coordinate of a point where the graph intersects an axis. Here the graph crosses the T-axis at $(0, 5)$, so the T-intercept is 5. The graph contains $(-2.5, 0)$, so its h-intercept is -2.5.

The slope of the line is the rate of change, 2° per hour. To test this, find the slope between two points on the line. Trying $(0, 5)$ and $(3, 11)$ with the slope formula gives

$$\frac{11 - 5}{3 - 0} = \frac{6}{3} = 2.$$

Notice that in $T = 2h + 5$, the slope is 2 and 5 is the y-intercept.

LESSON 3-1 Constant Increase or Decrease 127

of the linear increase or decrease is graphed. Likewise, the constant rate of change is the slope of the linear graph.

Alternate Approach
One way to illustrate the ideas of constant increase and decrease is to use physical objects, such as paper clips or chalk. Place a few objects on a desk top to illustrate an initial condition. Then, have every student add two more objects to the initial group. Draw a graph on the chalkboard to show how the number of objects on the desk increases with the number of students. A constant decrease can be illustrated by reversing the process described above.

Making Connections
Point out to students that the graph of $y = mx + b$ is the image of the direct variation $y = mx$ under the translation b units up or down. This idea will be applied in later chapters to raise or lower any graph.

In general, any constant increase or constant decrease situation can be modeled by an equation of the form $y = mx + b$. The graph of $y = mx + b$ is a line with slope m and y-intercept b. The slope m corresponds to the rate of change in the situation. The **y-intercept b**, which is the value of y when x is 0, corresponds to the initial value of the dependent variable. The form $y = mx + b$ is called the **slope-intercept form** of an equation for a line.

Example 2 describes a situation of constant decrease.

Example 2

At the beginning of the month, Katie buys a 50-pound sack of wild-bird feed. She puts $\frac{2}{3}$ pound in the bird feeder each morning.
a. Let y (the dependent variable) be the number of pounds left in the sack after x days. Write an equation relating y to x in slope-intercept form.
b. Graph the equation from part a.
c. How long will it be until the supply runs out?

Solution
a. This is an instance of constant decrease. So the equation is

$$y = mx + b,$$

and m and b need to be found. The rate of change m is $\frac{2}{3}$ pound per day. Because the amount of feed in the sack is decreasing, $m = -\frac{2}{3}$. The initial amount of food is 50 pounds. Because 50 is the value of y when $x = 0$, the y-intercept is 50, and the equation is

$$y = -\frac{2}{3}x + 50.$$

b. Make a table with some of the solutions.

x	0	3	6	9	12
y	50	48	46	44	42

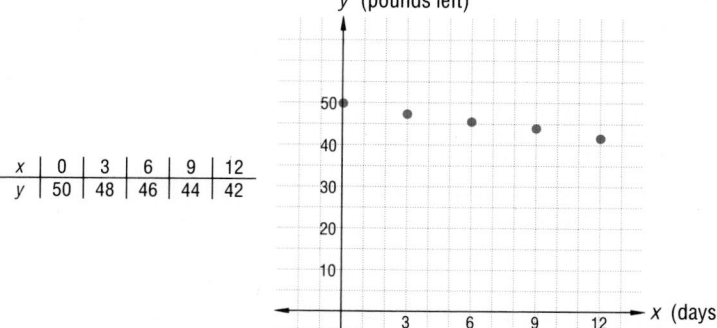

128

c. The supply runs out when $y = 0$. Substitute this into the equation and solve for x.

Substitute	$0 = -\frac{2}{3}x + 50$
Multiply by 3 to clear fractions	$0 = -2x + 150$
Add $2x$ to both sides.	$2x = 150$
Multiply both sides by $\frac{1}{2}$.	$x = 75$

The supply will last 75 days.

Check Although our graph does not extend far enough to show it, the point (75, 0) is on the graph of this equation.
The rate of change between any two points should be the slope, $-\frac{2}{3}$.
Using (0, 50) and (6, 46) gives a slope of

$$\frac{50 - 46}{0 - 6} = \frac{4}{-6} = -\frac{2}{3}.$$

In cases of constant increase, as in Example 1, the graph of the line slants up from left to right, indicating a positive slope. In cases of constant decrease, as in Example 2, the graph slants down from left to right, indicating a negative rate of change. This makes it easy to tell at a glance whether a graph represents a linear increase or decrease.

Questions

Covering the Reading

In 1–4, refer to Example 1.
1. In $T = 2h + 5$, name:
   a. the independent variable   *h*
   b. the dependent variable   *T*

2. What is the temperature after $3\frac{1}{2}$ hours?   **12°C**

3. In the equation $T = 2h + 5$, 5 represents the __?__ on the graph and the __?__ in the problem.   **T-intercept; initial temperature**

4. *True or false* The 2° increase per hour is the slope of the line.   **True**

5. *True or false* All instances of constant increase can be modeled by the equation $y = mx + b$.   **True**

In 6 and 7, refer to the equation $y = mx + b$.
6. The coefficient of x tells you the __?__ of the line.   **slope**

7. In cases of constant increase or constant decrease, the y-intercept b corresponds to __?__.   **the initial condition**

NOTES ON QUESTIONS

Question 17: This question illustrates the idea that direct linear variations are also constant increase or decrease situations whose initial value is zero. Students reviewed slope in Chapter 2 when graphing $y = kx$, so that they may want to extend this concept to graphs of constant increase or decrease situations. If so, have them explain their methods in class before beginning Lesson 3-2.

ADDITIONAL ANSWERS

11.a. 6   b. -5

12.a. $-\frac{3}{4}$ b. $\frac{2}{5}$

13.a. 1   b. 3

14.a. k b. 0

15.a. (4, 10) is on the graph if it satisfies $y = \frac{3}{4}x + 7$.
Does $10 = \frac{3}{4} \cdot 4 + 7$? Yes.

b. $\frac{3}{4}$

c. $m = \frac{y_2 - y_1}{x_2 - x_1} = \frac{10 - 7}{4 - 0} = \frac{3}{4}$

d. 7

16.b.

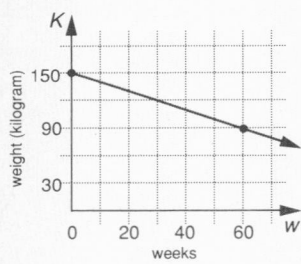

17.b.

x	-2	-1	0	1	2
y	-7	$-\frac{7}{2}$	0	$\frac{7}{2}$	7

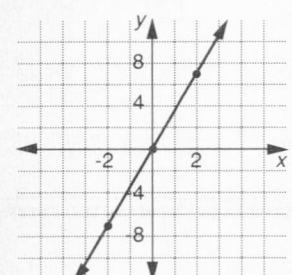

In 8 and 9, refer to Example 2.

8. How many pounds of bird feed are left after 10 days? $43\frac{1}{3}$ lb

9. How long will it take for the supply of bird feed to get below 15 pounds?   **53 days**

10. The graph below represents an example of constant __?__.
increase

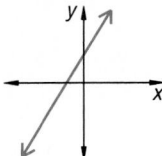

M3-1,10

In 11–14, identify: (a) the slope; (b) the y-intercept.   **See margin.**

11. $y = 6x - 5$

12. $y = \frac{2}{5} - \frac{3}{4}x$

13. $y = x + 3$

14. $y = kx$

Applying the Mathematics

15. The equation $y = \frac{3}{4}x + 7$ is graphed below.   **See margin.**
   a. Verify that (4, 10) is on the graph.
   b. From the equation, what should the slope be?
   c. Use the points (0, 7) and (4, 10) to verify your answer to part b.
   d. What is the y-intercept?

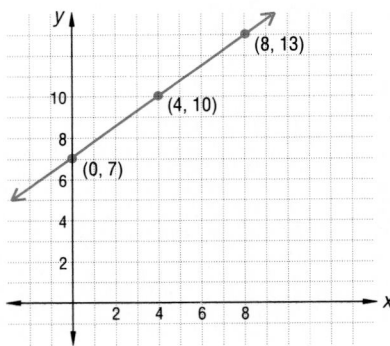

16. Refer to situation C, about the man on a diet, on page 126. $K =$
   a. Find an equation relating weight K and number of weeks w.   **150 -w**
   b. Graph your equation from part a.   **See margin.**

17. Suppose y varies directly as x, and that y is 7 when x is 2.
   a. Find the constant of variation and write an equation describing the variation. $y = \frac{7}{2}x$
   b. Make a table of values and graph the equation.   **See margin.**
   c. Verify that this direct variation equation fits the $y = mx + b$ model by identifying the slope and y-intercept. $m = \frac{7}{2}, b = 0$
   d. Does this variation represent constant increase or constant decrease?   **constant increase**

130

18. *Skill sequence* Solve for x. *(Lessons 1-7, 1-9)*
a. $-3x = 1.8$ -.6
b. $9 - 3x = 1.8$ 2.4
c. $2 - (9 - 3x) \le 1.8$ $x \le 2.9\overline{3}$
d. $2 - (9 - 3x) \le 1.8 - x$ $x \le 2.2$

19. Solve for y: $x + 2y = 5$. *(Lesson 1-7)* $y = -\frac{1}{2}x + \frac{5}{2}$

20. Suppose B ounces of blended fruit juice is 10% apple juice. How many ounces of juices other than apple juice are in the blend? *(Lesson 1-5)*   0.9B

21. a. Find the area of a circle inscribed in a square with side 6 cm long. 9π cm²
b. Find the area of a circle inscribed in a square with side x cm long. *(Previous course)* $\frac{1}{4}\pi x^2$ cm²

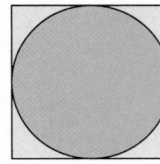

22. Given $a_n = 2 + 5(n - 1)$. What is the first value of n which makes $a_n \ge 51$? *(Lessons 1-3, 1-9)*   11

23. Simplify $\dfrac{1}{\frac{1}{a}}$. *(Lesson 1-5)*   a

24. Simplify $\dfrac{\frac{x}{y}}{\frac{x}{y}}$. *(Lesson 1-5)*   1

25. What place in the world would you most like to visit? Find out how much it would cost to go there by air, and estimate how much your average daily expenses would be. Write an equation that can be used to calculate the total cost T of your visit if you stayed for n days.
Many answers are possible.

FOLLOW-UP

MORE PRACTICE
For more questions on SPUR Objectives, use *Lesson Master 3-1*, shown below.

EXTENSION
An interesting situation to discuss is that of the pressure in a tire with a slow leak. Ask students if this is a true constant decrease situation. (No, because the rate of loss in pressure is related to the amount of pressure.) Later in this course, students will study situations in which the rate is not constant. In this lesson, it should be stressed that the rate is always constant in a linear situation. One point that can be brought out in this discussion is that one needs to choose mathematical models carefully, and that a model may be a good predictor only over a limited domain.

NAME _____

LESSON **MASTER   3-1**
QUESTIONS ON **SPUR** OBJECTIVES

■**SKILLS**   *Objective A (See pages 176-179 for objectives.)*
In 1–5, complete the chart below.

	Equation	Slope	y-intercept
1.	$y = -2x + 5$	-2	5
2.	$y = \frac{1}{2}x - 7$	$\frac{1}{2}$	-7
3.	$y = -4x$	-4	0
4.	$y = \frac{1}{2} - \frac{5}{2}x$	$-\frac{5}{2}$	$\frac{1}{2}$
5.	$y = -\frac{3}{8}x$	$-\frac{3}{8}$	0

■**USES**   *Objective H*
In 6–8, a box weighs 0.5 lb when empty and is filled with apples weighing 0.3 lb each.

6. Write an equation relating the weight w and the number n of apples. $w = (0.5 + 0.3n)$ lb

7. Find the weight when there are 37 apples in the crate   11.6 lb

8. If the weight capacity of the box is 15 lb, what is the maximum number of apples it can hold?   50

In 9 and 10, a trucker drives a 900-mile run, averaging 50 mph.

9. After h hours, how much farther must the trucker drive to finish the run? $(900 - 50n)$ miles

10. How many hours must the trucker drive to be 200 miles from the end of the run?   14

26   *Advanced Algebra © Scott, Foresman and Company*

RESOURCES
- Lesson Master 3-2
- Visual for Teaching Aid 10 provides the graph that is used to prove the theorem that two lines with the same slope are parallel.
- Computer Master 3

OBJECTIVES

C Convert linear equations to slope-intercept form.

E Recognize that two lines are parallel if and only if they have the same slope.

F Identify the properties of the slope-intercept form of a linear relation.

L Graph linear equations using slope and y-intercept.

TEACHING NOTES

Reading Proofs for the two theorems concerning parallel lines may be difficult for some students. Encourage them to read this material slowly, locating in the diagram each line, angle, and triangle as it is referenced.

Making Connections
You may wish to go through the proof that equal slopes imply parallel lines as it uses SAS Congruence. Students appreciate seeing that an idea they learned in one mathematics course is useful in another course. The proof of the converse of the statement that equal slopes imply parallel lines, namely that parallel lines imply equal slopes, uses ASA Congruence.

LESSON

3-2

The Graph of $y = mx + b$

The mathematical terms slope *and* intercept *invoke design considerations.*

As you saw in the last section, the solutions to an equation of the form $y = mx + b$ lie on a line with slope m and y-intercept b. The slope and y-intercept give you a powerful and efficient way to graph any equation in this form.

Example 1 Graph the line $y = 4x + 7$ using its slope and y-intercept.

Solution The y-intercept is 7, so the line contains $(0, 7)$. Use the slope to locate another point. The slope 4 means that every horizontal change of one unit to the right corresponds to a vertical change of four units up. Starting at $(0, 7)$, count 1 unit right and 4 up. This gives the new point $(0 + 1, 7 + 4) = (1, 11)$. Plot $(1, 11)$ and draw the line.

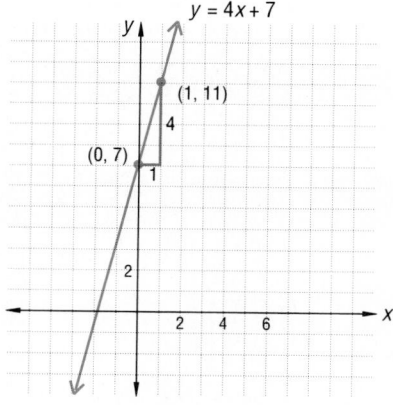

Check 1 The point $(1, 11)$ satisfies the equation $y = 4x + 7$, since $11 = 4 \cdot 1 + 7$. Since the two points $(0, 7)$ and $(1, 11)$ determine a line, the graph must be correct.

Check 2 The point $(-1, 3)$ satisfies the equation. This point also lies on the line determined by $(0, 7)$ and $(1, 11)$.

132

The line $y = 4x - 2$ is graphed below, along with $y = 4x + 7$. Both lines have slope 4. On each line, as you move 1 unit to the right, the line moves up 4 units. Right triangles ABC and DEF are congruent by SAS Congruence, so these lines form congruent angles at A and D with the y-axis. Consequently, $\overleftrightarrow{AB}$ and $\overleftrightarrow{DE}$ are parallel. This argument can be repeated with any two lines that have the same slope. Thus, the following theorem can be proved.

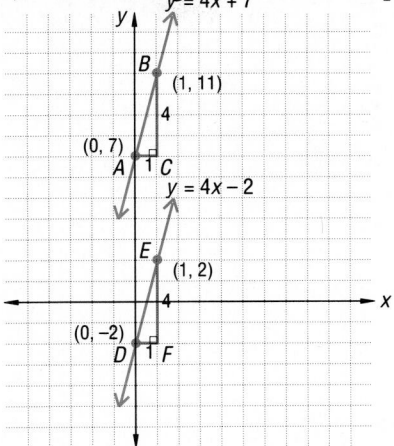

Theorem:

If two lines have the same slope, then they are parallel.

You can also prove the converse of this theorem. Parallel lines are drawn below, with slopes m_1 and m_2, and transversal l is parallel to the y-axis. Recall that corresponding angles formed by parallel lines and a transversal are congruent. So the corresponding angles, $\angle 1$ and $\angle 2$, are congruent. Also, line l forms right angles with $\overleftrightarrow{GH}$ and $\overleftrightarrow{JK}$. So the triangles are congruent by the ASA Congruence. Consequently, $m_1 = m_2$ and the slopes are equal. Since this proof used lines that intersect the y-axis, we have proved the converse, which is stated at the top of page 134.

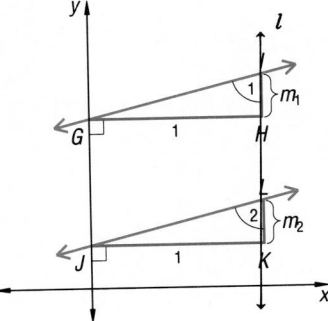

LESSON 3-2   The Graph of $y = mx + b$ **133**

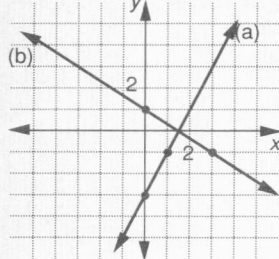
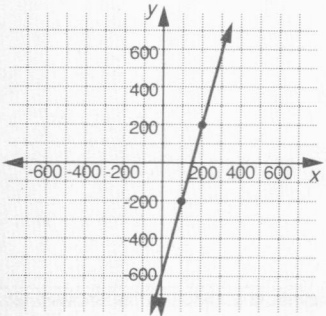
Theorem:

> If two nonvertical lines are parallel, then they have the same slope.

Graphing a line by using its slope and y-intercept can be much faster than first constructing a table of solutions. However, at times an equation for a line may need to be rewritten before it is in slope-intercept form. Example 2 illustrates this.

Example 2   Graph the line $2y = -3x + 10$ using its slope and y-intercept.

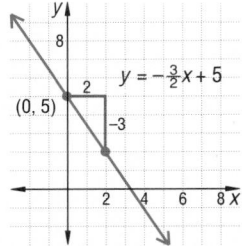

Solution   The equation is solved for $2y$, thus it is not in slope-intercept form. To solve for y, divide both sides by 2.

$$y = -\frac{3}{2}x + 5$$

From this form you can see that the slope is $-\frac{3}{2}$ and the y-intercept is 5. Again, first plot the y-intercept. A slope of $-\frac{3}{2}$ means a vertical change of $-\frac{3}{2}$ unit for every horizontal change of 1 unit, which is the same as 3 units down for every 2 units to the right.
Start at (0, 5) to get the new point $(0 + 2, 5 - 3) = (2, 2)$.

Check   Substitute (2, 2) into the equation.
Does $2 = -\frac{3}{2}(2) + 5$? Yes.

Lines with negative slope go down to the right. Lines with positive slope go up to the right. Lines with slope 0 are horizontal. Vertical lines are a different matter; they are discussed in Lesson 3-4.

134

Example 3 Graph the line $y = -2$.

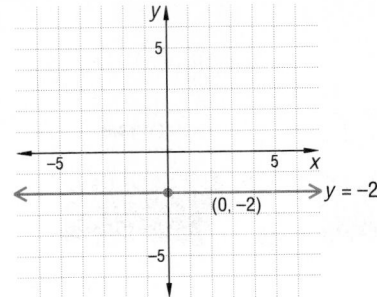

Solution The equation $y = -2$ is the same as $y = 0x - 2$. This shows that the y-intercept is -2. So the line contains $(0, -2)$ and the slope is 0. A slope of 0 means that for a horizontal change of 1 unit there is a vertical change of 0 units. In other words, there is no vertical change, and the graph is a horizontal line.

Check Any value of x in $y = 0x - 2$ yields a y-value of -2. In other words, all points on the line have -2 as their second coordinate.

In general, a line is horizontal if and only if it has an equation of the form $y = b$. Its slope is 0 and its y-intercept is b.

Questions

Covering the Reading

1. The equation $y = mx + b$ is called the __?__ form of an equation for a line.   **slope-intercept**

2. A slope of 7 means a __?__ change of __?__ units for every horizontal change of one unit.   **vertical; 7**

3. *Multiple choice* A slope of $-\frac{5}{6}$ means   **b**
   (a) a vertical change of -6 units for a horizontal change of 5 units.
   (b) a vertical change of $-\frac{5}{6}$ unit for every horizontal change of 1 unit.
   (c) a vertical change of 6 units for a horizontal change of -5 units.
   (d) a vertical change of 1 unit for a horizontal change of $-\frac{5}{6}$ units.

4. Refer to the line of Example 1. Start at the point $(1, 11)$.   **(2, 15)**
   a. Going 1 unit to the right and 4 units up puts you at what point?
   b. Verify that your answer to part a lies on the line.   **See margin.**

5. Refer to the line of Example 2. It appears that $(4, -1)$ lies on the line. Verify that this is true using the given equation for the line.
   See margin.

NOTES ON QUESTIONS
Question 14: The two equations are confused by some students. Point out that in the equation $y = 2x$, one can see that as the value of x changes, so does the value of y. The y-value can not be determined until the x-value is known. In the equation $y = 2$, however, the y-value is always 2, regardless of the value of x. It is helpful to write the equation $y = 2$ as $y = 0 \cdot x + 2$ to illustrate the independence of the value of y as the value of x changes.

Question 16: Some students may avoid this question because of the magnitude of the coordinates. These students think the problem is more difficult than it is. Point out that the properties of lines hold regardless of the values of the numbers and, with calculators, working with large or small numbers is not difficult.

Question 22: At first, it may seem that the question does not exemplify a constant decrease situation for the same reason as the tire-leak example used in the Extension for Lesson 3-1. However, water tanks are usually constructed to keep pressure constant at any water level.

Question 26: This question anticipates **Example 2** of the next lesson and should be discussed.

ADDITIONAL ANSWERS
4.b. Does $15 = 4 \cdot 2 + 7$? Yes.

5. Does $2(-1) = -3(4) + 10$? Yes, $-2 = -12 + 10$.

MORE PRACTICE
For more questions on SPUR Objectives, use *Lesson Master 3-2*, shown on page 137.

EXTENSION
Ask students if they think the slope can help determine the scales on the axes when graphing by hand. (yes) Use an example to illustrate this idea. The slope of the equation $25x + y = 75$ is -25. Numbering the *y*-axis by tens, twenties, or twenty-fives would be appropriate. The *y*-intercept is 75 and would be located easily on any one of these scales. Ask students if numbering by fives or fifties would be appropriate. (No; numbering by fives would make the graph too large and numbering by fifties, too small.)

EVALUATION
Alternative Assessment
In order to evaluate students' understanding of the relationship between the orientation of a line in a plane and its slope, use the following activity. Identify a horizontal and vertical edge of the chalkboard as the *x*- and *y*-axis of a coordinate plane. Then draw a line on the chalkboard and have students state whether the slope is positive, negative, or zero. After repeating this activity for five or six lines, call upon students to explain how to find the slope of any line.

ADDITIONAL ANSWERS
10.c.

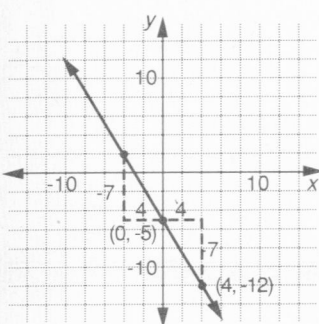

6. If two lines are parallel, what can be said about their slopes?
They are equal.

7. A line is parallel to $y = \frac{1}{3}x - 2$ and contains $(1, 5)$. What is the slope of this line? $\frac{1}{3}$

In 8 and 9, refer to triangles in this lesson.

8. Name the corresponding sides and angles that show $\triangle ABC$ to be congruent to $\triangle DEF$. $\overline{AC} \cong \overline{DF}$; $\angle C \cong \angle F$; $\overline{CB} \cong \overline{FE}$

9. Name the corresponding sides and angles that show $\triangle GHI \cong \triangle JKL$. $\angle HGI \cong \angle KJL$; $\angle GHI \cong \angle JKL$; $\overline{GH} \cong \overline{JK}$

10. Given the equation $4y = -7x - 20$.
a. Rewrite the equation in slope-intercept form. $y = \frac{-7}{4}x - 5$
b. Identify the slope and the *y*-intercept. **slope:** $\frac{-7}{4}$; *y*-intercept: -5
c. Graph the equation. **See margin.**

11. Graph the line whose equation is $y = 1$. **See margin.**

12. The equation $y = b$ represents a __?__ line with slope __?__.
horizontal; 0

13. **a.** Draw the line with *y*-intercept -6 and slope $\frac{2}{5}$. **See margin.**
b. Write the equation of this line in slope-intercept form. $y = \frac{2}{5}x - 6$
c. Use the equation to predict *x* when *y* is 3. Check to see if the point is on the line. $x = 22\frac{1}{2}$; yes

14. Graph the lines $y = 2$ and $y = 2x$ on the same set of axes.
See margin.

15. Consider the equation $5x + 2y = 24$.
a. Put the equation in slope-intercept form. $y = -\frac{5}{2}x + 12$
b. Identify the slope and the *y*-intercept. **slope:** $-\frac{5}{2}$; *y*-intercept: 12
c. Graph the line using the slope and intercept. **See margin.**

16. A line has no *x*-intercept and goes through the point $(17, -68)$. Give an equation for the line. $y = -68$

17. **a.** Graph the line $y = -3x + 1$. **See margin.**
b. Plot the point $(3,2)$, and draw a line through it parallel to the line $y = -3x + 1$. **See margin.**

18. Write an equation for the line with *y*-intercept 11 that is parallel to $y = \frac{4}{5}x + 7$. $y = \frac{4}{5}x + 11$

In 19–21, tell whether the line has a positive or negative slope. *(Lesson 3-1)*

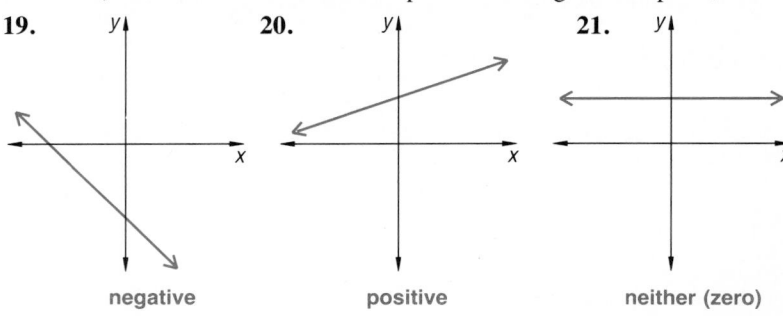

19. negative   **20.** positive   **21.** neither (zero)

136

22. A tank has a slow leak. The water level starts at 100 inches and falls $\frac{1}{2}$ inch per day.   **constant decrease**
  a. What kind of situation is this: constant increase or decrease?
  b. Write an equation relating day d and the water level L. $L = 100 - \frac{1}{2}d$
  c. After how many days will the tank be empty? *(Lesson 3-1)*
  200 days

23. Find Q_6 if $Q_n = 4000(1.05)^n$. *(Lesson 1-3)*   **5360.3825**

24. Find S_4 if $S_1 = 2$ and $S_n = 3 \cdot S_{n-1}$. *(Lesson 1-4)*   **54**

25. Solve: $-3x - 5(x - 9) > -6x$. *(Lesson 1-9)*   **x < 22.5**

11., 13.a., 14., 15.c., 17.a. and b., and 27.a.–f. See Additional Answers in the back of this book.

26. a. How much alcohol is in a 9-oz solution of water and alcohol that is 20% alcohol?   **1.8 oz**
  b. How much alcohol is in an x-oz solution of water and alcohol that is 20% alcohol?   **0.2x oz**
  c. How much water is in an x-oz solution of water and alcohol that is 20% alcohol? *(Previous course)*   **0.8x oz**

Exploration

27. A function grapher can save time on this question. Consider the lines with equations $y = \frac{1}{4}x$ and $y = 4x$.   **See margin.**
  a. Graph both lines on the same pair of coordinate axes.
  b. Find the slope of each line.
  c. Determine an equation for the bisector of the acute angles formed by these lines.
  d. Repeat parts a–c, using lines with equations $y = \frac{1}{3}x$ and $y = 3x$.
  e. Make a conjecture generalizing this problem and its results.
  f. Make and test a conjecture with an example where the lines have negative slopes.

RESOURCES
■ Lesson Master 3-3
■ Quiz for Lessons 3-1
  Through 3-3

OBJECTIVE

J Model situations leading to
linear combinations.

TEACHING NOTES

Remind students to consider
sensible substitutions for the
variables when graphing a
linear combination. They
should determine in which
quadrant a graph lies before
starting to draw the graph. At
this time, they should also
determine whether the graph
is discrete or continuous.

Error Analysis Students
often decide too quickly that
a situation can be modeled by
a linear combination. Encourage them to keep track of
units. For example, consider
the following situation: A car
gets 25 miles to a gallon of
gas while driving in the city
and 32 miles to a gallon on a
highway. The gas tank holds
14 gallons. If the car is driven
x miles in the city and y miles
on the highway and runs out
of gas, write an equation relating x and y and the size of
the tank.
  Explain that in this situation, the equation $25x +
32y = 14$ does not work.
Have students check this
using units: (25 miles per gallon) (x miles). The reciprocal
rates must be used to get an
answer in gallons. In the city,
the car uses 1/25 of a gallon
for each mile driven, and 1/32
of a gallon for each mile in
the country. Therefore, the
the equation is $\frac{x}{25} + \frac{y}{32} = 14$.

**LESSON
3-3**

Linear Combinations

Consider the following problem.

> Milton has C 20¢ stamps and E 25¢ stamps.
> Find the total value of his stamps.

The rate-factor model of multiplication gives C stamps at 20¢ per
stamp, for a total cost of $20C$ cents. Likewise, E stamps at 25¢ per
stamp cost $25E$ cents. Then the total value of the stamps is

$$20C + 25E.$$

This expression is called a **linear combination** of C and E. In a
linear combination, all variables are to the first power and are not
multiplied or divided by each other.

Linear combinations occur in a wide variety of real situations.

■ ■ ■ ■ ■ ■ ■ ■

Example 1 In professional hockey a win is worth 2 points, a tie is worth 1 point,
and a loss is worth 0 points. The Eagle hockey team has earned a
total of 35 points.
  a. Write an equation to express the relationship between the number
  of wins W, ties T, losses L, and the total points of the Eagle team.
  b. If the team had 12 wins, how many ties did it have?

Solution

a. Each win is worth 2 points, so W wins are worth $2W$ points. A tie is worth 1 point, so T ties are worth $1T$ points. Because losses are worth 0 points, L losses add $0L$ to the total. This total is 35, so

$$2W + 1T + 0L = 35.$$

Simplify. $\quad\quad\quad\quad\quad 2W + T = 35$

b. Substituting 12 for W into the equation found in part a gives

$$2 \cdot 12 + T = 35.$$

Solve for T. $\quad\quad\quad\quad T = 11$

So when the team had 12 wins, it also had 11 tie games.

Check The 12 wins are worth 24 points, and 11 ties are worth 11 points. This is 35 points altogether.

■ ■ ■ ■ ■ ■ ■ ■ ■

Example 2 A chemist mixes x ounces of a 20% alcohol solution with y ounces of a 30% alcohol solution. The final mixture contains 9 ounces of alcohol.
a. Write an equation relating x, y, and the total number of ounces of alcohol.
b. How many ounces of the 30% alcohol solution must be added to 2.7 ounces of the 20% alcohol solution to get 9 ounces of alcohol in the final mixture?

Solution

a. A 20% alcohol solution means that 20% of the x ounces are alcohol and 20% of x is $0.2x$. Similarly, 30% of the y ounces are alcohol, which is $0.3y$. The linear combination $0.2x + 0.3y$ gives the total number of ounces of alcohol. There are 9 ounces of alcohol, so an equation is $0.2x + 0.3y = 9$.

b. Substitute 2.7 for x.

$$0.2(2.7) + 0.3y = 9$$
$$0.54 + 0.3y = 9$$
$$0.3y = 8.46$$
$$y = 28.2$$

So the mixture contains 28.2 ounces of the 30% alcohol solution.

The equation $0.2x + 0.3y = 9$ can be graphed. Solving for y shows that the graph is a line and puts the equation in slope-intercept form.

Multiply both sides by 10 to clear fractions. $\quad 2x + 3y = 90$
Subtract 2x from both sides. $\quad\quad\quad\quad\quad 3y = -2x + 90$

Divide both sides by 3. $\quad\quad\quad\quad\quad\quad\quad y = -\frac{2}{3}x + 30$

1. Many elevators have a capacity of one metric ton (1000 kg). If a child's weight averages 35 kg (77 lb) and an adult's weight averages 75 kg (165 lb), how many children C and adults A can the elevator hold?
Any C and A are correct as long as they satisfy $35C + 75A \leq 1000$. The answer is found by using an inequality because the elevator can hold less than its capacity. If the question had asked "How many children and adults can the elevator hold at most?," then the equation $35C + 75A = 1000$ would provide the answer.

2. A lawn maintenance worker combines two kinds of solutions, each a mixture of weed killer and water. Mixture A is 5% weed killer and mixture B is 15% weed killer.
a. Write an equation relating A, B, and the total amount T of weed killer.
$0.05A + 0.15B = T$
b. The lawn worker wants 12 ounces of weed killer in the final mixture. Draw a graph to illustrate the possible combinations.

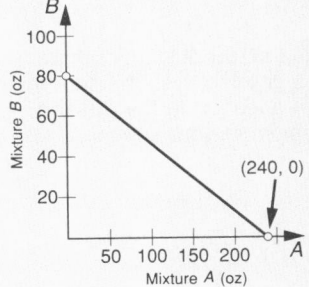

Thus, the slope of the line is $-\frac{2}{3}$ and the y-intercept is 30. The graph is shown below.

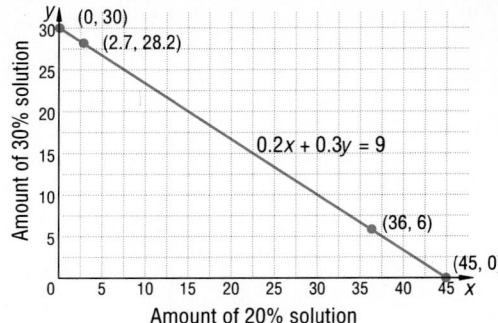

The graph is continuous because the number of ounces of either solution may be any nonnegative real number. It is a segment because the amount of each solution cannot be negative.

Each point on the segment refers to a different mixture of the alcohol solutions. The point (2.7, 28.2) stands for 2.7 oz of 20% solution and 28.2 oz of 30% solution. The point (36, 6) means that 36 oz of the 20% solution could be mixed with 6 oz of the 30% solution to yield 9 oz of alcohol.

Any linear-combination situation in two variables is modeled by an equation whose graph is a line or a part of a line. This fact is the origin of the phrase "linear combination."

Questions

Covering the Reading

1. The expression $20C + 25E$ is called a __?__ of C and E.
   linear combination
2. At a sale Greta Diehl bought B blouses at $7 each, S skirts at $14 each, and H pairs of shoes at $19 each. Write a linear combination to find the amount spent at the sale. $7B + 14S + 19H$

In 3 and 4, refer to Example 1.

3. The team has W wins, T ties and L losses. How many points were earned by the team? $2W + T$

4. With T as the dependent variable, (4, 27) is a solution to $2W + T = 35$. This solution means the team won __?__ games, tied __?__ games, and earned a total of __?__ points.   4; 27; 35

5. $40x + 8y$ is a __?__ of x and y.   linear combination

6. The graph of $Ax + By = C$ is a __?__.   line

140

140

7. Suppose that S ounces of a solution that is 60% alcohol are combined with N ounces of a 90% alcohol solution. **7d) .6S + .9N = 18**
   a. How many ounces of alcohol are in the 60% solution? **.6S**
   b. How many ounces of alcohol are in the 90% solution? **.9N**
   c. How many total ounces of alcohol are in the combination? **.6S + .9N**
   d. If Alice Seawell wants 18 ounces of alcohol in the final mixture, what equation relates S, N, and the 18 total ounces of alcohol?
   e. Solve the equation of part a for N. Graph the solutions to the equation, plotting S on the horizontal axis. **See margin.**
   f. How many ounces of the 90% solution must be added to 9 ounces of the 60% solution to get 18 ounces of alcohol in the final mixture? **14 oz**

8. In a store, lettuce sells for 89¢ a head and tomatoes for 59¢ per pound.
   a. What will be the cost of 6 heads of lettuce and 8 pounds of tomatoes? **$10.06**
   b. What will be the cost of H heads of lettuce and P pounds of tomatoes? **.89H + .59P dollars**
   c. Write an equation indicating the amounts of lettuce H and tomatoes P you can buy for $5.00. **.89H + .59P = 5**

9. William Bates Green spent Saturday mowing lawns. He charged $5 for small lawns and $10 for large lawns and earned $70. Let S be the number of small lawns and L be the number of large lawns. **See margin.**
   a. What type of numbers make sense for S and L in this context?
   b. Write an equation relating S, L, and the amount of money earned.
   c. Graph the equation of part a.
   d. Give all possible pairs of numbers of large and small lawns Will could have mowed.

10. The Ironman triathlon is a sporting event made up of a 2.4-mile swim, a 112-mile bicycle race, and a marathon run of 26.2 miles. If a competitor takes S minutes per mile swimming, B minutes per mile biking, and R minutes per mile running, what will be the competitor's total time for the triathlon? **2.4S + 112B + 26.2R**

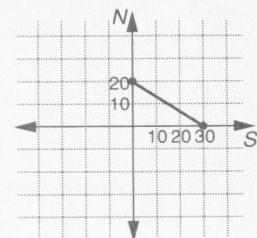

9.a. nonnegative numbers
b. $5S + 10L = 70$
c.

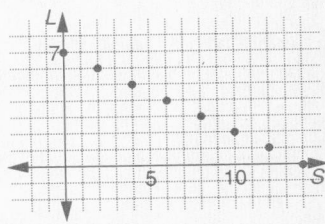

d. 7 and 0, 6 and 2, 5 and 4, 4 and 6, 3 and 8, 2 and 10, 1 and 12, 0 and 14

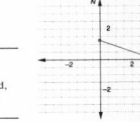

FOLLOW-UP

MORE PRACTICE
For more questions on SPUR Objectives, use *Lesson Master 3-3,* shown on page 141.

EVALUATION
A quiz covering Lessons 3-1 through 3-3 is provided in the Teacher's Resource File.

ADDITIONAL ANSWERS
19.

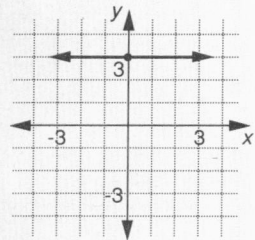

20.

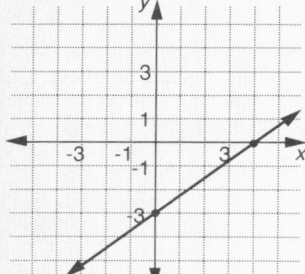

Review

11. For the line graphed below, determine: $y = \frac{2}{3}x - 4$
a. its slope $\frac{2}{3}$ **b.** its y-intercept 4 **c.** an equation *(Lessons 3-1, 3-2)*

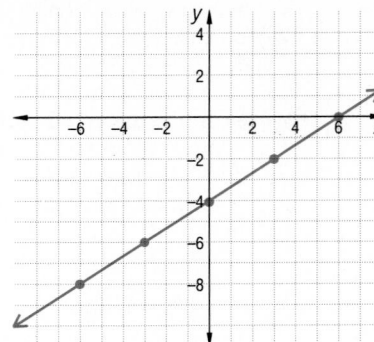

12. A line is parallel to $5y = 20 - 30x$. What is its slope? *(Lesson 3-2)* -6

In 13–18, find the distance between the given points. *(Previous course)*

13. (1, 3) and (6, 15) 13
14. (4, 5) and (-4, 5) 8
15. (2, 11) and (2, -7) 18
16. (-3, -2) and (6, 0) $\sqrt{85}$
17. (a, b) and (c, d) $\sqrt{(a-c)^2 + (b-d)^2}$
18. $(k, 0)$ and $(0, k)$ $\sqrt{2k^2}$

In 19 and 20, graph on a coordinate plane. *(Lesson 3-2)* **See margin.**

19. $y = 3$
20. $y = \frac{3}{4}x - 3$

21. The math department at a school has 100 reams of paper at the start of the school year (a ream of paper contains 500 sheets). Each school day the department uses about $\frac{2}{3}$ of a ream.
a. Let d be the number of school days from the start of the year and R be the number of reams remaining. Write a formula for R in terms of d. $R = 100 - \frac{2}{3}d$
b. When the supply gets down to 10 reams, a new supply of paper needs to be ordered. After how many school days will paper need to be ordered? *(Lesson 3-1)* **135 days**

22. 20% of 80 is what percent of 200? *(Previous course)* **8%**

Exploration

23. In many schools, a student's grade-point average is calculated using linear combinations. Some schools give 4 points for each A, 3 points for each B, 2 points for each C, and 1 point for each D. Suppose a student gets 7 As, 3 Bs, and 2 Cs.
a. Calculate this student's total number of points. **41 points**
b. Divide your answer in part a by the total number of classes (12) to get the grade point average. **approximately 3.42**
c. Calculate your own grade point average for last year using this scheme. **Many answers are possible.**

142

LESSON

3-4

The Graph of
$Ax + By = C$

OBJECTIVES

C Convert linear equations from standard form to slope-intercept form, and vice versa.
F Identify properties of the standard form of a linear relation.
L Graph a linear equation in standard form using its x- and y-intercepts.

The set of all points with x-coordinate equal to 2 is a vertical line, as the graph below shows. This line can be described by the equation $x = 2$. Sometimes it is useful to think of the equivalent form

$$x + 0 \cdot y = 2$$

to stress that y can take on any value.

TEACHING NOTES

Reading Students frequently confuse the graphs of $x = a$ and $y = b$. One way to eliminate this confusion is to have students read the equations as "x-value equals a" and "y-value equals b."

Students also confuse the slopes of $x = a$ and $y = b$. Have students think of an application, for instance, the steepness of a ski hill. A horizontal line corresponds to flat land, no tilt at all; slope 0. A vertical line could be thought of as an impossible slope to ski, the tilt is infinitely large; undefined slope.

Encourage students to determine x- and y-intercepts *mentally* when possible. Explain that when an equation is in standard form, $Ax + By = C$, and when either or both values A and B divide C, then intercepts can be found quickly. Since substituting 0 for x has the effect of eliminating the x-term, have students cover the x-term with a finger and mentally solve the resulting

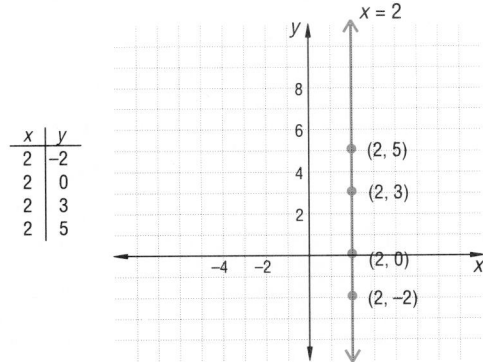

x	y
2	-2
2	0
2	3
2	5

What is the slope of the line $x = 2$? Calculating the slope by using the points $(2, 0)$ and $(2, 3)$ results in a denominator of 0.

$$m = \frac{3 - 0}{2 - 2} = \frac{3}{0}$$

You know that division by 0 is undefined, so the slope is said to be undefined. By the same argument, the slope of any vertical line $x = a$ is undefined.

LESSON 3-4 The Graph of $Ax + By = C$ 143

Here is a summary of some important properties of lines with which you are familiar.

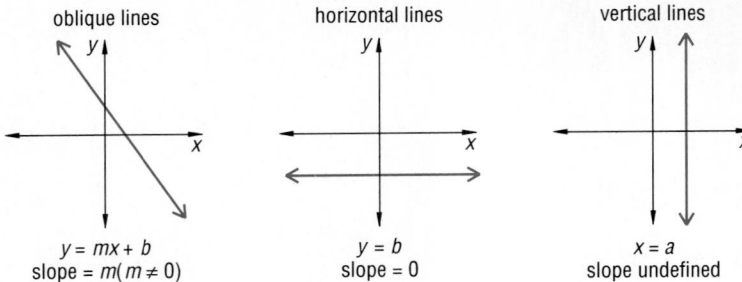

oblique lines	horizontal lines	vertical lines
$y = mx + b$	$y = b$	$x = a$
slope $= m(m \neq 0)$	slope $= 0$	slope undefined

Vertical lines cannot have equations of the form $y = mx + b$ because for a vertical line, the coefficient of y must be 0. But there is an equation form which includes all these instances. The form is $Ax + By = C$, where A and B are not both zero. This is called the **standard form of a linear equation.** The following argument shows why the standard form of a linear equation describes all possible lines.

When $B \neq 0$: The equation $Ax + By = C$ can be rewritten in slope-intercept form.

Add -Ax. $\qquad\qquad By = -Ax + C$

Multiply by $\frac{1}{B}$ ($B \neq 0$). $\quad y = -\frac{A}{B}x + \frac{C}{B}$

This is an equation of a line with slope $-\frac{A}{B}$ and y-intercept $\frac{C}{B}$.

1. If $A \neq 0$, then the slope is not 0 and the line is *oblique*.

2. If $A = 0$, then $y = \frac{C}{B}$.

This is an equation of a *horizontal* line with slope 0 and y-intercept $\frac{C}{B}$.

When $B = 0$: The equation $Ax + By = C$ can be written in the following form:

$$Ax = C$$
$$x = \frac{C}{A}$$

This is an equation of a *vertical* line. A vertical line has no slope and has x-intercept $\frac{C}{A}$.

144

The above argument proves that if an equation is of the form $Ax + By = C$ (A and B not both 0), then it represents a line. The converse of that statement is "If an equation represents a line, then it is of the form $Ax + By = C$ (A and B not both 0)." This converse can be proved by reversing the steps in the argument. Both statements together can be expressed as a theorem.

Theorem:

> The graph of the equation $Ax + By = C$ (A and B not both 0) is a line.

The standard form of a linear equation arises in linear-combination situations. There is a shortcut in graphing an equation in this form by using its intercepts. The next example shows how to use the shortcut.

Example   Graph the equation $6x - 3y = 12$ by using its intercepts.

> **Solution**   The **x-intercept** is the value of x at the point where the line crosses the x-axis. This point has second coordinate 0. So substitute 0 for y and solve for x.
>
> $$6x - 3(0) = 12$$
> $$x = 2$$
>
> Thus the x-intercept is 2.
> To find the y-intercept, substitute 0 for x and solve for y.
>
> $$6(0) - 3y = 12$$
> $$y = -4$$
>
> Thus the y-intercept is -4.
> Plot (2, 0) and (0, -4). Draw the line between them, as shown below.

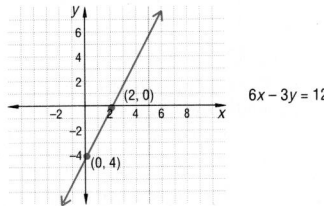

> **Check**   The point (1, -2) appears to be on the graph. Substitute to see if the coordinates satisfy the equation.
>
> Does $6(1) - 3(-2) = 12$?
> Does $6 + 6 = 12$? Yes

LESSON 3-4   The Graph of $Ax + By = C$ **145**

1. Graph the equation $5x + 3y = 15$ by using its intercepts.
Intercepts are (0, 5) and (3, 0).

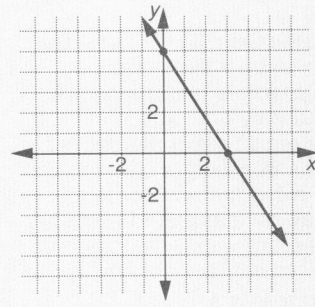

2. Give an equation in standard form for the line with y-intercept $\frac{2}{3}$ and slope -3.
$9x + 3y = 2$

3. A day-care center needs to build a fence around its playground. The operators of the center are not sure of the exact dimensions of the rectangular lot, but they have ordered 150 feet of fencing, posts, and gates. Since one side of the playground will be a wall of the day-care center, it needs no fencing.
a. Write a equation describing this situation.
$L + 2W = 150$
b. Graph the equation by using its intercepts.
Intercepts are (0, 75) and (150, 0).

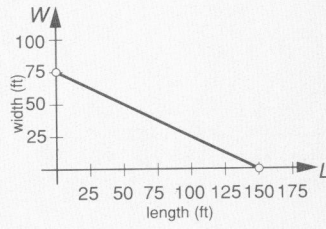

c. Give three possible dimensions for the rectangular lot.
(30, 60); (50, 50); (100, 25)

NOTES ON QUESTIONS
Question 17: Stress that when transforming an equation to standard form, it is a convention to write the leading coefficient as a positive number.

Question 21: Some students may think that the question is multiple choice and only one choice can be correct. That is not correct. This question is given to emphasize that the same slope may be interpreted in many different ways. Ask students to provide additional ways to express a slope of $-\frac{4}{3}$.

ADDITIONAL ANSWERS
7.a.

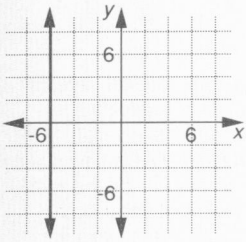

b. Slope is undefined.

12.c.

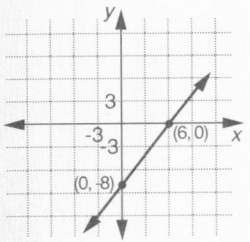

13.a.–c., 14.a.–c., 15.a.–c. See Additional Answers in the back of this book.

Covering the Reading

In 1–3, match the line with a description of its slope.
1. horizontal line   a   (a) 0 slope
2. vertical line   c   (b) non-zero slope
3. oblique line   b   (c) slope undefined

4. The line whose equation is of the form $y = mx + b$ is oblique when m __?__ 0. $\neq$

5. How many intercepts does an oblique line have?   2

6. The graph of $y = 7$ is a __?__ line with y-intercept __?__.
     horizontal; 7

7. **a.** Graph the line with equation $x = -6$.   See margin.
   b. What can be said about the slope of this line?   See margin.

In 8–10, refer to the general discussion of the graph of $Ax + By = C$.

8. **a.** If neither A nor B is 0, the equation can be written in slope-intercept form as __?__. $y = \frac{-A}{B}x + \frac{C}{B}$
   b. The slope of the line is __?__. $\frac{-A}{B}$
   c. The y-intercept of the line is __?__. $\frac{C}{B}$

9. If $A = 0$ and $B \neq 0$, then the line is __?__ and has __?__ slope.
   horizontal; 0

10. If $A \neq 0$ and $B = 0$, then the line is __?__ and has __?__ slope.
   vertical; undefined

11. To find the x-intercept of a line, for which variable should you substitute 0?   y

12. Consider the graph of the equation $4x - 3y = 24$.
   a. Find its x-intercept.   6
   b. Find its y-intercept.   -8
   c. Graph the line using the points from parts a and b.   See margin.

Applying the Mathematics

In 13–15, (a) tell whether each line is vertical, horizontal, or oblique; (b) give all intercepts for each line; (c) graph each equation.   See margin.

13. $y = 4$ 14. $2x - 3y = 18$ 15. $2x = 16$

16. Meg combines N oz of a solution that is 10% alcohol with Y oz of a solution that is 20% alcohol. She ends up with a mixture that contains 1.2 oz of alcohol.
   a. Write an equation relating N, Y, and the amount of alcohol in the mixture.   1.2 = .1N +.2Y
   b. Graph the equation you obtained in part (a) by finding the N- and Y- intercepts. Consider N the independent variable.   See margin.
   c. Use your graph to find out how many ounces of the 20% solution must be added to 8 oz of the 10% solution to get the final mixture.
   2 oz

17. Give an equation in standard form for the line with y-intercept $-\frac{1}{5}$ and slope 2.   10x − 5y = 1

146

18. A 3-line classified advertisement in a local paper costs $10.20 for five weekdays and $12.35 for a weekend edition. What is the cost of x ads during the week and y ads on the weekend? *(Lesson 3-3)*
10.20x + 12.35y

19. You have some money saved from your job. You invest S of it in a savings account that pays 8% interest and the rest R in a checking account that pays 6%. You earn $84 interest in one year. *(Lesson 3-3)*
    a. Write an equation relating S, R, and the total amount of interest.
    b. Give three possible pairs of values for R and S. **.08S + .06R = 84**
       samples: (1000, 300); (600, 600); (200, 900)

20. The city police department pays police officers $1500 per month and pays their supervisors $2400 per month. The total payroll for the month is $60,000. *(Lesson 3-3)*   **1500P + 2400S = 60,000**
    a. Write an equation relating the number of police officers P, the number of supervisors S, and the total monthly payroll.
    b. If there are 10 supervisors, how many police officers are there?
       24

21. A slope of $-\frac{4}{3}$ means which of the following? *(Lessons 2-4, 3-2)*   **b, c**
    (a) A vertical change of -3 units for a horizontal change of 4 units
    (b) A vertical change of -4 units for a horizontal change of 3 units
    (c) A vertical change of $-\frac{4}{3}$ units for a horizontal change of 1 unit
    (d) A vertical change of 1 unit for a horizontal change of $-\frac{4}{3}$ units

22. Solve for x. $x - 11 = \frac{7}{5}(x + 3)$ *(Lesson 1-7)*

23. Suppose you can get as many 22¢ stamps and 3¢ stamps as you want. You could make 24¢ using eight 3¢ stamps, but you cannot make 23¢ postage exactly. What is the largest value that *cannot* be made with these stamps?   **41¢**

24. **a.** Find the x- and y-intercepts of $\frac{x}{2} + \frac{y}{7} = 1$.   **2, 7**

    b. Find the x- and y-intercepts of $\frac{x}{-5} + \frac{y}{6} = 1$.   **-5, 6**

    c. Based on parts a and b above, make a conjecture about the x- and y-intercepts of $\frac{x}{a} + \frac{y}{b} = 1$. Either prove your conjecture or give a counterexample to it.   **a, b; when x = 0, y = b; when y = 0, x = a**

LESSON 3-4   The Graph of $Ax + By = C$ **147**

MORE PRACTICE
For more questions on SPUR Objectives, use *Lesson Master 3-4*, shown below.

EXTENSION
In the discussion of $Ax + By = C$, ask students to think about when $A = B = 0$. Discuss with students the two possibilities. When $C = 0$, the solution set is the entire coordinate plane. When $C \neq 0$, the solution set is null.

16.b.

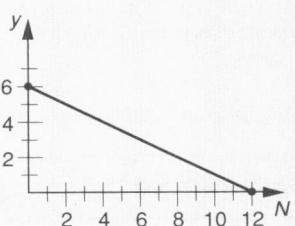

22. x = -38

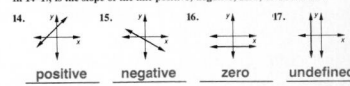

147

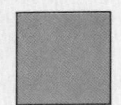

LESSON 3-5

OBJECTIVES

B Find an equation for a line given two points on it, or given a point on it and its slope.
F Identify properties of the point-slope form of a linear equation.
I In a real-world context, find an equation for a line containing two given points.

TEACHING NOTES

Go through **Example 3b** and the paragraph following it carefully. Students have difficulty with the idea that (x, y) is any point on the line, for they are so accustomed to finding particular values of x and y.

Many students have learned to use the slope-intercept form $y = mx + b$ to find the line through a given point with a given slope. They may want to use this form only. Stress the ease and quickness of using the point-slope equation. **Questions 7–9** are designed to help you make this point.

The notation (x_1, y_1) deserves a comment as the subscripts do not stand for terms in a sequence as in Chapter 1. Instead, the subscripts indicate a particular known point, as opposed to the general point (x, y).

LESSON

3-5

Finding an Equation of a Line

Two points determine a line. You use this idea every time you draw the line through two points with a ruler. It is a postulate from geometry. In algebra, this idea raises the question: What is an equation of the line through two given points? The next two examples show one way to get such an equation.

Example 1 Find an equation of the line L through (3, 5) and (6, -1).

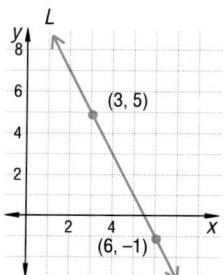

Solution Line L is oblique so it has an equation in slope-intercept form $y = mx + b$. First calculate the slope m.

$$m = \frac{-1 - 5}{6 - 3} = \frac{-6}{3} = -2$$

Substitute -2 for m:

$$y = -2x + b$$

Only the value of b is left to find. We can use either of the points to get b. Choose (3, 5) and substitute for x and y.

$$5 = -2 \cdot 3 + b$$

148

Solve for *b*: $\qquad\qquad$ *b* = 11

The work is done. Since *m* = -2 and *b* = 11, an equation for *L* is
y = -2*x* + 11.

Check From the graph above you can see that the *y*-intercept must
be greater than 8 and that the slope is indeed negative. This is a
quick check.
   For an exact check, substitute the other given point (6, -1) in the
equation to test if it works. Does -1 = -2 · 6 + 11? Yes, so the equation is correct.

If one of the given points is on the *y*-axis, then the *y*-intercept *b* is
already given, and all that is needed is *m*. This situation is illustrated
in Example 2.

Example 2 Suppose you remember that 0°C = 32°F and 100°C = 212°F, but you
have forgotten the conversion formula. You know that the formula is
linear. Reconstruct the formula with *C* as the first coordinate and *F* as
the second.

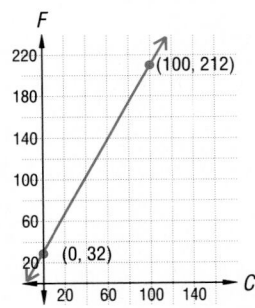

Solution With *C* as the independent variable, the formula will be of
the form *F* = *mC* + *b*. Values of *m* and *b* are needed. First find the
slope, using the given points (0, 32) and (100, 212).

$$m = \frac{212 - 32}{100 - 0} = \frac{180}{100} = 1.8$$

Because the line crosses the *F*-axis at (0, 32), *b* = 32. Substitute
these values into *F* = *mC* + *b*. The desired formula is *F* = 1.8*C* + 32.

Check Substitute (100, 212) in the equation. Does 212 = 1.8(100) +
32? Yes.

Recall Playfair's Parallel Postulate from geometry: *Through a point in a plane, there is exactly one line parallel to a given line.* This line can be found algebraically if you know the slope of the given line.

Example 3 A line l passes through the point (12, -5) and is parallel to the line $y = 4x$.
a. Graph l.
b. Find an equation for l in slope-intercept form.

Solution
a. Recall that parallel lines have the same slope. Because the line $y = 4x$ has slope 4, the line l through (12, -5) must also have slope 4. At the right, this slope is used to graph l. Notice that its intercepts are not easily read.

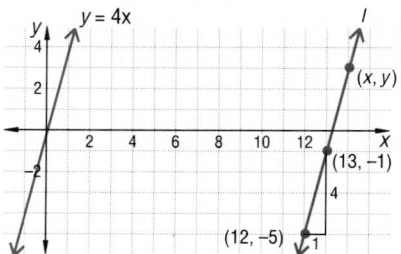

b. The line l contains (12, -5) and has slope 4. Let (x, y) be any other point on l. Substitute into the slope formula.

$$\frac{y - (-5)}{x - 12} = 4$$

To put the equation into slope-intercept form, multiply both sides by $(x - 12)$.

$$y - (-5) = 4(x - 12)$$
$$y + 5 = 4x - 48$$
$$y = 4x - 53$$

Check Is the point (13, -1) on the line? Does $-1 = 4(13) - 53$? Yes.

Each of the equations $y - (-5) = 4(x - 12)$ and $y = 4x - 53$ represents the line through (12, -5) with slope 4. The slope-intercept form is handy because it is a formula that you can use to calculate values of y quickly if you know x-values. However, the form $y - (-5) = 4(x - 12)$ is nice because the three constants in it are the given information: the coordinates of a point and the slope.

150

The method of Example 3 can be generalized.

Point-Slope Theorem:

If a line contains (x_1, y_1) and has slope m, then it has equation

$$y - y_1 = m(x - x_1).$$

Proof:

Let L be the line with slope m containing (x_1, y_1). If (x, y) is any other point on L, then by the definition of slope,

$$m = \frac{y - y_1}{x - x_1}.$$

Multiplying both sides by $x - x_1$ gives

$$m(x - x_1) = y - y_1.$$

This is the desired equation of the theorem.

The equation $y - y_1 = m(x - x_1)$ is called a **point-slope equation** for a line. The most convenient form to use for writing an equation depends on the information given. If you know the slope and y-intercept, use $y = mx + b$. If you know the slope and some other point, use $y - y_1 = m(x - x_1)$. If you know two points, find the slope and then use either the point-slope form or the slope-intercept form.

Questions

Covering the Reading

1. __?__ points determine a line.   2

2. A line contains $(6, 4)$ and $(2, 8)$.
   a. Find its slope.   -1
   b. Use the point $(6, 4)$ together with the slope to find the y-intercept.   10
   c. Write an equation for the line and check. $y = -x + 10$; $8 = -2 + 10$
   d. Does the point $(0.8, 9.8)$ satisfy the equation of part c?   no

3. Why is the slope-intercept form the most convenient one to use in Example 2?   The y-intercept is given.

4. State Playfair's Parallel Postulate.   Through a point in a plane, there is exactly one line parallel to a given line.

5. *True or false* A line is determined by its slope and any point on it.   True

6. The point-slope form of the equation for a line with slope m and passing through point (x_1, y_1) is __?__. $y - y_1 = m(x - x_1)$

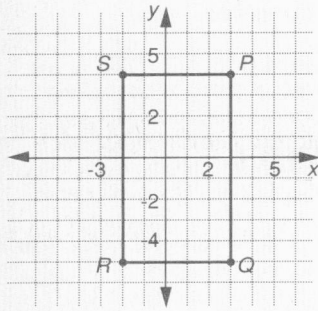
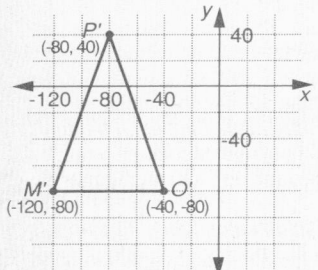
7. Which is easier to use, the point-slope form or the slope-intercept form for the given information?
   a. given the slope and a point other than the y-intercept **point-slope**
   b. given the y-intercept and the slope **slope-intercept**
   c. given two points **point-slope**

In 8 and 9, use the most convenient form of a linear equation to write an equation for the line with the given information.

8. slope 6 and y-intercept -1 $y = 6x - 1$

9. slope $\frac{2}{3}$ and passing through $(7, 1)$ $y - 1 = \frac{2}{3}(x - 7)$

In 10 and 11, a line passes through the points $(7, 12)$ and $(5, 16)$.

10. a. Find the slope of the line. -2
   b. Use the slope and the point $(7, 12)$ in the point-slope form to find an equation for the line. $y - 12 = -2(x - 7)$
   c. Put your solution to part b in standard form. $2x + y = 26$

11. Repeat Questions 10b and 10c with the point $(5, 16)$ and the slope from 10a. Do you get an equivalent equation? If not, why not?
See margin.

12. Find an equation for the line through $(-4, 5)$ parallel to $y = 6x + 10$.
$y - 5 = 6(x + 4)$

13. Scientists often use kelvins to measure temperature. On this scale, $32°F \approx 273.15$ kelvins and $212°F \approx 373.15$ kelvins. Let F represent Fahrenheit temperature and K represent the number of kelvins. The relationship is linear. Find an equation relating temperature in kelvins (dependent variable) and the Fahrenheit temperature.
$K - 273.15 = \frac{5}{9}(F - 32)$

14. A printer finds that it costs \$1290 to print 30 books and \$1335 to print 45 books. Let c be the cost of printing b books. Assume c is linearly related to b. $c - 1290 = 3(b - 30)$
   a. Find an equation relating cost to the number of books printed.
   b. How much will it cost to print 100 books? **\$1500**
   c. How much will it cost to print 0 books? (This is the set-up cost.) **\$1200**

15. Let $P = (3, 4)$, $Q = (3, -5)$, $R = (-2, -5)$, and $S = (-2, 4)$.
   a. Graph rectangle $PQRS$. **See margin.**
   b. Give equations for the four sides. **See margin.**
   c. Find the area of $PQRS$. *(Lesson 3-4, previous course)* **45 sq. units**

16. If $3x + 8 = 40$, find the value of $6x + 16$. *(Previous course)* **80**

In 17 and 18, refer to the following situation. Jamie is driving along a deserted country road. Her car uses one gallon of gas for every 27 miles she travels. Her gas tank holds 18 gallons. Let m be the number of miles she travels. Let g be the number of gallons of gas used. Let L be the amount left in the tank.

17. Find an equation relating g and L. $L = 18 - g$

18. Find an equation relating g and m. *(Lessons 3-1, 2-1, 1-1)* $\frac{1}{27}m = g$

152

19. As of November 1988, the greatest combined number of points ever scored in a professional basketball game was 370 by Denver and Dallas in 1983. A free throw is worth 1 point, a field goal 2 points, and there are 3-point shots. Suppose two opponents break this record with *A* free throws, *B* field goals and *C* 3-point shots. Write an equation or inequality that expresses this idea. *(Lesson 3-3)*   **A + 2B + 3C > 370**

20. Triangle *MOP* is shown below. Graph the reflection image over the *x*-axis of △*MOP*. Label the points *M'*, *O'*, and *P'* and state their coordinates. *(Previous course)*   **See margin.**

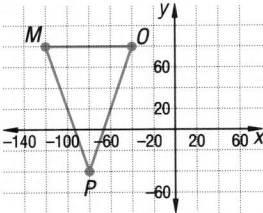

Exploration

21. In 1957, the world record in 800-meter freestyle swimming was about 10 minutes 30 seconds for women and 9 minutes 15 seconds for men. Between 1957 and 1980, these records had been decreasing at a rate of about 4 sec/yr for women and 3 sec/yr for men.   **See margin.**
   a. According to this information, what should the records have been in 1988?
   b. According to this information, what will the records be in the year 2000?
   c. Check a book of records and see if the predictions for 1988 were true.

MORE PRACTICE
For more questions on SPUR Objectives, use *Lesson Master 3-5,* shown below.

EVALUATION
Alternative Assessment
To verify that students understand how to find the equation of a line, ask various students to describe verbally at least one technique for obtaining the equation of a line given certain information. For example, describe how to find the equation of a line given the coordinates of any two points on the line.

NAME _____

LESSON **MASTER   3–5**
QUESTIONS ON **SPUR** OBJECTIVES

■**SKILLS**   *Objective B (See pages 176–179 for objectives.)*
In 1–8, find an equation for the line with the given information.

1. slope 5, through (-2, 8)	$y = 5x + 18$
2. slope $-\frac{1}{3}$, through (-36, 85)	$y = -\frac{1}{3}x + 73$
3. slope -2, through origin	$y = -2x$
4. slope .75, through origin	$y = .75x$
5. through (2, -5) and (0, 3)	$y = 4x + 3$
6. contains (-3, -5) and (-6, 1)	$y = 2x - 11$
7. through (9, -20) and (-2, -15)	$y = -\frac{5}{11}x - 15\frac{10}{11}$
8. parallel to $y = -\frac{1}{2}x - 4$, through (8, 2)	$y = -\frac{1}{2}x + 6$

■**PROPERTIES**   *Objective E*
9. Give the point-slope form of a linear equation. $y - y_1 = m(x - x_1)$

■**PROPERTIES**   *Objective F*
10. *True or false* The line with the equation $y - 8 = 6(x + 2)$ goes through the point (8, 2).   **false**

■**USES**   *Objective I*
11. An accountant finds it costs a business $5250 to make 160 pairs of eyeglasses and $7900 to make 210 pairs of glasses. Assuming the cost and number of glasses are linearly related, how much would it cost to make 320 pairs of glasses?   **$13,730**

12. Kelvin and Fahrenheit temperatures are related by a linear equation. Two pairs of corresponding temperatures are $0°K = -459.4°F$ and $255.2K = 0°F$. Write a linear equation relating K and F, and solve it for K.

$$K = \frac{255.2}{459.4}F + 255.2, \text{ or } K = .56F + 255.2$$

13. A rug company finds it costs $80 to install 1000 square feet of carpet and $120 to install 1800 square feet of carpet. Assuming a linear relationship between cost and the number of square feet installed, how much will it cost to install 3000 feet of carpeting?   **$180**

31

RESOURCES
■ Lesson Master 3-6
🖳 Computer Master 4

OBJECTIVES

D Describe arithmetic sequences using explicit formulas.
G Recognize properties of arithmetic sequences.
K Solve real-world problems using arithmetic sequences.

TEACHING NOTES

Remind students that a sequence is an ordered list. Ask them to list the next three reasonable terms of the following sequences:
(a) 15, 20, 25, 30, . . . (35, 40, 45)
(b) -12, -15, -18, -21, . . . (-24, -27, -30)
(c) 2, 3, 5, 7, . . . (11, 13, 17)

Point out to students that they should not assume a given sequence is arithmetic unless given a formula or told it is. Sequence (c) above is most frequently continued by students with the terms 9, 11, 13, 15, 17, . . . , but we meant the sequence of prime numbers, which is not an arithmetic sequence.

Before students begin to work the questions, discuss the relationship between b in the equation $y = mx + b$ and a_1 in the equation $a_n - a_1 = d(n - 1)$. Stress that the first term of an arithmetic sequence is a_1, and b is the term that should come right before the first term. In the arithmetic sequence 12, 15, 18, 21, . . . , $a_1 = 12$ and $b = 9$. Since b represents

LESSON

3-6

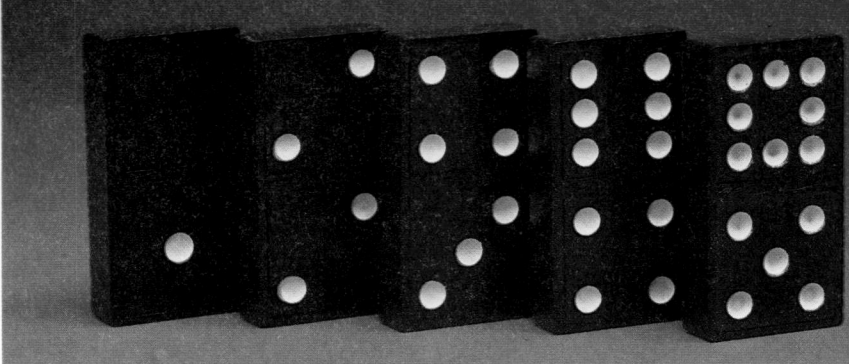

Arithmetic Sequences: Explicit Formulas

Some sequences are described by linear equations. Recall that the domain for a sequence is the set of natural numbers. If you substitute the natural numbers 1, 2, 3, 4, 5, ... for x in the linear equation

$$y = 4x - 5$$

you will generate the following sequence of values for y:

$$-1, 3, 7, 11, 15, \ldots$$

By substituting n for x and a_n for y you can generate a formula for a_n, the nth term of this sequence.

$$a_n = 4n - 5$$

Remember that n is now restricted to the set of natural numbers, $\{1, 2, 3, \ldots\}$.

Both the linear equation and the sequence equation are graphed below. On the graph of the linear equation, the ordered pairs are of the form (x, y), while on the graph of the sequence equation, the ordered pairs are of the form (n, a_n). The graph of $a_n = 4n - 5$ is part of the graph of $y = 4x - 5$. The sequence generates a set of discrete points because its domain is restricted to the natural numbers. Just as the line continues forever, so the graph of the sequence equation continues for all natural-number values of n.

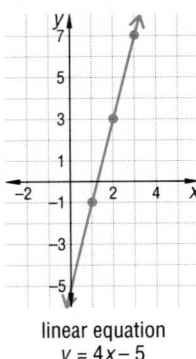

linear equation
$y = 4x - 5$

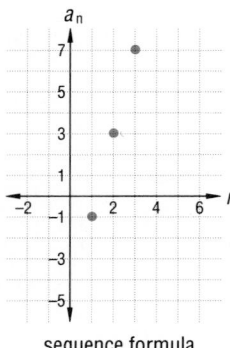

sequence formula
$a_n = 4n - 5$

In the sequence $a_n = 4n - 5$ there is a *constant difference* of 4 between successive terms. This difference is the slope of the graph. As a check, the ordered pairs (2, 3) and (3, 7) from the sequence graph give the slope:

$$m = \frac{7 - 3}{3 - 2} = \frac{4}{1} = 4$$

A sequence with a constant difference is called a **linear sequence** or **arithmetic sequence.** (Here the word *arithmetic* is used as an adjective; it is pronounced *arithmetic*.)

If you are given the first term and the constant difference for an arithmetic sequence, you can find an explicit formula for the *n*th term of that sequence. Finding this formula is just like finding an equation of a line using the point-slope form. Example 1 shows how this can be done.

■ ■ ■ ■ ■ ■ ■ ■ ■ ■

Example 1   Find a formula for the *n*th term of the arithmetic sequence 4, 11, 18, 25, ...

Solution   The constant difference between terms is $11 - 4$, or $18 - 11$, or $25 - 18$; it is the slope 7. The first term a_1 is 4, which gives the point (1, 4).

The point-slope form is
$$y - y_1 = m(x - x_1).$$

Substitute a_n for y, 4 for y_1, 7 for m, n for x, and 1 for x_1.

$$a_n - 4 = 7(n - 1)$$

Solve for a_n. $a_n - 4 = 7n - 7$
$$a_n = 7n - 3$$

This is a formula for the *n*th term of the sequence.

Check   Substitute values for n into the formula for a_n. Do you get the correct term? Try $n = 4$. Do you get $a_4 = 25$? $a_4 = 7 \cdot 4 - 3 = 25$. Yes.

The solution of Example 1 can be generalized to find an explicit formula relating the *n*th term, a_n, and the first term, a_1, of an arithmetic sequence. Each term is of the form (n, a_n) and the first term is the ordered pair $(1, a_1)$. The slope is just the constant difference, which we call d. Use these values in the point-slope form of the linear equation:

$$a_n - a_1 = d(n - 1)$$
Solve for a_n: $a_n = a_1 + (n - 1)d$

the *y*-intercept, when *x* is 0, we say that *b* represents the *zeroth* term in a sequence. This can be illustrated by the graphs on page 154. Point out that on the graph at the left, *b* is -5, the *y*-intercept. On the graph at the right, the first point shown is a_1. To get from a_1 to *b*, go left one unit and down four units.

ADDITIONAL EXAMPLES

1. Find a formula for the nth term of the arithmetic sequence

12, 14.5, 17, 19.5, ...

$a_n = 12 + 2.5(n - 1)$

2. Judy decides to begin a fitness program. She plans to run one-half mile on the first day, then will add one-tenth of a mile to her workout on each successive day. Write a formula to express how far Judy will be running on day n.

$a_n = .5 + .1(n - 1)$

It is appropriate to ask students if these formulas make sense for all positive values of n. Does Judy really want to become a marathon runner?

3. In an arithmetic sequence, $a_4 = 20$ and $a_7 = 56$. Find a formula for a_n.

$a_n - 20 = 12(n - 4)$, so $a_n = 12_n - 28$.

Error Analysis Students sometimes make the mistake of forgetting to multiply through by the negative number in a formula for a sequence that is decreasing. You may want to show several examples in which $d < 0$.

Students also sometimes start with an inappropriate formula when asked to find an equation formula for a_n, given terms other than the first term. If the fifth term is given, they might write $a_n = a_5 + (n - 5)d$.

Encourage students to check their formulas by substituting known values, so they can catch such errors.

This short argument proves the following theorem.

Theorem:

The nth term a_n of an arithmetic sequence with first term a_1 and constant difference d is given by the explicit formula

$$a_n = a_1 + (n - 1)d.$$

Example 2 Find the 40th term of the arithmetic sequence 100, 97, 94, 91, ...

Solution The first term $a_1 = 100$, and the constant difference is -3. Since the 40th term is to be found, substitute $n = 40$ into the formula of the theorem:

$$a_{40} = 100 + (40 - 1) \cdot \text{-}3 = 100 + 39 \cdot \text{-}3 = \text{-}17$$

The 40th term is -17.

Example 3 In a concert hall the first row has 10 seats in it, and each subsequent row has two more seats than the row in front of it. If the last row has 64 seats, how many rows are in the concert hall?

Solution Because each succeeding row has two additional seats, the number of seats in each row generates the sequence

$$10, 12, 14, 16, ..., 64.$$

Thus, you know that $a_1 = 10$, $d = 2$, and $a_n = 64$, where n is the number of rows. To find n, substitute the known values into $a_n = a_1 + (n - 1)d$ and solve.

$$64 = 10 + (n - 1)2$$
$$54 = 2(n - 1)$$
$$27 = n - 1$$
$$28 = n$$

There are 28 rows of seats in the concert hall.

Check 1 Substitute $a_1 = 10$, $d = 2$, and $n = 28$ into $a_n = a_1 + (n - 1)d$.

$$a_{28} = 10 + (28 - 1)2 = 10 + 54 = 64$$

The last row has the correct number of seats.

Check 2 You could also check your answer by writing the first 28 terms of the sequence to verify that $a_{28} = 64$.

Questions

Covering the Reading

1. Suppose $a_n = 5n + 2$.
   a. The domain for n is ___?___.   the set of natural numbers
   b. Graph the sequence.   See margin.

In 2 and 3, (a) write the first three terms of the sequence; (b) find the constant difference between the terms; (c) graph.   See margin.

2. $a_n = 3n$ **3.** $a_n = \frac{1}{2}n - 7$

4. How is the constant difference of a linear sequence related to the slope of its graph?   They are the same number.

5. The nth term of an arithmetic sequence with first term a_1 and constant difference d is ___?___. $a_1 + (n - 1)d$

6. a. Find a formula for the nth term of the sequence 13, 15, 17, 19, 21, ... $a_n = 13 + (n - 1)2$
   b. Calculate the 51st term of this sequence.   113

In 7 and 8, (a) find a formula for the nth term of the sequence; (b) find the 100th term.

7. 6, 15, 24, 33, ...   **8.** 16, 14.5, 13, 11.5, ...
   a) $a_n = 6 + (n - 1)9$; b) 897   a) $a_n = 16 - (n - 1)1.5$; b) -132.5

ADDITIONAL ANSWERS
1.b.

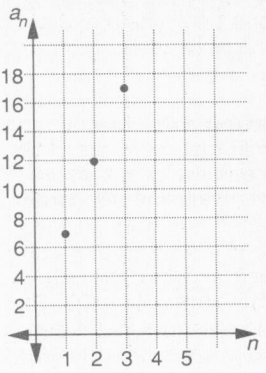

2.a. 3, 6, 9   b. 3
c.

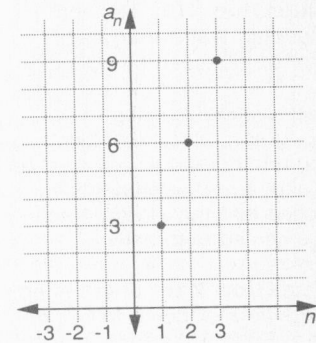

3.a. $-6\frac{1}{2}$, -6, $-5\frac{1}{2}$
b. $\frac{1}{2}$
c.

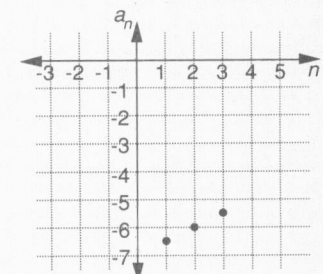

NOTES ON QUESTIONS
Questions 14 and 15:
These questions can either be done by thinking of a sequence or by thinking of a line.

Question 16: Mention to students that there are times when one wants to think of discrete situations as continuous and use the equations for x and y instead of n and a_n, such as when the values become extremely large. Explain to students that if they tried to make 5000 discrete points on a piece of graph paper, the graph would look continuous.

Question 18: Remind students that the equation can be obtained by noting that the y-intercept is $(0, 0)$, determining the slope from the graph, and substituting the numbers in $y = mx + b$. Make sure that students notice that the x- and y-axis are scaled differently.

Question 23: There is no algorithm for doing this question. Explain that one way is to examine the differences of consecutive terms. This gives $2, 4, 8, 16, \ldots$, and suggests that the sequence has a formula involving 2^n.

9. Refer to Example 3. Suppose that in some other concert hall the first row has 40 seats, each subsequent row has two more seats than the row in front of it, and the last row has 70 seats. How many rows of seats are there?   **16 rows**

10. *Multiple choice* Which sequence is *not* an arithmetic sequence?   **b**
    (a) 5, 9, 13, 17, ...   (b) 3, 6, 12, 24, ...
    (c) $\frac{1}{2}$, 1, $\frac{3}{2}$, 2, $\frac{5}{2}$, ...   (d) 0, -1, -2, -3, -4, ...

11. **a.** Does the graph of an arithmetic sequence have an intercept?   **no**
    b. If yes, how can you find it from a formula for the nth term? If not, why not?   **The domain is the set of natural numbers.**

12. **a.** What numbers will the following BASIC program print when run, if you input 15 for A and 3 for D in line 10?   **15, 18, 24, 33, 45, 60**

```
10 INPUT A, D
20 FOR N = 1 TO 6
30    A = A + D * (N − 1)
40    PRINT A
50 NEXT N
60 END
```

   b. If line 20 is changed to FOR N = 1 TO 100, and the user inputs 15 for A and 3 for D, what will be the last number printed?
   312

13. Stu and Perri start biking each week for training. They start by biking 14 miles the first week. By the twenty-fifth week they want to bike 74 miles a week. If the number of miles biked each week is to form an arithmetic sequence, what should be their weekly increase? $\frac{5}{2}$ **mi**

In 14 and 15, a local radio station is holding a contest to give away cash. The announcer calls a number and if the person who answers guesses the correct amount of money in the pot, he or she wins the money. If the resident misses, $20 is added to the money pot.

14. On the 12th call, a contestant won $675. How much was in the pot at the beginning?   **$455**

15. Suppose the pot starts with $150. On what call would the winner receive $1110?   **49th**

158

16. A business finds that it costs $950 to make 300 pillows and $1475 to make 650 pillows. Assuming a linear relationship between cost and number of pillows, find the cost of making 5000 pillows. *(Lesson 3-5)*
$8000

17. Find an equation for the line that goes through $(-6, -8)$ and $(9, 2)$. *(Lesson 3-5)* $y = \frac{2}{3}x - 4$

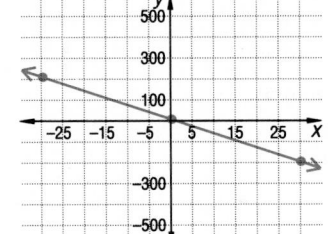

18. Find an equation for the line graphed at the right. *(Lesson 3-5)* $y = \frac{-20}{3}x$

19. Find an equation of the line passing through $(-7, 8)$ and parallel to $y = \frac{3}{5}x - 2$. *(Lesson 3-5)* $y = \frac{3}{5}x + \frac{61}{5}$

20. Give the distance between $(0, 0)$ and $(-3, -4)$. *(Previous course)* 5

Multiple choice In 21 and 22, refer to the graphs below. *(Lessons 2-4, 2-5, 2-7)*

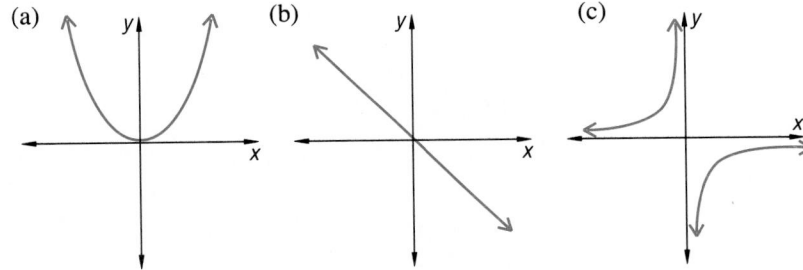

21. Which graph does not represent a direct variation? c

22. Which graph represents a situation in which the constant of variation is positive? a

23. Here is a sequence that is *not* a linear sequence.

$$3, 5, 9, 17, 33, 65, 129, 257, 513, \ldots$$

b) $a_1 = 3;\ a_n = a_{n-1} + 2^{n-1}$ for $n > 1$

a. What is the next term? 1025
b. Find a recursive formula for the nth term.
c. Find an explicit formula for the nth term. $a_n = 2^n + 1$

LESSON 3-6 Arithmetic Sequences: Explicit Formulas 159

OBJECTIVE

D Describe arithmetic sequences using recursive formulas.

TEACHING NOTES

Remind students that a recursive formula for a sequence has two parts, the statement of the first term and the formula to generate the rest of the sequence.

Reading It is often helpful to have students translate a recursive formula into words. For the arithmetic sequence $a_1 = -5$, $a_n = a_{n-1} + 3$, the translation is, "The first term is -5. To get the nth term in the sequence, add 3 to the previous term." A translation of the general formula is, "The first term is a_1; all other terms of the sequence are found by adding d to the previous term."

ADDITIONAL EXAMPLES
1. What sequence is generated by
$$\begin{cases} a_1 = 53 \\ a_n = a_{n-1} - 7, n > 1? \end{cases}$$
53, 46, 39, 32, 25, . . .

2. Consider the arithmetic sequence 112, 120, 128, 136, ...
a. Find a recursive formula.
$$\begin{cases} a_1 = 112 \\ a_n = a_{n-1} + 8, n > 1 \end{cases}$$
b. Find an explicit formula.
$$a_n = 8n + 104$$

LESSON

3-7

Arithmetic Sequences: Recursive Formulas

Recall from Lesson 1-4 that a recursive formula gives a rule for finding the nth term of a sequence from one or more of the previous terms. Consider this recursive formula:

$$\begin{cases} a_1 = -5 \\ a_n = a_{n-1} + 3, \text{ for } n > 1 \end{cases}$$

The first few terms of this sequence are

$$-5, -2, 1, 4, 7, 10, \ldots .$$

This is an arithmetic sequence because there is a constant difference of 3 between successive terms.

The key that this is an arithmetic sequence is in the second line. Suppose 3 is replaced by d. Then

$$a_n = a_{n-1} + d, \text{ for } n > 1.$$

Subtracting a_{n-1} from each side gives $a_n - a_{n-1} = d$. That is, d is the difference between the nth term and the $(n - 1)$st term. If d is constant, then the sequence has a constant difference and is arithmetic. This proves the following theorem.

Theorem:

If d is constant, the recursive formula

$$\begin{cases} a_1 \\ a_n = a_{n-1} + d, \text{ for } n > 1 \end{cases}$$

generates the arithmetic sequence with first term a_1 and constant difference d.

Example 1 What sequence is generated by $\begin{cases} a_1 = 1000 \\ a_n = a_{n-1} - 40, n > 1? \end{cases}$

Solution The first term is 1000. The difference is -40. So the sequence is

$$1000, 960, 920, 880, \ldots .$$

It is useful to be able to find both explicit and recursive formulas for arithmetic sequences.

160

3. Due to an increasing population, the town of Valley Heights was concerned about its water supply. The town council voted to add 20,000 acre-feet of water immediately to its reservoir capacity of 3 million acre-feet, and an additional 20,000 acre feet of water each year. Write a recursive formula to express the capacity of the reservoir in n years.

$$\begin{cases} a_1 = 3{,}020{,}000 \\ a_n = a_{n-1} + 20{,}000, n > 1 \end{cases}$$

NOTES ON QUESTIONS
Question 9: Due to the abstract nature of the question, students may need help. Have them say to themselves, "To get the next term, add 3x to the previous term."

Questions 11–13: The programs may use either recursive or explicit formulas.

Question 18: If done by hand, the graph is easily done if the x-axis is numbered by tens, twenty-fives or fifties, and the y-axis is numbered by ones or twos. Remind students of two ways to make this decision:
(1) Solve for y and use the slope and y-intercept as scale indicators.
(2) Write the equation in standard form and find both the x- and y-intercepts.

Question 19: Students are asked to graph over a limited domain. This concept is incorporated into the discussion of piecewise linear graphs in Lesson 3-8.

Question 22: If students find one other positive integer satisfying the conditions, they should be commended. They are usually surprised to find that all the numbers form an arithmetic sequence.

Example 2

Steve borrowed $370 from his parents for airfare to visit his sister in college. He will pay them back at the rate of $30 each month. Let a_n be the amount he still owes after n months. Find (a) a recursive formula and (b) an explicit formula for a_n.

Solution

a. After 1 month he owes $340, so $a_1 = 340$. Each month he pays back $30, so $d = -30$. The recursive formula is then

$$\begin{cases} a_1 = 340 \\ a_n = a_{n-1} - 30, n > 1. \end{cases}$$

b. For an explicit formula, $a_n = a_1 + (n - 1)d$
$$a_n = 340 + (n - 1) \cdot -30$$
$$a_n = 340 - 30n + 30$$
$$a_n = 370 - 30n$$

Check Each formula generates the sequence 340, 310, 280, 250, ...

Computers can generate sequences using either explicit or recursive formulas. The BASIC programs below each generate the first 10 terms of the sequence of Example 2.

Recursive
```
10 LET A = 340
20 FOR N = 1 TO 10
30   PRINT A
40   A = A - 30
50 NEXT N
60 END
```

Explicit
```
11 FOR N = 1 TO 10
21   LET AN = 340 - 30 * (N - 1)
31   PRINT AN
41 NEXT N
51 END
```

161

Questions

Covering the Reading

1. A recursive formula gives you a rule for finding the nth term if you already know ___?___.   one or more of the previous terms

2. A recursive formula for an arithmetic sequence with first term a_1 and constant difference d is ___?___. $a_1; a_n = a_{n-1} + d$ for $n > 1$

3. a. What are the first four terms of the sequence generated by this formula?

$$\begin{cases} a_1 = 1 \\ a_n = a_{n-1} + 6, \text{ for } n > 1 \end{cases}$$ 1, 7, 13, 19

b. Write a computer program to generate the first 25 terms of this sequence.   See margin.

4. Refer to Example 2. Suppose Steve borrowed $325 and repaid $25 per month. Find (a) a recursive formula and (b) an explicit formula for the amount a_n owed n months after payment begins.   See margin.

5. Write (a) a recursive formula and (b) an explicit formula for the arithmetic sequence 13, 19, 25, 31, ...   See margin.

6. The BASIC program below generates several terms of a sequence using a recursive formula.

```
10 LET A = 15
20 FOR N = 1 TO 7
30    PRINT A
40    A = A + 3.5
50 NEXT N
60 END
```
                                    15, 18.5, 22, 25.5,
                                    29, 32.5, 36
a. What sequence is printed when the program is run?
b. Change this program so that the sequence is defined explicitly.
See margin.

Applying the Mathematics

7. Write a recursive formula for the arithmetic sequence with explicit formula $a_n = 10.8 + 2.4n$. $a_1 = 13.2; a_n = a_{n-1} + 2.4$ for $n > 1$

In 8 and 9, rewrite each recursive formula in explicit form.   See margin.

8. $\begin{cases} a_1 = 8.1 \\ a_n = a_{n-1} + 1.7, \text{ for } n > 1 \end{cases}$ **9.** $\begin{cases} a_1 = -x \\ a_n = a_{n-1} + 3x, \text{ for } n > 1 \end{cases}$

10. Jennifer's grandparents opened a savings account for their granddaughter. They started the account with $500 on her first birthday, and each subsequent year on her birthday they deposited $150.
a. Write an explicit formula for the amount a_n in the account after n birthdays. $a_n = 150n + 350$
b. Write a recursive formula for a_n.
$a_1 = 500: a_n = a_{n-1} + 150$ for $n > 1$

162

In 11–13, write a computer program to generate: **See margin.**

11. the first 1000 odd numbers.

12. the first 500 multiples of 11.

13. the sequence of Question 4.

Review

14. Find the 400th positive integer in the arithmetic sequence 9, 19, 29, 39, ... *(Lesson 3-6)* **3999**

15. If $t_n = 10 + 7(n - 1)$ find t_{89}. *(Lesson 3-6)* **626**

16. In a contest the first-place winner gets $100,000 and the tenth-place winner gets $23,500. If the winning amounts form an arithmetic sequence, find the cash difference between prizes. *(Lesson 3-6)* **$8500**

17. Find an equation of the line containing (-2, 4) parallel to $2x + y = 12$. *(Lesson 3-5)*
$2x + y = 0$

18. Graph $6(-3x + 50y) = 2400$. Be careful! You will need to choose your scales carefully in order to show the intercept and slope clearly. *(Lesson 3-4)* **See margin.**

19. Use $y = 3 - x$ *(Lessons 3-2, 1-1; Previous course)* **See margin.**
  a. Graph only the part of the graph between the x- and y-intercepts.
  b. What is the domain? **$0 \le x \le 3$**
  c. Find the midpoint of the segment you graphed in part a. **(1.5, 1.5)**

In 20 and 21, let $A = (\frac{1}{2}, \frac{2}{3})$ and $B = (-\frac{5}{2}, -\frac{11}{3})$. *(Lessons 1-4, 1-5, 3-1)*

20. Find the length of $\overline{AB}$. **21.** Find the slope of $\overline{AB}$.
  $\frac{5\sqrt{10}}{3}$ $\frac{13}{9}$

Exploration

22. Find all the positive integers that meet all three of these conditions at the same time: (a) They leave a remainder of 1 when divided by 2. (b) They leave a remainder of 3 when divided by 4. (c) They leave a remainder of 5 when divided by 6. (Hint: 35 is one such number.)
positive integers of the form $12n - 1$

FOLLOW-UP

MORE PRACTICE
For more questions on SPUR Objectives, use *Lesson Master 3-7*, shown below.

EVALUATION
A quiz covering Lessons 3-4 through 3-7 is provided in the TRF.

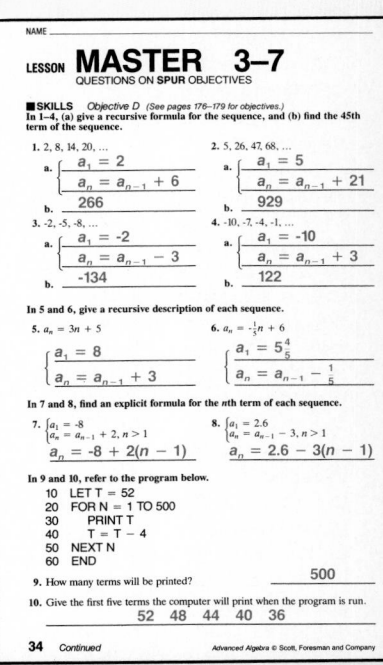

LESSON 3-8

RESOURCES
■ Lesson Master 3-8
▣ Visual for Teaching Aid 11 displays the piecewise linear graph of Horace's bicycle trip. Use with Additional Example 1.
▣ Visual for Teaching Aid 12 displays Additional Example 2.
▣ Visual for Teaching Aid 13 displays the graph for **Questions 9-12**.
▣ Computer Master 5

OBJECTIVE

M Graph and describe piecewise linear situations.

TEACHING NOTES

Explain to students that in order to describe a situation by a piecewise linear graph, the situation must be one that can be described by segments or rays, each having a constant rate of change.

At first, students may find the task of determining equations for a piecewise linear graph difficult. Encourage students to use a classic problem-solving strategy—that is, *divide a difficult problem into simpler parts and then solve each part*. Have them use the endpoints of each segment to calculate the slope of that segment; then they can use either endpoint and the point-slope form to find the equation of that segment. If the section is a ray, they should use the endpoint and any other point on the ray to determine the slope. Using the endpoints of segments or rays stresses the domain limitations for each equation.

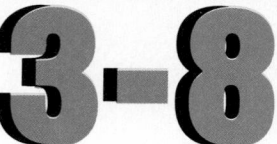

As you know, graphs can convey a great deal of information in a small amount of space. Horace made the graph below to describe his bicycle trip, which included two stops. It gives his distance D, in miles from home, t hours after leaving home.

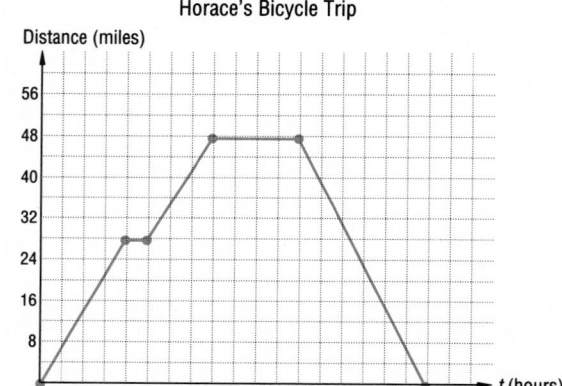

This graph is made up of five segments. Because each of these five segments is a piece of a line, the graph is called **piecewise linear.** The graph shows that Horace started from home and bicycled at a constant rate for 2 hours, winding up 28 miles from home. After a half-hour stop, he traveled for another hour and a half, until he was 48 miles from home. Then he stopped again, this time for two hours. Finally, he returned home traveling at a constant rate and reached home 9 hours after starting out.

Sometimes it is efficient to have equations for each part of a piecewise linear graph. Such situations can occur when large numbers of items are bought or used. If the cost or rate changes, the graph may be piecewise linear. This can happen with food or utility bills.

164

Example 1 An electric company calculates bills for its residential customers based on these charges:

> $10.00 monthly service fee;
> $.07 per kwh energy charge for the first 400 kwh;
> $.04 per kwh energy charge for each kwh over 400.

a. Calculate the monthly electric bill for a family that uses 300 kwh.
b. Calculate the monthly electric bill for a family that uses 600 kwh.
c. Draw a graph showing how cost C (in dollars) is related to usage k (in kwh).

Solution

a. Add the service fee to the charge for the electricity used.
$$C = 10 + .07(300)$$
$$C = 10 + 21$$
$$C = 31$$

The family must pay $31 for 300 kwh.

b. The cost changes when more than 400 kwh are used. There are three things to be considered.

$$C = 10 \quad + \quad .07(400) \quad + \quad .04(200)$$
$$\downarrow \qquad\qquad \downarrow \qquad\qquad \downarrow$$
service   charge for   charge for
fee   first 400 kwh   kwh over 400

$$C = 10 + 28 + 8 = 46$$

The family must pay $46 for 600 kwh.

c. For the first 400 kwh the increase is constant. This piece of the graph is a segment with one endpoint (0, 10) and a slope of $.07 per kwh. The other endpoint is the point at $k = 400$. When $k = 400$, $C = 10 + .07(400) = 38$.

At (400, 38) a new constant rate of increase begins. Because the slope of $.04 per kwh is less for this piece of the graph, it increases more slowly. This part of the graph is a ray, since the rate of $.04 per kwh applies to all values of k greater than 400. The graph is shown below.

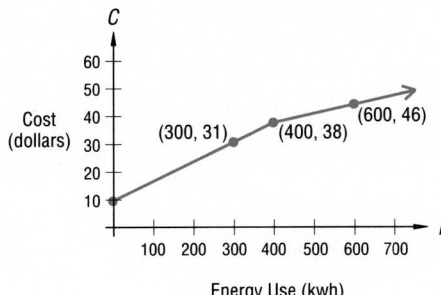

Monthly Electric Costs

LESSON 3-8   Piecewise Linear Graphs   **165**

Remind students that when they are asked for the equations of a piecewise linear graph, they must list the domain for each equation.

ADDITIONAL EXAMPLES
1. Refer to the graph of Horace's bicycle trip. Describe algebraically Horace's distance from home during his trip.

$$\begin{cases} y = 14x & 0 \le x \le 2 \\ y = 28 & 2 < x < 2.5 \\ y = \dfrac{40}{3}x - \dfrac{16}{3} & 2.5 \le x \le 4 \\ y = 48 & 4 < x < 6 \\ y = -16x + 144 & 6 \le x \le 9 \end{cases}$$

2. Below is a graph that describes baby Leah's weight over the first 16 weeks of her life.

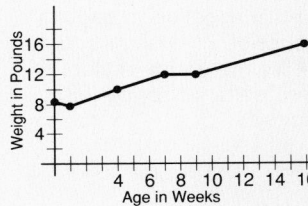

a. How much did the baby weight at birth?
about $8\frac{1}{2}$ lb
b. For how long did the baby lose weight?
1 week
c. What was the baby's actual weight change during weeks 2 through 7?
about 3 lbs
d. At what rate did the baby's weight change during weeks 2 through 7?
$\frac{3}{5}$ lb/wk

Question 13: If students have seen a definition for the absolute value function, the graph may come rather easily. The graph is the same as that of $y = -|x|$.

Question 16: The question introduces a parabolic section to a piecewise graph. This type of graph could model the flight of an eagle scooping down to catch a mouse, the path of the center of a wheel as it moves into and out of a pothole, the shape of a cross-section of a trough, and so on. Point out to students that this graph is a piecewise graph but not a piecewise linear graph.

Question 21: You could use this question to begin a discussion of Lesson 3-9. Ask for the graph of all ordered pairs satisfying the inequality.

ADDITIONAL ANSWERS
13.

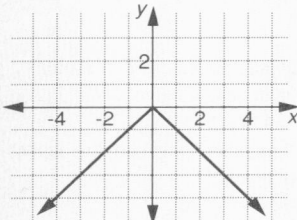

15.a.

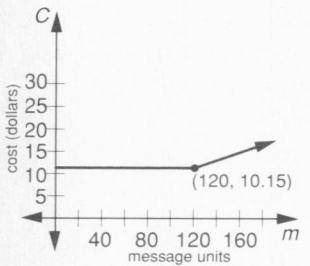

b. $C = 10.15$ for $0 \le m \le 120$; $C = 10.15 + .035m$ for $m > 120$

16. See margin on page 168.

Piecewise linear graphs can be described algebraically by using the following procedure. First, write an equation for each segment or ray that is part of the graph. Then list the equation for each piece of the graph together with the domain over which that equation is defined.

Example 2 In the situation of Example 1, describe algebraically how the cost C depends on k.

Solution The slope of the segment from the point $(0, 10)$ to the point $(400, 38)$ is .07.
Thus,

$$C = .07k + 10 \text{ for } 0 \le k \le 400.$$

An equation for the ray through $(400, 38)$ with slope .04 is given in point-slope form:

$$C - 38 = .04(k - 400)$$
$$C = .04(k - 400) + 38$$
$$C = .04k + 22$$

In summary, this situation is described algebraically as follows:

$$\begin{cases} C = .07k + 10, \text{ for } 0 \le k \le 400 \\ C = .04k + 22, \text{ for } k > 400. \end{cases}$$

Notice that the final description contains an equation for each segment or ray together with the domain over which that equation is defined.

Questions

Covering the Reading

1. A graph that is composed of pieces of lines is called __?__.
   piecewise linear

In 2–6, refer to the graph of Horace's Bicycle Trip.

2. How many line segments are drawn in this graph? 5

3. What is the total amount of time that Horace stopped during his trip?
   $2\frac{1}{2}$ hr

4. What was the farthest Horace was away from home on this trip?
   48 mi

5. How fast was Horace going during the first two hours of his trip?
   14 mph

6. How fast was Horace going during the last three hours of his trip?
   16 mph

166

In 7 and 8, refer to Example 1.

7. Find the monthly electric bill for a family that uses 500 kwh. **$42**

8. *Multiple choice* The formula $C = .07k + 10$ gives the cost of k kwh of electricity **b**
(a) for $k > 0$.   (b) for $0 \le k \le 400$.   (c) for $k \ge 400$.

In 9–12, refer to the following graph. Carmen walks to school, to her job after school, and then home. Let M be the number of miles she is from home at time T.

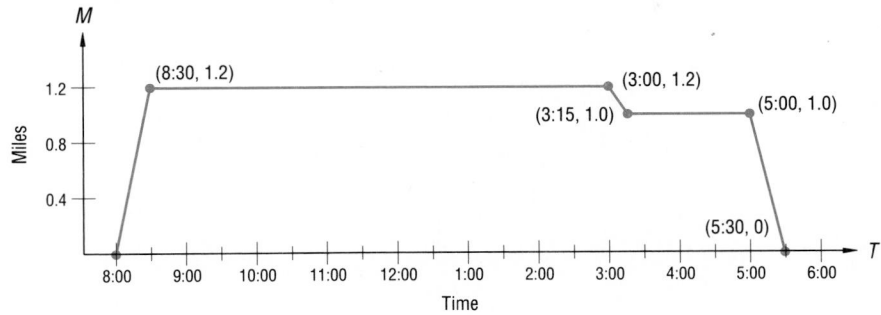

9. How far is school from home?   **1.2 mi**

10. During what time period is Carmen at work?   **3:15 to 5:00**

11. How long does it take Carmen to walk to school? $\frac{1}{2}$ **hr**

12. a. Find the slope of the segment from (8:00, 0) to (8:30, 1.2) using hours as the unit for time.   **2.4**
 b. What does this slope represent?
 Carmen's rate, in mph, walking to school

13. Draw a graph of the following situation:
$$\begin{cases} y = x, & \text{for } x \le 0 \\ y = -x, & \text{for } x > 0 \end{cases}$$ **See margin.**

In 14 and 15, use the following phone rates: A customer is allowed to use a maximum of 120 message units per month for a $10.15 fee. Each local call after the 120th is billed at a rate of $0.035 per message unit.

14. Find the monthly phone bill for a family using
 a. 100 message units   **$10.15**
 b. 120 message units   **$10.15**
 c. 160 message units.   **$11.55**

15. a. Draw a graph of the relation between the cost C and the number of message units m.   **See margin.**
 b. Describe this situation algebraically by finding an equation for each segment or ray.   **See margin.**

16. Draw a graph of the following situation. When $x < -2$, $y = 4$. When $-2 \le x \le 2$, $y = x^2$. When $x > 2$, $y = 4$.   **See margin.**

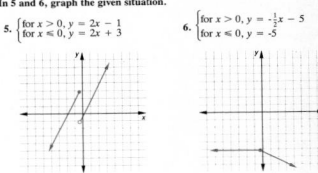
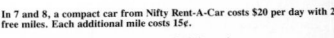
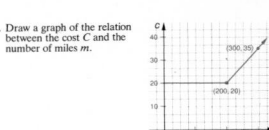
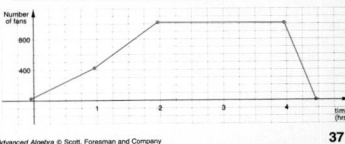

168

FOLLOW-UP

MORE PRACTICE
For more questions on SPUR Objectives, use *Lesson Master 3-8*, shown on page 167.

EXTENSION
Piecewise definitions for graphs enable polygons to be described algebraically. For instance,

$$\begin{cases} y = 1 & \text{for } -1 \leq x \leq 1, \\ y = -1 & \text{for } -1 \leq x \leq 1, \\ x = 1 & \text{for } -1 \leq y \leq 1, \\ x = -1 & \text{for } -1 \leq y \leq 1 \end{cases}$$

describes a square. (The single equation $|x| + |y| = 1$ describes a square also.) Ask students to explore the idea of a set of equations that describe a tilted square, or a rectangle, or a parallelogram.

ADDITIONAL ANSWERS
16.

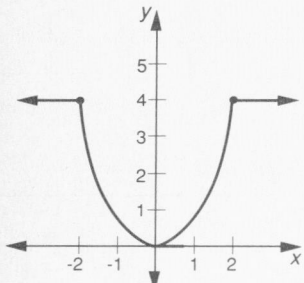

29.

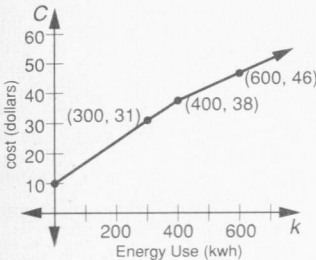

---

17. For the arithmetic sequence 2, -3, -8, -13, ... ,
  a. write an explicit formula. *(Lesson 3-6)* $a_n = 7 - 5n$
  b. write a recursive formula. *(Lesson 3-7)* $a_1 = 2; a_n = a_{n-1} - 5$ for $n > 1$

18. Find a recursive formula for the sequence described by $a_n = -1.5 + 2.5n$. *(Lesson 3-7)* $a_1 = 1.0; a_n = a_{n-1} + 2.5$ for $n > 1$

19. A store displays cans stacked in rows. The top row has 1 can, each subsequent row has 3 more cans than the row above it, and the bottom row has 37 cans. How many rows of cans are there? *(Lesson 3-6)* **13 rows**

20. Find an equation for the line through $(\frac{1}{2}, \frac{3}{4})$ parallel to the line through $(5, 7)$ and $(6, -8)$. *(Lesson 3-5)* $60x + 4y = 33$

21. Solve for y: $5x - 8y < -18$. *(Lesson 1-9)* $y > \frac{5}{8}x + \frac{9}{4}$

In 22–27, use the figures below. The triangles are congruent and segments that look parallel are. Fill in the blank with one of the words translation, rotation, or reflection. *(Previous course)*

22. B is a __?__ image of A. **reflection**

23. C is a __?__ image of B. **translation**

24. A is a __?__ image of B. **reflection**

25. D is a __?__ image of B. **rotation**

26. B is a __?__ image of C. **translation**

27. D is a __?__ image of C. **rotation**

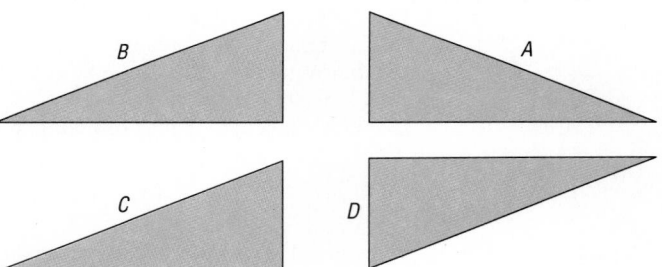

28. Find the gas or electric rates for a home or apartment in your local area. Make a graph like that in Example 1 for the rates you find.
  Many answers are possible.

29. Most function graphers allow more than one graph to be shown at a time. Graph the monthly electric costs from Example 1, using a function grapher, by splitting the graph into its two linear parts.
  See margin.

Take a linear equation and replace the = sign with <, ≤, >, or ≥. The result is a **linear inequality.** Here are some examples.

$$x \geq 5 \qquad y > 2x + 7 \qquad x + 3y \leq 12$$

There are usually more solutions to these sentences than are practical to list. However, the solutions can readily be seen when they are graphed.

In any graph of a line in a plane, the line separates the plane into two distinct regions. They are called **half-planes.** The line itself is the **boundary** of the two regions. In a linear inequality, the solutions are located in one of the half planes and sometimes include points on the boundary.

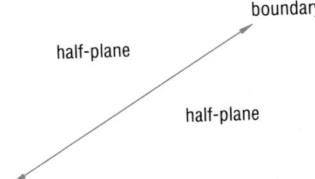

Inequalities with horizontal or vertical boundaries can be quickly graphed.

Example 1 Graph the linear inequality $x \geq 5$ in the coordinate plane.

Solution This half-plane is the collection of all points where the x-coordinate is equal to or greater than 5. The graph includes the line $x = 5$ and every point to the right of that line. These points are shaded in the graph.

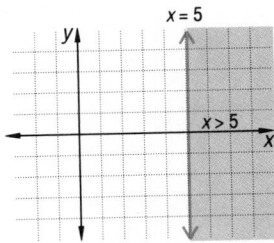

Check Pick a point in the shaded region. Its coordinates should satisfy $x \geq 5$. We pick (7, 1). Is $7 \geq 5$? Yes. So (7, 1) is in the solution set.

If you pick a point in the non-shaded region its coordinates should not satisfy the inequality. We pick (1, 4). Is $1 \geq 5$? No. Therefore (1, 4) is not in the solution set.

RESOURCES
■ Lesson Master 3-9

OBJECTIVE

L Graph linear inequalities.

TEACHING NOTES

Encourage students to use (0, 0) as a test point because of its ease of substitution in most inequalities. Stress, however, that (0, 0) should not be used when it is on the boundary since a point on the boundary will not enable the student to determine which half-plane is in the solution set.

Reading Point out to students that **Example 1** explains how to graph $x \geq 5$ by reading it as "the set of all points where the x-coordinate is equal to or greater than 5." Encourage students to utilize this reading technique with other inequalities. For example, read **Example 2**, $y > 2x + 7$, as "the set of all points where the y-coordinates are greater than $2x + 7$." Such a reading helps students realize that the half-plane of the solution set is the half-plane where the y-values are larger, that is, the half-plane above the boundary.

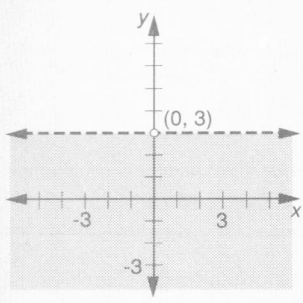

2. Graph the linear inequality $y \leq -\frac{4}{3}x + 5$.

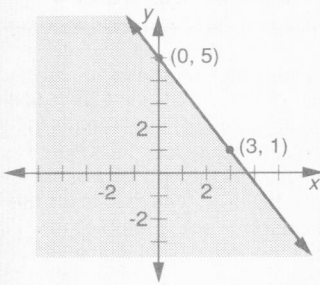

3. An ounce of hamburger beef yields about 80 calories, and a french fry about 11. If you want less than 500 calories, what combinations of beef and french fries are possible?
Graph $80h + 11f < 500$.
Point out that points on the boundary segment indicate combinations of hamburger and fries that total exactly 500 calories. Note also the restricted domain on both independent and dependent variables.

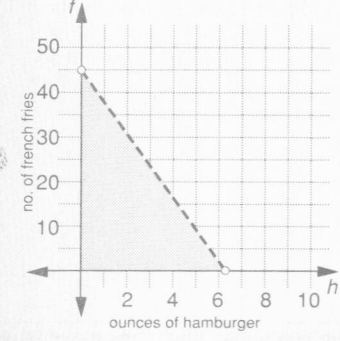

Example 2 illustrates graphing inequalities with oblique boundaries.

Example 2 Graph the linear inequality $y > 2x + 7$.

Solution Many ordered pairs satisfy this inequality. To picture them, first locate the boundary $y = 2x + 7$. This equation is in slope-intercept form. Plot the y-intercept 7 and use the slope to get another point (1, 9). These points must be connected with a dashed line because the sign is $>$, not $\geq$. This means that the boundary points do not satisfy the inequality. The boundary line is shown below at the left.

Step 1

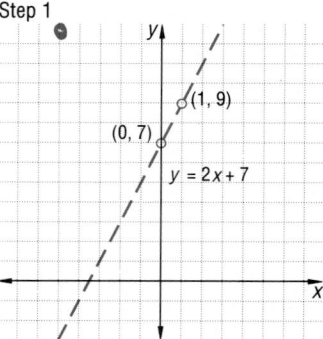

Step 2

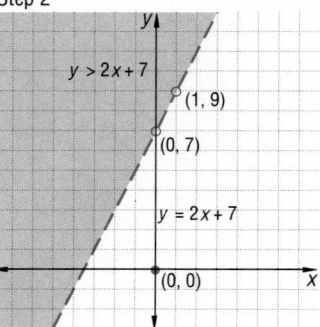

To see which half-plane contains the solutions, test a point. Usually (0, 0) is an easy point to test. Substitute (0, 0) into $y > 2x + 7$. Is $0 > 2(0) + 7$? No. So (0, 0) is not included in the points that are possible solutions to $y > 2x + 7$. The graph should be shaded in the half-plane on the other side of the line as shown at the right above.

Check Pick a point in the shaded region. We pick (-3, 6). Do the coordinates satisfy $y > 2x + 7$? Is $6 > 2(-3) + 7$? Yes.

Linear inequalities often arise from real situations.

Example 3 A ferry boat transports cars and buses across a river. It has space for 12 cars, and a bus takes up the space of 3 cars. Draw a graph showing how many cars and buses can be taken in one crossing.

Solution This is a linear-combination situation. A car occupies 1 space, so x cars need x spaces. A bus occupies 3 spaces, so y buses need $3y$ spaces. The ferry has only 12 spaces; so a sentence describing the situation is

$$x + 3y \leq 12.$$

170

First, locate the boundary $x + 3y = 12$. This equation is in standard form; so use the intercepts, (0, 4) and (12, 0). Some points on the boundary go through lattice points (points with integer coordinates) and do satisfy the inequality.

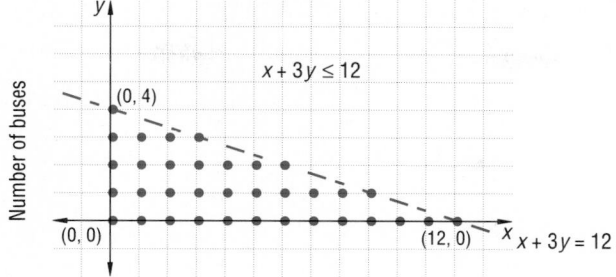

To determine in which half-plane the solutions lie, try an ordered pair. Substituting (0, 0) gives $0 + 3(0) \leq 12$. This is true; so (0, 0) is in the solution set, and the half-plane of solutions is *below the boundary line.* Because x and y represent numbers of cars and buses, they must be whole numbers. Thus the graph consists of only those points on or below the line $x + 3y = 12$ whose coordinates are whole numbers. Because this is a discrete set, the solutions are represented by the dots in the graph. On the boundary, dots are shown only for the points with whole-number coordinates. The solution set is shown in the graph above. Notice that there are 35 combinations of cars and buses that can be taken by the ferry.

Check   To check that the correct half-plane was chosen, pick a point in the other half-plane. It should not work in the inequality. We choose (10, 5). Substitute into the inequality. Is $10 + 3(5) \leq 12$? No; so the solution checks.

In Example 3 the solutions can be identified individually. But in Example 2, the number of solutions is infinite. So the graph for Example 2 must be shaded because the solutions cannot be individually identified.

In summary, to graph a linear inequality:

1. Graph the appropriate boundary line, either dotted or solid for the corresponding linear equation.
2. Test a point in one half-plane to see if the point satisfies the inequality. The point (0, 0) is often used, if possible.
3. Shade the half-plane that satisfies the inequality, or plot points if the situation is discrete.

NOTES ON QUESTIONS
Question 14: It is interesting to focus on the difference between the mathematical domain and range and a realistic domain and range, which takes into account the real-world restrictions of the problem itself, such as the fact that wins and losses cannot be negative. Some students' graphs for this problem will have infinite domains and ranges, while others will restrict theirs. We consider both of these graphs correct and useful.

Error Analysis for Question 15: Students may have problems choosing the correct inequality. A common error is to use the wrong inequality sign. For example, students will write $y > -\frac{3}{4}x - 4$ as the answer instead of $y < -\frac{3}{4}x - 4$. To avoid this error, tell students to use either the slope-intercept form or the point-slope form. If the point-slope form is used, students should solve for y. Isolating y makes it easier for students to choose the correct inequality sign.

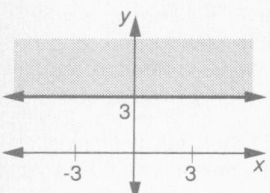
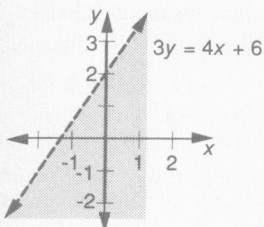
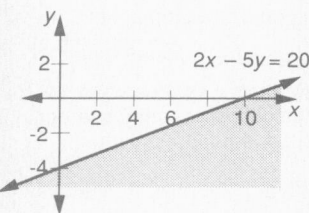
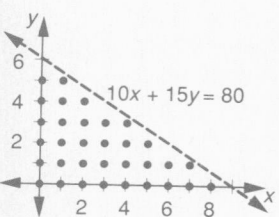
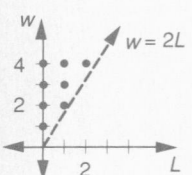
Questions

1. A linear inequality is formed by replacing the = sign in a linear equation with __?__, __?__, __?__, or __?__.   >, <, ≥, ≤

2. A line separates a plane into two distinct regions called __?__. The line itself is called the __?__ of these regions.
   half-planes; boundary

3. The graph of all solutions to $x < -2$ consists of points to the __?__ of the line $x = -2$.   **left**

4. Graph the set of all ordered pairs that satisfy $y \geq 3$.   **See margin.**

In 5–7, refer to Example 2. Justify your answer.

5. *True or false* The ordered pair (-4, 3) is a solution to the inequality.
   True; 3 > -1

6. Why is the boundary line dotted rather than solid?
   The sign is >, not ≥.

7. How would the graph change if the inequality were $y < 2x + 7$?
   The other half-plane would be shaded.

In 8–10, refer to Example 3.

8. Why are there no points in the solution set in the second, third, or fourth quadrants?
   A negative number of cars or buses does not make sense.

9. a. In how many ways can the ferry cross the river full?   **5**
   b. List them.   **(0, 4); (3, 3); (6, 2); (9, 1); (12, 0)**
   c. On which part of the graph are these solutions found?
   on the boundary line, x + 3y = 12

10. a. In how many ways can the ferry cross the river with empty space?   **30**
    b. List four of them.   **See margin.**
    c. Where are these solutions found on the graph?   **See margin.**

In 11 and 12, graph each inequality.   **See margin.**

11. $3y < 4x + 6$ 12. $2x - 5y \geq 20$

13. A person wants to buy x pencils at 10¢ each and y erasers at 15¢ each. The total spent must be less than 90¢.
    a. What inequality must x and y satisfy?   **10x + 15y < 90**
    b. Graph all solutions.   **See margin.**
    c. How many solutions are there?   **33**

14. The players on the Dunkers basketball team must win at least twice as many games as they lose to make the playoffs. Graph the set of points (L, W) that satisfy these conditions.   **See margin.**

15. Write an inequality that describes the region graphed below.
    $y < -\frac{3}{4}x - 4$

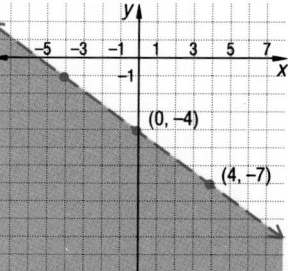

16. Philip David Bayusun fills the bathtub slowly at a constant rate. He turns off the water, then gets in the tub and bathes. After a few minutes he gets out of the tub and pulls the plug. The water drains quickly. Which of the graphs below shows the relation between the volume V of water in the tub and time t? *(Lesson 3-8)*   **a**

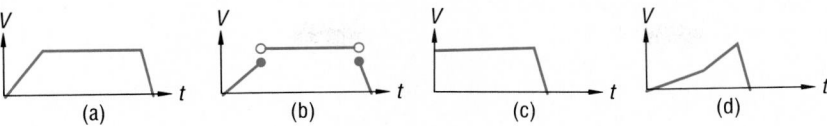

(a)   (b)   (c)   (d)

17. Draw a graph of the following situation:

$$\begin{cases} y = 6, \text{ for } x > 2 \\ y = 3x, \text{ for } 0 \le x \le 2 \\ y = -\tfrac{1}{2}x, \text{ for } x \le 0 \end{cases}$$ *(Lesson 3-8)*   **See margin.**

18. Write a recursive formula for the sequence described by $a_n = 3n + 11$. *(Lesson 3-7)* $a_1 = 14; a_n = a_{n-1} + 3$ for $n > 1$

19. Write equations for the lines graphed below. *(Lessons 3-4, 3-5)*
a) $y = x + 250;$ **b)** $y = -50$

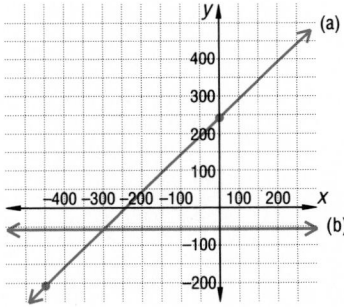

20. Two figures have equal areas. Must they be congruent if the figures are: *(Previous course)*
a. squares **b.** triangles **c.** octagons **d.** circles?
yes   no   no   yes

21. In this chapter you have graphed many lines that came from real situations.
a. Pick one of the situations and reword it so that it leads to a linear inequality, as in Example 3.   **Many answers are possible.**
b. Graph the inequality.   **Many answers are possible.**

FOLLOW-UP

MORE PRACTICE
For more questions on SPUR Objectives, use *Lesson Master 3-9,* shown below.

17.

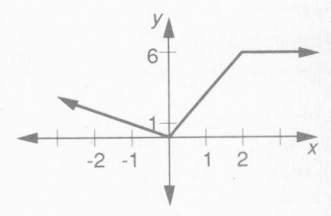

NAME

LESSON **MASTER 3–9**
QUESTIONS ON **SPUR** OBJECTIVES

■ **PROPERTIES** *Objective E (See pages 176–179 for objectives.)*

1. How does the graph of $y \le -2x + 5$ differ from the graph of $y = -2x + 5$?
   The half-plane below $y = -2x + 5$ is shaded in the graph of $y \le -2x + 5$.

In 2–5, is the point (-2, -2) in the solution set of the inequality?
Write yes or no.

2. $y < x$ no   3. $y \ge x$ yes
4. $y > 3x + 4$ no   5. $y \le -5x - 10$ yes

■ **USES** *Objective J*

6. A chemist combines x liters of water that is 8% acid and y liters of water that is 3% acid.
   a. How much water is there altogether? $x + y$ liters
   b. How much acid is there altogether? $.08x + .03y$
   c. Write an inequality stating that the combined solutions should contain no more than 3 liters of acid. $.08x + .03y \le 3$
   d. Use your answer in part (c) to determine the largest amount of the 8% solution that could be mixed with 50 liters of the 3% solution.   18.75 liters

■ **REPRESENTATIONS** *Objective L*

7. Graph the set of points that satisfy $2x - 3y < 15$.
8. Graph the set of points that satisfy $y \ge 3x$.

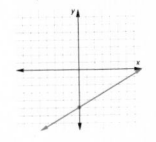

38   Advanced Algebra © Scott, Foresman and Company

SUMMARY

The Summary gives an overview of the entire chapter
and provides an opportunity
for students to consider the
material as a whole. Thus,
the Summary can be used to
help students relate the concepts presented in the
chapter.

VOCABULARY

Terms, symbols, and properties are listed by lesson to
provide a checklist of things
a student must know. Em-
phasize to students that they
should read the vocabulary
list carefully before starting
the Progress Self-Test. If students do not understand the
meaning of a term, they
should refer back to the indicated lesson.

Definitions or descriptions of
all terms in the vocabulary
list may be found in the
Glossary.

Summary

A linear equation in two variables is one that is equivalent to an equation of the form $Ax + By = C$. The graph of a linear equation is a line. If the line is not vertical, then its equation can be put into the form $y = mx + b$, with slope m and y-intercept b. Horizontal lines have slope 0 and equations of the form $y = b$. Slope is not defined for vertical lines, which have equations of the form $x = a$.

Linear equations result from two basic kinds of situations: constant increase or decrease, and linear combination. Sequences with a constant increase or decrease have a constant difference between terms. Their graphs are collinear points, and they are called linear, or arithmetic, sequences. If a_n is the nth term of an arithmetic sequence with constant difference d, then the sequence can be described explicitly as

$$a_n = a_1 + (n - 1)d$$

or recursively as

$$\begin{cases} a_1 \\ a_n = a_{n-1} + d, \text{ for } n > 1. \end{cases}$$

A graph that is the union of segments and rays is called piecewise linear. Piecewise linear graphs result from situations in which rates are constant for a while but change at known points.

A linear inequality in two variables is one that is equivalent to $Ax + By < C$ or $Ax + By \leq C$. The graph of a linear inequality is a half-plane, the set of points on one side of a line. Linear inequalities can arise from any of the situations that lead to linear equations.

Vocabulary

Below are the most important terms and phrases for this chapter. You should be able to give a definition for those terms marked with *. For all other terms you should be able to give a general description or a specific example.

Lesson 3-1
constant-increase, constant-decrease situation
slope-intercept form of a linear equation:
$y = mx + b$
* y-intercept

Lesson 3-3
linear-combination situation

Lesson 3-4
vertical line, oblique line, horizontal line
standard form of a linear equation: $Ax + By = C$
* x-intercept

Lesson 3-5
point-slope form of a linear equation: $y - y_1 = m(x - x_1)$

Lesson 3-6
* linear sequence, arithmetic sequence
* explicit formula for an arithmetic sequence:
$a_n = a_1 + (n - 1)d$

Lesson 3-7
recursive formula for an arithmetic sequence:

Lesson 3-8
piecewise linear graph

Lesson 3-9
linear inequality
half-plane
boundary

174

Progress Self-Test

Take this test as you would take a test in class. Use graph paper, a ruler, and a calculator. Then check your work with the solutions in the Selected Answers section in the back of the book. See margin.

1. Graph the line with equation $y = 3x - 5$.

2. Graph the line with equation $y = 40$. See margin.

3. Graph the set of points satisfying $x + 2y > 6$. See margin.

4. Consider the line with equation $4x - 5y = 12$.
   a. What is its slope? $\frac{4}{5}$
   b. What are its x- and y-intercepts? $3, -\frac{12}{5}$

5. The equation $y = mx + b$ models a constant-decrease situation for what values of m? negative

6. Give an equation for the line through (4, 2) and (-5, 3). $y - 2 = -\frac{1}{9}(x - 4)$

7. Give an equation of the line parallel to $y = \frac{5}{3}x + 4$ that goes through (5, -1). $5x + 3y = 28$

8. a. For what kind of lines is slope not defined?
   b. Which lines have a slope of zero?
   a) vertical lines; b) horizontal lines

In 9 and 10, a company makes 36″ and 48″ shoelaces by cutting off lengths from a spool of cord. Let S be the number of 36″ laces and L be the number of 48″ laces made.

9. How much cord will be used in making S short and L long laces? $36S + 48L$ in.

10. If a spool has 3000 inches of cord and 50 short laces are made, how many long laces can be made? 25 long laces

In 11 and 12, a scuba diver is 40 m below the surface. She ascends at a constant rate of 0.8 m/sec.

11. What will be her depth after t seconds? $-40 + .8t$

12. How long will it take to reach a depth of 10 m? 37.5 sec

13.
```
10 LET A = 1
20 FOR N = 1 TO 12
30    PRINT A
40    A = A + 5
50 NEXT N
60 END
```
1, 6, 11, 16, 21, 26, 31, 36, 41, 46, 51, 56
   a. What sequence is generated?
   b. Is the sequence arithmetic? Yes

14. Rewrite $y = \frac{1}{3}x + 2$ in standard form. $x - 3y = -6$

15. *Multiple choice* A store charges for copies:

For		
1–50 copies		5¢ each
51–200 copies		4¢ each
more than 200 copies		3¢ each

Which graph most closely describes the total cost C for printing n copies? a

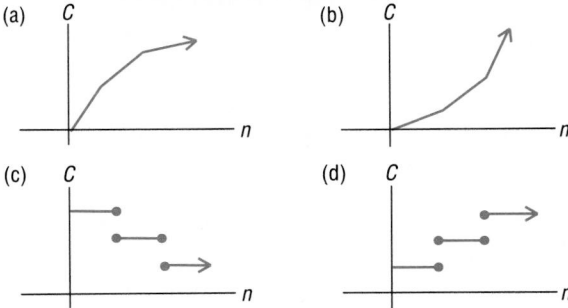

In 16 and 17, -7, -10, -13, -16, ... is an arithmetic sequence. See margin.

16. Write an explicit formula for the sequence.

17. Write a recursive formula for the sequence.

18. a. Is the origin in the solution set for the graph of $y > -3x$? Justify your answer.
    b. Is (2, -1) in the graph of $3x - 5y < 8$? Justify your answer. See margin.

19. Carlos began by swimming 20 min every day for the first week. Each week he increased his daily swim time by 15 min. After how many weeks was he swimming 110 min daily? 7 weeks

20. The graph below represents the height and horizontal distance moved by a ski lift.

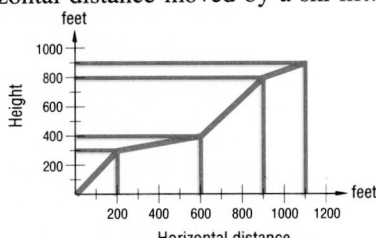

Horizontal distance

   a. What is the slope of the section whose horizontal distance goes from 600 to 900 feet? $\frac{4}{3}$
   b. Write an equation for the section in part a.

$y = \frac{4}{3}x - 400$

PROGRESS SELF-TEST

We cannot overemphasize the importance of these end-of-chapter materials. It is at this point that the material "gels" for many students, allowing them to solidify skills and understanding. In general, student performance should be markedly improved after these pages.

USING THE PROGRESS SELF-TEST
Assign the Progress Self-Test as a one-night assignment. Worked-out *solutions* for all questions are in the Selected Answers section of the student book. Encourage students to take the Progress Self-Test honestly, grade themselves, and then be prepared to discuss the test in class.

Advise students to pay special attention to those Chapter Review questions (pages 176–179) which correspond to questions missed on the Progress Self-Test. A chart provided with the Selected Answers keys the Progress Self-Test questions to the lettered SPUR Objectives in the Chapter Review or to the Vocabulary. It also keys the questions to the corresponding lessons where the material is covered.

ADDITIONAL ANSWERS
1.

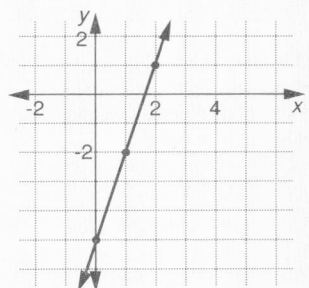

2., 3., 16., 17., and 18. See Additional Answers in the back of this book.

175

Chapter Review

Questions on **SPUR** Objectives

CHAPTER REVIEW

The main objectives for the chapter are organized here into sections corresponding to the four main types of understanding this book promotes: Skills, Properties, Uses, and Representations.

USING THE CHAPTER REVIEW
Whereas end-of-chapter material may be considered optional in some texts, in *Advanced Algebra* we have selected these objectives and questions with the expectation that they will be covered. Students should be able to answer these questions with about 85% accuracy after studying the chapter.

You may assign these questions over a single night to help students prepare for a test the next day, or you may assign the questions over a two-day period.

If you work the questions over two days, then we recommend assigning the *evens* for homework the first night so that students get feedback in class the next day, then assigning the *odds* the night before the test so students can use the answers provided in the book.

ADDITIONAL ANSWERS
11. $y - 2 = -\frac{3}{2}(x + 1)$

17.a. $a_n = 7 + 5(n - 1)$
b. $a_1 = 7$; $a_{n-1} + 5$ for $n > 1$
c. 377

18.a. $a_n = 8 - 6(n - 1)$
b. $a_1 = 8$; $a_n = a_{n-1} - 6$ for $n > 1$
c. -436

SPUR stands for **S**kills, **P**roperties, **U**ses, and **R**epresentations. The Chapter Review questions are grouped according to the SPUR Objectives for this chapter.

See margin for answers not shown on this page.

SKILLS deal with the procedures used to get answers.

■ **Objective A:** *Determine the slope and intercepts of a line given its equation. (Lessons 3-1, 3-2, 3-4)*

In 1–3, give: (a) the slope; (b) the *y*-intercept.

1. $y = 7x - 2$ a) 7; b) -2

2. $500x + 700y = 1200$ a) $-\frac{5}{7}$; b) $\frac{12}{7}$

3. $y = 4$ a) 0; b) 4

In 4–6, find: (a) the *x*-intercept; (b) the *y*-intercept.

4. $3x + 5y = 45$ a) 15; b) 9

5. $x = -4.7$ a) -4.7; b) none

6. $6y = 8x$ a) 0; b) 0

■ **Objective B:** *Find an equation for a line given two points on it, or given a point on it and its slope. (Lesson 3-5)*

7. Find an equation for the line with slope 8 containing (40, 75). $y = 8x - 245$

8. Find an equation for the line with slope -0.25 through the origin. $y = -0.25x$

9. Find an equation for the line through (2, 4) and (-1, 6). $y - 4 = -\frac{2}{3}(x - 2)$

10. Find an equation for the line through (5,-9) and (5, 14). $x = 5$

11. Find an equation for the line parallel to $3x + 2y = 9$ and passing through (-1, 2).

12. Find an equation for the line parallel to $y = 4x$, containing (11, 0). $y = 4x - 44$

■ **Objective C:** *Convert linear equations from standard form to slope-intercept form, and vice-versa. (Lessons 3-2, 3-4)*

In 13 and 14, put into slope-intercept form.

13. $2x + 6y = 12$ $y = -\frac{1}{3}x + 2$

14. $x - y = 4$ $y = x - 4$

In 15 and 16, put into standard form $Ax + By = C$ with A, B, and C integers.

15. $y = \frac{2}{3}x - \frac{5}{3}$ $2x - 3y = 5$

16. $2y - 4 = 5x$ $5x - 2y = -4$

■ **Objective D:** *Describe arithmetic sequences, both explicitly and recursively. (Lessons 3-6, 3-7)*

In 17 and 18, describe the *n*th term of each sequence: (a) in explicit form; (b) in recursive form. Then (c) find the 75th term of the sequence.

17. 7, 12, 17, 22, …

18. 8, 2, -4, -10, …

19. Give a recursive description of the sequence $a_n = 2n - 11$ $a_1 = -9$; $a_n = a_{n-1} + 2$ for $n > 1$

20. Find an explicit formula for the *n*th term of the sequence $a_n = \frac{1}{2} + (n - 1)4$
$$\begin{cases} a_1 = \frac{1}{2} \\ a_n = a_{n-1} + 4, \text{ for } n > 1. \end{cases}$$

The Chambered Nautilus shows recursive growth.

In 21 and 22, (a) find how many terms will be printed, and (b) give the first five terms the computer will print when the program is run.

21.
```
20 LET A = 100
30 FOR N = 1 TO 1000
40    PRINT A
50    A = A + 1
60 NEXT N
70 END
```
a) 1000; b) 100, 101, 102, 103, 104

22.
```
25 FOR N = 1 TO 10
35    LET AN = 2*N + 3
45    PRINT AN
55 NEXT N
65 END
```
a) 10; b) 5, 7, 9, 11, 13

PROPERTIES deal with the principles behind the mathematics.

■ **Objective E:** *Recognize properties of graphs of linear relations.* (*Lessons 3-2, 3-4, 3-5, 3-9*)

In 23–25, state whether the line is vertical, horizontal, or oblique.

23. $y = -4$ horizontal

24. $2x - 3y = 8$ oblique

25. $4x = 12$ vertical

26. Parallel lines have the same __?__.   slope

27. *Multiple choice* Which of the following does not mean a slope of $-\frac{4}{3}$?   a
(a) a vertical change of -3 units for a horizontal change of 4 units
(b) a vertical change of -4 units for a horizontal change of 3 units
(c) a vertical change of $-\frac{4}{3}$ units for a horizontal change of 1 unit
(d) a vertical change of $\frac{4}{3}$ units for a horizontal change of -1 unit

28. *True or false* The line with the equation $y - 5 = 3(x - 2)$ goes through the point $(5, 2)$.   **False**

29. How does the graph of $y > 2x - 7$ differ from the graph of $y = 2x - 7$?

In 30–32, tell whether the point $(3, 3)$ is in the solution set of the inequality.

30. $y \geq x$ yes

31. $y < x$ no

32. $y < 2x - 7$ no

■ **Objective F:** *Identify properties of the three general forms of linear relations.* (*Lessons 3-2, 3-4, 3-5*)

In 33–35, use the equation $y = mx + b$.

33. It models a constant increase if m is __?__.   positive

34. What constant represents the initial amount?   b

35. What is this form of a linear equation called?   slope-intercept

In 36 and 37, use the equation $Ax + By = C$.

36. To find the x-intercept, substitute __?__ for __?__.   0; y

37. If $A = 0$ and $B \neq 0$, the graph of this equation is a __?__ line.   horizontal

38. Give the point-slope form of a linear equation.

■ **Objective G:** *Recognize properties of arithmetic sequences.* (*Lessons 3-6, 3-7*)

39. Arithmetic sequences are formed by __?__ a __?__ to the previous term.

40. *Multiple choice* Which is not true of the graph of an arithmetic sequence?   c
(a) The graph consists of discrete points.
(b) All points on the graph are collinear.
(c) The graph is a half-plane.

In 41–44, tell whether the numbers could be the first four terms of an arithmetic sequence.

41. 1.2, 1.4, 1.6, 1.8, ...   yes

42. $\pi + 1, \pi + 2, \pi + 3, \pi + 4, ...$ yes

43. -9, -11, -13, -15, ...   yes

44. 4, 2, $\frac{1}{2}$, $\frac{1}{4}$, ...   no

29. The graph of $y > 2x - 7$ is the half-plane to the left of and above the line $y = 2x - 7$.

38. The line through (x_1, y_1) with slope m has equation $y - y_1 = m(x - x_1)$.

39. adding; constant difference

60.

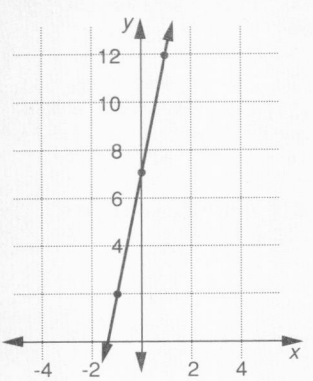

61.

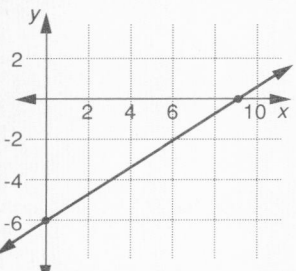

62.

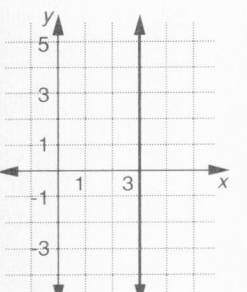

63.

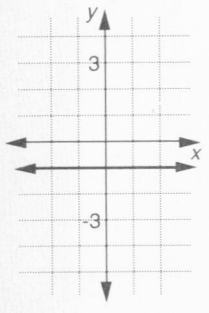

In 45–48, does the formula generate an arithmetic sequence?

45. $\begin{cases} a_1 = 1.5 \\ a_n = a_{n-1} + 13, \text{ for } n > 1 \end{cases}$ **yes**

46. $\begin{cases} a_1 = 9 \\ a_n = 2a_{n-1} \text{ for } n > 1 \end{cases}$ **no**

47. $a_n = 3n^2 + 2$ **no**

48. $a_n = 11n + 4$ **yes**

USES deal with applications of mathematics in real situations.

■ **Objective H:** *Model constant increase or constant decrease situations. (Lesson 3-1)*

In 49 and 50, a crate weighs 3 kilograms (kg) when empty. It is filled with grapefruit weighing 0.2 kg each.

49. Write an equation relating the weight w and the number n of grapefruit. $w = 3 + .2n$

50. Find the weight when there are 22 grapefruit in the crate. **7.4 kg**

In 51 and 52, a math teacher has a ream of 500 sheets of graph paper. Each week the advanced algebra class uses about 30 sheets.

51. About how many sheets are left after w weeks? $500 - 30w$

52. After how many weeks will there be 50 sheets left? **15 weeks**

■ **Objective I:** *In a real-world context, find an equation for a line containing two given points. (Lesson 3-5)*

53. Woody Bench finds that it costs his business $7,600 to make 30 desks and $16,000 to make 100 desks. Assuming a linear relationship between the cost and the number of desks, how much will it cost to make 1000 desks? **$124,000**

54. Celsius temperature and Réaumur temperature are related by a linear equation. Two pairs of corresponding temperatures are $0°C = 0°R$ and $100°C = 80°R$. Write a linear equation relating R and C, and solve it for R. $R = \frac{4}{5}C$

55. Charlotte's business finds that the cost of making shoes is linearly related to the number of shoes it makes. It costs $1450 to make 150 pairs of shoes and $1675 to make 225 pairs of shoes. $C = 3p + 1000$

a. Let C = the cost of making p pairs of shoes. Write a formula relating C to p.

b. How much will it cost to make 500 pairs of shoes? **$2500**

■ **Objective J:** *Model situations leading to linear combinations. (Lessons 3-3, 3-5, 3-9)*

56. Lubbock Lumber sells 6-foot 2-by-4s for $1.70 each and 8-foot 2-by-6s for $2.50 each. Last week they sold $250 worth of these boards. Let F be the number of 2-by-4s and S be the number of 2-by-6s.

a. Write an equation to model this situation. $1.7F + 2.5S = 250$

b. If 100 2-by-4s were sold, how many 2-by-6s were sold? **32**

57. A maintenance engineer of a swimming pool combines A gallons of water that is 6% chlorine and B gallons of water that is 8% chlorine. $A + B$ gal

a. How much water is there altogether?

b. How much chlorine is there altogether? .06A

c. At least 2 gallons of chlorine are needed .08B in the pool. Write an inequality that describes this situation. $.06A + .08B \geq 2$

■ **Objective K:** *Solve real-world problems using arithmetic sequences. (Lessons 3-6, 3-7)*

58. The number of feet traveled during each second of free fall is given by the formula $a_n = 16 + 32(n - 1)$. What distance is traveled during the eighth second? **240 ft**

59. When Florence Flask joined a laboratory she was given a $26,000 salary and promised at least an $1800 raise each year. What is the longest it could take for her salary to reach $35,000? **5 years**

178

REPRESENTATIONS deal with pictures, graphs, or objects that illustrate concepts.

■ **Objective L:** *Graph linear equations and linear inequalities. (Lessons 3-2, 3-4, 3-9)*

60. Graph the line with slope 5 and *y*-intercept 7. **See margin for 60–65.**

61. Graph the line $4x - 6y = 36$.

62. Graph $x = 3$ in the coordinate plane.

63. Graph $y = -1$ in the coordinate plane.

64. Graph the set of points that satisfy $5x + 4y \leq 40$.

65. Graph the set of points that satisfy $y < 2x$.

In 66–68, tell whether the slope of the line is positive, negative, zero, or undefined.

66.
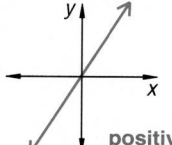
positive

67.
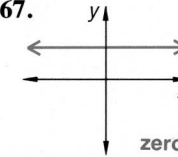
zero

68.
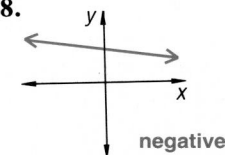
negative

69. What is an equation for the line graphed below? **x + 2y = 4**

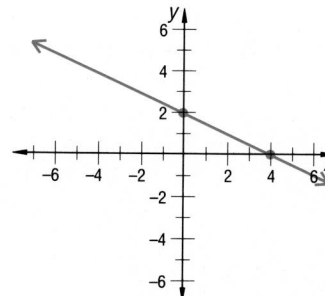

■ **Objective M:** *Graph and describe piecewise linear situations. (Lessons 3-8)*

In 70–72, refer to the graph below. Cory traveled from her cousin's house to her grandmother's and then back home.

Cory's Distance from Home

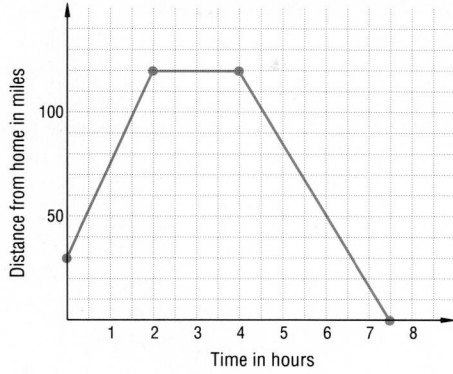

70. How far from home did Cory start? **30 mi**

71. How fast did Cory travel during the first two hours? **45 mph**

72. What was the total distance Cory traveled this day? **210 mi**

73. Graph the situation described by:
$$\begin{cases} y = x + 3, \text{ for } x > 0 \\ y = -x + 3, \text{ for } x \leq 0 \end{cases}$$ **See margin.**

74. A cheetah trots along at 5 mph for a minute, spies a small deer and speeds up to 60 mph in just 6 seconds. After chasing the deer at this speed for 30 seconds, the cheetah gives up and, over the next 20 seconds, slows to a stop. Graph this situation plotting time on the horizontal axis and speed on the vertical axis. **See margin.**

64.

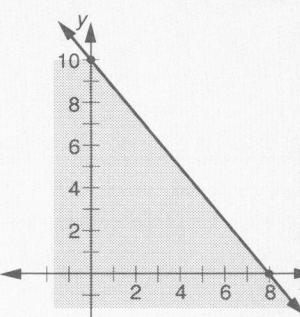

65.

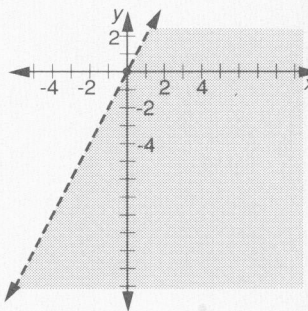

73. and 74. See Additional Answers in the back of this book.

EVALUATION
Three forms of a Chapter Test are provided in the Teacher's Resource File. Chapter 3 Test, Forms A and B cover just Chapter 3. The third test is Chapter 3 Test, Cumulative Form. About 50% of this test covers Chapter 3, 25% covers Chapter 2, and 25% covers Chapter 1. A fourth test, Comprehensive Test, Chapters 1–3, that is primarily multiple choice in format, is also provided. For information on grading, see *General Teaching Suggestions: Grading* on page T44 in the Teacher's Edition.

ASSIGNMENT RECOMMENDATION
We strongly recommend that you assign Lesson 4-1, both reading and some questions, for homework the evening of the test. It gives students work to do after they have completed the test and keeps the class moving. If you do not do this, you may cover one less *chapter* over the course of the year.

CHAPTER 4 ■ MATRICES

DAILY PACING CHART ■ CHAPTER 4

Students in the Full Course should complete all but one of the chapters by the end of the year. Students in the Minimal Course will spend more time on quizzes and the Chapter Review. As such, these students should complete about ten or eleven chapters.

DAY	MINIMAL COURSE	FULL COURSE
1	4-1	4-1
2	4-2	4-2
3	4-3	4-3
4	4-4	4-4
5	Quiz (TRF); Start 4-5.	Quiz (TRF); 4-5
6	Finish 4-5.	4-6
7	4-6	4-7
8	4-7	Quiz (TRF); 4-8
9	Quiz (TRF); Start 4-8.	4-9
10	Finish 4-8.	4-10
11	4-9	Progress Self-Test
12	4-10	Chapter Review
13	Progress Self-Test	Chapter Test (TRF)
14	Chapter Review	
15	Chapter Review	
16	Chapter Test (TRF)	

TESTING OPTIONS

TESTING OPTIONS
■ Quiz for Lessons 4-1 Through 4-4   ■ Chapter 4 Test, Form A   ■ Chapter 4 Test, Cumulative Form
■ Quiz for Lessons 4-5 Through 4-7   ■ Chapter 4 Test, Form B

INDIVIDUAL DIFFERENCES

PROVIDING FOR INDIVIDUAL DIFFERENCES

The student text is written for the *average* student. The program, however, can be adapted for both less capable and for more capable students.

A blackline master (in the Teacher's Resource File) is provided for each lesson for those students who need more practice. The Teacher's Edition frequently provides Error Analysis and Alternate Approach features to provide additional instructional strategies.

For students who require additional challenge, Extension activities are regularly provided in the Teacher's Edition.

OBJECTIVES ■ CHAPTER 4

Students should master the chapter objectives by the time they complete the chapter.
To ensure mastery, there is continual review built into each set of lesson questions.
After students complete the chapter lessons, they assess their mastery on the Progress
Self-Test. Then they do the Chapter Review and pay special attention to those questions
that match the objectives missed on the Progress Self-Test. Students can get extra
practice on these objectives by using the master for each lesson in the Teacher's
Resource File.

OBJECTIVES FOR CHAPTER 4 (Organized into the SPUR categories—Skills, Properties, Uses, and Representations)	Progress Self-Test Questions	Chapter Review Questions	Lesson Master from Teacher's Resource Book*
SKILLS			
A Perform matrix operations.	4–5, 15	1 through 11	4-2, 4-9
B Determine equations of lines perpendicular to given lines.	10	11 through 15	4-8
PROPERTIES			
C Recognize properties of operations on matrices.	3, 9	16 through 20	4-2, 4-6
USES			
D Use matrices to store data	2	21 through 23	4-1
E Use matrix addition, matrix multiplication, and scalar multiplication to solve real-world problems.	13	24 through 27	4-2, 4-9
REPRESENTATIONS			
F Relate transformations to matrices, and vice versa.	11–12, 16–18	28 through 32	4-3, 4-4, 4-5, 4-6, 4-7
G Use matrices to perform transformations.	6–8, 20	33 through 39	4-3, 4-4, 4-5, 4-6, 4-7
H Graph figures and their transformation images.	1, 19	40 through 44	4-1, 4-3, 4-4, 4-5, 4-6, 4-7

* **The masters are numbered to match the lessons.**

OVERVIEW ■ CHAPTER 4

The content of Chapter 4 will be new to most students. However, with the increase in importance of linear algebra and computers, it is content with which students need to be familiar.

There are two broad goals for Chapter 4. One goal is to study matrices as a means for storing data and solving problems. A second goal is to use matrices to review geometric transformations. The language of reflections, rotations, translations, size changes, and scale changes appears again in Chapters 5, 6, 7, 10, 12, and 14.

The chapter consists of several groups of lessons. Lessons 4-1 and 4-2 introduce students to the vocabulary and notation for matrices, their use in storing data, and the definition of matrix multiplication. Lessons 4-3 and 4-4 discuss matrices used for size and scale changes, together with those properties preserved or not preserved under such transformations. Lessons 4-5, 4-6, and 4-7 introduce matrices used for reflections and rotations. Rotations are presented as the composite of two reflections. These lessons provide

the mathematics necessary to prove the relationship between slopes of perpendicular lines that is presented in Lesson 4-8. The final two lessons deal with matrix addition and its application to the study of translations. A summary page at the end of the chapter contains all the transformation matrices presented in Chapter 4.

PERSPECTIVES ■ CHAPTER 4

The Perspectives provide the rationale for the inclusion of topics or approaches, provide mathematical background, and make connections within UCSMP.

4-1

STORING DATA IN MATRICES

The material in this lesson should be fairly easy and interesting to most students. It consists of definitions, a data storage model, and the definition of a point matrix. The lesson is important because it lays the groundwork for the rest of the chapter.

4-2

MATRIX MULTIPLICATION

There are four common elementary applications for matrix multiplication: business situations, given in this lesson; transformation applications, treated in Lesson 4-3; applications to systems, discussed in Chapter 5; and applications to networks, which are not covered in this book.

We purposely delay a discussion of systems applications because it would not introduce any new ideas. The business applications provide more interesting material.

4-3

SIZE CHANGES

Lesson 4-3 begins a study of relations between transformations and matrices. Size changes may be familiar to students from their work in geometry. For students who have studied transformations, this lesson can be covered quickly and thus provide additional time to work with matrix multiplication, if necessary.

A size change or size transformation is sometimes called a *dilatation,* or *dilation,* an *expansion* or *contraction,* or a *homothety.* In this material, the use of subscripts provide the magnitude of the size change.

4-4

SCALE CHANGES

Size changes stretch or shrink a figure by the same amount in both the horizontal and vertical directions. In contrast, a scale change can affect the figure by different amounts in the two directions. Therefore, two subscripts are needed to identify the scale change.

Note that we require magnitudes on both size changes and scale changes to be positive. This does not have to be the case; there can be negative scale changes. If one factor is negative, a reflection is performed; if both factors are negative, then a 180° rotation is performed. Our reason for keeping the magnitudes positive is for simplicity of the properties. In Chapter 12, scale changes are used to relate circles to ellipses.

4-5

REFLECTIONS

One reason that reflections are such important transformations is that the preimage and image figures are congruent. The image looks backwards because orientation is reversed. Another reason reflections are important is their intimate connection with bilateral symmetry, so common in the real world and in mathematics (it is a property of all the conics and of sine waves). A third reason is that the graphs of inverse functions are reflection images of each other over the line $y = x$, which is discussed in Chapter 7.

4-6

TRANSFORMATIONS AND MATRICES
This lesson groups size changes, scale changes, reflections, and rotations under the general heading of transformations. The student text does not use the word function to describe transformations, but they are certainly functions. Each transformation has a domain (the entire plane), a rule for the function, and a range (the entire plane again). Each preimage point has a clearly defined image point.

Composition of transformations and its notation are also introduced. The concept of composition will be further developed with functions in Chapter 7. Students familiar with transformations should not have a difficult time relating transformations and their composites to matrices. Other students may need more practice with composites of transformations.

4-7

ROTATIONS
By this point in the chapter, most students should feel comfortable with transformations and the matrices which represent them. Rotations are interesting examples of transformations that will give students more practice with matrices.

It is important not to skip this lesson. Rotations are used in the next lesson to prove the theorem that states that the product of slopes of two perpendicular lines is negative one. And in Chapter 10, these transformations form the basis for the definition of cos x and sin x.

In this lesson, we consider matrices only for rotations whose magnitudes are integral multiples of 90°. But other rotations have matrices also. All the matrices in this lesson are special cases of the matrix $\begin{bmatrix} \cos \theta & -\sin \theta \\ \sin \theta & \cos \theta \end{bmatrix}$ for R_θ.

4-8

PERPENDICULAR LINES
The major concept of this lesson is the theorem which expresses the relationship between the slopes of two perpendicular lines. The proof of this theorem is demonstrated by using the rotation of 90°.

Although this particular proof is not used in some books, we believe that it best explains the situation. Stress that $R_{90}(x, y) = (-y, x)$; thus, R_{90} switches coordinates and changes the sign on the second coordinate. When the same changes are made to both pairs of coordinates (x_1, y_1) and (x_2, y_2) in the formula for the slope m of the original line, the result is the slope of the perpendicular line. This slope turns out to be the negative reciprocal of the original slope—that is, $-\frac{1}{m}$.

4-9

MATRIX ADDITION
This lesson introduces the operation of matrix addition and subtraction. The other main idea presented in this lesson is the concept of scalar multiplication. The definition is natural and easy to understand. Students should realize that multiplying by a scalar k is equivalent to multiplying by a matrix for a size change.

Both addition and scalar multiplication of matrices are fundamental operations in linear algebra. Our goal in this lesson is simply to introduce these operations so that

(1) students will see how matrices can represent translations (this is done in Lesson 4-10); and (2) the next time these operations are encountered, students will feel familiar with them.

4-10

TRANSLATIONS
Translations provide the most basic way to modify graphs. After completing this lesson, students should be able to view many of the graphs they will encounter in mathematics as translations of basic graphs. For instance:

The line $y = mx + b$ is the image of $y = mx$ under $T_{0, b}$.

The sine curve $y = \sin(x - b)$ is the image of $y = \sin x$ under $T_{b, 0}$.

The parabola $y = a(x - h)^2 + k$ is the image of $y = ax^2$ under $T_{h, k}$.

The circle $(x - h)^2 + (y - k) = r^2$ is the image of $x^2 + y^2 = r^2$ under $T_{h, k}$.

It is from the last two of these that we have chosen the letters to represent the general slide $T_{h, k}$.

This lesson emphasizes the algebraic definition of a translation because it is independent of the figure being translated, whereas with the matrix description, the dimensions of $T_{h, k}$ depend on the dimensions of the preimage polygon. Also, in Lesson 6-4, students will encounter the Graph-Translation Theorem. Understanding that theorem requires that students know the algebraic definition of $T_{h, k}$.

CHAPTER 4

We recommend 13 to 16 days for this chapter: 10 to 12 on the lessons; 1 for the Progress Self-Test; 1 or 2 for the Chapter Review; and 1 for a Chapter test. (See the Daily Pacing Chart on page 180A.) If you spend more than 16 days on this chapter, you are moving too slowly. Keep in mind that each lesson includes Review questions to help students firm up content studied previously.

USING PAGES 180-181

The study of matrices can be introduced by discussing with students the need to store and manipulate data. Point out that many problems in the real world are very complex because they require the manipulation of large quantities of data. For example, predictions of how the U.S. economy will perform in the future are based upon the analysis of very large quantities of data. Matrices are used to make these kinds of predictions.

A second use of matrices is to describe geometric *transformations*. Transformations are not only mathematically interesting, but they also enable the geometry of congruence and similarity to be applied in algebra.

Matrices

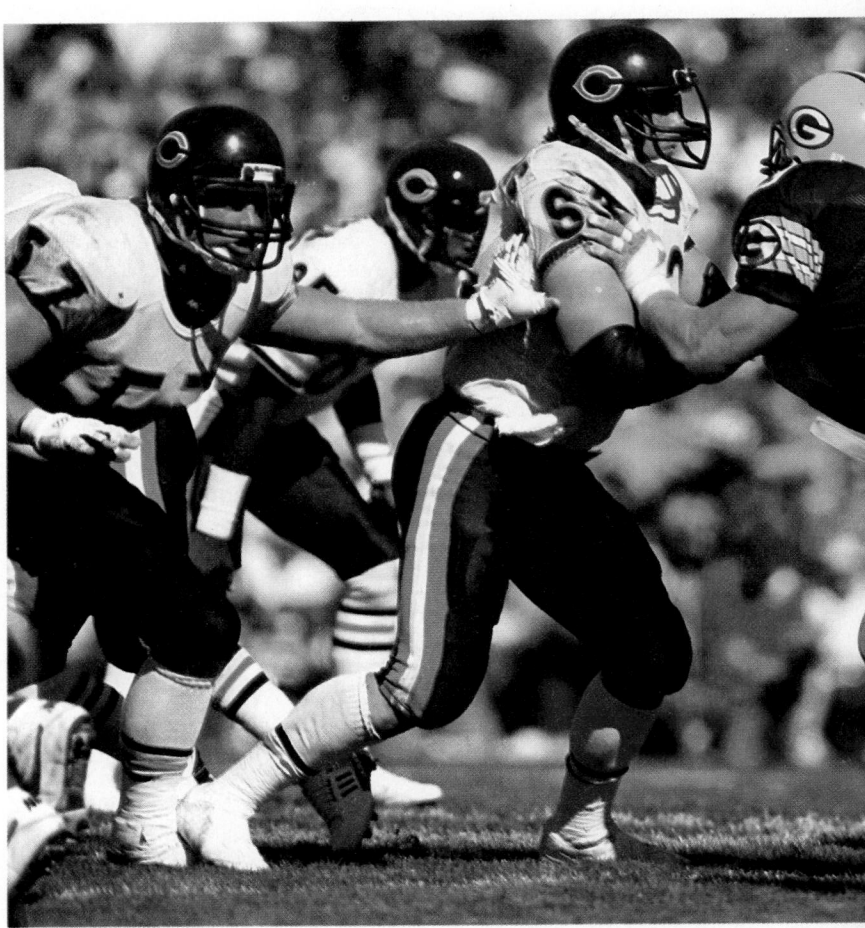

180

A *matrix* is a rectangular arrangement of objects, each of which is called an *element* of the matrix. The plural of "matrix" is "matrices." One use of matrices is to store data. In the matrix below, the elements are numbers representing the performance of five professional football teams in the 1985 season. The titles of the rows and columns are not part of the matrix.

National Football Conference
Central Division Results
1985

	W	L	Pts. Earned	Opponents' Pts.
Chicago	15	1	456	198
Green Bay	8	8	337	355
Minnesota	7	9	346	359
Detroit	7	9	307	366
Tampa Bay	2	14	294	448

A second use of matrices is to describe transformations of various geometric figures. On the graph, *QUAD* has been reflected over the *x*-axis. The vertices of *QUAD* may be described by a matrix. You will learn that the image *Q'U'A'D'* can be calculated by multiplying two matrices.

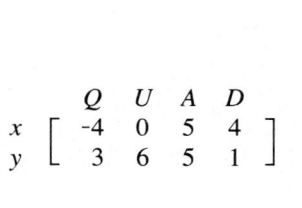

$$
\begin{array}{c}
\quad\; Q \;\; U \;\; A \;\; D \\
x \begin{bmatrix} -4 & 0 & 5 & 4 \\ 3 & 6 & 5 & 1 \end{bmatrix} \\
y
\end{array}
$$

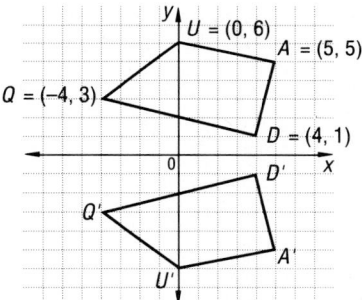

A third use of matrices, which is even more geometric, is to describe the pictures you see on television screens and computer monitors. These matrices are rectangular arrays of square dots.

In this chapter you will study various operations using matrices and how those operations can be applied to geometric transformations and real life situations.

RESOURCES
■ Lesson Master 4-1
▨ Visual for Teaching Aid 14 provides the matrices used in Additional Examples 1 and 2.
▨ Visual for Teaching Aid 15 displays the heptagon used in Additional Example 3.

OBJECTIVES

D Use matrices to store data.
H Graph a figure denoted by a matrix.

TEACHING NOTES

It is important that students understand that the dimensions of a matrix denote the number of rows and columns and do not refer to the values of the elements. Point out to students that in everyday language, both rows and columns of a matrix are "in a row," but only the column is "in a column."

When discussing **Example 1,** stress the definition of equality for matrices. If two matrices do not have the same dimensions, they cannot be equal. Although M_1 and M_2 are each acceptable ways to store the same data, they are not equal matrices.

Explain that point matrices are of dimension $2 \times n$, where n is the number of points represented by the matrix. Stress that a $2 \times n$ matrix can stand for other things as well, for instance, n pieces of information on two people. When a $2 \times n$ matrix is used as a point matrix, this will be stated or easily inferred from the context of a problem.

LESSON

Storing Data in Matrices

Information is often stored in matrices. The inventory of athletic clothing owned by a high-school cross-country team is shown in the matrix below.

	sweat pants	sweat shirts	shorts	
small	9	10	8	row 1
medium	18	20	19	row 2
large	20	24	23	row 3
x-large	11	11	(12)	row 4
	column 1	column 2	column 3	

the element in the 4th row and 3rd column

The elements of this matrix are enclosed by large square brackets. (Sometimes large parentheses are used in place of brackets.) This matrix has 4 rows and 3 columns. It is said to have *dimensions* 4 by 3, written 4×3. In general, a matrix with m rows and n columns has **dimensions $m \times n$.**

182

Example 1 The Matterhorn Company produced 1500 trumpets and 1200 French horns in September; 2000 trumpets and 1400 French horns in October; 900 trumpets and 700 French horns in November.
  a. Store the company's production in a matrix.
  b. What are the dimensions of the matrix?

Solution
  a. There are two matrices that can be written. Matrix M_1 has the months as rows and matrix M_2 has the months as columns. Either matrix is an acceptable way to store the data.

Matrix M_1

$$\begin{array}{c} \\ \text{Sept.} \\ \text{Oct.} \\ \text{Nov.} \end{array} \begin{array}{cc} \text{trumpets} & \text{French horns} \\ \left[\begin{array}{cc} 1500 & 1200 \\ 2000 & 1400 \\ 900 & 700 \end{array}\right] \end{array}$$

Matrix M_2

$$\begin{array}{c} \\ \text{trumpets} \\ \text{French horns} \end{array} \begin{array}{ccc} \text{Sept.} & \text{Oct.} & \text{Nov.} \\ \left[\begin{array}{ccc} 1500 & 2000 & 900 \\ 1200 & 1400 & 700 \end{array}\right] \end{array}$$

  b. Matrix M_1 has 3 rows and 2 columns, so its dimensions are 3×2. Matrix M_2 has 2 rows and 3 columns, so its dimensions are 2×3.

Although matrices M_1 and M_2 are equivalent ways to store the data, the two matrices are not considered equal. Two **matrices are equal** if and only if they have the same dimensions and corresponding elements are equal.

Points and polygons can also be represented by matrices. The ordered pair (x, y) is generally represented by the matrix

$$\left[\begin{array}{c} x \\ y \end{array}\right].$$

This 2×1 matrix is called a **point matrix.** Notice that the element in the first row is the x-coordinate and the element in the second row is the y-coordinate. Thus the point $(5, -1)$ is represented by the matrix

$$\left[\begin{array}{c} 5 \\ -1 \end{array}\right].$$

Similarly, polygons can be written as matrices. The first row of the matrix contains the x-coordinates of the vertices in the order in which the polygon is named. The second row contains the corresponding y-coordinates. Example 2 on page 184 illustrates this.

LESSON 4-1 Storing Data in Matrices 183

1. Use the matrix below to answer the questions.

Medals Won in 1984 Summer Olympic Games

	Gold	Silver	Bronze	Total
U.S.	83	61	30	174
W. Ger.	17	19	23	59
Romania	20	16	17	53
Canada	10	18	16	44
Britain	5	10	22	37
China	15	8	9	32
Italy	14	6	12	32
Japan	10	8	14	32
France	5	7	15	27
all others	47	66	84	197

a. What are the dimensions of the matrix?
10 × 4
b. What does the element in the 5th row and 2nd column indicate?
The number of silver medals won by Britain was 10.
c. To what does the element 83 refer?
the number of U.S. gold medals
d. How many bronze medals did France win?
15
e. What are the dimensions of the matrix obtained when the rows and columns are interchanged?
4 × 10

2. The following is a matrix of temperatures in degrees Fahrenheit from selected cities on August 1, 1987.

	High	Low
Paris	66	59
London	70	57
Moscow	75	57
Beijing	86	70
Lima	69	57
Montreal	76	53

a. What are the dimensions of this matrix?
6 × 2
b. What does the element in the 3rd row and 2nd column represent?
the low temperature in Moscow on August 1, 1987
c. What does the element 76 tell you?
the high temperature in Montreal on August 1, 1987

d. What was the low temperature in Lima on August 1, 1987?
57° F

e. Represent the same data in a 2 × 6 matrix.

sample:

	Par. Lon.	Mos.	Beij.	Lima	Mon.
H:	66	70	75	86	69 76
L:	59	57	57	70	57 53

$$\text{H:} \begin{bmatrix} 66 & 70 & 75 & 86 & 69 & 76 \\ 59 & 57 & 57 & 70 & 57 & 53 \end{bmatrix}$$

3. Use the heptagon below to answer the questions.

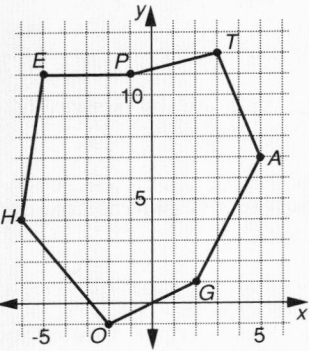

a. Give the matrix for polygon *HEPTAGO*.

$$\begin{bmatrix} -6 & -5 & -1 & 3 & 5 & 2 & -2 \\ 4 & 11 & 11 & 12 & 7 & 1 & -1 \end{bmatrix}$$

b. Give the matrix for polygon *TAGOHEP*.

$$\begin{bmatrix} 3 & 5 & 2 & -2 & -6 & -5 & -1 \\ 12 & 7 & 1 & -1 & 4 & 11 & 11 \end{bmatrix}$$

c. Are the two matrices for parts (a) and (b) equal? Why or why not?
No; corresponding elements are not equal.

ADDITIONAL ANSWERS
3.a. 5   b. 4   c. 5 × 4

4.a. 2   b. 5   c. 2 × 5

$$8. \begin{bmatrix} 1500 & 1200 \\ 2000 & 1400 \\ 900 & 700 \\ 2500 & 3800 \end{bmatrix}$$

11.b. No, corresponding elements are not equal.

$$12. \quad \begin{array}{ccc} & T & R & I \end{array}$$
$$x \begin{bmatrix} -1 & 2 & -2 \\ -2 & 3 & 4 \end{bmatrix} y$$

Example 2
a. Write pentagon *PENTA* as a matrix.
b. Write pentagon *NEPAT* as a matrix.
c. Are the two matrices equal?

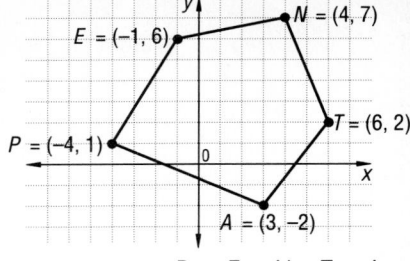

Solution
a. Starting with the coordinates of *P*, write the *x*-coordinates in the first row and the *y*-coordinates in the second row.

$$\begin{array}{cccccc} & P & E & N & T & A \end{array}$$
$$\begin{array}{c} x \\ y \end{array} \begin{bmatrix} -4 & -1 & 4 & 6 & 3 \\ 1 & 6 & 7 & 2 & -2 \end{bmatrix}$$

b. Start with the coordinates of *N*.

$$\begin{array}{cccccc} & N & E & P & A & T \end{array}$$
$$\begin{array}{c} x \\ y \end{array} \begin{bmatrix} 4 & -1 & -4 & 3 & 6 \\ 7 & 6 & 1 & -2 & 2 \end{bmatrix}$$

c. The two matrices are not equal because all corresponding elements are not equal. However, both matrices are valid ways to represent the polygon.

Questions

Covering the Reading

1. What is a matrix?   **A rectangular arrangement of objects**

2. *True or false* Each element in a matrix must be a number.   **False**

In 3 and 4, for each matrix state: (a) the number of rows; (b) the number of columns; and (c) the dimensions.

3. the National Football League matrix on page 181.   **See margin.**

4. the matrix for pentagon *PENTA* above.   **See margin.**

In 5–7, refer to the clothing matrix at the start of this lesson.

5. How many large sweatshirts did the cross-country team have?   **24**

6. What type of clothing does the element in the 2nd row, 3rd column represent?   **medium shorts**

7. What does the sum of the elements in the 3rd column represent?
total number of shorts

8. Refer to Example 1. Suppose the Matterhorn Company produces 2500 trumpets and 3800 French horns in December. Construct a 4 × 2 matrix that gives the company's production through December.
See margin.

184

9. The ordered pair (a, b) can be represented by the matrix __?__. This matrix is called a __?__ matrix. $\begin{bmatrix} a \\ b \end{bmatrix}$; **point**

10. *Multiple choice* Which represents the point $(-1, 4)$?   **c**

    (a) $\begin{bmatrix} -1 & 4 \end{bmatrix}$ (b) $\begin{bmatrix} 4 & -1 \end{bmatrix}$

    (c) $\begin{bmatrix} -1 \\ 4 \end{bmatrix}$ (d) $\begin{bmatrix} 4 \\ -1 \end{bmatrix}$

11. Refer to Example 2. $\begin{bmatrix} -1 & -4 & 3 & 6 & 4 \\ 6 & 1 & -2 & 2 & 7 \end{bmatrix}$
    a. Write pentagon EPATN as a matrix.
    b. Are the matrices for EPATN and PENTA equal? Why or why not?
    See margin.

Applying the Mathematics

12. Write $\triangle TRI$ as a matrix.   **See margin.**

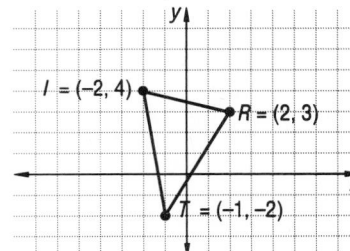

13. The matrix below gives the numbers of active duty U.S. military personnel as of 1986.

	Commissioned Officers	Enlisted Personnel
Army	105,060	731,905
Navy	70,291	500,810
Marines	20,175	177,850
Air Force	108,400	488,600

    b) the total number of enlisted Navy personnel
    a. What are the dimensions of this matrix?   **4 × 2**
    b. What does the sum of the elements in row 2 represent?
    c. What does the sum of the elements in column 1 represent?
    the total number of commissioned officers

14. If $\begin{bmatrix} 7 & 4 \\ y & 2 \end{bmatrix} = \begin{bmatrix} x & 4 \\ 8 & 2 \end{bmatrix}$, then $x =$ __?__ and $y =$ __?__.   **7, 8**

15. If $\begin{bmatrix} 3a + 1 \\ b + 4 \end{bmatrix} = \begin{bmatrix} 7 \\ 4 \end{bmatrix}$, then $a =$ __?__ and $b =$ __?__.   **2, 0**

NAME _____

■ **USES**   *Objective D (See pages 241–243 for objectives.)*

1. According to the Census Bureau, in 1986, 13.8% of elementary school teachers were men and 86.2% were women. In the middle grades, 38.6% were men and 61.4% were women. In high school, 53% were men and 47% were women. Store this information in a 3 × 2 matrix.

	men	women
elementary school	13.8	86.2
middle grades	38.6	61.4
high school	53.0	47.0

2. A poll conducted by the Lincoln High School newspaper found that the average weekly allowance for freshmen boys is $4, freshmen girls is $3.50, sophomore boys is $6, sophomore girls is $5, junior boys is $6.50, junior girls is $7, senior boys is $8.25, and senior girls is $8.50. Store the data in a 4 × 2 matrix.

	boys	girls
freshman	4.00	3.50
sophomore	6.00	5.00
junior	6.50	7.00
senior	8.25	8.50

3. The matrix at the right gives Census Bureau figures on the average earnings of workers in thousands of dollars. What element gives the earnings of a woman machine operator?

	Men	Women
executive	35.0	21.4
salesperson	26.8	12.9
machine operator	20.6	12.3
farmer	10.7	8.0

the element in the 3rd row, 2nd column: 12.3

NAME _____
Lesson MASTER 4–1 (page 2)

■ **REPRESENTATIONS**   *Objective H*

4. Draw the polygon described by the matrix $\begin{bmatrix} -1 & 5 & 3 \\ 1 & 3 & -5 \end{bmatrix}$

5. Draw the polygon described by the matrix $\begin{bmatrix} 1 & 4 & -2 & -2 \\ -3 & -2 & -6 & 1 \end{bmatrix}$

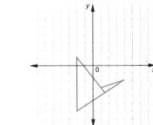

In 6 and 7, write a matrix for the given polygon.

6.

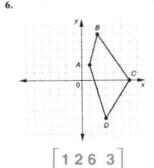

7.

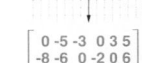

$\begin{bmatrix} 1 & 2 & 6 & 3 \\ 2 & 6 & 0 & -5 \end{bmatrix}$ $\begin{bmatrix} 0 & -5 & -3 & 0 & 3 & 5 \\ -8 & -6 & 0 & -2 & 0 & 6 \end{bmatrix}$

Question 18: You may wish to have students sketch special cases of $y = kx$ by hand or with an automatic grapher before they attempt to answer this question.

Question 20: You may need to point out the relationship $y = \frac{36}{x}$ between x and y.

MORE PRACTICE
For more questions on SPUR Objectives, use *Lesson Master 4-1,* shown on page 185.

ADDITIONAL ANSWERS
16.a. sample:

	from Adam	from Barbara	from Clem
to Adam	0	2	5
to Barbara	3	0	3
to Clem	1	4	0

Rows and columns could be interchanged.
b. Adam wrote 4; Barbara wrote 6; Clem wrote 8.

17.

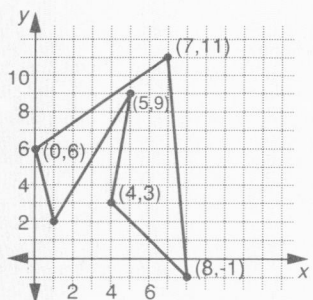

18a. The line becomes very steep but rotates no more than 45°.
b. The line becomes very flat but rotates no more than 45°.

---

16. Three cousins, Adam, Barbara, and Clem, write to each other from time to time. Last year Adam received 2 letters from Barbara and 5 from Clem; Barbara received 3 from Adam and 3 from Clem. Clem received 1 from Adam and 4 from Barbara.   See margin.
    a. Organize this information in a 3 × 3 matrix. (Hint: There are three 0s in the matrix.)
    b. How many letters did each cousin write?

17. The matrix $\begin{bmatrix} 7 & 8 & 4 & 5 & 1 & 0 \\ 11 & -1 & 3 & 9 & 2 & 6 \end{bmatrix}$ describes a hexagon.

    Graph this hexagon.   See margin.

Review

18. Consider the line $y = kx$ graphed on a coordinate plane in which the scales on the x- and y-axes are the same. In one sentence, describe how the position of the line $y = kx$ changes as k changes from the number 1 to:
    a. a large positive real number,   See margin.
    b. a very small positive fraction,   See margin.
    c. a negative real number. *(Lesson 2-4)*
       The line rotates clockwise between 45° and 135°.
19. Which four of the following describe the graph of $y = -4x^2$? *(Lesson 2-5)*
    a. hyperbola   b. direct variation
    c. parabola   d. inverse variation
    e. continuous   f. symmetric to y-axis   b, c, e, f

20. Find the next two terms in the following inverse-variation sequence: *(Lessons 1-3, 2-7)*
    $(1, 36), (2, 18), (3, 12), (4, 9), (5, 7.2)$.   (6, 6), (7, 5.14)

Exploration

21. Sports results in newspapers are often tabulated as matrices. Look in a newspaper to find an example of a matrix different from that in this lesson.   Many answers are possible; baseball, basketball, soccer, and hockey statistics are often given in matrices.

LESSON
4-2

Matrix Multiplication

RESOURCES
■ Lesson Master 4-2
▣ Visual for Teaching Aid 16 displays the matrices of **Examples 1 and 2.**
▣ Visuals for Teaching Aids 17 and 18 provide the matrices for **Questions 4, 5, 8, 10, 11, 13, 14, and 16.**

OBJECTIVES

A Multiply matrices.
C Recognize properties of matrix multiplication.
E Use matrix multiplication to solve real-world problems.

TEACHING NOTES

We recommend the following approach when teaching matrix multiplication. First, explain multiplying a row by a column. Then, point out that matrices can be multiplied only when the number of columns of the left matrix equals the number of rows of the right matrix. Next, show how to determine the dimensions of the product. Then, find each element of the product matrix as the product of the row and the column that element is in.

Emphasize the pairing of the elements in a row with the elements in a column. When multiplying

$$[4\ 6\ 3] \cdot \begin{bmatrix} 2 \\ 9 \\ 1 \end{bmatrix},$$

students should see that every element in the row has a corresponding element in the column. In contrast, if

In linear-combination applications, it is quite useful to store data in matrices which can then be multiplied. For instance, a movie theater charges $5 for adults over 17, $2 for students 13–17 years old, and $1 for children 12 or under. What is the cost for 7 adults, 4 students, and 3 children under 12 to enter this theater?

The answer is $7 \cdot \$5 + 4 \cdot \$2 + 3 \cdot \$1 = \$46$. This is the same arithmetic needed to calculate the *product* of these two matrices.

$$[\ 7\quad 4\quad 3\ ] \quad \cdot \quad \begin{bmatrix} 5 \\ 2 \\ 1 \end{bmatrix}$$

number of people   cost per
in each category   category

Matrix multiplication is done by multiplying a row by a column. Multiply the first element in the row by the first element in the column, the second element in the row by the second element in the column, and so on. Finally, add the resulting products. The product is the 1×1 matrix [46], corresponding to the $46 total cost for the movie.

$$[\ 7\quad 4\quad 3\ ] \cdot \begin{bmatrix} 5 \\ 2 \\ 1 \end{bmatrix} = [\ 7 \cdot 5 + 4 \cdot 2 + 3 \cdot 1\ ] = [\ 46\ ]$$

If the left matrix has 2 rows and the right matrix 3 columns, then there are 6 ways to multiply a row by a column. That is exactly what is done to multiply two larger matrices. The 6 numbers are put in 2 rows and 3 columns in a natural way.

Example 1 Let $A = \begin{bmatrix} 8 & -2 \\ 4 & 1 \end{bmatrix}$ and $B = \begin{bmatrix} 1 & 3 & 5 \\ 0 & 4 & 2 \end{bmatrix}$. Find AB.
               2×2 2×3

LESSON 4-2 Matrix Multiplication   **187**

$$[4 \; 6 \; 3 \; 8] \cdot \begin{bmatrix} 2 \\ 9 \\ 1 \end{bmatrix},$$

they cannot do so because 8 has no corresponding element.

ADDITIONAL EXAMPLES

In **1** and **2,** write the product as one matrix.

1. $\begin{bmatrix} 2 & 1 & 9 \\ 8 & 5 & -6 \end{bmatrix} \cdot \begin{bmatrix} 1 & 4 \\ -3 & 7 \\ 5 & 3 \end{bmatrix}$

$\begin{bmatrix} 44 & 42 \\ -37 & 49 \end{bmatrix}$

2. $\begin{bmatrix} 1 & 4 \\ -3 & 7 \\ 5 & 3 \end{bmatrix} \cdot \begin{bmatrix} 2 & 1 & 9 \\ 8 & 5 & -6 \end{bmatrix}$

$\begin{bmatrix} 34 & 21 & -15 \\ 50 & 32 & -69 \\ 34 & 20 & 27 \end{bmatrix}$

3. Joe and Bob both tutor mathematics. They each charge $10 per hour for one person and $25 an hour for a small group. Each week Joe tutors 3 people individually and works with 2 small groups. Bob tutors 5 people individually and works with 1 small group.
a. Write a matrix C representing their charges.

$C = \begin{array}{l} \text{individual} \\ \text{small group} \end{array} \begin{bmatrix} 10 \\ 25 \end{bmatrix}$

b. Write a matrix T representing the number they tutor each week.

$T = \begin{array}{l} \text{Joe} \\ \text{Bob} \end{array} \begin{bmatrix} 3 & 2 \\ 5 & 1 \end{bmatrix}$

c. Find TC.
$TC =$

$\begin{bmatrix} 3 & 2 \\ 5 & 1 \end{bmatrix} \begin{bmatrix} 10 \\ 25 \end{bmatrix} = \begin{bmatrix} 80 \\ 75 \end{bmatrix} \begin{array}{l} \text{Joe} \\ \text{Bob} \end{array}$

d. What does TC represent?
TC represents the total amount earned by each tutor.

Solution Find the dimensions of AB. The product has the same number of rows as the first matrix and the same number of columns as the second matrix. So AB has 2 rows and 3 columns. Now fill in AB. The product of row 1 of A and column 1 of B is

$$8 \cdot 1 + -2 \cdot 0 = 8.$$

This is put in the 1st row and 1st column of the answer. Thus far we have

$$\begin{bmatrix} \boxed{8} & -2 \\ 4 & 1 \end{bmatrix} \begin{bmatrix} \boxed{1} & 3 & 5 \\ \boxed{0} & 4 & 2 \end{bmatrix} = \begin{bmatrix} \boxed{8} & \text{—} & \text{—} \\ \text{—} & \text{—} & \text{—} \end{bmatrix}.$$

The product of row 1 of A and column 2 of B is $8 \cdot 3 + -2 \cdot 4 = 16$. Now you know the element in the 1st row and 2nd column of the answer.

$$\begin{bmatrix} \boxed{8} & -2 \\ 4 & 1 \end{bmatrix} \begin{bmatrix} 1 & \boxed{3} & 5 \\ 0 & \boxed{4} & 2 \end{bmatrix} = \begin{bmatrix} 8 & \boxed{16} & \text{—} \\ \text{—} & \text{—} & \text{—} \end{bmatrix}$$

The other four elements of P are found using this

row ☐ by column ☐ pattern.

For instance, the element in the 2nd row, 3rd column of AB is found by multiplying the 2nd row of A by the 3rd column of B, shown here along with the final result.

$$\begin{bmatrix} 8 & -2 \\ \boxed{4} & \boxed{1} \end{bmatrix} \begin{bmatrix} 1 & 3 & \boxed{5} \\ 0 & 4 & \boxed{2} \end{bmatrix} = \begin{bmatrix} 8 & 16 & 36 \\ 4 & 16 & \boxed{22} \end{bmatrix}$$

Definition of matrix multiplication:

Suppose A is an $m \times n$ matrix and B is an $n \times p$ matrix. Then the product $A \cdot B$ or AB is the $m \times p$ matrix whose element in row i and column j is the product of row i of A and column j of B.

Notice that the product of two matrices exists only if the rows of the left matrix can be multiplied by the columns of the right matrix. Thus *the product of two matrices A and B exists only when the number of columns of A equals the number of rows of B.* So if A is $m \times n$, B must be $n \times p$ in order for AB to exist.

$$\begin{bmatrix} 8 & -2 \\ 4 & 1 \end{bmatrix} \begin{bmatrix} 1 & 3 & 5 \\ 0 & 4 & 2 \end{bmatrix} \qquad \begin{bmatrix} 1 & 3 & 5 \\ 0 & 4 & 2 \end{bmatrix} \begin{bmatrix} 8 & -2 \\ 4 & 1 \end{bmatrix}$$

$2 \times 2 \qquad 2 \times 3 \qquad\qquad 2 \times 3 \qquad 2 \times 2$

equal   not equal

These matrices can be multiplied.   These matrices cannot be multiplied.

188

These two cases indicate that in general, *multiplication of matrices is not commutative.*

The following example illustrates a situation requiring multiplication of more than two matrices.

Example 2

Costumes have been designed for the school play. Each boy's costume requires 5 yards of fabric, 4 yards of ribbon, and 3 packets of sequins. Each girl's costume requires 6 yards of fabric, 5 yards of ribbon, and 2 packets of sequins. Fabric costs $4 per yard; ribbon costs $2 per yard; and sequins cost $.50 per packet. Costumes are needed for 8 boys and 10 girls. Find the total cost of making these costumes.

Solution The information can be stored in three matrices.

$$
\begin{array}{c} \text{Boys}\;\;\text{Girls} \\ \begin{bmatrix} 8 & 10 \end{bmatrix} \\ \text{number of} \\ \text{costumes} \end{array}
\begin{array}{c} \text{Fabric}\;\;\text{Ribbon}\;\;\text{Sequins} \\ \begin{bmatrix} 5 & 4 & 3 \\ 6 & 5 & 2 \end{bmatrix} \\ \text{materials for} \\ \text{one costume} \end{array}
\begin{array}{c} \text{cost} \\ \begin{bmatrix} 4 \\ 2 \\ .50 \end{bmatrix} \\ \text{unit cost} \\ \text{of material} \end{array}
$$

The total cost of making the costumes is given by the product of these three matrices. To multiply more than two matrices, multiply two at a time using the definition given earlier.

$$
\begin{bmatrix} 8 & 10 \end{bmatrix} \left(\begin{bmatrix} 5 & 4 & 3 \\ 6 & 5 & 2 \end{bmatrix} \begin{bmatrix} 4 \\ 2 \\ .50 \end{bmatrix} \right)
$$

$$
= \begin{bmatrix} 8 & 10 \end{bmatrix} \begin{bmatrix} 5 \cdot 4 + 4 \cdot 2 + 3 \cdot .50 \\ 6 \cdot 4 + 5 \cdot 2 + 2 \cdot .50 \end{bmatrix}
$$

$$
= \begin{bmatrix} 8 & 10 \end{bmatrix} \begin{bmatrix} 29.50 \\ 35 \end{bmatrix}
$$

$$
= \begin{bmatrix} 8 \cdot 29.50 + 10 \cdot 35 \end{bmatrix}
$$

$$
= \begin{bmatrix} 586 \end{bmatrix}
$$

The total cost is $586.

Notice that in Example 2 we calculated the cost of making one boy's costume ($29.50) and one girl's costume ($35) and then multiplied this matrix by the matrix representing the number of boy's and girl's costumes needed. In Question 8, you are asked to verify that the result is the same if you first find the total amount of material needed for all costumes and then multiply by the matrix giving the unit cost of each item. You will be verifying an instance that, in general, *matrix multiplication is associative.*

Questions

In 1 and 2, multiply the column by the row.

1. $\begin{bmatrix} 3 & 5 & 7 \end{bmatrix} \begin{bmatrix} 1 \\ 0 \\ -2 \end{bmatrix} = \begin{bmatrix} \underline{\ ?\ } \end{bmatrix} \begin{bmatrix} -11 \end{bmatrix}$

2. $\begin{bmatrix} 1 & -1 & 1 & -1 \end{bmatrix} \begin{bmatrix} 10 \\ 9 \\ 8 \\ 7 \end{bmatrix} = \begin{bmatrix} \underline{\ ?\ } \end{bmatrix} \begin{bmatrix} 2 \end{bmatrix}$

In 3 and 4, (a) determine the dimensions of each matrix; (b) decide if the product can or cannot be found; and (c) if so, find the product; if not, tell why not.

3. $\begin{bmatrix} 8 & 1 & 0 \\ 6 & 3 & -4 \end{bmatrix} \begin{bmatrix} 2 & 8 \\ 5 & 4 \end{bmatrix}$
See margin.

4. $\begin{bmatrix} 9 & 4 & 8 & 6 \\ 2 & 0 & 3 & 1 \\ 1 & -2 & 5 & 0 \end{bmatrix} \begin{bmatrix} 12 & 2 \\ 15 & 1 \\ 3 & 9 \\ 8 & 11 \end{bmatrix}$
See margin.

5. Let $M = \begin{bmatrix} 6 & 2 \\ 0 & 3 \end{bmatrix}$ and $N = \begin{bmatrix} 5 & 8 & -2 \\ -4 & 1 & 0 \end{bmatrix}$. Find the

elements in $MN = \begin{bmatrix} \underline{\ ?\ } & \underline{\ ?\ } & \underline{\ ?\ } \\ \underline{\ ?\ } & \underline{\ ?\ } & \underline{\ ?\ } \end{bmatrix}$. $\begin{bmatrix} 22 & 50 & -12 \\ -12 & 3 & 0 \end{bmatrix}$

6. If A has dimensions 11×15 and B has dimensions 15×19, what are the dimensions of AB? $\quad 11 \times 19$

7. If A is $m \times n$ and B is $p \times q$, when does AB exist? $\quad$ when $n = p$

In 8 and 9, refer to Example 2.

8. Verify that $\left(\begin{bmatrix} 8 & 10 \end{bmatrix} \begin{bmatrix} 5 & 4 & 3 \\ 6 & 5 & 2 \end{bmatrix} \right) \begin{bmatrix} 4 \\ 2 \\ .50 \end{bmatrix} = \begin{bmatrix} 586 \end{bmatrix}$.
See margin.

9. What property is verified using the results from Example 2 and Question 8? $\quad$ Matrix multiplication is associative.

In 10 and 11, suppose $X = \begin{bmatrix} 3 & 0 & 5 \\ -1 & 4 & 2 \end{bmatrix}$ and $Y = \begin{bmatrix} 2 & -2 \\ 0 & 1 \\ -3 & 4 \end{bmatrix}$.

Calculate each product.

10. XY $\begin{bmatrix} -9 & 14 \\ -8 & 14 \end{bmatrix}$

11. YX $\begin{bmatrix} 8 & -8 & 6 \\ -1 & 4 & 2 \\ -13 & 16 & -7 \end{bmatrix}$

12. *True or false* Matrix multiplication is commutative. $\quad$ False

190

13. The matrix $\begin{bmatrix} 1 & 0 \\ 0 & 1 \end{bmatrix}$ is called the **2 × 2 identity matrix** for

multiplication. To see why, calculate the products in parts a and b.

a. $\begin{bmatrix} 1 & 0 \\ 0 & 1 \end{bmatrix}\begin{bmatrix} a & b \\ c & d \end{bmatrix}\quad\begin{bmatrix} a & b \\ c & d \end{bmatrix}$

b. $\begin{bmatrix} a & b \\ c & d \end{bmatrix}\begin{bmatrix} 1 & 0 \\ 0 & 1 \end{bmatrix}\quad\begin{bmatrix} a & b \\ c & d \end{bmatrix}$

c. *True or false* Matrix multiplication with the identity matrix is commutative.   **True**

In 14 and 15, the matrix D below gives the daily delivery of cases of bakery products to two restaurants.

	whole wheat	white	rye	English muffins
Shorty's	5	10	3	5
Slim's	0	15	8	10

The matrix C below gives the unit cost for each item in the bakery.

whole wheat	.70
white	.70
rye	.65
English muffin	.80

14. a. Find DC. $\begin{bmatrix} 16.45 \\ 23.70 \end{bmatrix}$
b. What is the daily cost of bakery products at Shorty's?   **$16.45**

15. Shorty's restaurant is open 20 days this month and Slim's is open 25 days. Let M = [20 25]. Find the total cost of bakery items for the month at these two restaurants.   **$921.50**

16. Solve for x. $\begin{bmatrix} 3 & 1 \\ 0 & 2 \end{bmatrix}\begin{bmatrix} x \\ 9 \end{bmatrix} = \begin{bmatrix} 10 \\ 18 \end{bmatrix}$ $\frac{1}{3}$

---

8. $[8\ 10]\begin{bmatrix} 5 & 4 & 3 \\ 6 & 5 & 2 \end{bmatrix} =$
[100 82 44];

[100 82 44] $\begin{bmatrix} 4 \\ 2 \\ .50 \end{bmatrix} = $ **[586]**

NAME

LESSON MASTER 4–2
QUESTIONS ON **SPUR** OBJECTIVES

■**SKILLS** *Objective A* *(See pages 241–243 for objectives.)*
In 1–4, calculate the product.

1. $[3\ 8\ -2]\begin{bmatrix} 5 \\ 1 \\ 0 \end{bmatrix} =$ **23**   **2.** $\begin{bmatrix} 7 & 2 \\ 1 & 11 \end{bmatrix}\begin{bmatrix} 6 & 3 \\ 1 & -5 \end{bmatrix} = \begin{bmatrix} 44 & 11 \\ 17 & -52 \end{bmatrix}$

3. $\begin{bmatrix} 1 & 6 \\ -3 & 2 \end{bmatrix}\begin{bmatrix} -2 & \frac{1}{2} \\ 0 & 5 \end{bmatrix} = \begin{bmatrix} -2 & 30\frac{1}{2} \\ 6 & 8\frac{1}{2} \end{bmatrix}$

4. $\left([1\ -8\ 5]\begin{bmatrix} 3 & 9 \\ 5 & 2 \\ 1 & 8 \end{bmatrix}\right)\begin{bmatrix} 1 & -10 \\ 3 & 5 \end{bmatrix} =$ **[67 485]**

■**PROPERTIES** *Objective C*

5. $\begin{bmatrix} 7 & 8 \\ 0 & 2 \\ 1 & 13 \end{bmatrix} \times A = \begin{bmatrix} -14 & 24 \\ 0 & 6 \\ -2 & 39 \end{bmatrix}$ What are the dimensions of A? **2 × 2**

6. a. *True or false* Matrix multiplication is always commutative. **false**

b. Use $\begin{bmatrix} 8 & -2 \\ 6 & -5 \end{bmatrix}$ and $\begin{bmatrix} -2 & 1 \\ 3 & -8 \end{bmatrix}$ to support your answer to part (a).

$\begin{bmatrix} 8 & -2 \\ 6 & -5 \end{bmatrix}\begin{bmatrix} -2 & 1 \\ 3 & -8 \end{bmatrix} = \begin{bmatrix} -22 & -8 \\ -27 & -34 \end{bmatrix}$ and

$\begin{bmatrix} -2 & 1 \\ 3 & -8 \end{bmatrix}\begin{bmatrix} 8 & -2 \\ 6 & -5 \end{bmatrix} = \begin{bmatrix} -10 & -1 \\ 72 & -46 \end{bmatrix}$

In 7 and 8, state whether the product exists. Do not actually perform a computation. Write yes or no.

7. $\begin{bmatrix} 5 & 7 & 8 \\ -12 & 1 & -5 \end{bmatrix}\begin{bmatrix} 2 \\ 0 \end{bmatrix}$ **no**   **8.** $\begin{bmatrix} 21 & 8 \\ 0 & -1 \\ 5 & 9 \end{bmatrix}\begin{bmatrix} 6 & 5 \\ 0 & 3 \end{bmatrix}$ **yes**

NAME
Lesson MASTER 4–2 (page 2)

9. X and Y are matrices. X has dimensions $w \times v$ and Y has dimensions $v \times t$.
a. Which product exists, XY or YX? **XY**
b. What are the dimensions of your answer in part (a)? **w × t**

10. What 3 × 3 matrix is the identity for multiplication? $\begin{bmatrix} 1 & 0 & 0 \\ 0 & 1 & 0 \\ 0 & 0 & 1 \end{bmatrix}$

■**USES** *Objective E*

11. When a volleyball team wins, they go to Burgerama. A single hamburger costs $2.10, a double costs $2.85, and a triple costs $3.60. The team's order for their first victory consisted of 2 singles, 8 doubles, and 4 triples. After their second victory, they ordered 1 single, 7 doubles, and 6 triples. Write matrices C and N for the costs and numbers ordered, then find CN to determine the total costs of the orders.

$C = [2.10\ 2.85\ 3.60]$ $N = \begin{bmatrix} 2 & 1 \\ 8 & 7 \\ 4 & 6 \end{bmatrix}$

$CN =$ **[$41.40 $43.65]; first order: $41.40; second order: $43.65**

12. An athletic shoe manufacturer compiled data on the performance of their largest outlets. Sales (in thousands of pairs) of the company's three main products are summarized below.

	Outlet A	Outlet B	Outlet C
running shoes	72	12	25
basketball shoes	38	8	21
tennis shoes	51	15	38

Running shoes cost $25, basketball shoes cost $35, and tennis shoes cost $30. Use matrix multiplication to find the total revenue of each outlet.

Multiply by $\begin{bmatrix} 25 \\ 35 \\ 30 \end{bmatrix}$; **[4660 1030 2500]**

Outlet A: $4660.00; Outlet B: $1030.00; Outlet C: $2500.00

ADDITIONAL ANSWERS
17.

$$\begin{bmatrix} 50 & 40 & 17 \\ 100 & 80 & 3 \\ 42 & 58 & 5 \end{bmatrix}, \begin{bmatrix} 50 & 100 & 42 \\ 40 & 80 & 58 \\ 17 & 3 & 5 \end{bmatrix}$$

18.a.

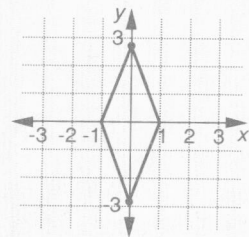

c.

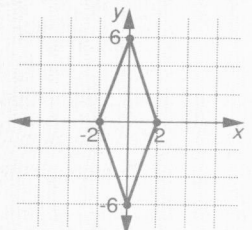

**19. The distance between
(1, 5) and (7, 6) is $\sqrt{37}$;
between (1, 5) and (-5, 4)
is $\sqrt{37}$. The triangle is
isosceles.**

Review

17. In June, the Faucets & Fixtures Company produced 50 porcelain sinks, 40 stainless steel sinks, and 17 molded plastic sinks. In July, they produced 100 porcelain, 80 stainless steel, and 3 molded plastic sinks. In August they produced 42 porcelain, 58 stainless steel, and 5 molded plastic sinks. Write two different 3×3 matrices to store these data. *(Lesson 4-1)*   See margin.

18. Use the matrix $\begin{bmatrix} 0 & -1 & 0 & 1 \\ 3 & 0 & -3 & 0 \end{bmatrix}$.

   a. Graph the polygon represented by the matrix. *(Lesson 4-1)*   See margin.
   b. What kind of polygon is it? *(Previous course)*   rhombus
   c. Graph the image of this polygon under a size change of magnitude 2. *(Previous course)*   See margin.

19. The matrix $\begin{bmatrix} 1 & 7 & -5 \\ 5 & 6 & 4 \end{bmatrix}$ can represent a triangle. Use the distance formula to show that this triangle is isosceles. *(Lesson 4-1, previous course)*   See margin.

20. In this figure, $\triangle ADB \sim \triangle AEC$. If $DE = 12$, find BC and CE. *(Previous course)*   BC = 9, CE = 6

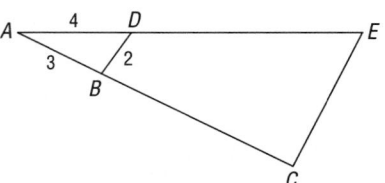

Exploration

21. In Question 13 you worked with the 2×2 identity matrix. Make a conjecture regarding the 3×3 identity matrix for multiplication. Test your conjecture on the general 3×3 matrix.

$$\begin{bmatrix} a & d & g \\ b & e & h \\ c & f & i \end{bmatrix}$$

$$\begin{bmatrix} 1 & 0 & 0 \\ 0 & 1 & 0 \\ 0 & 0 & 1 \end{bmatrix} \begin{bmatrix} a & d & g \\ b & e & h \\ c & f & i \end{bmatrix} = \begin{bmatrix} a & d & g \\ b & e & h \\ c & f & i \end{bmatrix} \begin{bmatrix} 1 & 0 & 0 \\ 0 & 1 & 0 \\ 0 & 0 & 1 \end{bmatrix} = \begin{bmatrix} a & d & g \\ b & e & h \\ c & f & i \end{bmatrix}$$

192

LESSON 4-3

Size Changes

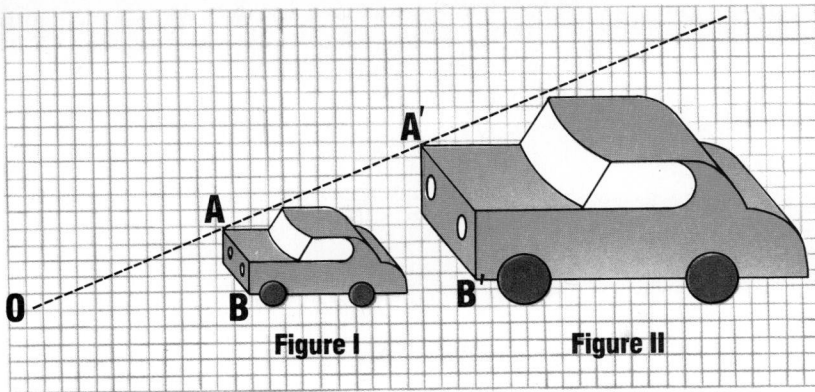

Figure I   **Figure II**

In the drawing above, figure I and point O were given. We call figure I the **preimage**. The points on figure II are located in the following way. For each point A on figure I, a corresponding point A' (read "A prime") is found for figure II. The position of A' is determined by the following rules:

$$A' \text{ is on } \overleftrightarrow{OA}$$

$$\frac{OA'}{OA} = 2$$

This procedure was repeated with point B to find B' and with all other key points on the smaller car.

The resulting figure II is called a **size change image** of figure I. Specifically, the above size change has center O and magnitude 2. The two figures are similar with the ratio of similitude being 2.

Size changes with centers at (0, 0) are easy to do using matrices.

As you have seen, matrices can represent geometric figures. For example, if $P = (3, 1)$, $Q = (-4, 0)$, and $R = (-3, -2)$, then $\triangle PQR$ can be represented by the matrix

$$\begin{bmatrix} 3 & -4 & -3 \\ 1 & 0 & -2 \end{bmatrix}.$$

Notice what happens when this matrix is multiplied by $\begin{bmatrix} 3 & 0 \\ 0 & 3 \end{bmatrix}$.

$$\begin{bmatrix} 3 & 0 \\ 0 & 3 \end{bmatrix} \begin{bmatrix} 3 & -4 & -3 \\ 1 & 0 & -2 \end{bmatrix} = \begin{bmatrix} 9 & -12 & -9 \\ 3 & 0 & -6 \end{bmatrix}$$
$$\quad\quad\quad\quad P \quad Q \quad R \quad\quad\quad\quad\quad P' \quad Q' \quad R'$$

LESSON 4-3

RESOURCES
■ Lesson Master 4-3

OBJECTIVES

F Relate size changes to matrices, and vice versa.
G Perform size changes with center (0, 0) using matrices.
H Graph figures and their size change images.

TEACHING NOTES

Encourage students to draw preimage and image figures. Have students calculate lengths of sides to verify that the ratio of image length to preimage length is the magnitude of the size change. By determining angle measurements and slopes of segments, students can verify that these quantities are preserved under size changes.

Because corresponding angle measurements are equal and corresponding lengths are in the same ratio (size change magnitude), the preimage and image are similar. Thus, size changes are similarity transformations. The magnitude of the size transformation is the ratio of similitude.

LESSON 4-3 Size Changes   **193**

193

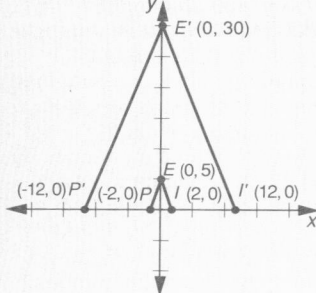
The product can also be considered as a triangle. We call it $\triangle P'Q'R'$, (read "triangle P prime, Q prime, R prime"). Multiplying by

$$\begin{bmatrix} 3 & 0 \\ 0 & 3 \end{bmatrix}$$

has transformed the original triangle. $\triangle PQR$ is the preimage; $\triangle P'Q'R'$ is its image.

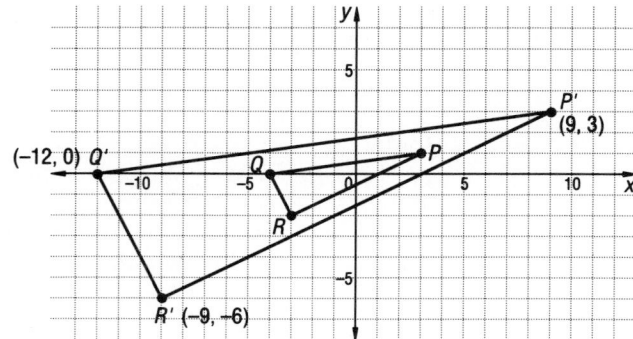

Recall from geometry that this transformation is called a **size change of magnitude** or **scale factor** 3. We denote this size change by S_3. We write

$$S_3 (3, 1) = (9, 3)$$
$$S_3 (-4, 0) = (-12, 0)$$
$$S_3 (-3, -2) = (-9, -6)$$

We read the first one as "A size change of magnitude 3 maps (3, 1) onto (9, 3)." Since $\begin{bmatrix} 3 & 0 \\ 0 & 3 \end{bmatrix} \begin{bmatrix} x \\ y \end{bmatrix} = \begin{bmatrix} 3x \\ 3y \end{bmatrix}$, in general

$$S_3 (x, y) = (3x, 3y).$$

We read this as "A size change of magnitude 3 maps any point (x, y) onto the point $(3x, 3y)$."

In general, S_k represents the size change with center (0, 0) and magnitude $k \neq 0$. In earlier courses, you may have learned that $S_k(x, y) = (kx, ky)$. Now, with matrix multiplication,

$$\begin{bmatrix} k & 0 \\ 0 & k \end{bmatrix} \begin{bmatrix} x \\ y \end{bmatrix} = \begin{bmatrix} kx + 0y \\ 0x + ky \end{bmatrix}$$

$$= \begin{bmatrix} kx \\ ky \end{bmatrix}.$$

This proves the following theorem.

194

Theorem:

$$\begin{bmatrix} k & 0 \\ 0 & k \end{bmatrix} \text{ is the matrix for } S_k.$$

Example Given *ABCD* with *A* = (0, 3), *B* = (-2, -4), *C* = (-6, -4), and *D* = (-6, 4), find the image *A'B'C'D'* under S_5.

Solution Write *ABCD* and S_5 in matrix form and multiply.

$$\underset{S_5}{\begin{bmatrix} 5 & 0 \\ 0 & 5 \end{bmatrix}} \underset{(ABCD)}{\begin{bmatrix} 0 & -2 & -6 & -6 \\ 3 & -4 & -4 & 4 \end{bmatrix}} = \underset{A'B'C'D'}{\begin{bmatrix} 0 & -10 & -30 & -30 \\ 15 & -20 & -20 & 20 \end{bmatrix}}$$

Thus *A'B'C'D'* has vertices *A'* = (0, 15), *B'* = (-10, -20), *C'* = (-30, -20), and *D'* = (-30, 20).

Check Graph the preimage and image. They should look similar, and they do.

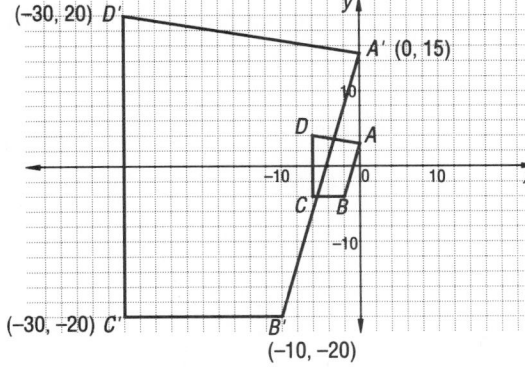

In similar figures, (1) corresponding angles are congruent and (2) ratios of corresponding segments equal the ratio of similitude. Referring back to the Example, (1) $\angle D \cong \angle D'$ and (2) $\dfrac{D'C'}{DC} = \dfrac{40}{8} = 5$.

The ratio of similitude is thus the same as the magnitude of the size change. Any two other corresponding distances will have the same ratio. For instance,

$$AB = \sqrt{(-2 - 0)^2 + (-4 - 3)^2} = \sqrt{53}$$

and $A'B' = \sqrt{(-10 - 0)^2 + (-20 - 15)^2} = \sqrt{1325}.$

Thus $\dfrac{A'B'}{AB} = \dfrac{\sqrt{1325}}{\sqrt{53}} = 5,$

which is the scale factor.

In general, a size change of magnitude *k* multiplies distances by *k* so that the ratio of image lengths to preimage lengths is *k*.

LESSON 4-3 Size Changes **195**

6. Find the slope of each side of $\triangle PIE$ and $\triangle P'I'E'$.
slope of $\overline{PI}$ = slope of $\overline{P'I'}$ = 0
slope of $\overline{IE}$ = slope of $\overline{IE}$ = $-\frac{5}{2}$
slope of $\overline{EP}$ = slope of $\overline{E'P'}$ = $\frac{5}{2}$

7. *True or false*
Corresponding sides of $\triangle PIE$ and $\triangle P'I'E'$ are parallel.
true

8. Is $\triangle PIE \sim \triangle P'I'E'$? Why or why not?
Yes; corresponding sides are in proportion.

9. Find the area of $\triangle PIE$.
$A = \frac{1}{2}$ (4)(5) = 10

10. Find the area of $\triangle P'I'E'$.
$A = \frac{1}{2}$ (24)(30) = 360

11. Find the ratio of the larger area to the smaller area.
36:1

Additional Example 11 is worthy of discussion as it is a demonstration that the ratio of area of image to area of preimage is the magnitude squared.

NOTES ON QUESTIONS

Question 11: Encourage students to make a sketch. It will help them to see that the equation of the line is in the form $y = kx$ and that the slope is $\frac{4}{3}$.

Questions 17 and 18: Note again instances showing that matrix multiplication is not commutative. In **Question 17c,** the product can only be calculated in one order. Although both *MN* and *NM* exist in **Question 18,** they are not equal.

ADDITIONAL ANSWERS

1. A size change of magnitude 3 maps (3, 1) onto (9, 3).

2. triangle *P*-prime, *Q*-prime, *R*-prime

10.b.

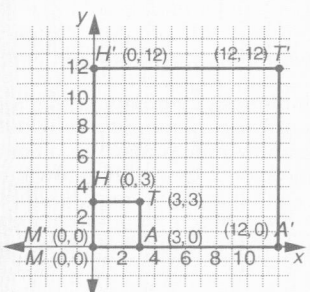

12. $\triangle ABC = \begin{bmatrix} 6 & -4 & 2 \\ 8 & 2 & -2 \end{bmatrix}$

$\triangle A'B'C' = \begin{bmatrix} 3 & -2 & 1 \\ 4 & 1 & -1 \end{bmatrix}$

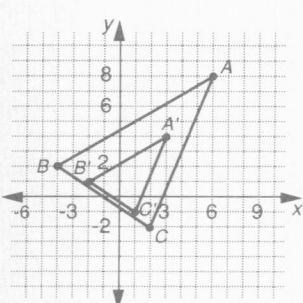

| Covering the Reading |

In 1 and 2, how is the expression read?

1. $S_3: (3, 1) = (9, 3)$ See margin.

2. $\triangle P'Q'R'$ See margin.

3. Refer to $\triangle PQR$ and $\triangle P'Q'R'$ in this lesson.
   a. $\triangle P'Q'R'$ is the image of $\triangle PQR$ under what transformation? S_3
   b. What is the matrix for this transformation? $\begin{bmatrix} 3 & 0 \\ 0 & 3 \end{bmatrix}$

4. The matrix $\begin{bmatrix} k & 0 \\ 0 & k \end{bmatrix}$ is associated with a(n) __?__ change with center __?__ of magnitude __?__.   size; (0, 0); $k \neq 0$

In 5 and 6, refer to the Example in the lesson.

5. What are the coordinates of the image of point *B*?   (-10, -20)

6. What is the scale factor?   5

True or false In 7–9, under a size change,

7. an angle and its image are congruent.   True

8. a segment and its image are congruent.   False

9. a figure and its image are similar.   True

10. Let the quadrilateral *MATH* be represented by the matrix $\begin{bmatrix} 0 & 3 & 3 & 0 \\ 0 & 0 & 3 & 3 \end{bmatrix}$.

   a. Calculate the image $M'A'T'H'$ of this quadrilateral under $\begin{bmatrix} 4 & 0 \\ 0 & 4 \end{bmatrix}$. $\begin{bmatrix} 0 & 12 & 12 & 0 \\ 0 & 0 & 12 & 12 \end{bmatrix}$

   b. Graph the preimage and image.   See margin.
   c. What type of quadrilateral is *MATH*?   square
   d. What type of quadrilateral is $M'A'T'H'$?   square

| Applying the Mathematics |

11. Suppose $P = (3, 4)$ and P' is the image of P under a size change with center $O = (0, 0)$ and magnitude 2.5.

   a. Verify that $\dfrac{OP'}{OP} = 2.5$. $P' = (7.5, 10); \dfrac{OP'}{OP} = \dfrac{12.5}{5} = 2.5$
   b. Give an equation for the line containing O, P, and P'. $y = \frac{4}{3}x$

12. $\triangle ABC$ has matrix $\begin{bmatrix} 6 & -4 & 2 \\ 8 & 2 & -2 \end{bmatrix}$. Graph $\triangle ABC$ and its image $\triangle A'B'C'$ under $S_{1/2}$.   See margin.

13. Refer to the Example in the lesson.
  a. Find the slope of $\overline{AB}$. $\frac{7}{2}$
  b. Find the slope of $\overline{A'B'}$. $\frac{7}{2}$
  c. Is $\overline{AB}$ parallel to $\overline{A'B'}$? Why or why not? Yes, because the slopes are equal.
  d. Is $\overline{AD} \parallel \overline{A'D'}$? Justify your answer. Yes, because slopes are $\frac{-1}{6}$.

14. In the example, verify that $\frac{A'D'}{AD} = 5$. $\frac{A'D'}{AD} = \frac{\sqrt{925}}{\sqrt{37}} = 5$

15. A 4 × 5 drawing is enlarged to 8 × 10 by using a size change. $\begin{bmatrix} 2 & 0 \\ 0 & 2 \end{bmatrix}$

  a. What is the matrix for the size change?
  b. The three people in the drawing have noses located at points (1, 3.5), (1.5, 3.1), and (2, 4.1). Write a matrix for the location of their noses in the enlargement.
  c. The noses in the enlargement are how many times as long as the noses in the original drawing? twice as long 15b) $\begin{bmatrix} 2 & 3 & 4 \\ 7 & 6.2 & 8.2 \end{bmatrix}$

Review

16. A matrix lists the vertices of an *n*-gon. What are the dimensions of the matrix? *(Lesson 4-1)* 2 × n

17. A clothing manufacturer has factories in Chicago, Minneapolis, and Syracuse. Sales (in thousands) can be summarized by the following matrix S.

	Blouses	Dresses	Skirts	Slacks
Chicago	9	14	12	18
Minneapolis	5	7	7	10
Syracuse	3	3	2	4

  a. What are the dimensions of S? 3 × 4
  b. The selling price of a blouse is $25, of a dress is $70, of a skirt is $30, and of a pair of slacks is $30. Write a 4 × 1 matrix representing the selling prices of the items. See margin.
  c. Use matrix multiplication to determine the total revenue of each factory. *(Lessons 4-1, 4-2)* See margin.

18. Let $M = \begin{bmatrix} 1 & 3 \\ 5 & 7 \end{bmatrix}$ and $N = \begin{bmatrix} -8 & -6 \\ -4 & -2 \end{bmatrix}$. Calculate:

  a. *MN* See margin.   **b.** *NM* *(Lesson 4-2)* See margin.

19. Solve for *a* and *b*: $\begin{bmatrix} 2 & a \\ 3 & b \end{bmatrix} \begin{bmatrix} 5 \\ 6 \end{bmatrix} = \begin{bmatrix} 7 \\ 8 \end{bmatrix}$. $a = \frac{-1}{2}$; $b = \frac{-7}{6}$ *(Lesson 4-2)*

LESSON 4-3 Size Changes **197**

NOTES ON QUESTIONS
Question 20: In geometry, you might answer this question by using the Fundamental Theorem of Similarity: The ratio of areas of similar figures is the square of the ratio of similitude. In this course, you might use the equivalent direct variation formulation: If figures are similar, then their areas vary as the square of corresponding sides.

Question 23: It is helpful for students to draw graphs when trying to compute the new areas.

17.b. $\begin{bmatrix} 25 \\ 70 \\ 30 \\ 30 \end{bmatrix}$

c. Chicago: $2,105,000
Minneapolis: $1,125,000
Syracuse: $465,000

18.a. $MN = \begin{bmatrix} -20 & -12 \\ -68 & -44 \end{bmatrix}$

b. $NM = \begin{bmatrix} -38 & -66 \\ -14 & -26 \end{bmatrix}$

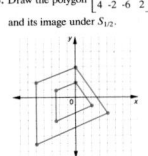
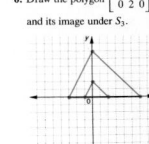

MORE PRACTICE
For more questions on SPUR
Objectives, use *Lesson Master 4-3*, shown on page 197.

ADDITIONAL ANSWERS
21.

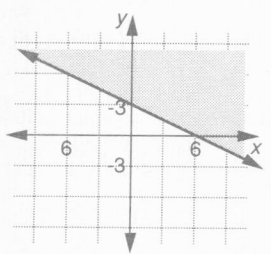

23.a. $\begin{bmatrix} 0 & 4 & 4 & 0 \\ 0 & 0 & 4 & 4 \end{bmatrix}$

b. $\begin{bmatrix} 0 & 6 & 6 & 0 \\ 0 & 0 & 6 & 6 \end{bmatrix}$

c. $\begin{bmatrix} 0 & 8 & 8 & 0 \\ 0 & 0 & 8 & 8 \end{bmatrix}$

d. $\begin{bmatrix} 0 & 10 & 10 & 0 \\ 0 & 0 & 10 & 10 \end{bmatrix}$

e.

Original Area	Matrix	New Area
4 units²	$\begin{bmatrix} 2 & 0 \\ 0 & 2 \end{bmatrix}$	16 units²
4 units²	$\begin{bmatrix} 3 & 0 \\ 0 & 3 \end{bmatrix}$	36 units²
4 units²	$\begin{bmatrix} 4 & 0 \\ 0 & 4 \end{bmatrix}$	64 units²
4 units²	$\begin{bmatrix} 5 & 0 \\ 0 & 5 \end{bmatrix}$	100 units²

f. The new area equals the original area times the square of the magnitude of the size change, or New Area = Original Area · k^2.

---

20. Two figures, F and G, are similar. The perimeter of F is 20 cm and of G is 15 cm. If the area of F is 100 cm², what is the area of G? *(Previous course)*   56.25 cm²

21. Graph $2x + 4y \geq 12$. *(Lesson 3-9)*   See margin.

22. Refer to the graph below. The graph shows the location of an elevator over a one minute period. *(Lessons 2-4, 3-8)*

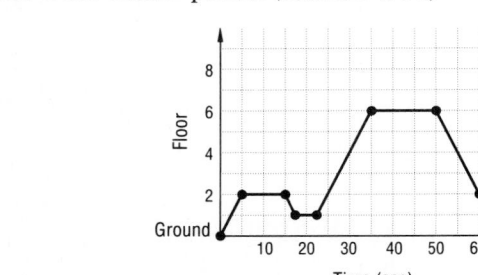

22a) from the 35th to the 50th second

a. When is the elevator on the sixth floor?   from the 35th to the 50th second
b. At what rate does the elevator ascend?   1 floor/2.5 sec, or .4 floor/sec
c. Does the elevator descend at the same rate it ascends?   Yes

Exploration

23. $ABCD$ is the square defined by the matrix $\begin{bmatrix} 0 & 2 & 2 & 0 \\ 0 & 0 & 2 & 2 \end{bmatrix}$.

Transform $ABCD$ by multiplying its matrix by each of the following size-change matrices (and by some others of your own choice).
See margin.

a. $\begin{bmatrix} 2 & 0 \\ 0 & 2 \end{bmatrix}$ **b.** $\begin{bmatrix} 3 & 0 \\ 0 & 3 \end{bmatrix}$ **c.** $\begin{bmatrix} 4 & 0 \\ 0 & 4 \end{bmatrix}$ **d.** $\begin{bmatrix} 5 & 0 \\ 0 & 5 \end{bmatrix}$

e. Find the area of each new shape. Enter your results in a table like this one:

Original Area	Matrix	New Area
4 units²	$\begin{bmatrix} 2 & 0 \\ 0 & 2 \end{bmatrix}$	_?_ units²
4 units²	$\begin{bmatrix} 3 & 0 \\ 0 & 3 \end{bmatrix}$	_?_ units²
_?_	$\begin{bmatrix} 4 & 0 \\ 0 & 4 \end{bmatrix}$	_?_
_?_	$\begin{bmatrix} 5 & 0 \\ 0 & 5 \end{bmatrix}$	_?_

f. There is a connection between the entries of a matrix associated with a size change and the effect the matrix has on the area of a shape. What is this connection?

198

Scale Changes

In contrast to a size change, which you studied in the previous lesson, a **scale change** can change a figure by stretching or shrinking it in either a horizontal direction only, in a vertical direction only, or in both directions.

| Original | Horizontal scale change of magnitude 2 (a stretch) | Vertical scale change of magnitude ⅓ (a shrink) | Horizontal and Vertical scale change |

The scale change $S_{a,b}$ combines a horizontal scale change of magnitude a with a vertical scale change of magnitude b. Here we require the magnitudes a and b to be positive. If a magnitude is larger than 1, the scale change is a *stretch* in that direction. When a magnitude is less than 1, the scale change is a *shrink* in that direction.

Definition:

The scale change $S_{a,b}$ is the transformation that maps (x, y) onto (ax, by).

Example 1

Given $\triangle ABC$ with $A = (0, 3)$, $B = (-2, -4)$, and $C = (4, 0)$. Find the image $\triangle A'B'C'$ of $\triangle ABC$ under $S_{2,5}$.

Solution $S_{2,5}(x, y) = (2x, 5y)$. That is, each image point is found by multiplying the x-coordinate of the preimage by 2 and the y- coordinate by 5.

$S_{2,5}(0, 3) = (0, 15)$
$S_{2,5}(-2, -4) = (-4, -20)$
$S_{2,5}(4, 0) = (8, 0)$

$\triangle A'B'C'$ has vertices $A' = (0, 15)$, $B' = (-4, -20)$, and $C' = (8, 0)$.

LESSON 4-4   Scale Changes   199

RESOURCES
■ Lesson Master 4-4
■ Quiz for Lessons 4-1 Through 4-4

OBJECTIVES

F Relate scale changes to matrices, and vice versa.
G Perform scale changes using matrices.
H Graph figures and their scale change images.

TEACHING NOTES

Name a rectangle
$\begin{bmatrix} 0 & 4 & 4 & 0 \\ 0 & 0 & 3 & 3 \end{bmatrix}$ *QUAD* and
have students compare it to its image under $S_{2,5}$. Students should see that the ratios of lengths of sides and their images are not the same. Stress that scale changes are not similarity transformations.

It is important that students understand that $S_{a,b} \neq S_{b,a}$. Have them graph the rectangle *QUAD* and sketch its image under $S_{2,5}$ and then under $S_{5,2}$. They should see that the transformations are not the same.

Stress that a positive magnitude less than one produces a shrink and a magnitude greater than one produces a stretch in that particular direction. The magnitude 1 is an identity magnitude, producing neither a stretch nor a shrink.

The size change transformations studied in Lesson 4-3 are special cases of scale change transformations. Explain that they are scale changes with equal horizontal and vertical magnitudes.

1. Given $\triangle DEF$ with $D = (-3, 0)$, $E = (1, 4)$, and $F = (2, -3)$, find the image $\triangle D'E'F'$ of $\triangle DEF$ under $S_{3,2}$. Draw the graphs of the pre-image and image.

$S_{3,2}(-3, 0) = (-9, 0)$
$S_{3,2}(1, 4) = (3, 8)$
$S_{3,2}(2, -3) = (6, -6)$
$\triangle D'E'F'$ has vertices $D' = (-9, 0)$, $E' = (3, 8)$, and $F' = (6, -6)$.

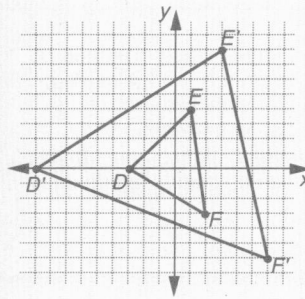

Note that sides and their images are not parallel.

2. Quadrilateral $ABCD$ is represented by the matrix $\begin{bmatrix} -3 & -1 & 3 & 1 \\ 1 & 5 & 7 & -2 \end{bmatrix}$. Use matrix multiplication to find its image under $S_{5,9}$.

The scale change matrix is $\begin{bmatrix} 5 & 0 \\ 0 & 9 \end{bmatrix}$.

$\begin{bmatrix} 5 & 0 \\ 0 & 9 \end{bmatrix}\begin{bmatrix} -3 & -1 & 3 & 1 \\ 1 & 5 & 7 & -2 \end{bmatrix}$

$= \begin{bmatrix} -15 & -5 & 15 & 5 \\ 9 & 45 & 63 & -18 \end{bmatrix}$

Check The graphs of the preimage and image are shown below.

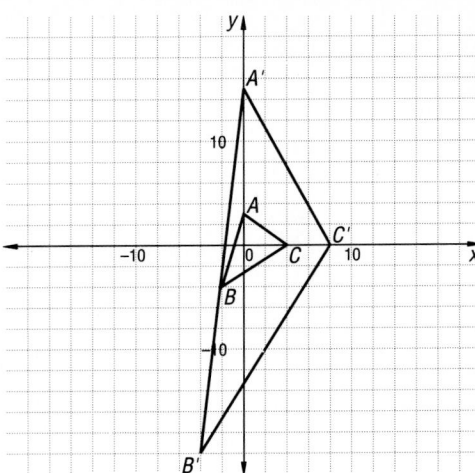

Example 1 shows that a scale change is not necessarily a similarity transformation. The ratios of the lengths of corresponding sides in $\triangle ABC$ and $\triangle A'B'C'$ are *not* equal.

$$\frac{A'B'}{AB} = \frac{\sqrt{(-20 - 15)^2 + (-4 - 0)^2}}{\sqrt{(-4 - 3)^2 + (-2 - 0)^2}} = \frac{\sqrt{1241}}{\sqrt{53}} \approx 4.84$$

and

$$\frac{B'C'}{BC} = \frac{\sqrt{(0 - -20)^2 + (8 - -4)^2}}{\sqrt{(0 - -4)^2 + (4 - -2)^2}} = \frac{\sqrt{544}}{\sqrt{52}} \approx 3.23$$

Because the ratios are different, the two triangles are not similar.

Because a size change has a 2×2 matrix, it is reasonable to expect that a scale change also has one. Suppose that $S_{a,b}$ has the matrix

$$\begin{bmatrix} e & f \\ g & h \end{bmatrix},$$

where e, f, g, and h are real numbers. Because $(x, y) \to (ax, by)$ under $S_{a,b}$, we want to find e, f, g, and h such that

$$\begin{bmatrix} e & f \\ g & h \end{bmatrix}\begin{bmatrix} x \\ y \end{bmatrix} = \begin{bmatrix} ax \\ by \end{bmatrix}.$$

200

Theorem:

$\begin{bmatrix} a & 0 \\ 0 & b \end{bmatrix}$ is the matrix for $S_{a,b}$.

Proof:

By matrix multiplication,

$$\begin{bmatrix} a & 0 \\ 0 & b \end{bmatrix} \begin{bmatrix} x \\ y \end{bmatrix} = \begin{bmatrix} ax \\ by \end{bmatrix},$$

which proves the theorem.

■ ■ ■ ■ ■ ■ ■ ■

Example 2 Refer to $\triangle ABC$ from Example 1. Use matrix multiplication to find the image $\triangle A'B'C'$ under $S_{2,5}$.

Solution Write $S_{2,5}$ and $\triangle ABC$ in matrix form.

$$\overset{S_{2,5}}{\begin{bmatrix} 2 & 0 \\ 0 & 5 \end{bmatrix}} \overset{\triangle ABC}{\begin{bmatrix} 0 & -2 & 4 \\ 3 & -4 & 0 \end{bmatrix}} = \overset{\triangle A'B'C'}{\begin{bmatrix} 0 & -4 & 8 \\ 15 & -20 & 0 \end{bmatrix}}$$

Check The product matrix gives the same result for $\triangle A'B'C'$ that was found in Example 1.

Notice that a scale change may stretch or shrink by different amounts in the horizontal and vertical directions. If the amounts are the same in both directions, then the scale change matrix has the form $\begin{bmatrix} a & 0 \\ 0 & a \end{bmatrix}$ and is really just a size change. Thus a size change is a special type of scale change. This can be stated in symbols as $S_{k,k} = S_k$.

Questions

1. $S_{a,b}$ maps (x, y) onto __?__.   **(ax, by)**

2. What is the image of $(1, -2)$ under $S_{2,5}$?   **(2, -10)**

3. If the horizontal and vertical scale change of the right-most drawing of the person at the beginning of this lesson were to be done by applying $S_{a,b}$, what are the values of a and b? $a = 1, b = \frac{1}{3}$

4. a. Multiply $\left(\begin{bmatrix} 100 & 0 \\ 0 & 200 \end{bmatrix} \begin{bmatrix} 7 \\ 9 \end{bmatrix} \right)$ $\begin{bmatrix} 700 \\ 1800 \end{bmatrix}$

   b. You have found the image of __?__ under __?__. $\begin{bmatrix} 7 \\ 9 \end{bmatrix}$; $S_{100,200}$

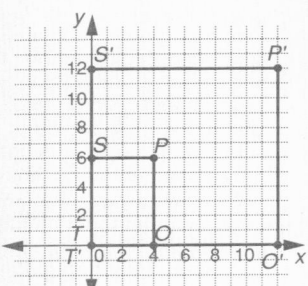
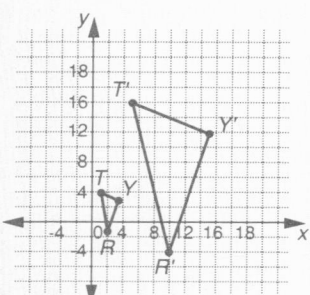
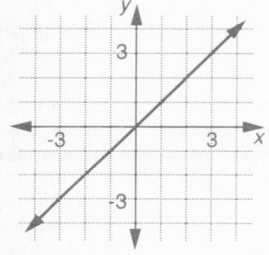
5. The scale change with matrix $\begin{bmatrix} 0.5 & 0 \\ 0 & 1.5 \end{bmatrix}$ is a horizontal __?__ and a vertical __?__.   **shrink, stretch**

6. *True or false* A size change is a special type of scale change.   **True**

7. Refer to Example 1.
   a. Find the slope of $\overline{AB}$. $\frac{7}{2}$
   b. Find the slope of $\overline{A'B'}$. $\frac{35}{4}$
   c. Is $\overline{AB}$ parallel to $\overline{A'B'}$? Justify your answer.   **No; the slopes are different**
   d. Under a scale change, is a line necessarily parallel to its image?   **No**

In 8–10, determine whether a size change or a scale change is needed. Write the matrix that could be associated with each change.

8. A 4×6 photograph is to be enlarged to 10×12.   **scale change,** $\begin{bmatrix} 2.5 & 0 \\ 0 & 2 \end{bmatrix}$

9. A cabinet maker wants to make a new bookcase twice as tall and twice as wide as the original.   **size change,** $\begin{bmatrix} 2 & 0 \\ 0 & 2 \end{bmatrix}$

10. A drawing that fills an $8'' \times 10\frac{1}{2}''$ regular notebook paper is enlarged for $8\frac{1}{2}'' \times 11''$ college-size notebook paper.   **scale change,** $\begin{bmatrix} 1\frac{1}{16} & 0 \\ 0 & 1\frac{1}{21} \end{bmatrix}$

11. a. Quadrilateral *TOPS* is represented by the matrix

$$\begin{bmatrix} 0 & 4 & 4 & 0 \\ 0 & 0 & 6 & 6 \end{bmatrix}.$$ What type of quadrilateral is *TOPS*?   **rectangle**

   b. Find the matrix of the image of quadrilateral *TOPS* under

$$\begin{bmatrix} 3 & 0 \\ 0 & 2 \end{bmatrix}.$$ **See margin.**

   c. What type of quadrilateral is $T'O'P'S'$?   **square**
   d. Graph the preimage and image of the quadrilateral.   **See margin.**

12. Consider the matrix equation below.

$$\overset{S_{a,b}}{\begin{bmatrix} a & 0 \\ 0 & b \end{bmatrix}} \overset{\triangle TRY}{\begin{bmatrix} 1 & 2 & 3 \\ 4 & -1 & 3 \end{bmatrix}} = \overset{\triangle T'R'Y'}{\begin{bmatrix} 5 & 10 & 15 \\ 16 & -4 & 12 \end{bmatrix}}$$

   a. What scale change is represented by this equation? $S_{5,4}$
   b. Draw the preimage and the image of $\triangle TRY$.   **See margin.**
   c. Find $\dfrac{T'R'}{TR}$ and $\dfrac{T'Y'}{TY}$. ≈ 4.04; ≈ 4.82
   d. Should the ratios be the same? Why or why not?   **No; scale changes do not preserve distances**

13. Consider the line with equation $y = x$.
   a. Graph this line using the same scales for the x- and y-axes.   **See margin.**
   b. What is the measure of the angle that the line makes with the positive x-axis? *(Previous course, Lesson 2-4)* $45°$

14. Evaluate $P_n = 500(2)^{n-1}$ when $n = 1$. *(Lesson 1-2)* $P_1 = 500$

202

15. Find AX when $X = \begin{bmatrix} 2 & -1 & -2 \\ 0 & 1 & -3 \\ 3 & 4 & 0 \end{bmatrix}$ and $A = \begin{bmatrix} 3 & 2 & 1 \\ 1 & 0 & 1 \\ -3 & -2 & 0 \end{bmatrix}$ See margin.
(Lesson 4-2)

16. The matrix below gives the daily delivery of boxes of apples and pears to two markets.

$$\begin{array}{c} \\ \text{apples} \\ \text{pears} \end{array} \begin{array}{cc} \text{Troy's} & \text{Abby's} \\ \begin{bmatrix} 5 & 4 \\ 1 & 2 \end{bmatrix} \end{array}$$

During peak season the markets triple their demand for fruit.
a. What size change is needed to meet the increased demand? Represent the size change by a matrix.
b. Multiply the original matrix by the size-change matrix to find the new matrix which meets the increased demand. *(Lesson 4-3)*

a) $\begin{bmatrix} 3 & 0 \\ 0 & 3 \end{bmatrix}$ b) $\begin{bmatrix} 15 & 12 \\ 3 & 6 \end{bmatrix}$

17. a. Solve $\dfrac{\frac{x}{3}}{5} = 15$. b. Solve $\dfrac{\frac{y}{3}}{\frac{5}{9}} = 15$. *(Lesson 1-5)*

$x = 225$ $y = 25$

18. $ABCD$ is the square defined by the matrix $\begin{bmatrix} 0 & 2 & 2 & 0 \\ 0 & 0 & 2 & 2 \end{bmatrix}$.

Transform $ABCD$ by multiplying its matrix by each of the following matrices (and by some others of your own choice).

a. $\begin{bmatrix} 3 & 0 \\ 0 & 4 \end{bmatrix} \begin{bmatrix} 0 & 6 & 6 & 0 \\ 0 & 0 & 8 & 8 \end{bmatrix}$ b. $\begin{bmatrix} 3 & 0 \\ 0 & 1 \end{bmatrix} \begin{bmatrix} 0 & 6 & 6 & 0 \\ 0 & 0 & 2 & 2 \end{bmatrix}$

c. $\begin{bmatrix} 3 & 0 \\ 0 & 2 \end{bmatrix} \begin{bmatrix} 0 & 6 & 6 & 0 \\ 0 & 0 & 4 & 4 \end{bmatrix}$ d. $\begin{bmatrix} 2 & 0 \\ 0 & 1 \end{bmatrix} \begin{bmatrix} 0 & 4 & 4 & 0 \\ 0 & 0 & 2 & 2 \end{bmatrix}$

e. Find the area of each new shape. Enter your results in a table like this one: See margin.

Original Area	Matrix	New Area
4 units^2	$\begin{bmatrix} 3 & 0 \\ 0 & 4 \end{bmatrix}$	units^2
4 units^2	$\begin{bmatrix} 3 & 0 \\ 0 & 1 \end{bmatrix}$	units^2
?	$\begin{bmatrix} 3 & 0 \\ 0 & 2 \end{bmatrix}$	?
?	$\begin{bmatrix} 2 & 0 \\ 0 & 1 \end{bmatrix}$	?

f. There is a connection between the elements a and b of the scale-change matrix $\begin{bmatrix} a & 0 \\ 0 & b \end{bmatrix}$ and the effect the scale change has on the area of a shape. What is this connection? See margin.

LESSON 4-4 Scale Changes **203**

FOLLOW-UP

MORE PRACTICE
For more questions on SPUR Objectives, use *Lesson Master 4-4,* shown below.

EVALUATION
A quiz covering Lessons 4-1 through 4-4 is provided in the Teacher's Resource File.

15. $\begin{bmatrix} 9 & 3 & -12 \\ 5 & 3 & -12 \\ -6 & 1 & 12 \end{bmatrix}$

18.e.

Original Area	Matrix	New Area
4 units^2	$\begin{bmatrix} 3 & 0 \\ 0 & 4 \end{bmatrix}$	48 units^2
4 units^2	$\begin{bmatrix} 3 & 0 \\ 0 & 1 \end{bmatrix}$	12 units^2
4 units^2	$\begin{bmatrix} 3 & 0 \\ 0 & 2 \end{bmatrix}$	24 units^2
4 units^2	$\begin{bmatrix} 2 & 0 \\ 0 & 1 \end{bmatrix}$	8 units^2

f. The new area equals the original area times the product of the magnitudes of the horizontal and vertical scale changes, or New Area = Original Area · ab.

 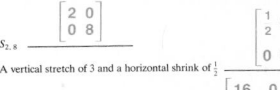
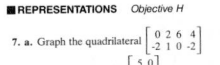

LESSON 4-5

RESOURCES
■ Lesson Master 4-5

OBJECTIVES

F Relate reflections to matrices, and vice versa.
G Perform reflections using matrices.
H Graph figures and their reflection images.

TEACHING NOTES

To introduce or review the idea of a reflection, have students reflect each of the points (0, 5), (3, 4), (-2, 1), (4, -6), and (-5, 0) over the y-axis. Once they have done this, students should have little trouble concluding that the reflection image of (x, y) over the y-axis is (-x, y).

Reflect the same points over the x-axis and over the line y = x. Students should have little difficulty observing that the image of (x, y) when reflected over the x-axis is (x, -y), and that the image is (y, x) when the reflection is over the line y = x.

Alternate Approach
Ask students for their definition of symmetry. Introduce the term *reflection* using real-world applications. For example, suggest that students think of their own mirror images. Draw a figure in quadrant 1. Then have students draw its reflection image over the lines x = 0 and y = 0.

Label the points of your drawing, and have students label the points of the other two figures. In both cases, ask for the line of symmetry.

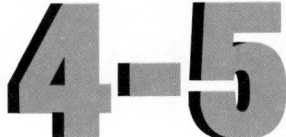

Reflections

Recall from geometry that the **reflection image of a point A over a line m** is:
1. the point A, if A is on m;
2. the point A' such that m is the perpendicular bisector of $\overline{AA'}$, if A is not on m.

The line m is called the **reflecting line** or **line of reflection.** The figure below shows the reflection image of an insect over the line m.

Suppose the reflecting line is the y-axis, as shown below. If $A = (x, y)$, its reflection image has the opposite first coordinate but the same second coordinate. So $A' = (-x, y)$.

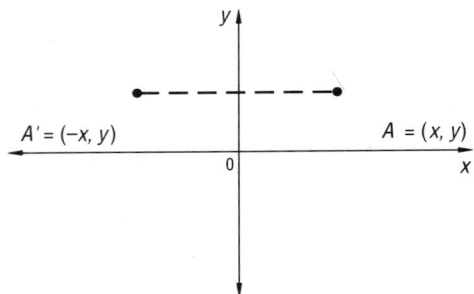

You can verify that the y-axis is the perpendicular bisector of $\overline{AA'}$. Reflection over the y-axis can be denoted $r_{y\text{-axis}}$ or r_y. In this book we use r_y. So we can write

$$r_y(x, y) = (-x, y).$$

We read this as "the reflection over the y-axis maps point (x, y) onto point $(-x, y)$."

Can a matrix associated with r_y be found? Notice that

$$\begin{bmatrix} -1 & 0 \\ 0 & 1 \end{bmatrix} \begin{bmatrix} x \\ y \end{bmatrix} = \begin{bmatrix} -1 \cdot x + 0 \cdot y \\ 0 \cdot x + 1 \cdot y \end{bmatrix} = \begin{bmatrix} -x \\ y \end{bmatrix}.$$

This proves the following theorem

Theorem:

$$\begin{bmatrix} -1 & 0 \\ 0 & 1 \end{bmatrix}$$ is the matrix for r_y.

Example 1   If $A = (1, 2)$, $B = (1, 4)$, and $C = (2, 4)$, find the image of $\triangle ABC$ under the transformation r_y.

Solution   Represent r_y and $\triangle ABC$ as matrices and multiply.

$$\overset{r_y}{\begin{bmatrix} -1 & 0 \\ 0 & 1 \end{bmatrix}} \overset{\triangle ABC}{\begin{bmatrix} 1 & 1 & 2 \\ 2 & 4 & 4 \end{bmatrix}} = \begin{bmatrix} -1 & -1 & -2 \\ 2 & 4 & 4 \end{bmatrix}$$

The image $\triangle A'B'C'$ has $A' = (-1, 2)$, $B' = (-1, 4)$, and $C' = (-2, 4)$.

Check   The preimage and image are graphed here.

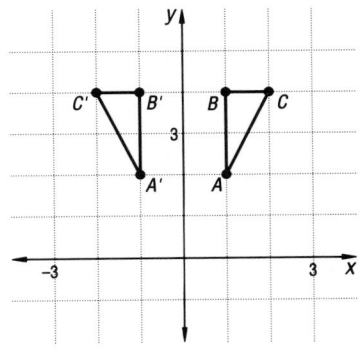

Two other important reflecting lines are the x-axis and the line with equation $y = x$. Reflection over the x-axis is denoted by r_x; and reflection over the line $y = x$, by $r_{y=x}$. You can verify the following results:

$$r_x: (x, y) \rightarrow (x, -y)$$
$$r_{y=x}: (x, y) \rightarrow (y, x)$$

The graphs on the top of page 206 show the effects of r_x and $r_{y=x}$ on $\triangle ABC$ of Example 1.

Have students identify which coordinates changed. Following this discussion, remind students which 2 × 2 matrix is associated with each reflection. Once r_y and r_x are understood, introduce $r_{y=x}$.

ADDITIONAL EXAMPLES
1. If $D = (-3, -1)$, $E = (-3, -4)$, and $F = (-1, -1)$, graph the image of $\triangle DEF$ under

a. r_y

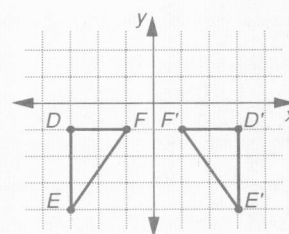

b. r_x

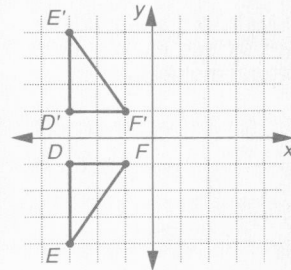

c. $r_{y=x}$

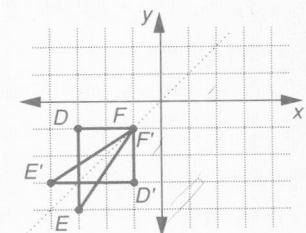

2. Use matrix multiplication to find the reflection image of the pentagon *NIFTY* over the line $y = x$ if $N = (-1, 5)$, $I = (7, 2)$, $F = (6, -3)$, $T = (0, -5)$, and $Y = (-5, -5)$. Graph the image and preimage.

$$\begin{bmatrix} 0 & 1 \\ 1 & 0 \end{bmatrix} \begin{bmatrix} -1 & 7 & 6 & 0 & -5 \\ 5 & 2 & -3 & -5 & -5 \end{bmatrix}$$

$$= \begin{bmatrix} 5 & 2 & -3 & -5 & -5 \\ -1 & 7 & 6 & 0 & -5 \end{bmatrix}$$

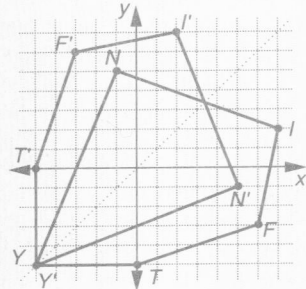

3. Multiply the matrix for $r_{y=x}$ by itself and explain the result geometrically.

$$\begin{bmatrix} 0 & 1 \\ 1 & 0 \end{bmatrix} \begin{bmatrix} 0 & 1 \\ 1 & 0 \end{bmatrix} = \begin{bmatrix} 1 & 0 \\ 0 & 1 \end{bmatrix}$$

The result of the multiplication is the 2 × 2 identity matrix. This means that reflecting a figure over $y = x$ and then reflecting the image over $y = x$ yields the original preimage. In general, if a figure is reflected over any line and the image is reflected in that same line, the result is the original figure.

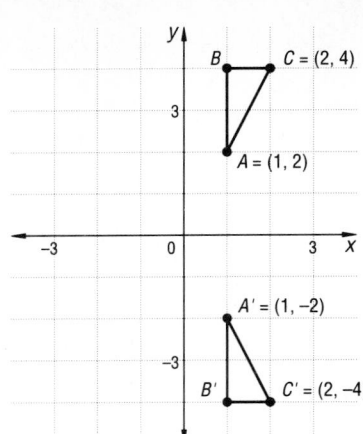

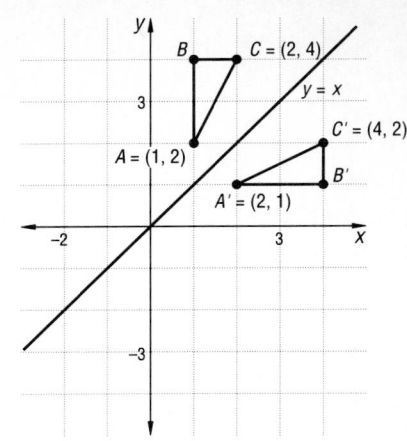

The matrices for r_x and $r_{y=x}$ also involve only 0s, 1s, and -1s.

Theorem:

$$\begin{bmatrix} 1 & 0 \\ 0 & -1 \end{bmatrix}$$ is the matrix for r_x.

Proof:

$$\begin{bmatrix} 1 & 0 \\ 0 & -1 \end{bmatrix} \begin{bmatrix} x \\ y \end{bmatrix} = \begin{bmatrix} 1 \cdot x + 0 \cdot y \\ 0 \cdot x + -1 \cdot y \end{bmatrix} = \begin{bmatrix} x \\ -y \end{bmatrix}$$

Theorem:

$$\begin{bmatrix} 0 & 1 \\ 1 & 0 \end{bmatrix}$$ is the matrix for $r_{y=x}$.

Proof:

You are asked to do this proof in Question 13.

· · ■ ■ ■

Example 2 Find the reflection image of pentagon *WEIRD* over the line $y = x$ if $W = (-1, -1)$, $E = (3, -2)$, $I = (6, 0)$, $R = (6, 5)$, and $D = (-1, 7)$.

Solution Represent $r_{y=x}$ and *WEIRD* by matrices and multiply.

$$\overset{r_{y=x}}{\begin{bmatrix} 0 & 1 \\ 1 & 0 \end{bmatrix}} \overset{WEIRD}{\begin{bmatrix} -1 & 3 & 6 & 6 & -1 \\ -1 & -2 & 0 & 5 & 7 \end{bmatrix}} = \overset{W'E'I'R'D'}{\begin{bmatrix} -1 & -2 & 0 & 5 & 7 \\ -1 & 3 & 6 & 6 & -1 \end{bmatrix}}$$

$W'E'I'R'D'$ is represented by the product matrix.

206

Check *WEIRD* and *W'E'I'R'D'* are graphed below.

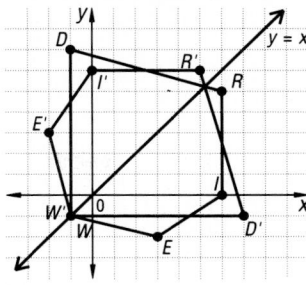

It is important to note one significant way that reflections differ from size and scale changes. Reflection images are *congruent* to their preimages. For instance, in Example 1 $\triangle ABC \cong \triangle A'B'C'$. Under size changes, preimages and images are similar but not necessarily congruent.

At this point you have learned matrices for some size changes, some scale changes, and three reflections. You may wonder: How do I remember them? Question 11 will help you.

Questions

Covering the Reading

1. Suppose that A is not on line m and that A' is the reflection image of A over m. Then m is the __?__ of $\overline{AA'}$.   **Perpendicular bisector.**

2. **a.** What is the reflection image of a point A over a line m if A is on m?   **It is the same point.**
   b. Which vertex on pentagon *WEIRD* shows this?   **W**

3. Refer to Example 1. Use matrices to find the image of $\triangle ABC$ under $r_{y=x}$. Graph $\triangle ABC$ and this image.   **See margin.**

4. How can the following sentence be read?   **See margin.**

$$r_x (x, y) = (x, -y)$$

Multiple choice In 5–7, choose the matrix that corresponds to the given reflection.

(a) $\begin{bmatrix} 1 & 0 \\ 0 & -1 \end{bmatrix}$ (b) $\begin{bmatrix} -1 & 0 \\ 0 & 1 \end{bmatrix}$ (c) $\begin{bmatrix} -1 & 0 \\ 0 & -1 \end{bmatrix}$

(d) $\begin{bmatrix} 0 & 1 \\ 1 & 0 \end{bmatrix}$ (e) $\begin{bmatrix} 0 & -1 \\ -1 & 0 \end{bmatrix}$

5. r_x **a**   6. r_y **b**   7. $r_{y=x}$ **d**

8. Refer to Example 2. Find the matrix for the reflection image of *WEIRD* over the y-axis. Graph *WEIRD* and its image $W''E''I''R''D''$.
   See margin.

LESSON 4-5 Reflections   **207**

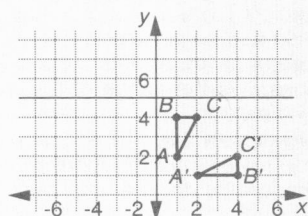
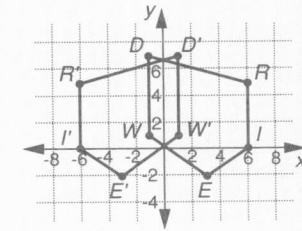

9. *True or false* Reflection images are congruent to their preimages.
   True
10. Translate the matrix equation below by filling in the blanks.

$$\begin{bmatrix} -1 & 0 \\ 0 & 1 \end{bmatrix}\begin{bmatrix} 2 \\ 3 \end{bmatrix} = \begin{bmatrix} -2 \\ 3 \end{bmatrix}$$

The reflection image of the point __?__ over the line __?__ is the point
__?__.   (2, 3); $x = 0$; (-2, 3)

11. Let $F = (1, 0)$ and $S = (0, 1)$.
    a. Find their images under the transformation with matrix

    $\begin{bmatrix} a & b \\ c & d \end{bmatrix}$. $F' = (a, c), S' = (b, d)$

    b. The image of (1, 0) is the first __?__ of this matrix.   column
    c. The image of (0, 1) is the second __?__ of this matrix.   column
    d. Explain how this idea leads to a way of remembering the 2 × 2 matrix for any transformation that has one.   See margin.

12. Write the matrices for r_x, r_y, and $r_{y=x}$. Multiply each matrix by itself and explain your results.   See margin.

13. Prove that $\begin{bmatrix} 0 & 1 \\ 1 & 0 \end{bmatrix}$ is the matrix for reflection over the line
    $y = x$.   See margin.

14. Let $P = (x, y)$, $Q = (y, x)$,   See margin.
    and let *R* be any point on the line
    $y = x$. Then $R = (a, a)$.
    a. Verify that $PR = QR$.
    b. From part a, what theorem from geometry allows you to conclude that the line $y = x$ is the perpendicular bisector of $\overline{PQ}$?

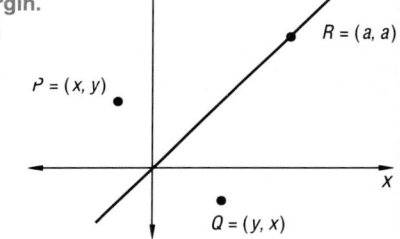

15. Recall from geometry that the area of a parallelogram varies jointly as the length of the base and the height. What happens to the area of the parallelogram when both the length and height are tripled? Prove your conjecture. *(Lesson 2-3)*   See margin.

16. Find the change in the area of the polygon represented by

$\begin{bmatrix} 3 & 2 & 5 & -3 \\ 4 & -1 & 0 & 1 \end{bmatrix}$ when it is multiplied on the left by

$\begin{bmatrix} 3 & 0 \\ 0 & 3 \end{bmatrix}$.   *(Lesson 4-3, previous course)*   The area is multiplied by 9.

208

17. Refer to the diagram below. Find y given $\ell \parallel m$. *(Previous courses)*   110°

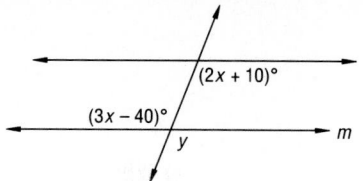

18. Find an equation for the line parallel to $y = 3x - 4$ and containing the point $(2, -5)$. *(Lesson 3-2)* $y = 3x - 11$

19. Trace the figure below. Point H on pentagon *HOUSE* has been rotated 90° about point C to the position of H'. Rotate the other vertices of *HOUSE* 90° about C and draw $H'O'U'S'E$. *(Previous course)*   **See margin.**

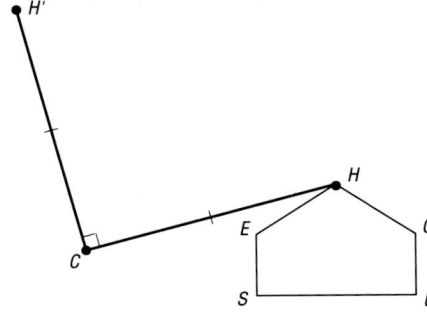

MORE PRACTICE
For more questions on SPUR Objectives, use *Lesson Master 4-5*, shown below.

19.

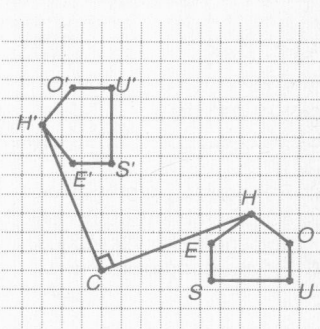

20. Let $r_{y=-x}$ denote reflection over the line $y = -x$.
   a. By graphing and testing points, complete this sentence.
   $r_{y=-x}\,(x, y) = \underline{\ ?\ }$. $(-y, -x)$
   b. Find the 2×2 matrix associated with $r_{y=-x}$. $\begin{bmatrix} 0 & -1 \\ -1 & 0 \end{bmatrix}$

Exploration

■ **REPRESENTATIONS**   *Objective F (See pages 241–243 for objectives.)*
In 1 and 2, use each matrix equation to complete the sentence.

1. $\begin{bmatrix} 0 & 1 \\ 1 & 0 \end{bmatrix}\begin{bmatrix} -3 \\ 8 \end{bmatrix} = \begin{bmatrix} 8 \\ -3 \end{bmatrix}$ The reflection image of the point ___(-3, 8)___
over the line ___$y = x$___ is the point ___(8, -3)___ .

2. $\begin{bmatrix} -1 & 0 \\ 0 & 1 \end{bmatrix}\begin{bmatrix} 2 \\ 1 \end{bmatrix} = \begin{bmatrix} -2 \\ 1 \end{bmatrix}$ The reflection image of the point ___(2, 1)___
over the line ___$x = 0$___ is the point ___(-2, 1)___ .

3. Multiply the matrix r_x by itself and explain your results.
$\begin{bmatrix} 1 & 0 \\ 0 & -1 \end{bmatrix}\begin{bmatrix} 1 & 0 \\ 0 & -1 \end{bmatrix} = \begin{bmatrix} 1 & 0 \\ 0 & 1 \end{bmatrix}$; Identity matrix is formed.

■ **REPRESENTATIONS**   *Objective G*
In 4–7, find the matrix for each transformation.

(a) $\begin{bmatrix} 6 & 0 \\ 0 & 6 \end{bmatrix}$ (b) $\begin{bmatrix} -1 & 0 \\ 0 & 1 \end{bmatrix}$ (c) $\begin{bmatrix} 6 & 0 \\ 0 & 2 \end{bmatrix}$ (d) $\begin{bmatrix} 0 & 1 \\ 1 & 0 \end{bmatrix}$ (e) $\begin{bmatrix} 1 & 0 \\ 0 & -1 \end{bmatrix}$

4. r_x ___(e)___   5. $r_{y=-x}$ ___(d)___   6. r_y ___(b)___   7. S_6 ___(a)___

8. Find the image of $\begin{bmatrix} 8 & 0 & .3 & 1 \\ -2 & 1 & 0 & -5 \end{bmatrix}$ 9. Find the image of $\begin{bmatrix} 3 & -2 & 2 & 0 \\ 1 & 0 & -9 & 5 \end{bmatrix}$
under r_x.   under $r_{y=-x}$.
$\begin{bmatrix} 8 & 0 & .3 & 1 \\ 2 & -1 & 0 & 5 \end{bmatrix}$ $\begin{bmatrix} 1 & 0 & .9 & 5 \\ 3 & -2 & 2 & 0 \end{bmatrix}$

■ **REPRESENTATIONS**   *Objective H*

10. Parallelogram *ALGE* is represented by the matrix
$\begin{bmatrix} -5 & -6 & 0 & 1 \\ -2 & -6 & -5 & -1 \end{bmatrix}$. Graph the
preimage and image under r_y.

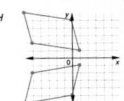

OBJECTIVES

C Recognize properties of transformation composition and matrix multiplication.
F Relate composites of transformations to products of matrices, and vice versa.
G Perform composites of transformations using matrices.
H Graph figures and their images under composites of transformations.

TEACHING NOTES

Reading Students may find the notation for composition of transformations confusing. In English, we read from left to right, but in mathematics we sometimes read from right to left. Stress that the symbol ∘ should be read as "following." Thus, $r_{y=x} \circ r_x$ means $r_{y=x}$ following r_x. First, r_x is applied and then $r_{y=x}$ is applied to the result.

After discussing the **Example**, distinguish between the words *composite* and *composition*. They are as different as *sum* and *addition*. The latter in each case refers to the operation; the former, to the result of performing the operation.

Transformations and Matrices

A **transformation** is a one-to-one correspondence between sets of points. Transformations are described by rules. These rules may be algebraic (by a formula), geometric (by giving the location of image points), or arithmetic (by a matrix). In the past three lessons, you have encountered the 2×2 matrices for transformations known as size changes, scale changes, and reflections. Here we summarize some of the properties of multiplication of 2×2 matrices, and discuss how they are related to transformations.

It is reasonable to compare multiplication of 2×2 matrices with multiplication of real numbers.

1. (closure) *The set of 2×2 matrices is closed under multiplication.*
   Closure means: If you multiply two 2×2 matrices, the result is a 2×2 matrix. This property follows from the definition of multiplication of matrices.

2. (noncommutativity) *In general, multiplication of 2×2 matrices is not commutative.*
   As you will learn in the questions, multiplication with some 2×2 matrices is commutative. But in general, you cannot assume $AB = BA$.

3. (associativity) *Multiplication of 2×2 matrices is associative.*

210

Proof:

Remember that, for real numbers, associativity of multiplication means

$$(ab)c = a(bc).$$

For matrices, therefore, it must be shown that

$$(AB)C = A(BC).$$

The calculation must work for all 2×2 matrices, so let

$$A = \begin{bmatrix} a & b \\ c & d \end{bmatrix}, \quad B = \begin{bmatrix} e & f \\ g & h \end{bmatrix}, \quad C = \begin{bmatrix} i & j \\ k & l \end{bmatrix}.$$

Now it is only a matter of some manipulation, which is left for you in Question 5.

---

4. (identity) *The matrix* $\begin{bmatrix} 1 & 0 \\ 0 & 1 \end{bmatrix}$ *is the identity for multiplication of* 2×2 *matrices.*

Proof:

For the real numbers, 1 is the identity for multiplication: For all a, $1 \cdot a = a \cdot 1 = a$. Therefore, we need to find a 2×2 matrix that we will call I, such that for all 2×2 matrices A,

$$I \cdot A = A \cdot I = A.$$

The matrix for a size change of magnitude 1, $\begin{bmatrix} 1 & 0 \\ 0 & 1 \end{bmatrix}$,

serves this purpose.

$$\begin{bmatrix} 1 & 0 \\ 0 & 1 \end{bmatrix} \begin{bmatrix} a & b \\ c & d \end{bmatrix} = \begin{bmatrix} a & b \\ c & d \end{bmatrix} \quad \text{and}$$

$$\begin{bmatrix} a & b \\ c & d \end{bmatrix} \begin{bmatrix} 1 & 0 \\ 0 & 1 \end{bmatrix} = \begin{bmatrix} a & b \\ c & d \end{bmatrix}$$

(Both multiplications are needed because multiplication is not always commutative.)

The proof of the identity property illustrates the close relationship between transformations and matrices. When the matrix $\begin{bmatrix} x \\ y \end{bmatrix}$ is multiplied on the left by $\begin{bmatrix} 1 & 0 \\ 0 & 1 \end{bmatrix}$, each point (x, y) coincides

1. Graph the rectangle determined by the points (3, 1), (3, 2), (6, 2), and (6, 1). Label the vertices *ALEX*. Find its image under the transformation $r_x \circ r_{y=x}$.
Solution 1: Do it geometrically, without matrices.

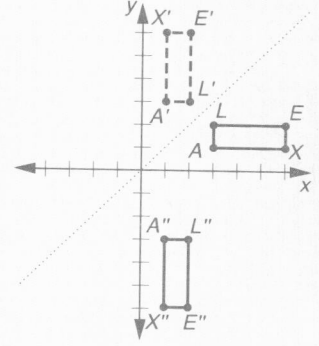

Solution 2: Represent the rectangle by a matrix and multiply by the transformation matrices.

$$\underset{r_x}{\begin{bmatrix} 1 & 0 \\ 0 & -1 \end{bmatrix}} \underset{r_{y=x}}{\begin{bmatrix} 0 & 1 \\ 1 & 0 \end{bmatrix}} \overset{A\ L\ E\ X}{\begin{bmatrix} 3 & 3 & 6 & 6 \\ 1 & 2 & 2 & 1 \end{bmatrix}}$$

$$\underset{r_x \circ r_{y=x}}{\begin{bmatrix} 0 & 1 \\ -1 & 0 \end{bmatrix}} \overset{A\ L\ E\ X}{\begin{bmatrix} 3 & 3 & 6 & 6 \\ 1 & 2 & 2 & 1 \end{bmatrix}}$$

$$\overset{A''\ L''\ E''\ X''}{\begin{bmatrix} 1 & 2 & 2 & 1 \\ -3 & -3 & -6 & -6 \end{bmatrix}}$$

2. If $T_1 = r_x$ and $T_2 = r_y$, find a single matrix to describe the composite transformation $T_2 \circ T_1$.
$T_2 \circ T_1 = r_y \circ r_x$

$$\underset{r_y}{\begin{bmatrix} -1 & 0 \\ 0 & 1 \end{bmatrix}} \underset{r_x}{\begin{bmatrix} 1 & 0 \\ 0 & -1 \end{bmatrix}} = \begin{bmatrix} -1 & 0 \\ 0 & -1 \end{bmatrix}$$

with its image. Thus $\begin{bmatrix} 1 & 0 \\ 0 & 1 \end{bmatrix}$ is called the **identity transformation.**

$$\begin{bmatrix} 1 & 0 \\ 0 & 1 \end{bmatrix} \begin{bmatrix} x \\ y \end{bmatrix} = \begin{bmatrix} 1 \cdot x + 0 \cdot y \\ 0 \cdot x + 1 \cdot y \end{bmatrix} = \begin{bmatrix} x \\ y \end{bmatrix}$$

Properties of matrices correspond to properties of transformations. The example shows how the product of two matrices is related to the corresponding transformations.

Example The flag F has key points at $A = (1, 2)$, $B = (1, 6)$, and $C = (3, 6)$. First, reflect this flag over the x-axis. Then reflect the image about the line $y = x$.

Solution 1 A', B', and C' are key points on the first image over the x-axis. A'', B'', and C'' are on the final image found by reflecting A', B', and C' over the line $y = x$.

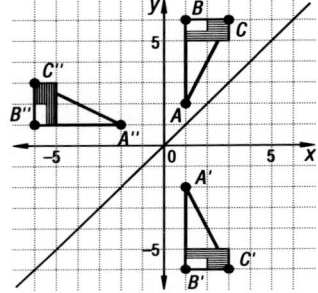

Solution 2 Represent A, B, and C by the matrix $\begin{bmatrix} 1 & 1 & 3 \\ 2 & 6 & 6 \end{bmatrix}$.

To find the first image, multiply this matrix on the left by the matrix for r_x.

$$\overset{r_x}{\begin{bmatrix} 1 & 0 \\ 0 & -1 \end{bmatrix}} \overset{ABC}{\begin{bmatrix} 1 & 1 & 3 \\ 2 & 6 & 6 \end{bmatrix}} = \overset{A'B'C'}{\begin{bmatrix} 1 & 1 & 3 \\ -2 & -6 & -6 \end{bmatrix}}$$

To find the second image, multiply the matrix for A', B', and C' by the matrix for $r_{y=x}$.

$$\overset{r_{y=x}}{\begin{bmatrix} 0 & 1 \\ 1 & 0 \end{bmatrix}} \overset{A'B'C'}{\begin{bmatrix} 1 & 1 & 3 \\ -2 & -6 & -6 \end{bmatrix}} = \overset{A''B''C''}{\begin{bmatrix} -2 & -6 & -6 \\ 1 & 1 & 3 \end{bmatrix}}$$

The points $A'' = (-2, 1)$, $B'' = (-6, 1)$, and $C'' = (-6, 3)$ enable the final flag to be drawn.

Check The coordinates for the flag determined by using matrix methods are the same as the coordinates in the graph of the final image.

212

We call the final flag the image of the original flag under the **composite** of the reflections r_x and $r_{y=x}$.

Definition:

Suppose transformation T_1 maps figure F onto figure F', and transformation T_2 maps figure F' onto figure F''. The transformation that maps F onto F'' is called the composite of T_1 and T_2, written $T_2 \circ T_1$.

The symbol $\circ$ means "following." Thus in the example, the composite is

$$r_{y=x} \circ r_x.$$

To describe the composite, ignore the first image and look only at the preimage and the final image.

How are the two flags related?

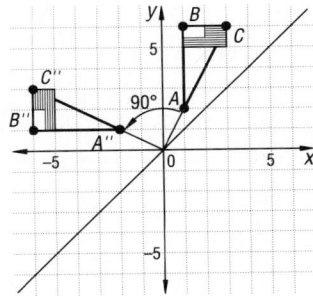

The graph shows that the composite is neither a reflection nor a size or scale change. Recall from geometry that the preimage and image are related by a different type of transformation called a **rotation.** This rotation has center $(0, 0)$. If the preimage flag is turned $90°$ about $(0, 0)$ in a counterclockwise direction, the image flag results. We denote this rotation by R_{90}. This rotation is the composite of the two reflections.

$$R_{90} = r_{y=x} \circ r_x$$

How do we find the matrix associated with R_{90}? Notice that the composition of transformations of the example led to the following matrix multiplication.

$$
\overset{r_{y=x}}{\begin{bmatrix} 0 & 1 \\ 1 & 0 \end{bmatrix}} \left(\overset{r_x}{\begin{bmatrix} 1 & 0 \\ 0 & -1 \end{bmatrix}} \overset{\triangle ABC}{\begin{bmatrix} 1 & 1 & 3 \\ 2 & 6 & 6 \end{bmatrix}} \right)
$$

ADDITIONAL ANSWERS

2. sample:

$\begin{bmatrix} 1 & 0 \\ 0 & 1 \end{bmatrix}\begin{bmatrix} a & c \\ b & d \end{bmatrix} = \begin{bmatrix} a & c \\ b & d \end{bmatrix}$;

$\begin{bmatrix} a & c \\ b & d \end{bmatrix}\begin{bmatrix} 1 & 0 \\ 0 & 1 \end{bmatrix} = \begin{bmatrix} a & c \\ b & d \end{bmatrix}$

3. sample:

$\begin{bmatrix} 1 & 0 \\ 2 & 1 \end{bmatrix}\begin{bmatrix} 2 & 2 \\ 0 & 3 \end{bmatrix} = \begin{bmatrix} 2 & 2 \\ 4 & 7 \end{bmatrix}$;

$\begin{bmatrix} 2 & 2 \\ 0 & 3 \end{bmatrix}\begin{bmatrix} 1 & 0 \\ 2 & 1 \end{bmatrix} = \begin{bmatrix} 6 & 2 \\ 6 & 3 \end{bmatrix}$

4.a. $(XY)Z$ =

$\left(\begin{bmatrix} 1 & -2 \\ 3 & 4 \end{bmatrix}\begin{bmatrix} 0 & 1 \\ 4 & -2 \end{bmatrix}\right)\begin{bmatrix} \frac{1}{2} & 1 \\ 0 & 1 \end{bmatrix}$ =

$\begin{bmatrix} -8 & 5 \\ 16 & -5 \end{bmatrix}\begin{bmatrix} \frac{1}{2} & 1 \\ 0 & 1 \end{bmatrix} = \begin{bmatrix} -4 & -3 \\ 8 & 11 \end{bmatrix}$

$X(YZ)$ =

$\begin{bmatrix} 1 & -2 \\ 3 & 4 \end{bmatrix}\left(\begin{bmatrix} 0 & 1 \\ 4 & -2 \end{bmatrix}\begin{bmatrix} \frac{1}{2} & 1 \\ 0 & 1 \end{bmatrix}\right)$ =

$\begin{bmatrix} 1 & -2 \\ 3 & 4 \end{bmatrix}\begin{bmatrix} 0 & 1 \\ 2 & 2 \end{bmatrix} = \begin{bmatrix} -4 & -3 \\ 8 & 11 \end{bmatrix}$

5.a. $(AB)C$ =

$\left(\begin{bmatrix} a & b \\ c & d \end{bmatrix}\begin{bmatrix} e & f \\ g & h \end{bmatrix}\right)\begin{bmatrix} i & j \\ k & l \end{bmatrix}$ =

$\begin{bmatrix} ae + bg & af + bh \\ ce + dg & cf + dh \end{bmatrix}\begin{bmatrix} i & j \\ k & l \end{bmatrix}$ =

$\begin{bmatrix} aei+bgi+afk+bhk & aej+bgj+afl+bhl \\ cei+dgi+cfk+dhk & cej+dgj+cfl+dhl \end{bmatrix}$

b. $A(BC)$ =

$\begin{bmatrix} a & b \\ c & d \end{bmatrix}\left(\begin{bmatrix} e & f \\ g & h \end{bmatrix}\begin{bmatrix} i & j \\ k & l \end{bmatrix}\right)$ =

$\begin{bmatrix} a & b \\ c & d \end{bmatrix}\begin{bmatrix} ei+fk & ej+fl \\ gi+hk & gj+hl \end{bmatrix}$ =

$\begin{bmatrix} aei+afk+bgi+bhk & aej+afl+bgi+bhl \\ cei+cfk+dgi+dhk & cej+cfl+dgi+dhl \end{bmatrix}$

6. $\begin{bmatrix} \pi & \sqrt{2} \\ -3 & \frac{3}{4} \end{bmatrix}$

12. $\begin{bmatrix} 0 & -2 \\ -2 & 0 \end{bmatrix}$

13.a $\begin{bmatrix} 0 & 1 \\ -1 & 0 \end{bmatrix}$

c. not the same;

$r_{y=x} \circ r_x = R_{90}$

Because matrix multiplication is associative, this product could be computed as follows:

$$= \left(\overset{r_{y=x}}{\begin{bmatrix} 0 & 1 \\ 1 & 0 \end{bmatrix}} \overset{r_x}{\begin{bmatrix} 1 & 0 \\ 0 & -1 \end{bmatrix}} \right) \overset{\triangle ABC}{\begin{bmatrix} 1 & 1 & 3 \\ 2 & 6 & 6 \end{bmatrix}}$$

$$= \begin{bmatrix} 0 & -1 \\ 1 & 0 \end{bmatrix} \overset{\triangle ABC}{\begin{bmatrix} 1 & 1 & 3 \\ 2 & 6 & 6 \end{bmatrix}}$$

$$= \overset{\triangle A''B''C''}{\begin{bmatrix} -2 & -6 & -6 \\ 1 & 1 & 3 \end{bmatrix}}$$

Multiplying the two reflection matrices gives the single matrix

$\begin{bmatrix} 0 & -1 \\ 1 & 0 \end{bmatrix}$. Applying this matrix to A, B, and C results in the

final images A'', B'', and C''. Thus the single matrix $\begin{bmatrix} 0 & -1 \\ 1 & 0 \end{bmatrix}$

can be used to do the composition $r_{y=x} \circ r_x$. The general idea is summarized in the following theorem.

Theorem:

If transformation T_1 has matrix M_1 and transformation T_2 has matrix M_2, then $T_2 \circ T_1$ has matrix M_2M_1.

Questions

Covering the Reading

1. When a 2×2 matrix is multiplied by a 2×2 matrix, what are the dimensions of the product matrix? 2×2

2. Give an example to show that multiplication of 2×2 matrices is sometimes commutative.   See margin.

3. Find two 2×2 matrices A and B such that $AB \neq BA$.   See margin.

4. Let $X = \begin{bmatrix} 1 & -2 \\ 3 & 4 \end{bmatrix}$, $Y = \begin{bmatrix} 0 & 1 \\ 4 & -2 \end{bmatrix}$, and $Z = \begin{bmatrix} \frac{1}{2} & 1 \\ 0 & 1 \end{bmatrix}$.

   a. Show that $(XY)Z = X(YZ)$.   See margin.
   b. The answer to part a is an instance of what property?
      multiplication of 2×2 matrices is associative.
5. Finish the proof (on page 211) that multiplication of 2×2 matrices is associative, by calculating the following:
   a. $(AB)C$ See margin.   b. $A(BC)$.   See margin.

214

6. Multiply $\begin{bmatrix} 1 & 0 \\ 0 & 1 \end{bmatrix}$ by $\begin{bmatrix} \pi & \sqrt{2} \\ -3 & \frac{3}{4} \end{bmatrix}$. **See margin.**

7. The identity transformation maps each point onto __?__.   **itself**

8. The symbol ∘ means __?__.   **following**

9. In the rotation $r_{y=x} \circ r_x$, which reflection is done first, $r_{y=x}$ or r_x? r_x

10. R_{90} represents a rotation of __?__ degrees around __?__ in a(n) __?__ direction.   **90, the origin, counterclockwise**

11. What property of matrix multiplication justifies that

$$\begin{bmatrix} 0 & 1 \\ 1 & 0 \end{bmatrix} \left(\begin{bmatrix} 1 & 0 \\ 0 & -1 \end{bmatrix} \begin{bmatrix} 1 & 1 & 3 \\ 2 & 6 & 6 \end{bmatrix} \right) =$$

$$\left(\begin{bmatrix} 0 & 1 \\ 1 & 0 \end{bmatrix} \begin{bmatrix} 1 & 0 \\ 0 & -1 \end{bmatrix} \right) \begin{bmatrix} 1 & 1 & 3 \\ 2 & 6 & 6 \end{bmatrix}.$$

Associative property of matrix multiplication

12. If T_1 has matrix $\begin{bmatrix} -2 & 0 \\ 0 & 2 \end{bmatrix}$ and T_2 has matrix $\begin{bmatrix} 0 & 1 \\ -1 & 0 \end{bmatrix}$, what is a matrix for $T_1 \circ T_2$?   **See margin.**

Applying the Mathematics

13. a. Find the matrix for $r_x \circ r_{y=x}$.   **See margin.**
   b. To what single transformation is $r_x \circ r_{y=x}$ equivalent? R_{270}
   c. How does your answer to part b compare with $r_{y=x} \circ r_x$?
   See margin.

14. Graph the image of the flag of this lesson under the transformation $S_2 \circ r_y$.   **See margin.**

15. a. Prove that if C is any 2×2 matrix, then $S_k \cdot C = C \cdot S_k$.   **See margin.**
   b. What does part a imply is true about size-change transformations?
   See margin.

---

14. $\triangle ABC = \begin{bmatrix} 1 & 1 & 3 \\ 2 & 6 & 6 \end{bmatrix}$.

$\triangle A'B'C' = \begin{bmatrix} -2 & -2 & -6 \\ 4 & 12 & 12 \end{bmatrix}$

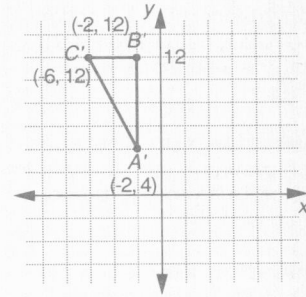

15.a. $S_k \cdot C =$

$\begin{bmatrix} k & 0 \\ 0 & k \end{bmatrix} \begin{bmatrix} m & n \\ p & q \end{bmatrix} =$

$\begin{bmatrix} km & kn \\ kp & kq \end{bmatrix}$

$C \cdot S_k = \begin{bmatrix} m & n \\ p & q \end{bmatrix} \begin{bmatrix} k & 0 \\ 0 & k \end{bmatrix} =$

$\begin{bmatrix} km & kn \\ kp & kq \end{bmatrix}$

b. Size change transformations are commutative.

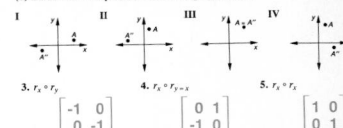

16. $\triangle BAT$ can be represented by $\begin{bmatrix} 0 & 3 & -1 \\ 5 & -2 & -1 \end{bmatrix}$.

 a. Find a matrix to represent the image $\triangle B'A'T'$ under r_x.   **See margin.**
 b. *True or false* $\triangle BAT \cong \triangle B'A'T'$. *(Lesson 4-5)*   **True**

17. a. What kind of triangle is represented by $\begin{bmatrix} -7 & 7 & 0 \\ 0 & 0 & 7 \end{bmatrix}$?
    isosceles right triangle
 b. What matrix describes the image of the triangle in part a under

   $\begin{bmatrix} 4 & 0 \\ 0 & 1 \end{bmatrix}$?   **See margin.**

 c. What special kind of triangle is the image?   **isosceles**
 d. Find the areas of the two triangles. *(Previous course; Lessons 4-1, 4-4)*
    49 units², 196 units²

18. Each month the population of Boomtown increases by 50 people. In contrast, the population of Bustville has been decreasing by 80 people/month. Suppose Boomtown now has 25,620 people and Bustville 31,250, and these growth rates continue.
 a. In how many months will Boomtown have more people?   **44 mo**
 b. What will the population be then? *(Lesson 1-7)*
    27,820 in Boomtown; 27,730 in Bustville

19. *Multiple choice* Which expression equals $-(x_1 - x_2)$? *(Previous course)*   **a**
    a. $x_2 - x_1$ b. $x_1 - x_2$ c. $x_1 + x_2$
    d. $-x_{-1}$ e. none of these

20. Explore whether multiplication of 3 × 3 matrices has properties identical or similar to the properties for multiplication of 2 × 2 matrices given in this lesson.

 Properties are the same, with $\begin{bmatrix} 1 & 0 & 0 \\ 0 & 1 & 0 \\ 0 & 0 & 1 \end{bmatrix}$ **as the identity matrix.**

216

Rotations are closely related to angles. The arcs used to denote angles suggest turns. Angles with larger measure require more turn.

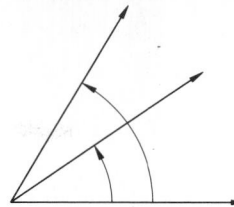

Rotations often occur one after the other, as when going from one frame to another in animated cartoons or in computer generated images.

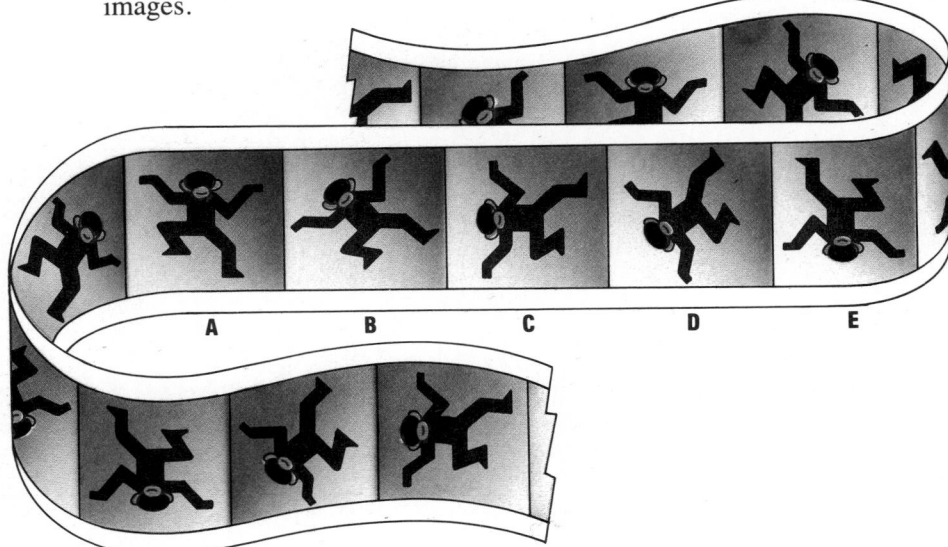

In these frames, the monkey undergoes a series of 45° counterclockwise rotations. Notice that monkeys two frames apart are turned 90°. This is a result of a fundamental property of rotations which itself is derived from the Angle Addition Postulate in geometry.

Theorem:

A rotation of $x°$ following one of $y°$ results in a rotation of $(x + y)°$. In symbols: $R_x \circ R_y = R_{x+y}$.

Notice that $\begin{bmatrix} a & b \\ c & d \end{bmatrix} \begin{bmatrix} 0 \\ 0 \end{bmatrix} = \begin{bmatrix} 0 \\ 0 \end{bmatrix}$ for all a, b, c, and d.

So any transformations with a 2×2 matrix must map $(0, 0)$ onto itself. Thus the only rotations that can have 2×2 matrices are those with center $(0, 0)$.

OBJECTIVES

F Relate rotations to matrices, and vice versa.
G Rotate figures using matrices.

TEACHING NOTES

Students should be able to determine the matrices for R_{90}, R_{180}, and R_{270}. They can either memorize them, learn the matrix for R_{90} and obtain the others through matrix multiplication, or they can determine them by examining the images of $(1, 0)$ and $(0, 1)$. The last of these options is presented at the end of this lesson and is preferable.

Have students predict the matrix for R_{360}. Then have them derive it through repeated multiplication. It will be the 2×2 identity matrix $\begin{bmatrix} 1 & 0 \\ 0 & 1 \end{bmatrix}$, since a 360° rotation is equivalent to a 0° rotation. Thus, another name for this rotation is R_0.

Reading Stress to students that an expression of the form $R_y \circ R_x$ means to rotate by x and then rotate by y; thus, we are reading from right to left instead of left to right as we would with most expressions.

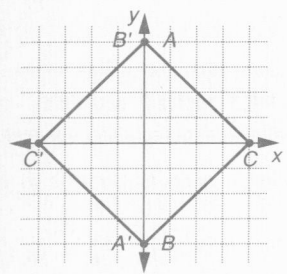
In Lesson 4-6, you learned the following theorem.

Theorem:

$$\begin{bmatrix} 0 & -1 \\ 1 & 0 \end{bmatrix}$$ is the matrix for R_{90}.

By composing two 90° rotations, a matrix for R_{180} can be found.

Example Find the matrix for R_{180}.

Solution A rotation of 180° can be considered as a 90° rotation followed by another 90° rotation. That is,

$$R_{90} \circ R_{90} = R_{180}.$$

In matrix form,

$$\begin{bmatrix} 0 & -1 \\ 1 & 0 \end{bmatrix} \begin{bmatrix} 0 & -1 \\ 1 & 0 \end{bmatrix} = \begin{bmatrix} -1 & 0 \\ 0 & -1 \end{bmatrix}.$$

The matrix for R_{180} is $\begin{bmatrix} -1 & 0 \\ 0 & -1 \end{bmatrix}$.

Check Apply this matrix to a figure. We use A, B, and C from the last lesson.

$$\begin{matrix} R_{180} & \triangle ABC & \triangle A^*B^*C^* \\ \begin{bmatrix} -1 & 0 \\ 0 & -1 \end{bmatrix} & \begin{bmatrix} 1 & 1 & 3 \\ 2 & 6 & 6 \end{bmatrix} = & \begin{bmatrix} -1 & -1 & -3 \\ -2 & -6 & -6 \end{bmatrix}. \end{matrix}$$

The graph verifies that each point of $\triangle ABC$ has been rotated 180° to the corresponding image point of $\triangle A^*B^*C^*$.

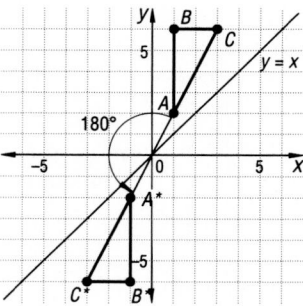

In Question 8 of this lesson you will be asked to show, in a similar way, that the matrix for R_{270} is $\begin{bmatrix} 0 & 1 \\ -1 & 0 \end{bmatrix}$.

218

Rotations in the clockwise direction have negative magnitudes. So R_{-90} represents a 90° turn clockwise. Because a rotation of -90° has the same image as a rotation of 270°, R_{-90} equals R_{270}.

Here is a summary of the rotations of this lesson:

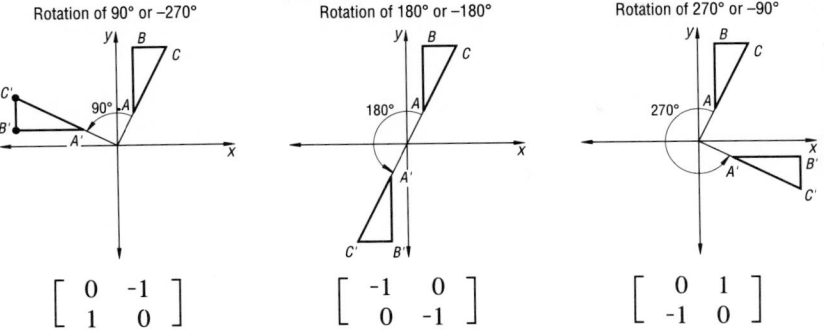

Rotation of 90° or −270°	Rotation of 180° or −180°	Rotation of 270° or −90°
$\begin{bmatrix} 0 & -1 \\ 1 & 0 \end{bmatrix}$	$\begin{bmatrix} -1 & 0 \\ 0 & -1 \end{bmatrix}$	$\begin{bmatrix} 0 & 1 \\ -1 & 0 \end{bmatrix}$

These matrices make it possible to get algebraic formulas for rotation images. For instance, for R_{90},

$$\begin{bmatrix} 0 & -1 \\ 1 & 0 \end{bmatrix} \begin{bmatrix} x \\ y \end{bmatrix} = \begin{bmatrix} 0 \cdot x + -1 \cdot y \\ 1 \cdot x + 0 \cdot y \end{bmatrix} = \begin{bmatrix} -y \\ x \end{bmatrix}.$$

Thus $R_{90}(x, y) = (-y, x)$.

You have learned matrices for many transformations in this chapter. To remember the 2 × 2 matrix for a particular transformation T, use this rule: The first column is the image of (1, 0) under T. The second column is the image of (0, 1). So, for example, to remember the matrix for R_{90}, use the picture below and record the images as shown in the matrix.

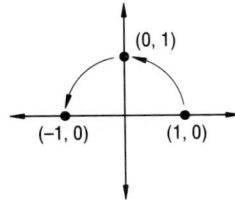

Questions

Covering the Reading

1. The composite of a rotation of 45° and a rotation of 90° is a rotation of ___?___. **135°**

2. In general, $R_x \circ R_y = $ ___?___. **R_{x+y}**

3. How much of a turn did the monkey pictured in the lesson undergo from the first frame to the last frame? **180° clockwise**

LESSON 4-7 Rotations   219

NOTES ON QUESTIONS
Question 15: Drawing a picture will confirm the result of this question. Pick any figure and show that its image under the composite equals its image under r_x.

Question 16: This question is more easily done by graphing than by using matrices. Remind students they could confirm that these points are on the circle by using the Distance Formula.

Question 22: The transformation is a composite of a reflection and a size change.

Questions 25 and 26: Be sure to stress these questions. They are meant to be groundwork for Lesson 4-8.

Question 29: This is meant to be an estimation question. Have the students pick a point, use the matrix R_x to find the image point, and use a protractor to estimate carefully the angle of rotation.

8. $\begin{bmatrix} -1 & 0 \\ 0 & -1 \end{bmatrix}\begin{bmatrix} 0 & -1 \\ 1 & 0 \end{bmatrix} = \begin{bmatrix} 0 & 1 \\ -1 & 0 \end{bmatrix}$

14. $MATH = \begin{bmatrix} 0 & 5 & 5 & -1 \\ 0 & 0 & 7 & 3 \end{bmatrix}$

$M'A'T'H = \begin{bmatrix} 0 & -5 & -5 & 1 \\ 0 & 0 & -7 & -3 \end{bmatrix}$

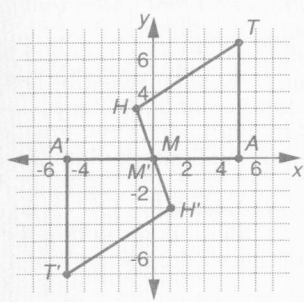

16.a. and b.

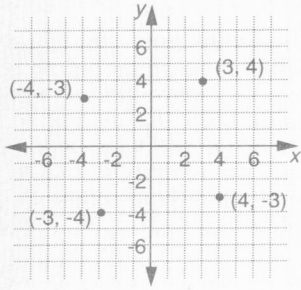

(3, 4)
(-4, -3)
(-3, -4)
(4, -3)

17.a. and b.

$\triangle ABC = \begin{bmatrix} -5 & -1 & -1 \\ 0 & 2 & 4 \end{bmatrix}$

$\triangle A'B'C' = \begin{bmatrix} 5 & 1 & 1 \\ 0 & -2 & -4 \end{bmatrix}$

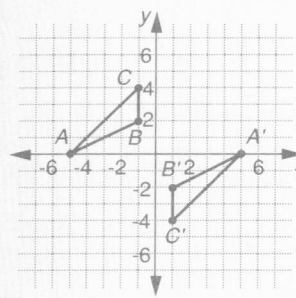

4. A rotation of negative magnitude is in what direction?   clockwise

In 5–7, identify the matrix for the given rotation.

a. $\begin{bmatrix} 0 & -1 \\ 1 & 0 \end{bmatrix}$ **b.** $\begin{bmatrix} 0 & -1 \\ -1 & 0 \end{bmatrix}$ **c.** $\begin{bmatrix} -1 & 0 \\ 0 & -1 \end{bmatrix}$

d. $\begin{bmatrix} 0 & 1 \\ -1 & 0 \end{bmatrix}$ **e.** $\begin{bmatrix} -1 & 0 \\ 0 & 1 \end{bmatrix}$

5. R_{90} a   **6.** R_{-90} d   **7.** R_{180} c

8. Consider a rotation of 270° as being a rotation of 90° followed by a rotation of 180°. Using the method of the example, show that

$\begin{bmatrix} 0 & 1 \\ -1 & 0 \end{bmatrix}$ is the matrix for R_{270}.   See margin.

In 9–12, find each image.

9. $R_{90}(3, 5)$ (-5, 3)   **10.** $R_{180}(3, 5)$ (-3, -5)

11. $R_{270}(3, 5)$ (5, -3)   **12.** $R_{90}(-2, -1)$ (1, -2)

Applying the Mathematics

13. What is the matrix for R_0? $\begin{bmatrix} 1 & 0 \\ 0 & 1 \end{bmatrix}$

14. Quadrilateral $MATH$ has coordinates $M = (0, 0)$, $A = (5, 0)$, $T = (5, 7)$, and $H = (-1, 3)$. Graph $MATH$ and its image under R_{180}. See margin.

15. a. Calculate a matrix for $R_{180} \circ r_y$. $\begin{bmatrix} 1 & 0 \\ 0 & -1 \end{bmatrix}$
b. To what transformation does the matrix in part a correspond? r_x
See margin.

16. The point (3, 4) lies on the circle with center (0, 0) and radius 5.
a. Rotate this point 90°, 180°, and 270° around (0, 0) to find the coordinates of 3 other points on this circle.
b. Graph all 4 points.

17. a. Graph triangle ABC with vertices $A = (-5, 0)$, $B = (-1, 2)$, and $C = (-1, 4)$. See margin.
b. Graph the image of $\triangle ABC$ under $r_y \circ r_x$. See margin.
c. The triangle in part a is the image of $\triangle ABC$ under what rotation? R_{180}

Review

In 18–21, write the matrix for each transformation. *(Lessons 4-3, 4-4, 4-5, 4-6)*

18. the size change of magnitude 3, center (0, 0) $\begin{bmatrix} 3 & 0 \\ 0 & 3 \end{bmatrix}$

19. the identity transformation $\begin{bmatrix} 1 & 0 \\ 0 & 1 \end{bmatrix}$

20. $r_{y=x}$ $\begin{bmatrix} 0 & 1 \\ 1 & 0 \end{bmatrix}$ **21.** $(x, y) \rightarrow (x, 3y)$ $\begin{bmatrix} 1 & 0 \\ 0 & 3 \end{bmatrix}$

22. a. Let $T = (-2, 3)$, $R = (5, 3)$, $A = (5, 0)$, and $P = (3, 0)$. Graph polygon *TRAP*.   See margin.
   b. Graph the image of *TRAP* under the transformation with matrix

$$\begin{bmatrix} 2 & 0 \\ 0 & -2 \end{bmatrix}.$$ See margin.

   c. Describe the transformation. *(Lessons 4-1, 4-4, 4-6)*   See margin.

23. If y varies inversely as the square of x and $y = 10$ when $x = 5$, what is y when $x = 6$? *(Lesson 2-2)*   6.94

24. Calculate the coordinates of the midpoint of the segment joining $(-4, 6)$ and $(2, 3)$. *(Previous course)* $(-1, 4\frac{1}{2})$

25. What is the definition of "perpendicular lines"? *(Previous course)*   See margin.

26. Show that the matrix $\begin{bmatrix} 5 & -3 & 0 \\ 3 & 5 & 0 \end{bmatrix}$ represents a right triangle by

using the Pythagorean theorem. *(Lesson 4-1, Previous course)*   See margin.

27. Use the figure below. Describe the transformation that maps *ABCDE* onto $A'B'C'D'E'$.
   a. in words.   The reflection over the y-axis
   b. by a matrix.   See margin.
   c. with an algebraic formula.
      (Lesson 4-5)   R(x, y) = (-x, y)

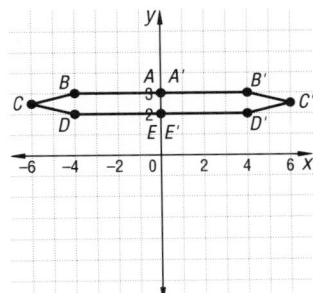

Exploration

28. The matrix for R_{30} is $\begin{bmatrix} \frac{\sqrt{3}}{2} & \frac{-1}{2} \\ \frac{1}{2} & \frac{\sqrt{3}}{2} \end{bmatrix}$.   Use this information to

determine matrices for some other rotations.   See margin.

29. The matrix $\begin{bmatrix} 0.6 & -0.8 \\ 0.8 & 0.6 \end{bmatrix}$ is a matrix for a rotation R_x. By

carefully plotting points and their images, estimate x, the magnitude of the rotation.   See margin.

MORE PRACTICE
For more questions on SPUR Objectives, use *Lesson Master 4-7*, shown below.

EVALUATION
A quiz covering Lessons 4-5 through 4-7 is provided in the Teacher's Resource File.

22.a. and b.

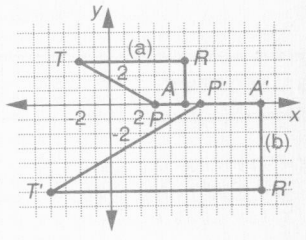

c. reflection about x-axis, stretch by 2

25., 26., 27.b., 28., and 29. See Additional Answers in the back of this book.

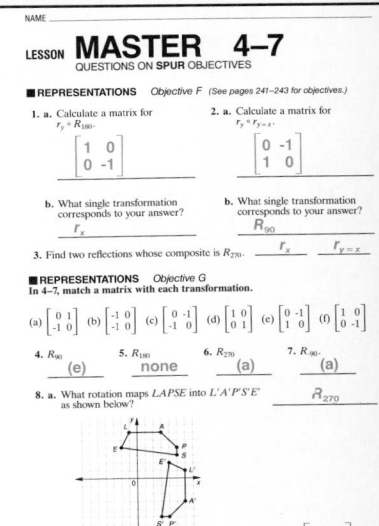

OBJECTIVE

B Determine equations of
lines perpendicular to
given lines.

TEACHING NOTES

Begin the lesson by discussing **Example 1** with the
class. This example reviews
rotations and at the same
time validates the perpendicular line slope theorem.
Next, discuss the theorem
itself. The proof of this
theorem in the text is algebraic and much simpler for
students than it looks.

Error Analysis In a problem, such as **Example 2**,
where two lines are involved,
students may confuse the
slopes of the lines. If this
happens, encourage them to
label the lines and their
slopes using subscripts. For
example, $L_1: y = -\frac{3}{2}x + 2$
has slope $m_1 = -\frac{3}{2}$;
$L_2: y - 1 = \frac{2}{3}(x + 4)$ has
slope $m_2 = \frac{2}{3}$. The subscripts
relate the lines and their
slopes.

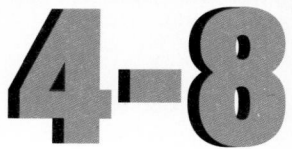

Perpendicular Lines

*The rotation of this carnival ride combines two perpendicular
forces: centripetal force (toward the center) and centrifugal
force (tangent to the circular movement).*

In this lesson, ideas about rotations help to deduce an important
theorem about the slopes of perpendicular lines. Recall from
geometry that two lines are perpendicular if and only if they form a
90° angle. In the last section you learned that $R_{90}(x, y) = (-y, x)$.
We can use R_{90} to rotate a line 90° by taking any two points P and
Q on the line and rotating them 90° about the origin. The line drawn
through the two image points P' and Q' will then be perpendicular
to the original line.

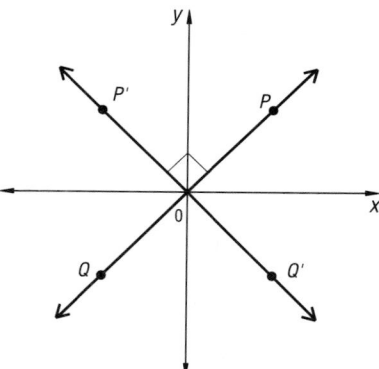

Example 1 Given $A = (4, 1)$ and $B = (-5, -3)$:
  a. Rotate $\overleftrightarrow{AB}$ 90°.
  b. Graph $\overleftrightarrow{AB}$ and its image $\overleftrightarrow{A'B'}$.
  c. Find the slopes of $\overleftrightarrow{AB}$ and $\overleftrightarrow{A'B'}$.
  d. What relationship exists between the two slopes?

222

Solution

a. Use $R_{90}(x, y) = (-y, x)$.
  $A' = R_{90}(A) = R_{90}(4, 1) = (-1, 4)$
  $B' = R_{90}(B) = R_{90}(-5, -3) = (3, -5)$
  Thus two points on the image line are $A' = (-1, 4)$ and $B' = (3, -5)$.

b. The preimage $\overleftrightarrow{AB}$ and image $\overleftrightarrow{A'B'}$ are graphed below.

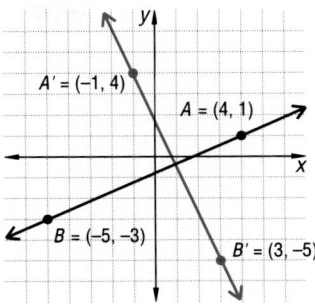

c. The slope of $\overleftrightarrow{AB}$: $\dfrac{-3 - 1}{-5 - 4} = \dfrac{4}{9}$; the slope of $\overleftrightarrow{A'B'}$: $\dfrac{-5 - 4}{3 - (-1)} = -\dfrac{9}{4}$.

d. The slopes are negative reciprocals of each other. Another way to say that is to say that the product of the slopes is -1.

Example 1 is an instance of the following theorem.

Theorem:

If two lines with slopes m_1 and m_2 are perpendicular, then $m_1 \cdot m_2 = -1$.

The following argument proves that if the two lines are perpendicular, then the product of their slopes is -1. We are given lines with slopes m_1 and m_2. We must find values for m_1 and m_2 and multiply those values. The given lines are parallel to lines with the same slopes that intersect at the origin. We prove the theorem for two lines through the origin; this proves the property for perpendicular lines elsewhere.

1. Determine whether the lines with equations (a) $2x - 4y = 1$ and (b) $x - 2y = 2$ are parallel, perpendicular, or neither.
slope of (a) = slope of (b) $= \frac{1}{2}$; the lines are parallel.

2. Line l is defined by $5x + 4y = 7$; line n contains $(3, 8)$; and $n \perp l$. Find an equation for line n.
$y - 8 = \frac{4}{5}(x - 3)$

3. Find an equation for the perpendicular bisector of the segment joining $A = (-6, 7)$ and $B = (-8, -3)$.
$y - 2 = -\frac{1}{5}(x + 7)$

4. Find the value of h if the line determined by $(4, h)$ and $(6, 9)$ is perpendicular to the line $y = -\frac{4}{3}x + 7$.
$\frac{h - 9}{4 - 6} = \frac{3}{4}$, so $h = 7\frac{1}{2}$.

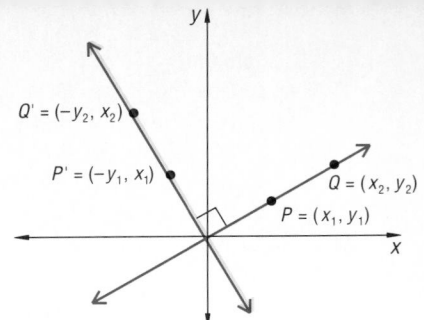

Proof

Let $P = (x_1, y_1)$ and $Q = (x_2, y_2)$
be two points on a line $\overleftrightarrow{PQ}$ that contains the origin.
Since $R_{90}(x, y) = (-y, x)$ for all (x, y),
$$R_{90}(x_1, y_1) = (-y_1, x_1)$$
and $$R_{90}(x_2, y_2) = (-y_2, x_2).$$

The image line contains $P' = (-y_1, x_1)$ and $Q' = (-y_2, x_2)$.
Let the slopes of the lines be m_1 and m_2.

$$m_1 = \text{slope of } \overleftrightarrow{PQ} = \frac{y_2 - y_1}{x_2 - x_1}$$

$$m_2 = \text{slope of } \overleftrightarrow{P'Q'} = \frac{x_2 - x_1}{-y_2 - (-y_1)} = \frac{x_2 - x_1}{-(y_2 - y_1)} = -\frac{x_2 - x_1}{y_2 - y_1}$$

The product of the slopes is

$$m_1 \cdot m_2 = \frac{y_2 - y_1}{x_2 - x_1} \cdot \left(-\frac{x_2 - x_1}{y_2 - y_1} \right)$$
$$= -1.$$

Example 2 Line n goes through $(-4, 1)$ and is perpendicular to line l whose equation is $y = -\frac{3}{2}x + 2$. Find an equation for line n.

Solution The situation is graphed at the right. Line l is in slope-intercept form; its slope is $-\frac{3}{2}$. Any line perpendicular to it has slope $\frac{2}{3}$, since $-\frac{3}{2} \cdot \frac{2}{3} = -1$. An equation for line n having slope $\frac{2}{3}$ and going through $(-4, 1)$ is

$$y - 1 = \frac{2}{3}(x + 4).$$

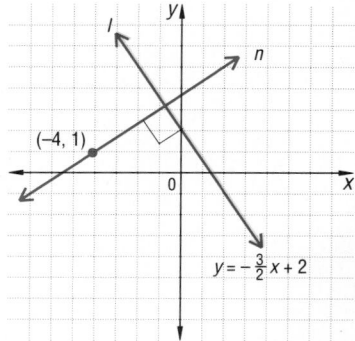

224

Recall from geometry that all points on the perpendicular bisector of a segment AB are equidistant from the endpoints A and B. This idea is used in the next example.

Example 3 Find an equation for the set of points equidistant from $Y = (-2, -5)$ and $C = (6, 5)$.

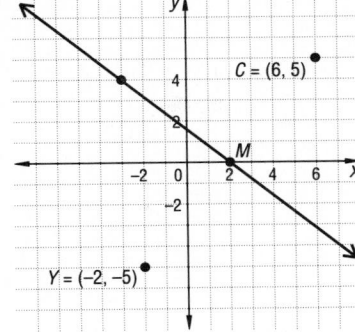

Solution The set of points equidistant from Y and C is the perpendicular bisector of $\overline{YC}$. To find the equation, first find the coordinate of M, the midpoint of $\overline{YC}$.

$$M = \left(\frac{-2 + 6}{2}, \frac{-5 + 5}{2}\right) = (2, 0)$$

Then find the slope m of any line perpendicular to $\overline{YC}$.

$$m = \frac{5 - (-5)}{6 - (-2)} = \frac{10}{8} = \frac{5}{4}$$

The slope of any perpendicular to $\overline{YC}$ is $-\frac{4}{5}$.
Now use the point-slope formula to write an equation for the line through $(2, 0)$ with slope $-\frac{4}{5}$.

$$y - 0 = -\tfrac{4}{5}(x - 2)$$

Check Let $x = -3$. Then $y = 4$. Does the line seem to go through $(-3, 4)$? Yes.

Suppose line l_1 has slope m_1, line l_2 has slope m_2, and $m_1m_2 = -1$. Are l_1 and l_2 perpendicular? The answer is yes, by the following argument. Any line l_3 perpendicular to l_1 has slope m_3, where $m_1m_3 = -1$. Thus $m_1m_3 = m_1m_2$, which means that $m_3 = m_2$. Therefore l_3 and l_2 have the same slope; so $l_3 \parallel l_2$. But we know that $l_1 \perp l_3$. We also know that if a line is perpendicular to one of two parallel lines, it must be perpendicular to the other. Thus, $l_1 \perp l_2$. We have proved the converse of the previous theorem:

Theorem:

If two lines have slopes m_1 and m_2 and $m_1m_2 = -1$, then the lines are perpendicular.

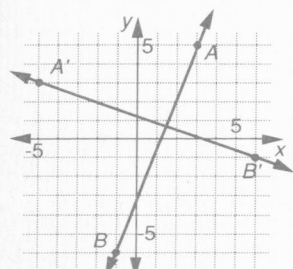
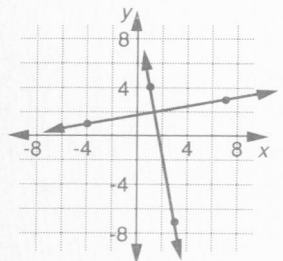
Covering the Reading

1. Under R_{90}, the image of (x, y) is __?__. $(-y, x)$

2. Let $\overleftrightarrow{AB}$ contain points $A = (3, 5)$ and $B = (-1, -6)$.
   a. Find two points on the image of $\overleftrightarrow{AB}$ under R_{90}. samples: (-5, 3),(6, -1)
   b. Graph $\overleftrightarrow{AB}$ and its image $\overleftrightarrow{A'B'}$. See margin.
   c. Find the slopes of $\overleftrightarrow{AB}$ and of $\overleftrightarrow{A'B'}$. $\frac{11}{4}, -\frac{4}{11}$ respectively
   d. The product of the slopes is __?__. $\frac{11}{4} \cdot -\frac{4}{11} = -1$

3. Two lines with nonzero slopes m_1 and m_2 are perpendicular if and only if __?__. $m_1m_2 = -1$

4. Refer to the proof of the first theorem in this lesson.
   a. What rotation maps points on $\overleftrightarrow{PQ}$ onto corresponding points on $\overleftrightarrow{P'Q'}$? R_{90}
   b. The slope of $\overleftrightarrow{PQ}$ is __?__. $\frac{y_2 - y_1}{x_2 - x_1}$
   c. The slope of $\overleftrightarrow{P'Q'}$ is __?__. $-\frac{x_2 - x_1}{y_2 - y_1}$

5. Given the line with equation $2x + 6y = 1$ and the point $P = (7, -2)$:
   a. Find the slope of a line perpendicular to the given line. 3
   b. Find an equation for the line through P and perpendicular to the given line. $y + 2 = 3(x - 7)$

6. Find an equation of the line through $(6, 1)$ and perpendicular to the line $y = \frac{4}{3}x - 2$. $y - 1 = -\frac{3}{4}(x - 6)$

7. Suppose Y is $(1, -4)$ and C is $(-3, 10)$. What is an equation for the perpendicular bisector of $\overline{YC}$? $y - 3 = \frac{2}{7}(x + 1)$

8. $\overline{CD}$ has endpoints $C = (9, 5)$ and $D = (-7, 11)$. Find an equation for the perpendicular bisector of $\overline{CD}$. $y - 8 = \frac{8}{3}(x - 1)$

Applying the Mathematics

9. *Multiple choice* A line perpendicular to the line with equation $x = 7$ has a
   (a) slope 0.   (b) undefined slope.   (c) slope $\frac{1}{7}$.   (d) slope 7.

10. Why do the statements of the theorems in this lesson apply only to lines with nonzero slopes? Reciprocal of zero is not defined.

11. Find an equation for the line through $(6, 2)$ and perpendicular to $y = 4$. $x = 6$

12. Given the line containing points $A = (7, 3)$ and $B = (-4, 1)$:
    a. Find the coordinates of A' and B' under R_{270}. $A' = (3, -7); B' = (1, 4)$
    b. Graph both the preimage and the image. See margin.
    c. Find the slopes of $\overleftrightarrow{AB}$ and $\overleftrightarrow{A'B'}$. See margin.
    d. What relationship exists between the slopes? What does this tell you about the lines? See margin.
    e. A counterclockwise rotation of 270° is the same as a clockwise rotation of __?__. See margin.

13. Fill each blank with ∥ or ⊥. Assume all lines lie in the same plane.
  a. If $l \parallel m$ and $m \parallel n$, then $l \underline{\ ?\ } n$.   ∥
  b. If $l \parallel m$ and $m \perp n$, then $l \underline{\ ?\ } n$.   ⊥
  c. If $l \perp m$ and $m \parallel n$, then $l \underline{\ ?\ } n$.   ⊥
  d. If $l \perp m$ and $m \perp n$, then $l \underline{\ ?\ } n$.   ∥

Review

14. a. Find the matrix for the image of the triangle defined by

$$\begin{bmatrix} 1 & 1 & 3 \\ 2 & 6 & 7 \end{bmatrix} \text{ under } R_{270}. \quad \begin{bmatrix} 2 & 6 & 7 \\ -1 & -1 & -3 \end{bmatrix}$$

  b. Graph the preimage and image. *(Lesson 4-7)*   **See margin.**

15. a. Calculate a matrix for $r_y \circ R_{180}$. $\begin{bmatrix} 1 & 0 \\ 0 & -1 \end{bmatrix}$
  b. To what transformation does this matrix correspond? *(Lesson 4-7)* r_x

16. Matrix D gives the daily delivery of fish to two markets. Matrix C gives the unit cost for each item in the market.

	cod	perch	grouper
Albert's	12	6	20
Carlita's	8	5	32

$= D$

	unit cost
cod	2.89
perch	2.59
grouper	1.98

$= C$

  a. Find DC. $\begin{bmatrix} 88.82 \\ 99.43 \end{bmatrix}$
  b. What is the daily cost of fish at Carlita's? *(Lesson 4-2)*   **$99.43**

17. Find the first five terms of the sequence $\begin{cases} S_1 = 1 \\ S_n = S_{n-1} + n^3 \text{ for } n > 1. \end{cases}$
  (Lesson 1-4)   **1, 9, 36, 100, 725**

18. a. Solve for x: $u + vx = w + yx$. $\dfrac{w - u}{v - y}$
  b. When does the equation in part a have no solution? *(Lesson 1-8)*   **if $v = y$**

19. Wee Willie Winkle determined that he gets about $\frac{1}{4}$ of his daily calories from breakfast, $\frac{1}{5}$ from lunch, $\frac{1}{3}$ from dinner, and 500 calories from snacks. About how many calories does he consume daily? *(Lesson 1-8)*   **2300**

Exploration

20. Begin with the line $y = 2x + 7$. Choose five different transformations. Find an equation for the image of this line under each transformation you have chosen.   **See margin.**

FOLLOW-UP

MORE PRACTICE
For more questions on SPUR Objectives, use *Lesson Master 4-8*, shown below.

14.b.
$$\triangle A'B'C' = \begin{bmatrix} 2 & 6 & 7 \\ -1 & -1 & -3 \end{bmatrix}$$

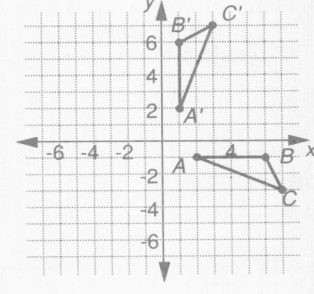

20. Many answers are possible.

NAME _____

LESSON **MASTER** **4–8**
QUESTIONS ON **SPUR** OBJECTIVES

■ SKILLS   *Objective B   (See pages 241–243 for objectives.)*
In 1–4, find an equation for the line that goes through the given point and is perpendicular to the given line.

1. $(2, -6); y = \frac{3}{2}x - 10$ **2.** $(3, 7); 4x + y = 2$

  $y = -\frac{2}{3}x - 4\frac{2}{3}$ $y = \frac{1}{4}x + 6\frac{1}{4}$

3. $(4, -7); y = -2$ **4.** $(8, 0); x = 12$

  $x = 4$ $y = 0$

In 5 and 6, find an equation for the set of points that are equidistant from the two given points.

5. $(3, -2); (1, 6)$ **6.** $(7, -4); (-7, 16)$

  $y = \frac{1}{4}x + \frac{3}{2}$ $y = \frac{7}{10}x + 6$

7. Given $M = (4, -10)$ and $N = (-6, -5)$, find an equation for the perpendicular bisector of $\overline{MN}$. $y = 2x - 5\frac{1}{2}$

8. Suppose l, m, and n are three lines.
  a. Fill in the blank with ∥ or ⊥.
    If $l \parallel m$ and $m \perp n$, then $l \underline{\ \perp\ } n$.
  b. Make a sketch of how these lines may be arranged.
    Sample:

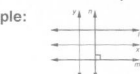

48   Advanced Algebra © Scott, Foresman and Company

227

LESSON

4-9

Matrix Addition

There are many situations which require adding the information stored in matrices. For instance, suppose matrix *C* represents the current inventory of Elizabeth's Boutique Department.

$$
\begin{array}{c}
\textbf{sizes}\\
\begin{array}{cccccc}
 & 8 & 10 & 12 & 14 & 16 \\
\text{dresses} & 5 & 7 & 8 & 10 & 9 \\
\text{suits} & 3 & 4 & 6 & 2 & 2 \\
\text{skirts} & 15 & 20 & 18 & 23 & 7 \\
\text{blouses} & 12 & 18 & 14 & 21 & 11
\end{array} = C
\end{array}
$$

The boutique receives a delivery of new items represented by matrix *D*.

$$
\begin{array}{c}
\textbf{sizes}\\
\begin{array}{cccccc}
 & 8 & 10 & 12 & 14 & 16 \\
\text{dresses} & 3 & 2 & 4 & 3 & 1 \\
\text{suits} & 1 & 2 & 3 & 4 & 2 \\
\text{skirts} & 5 & 6 & 4 & 3 & 5 \\
\text{blouses} & 4 & 3 & 5 & 7 & 6
\end{array} = D
\end{array}
$$

The new inventory is found by taking the sum of matrices *C* and *D*. This **matrix addition** is performed according to the following rule.

> **Definition:**
>
> If two matrices *A* and *B* have the same dimensions, their sum *A* + *B* is the matrix in which each element is the sum of the corresponding elements in *A* and *B*.

228

For the matrices above, the sum $C + D$ is a 4 × 5 matrix. Add corresponding elements of C and D to find the elements of $C + D$. We have circled one set of corresponding elements.

$$C + D = \begin{bmatrix} 8 & 9 & 12 & 13 & 10 \\ 4 & 6 & 9 & 6 & 4 \\ 20 & 26 & 22 & \boxed{26} & 12 \\ 16 & 21 & 19 & 28 & 17 \end{bmatrix}$$

Because addition of real numbers is commutative, *addition of matrices is commutative.* Thus for any two matrices A and B with the same dimensions, $A + B = B + A$. Also, for all matrices A, B, and C, $(A + B) + C = A + (B + C)$; *addition of matrices is associative.*

Subtraction of matrices is defined in a similar manner: Given two matrices A and B, their difference $A - B$ is the matrix whose element in each position is the difference of the corresponding elements in A and B.

■ ■ ■ ■ ■ ■ ■ ■

Example 1 The matrix $W1$ below represents the costs of 1 dozen each of eggs and oranges in three different markets during one week. The matrix $W2$ represents the cost of these same items in the same stores during another week.

market

$$W1 = \begin{array}{cc} & \begin{array}{ccc} 1 & 2 & 3 \end{array} \\ & \begin{bmatrix} .97 & .90 & .95 \\ 1.99 & 1.79 & 1.59 \end{bmatrix} \begin{array}{l} \text{eggs} \\ \text{oranges} \end{array} \end{array}$$

market

$$W2 = \begin{array}{cc} & \begin{array}{ccc} 1 & 2 & 3 \end{array} \\ & \begin{bmatrix} .97 & .85 & 1.05 \\ 1.49 & 1.79 & 1.89 \end{bmatrix} \begin{array}{l} \text{eggs} \\ \text{oranges} \end{array} \end{array}$$

a. Find $W2 - W1$.
b. Which of the markets had the greatest change in the price of oranges from Week 1 to Week 2?

Solution

a.

$$\begin{array}{ccc} W2 & W1 & W2 - W1 \\ \begin{bmatrix} .97 & .85 & 1.05 \\ 1.49 & 1.79 & 1.89 \end{bmatrix} - \begin{bmatrix} .97 & .90 & .95 \\ 1.99 & 1.79 & 1.59 \end{bmatrix} = \begin{bmatrix} 0 & -.05 & .10 \\ -.50 & 0 & .30 \end{bmatrix} \end{array}$$

b. The changes in prices of oranges are given in row 2 of the matrix $W2 - W1$. The greatest change in prices occurred with oranges in market 1. The price of oranges decreased $.50 per dozen in this period.

LESSON 4-9   Matrix Addition   **229**

day. What was their delivery on the day of the festival?

$$\begin{bmatrix} 50 & 34 & 100 \\ 60 & 40 & 124 \end{bmatrix}$$

Matrix addition is related to a special type of matrix multiplication called *scalar multiplication*. Consider

$$\begin{bmatrix} 7 & 8 \\ 4 & 2 \end{bmatrix} + \begin{bmatrix} 7 & 8 \\ 4 & 2 \end{bmatrix} + \begin{bmatrix} 7 & 8 \\ 4 & 2 \end{bmatrix} = \begin{bmatrix} 21 & 24 \\ 12 & 6 \end{bmatrix}.$$

Notice that in the final result, every element of the original matrix has been multiplied by 3. We rewrite this as $3\begin{bmatrix} 7 & 8 \\ 4 & 2 \end{bmatrix}$. The constant 3 is called a **scalar. Scalar multiplication** is defined as follows.

Definition:

The product of a scalar k and a matrix A is the matrix kA in which each element is k times the corresponding element in A.

■ ■ ■ ■ ■ ■ ■ ■

Example 2   Find the product $5\begin{bmatrix} 7 & 2 & -1 \\ 4 & 9 & 11 \end{bmatrix}$.

Solution   Every element in the matrix must be multiplied by 5.

$$5\begin{bmatrix} 7 & 2 & -1 \\ 4 & 9 & 11 \end{bmatrix} = \begin{bmatrix} 5 \cdot 7 & 5 \cdot 2 & 5 \cdot (-1) \\ 5 \cdot 4 & 5 \cdot 9 & 5 \cdot 11 \end{bmatrix} = \begin{bmatrix} 35 & 10 & -5 \\ 20 & 45 & 55 \end{bmatrix}$$

Questions

Covering the Reading

1. What must be true about the dimensions of two matrices in order for addition or subtraction to be possible?
   They must have the same dimensions.

In 2 and 3, refer to the clothing matrices C and D at the beginning of this lesson.

2. Does $C + D = D + C$?   Yes

3. Suppose the shop gets another delivery described by matrix P below. Find the new inventory $P + C + D$.   See margin.

sizes

$$P = \begin{array}{c} \\ \begin{bmatrix} 5 & 2 & 1 & 0 & 3 \\ 4 & 1 & 1 & 1 & 2 \\ 3 & 6 & 4 & 10 & 5 \\ 4 & 2 & 5 & 11 & 12 \end{bmatrix} \end{array} \begin{array}{l} \text{dresses} \\ \text{suits} \\ \text{skirts} \\ \text{blouses} \end{array}$$

with column headers: 8 10 12 14 16

NOTES ON QUESTIONS
Questions 6 and 7:
These two questions illustrate that, like subtraction of real numbers, subtraction of matrices is not commutative.

Questions 12–14: Remind students that when matrices represent real-world data, the matrices need to be labeled in order that the data be easily identifiable. These questions illustrate good examples of labeling.

4. Refer to Example 1.
   a. In which market did the price of a dozen eggs change the most from Week 1 to Week 2?   3
   b. Was that change an increase or decrease?   increase

In 5–7, let $A = \begin{bmatrix} 3 & 5 \\ 0 & -3 \end{bmatrix}$, $B = \begin{bmatrix} 4 & -5 \\ -2 & 1 \end{bmatrix}$, and

$C = \begin{bmatrix} 1 & -1 \\ -6 & 3 \end{bmatrix}$. Find:

5. $6C$ $\begin{bmatrix} 6 & -6 \\ -36 & 18 \end{bmatrix}$ 6. $A - B$ $\begin{bmatrix} -1 & 10 \\ -2 & 4 \end{bmatrix}$ 7. $B - A$ $\begin{bmatrix} 1 & -10 \\ -2 & 4 \end{bmatrix}$

8. *True or false* Subtraction of matrices is commutative.   **False**

9. Use the matrices in Questions 5–7.
   a. Find $(A + B) + C$.   a) $\begin{bmatrix} 8 & -1 \\ -1 & 1 \end{bmatrix}$ b) $\begin{bmatrix} 8 & -1 \\ -8 & 1 \end{bmatrix}$
   b. Find $A + (B + C)$.
   c. What property is illustrated by the results of parts a and b?
      Addition of matrices is associative.

Applying the Mathematics

10. Let $M = \begin{bmatrix} 2 & 1 \\ 0 & -2 \end{bmatrix}$, $N = \begin{bmatrix} -2 & 3 \\ -5 & 0 \end{bmatrix}$, and $P = \begin{bmatrix} 1 & -4 \\ 1 & 2 \end{bmatrix}$.
   a. Compute $M(N + P)$.   a) $\begin{bmatrix} -6 & 0 \\ 8 & -4 \end{bmatrix}$ b) $\begin{bmatrix} -6 & 0 \\ 8 & -4 \end{bmatrix}$
   b. Compute $MN + MP$.
   c. Is matrix multiplication distributive over matrix addition in this case?   Yes

11. Solve for a, b, c, and d. $a = 8$; $b = -\frac{3}{5}$; $c = 21$; $d = 24.5$

$$3 \begin{bmatrix} a & -1 \\ c & 4 \end{bmatrix} - 5 \begin{bmatrix} 3 & b \\ 11 & -2.5 \end{bmatrix} = \begin{bmatrix} 9 & 0 \\ 8 & d \end{bmatrix}$$

12. The matrices N, C, and S give the enrollments by sex and grade at North, Central, and South high schools. In each matrix Row 1 gives the number of boys and Row 2 the number of girls. Columns 1 to 4 give the number of students in grades 9 through 12, respectively. Calculate entries in the matrix T that shows the total enrollment by sex and grade in the three schools.   See margin.

	9	10	11	12	
$N =$	250	245	240	235	boys
	260	250	240	230	girls

$$C = \begin{bmatrix} 200 & 190 & 180 & 170 \\ 200 & 195 & 190 & 185 \end{bmatrix}$$

$$S = \begin{bmatrix} 140 & 135 & 130 & 125 \\ 130 & 130 & 125 & 120 \end{bmatrix}$$

LESSON 4-9   Matrix Addition   231

EXTENSION
Ask students to prove that for 2×2 matrices, addition is commutative. Have them calculate the sums on the left- and right-hand sides of the expression below to show that the equality is true.

$$\begin{bmatrix} e & f \\ g & h \end{bmatrix} + \begin{bmatrix} a & b \\ c & d \end{bmatrix} =$$

$$\begin{bmatrix} a & b \\ c & d \end{bmatrix} + \begin{bmatrix} e & f \\ g & h \end{bmatrix}$$

They might also prove for 2×2 matrices that addition is associative, and that multiplication is distributive over addition.

ADDITIONAL ANSWERS

13.a.
$$\begin{bmatrix} -1 & 5 & -4 & -6 \\ -7 & 16 & -9 & -23 \\ 10 & -4 & -6 & 14 \\ 8 & -6 & -2 & 14 \\ 9 & -12 & 3 & 21 \end{bmatrix}$$

b. how many more points each team had in 1983–84 than in 1982–83
c. how many more wins, losses, ties, and total points Boston had in 1983–84 than in 1982–83

14. $\begin{bmatrix} 7 & 13 & 23 \\ 16 & 29 & 12 \end{bmatrix}$

15.a. $y - 0 = \frac{1}{2}(x - 3)$
b. $y - 0 = -2(x - 3)$

23.b. and c. See Additional Answers in the back of this book.

---

13. The results of the National Hockey League Adams Division for 1982–1983 and 1983–1984 are given in the matrices below.

1982–1983

	W	L	T	Pts.
Boston	50	20	10	110
Montreal	42	24	14	98
Buffalo	38	29	13	89
Quebec	34	34	12	80
Hartford	19	54	7	45

1983–1984

	W	L	T	Pts.
Boston	49	25	6	104
Montreal	35	40	5	75
Buffalo	48	25	7	103
Quebec	42	28	10	94
Hartford	28	42	10	66

a. Subtract the top matrix from the bottom matrix. Call the difference M. See margin.
b. What is the meaning of the 4th column of M? See margin.
c. What is the meaning of the 1st row of M? See margin.

14. Mr. Toi makes handcrafted toys for children. His output last year is represented by the matrix at the right. He wants to increase his output by 30%. Find the matrix that describes the needed output. Round elements to the nearest whole number. See margin.

	sm	med	lg
dolls	5	10	18
stuffed animals	12	22	9

Review

15. Let l be the line $x - 2y = -4$ and let $P = (3, 0)$. Find an equation for the line through P: See margin.
a. parallel to l.
b. perpendicular to l.
(Lessons 3-5, 4-8)

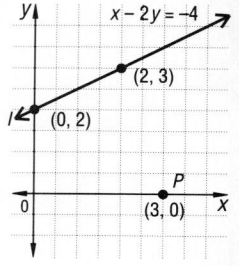

232

16. Match each numbered item on the right with the best lettered choice on the left. *(Lessons 4-1, 4-6, 4-7)*   **a) ii; b) i; c) iv; d) iii**

a. $\begin{bmatrix} 2 \\ 3 \end{bmatrix}$ (i) identity

b. $\begin{bmatrix} 1 & 0 \\ 0 & 1 \end{bmatrix}$ (ii) point

c. $\begin{bmatrix} 0 & 1 \\ -1 & 0 \end{bmatrix}$ (iii) R_{90}

d. $\begin{bmatrix} 0 & -1 \\ 1 & 0 \end{bmatrix}$ (iv) R_{-90}

In 17–20, give the 2 × 2 matrix for the transformation. *(Lessons 4-3, 4-4, 4-5, 4-7)*

17. r_x $\begin{bmatrix} 1 & 0 \\ 0 & -1 \end{bmatrix}$ **18.** S_2 $\begin{bmatrix} 2 & 0 \\ 0 & 2 \end{bmatrix}$ **19.** $S_{3,4}$ $\begin{bmatrix} 3 & 0 \\ 0 & 4 \end{bmatrix}$ **20.** R_{180} $\begin{bmatrix} -1 & 0 \\ 0 & -1 \end{bmatrix}$

21. Scenic City and Watertown are both along Raging River. A bridge is to be built across the river and be equidistant from the two cities. If Scenic City is at (-12, 8) and Watertown is at (22, 34), on what line should the bridge be built? *(Lesson 4-8)*
on $y - 21 = -\frac{17}{13}(x - 5)$

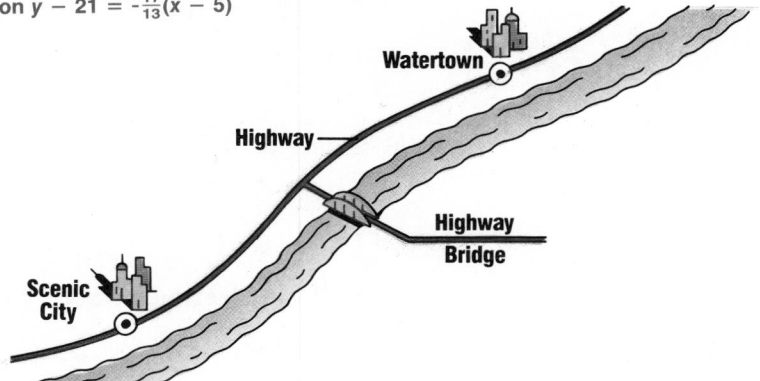

22. Approximate the solution to $\sqrt{3}(5 - .7x) = 19.04$ to the nearest hundredth. *(Lesson 1-7)* ≈-8.56

Exploration

23. Yet another operation with matrices is powering. Consider the matrix
$$M = \begin{bmatrix} 0.7 & 0.3 \\ 0.6 & 0.4 \end{bmatrix}.$$ **See margin.**

a. Calculate $M \cdot M$. Call it M^2. $\begin{bmatrix} .67 & .33 \\ .66 & .34 \end{bmatrix}$
b. Write a computer program to calculate M^3, M^4, and so on, up to M^{20}. **See margin.**
c. What matrix does M^n seem to approach as n gets larger and larger? **See margin.**

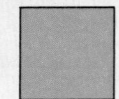

RESOURCES
■ Lesson Master 4-10

In this chapter you have found transformation images by multiplying matrices. There is one transformation for which images can be found by adding matrices. Consider △ABC and △A'B'C' below. △A'B'C' is a *slide* or **translation** image of the preimage △ABC. The matrices M and M' for these triangles are given at the left.

OBJECTIVE

H Graph figures and their translation images.

Translations

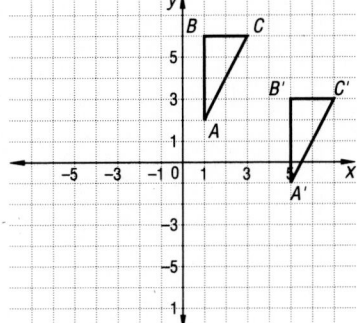

$$\triangle ABC$$
$$M = \begin{bmatrix} 1 & 1 & 3 \\ 2 & 6 & 6 \end{bmatrix}$$

$$\triangle A'B'C'$$
$$M' = \begin{bmatrix} 5 & 5 & 7 \\ -1 & 3 & 3 \end{bmatrix}$$

TEACHING NOTES

It may help students to visualize the image of a figure under the translation $T_{h,k}$ if they think of $T_{h,k}$ as "sliding" the figure *h* units to the right (to the left if *h* is negative) and *k* units up (down if *k* is negative). However, emphasize to students that there is no physical sliding. The translation, like all other transformations, is simply a correspondence between a figure and its image.

This is a good time to summarize the ideas of the chapter. Review with students that transformations may be described *algebraically* (with a formula for the image (x', y') in terms of (x, y)), *arithmetically* (with a matrix), or *geometrically* (by indicating the location of image points without using coordinates). It may be worthwhile to discuss the strengths and weaknesses of each definition and why the algebraic definition is preferable with translations.

Point out to students that unlike the other transformations encountered in this chapter, translations cannot be done by multiplying by a 2 × 2 matrix. They should remember that any transformation with a 2 × 2 matrix must map (0, 0) onto itself, and the only translation that does so is $T_{0,0}$.

Now we calculate $M' - M$.

$$M' - M = \begin{bmatrix} 5 & 5 & 7 \\ -1 & 3 & 3 \end{bmatrix} - \begin{bmatrix} 1 & 1 & 3 \\ 2 & 6 & 6 \end{bmatrix} = \begin{bmatrix} 4 & 4 & 4 \\ -3 & -3 & -3 \end{bmatrix}$$

In $M' - M$, all the elements in the first row are equal and all the elements in the second row are equal. Thus, to get the image △A'B'C', add 4 to every x-coordinate and -3 to every y-coordinate of the preimage.

$$\overset{M}{\begin{bmatrix} 1 & 1 & 3 \\ 2 & 6 & 6 \end{bmatrix}} + \begin{bmatrix} 4 & 4 & 4 \\ -3 & -3 & -3 \end{bmatrix} = \overset{M'}{\begin{bmatrix} 5 & 5 & 7 \\ -1 & 3 & 3 \end{bmatrix}}$$

This leads to an algebraic definition of translation.

Definition:

The transformation that maps (x, y) onto (x + h, y + k) is a translation of *h* units horizontally and *k* units vertically and is denoted by $T_{h,k}$.

△A'B'C' was obtained from △ABC with the translation $T_{4,-3}$.

There is no single matrix for a translation because the dimensions of that matrix would depend on the figure being translated. Translations are easy to do using the formula $T_{h,k}(x, y) = (x + h, y + k)$.

234

■ ■ ■ ■ ■ ■

Example A quadrilateral has vertices $Q = (-4, 2)$, $U = (-2, 6)$, $A = (0, 5)$, and $D = (0, 3)$.
a. Find its image under the transformation $T_{3,5}$.
b. Graph the image and preimage on the same graph.

Solution
a. $T_{3,5}(x, y) = (x + 3, y + 5)$, so $T(-4, 2) = (-1, 7)$.
$T(-2, 6) = (1, 11)$
$T(0, 5) = (3, 10)$
$T(0, 3) = (3, 8)$

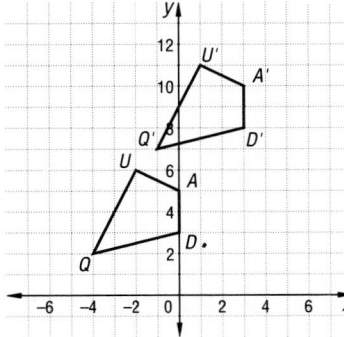

b. The image appears to be 3 units to the right and 5 units up, as it should.

Questions

Covering the Reading

In 1 and 2, refer to $\triangle ABC$ and $\triangle A'B'C'$ at the beginning of the lesson.
1. What translation maps $\triangle ABC$ onto $\triangle A'B'C'$? **T$_{4,-3}$**

2. What translation maps $\triangle A'B'C'$ onto $\triangle ABC$? **T$_{-4,3}$**

3. A translation is a transformation mapping (x, y) to __?__. **(x + h, y + k)**

4. $T_{h,k}$ is a translation __?__ units horizontally and __?__ units vertically.
h, k
5. Refer to the Example. Graph $QUAD$ and its image $Q'U'A'D'$ under $T_{4,7}$. **See margin.**

In 6–8, find the image of the point under $T_{-2,6}$.
6. $(0, 0)$ **(-2, 6)**   **7.** $(100, -98)$ **8.** (a, b) **(a − 2, b + 6)**
(98, -92)
9. A transformation T has a 2×2 matrix. If $T(1, 0) = (7, 11)$ and $T(0, 1) = (2, 3)$, what is the matrix for T? $\begin{bmatrix} 7 & 2 \\ 11 & 3 \end{bmatrix}$

LESSON 4-10 *Translations* **235**

ADDITIONAL EXAMPLES
1. A pentagon is to be translated under $T_{10,12}$. What matrix describes this translation?

$$\begin{bmatrix} 10 & 10 & 10 & 10 & 10 \\ 12 & 12 & 12 & 12 & 12 \end{bmatrix}$$

2. In triangle *POD*, $P = (4, 9)$, $O = (3, -1)$, and $D = (6, -4)$. It is to be translated using $T_{-1,1}$.
a. Find the translation matrix.

$$\begin{bmatrix} -1 & -1 & -1 \\ 1 & 1 & 1 \end{bmatrix}$$

b. Find the image matrix.

$$\begin{bmatrix} 3 & 2 & 5 \\ 10 & 0 & -3 \end{bmatrix}$$

c. Graph both the preimage and the image.

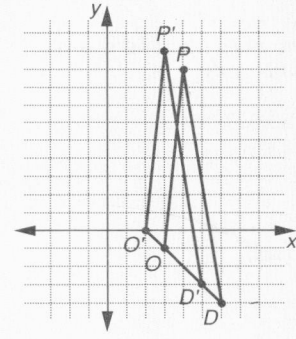

3. What translation undoes $T_{-6,4}$?
$T_{6,-4}$

ADDITIONAL ANSWERS
5. $QUAD = \begin{bmatrix} -4 & -2 & 0 & 0 \\ 2 & 6 & 5 & 3 \end{bmatrix}$

$Q'U'A'D' = T_{4,7} \begin{bmatrix} 0 & 2 & 4 & 4 \\ 9 & 13 & 12 & 10 \end{bmatrix}$

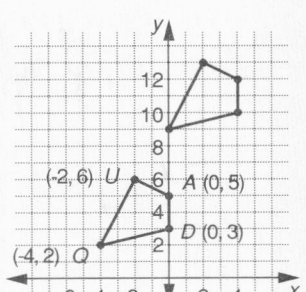

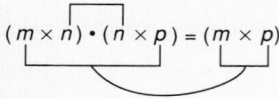
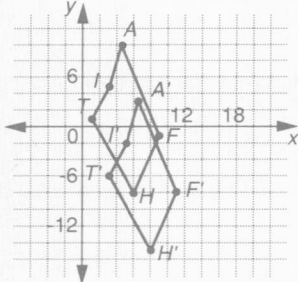
Applying the Mathematics

See margin.

10. Refer to the graph at the right.
    a. What translation maps $ABCDE$ onto $A'B'C'D'E'$?
    b. Verify that $\overline{CD} \cong \overline{C'D'}$.
    c. Verify that $\overline{BC} \parallel \overline{B'C'}$.

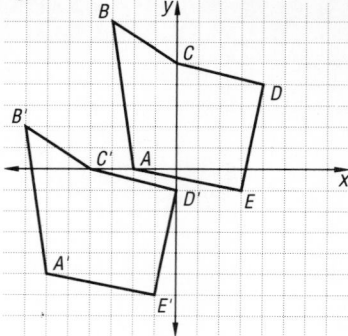

11. $\begin{bmatrix} 9 & 4 & 3 & 1 & 6 \\ -1 & 10 & 5 & 1 & -8 \end{bmatrix}$ represents pentagon *FAITH*.
    a. Apply the translation $T_{2,-7}$ to the pentagon. $\begin{bmatrix} 11 & 6 & 5 & 3 & 8 \\ -8 & 3 & -2 & -6 & -15 \end{bmatrix}$
    b. Graph the preimage and the image on the same set of axes.
    See margin.

12. $\triangle CUB$ is translated under $T_{4,9}$ to get $\triangle C'U'B'$. $\triangle C'U'B'$ is then translated under $T_{6,5}$ to get $\triangle C''U''B''$. What single translation will give the same result as $T_{6,5} \circ T_{4,9}$? $T_{10,14}$

Review

13. The matrices below represent U.S. foreign trade with other countries in millions of dollars.

	1982		1983	
	Exports	Imports	Exports	Imports
Western Hemisphere	67,312	84,467	63,970	93,873
Europe	63,664	53,413	59,590	55,243
Asia	64,822	85,170	63,813	91,464
Africa	10,271	8,768	17,770	14,425
Oceania	5,700	4,827	3,131	3,044

    a. Find the growth in the foreign trade from 1982 to 1983. **See margin.**
    b. From which area did the imports increase the most? *(Lesson 4-8)*
    Western Hemisphere

$$\begin{bmatrix} 0 & -1 \\ -5 & -6 \end{bmatrix}$$

14. Find a single matrix equal to

$$\begin{bmatrix} 1 & -1 & 2 \\ 0 & 2 & 1 \end{bmatrix} \begin{bmatrix} 2 & 8 \\ -1 & 0 \\ 1 & -2 \end{bmatrix} - \begin{bmatrix} 5 & 5 \\ 4 & -4 \end{bmatrix}.$$ *(Lessons 4-8, 4-2)*

15. By what must you multiply $\begin{bmatrix} 5 & 0 & -1 \\ 2 & 6 & -4 \end{bmatrix}$ to get

$\begin{bmatrix} -10 & 0 & 2 \\ 1 & 3 & -2 \end{bmatrix}$? *(Lesson 4-4)* See margin.

16. $H = (5, 1)$ and $I = (-3, -1)$.
  a. Find the image $\overline{H'I'}$ under r_y. $H' = (-5, 1); I' = (3, -1)$
  b. Find $\overline{HI}$ and $\overline{H'I'}$ and compare the two lengths.   Both equal $2\sqrt{17}$.
  c. Are $\overline{HI}$ and $\overline{H'I'}$ perpendicular? Justify your answer. *(Lessons 4-5, 4-7)*   No; the product of their slopes is not -1.

In 17–22, (a) give the matrix for the transformation; (b) give the image of (a, b). *(Lessons 4-3, 4-4, 4-5, 4-6)*   See margin.

17. $R_{270°}$ **18.** r_x

19. a size change of magnitude 4

20. $S_{1,6}$ **21.** $R_{180°}$

22. reflection over the line $y = x$

Exploration

23. A transformation has the following rule: The image of (x, y) is $(3x, y + 2)$. Find images of a figure of your own choosing. Geometrically describe what the transformation does to a figure.
The chosen figure is stretched by a factor of 3 in the horizontal direction and raised 2 units in the vertical direction.

FOLLOW-UP

MORE PRACTICE
For more questions on SPUR Objectives, use *Lesson Master 4-10*, shown below.

EXTENSION
The geometric definition of a translation is not given in this book. However, if you wish to share it with your students it is as follows: Let T be the translation that maps A onto B. Then $T(C) = D$ if and only if $ACDB$ is a parallelogram.

19.a. $\begin{bmatrix} 4 & 0 \\ 0 & 4 \end{bmatrix}$

b. $(4a, 4b)$

20.a. $\begin{bmatrix} 1 & 0 \\ 0 & 6 \end{bmatrix}$

b. $(a, 6b)$

21.a., b., 22.a., b., and 23. See Additional Answers in the back of this book.

NAME _____

237

Summary

A matrix is a rectangular array for storing data. The product of two matrices contains the sums of linear combinations of the rows and columns being multiplied. Not all matrices can be multiplied; the number of columns of the left matrix must equal the number of rows of the right matrix. Matrix multiplication is associative but not commutative.

Matrices can be added if they have the same dimensions. Any matrix can be multiplied by a number called a scalar.

Matrices with 2 rows can represent points and figures in the coordinate plane. Multiplying such a matrix by a 2×2 matrix on the left may yield a transformation image of the figure. Transformations for which matrices are found in this chapter include reflections, rotations, size changes, and scale changes. A summary is given below. The rotation of 90° about the origin is a particularly important transformation. From it, we proved that two nonvertical lines are $\perp$ if and only if the product of their slopes is -1.

The set of 2×2 matrices under multiplication has many properties. It is closed; though not commutative, it is associative; there is an identity $\begin{bmatrix} 1 & 0 \\ 0 & 1 \end{bmatrix}$.

Transformations Yielding Images Congruent to Preimages

Reflections:

over the *x*-axis
$$\begin{bmatrix} 1 & 0 \\ 0 & -1 \end{bmatrix}$$
$r_x(x, y) = (x, -y)$

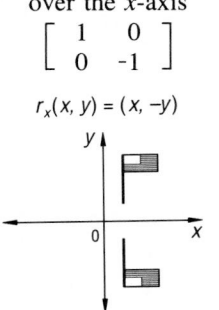

over the *y*-axis
$$\begin{bmatrix} -1 & 0 \\ 0 & 1 \end{bmatrix}$$
$r_x(x, y) = (-x, y)$

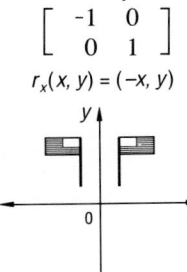

over the line $x = y$
$$\begin{bmatrix} 0 & 1 \\ 1 & 0 \end{bmatrix}$$
$r_x(x, y) = (y, x)$

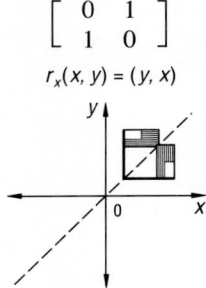

Rotations with center (0, 0):

magnitude 90°
$$\begin{bmatrix} 0 & -1 \\ 1 & 0 \end{bmatrix}$$
$R_{90}(x, y) = (-y, x)$

magnitude 180°
$$\begin{bmatrix} -1 & 0 \\ 0 & -1 \end{bmatrix}$$
$R_{180}(x, y) = (-x, -y)$

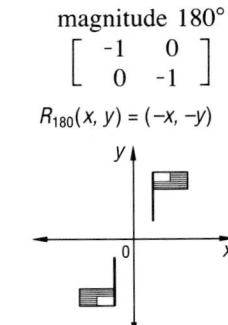

magnitude 270°
$$\begin{bmatrix} 0 & 1 \\ -1 & 0 \end{bmatrix}$$
$R_{270}(x, y) = (y, -x)$

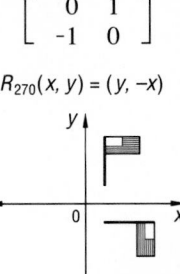

238

Translations:
No general matrix, $T_{h,k} = (x + h, y + k)$.

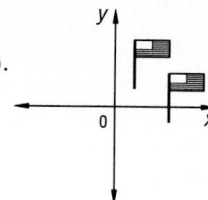

**Transformations Yielding Images
Similar to Preimages**

Size changes with center $(0, 0)$, magnitude k:

$$\begin{bmatrix} k & 0 \\ 0 & k \end{bmatrix}$$

$S_k(x, y) = (kx, ky)$

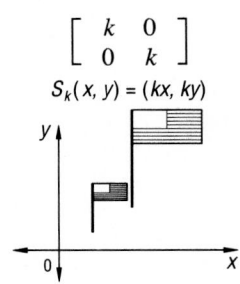

Other Transformations

Scale changes with horizontal magnitude a and
vertical magnitude b:

$$\begin{bmatrix} a & 0 \\ 0 & b \end{bmatrix}$$

$S_{a,b}(x, y) = (ax, by)$

The identity transformation maps any figure onto itself. It can be considered as the size change S_1, the rotation R_0, or the translation $T_{0,0}$.

Vocabulary

Below are the most important terms and phrases for this chapter.
You should be able to give a definition or general description
and a specific example of each.

Lesson 4-1
*matrix, element of a matrix, dimensions $m \times n$,
equal matrices, point matrix

Lesson 4-2
matrix multiplication

Lesson 4-3
*size change, image, preimage,
scale factor, magnitude of size change

Lesson 4-4
*scale change, horizontal scale change,
vertical scale change, stretch, shrink

Lesson 4-5
*reflection

Lesson 4-6
*transformation, *identity transformation,
*composite of transformations, composition,
rotation

Lesson 4-9
*matrix addition, matrix subtraction,
scalar, scalar multiplication

Lesson 4-10
*translation

CHAPTER 4   Summary and Vocabulary   **239**

Progress Self-Test

Answers not given on this page can be found in the Additional Answers section in the back of this book. Take this test as you would take a test in class. Use graph paper. Then check your work with the solutions in the Selected Answers section in the back of the book.

1. Graph the polygon described by the matrix

$$\begin{bmatrix} 3 & -5 & -6 & -5 & -1 & 5 \\ 4 & 2 & 0 & -2 & -3 & -4 \end{bmatrix}$$ **See margin.**

2. One day on Fruhtair flying from Appleton there were 14 first-class and 120 economy passengers going to Peachport; 3 first-class and 190 economy passengers bound for Bananasville; and 8 first-class and 250 economy passengers flying to Grapetown. Write a 2 × 3 matrix to store this information. **See margin.**

In 3–9, use matrices *A*, *B* and *C* below.

$$A = \begin{bmatrix} 5 & -2 \\ 4 & -2 \\ -1 & 0 \end{bmatrix} \quad B = \begin{bmatrix} 2 & 0 \\ 1 & 5 \end{bmatrix} \quad C = \begin{bmatrix} 8 & 6 \\ -2 & 2 \end{bmatrix}$$

3. Which product exists, *AB* or *BA*? **AB**

4. Find *BC*. $\begin{bmatrix} 16 & 12 \\ -2 & 16 \end{bmatrix}$ **5.** Find *B* − *C*.

6. Find the image of *B* under r_y. $\begin{bmatrix} -6 & -6 \\ 3 & 3 \end{bmatrix}$

7. Find the image of *C* under R_{90}.

8. Calculate 7*B*.

9. Why is $\begin{bmatrix} 1 & 0 \\ 0 & 1 \end{bmatrix}$ called the identity matrix? **The image is identical to the preimage.**

10. Find an equation for the line through (3, -2.5) that is perpendicular to $y = 5x - 3$.

11. Calculate the matrix for $r_x \circ R_{270}$.

12. Refer to the graph below. What translation maps *FIGURE* onto *F'I'G'U'R'E'*? $T_{8,-8}$

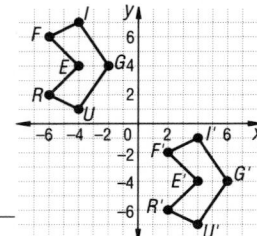

13. A shoe manufacturer has factories in Los Angeles, Tucson, and Santa Fe. One year's sales (in thousands) can be summarized by the following matrix.

	Deck shoes	Pumps	Sandals	Boots
Los Angeles	23	8	10	5
Tucson	11	5	10	15
Santa Fe	2	3	15	15

The selling prices of deck shoes, pumps, sandals, and boots are $18, $58, $12, and $76, respectively. Use matrix multiplication to determine the total revenue of each factory.

14. Two pet stores merge and combine inventories. If the matrices below represent each store's inventory before the merger, what will be their inventory after the merger? **See margin.**

	Lois's Pet Shop		Doug's Pet Shop	
	Males	Females	Males	Females
Dogs	8	11	10	14
Cats	5	4	11	13
Birds	15	16	7	9
Monkeys	2	0	0	3

15. Solve for *a* and *b*.

$$\begin{bmatrix} a & 0 \\ 0 & b \end{bmatrix}\begin{bmatrix} -9 \\ -7 \end{bmatrix} = \begin{bmatrix} -3 \\ 14 \end{bmatrix} \quad \begin{array}{l} a = \frac{1}{3}; \\ b = -2 \end{array}$$

In 16 and 17, give the matrix you might use if you wanted to perform the given transformation.

16. a horizontal stretch of magnitude 2 and a vertical shrink of magnitude $\frac{1}{2}$

17. a reflection over the line $y = x$

18. What is the image of (x, y) under a translation 4 units left and 12 units up?

19. Let $A = (7, 6)$, $B = (-1, 2)$, and $C = (3, -4)$. Graph $\triangle ABC$ and $R_{90}(\triangle ABC)$. **See margin.**

20. The transformation with matrix $\begin{bmatrix} .5 & 0 \\ 0 & .5 \end{bmatrix}$ is applied to $\triangle PQR$ with sides 3 cm, 4 cm, and 5 cm long. What are the lengths of the sides of $\triangle P'Q'R'$? **1.5 cm; 2 cm; 2.5 cm**

240

Chapter Review

Answers not given on this page can be found in the Additional Answers.

Questions on **SPUR** Objectives

SPUR stands for **S**kills, **P**roperties, **U**ses, and **R**epresentations.
The Chapter Review questions are grouped according to the
SPUR Objectives for this chapter.

SKILLS deals with the procedures used to get answers.

■ **Objective A:** *Perform matrix operations.* *(Lessons 4-2, 4-8, 4-9)*

In 1–3, calculate the product.

1. $\begin{bmatrix} 6 & -1 & -4 \end{bmatrix} \begin{bmatrix} 8 \\ -3 \\ -2 \end{bmatrix}$ $\begin{bmatrix} 59 \end{bmatrix}$

2. $\begin{bmatrix} 2 & 3 \\ -3 & 5 \end{bmatrix} \begin{bmatrix} 4 & 9 \\ 7 & 6 \end{bmatrix}$ $\begin{bmatrix} 29 & 36 \\ 23 & 3 \end{bmatrix}$

3. $\left(\begin{bmatrix} 1 & 2 & 3 \end{bmatrix} \begin{bmatrix} 4 & 7 \\ 5 & 8 \\ 6 & 9 \end{bmatrix} \right) \begin{bmatrix} 16 & 0 \\ 0 & 4 \end{bmatrix}$ $\begin{bmatrix} 512 & 200 \end{bmatrix}$

4. What matrix must you multiply by
$\begin{bmatrix} 5 & 3 & 1 \\ 1 & 2 & 0 \end{bmatrix}$ to get $\begin{bmatrix} 1 & .6 & .2 \\ -.5 & -1 & 0 \end{bmatrix}$? $\begin{bmatrix} .2 & 0 \\ 0 & -.5 \end{bmatrix}$

5. Find a single matrix for
$\begin{bmatrix} 8 & 6 \\ 3 & -2 \\ 4 & -1 \end{bmatrix} - \begin{bmatrix} -3 & 0 \\ -1 & 6 \\ -4 & -3 \end{bmatrix}$. $\begin{bmatrix} 11 & 6 \\ 4 & -8 \\ 8 & 2 \end{bmatrix}$

In 6 and 7, let
$A = \begin{bmatrix} 2 & 3 & 4 \\ 7 & 5 & -1 \\ 1 & 2 & 0 \end{bmatrix}$ and $B = \begin{bmatrix} 1 & -6 & 0 \\ 2 & 3 & 1 \\ 4 & 9 & 2 \end{bmatrix}$.

6. Find $2A + B$. **See margin.**
7. Find $3A - 4B$. **See margin.**

In 8–11, solve for a and b.

8. $\begin{bmatrix} a & 16 \\ 10 & b \end{bmatrix} + \begin{bmatrix} .4 & -1 \\ -10 & 3.1 \end{bmatrix} = \begin{bmatrix} 2 & 15 \\ 0 & -7 \end{bmatrix}$

9. $2\begin{bmatrix} -1 & 9 \\ b & -.5 \end{bmatrix} - \begin{bmatrix} a & 7 \\ -3 & 3 \end{bmatrix} = \begin{bmatrix} 6 & 11 \\ 13 & -4 \end{bmatrix}$

10. $\begin{bmatrix} a & 0 \\ 0 & b \end{bmatrix} \begin{bmatrix} 2 \\ -9 \end{bmatrix} = \begin{bmatrix} 10 \\ 27 \end{bmatrix}$

11. $\begin{bmatrix} 0 & -1 \\ 1 & 0 \end{bmatrix} \begin{bmatrix} a \\ b \end{bmatrix} = \begin{bmatrix} -5 \\ 8 \end{bmatrix}$

10) $a = 5$; $b = -3$; 11) $a = 8$; $b = 5$

■ **Objective B:** *Determine equations of lines perpendicular to given lines.* *(Lesson 4-8)*

12. Find an equation for the line through $(3, -1)$ and perpendicular to $y = -\frac{1}{2}x + 4$.

13. Find an equation for the line through $(7, 8)$ and perpendicular to $x = -4$.

14. Find an equation for the set of all points which are equidistant from $(8, 7)$ and $(-2, 9)$. $y - 8 = 5(x - 3)$

15. Given $A = (6, 1)$ and $B = (-2, 3)$. Find an equation for the perpendicular bisector of $\overline{AB}$. $y - 2 = 4(x - 2)$

PROPERTIES deal with the principles behind the mathematics.

■ **Objective C:** *Recognize properties of operations on matrices.* *(Lessons 4-2, 4-6, 4-8)*

In 16 and 17, (a) is the statement true or false?
(b) Give an example to back up your answer.

16. Matrix addition is commutative. **See margin.**
17. Matrix multiplication is associative. **See margin.**

18. Determine whether the following products exist.

a. $\begin{bmatrix} 1 & 6 & 4 \end{bmatrix} \begin{bmatrix} 2 \\ 8 \end{bmatrix}$ **No**

b. $\begin{bmatrix} 3 & 1 & 6 \\ 5 & 8 & -2 \end{bmatrix} \begin{bmatrix} 1 & -1 & 0 & 7 \\ 1 & 0 & 0 & 0 \\ 0 & 1 & 5 & 2 \end{bmatrix}$ **Yes**

CHAPTER 4 Chapter Review **241**

RESOURCES
■ Chapter 4 Test, Form A
■ Chapter 4 Test, Form B
■ Chapter 4 Test, Cumulative Form

CHAPTER REVIEW

The main objectives for the chapter are organized here into sections corresponding to the four main types of understanding this book promotes: Skills, Properties, Uses, and Representations.

USING THE CHAPTER REVIEW
Whereas end-of-chapter material may be considered optional in some texts, in *Advanced Algebra* we have selected these objectives and questions with the expectation that they will be covered. Students should be able to answer these questions with about 85% accuracy after studying the chapter.

If you work the questions over two days, then we recommend assigning the *evens* for homework the first night so that students get feedback in class the next day, then assigning the *odds* the night before the test so students can use the answers provided in the book.

ADDITIONAL ANSWERS

6. $\begin{bmatrix} 5 & 0 & 8 \\ 16 & 13 & -1 \\ 6 & 13 & 2 \end{bmatrix}$

7. $\begin{bmatrix} 2 & 33 & 12 \\ 13 & 3 & -7 \\ -13 & -30 & -8 \end{bmatrix}$

8. $a = 1.6$; $b = -10.1$

9. $a = -8$; $b = 5$

12. $y + 1 = 2(x + 3)$

13. $y - 8 = \frac{1}{4}(x - 7)$

16.a. true
b. Many answers are possible.

17.a. true
b. Many answers are possible (see Question 5, Lesson 4-6).

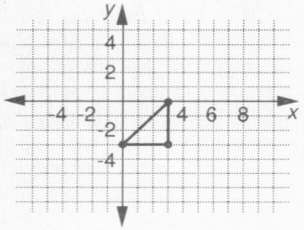
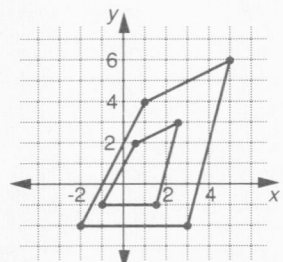
19. N and T are matrices. N has dimensions $r \times p$ and T has dimensions $q \times r$.
  a. Which product exists, NT or TN? **TN**
  b. What are the dimensions of your answer in part a? *q × p*

20. What 2×2 matrix is the identity for multiplication? $\begin{bmatrix} 1 & 0 \\ 0 & 1 \end{bmatrix}$

USES deal with applications of mathematics in real situations.

▪ **Objective D:** *Use matrices to store data.* (Lesson 4-1)

21. Chuck makes handcrafted furniture. Last year he made 5 oak tables, 10 oak chairs, 3 pine tables, 12 pine chairs, 1 maple table, and 6 maple chairs. Store this data in a 2×3 matrix. **See margin.**

22. Bogus High School has 490 freshmen boys, 487 freshmen girls, 402 sophomore boys, 416 sophomore girls, 358 junior boys, 344 junior girls, 293 senior boys, and 300 senior girls. Write a 4×2 matrix to describe the school's enrollment. **See margin.**

23. The matrix at the right gives the cost of several items at three different markets. Which element gives the cost of plums in Market 1?

	Market 1	Market 2	Market 3
eggs	.89	.95	.99
plums	.90	.79	.82
peaches	1.49	1.50	1.59
bananas	.33	.28	.25

element in 2nd row and 1st column

▪ **Objective E:** *Use matrix addition, matrix multiplication, and scalar multiplication to solve real-world problems.* (Lessons 4-2, 4-9)

24. A large pizza costs \$12.50, a medium pizza costs \$8.90, and a small pizza \$5.20. An order for a Journalism Club party consists of 7 large pizzas, 2 medium pizzas, and 4 small pizzas. Write matrices C and N for the cost and number ordered, then calculate CN to find the total cost of the order. **See margin.**

$\begin{bmatrix} 249 & 403.20 & 154.80 \\ 118.80 & 236.40 & 65.40 \end{bmatrix}$

25. An electronics manufacturer has two factories. Sales (in thousands) can be summarized by the following matrix.

	Factory 1	Factory 2
VHS	15	6
TV	10	8
CD	2	1

See margin.

The selling price of a VHS recorder is \$270, a TV is \$320, and a compact disc player is \$210. Use matrix multiplication to determine the total revenue of each factory.

26. A book company has two presses, and print runs for two years are given in the matrices below.

1987

	textbooks	novels	nonfiction
Press 1	250,000	125,000	312,000
Press 2	60,000	48,000	90,000

1988

	textbooks	novels	nonfiction
	190,000	100,000	140,000
	45,000	60,000	72,000

  a. Calculate the matrix that represents the growth in production of each press from 1987 to 1988. **See margin.**
  b. Which type of book decreased the most in production? **nonfiction**

27. Normal fares (in \$) of an airline to three cities are given in the matrix below.

	city 1	city 2	city 3
first class	415	672	258
economy	198	394	109

To increase air travel, the airline plans to reduce fares by 40%. Find the new fares for travel to these three cities.

242

REPRESENTATIONS deal with pictures, graphs, or objects that illustrate concepts.

■ **Objective F:** *Relate transformations to matrices, and vice versa. (Lessons 4-3, 4-4, 4-5, 4-6, 4-7, 4-10)*

28. Translate the following matrix equation into English by filling in the blanks.

$$\begin{bmatrix} 0 & 1 \\ 1 & 0 \end{bmatrix} \begin{bmatrix} 5 \\ -2 \end{bmatrix} = \begin{bmatrix} -2 \\ 5 \end{bmatrix}$$

The reflection image of the point __?__ over the line __?__ is the point __?__. **See margin.**

29. Multiply the matrix for r_y by itself, and explain your answer in terms of the transformation it represents. **See margin.**

30. The matrix $\begin{bmatrix} 6 & 0 \\ 0 & 6 \end{bmatrix}$ is associated

with a __?__ change with center __?__ and magnitude __?__. **size; (0, 0); 6**

31. **a.** Calculate a matrix for $r_x \circ R_{180}$. $\begin{bmatrix} -1 & 0 \\ 0 & 1 \end{bmatrix}$
    b. What single transformation corresponds to your answer? r_y

32. Find two reflections whose composite is R_{180}. $r_x \circ r_y$

■ **Objective G:** *Use matrices to perform transformations. (Lessons 4-3, 4-4, 4-5, 4-7, 4-8, 4-9)*

In 33–35, match a matrix with each transformation.

a. $\begin{bmatrix} 1 & 0 \\ 0 & 1 \end{bmatrix}$ **b.** $\begin{bmatrix} 1 & 0 \\ 0 & -1 \end{bmatrix}$

c. $\begin{bmatrix} 0 & 1 \\ 1 & 0 \end{bmatrix}$ **d.** $\begin{bmatrix} 4 & 0 \\ 0 & 6 \end{bmatrix}$

e. $\begin{bmatrix} 0 & -1 \\ 1 & 0 \end{bmatrix}$ **f.** $\begin{bmatrix} 0 & 1 \\ -1 & 0 \end{bmatrix}$

33. $r_{y=x}$ **c**   34. $S_{4,6}$ **d**   35. R_{90} **e**

36. Find the image of $\begin{bmatrix} -1 & 0 & 4 & 0 \\ 3 & .5 & -1 & 5 \end{bmatrix}$

    under r_y. $\begin{bmatrix} 1 & 0 & -4 & 0 \\ 3 & .5 & -1 & 5 \end{bmatrix}$

37. *GOLD* has coordinates G (0, 0), O (4, 1), L (3, 5), and D (-1, 4). Find the matrix of the image of *GOLD* under R_{270}. **See margin.**

38. Find the matrix of the image of

    $\begin{bmatrix} 6 & 8 & 2 \\ 0 & 4 & 0 \end{bmatrix}$ under $S_{\frac{1}{2}}$. $\begin{bmatrix} 3 & 4 & 1 \\ 0 & 2 & 0 \end{bmatrix}$

39. What translation maps *PEAR* onto *P'E'A'R'* as shown at the right? $T_{2,-1}$

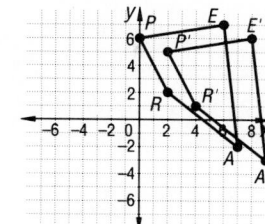

■ **Objective H.** *Graph figures and their transformation images. (Lessons 4-1, 4-3, 4-4, 4-5, 4-6, 4-9)*

40. Draw the polygon described by the matrix

    $\begin{bmatrix} 3 & 0 & 3 \\ -3 & -3 & 0 \end{bmatrix}$. **See margin.**

41. Refer to the graph at the right. Write quadrilateral *HOPE* as a matrix. **See margin.**

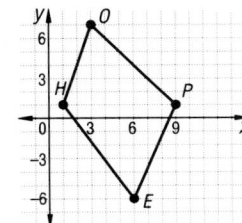

42. Draw the polygon $\begin{bmatrix} 1 & 5 & 3 & -2 \\ 4 & 6 & -2 & -2 \end{bmatrix}$

    and its image under $S_{\frac{1}{2}}$. **See margin.**

43. Trapezoid *ABCD* is represented by

    $\begin{bmatrix} -1 & 6 & 5 & 0 \\ 0 & 0 & 4 & 4 \end{bmatrix}$. Graph the preimage

    and image under r_y. **See margin.**

44. Consider the quadrilateral defined by the

    matrix $\begin{bmatrix} 0 & -1 & 0 & 1 \\ 1 & 0 & -1 & 0 \end{bmatrix}$.

    a. Graph the quadrilateral and its image

    under $\begin{bmatrix} 3 & 0 \\ 0 & 3 \end{bmatrix}$. **See margin.**

    b. Are the image and preimage similar? **Yes**
    c. Are they congruent? **No**

CHAPTER 4 Chapter Review **243**

EVALUATION
Three tests are provided for this chapter in the Teacher's Resource File. Chapter 4 Test, Forms A and B cover just Chapter 4. The third test is Chapter 4 Test, Cumulative Form. About 50% of this test covers Chapter 4, 25% covers Chapter 3, and 25% covers previous chapters. For information on grading, see *General Teaching Suggestions: Grading* on page T44 in the Teacher's Edition.

ASSIGNMENT RECOMMENDATION
We strongly recommend that you assign Lesson 5-1, both reading and some questions, for homework the evening of the test.

43.

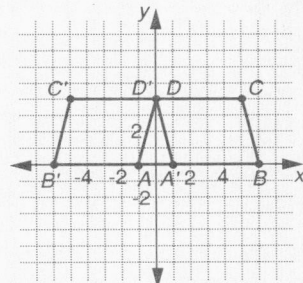

44.a.

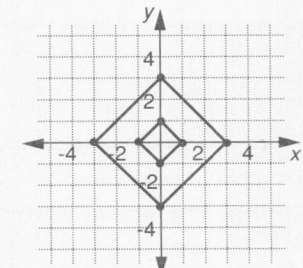

CHAPTER 5 ■ SYSTEMS

DAILY PACING CHART ■ CHAPTER 5

Students in the Full Course should complete all but one of the chapters by the end of the year. Students in the Minimal Course will spend more time on quizzes and the Chapter Review. As such, these students should complete about ten or eleven chapters.

DAY	MINIMAL COURSE	FULL COURSE
1	5-1	5-1
2	5-2	5-2
3	5-3	5-3
4	Quiz (TRF); Start 5-4.	Quiz (TRF); 5-4
5	Finish 5-4.	5-5
6	5-5	5-6
7	5-6	5-7
8	5-7	Quiz (TRF); 5-8
9	Quiz (TRF); Start 5-8.	5-9
10	Finish 5-8.	Progress Self-Test
11	5-9	Chapter Review
12	Progress Self-Test	Chapter Test (TRF)
13	Chapter Review	
14	Chapter Review	
15	Chapter Test (TRF)	

TESTING OPTIONS
■ Quiz for Lessons 5-1 Through 5-3   ■ Chapter 5 Test, Form A   ■ Chapter 5 Test, Cumulative Form
■ Quiz for Lessons 5-4 Through 5-7   ■ Chapter 5 Test, Form B

PROVIDING FOR INDIVIDUAL DIFFERENCES
The student text is written for the *average* student. The program, however, can be adapted for both less capable and for more capable students.

A blackline master (in the Teacher's Resource File) is provided for each lesson for those students who need more practice. The Teacher's Edition frequently provides Error Analysis and Alternate Approach features to provide additional instructional strategies.

For students who require additional challenge, Extension activities are regularly provided in the Teacher's Edition.

OBJECTIVES ■ CHAPTER 5

Students should master the chapter objectives by the time they complete the chapter.
To ensure mastery, there is continual review built into each set of lesson questions.
After students complete the chapter lessons, they assess their mastery on the Progress
Self-Test. Then they do the Chapter Review and pay special attention to those questions
that match the objectives missed on the Progress Self-Test. Students can get extra
practice on these objectives by using the master for each lesson in the Teacher's
Resource Book.

OBJECTIVES FOR CHAPTER 5 (Organized into the SPUR categories—Skills, Properties, Uses, and Representations)	Progress Self-Test Questions	Chapter Review Questions	Lesson Master from Teacher's Resource File*
SKILLS			
A Solve systems using the linear-combination or substitution method.	4–5	1 through 9	5-3, 5-4
B Find the inverse and determinant of a 2 × 2 matrix.	7	10 through 15	5-5
C Use matrices to solve systems of equations.	8	16 through 19	5-6
PROPERTIES			
D Recognize properties of systems of equations.	3	20 through 27	5-2, 5-3, 5-6
E Recognize properties of systems of inequalities.	9, 13	28 through 32	5-7, 5-8
USES			
F Use linear systems to solve real-world problems.	6	33 through 35	5-3, 5-4
G Use linear programming to solve problems in the real world.	10, 12	36, 37	5-8, 5-9
REPRESENTATIONS			
H Graph compound sentences.	1	38 through 44	5-1
I Solve systems of inequalities by graphing.	11	45 through 47	5-1, 5-7
J Estimate solutions to systems by graphing.	2	48 through 51	5-2, 5-7

* The masters are numbered to match the lessons.

OVERVIEW ■ CHAPTER 5

Chapter 5 reviews and extends methods of solving systems of equations from first-year algebra, and then introduces two new concepts: solving systems using matrices and linear programming. Linear programming problems are an important application, and the chapter is structured so that students can master all the prerequisite skills before having to solve such problems.

The first two lessons review the graphing associated with systems. Lesson 5-1 compares and contrasts solutions to compound sentences connected by *and* and *or*, and relates them to intersections and unions of sets. Graphs are made both on the number line and in the coordinate plane. Lesson 5-2 reviews graphing 2 × 2 linear systems to find the solution for the system and extends the technique to nonlinear systems, using familiar curves such as the parabola and rectangular hyperbola. (The algebraic solution of quadratic systems is delayed until Chapter 12.)

Lessons 5-3 and 5-4 review the linear combination and substitution methods, and extend these techniques to simple nonlinear or 3 × 3 linear systems.

Lessons 5-5 and 5-6 introduce a method of solving systems by using matrices. In Lesson 5-5, students are taught how to find the inverse of a 2 × 2 matrix and then how to use the inverse to solve a system. In Lesson 5-6, 3 × 3 systems are solved by matrices, but the inverse is always given.

Lessons 5-7 through 5-9 develop the topic of linear programming. Lesson 5-7 extends systems of inequalities, introduced in Lesson 5-1, to oblique lines. Lesson 5-8 introduces linear programming problems by giving students the inequalities or graph of the feasible region. In Lesson 5-9, the constraints are given to the student in prose form.

PERSPECTIVES ■ CHAPTER 5

The Perspectives provide the rationale for the inclusion of topics or approaches, provide mathematical background, and make connections within UCSMP.

5-1

COMPOUND SENTENCES

The ideas in this lesson should be easy for many students because they build on concepts studied in first-year algebra. These concepts were reviewed earlier in this course: solutions to inequalities on the number line (Lesson 1-9), solutions to inequalities in the coordinate plane (Lesson 3-9), and solutions to linear equations in the plane (Lessons 3-2 and 3-4). However, this lesson requires attention to detail, and even students who know the concepts will need to pay close attention when answering the questions.

The purpose of Lesson 5-1 is to compare and contrast solutions to compound sentences using the words *and* and *or,* and to represent the solutions using one- and two-dimensional graphs. Set notation and the symbols ∪ and ∩, for union and intersection, respectively, are introduced.

5-2

REPRESENTING SYSTEMS

In contrast to Lesson 5-1, this lesson focuses only on *systems,* that is, compound sentences using the word *and.* The lesson reviews the idea that the solution to a system of equations is represented by the point(s) of intersection of the graphs of the equations.

Notice that we usually find the intersection of two or more curves by first graphing their union.

Graphing by hand is of limited value in finding exact solutions. Accurate solutions are often difficult or impossible to read from hand-drawn graphs. However, they provide important information by allowing us to discover whether there are any solutions and, if so, how many there are.

Sometimes the words *dependent* and *independent* are used to describe systems. Since these words have specific meanings in linear algebra, it may be confusing to use them in a different way now.

Students who have taken UCSMP *Algebra* and *Geometry* have studied linear systems twice. The material of this and the next two lessons should be very easy for them.

5-3

THE LINEAR-COMBINATION METHOD

Lesson 5-3 shows how the Addition and Multiplication Properties of Equality can be used to find solutions to certain systems.

This method is called the *linear-combination* method because the resulting equation is a linear combination of the given equations. In general, given

$$ax + by = e$$
$$\text{and} \quad cx + dy = f$$

that intersect in a single point, *any* linear combination of these equations

$$m(ax + by) + n(cx + dy) = me + nf$$

will contain that point. The multipliers *m* and *n* are chosen so that the resulting combination has only *x* or only *y* in it. That is, the combination will be a horizontal or vertical line containing the point of intersection.

Application of this method to solving higher order linear systems can involve extensive algebraic manipulations. Except for Question 18, we delay this work until Chapter 11. The substitution method is used to solve higher order linear systems in Lesson 5-4.

5-4
THE SUBSTITUTION METHOD

Lesson 5-4 reviews the substitution method for solving systems of equations. The use of this technique for 2 × 2 linear systems should be familiar to students. Using the substitution method for solving higher order systems is most likely new content.

Substitution is a more powerful method than the linear-combination method, but the manipulation can be more complicated. To solve a system with one linear and one nonlinear equation, the substitution method is often the method of choice, as illustrated in Example 3.

5-5
INVERSE OF MATRICES

Lesson 5-5 and 5-6 relate the matrix concepts studied in Chapter 4 to systems of equations. In this lesson, the inverse of a 2 × 2 matrix is found. In the next lesson, the inverse is used to solve systems of linear equations.

A system of linear equations can be considered as a *single* matrix equation $AX = B$, where A is a matrix of coefficients, X is a matrix of variables to be found, and B is the matrix of constants. This equation is solved by multiplying both sides by the multiplicative inverse of the matrix A.

5-6
USING MATRICES TO SOLVE SYSTEMS

This lesson illustrates how to solve 2 × 2 and 3 × 3 linear systems by representing the system as a matrix equation, and multiplying each side of the matrix equation by the inverse of the coefficient matrix.

For the 2 × 2 case, students can use the Inverse-Matrix Theorem from Lesson 5-5 to find the inverse of the coefficient matrix when it exists.

For the 3 × 3 case, students are always given the inverse of the coefficient matrix. The methods for finding the inverse of a 3 × 3 matrix are beyond the scope of this course.

With the availability of computers, and the ease with which computers can do matrix calculations, matrix methods for solving systems are used widely. By the end of the chapter, students should be able to solve 2 × 2 and 3 × 3 systems (when the inverse of the coefficient matrix is given) with matrix methods.

5-7
SYSTEMS OF LINEAR INEQUALITIES

This lesson teaches students to solve systems of linear inequalities using their knowledge of graphs of inequalities (Lessons 3-9 and 5-1) and of systems of equations (Lessons 5-2 through 5-4). It introduces the words *feasible set* or *feasible region* for the solution set of a system of inequalities and lays the groundwork for the solution of problems using the linear programming method discussed in Lessons 5-8 and 5-9.

5-8
LINEAR PROGRAMMING I

This is the first of two lessons devoted to linear programming. Initially, the problems may seem formidable to students. However, when students realize how the mathematics they know can be applied to solve such seemingly complex problems, they usually enjoy these lessons.

The Linear-Programming Theorem gives a numerical shortcut for finding the maximum or minimum value of an expression without having to graph a family of lines. The linear-combination expression to be maximized or minimized is often called the *objective function*.

Linear-programming problems take a long time to do. We suggest giving no more than two such problems in an assignment, though you may wish to assign other questions at the same time.

5-9
LINEAR PROGRAMMING II

In Lessons 5-7 and 5-8, most situations presented to students included a set of inequalities. In this lesson, students must translate a given situation into a system of inequalities which represent the constraints of the problem, and an expression to be maximized or minimized in order to solve the problem.

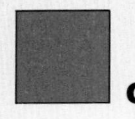

CHAPTER 5

We recommend 12 to 15 days for this chapter: 9 to 11 on the lessons; 1 for the Progress Self-Test; 1 or 2 for the Chapter Review; and 1 for a Chapter test. (See the Daily Pacing Chart on page 244A.) If you spend more than 15 days on this chapter, you are moving too slowly. Keep in mind that each lesson includes Review questions to help students firm up content studied previously.

USING PAGES 244-245
Discuss the ways that the words *and* and *or* are used in ordinary language and in mathematics. Introduce the term *system* by using the example given, and ask students to explain the meaning of the word *conditions*.

The history of the development of mathematical ideas can be used to motivate the introduction of new ideas for students. Read through the paragraph that outlines how the procedures for solving systems were developed. Then discuss the applications that Gauss, Kantorovich, and Stigler used to study systems.

CHAPTER 5

Systems

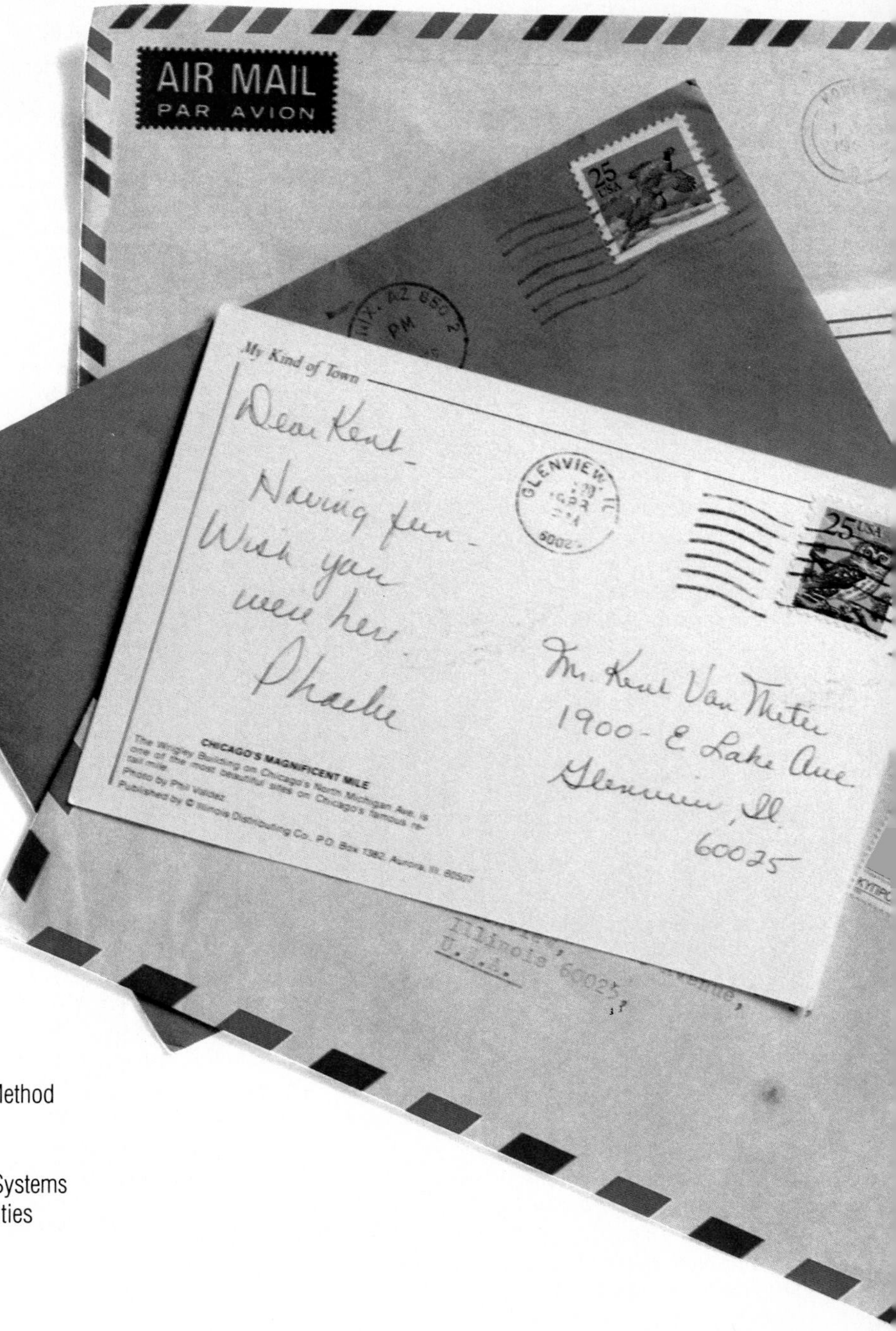

In ordinary language, you can use the words *and* and *or* as conjunctions to join two or more clauses. In mathematics, these two words are used in a similar way. A sentence in which two clauses are connected by the word *and* or by the word *or* is a *compound sentence*.

For instance, here are postal regulations for the minimum size packages that can be sent through the mails.

> All pieces must be at least 0.007 of an inch thick, *and*
> all pieces (except keys and identification devices) that are $\frac{1}{4}$ inch
> or less thick must be $\begin{cases} \text{rectangular in shape, } and \\ \text{at least } 3\frac{1}{2} \text{ inches high, } and \\ \text{at least 5 inches long.} \end{cases}$

Mathematically, we could say the conditions are: (1) thickness $T \geq 0.007''$ and (2) if $T \leq 0.25''$, then the parcel must be a rectangular solid with other dimensions $h \geq 3.5''$ and $\ell \geq 5''$. Notice that constraints may involve just one variable *(T)* or many variables $(T, h, \text{and } \ell)$.

When mathematical conditions are joined by the word *and*, the set of conditions or sentences is called a *system*. Thus, a system is a special kind of compound sentence. You have seen the most common type, systems of linear equations, in earlier mathematics courses. Here is an example:

$$\begin{cases} 3x + 4y = 12 \\ x - 7y = 15 \end{cases}$$

The history of solving systems has included some of the greatest mathematicians of all time. An efficient procedure for solving systems of linear equations with any number of variables was developed by the German mathematician Karl Friedrich Gauss in 1819. He adapted the linear combination method you will study in Lesson 5-3. In 1821, the French mathematician Jean Baptiste Joseph Fourier considered systems of linear inequalities and proved the theorem mentioned in Lesson 5-8. Solving systems by using matrices, found in Lesson 5-6, was known to Cayley in the middle of the last century.

Solving systems has always had many applications, and new ones have been developed in recent times. Gauss was trying to calculate the orbits of planets and asteroids from the sightings made by a few astronomers. In 1939, the Russian mathematician L.V. Kantorovich was the first to announce that large systems might have applications for production planning in industry. In 1945, George Stigler used systems to determine a best diet for the least cost. For these works, Kantorovich received a Nobel Prize in 1975; Stigler in 1982. (Both prizes were in economics; there is no Nobel Prize in mathematics.) You will study simplified examples of these kinds of problems in the last three lessons of this chapter.

LESSON 5-1

OBJECTIVES

H Graph compound sentences in one variable on the number line.
I Solve systems of inequalities by graphing.

TEACHING NOTES

Sometimes students are unsure whether a sentence should be graphed on a number line or on a coordinate plane. Point out that when a sentence is expressed in set notation, the variables preceding the colon indicate whether a solution is to be found in one dimension or two. For example,
   s in $\{s: 45 \le s \le 55\}$
and (x, y) in $\{(x, y): x \ge 3\}$.

The distinction between *or* and *and,* and *union* and *intersection* are key concepts in this lesson. To distinguish union and intersection, suggest that students think of a labor union wanting as many members as possible and street intersections containing only those points that are in both crossing streets. Point out that the symbol ∪ looks like a U for union.

Compound Sentences

You are already familiar with the use of compound sentences to describe intervals on the number line. For example, the sentence $4 < x < 8$ means $4 < x$ *and* $x < 8$.

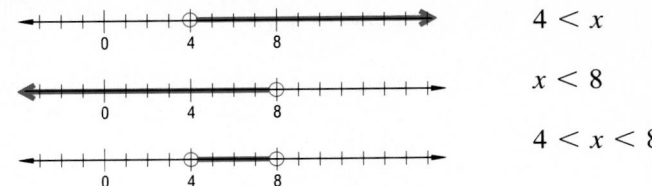

$$4 < x$$
$$x < 8$$
$$4 < x < 8$$

The solution set for a compound sentence using *and* consists of the **intersection** of the solution sets to the individual sentences. The intersection of two sets is the set consisting of those values common to both sets. The graph of the intersection consists of the points common to the graphs of the individual sets. Of the three graphs above, the bottom is the intersection of the other two.

The symbol used for intersection is ∩. $A \cap B$ is the intersection of sets A and B. Thus,

$$\{x: 4 < x < 8\} = \{x: x > 4\} \cap \{x: x < 8\}.$$

This line can be read "The set of x between 4 and 8 equals the intersection of the set of x greater than 4 and the set of x less than 8."

In contrast, the solution set for a compound sentence using *or* consists of the **union** of the solution sets to the individual sentences. The union of two sets is the set consisting of those values in either one or both sets. In other words, all points of either set are in the final graph. This meaning of the word *or* is inclusive, which is somewhat different from the ordinary, exclusive, meaning that usually implies *either, but not both*. The symbol often used for union is ∪. $A \cup B$ is the union of sets A and B. For instance, the sets of ages A which do not pay full fare on buses might be

$$\{A: A < 12 \text{ or } A > 65\}.$$

The graph is the union of the graphs of the individual parts.

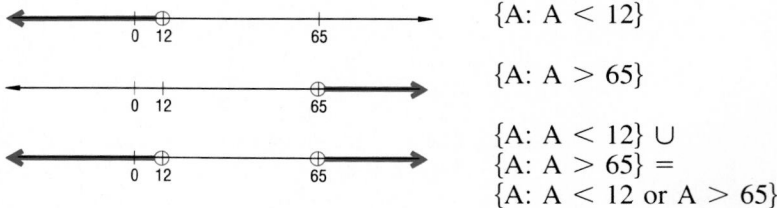

$$\{A: A < 12\}$$
$$\{A: A > 65\}$$
$$\{A: A < 12\} \cup$$
$$\{A: A > 65\} =$$
$$\{A: A < 12 \text{ or } A > 65\}$$

246

Compound sentences have many uses.

■ ■ ■ ■ ■ ■ ■ ■

Example 1 On some interstate highways you must drive at least 45 mph but no more than 55 mph. Let *s* represent the speed.
a. Graph the possible legal speeds.
b. Write the possible legal speeds in set notation.

Solution
a. The legal speeds must satisfy both conditions at the same time, so this is an example of the intersection of the two solution sets.
b. An appropriate expression in set notation is $\{s: 45 \le s \le 55\}$. This can be read "The set of numbers *s* such that *s* is between 45 and 55, inclusive."

"At least 45" means $s \ge 45$.

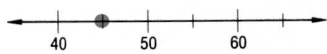

"No more than 55" mph means $s \le 55$.

So, $s \ge 45$ and $s \le 55$.

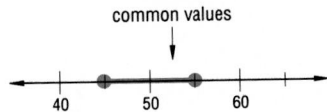

Another possible answer in set notation is $\{s: s \ge 45\} \cup \{s: s \le 55\}$.

Compound sentences may also describe graphs in the coordinate plane. For instance, in the coordinate plane the graph of $x = 3$ is a vertical line and the graph of $y = 2$ is a horizontal line. The ordered pair (3, 2) is the intersection of these two lines. It is the only point for which $x = 3$ *and* $y = 2$.

LESSON 5-1 Compound Sentences   247

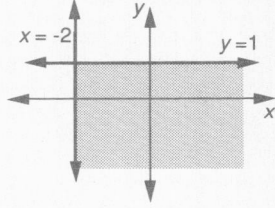

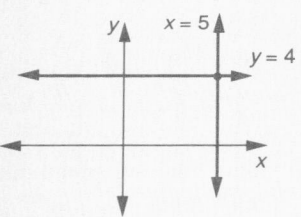
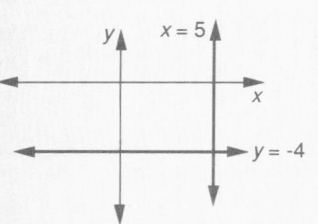
Example 2 Graph the set of all points (x, y) in a plane for which
a. $x \geq 3$ or $y \geq 2$;
b. $x \geq 3$ and $y \geq 2$.

Solution

$\{(x, y): x \geq 3\}$ has the graph:

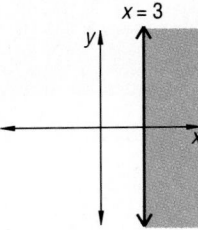

$\{(x, y): y \geq 2\}$ has the graph:

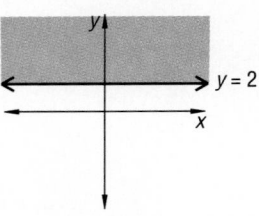

a. *Or* tells you to find all values satisfying either one or both sentences. The result is the union of the above sets. The graph of $\{(x, y): x \geq 3 \text{ or } y \geq 2\}$ is the shaded region shown below.

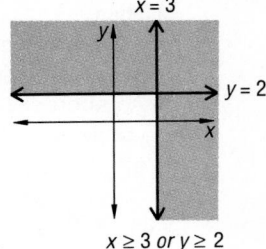

$x \geq 3 \text{ or } y \geq 2$

b. *And* tells you to find all values satisfying both sentences simultaneously. The result is all the common values, that is, the intersection of the sets $\{(x, y): x \geq 3\}$ and $\{(x, y): y \geq 2\}$. The graph of $\{(x, y): x \geq 3 \text{ and } y \geq 2\}$ is the shaded region shown below.

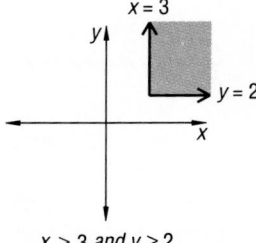

$x \geq 3 \text{ and } y \geq 2$

248

Questions

1. A sentence consisting of clauses joined by the words *and* or *or* is called a __?__.   **compound sentence**

2. The solution set to a compound sentence using *or* consists of the __?__ of the solution sets to the individual sentences.   **union**

3. Graph on a number line the solution set to the sentence $x < 6$ *or* $x > 11$.   **See margin.**

4. $-2 < x < 3$ means $-2 < x$ __?__ $x < 3$.   *and*

5. The solution set to a compound sentence using *and* consists of the __?__ of the solution sets to the individual sentences.   **intersection**

6. Graph on a number line the solution set to the sentence $n \geq 2.95$ *and* $n \leq 3.005$.   **See margin.**

7. Translate using set notation: the set of numbers x between 0 and 10 equals the intersection of the set of numbers x greater than 0 and the set of numbers x less than 10. $\{x: 0 < x < 10\} = \{x: x > 0\} \cap \{x: x < 10\}$

8. Refer to Example 1. Recently some states have changed the maximum speed limit to 65 mph, while maintaining a minimum speed of 45 mph.
   a. Graph the possible legal speeds on a number line.   **See margin.**
   b. Write the possible legal speeds in set notation. $\{x: 45 \leq x \leq 65\}$

9. In a coordinate plane, graph   **See margin.**
   a. the intersection of the lines with equations $x = 5$ and $y = 4$.
   b. the union of the line with equation $x = 5$ and the line with equation $y = -4$.   **See margin.**

10. **a.** Graph $\{(x, y): x \geq 7\} \cup \{(x, y): y \leq -9\}$.   **See margin.**
    b. Graph $\{(x, y): x \geq 7\} \cap \{(x, y): y \leq -9\}$.   **See margin.**

11. Why did the mathematician Gauss become interested in solving systems of equations?   **See margin.**

12. Name two persons who received Nobel prizes for finding new applications for systems, and describe their applications.   **See margin.**

13. Match each set at the left with its graph at the right.
    a. $\{x: x > 1$ *and* $x < 4\}$ ii   (i)

    b. $\{x: x > 1$ *or* $x < 4\}$ iv   (ii)
    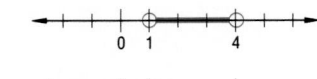

    c. $\{x: x < 1$ *or* $x > 4\}$ i   (iii)

    d. $\{x: x < 1$ *and* $x > 4\}$ v   (iv)
    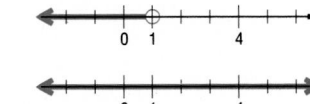

    (v)

LESSON 5-1 Compound Sentences   **249**

NAME _____

LESSON **MASTER 5–1**
QUESTIONS ON **SPUR** OBJECTIVES

■ **REPRESENTATIONS**   *Objective H*   (See pages 302–305 for objectives.)
In 1–6, graph on the number line.

1. $\{y: 0 < y \leq 10\}$ 2. $\{w: -6 \leq w$ and $w \leq 1\}$

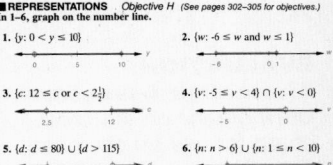

3. $\{c: 12 \leq c$ or $c < 2\frac{1}{2}\}$ 4. $\{v: -5 \leq v < 4\} \cap \{v: v < 0\}$

5. $\{d: d \leq 80\} \cup \{d > 115\}$ 6. $\{n: n > 6\} \cup \{n: 1 \leq n < 10\}$

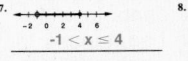

In 7 and 8, write a compound sentence in the variable x that describes the given graph.

7.
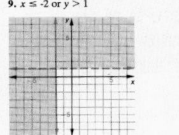
$-1 < x \leq 4$

8.
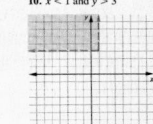
$x < -18$ or $x > -13$

■ **REPRESENTATIONS**   *Objective I*
In 9 and 10, graph each compound sentence in the coordinate plane.

9. $x \leq -2$ or $y > 1$ 10. $x < 1$ and $y > 3$

52 *Continued*   *Advanced Algebra © Scott, Foresman and Company*

NAME _____
Lesson MASTER 5–1 (page 2)

In 11 and 12, describe each graph using a compound sentence.

11.
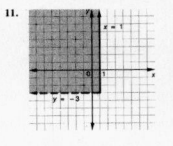
$x \leq 1$ and $y > -3$

12.
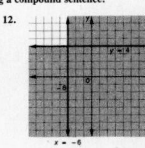
$y \leq 8$ or $x \geq -6$

Advanced Algebra © Scott, Foresman and Company   **53**

MORE PRACTICE
For more questions on SPUR
Objectives, use *Lesson Master 5-1,* shown on page 249.

EXTENSION
Some students may be interested in learning some history of mathematics. Suggest that a good topic is a brief report on one of the mathematicians mentioned on page 245.

EVALUATION
Alternative Assessment
Draw graphs on the chalkboard (or use an overhead projector) that illustrate the union or intersection of sets of points on the number line. Call upon students to write the compound sentences that describe the graphs. Whether or not the response is correct, ask the student to describe verbally his or her reason for the sentence written.

ADDITIONAL ANSWERS
14.b., 17.a., 18.a., 22. and 29. See Additional Answers in the back of this book.

15. should use "or," not "and"

17.b. a rectangle with dimensions 3 × 5 and its interior

18.b. a region of the plane that represents all combinations of acceptable dimensions for length and height

25. samples: "To be and not to be, that is the question"; "Truth and consequences"; "of the people, by the people, or for the people."

Applying the Mathematics

14. Louise wants to buy a car. She will spend more than $8000 but less than $11,000 on a new car, or she will buy a good used car for no more than $5000. Let c represent the cost of the car she will buy.
   a. Write a sentence using set notation describing the amount she may spend.   {c: 8000 < c < 11,000} ∪ {c: 0 < c < 5000}
   b. Graph the possible values of c on a number line.   See margin.

15. Willard solved $x^2 = 4$ and wrote "$x = 2$ *and* $x = $ -2." What is wrong with Willard's answer?   See margin.

16. The set $\{(x, y): x > 0 \text{ and } y > 0\}$ describes the first quadrant of the coordinate plane. What set describes the second quadrant?
   {(x, y): x < 0 and y > 0}

17. **a.** Graph $\{(x, y): 2 \le x \le 5 \text{ and } -2 \le y \le 3\}$.   See margin.
   b. Describe the graph geometrically. See margin.

18. Consider the postal regulations on the first page of this chapter.
   a. Graph $\{(\ell, h): \ell \ge 5 \text{ and } h \ge 3.5\}$.   See margin.
   b. What have you graphed?   See margin.

19. The words AND and OR in BASIC have the same meaning as in algebra. Consider the program below.

```
10 FOR X = 1 TO 100
20      LET Y = 3*X
30      IF Y < 250 AND Y > 200 THEN PRINT X
40 NEXT X
50 END
```
                                              67, 68, 69, ... , 83
   a. What numbers will be printed when this program is run?
   b. What numbers would be printed if the word AND were changed to OR in line 30?   1, 2, 3, ... , 100

Review

20. An equation relating the total surface area T of a cylinder with height h and radius r is $T = 2\pi r^2 + 2\pi rh$. Solve this equation for h. *(Lesson 1-8)* $h = \dfrac{T}{2\pi r} - r$

21. If y varies inversely as x^3, how is the value of y changed if x is:
   a. quadrupled?   y is divided by 64.   **b.** halved? *(Lesson 2-3)*
                                           y is multiplied by 8.
22. Graph the line with equation $8x - 4y = 16$. *(Lesson 3-4)*   See margin.

23. Triangle ABC has coordinates $A = (1, -2)$, $B = (4, 0)$, and $C = (-3, 3)$. Graph and write the matrix of the image of $\triangle ABC$ under R_{180}. *(Lesson 4-6)*   See margin.

Exploration

24. Normal weights are often given in a table as a range of values depending on height. Find such a table in a health book or almanac. Graph the interval of normal weights for your height.
   Many answers are possible.
25. In ordinary usage, replacing *or* by *and* can dramatically change a sentence. For instance, "Give me liberty and give me death." only differs from Patrick Henry's famous saying by that one word. Find examples of other sayings whose meaning is changed by replacing "and" with "or," or vice-versa.   See margin.

250

5-2

Representing Systems

In the previous lesson you worked with compound sentences that represent situations satisfying more than one condition. A **system,** which is a set of conditions joined by the word *and*, is a special kind of compound sentence. A system is often denoted by a brace. Thus the compound sentence

$$y = 5x + 40 \text{ and } y = 9x$$

can be written as this system:

$$\begin{cases} y = 5x + 40 \\ y = 9x \end{cases}$$

Systems with one or two variables can be represented graphically. The **solution set for a system** is the intersection of the solution sets for the individual sentences.

Example 1   The system

$$\begin{cases} y = 5x + 40 \\ y = 9x \end{cases}$$

is graphed below.
a. How many solutions are there?
b. Find the solution(s) from the graph.

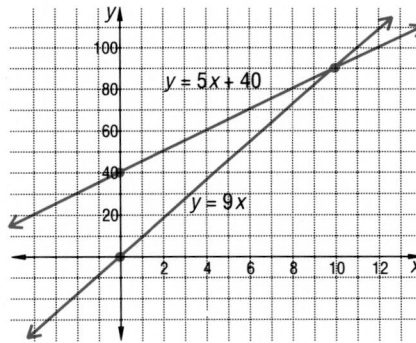

Solution   a. The solution consists of all points of intersection. The two lines intersect in only one point, so there is only one solution.
b. The lines seem to intersect when $x = 10$ and $y = 90$.

Check   Substitute the point (10, 90) into both sentences.
Is $90 = 5(10) + 40$? Yes.
Is $90 = 9(10)$? Yes.
The single solution is the point (10, 90).

RESOURCES
■ Lesson Master 5-2
▣ Visual for Teaching Aid 24 displays the graph of **Example 2.**
▣ Computer Master 7

OBJECTIVES

J Estimate solutions to systems of equations by graphing.
D Recognize properties of systems of equations.

TEACHING NOTES

The words *consistent* and *inconsistent* as used in mathematics may be new to many students. For students who might be confused by a system such as the one in **Example 5**, stress that it is useful to know that one equation is equivalent to another. Point out that a quick check to see if the equations can be algebraically transformed into identical form can help identify this type of system.

Alternate Approach   If some students are having difficulties identifying the graphs of systems as being consistent or inconsistent, let these students work together in pairs. Have one student draw a system of lines on graph paper while the other student tries to classify the system. Suggest that students check their work by using the textbook.

Making Connections   A more detailed discussion of consistent systems with infinitely many solutions occurs in the Extension in Lesson 5-3 on page 262.

The three ways of describing solutions to individual sentences also apply to systems. The solution to the system of Example 1 could be expressed in any of the following ways.

1. listing the solution: (10, 90)
2. writing the solution set: {(10, 90)}
3. writing a simplified equivalent system: $\begin{cases} x = 10 \\ y = 90 \end{cases}$

Graphing a system can quickly indicate the number of solutions, but does not always give an exact answer. As Example 2 shows, graphing helps to approximate the solutions.

Example 2   Bobbi owns land on a straight stretch of the Old Man River. She plans to fence in a rectangular piece of land along the river. She has 80 m of fencing material, and she wants to enclose an area of 500 square meters. The stretch along the river does not need to be fenced. What can the dimensions of this region be?

Solution   Let W and S be the lengths of the width and sides, respectively. The perimeter of fencing is one width plus two sides. Then

$$\begin{cases} W + 2S = 80 & \text{(fencing)} \\ WS = 500 & \text{(area)} \end{cases}$$

Graph each sentence. (Key points are identified in the graph below.) Since W and S must be positive because they represent lengths, it is not necessary here to draw the third-quadrant branch of the hyperbola.

The graphs intersect at two points. So there are two solutions. One looks to be near (65, 8) and the other is near (15, 32). Bobbi can make the width about 65 m long and the other two sides about 8 m long, or she can make the width 15 m long and the other two sides 32 m long.

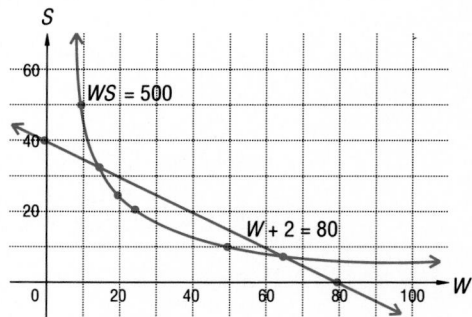

252

252

Check Because the solutions are estimates, a check is very important. Substitute (65, 8) into both sentences.

$$65 + 2 \cdot 8 = 81 \approx 80$$
$$65 \cdot 8 = 520 \approx 500$$

The check shows that (65, 8) is an approximate solution, not an exact solution. The check of (15, 32) is left to you in Question 6. The set of approximate solutions is {(65, 8), (15, 32)}.

If you have an automatic grapher, you can estimate the solutions to a system to a high degree of accuracy for rescaling or zooming around each point of intersection. For instance, the screen below, from a function grapher, shows that a more accurate solution to the system in Example 2 is $W = 64.5$ and $S = 7.8$.

$$64.5 + 2(7.8) = 80.1 \approx 80$$
$$64.5 \cdot 7.8 \quad = 503.2 \approx 500$$

To get a solution accurate to the nearest hundredth, you would have to zoom or rescale again.

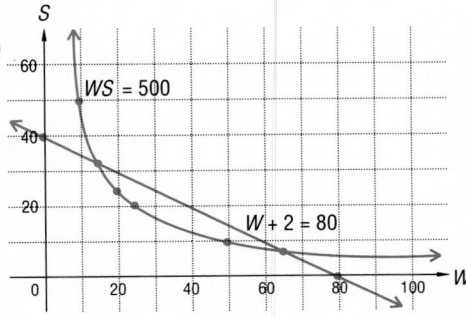

Systems are classified into two groups depending on whether or not solutions exist. If a system has solutions, it is called **consistent**; if it has no solutions, it is **inconsistent**.

When two individual sentences are lines, there are three possibilities for the system. The lines can intersect in one point, they can be parallel and nonintersecting, or they can be identical. The possibilities are shown in the next three examples.

■ ■ ■ ■ ■ ■ ■ ■

Example 3   Is the system $\begin{cases} x + y = 5 \\ 2x - y = 4 \end{cases}$ inconsistent or consistent?

Solution For $x + y = 5$, the slope is -1. For $2x - y = 4$, the slope is 2. The two lines intersect, so the system is consistent.

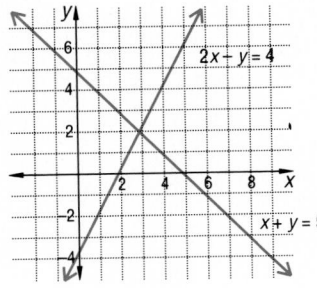

---

2. Fred is planting a garden in a contest. He has 70 meters of fencing, and to be eligible to win he must have a garden of 400 square meters. To obtain this area by using only 70 meters of fencing, Fred finds that he must use a wall of his barn as one side of the garden. What can the dimensions of the garden be?

Let W and S be the lengths of the widths and sides, respectively.

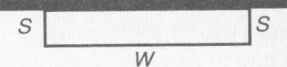

W + 2S = 70 and WS = 400

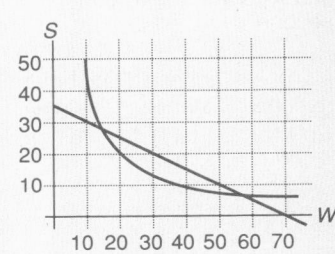

Estimated solutions near (14, 28) and (56, 7).

Questions 12-14: It is important to discuss the systems and their graphs when working with these questions. Emphasize that although there may be cases in which exact solutions can be read directly from a graph, in most cases solutions read from a graph are approximations.

Question 17: It may be helpful to make a chart that shows the distances of the father and daughter from the starting point after each second.

Seconds	Father's Distance	Daughter's Distance
0	0	40
1	9	45
2	18	50
3	27	55
.	.	.
.	.	.
.	.	.

Example 4   Is the system $\begin{cases} 4x + 3y = 24 \\ 12x + 9y = 36 \end{cases}$ inconsistent or consistent?

Solution   For $4x + 3y = 24$, the slope is $-\frac{4}{3}$. For $12x + 9y = 36$, the slope is also $-\frac{4}{3}$. Thus the lines are parallel. The y-intercept of the first line is 8; for the second line, it is 4. There are no points that satisfy both equations, so the system is inconsistent.

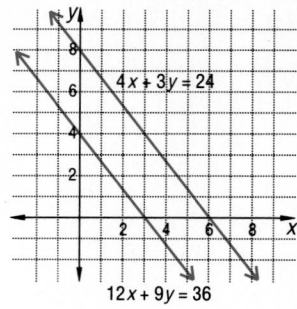

Example 5   Is the system $\begin{cases} 4x + 3y = 24 \\ 8x + 6y = 48 \end{cases}$ inconsistent or consistent?

Solution   Both lines have slope of $-\frac{4}{3}$ and y-intercept of 8. So the two equations represent the same line. Every point satisfying one equation satisfies the other one. The system is consistent and there are infinitely many solutions.

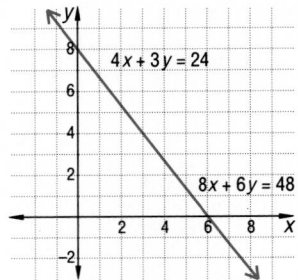

Questions

Covering the Reading

1. *Multiple choice* The solution to a system consists of   b
   (a) the union of the solution sets of the individual sentences.
   (b) the intersection of the solution sets of the individual sentences.
   (c) all points satisfying at least one of the individual sentences.

In 2 and 3, consider this system: $\begin{cases} y = 3x + 2 \\ y = 20 \end{cases}$

2. *Multiple choice* The system means   a
   (a) $y = 3x + 2$ *and* $y = 20$
   (b) $y = 3x + 2$ *or* $y = 20$.

3. **a.** The solution to the system is __?__.   (6, 20)
   b. Verify that the ordered pair you found in part a is the solution.
   (6, 20) satisfies both equations.

254

In 4–6, refer to Example 2.

4. *Multiple choice* WS = 500 represents a relationship involving: **b**
   (a) perimeter   (b) area   (c) volume

5. Why do you not need to draw the third-quadrant branch of the hyperbola? *See margin.*

6. Show that (15, 32) is an approximate solution to the system.
   See margin.

7. Give an example of a system with infinitely many solutions.
   See margin.

8. *True or false* If two lines have the same slope, then they represent inconsistent systems. **False**

In 9–11, the graph of a system is described. Is the system consistent or inconsistent?

9. parallel, different lines **inconsistent**

10. lines intersecting at one point **consistent**

11. identical lines **consistent**

In 12–14, use the given systems and their graphs.
(a) Tell how many solutions the system has.
(b) Identify the system as inconsistent or consistent.
(c) Estimate the solutions, if there are any.
(d) Verify that your solutions satisfy all equations of the system.

12. $\begin{cases} y = x^2 \\ y = x - 5 \end{cases}$ *See margin.*

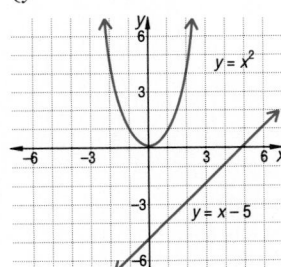

13. $\begin{cases} xy = 2 \\ 2x - y = 3 \end{cases}$ *See margin.*

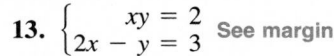
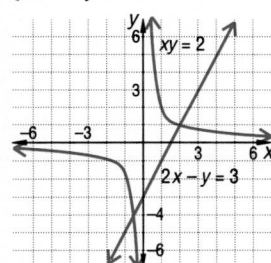

14. $\begin{cases} y = x^2 \\ xy = 8 \end{cases}$ *See margin.*

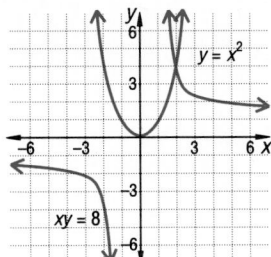

NOTES ON QUESTIONS
Computer for Question 20: This question shows the relationship between hand-drawn graphing and the use of automatic graphers. Point out that each complements the other. The automatic grapher gives a more accurate solution. However, hand graphing initially helps to "zero in" on the solution set and allows us to shorten computer running time.

Question 23: This question reviews the translation of a problem in English into mathematical symbols. Be certain to discuss this problem. It is preparation for Lesson 5-3, which explains how to use linear combinations to solve systems of equations.

ADDITIONAL ANSWERS
5. Because W and S represented lengths, we are interested only in positive values for W and S. Therefore, the third-quadrant branch of the hyperbola can be ignored because any point in the third quadrant would yield negative values for W and S.

6. Substitute the point (15, 32) into both sentences of the system:
$15 + 2 \cdot 32 = 79 \approx 80$;
$15 \cdot 32 = 480 \approx 500$.

7. sample: $\begin{cases} x - y = 5 \\ -2x + 2y = -10 \end{cases}$

12.a. zero
b. inconsistent

13.a. two   b. consistent
c. (2, 1); $\left(-\frac{1}{2}, -4\right)$
d. Substitute both points back into both sentences of the system:
$2 \cdot 1 = 2, 2 \cdot 2 - 1 = 3$;
$\left(-\frac{1}{2}\right) \cdot (-4) = 2$,
$2 \cdot \left(-\frac{1}{2}\right) - (-4) = 3$.

14.a. one   b. consistent
c. (2, 4)
d. Substitute this point back into both sentences in the system: $4 = 2^2$;
$2 \cdot 4 = 8$.

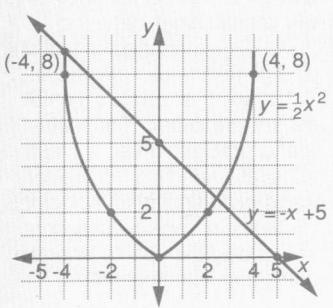
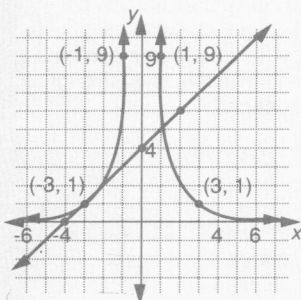
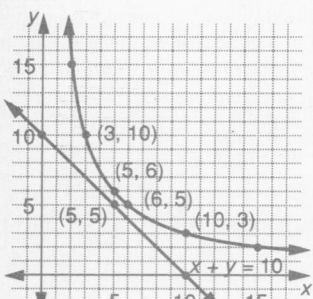
In 15 and 16, (a) graph each system; (b) tell how many solutions the system has; and (c) estimate any solutions.

15. $\begin{cases} y = \frac{1}{2}x^2 \\ y = -x + 5 \end{cases}$ See margin.

16. $\begin{cases} y = \dfrac{9}{x^2} \\ y = x + 4 \end{cases}$ See margin.

17. The system of Example 1 could represent the following situation: A child challenged her father to a race. The father gave her a head start of 40 m. He ran at 9 meters per second. She ran at 5 meters per second. Let y be distance and x be time in seconds.
   a. Which equation represents the father's distance from the start after x seconds? $y = 9x$
   b. After 1 second, how far was the father from the start? How far was the daughter? father: 9 m; daughter: 45 m
   c. When did the father catch up to his daughter? 10 sec
   d. When the father caught up to her, how far from the start were they? 90 m

18. Phillip has 150 m of fencing material and wants to surround all four sides of a rectangle with area 1300 square meters. Use graphing to estimate the dimensions of this region. See margin.

19. Use a graph to show that there do not exist two real numbers x and y whose product is 30 and whose sum is 10. See margin.

20. Graphing can be the first step in helping to solve complicated systems by search procedures. Consider the system $\begin{cases} y = 3x^2 \\ y = 4x + 10. \end{cases}$
A rough graph shows a solution between $x = -2$ and $x = 0$. By restricting the domain in the FOR ... NEXT loop, you can get closer and closer approximations of solutions.

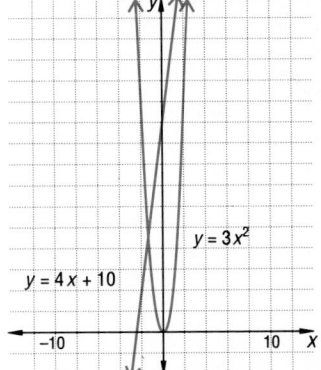

```
10 PRINT "X", "Y1", "Y2"
20 FOR X = -2 TO 0 STEP .01
30    Y1 = 3 * X ^ 2
40    Y2 = 4 * X + 10
50    PRINT X, Y1, Y2
60 NEXT X
70 END
```

$y = 3x^2$

$y = 4x + 10$

(Different scales on the two axes) $x = -1.28; y = 4.92$
a. Run the program and find the solution to two decimal places.
b. Change line 20 to find the other solution, which is between $x = 2$ and $x = 3$. $x = 2.61; y = 20.44$

Review

21. Graph the solution set on a number line.
$\{x: -0.5 \le x < 4\}$ *(Lesson 5-1)*   See margin.

22. a. Graph $\{x: x > 4 \text{ or } x > -2\}$.   See margin.
    b. Graph $\{x: x > 4 \text{ and } x > -2\}$. *(Lesson 5-1)*   See margin.

23. Angela has x \$5.99 records, y \$6.25 records, and z \$7.99 records. If the total value is T, write an equation relating all these variables. *(Lesson 3-3)*
$5.99x + 6.25y + 7.99z = T$

24. Let $A = (-2, 6)$ and $B = (3, 7)$.
    a. Find AB.   about 5.099
    b. Find the midpoint of $\overline{AB}$. *(Previous course)* $(\frac{1}{2}, 6\frac{1}{2})$

Exploration

25. Consider both branches of the hyperbola with equation $y = \frac{1}{x}$. Is there any line that intersects this hyperbola in exactly one point?
Any line tangent to either branch will intersect the hyperbola in exactly one point. One such line is $y = -x + 1$.

FOLLOW-UP

MORE PRACTICE
For more questions on SPUR Objectives, use *Lesson Master 5-2*, shown below.

EXTENSION
Have students consider each of the following pairs of geometric figures and tell the greatest number of solutions possible: circle, line (2); parabola, line (2); parabola, circle (4); hyperbola, line (2); ellipse, line (2); square, line (2); triangle, line (2).

21.

22.a.

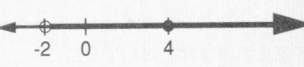

b.

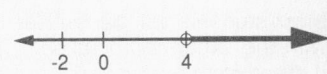

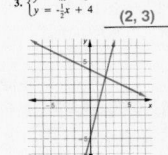 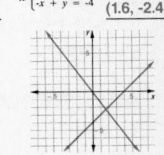
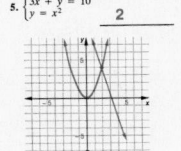 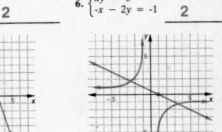

RESOURCES
■ Lesson Master 5-3
■ Quiz on Lessons 5-1
   Through 5-3

OBJECTIVES

A Solve systems using the
   linear-combination method.
D Recognize properties of
   linear systems.
F Use linear systems to
   solve real-world problems.

TEACHING NOTES

Most students will be familiar
with the linear-combination
method from their previous
algebra course. Stress the
need to work accurately. Encourage students to organize
their work on the page.

Error Analysis Most mistakes that students make in
solving systems using linear
combinations are careless
rather than conceptual. Encourage students to use the
format shown in **Example
2.** Illustrate the use of the
format by working several
examples.

ADDITIONAL EXAMPLES
1. Solve each system. Check
the answers by substituting
them in the original system
or by making a quick sketch
to see that the answers are
reasonable.
a. $\begin{cases} 3x + 2y = 22 \\ 9x - 8y = -4 \end{cases}$
$x = 4, y = 5$
b. $\begin{cases} 5x + 3y = 7 \\ 3x + 5y = -23 \end{cases}$
$x = 6.5, y = -8.5$

LESSON

5-3

The Linear-Combination Method

In the last lesson you graphed systems to estimate or find solutions.
Graphing works for estimating, but does not often give exact solutions. To find exact solutions, you usually need to use algebraic
techniques. The next several lessons discuss algebraic techniques.

Systems are **equivalent** if and only if they have the same solutions.
For example, the two systems below are equivalent because they
have the same solution (-1, 4).

$$\begin{cases} 3a + 2b = 5 \\ 7a + 4b = 9 \end{cases} \qquad \begin{cases} a + b \le 10 \\ -14a - 3b = 2 \\ 2a - b = -6 \end{cases}$$

The goal in solving is to take a more complicated system like either
of those above and find the simplest equivalent system,

$$\begin{cases} a = -1 \\ b = 4. \end{cases}$$

One technique for solving equations uses the Addition Property of
Equality.

■ ■ ■ ■ ■ ■ ■ ■

Example 1   Solve the system $\begin{cases} x + y = 9 \\ 2x - y = 2 \end{cases}$.

Solution   Notice that the coefficients of y are 1 and -1 which add to
zero. Adding the sides of the two equations gives an equation in one
variable.

$$3x = 11$$

Thus $x = \frac{11}{3}$ or $3\frac{1}{3}$.

Substitute the value of x into either of the two original equations to
solve for y. We choose the first equation.

$$\frac{11}{3} + y = 9$$
$$y = \frac{16}{3}$$

The solution is $(\frac{11}{3}, \frac{16}{3})$.

Check 1   Verify that $(\frac{11}{3}, \frac{16}{3})$ satisfies each of the given sentences.

Does $\frac{11}{3} + \frac{16}{3} = 9$?   Yes.

Does $2 \cdot \frac{11}{3} - \frac{16}{3} = 2$?   Yes, so it checks.

258

Check 2 Graph the lines $x + y = 9$ and $2x - y = 2$. The coordinates $(\frac{11}{3}, \frac{16}{3})$ are reasonable for the point of intersection.

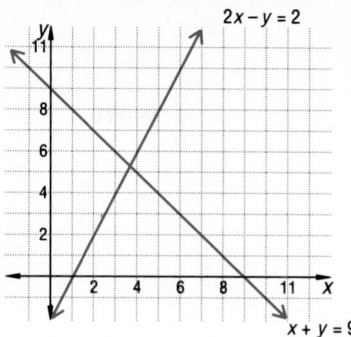

In Example 1, the coefficients of one variable were opposites. In many systems, the coefficients are not so convenient. Example 2 shows how such systems can be solved using both the Multiplication and Addition Properties of Equality.

Example 2 Solve the system $\begin{cases} 6s + 8p = 22 \\ 4s + 3p = 10 \end{cases}$.

Solution To use the addition method of Example 1, the coefficients of one of the variables must be opposites. Notice that the least common multiple of 6 and 4 (the coefficients of s) is 12. Use the Multiplication Property of Equality to multiply the first equation by 2 and the second equation by -3 to get opposite coefficients for s.

$$
\begin{array}{llll}
6s + 8p & = 22 & \text{(multiply by 2)} & \Rightarrow \quad 12s + 16p = 44 \\
4s + 3p & = 10 & \text{(multiply by -3)} & \Rightarrow \quad \underline{-12s - 9p = -30} \\
& & \text{Add} & \qquad\qquad 7p = 14 \\
& & & \qquad\qquad\ p = 2.
\end{array}
$$

Substitute $p = 2$ into either equation and solve for s. We substitute into $6s + 8p = 22$.

$$6s + 8(2) = 22$$
$$s = 1$$

Check Substitute $p = 2$ and $s = 1$ into the other sentence, $4s + 3p = 10$. Does $4(1) + 3(2) = 10$? Yes.

In Example 2, we could have found the least common multiple for the coefficients of p, which is 24. Then the first equation would be multiplied by 3 (because $8 \cdot 3 = 24$), and the second equation would be multiplied by -8 (because $3 \cdot -8 = -24$). Solving the system in this way would still result in the same solution.

---

2. A park district rents its swimming pool to residents for private parties. The rental charge consists of two parts. The first part is a charge for fixed costs. This charge remains the same regardless of the number of guests. The second part of the fee is a cost per guest. For a party of 40, the total charge is $230, and for a party of 125 people, the cost is $400. Find the fixed cost and the cost per guest.
Let g represent the cost per guest and f represent the fixed cost. The equations are 40g + f = 230 and 125g + f = 400. The fixed cost is $150 and the cost per guest is $2.00.

Ration stamps were used to distribute scarce goods.

Systems arise in important practical endeavors. During World War II, the United States (and many other countries) had to ration certain foods. Mathematicians were involved in determining diets that met the minimum requirements of protein, vitamins, and minerals. Here is a simplified example.

The table shows the protein and calcium contents for a serving of spaghetti and peas. How many servings of each are needed to get 22 g of protein and 100 mg of calcium?

	SPAGHETTI	PEAS
protein (g) per serving	6	8
calcium (mg) per serving	40	30

To solve, let s be the number of servings of spaghetti and let p be the number of servings of peas. Then the grams of protein must satisfy

$$6s + 8p = 22,$$

and the milligrams of calcium must satisfy

$$40s + 30p = 100.$$

If you divide the second equation by 10, the system of Example 2 results.

In Chapter 3 you learned that $Ax + By = C$ is called a linear combination in two variables x and y. The method used to solve the problems in this lesson is often called the **linear-combination method** of solving systems because it involves adding multiples of the given equations.

The systems in the examples above are consistent, and each has a unique solution. The linear-combination method gives interesting results for inconsistent systems or ones with infinitely many

260

solutions. In Lesson 5-2, for example, graphing showed that $\begin{cases} 4x + 3y = 24 \\ 12x + 9y = 36 \end{cases}$ represents an inconsistent system. These results could have been found by the linear-combination method. Multiply the first equation by -3 and add:

$$
\begin{aligned}
-12x - 9y &= -72 \\
12x + 9y &= 36 \\
\hline
0 &= -36
\end{aligned}
$$

The result $0 = -36$ is false. This indicates the original system is always false; it has no solutions. The two lines are parallel.

Graphing also showed that the system $\begin{cases} 4x + 3y = 24 \\ 8x + 6y = 48 \end{cases}$ has infinitely many solutions. Again this could have been found by the linear-combination method. Multiply the first equation by -2.

$$
\begin{aligned}
-8x - 6y &= -48 \\
8x + 6y &= 48 \\
\hline
0 &= 0
\end{aligned}
$$

The result $0 = 0$ is always true. This indicates that the original system is always true; there are infinitely many solutions. Any (x, y) satisfying $4x + 3y = 24$ solves the system. The two equations represent the same line.

Questions

Covering the Reading

1. When are systems of equations equivalent?
   when they have the same solution set

In 2 and 3, refer to Example 1.

2. The equation $3x = 11$ is the result of __?__ the two original equations.
   adding

3. Why is the method of solving by graphing unsatisfactory for this problem? We want techniques that provide exact solutions.

4. Refer to Example 2. Multiply the first equation by 3 and the second equation by -8. Solve the resulting system to show that the solution is still $p = 2$ and $s = 1$. See margin.

5. Lynne wants to get 26 grams of protein and 17.5 grams of fat from one meal of beef stew and bread. How many servings of each does she need to eat? $1\frac{1}{2}$ servings of stew; 1 slice of bread

	Beef stew with vegetables	Bread
protein (g) per serving	16	2
fat (g) per serving	11	1

LESSON 5-3 The Linear-Combination Method 261

NOTES ON QUESTIONS
Question 12: Point out that multiplying both sides of the second equation by 100 will clear the decimals. This should be done before proceeding with a linear-combination solution.

Questions 13 and 14: These questions can lead to a discussion of the relationship between constants and consistency. The criterion will be discussed in Lesson 5-6. However, you could extend the discussion at this time (see the Extension for this lesson).

Question 17: This question uses linear combinations in a chemistry application that students may also encounter in their science classes.

Question 18: The linear-combination method is extended to quadratic systems in this question. The first equation is a hyperbola and the second is an ellipse, as shown on the graph below. These systems are discussed in Chapter 11.

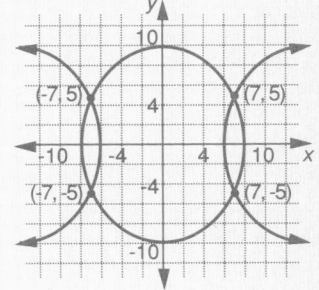

ADDITIONAL ANSWERS
4.
$6s + 8p = 22$
(mult. by 3)
$4s + 3p = 10$ (mult. by -8)
$18s + 24p = 66$
$-32s - 24p = -80$
$\overline{-14s = -14}$
$s = 1$
Substitute $s = 1$ into
$4s + 3p = 10$
$4(1) + 3p = 10$
$3p = 6$
$p = 2$

EXTENSION
You could discuss consistent systems with infinitely many solutions and inconsistent systems in more detail than is given in the text. Two equations in which one is a nonzero multiple of the other form a system with infinitely many solutions. The systems

$$\begin{cases} 3x + 4y = 5 \\ 9x + 12y = 15 \end{cases}$$

and $\begin{cases} y = x^2 \\ \pi y = \pi x^2 \end{cases}$

have infinitely many solutions because the second equation is a nonzero multiple of the first. Likewise,

$$\begin{cases} 4x + 8y = 12 \\ 5x + 10y = 15 \end{cases}$$

has infinitely many solutions; each equation is a multiple of $x + 2y = 3$.

Linear equations in which the coefficients are multiples of each other but the constants are not are inconsistent; their graphs are parallel lines with different intercepts. Thus, students should recognize that

$$\begin{cases} 3x + 5y = 18 \\ 6x + 10y = 20 \end{cases}$$

and $\begin{cases} 4x + 4y = 20 \\ 3x + 3y = -6 \end{cases}$

are inconsistent systems without doing any algebraic manipulations. The concept of seeing the coefficients as a unit and the constants as a unit will help in Lesson 5-6, when these units are written as separate matrices.

EVALUATION
A quiz covering Lessons 5-1 through 5-3 is provided in the Teacher's Resource File.

6. Morris was solving a system and got $0 = 0$ after adding the equations together. This result means that Morris has what kind of system?
consistent, with infinitely many solutions

In 7–12, use the linear-combination method to solve the system.

7. $\begin{cases} 5x - 6y = 3 \\ 2x + 12y = 12 \end{cases}$ **(1.5, .75)**

8. $\begin{cases} 2v + w = 47 \\ 8v - 4w = 28 \end{cases}$ **(13.5, 20)**

9. $\begin{cases} x + 3y = 12 \\ 4x + 12y = 48 \end{cases}$ **infinitely many**

10. $\begin{cases} 1000x + 30y = 500 \\ x - 2y = 11 \end{cases}$ $\left(\frac{19}{29}, \frac{-150}{29}\right)$

11. $\begin{cases} a + b = \frac{1}{3} \\ a - b = \frac{1}{4} \end{cases}$ $\left(\frac{7}{24}, \frac{1}{24}\right)$

12. $\begin{cases} 5u + 4v = -18 \\ 0.04u - 0.12v = 0.16 \end{cases}$ **(-2, -2)**

In 13–15, use the linear-combination method to determine whether the system is inconsistent or consistent. *(Lesson 5-2)*

13. $\begin{cases} 2x + 3y = 4 \\ 5x + 6y = 7 \end{cases}$ **consistent**

14. $\begin{cases} 2x + 3y = 4 \\ 4x + 6y = 8 \end{cases}$ **consistent**

15. $\begin{cases} 2x + 3y = 4 \\ 4x + 6y = 9 \end{cases}$ **inconsistent**

Applying the Mathematics

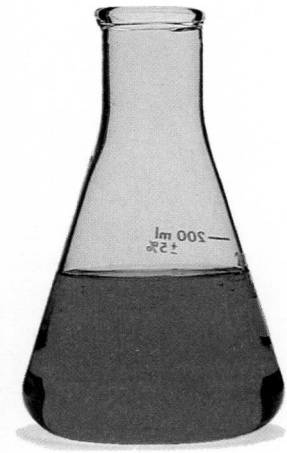

16. At the zoo, Jay and Terri bought food for themselves and a friend. Jay bought 3 slices of pizza and 1 lemonade for $4.50. Terri paid $4.00 for 2 slices of pizza and 2 lemonades. What should their friend reimburse Terri for his lemonade? **75¢**

17. N ml of a 60% salt solution are mixed with S ml of an 80% salt solution. The result is 35 ml of a 72% salt solution.
   a. Write an equation relating N, S, and the total number of ml. **$N + S = 35$**
   b. The amount of salt in the 72% solution is $0.72(35) = 25.2$ ml. Write an equation relating the amount of salt in the 60%, 80%, and 72% solutions. **$N(.60) + S(.80) = 25.2$**
   c. Solve the system represented by your answers in parts a and b. How many ml of the 60% and the 80% solutions are needed? **$S = 21$, $N = 14$**

262

18. Solve by the linear-combination method.
$$\begin{cases} 9x^2 - 6y^2 = 291 \\ 3x^2 + 2y^2 = 197 \end{cases}$$ (-7, -5); (7, 5): (-7, 5); (7, -5)

Review

19. Graph the solution set of this compound sentence in a coordinate plane. *(Lesson 5-1)*

$$x \geq 9 \ or \ y < \tfrac{1}{2} \quad \text{See margin.}$$

20. Graph the solution set of each sentence in the system below and approximate the solutions. *(Lesson 5-2)*

$$\begin{cases} y = \tfrac{1}{2}x^2 \\ y = \tfrac{1}{3}x + 1 \end{cases} \quad \text{See margin.}$$

21. Consider the system
$$\begin{cases} 5x - 3y = 6 \\ x - y = 2 \end{cases}$$
graphed below.
  a. How many solutions does the system have? one
  b. Is the system inconsistent or consistent? *(Lesson 5-2)* consistent

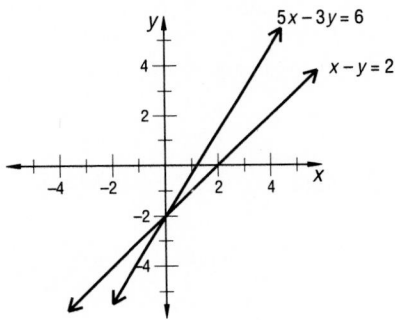

Exploration

24. Look up the suggested daily number of grams of protein, vitamin A, and calcium recommended for your age. Find some combinations of food that will give you the recommended amounts.
Many answers are possible.

ADDITIONAL ANSWERS
19.

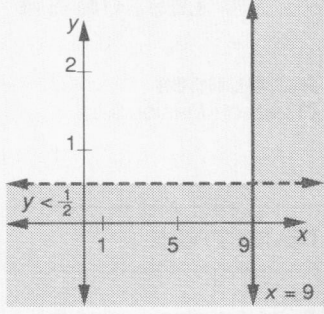

20.

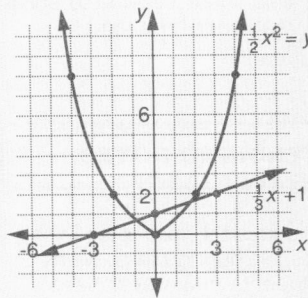

The points of intersection are approximately (1.8, 1.6) and (-1.1, 0.6).

OBJECTIVES

A Solve systems using the substitution method.
F Use linear sysems to solve real-world problems.

TEACHING NOTES

Discuss the examples in this lesson during class. Many students may never have seen a system with more than two equations. **Example 2** is an excellent illustration of a system of three equations that is easily solved by substitution.

Example 3 shows the solution of a nonlinear system. This is most likely the first system of equations with more than one solution that the students have seen. Relate the solutions to the graph of the system. Stress that the graph indicates that there are two solutions. Since the graph of the equations will not intersect again, it is important for students to understand that there are only two solutions.

LESSON

5-4

The Substitution Method

If $a = b$, then a can be substituted for b in any arithmetic or algebraic expression. This, the Substitution Property of Equality, is obvious when $a = 10$ and $b = 7 + 3$. It is not so obvious that when $y = 6x - 17$, for example, you can substitute $6x - 17$ for y. This second application of the Substitution Property is useful in solving systems.

Example 1 Solve the system $\begin{cases} y = 6x - 17 \\ 21x - 4y = 10. \end{cases}$

Solution Substitute $6x - 17$ for y in the second equation.

$$21x - 4(6x - 17) = 10$$

The equation now has only one variable. Solve for x.

$$21x - 24x + 68 = 10$$
$$-3x = -58$$
$$x = \frac{58}{3}$$

Now substitute in either equation to find y. We use the first because it is solved for y. (The other equation will be the check.)

$$y = 6 \cdot \frac{58}{3} - 17$$
$$= 116 - 17$$
$$= 99$$

Check Use the second equation. Does $21 \cdot \frac{58}{3} - 4 \cdot 99 = 10$? Yes, $406 - 396 = 10$.

Another situation where substitution can be used conveniently is when there are more than two variables and two equations, as Example 2 illustrates.

264

Example 2 An end zone has a seating capacity of 4216. There are four times as many lower-level seats as there are upper-level seats. Also, there are three times as many mezzanine seats as there are upper-level seats. How many seats of each type are there?

Solution

Let L = the number of lower-level seats,
M = the number of mezzanine seats,
U = the number of upper-level seats.

Then the system is

$$\begin{cases} L + M + U = 4216 \\ L = 4U \\ M = 3U. \end{cases}$$

Substitute the expressions for L and M into the first equation.

$$4U + 3U + U = 4216$$
$$8U = 4216$$

Thus,
$$U = 527$$
$$L = 4 \cdot 527 = 2108$$
$$M = 3 \cdot 527 = 1581.$$

There are 527 upper-level seats, 2108 lower-level seats, and 1581 mezzanine seats.

Check The total number of seats should add to 4216. It does: $527 + 2108 + 1581 = 4216$.

The substitution method generally works with any system which has a linear equation and a nonlinear equation. Substitute an expression from the linear equation into the nonlinear equation. Example 3 illustrates this.

Example 3 Solve the system $\begin{cases} y = 3x \\ xy = 48. \end{cases}$

Solution Substitute $3x$ for y in the second equation.

$$x(3x) = 48$$
$$3x^2 = 48$$
$$x^2 = 16$$
$$x = 4 \text{ or } x = -4$$

(Note the word *or*. The solution set is the union of all possible answers.) Each value of x yields a value of y. Substitute each value of x into either of the original equations. We substitute into $y = 3x$. If $x = 4$, then $y = 3(4) = 12$. If $x = -4$, then $y = 3(-4) = -12$. The solution set is $\{(4, 12), (-4, -12)\}$.

Error Analysis When using the substitution method, most students will solve for one variable correctly. However, some students will not multiply through by the variable's coefficient after the substitution is made into the second equation. In **Example 1**, for instance, when $6x - 17$ is substituted for y in the second equation, $21x - 4y = 10$, the new equation may become $21x - (6x - 17) = 10$. Stress the importance of the variable's coefficient.

Another difficulty is multiplying by using the Distributive Property, especially when the coefficient is negative. In this case, students often make careless errors in sign. Remind them to work more accurately.

ADDITIONAL EXAMPLES

1. Solve using substitution.

a. $\begin{cases} x + y = 6 \\ y = x + 2 \end{cases}$

$x = 2, y = 4$

b. $\begin{cases} 2x - y = -9 \\ 3x - 8y = -7 \end{cases}$

$x = -5, y = -1$

2. In news reports, profits of a company this year (T) are often compared to those from last year (L), but the actual values are sometimes not stated. Suppose that this year a company made \$8 million more than last year, and that profits were up 20%. Determine T and L.

$T = L + 8 \cdot 10^6$ and $T = 1.20L$. L = \$40 million and T = \$48 million.

3. Solve the system.
$\begin{cases} y = 4x \\ xy = 36 \end{cases}$

The solutions are (3, 12) and (-3, -12).

Check 1 Substitute the coordinate of each point into each equation. For (4, 12): Does $12 = 3 \cdot 4$? Yes. Does $4 \cdot 12 = 48$? Yes. In the Questions, you are asked to check the other point.

Check 2 Graph the equations. The graph below shows that there are two solutions. One solution seems near $(4, 12)$; the other near $(-4, -12)$.

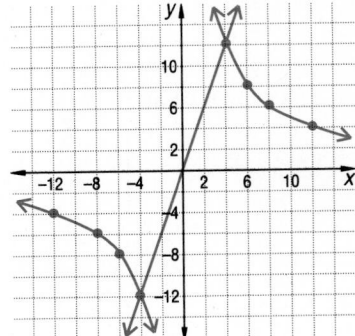

The examples of this lesson illustrate that substitution may be an appropriate method when:
1. at least one of the equations has been or can easily be solved for one of the variables;
2. there are three or more equations and three or more variables; or
3. the system has one linear and one nonlinear equation.

Questions

Covering the Reading

1. Write the Substitution Property of Equality.   See margin.

2. Solve the system $\begin{cases} y = 3x + 5 \\ 4x - 3y = 12. \end{cases}$ $(\frac{-27}{5}, \frac{-56}{5})$

In 3 and 4, refer to Example 2.

3. After the expressions in the second and third equations were substituted into the first equation, how many variables were in this new equation?   one

4. A second stadium was built to the same specifications but has a seating capacity of 6904. How many upper level seats are there?   863

5. Solve the system $\begin{cases} 3x + 2y + z = 24 \\ x = 5z - 20 \\ y = -2z. \end{cases}$ $(15, -14, 7)$

266

In 6 and 7, refer to Example 3.

6. Verify that (-4, -12) is a solution to the system. **See margin.**

7. The graph of $y = 3x$ is a __?__ and the graph of $xy = 48$ is a __?__ .
line; hyperbola

8. Solve the system $\begin{cases} y = 3x \\ xy = 75. \end{cases}$ **(5, 15); (-5, -15)**

In 9 and 10, refer to the following systems.

(a) $y = 3x + 1$
$4x - 3y = 12$
(c) $3x + 2y + z = 7$
$x = 5z$
$y = -2z$

(b) $5x - 7y = 12$
$-12x + 8y = 19$
(d) $x + 5y = 12$
$4x - 7y = 13$

9. Which systems are written in a form that is convenient to be solved using linear combinations? **b, d**

10. Which systems can be solved conveniently using substitution? **a, c**

Applying the Mathematics

11. A sports stadium seats 60,000 people. The home team gets 4 times as many tickets as the visiting team. Let H be the number of tickets for the home team and V be the number of tickets for the visiting team.
  a. *Multiple choice* Which system represents the given conditions? **iii**

  (i) $\begin{cases} 4H + 4V = 60{,}000 \\ H = 4V \end{cases}$ (ii) $\begin{cases} H + V = 60{,}000 \\ V = 4H \end{cases}$

  (iii) $\begin{cases} H = 4V \\ H + V = 60{,}000 \end{cases}$

  b. Solve the correct system for H and V.   **H = 48,000; V = 12,000**

12. FASTPIC offers to process a roll of film for 30¢ per print with free developing. A competitor, QUALIPRINT, will process a roll for 25¢ per print plus a $2.00 developing charge.
  a. For what number of prints will the cost be the same at FASTPIC and QUALIPRINT?   **40 prints**
  b. What is the cost for this number of prints?   **$12.00**

13. A recipe that makes 7 cups of French dressing uses tomato juice, vinegar, and olive oil. It calls for 3 times as much vinegar as tomato juice and $4\frac{1}{2}$ times as much olive oil as vinegar. How much of each ingredient should be used?   **juice: .4 C; vinegar: 1.2 C; oil: 5.4 C**

14. Six towns on a train line are in order: Achilles, Bacchus, Calypso, Daedalus, Electra, and Fates. The distance from Achilles to Bacchus is twice the distance from Bacchus to Calypso, which is three times the distance from Calypso to Daedalus. The distance from Daedalus to Electra is two miles less than the distance from Daedalus to Electra to Fates, which is twelve times longer than the distance from Daedalus to Electra. The total distance from Achilles to Fates is 112 miles. What is the distance between Achilles and Daedalus? $109\frac{9}{11}$ **miles**

LESSON 5-4   The Substitution Method   **267**

NOTES ON QUESTIONS
Questions 9 and 10:
These questions are important in helping students apply guidelines to analyze a given problem and choose an appropriate solution method before the computation becomes cumbersome.

Questions 17 and 18:
These questions review multiplication of matrices. Students should recognize that the first matrix in **Question 17** is the 3 × 3 identity matrix. Identity matrices are important for Lessons 5-5 and 5-6.

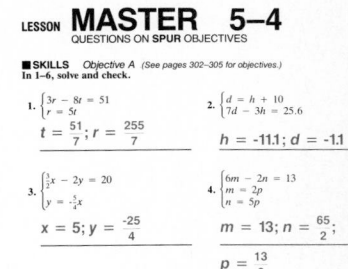

NAME _____

LESSON **MASTER   5-4**
QUESTIONS ON **SPUR** OBJECTIVES

■**SKILLS**   *Objective A (See pages 302–305 for objectives.)*
In 1–6, solve and check.

1. $\begin{cases} 3r - 8t = 51 \\ r = 5t \end{cases}$
   $t = \frac{51}{7}; r = \frac{255}{7}$

2. $\begin{cases} d = h + 10 \\ 7d - 3h = 25.6 \end{cases}$
   $h = -11.1; d = -1.1$

3. $\begin{cases} \frac{3}{2}x - 2y = 20 \\ y = -\frac{5}{4}x \end{cases}$
   $x = 5; y = \frac{-25}{4}$

4. $\begin{cases} 6m - 2n = 13 \\ m = 5p \\ n = 5p \end{cases}$
   $m = 13; n = \frac{65}{2};$
   $p = \frac{13}{2}$

5. $\begin{cases} d = 6e + 5 \\ e = -2f - 8 \\ f = -3 \end{cases}$
   $d = -7, e = -2, f = -3$

6. $\begin{cases} 3y = 2x \\ 10y + 5x = 70 \end{cases}$
   $x = 6; y = 4$

■**USES**   *Objective F*
7. Arthur Dekko, a furniture maker, uses a secret formula for paint. He combines a certain amount of Nu Blue with 3 times as much Dread Red. His mixture totals about 2 gallons (about 128 oz). How much of each kind of paint does he use?
32 oz of Nu Blue; 96 oz of Dread Red

8. Kleener Dry Cleaning charges $.85 to launder a shirt. Fancy Laundry charges $.95 per shirt, but gives a $1 discount for 5 shirts or more.
  a. For what number of shirts will the cost at Kleener be the same as at Fancy?   **10 shirts**
  b. What is the cost for this number of shirts?   **$8.50**

ADDITIONAL ANSWERS
16.

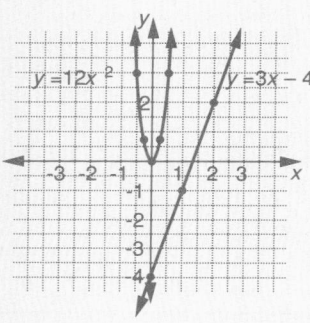

inconsistent; no solution

17. $\begin{bmatrix} 2 & \sqrt{3} & -1 \\ 0 & 5.1 & 0 \\ -4 & 11 & -2 \end{bmatrix}$

18. $\begin{bmatrix} 58 \\ -10 \end{bmatrix}$

19. $\angle ROC = 70°$, $\angle CKR = 60°$, $\angle KRO = 80°$, $\angle OCK = 150°$

20. In the second
condition, you are taking
away 2 citrons and adding
2 wood apples to get a
total cost which is 6 less
than the original. This
means that each wood
apple must cost 3 less
than each citron. So find
two whole numbers with a
difference of 3 such that
the sum of their respective
multiples of 9 and 7 is 107.
Thus, there are 8 citrons
and 5 wood apples.

Review

15. Solve the system $\begin{cases} 4x - 3y = 1 \\ 5x - 6y = 9. \end{cases}$ *(Lesson 5-3)* $\left(\frac{-7}{3}, \frac{-31}{9}\right)$

16. Solve by graphing $\begin{cases} y = 12x^2 \\ y = 3x - 4. \end{cases}$ *(Lesson 5-2)* **See margin.**

In 17 and 18, multiply. *(Lesson 4-2)*

17. $\begin{bmatrix} 1 & 0 & 0 \\ 0 & 1 & 0 \\ 0 & 0 & 1 \end{bmatrix} \begin{bmatrix} 2 & \sqrt{3} & -1 \\ 0 & 5.1 & 0 \\ -4 & 11 & -2 \end{bmatrix}$ **See margin.**

18. $\begin{bmatrix} 2 & 4 \\ -3 & 1 \end{bmatrix} \begin{bmatrix} 7 \\ 11 \end{bmatrix}$ **See margin.**

19. Find the measures of all four angles of quadrilateral *ROCK*
drawn below. *(Previous course)* **See margin.**

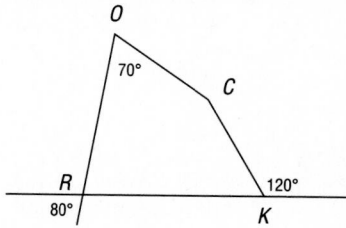

Exploration

20. This problem was made up by the Indian mathematician Mahavira and
dates from about 850 A.D. "The price of nine citrons and seven fragrant wood apples is 107; again, the mixed price of seven citrons and
nine fragrant wood apples is 101. Oh you arithmetician, tell me
quickly the price of a citron and a wood apple here, having distinctly
separated these prices well." At this time algebra had not been developed yet. How could this question be answered by someone without
algebra? **See margin.**

268

Inverses of Matrices

In this chapter you have seen three methods of solving systems: graphing, linear combination, and substitution. A fourth method makes use of matrices.

Recall that real numbers a and b are multiplicative inverses if and only if $ab = ba = 1$. Recall also that the real number 0 does not have a multiplicative inverse.

Similarly, 2×2 matrices M and N are **inverse matrices** if and only if their product is the 2×2 identity matrix for multiplication,

$$MN = NM = \begin{bmatrix} 1 & 0 \\ 0 & 1 \end{bmatrix}.$$

There are many such pairs of matrices. For instance, the inverse of

$$\begin{bmatrix} 4 & 0 \\ 0 & 3 \end{bmatrix} \text{ is } \begin{bmatrix} \frac{1}{4} & 0 \\ 0 & \frac{1}{3} \end{bmatrix} \text{ because}$$

$$\begin{bmatrix} 4 & 0 \\ 0 & 3 \end{bmatrix} \begin{bmatrix} \frac{1}{4} & 0 \\ 0 & \frac{1}{3} \end{bmatrix} = \begin{bmatrix} 1 & 0 \\ 0 & 1 \end{bmatrix} \text{ and}$$

$$\begin{bmatrix} \frac{1}{4} & 0 \\ 0 & \frac{1}{3} \end{bmatrix} \begin{bmatrix} 4 & 0 \\ 0 & 3 \end{bmatrix} = \begin{bmatrix} 1 & 0 \\ 0 & 1 \end{bmatrix}.$$

Recall that $\begin{bmatrix} 4 & 0 \\ 0 & 3 \end{bmatrix}$ is the matrix for the scale change $S_{4,3}$.

To undo the effect of $S_{4,3}$ on a figure, apply the scale change $S_{\frac{1}{4},\frac{1}{3}}$.

That scale change is associated with the matrix $\begin{bmatrix} \frac{1}{4} & 0 \\ 0 & \frac{1}{3} \end{bmatrix}$.

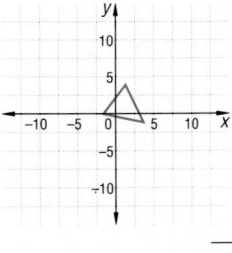

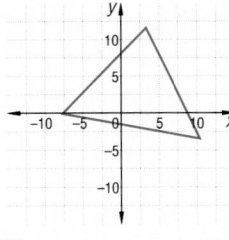

$S_{4,3}$

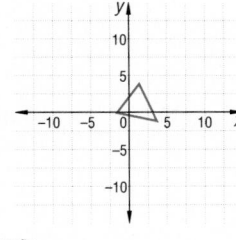

$S_{1/4,\,1/3}$

LESSON 5-5

RESOURCES
■ Lesson Master 5-5

OBJECTIVE

B Find the inverse and determinant of a 2×2 matrix.

TEACHING NOTES

Point out that the inverse of a 2×2 matrix is also a 2×2 matrix, which allows the two matrices to be multiplied in either order. Have students verify the matrix multiplications at the top of page 270 and in the proof of the Inverse Matrix Theorem.

An easy algorithmic way for students to remember the Inverse-Matrix Theorem is as follows. To find M^{-1}, the inverse of M, a 2×2 matrix of the form $\begin{bmatrix} a & b \\ c & d \end{bmatrix}$:
(1) Find det M. If det $M = 0$, the inverse does not exist.
(2) Reverse the positions of a and d.
(3) Take the opposites of b and c.
(4) Divide each element of the new matrix by det M.

1. Find the inverse of the matrix.

a. $\begin{bmatrix} 4 & -3 \\ 2 & 1 \end{bmatrix}$

$\begin{bmatrix} \frac{1}{10} & \frac{3}{10} \\ -\frac{1}{5} & \frac{2}{5} \end{bmatrix}$

b. $\begin{bmatrix} 6 & -4 \\ 3 & -2 \end{bmatrix}$

No inverse exists.

c. $\begin{bmatrix} 11 & 3 \\ 7 & 2 \end{bmatrix}$

$\begin{bmatrix} 2 & -3 \\ -7 & 11 \end{bmatrix}$

2. Just as two real numbers 1 and -1 are their own multiplicative inverses, the identity matrix is its own inverse. Find another 2 × 2 matrix which is its own inverse. **Think of the relationship between transformations and matrices. Which transformations are their own inverse? Matrices for reflections, such as** $\begin{bmatrix} 0 & -1 \\ -1 & 0 \end{bmatrix}$ **and** $\begin{bmatrix} 0 & 1 \\ 1 & 0 \end{bmatrix}$**.**

Other inverses may not be so obvious. The inverse of

$$\begin{bmatrix} 2 & 5 \\ 3 & 8 \end{bmatrix} \text{ is } \begin{bmatrix} 8 & -5 \\ -3 & 2 \end{bmatrix}.$$

This result can be verified by matrix multiplication.

$$\begin{bmatrix} 8 & -5 \\ -3 & 2 \end{bmatrix}\begin{bmatrix} 2 & 5 \\ 3 & 8 \end{bmatrix} = \begin{bmatrix} 8(2) + -5(3) & 8(5) + -5(8) \\ -3(2) + 2(3) & -3(5) + 2(8) \end{bmatrix} = \begin{bmatrix} 1 & 0 \\ 0 & 1 \end{bmatrix}$$

Similarly, multiplication in the other order also results in the identity.

$$\begin{bmatrix} 2 & 5 \\ 3 & 8 \end{bmatrix}\begin{bmatrix} 8 & -5 \\ -3 & 2 \end{bmatrix} = \begin{bmatrix} 1 & 0 \\ 0 & 1 \end{bmatrix}$$

How can the inverse of a matrix be found? The following powerful theorem tells when an inverse matrix exists, and gives you a formula to find that inverse.

Inverse-Matrix Theorem:

If $ad - bc \neq 0$, the inverse of $\begin{bmatrix} a & b \\ c & d \end{bmatrix}$ is

$$\begin{bmatrix} \dfrac{d}{ad - bc} & \dfrac{-b}{ad - bc} \\ \dfrac{-c}{ad - bc} & \dfrac{a}{ad - bc} \end{bmatrix}.$$

Proof:

We need only to show that the product of the two matrices in either order is the identity matrix.

$$\begin{bmatrix} a & b \\ c & d \end{bmatrix}\begin{bmatrix} \dfrac{d}{ad - bc} & \dfrac{-b}{ad - bc} \\ \dfrac{-c}{ad - bc} & \dfrac{a}{ad - bc} \end{bmatrix}$$

$$= \begin{bmatrix} \dfrac{ad}{ad - bc} + \dfrac{-bc}{ad - bc} & \dfrac{-ab}{ad - bc} + \dfrac{ab}{ad - bc} \\ \dfrac{cd}{ad - bc} - \dfrac{cd}{ad - bc} & \dfrac{-bc}{ad - bc} + \dfrac{ad}{ad - bc} \end{bmatrix} \quad \text{matrix multiplication}$$

$$= \begin{bmatrix} \dfrac{ad - bc}{ad - bc} & \dfrac{0}{ad - bc} \\ \dfrac{0}{ad - bc} & \dfrac{ad - bc}{ad - bc} \end{bmatrix} \quad \begin{array}{l}\text{addition of fractions and} \\ \text{definition of subtraction}\end{array}$$

$$= \begin{bmatrix} 1 & 0 \\ 0 & 1 \end{bmatrix} \quad \text{simplification}$$

270

In Question 2, you are asked to verify the multiplication in reverse order.

■ ■ ■ ■ ■ ■ ■ ■

Example 1 Use the theorem to find the inverse of the matrix $\begin{bmatrix} 0 & -2 \\ 3 & 1 \end{bmatrix}$.

Solution In $\begin{bmatrix} 0 & -2 \\ 3 & 1 \end{bmatrix}$, $a = 0$, $b = -2$, $c = 3$, and $d = 1$.

So $ad - bc = 0(1) - (-2)(3) = 6$. Substitute into the formula to get

$$\begin{bmatrix} \frac{1}{6} & \frac{2}{6} \\ -\frac{3}{6} & \frac{0}{6} \end{bmatrix}, \text{ which can be written as } \begin{bmatrix} \frac{1}{6} & \frac{1}{3} \\ -\frac{1}{2} & 0 \end{bmatrix}.$$

The multiplicative inverse of a real number x is sometimes written as x^{-1}. In the same way, the multiplicative inverse of a matrix M can be written as M^{-1}.

Only **square matrices**, that is, ones with the same number of rows and columns can have inverses. However, not all square matrices have inverses. If $M = \begin{bmatrix} a & b \\ c & d \end{bmatrix}$ and $ad - bc = 0$, then $\frac{1}{ad - bc}$

is undefined, so M^{-1} cannot exist.

■ ■ ■ ■ ■ ■ ■ ■

Example 2 Verify that $\begin{bmatrix} 3 & 1 \\ 6 & 2 \end{bmatrix}$ does not have an inverse.

Solution Suppose $\begin{bmatrix} 3 & 1 \\ 6 & 2 \end{bmatrix}$ had an inverse $\begin{bmatrix} a & b \\ c & d \end{bmatrix}$. Then

$$\begin{bmatrix} 3 & 1 \\ 6 & 2 \end{bmatrix} \begin{bmatrix} a & b \\ c & d \end{bmatrix} = \begin{bmatrix} 1 & 0 \\ 0 & 1 \end{bmatrix}.$$

Then $3a + c = 1$ and $6a + 2c = 0$. This system has no solution, so the matrix can have no inverse.

Check In this matrix $a = 3$, $b = 1$, $c = 6$, and $d = 2$. Thus $ad - bc = 3 \cdot 2 - 1 \cdot 6 = 0$. This means there is no inverse.

Question 23: The coding scheme in this question makes use of modular arithmetic. Explain to students that any two integers that differ by 26 are associated with the same letter of the alphabet. Thus, 1, 27, 53, . . . , and -25, -51, . . . are all associated with *A*. The positive integers associated with any letter form a linear sequence with constant difference 26. Whereas students might associate codes with spies, codes are used today to keep private financial records of people and companies, and to make certain that numbers are used accurately.

271

The expression $ad - bc$ that is associated with the 2×2 matrix

$A = \begin{bmatrix} a & b \\ c & d \end{bmatrix}$ is called the **determinant** of the matrix A, since it determines whether or not matrix A has an inverse. We abbreviate the word *determinant* as *det*. For instance, $\det \begin{bmatrix} 3 & 2 \\ -5 & 4 \end{bmatrix} =$

$3 \cdot 4 - 2 \cdot -5 = 22$. The idea of the determinant was first used by the German mathematician Gottfried Leibniz (1646–1716), who is also known as one of the inventors of calculus. Using this notation and scalar multiplication, the Inverse-Matrix Theorem can be written as:

If $M = \begin{bmatrix} a & b \\ c & d \end{bmatrix}$ and $\det M \neq 0$, then $M^{-1} = \dfrac{1}{\det M} \begin{bmatrix} d & -b \\ -c & a \end{bmatrix}$.

Questions

Covering the Reading

1. **a.** If a and b are real numbers that are multiplicative inverses of each other, what does ab equal?   1
   b. If M and N are 2×2 matrices that are multiplicative inverses of each other, what does MN equal?   See margin.

2. Verify the second part of the proof of the Inverse-Matrix Theorem. That is, show that the identity matrix is the product of the two matrices in the reverse order.   See margin.

In 3 and 4, is the statement true or false?

3. Only square matrices have inverses.   True

4. All square matrices have inverses.   False

5. M is a matrix with nonzero determinant. What is denoted by M^{-1}?   the inverse of M

6. Give an expression for $\det \begin{bmatrix} a & b \\ c & d \end{bmatrix}$. $ad - bc$

7. In Example 1, what is the determinant of the given matrix?   6

8. Give an example of a matrix not mentioned in this lesson that does not have an inverse.   See margin.

In 9–12, a matrix is given. (a) Find its determinant. (b) Find its inverse, if it has one. (c) Check your answer to part b by multiplying.   See margin.

9. $\begin{bmatrix} 5 & 4 \\ 2 & 2 \end{bmatrix}$ 10. $\begin{bmatrix} -1 & -3 \\ 4 & -8 \end{bmatrix}$ 11. $\begin{bmatrix} a & 0 \\ 0 & b \end{bmatrix}$ 12. $\begin{bmatrix} \frac{1}{2} & \frac{1}{2} \\ \frac{1}{2} & \frac{1}{2} \end{bmatrix}$

272

13. If $A = \begin{bmatrix} -7 & 4 \\ -9 & -4 \end{bmatrix}$ and $B = \begin{bmatrix} 3 & 3 \\ 0 & 3 \end{bmatrix}$, find

    a. det A. 64   **b.** det B. 9   **c.** det AB. 576

14. a. Find the inverse of the matrix for R_{90}. See margin.
    b. Explain the result to part a geometrically. See margin.

15. The inverse of a 2×2 matrix can be found by solving a pair of

systems. Here is how. If the inverse of $\begin{bmatrix} 0 & -2 \\ 3 & 1 \end{bmatrix}$ is $\begin{bmatrix} e & f \\ g & h \end{bmatrix}$,

then $\begin{bmatrix} 0 & -2 \\ 3 & 1 \end{bmatrix} \begin{bmatrix} e & f \\ g & h \end{bmatrix} = \begin{bmatrix} 1 & 0 \\ 0 & 1 \end{bmatrix}$.

This yields the systems $\begin{cases} 0e - 2g = 1 \\ 3e + g = 0 \end{cases}$ and $\begin{cases} 0f - 2h = 0 \\ 3f + h = 1 \end{cases}$.

See margin.
    a. Solve the systems above and determine the inverse matrix.
    b. Check your answer to part a by finding the inverse matrix using
      the Inverse-Matrix Theorem. See margin.

16. a. Solve the following system by adding: $\begin{cases} 5x - 3y = 15 \\ 5x + 3y = 15 \end{cases}$ (3, 0)
    b. It can just as easily be solved by subtracting. Solve by subtracting
      to check your answer. *(Lesson 5-3)* (3, 0)

In 17 and 18, solve the system. *(Lessons 5-3, 5-4)*

17. $\begin{cases} y = 4x \\ 3x + 2y = 22 \end{cases}$ (2, 8)   **18.** $\begin{cases} 2x - 8y = 6 \\ -x + 4y = 3 \end{cases}$ no solution

19. Name two situations in which it is convenient to solve a system by
    substituting. *(Lesson 5-4)* See margin.

20. Alan Aska wants to purchase a new air conditioner. One brand costs
    $540 to purchase and $20 a month to operate. A less efficient brand
    costs $320 to purchase and $24 a month to operate. See margin.
    a. Plot the costs over time of both brands on a single graph.
    b. What does the point of intersection denote? *(Lessons 5-2, 5-3)*

21. Graph the set of ordered pairs satisfying $2y < 3x - 6$. *(Lesson 3-9)*
    See margin.

22. a. Find the area of the triangle with vertices $(0, 0)$, $(-3, 0)$, and
      $(-7, 8)$. 12 sq units

    b. Calculate $\frac{1}{2}\det \begin{bmatrix} -3 & -7 \\ 0 & 8 \end{bmatrix}$. -12
                                     11 sq units

    c. Find the area of the triangle with vertices $(0, 0)$, $(5, 2)$, and $(4, 6)$.

    d. Calculate $\frac{1}{2}\det \begin{bmatrix} 5 & 4 \\ 2 & 6 \end{bmatrix}$. 11

    e. Generalize parts a–d. See margin.
    f. Test your generalization with another example. See margin.

LESSON 5-5 Inverses of Matrices   **273**

15.a. $e = \frac{1}{6}$; $f = \frac{1}{3}$; $g = -\frac{1}{2}$; $h = 0$
b. $ad - bc = 6$;

$\begin{bmatrix} \frac{1}{6} & \frac{2}{6} \\ -\frac{3}{6} & \frac{0}{6} \end{bmatrix} = \begin{bmatrix} \frac{1}{6} & \frac{1}{3} \\ -\frac{1}{2} & 0 \end{bmatrix}$

19. when at least one of the equations has been or can easily be solved for one variable, or when the system has one linear and one nonlinear equation, or when there are more than two variables and equations

20.a.

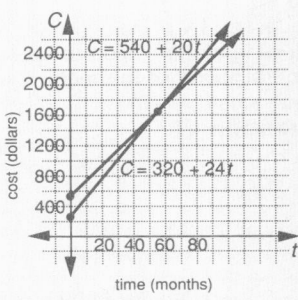

20.b., 21., 22.e., f. See Additional Answers in the back of this book.

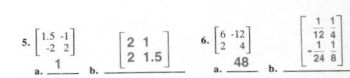
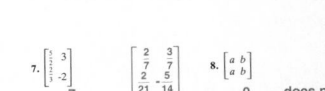

EXTENSION
Notice that the proof of the Inverse-Matrix Theorem does not tell how we knew in advance that

$$\begin{bmatrix} \dfrac{d}{ad-bc} & \dfrac{-b}{ad-bc} \\ \dfrac{-c}{ad-bc} & \dfrac{a}{ad-bc} \end{bmatrix} \text{ was}$$

indeed the inverse of
$\begin{bmatrix} a & b \\ c & d \end{bmatrix}$. You can extend the lesson by presenting the following ideas, which are a generalization of the technique illustrated in **Question 15**.

If the inverse of $\begin{bmatrix} a & b \\ c & d \end{bmatrix}$ exists, it must be a 2×2 matrix. Call the inverse $\begin{bmatrix} w & x \\ y & z \end{bmatrix}$. Then we need to find w, x, y, and z such that $\begin{bmatrix} a & b \\ c & d \end{bmatrix}\begin{bmatrix} w & x \\ y & z \end{bmatrix}$
$= \begin{bmatrix} 1 & 0 \\ 0 & 1 \end{bmatrix}$.

Multiplying the matrices on the left and equating the entries yields the system below.

$$\begin{cases} aw + by = 1 \\ ax + by = 0 \\ cw + dy = 0 \\ cx + dz = 1 \end{cases}$$

By using linear-combination techniques, we can solve for w, x, y, and z. For instance, if the first equation is multiplied by c, and the third by $-a$, and the resulting equations are added, then we can solve for y.

$$y = \dfrac{c}{bc-ad} = \dfrac{-c}{ad-bc}$$

Other linear combinations can be used to find w, x, and z. Some motivated students might enjoy working through the complete derivation.

---

23. In 1929–31, the mathematician Lester Hill devised a method of encoding messages using matrices. Every integer is assigned a letter according to the scheme:

$1 = A, 2 = B, 3 = C, \dots , 25 = Y, 26 = Z, 27 = A, 28 = B, \dots ,$
and $0 = Z, -1 = Y, \dots, -24 = B, -25 = A, -26 = Z, \dots$.

To code or encipher the word *FOUR*, follow these steps.

Step 1. Put the letters into a matrix four at a time. With $6 = F$, $15 = O$, $21 = U$, $18 = R$, use the matrix

$$\begin{bmatrix} 6 & 15 \\ 21 & 18 \end{bmatrix}.$$

Step 2. Multiply each 2×2 matrix by the *coding* or *key matrix*, such as $\begin{bmatrix} 0 & 1 \\ 1 & 2 \end{bmatrix}$.

$$\begin{bmatrix} 0 & 1 \\ 1 & 2 \end{bmatrix}\begin{bmatrix} 6 & 15 \\ 21 & 18 \end{bmatrix} = \begin{bmatrix} 21 & 18 \\ 48 & 51 \end{bmatrix}$$

Step 3. Change the matrix $\begin{bmatrix} 21 & 18 \\ 48 & 51 \end{bmatrix}$

back to letters to write the coded message: *URVY*.

Step 4. Repeat this as many times as necessary to encode a longer message.

a. Code *MEET ME AT* using the key $\begin{bmatrix} 0 & 1 \\ 1 & 2 \end{bmatrix}$. **ETWSATOS**

To decode or decipher a message,

Step 1. Break the message up into groups of four letters and write as matrices using the corresponding numbers. Each letter-group matrix should be: $\begin{bmatrix} \text{1st letter} & \text{2nd letter} \\ \text{3rd letter} & \text{4th letter} \end{bmatrix}$.

Step 2. Find the inverse of the key matrix and multiply each letter-group matrix by the inverse.

b. The following message was also enciphered using the key

$$\begin{bmatrix} 0 & 1 \\ 1 & 2 \end{bmatrix}:$$

YTKOFOTISBGVITWKOULO.

What is the original message? **MAY THE FOURS BE WITH YOU**

c. Make up a code matrix and a coded message of your own. The inverse of your coding matrix must have a determinant of 1. **Many answers are possible.**

LESSON 5-6

Using Matrices to Solve Systems

Notice that $\begin{bmatrix} 1 & 3 \\ 2 & -1 \end{bmatrix} \begin{bmatrix} x \\ y \end{bmatrix} = \begin{bmatrix} x + 3y \\ 2x - y \end{bmatrix}$.

This means that it is possible to represent the system $\begin{cases} x + 3y = 22 \\ 2x - y = 2 \end{cases}$ as a matrix equation:

$$\begin{bmatrix} 1 & 3 \\ 2 & -1 \end{bmatrix} \begin{bmatrix} x \\ y \end{bmatrix} = \begin{bmatrix} 22 \\ 2 \end{bmatrix}$$

This is the **matrix form of the system.** The matrix $\begin{bmatrix} 1 & 3 \\ 2 & -1 \end{bmatrix}$ represents the coefficients of the variables, so it is called the **coefficient matrix**. The matrix $\begin{bmatrix} 22 \\ 2 \end{bmatrix}$ contains the constants on the right sides of the equations. It is called the **constant matrix** for this system.

A system in matrix form can be solved using matrix multiplication. Just as the Multiplication Property of Equality allows both sides of an equation to be multiplied by any number, both sides of a matrix equation can be multiplied by any matrix. To solve, we multiply by the inverse of the coefficient matrix. By the theorem in Lesson 5-5,

the inverse of $\begin{bmatrix} 1 & 3 \\ 2 & -1 \end{bmatrix}$ is found to be $\begin{bmatrix} \frac{1}{7} & \frac{3}{7} \\ \frac{2}{7} & -\frac{1}{7} \end{bmatrix}$.

Multiply both sides of the matrix equation by this inverse of the coefficient matrix. Because matrix multiplication is not commutative, the inverse matrix must be at the left on *each* side of the equation.

$$\begin{bmatrix} \frac{1}{7} & \frac{3}{7} \\ \frac{2}{7} & -\frac{1}{7} \end{bmatrix} \begin{bmatrix} 1 & 3 \\ 2 & -1 \end{bmatrix} \begin{bmatrix} x \\ y \end{bmatrix} = \begin{bmatrix} \frac{1}{7} & \frac{3}{7} \\ \frac{2}{7} & -\frac{1}{7} \end{bmatrix} \begin{bmatrix} 22 \\ 2 \end{bmatrix}$$

After the matrices are multiplied, the equation becomes

$$\begin{bmatrix} 1 & 0 \\ 0 & 1 \end{bmatrix} \begin{bmatrix} x \\ y \end{bmatrix} = \begin{bmatrix} 4 \\ 6 \end{bmatrix}.$$

The presence of the identity matrix verifies that the inverse matrix was calculated correctly. Thus

$$\begin{bmatrix} x \\ y \end{bmatrix} = \begin{bmatrix} 4 \\ 6 \end{bmatrix},$$

or $x = 4$ and $y = 6$. You are asked to check this solution in Question 3 at the end of this lesson.

RESOURCES
■ Lesson Master 5-6
■ Quiz for Lessons 5-4 Through 5-6

OBJECTIVE

C Use matrices to solve systems of equations.

TEACHING NOTES

Students will appreciate an introduction to the method of using matrices to solve systems of equations before they read the text. Use a system they have recently solved, such as **Example 1** from Lesson 5-3.

Stress that each equation must be in the form $ax + by = c$ or $ax + by + cz = d$ before the matrix method of solution can be applied. Emphasize that when solving a 3×3 system, the inverse matrix must be to the left of the constant matrix, otherwise the multiplication cannot be done.

Students may wonder why they are using matrices to solve systems they could solve by other means. You can give them many reasons: (1) these methods generalize the solving of systems with many equations and many variables; (2) these are the methods used by computers; (3) these methods indicate exactly when a system has a solution; and (4) the Matrix-Solution Theorem works with any linear system of n equations and n variables.

In general, to solve the system $\begin{cases} ax + by = e \\ cx + dy = f \end{cases}$ by using matrices, rewrite the system as a matrix equation

$$\begin{bmatrix} a & b \\ c & d \end{bmatrix} \begin{bmatrix} x \\ y \end{bmatrix} = \begin{bmatrix} e \\ f \end{bmatrix},$$

which is of the form

$$M \begin{bmatrix} x \\ y \end{bmatrix} = K.$$

Then multiply both sides of the equation by M^{-1}.

$$M^{-1}M \begin{bmatrix} x \\ y \end{bmatrix} = M^{-1}K$$

$$\begin{bmatrix} 1 & 0 \\ 0 & 1 \end{bmatrix} \begin{bmatrix} x \\ y \end{bmatrix} = M^{-1}K$$

$$\begin{bmatrix} x \\ y \end{bmatrix} = M^{-1}K$$

The last equation shows that the solution of a system is the product of the inverse of the coefficient matrix and the constant matrix.

■ ■ ■ ■ ■ ■ ■

Example 1 Use matrices to solve $\begin{cases} 9x = 3 + y \\ 2x - 3y = 5. \end{cases}$

Solution Rewrite the first equation so that it can be put in matrix form.

$$\begin{cases} 9x - y = 3 \\ 2x - 3y = 5 \end{cases}$$

This is equivalent to the matrix equation

$$\begin{bmatrix} 9 & -1 \\ 2 & -3 \end{bmatrix} \begin{bmatrix} x \\ y \end{bmatrix} = \begin{bmatrix} 3 \\ 5 \end{bmatrix}.$$

The inverse of the coefficient matrix is $\begin{bmatrix} \frac{3}{25} & \frac{-1}{25} \\ \frac{2}{25} & \frac{-9}{25} \end{bmatrix}$, or $\begin{bmatrix} .12 & -.04 \\ .08 & -.36 \end{bmatrix}$.

Multiply both sides of the matrix equation by the inverse matrix; the inverse matrix is always placed *on the left.*

$$\begin{bmatrix} .12 & -.04 \\ .08 & -.36 \end{bmatrix} \begin{bmatrix} 9 & -1 \\ 2 & -3 \end{bmatrix} \begin{bmatrix} x \\ y \end{bmatrix} = \begin{bmatrix} .12 & -.04 \\ .08 & -.36 \end{bmatrix} \begin{bmatrix} 3 \\ 5 \end{bmatrix}$$

$$\begin{bmatrix} 1 & 0 \\ 0 & 1 \end{bmatrix} \begin{bmatrix} x \\ y \end{bmatrix} = \begin{bmatrix} .16 \\ -1.56 \end{bmatrix}$$

So the solution is $x = .16$ and $y = -1.56$.

Check Does $9 \cdot .16 = 3 + -1.56$? Yes, both sides equal 1.44.
Does $2 \cdot .16 - 3 \cdot -1.56 = 5$? Yes.

Matrices provide an easy way to tell when linear systems have exactly one solution. The system

$$\begin{cases} ax + by = e \\ cx + dy = f \end{cases}$$

has exactly one solution only if the inverse of $\begin{bmatrix} a & b \\ c & d \end{bmatrix}$ exists.

This inverse exists if and only if its determinant, $ad - bc$, is not zero. This leads to the following theorem.

Matrix-Solution Theorem:

A 2 × 2 system has exactly one solution if and only if the determinant of the coefficient matrix is *not* zero.

When the determinant of the coefficient matrix is 0, there is no unique solution. To determine whether the system has infinitely many solutions or none at all, you should find a solution to one of the equations and test it in the other one. Consider the system

$$\begin{cases} 6x - 9y = 10 \\ 62x - 93y = 310 \end{cases}.$$

The determinant is $ad - bc = 6 \cdot (-93) - (-9) \cdot (62) = 0$; so there is no unique solution. The point $(\frac{5}{3}, 0)$ satisfies the first equation, but not the second. Thus the system has no solution; it is inconsistent.

Computer programs can find inverses of large matrices (often with dozens or hundreds of variables) to solve linear systems. Without such programs, you will solve a system of three equations with three variables using 3 × 3 matrices. The identity matrix for 3 × 3 matrices is

$$I = \begin{bmatrix} 1 & 0 & 0 \\ 0 & 1 & 0 \\ 0 & 0 & 1 \end{bmatrix}.$$

The calculation of the inverse of a 3 × 3 matrix is complicated, so we give it.

Example 2 Solve this system

$$\begin{cases} 2x - y + 3z = 9 \\ x + 2z = 3 \\ 3x + 2y + z = 10 \end{cases}$$

by using the coefficient matrix M and its inverse M^{-1} shown below.

$$M = \begin{bmatrix} 2 & -1 & 3 \\ 1 & 0 & 2 \\ 3 & 2 & 1 \end{bmatrix} \qquad M^1 = \begin{bmatrix} \frac{4}{7} & -1 & \frac{2}{7} \\ -\frac{5}{7} & 1 & \frac{1}{7} \\ -\frac{2}{7} & 1 & -\frac{1}{7} \end{bmatrix}$$

Solution Rewrite the system as a matrix equation.

$$\begin{bmatrix} 2 & -1 & 3 \\ 1 & 0 & 2 \\ 3 & 2 & 1 \end{bmatrix} \begin{bmatrix} x \\ y \\ z \end{bmatrix} = \begin{bmatrix} 9 \\ 3 \\ 10 \end{bmatrix}$$

Multiply both sides on the left by M^{-1} and simplify.

$$\begin{bmatrix} \frac{4}{7} & -1 & \frac{2}{7} \\ -\frac{5}{7} & 1 & \frac{1}{7} \\ -\frac{2}{7} & 1 & -\frac{1}{7} \end{bmatrix} \begin{bmatrix} 2 & -1 & 3 \\ 1 & 0 & 2 \\ 3 & 2 & 1 \end{bmatrix} \begin{bmatrix} x \\ y \\ z \end{bmatrix} = \begin{bmatrix} \frac{4}{7} & -1 & \frac{2}{7} \\ -\frac{5}{7} & 1 & \frac{1}{7} \\ -\frac{2}{7} & 1 & -\frac{1}{7} \end{bmatrix} \begin{bmatrix} 9 \\ 3 \\ 10 \end{bmatrix}$$

$$\begin{bmatrix} 1 & 0 & 0 \\ 0 & 1 & 0 \\ 0 & 0 & 1 \end{bmatrix} \begin{bmatrix} x \\ y \\ z \end{bmatrix} = \begin{bmatrix} 5 \\ -2 \\ -1 \end{bmatrix}$$

$$\begin{bmatrix} x \\ y \\ z \end{bmatrix} = \begin{bmatrix} 5 \\ -2 \\ -1 \end{bmatrix}$$

So the solution is $x = 5$, $y = -2$, and $z = -1$. This is easily checked.

You are not expected to find the inverse matrix for a 3×3 system in this chapter. It will always be given.

Questions

Covering the Reading

In 1–3, refer to the system at the start of this lesson.

1. What does the matrix $\begin{bmatrix} 1 & 3 \\ 2 & -1 \end{bmatrix}$ represent?   the coefficients of the variables

2. Noel Issen found the inverse $\begin{bmatrix} \frac{1}{7} & \frac{3}{7} \\ \frac{2}{7} & \frac{-1}{7} \end{bmatrix}$ and multiplied as shown here.

$$\begin{bmatrix} 1 & 3 \\ 2 & -1 \end{bmatrix} \begin{bmatrix} \frac{1}{7} & \frac{3}{7} \\ \frac{2}{7} & \frac{-1}{7} \end{bmatrix} \begin{bmatrix} x \\ y \end{bmatrix} = \begin{bmatrix} 22 \\ 2 \end{bmatrix} \begin{bmatrix} \frac{1}{7} & \frac{3}{7} \\ \frac{2}{7} & \frac{-1}{7} \end{bmatrix}$$

What did Noel do wrong?   He multiplied by the inverse on the right rather than on

3. Check that (4, 6) is the solution of the system.
$4 + 3(6) = 22; 2(4) - 6 = 2$

4. Solve the system of Example 1, using inverse matrices, if the order of equations is reversed.   See margin.

5. How many solutions does the following system have?

$$\begin{cases} 4x + y = 2 \\ 9x - 2y = 4 \end{cases} \quad \text{one}$$

Justify your answer.
The determinant of the coefficient matrix is different from 0.

6. Tell whether the following system has no solutions or infinitely many solutions.

$$\begin{cases} 30x - 18y = 67 \\ 35x - 21y = 76 \end{cases} \quad \text{no solutions}$$

In 7–9, M stands for the coefficient matrix of each system. What matrix does $M^{-1} \cdot M$ equal for the following systems?

7. a system with two equations and two unknowns such as $\begin{cases} ax + by = c \\ dx + ey = f \end{cases}$
the 2 × 2 identity matrix

8. the system $\begin{cases} 4x - 2y + 3z = 1 \\ 8x - 3y + 5z = 4 \\ 7x - 2y + 4z = 5 \end{cases}$ the 3 × 3 identity matrix

9. a 3 × 3 system   the 3 × 3 identity matrix

In 10 and 11, solve each system using matrices.

10. $\begin{cases} -8A - 3B = 10 \\ 4A + 6B = 5 \end{cases}$ $(\frac{-25}{12}, \frac{20}{9})$

11. $\begin{cases} 10x + 15y = 30 \\ 4x + 6y = 12 \end{cases}$ infinitely many solutions

Question 21: This question implies a one-dimensional, or number line, graph. Explain to students that a coordinate plane graph would be indicated by the notation $\{(x, y): x > 11\} \cap \{(x, y): x > 12\}$. The solution would then be the vertical strip from $x = 11$ to $x = 12$ including the right but not the left boundary line.

ADDITIONAL ANSWERS
4. $2x - 3y = 5$
   $9x - y = 3$

$\begin{bmatrix} 2 & -3 \\ 9 & -1 \end{bmatrix} \begin{bmatrix} x \\ y \end{bmatrix} = \begin{bmatrix} 5 \\ 3 \end{bmatrix}$

$\begin{bmatrix} -.04 & .12 \\ -.36 & .08 \end{bmatrix} \begin{bmatrix} 2 & -3 \\ 9 & -1 \end{bmatrix} \begin{bmatrix} x \\ y \end{bmatrix} =$

$\begin{bmatrix} -.04 & .12 \\ -.36 & .08 \end{bmatrix} \begin{bmatrix} 5 \\ 3 \end{bmatrix}$

$\begin{bmatrix} 1 & 0 \\ 0 & 1 \end{bmatrix} \begin{bmatrix} x \\ y \end{bmatrix} = \begin{bmatrix} .16 \\ -1.56 \end{bmatrix}$

$x = .16, y = -1.56$

EXTENSION
You may wish to show students how to create their own 3 × 3 examples. Recall that the inverse M^{-1} of the matrix

$$M = \begin{bmatrix} a_{11} & a_{12} & a_{13} \\ a_{21} & a_{22} & a_{23} \\ a_{31} & a_{32} & a_{33} \end{bmatrix}$$

exists if and only if det $M \neq 0$. If det $M \neq 0$, then the inverse of

$$M = \begin{bmatrix} \dfrac{C_{11}}{\det M} & \dfrac{C_{12}}{\det M} & \dfrac{C_{13}}{\det M} \\ \dfrac{C_{21}}{\det M} & \dfrac{C_{22}}{\det M} & \dfrac{C_{23}}{\det M} \\ \dfrac{C_{31}}{\det M} & \dfrac{C_{32}}{\det M} & \dfrac{C_{33}}{\det M} \end{bmatrix}$$

where the cofactor C_{ij} of the component a_{ij} is the product of $(-1)^{i+j}$ and the determinant of the 2 × 2 submatrix of M is determined by deleting the ith row and the jth column. Also, det $M = a_{11}C_{11} + a_{12}C_{12} + a_{13}C_{13}$. For generalizations of these formulas to higher-order $n \times n$ systems, consult any standard linear algebra text.

EVALUATION
A quiz covering Lessons 5-4 through 5-6 is provided in the Teacher's Resource File.

ADDITIONAL ANSWERS
12.b. $4(1) - 2(3) + 3(1) = 1$
$\qquad\qquad 4 - 6 + 3 = 1$
$\qquad\qquad\qquad\quad 1 = 1$
$\qquad 8(1) - 3(3) + 5(1) = 4$
$\qquad\qquad 8 - 9 + 5 = 4$
$\qquad\qquad\qquad\quad 4 = 4$
$\qquad 7(1) - 2(3) + 4(1) = 5$
$\qquad\qquad 7 - 6 + 4 = 5$
$\qquad\qquad\qquad\quad 5 = 5$

15.b.
$w + 2y = 5 \quad x + 2z = 6$
$3w + 4y = 7 \quad 3x + 4z = 8$

---

12. Refer to Example 2.

a. Solve the system $\begin{cases} 4x - 2y + 3z = 1 \\ 8x - 3y + 5z = 4 \\ 7x - 2y + 4z = 5 \end{cases}$ using matrices. The coefficient matrix and its inverse are given here.

$$M = \begin{bmatrix} 4 & -2 & 3 \\ 8 & -3 & 5 \\ 7 & -2 & 4 \end{bmatrix} \qquad M^{-1} = \begin{bmatrix} -2 & 2 & -1 \\ 3 & -5 & 4 \\ 5 & -6 & 4 \end{bmatrix} \quad (1, 3, 1)$$

b. Check your answer.   See margin.

Applying the Mathematics

In 13–14, for what value of n does

13. $\begin{cases} 2x + 4y = n \\ x + 2y = 7 \end{cases}$ have infinitely many solutions? $n = 14$

14. $\begin{cases} 4x - 6y = 5 \\ 2x + ny = 2 \end{cases}$ have no solution? $n = -3$

15. a. Solve this matrix equation. $w = -3, x = -4, y = 4, z = 5$
$\begin{bmatrix} 1 & 2 \\ 3 & 4 \end{bmatrix} \begin{bmatrix} w & x \\ y & z \end{bmatrix} = \begin{bmatrix} 5 & 6 \\ 7 & 8 \end{bmatrix}$

b. What two systems does part a simultaneously solve?   See margin.

Review

In 16 and 17, solve using any method. *(Lessons 5-3, 5-4)*

16. $\begin{cases} 3x - 2 = z \\ \quad x = y + 9 \\ \quad z = 8x \end{cases}$ $(-\frac{2}{5}, -\frac{47}{5}, \frac{-16}{5})$

17. $\begin{cases} a = 20b + 11 \\ a = 3b - 6 \end{cases}$ $(-9, -1)$

In 18 and 19, two cake mixes contain percents of the U.S. RDA (recommended daily amounts) of vitamin C as given here. *(Lesson 5-3)*

Mix	Vitamin C
A	2.0%
B	1.2%

18. Duncan Crocker wants to mix some of each kind to obtain 200 oz of mixture that contains 1.5% of the U.S. RDA of vitamin C. How much of each should he use?   mix A: 75 oz; mix B: 125 oz

19. Betty Hines wants 100 oz of a mixture that contains 1.8% of the U.S. RDA of vitamin C. How should she make the mixture?
mix A: 75 oz; mix B: 25 oz

20. Write an inequality for the graph below. *(Lesson 3-9)* **y > x**

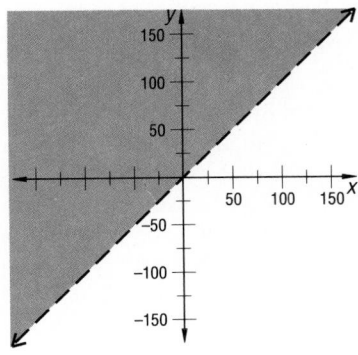

21. Graph $\{x: x > 11\} \cap \{x: x > 12\}$. *(Lesson 5-1)* **See margin.**

Exploration

22. a. Show how the two systems

$$\begin{cases} 3w + 4y = 5 \\ w + 2y = 0 \end{cases} \qquad \begin{cases} 3x + 4z = 1 \\ x + 2z = 3 \end{cases}$$

can be rewritten as a single equation using three 2×2 matrices.
See margin.

b. When can two 2×2 systems be rewritten as in part a?
when the coefficient matrices are equal

c. Can three 2×2 systems ever be rewritten as a single matrix equation?   **when the coefficient matrices are equal**

21.

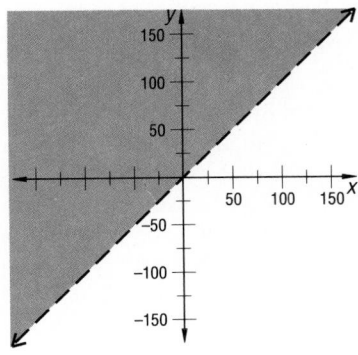
(number line with filled point near 12, marks 4 6 8 10 12 14 16)

22.a.

$$\begin{bmatrix} 3 & 4 \\ 1 & 2 \end{bmatrix}\begin{bmatrix} w & x \\ y & z \end{bmatrix} = \begin{bmatrix} 5 & 1 \\ 0 & 3 \end{bmatrix}$$

NAME _____

■**SKILLS**   *Objective C (See pages 302–305 for objectives.)*
In 1–4, solve each system using matrices.

1. $\begin{cases} 7x + 2y = 24 \\ 5x - 3y = -36 \end{cases}$ **2.** $\begin{cases} 3m - 7n = -19 \\ 7m - 4n = 5 \end{cases}$

  $x = 0, y = 12$ $m = 3, n = 4$

3. $\begin{cases} 3p = q - 6 \\ 5p = 3q + 6 \end{cases}$ **4.** $\begin{cases} \frac{11}{x} = 3x + 2y \\ -2 = 5x - y \end{cases}$

  $p = -6, q = -12$ $x = \frac{1}{5}, y = 3$

5. Solve using the given coefficient matrix and its inverse.

$\begin{cases} 3x + 4y = 19 \\ 2y + 3z = 8 \\ 4x - 5z = 7 \end{cases}$ $M = \begin{bmatrix} 3 & 4 & 0 \\ 0 & 2 & 3 \\ 4 & 0 & -5 \end{bmatrix}$ $M^{-1} = \begin{bmatrix} \frac{5}{6} & \frac{10}{9} & \frac{2}{3} \\ \frac{1}{3} & -\frac{5}{6} & -\frac{1}{3} \\ -\frac{4}{9} & \frac{8}{9} & \frac{1}{3} \end{bmatrix}$

  $(x, y, z) = (3, \frac{5}{2}, 1)$

■**PROPERTIES**   *Objective D*
In 6–8, find the value of k for which the given system has infinitely many solutions.

6. $\begin{cases} 9x - \frac{5}{3}y = 2 \\ 27x - 5y = k \end{cases}$ **7.** $\begin{cases} 3x + 4y = -6 \\ kx - 36y = 54 \end{cases}$ **8.** $\begin{cases} 2y - 8x = -84 \\ 20x - 5y = k \end{cases}$
  $k = -6$ $k = -27$ $k = 210$

In 9 and 10, find a value of n for which the given system has no solutions.

9. $\begin{cases} -12x - 9y = n \\ 16x + 12y = 28 \end{cases}$ **10.** $\begin{cases} 24x - 42y = 18 \\ 10x - 17.5y = n \end{cases}$

  any value of n any value of n
  except $n = -21$ except $n = 7.5$

RESOURCES
■ Lesson Master 5-7
▣ Visual for Teaching Aid 25 displays the solution and graph for **Example 2**.
▣ Visual for Teaching Aid 26 provides the question for Additional Example 2.
▣ Visual for Teaching Aid 27 displays **Question 14** and the grid for graphing the results.

OBJECTIVES

E Recognize properties of systems of inequalities.
I Solve systems of inequalities of graphing.

TEACHING NOTES

As in the case of graphing lines and curves (Lesson 5-2), we usually find the intersection of the solution sets by first graphing their union. However, point out to students that in this lesson the feasible region is highlighted by redrawing it with only the points that belong to the intersection. Students do not have to draw two figures as in **Example 1**; the left drawing is sufficient.

It is helpful to discuss **Example 2** in class. Engage the class in a discussion of how the inequalities are derived. Graph the feasible set together, and use what has been learned about solving systems of equations to find the vertices. Emphasize that the feasible set includes *all* the points that satisfy the conditions stated in the inequalities and *only* those points.

LESSON

5-7

Systems of Linear Inequalities

The graph of a linear inequality in two variables is a half-plane. So the graph of the solution to a system of linear inequalities is the intersection of coplanar half-planes. The set of solutions to a system of linear inequalities is called the **feasible set** or **feasible region** for that system. Such feasible sets are often the interiors of angles or polygons. Sometimes boundaries are included in the sets and sometimes not. The intersections of the boundaries are called **vertices** of the feasible sets.

■ ■ ■ ■ ■ ■ ■■

Example 1 Graph the feasible set of the system $\begin{cases} y > -2x + 6 \\ y \leq \frac{1}{4}x - 3. \end{cases}$

Solution Graph each inequality on the same set of axes. The graph of $y > -2x + 6$ is the set of points above and to the right of the line with equation $y = -2x + 6$. In the graphs below, this set is indicated by the shading ▨. The graph of $y \leq \frac{1}{4}x - 3$ consists of points on or below the line with equation $y = \frac{1}{4}x - 3$, indicated by the shading ▢. The part of the plane marked with both types of shading is the feasible set for this system. As shown in the graph at the bottom, in this example the feasible set is the interior and one side of an angle.

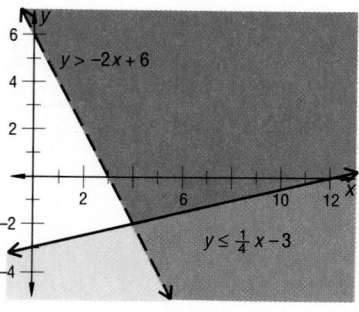

Feasible Set

282

Check Find the vertex of the feasible set by solving the system of equations

$$\begin{cases} y = -2x + 6 \\ y = \tfrac{1}{4}x - 3. \end{cases}$$

This vertex is (4, -2), which checks with the graph. Pick a point in the shaded region, such as (8, -5), and substitute it into each inequality.

Is -5 > -2(8) + 6? Yes.
Is -5 ≤ $\tfrac{1}{4}$ (8) − 3? Yes. So the solution checks.

You should also try points outside the region to show they do not work. However, this is not a fool-proof check.

The applications of systems to production planning in industry, discovered by Kantorovich in 1939, may involve systems with thousands of variables. Computers are needed to work out the problems. But simple examples can be done by hand. Here is a simplified example of a business application.

■ ■ ■ ■ ■ ■ ■ ■

Example 2 The Biltrite Furniture company makes wooden desks and chairs. Carpenters and finishers work on each item. On the average the carpenters spend four hours working on each chair and eight hours on each desk. There are enough carpenters for up to 8000 worker-hours per week. The finishers spend about two hours on each chair and one hour on each desk. There are enough finishers for a maximum of 1300 worker-hours per week. Given the above constraints, find the feasible region for the number of chairs and desks that can be made per week.

1. Graph the feasible set of the system

$$\begin{cases} x + 2y \le 12 \\ 2x + y \le 12 \\ \quad x \ge 0 \\ \quad y \ge 0 \end{cases}$$

and give the coordinates of its vertices.

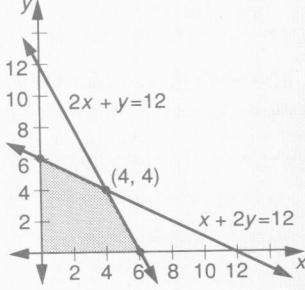

Vertices are (0, 6), (6, 0), (4, 4), and (0, 0).

2. (This question is adapted from the CPA exam May, 1975.) The Random Company manufactures two products, Zeta and Beta. Each product must pass through two processing operations. Zeta takes one hour each on processes number one and two. Beta takes 2 hours on process one and 3 hours on process two. Process one has a total capacity of 1000 hours per day, process two, 1275 hours per day.
a. Make a table to illustrate the information.

	# Zeta	# Beta	Total Hours Available
hours of process 1	1	2	1000
hours of process 2	1	3	1275

b. Identify the variables.
Let x = number of Zetas to be made each day.
Let y = number of Betas to be made each day.
c. Write sentences to model each step in the process.

$$\begin{cases} x + 2y \le 1000 \\ x + 3y \le 1275 \\ \quad x \ge \quad 0 \\ \quad y \ge \quad 0 \end{cases}$$

d. Graph the solution to the system.

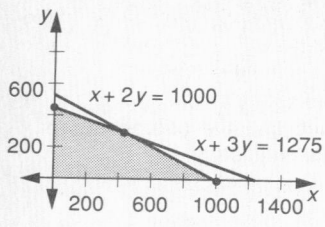

e. Identify the vertices of the feasible region.
Vertices are (0, 425), (0, 0), (1000, 0), and (450, 275).

Solution   Make a table to illustrate the information.

	CHAIRS	DESKS	TOTAL HOURS AVAILABLE
Hours of carpentry per piece	4	8	8000
Hours of finishing per piece	2	1	1300

Then identify the variables.
Let x = number of chairs to be made per week,
   y = number of desks to be made per week.

Write sentences to model each aspect of the manufacturing process. Because x and y represent pieces of furniture, they must be any non-negative integers; that is,

$$x \geq 0 \text{ and } y \geq 0.$$

The carpentry hours must satisfy

$$4x + 8y \leq 8000.$$

The finishing hours must satisfy

$$2x + y \leq 1300.$$

Thus the feasible region for this situation is the solution of the system

$$\begin{cases} x \geq \quad 0 \\ y \geq \quad 0 \\ 4x + 8y \leq 8000 \\ 2x + y \leq 1300. \end{cases}$$

Now graph the solution to the system. The first two inequalities indicate all solutions are in the first quadrant or on the positive axes. So it is sufficient to graph the last two inequalities only in the first quadrant to find the feasible region. Although only integer values are solutions, shading is used because it would be too difficult to show all the dots. In this case and many others, the context of the situation is necessary to interpret the graph accurately.

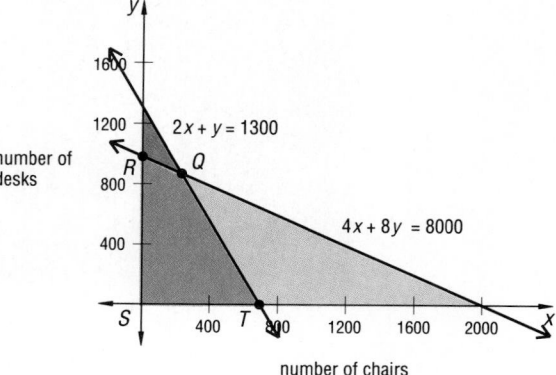

284

The intersection of the half-planes is the feasible region. This region is the union of the quadrilateral QRST and its interior. You can find the coordinates of each vertex of the quadrilateral by solving a system of equations. For instance, Q is the solution of the system

$$\begin{cases} 4x + 8y = 8000 \\ 2x + y = 1300. \end{cases}$$

Check   Choose any point in the feasible region and see if it is a solution of each inequality of the system. We choose (400, 200).

Is $400 \geq 0$? Yes.
Is $200 \geq 0$? Yes.
Is $4(400) + 8(200) \leq 8000$? Yes.
Is $2(400) + 200 \leq 1300$? Yes.

So one option available to the Biltrite Furniture Company is to make 400 chairs and 200 desks per week.

As a further check, choose a point outside the shaded region, like (700, 400), and show that there is at least one inequality in which it does not work.

Questions

Covering the Reading

1. The solution to a system of linear inequalities can be represented by the ___?___ of half-planes.   **intersection**

2. What is the solution to a system of linear inequalities often called?
feasible set or feasible region

In 3–5, refer to Example 1. Verify that:

3. (10, -6) is a solution to the system.   **See margin.**

4. (5, 0) is *not* a solution to the system.   **See margin.**

5. (4, -2) is the vertex of the feasible set for the system.   **See margin.**

In 6–10, refer to Example 2.

6. Which inequality expresses the amount of time that the company can have its finishers working?   **$2x + y \leq 1300$**

7. Why is it sufficient to consider only the first quadrant in graphing the feasible set?   **The number of pieces of furniture will be nonnegative.**

8. Find the coordinates of vertex Q.   **(200, 900)**

9. What system of equations gives vertex R as its solution?   **See margin.**

10. Could the company manufacture 600 chairs and 200 desks per week under the given operating conditions?   **no**

NOTES ON QUESTIONS
Questions 14 and 15:
Stress the importance of using a table to illustrate the information in each problem. Because mathematical prose is often very terse, the use of a table helps students to separate and clarify the given information.

Making Connections for Question 21: The definition of a convex region is contained in this question. The concept is an important one in preparation for the Linear-Programming Theorem to be discussed in Lessons 5-8 and 5-9. Every feasible region to a system of linear inequalities is convex.

ADDITIONAL ANSWERS
3. Is $-6 > -2(10) + 6$? Yes.
Is $-6 \leq \frac{1}{4}(10) - 3$? Yes, so the solution checks.

4. Is $0 > -2(5) + 6$? Yes.
Is $0 \leq \frac{1}{4}(10) - 3$? No, so this is not a solution.

5. Is $-2 = -2(4) + 6$? Yes.
Is $-2 = \frac{1}{4}(4) - 3$? Yes, so this is a solution for the vertex of the feasible set.

9. $\begin{cases} 4x + 8y = 8000 \\ x \geq 0 \end{cases}$

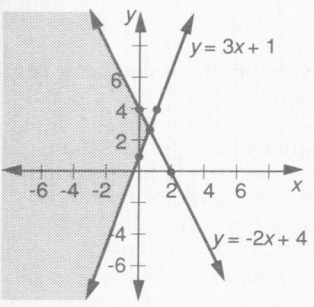
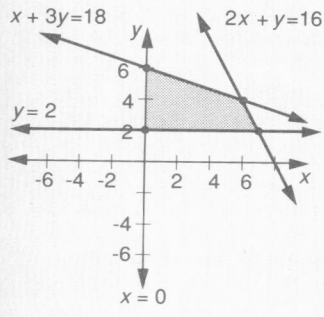
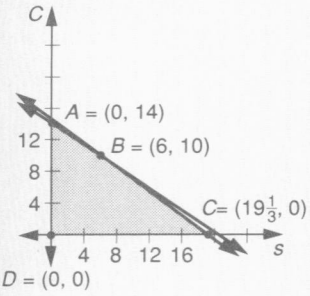
Applying the Mathematics

11. Refer to the graph below.
 a. Find the coordinates of vertex B of the feasible set.   (4, 5)
 b. Write a system of inequalities represented by this feasible set.
   See margin.

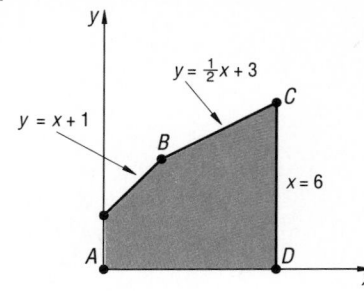

In 12 and 13, (a) graph the feasible region of each system of inequalities; and (b) find the coordinates of each vertex.   See margin.

12. $\begin{cases} y \geq 3x + 1 \\ y \leq -2x + 4 \end{cases}$

13. $\begin{cases} x + 3y \leq 18 \\ 2x + y \leq 16 \\ x \geq 0 \\ y \geq 2 \end{cases}$

14. A clothier makes women's suits and coats from nylon and wool. Each suit requires 2 yards of nylon lining and 3 yards of wool. Each coat requires 3 yards of nylon lining and 4 yards of wool. Only 42 yards of nylon lining and 58 yards of wool are in stock.

 a. Let s be the number of suits and c be the number of coats. Complete the translation of this situation into a system of inequalities:
   $s \geq$ __?__ ; c __?__ 0; $2s + 3c \leq$ __?__ ; __?__ ≤ 58 0; $\geq$; 42; 3s + 4c
 b. Graph the feasible region for this system and label the vertices.
   (Let s be the independent variable.)   See margin.

15. An electronics firm makes two kinds of televisions: black-and-white and color. The firm has enough equipment to make as many as 1000 black-and-white sets per month or 600 color sets per month. It takes 20 worker-hours to make a black-and-white set and 30 worker-hours to make a color set. The firm has up to 24,000 worker-hours of labor available each month. Let x be the number of black-and-white TVs and y be the number of color TV's made in a month.
 a. Translate this situation into a system of inequalities.   See margin.
 b. Graph the feasible set for this system, and label the vertices.
   See margin.

Review

16. Name four methods of solving systems of equations. (*Lessons 5-2, 5-3, 5-4, 5-6*)   See margin.

In 17–19, (a) state a method which would solve each system conveniently and (b) solve each system. (*Lessons 5-2, 5-3, 5-4, 5-6*)   See margin.

17. $\begin{cases} y = 4x \\ 8x + 7y = 18 \end{cases}$

18. $\begin{cases} 5x + 6y = 18 \\ -5x + 7y = 21 \end{cases}$

19. $\begin{cases} y = \dfrac{8}{x} \\ y = x^2 \end{cases}$

20. Solve the following matrix equation. *(Lesson 5-6)*

$$\begin{bmatrix} -1 & 2 \\ 3 & 4 \end{bmatrix} \begin{bmatrix} x \\ y \end{bmatrix} = \begin{bmatrix} -6 \\ 8 \end{bmatrix}$$ **(4, -1)**

21. A region of the plane is said to be **convex** if and only if any two points of the region can be connected by a line segment which is itself entirely within the region. The pentagon below is convex but the quadrilateral is not. **a, c, d**

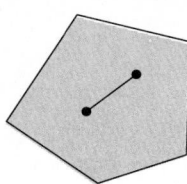   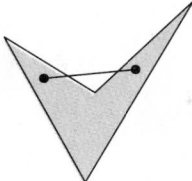

Convex   **Not convex**

Which of the following shaded regions are convex? *(Previous course)*

(a) 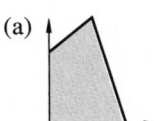   (b) 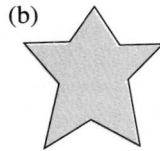   (c) 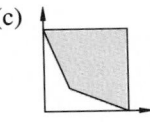   (d)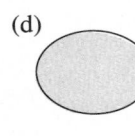

22. Solve. *(Previous course)*
 a. $x^2 + 7 = 56$ **x = 7 or x = -7**
 b. $(y - 3)^2 = 81$ **y = 12 or y = -6**

Exploration

23. a. At most how many pieces can you get out of a circular pie with 4 straight cuts? How many of these pieces are convex?   **11; 11**
 b. At most how many pieces can you get out of a circular pie with *n* straight cuts? How many of these pieces are convex?
 $\dfrac{n^2 + n + 2}{2}$; **all of them**

MORE PRACTICE
For more questions on SPUR Objectives, use *Lesson Master 5-7*, shown below.

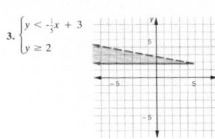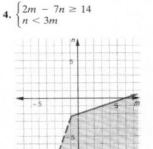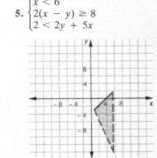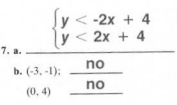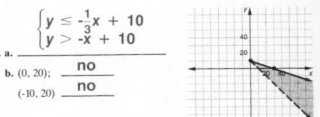

LESSON 5-8

RESOURCES

■ Lesson Master 5-8
▣ Visual for Teaching Aid 28 displays the system and graph of the lesson's **Example**.
▣ Visual for Teaching Aid 29 reproduces the question of the Additional Example.
▣ Computer Master 8

OBJECTIVE

G Use linear programming to solve problems in the real world, given the inequalities or graph of the feasible region.

TEACHING NOTES

Before assigning any reading in Lesson 5-8, motivate the Linear-Programming Theorem with a problem from Lesson 5-7, such as Question 14. Students should have found that the system

$$\begin{cases} s \geq 0 \\ c \geq 0 \\ 2s + 3c \leq 42 \\ 3s + 4c \leq 58 \end{cases}$$

models the situation, and that the vertices of the feasible region are (0, 14), (6, 10), (0, 0), and $\left(19\frac{1}{3}, 0\right)$. However, $19\frac{1}{3}$ must be rounded *down* to 19, as only whole numbers of suits can be made. Now, ask students the question: "Suppose the clothier makes a profit of $20 on each suit and $40 on each coat. How many suits and how many coats must be made to *maximize* the profit?" By graphing the family of lines determined by equations of the form $20s + 40c = P$, you can show that the greatest profit will occur at the vertex (0, 14).

5-8

Linear Programming I

In Example 2 of Lesson 5-7, a system of linear inequalities models some of the manufacturing operations of the Biltrite Furniture Company. The feasible set describes various linear combinations of chairs and desks that the company can make with the given constraints. Now suppose that the company also knows that it earns a profit of $15 on each chair and $20 on each desk it makes. Given the known constraints, how can the production schedule be set up to maximize the profit?

If x chairs and y desks are sold, the profit P is given by the formula

$$15x + 20y = P.$$

For instance, the solutions to

$$15x + 20y = 3000$$

are ordered pairs that will yield a $3000 profit.

The figure below again shows the feasible region for Biltrite's system of inequalities. The figure also shows the graphs of some lines that result from substituting different values of P into the profit formula.

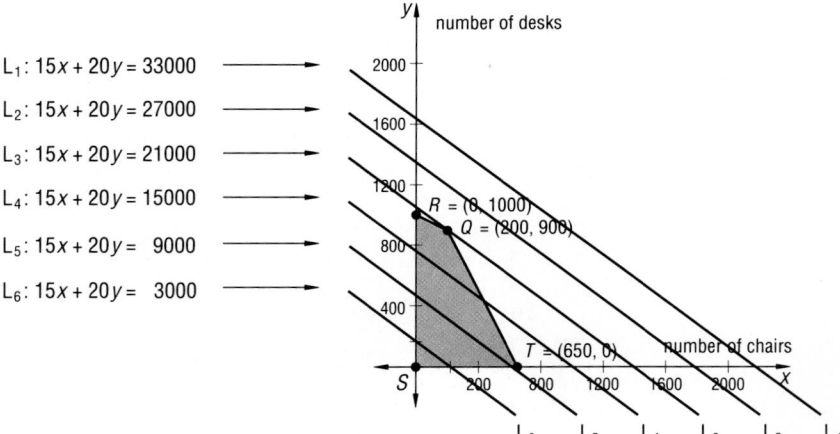

L_1: $15x + 20y = 33000$

L_2: $15x + 20y = 27000$

L_3: $15x + 20y = 21000$

L_4: $15x + 20y = 15000$

L_5: $15x + 20y = 9000$

L_6: $15x + 20y = 3000$

288

288

All lines with equations of the form $15x + 20y = P$ are parallel because each has slope $-\frac{3}{4}$. Some of these lines intersect the feasible region and some do not. In the figure above, the lines above L_3 do not intersect the feasible set. Lines that do intersect the feasible region represent possible profits. The greatest profit will occur when the line with equation $15x + 20y = P$ is as high as possible, but still intersects the feasible region. This will happen when the profit line passes through vertex $Q = (200, 900)$. This is the line L_3. Thus to maximize profits, the company should manufacture 200 chairs and 900 desks per week. So the maximum profit under these conditions is $21,000.

Problems such as this one, which lead to systems of linear inequalities, are called **linear-programming problems.** The word "programming" does not refer to a computer; it means that the solution gives a "program," or course of action, to follow. The most profitable "program" for Biltrite Furniture Company is to make 200 chairs and 900 desks per week.

In 1826, the French mathematician Joseph Fourier proved the following theorem:

Linear-Programming Theorem:

> The feasible region of a linear programming problem is convex, and the maximum or minimum quantity is determined at one of the vertices of the region.

The Linear-Programming Theorem tells you where to look for the greatest or least value of a linear combination expression in a linear-programming situation, without having to draw many lines through the feasible region.

In 1945, George Stigler (then at Columbia University, now at the University of Chicago) was looking for the cheapest diet that would provide a person's daily needs of calories, proteins, calcium, iron, vitamin A, thiamine, riboflavin, niacin, and ascorbic acid. He considered 70 possible foods and found that the lowest-cost diet was a combination of wheat flour, cabbage, and pork liver. By mixing amounts of these, a person was thought to be able to live in good health for $59.88 a year (then). Costs today are higher, so it might now cost $400 a year for that diet.

Here is a simplified diet problem, of the type first considered by Stigler.

ADDITIONAL EXAMPLE

Use linear programming to solve the following problem. Jeano's candy factory packages bags of mixed nuts. Jeano has 75 pounds of cashews and 120 pounds of peanuts. They are to be mixed in 1-pound packages in the following way: a lower-grade package that contains 4 ounces of cashews and 12 ounces of peanuts and a higher grade mixture that contains 8 ounces of cashews and 8 ounces of peanuts. A profit of $0.35 per package will be made on the low-grade mixture, and a profit of $0.55 per package will be made on the high-grade mixture. How many packages of each mixture should Jeano make to obtain the maximum profit? (Hint: Use 75 lb = 1200 oz.)

	Low-grade Mix	High-grade Mix	Max. Available
C	4 oz	8 oz	1200 oz
P	12 oz	8 oz	1920 oz

Let **L** = number of packages of low-grade mixture. Let **H** = number of packages of high-grade mixture.

$$\begin{cases} 4L + 8H \le 1200 \\ 12L + 8H \le 1920 \\ L \ge 0 \\ H \ge 0 \end{cases}$$

$P = .35L + .55H$

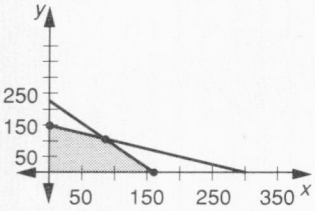

Vertices of the feasible region are (0, 0), (0, 150), (160, 0), and (90, 105). The maximum profit of $86.50 is at (90, 105).

Example Stuart Dent decided to investigate one of his typical meals, fried chicken and corn on the cob. He compiled the data in the following table.

	Vitamin A	Potassium (mg)	Iron (mg)	Calories
Fried Chicken	100	0	1.2	122
Corn	310	151	1.0	70

Stu let f = the number of pieces of chicken and e = the number of ears of corn. After deciding the minimum amounts of each needed from this meal he wrote the system:

$$\begin{cases} f \ge 0 \\ e \ge 0 \\ 100f + 310e \ge 1000 \quad \text{(at least 1000 units vitamin A)} \\ 151e \ge 200 \quad \text{(at least 200 mg potassium)} \\ 1.2f + e \ge 6 \quad \text{(at least 6 mg iron)} \\ 122f + 70e \ge 600 \quad \text{(at least 600 Calories)} \end{cases}$$

His graph is shown below.

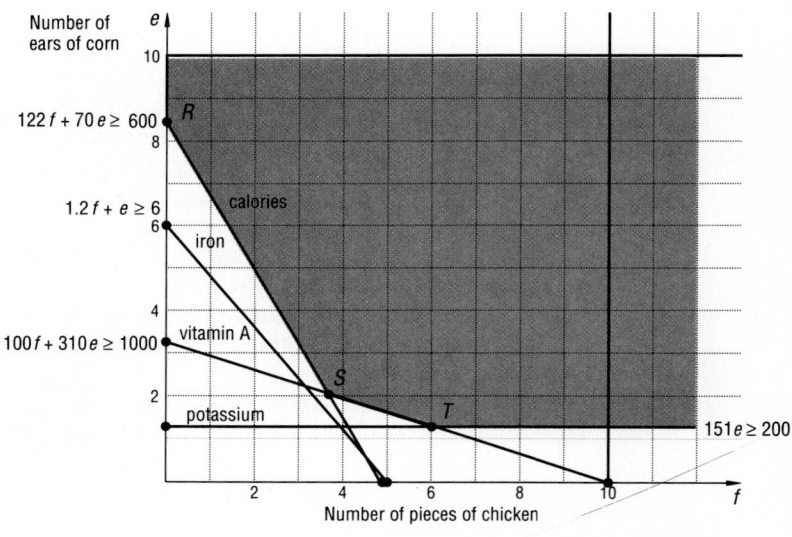

a. Find the vertices of the feasible region.

b. Apply the Linear-Programming Theorem to determine the values of f and e that will meet the nutritional requirements above at the lowest cost C, where $C = .90f + .75e$. (That is, each piece of chicken costs 90¢ and an ear of corn costs 75¢.)

290

Solution **a.** There are three vertices: R, S, and T. Vertex R is the e-intercept of the line with equation $122f + 70e = 600$. Substituting 0 for f gives

$$122(0) + 70e = 600.$$
$$e \approx 8.6$$

So the coordinates of R are about $(0, 8.6)$.

Vertex S is the intersection of the lines with equations $122f + 70e = 600$ and $100f + 310e = 1000$. First divide each equation so the coefficient of f becomes 1 or -1; then solve by the linear-combination method.

$122f + 70e = 600$	(divide by 122) $\Rightarrow$	$f + .57e \approx 4.92$
$100f + 310e = 1000$	(divide by -100) $\Rightarrow$	$-f - 3.10e = -10$
	(add) $\Rightarrow$	$-2.53e \approx -5.08$
		$e \approx 2$

Substituting 2 for e into either equation gives $f \approx 3.8$; so the coordinates of S are about $(3.8, 2)$.

Finally, T is the intersection of $100f + 310e = 1000$ and $151e = 200$. By solving the second equation and substituting into the first, Stuart found that the coordinates of T are about $(6, 1.3)$.

b. The feasible region is a convex set. The Linear-Programming Theorem says that the minimum of $C = .90f + .75e$ occurs at a vertex. Stuart evaluated C at each vertex to see which combination of f and e gave the minimum cost. To make sense in this context, the coordinates of each vertex must be rounded off to the next highest integer. Thus $R = (0, 9)$, $S = (4, 2)$, and $T = (6, 2)$.

$$\text{At } R = (0, 9): \quad C = .90(0) + .75(9) = 6.75$$
$$\text{At } S = (4, 2): \quad C = .90(4) + .75(2) = 5.10$$
$$\text{At } T = (6, 2): \quad C = .90(6) + .75(2) = 6.90$$

Thus the minimum value of C is \$5.10. It occurs at vertex S, that is, when Stuart has 4 pieces of chicken and 2 ears of corn.

Of course many other vitamins, minerals, and foods are taken into account by dietitians planning well-balanced meals. Stigler could not consider a greater number of possible foods nor consider more health needs because computers were not available in 1945. Today it is possible to consider hundreds of foods and many more daily needs than he did.

ADDITIONAL ANSWERS
9.a.

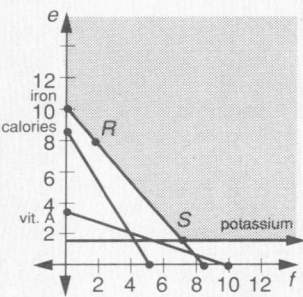

13.

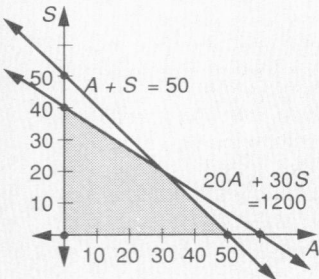

15.a.

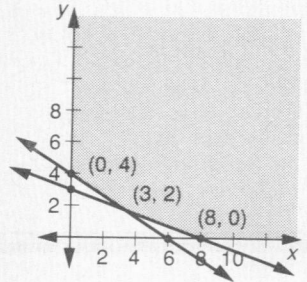

Questions

Covering the Reading

In 1–5, refer to the discussion of the Biltrite Furniture Company at the beginning of this lesson.

1. What is the company trying to maximize?   **profit**

2. What do 15 and 20 represent in the profit equation?
   profit per chair; profit per desk

3. *True or false* If a line with equation $15x + 20y = P$ intersects the feasible region for the system of inequalities, it is possible for Biltrite to make a profit of P dollars.   **True**

4. The maximum weekly profit Biltrite can earn is __?__. This occurs when the company produces __?__ chairs and __?__ desks.
   $21,000; 200; 900

5. Find the profit if 199 chairs and 899 desks are made.   **$20,965**

6. To what does the word "program" refer in a linear-programming problem?   **a course of action to follow**

7. In a linear-programming problem, why is it necessary to find the vertices of the feasible region?   **Maximums or minimums occur at vertices.**

In 8 and 9, refer to the example in this lesson.

8. **a.** Which linear combination must be minimized? $C = .90f + .75e$
   b. The minimum value of C satisfying the constraints of the problem is __?__. It occurs at vertex __?__.   **510; $S = (4, 2)$**

9. If Stuart had needed more iron in his diet he might have written the linear combination for iron as $1.2f + e \geq 10$.
   a. Regraph the feasible region of the system with this new iron requirement.   **See margin.**
   b. In the new feasible region, which vertex yields the minimum cost?
   in rounded values, (7, 1)

10. **a.** A diet problem like the one in the example was first modeled mathematically by whom and in what year?   **George Stigler; 1945**
    b. Why can more variables be dealt with now than could be considered when diet problems were first done?
    Computers can handle more variables

Applying the Mathematics

11. Use the feasible set graphed at the right. Which vertex maximizes the given profit equation, $P = 3x + 4y + 250$? $T = (50, 70)$

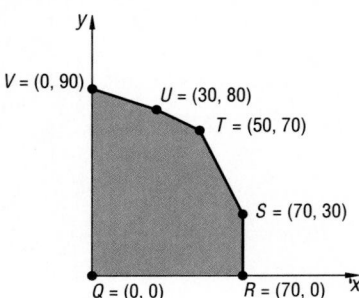

292

In 12–14, suppose that a farmer has no more than 50 acres for planting alfalfa and soy beans and has a maximum of $1200 to spend on the planting. It costs $20 per acre to plant alfalfa and $30 per acre to plant soy beans. The profit per acre for alfalfa is $250 and for soy beans is $300. If A is the number of acres of alfalfa and S is the number of acres of soy beans that the farmer plants, the system for this problem is:

$$\begin{cases} A + S \le 50 \\ 20A + 30S \le 1200 \\ A \ge 0 \\ S \ge 0 \end{cases}$$

12. Match each inequality in the system with its meaning.
    a. $A + S \le 50$ ii
    b. $20A + 30S \le 1200$ iii
    c. $A \ge 0$ iv
    d. $S \ge 0$ i

    (i) The number of acres of soybeans is not negative.
    (ii) The total number of acres is not more than 50.
    (iii) The cost of planting must be no more than $1200.
    (iv) The least number of acres of alfalfa is zero.

13. Graph the feasible region. Let A be the independent variable.
    See margin.
14. a. Find the vertices of the feasible region.   (0, 0); (0, 40); (30, 20); (50, 0)
    b. The profit formula is $P = 250A + 300S$. At which vertex is P maximized?   (30, 20)

15. A landscaping contractor uses a combination of two brands of fertilizers, each containing different amounts of phosphates and nitrates, as shown in the table below. A certain lawn requires a mixture of at least 24 lb of phosphates and at least 16 lb of nitrates.

	Phosphate content per package	Nitrate content per package
Brand A	4 lb	2 lb
Brand B	6 lb	5 lb

If x is the number of packages of Brand A and y is the number of packages of Brand B, then the conditions of the problem can be modeled by the following system of inequalities:

$$\begin{cases} x \ge 0 \\ y \ge 0 \\ 4x + 6y \ge 24 \\ 2x + 5y \ge 16 \end{cases}$$

a. Graph the feasible region.   See margin.
b. If a package of Brand A costs $6.99 and a package of Brand B costs $17.99, then the cost C is found by the equation $C = 6.99x + 17.99y$. Which pair (x, y) in the feasible region gives the lowest cost?   (8, 0)

LESSON 5-8   Linear Programming I   293

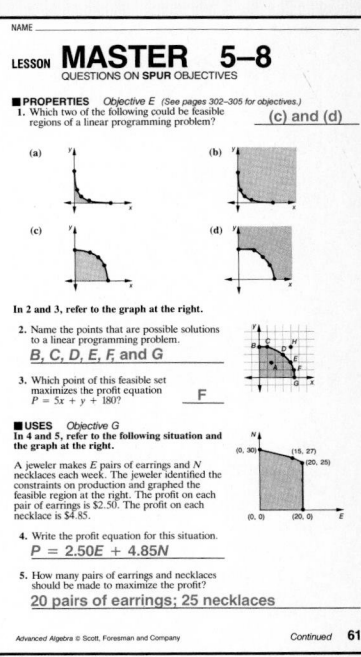

16. Refer to Question 15 in Lesson 5–7. Suppose the electronics firm earns a profit of $25 on each black-and-white TV and $40 on each color TV.
  a. Write a formula for the monthly profit earned. $P = 25x + 40y$
  b. What combination of black-and-white and color TV's will maximize profit?   (300, 600)

Review

17. Find an equation of the line through the points (-2, -4) and (5, 7).
  (Lesson 3-5) $y - 7 = \frac{11}{7}(x - 5)$

18. *Multiple choice* Which of the following systems describes the graph below? *(Lesson 5-7)*   b

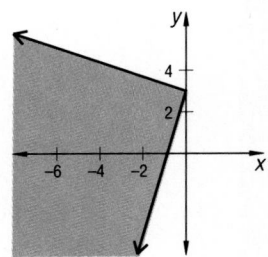

  (a) $2y + x \geq 6$ (b) $2y + x \leq 6$ (c) $2y + x < 6$
     $y - 3x \leq 3$ $y - 3x \geq 3$ $y - 3x > 3$

19. The strength S of a rectangular beam varies directly as its width w and the square of its depth d, and varies inversely as its length L. Suppose a beam can support 1750 pounds, and its dimensions are $w = 4''$, $d = 8''$, and $L = 20$ feet. What is the strength of a beam of the same material where $w = 4''$, $d = 8''$, and $L = 25$ feet? *(Lesson 2-9)*   1400 lb

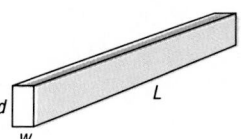

Exploration

20. Suppose $a + b + c + d = 100$, and a, b, c, and d are all nonnegative. What are the largest and smallest possible values of $abcd$?
  See margin.

294

LESSON 5-9

Linear Programming II

In Lesson 5–8, you practiced using the Linear-Programming Theorem for a given feasible region and linear combination expression to be maximized or minimized. In this lesson you will learn to solve linear-programming problems from scratch. Because linear-programming problems are long and involved, you must be very organized and neat. To solve a linear programming problem:

1. Identify the variables.
2. Translate the constraints of the problem into a system of inequalities relating the variables. If necessary, make a table.
3. Graph the system of inequalities; find the vertices of the feasible set.
4. Write a formula or an expression to be maximized or minimized.
5. Apply the Linear-Programming Theorem.
6. Interpret the results.

The bolder type in the solution to the example is what you should write. The rest is explanation, or what you might think as you solve the problem.

Example Some students make necklaces and bracelets in their spare time and sell all that they make. Every week they have available 10,000 g of metal and 20 hours to work. It takes 50 g of metal to make a necklace and 200 g to make a bracelet. Each necklace takes 30 minutes to make and each bracelet takes 20 minutes. The profit on each necklace is $3.50, and the profit on each bracelet is $2.50. The students want to earn as much money as possible. Because you are taking this algebra course, they ask you to give them advice. What numbers of necklaces and bracelets should they make each week?

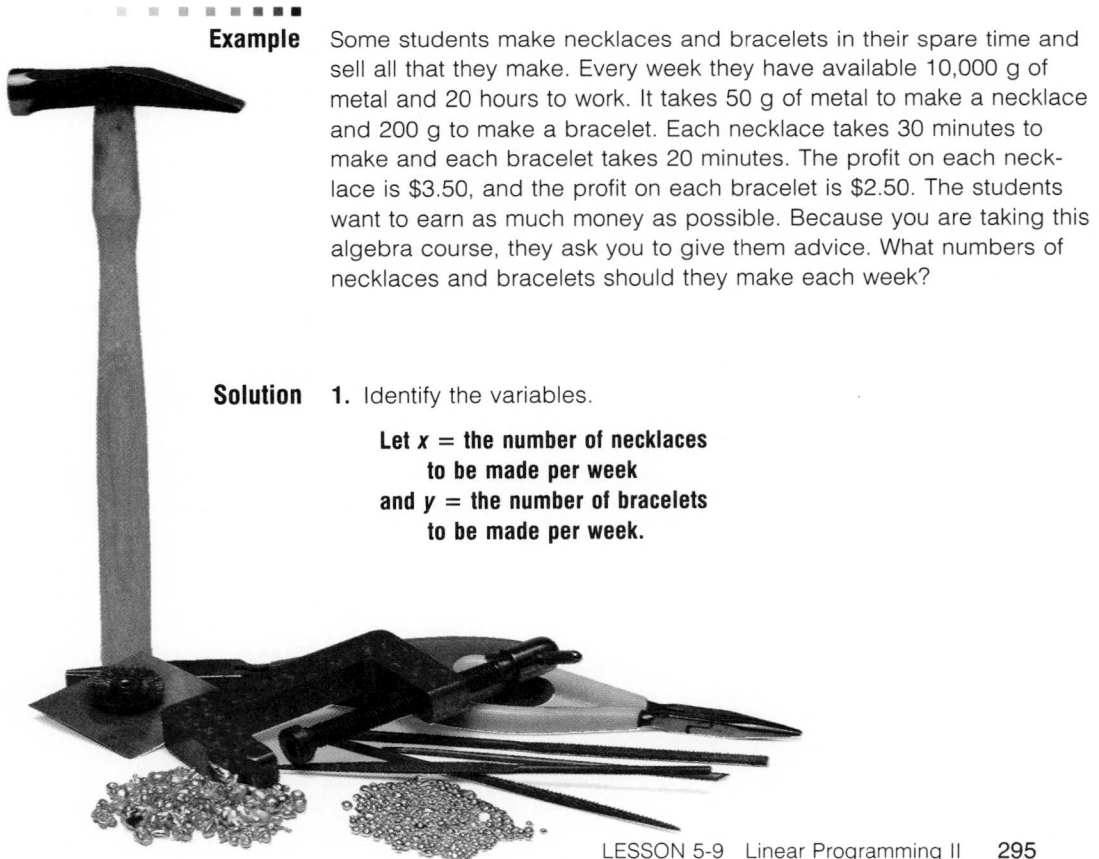

Solution 1. Identify the variables.

Let x = the number of necklaces to be made per week
and y = the number of bracelets to be made per week.

RESOURCES
■ Lesson Master 5-9
▣ Visual for Teaching Aid 30 displays the table, the system, and the graph for the lesson's **Example**.

OBJECTIVE

G Use linear programming to solve problems in the real world.

TEACHING NOTES

If you have discussed several examples from Lessons 5-7 and 5-8 in class, students will probably not need any additional examples before reading Lesson 5-9. What they will need now is time to work either individually or in **small groups** on the questions in this lesson. Notice that there is only one Applying the Mathematics question. Experience shows that no more than two complete linear-programming problems and some shorter questions are a reasonable nightly assignment for students at this level.

Error Analysis The problems in this lesson contain a great deal of information. Students may have trouble separating the information which gives the constraints of the problem from the information involved in the objective function. Stress to them that the latter information is usually in the form of a monetary amount—either a cost or a profit. It may help students to identify the objective function first, and then to find the constraints from the remaining information.

2. The following table summarizes the information about production.

	Metal Used	Time to Make
for each necklace	50 g	30 min
for each bracelet	200 g	20 min
Total available	10,000 g	20 hours

Translate the constraints into a system.
Negative numbers cannot be used; thus:

$$x \geq 0$$
$$y \geq 0$$

The amount of metal (in grams) used satisfies

$$50x + 200y \leq 10,000.$$

The amount of time (in minutes) needed satisfies

$$30x + 20y \leq 1200.$$

3. Graph the system and find the vertices. Only the feasible set is shown below.

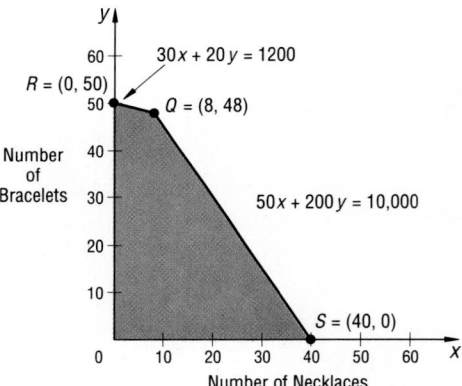

The vertices are found by solving systems of equations. For instance, Q is found by solving $50x + 200y = 10,000$ *and* $30x + 20y = 1200$.

4. Write a formula to be maximized. The profit formula is

$$P = 3.50x + 2.50y.$$

P is to be maximized.

296

5. Apply the Linear-Programming Theorem. Substitute the coordinates of each vertex into the profit formula.

For (0,0)	$P = 3.5(0) + 2.5(0)$	$= 0$
For (40, 0)	$P = 3.5(40) + 2.5(0)$	$= 140$
For (8, 48)	$P = 3.5(8) + 2.5(48)$	$= 148$
For (0, 50)	$P = 3.5(0) + 2.5(50)$	$= 125$

6. Interpret the results. The maximum profit of $148 occurs at vertex $Q = (8, 48)$. If they want to satisfy all the conditions, **the students should make 8 necklaces and 48 bracelets each week**.

Linear programming is often used in industries in which all the competitors make the same product (such as oil, gasoline, paper, milk, and so on). Efficiency in the use of labor and materials determines the amount of profit. These situations can involve as many as 5000 variables and 10,000 inequalities. Although we use graphing to solve linear programming problems in this book, more efficient methods of solution are used by computers. The most important procedure is the *simplex algorithm* invented in 1947 by the econometrician Leonid Hurwicz and the mathematicians George Dantzig and T.C. Koopmans, all from the United States. For this work, Koopmans shared the Nobel Prize with Kantorovich in 1982.

Questions

Covering the Reading

In 1–4, refer to the example in this lesson.
1. What are the students trying to find?
   number of necklaces and bracelets to maximize profits
2. What is the x-intercept of the equation that limits the amount of metal to be used? Is it in the feasible region?   **200; no**

3. How much more profit do the students make with the linear combination at (8,48) than at the next best vertex?   **$8.00**

4. **a.** What would be the profit if the students made 9 necklaces and 47 bracelets?   **$149.00**
   b. Why can they not do this?
   The point does not meet the time constraint.

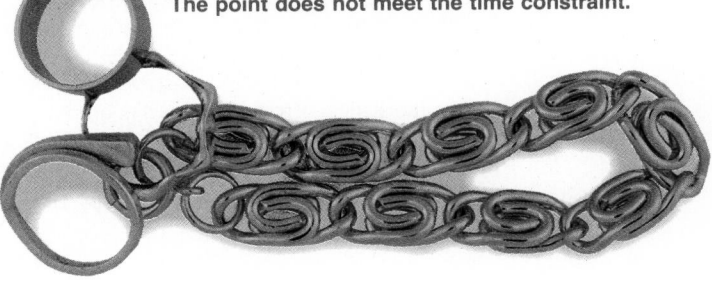

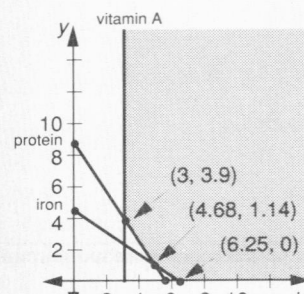

NOTES ON QUESTIONS

Question 7: This question combines all of Lessons 5-7, 5-8, and 5-9. The question is worded in such a way (steps (a) through (f)) as to provide direction to the insecure students as they work their way through the problem. Encourage them to do as complete a solution as possible on their own.

Question 8: Emphasize that the solution for this question (a maximization problem) should follow the same steps as that for **Question 7** (a minimization).

Question 11: The graph for this question is a piecewise linear one. You may want to give students this hint before they start the assignment.

Question 12: This skill sequence reviews solving simple quadratic equations in preparation for Chapter 6.

ADDITIONAL ANSWERS
7.b.

	Iron (mg)	Vit. A (units)	Prot. (g)
hamburger	.8	10	6.5
potato	1.1	0	4
required constraints	5	30	35

$$\text{Then,} \begin{cases} h \geq 0 \\ p \geq 0 \\ .8h + 1.1p \geq 5 \\ 10h + 0p \geq 30 \\ 6.5h + 4p \geq 35 \end{cases}$$

c.

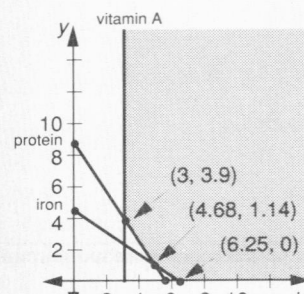

5. Suppose the students in the example decide to put semi-precious gems in their jewelry: six in each necklace and one in each bracelet. They can use 150 gems each week.
   a. Translate this constraint into an inequality. $6x + y \leq 150$
   b. The entire system, including this new constraint, is graphed below. Find the new vertices, T and U. $T = (20, 30); U = (25, 0)$
   c. Do the students need to change their program to keep profits at a maximum? Justify your answer.   **No; profit is still maximized at Q.**

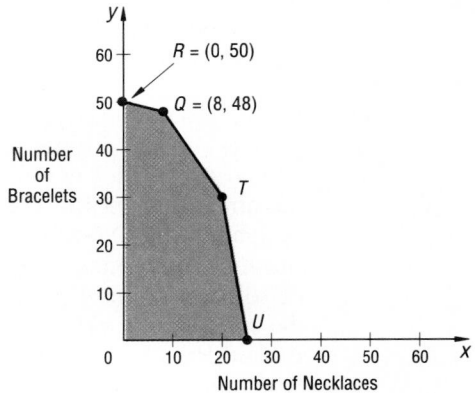

6. a. Name a method for solving linear programming problems without graphing.   **the simplex algorithm**
   b. Who developed this method, and when?
   Hurwicz, Dantzig, Koopmans; 1947

7. Some parents shopping for their family want to know how much hamburger and how many potatoes to buy. From a food-value table they find that one ounce of hamburger has .8 mg of iron, 10 units of vitamin A, and 6.5 grams of protein. One medium potato has 1.1 mg of iron, 0 units of vitamin A, and 4 grams of protein. For this meal the parents want to serve at least 5 mg of iron, 30 units of vitamin A, and 35 grams of protein. One potato costs \$0.05 and 1 ounce of hamburger costs \$0.11. The parents want to be economical (minimize their costs), yet meet daily requirements. They need a program for the quantity of hamburger and potatoes to buy for the family.
   a. Identify the variables for this problem.   **h: oz of hamburger; p: potatoes**
   b. Translate the constraints of the problem into a system of inequalities. (You should have five inequalities; a table may help.)   **See margin.**
   c. Graph the system of inequalities in part b, and find the vertices of the feasible set.   **See margin.**
   d. Write an expression for the cost (to be minimized).   **.11h + .05p**
   e. Apply the Linear-Programming Theorem to determine which vertex minimizes the cost expression of part d.   **(3, 4)**
   f. Interpret your answer to part e. What is the best program for this family?   **3 oz of hamburger; 4 potatoes**

298

8. A company makes two kinds of tires: model R (regular) and model S (snow). Each tire is processed on three machines, A, B, and C. To make one model R requires $\frac{1}{2}$ hour on machine A, 2 hours on B, and 1 hour on C. To make one model S requires 1 hour on A, 1 hour on B, and 4 hours on C. During the next week machine A will be available for at most 20 hours, machine B for at most 60 hours, and machine C for at most 60 hours. If the company makes a $10 profit on each model R tire and a $15 profit on each model S tire, about how many of each tire should be made to maximize the company's profit? *(Lesson 5-8)* **26 regular and 7 snow tires**

9. An alloy containing 65% aluminum is made by melting together two alloys that are 25% aluminum and 75% aluminum. How many kilograms of each alloy must be used to produce 160 kilograms of the 65% alloy? *(Lesson 5-3)* **25% aluminum: 32 kg; 75% aluminum: 128 kg**

10. A formula for the nth term of a sequence is

$$a_n = 10 - .5(n - 1).$$

a. Write the first three terms. **10, 9.5, 9** $a_1 = 10; a_n =$
b. Write a recursive formula for this sequence. $a_{n-1} - .5$ for $n > 1$
c. Solve the explicit formula for n. $-2a_n + 21 = n$
d. One term of the sequence is -39. Which term is it? *(Lessons 1-3, 1-4, 1-8)* **99th**

11. In the NFL passer rating system, a quarterback who completes $x\%$ of his passes is awarded p points as follows:

if $x \leq 30$, $p = 0$
if $30 < x < 77.5$, $p = \frac{1}{20}(x - 30)$
if $x \geq 77.5$, $p = 2.375$.

Graph the ordered pairs (x, p). (Note: Quarterbacks also get points for touchdowns and yards gained and lose points for interceptions.) *(Lesson 3-8)* **See margin.**

12. *Skill sequence* Solve. *(Previous course)*
a. $x^2 = 49$ **b.** $x^2 + 2 = 51$ **c.** $x^2 + 2 = 49$
  $x = 7$ or $x = -7$ $x = 7$ or $x = -7$ $x = \sqrt{47}$ or $x = -\sqrt{47}$

13. In this and the last lesson, several situations are given that lead to linear-programming problems. For instance, one situation is found in the example of this lesson, and one is in Question 7 above. Make up another situation that would lead to this kind of problem. **Many answers are possible.**

FOLLOW-UP

MORE PRACTICE
For more questions on SPUR Objectives, see *Lesson Master 5-9*, shown below.

11. See Additional Answers in the back of this book.

NAME _____

LESSON **MASTER** **5-9**
QUESTIONS ON **SPUR** OBJECTIVES

■**USES** *Objective G (See pages 302–305 for objectives.)*
In 1–4, refer to the following situation.

Some investors want to build a large complex of 1- and 2-bedroom apartments. At most, 160 apartments can be created, and operating expenses may be no more than $30,000 per month. Maintaining a 1-bedroom unit costs the building owners $150 per month; a 2-bedroom apartment costs $250 per month. Each 1-bedroom apartment nets the owners $8 per month profit. Two-bedroom apartments result in a $12-per-month profit.

1. Let S be the number of single-bedroom apartments, and let T be the number of two-bedroom apartments. Translate the constraints into a system of inequalities.
$$S \geq 0$$
$$T \geq 0$$
$$S + T \leq 160$$
$$150S + 250T \leq 30,000$$

2. Graph the system with S as the independent variable. List the vertices of the feasible set.
(0, 120); (100, 60); (160, 0)

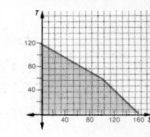

3. Write an expression to be maximized.
Profit = $8S + 12T$

4. Apply the Linear Programming Theorem and interpret its results.
Maximum profit is $1520 per month by making 100 1-bedroom apts. and 60 2-bedroom apts.

Advanced Algebra © Scott, Foresman and Company   *Continued* **63**

NAME _____
Lesson MASTER 5-9 (page 2)

In 5 and 6, refer to the following situation.

A cannery makes soup and fruit. A can of soup costs $0.30 to produce and a can of fruit costs $0.20. The per-hour cost of producing these items cannot exceed $1000. A total of 4000 cans can be produced per hour, and no more than 2500 of these can be soup. The cannery makes $0.15 on each can of soup and $0.08 on each can of fruit.

5. Use linear programming to determine how many cans of soup and how many cans of fruit should be produced per hour for maximum profit?

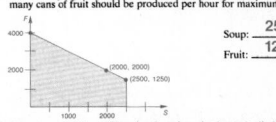

Soup: 2500
Fruit: 1250

6. Suppose a machine malfunction forced production to be limited to no more than 3000 cans of fruit per hour. Would the number of each kind of can produced need to change for maximum profit? Justify your answer.
Yes; at the old constraint, 3750 cans were produced for maximum profit. This is too many under the new constraint. Now, 3000 cans will be produced, 2500 soup and 500 fruit.

64   Advanced Algebra © Scott, Foresman and Company

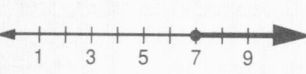
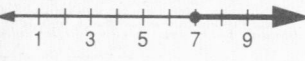
Summary

When two or more sentences are joined by the words *and* or *or,* a compound sentence results. The solution set to *A or B* is the union of the solution sets of *A* and *B*. If the word joining them is *and,* the compound sentence is called a system. The solution set to *A and B* is the intersection of the solution sets of *A* and *B*.

Systems have many applications and may contain any number of variables. If the system contains one variable, then its solutions can be graphed on a number line. If the system contains two variables, then its solutions can be graphed in the plane. Graphing in the plane often tells you the number of solutions but may not yield the exact solutions.

This chapter deals primarily with ways of solving systems of linear equations and inequalities in two variables. Three methods for solving linear equations use linear combinations, substitution, and matrices. The matrix method converts a system of two equations in two unknowns to a single matrix equation. To get the solution, both sides of the equation are then multiplied by the inverse of the coefficient matrix.

The graph of a single linear inequality is a half-plane. For a system of two linear inequalities, if the boundary lines intersect, then the graph is the interior of an angle and perhaps one or both of its sides.

Systems with two variables but more than two inequalities arise in linear-programming problems. In a linear-programming problem, you look for a solution to the system that maximizes or minimizes the value of a particular expression. You first find the set of solutions to the system. This feasible set is always a convex region. The Linear-Programming Theorem states that the desired point must be a vertex of the feasible set, so all vertices are tried. Applications of linear programming are a recent development in mathematics and are quite important in industry.

Vocabulary

Below are the most important terms and phrases for this chapter. You should be able to give a definition for those terms marked with *. For all other terms you should be able to give a general description and a specific example.

Lesson 5-1
compound sentence, * union of sets
*intersection of sets

Lesson 5-2
system, *solution set for a system
consistent, inconsistent system

Lesson 5-3
*equivalent systems
linear-combination method

Lesson 5-4
substitution method

Lesson 5-5
*inverse M^{-1} of a matrix M
Inverse-Matrix Theorem, square matrix
*determinant of a 2×2 matrix M, det M

Lesson 5-6
matrix form of a system
coefficient matrix, constant matrix
Matrix-Solution Theorem

Lesson 5-7
*feasible set, feasible region
*vertices of feasible region
convex region

Lesson 5-8
linear-programming problem
Linear-Programming Theorem

300

Progress Self-Test

Answers in the back of this book.

Take this test as you would take a test in class. Use graph paper and a calculator. Then check your work with the solutions in the Selected Answers section in the back of the book.

1. On a number line, graph $\{x: x \geq -5\} \cap \{x: x \geq 7\}$.   **See margin.**

2. A graph of the system $\begin{cases} y = .5x - 2 \\ y = -x^2 \end{cases}$ is shown below. Approximate the solutions to the system.   **(-1.7, -2.9); (1.2, -1.4)**

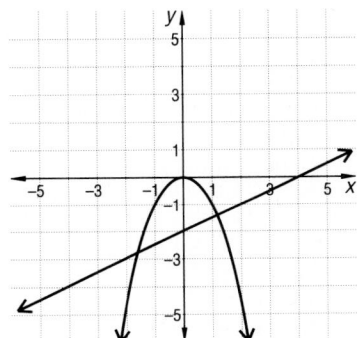

3. Consider the system $\begin{cases} 2x - 9y = 8 \\ 2x - 9y = -7. \end{cases}$
   a. Is this system inconsistent?   **Yes**
   b. Why or why not?
      The lines do not intersect.

In 4 and 5, solve each system.

4. $\begin{cases} s = 4t \\ r = t + 11 \\ 3r - 8s = 4 \end{cases}$ 5. $\begin{cases} -3x + 3y = 2 \\ -4x - 2y = 3 \end{cases}$
   4. (12, 4, 1)   5. $(-\frac{13}{18}, -\frac{1}{18})$

6. At Eggs-N-Links Restaurant you can get a Double Duo Breakfast of 2 eggs with 2 sausage links for $2.78 and a Triple Quad Breakfast of 3 eggs with 4 sausage links for $4.99. From this information, what might Eggs-N-Links charge for 1 egg?   **57¢**

In 7 and 8, consider the system $\begin{cases} 8x + 3y = 41 \\ 6x + 5y = 39. \end{cases}$

7. Find the inverse of the coefficient matrix.

8. Use a matrix equation to solve the system.

9. *Multiple choice* The graph below shows the feasible set for which system?   **c**
   (a) $\begin{cases} y \leq x \\ x \geq 2) \end{cases}$ (b) $\begin{cases} y > x \\ x \leq 2 \end{cases}$
   (c) $\begin{cases} y \leq x \\ x < 2 \end{cases}$ (d) $\begin{cases} y < x \\ x < 2 \end{cases}$

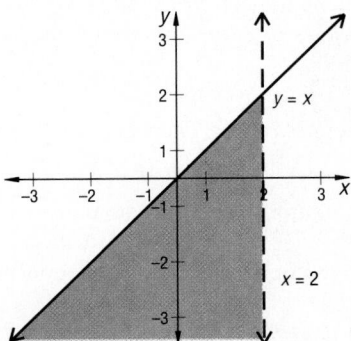

In 10–12, a furniture manufacturer makes upholstered chairs and sofas. On the average it takes carpenters 7 hours to build a chair and 4 hours to build a sofa. There are enough carpenters for no more than 133 worker-hours per day. Upholsterers average 2 hours per chair and 6 hours per sofa. There are enough upholsterers for no more than 72 worker-hours per day. The profit per chair is $80 and the profit per sofa is $70. How many sofas and chairs should be made per day to maximize the profit?   **See margin.**

10. Translate the constraints into a system of linear inequalities.

11. Graph the system of inequalities and find the vertices of the feasible set.

12. Apply the Linear-Programming Theorem and interpret the results.

13. Which boundary is included in the solution set of $\begin{cases} y \leq 7 \\ y > x + 2 \end{cases}$? $y = 7$

PROGRESS SELF-TEST

We cannot overemphasize the importance of these end-of-chapter materials. It is at this point that the material "gels" for many students, allowing them to solidify skills and understanding. In general, student performance should be markedly improved after these pages.

USING THE PROGRESS SELF-TEST
Assign the Progress Self-Test as a one-night assignment. Worked-out *solutions* for all questions are in the Selected Answer section of the student book. Encourage students to take the Progress Self-Test honestly, grade themselves, and then be prepared to discuss the test in class.

Advise students to pay special attention to those Chapter Review questions (pages 302–305) which correspond to questions missed on the Progress Self-Test. A chart provided with the Selected Answers keys the Progress Self-Test questions to the lettered SPUR Objectives in the Chapter Review or to the Vocabulary. It also keys the questions to the corresponding lessons where the material is covered.

8. $\begin{bmatrix} \frac{5}{22} & \frac{-3}{22} \\ \frac{-6}{22} & \frac{8}{22} \end{bmatrix} \begin{bmatrix} 8 & 3 \\ 6 & 5 \end{bmatrix} \begin{bmatrix} x \\ y \end{bmatrix}$

$= \begin{bmatrix} \frac{5}{22} & \frac{-3}{22} \\ \frac{-3}{11} & \frac{4}{11} \end{bmatrix} \begin{bmatrix} 41 \\ 39 \end{bmatrix}$;

$\begin{bmatrix} x \\ y \end{bmatrix} = \begin{bmatrix} 4 \\ 3 \end{bmatrix}$

So the solution to the system is x = 4 and y = 3.

10., 11., 12., and 13. See Additional Answers in the back of this book.

Chapter Review

Questions on **SPUR** Objectives

For answers not shown, see Additional Answers.

SPUR stands for **S**kills, **P**roperties, **U**ses, and **R**epresentations.
The Chapter Review questions are grouped according to the
SPUR Objectives for this chapter.

SKILLS deal with the procedures used to get answers.

■ **Objective A:** *Solve systems using the linear-combination or substitution method. (Lessons 5-3, 5-4)*

1. *Multiple choice* The system $\begin{cases} 2x + 3y = 19 \\ 4x - y = 17 \end{cases}$
becomes $-7y = -21$ if you: **a**
(a) multiply the first equation by -2 and add.
(b) multiply the second equation by 3 and add.
(c) multiply the first equation by 2, the second equation by -1 and add.
(d) multiply the second equation by 3 and subtract.

2. Which choice in Question 1 does not help to solve the system? **d**

In 3–8, solve and check.

3. $\begin{cases} 2a - 4b = 18 \\ 3a - b = 22 \end{cases}$ (7, -1)

4. $\begin{cases} 3m + 10n = 16 \\ m = -6n \end{cases}$ (12, -2)

5. $\begin{cases} y = x - 4 \\ 2x - y = -2.5 \end{cases}$ (-6.5, -10.5)

6. $\begin{cases} 3x + 6y = -3 \\ -5x - 8y + 22 = 0 \end{cases}$ (26, -13.5)

7. $\begin{cases} 2r + 15t = 6 \\ r = 3s \\ t = \frac{2}{5}s \end{cases}$ $(\frac{3}{2}, \frac{1}{2}, \frac{1}{5})$

8. $\begin{cases} a = 3b - 2 \\ b = 4c + 5 \\ c = 5a + 1 \end{cases}$ $(\frac{-25}{59}, \frac{31}{59}, \frac{-66}{59})$

9. Consider the system $\begin{cases} y = 5x \\ -3x + 2y = -28. \end{cases}$
   a. Name three methods you can use to solve this system.   See margin.
   b. Solve and check the system.   (-4, -20)

■ **Objective B:** *Find the inverse and determinant of a 2 × 2 matrix. (Lesson 5-5)*

In 10–15, give: (a) the determinant; (b) the inverse, if it exists.   See margin.

10. $\begin{bmatrix} 1 & 9 \\ -7 & 6 \end{bmatrix}$ 11. $\begin{bmatrix} 2 & 0 \\ 0 & 1 \end{bmatrix}$

12. $\begin{bmatrix} 6 & 4 \\ -3 & 2 \end{bmatrix}$ 13. $\begin{bmatrix} 1 & 4 \\ -3 & 6 \end{bmatrix}$

14. $\begin{bmatrix} 2 & -4 \\ 5 & -10 \end{bmatrix}$ 15. $\begin{bmatrix} a & b \\ c & d \end{bmatrix}$

■ **Objective C:** *Use matrices to solve systems of equations. (Lesson 5-6)*

In 16–18, solve each system using matrices.

16. $\begin{cases} 2x - 9y = 14 \\ 6x - y = 42 \end{cases}$ (7, 0)

17. $\begin{cases} 4a - 5b = -19 \\ 3a + 7b = 18 \end{cases}$ (-1, 3)

18. $\begin{cases} 3m = 4n + 5 \\ 2m = 3n - 6 \end{cases}$ (39, 28)

19. $\begin{cases} \frac{1}{2} = 3x - 4y \\ 3 = x + 8y \end{cases}$ $(\frac{4}{7}, \frac{17}{56})$

Left margin

CHAPTER REVIEW

The main objectives for the chapter are organized here into sections corresponding to the four main types of understanding this book promotes: Skills, Properties, Uses, and Representations.

USING THE CHAPTER REVIEW
Whereas end-of-chapter material may be considered optional in some texts, in *Advanced Algebra* we have selected these objectives and questions with the expectation that they will be covered. Students should be able to answer these questions with about 85% accuracy after studying the chapter.

You may assign these questions over a single night to help students prepare for a test the next day, or you may assign the questions over a two-day period.

If you work the questions over two days, then we recommend assigning the *evens* for homework the first night so that students get feedback in class the next day, then assigning the *odds* the night before the test so students can use the answers provided in the book.

ADDITIONAL ANSWERS
9.a. substitution, graphing, linear combination, use of matrices

10.a. 69

b. $\begin{bmatrix} \frac{2}{23} & -\frac{3}{23} \\ \frac{7}{69} & \frac{1}{69} \end{bmatrix}$

11.a. 2

b. $\begin{bmatrix} \frac{1}{2} & 0 \\ 0 & 1 \end{bmatrix}$

PROPERTIES deal with the principles behind the mathematics.

■ Objective D: *Recognize properties of systems of equations. (Lessons 5-2, 5-3, 5-4, 5-6)*

20. Are the systems $\begin{cases} 3x - y = 19 \\ 5x + 2y = 39 \end{cases}$ and
$\begin{cases} x = 7 \\ x + y = 9 \end{cases}$ equivalent?   Yes

21. Give the simplest system equivalent to $3x = 6$ and $x + y = 10$.

22. A system with no solutions is called __?__.
   inconsistent

In 23–25, (a) identify each system as inconsistent or consistent; (b) give the number of solutions.   **See margin.**

23. $\begin{cases} 3x + 5y = 15 \\ 3x + 5y = 45 \end{cases}$ **24.** $\begin{cases} 6m - 4n = 9 \\ -3m = -2n - \frac{9}{2} \end{cases}$

25. $\begin{cases} 8a - 5b = 40 \\ 2a + b = -6 \end{cases}$

26. For what value of k does $\begin{cases} 2x + ky = 6 \\ 14x + 7y = 42 \end{cases}$
   have infinitely many solutions? $k = 1$

27. For what value of t does $\begin{cases} 3x + 9y = t \\ 4x + 12y = 7 \end{cases}$
   have infinitely many solutions? $t = \frac{21}{4}$

■ Objective E: *Recognize properties of systems of inequalities. (Lessons 5-7, 5-8)*

28. *True or false* The boundaries are included
   in the solution set of $\begin{cases} y > 2 \\ y < 4 - x. \end{cases}$ **False**

29. Which two of the following could be feasible regions in a linear-programming situation?   **a, c**

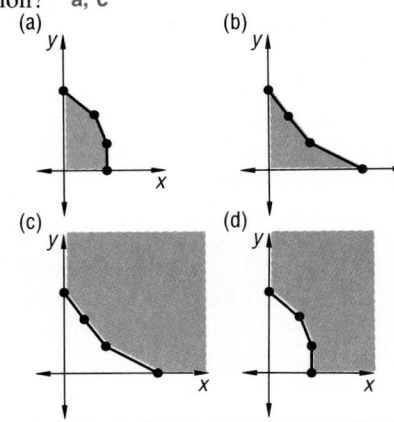
(a)   (b)
(c)   (d)

30. A system of inequalities was graphed as shown below. Are the coordinates listed below possible solutions to the system? Justify your answers.
   a. (3, 2)   Yes; (3, 2) is in the feasible region.
   b. (6, 2)   No; (6, 2) is not in the feasible region.

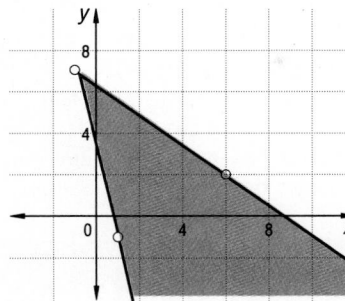

31. Where in a feasible set are the possible solutions to a linear-programming problem? at the verti

32. Does the point M in the region below represent a possible solution to a linear-programming problem?   **Yes**

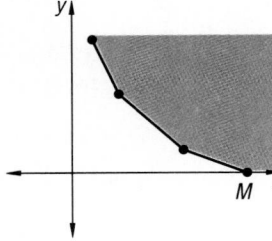

12.a. 24

b. $\begin{bmatrix} \frac{1}{12} & -\frac{1}{6} \\ \frac{1}{8} & \frac{1}{4} \end{bmatrix}$

13.a. 18

b. $\begin{bmatrix} \frac{1}{3} & -\frac{2}{9} \\ \frac{1}{6} & \frac{1}{18} \end{bmatrix}$

14.a. 0
b. Inverse does not exist.

15.a. $ad - bc$

$\begin{bmatrix} \frac{d}{ad-bc} & \frac{-b}{ad-bc} \\ \frac{-c}{ad-bc} & \frac{a}{ad-bc} \end{bmatrix}$

21. $x = 2$ and $y = 8$

23.a. inconsistent
b. no solutions

24.a. consistent
b. many solutions

25.a. consistent
b. one solution

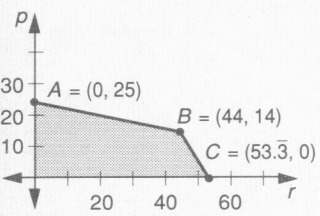

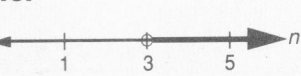

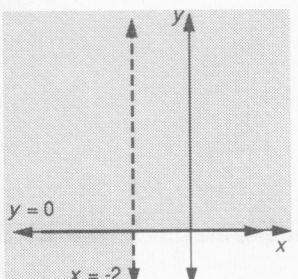
USES deal with applications of mathematics in real situations.

■ **Objective F:** *Use linear systems to solve real-world problems.* (*Lessons 5-3, 5-4*)

33. At Kit's Kitchen, the Big Deal costs $3.50 for two hamburgers and one order of fries. The family pack costs $12.00 for six burgers and six orders of fries. If the prices are constant, how much does one hamburger cost? **$1.50**

34. One night at the circus the big-top attraction sold out, selling all 3,050 seats. There are four times as many lower-level seats as upper-level seats. How many upper-level seats are there? **610 upper-level seats**

35. Billy likes to mix two cereals for breakfast. He wants to reduce his sugar intake without giving up Sugar-O's, his favorite cereal. Sugar-O's contains 20% sugar while Health-Nut contains 5% sugar. How much of each cereal should he eat to fill a bowl with a 25 g mixture which is 10% sugar?
Sugar-O's: $8\frac{1}{3}$ g; Health-Nut: $16\frac{2}{3}$ g

■ **Objective G:** *Use linear programming to solve problems in the real world.* (*Lessons 5-8, 5-9*)

36. Jocelyn's Jewelry Store makes rings and pendants. Every week the staff uses at most 500 g of metal and spends at most 80 hours making jewelry. It takes 5 g of metal to make a ring and 20 g to make a pendant. Each ring takes 1.5 hours to make and each pendant takes 1 hour. The profit on each ring is $90 and the profit on each pendant $40. The store wants to earn as much profit as possible. **See margin.**
  a. Identify the variables and translate the constraints into a system of inequalities.
  b. Graph the system and find the vertices of the feasible set.
  c. Write an expression to be maximized.
  d. Apply the Linear-Programming Theorem and interpret the results.

37. Brendan is studying hard for two final exams, one in his Spanish class, the other in algebra. He figures that each Spanish vocabulary word he learns will mean an increased score of about 0.04 point. (That is, he expects that about 1 in 25 words will be on the test.) Each algebra question he reviews will mean an increased score of about 0.10 point. (About 1 in 10 questions will be on the test.) He has two difficulties: there are only 4 hours to study between now and the test and he has only 12 sheets of notebook paper, each with 35 lines. Each new vocabulary word takes about 2 minutes to learn. An algebra question averages about 4 minutes. A vocabulary word takes 3 lines of notebook paper (he writes them down again and again to work on them). A typical algebra question takes 10 lines.
  a. How much time should Brendan spend on Spanish and how much on algebra to maximize the increase in his total score?
  Spanish: 90 min; algebra: 15 min
  b. If he spends the time, what increase in score can he expect in Spanish and what increase in algebra?
  Spanish: 3.6 points; algebra: 1.5 points

304

REPRESENTATIONS deal with pictures, graphs, or objects that illustrate concepts.

■ **Objective H:** *Graph compound sentences. (Lesson 5-1)*

In 38–41, graph on a number line.　**See margin.**

38. $\{x: x > 9 \text{ and } x < 14\}$

39. $\{t: -2 \le t < 7\} \cap \{t: t \ge 0\}$

40. $\{n: n > 5\} \cup \{n: n > 3\}$

41. $\{y: y \le 4\} \cup \{y: 5 \le y \le 6\}$

42. Write the compound sentence in the variable x that is graphed below.
$x \le -1 \text{ or } x > 3$

See margin.

In 43 and 44, graph on a coordinate plane.

43. $x < -2 \text{ or } y \ge 0$　　**44.** $x \ge 5 \text{ and } y \ge 12$

45. Use a compound sentence to describe the region graphed below.
$x \le -3$
$y \le -1$

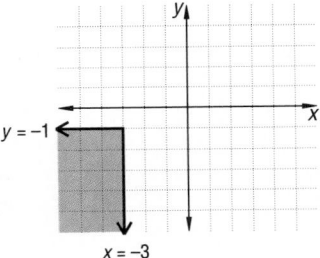

■ **Objective I:** *Solve systems of inequalities by graphing. (Lessons 5-1, 5-7)*

In 46–48, graph the solution set.　**See margin.**

46. $\begin{cases} x \ge 2 \\ y \le -3 \end{cases}$

47. $\begin{cases} 7c + 3d < 21 \\ 7c - 3d > -1) \end{cases}$

48. $\begin{cases} 5x \ge -10 \\ 3(x + y) \le 6 \\ 6 > y - 4x \end{cases}$

■ **Objective J:** *Estimate solutions to systems by graphing. (Lesson 5-2)*

In 49 and 50, estimate all solutions by graphing.

49. $\begin{cases} x - 2y = -4 \\ y = x^2 \end{cases}$　**50.** $\begin{cases} 3x + 5y = -20 \\ xy = 6 \end{cases}$　**See margin.**

51. *Multiple choice* Which of the following systems describes the region below?　**c**

(a) $\begin{cases} y < \frac{1}{2}x + 2 \\ y < \frac{1}{2}x - 3 \end{cases}$

(b) $\begin{cases} y > 2x + 2 \\ y < 2x - 3 \end{cases}$

(c) $\begin{cases} y \le 2x + 2 \\ y \ge 2x - 3 \end{cases}$

(d) $\begin{cases} y \le 2x - 1 \\ y \ge 2x + 1.5 \end{cases}$

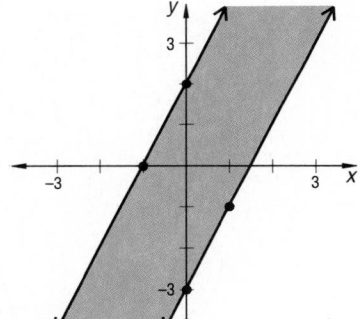

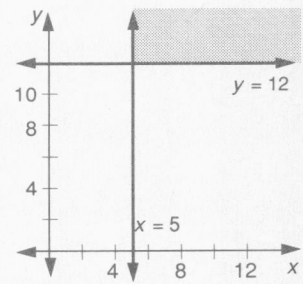
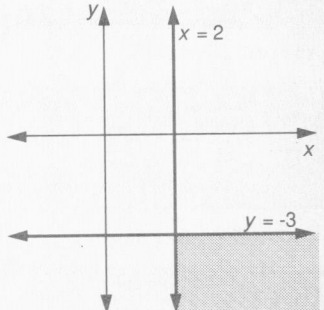

CHAPTER 6 ■ PARABOLAS AND QUADRATIC EQUATIONS

DAILY PACING CHART ■ CHAPTER 6

Students in the Full Course should complete all but one of the chapters by the end of the year. Students in the Minimal Course will spend more time on quizzes and the Chapter Review. As such, these students should complete about ten or eleven chapters.

DAY	MINIMAL COURSE	FULL COURSE
1	6-1	6-1
2	6-2	6-2
3	6-3	6-3
4	Quiz (TRF); Start 6-4.	Quiz (TRF); 6-4
5	Finish 6-4.	6-5
6	6-5	6-6
7	6-6	Quiz (TRF); 6-7
8	Quiz (TRF); Start 6-7.	6-8
9	Finish 6-7.	6-9
10	6-8	6-10
11	6-9	Progress Self-Test
12	6-10	Chapter Review
13	Progress Self-Test	Chapter Test (TRF)
14	Chapter Review	Comprehensive Test (TRF)
15	Chapter Review	
16	Chapter Test (TRF)	
17	Comprehensive Test (TRF)	

TESTING OPTIONS
■ Quiz for Lessons 6-1 Through 6-3   ■ Chapter 6 Test, Form A   ■ Chapter 6 Test, Cumulative Form
■ Quiz for Lessons 6-4 Through 6-6   ■ Chapter 6 Test, Form B   ■ Comprehensive Test, Chapters 1-6

PROVIDING FOR INDIVIDUAL DIFFERENCES
The student text is written for the *average* student. The program, however, can be adapted for both less capable and for more capable students.

A blackline master (in the Teacher's Resource File) is provided for each lesson for those students who need more practice. The Teacher's Edition frequently provides Error Analysis and Alternate Approach features to provide additional instructional strategies.

For students who require additional challenge, Extension activities are regularly provided in the Teacher's Edition.

OBJECTIVES ■ CHAPTER 6

Students should master the chapter objectives by the time they complete the chapter. To ensure mastery, there is continual review built into each set of lesson questions. After students complete the chapter lessons, they assess their mastery on the Progress Self-Test. Then they do the Chapter Review and pay special attention to those questions that match the objectives missed on the Progress Self-Test. Students can get extra practice on these objectives by using the master for each lesson in the Teacher's Resource File.

OBJECTIVES FOR CHAPTER 6 (Organized into the SPUR categories—Skills, Properties, Uses, and Representations)	Progress Self-Test Questions	Chapter Review Questions	Lesson Master from Teacher's Resource File*
SKILLS			
A Expand squares of binomials.	23–24	1 through 6	6-1
B Transform quadratic equations from vertex form to standard form, and vice versa.	1	7 through 11	6-5
C Simplify expressions involving imaginary numbers.	4–6	12 through 19	6-8, 6-10
D Solve quadratic equations.	12–14	20 through 33	6-6, 6-8, 6-10
E Perform operations with complex numbers.	7–8	34 through 41	6-9
PROPERTIES			
F Use the Graph-Translation Theorem to interpret equations and graphs.	9, 25	42 through 48	6-3, 6-4
G Use the discriminant of a quadratic equation to determine the nature of the solutions to the equation.	17b	49 through 53	6-7
H Classify complex numbers.	15–16	54 through 61	6-9
USES			
I Use quadratic equations to solve problems dealing with velocity and acceleration.	18–20	62 through 65	6-2
J Solve area problems which can be modeled by quadratic equations.	21	66, 67	6-1
REPRESENTATIONS			
K Graph parabolas and interpret them.	2–3, 10–11	68 through 75	6-2, 6-4, 6-6
L Use the discriminant of a quadratic equation to determine the number of x-intercepts of the graph.	17a	76 through 79	6-7
M Find points of a parabola given its focus and directrix.	22	80, 81	6-3

* The masters are numbered to match the lessons.

OVERVIEW ■ CHAPTER 6

This chapter continues the study of quadratic equations introduced in Chapter 2 with a discussion of $y = kx^2$. By the end of the chapter, students should be able to find the solutions to any quadratic equation in one variable. We balance traditional paper-and-pencil skills of manipulating expressions and solving equations along with an analysis of the relationship between parameters of equations and the properties of graphs.

In Lesson 6-1, students learn to solve equations of the form $ax^2 = k$ by applying the theorem $\sqrt{x^2} = |x|$.

Lesson 6-2 is devoted to graphing equations of the form $y = ax^2 + bx + c$ and to applications involving distance, time, velocity, and acceleration.

Lesson 6-3 introduces the parabola geometrically, that is, as the set of points equidistant from a given point and a given line. This approach enables us to prove that $y = x^2$ is indeed a parabola. The Graph-Translation Theorem is then introduced in Lesson 6-4 to derive the vertex form of the parabola, $y - k = a(x - h)^2$. In Lesson 6-5, students complete the square to rewrite equations of the form $y = ax^2 + bx + c$ in vertex form.

Lessons 6-6 and 6-7 are devoted to studying the Quadratic Formula. In Lesson 6-6, the formula is derived and used to solve equations. In Lesson 6-7, the discriminant is used to determine the number of real solutions of a quadratic equation, and to analyze the relation between the graph of $y = ax^2 + bx + c$ and its x-intercepts.

Lessons 6-8 and 6-9 introduce imaginary numbers and complex numbers, respectively, paving the way for Lesson 6-10, in which the Quadratic Formula is used to solve all types of quadratic equations with real coefficients.

In this chapter, quadratic equations are not solved by factoring trinomials. The reason is to teach students problem-solving strategies that generalize easily, and because few realistic applications are modeled by equations that can be solved by factoring over the rationals. Factoring trinomials and the Factor Theorem are discussed in Chapter 11.

The microcomputer is a powerful tool for generating tables of values and graphs of equations. We strongly suggest that if you do not have a computer available on a daily basis, you reserve one for use at least twice during this chapter. You will find automatic graphers very useful. Two optimal places for its use are in Lessons 6-2 and 6-4.

PERSPECTIVES ■ CHAPTER 6

The Perspectives provide the rationale for the inclusion of topics or approaches, provide mathematical background, and make connections within UCSMP.

6-1

SQUARES AND SQUARE ROOTS

This lesson reviews several concepts necessary for the discussions in the rest of the chapter. First is the relationship between square roots and absolute value: $\sqrt{x^2} = |x|$. This idea is needed for changing distance (which involves absolute value) into squares in the derivation of equations of parabolas.

Second is the application of squares to areas. This generates a type of problem which reoccurs throughout the chapter.

Third is a review of the Binomial-Square Theorem. The theorem is needed for completing the square in Lesson 6-5, but it will be helpful to students in each lesson.

6-2

GRAPHING $y = ax^2 + bx + c$

This lesson presents applications of projectile motion subject to constant acceleration; that is, objects whose height h at time t is given by an equation of the form

$$h = -\tfrac{1}{2}gt^2 + v_0t + h_0.$$

Applications of this type were first analyzed by Tartaglia and Galileo in the 16th century and are important historically. Their work led to the invention of calculus by Newton and Leibniz and paved the way for modern physics and mechanics. Newton identified a gravitational constant as the force attracting objects to Earth.

6-3

THE PARABOLA

In this lesson, a locus definition for the parabola is introduced and used to derive an equation for particular parabolas with focus of the form $(0, k)$ and horizontal directrix $y = -k$, yielding an equation of the form $y = ax^2$, where $a = \frac{1}{4k}$.

We do not derive the general equation of the parabola from the locus definition; however, an equation for any parabola with a vertical line of symmetry is derived by using the Graph-Translation Theorem in the next lesson. The algebraic definition of a parabola as the set of points that satisfies a general equation, and the geometric definition as a conic section are discussed in Chapter 12.

6-4

THE GRAPH-TRANSLATION THEOREM

The Graph-Translation Theorem is a very powerful theorem that can be used repeatedly in a student's later work in mathematics. This lesson emphasizes the application of the theorem to parabolas. Having found in the previous lesson that $y = ax^2$ is a parabola with vertex (0, 0) symmetric to the y-axis ($x = 0$), in this lesson, the parabola is translated h units to the right and k units up to get $y - k = a(x - h)^2$, with vertex (h, k) and line of symmetry $x = h$.

6-5

COMPLETING THE SQUARE

The technique called *completing the square* is introduced for two reasons: (1) to find the vertex of a parabola whose equation has been expanded; (2) to derive the quadratic formula (done in Lesson 6-6).

In this lesson, we show that the vertex form of an equation of a parabola can be rewritten in expanded form and vice versa. Students practice rewriting standard forms as vertex forms in order to make graphs and solve problems about maxima or minima.

Solving quadratic equations by completing the square is not an objective of this book. Completing the square to solve quadratics is also not in UCSMP *Algebra*. Since the Quadratic Formula is the general theorem, it is not necessary to derive individual cases.

6-6

THE QUADRATIC FUNCTION

This lesson motivates, proves, and shows a simple application of the Quadratic Formula Theorem. The central concept is that the solutions to $ax^2 + bx + c = 0$ when $a \neq 0$ are given by substitution in the formula $x = \dfrac{-b \pm \sqrt{b^2 - 4ac}}{2a}$, and that any quadratic equation may be solved in this manner.

Students who have studied from UCSMP *Algebra* and *Geometry* have already worked with this formula. In this course, students should understand how the formula is derived.

The Quadratic Formula Theorem is important because it solves *any* quadratic equation. It is one of the most important theorems in this course, and it should be memorized by students.

6-7

ANALYZING SOLUTIONS TO A QUADRATIC

This lesson serves three purposes. It gives students an extra day to practice calculating solutions to quadratic equations. It introduces the concept of the discriminant and its relation to the number and nature of the roots of a quadratic equation. And, it sets up Lessons 6-8 and 6-9, where students will be dealing with nonreal solutions to quadratics.

Discriminants will be used again in Lesson 12-6 to identify quadratic relations as ellipses, parabolas, or hyperbolas.

6-8

THE IMAGINARY NUMBER *i*

For many years, the concept of imaginary number was difficult for mathematicians to accept and explain logically, even though they were able to devise rules that made computation with such numbers relatively easy. Now such numbers are considered as "real" as real numbers.

In this lesson, students are introduced to the definition of i. They learn how to use i to rewrite $\sqrt{-b}$ when $b > 0$, and how to square numbers of the form ki. In the next lesson, complex numbers are introduced.

The questions in this lesson are short and relatively easy. They will give students plenty of practice to reinforce the new concepts in the lesson.

6-9

COMPLEX NUMBERS

This lesson defines and introduces operations on the set of complex numbers. Addition, subtraction, and multiplication of complex numbers are covered. Although we do not consider it vital for students to learn division of complex numbers in their first exposure to them, Questions 24 and 25 cover this skill, should a teacher wish to include it.

Many books *define* addition and multiplication of complex numbers and then deduce their properties. We take another approach: we assume, as we did with real numbers, that the complex numbers possess the customary (field) properties, and from those assumptions deduce the operations of complex addition and multiplication.

6-10

SOLVING ALL QUADRATICS

The Quadratic Formula may be applied to any quadratic equation. However, in this lesson, we restrict our attention to those quadratic equations with real coefficients.

When the solutions to a quadratic equation are rational, they can be checked by substitution without much difficulty. But when the solutions are of the form $m \pm \sqrt{n}$, the Sum and Product of Roots Theorem is a much simpler check. The sum $2m$, and the product, $m^2 - n^2$ (if n is positive) or $m^2 + n^2$ (if n is negative), are easy to calculate and easy to relate to $\frac{-b}{a}$ and $\frac{c}{a}$.

CHAPTER 6

We recommend 14 to 17 days for this chapter: 10 to 12 on the lessons; 1 for the Progress Self-Test; 1 or 2 for the Chapter Review; 1 for a Chapter test. There is also a Comprehensive Test, which can serve as a quarterly or semester exam. (See the Daily Pacing Chart on page 306A.) If you spend more than 17 days on this chapter, you are moving too slowly. Keep in mind that each lesson includes Review questions to help students firm up content studied previously.

USING PAGES 306–307

Introduce the term *quadratic expression* by using the examples given in the book. Then show students some examples of quadratic equations. Point out that quadratic equations can be used to solve many types of real-world problems, such as finding the distance an object travels given certain conditions.

Discuss the distance formula briefly, and introduce the term *parabola* as the graph of a quadratic equation. Draw a few parabolas on the chalkboard to give students an idea of the shape of the curve.

Parabolas and Quadratic Equations

Quadratic expressions are expressions that contain one or more terms in x^2, y^2, or xy, but no higher powers of x or y. An expression that can be simplified into the form $ax^2 + bx + c$ is called a *quadratic expression in the variable x*. Equations that involve quadratic expressions are called *quadratic equations*. You have probably solved quadratic equations in previous courses.

Many diverse situations lead to quadratic expressions. The area formulas $A = s^2$ (for a square) and $A = \pi r^2$ (for a circle) obviously involve quadratic expressions. All other area formulas also involve the product of two lengths. Even the area of a rectangle with length x and width y is a quadratic expression in the two variables x and y. You will study quadratics and area in Lesson 6-1.

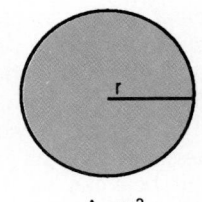

$A = \pi r^2$

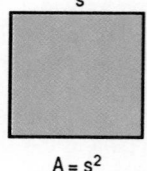

$A = s^2$

Quadratic expressions also arise from studying the paths of objects. The distance an object such as a basketball travels depends on its velocity and acceleration. Lesson 6-2 discusses equations which arise from velocity and acceleration.

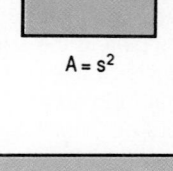

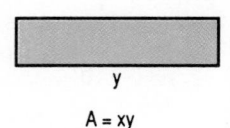

$A = xy$

306

The formula for the distance d between two points (x_1, y_1) and (x_2, y_2) is

$$d = \sqrt{(x_2 - x_1)^2 + (y_2 - y_1)^2}.$$

Underneath the radical sign are two quadratic expressions. The curve known as the *parabola* can be defined in terms of distance and, as a result, all parabolas can be described by quadratic equations. You will see how this is done in Lesson 6-3.

The remainder of the chapter is devoted to quadratic equations and the parabolas which are their graphs. The study of quadratic equations began in ancient times and is related to some of the most important developments in all of mathematics. As you learn about quadratic equations, you will also learn some of the history of mathematics.

LESSON 6-1

Squares and Square Roots

The simplest quadratic equations are of the form $x^2 = k$. As you know, if $k \geq 0$ the solutions to $x^2 = k$ are called the **square roots** of k, namely $\sqrt{k}$ and $-\sqrt{k}$.

Caution: The square root or radical sign $\sqrt{}$ stands only for the *non-negative* square root of a number; $\sqrt{16} = 4$. To write the negative square root, write $-\sqrt{16} = -4$.

A particularly tricky expression is $\sqrt{x^2}$. It can be simplified, but cases must be considered separately.

$$\text{If } x \text{ is positive, then } \sqrt{x^2} = x.$$
$$\text{If } x \text{ is negative, then } \sqrt{x^2} = -x.$$
$$\text{If } x = 0, \text{ then } \sqrt{x^2} = 0.$$

This proves a surprising relationship between square roots and absolute value.

Theorem:

For all real numbers x, $\sqrt{x^2} = |x|$.

For example, $\sqrt{(-4)^2} = \sqrt{16} = 4$ and $|-4| = 4$.
$\sqrt{(8.18)^2} = \sqrt{66.9124} = 8.18$ and $|8.18| = 8.18$

Questions about squares intrigued the ancient Greeks. They wondered: What should be the radius of a circle if it is to have the same area as a given square? With algebra, it is easy to answer this question.

■ ■ ■ ■ ■ ■ ■■

Example 1 A square and circle have the same area. The square has side of length 10. What is the radius of the circle?

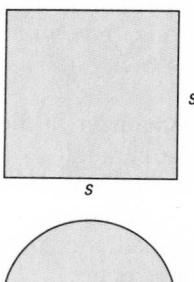

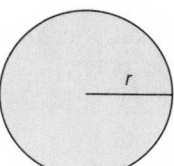

308

Solution The area of the square is 100. Thus, if r is the radius of the circle with area 100, we find r as follows:

$$\pi r^2 = 100$$

$$r^2 = \frac{100}{\pi}$$

$$|r| = \sqrt{\frac{100}{\pi}}$$

$$r = \pm\sqrt{\frac{100}{\pi}}$$

We can ignore the negative solution here. A calculator gives $r \approx 5.64$.

Check The diameter of the circle should be greater than the side of the square. Since $d = 2r$, $d \approx 11.28$, which is greater than 10.

Expressions you might write for finding areas of rectangles are quadratic expressions.

Example 2 Suppose a swimming pool 50 m by 20 m is to be built with a walkway around it. If the walkway is w meters wide, write an expression for the total area of the pool and walkway.

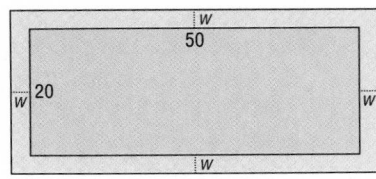

Solution Draw a picture. The pool with walkway occupies a rectangle with length $50 + 2w$ meters and width $20 + 2w$ meters. The area of this rectangle is $(50 + 2w)(20 + 2w)$ square meters.

By using the distributive property, the expression $(50 + 2w)(20 + 2w)$ can be expanded. You have done this kind of multiplication in your earlier study of algebra. Remember that the idea is to think of $(50 + 2w)$ as a single quantity.

$$(50 + 2w)(20 + 2w) = (50 + 2w) \cdot 20 + (50 + 2w) \cdot 2w$$

Again use the distributive property.

$$= 1000 + 40w + 100w + 4w^2$$
$$= 1000 + 140w + 4w^2$$

The expanded expression is in the familiar form $ax^2 + bx + c$.

Alternate Approach
Some students find it easier to understand and use the Binomial-Square Theorem if it is presented as a verbal statement in addition to its formula statement. The theorem would read: To square a binomial, square the first term, add (or subtract) twice the product of the two terms, and then add the square of the second term.

The expressions $50 + 2w$ and $20 + 2w$ are binomials. If the two binomials to be multiplied are equal, then the result is the square of the binomial.

Example 3   Expand $(x + y)^2$.

Solution

$$
\begin{aligned}
(x + y)^2 &= (x + y)(x + y) && \text{definition of 2nd power}\\
&= (x + y)x + (x + y)y && \text{Distributive Property}\\
&= x^2 + yx + xy + y^2 && \text{Distributive Property}\\
&= x^2 + 2xy + y^2. && \text{Commutative Property of}\\
& && \text{Multiplication and}\\
& && \text{Distributive Property}
\end{aligned}
$$

This expansion occurs so often it is identified as a theorem.

Binomial-Square Theorem:

For all real numbers x and y:

$$(x + y)^2 = x^2 + 2xy + y^2$$
$$(x - y)^2 = x^2 - 2xy + y^2.$$

You are asked to prove the second part of the theorem in Question 12. Of course, the theorem holds for any numbers or expressions. It is important that you be able to apply it rather automatically.

Example 4   Expand $\left(3x - \frac{k}{4}\right)^2$.

Solution   The idea is to use the second part of the Binomial-Square Theorem, with $3x$ in place of x and $\frac{k}{4}$ in place of y.

$$\left(3x - \frac{k}{4}\right)^2 = (3x)^2 - 2(3x)\left(\frac{k}{4}\right) + \left(\frac{k}{4}\right)^2$$

$$= 9x^2 - \frac{3k}{2}x + \frac{k^2}{16}$$

Check   Let $x = 3$ and $k = 8$. The left side is then 7^2 or 49. The right side is

$$9 \cdot 3^2 - \frac{3 \cdot 8}{2} \cdot 3 + \frac{8^2}{16}.$$

You should do the calculation to verify that its value is 49.

310

Squares of binomials occur in the formula for the distance d between two points (x_1, y_1) and (x_2, y_2) in the plane.

$$d = \sqrt{(x_2 - x_1)^2 + (y_2 - y_1)^2}$$

If the points are on the same horizontal line, then $y_2 = y_1$ and so $y_2 - y_1 = 0$. Then $(y_2 - y_1)^2 = 0$ and the formula can be simplified to

$$d = \sqrt{(x_2 - x_1)^2}.$$

By the theorem on page 308, this is equivalent to the formula

$$d = |x_2 - x_1|,$$

which you learned in geometry as the formula for the distance between two points on a number line. For instance, the distance between $(17, 5)$ and $(3, 5)$ is:

$$
\begin{aligned}
&\sqrt{(3 - 17)^2 + (5 - 5)^2} \\
&= \sqrt{(3 - 17)^2} \\
&= \sqrt{(-14)^2} \\
&= 14
\end{aligned}
$$

The result, 14, is the same as $|3 - 17|$. In this way absolute value, distance, squares, and square roots are closely related.

Questions

Covering the Reading

1. *Multiple choice* Which is not a quadratic equation? **d**
   a. $y = \frac{1}{2}x^2$ **b.** $xy = 4$ **c.** $x^2 + y^2 = 10$ **d.** $y = 2x$

2. The square roots of 5 are __?__ and __?__. $\sqrt{5}, -\sqrt{5}$

3. Solve for t: $t^2 = 400$. **20, -20**

4. A circle has the same area as a square of side 6. What is the radius of the circle? $\sqrt{\dfrac{36}{\pi}}$

5. A swimming pool 50 m by 25 m is to be built with a walkway w meters wide around it. Write the total area of the pool and walkway in expanded form. **1250 + 150w + 4w²**

NOTES ON QUESTIONS

Question 23: The expression on the left side of the equation is the result of calculating the distance between (x, y) and $(3, y)$ using the Pythagorean Distance Formula. This kind of expression will also occur in the derivation of equations for parabolas given the focus and directrix. To answer the question, have students simplify the left side. For all n, $\sqrt{n^2} = |n|$. Replacing n with $x - 3$, we find that $\sqrt{(x - 3)^2} = |x - 3|$. If $|x - 3| = |k|$, then $\pm k = x - 3$. So $k = \pm(x - 3)$.

Error Analysis for Question 26: Some students will try to multiply both $x + 1$ and $2x + 1$ by $\frac{1}{6}x$. Ask them to multiply $(4)(2)(5)$ and they will quickly see their error. Remind them that multiplication is associative and that they may do the multiplications in any order they wish, although most will choose to multiply the binomials as a first step.

Question 29: Encourage students to make a sketch for this question.

Question 30: Remind students that there are always two solutions to an equation of the form $x^2 + a = b$, when $a < b$. Emphasize that the solution of an equation includes all numbers from the domain that make the original sentence true.

Questions 33 and 34: These questions review geometric skills that will be used in Lesson 6-3.

ADDITIONAL ANSWERS

6. $8x^2 + 14xy + 3y^2$

7. $x^2 - x - 2$

8. $6 - 5y + y^2$

9. $x^2 + 2xy + y^2$

10. $x^2 - 2xy + y^2$

11. $25n^2 + 80np + 64p^2$

12. $a^2 - 16a + 64$

13. $4w^2 - 2w + \frac{1}{4}$

14. $x^2 - 2x + 2$

15. $(x - y)^2$
$= (x - y)(x - y)$
   Definition of 2nd power
$= (x - y)x - (x - y)y$
   Distributive Prop.
$= x^2 - yx - xy + y^2$
   Distributive Prop.
$= x^2 - 2xy + y^2$
   Commutative Prop. and
   Distributive Prop.

19. $\sqrt{(a - c)^2 + (b - d)^2}$

31.

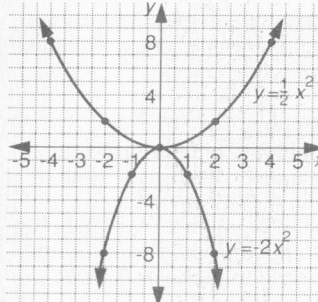

In 6–14, expand and simplify. **See margin.**

6. $(4x + y)(2x + 3y)$ **7.** $(x + 1)(x - 2)$ **8.** $(2 - y)(3 - y)$

9. $(x + y)^2$ **10.** $(x - y)^2$ **11.** $(5n + 8p)^2$

12. $(a - 8)^2$ **13.** $(2w - \frac{1}{2})^2$ **14.** $(x - 1)^2 + 1^2$

15. Prove the second part of the Binomial-Square Theorem. **See margin.**

16. Calculate:
   a. $|3|$ 3   **b.** $|-3|$ 3   **c.** $-|-3|$ -3   **d.** $-(-3)$ 3

17. When $x < 0$, $\sqrt{x^2} = \underline{\ ?\ }$. -x

18. When $x < 0$, $|x| = \underline{\ ?\ }$. -x

In 19–22, give the distance between the two points.

19. (a, b) and (c, d) **20.** $(8, 2)$ and $(-3, 2)$ 11
   See margin.
21. $(1, 5)$ and $(-1, -5)$ $\sqrt{104}$ **22.** $(0, 0)$ and $(5, 12)$ 13

23. If $\sqrt{(x - 3)^2} = |k|$, then $k = \underline{\ ?\ }$. x − 3 or 3 − x

24. Refer to the walkway around the swimming pool mentioned in this lesson. What is the area of the walkway? $140w + 4w^2$

In 25–27, expand.

25. $\frac{1}{2}n(n + 1)$, the sum of integers from 1 to n $\frac{1}{2}n^2 + \frac{1}{2}n$

26. $\frac{1}{6}x(x + 1)(2x + 1)$, the sum of the squares of the integers from 1 to x
                                            $\frac{1}{3}x^3 + \frac{1}{2}x^2 + \frac{1}{6}x$

27. $(x + y)^2 - (x - y)^2$ 4xy

28. Find the perimeter of the triangle with vertices at $(0, 0)$, $(0, 1)$, and $(2, 3)$. $1 + 2\sqrt{2} + \sqrt{13}$

29. On a brand-name pizza box, the directions read: "Spread dough to edges of pizza pan or onto a 10″ by 14″ rectangle on cookie sheet." How big a circular pizza could you make with this dough, assuming it is spread the same thickness as for the rectangular pizza?

30. Solve: $x^2 + 36 = 49$. $x = \sqrt{13}$ or $-\sqrt{13}$ $r = \sqrt{\dfrac{140}{\pi}} \approx 6.7$ inches

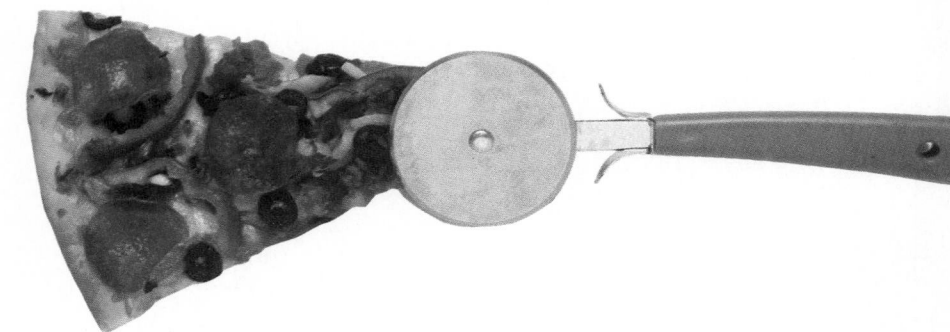

312

31. Graph $y = \frac{1}{2}x^2$ and $y = -2x^2$ on the same set of axes. *(Lesson 2-5)*
See margin.

32. Find an equation for line l which goes through $(5, 2)$ perpendicular to the line with equation $3x - 4y = 12$. *(Lesson 4-6)* $4x + 3y = 26$

33. Use the drawing below. Draw the segment whose length is the distance from point P to line l. *(Previous course)*   See margin.

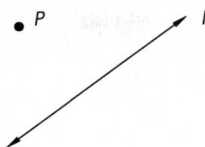

34. Copy the figure below.
  a. Draw or construct a line m through Q perpendicular to l.
  b. Find a point P on m so that $FQ = QP$. *(Previous course)*   See margin.

35. Let $A = \begin{bmatrix} 3 & 4 \\ -1 & 2 \end{bmatrix}$ and $B = \begin{bmatrix} 0.2 & -0.4 \\ 0.1 & 0.3 \end{bmatrix}$.
  a. Find AB. $\begin{bmatrix} 1 & 0 \\ 0 & 1 \end{bmatrix}$
  b. How are A and B related? *(Lesson 5-5)*   inverses

36. In classical times the problem of finding a square with the same area as a circle was called "squaring the circle" by the Greeks. Another problem they were interested in was called "duplicating a cube." Determine what this problem was.
Given a cube with volume V, find the side of a cube with volume 2V.

MORE PRACTICE
For more questions on SPUR Objectives, use *Lesson Master 6-1*, shown below.

33.

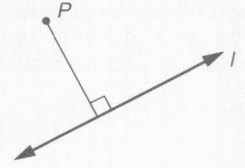

34.

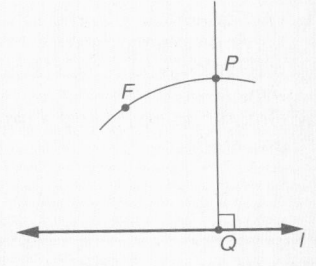

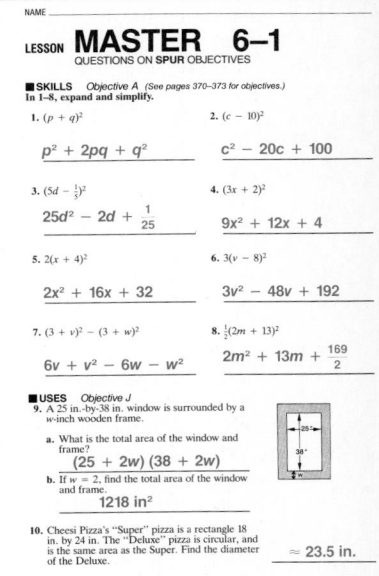

NAME _____

LESSON **MASTER   6–1**
QUESTIONS ON **SPUR** OBJECTIVES

■SKILLS   *Objective A   (See pages 370–373 for objectives.)*
In 1–8, expand and simplify.

1. $(p + q)^2$

$$p^2 + 2pq + q^2$$

2. $(c - 10)^2$

$$c^2 - 20c + 100$$

3. $(5d - \frac{1}{5})^2$

$$25d^2 - 2d + \frac{1}{25}$$

4. $(3x + 2)^2$

$$9x^2 + 12x + 4$$

5. $2(x + 4)^2$

$$2x^2 + 16x + 32$$

6. $3(v - 8)^2$

$$3v^2 - 48v + 192$$

7. $(3 + v)^2 - (3 + w)^2$

$$6v + v^2 - 6w - w^2$$

8. $\frac{1}{2}(2m + 13)^2$

$$2m^2 + 13m + \frac{169}{2}$$

■USES   *Objective J*
9. A 25 in.-by-38 in. window is surrounded by a w-inch wooden frame.

  a. What is the total area of the window and frame?
  $$(25 + 2w)(38 + 2w)$$
  b. If $w = 2$, find the total area of the window and frame.
  $$1218 \text{ in}^2$$

10. Cheesi Pizza's "Super" pizza is a rectangle 18 in. by 24 in. The "Deluxe" pizza is circular, and is the same area as the Super. Find the diameter of the Deluxe. ≈ 23.5 in.

LESSON 6-2

OBJECTIVES

I Use quadratic equations to solve problems dealing with velocity and acceleration.

K Graph parabolas and interpret them.

TEACHING NOTES

The move from the discrete graph in **Example 1** to the continuous graph may not be obvious. Explain to students why the curve is drawn through the points in the order from left to right. Ask students to find the values of h when $t = .5$, $t = 1.5$, $t = 2.5$, and so on.

Students may wonder how to determine where the parabola turns—that is, the location of its vertex. For now, they may estimate this point from the graph. The exact determination will be covered in Lesson 6-5. In this lesson, we expect students to estimate x-intercepts from the graph and to check by substitution that at this value of x, y equals 0. After studying the Quadratic Formula in Lesson 6-6, they should be able to determine the x-intercepts precisely.

Graphing $y = ax^2 + bx + c$

Should a thunderstorm travel 30 mph in an easterly direction for $2\frac{1}{2}$ hours, it will wind up 75 miles east of where it started. In general, if it travels at a velocity v for t hours, its distance d in miles from the start equals vt.

In the 17th century, Isaac Newton discovered that the same idea holds for objects thrown into the air or moving in space—but with an additional term needed. He found that if a ball is thrown straight up at a velocity of 44 feet per second (which is 30 mph), after t seconds it will go up

$$44t \text{ feet,}$$

except that a force he called *gravity* would reduce its height by $16t^2$ feet. Thus after t seconds, its height h in feet would be

$$44t - 16t^2 \text{ feet.}$$

If the thrower's hand was 5 feet above the ground when the ball was released, the height in feet above ground would be

$$44t - 16t^2 + 5.$$

We usually write this as $h = -16t^2 + 44t + 5$, with the powers of t in decreasing order. By substituting values for t, the height h can be found after any number of seconds. The pairs (t, h) can be graphed.

314

Example 1 If $h = -16t^2 + 44t + 5$,

    a. find h when $t = 0, 1, 2,$ and 3,

    b. graph the pairs (t, h), and

    c. interpret the graph in the situation of throwing a ball.

Solution

a. When $t = 0$, $h = 5$.

    When $t = 1$, $h = -16 \cdot 1^2 + 44 \cdot 1 + 5$

                   $= 33$.

    When $t = 2$, $h = -16 \cdot 2^2 + 44 \cdot 2 + 5$

                   $= 29$.

    When $t = 3$, $h = -7$.

b. The points are plotted at the right.

c. $(0, 5)$ means that at 0 seconds, the time of release, the ball is 5 feet above the ground. The solution $(1, 33)$ means the ball is 33 feet high after 1 second, and $(2, 29)$ means the ball is 29 feet high after 2 seconds (it is already on its way down). After 3 seconds, the value of h is 7 feet below ground level. Unless the ground is not level, it has already hit the ground.

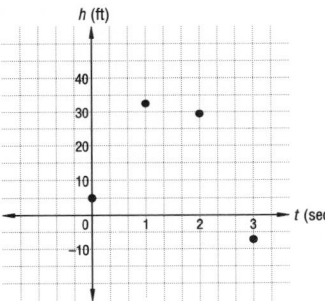

The points in Example 1 do not lie on a line and, in fact, do not tell much about the shape of the graph. More points are needed. By calculating h for other values of t, or letting a function grapher do the work, you can obtain a graph similar to the one below.

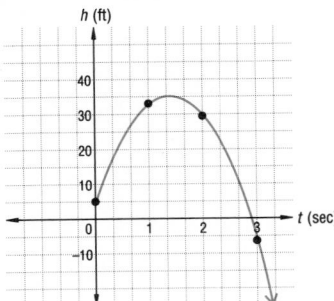

Note that the domain of the graph is the set of nonnegative real numbers.

LESSON 6-2 Graphing $y = ax^2 + bx + c$ **315**

1.a. From the graph of $h = -16t^2 + 44t + 5$ on page 315, estimate at what times the height of the ball is 20 ft.
approximately .4 and 2.4 seconds after being thrown
b. Use the formula and your calculator to determine the height of the ball one-half second after it was thrown.
23 feet

2. Suppose a toy rocket is launched so that its height h in meters after t seconds is given by $h = -4.9t^2 + 20t + 1.5$.
a. How high is the rocket after one second?
16.6 m
b. How high is the rocket when launched?
At launching, $t = 0$, so height is 1.5 m.
c. How high is the rocket after 12 seconds?
Since $t = 12$ gives $h = -464.1$, the rocket is no longer in the air. It has returned to the ground.

3. Graph $y = x^2 + 2x - 1$ for values between 3 and -3.

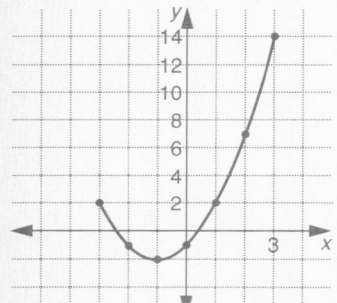

The graph is part of a parabola. In fact, if $h = -16t^2 + 44t + 5$ is graphed for all real numbers t, it is a translation image of the graph of $y = -16x^2$.

Two natural questions about the thrown ball are related to questions about this parabola: **1.** How high does the ball get? That asks for the largest possible value of h. From the graph, it seems to be about 35 feet. **2.** When does the ball hit the ground? That asks for the larger t-intercept of the graph. It is between 2 and 3, nearer 3. In later lessons, you will learn how to determine more precise answers to these questions.

Newton found a general formula for the height h of an object at time t with an initial upward velocity v_0 and initial height h_0. That formula is

$$h = -\tfrac{1}{2}gt^2 + v_0 t + h_0,$$

where g is the *gravitational constant,* also called the **acceleration due to gravity.** Recall that velocity is based on speed. It is the rate of change of distance with respect to time. Velocity involves units like miles per hour, feet per second, or meters per second. Acceleration measures how fast the velocity changes. This "rate of a rate" involves units like feet per second per second or meters per second^2. The acceleration due to gravity varies depending on how close the object is to the center of a massive object. Near the surface of the earth, the earth's gravitational constant is about 32 ft/sec^2 or 9.8 m/sec^2.

Caution! The equation

$$h = -\tfrac{1}{2}gt^2 + v_0 t + h_0$$

represents the height h of the ball at time t. It *does not* describe the path of the ball. However, the actual path of a ball thrown up into the air at any angle except straight up or straight down is almost parabolic, and an equation for the path is similar to the ones studied in this lesson.

Some parabolas have simpler equations. For instance, when a ball is dropped (not thrown downward), its initial velocity is 0. Thus $v_0 = 0$, and the formula $h = -\tfrac{1}{2}gt^2 + v_0 t + h_0$ becomes $h = -\tfrac{1}{2}gt^2 + h_0$.

■ ■ ■ ■ ■ ■ ■

Example 2   A ball is dropped from the top of a building 20 meters tall.
    a. Find an equation describing the relation between h, the ball's height above the ground, and time t.
    b. Graph its height h after t seconds.
    c. Estimate how much time it takes the ball to fall to the ground.

316

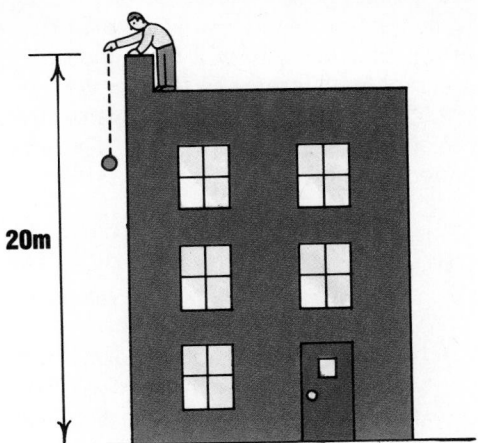

20m

Solution

a. Because the unit of height is meters, use $g = 9.8$ m/sec². The ball is dropped, so $v_0 = 0$. Because the ball started 20 meters up, $h_0 = 20$. So the height in this situation is determined by the equation

$$h = -\tfrac{1}{2}(9.8)t^2 + (0)t + 20$$

or $\qquad h = -4.9t^2 + 20.$

b. Negative values of t are not in the domain of t, so the graph is to the right of the vertical axis.

t	$h = -4.9t^2 + 20$
0	20
1	15.1
2	0.4
3	-24.1
0.5	18.775
1.5	8.975

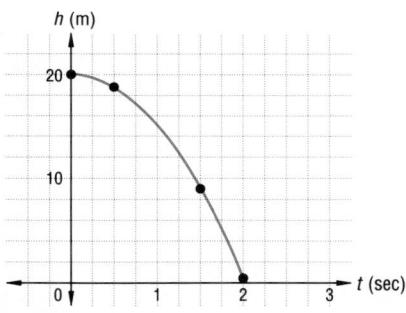

c. At $t = 2$ the ball is 0.4 m above the ground; at $t = 3$, according to the equation, the ball will be 24.1 m below ground. The ball hits the ground just after 2 seconds.

Notice that the rate of change of the curve becomes more and more negative as t increases from 0 to 2. This reflects the increasing speed of the ball as it falls.

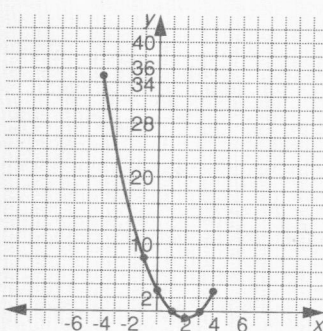
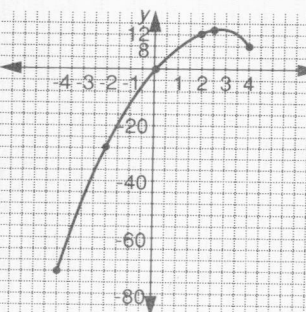
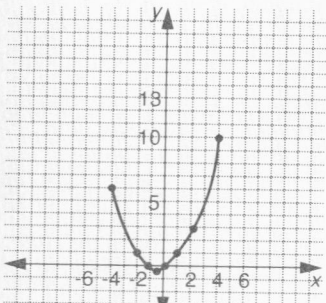
The equations $h = -16t^2 + 44t + 5$ and $h = -4.9t^2 + 20$ are of the form $y = ax^2 + bx + c$, a **quadratic equation** when $a \neq 0$. Later in this chapter, you will learn that the graph of $y = ax^2 + bx + c$ is a parabola congruent to the graph of $y = ax^2$. Recall that when $a < 0$ the graph of $y = ax^2$ opens down; when the coefficient $a > 0$, the parabola opens up. The graph of $h = -16t^2 + 28t + 3$ is congruent to the graph of $h = -16t^2$, so it opens down.

Example 3   Graph $y = x^2 - 3x + 2$ for values of x between -4 and 4.

Solution   Make a table of values by substituting for x and finding y. Adjust the scale on the y-axis so that the entire curve is included. Plot points by hand or use a function grapher.

x	y
-4	30
-3	20
-2	12
-1	6
0	2
1	0
2	0
3	2
4	6

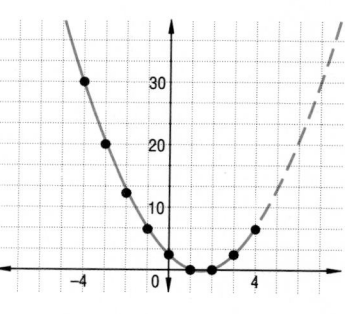

Check   The graph looks like the parabolic graph of $y = x^2$.

The parabola will continue as indicated by the dashed extension. The entire parabola, which extends forever, is reflection-symmetric. The line of symmetry in Example 3 is the vertical line with equation $x = 1\frac{1}{2}$, midway between the two points of intersection with the x-axis.

Questions

Covering the Reading

1. If an object travels at a velocity v for t seconds, how far will it go?
vt

In 2–4, use the equation $h = -\frac{1}{2}gt^2 + v_0t + h_0$.

2. Give the meaning of each of the following variables.   See margin.
a. h **b.** h_0 **c.** v_0 **d.** t **e.** g

3. If v_0 is measured in meters per second, what value of g should be used?   9.8 m/sec²

318

4. What is the value of v_0 if a ball is dropped?   0

In 5–7, refer to the graph of Example 1.

5. About how high is the ball after 2.5 seconds?   15 ft

6. When the ball hits the ground, the value of h is __?__.   0

7. About when will the ball be 15 feet from the ground? (There are two answers.) $t \approx \frac{1}{4}$ or $t \approx 2.5$

In 8 and 9, refer to Example 2.

8. What point corresponds to the time the ball is dropped?   (0, 20)

9. Tell whether the ball is above or below ground at $t = 2.1$. Justify your answer.   See margin.

10. In Example 3, (a) give an equation for the line of symmetry of the graph and (b) estimate the coordinates of the lowest point on the graph.   a) $x = \frac{3}{2}$ b) $\left(\frac{3}{2}, -\frac{1}{4}\right)$

In 11–14, graph the given equation for $-4 \le x \le 4$. If you use a function grapher, copy its graph onto your own paper.   See margin.

11. $y = x^2 - 4x + 3$

12. $y = -2x^2 + 10x$

13. $y = \frac{1}{2}x^2 + \frac{x}{2}$

14. $y = -\frac{x^2}{4} + 2$

Applying the Mathematics

15. A certain circus juggler throws a ball from her hand at a height of 1 m with an initial upward velocity of 10 meters per second.
    a. Write an equation to describe the height of the ball after t seconds. $h = -4.9t^2 + 10t + 1$
    b. How high will the ball be after 1 second?   6.1 m
    c. Graph the equation from part a.   See margin.
    d. Estimate the maximum height the ball reaches.
       about 6.1 m

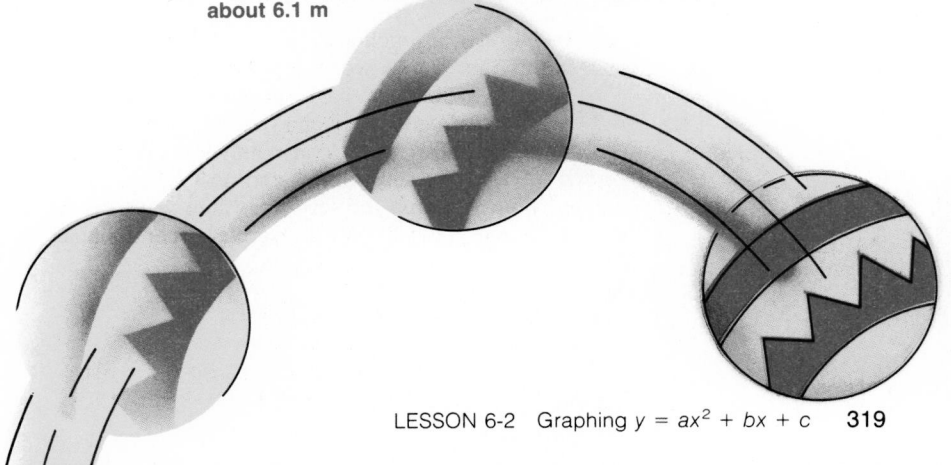

LESSON 6-2   Graphing $y = ax^2 + bx + c$ **319**

NOTES ON QUESTIONS
Question 16: If students have difficulty writing the equation for part (a), remind them of the meaning of the variables in the height formula. In this case, v_0, the initial velocity, is 0, and h_0, initial height, is 21,980 ft. In part (c), they should solve the equation for t when h, the height when he landed, is zero.

Question 17: Encourage students to use a diagram for this question. Although they have not yet been asked to find perimeter in a similar problem, if they can answer part (a), they will more likely be able to answer part (b) without difficulty.

Question 18: This is an order-of-operations question. Have students read some of the problem out loud if they are having difficulty. Compare and contrast similar problems. For example, (b) reads "the absolute value of the opposite of x," while (d) reads "the opposite of the absolute value of x."

14.

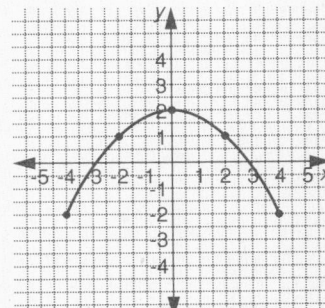

15.c.

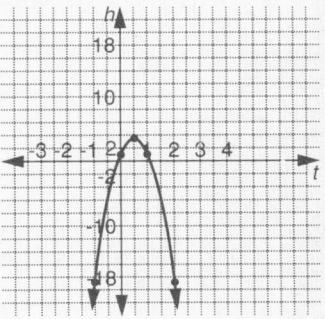

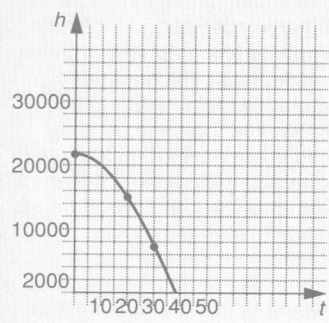
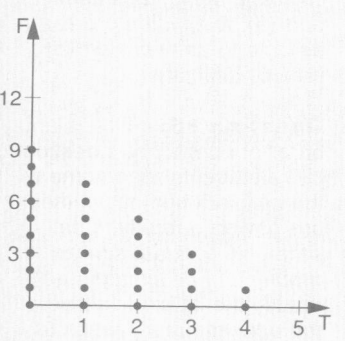
Review

16. I. M. Chisov of the USSR set a record in January 1942 for the highest altitude from which someone survived after bailing out of an airplane without a parachute. He bailed out at 21,980 feet. $h = -16t^2 + 21{,}980$
    a. Write an equation describing his height at t seconds.
    b. Graph the equation in part a. See margin.
    c. About how long did his fall take? ≈37 seconds

17. A picture frame w inches wide is to surround a picture that is 8″ by 12″. $96 + 40w + 4w^2$
    a. What is the area of the picture with its frame? *(Lesson 6-1)*
    b. What is the perimeter of the picture frame? *(Previous course)*
       $40 + 8w$

18. Evaluate for $x = -0.5$. *(Lesson 6-1)*
    a. $|x|$ 0.5   b. $|-x|$ 0.5   c. $-(-x)$ -0.5   d. $-|x|$ -0.5
    e. x^2 0.25   f. $(-x)^2$ 0.25   g. $\sqrt{x^2}$ 0.5   h. $-\sqrt{x^2}$ -0.5

19. Expand and simplify. *(Lesson 6-1)*
    a. $(x - 2)^2$ $x^2 - 4x + 4$ b. $3(x - 2)^2$ $3x^2 - 12x + 12$
    c. $3(x - 2)^2 - 12$ $3x^2 - 12x$

20. In football, a touchdown is worth 6 points, a field goal is worth 3 points, a safety is worth 2 points, and a point-after-touchdown (PAT) is worth 1 point. *(Lessons 3-3, 3-9, 2-5)* See margin.
    a. If a team gets T touchdowns, F field goals, S safeties, and P PATs, how many total points does it have?
    b. A team has no safeties and no PATs, and a total of at most 27 points. Graph the set of possible ways this could happen.
    c. Is the graph in part b discrete or continuous?

320

21. Given the feasibility region at the right, find the vertex at which $80x + 120y = P$ is maximized. *(Lesson 5-8)*   (15, 30)

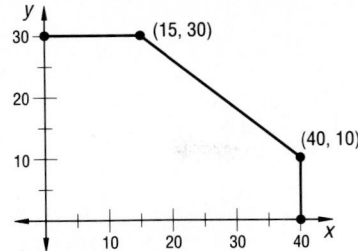

Exploration

22. Use this program, which generates values of quadratic expressions.

```
10 PRINT "VALUES OF Y = A * X ^ 2 + B * X + C"
20 INPUT "COEFFICIENTS A,B,C:"; A, B, C
30 PRINT "Y ="; A; "X ^ 2 +"; B; "X + "; C
40 PRINT "X", "Y"
50 FOR X = 0 TO 3 STEP 0.1
60    LET Y = A * X ^ 2 + B * X + C
70    PRINT X, Y
80 NEXT X
90 END
```

a. Use the program to generate the values of $y = -16x^2 + 44x + 5$ for the values of x from 0 to 3, increasing by 0.1. (Hint: For this equation, $A = -16$, $B = 44$, and $C = 5$.)

b. In part a, change the value of C from 5 to some other value. Run the program again and compare your results with those from part a. Relate the results you get to the situation of Example 1.

22a) The program prints a table with 31 ordered pairs (0, 5); (0.1, 9.24), (0.2, 13.16), ..., (3, -7).
22b) The x-values in the table will be the same as those in part a. The corresponding y-values will differ from those in part a by |5 − c|, where c is the number input in line 20. The graph of these (x, y) values will be an image of the graph in Example 1 under a vertical translation.

LESSON 6-2   Graphing $y = ax^2 + bx + c$ **321**

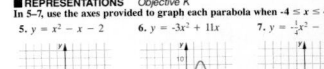
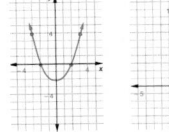
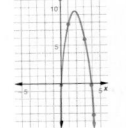

RESOURCES
■ Lesson Master 6-3
■ Quiz for Lessons 6-1
  Through 6-3
■ Visual for Teaching Aid 32
  can be used when dis-
  cussing the definition of a
  parabola.

OBJECTIVE

M Find points on a parabola
given its focus and
directrix.

TEACHING NOTES

Begin the lesson by asking
students to describe the set
of points equidistant from two
points. (the ⊥ bisector of the
segment joining them) Then
ask for the set of points equidistant from two parallel
lines. (the line parallel halfway between) This requires
knowing the distance be-
tween a point and a line.
Now ask: What is the set of
points equidistant from two
intersecting lines? (the bisec-
tors of the angles formed by
the lines) Then introduce the
parabola as the set of points
equidistant from a point and
a line.

An algorithm for finding
points on a parabola with
focus F and directrix l is
given in **Example 1**.
(1) Draw the line at a distance r from l on the same
side as F.
(2) Draw a circle with center
F and radius r. If r is large
enough, the line and circle
will intersect in two points
that are on the parabola. By
picking other values of r, as
many other points on the
parabola as desired can be
found.

The Parabola

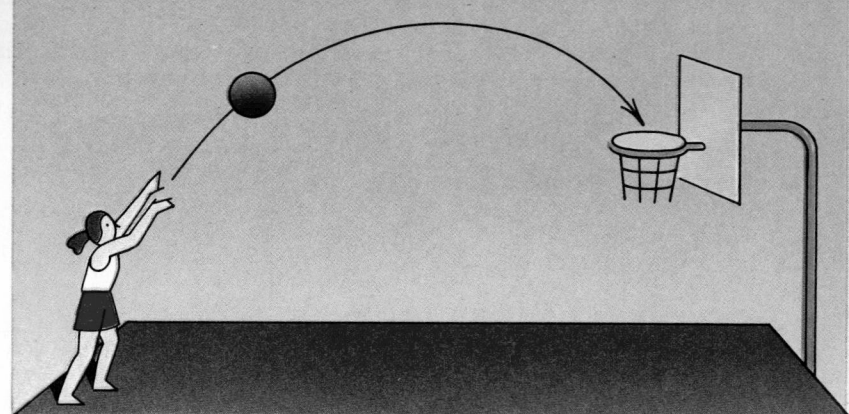

We have asserted that the path of a tossed object is a parabola. For
instance, the path of a basketball shot is part of a parabola from the
time it leaves the shooter's hands until it hits some other object.

In order to determine whether a curve is or is not a parabola, a
definition of **parabola** is necessary. Parabolas can be defined
geometrically.

Definition:

> Let ℓ be a line and F be a point not on ℓ. A parabola is the
> set consisting of every point in the plane of F and ℓ whose
> distance from F equals its distance from ℓ.

F is called the **focus** and ℓ the **directrix** of the parabola. Thus a
parabola is the set of points in a plane equidistant from its focus
and its directrix. Neither the focus nor directrix is on the parabola.
Below is a sketch of a parabola. Four points V, P_1, P_2, and P_3 are
identified on the parabola. Note that each is equidistant from the
focus F and the directrix ℓ.

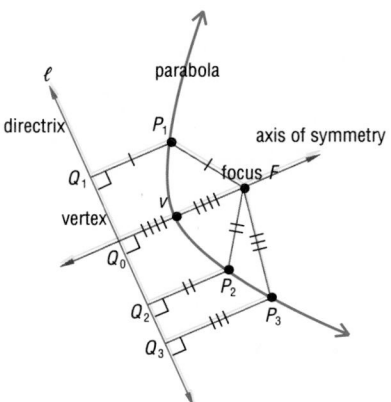

322

To understand the definition, you must remember that the distance from a point P to a line ℓ is the length of the perpendicular from P to ℓ. In the sketch, $\overline{P_1Q_1} \perp \ell$ and $P_1Q_1 = P_1F$. Also, $\overline{P_2Q_2} \perp \ell$ and $P_2Q_2 = P_2F$, and so on. The point V is special. It lies on the line from F perpendicular to line ℓ and is called the **vertex** of the parabola.

Example 1   Trace the figure. Find five points on the parabola with focus G and directrix m.

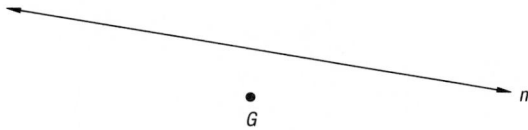

Solution   Five points V, P_1, P_2, P_3, and P_4 are shown.

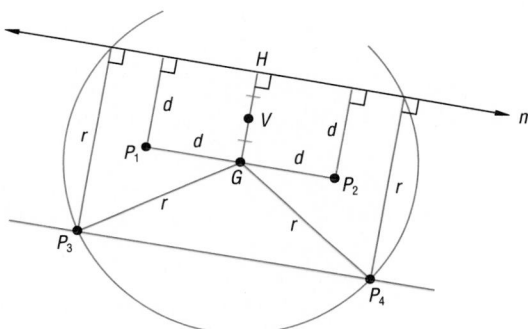

1. The vertex V is the midpoint of the perpendicular segment $\overline{GH}$ from G to m.
2. Points P_1 and P_2 are third vertices of squares with $\overline{GH}$ as one side. Each is the same distance d from G as from m.
3. To find P_3 and P_4, first draw a circle with center G and with any radius $r > \dfrac{d}{2}$. Then draw a line that is parallel to m and a distance r from it. The intersection of that line with the circle gives two points on the parabola.

To find other points, use circles with different radii (always $> \dfrac{d}{2}$).

The definition of a parabola is used to find an equation of a parabola in **Example 2**. Work through this solution with students as it is a difficult derivation.

ADDITIONAL EXAMPLES
1. Find an equation for the parabola with focus (0, -3) and directrix $y = 3$.

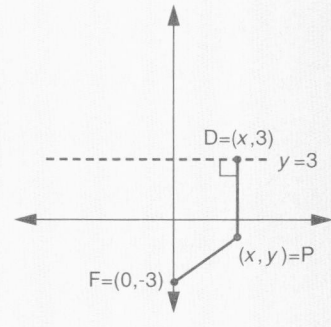

$y = -\frac{1}{12}x^2$

2. Verify that the point (60, -300) is equidistant from the focus and directrix in the above parabola.
Solution 1: Since (60, -300) satisfies $y = -\frac{1}{12}x^2$, it is equidistant from the focus and the directrix by the definition of a parabola.
Solution 2: Use the figure from the previous example. Let $P = (60, -300)$. Then $PF = 303 = PD$.

To find an equation for a parabola, the distance from a point to a line in the coordinate plane must be calculated. Notice that the distance d from (x, y) to the line $y = k$ is the distance from (x, y) to (x, k). By the distance formula,

$$d = \sqrt{(x - x)^2 + (y - k)^2}$$
$$= \sqrt{(y - k)^2}.$$

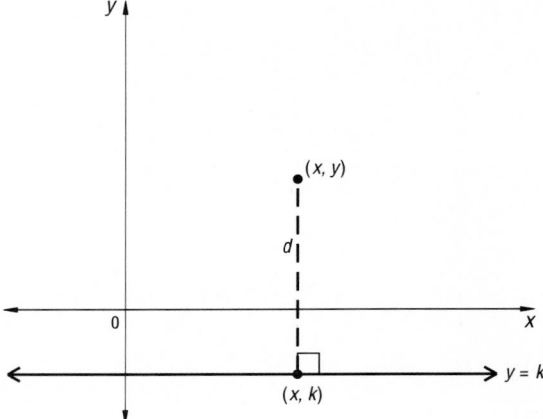

This idea is used in the next example, with $k = -5$.

■ ■ ■ ■ ■ ■ ■ ■

Example 2 Find an equation for the parabola with focus $(0, 5)$ and directrix $y = -5$.

Solution Draw a picture. Let $P = (x, y)$ be any point on the parabola. If $Q = (x, -5)$, then $PF = PQ$.

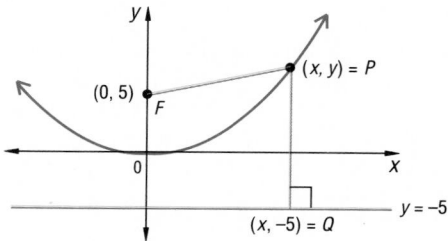

Definition of a parabola	$PF = PQ$
The Distance Formula	$\sqrt{(x - 0)^2 + (y - 5)^2} = \sqrt{(x - x)^2 + (y - -5)^2}$
Square both sides.	$x^2 + (y - 5)^2 = (y + 5)^2$
Expand.	$x^2 + y^2 - 10y + 25 = y^2 + 10y + 25$
Add $-y^2 - 25$ to both sides.	$x^2 - 10y = 10y$
Add $10y$ to both sides.	$x^2 = 20y$
Solve for y.	$y = \frac{1}{20}x^2$

324

Check We need to verify that a point on $y = \frac{1}{20}x^2$ is equidistant from $(0, 5)$ and $y = -5$. We use $A = (30, 45)$.

$$AF = \sqrt{(30 - 0)^2 + (45 - 5)^2} = \sqrt{30^2 + 40^2} = \sqrt{2500} = 50$$

The distance from A to $y = -5$ is the distance from $(30, 45)$ to $(30, -5)$, which is 50 also.

In Example 2, if you were to replace $(0, 5)$ by $(0, \frac{1}{4})$ and $y = -5$ by $y = -\frac{1}{4}$, the equation for the parabola would be $y = x^2$. If $(0, 5)$ is replaced by $\left(0, \dfrac{1}{4a}\right)$ and $y = -5$ is replaced by $y = -\dfrac{1}{4a}$, then the parabola has equation $y = ax^2$. The derivation for both of these follows the idea in Example 2 and demonstrates the following theorem.

Theorem:

The graph of $y = ax^2$ is a parabola.

When $a < 0$, you have learned that the parabola opens down. In that case the directrix is above the x-axis, the focus below.

If a parabola is rotated in space around its line of symmetry, the three-dimensional figure it creates is called a **paraboloid**. The focus of a paraboloid is the focus of the rotated parabola. Two examples are:

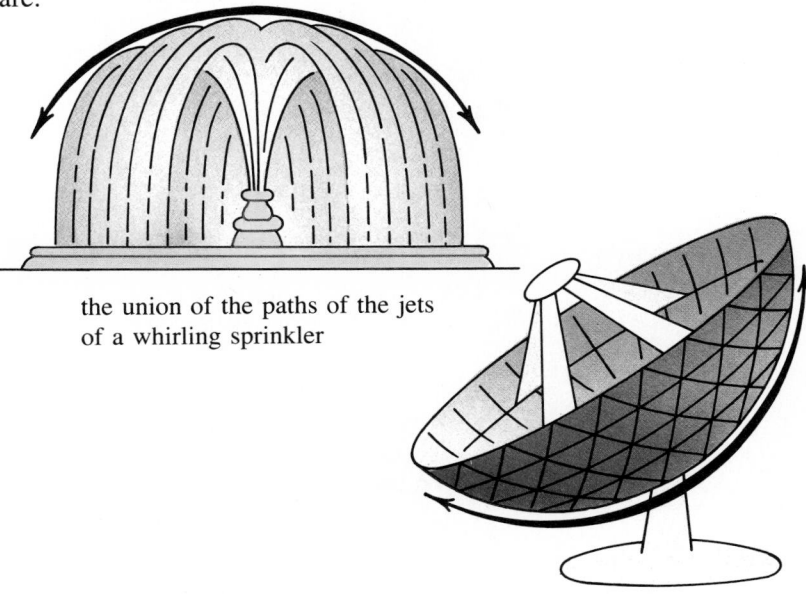

the union of the paths of the jets of a whirling sprinkler

a satellite receiving dish

LESSON 6-3   The Parabola   **325**

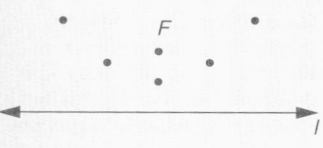
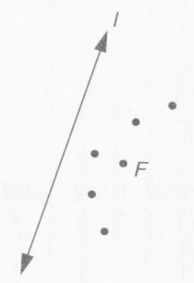
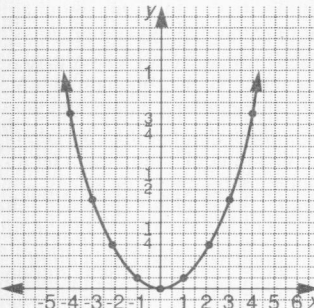
Questions

1. Define parabola.   See margin.

In 2 and 3, trace the figure and draw five points on the parabola with focus F and directrix ℓ.   See margin.

2.

3.

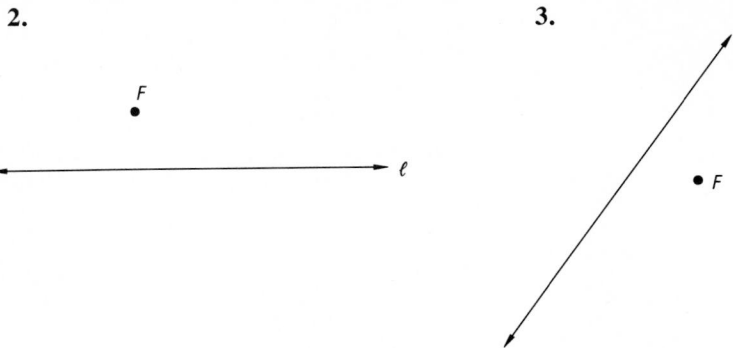

In 4–6, refer to the parabola below. F is its focus, ℓ its directrix.

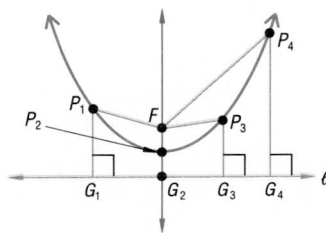

4. *True or false*
 a. $P_1F = P_3G_3$ False   **b.** $FP_4 = G_4P_4$ True

5. Name the vertex. P_2

6. Are the focus and directrix on the parabola?   No

7. a. Graph the parabola with equation $y = \frac{1}{20}x^2$.   See margin.
 b. Give its focus, vertex, and directrix.   See margin.
 c. Verify that the point (2, 0.2) is equidistant from the focus and directrix.   See margin.

8. Verify that the graph of $y = x^2$ is a parabola with focus $(0, \frac{1}{4})$ and directrix $y = -\frac{1}{4}$ by choosing a point on the graph and showing that two appropriate distances are equal.   See margin.

In 9–11, tell whether the parabola opens up or down.

9. $y = 4x^2$ up   **10.** $y = -4x^2$ down   **11.** $y = \frac{1}{4}x^2$ up

12. a. What is a paraboloid?   See margin.
 b. Give an example from the real world.   Satellite dish

326

326

In 13 and 14, use the information given in Question 8.

13. The graph of $y = x^2 + 3$ is a parabola congruent to and three units above the graph of $y = x^2$. What are the focus and directrix of $y = x^2 + 3$? **See margin.**

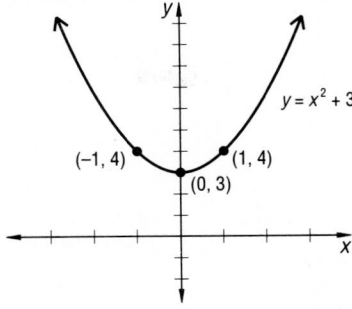

$y = x^2 + 3$

$(-1, 4)$ $(1, 4)$

$(0, 3)$

14. Give the focus, vertex, and directrix of the parabola with equation $y = -x^2$. **See margin.**

15. Given $F = (0, 2)$ and line ℓ with equation $y = -2$.
    a. What is an equation for the set of points equidistant from F and ℓ?
    b. Check your answer. **See margin.**

$y = \dfrac{x^2}{8}$

16. Consider the parabola with focus $F = (0, 3)$ and directrix $y = -3$.

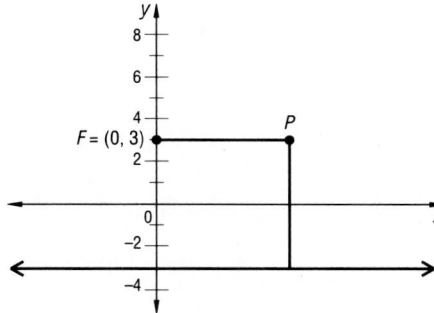

$F = (0, 3)$ P

a. What are the coordinates of its vertex? The drawing can help you. **(0, 0)**
b. A square has been drawn. The focus and a point P on the parabola are two vertices of the square. Find the coordinates of P. **(6, 3)**
c. Use symmetry to find the coordinates of another point on the parabola. **(-6, 3)**
d. Trace the figure and sketch the parabola. **See margin.**
e. Find an equation for this parabola. $y = \frac{1}{12}x^2$

13. Focus is $\left(0, 3\frac{1}{4}\right)$; directrix is $y = 2\frac{3}{4}$.

14. Focus is $\left(0, -\frac{1}{4}\right)$; vertex is $(0, 0)$; directrix is $y = \frac{1}{4}$.

15.b. $(4, 2)$ is on $y = \frac{x^2}{8}$.

The distance between $(0, 2)$ and $(4, 2)$ is 4, and the distance between $y = -2$ and $(4, 2)$ is 4.

16.d.

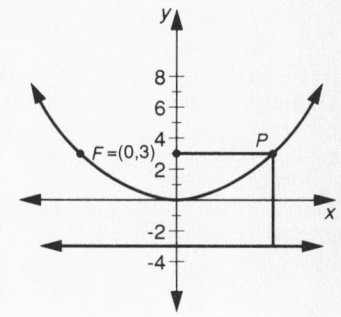

$F = (0,3)$ P

$y = \dfrac{x^2}{8}$

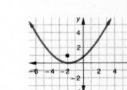
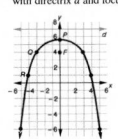
327

ADDITIONAL ANSWERS
17.a. $A = \pi(r + h)^2 - \pi r^2$
  $= 2\pi rh + \pi h^2$
b. C (large) $= 2\pi(r + h) =$
$2\pi r + 2\pi h$
C (small) $= 2\pi r.$ Then
$(2\pi r + 2\pi h) - (2\pi r) = 2\pi h$

18.a.

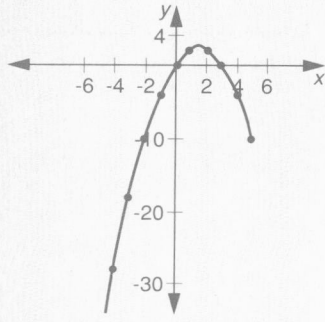

20.

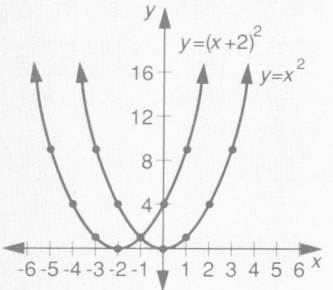

**21. See Additional
Answers in the back of this
book.**

25.a. *P* is the focus; the
bottom edge of the paper
is the directrix.
b. *Q* is the focus; the
bottom edge of the paper
is the directrix.

Review

17. Two concentric circles are shown at the right. The smaller has radius
r, and the larger has radius $r + h$.
    a. Find the area of the shaded region.   See margin.
    b. Prove that the circumference of the larger is $2\pi h$ more than the
       circumference of the smaller. *(Previous course, Lesson 6-1)*   See margin.

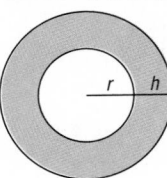

18. a. Graph $y = 3x - x^2$ for values of x between -5 and 5.   See margin.
    b. Estimate the coordinates of the vertex of the graph. *(Lesson 6-2)*
       $(1\frac{1}{2}, 2\frac{1}{4})$

19. The KTHI-TV transmitting tower between Fargo and Blanchard, North
    Dakota, is about 629 meters tall.
    a. If a hammer were dropped from the top, what will its height be
       after t seconds? $h = -4.9t^2 + 629$
    b. In about how many seconds would it hit the ground? *(Lesson 6-2)*
       11 seconds

In 20 and 21, graph both sentences by hand, by computer, or by graphing
calculator. Compare the graphs. *(Lesson 6-2)*

20. $y = x^2$ and $y = (x + 2)^2$ See margin.

21. $y = x^2 - 6$ and $y = (x - 5)^2 - 6$ See margin.

In 22–24, recall that for all real numbers a and b, $\sqrt{a}\sqrt{b} = \sqrt{ab}$. Use
this property to simplify each expression. *(Previous course)*

22. $\sqrt{3}\sqrt{12}$ 6   23. $\sqrt{20}\sqrt{50}$ $10\sqrt{10}$ 24. $(\sqrt{7})^2$ 7

Exploration

25. Parabolas can be formed without equations
    or graphs. Follow these steps to see how
    to make a parabola by folding paper.
    a. Take a sheet of unlined paper. Fold it
       in half as shown at the right. Cut or tear
       along the fold to make two congruent
       pieces. On one piece mark a point P
       about one inch above the center of the
       lower edge. Fold the paper so that the
       lower edge touches $P,$ and crease well
       as shown at the right. Repeat 10 to 15
       times, each time folding in a different
       direction. The creases represent the
       tangents to a parabola. What are its
       focus and directrix?   See margin.
    b. On the other piece of paper mark a point Q approximately in the
       center. Repeat the procedure used in part a. Where are the focus
       and directrix for this parabola?   See margin.
    c. The two parabolas formed in parts a and b illustrate the property
       that as the distance between the focus and the directrix __?__ , the
       parabola opens more slowly.   **increases**

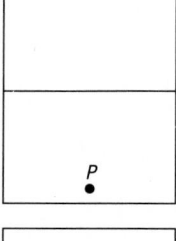

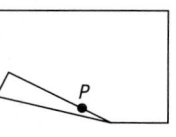

6-4

The Graph-Translation Theorem

LESSON 6-4

RESOURCES
■ Lesson Master 6-4
▣ Visual for Teaching Aid 33
  displays the parabola and
  its image for **Example 1**.
▣ Computer Master 10

The equation $x^2 = 9$ has two solutions, 3 and -3. Now consider the related equation

$$(x - 8)^2 = 9.$$

To solve this equation, a first idea might be to expand $(x - 8)^2$, but that is the hard way. The easier way is to take the square roots of each side. If $(x - 8)^2$, then there are four possibilities: $x - 8 = 3$, $x - 8 = -3$, $-(x - 8) = 3$, or $-(x - 8) = -3$. Two of the pairs are equivalent; so

$$x - 8 = 3 \text{ or } x - 8 = -3.$$

To solve these equations, add 8 to each side.

$$x = 11 \text{ or } x = 5$$

The solutions to $(x - 8)^2 = 9$ are larger by 8 than the solutions to $x^2 = 9$. This is to compensate for subtracting 8 in that equation. When the solutions are graphed on the number line, they are 8 units to the right. In other words, the solutions to $(x - 8)^2 = 9$ are the images of the solutions to $x^2 = 9$ under a translation 8 to the right.

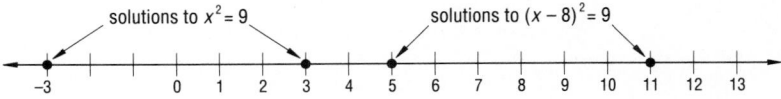

In general, the following theorem holds.

Theorem:

In a sentence to be solved for x, replacing x by $x - h$ increases the solutions by h.

OBJECTIVE

F Use the Graph-Translation Theorem to interpret equations and graphs.

TEACHING NOTES

Point out that the corollary to the Graph-Translation Theorem tells how to graph any parabola that is a translation image of $y = ax^2$ (which they learned to graph in Chapter 2). Emphasize that in the vertex form of a parabola, there are three important constants: h, k, and a. Because translations are isometries, the graphs of $y = ax^2$ and $y - k = a(x - h)^2$ are congruent, and a determines whether the parabola opens up or down and its "width."

There is no substitute for substitution. Go through **Example 1**. Find any point on $y = 3x^2$, for example, (-2, 12). Show that there is a corresponding point, for example, (4, 19) on the graph of the equation $y - 7 = 3(x - 6)^2$. Only with actual substitution does the Graph-Translation Theorem seem reasonable. Students should see that the subtraction of h and k compensates for the larger values that are substituted for x and y.

ADDITIONAL EXAMPLES

1. Sketch the graph of $y - 2 = -2(x + 3)^2$.

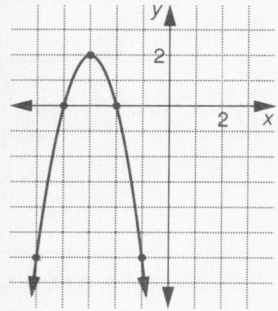

This is the image of $y = -2x^2$ under a translation 3 units to the left and 2 units up.

2. Sketch the image of $y + 3 = \frac{1}{2}x^2$.

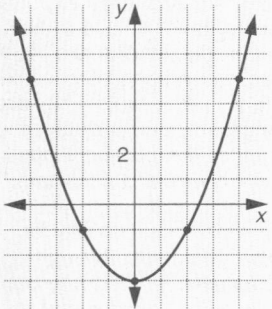

This is the graph of $y = \frac{1}{2}x^2$ translated 3 units down.

Remember that if h is negative, the translation can be viewed as being "negative right," which is left.

The direction of the translation may seem the reverse of what you expect. But consider the two parabolas $y = x^2$ and $y = (x - 8)^2$. The first has vertex $(0, 0)$. The second has vertex $(8, 0)$. The graph of $y = (x - 8)^2$ is a translation image of $y = x^2$, 8 units to the right. The graphs are congruent parabolas.

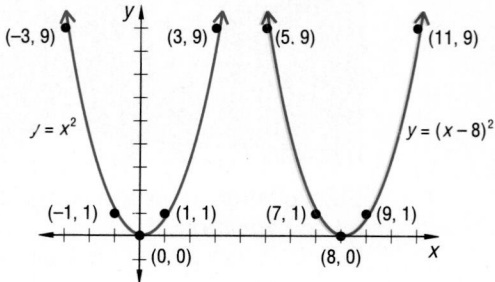

Translations of graphs up and down result from replacing y by $y - k$. For example, the equation

$$y - 3 = x^2$$

is equivalent to $y = x^2 + 3$. Its graph is 3 units above $y = x^2$. Again, if k is negative, then the translation is "negative up," which is down.

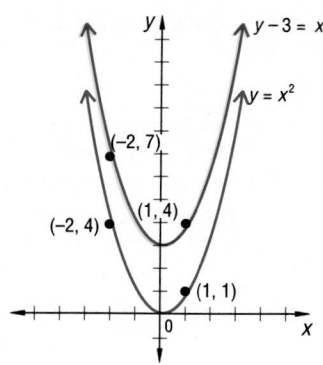

Translations can be done horizontally and vertically at the same time. The general idea is simple yet very powerful. Recall that the translation $T_{h,k}$ slides a figure h units to the right and k units up.

Graph-Translation Theorem:

In a sentence for a graph, replacing x by $x - h$ and y by $y - k$ causes the graph to undergo the translation $T_{h,k}$.

330

A **corollary** is a theorem that follows immediately from another theorem. The Graph-Translation Theorem has many corollaries.

Corollary:

The image of the parabola $y = ax^2$ under the translation $T_{h,k}$ is $y - k = a(x - h)^2$.

■ ■ ■ ■ ■ ■ ■ ■ ■ ■

Example 1   Sketch the graph of $y - 7 = 3(x - 6)^2$.

Solution   The graph is 6 units to the right and 7 units above $y = 3x^2$. So the graph is a parabola with vertex (6, 7). Because $y = 3x^2$ opens up, the parabola opens up. To find some other points start with the vertex and use symmetry. The x-value 1 unit to the left of the axis of symmetry is $x = 5$. Substitute $x = 5$ into the equation of the parabola to get $y = 10$. Then by symmetry a point 1 unit to the right of the axis of symmetry is (7, 10). In a similar manner you can verify that (4, 19) and (8, 19) are on the parabola. The graph is below.

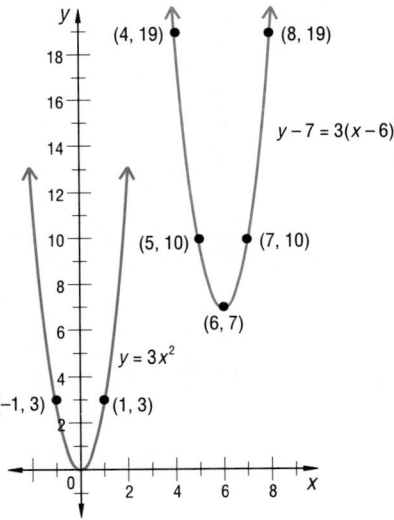

The equation $y - k = a(x - h)^2$ is the **vertex form of an equation for a parabola.** The parabola has vertex (h, k). If $a > 0$, then the parabola opens up and the graph has a minimum. If $a < 0$, then the parabola opens down and the graph has a maximum. When the equation for a parabola is in vertex form, the parabola can be graphed quickly.

NOTES ON QUESTIONS
Question 9:   When discussing this question, point out that the second equation is identical to the first except that x has been replaced by $x - 4$. This translates the solutions four units to the right, so the solutions to the second equation are four greater than those to the first. The students should be able to extend this idea to answer **Question 10.** In both questions, encourage students to check their answers by substitution.

Questions 12 and 13:   If an automatic grapher is available, use it to check students' answers.

Question 14:   This question extends the Graph-Translation Theorem to obtain the point-slope equation for a line.

Question 16a: If students have difficulty locating the vertex of the parabola, have them make a sketch. The vertex is halfway between the focus and the directrix.

331

MORE PRACTICE
For more questions on SPUR Objectives, use *Lesson Master 6-4*, shown on page 333.

EXTENSION
Present the following proof of the Graph-Translation Theorem:
$T_{h,k}: (x', y') = (x + h, y + k)$
Thus,
$x' = x + h$ and $y' = y + k$
from which
$x = x' - h$ and $y = y' - k$.
Stress to students that a relationship between x and y is known. They can substitute $x' - h$ for x and $y' - k$ for y. The result is a relationship involving the coordinates of the image points under this translation. The only reason we do not see the x' and y' in the image is that we customarily drop the prime symbols.

The Graph-Translation Theorem can be used frequently throughout the rest of *Advanced Algebra*. If, for instance, a student knows how to make a quick sketch of $y = \dfrac{36}{x}$. Then it is easy to make a sketch of
$y - 4 = \dfrac{36}{x} - 3$ using
this theorem.

ADDITIONAL ANSWERS
1.a. $x = 10$, $x = -10$
b. $x = 13$, $x = -7$

2.a. $y = \sqrt{6}$, $y = -\sqrt{6}$
b. $y = \sqrt{6} + 5$,
$y = -\sqrt{6} + 5$

3. The graph of $y = (x - 8)^2$ is a translation of $y = x^2$ eight units to the right.

7.d.

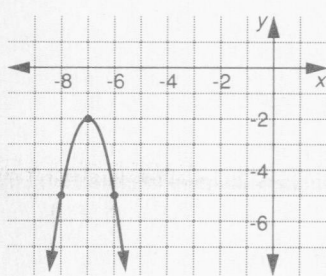

Example 2 Sketch the graph of $y = \frac{1}{2}(x + 2)^2$.

Solution Put the equation in vertex form: $y - 0 = \frac{1}{2}(x - -2)^2$. The graph is the parabola two units to the left of $y = \frac{1}{2}x^2$. Thus it opens upward, and its vertex is $(-2, 0)$. The minimum value is $y = 0$. Find other points by substituting values near -2 for x.

x	y
-2	0
-1	$\frac{1}{2}$
-3	$\frac{1}{2}$
0	2
-4	2

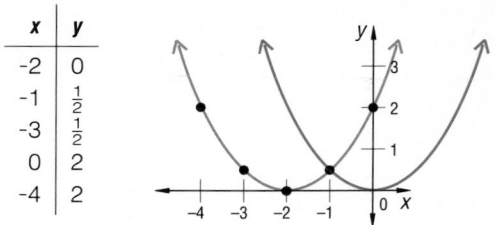

Check Use an automatic grapher to plot solutions to $y = \frac{1}{2}x^2$ and $y = \frac{1}{2}(x + 2)^2$ on the same set of axes.

Questions

Covering the Reading

1. Solve: **a.** $x^2 = 100$; **b.** $(x - 3)^2 = 100$.   See margin.

2. Solve: **a.** $y^2 = 6$; **b.** $(y - 5)^2 = 6$.   See margin.

3. How are the graphs of $y = x^2$ and $y = (x - 8)^2$ related?   See margin.

4. The graph of $y - k = a(x - h)^2$ is __?__ units above and __?__ units to the right of the graph of $y = ax^2$.   k, h

5. Refer to Example 1.
   a. The focus of $y = 3x^2$ is $(0, \frac{1}{12})$. What is the focus of
   $$y - 7 = 3(x - 6)^2?   (6, 7\frac{1}{12})$$

   b. The directrix of $y = 3x^2$ is $y = -\frac{1}{12}$. What is the directrix of
   $$y - 7 = 3(x - 6)^2?   y = 6\frac{11}{12}$$

6. **a.** The equation $y - k = a(x - h)^2$ is in the __?__ form of an equation for a parabola.   vertex
   b. The vertex is __?__.   (h, k)

7. Use the equation $y + 2 = -3(x + 7)^2$.
   a. Give the coordinates of the vertex.   (-7, -2)
   b. Give an equation for the axis of symmetry.   x = -7
   c. Tell whether the parabola opens up or down.   down
   d. Graph the solution set to the equation.   See margin.

8. Suppose the parabola with equation $y = 2x^2$ undergoes the translation $T_{2,-3}$. Find an equation for its image. $y + 3 = 2(x - 2)^2$

9. One solution to $x^2 + 5x + 3 = 87$ is 7. Use that information to get a solution to $(x - 4)^2 + 5(x - 4) + 3 = 87$. $x = 11$

10. One solution to $39x - 21y = 1200$ is (41, 19). Use this information to get a solution to $39(x - 5) - 21(y - 3) = 1200$.   (46, 22)

11. Solve: **a.** $|z| = 34$ $z = \pm34$ **b.** $|z + 1| = 34$ 33 or -35.

12. The parabola graphed at the right is congruent to $y = 3x^2$ and has vertex (-2, 2). What is an equation for it?
$y - 2 = 3(x + 2)^2$.

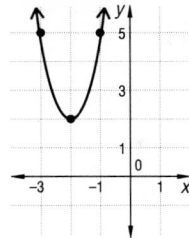

13. A parabola has vertex (2, -5) and opens down. If the parabola is congruent to $y = 7x^2$, what is an equation for the parabola?
$y + 5 = -7(x - 2)^2$

14. The point-slope form of a line, $y - y_1 = m(x - x_1)$, can be thought of as the image of the line with equation ___?___ under the translation $T_{a,b}$, where $a = $ ___?___ and $b = $ ___?___. $y = mx, x_1, y_1$

15. Define: parabola. *(Lesson 6-3)*   See margin.

16. A parabola has focus (0, 1) and directrix $y = -1$.
  a. What is its vertex?   (0, 0)
  b. State whether the vertex is a maximum or a minimum.   minimum
  c. Give the coordinates of two other points on the parabola. *(Lesson 6-3)*   (2, 1), (-2, 1)

17. Expand.   See margin.
  a. $(x + 4)^2$ **b.** $2(x + 4)^2$ **c.** $2(x + 4)^2 + 3$ *(Lesson 6-1)*

18. A rectangular lot 100' by 60' is in a town that allows no building closer than 2 feet to the edge of a lot.
  a. How much room is there to build?   5376 sq ft
  b. If no building closer than x feet were allowed, how much room would be left? *(Lesson 6-1)* $6000 - 320x + 4x^2$

19. It takes $\frac{1}{2}n(n - 1)$ handshakes for each of n people at a party to shake hands with everyone else. Expand this expression. *(Lesson 1-5)* $\frac{1}{2}n^2 - \frac{1}{2}n$

20. The parabola with equation $x = y^2$ is graphed at the right.   See margin.
  a. Give the coordinates of five points on this parabola.
  b. Graph its image under the translation $T_{3,-1}$.
  c. Write an equation for the image.
  d. Does the Graph-Translation Theorem hold for parabolas that open to the side?

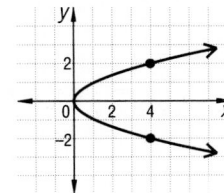

---

15. A parabola is the set of all points in the plane which are equidistant from a line *l* and a point *F* not on that line.

17.a. $x^2 + 8x + 16$
b. $2x^2 + 16x + 32$
c. $2x^2 + 16x + 35$

20.a. (0, 0), (1, 1), (1, -1), (4, 2), (4, -2)
b.

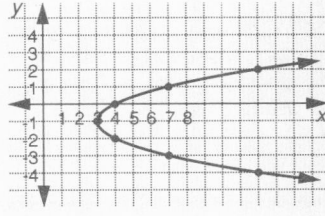

c. $x - 3 = (y + 1)^2$
d. yes

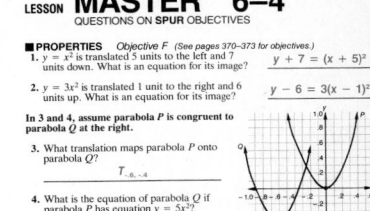
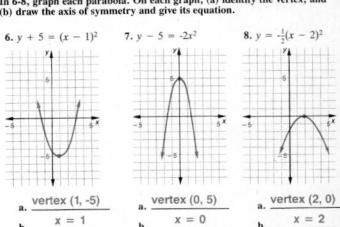
333

OBJECTIVE

B Transform quadratic equations from vertex form to standard form, and vice versa.

TEACHING NOTES

Begin the lesson by having students guess the number that needs to be added to an expression in the form $x^2 + bx$ in order to complete the square. Some binomials that can be used are $x^2 + 8x$, $x^2 - 2x$, or $x^2 + 30x$. Most students will begin to see the pattern. Ask students to verbalize the pattern by giving the term needed to complete $x^2 + 7x$. The odd coefficient of x will force students to isolate the steps in the method they are using to find the term $\left(\frac{b}{2}\right)^2$.

The complete-the-square method is applied in **Example 3**. Explain that this method changes the form of an equation that is relatively difficult to graph by hand to an equivalent form that is easier to graph with the Graph-Translation Theorem. Note that most function graphers can plot $y = ax^2 + bx + c$ and $y = a(x - h)^2 + k$ equally easily.

LESSON

Completing the Square

You have now seen two forms for an equation of a parabola.

$$y = ax^2 + bx + c \quad \text{expanded form}$$
$$y - k = a(x - h)^2 \quad \text{vertex form}$$

The vertex form, as its name suggests, shows the vertex and so gives the maximum or minimum point on the parabola. In the next lesson, you will learn that the expanded form is more convenient for finding the intercepts of the graph. Because each form is useful, converting from one form to the other is helpful.

Example 1 Convert $y - 3 = 4(x + 6)^2$ to expanded form.

Solution Expand the binomial.

$$y - 3 = 4(x^2 + 12x + 36)$$
$$= 4x^2 + 48x + 144$$

So $\qquad y = 4x^2 + 48x + 147.$

To convert from expanded form to vertex form, a process known as **completing the square** is used. Remember that

$$(x + h)^2 = x^2 + 2hx + h^2.$$

The trinomial $x^2 + 2hx + h^2$ is called a **perfect-square trinomial.**

Example 2 What number should be added to $x^2 + 10x$ to make a perfect-square trinomial?

Solution Compare $x^2 + 10x + \underline{\ ?\ }$ with the perfect-square trinomial $x^2 + 2hx + h^2$. The first terms, x^2, are identical. To make the second terms equal, set

$$10x = 2hx.$$

So $\qquad h = 5.$

The term added should be h^2 or 25.

Check $x^2 + 10x + 25 = (x + 5)^2.$

334

To generalize Example 2, consider the expression

$$x^2 + bx + \underline{\ ?\ }.$$

What must be put in the blank so the result is a perfect-square trinomial?

$$x^2 + bx + \underline{\ ?\ } = x^2 + 2hx + h^2$$

Since $b = 2h$, $h = \frac{1}{2}b$. Then $h^2 = (\frac{1}{2}b)^2$. This proves:

Theorem:

To complete the square on $x^2 + bx$, add $(\frac{1}{2}b)^2$.

Now you are ready to find the vertex of a parabola from its expanded-form equation.

Example 3 Find the vertex of the parabola with equation $y = x^2 + 10x + 8$.

Solution
Step 1) Rewrite the equation so that only terms with x are on one side.

$$y - 8 = x^2 + 10x + \underline{\ ?\ }$$

Step 2) Complete the square on x. Here $b = 10$, so $(\frac{1}{2}b)^2 = 25$.
Step 3) Add 25 to both sides. $y - 8 + 25 = x^2 + 10x + 25$
Step 4) Put in vertex form. $y + 17 = (x + 5)^2$
The vertex of the parabola is $(-5, -17)$.

Check If the graph has vertex $(-5, -17)$, the parabola can be sketched. Now let $x = -4$. Then

$$y = (-4)^2 + 10 \cdot -4 + 8 = -16.$$

If $x = -6$, $y = -16$ also. This indicates that $(-5, -17)$ is the lowest point on the parabola.

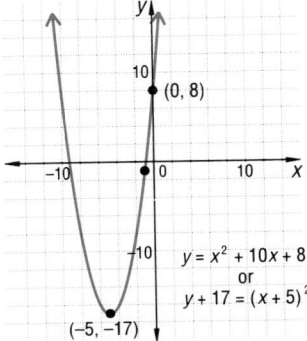

$$y = x^2 + 10x + 8$$
or
$$y + 17 = (x + 5)^2$$

Completing the square on an expression whose x^2 coefficient is not 1 is difficult for some students. Work through **Example 4** slowly, and guide students through a few more problems of this type. The form used in this example parallels the form used to complete the square in the proof of the quadratic formula in Lesson 6-7.

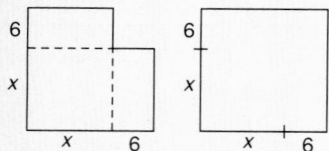
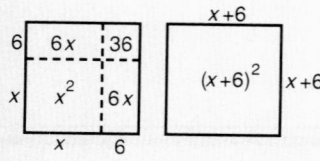
Example 2 and Example 3 indicate how to complete the square on an expression of the form $x^2 + bx$, where the coefficient of x^2 is 1. If the coefficient of x^2 is not 1, two extra steps are needed.

▪ ▫ ▪ ▫ ▪ ▪ ▪▪

Example 4   Find the vertex of the parabola with equation $y = 2x^2 - 5x - 9$.

Solution   Again complete the square.

1. Add 9 to both sides, as before, to remove a constant term from the right side.

$$y + 9 = 2x^2 - 5x$$

2. Divide both sides of the equation by 2, the coefficient of x^2.

$$\frac{y + 9}{2} = x^2 - \frac{5}{2}x$$

3. Complete the square on the right side. Here $b = -\frac{5}{2}$, so $\left(\frac{b}{2}\right)^2 = (-\frac{5}{4})^2 = \frac{25}{16}$. This number must be added to both sides.

$$\frac{y + 9}{2} + \frac{25}{16} = x^2 - \frac{5}{2}x + \frac{25}{16}$$
$$\frac{y + 9}{2} + \frac{25}{16} = \left(x - \frac{5}{4}\right)^2$$

4. It looks complicated, but do not fear! Multiply both sides by the same number 2 you divided by in step 2. This makes the coefficient of y again equal to 1.

$$y + 9 + \frac{25}{8} = 2(x - \frac{5}{4})^2$$

5. Put the equation into vertex form.

$$y + \frac{97}{8} = 2(x - \frac{5}{4})^2$$

6. Read the vertex from the vertex form. The vertex is $(\frac{5}{4}, -\frac{97}{8})$.

Check 1   Substitute $\frac{5}{4}$ for x in the original equation. Does $y = -\frac{97}{8}$?

$$2(\tfrac{5}{4})^2 - 5 \cdot \tfrac{5}{4} - 9 = 2 \cdot \tfrac{25}{16} - \tfrac{25}{4} - 9$$
$$= \tfrac{25}{8} - \tfrac{25}{4} - 9$$
$$= \tfrac{25}{8} - \tfrac{50}{8} - \tfrac{72}{8}$$
$$= -\tfrac{97}{8}$$

If the vertex is at $x = \frac{5}{4}$, then $x = 1$ and $x = 1.5$ should give the same values of y. Try them.

Check 2   Graph the parabola. This is left for you to do also.

336

Completing the square helps to find key points on graphs involving quadratic expressions. Its most important application is in the proof of the Quadratic Formula, which you shall see in the next lesson.

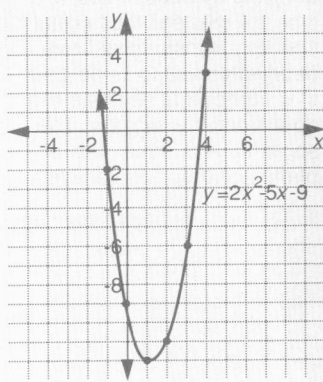

Questions

Covering the Reading

In 1–4, convert the equation to expanded form.

1. $y = (x + 3)^2 + 2$
$y = x^2 + 6x + 11$

2. $y = \left(x - \dfrac{b}{2}\right)^2$ $y = x^2 - bx + \dfrac{b^2}{4}$

3. $y = 2(x - 4)^2 - 1$
$y = 2x^2 - 16x + 31$

4. $\dfrac{y}{6} = (x + \frac{1}{2})^2$ $y = 6x^2 + 6x + \frac{3}{2}$

In 5–7, find a number to put in each blank to make each expression a perfect-square trinomial.

5. $x^2 + 18x +$ __?__   **6.** $z^2 - 3z +$ __?__ $\frac{9}{4}$ **7.** $x^2 + bx +$ __?__ $\dfrac{b^2}{4}$
81

In 8–11, find the vertex of the parabola represented by each equation.

8. $y = x^2 + 18x + 6$
(-9, -75)

9. $y = x^2 - 3x + 1$ $(\frac{3}{2}, -\frac{5}{4})$

10. $y = 2x^2 - 6x + 4$ $(\frac{3}{2}, -\frac{1}{2})$

11. $y = 3x^2 + 4x + 5$ $(-\frac{2}{3}, \frac{11}{3})$

Applying the Mathematics

12. Finish Check 2 of Example 4.   See margin.

13. a. Find the vertex of the parabola $h = -16t^2 + 44t + 5$ graphed in Lesson 6-2. $(\frac{11}{8}, \frac{141}{4})$
b. What is the maximum height of the ball?   35.25 feet

14. What term must be added to the expression $a^2 + 7ay +$ __?__ to make a perfect square? $\dfrac{49y^2}{4}$

15. A student stated that $y^2 - 6y + 9 = (y - 3)^2$. Another student stated that $y^2 - 6y + 9 = (3 - y)^2$. Their teacher stated that both students were correct. Explain this mystery. $(y - 3)^2 = (3 - y)^2$

16. a. Give the sum of the areas of the three rectangles. $x^2 + 12x$
b. What number must be added to this sum to complete the square?   36
c. Interpret your answer to part b geometrically.   See margin.

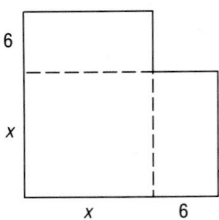

Review

In 17–19, solve. *(Previous course, Lesson 6-4)*   **See margin.**

17. $(x + 16)^2 = 36$ **18.** $y^2 + 16 = 36$ **19.** $(z - 5)^2 = 2$

In 20 and 21, refer to the graph of a bird's flight shown below. *(Lesson 3-8)*

20. When was the bird on the ground?   **See margin.**

21. What was the bird's average speed during its first descent?   **200 ft/min**

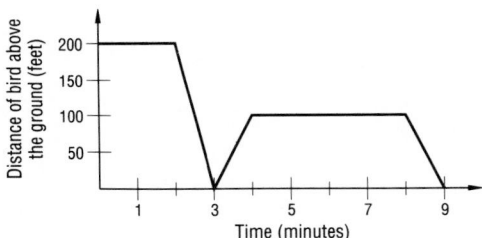

22. Graphed at the right is $y = x^2$ and its directrix $y = -\frac{1}{4}$.
   a. What are the coordinates of the focus F? $(0, \frac{1}{4})$
   b. Calculate $d_1, d_2, d_3,$ and d_4. *(Lesson 6-3)*   **See margin.**

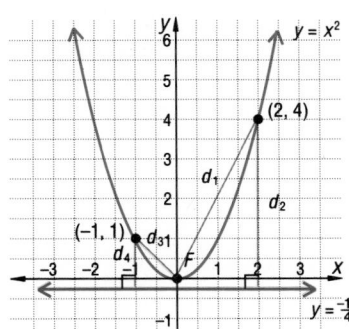

In 23–25, is the statement true or false? *(Previous course)*

23. $\sqrt{40,000} = 200$ **24.** $\sqrt{50} = 5\sqrt{10}$ **25.** $\sqrt{48} = 4\sqrt{3}$

26. *ABCD* is a square of sides $a + b + c$. The areas of three regions inside have been given.
   a. Find the areas of the other six rectangles.
   b. Use the drawing to expand $(a + b + c)^2$.
   c. Show a drawing to expand $(a + b + c + d)^2$.
   d. Generalize parts b and c.

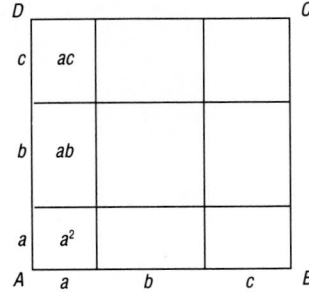

FOLLOW-UP

MORE PRACTICE
For more questions on SPUR Objectives, use *Lesson Master 6-5*, shown below.

EXTENSION
Exploration **Question 26** can be extended by having students substitute *a*, *b*, and *c* to expand expressions such as $(3x - 4y + 5)^2$.

NAME _____

LESSON **MASTER   6–5**
QUESTIONS ON **SPUR** OBJECTIVES

■**SKILLS**   *Objective B   (See pages 370–373 for objectives.)*
In 1–3, transform each equation into expanded form.

1. $y = 5(x - 2)^2 + 18$ **2.** $y - 6 = -3(x + 9)^2$ **3.** $y + 2 = \frac{1}{2}(x - 12)^2$

$y = 5x^2 - 20x + 38$ $y = -3x^2 - 54x - 237$ $y = \frac{1}{2}x^2 - 12x + 70$

In 4–7, transform each equation into vertex form.

4. $y = x^2 - 12x + 1$ **5.** $y = x^2 - 7x + 5$

$y + 35 = (x - 6)^2$ $y + \frac{29}{4} = (x - \frac{7}{2})^2$

6. $y = 3x^2 - 12x - 10$ **7.** $15y = 5x^2 - 30x - 21$

$y + 22 = 3(x - 2)^2$ $15y + 66 = 5(x - 3)^2$

In 8–11, match each equation with its equivalent.

8. $y = x^2 - 6x + 11$ ___IV___   **I.** $y + 3 = -(x + 1)^2$
9. $y - 4 = 2(x - 2)^2$ ___II___   **II.** $y = 2x^2 - 8x + 12$
10. $y + \frac{21}{4} = (x + \frac{5}{2})^2$ ___III___   **III.** $y = x^2 + 5x + 1$
11. $y = -x^2 - 2x - 4$ ___I___   **IV.** $y - 2 = (x - 3)^2$

Advanced Algebra © Scott, Foresman and Company   **69**

RESOURCES
■ Lesson Master 6-6
■ Quiz for Lessons 6-4
   Through 6-6
▣ Visual for Teaching Aid 34
   can be used to introduce
   the Quadratic Formula and
   to discuss Additional Ex-
   ample 3.
▣ Visual for Teaching Aid 35
   displays the proof of the
   Quadratic Formula.

OBJECTIVE

D Solve quadratic equations
using the Quadratic For-
mula.

TEACHING NOTES

When discussing the
Quadratic-Formula Theorem,
emphasize that one side of
the equation must be zero.
This discourages students
from incorrectly misapplying
the formula.

Since most students have
studied this theorem in previous courses, expect them to
follow the proof in this lesson
and to memorize the theorem
quickly.

Stress that the $\pm$ sign in the
formula means that there are
possibly two solutions. Encourage students to separate
the solutions as is done in
the examples for this lesson.

This lesson provides a good
opportunity to review how to
simplify square root ex-
pressions and to help
students use their calculators
efficiently.

LESSON

6-6

The Quadratic Formula

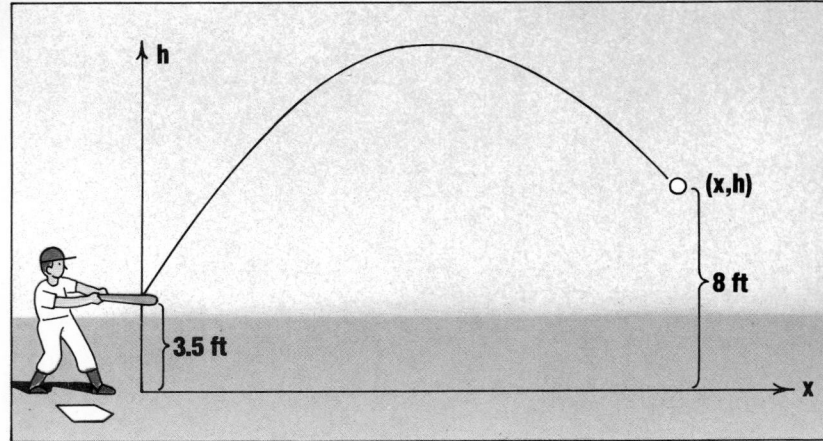

Pop Fligh, the famous baseball player, hits a pitch that is 3.5 ft
high. The ball travels towards the outfield along a nearly parabolic
path, described by the equation

$$h = -.005x^2 + 2x + 3.5,$$

where x is the distance (in feet) of the ball from home plate, and h
is the height (in feet) of the ball at that instant. When is the ball 8
feet high?

Because we wish to know the horizontal distance x when the height
is 8, substitute 8 for h in the above equation.

$$8 = -.005x^2 + 2x + 3.5$$

By adding -8 to each side, the equation is put in standard form
$ax^2 + bx + c = 0$.

$$0 = -.005x^2 + 2x - 4.5$$

This equation can be solved by rewriting it in vertex form, but the
arithmetic is messy. It is much easier to solve the general equation
$ax^2 + bx + c = 0$. The result is called the **Quadratic Formula**.
This formula is very important—*you must memorize it*. The Quadratic
Formula is a theorem; that is, it can be proved from the basic
properties of algebra.

Quadratic-Formula Theorem:

If $ax^2 + bx + c = 0$ and $a \neq 0$, then $x = \dfrac{-b \pm \sqrt{b^2 - 4ac}}{2a}$.

The proof of the Quadratic Formula requires completing the square.

340

340

Proof

Given is the equation $ax^2 + bx + c = 0$, where $a \neq 0$.

1. Divide both sides by a so the coefficient of x^2 is 1. On the right side, $\frac{0}{a} = 0$.

$$x^2 + \frac{b}{a}x + \frac{c}{a} = 0$$

2. Add $-\frac{c}{a}$ to each side.

$$x^2 + \frac{b}{a}x = -\frac{c}{a}$$

3. To complete the square, add $\left(\frac{1}{2} \cdot \frac{b}{a}\right)^2$ to both sides.

$$x^2 + \frac{b}{a}x + \frac{b^2}{4a^2} = \frac{b^2}{4a^2} - \frac{c}{a}$$

4. Write the left side as a binomial squared.

$$\left(x + \frac{b}{2a}\right)^2 = \frac{b^2}{4a^2} - \frac{c}{a}$$

5. Add the fractions on the right side.

$$\left(x + \frac{b}{2a}\right)^2 = \frac{b^2 - 4ac}{4a^2}$$

6. Take the square root of each side.

$$x + \frac{b}{2a} = \frac{\pm\sqrt{b^2 - 4ac}}{2a}$$

7. Add $-\frac{b}{2a}$ to both sides.

$$x = \frac{-b \pm \sqrt{b^2 - 4ac}}{2a}$$

Example 1   Solve $3x^2 + 11x - 4 = 0$.

Solution   The Quadratic Formula lets you solve any quadratic equation. Here $a = 3$, $b = 11$, and $c = -4$.

$$x = \frac{-b \pm \sqrt{b^2 - 4ac}}{2a}$$
$$= \frac{-11 \pm \sqrt{11^2 - 4 \cdot 3 \cdot -4}}{2 \cdot 3}$$
$$= \frac{-11 \pm \sqrt{121 - -48}}{6}$$
$$= \frac{-11 \pm \sqrt{169}}{6}$$
$$= \frac{-11 \pm 13}{6}$$

The $\pm$ sign here means there are two solutions, one with the $+$ sign, one with the $-$ sign.

$$x = \frac{-11 + 13}{6} \quad \text{or } x = \frac{-11 - 13}{6}$$

So $\qquad\qquad x = \frac{1}{3} \qquad\qquad$ or $x = -4$

Check   Each solution should be checked.
Does $3 \cdot (\frac{1}{3})^2 + 11 \cdot \frac{1}{3} - 4 = 0$? Yes, $\frac{1}{3} + \frac{11}{3} - 4 = 0$.
Does $3 \cdot (-4)^2 + 11 \cdot -4 - 4 = 0$? Yes, $48 - 44 - 4 = 0$.

Computer   Use an automatic grapher to plot solutions to the equation $h = .005x^2 + 2x + 3.5$ for Pop Fligh's ball. A convenient window is $0 \leq x \leq 400$; $0 \leq y \leq 250$. By zooming or rescaling, illustrate the geometric interpretation to **Example 3**.

ADDITIONAL EXAMPLES
1. Solve $10x^2 - 13x - 3 = 0$.
$x = \frac{3}{2}$ or $x = -\frac{1}{5}$

2. Accounting for a driver's reaction time, the minimal distance d in feet it takes for a car to stop is approximated by the formula $d = .042s^2 + 1.1s$, where s is the speed in miles per hour. If a car took 200 feet to stop, about how fast was it going?
about 57 mph

3. Solve Pop Fligh's problem to find out when the ball is 50 feet high.
The equation to be solved is $50 = -.005x^2 + 2x + 3.5$, which after some manipulation can be rewritten as $x^2 - 400x + 9300 = 0$. The solutions are $200 \pm \sqrt{30700}$, indicating that there are two places where the ball is 50 feet high: about 25 feet from home plate and about 375 feet from home plate.

■ ■ ■ ■ ■ ■ ■ ■

Example 2 The 3-4-5 right triangle has sides whose lengths are consecutive integers. Are there any other right triangles with this property?

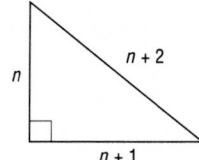

Solution If n is an integer, then n, $n + 1$, and $n + 2$ are consecutive integers. By the Pythagorean Theorem, we get

$$n^2 + (n + 1)^2 = (n + 2)^2.$$

Therefore

$$n^2 + n^2 + 2n + 1 = n^2 + 4n + 4.$$
or
$$2n^2 + 2n + 1 = n^2 + 4n + 4.$$

To rewrite the equation in standard form, add $-n^2 - 4n - 4$ to each side.

$$n^2 - 2n - 3 = 0$$

Now the quadratic formula can be used. Here $a = 1$, $b = -2$, and $c = -3$. Therefore

$$n = \frac{-(-2) \pm \sqrt{(-2)^2 - 4(1)(-3)}}{2(1)}$$

$$= \frac{2 \pm \sqrt{16}}{2}$$

$$= \frac{2 \pm 4}{2}.$$

So $n = \dfrac{2 + 4}{2} = 3$ or $n = \dfrac{2 - 4}{2} = -1$.

If $n = 3$, $n + 1 = 4$, and $n + 2 = 5$. The second solution must be rejected because a side of a triangle must have positive length. Thus the only right triangle with consecutive-integer dimensions is the 3-4-5 right triangle.

In Examples 1 and 2, the number $b^2 - 4ac$ under the radical sign is a perfect square; so the solutions are integers or simple fractions. In applications, however, the numbers are not always so nice. Still the Quadratic Formula works, but a calculator is needed. Here is the problem posed at the beginning of this lesson.

Example 3 Find out when Pop Fligh's baseball is 8 feet high.

Solution We need to solve $-.005x^2 + 2x - 4.5 = 0$, Thus, in this situation $a = -.005$, $b = 2$, and $c = -4.5$. Substitute into the formula:

$$x = \frac{-2 \pm \sqrt{2^2 - 4 \cdot (-.005) \cdot (-4.5)}}{2 \cdot (-.005)}$$

$$= \frac{-2 \pm \sqrt{4 - .09}}{-.01}$$

$$= \frac{-2 \pm \sqrt{3.91}}{-.01}$$

Use a calculator to estimate the square root and separate the two solutions.

$$x \approx \frac{-2 + 1.977}{-.01} \quad \text{or} \quad x \approx \frac{-2 - 1.977}{-.01}$$

So $\qquad x \approx 2.3 \qquad$ or $x \approx 397.7$.

As you might expect, there are two places where the ball is 8 ft high. The first is when the ball is about 2.3 ft away from home plate and on the way up. The second is when the ball is about 398 ft away from home plate and on the way down.

Questions

Covering the Reading

1. If $ax^2 + bx + c = 0$, give the two values of x in terms of a, b, and c.   **See margin.**

2. The proof of the Quadratic Formula is based on what idea?
   completing the square
3. *Multiple choice* The Quadratic Formula is a   a
   (a) theorem.   (b) postulate.   (c) definition.

In 4–6, refer to the proof of the quadratic formula.

4. Expand $\left(x + \dfrac{b}{2a}\right)^2$. $x^2 + \dfrac{b}{a}x + \dfrac{b^2}{4a^2}$

5. Write a fraction equal to $\dfrac{c}{a}$ but with denominator $4a^2$. $\dfrac{4ac}{4a^2}$

6. One square root of $\left(x + \dfrac{b}{2a}\right)^2$ is $x + \dfrac{b}{2a}$. What are the square roots of $\dfrac{b^2 - 4ac}{4a^2}$? $\dfrac{\sqrt{b^2 - 4ac}}{2a}, -\dfrac{\sqrt{b^2 - 4ac}}{2a}$

NOTES ON QUESTIONS
Question 16: This question can be solved without using the quadratic formula by rewriting the expression as a binomial squared, then finding the square root of both sides of the equation. This method gives students a clear idea of when the quadratic formula gives a single root.

Question 21: This question highlights the two meanings of $\pm$, one being the two operations performed in the quadratic formulas, the other being the meaning of the key on a calculator.

Question 22: This question gives an algorithm for using a calculator to solve a quadratic equation. You may want to spend some time helping students use their calculators' memories and recall buttons.

Question 27: To justify their answers, students may complete the square on the first equation, or expand the second.

ADDITIONAL ANSWERS
1. $x = \dfrac{-b + \sqrt{b^2 - 4ac}}{2a}$ or
   $x = \dfrac{-b - \sqrt{b^2 - 4ac}}{2a}$

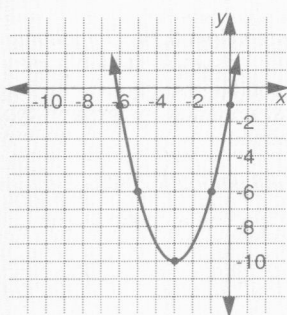
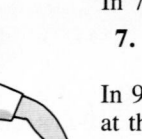

In 7 and 8, find all solutions using the Quadratic Formula.

7. $10x^2 + 13x + 3 = 0$ **8.** $6v^2 - 5v - 3 = 0$ $\frac{5 \pm \sqrt{97}}{12}$
$-1, -\frac{3}{10}$

In 9–11, consider the equation $h = -.005x^2 + 2x + 3.5$ and the situation at the start of this lesson.

9. What do *h* and *x* represent?   See margin.

10. Manny Walker is the pitcher on the team playing against Pop. Manny is standing on the pitcher's mound, about 60 ft from home plate. How high is the ball when it is over Manny's head?   105.5 ft

11. When will Pop's hit be 100 ft high?
See margin.

12. In Example 3, we could have multiplied both sides of the equation by -1 and solved $.005x^2 - 2x + 4.5 = 0$. Find the solutions to this equation to the nearest tenth. $x = 397.7$ or 2.3

13. Refer to Example 2. If *n* is the first of three consecutive integers, what are the other two? $n + 1, n + 2$

Applying the Mathematics

14. Find all right triangles whose sides are consecutive *even* integers *n*, $n + 2$, and $n + 4$.   6, 8, 10

In 15–17, (a) put the equation in standard form and identify *a*, *b*, *c*; (b) solve the equation using the quadratic formula.   See margin.

15. $0 = -11x^2 + 20x + 4$

16. $n^2 + 9 = 6n$

17. $4(m^2 - 3m) = -9$.

18. **a.** Why cannot *a* equal 0 in the quadratic formula?
  b. Solve $0x^2 + bx + c = 0$.   See margin.

19. Consider the equation $ax^2 + bx + c = 0$, where $c = 0$.
  a. Solve for *x* in this special case. $x = 0$ or $x = -\frac{b}{a}$
  b. Solve $5y^2 + 8y = 0$. $y = 0$ or $y = -\frac{8}{5}$

20. Consider the parabola with equation $y = x^2 + 6x - 1$.
  a. Find the values of *x* for which $y = 0$. On a graph these points are called the __?__. $x = -3 + \sqrt{10}$ or $x = -3 - \sqrt{10}$; *x*-intercepts
  b. Find the vertex of this parabola. $(-3, -10)$
  c. Graph the parabola.   See margin.
  d. Give an equation for the axis of symmetry. $x = -3$

21. Alice tried to solve the equation

$$3x^2 - 8x + 5 = 0$$

using the quadratic formula and the calculator key sequence:

$8\,\boxed{\pm}\,\boxed{(}\,8\,\boxed{x^2}\,\boxed{-}\,4\,\boxed{\times}\,3\,\boxed{\times}\,5\,\boxed{)}\,\boxed{\sqrt{x}}\,\boxed{\div}\,2\,\boxed{\times}\,3\,\boxed{=}$.
 $*$ $*$

Her friends, Lois and Carol, starred the two places where she made mistakes. Correct Alice's mistakes.   See margin.

344

22. Madilyn Hadder said that she solved the equation

$$3x^2 - 8x + 5 = 0$$

in three steps.

Step 1) Calculate the square root first and store it in the memory:

$$8 \boxed{x^2} \boxed{-} 4 \boxed{\times} 3 \boxed{\times} 5 \boxed{=} \boxed{\sqrt{x}} \boxed{STO}$$

Step 2) Find $\dfrac{-b + \sqrt{}}{2a}$:

$$8 \boxed{+} \boxed{RCL} \boxed{=} \boxed{\div} \boxed{(} 2 \boxed{\times} 3 \boxed{)} \boxed{=}$$

Step 3) Find $\dfrac{-b - \sqrt{}}{2a}$:

$$8 \boxed{-} \boxed{RCL} \boxed{=} \boxed{\div} \boxed{(} 2 \boxed{\times} 3 \boxed{)} \boxed{=}$$

a. What are the two answers M. Hadder's key sequences give? Are they the correct solutions? $x = 1.667, x = 1$; they are correct.
b. Solve $5x^2 - 7x - 12 = 0$ using the key sequences above. You may need to use $\boxed{M+}$ for $\boxed{STO}$ and $\boxed{MR}$ for $\boxed{RCL}$. $x = -1$ or $x = 2.4$

Review

In 23–25, find the slope of the line:

23. containing the points $(8, 9)$ and $(-5, 2)$; $\frac{7}{13}$

24. with equation $2y = 1.2x - 3$; 0.6

25. through $(1, -4)$ and parallel to the x-axis. *(Lessons 3-1, 3-2)* 0

26. a. Graph the solution sets to $y = \dfrac{36}{x}$ and $y + 2 = \dfrac{36}{x}$ on the same axes. **See margin.**
b. Find equations for the lines of symmetry for the image and pre-image. **See margin.** *(Lessons 2-5, 6-5)*

27. Without graphing, explain why the equations $y = 3x^2 + 24x + 50$ and $y - 2 = 3(x + 4)^2$ have the same graph. *(Lessons 6-4, 6-5)*
The two equations are equivalent.

Exploration

28. Make up some questions you could ask about the path of the ball hit by Pop Fligh in this lesson. If you can, answer those questions.
Many answers are possible.

FOLLOW-UP

MORE PRACTICE
For more questions on SPUR Objectives, use *Lesson Master 6-6*, shown below.

EVALUATION
A quiz covering Lessons 6-4 through 6-6 is provided in the Teacher's Resource File.

26.a.

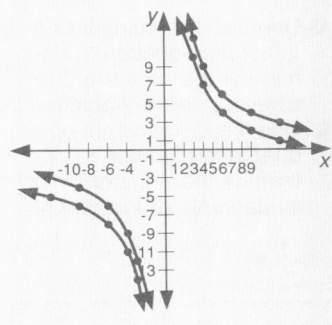

b. preimage: $y = x$, $y = -x$
image: $y = x - 2$, $y = -x - 2$

NAME _____

LESSON **MASTER 6–6**
QUESTIONS ON **SPUR** OBJECTIVES

■ SKILLS *Objective D (See pages 370–373 for objectives.)*
In 1–8, solve.

1. $x^2 + 2x - 3 = 0$ 2. $9n^2 + 30n = -24$

   $x = -3$ or 1 $n = -2, \frac{-4}{3}$

3. $w^2 - 10w + 5 = -20$ 4. $r^2 = 6r - 4$

   $w = 5$ $r = 3 + 2\sqrt{5}$ or $3 - 2\sqrt{5}$

5. $t(t - 5) = 40$ 6. $4 = 6k - k^2$

   $t = \frac{1}{2}(5 + \sqrt{185})$ or $k = 3 + \sqrt{5}$ or $3 - \sqrt{5}$

   $\frac{1}{2}(5 - \sqrt{185})$
7. $3p^2 - 4p - 10 = 2p^2 + 4p - 25$ 8. $3(5a^2 - 1) = 6(a + 2)$

   $p = 3$ or 5 $a = \frac{1 + \sqrt{26}}{5}$ or $\frac{1 - \sqrt{26}}{5}$

■ REPRESENTATIONS *Objective K*
In 9 and 10, (a) find the values of x for which $y = 0$ and (b) graph the parabola identifying its x-intercepts.

9. a. $y = x^2 - 3x - 1$ 10. a. $y = -3x^2 + 5x - 2$

   $x = \frac{3 + \sqrt{13}}{2}$ or $\frac{3 - \sqrt{13}}{2}$ $x = \frac{2}{3}$ or 1

b. 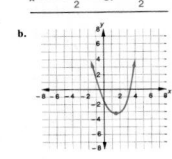   b.

OBJECTIVES

G Use the discriminant of a quadratic equation to determine the nature of the solutions to the equation.
L Use the discriminant of a quadratic equation to determine the number of x-intercepts of the graph.

TEACHING NOTES

Be sure students note that the discriminant of $ax^2 + bx + c = 0$ is $b^2 - 4ac$ and *not* $\sqrt{b^2 - 4ac}$.

Explain to students that if the coefficients are rational and the discriminant is a perfect square, there are two rational roots.

Stress the connection between the nature of the solutions to the quadratic equation $ax^2 + bx + c = 0$ and the x-intercepts of the graph of $y = ax^2 + bx + c$, as shown on page 349.

Reading This is a good time to discuss how the meaning a word can have in mathematics is different from the meaning it can have in general. For example, there is nothing "irrational" about irrational numbers. Nor is there anything "negative" about negative numbers. Later, in Lesson 6-8, you can refer to this discussion when introducing imaginary numbers.

LESSON

6-7

Solving
$ax + b < cx + d$

Even as early as 1700 B.C., ancient mathematicians considered geometry problems that today we would solve using quadratic equations. However, the ancients did not have our modern notation. Euclid, who lived around 300 B.C., would have phrased the problem $x^2 - 5x = 20$ geometrically:

"If a certain straight line be diminished by five, the rectangle of the whole and the diminished segment equals twenty."

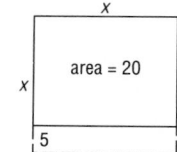

Five hundred years after Euclid, in about 250 A.D., the Greek mathematician Diophantus was the first to use symbols. Diophantus had no single symbol for an unknown: x is ζ and x^2 is Λγ. He would have written the equation $x^2 - 5x = 20$ as follows:

$$\Lambda\gamma \qquad \wedge \qquad \zeta\eta \qquad \epsilon\sigma\tau\iota \qquad \kappa$$
square of x less $5x$ equals 20

One of the first general descriptions of a method to solve quadratic equations was given by the Arab mathematician Al-Khowarizmi in 825 A.D., in a book entitled *Hisab al-jabr w'al muqabalah*. Our modern word "algebra" is derived from the second word of the title. Khowarizmi solved quadratics by completing the square, but his solutions were entirely in words. Around 1200 this book was translated into Latin by Fibonacci and European mathematicians had a method for solving quadratics.

346

The first to use letters and coefficients the way we do was Francois Vieté, a French mathematician, in the late 1500s. For $x^2 - 5x = 20$, Vieté would write "IAQ − 5A aequatur 20". Our modern notation, with exponents, is first found in a book by René Descartes published in 1637. Today's notation makes it relatively easy to solve any quadratic equations.

The history of quadratic equations is connected to the history of number ideas. Recall that a **real number** is a number that can be represented as a decimal and so graphed on a number line. Real numbers are either positive, negative, or zero. The Greeks thought there was only one solution to $x^2 = 9$, the "square root of 9." They did not consider negative numbers because to them the unknown could stand only for a length.

The Greeks at first thought that all numbers could be written as **simple fractions** in the form $\frac{p}{q}$ where p and q are integers, $q \neq 0$.

However, the Pythagoreans discovered that their solution to an equation like $x^2 = 8$ could not be represented as a simple fraction. They called these numbers *irrational*. Today we know that any square root of a whole number that is not a perfect square is irrational. Irrational numbers are exactly those numbers that have infinite nonrepeating decimals. Every real number is either rational or irrational.

real number	as a fraction	as a decimal	examples
rational	can be written as a simple fraction	is either finite or infinitely repeating	977.54, $\frac{-2}{3}$, $8.\overline{12}$, $17\frac{3}{32}$, $\sqrt{9}$
irrational	cannot be written as a simple fraction	is infinite and non-repeating	$\sqrt{2}$, π, $-3 + \sqrt{45}$

Due to their geometric origins, solutions to quadratic (and some other) equations are sometimes called *roots*. The roots of even the simplest quadratic equations include all types of numbers.

equation	number of real roots	type
$x^2 = 9$	2	rational
$x^2 = 8$	2	irrational
$x^2 = 0$	1	rational
$x^2 = -4$	0	

Computer Again, an automatic grapher is useful for generating multiple instances quickly and easily.

ADDITIONAL EXAMPLES

1. Determine the number of real roots of each of the following equations:

a. $3x^2 + 3x + 8 = 0$
none

b. $15x^2 + 2x - 1 = 0$
two

c. $16x^2 - 72x + 81 = 0$
one

d. $x^2 + 7x + 1 = 0$
two

2. Does the graph of $y = 6x^2 + 5x - 2$ have any x-intercepts?
Yes; $b^2 - 4ac > 0$ so there are two intercepts.

3. Does $10x^2 - x - 3 = 0$ have any rational solutions? If so, find them.
Yes; $b^2 - 4ac = 121$, a perfect square. The solutions are $x = \frac{3}{5}$ and $x = -\frac{1}{2}$.

When the quadratic equation is more complicated, the roots can still be counted and classified without completely solving the equation. Suppose a, b, and c are real numbers with $a \neq 0$, and $ax^2 + bx + c = 0$. Then the Quadratic Formula gives

$$x = \frac{-b \pm \sqrt{b^2 - 4ac}}{2a}.$$

If $b^2 - 4ac$ is positive, there are two real solutions, as you found in the last lesson. If $b^2 - 4ac$ is negative, then the Quadratic Formula results in the square root of a negative number. So there are no real solutions. If $b^2 - 4ac = 0$, then

$$x = \frac{-b \pm 0}{2a}$$

and there is only one solution, $x = \dfrac{-b}{2a}$.

Thus the expression $b^2 - 4ac$ determines the number of real roots. Accordingly, $b^2 - 4ac$ is called the **discriminant** of the quadratic equation $ax^2 + bx + c = 0$.

Discriminant Theorem:

If a, b, and c are real and $a \neq 0$, then the equation $ax^2 + bx + c = 0$ has:

    a. two real roots, if $b^2 - 4ac > 0$
    b. one real root, if $b^2 - 4ac = 0$
    c. zero real roots, if $b^2 - 4ac < 0$.

Example 1 Determine the number of real roots of the equation $4x^2 - 12x + 9 = 0$.

Solution Use the Discriminant Theorem. Here $a = 4$, $b = -12$, and $c = 9$. The discriminant $b^2 - 4ac$ is

$$(-12)^2 - 4(4)(9) = 0.$$

Thus, there is one real solution or root.

Example 2 How many real roots does $2x^2 + 3x + 4 = 0$ have?

Solution Here $a = 2$, $b = 3$, and $c = 4$, so $b^2 - 4ac = 9 - 4 \cdot 2 \cdot 4 < 0$. There are no real roots.

348

The x-intercepts of the graph of $y = ax^2 + bx + c$ are the roots of $ax^2 + bx + c = 0$. It should therefore not be surprising that the discriminant has information about the graph of $y = ax^2 + bx + c$. The number of real solutions to $ax^2 + bx + c = 0$ is equal to the number of x-intercepts of the graph of $y = ax^2 + bx + c$.

The following are graphs of parabolas whose equations are related to Examples 1 and 2 on page 348.

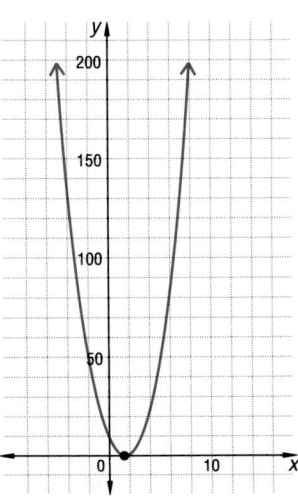

$$y = 4x^2 - 12x + 9$$
$$b^2 - 4ac = 0$$
One x-intercept: 1.5

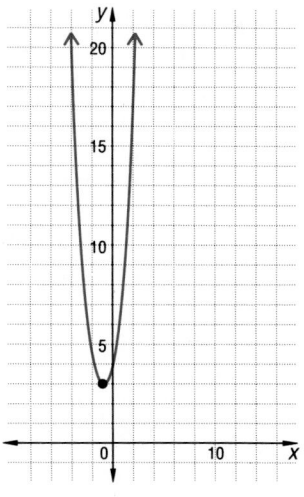

$$y = 2x^2 + 3x + 4$$
$$b^2 - 4ac < 0$$
no x-intercepts

If a, b, and c are *rational* and $b^2 - 4ac$ is a perfect square and all coefficients are rational, such as 49 or $\frac{16}{25}$, then $\sqrt{b^2 - 4ac}$ is rational and both roots are rational. Thus the discriminant tells you quickly much information about the nature of the solutions to a quadratic equation.

Example 3   Does $10t^2 - 3t = 4$ have any rational solutions?

Solution   First, rewrite the equation in standard form.
$$10t^2 - 3t - 4 = 0$$

Evaluate the discriminant. Here $a = 10$, $b = -3$, and $c = -4$. So $b^2 - 4ac = 9 - 4 \cdot 10 \cdot -4 = 169$. Since 169 is positive and is a perfect square, there are two real solutions, both rational.

Check   Finish solving the equation. $t = \dfrac{3 \pm \sqrt{169}}{20} = \dfrac{3 \pm 13}{20}$; so $t = \dfrac{4}{5}$ or $t = -\dfrac{1}{2}$. Do these numbers work in the original equation?

That is left for you to check.

Covering the Reading

In 1–4, match the idea at the left with the estimated length of time it has been known.

1. completing the square   d
2. today's notation for quadratics   e
3. problems leading to quadratics   a
4. first use of symbols for unknowns   c

   a. about 3700 years
   b. about 2300 years
   c. about 1750 years
   d. about 1150 years
   e. about 350 years

5. The word "algebra" is descended from the Arabic word __?__.   al-jabr

In 6–11, tell whether the number is (a) real and rational, (b) real and irrational, or (c) not real.

6. $\sqrt{10}$ b

7. $\sqrt{100}$ a

8. -5   a

9. $\frac{203}{317}$ a

10. $\sqrt{-4}$ c

11. 0   a

12. Give (a) the discriminant and (b) the roots of the quadratic equation $ax^2 + bx + c = 0$.   See margin.

13. Why are there no real roots when the discriminant to a quadratic equation is negative?   See margin.

In 14 and 15, what does the discriminant tell you about the roots to the equation?

14. $3x^2 - 4x + 5 = 0$ no real roots

15. $5y^2 - 10y + 5 = 0$ one real root

16. What information does the discriminant give you about the graph of $y = ax^2 + bx + c$?   number of x-intercepts

17. The discriminant of the equation of a parabola is -1000. What do you know about the graph?   It does not intercept the x-axis.

In 18 and 19, determine the number of x-intercepts the graph has, and whether they are rational or irrational.

18. $y = -3x^2 + 2x + 1$ 2, rational

19. $y = x^2 + 12x + 36$ 1, rational

In 20 and 21, *true or false*. If true, prove the statement; if false, give a counterexample.

20. Every parabola that has an equation of the form $y = ax^2 + bx + c$ has a *y*-intercept. **True; the graph must contain (0, c).**

21. By symmetry, whenever a parabola has one *x*-intercept, it also has a second *x*-intercept.
False; if discriminant = 0, the graph has exactly 1 x-intercept.

22. Pop Fligh wanted to know if the ball he hit (in Lesson 6-6) went higher than the top of the stadium, 200 feet high. He knew that the ball was *h* feet high *x* feet from home plate, where $h = -.005x^2 + 2x + 3.5$. Was the ball ever 200 feet high? (Hint: You can do this without finding the vertex.) **See margin.**

23. Find the value(s) of *k* for which the graph of the quadratic equation $y = x^2 + kx + 9$ will have exactly one *x*-intercept. (Hint: When is the discriminant zero?) **k = 6 or k = -6**

In 24 and 25, the following program in BASIC uses the discriminant to solve quadratic equations of the form $ax^2 + bx + c = 0$, where $a \neq 0$.

```
 90 PRINT "SOLVE A*X^2 + B*X + C = 0."
100 INPUT "COEFFICIENTS"; A, B, C
200 DISC = B^2 - 4*A*C
250 IF DISC < 0 THEN 700
300 X1 = (-B + SQR(DISC))/(2*A)
400 X2 = (-B - SQR(DISC))/(2*A)
500 PRINT "THE ROOTS ARE ";X1;" OR ";X2;"."
600 GO TO 999
700 PRINT "THERE ARE NO REAL ROOTS."
999 END
```

24. Check to see that this BASIC program gives the correct solutions to the equations.
   a. $-2x^2 + 40x = 0$ **The roots are 20 or 0.**
   b. $5x^2 - 150x + 1185 = 0$ **There are no real roots.**
   (Note: If your computer does not recognize ''-B'' in lines 300 and 400 and gives you an error message, try ''-1*B'' instead.)

25. a. Describe what happens when you input $a = 0$. **error message in line 300**
   b. Modify the program so it tests whether *a* is 0, and prints "NOT A QUADRATIC EQUATION" when $a = 0$. **See margin.**

Question 33b: This question can be an interesting class discussion question since there are two solutions to the equation
$8128 = \dfrac{n(n + 1)}{2}$. Emphasize that figurate numbers have a positive representation only.

ADDITIONAL ANSWERS

12.a. $b^2 - 4ac$

b. $x = \dfrac{-b \pm \sqrt{b^2 - 4ac}}{2a}$

13. The square root of a negative number is not a real number.

22. Yes. The discriminant for 200 = -.005x² + 2x + 3.5 is greater than 0, so there is a real solution.

25.b. Add lines:
110 IF A=0, THEN 610
610 PRINT "NOT A
    QUADRATIC EQUATION"
620 GO TO 999

MORE PRACTICE
For more questions on SPUR
Objectives, use *Lesson Master 6-7*, shown on page 351.

Review

26. Solve the quadratic equation in Question 15. *(Lesson 6-6)*   y = 1

27. Find the lengths of the sides of the rectangle shown at the beginning of this lesson. *(Lesson 6-6)*   7.62, 2.62

   x = 4, -16

28. a. Solve the quadratic equation $x^2 + 12x + 36 = 100$.
   b. What do the solutions have to do with the parabola of Question 19? *(Lessons 6-2, 6-6)*   It is a translation (100 units down).

29. Janice did not want to deal with a fraction when solving $n^2 - 5n + \frac{25}{4} = 0$, so she multiplied both sides by 4 and solved $4n^2 - 20n + 25 = 0$ instead. Do both equations have the same roots? Why or why not? *(Previous course, Lesson 1-6)*
   They have the same roots because the two equations are equivalent.

In 30–32, simplify. *(Previous course)*

30. $\sqrt{20}\sqrt{5}$ 10   **31.** $\dfrac{\sqrt{63}}{\sqrt{9}}$ $\sqrt{7}$ **32.** $\dfrac{\sqrt{84}}{2}$ $\sqrt{21}$

33. Thousands of years ago the Pythagoreans investigated *figurate numbers*. You are familiar with the sequence of squares,

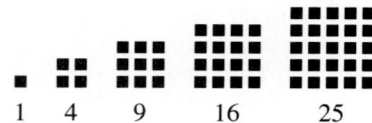

1   4   9   16   25

The *n*th square number is n^2. The *triangular numbers* are

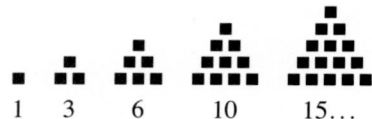

1   3   6   10   15...

T_n, the *n*th triangular number, is $\dfrac{n(n + 1)}{2}$.

   a. Find the 15th triangular number.   120
   b. Which triangular number is 8128? *(Lessons 1-3, 6-6)*   127

Exploration

34. Each of these words or phrases is named after a mathematician who is mentioned in this lesson. Tell its meaning and the name of the mathematician. (Look in a reference book, if necessary.)
   a. algorithm **b.** Diophantine equation **c.** Cartesian coordinate
   34a) a series of precise instructions for carrying out a process step-by-step; Al-Khowarizmi
   34b) a problem with solutions that are integers; Diophantes
   34c) a rectangular coordinate in the *xy*-plane; René Descartes

The Imaginary Number *i*

Imagine your surprise if you picked a number from a machine and got $\sqrt{-1}$. Until the 1500s, mathematicians were also puzzled by square roots of negative numbers. They knew that if they solved certain quadratics, they would get negative numbers under the radical sign. They did not know what to do with them.

One of the first to work with these numbers was Girolamo Cardano in a book called *Ars Magna* ("Great Art") published in 1545. He and other mathematicians of his time reasoned as follows:

When k is positive, the equation $x^2 = k$ has two solutions, $\sqrt{k}$ and $-\sqrt{k}$. If we solve the equation $x^2 = -k$ in the same way, then the two solutions are $\sqrt{-k}$ and $-\sqrt{-k}$. In this way, they defined symbols for the square roots of negative numbers.

Definition:

For $k > 0$, the two solutions to $x^2 = -k$ are denoted $\sqrt{-k}$ and $-\sqrt{-k}$.

By the definition, $(\sqrt{-k})^2 = -k$. This means that we can say, for *all* real numbers r,

$$\sqrt{r} \cdot \sqrt{r} = r.$$

Cardano and others then assumed that these numbers had the same properties as other numbers (but with certain exceptions, as you shall soon see). Descartes called these square roots of negatives **imaginary numbers**, in contrast to the numbers everyone understood which he called "real numbers." In his famous *Algebra* of 1777, Euler used the symbol *i* to denote $\sqrt{-1}$.

Definition:

$i = \sqrt{-1}.$

RESOURCES
■ Lesson Master 6-8

OBJECTIVE

C Simplify expressions involving imaginary numbers.

TEACHING NOTES

Explain to students that the use of the word *imaginary* to describe the square root of a negative number is unfortunate, for they have applications to solving equations and to some real-world applications. Emphasize that the term *imaginary number* is used to describe only the nonreal numbers that can be written in the form *bi*. The term *complex number* is broader, describing all numbers that can be written in the form *a* + *bi*. The latter term is introduced in Lesson 6-9, and is universally used by mathematicians.

Be sure to discuss **Example 2** with students. Encourage them to write out all the steps when multiplying or dividing square roots of negatives, as is done in this lesson, to avoid error.

Error Analysis Even after discussing **Example 2** in class, many students will multiply imaginary numbers under square root signs before taking the square root. You may need to stress several times that the imaginary numbers are different than real numbers, and thus we cannot assume that properties which hold true for real numbers will also hold true for imaginary numbers.

ADDITIONAL EXAMPLES
1. Show that $i\sqrt{7}$ is a square root of -7.
$i\sqrt{7} \cdot i\sqrt{7} = i^2 \cdot 7 = -7$

2. Simplify and state whether the number is real or imaginary.
a. $(8i)^2$
-64, real
b. $-3\sqrt{-49}$
-21i, imaginary
c. $\sqrt{-9} \cdot \sqrt{-121}$
-33, real

3. Solve.
a. $2x^2 - 100 = 0$
$\pm \sqrt{50} = \pm 5\sqrt{2}$
b. $2x^2 + 100 = 0$
$\pm \sqrt{-50} = \pm 5i\sqrt{2}$

That is, $i^2 = -1$. Now consider multiples of i, such as $5i$. By the definition of i, $5i = 5\sqrt{-1}$. If we assume that multiplication is commutative and associative, then

$$(5i)^2 = 5i \cdot 5i$$
$$= 5^2 \cdot i^2$$
$$= 25 \cdot -1$$
$$= -25.$$

Thus $5i$ is a square root of -25. We say that $5i = \sqrt{-25}$ and then $-5i = -\sqrt{-25}$. In general, if $k > 0$, $\sqrt{-k} = i\sqrt{k}$ and so the square roots of any negative number are multiples of i.

Example 1 Show that $i\sqrt{3}$ is a square root of -3.

Solution Multiply $i\sqrt{3}$ by itself.
$$i\sqrt{3} \cdot i\sqrt{3} = i \cdot i \cdot \sqrt{3} \cdot \sqrt{3}$$
$$= i^2 \cdot 3$$
$$= -1 \cdot 3$$
$$= -3$$

The other square root of -3 is $-i\sqrt{3}$.

Due to the long history of quadratics, solutions to them are described in different ways. The following all refer to the same numbers.

the solutions to $x^2 = -41$
the square roots of -41
$\sqrt{-41}$ and $-\sqrt{-41}$
$i\sqrt{41}$ and $-i\sqrt{41}$

The next example shows how to multiply square roots of negative numbers expressed in radical form. Notice that square roots are taken before multiplying.

Example 2 Simplify $\sqrt{-16}\sqrt{-25}$.

Solution Convert to multiples of i.
$$\sqrt{-16} \cdot \sqrt{-25} = i\sqrt{16} \cdot i\sqrt{25}$$
$$= 4i \cdot 5i$$
$$= 20i^2$$
$$= -20$$

354

You are familiar with the property $\sqrt{ab} = \sqrt{a}\,\sqrt{b}$ for *positive* real numbers a and b. Does this property hold when a and b are both negative? Consider Example 2. If we assume $\sqrt{a}\,\sqrt{b} = \sqrt{ab}$, then

$$\sqrt{-16}\,\sqrt{-25} = \sqrt{(-16)(-25)}$$
$$= \sqrt{400}$$
$$= 20.$$

Clearly, this is different from the answer in Example 2. This counterexample shows that

$$\sqrt{ab} \ne \sqrt{a}\,\sqrt{b}.$$

when a and b are negative numbers.

If you try to evaluate a number like $\sqrt{-16}$ on most calculators, an error message will be displayed because most scientific calculators are programmed to operate only with real numbers. So you must understand the principles of computation with imaginary numbers. The commutative, associative, and distributive postulates of addition and multiplication hold for imaginary numbers, as do all theorems based on these postulates. Consequently, working with multiples of i is much like working with any other numbers. For instance,

$$\sqrt{-9} - \sqrt{-25} = 3i - 5i = -2i$$

and
$$\frac{\sqrt{-9}}{\sqrt{-25}} = \frac{3i}{5i} = \frac{3}{5}.$$

Questions

Covering the Reading

Euler

1. *Multiple choice* About when did mathematicians begin to use roots of negative numbers as solutions to equations? c
   (a) sixth century   (b) twelfth century
   (c) sixteenth century   (c) twentieth century

2. Name the solutions of $x^2 + 1 = 0$. $x = i, -i$

3. *True or false* Not all negative numbers have square roots. **False**

4. $\sqrt{-b} = i\sqrt{b}$ when b _?_ 0.   >

5. Who first used the term "imaginary number"? **Descartes**

6. Who was the first person to suggest using i for $\sqrt{-1}$? **Euler**

7. Show that $i\sqrt{5}$ is a square root of -5. $(i\sqrt{5})(i\sqrt{5}) = i^2 \cdot 5 = -5$

8. Show that $-3i$ is a square root of -9. $(-3i)(-3i) = 9i^2 = -9$

In 9 and 10, solve for x. Write the solutions both with and without radical signs.

9. $x^2 + 16 = 0$
   $x = \pm 4\sqrt{-1}; x = \pm 4i$

10. $x^2 - 16 = 0$ $x = \pm\sqrt{16}; x = \pm 4$

LESSON 6-8   The Imaginary Number i **355**

**NOTES ON QUESTIONS
Questions 9, 10, and
26a and b:** Compare and
contrast the solutions to
these questions.

Question 27: You may
want to emphasize that
providing a counterexample
is an easy way to prove a
statement is false.

MORE PRACTICE
For more questions on SPUR
Objectives, use *Lesson Master 6-8*, shown on page 355.

ADDITIONAL ANSWERS
28.a. one **b.** one **c.** $m = \frac{1}{2}$

29.a. two **b.** zero
c. $x = \dfrac{-11 \pm \sqrt{41}}{20}$

In 11–16, write as real numbers or as multiples of i.

11. $\sqrt{-7}$ $i\sqrt{7}$ **12.** $\sqrt{-144}$ 12i **13.** $\sqrt{-2} \cdot \sqrt{2}$ 2i

14. $\sqrt{-3} \cdot \sqrt{-3}$ -3   **15.** $\sqrt{-6} \cdot \sqrt{-3}$ $-3\sqrt{2}$ **16.** $\sqrt{-96}$ $4i\sqrt{6}$

17. When does $\sqrt{xy} \neq \sqrt{x}\sqrt{y}$?   when $x < 0$ and $y < 0$

In 18–23, perform the indicated operations.

18. $3i + 4i$ 7i **19.** $8i - i$ 7i **20.** $2\sqrt{9} + \sqrt{49}$ 13

21. $2\sqrt{-9} + \sqrt{-49}$ 13i **22.** $\dfrac{\sqrt{-16}}{\sqrt{-4}}$ 2   **23.** $\dfrac{2i + 3i}{i}$ 5

Applying the Mathematics

In 24 and 25, simplify.

24. $\sqrt{-434281}$ 659i **25.** $\sqrt{-8} + \sqrt{-2}$ $3i\sqrt{2}$

26. Solve.
  a. $x^2 + 15 = 6$ $x = \pm 3i$ **b.** $(x - 3)^2 + 15 = 6$ $x = 3 \pm 3i$

27. *True or false* If false, give a counterexample.   False: $2i + (-2i) = 0$
  a. The sum of two imaginary numbers is imaginary.
  b. The product of two imaginary numbers is imaginary.
  False: $(2i)(3i) = -6$

Review

In 28 and 29, (a) give the number of real solutions to the quadratic, (b) give the number of rational solutions, and (c) find all solutions. *(Lessons 6-6, 6-7)*

28. $4m^2 - 4m + 1 = 0$ **29.** $10x^2 + 11x + 2 = 0$ See margin.
  See margin.

30. A ball is thrown upwards from a height of 3 feet with an initial velocity of 28 feet per second. $h = -16t^2 + 28t + 3$
  a. What is the height of the ball after t seconds? *(Lesson 6-2)*
  b. What is the maximum height of the ball? *(Lesson 6-5)*   15.25 ft
  c. When does the ball hit the ground? *(Lesson 6-6)*   After 1.85 seconds

In 31 and 32, let $y = \dfrac{\dfrac{x - 1}{2}}{\dfrac{x - 2}{3}}$.

Exploration

31. When $x = \frac{1}{3}$, is y positive or negative? *(Lesson 1-5)*   positive

32. Give the value of y when $x = 6$. *(Lesson 1-5)* $\frac{15}{8}$

33. By definition you know that $i^2 = -1$. So $i^3 = i^2 \cdot i = -1 \cdot i = -i$ and $i^4 = i^3 \cdot i = -i \cdot i = -i^2 = -(-1) = 1$.
  a. Continue this pattern to evaluate and simplify each of i^5, i^6, i^7, and i^8. $i^5 = i$; $i^6 = -1$; $i^7 = -i$; $i^8 = 1$
  b. Generalize your result to predict the value of i^{1988}, i^{1989}, and i^{2001}. $i^{1988} = 1$; $i^{1989} = i$; $i^{2001} = i$

356

LESSON 6-9

Complex Numbers

The oasis in this picture is a mirage. A mirage is an optical illusion—it does not exist. Many years ago mathematicians thought imaginary numbers didn't exist.

In the last lesson you studied a set of numbers of the form bi, called imaginary numbers. When a real number and an imaginary number are added, the sum is called a **complex number.**

Definition:

A complex number is a number of the form $a + bi$ where a and b are real numbers and $i = \sqrt{-1}$; a is called the real part and b is called the imaginary part.

For example, the **real part** of $-3 + 4i$ is -3; the **imaginary part** is 4 (not $4i$).

Two complex numbers $a + bi$ and $c + di$ are **equal** if and only if their real parts are equal and their imaginary parts are equal. That is, $a + bi = c + di$ if and only if $a = c$ and $b = d$. For example, if $x + yi = 2i - 3$, then $x = -3$ and $y = 2$.

All postulates for real numbers except those for inequality (see the appendices) also hold for the set of complex numbers. Thus, we can use these properties to operate with complex numbers in a manner consistent with real-number operations.

Example 1 Simplify: $(3 + 4i) + (7 + 8i)$.

Solution Addition of complex numbers is performed by adding real parts together and adding imaginary parts together.

$(3 + 4i) + (7 + 8i) = (3 + 7) + (4i + 8i)$ Associative and Commutative Properties of Addition
$= 10 + (4 + 8)i$ Distributive Property
$= 10 + 12i$ arithmetic

The Distributive Property can be used to multiply a complex number by a real number or by an imaginary number.

LESSON 6-9 Complex Numbers   357

LESSON 6-9

RESOURCES
- Lesson Master 6-9
- Visual for Teaching Aid 36 displays the complex number system.

OBJECTIVES

E Perform operations with complex numbers.
H Classify complex numbers.

TEACHING NOTES

Emphasize that just as a rational number, $\frac{a}{b}$, is determined by an ordered pair (a, b) of *integers*, a complex number, $a + bi$, is determined by an ordered pair (a, b) of *real numbers*. The form $a + bi$ makes it easy for us to remember the arithmetic and algebraic rules for operations with complex numbers.

You may wish to use a Venn diagram to illustrate the relationship between complex, real, and imaginary numbers.

COMPLEX NUMBERS

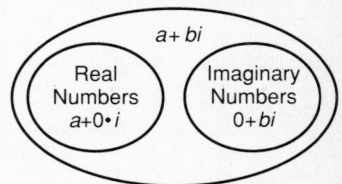

It is customary to write the answer to a complex number computation in the form $a + bi$, as the set of complex numbers is closed under the operations of addition, subtraction, multiplication, and division.

357

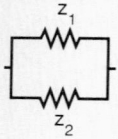 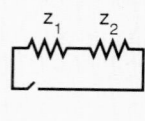
Example 2 Perform the operations: $2i(8 + 5i)$.

Solution
$$2i(8 + 5i) = 2i(8) + 2i(5i)$$ Distributive Property

$$= i(2 \cdot 8) + (2 \cdot 5)(i \cdot i)$$ Associative and Commutative Properties of Multiplication

$$= i(16) + 10\,(i^2)$$ arithmetic

$$= 16i + 10(-1)$$ Commutative Property of Multiplication and definition of i

$$= -10 + 16i$$ arithmetic and Commutative Property of Addition

In Example 2 notice that i^2 was simplified using the fact that $i^2 = -1$. In an answer, i should never be left to any power other than the first. Generally, all answers to complex number operations should be put in the form $a + bi$. This makes it easy to identify the real and imaginary parts.

Example 3 illustrates how the FOIL Theorem is used to multiply two complex numbers.

Example 3 Perform the operations: $(10 - 7i)(4 + 9i)$.

Solution Use the FOIL Theorem.
$$(10 - 7i)(4 + 9i) = 10 \cdot 4 + 10 \cdot 9i - 7i \cdot 4 - 7i \cdot 9i$$ FOIL Theorem

$$= 40 + 90i - 28i - 63i^2$$ arithmetic

$$= 40 + 62i - 63i^2$$ combining like terms

$$= 40 + 62i - 63(-1)$$ definition of i

$$= 103 + 62i$$ arithmetic

The previous examples illustrate the following theorem:

Theorem:

Given two complex numbers $a + bi$ and $c + di$.
complex addition:
$$(a + bi) + (c + di) = (a + c) + (b + d)i$$
complex multiplication:
$$(a + bi)(c + di) = (ac - bd) + (ad + bc)i$$

It is not necessary to memorize this theorem. Rather, remember to combine like terms when adding and to use the FOIL Theorem when multiplying.

358

Example 4 Multiply and simplify: $(8 - 5i)(8 + 5i)$.

Solution $(8 - 5i)(8 + 5i) = 64 + 40i - 40i - 25i^2$ FOIL Theorem

$= 64 - 25i^2$ combining like terms

$= 64 - 25(-1)$ definition of i

$= 89$ arithmetic

The complex numbers in Example 4 are called complex conjugates of each other. In general, the **complex conjugate** of $a + bi$ is $a - bi$. The product of two complex conjugates is a real number.

Every real number a is a complex number because $a = a + 0i$. Thus, the real numbers are a subset of the complex numbers. Likewise, every imaginary number bi equals $0 + bi$, so the imaginary numbers are also a subset of the complex numbers.

This diagram shows how various kinds of complex numbers are related.

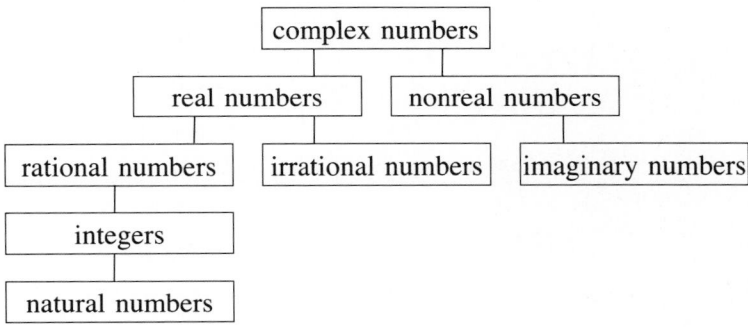

The first use of the term ''complex number'' is generally credited to Carl Friedrich Gauss (1777–1855). Gauss applied complex numbers to the study of electricity. Later in the 19th century, applications were found in geometry and acoustics. New applications continue to be discovered; since 1975 a new field called *dynamical systems* has arisen, in which complex numbers play a pivotal role. Among the offshoots of this field are gorgeous computer-generated drawings which have won awards in art competitions.

359

NOTES ON QUESTIONS

Questions 11 and 21:
Students are expected to recognize names of properties when they do these questions.

Questions 24 and 25:
Although division of complex numbers is not a mastery objective for this lesson, it is introduced with these questions. You may wish to spend some class time discussing division.

Question 32: Each side of the equation in this question may be divided by 2 before using the Quadratic Formula. Although it is not necessary to do so, most students prefer to work with integers of the smallest possible magnitude.

ADDITIONAL ANSWERS
23. $(a - bi)(a + bi) = a^2 - b^2i^2 + (ab - ab)i = a^2 + b^2$

27.c.

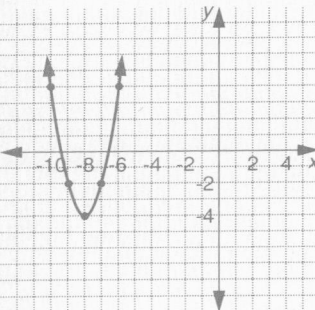

33.a. and b.

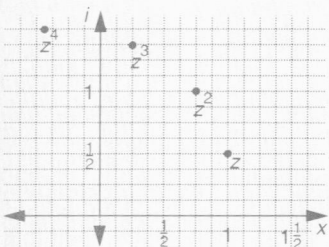

$z^2 = \left(\frac{3}{4}, 1\right)$, $z^3 = \left(\frac{1}{4}, \frac{11}{8}\right)$, $z^4 = \left(-\frac{7}{16}, \frac{3}{2}\right)$

c. appear to be on a spiral, $z^5 = \left(-\frac{19}{16}, \frac{41}{32}\right)$

Covering the Reading

1. A complex number is a number of the form __?__ where a, b are __?__ numbers. **$a + bi$, real**

2. The term "complex number" was coined by __?__. **Gauss**

In 3–5, give the real and imaginary parts of the complex number.

3. $14 + 5i$ **$a = 14, b = 5$**

4. $3 - i\sqrt{2}$ **$a = 3\ b = -\sqrt{2}$**

5. i **$a = 0, b = 1$**

6. The complex numbers $3 + 7i$ and $3 - 7i$ are called __?__.
   complex conjugates

In 7–10, perform the operations and write your answer in $a + bi$ form.

7. $(11 - 4i) + (18 - 3i)$
   $29 - 7i$

8. $3i(2 + 9i)$ **$-27 + 6i$**

9. $(2 - i)(2 + i)$ **5**

10. $(-8 + i)(5 - 3i)$ **$-37 + 29i$**

11. Provide reasons for each step.

$$(12 + 7i)(8 + 4i) = 96 + 48i + 56i + 28i^2$$
$$= 96 + 104i + 28i^2$$
$$= 96 + 104i + 28(-1)$$
$$= 96 + -28 + 104i$$
$$= 68 + 104i$$

a. __?__ **FOIL**
b. __?__ **Dist. Prop.**
c. __?__ **$i^2 = -1$**
d. __?__ **Comm. Prop.**
arithmetic

12. If $x + 12i = 7 - yi$, find x and y. **$x = 7, y = -12$**

13. *True or false* Every real number is also a complex number. **True**

14. Name two fields of technology in which complex numbers are applied. **Electricity, acoustics**

In 15–20, let $z = 9 - 4i$, $w = 16 + 2i$, and $v = 5 + 13i$. Write the following in $a + bi$ form.

15. $z + w$ **$25 - 2i$**

16. $z - v$ **$4 - 17i$**

17. $v - z$ **$-4 - 17i$**

18. $2v + 3w$ **$58 + 32i$**

19. w^2 **$252 + 64i$**

20. $vz + wz$ **$249 + 51i$**

Applying the Mathematics

21. a. The additive identity for the complex numbers is __?__. **$0 + 0i$**
    b. The multiplicative identity for the complex numbers is __?__.
    $1 + 0i$

22. Write $\sqrt{-9}$ in $a + bi$ form. **$0 + 3i$**

23. Consider the complex conjugates $a - bi$ and $a + bi$.
    a. Calculate their sum. **$2a$**
    b. Prove that their product is $a^2 + b^2$. **See margin.**

Division by complex numbers is performed by multiplying both numerator and denominator by the conjugate of the denominator. For example,

$$\frac{3-4i}{2+5i} = \frac{3-4i}{2+5i} \cdot \frac{2-5i}{2-5i} = \frac{6-15i-8i+20i^2}{4-10i+10i-25i^2} = \frac{-14-23i}{29} = \frac{-14}{29} - \frac{23}{29}i$$

360

In 24 and 25, divide using that method.

24. $\frac{5}{6 - 2i}$ $\frac{3}{4} + \frac{1}{4}i$ **25.** $\frac{3 + i}{4 - 7i}$ $\frac{1}{13} + \frac{5}{13}i$

26. Let $z = 1 + i$.
a. Calculate z^2. **2*i***
b. Multiply z^2 by itself to calculate z^4. **-4**
c. From this, complete the sentence: $1 + i$ is a 4th root of __?__. **-4**

Review

27. a. Find the vertex of the parabola with equation $y + 4 = 2(x + 8)^2$. **(-8, -4)**
b. Find the x-intercepts of the parabola with equation $y + 4 = 2(x + 8)^2$. **$-16 \pm \sqrt{2}$**
c. Graph the parabola. *(Lessons 6-1, 6-2, 6-4)* **See margin.**

28. A ball is thrown upwards at a velocity of 10 meters per second from an initial height of 1.5 meters.
a. Write an equation for its height h after t seconds. **$h = -4.9t^2 + 10t + 1.5$**
b. When does the ball reach its maximum height? **1.02 seconds**
c. How high does it reach? *(Lessons 6-1, 6-5)* **6.6 meters**

29. Who was the first to work with square roots of negative numbers? *(Lesson 6-8)* **Girolamo Cardano**

30. *Multiple choice* Which is not a square root of -9? *(Lesson 6-8)* **c**
(a) $-3i$ (b) $3i$ (c) -3 (d) $\sqrt{-9}$

In 31 and 32, solve. *(Lesson 6-6)*

31. $x^2 + 3x = 2$ **$\frac{-3 \pm \sqrt{17}}{2}$** **32.** $4a^2 = 2 + 4a$ **$\frac{1 \pm \sqrt{3}}{2}$**

Exploration

33. A complex number $a + bi$ is graphed as the point (a, b) with the x-axis as the real axis and the y-axis as the imaginary axis.
a. Graph $z = 1 + i$ as the point (1, 1). **See margin.**
b. Compute and graph z^2, z^3, and z^4. **See margin.**
c. What pattern emerges? Can you predict where z^5 will be? **See margin.**

FOLLOW-UP

MORE PRACTICE

For more questions on SPUR Objectives, use *Lesson Master 6-9*, shown below.

EXTENSION

Follow up the Exploration Question by graphing integral powers of other complex numbers. Students should see that generally the powers fall in a spiral; that spiral is best seen if the original complex number (a, b) is just above or just below the x-axis and if $a^2 + b^2$ is just a little greater than 1, which is why part (a) of the question uses $1 + \frac{1}{2}i$. If $a^2 + b^2 = 1$, integral powers of the complex number lie on a circle with radius 1 and center at the origin. If $a^2 + b^2 < 1$, a spiral of decreasing radius is formed by increasing powers of the complex number.

NAME ____________

LESSON MASTER 6–9
QUESTIONS ON **SPUR** OBJECTIVES

■ SKILLS *Objective E (See pages 370–373 for objectives.)*
In 1–12, perform the operations and write the answer in $a + bi$ form.

1. $(8 + 2i) + (-1 + 5i)$ **$7 + 7i$**
2. $(-0.6 - 0.2i) + (1.5 + 0.3i)$ **$.9 + .1i$**
3. $(10 + i) - (10 - i)$ **$2i$**
4. $(-\frac{1}{2} + i) - (-\frac{1}{2} - i)$ **$2i$**
5. $i(7 - 12i)$ **$12 + 7i$**
6. $-3i(i - 1)$ **$3 + 3i$**
7. $(4 + i)(6 - i)$ **$25 + 2i$**
8. $(i - 0.3)(i - 0.2)$ **$-.94 - .5i$**
9. $3 + \sqrt{-1}$ **$3 + i$**
10. $4 + \sqrt{-8}$ **$4 + 2i\sqrt{2}$**
11. $\frac{6 - \sqrt{-16}}{2}$ **$3 - 2i$**
12. $\frac{10 + \sqrt{-40}}{5}$ **$2 + \frac{2}{5}i\sqrt{10}$**

In 13–16, suppose $m = 1 - 9i$ and $n = i + 7$. Evaluate and simplify.

13. nm **$16 - 62i$**
14. m^2 **$-80 - 18i$**
15. $5n - m$ **$34 + 14i$**
16. $im - 2n$ **$-5 - i$**

■ PROPERTIES *Objective H*
In 17–22, classify as rational (r), irrational (i), pure imaginary (pi), or other complex (c).

17. -8 **c**
18. $\sqrt{-10}$ **pi**
19. $\sqrt{16}$ **r**
20. $\sqrt{-1 + 5i}$ **c**
21. $\sqrt{2}$ **i**
22. $\frac{\pi}{2}$ **i**

 73

LESSON 6-10

RESOURCES
■ Lesson Master 6-10

OBJECTIVE

D Solve any quadratic equation with real coefficients.

TEACHING NOTES

You can begin this lesson by asking students to solve an equation such as $x^2 - 12x + 40 = 0$ which has nonreal solutions. Help students work through the problem until they arrive at the solutions, $x = 6 + 2i$ or $x = 6 - 2i$.

Students should realize that now they are able to solve any quadratic equation, although they will not always be able to simplify the solutions to an equation with complex coefficients. Emphasize that when the coefficients of $ax^2 + bx + c = 0$ are real, such as in the example above, any complex roots are complex conjugates. However, when the coefficients are not all real, any complex roots are not complex conjugates.

LESSON

Solving All Quadratics

In the past few lessons, you have studied the Quadratic Formula, which gives solutions to all quadratic equations (Lesson 6-6); the number i, which allows square roots of negatives to be considered (Lesson 6-8); and the complex numbers, which allow real numbers and square roots of negatives to be combined (Lesson 6-9). You now have the machinery which enables you to put any solution to a quadratic in $a + bi$ form.

■ ■ ■ ■ ■ ■ ■■

Example 1   Solve $5x^2 + 8x + 10 = 0$.

Solution   Use the Quadratic Formula:
$$x = \frac{-8 \pm \sqrt{8^2 - 4 \cdot 5 \cdot 10}}{2 \cdot 5}$$
$$= \frac{-8 \pm \sqrt{-136}}{10}$$

Now use the definition of i,
$$= \frac{-8 \pm i\sqrt{136}}{10}$$

So, in $a + bi$ form,
$$x = -\frac{4}{5} + \frac{i\sqrt{136}}{10} \text{ or } x = -\frac{4}{5} - \frac{i\sqrt{136}}{10}.$$

Check   Since $\sqrt{136} \approx 11.7$, $x \approx -0.8 + 1.2i$ or $x \approx -0.8 - 1.2i$.
These can be substituted into the original equation.
Is $5(-0.8 + 1.2i)^2 + 8(-0.8 + 1.2i) + 10 \approx 0$?
The operations you learned in Lesson 6-9 now help to check.
Is $5(0.64 - 1.92i - 1.44) - 6.4 + 9.6i + 10 \approx 0$?
Is $-4 - 9.6i - 6.4 + 9.6i + 10 \approx 0$?
The left side simplifies to -0.4, quite close.
Similarly, the other root can be checked.

One way of simplifying this arithmetic is to rewrite $\sqrt{136}$ as a multiple of a smaller integer-square root.
$$\sqrt{136} = \sqrt{2} \cdot \sqrt{68}$$
$$\sqrt{136} = \sqrt{4} \cdot \sqrt{34} = 2\sqrt{34}$$
$$\sqrt{136} = \sqrt{8} \cdot \sqrt{17}$$

The solutions in Example 1 can be written as follows.
$$x = -\frac{4}{5} + \frac{i\sqrt{136}}{10} \text{ or } x = -\frac{4}{5} - \frac{i\sqrt{136}}{10}$$
or
$$x = -\frac{4}{5} + \frac{2i\sqrt{34}}{10} \text{ or } x = -\frac{4}{5} - \frac{2i\sqrt{34}}{10}$$
or
$$x = -\frac{4}{5} + \frac{i\sqrt{34}}{5} \text{ or } x = -\frac{4}{5} - \frac{i\sqrt{34}}{5}$$

The last of these is not much simpler, but a little bit simpler.

362

We say "simplify $\sqrt{136}$" and then get $2\sqrt{34}$. Is $2\sqrt{34}$ really simpler than $\sqrt{136}$? It depends on the use you have. For evaluating the square root with a calculator, $\sqrt{136}$ is simpler. But for work with the quadratic formula as in Example 1, $2\sqrt{34}$ may be simpler.

Checking solutions to quadratic equations can be tedious, but there is an easier way to check than by substitution. The actual problem that led Cardano to deal with complex numbers provides the path to this new way of checking.

■ ■ ■ ■ ■ ■ ■ ■■

Example 2   Find two numbers whose sum is 10 and whose product is 40.

Solution   Let one number be x. Then the other is $10 - x$. Because their product is 40,

$$x(10 - x) = 40.$$

This is a quadratic equation. Rewrite it in standard form.

$$10x - x^2 = 40$$
$$-x^2 + 10x - 40 = 0$$

Multiply both sides by -1 to make the arithmetic easier.

$$x^2 - 10x + 40 = 0$$

Use the quadratic formula.

$$x = \frac{-(-10) \pm \sqrt{(-10)^2 - 4(1)(40)}}{2(1)} = \frac{10 \pm \sqrt{-60}}{2}$$

Now "simplify" $\sqrt{-60}$.

$$x = \frac{10 \pm 2i\sqrt{15}}{2} = \frac{10}{2} \pm \frac{2i\sqrt{15}}{2}$$

So $x = 5 + i\sqrt{15}$ or $x = 5 - i\sqrt{15}$.

When $x = 5 + i\sqrt{15}$, $10 - x = 5 - i\sqrt{15}$, so these two roots are the solutions to the problem.

Check   Is the sum of the numbers 10?

$$(5 - i\sqrt{15}) + (5 + i\sqrt{15}) = 10.$$

Is the product of the numbers 40?

$$(5 - i\sqrt{15})(5 + i\sqrt{15}) = (5)^2 - (i\sqrt{15})^2 = 25 - 15i^2 = 25 + 15 = 40.$$

Compare the equation in Example 2 to its roots. The sum and the product of the roots appear in the equation. These are instances of the following theorem first recorded in its general form by Francois Viète in 1591.

ADDITIONAL EXAMPLES
1. Solve.
a. $x^2 - 4x + 7 = 0$
$x = 2 + i\sqrt{3}$ or $x = 2 - i\sqrt{3}$
b. $9x^2 - 4x = -5$
$x = \frac{2}{9} + \frac{i\sqrt{41}}{9}$ or
$x = \frac{2}{9} - \frac{i\sqrt{41}}{9}$

2. Find two numbers whose sum is 4 and whose product is 22.
$x(4 - x) = 22,$
so $x = 2 \pm 3i\sqrt{2}.$

3. Use the Sum and Product Theorem to show that
$x = \frac{5 \pm \sqrt{17}}{4}$ are the solutions to $2x^2 - 5x + 1 = 0$.
The sum of the roots is $\frac{5}{2}$, which equals $-\frac{b}{a}$. The product is $\frac{25 - 17}{16}$, which equals $\frac{1}{2}$ and equals $\frac{c}{a}$.

Questions 3 and 4:
These questions follow the idea of **Example 2.**

Question 15: This question stresses the symmetry of the graph of the parabola. The mean of any pair of solutions to $ax^2 + bx + c = n$, where n is real, will give the x-coordinate of the vertex of $y = ax^2 + bx + c$, and thus also indicates the location of the axis of symmetry.

Question 16: Students may need assistance in the solution to this question. If so, help them to write the equation $\frac{w}{h} = \frac{h}{w-h}$, substitute 1 for h, and solve for w.

Question 21: You may want to point out that when the students have discovered that $\frac{\sqrt{2}}{2} + \frac{i\sqrt{2}}{2}$ is a solution to $x^2 = i$, they have also located a square root of i. If they square $\frac{\sqrt{2}}{2} - \frac{i\sqrt{2}}{2}$, they will find that although it is the conjugate of the first number, it is not also a square root of i. The solutions to $x^2 = i$ are not conjugates since the coefficients of $x^2 = i$ are not real.

Sum and Product of Roots Theorem:

The numbers r_1 and r_2 are the roots of the equation $ax^2 + bx + c = 0$, with $a \neq 0$, if and only if

$$r_1 + r_2 = -\frac{b}{a} \text{ and } r_1 r_2 = \frac{c}{a}.$$

Proof

To prove that if r_1 and r_2 are the roots, then $r_1 + r_2 = -\frac{b}{a}$ and $r_1 r_2 = \frac{c}{a}$, start with the roots

$$r_1 = \frac{-b + \sqrt{b^2 - 4ac}}{2a} \text{ and } r_2 = \frac{-b - \sqrt{b^2 - 4ac}}{2a}.$$

(1) $\quad r_1 + r_2 = \dfrac{-b + \sqrt{b^2 - 4ac}}{2a} + \dfrac{-b - \sqrt{b^2 - 4ac}}{2a}$

$$= \frac{-b + \sqrt{b^2 - 4ac} - b - \sqrt{b^2 - 4ac}}{2a}$$

$$= \frac{-2b}{2a}$$

$$= -\frac{b}{a}$$

(2) $\quad r_1 r_2 = \left(\dfrac{-b + \sqrt{b^2 - 4ac}}{2a} \right) \left(\dfrac{-b - \sqrt{b^2 - 4ac}}{2a} \right)$

$$= \frac{b^2 - (b^2 - 4ac)}{4a^2}$$

$$= \frac{4ac}{4a^2}$$

$$= \frac{c}{a}$$

To prove that if $r_1 + r_2 = -\frac{b}{a}$ and $r_1 r_2 = \frac{c}{a}$, then r_1 and r_2 are the roots of $ax^2 + bx + c = 0$, begin with

$$r_1 + r_2 = -\frac{b}{a} \text{ and } r_1 r_2 = \frac{c}{a}.$$

Multiplying both sides of both equations by a gives

$$ar_1 + ar_2 = -b \text{ and } ar_1 r_2 = c.$$

So $\qquad ar_1 = -b - ar_2 \text{ and } ar_1 r_2 = c.$

Substitute $-b - ar_2$ for ar_1: $(-b - ar_2)r_2 = c$.
Distribute and add $-c$ to both sides: $-br_2 - ar_2^2 - c = 0$.
Multiply both sides by -1 and put in standard form:

$$ar_2^2 + br_2 + c = 0$$

Thus r_2 is a solution to $ax^2 + bx + c = 0$.
Similarly r_1 is a solution, which completes the proof.

364

Example 3 Alonzo believes $\frac{2}{3}$ and $\frac{4}{3}$ are the solutions to $9x^2 - 18x + 8 = 0$. Is he correct?

Solution Here the sum of the roots is $\frac{6}{3}$ or 2 and their product is $\frac{8}{9}$. In the equation, $a = 9$, $b = -18$, and $c = 8$. So $-\frac{b}{a} = -\frac{-18}{9} = -(-2) = 2$ and $\frac{c}{a} = \frac{8}{9}$. The solutions check.

Questions

Covering the Reading

1. Solve for x and write the solutions in $a + bi$ form: $x^2 - 4x + 5 = 0$.
   $2 + i,\ 2 - i$
2. State the problem that caused Cardano to deal with complex numbers.
   Some quadratic equations had two real roots, yet others did not.
3. Find two numbers whose sum is 4 and whose product is 29.
   $2 + 5i,\ 2 - 5i$
4. Find two numbers whose sum is 10 and whose product is 24.   4, 6

In 5–7, simplify.

5. $\dfrac{20 + \sqrt{600}}{2}$ $\quad$ 6. $\dfrac{-6 \pm \sqrt{-288}}{3}$ $\quad$ 7. $\dfrac{-40 + \sqrt{3200}}{-60}$
   $\ \ 10 + 5\sqrt{6}$ $\qquad\qquad$ $-2 \pm 4i\sqrt{2}$ $\qquad\qquad$ $\dfrac{2 - 2\sqrt{2}}{3}$

8. Name a situation in which $3\sqrt{2}$ is not simpler than $\sqrt{18}$.
   See margin.
9. The sum of the roots of $ax^2 + bx + c = 0$ is __?__, and the product of the roots is __?__. $\dfrac{-b}{a},\ \dfrac{c}{a}$

10. What are the sum and product of the roots of $7x^2 - 3x - 2 = 0$?
    sum $= \frac{3}{7}$, product $= -\frac{2}{7}$

Applying the Mathematics

11. In a quadratic equation with real coefficients, the roots will be complex conjugates when the discriminant is __?__.   See margin.

In 12–14, solve.

12. $x^2 + 100 = 0$ $x = \pm 10i$ 13. $-7 - 3y^2 = 5y$ $\dfrac{-5 \pm i\sqrt{59}}{6}$

14. $9t^2 - 12t + 229 = 0$ $\dfrac{2 \pm 15i}{3}$
    $\qquad\qquad\qquad\qquad\qquad$ See margin.

15. **a.** Graph $y = x^2 - 10x + 30$. Observe that there are no x-intercepts.
    b. Write an equation for the axis of symmetry of this graph. $x = 5$
    c. Solve $x^2 - 10x + 30 = 0$. $x = 5 \pm i\sqrt{5}$
    d. How is the average of the roots from part c related to the equation from part b? See margin.
    e. Generalize part d.   See margin.

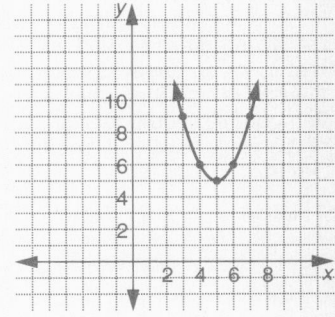
NAME _____

LESSON **MASTER 6–10**
QUESTIONS ON **SPUR** OBJECTIVES

■ **SKILLS** *Objective C (See pages 370–373 for objectives.)*
In 1–6, simplify.

1. $\sqrt{8}$ $\quad 2\sqrt{2}$ $\qquad$ 2. $6\sqrt{32}$ $\quad 24\sqrt{2}$

3. $\dfrac{\sqrt{27}}{3}$ $\quad i\sqrt{3}$ $\qquad$ 4. $\dfrac{12 \pm \sqrt{-36}}{3}$ $\quad 4 \pm 2i$

5. $\dfrac{-1 \pm \sqrt{-56}}{2}$ $\quad -\dfrac{1}{2} \pm i\sqrt{14}$ $\qquad$ 6. $\dfrac{-14 \pm \sqrt{-98}}{6}$ $\quad \dfrac{-14 \pm 7i\sqrt{2}}{6}$

Objective D
In 7–16, solve.

7. $x^2 + 49 = 0$ $\qquad\qquad$ 8. $z^2 + 961 = 0$

$\quad x = \pm 7i$ $\qquad\qquad$ $\quad z = \pm 31i$

9. $k^2 - 2k + 2 = 0$ $\qquad$ 10. $2w^2 + 6w + 5 = 0$

$\quad k = 1 \pm i$ $\qquad\qquad$ $\quad w = \dfrac{-3 \pm i}{2}$

11. $m^2 = 4m + 9$ $\qquad\qquad$ 12. $l^2 + 22 = 10l$

$\quad m = 2 \pm \sqrt{13}$ $\qquad$ $\quad l = 5 \pm \sqrt{3}$

13. $k^2 - 6k + 11.25 = 0$ $\qquad$ 14. $4x^2 + 49 = 0$

$\quad k = 3 \pm \dfrac{3}{2}i$ $\qquad\qquad$ $\quad x = \pm \dfrac{7}{2}i$

15. $4(t^2 - 7t) = 12(t - 9)$ $\quad$ 16. $5x^2 - 8x + 349 = -4x^2 + 4x + 120$

$\quad t = 5 \pm i\sqrt{2}$ $\qquad\qquad$ $\quad x = \dfrac{2}{3} \pm 5i$

74   $\qquad\qquad\qquad\qquad\qquad\qquad\qquad\qquad$ Advanced Algebra © Scott, Foresman and Company

365

MORE PRACTICE
For more questions on SPUR
Objectives, use *Lesson Mas-
ter 6-10*, shown on page 365.

EXTENSION
Have students edit the
BASIC program for finding
real roots on page 351 of
Lesson 6-7 so that it will also
find complex roots for quadratics that have real coefficients.

ADDITIONAL ANSWERS
16. $\frac{1 + \sqrt{5}}{2} \approx 1.618$ (the

other value is negative)

17. vertex: (1, 6)
x-intercept: (0, 3.45),
(0, –1.45)
axis of symmetry: x = 1

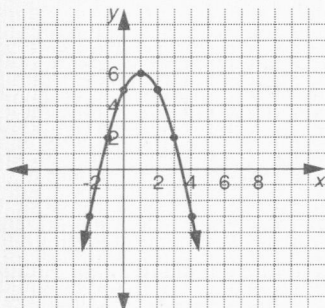

19.a. and b. See
Additional Answers in the
back of this book.

Review

16. Some Greek temples were constructed in the shape of a special rectangle. In such a rectangle, the ratio $\frac{w}{h}$ of width to height equals the ratio
$\frac{h}{w - h}$ of height to width after a square is removed. Let $h = 1$ unit
and find w, and thus find this ratio, known as the *golden ratio*. *(Lesson
6-6)* **See margin.**

17. Find the vertex, x-intercepts, and axis of symmetry of the parabola
$y = -x^2 + 2x + 5$. Graph this parabola. *(Lessons 6-2, 6-6)* **See margin.**

18. A coin is dropped into an empty well. If it takes 2 seconds for the
coin to hit the bottom, how deep is the well? *(Lesson 6-2)* **37.6 m**

19. The Paoli spin matrices $A = \begin{bmatrix} 0 & 1 \\ 1 & 0 \end{bmatrix}$, $B = \begin{bmatrix} 0 & -i \\ i & 0 \end{bmatrix}$,

and $C = \begin{bmatrix} 1 & 0 \\ 0 & -1 \end{bmatrix}$, where $i = \sqrt{-1}$, are used in studying

electron spin. Show that

a. $AB = \begin{bmatrix} -1 & 0 \\ 0 & -1 \end{bmatrix} \cdot BA$. **See margin.**

b. $CB = \begin{bmatrix} -1 & 0 \\ 0 & -1 \end{bmatrix} \cdot BC$. *(Lessons 6-9, 4-2)* **See margin.**

20. What is the 20th term of the arithmetic sequence $2 + i$, $5 + 3i$,
$8 + 5i$, ... ? *(Lessons 3-6, 6-9)* **59 + 39i**

Exploration

21. *Multiple choice* Which of these is a solution to the equation $x^2 = i$? **a**

(a) $\frac{\sqrt{2}}{2} + \frac{i\sqrt{2}}{2}$ (b) $\frac{\sqrt{2}}{2} - \frac{i\sqrt{2}}{2}$

(c) $\frac{1 + i}{2}$ (d) $\frac{1 - i}{2}$

Summary

Quadratic expressions involve one or more terms in x^2, y^2, or xy, but no higher powers of x or y. They arise from a number of situations; acceleration, paths of objects, distance, and area are the subject of problems in this chapter.

When a, b, and c are real numbers, $a \neq 0$, the graph of the equation $y = ax^2 + bx + c$ is a parabola. Using the process known as completing the square, this equation can be rewritten in vertex form $y - k = a(x - h)^2$. This parabola is a translation image of the parabola $y = ax^2$ you have seen in earlier chapters. Its vertex is (h, k), its line of symmetry is $x = h$, and it opens up if $a > 0$ and opens down if $a < 0$.

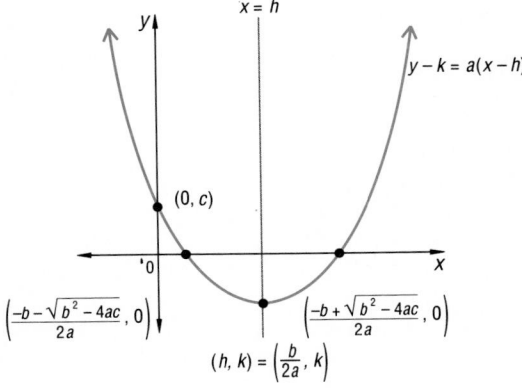

The parabola crosses the x-axis at the values of x for which $ax^2 + bx + c = 0$, the x-intercepts of the parabola. These values are found by the Quadratic Formula

$$x = \frac{-b \pm \sqrt{b^2 - 4ac}}{2a} .$$

The expression $b^2 - 4ac$ is the discriminant of the quadratic. If $b^2 - 4ac > 0$, there are two real solutions. That is the situation pictured at the left.

If the discriminant is zero, there is exactly one solution and the vertex of the parabola is on the x-axis. If a, b, and c are rational numbers and the discriminant is a perfect square, then the solutions are rational numbers.

If the discriminant is negative, there are no real solutions and the parabola does not intersect the x-axis. But there are two complex solutions, and if a, b, and c are real, these solutions are conjugates.

When k is positive, $\sqrt{-k} = i\sqrt{k}$. More specifically, $\sqrt{-1} = i$. Any complex number is of the form $a + bi$. Complex numbers are added and multiplied just like polynomials.

Skill with quadratics requires skill manipulating squares and square roots. Among the theorems reviewed in this chapter are the square of a binomial: for all x and y, $(x + y)^2 = x^2 + 2xy + y^2$. When x and y are positive, $\sqrt{xy} = \sqrt{x} \sqrt{y}$. But this does not hold when x and y are negative. In all quadratics, the sum of the roots is $\frac{-b}{a}$ and the product is $\frac{c}{a}$. These relationships can be used to check solutions to quadratics.

Vocabulary

Below are the most important terms and phrases for this chapter. You should be able to give a definition for those terms marked with a *. For all other terms you should be able to give a general description or a specific example.

Lesson 6-1
quadratic expression
quadratic equation
square root, radical sign
expanded form
Binomial-Square Theorem

Lesson 6-2
*quadratic equation
gravitational constant
$h = -\frac{1}{2}gt^2 + v_0t + h_0$
velocity
acceleration

Lesson 6-3
*parabola
directrix, focus
vertex
paraboloid

Lesson 6-4
Graph-Translation Theorem
vertex form of an equation of a parabola

Lesson 6-5
expanded form of an equation of a parabola
completing the square
perfect-square trinomial

Lesson 6-6
Quadratic Formula
standard form of a quadratic equation

Lesson 6-7
*root of an equation
real number
*rational number, *irrational number
*discriminant of a quadratic equation
Discriminant Theorem

Lesson 6-8
*$\sqrt{-x}$
*$\sqrt{-1}$, i
imaginary number

Lesson 6-9
*complex number
*real part, imaginary part
*equal complex numbers
*complex conjugate

Lesson 6-10
Sum and Product of Roots Theorem

ADDITIONAL ANSWERS
10.

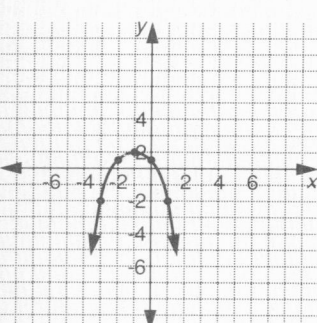

22.a. and b.

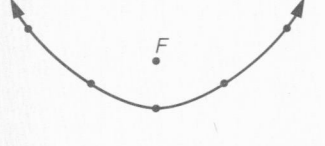

Progress Self-Test

Take this test as you would take a test in class. Use graph paper and a calculator. Then check your work with the solutions in the Selected Answers section in the back of the book.

In 1–3, consider the parabola with equation $y = x^2 - 8x + 12$.

1. Put the equation in vertex form. $y + 4 = (x - 4)^2$

2. What is the vertex of this parabola? (4, -4)

3. What are the x-intercepts of this parabola?
2, 6

In 4–7, perform the operations and simplify.

4. $2i \cdot i$ -2   **5.** $\sqrt{-8} \cdot \sqrt{-2}$ -4

6. $\dfrac{4 + \sqrt{-8}}{2}$ $2 + i\sqrt{2}$ **7.** $(3i + 2)(6i - 4)$ -26

8. If $z = 2 - 4i$ and $w = 1 + 5i$, what is $z - w$? $1 - 9i$

9. *Multiple choice* How does the graph of $y - 2 = -(x + 1)^2$ compare to the graph of $y = -x^2$?   c
 (a) It is 1 unit to the right and 2 units below.
 (b) It is 1 unit to the right and 2 units above.
 (c) It is 1 unit to the left and 2 units above.
 (d) It is 1 unit to the left and 2 units below.

10. Graph the solution set to $y - 2 = -(x + 1)^2$.
 See margin.

11. The vertex of the parabola below is (3, 5). The directrix is the line $y = 6$. What are the coordinates of the focus?   (3, 4)

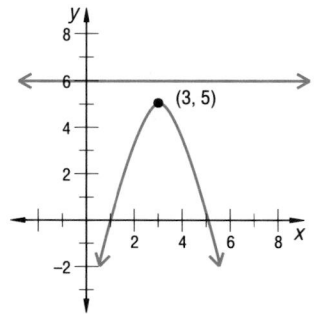

In 12 and 13, find all solutions.

12. $3x^2 + 14x - 5 = 0$ **13.** $(m + 40)^2 = 2$
 $\frac{1}{3}, -5$ $-40 \pm \sqrt{2}$

In 14 and 15, use the equation $y = ax^2 + bx + c$ for $a \neq 0$ and a, b, and c integers.

14. How many x-intercepts does the graph have
 a. if its discriminant is 0?
 b. if its discriminant is 1?
 a) 1; b) 2

15. If $y = 0$, describe the nature of the roots
 a. if its discriminant is 0.
 b. if its discriminant is -5.
 a) 1 integer root; b) 2 complex roots

In 16 and 17, expand.

16. $(a - 3)^2$ $a^2 - 6a + 9$

17. $(8v + 1)^2$ $64v^2 + 16v + 1$

18. A ball is thrown upwards from an initial height of 20 meters at an initial velocity of 10 meters per second. Write an equation for the height h of the ball at time t.
 $h = -4.9t^2 + 10t + 20$

In 19 and 20, the height in feet h of a ball at time t is given by $h = -16t^2 + 12t + 4$.

19. How high is the ball .5 seconds after it is thrown?   6 ft

20. When does the ball hit the ground?   after 1 sec

21. A rectangular piece of metal is 40 cm by 30 cm. Squares s cm on a side are cut from the corners so the metal can be bent and folded into an open box.
 a. What is the volume of that box in terms of s? $(40 - 2s)(30 - 2s)s$
 b. What is the volume of the box if it is 2 cm deep?   1872 cm³

22. a. Draw the figure below. Locate five points on the parabola with focus F and directrix ℓ.

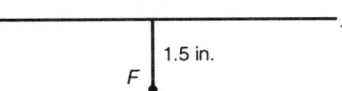

 b. Sketch the parabola.   See margin.

23. *Multiple choice* Which parabola is not congruent to the others?   a
 (a) $y = 2x^2$ (b) $y = x^2 + 2$
 (c) $y = (x + 2)^2$ (d) $y + 2 = x^2$

CHAPTER REVIEW

The main objectives for the chapter are organized here into sections corresponding to the four main types of understanding this book promotes: Skills, Properties, Uses, and Representations.

USING THE CHAPTER REVIEW
Whereas end-of-chapter material may be considered optional in some texts, in *Advanced Algebra* we have selected these objectives and questions that they will be covered. Students should be able to answer these questions with about 85% accuracy after studying the chapter.

You may assign these questions over a single night to help students prepare for a test the next day, or you may assign the questions over a two-day period.

If you work the questions over two days, then we recommend assigning the *evens* for homework the first night so that students get feedback in class the next day, then assigning the *odds* the night before the test so students can use the answers provided in the book.

ADDITIONAL ANSWERS
1. $a^2 + 2ax + x^2$

2. $y^2 - 22y + 121$

3. $9x^2 + 24x + 16$

4. $2x^2 - 8x + 8$

5. $9t^2 - 90t + 225$

6. $3a^2 + 6ab + 3b^2 - 4a + 4b$

Chapter Review

Questions on SPUR Objectives

SPUR stands for **S**kills, **P**roperties, **U**ses, and **R**epresentations. The Chapter Review questions are grouped according to the SPUR Objectives for this chapter.

SKILLS deal with the procedures used to get answers.

■ **Objective A:** *Expand squares of binomials.* (Lesson 6-1)

In 1–6, expand.   See margin.
1. $(a + x)^2$
2. $(y - 11)^2$
3. $(3x + 4)^2$
4. $2(x - 2)^2$
5. $9(t - 5)^2$
6. $3(a + b)^2 - 4(a - b)^2$

■ **Objective B:** *Transform quadratic equations from vertex form to standard form, and vice-versa.* (Lesson 6-5)

In 7 and 8, transform into standard form.
7. $y = 3(x + 2)^2 - 10$ $y = 3x^2 + 12x + 2$
8. $y + 8 = \frac{1}{2}(x - 4)^2$ $y = \frac{1}{2}x^2 - 4x$

In 9 and 10, transform each equation into vertex form.
9. $y = x^2 + 10x - 6$ $y + 31 = (x + 5)^2$
10. $4y = 2x^2 - 6x - 1$ $y + \frac{11}{8} = \frac{1}{2}(x - \frac{3}{2})^2$

11. *Multiple choice*   An equivalent form of the equation $y = 2x^2 - 4x + 3$ is   b
   a. $y - 1 = 2(x + 1)^2$
   b. $y - 1 = 2(x - 1)^2$
   c. $y - 3 = 2(x + 1)^2$
   d. $y - 2 = 2(I - 1)^2$

■ **Objective C:** *Simplify expressions involving imaginary numbers.* (Lessons 6-8, 6-10)

In 12–19, simplify.
12. $-i^2$ -1
13. $\sqrt{-36}$ 6i
14. $\sqrt{-16} \cdot \sqrt{-49}$ -28
15. $\sqrt{2} \cdot \sqrt{-2}$ 2i
16. $10\sqrt{-50}$ $50i\sqrt{2}$
17. $3i \cdot i$ -3
18. $\dfrac{4 \pm \sqrt{-80}}{2}$ $2 \pm 2i\sqrt{5}$
19. $\dfrac{-5 \pm \sqrt{-25}}{10}$ $-\frac{1}{2} \pm \frac{1}{2}i$

■ **Objective D:** *Solve quadratic equations.* (Lessons 6-6, 6-8, 6-10)

In 20–33, solve.
20. $(x - 3)^2 = 0$ 3
21. $d^2 - 48 = 0$ $\pm 4\sqrt{3}$
22. $z^2 = -8$ $\pm 2i\sqrt{2}$
23. $w^2 = -9$ $\pm 3i$
24. $x^2 + x - 1 = 0$ $x = \dfrac{-1 \pm \sqrt{5}}{2}$
25. $10y^2 - 7y = 6$ $y = \frac{6}{5}, -\frac{1}{2}$
26. $z^2 - 8z + 11 = -5$ $z = 4$
27. $0 = 4a^2 + 3a + 2$ $a = \dfrac{-3 \pm i\sqrt{23}}{8}$
28. $k^2 = 4k + 2$ $k = 2 \pm \sqrt{6}$
29. $3x^2 + 2x + 6 = 2x^2 + 4x - 3$ $x = 1 \pm 2i\sqrt{2}$
30. $x^2 + 25 = 0$ $x = \pm 5i$
31. $x(x + 1) = 1$ $x = \dfrac{-1 \pm 5}{2}$
32. $3 = 5p + 2p^2$ $p = -3, \frac{1}{2}$
33. $2(3n^2 + 2) = 4(n - 9)$ $n = \dfrac{1 \pm i\sqrt{59}}{3}$

370

■ **Objective E:** *Perform operations with complex numbers. (Lesson 6-9)*

In 34–37, perform the operations and write the answer in $a + bi$ form.

34. $(3 + 7i) + (-2 + 5i)$ $1 + 12i$

35. $(8 + i) - (8 - i)$ $0 + 2i$

36. $i(10 + 6i)$ $-6 + 10i$

37. $(4 + i)(9 - i)$ $37 + 5i$

In 38–41, suppose $u = 3 - i$ and $v = 8i + 5$. Evaluate and simplify.

38. uv $23 + 19i$

39. u^2 $8 - 6i$

40. $3u - v$ $4 - 11i$

41. $iu + v$ $6 + 11i$

PROPERTIES deal with the principles behind the mathematics.

■ **Objective F:** *Use the Graph-Translation Theorem to interpret equations and graphs. (Lessons 6-4, 6-5)*

42. The graph of $y = x^2$ is translated 7 units to the left and 5 units down. What is an equation for its image? $y + 5 = (x + 7)^2$

43. *Multiple choice* Which of the following is *not* true for the graph of the parabola with equation $y - 5 = -2(x + 1)^2$?   d
(a) The vertex is $(-1, 5)$.
(b) The maximum point is $(-1, 5)$.
(c) The equation of the axis of symmetry is $x = -1$.
(d) The graph opens up.

In 44 and 45, assume that parabola A is congruent to parabola B in the graph below.

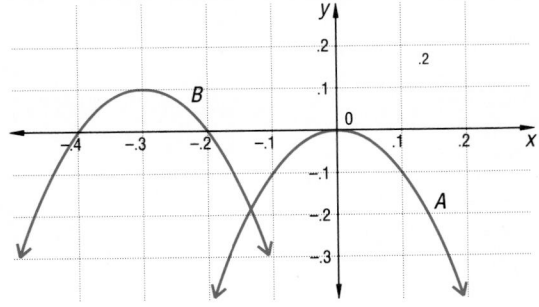

44. What translation maps parabola A onto B?
$T_{-.3,.1}$

45. What is the equation of parabola B if parabola A has equation $y = -10x^2$?
$y - 0.1 = -10(x + 0.3)$

46. Solve $6 = (x - 2)^2$ without expanding the binomial. $x = 2 \pm \sqrt{6}$

47. Solve $(k - 1)^2 = 36$. $k = 7, -5$

48. Solve $(3n + 11)^2 = 2$. $n = \dfrac{-11 \pm \sqrt{2}}{3}$

■ **Objective G:** *Use the discriminant of a quadratic equation to determine the nature of the solutions to the equation. (Lesson 6-7)*

In 49–52, **a.** evaluate the discriminant, **b.** give the number of real solutions, and **c.** tell whether the real solutions are rational or irrational.

49. $8x^2 + 9x + 6 = 0$ See margin.

50. $9 + 4y^2 - 12y = 0$ See margin.

51. $z^2 = 100z + 100$ See margin.

52. $6 + t = t^2 - 5$ See margin.

53. How many real solutions does $2y^2 = 3y$ have?   2

■ **Objective H:** *Classify complex numbers. (Lesson 6-8)*

In 54–61, tell whether the number is real, nonreal, rational, or irrational.

54. i nonreal

55. 17   real, rational

56. $-\frac{2}{3}$ real, rational

57. $\sqrt{45.3}$ real, irrational

58. $3 + i$ nonreal

59. $\sqrt{-4}$ nonreal

60. π real, irrational

61. 6.831   real, rational

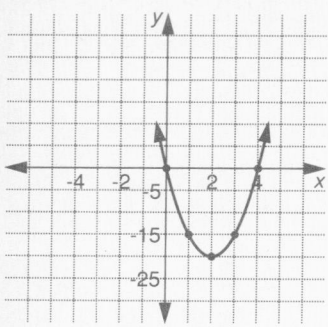

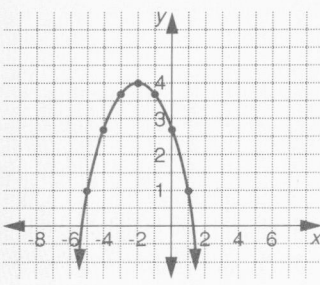

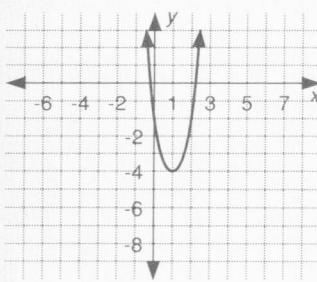

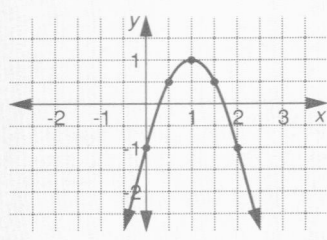

USES deal with applications of mathematics in real situations.

■ **Objective I:** *Use quadratic equations to solve problems dealing with velocity and acceleration.* (Lesson 6-2)

62. Suppose a ball is thrown upward from a height of 4.5 feet with an initial velocity of 21 feet per second.
  a. Write an equation relating the time t and height h of the ball. $h = -16t^2 + 21t + 4.5$
  b. When will the ball hit the ground? $t = 1.5$

63. A package of supplies is dropped from a helicopter hovering 100 m above the ground. Its parachute does not open. After how many seconds will the package reach the ground? (Neglect air resistance.)   **4.5 sec**

64. A ball is dropped from the roof of a house 25 feet high. To the nearest hundredth of a second, how long will it take the ball to hit the ground?   **1.25 seconds**

65. A ball is hit by a bat when 3 feet off the ground. It is caught at the same height 300 feet away from the batter. How far from the batter did it reach its maximum height?   **150 feet**

■ **Objective J:** *Solve area problems which can be modeled by quadratic equations.* (Lessons 6-1, 6-5)

66. A 20″ by 36″ picture is to be surrounded by a frame w inches wide.
  a. What is the total area of the picture and frame? $720 + 112w + 4w^2$
  b. If the total area is to be $\frac{4}{3}$ the area of the picture, how wide should the frame be?

67. Miriam wants to construct a rectangular pen alongside her house for her puppy Webster. Her father said she could use the 22 meters of chicken wire he had in the garage. What should be the dimensions of the pen if Miriam wants Webster to have as much running area as possible? $5\frac{1}{2}$ **by 11 meters**

REPRESENTATIONS deal with pictures, graphs or objects that illustrate concepts.

■ **Objective K:** *Graph parabolas and interpret them.* (Lessons 6-2, 6-3, 6-4, 6-6)

In 68–71, graph the parabola, identifying its vertex and x-intercepts.   **See margin.**

68. $y = 5x^2 - 20x$
69. $y - 4 = -\frac{1}{3}(x + 2)^2$
70. $y + 4 = 3(x - 1)^2$
71. $y = -2x^2 + 4x - 1$

In 72 and 73, refer to the parabolas shown below.

72. Which are *not* graphs of solutions to an equation of the form $y - k = a(x - h)^2$?
b, d

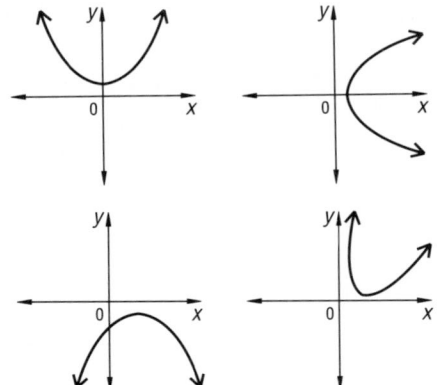

73. Given $y - k = a(x - h)^2$, for which of the above graphs is a negative? **c**

In 74 and 75, the height of a baseball thrown upwards at time t is shown on the graph below.
See margin.

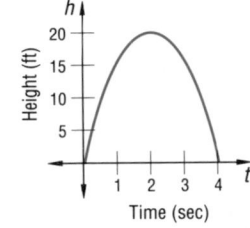

74. When did the ball reach its maximum height? About how high did it get?

75. When was the ball 10 feet high?
See margin.

■ **Objective L:** *Use the discriminant of a quadratic equation to determine the number of x-intercepts of the graph (Lesson 6-7)*

In 76 and 77, give the number of x-intercepts of the graph of the parabola.

76. $y = 3x^2 + 2x - 2$ **two**

77. $y = \frac{1}{2}(x + 5)^2 - 3$ **two**

78. Does the parabola $y = 6x^2 - 12x$ ever intersect the line $y = -5$? **Yes**

79. If the graph of $y = -\frac{1}{4}x^2$ has one x-intercept, how many x-intercepts does the graph of $y = -\frac{1}{4}(x - a)^2$ have? **one**

■ **Objective M:** *Find points on a parabola given its focus and directrix. (Lesson 6-3)*

80. Graph the set of points equidistant from the point (3, 2) and line $y = -2$ below.
See margin.

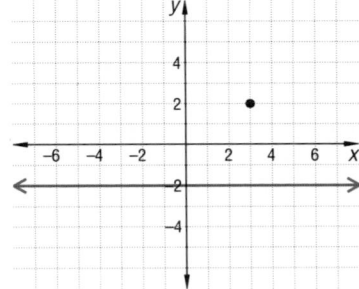

81. Find five points on the parabola with focus F and directrix d, including the vertex of the parabola. **See margin.**

74. maximum height at 2 sec; 20 ft high

75. at approximately 0.5 sec and 3.5 sec

80.

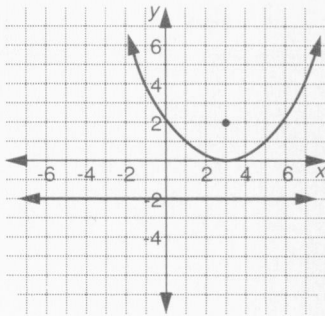

81.

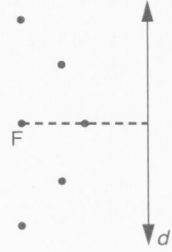

EVALUATION
Three forms of a Chapter Test are provided in the Teacher's Resource File. Chapter 6 Test, Forms A and B cover just Chapter 6. The third test is Chapter 6 Test, Cumulative Form. About 50% of this test covers Chapter 6, 25% covers Chapter 5, and 25% covers previous chapters. A fourth test, Comprehensive Test, Chapters 1–6, that is primarily multiple choice in format, is also provided. For information on grading, see *General Teaching Suggestions: Grading* on page T44 in the Teacher's Edition.

ASSIGNMENT RECOMMENDATION
We strongly recommend that you assign Lesson 7-1, both reading and some questions, for homework the evening of the test.

CHAPTER 7 ■ FUNCTIONS

DAILY PACING CHART ■ CHAPTER 7

Students in the Full Course should complete all but one of the chapters by the end of the year. Students in the Minimal Course will spend more time on quizzes and the Chapter Review. As such, these students should complete about ten or eleven chapters.

DAY	MINIMAL COURSE	FULL COURSE
1	7-1	7-1
2	7-2	7-2
3	7-3	7-3
4	7-4	7-4
5	Quiz (TRF); Start 7-5.	Quiz (TRF); 7-5
6	Finish 7-5.	7-6
7	7-6	7-7
8	7-7	Progress Self-Test
9	Progress Self-Test	Chapter Review
10	Chapter Review	Chapter Test (TRF)
11	Chapter Review	
12	Chapter Test (TRF)	

TESTING OPTIONS
■ Quiz for Lessons 7-1 Through 7-4   ■ Chapter 7 Test, Form B
■ Chapter 7 Test, Form A   ■ Chapter 7 Test, Cumulative Form

PROVIDING FOR INDIVIDUAL DIFFERENCES

The student text is written for the *average* student. The program, however, can be adapted for both less capable and for more capable students.

A blackline master (in the Teacher's Resource File) is provided for each lesson for those students who need more practice. The Teacher's Edition frequently provides Error Analysis and Alternate Approach features to provide additional instructional strategies.

For students who require additional challenge, Extension activities are regularly provided in the Teacher's Edition.

OBJECTIVES ■ CHAPTER 7

Students should master the chapter objectives by the time they complete the chapter.
To ensure mastery, there is continual review built into each set of lesson questions.
After students complete the chapter lessons, they assess their mastery on the Progress
Self-Test. Then they do the Chapter Review and pay special attention to those questions
that match the objectives missed on the Progress Self-Test. Students can get extra
practice on these objectives by using the master for each lesson in the Teacher's
Resource File.

OBJECTIVES FOR CHAPTER 7 (Organized into the SPUR categories—Skills, Properties, Uses, and Representations)	Progress Self-Test Questions	Chapter Review Questions	Lesson Master from Teacher's Resource File*
SKILLS			
A Find the value of a function.	1–3, 21–22	1 through 10	7-1, 7-4, 7-5
B Find the composite of functions.	6–7	11 through 16	7-3
C Read simple BASIC programs with special functions.	23	17 through 20	7-4, 7-5
D Obtain rules for inverses of functions.	12	21 through 24	7-6, 7-7
PROPERTIES			
E Determine whether a given relation is a function.	4–5	25 through 32	7-1, 7-2, 7-4, 7-5
F Determine the domain and range of simple functions given the function rule.	10, 20	33 through 39	7-2, 7-4, 7-5
G Determine relationships between a function and its inverse.	8, 11, 19	40 through 44	7-6, 7-7
USES			
H Find values of functions involving real data.	15	45 through 50	7-1, 7-4, 7-5
REPRESENTATIONS			
I Graph a function, given its rule.	9	51 through 58	7-2, 7-4, 7-5
J Determine the domain and range of a relation from its graph.	17	59 through 62	7-2
K Apply the vertical and horizontal line tests for a function and its inverse.	13–14	63 through 66	7-2, 7-6
L Graph the inverse of a function.	18	67–69	7-7

* The masters are numbered to match the lessons.

OVERVIEW ■ CHAPTER 7

Functions are a fundamental concept used to describe relationships among variables. Students will use functions in Chapters 8–14 of this book and in virtually every mathematics course they take after *Advanced Algebra*. The concept of function is one of the most important in mathematics.

Students of *Advanced Algebra* are already familiar with many relations. Some of these, such as variation equations, linear equations, and quadratic equations define functions. Others, such as vertical lines and linear inequalities, do not represent functions.

This chapter has two purposes: (1) to develop concepts and notation needed to discuss differences and similarities between known functions; and (2) to present several new functions. Although some questions in the chapter ask students to apply the Graph-Translation Theorem studied in Chapter 6, the major focus is on the "parent functions" pictured in the Chapter Summary on page 418.

The first three lessons introduce the vocabulary, notation, properties, and operations that apply to all functions. In Lesson 7-1, Euler's f(x) notation and a mapping notation for naming functions are introduced. Lesson 7-2 discusses the domain and range of a function, and the Vertical-Line Test for distinguishing between functions and nonfunctions. Lesson 7-3 covers composition of functions, and the notations (f ∘ g)(x) and f(g(x)). While students practice using the new vocabulary and notation, they review the linear, quadratic, and variation equations studied in Chapters 1–6.

In Lessons 7-4 and 7-5, three new classes of functions are introduced: greatest integer, absolute value, and powering functions, including the identity function. Students apply the vocabulary and notation learned in the first three lessons to these new functions.

The chapter ends with two lessons devoted to properties of functions. In Lesson 7-6, the inverse of a function is defined and the Horizontal-Line Test for Inverses is introduced. In Lesson 7-7, we introduce the notation f⁻¹ for the inverse function of f, and use the theorem which states that two functions are inverses of each other if and only if the composite in either order is the identity function.

As with the previous chapter, we believe that the presentation of this material can be enhanced by using function-plotting software or simple BASIC programs. If you do not have a computer available on a daily basis, we suggest borrowing one for demonstration purposes after completing Lesson 7-5.

PERSPECTIVES ■ CHAPTER 7

The Perspectives provide the rationale for the inclusion of topics or approaches, provide mathematical background, and make connections within UCSMP.

7-1

FUNCTION NOTATION

In this lesson, we introduce and define the concept of a *function* and present two commonly used notations for identifying functions.

We *describe* a function with the equation f(x) = x + 2, but we call the function f. We reserve f(x) to stand for the y-values of the function. Mapping notation, which is also used to describe functions, makes this clear, and it is consistent with the geometric applications of transformations in which r_m stands for a reflection over line m and $r_m(P)$ stands for the image of point P.

Mapping notation is used to stress the fact that a domain value determines a range value. The f(x) notation is used where there are sentences to solve. We call f(x) notation "Euler's f(x) notation" to emphasize that symbols are invented by people.

Students who have studied UCSMP *Algebra* have already used N(S) for the number of elements in a set and P(E) for the probability of an event. Students who have studied transformations in UCSMP Geometry have used r(P) for the reflection image of a point. However, f(x) notation may be new to other students.

7-2

GRAPHS OF FUNCTIONS

This lesson builds on students' knowledge of graphs to define the concepts of *domain* and *range* of a function and to provide a visual test (the vertical-line test) for deciding whether or not a relation is a function. If students have worked with a function grapher, then they have seen a visual display of a domain with the idea of *window*. The window for x defines the part of the domain of the function that can be seen. To see the entire function for that domain, the range must fall in the window.

7-3

COMPOSITION OF FUNCTIONS

In this lesson, we introduce the operation of compositions of functions. Given functions f and g, students are expected to (1) evaluate $f(g(c))$ for any given c such that the composites are defined, and (2) find an algebraic expression for $f(g(x))$ and $g(f(x))$.

Just as we distinguish between f (a function) and $f(x)$ (its value), so we distinguish between ∘ (an operation) and $f \circ g$ (the result of performing the operation). The operation is called *composition*; the result is called the *composite*.

Simple applications of composition of functions occur frequently in business contexts. The car discount rebate problem given at the beginning of this lesson is a good example that can be used to motivate the students and to preview key ideas about composition of functions.

7-4

STEP FUNCTIONS

In this lesson, students are introduced to the factorial function and an important class of functions called *step functions*. Step functions abound in real-life applications, and both the rounding down and rounding up functions are used frequently in computer science.

Sometimes step functions are called "ceiling" and "floor" functions, and have different symbols:

$\lceil x \rceil$ = the rounding up function = the smallest integer greater than or equal to x; $\lfloor x \rfloor$ = the greatest integer less than or equal to x = $[x]$ = INT(x).

7-5

OTHER SPECIAL FUNCTIONS

Although the vocabulary in Lesson 7-5 may be new to students, most will be familiar with the graphs. Thus, this is a good lesson for students to read on their own. It provides still another opportunity for practice with function notation and with the concepts of domain and range.

When examining a function, there are several characteristics to consider. In addition to domain and range, this lesson considers symmetry. Stress that symmetry is useful when evaluating a function, because one needs to calculate only the values for a portion of the domain; the other values can be found using that symmetry.

The terms "even function" and "odd function" derive from the power functions and are used to characterize functions which are not power functions but which have the same symmetries as well.

7-6

REFLECTIONS AND INVERSES

In this lesson, the inverse of a function is defined. Unlike the practice in some books, we allow every function to have an inverse. However, it should be emphasized that the inverse is not always a function.

This characterization allows us to discuss all the relations one gets by switching the x- and y-coordinates of a function. These relations, such as $x = y^2$, are important in their own right. Then later, when students feel more comfortable with the idea of exchanging x- and y-coordinates, they will be able to understand fully the procedure of restricting the domain of the inverse to make it a function.

7-7

INVERSE FUNCTIONS

In contrast to the previous lesson in which students studied inverses of all functions, Lesson 7-7 focuses only on those situations in which the inverse of a function is also a function. The Inverse Function Theorem is used to determine if two functions are inverses.

We could have used the symbol f^{-1} for the inverse of any function. But only when the inverse is a function could we use the symbol $f^{-1}(x)$. So we restrict use of f^{-1} to functions.

We recommend 10 to 12 days for this chapter: 7 to 8 on the lessons; 1 for the Progress Self-Test; 1 or 2 for the Chapter Review; and 1 for a Chapter test. (See the Daily Pacing Chart on page 374A.) If you spend more than 12 days on this chapter, you are moving too slowly.

USING PAGES 374–375
Introduce the term *correspondence*, and ask students if they have used this word in their everyday lives. Build upon students' responses, if possible, to arrive at the mathematical meaning of correspondence. Then define the concept of a function.

Review the meanings of the terms linear and quadratic. Ask students to suggest a few examples of both linear and quadratic functions. Tell students that the purposes of this chapter are to learn some language and notation for functions, and to study both some special functions and the properties of functions in general.

CHAPTER 7

Functions

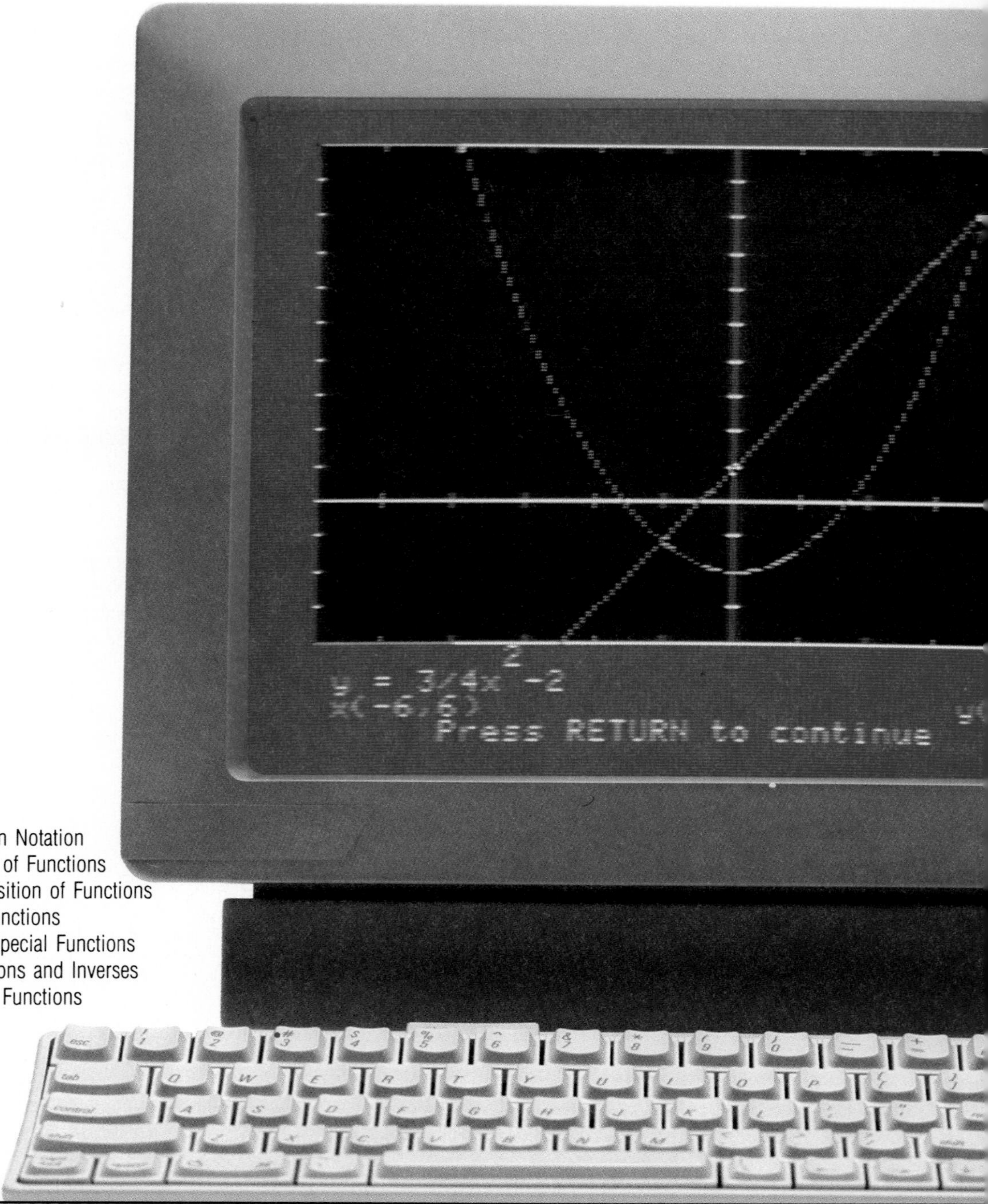

$$y = 3/4x^2 - 2$$
$$x(-6, 6)$$
Press RETURN to continue

374

A *function* is a correspondence between two variables such that each value of the first variable corresponds to exactly one value of the second variable.

You already know a great deal about many functions, though we have not used the name before. In Chapter 2 you studied functions of variation. In Chapter 3 you studied linear functions, and in Chapter 6 you studied quadratic functions.

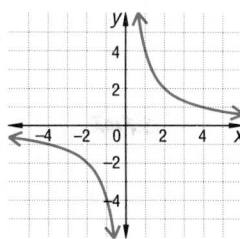

function of variation: $y = \dfrac{4}{x}$

The variable x corresponds to a second variable y whose value is four divided by x.

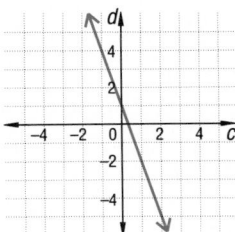

linear function: $d = -3c + 1$

In this function, each value of c corresponds to only one value of d which is found by multiplying c by -3 and then adding 1.

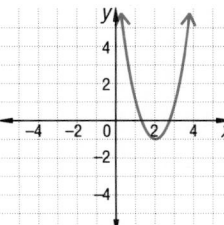

quadratic function: $y = 2x^2 - 8x + 7$

Since the value of y depends on the value of x, the second or dependent variable is y and the first or independent variable is x.

In this chapter you will learn about some other special functions and about general properties of functions.

CHAPTER 7 Functions   **375**

RESOURCES
■ Lesson Master 7-1
■ Visual for Teaching Aid 38 provides the graph for **Questions 16-18.**
■ Computer Master 12

LESSON

7-1

Function Notation

OBJECTIVES

A Find the value of a function.
E Determine whether a given relation is a function.
H Find values of functions involving real data.

TEACHING NOTES

Have students practice reading and evaluating functions using both Euler's notation and the mapping notation. Use **Example 3** to emphasize that they are two different notations that describe the same concept. For finite functions, there is a third notation, the list, as given in **Questions 14 and 15**.

Example 4 can be used to clarify the definition of a function. Stress the fact that a relation is any correspondence between a dependent variable and an independent variable (or any set of ordered pairs), but a function is a very special type of relation, one in which the dependent variable is uniquely determined by the independent variable.

The table of values below was distributed several years ago by the Highway Code of Great Britain. It gives information about three distances (thinking, braking, and stopping distances), each of which is a function of a car's speed.

Speed of car (mph)	10	20	30	40	50	60
Thinking distance (ft)	10	20	30	40	50	60
Braking distance (ft)	5	20	45	80	125	180
Stopping distance (ft)	15	40	75	120	175	240

The thinking distance is the distance a car travels after a driver is told to stop but before he or she applies the brakes. The braking distance is the distance the car needs in order to come to a complete stop after the driver applies the brakes. The stopping distance is the sum of the thinking and braking distances.

The data in the table above can be described with formulas.

Suppose   the car's speed (in mph) $= x$.

Then   the thinking distance (in feet) $= x$

and   the braking distance (in feet) $= \dfrac{x^2}{20}$

so   the stopping distance (in feet) $= x + \dfrac{x^2}{20}$.

If we let $y = x$, $y = \dfrac{x^2}{20}$, and $y = x + \dfrac{x^2}{20}$, all the x's and y's would be too confusing, so formulas often are written using Euler's **f(x) notation**. The notation f(x) is read "f of x." This notation is attributed to Leonard Euler (1707–1780, pronounced "oiler"), a Swiss mathematician who wrote one of the most influential algebra books of all time.

The thinking distance at speed x is

$\quad$ T$(x)= x$ $\qquad$ which is read "T of x equals x."

The braking distance at speed x is

$\quad$ B$(x)= \dfrac{x^2}{20}$ $\qquad$ which is read "B of x equals $\dfrac{x^2}{20}$."

The stopping distance at speed x is

$\quad$ S$(x)= x + \dfrac{x^2}{20}$ which is read "S of x equals $x + \dfrac{x^2}{20}$."

376

The parentheses in Euler's notation do not stand for multiplication. Instead, they enclose the independent variable. We say that T, B, and S are *functions*. The numbers T(x), B(x), and S(x) stand for the **values of these functions**, that is, the values of the dependent variable.

■ ■ ■ ■ ■ ■ ■ ■ ■

Example 1 Evaluate B(45).

Solution Substitute $x = 45$ into the equation B(x) = $\frac{x^2}{20}$.

$$B(45) = \frac{45^2}{20} = 101.25$$

Check Refer to the table on page 376. Braking distance for a car going 45 mph should be between that for cars going 40 mph and cars going 50 mph; that is, between 80 ft and 125 ft. The answer 101.25 feet is a reasonable value of the function at $x = 45$.

In addition to standard formulas and Euler's notation, functions may be described by the **arrow or mapping notation** used with transformations. Like Euler's notation, mapping notation states both the name of the function and the independent variable. For instance, if T, B, and S are names of the thinking, braking, and stopping distance functions, mapping notation for these functions is:

T: $x \rightarrow x$ which is read "T maps x onto x."

B: $x \rightarrow \frac{x^2}{20}$ which is read "B maps x onto $\frac{x^2}{20}$," and

S: $x \rightarrow x + \frac{x^2}{20}$ which is read "S maps x onto $x + \frac{x^2}{20}$."

■ ■ ■ ■ ■ ■ ■ ■

Example 2 Use the function S defined above to complete the statement:

$$S: 57 \rightarrow \underline{\ ?\ }.$$

Solution Substitute $x = 57$ into the mapping notation for stopping distance.

$$S: x \quad \rightarrow \quad x + \frac{x^2}{20}$$

$$S: 57 \quad \rightarrow \quad 57 + \frac{57^2}{20}$$

$$S: 57 \quad \rightarrow \quad 219.45$$

This is read "S maps 57 onto 219.45."

Check The stopping distance should be between 175 ft and 240 ft, so 219.45 is a reasonable value of the function.

You should be able to express formulas for functions with either Euler's notation or mapping notation.

LESSON 7-1 Function Notation **377**

NOTES ON QUESTIONS
Reading for Questions
2-4: These questions provide an opportunity to work
for a correct use of language.
Ask students to read aloud
what they have written on
their papers so that others in
the class can learn what language is appropriate, what is
not.

Question 21b-d: These
questions contain an idea
that is necessary for composition of functions, discussed in Lesson 7-3. Point
out that the x in f(x) can be
considered a placeholder.
Whatever is inside the parentheses gets substituted for
the independent variable in
the formula. For example, in
part (b), (x + 4) is substituted for x in the given
formula to get

$$f(x + 4) = \frac{9}{(x + 4)^2}.$$

Question 25: Another
correct answer is $\frac{1}{4}E + \frac{1}{8}E + \frac{1}{2}E + 5000 = E$, where E is
the value of Amy's estate.

Example 3 The number of diagonals d of a polygon with n sides is a function of n. Rewrite the formula

$$d = \frac{n(n - 3)}{2}$$

a. using Euler's notation;
b. using mapping notation.

Solution The independent variable is n. Let f be the function's name.

a. $f(n) = \frac{n(n - 3)}{2}$

b. $f: n \rightarrow \frac{n(n - 3)}{2}$

Notice that $d = f(n)$.

Every function is a **relation**, that is, a correspondence between a dependent and an independent variable. However, not all relations are functions. We can restate the definition of function given at the beginning of this chapter as follows.

Definition:

A function is a relation in which, for each ordered pair, the first coordinate has exactly one second coordinate.

Example 4 Does the table below represent a function? Why or why not?

x	0	3	4	5	4
y	5	4	3	0	-3

Solution This relation is not a function, because $x = 4$ is paired with two different y-values, $y = 3$ and $y = -3$.

Questions

Covering the Reading

1. A function is a relation in which for each value of the __?__ variable there is only one value of the __?__ variable. **independent; dependent**

In 2–4, how is each read?

2. $f(x)$ **f of x**

3. B: $x \rightarrow \frac{x^2}{20}$ **B maps x onto $\frac{x^2}{20}$**

4. $S(x) = x + \frac{x^2}{20}$ **S of x equals x + $\frac{x^2}{20}$**

In 5–7, refer to the functions in this lesson.

5. B: $50 \rightarrow$ __?__ **125**

6. $S(55) =$ __?__ **206.25**

7. $T(10) =$ __?__ **10**

8. The value of a function is a value of which variable, dependent or independent? **dependent**

9. The usual "rule of thumb" is to maintain one car length (about 16 feet) between your car and the car in front of you for every 10 mph. How realistic is this estimate at a speed of 60 mph? **See margin.**

In 10 and 11, refer to Example 3.

10. Evaluate f(12). **54**

11. State whether *n*, the number of sides, is the dependent or independent variable. **independent**

In 12 and 13, suppose that g: $x \rightarrow 5x - 2$.

12. Rewrite this formula using Euler's notation. **g(x) = 5x − 2**

13. g: $3 \rightarrow$ _?_ **13**

Applying the Mathematics

In 14 and 15, is the relation a function? Why or why not?

14.

x	0	1	-1	2	-2
y	0	1	1	4	4

Yes; for each value of *x* there is only one value of *y*.

15. {(16, 2), (8, 1), (0, 0), (8, -1), (16, -2)} **See margin.**

In 16–18, refer to the graphs at the right. The two graphs give information about the number of farms and the average size (in acres) of these farms across the United States from 1982 to 1987.

16. If the average size function is called A, then A: 1985 → _?_. **445**

17. If the number of farms function is called N, then N(1987) = _?_.
2,173,000

18. Show that 25.8 million acres of farmland were lost between 1982 and 1987 by multiplying A(1982) by N(1982) and then subtracting the product of A(1987) and N(1987).
See margin.

Farms: Larger, but less

The USA has lost 25.8 million acres of farmland since 1982. The average farm has increased by 33 acres, but more than 200,000 farms closed:

Average size in acres

461
428

460
450
440
430
420

Year '82 '83 '84 '85 '86 '87

Number of farms

2,401,000
2,173,000

2,400,000
2,300,000
2,200,000
2,100,000

'82 '83 '84 '85 '86 '87

In 19 and 20, Margo painted her bedroom. It took her 10 hours. Each hour she wrote down the percent of the job she thought she had finished.

Hours	1	2	3	4	5	6	7	8	9	10
Percent finished	5	20	35	50	50	65	70	80	95	100

19. If T(*h*) is the percent finished after *h* hours, what is T(5)? **50%**

20. If Margo began at 8 AM, in which hour did she not work at all?
noon to 1 PM

LESSON 7-1 Function Notation **379**

FOLLOW-UP

MORE PRACTICE
For more questions on SPUR Objectives, use *Lesson Master 7-1*, shown below.

EXTENSION
Have students research the recent application of Euler's work on the *clothoid* or *teardrop* curve. This curve is used in the construction of the latest roller coaster rides that take the rider upside down.

ADDITIONAL ANSWERS
9. 96 ft is not a realistic following distance since the stopping distance needed is about 240 ft.

15. No: the x-values of 8 and 16 are each paired with two different y-values.

18. 428(2,401,000) − 461(2,173,000) = 25,875,000 ≈ 25.9 million

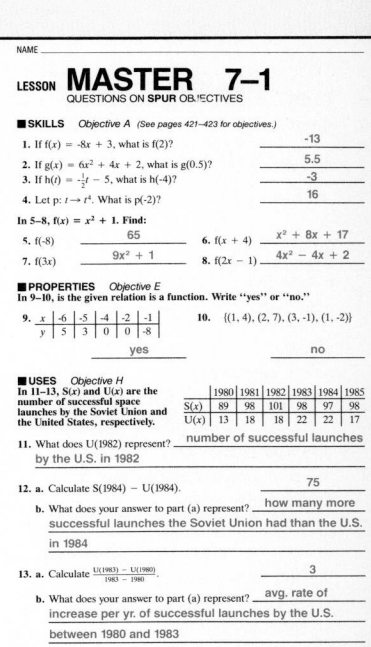

NAME _____

LESSON **MASTER 7–1**
QUESTIONS ON **SPUR** OBJECTIVES

■SKILLS   *Objective A (See pages 421–423 for objectives.)*

1. If f(x) = -8x + 3, what is f(2)? -13

2. If g(x) = 6x² + 4x + 2, what is g(0.5)? 5.5

3. If h(t) = -½t − 5, what is h(-4)? -3

4. Let p: t → t⁴. What is p(-2)? 16

In 5–8, f(x) = x² + 1. Find:

5. f(-8) 65

6. f(x + 4) x² + 8x + 17

7. f(3x) 9x² + 1

8. f(2x − 1) 4x² − 4x + 2

■PROPERTIES   *Objective E*
In 9–10, is the given relation a function. Write "yes" or "no."

9.

x	-6	-5	-4	-2	-1
y	5	3	0	0	-8

yes

10. {(1, 4), (2, 7), (3, -1), (1, -2)}

no

■USES   *Objective H*
In 11–13, S(x) and U(x) are the number of successful space launches by the Soviet Union and the United States, respectively.

	1980	1981	1982	1983	1984	1985
S(x)	89	98	101	98	97	98
U(x)	13	18	18	22	22	17

11. What does U(1982) represent? number of successful launches by the U.S. in 1982

12. a. Calculate S(1984) − U(1984). 75
  b. What does your answer to part (a) represent? how many more successful launches the Soviet Union had than the U.S. in 1984

13. a. Calculate $\frac{U(1983) - U(1980)}{1983 - 1980}$ 3
  b. What does your answer to part (a) represent? avg. rate of increase per yr. of successful launches by the U.S. between 1980 and 1983

Advanced Algebra © Scott, Foresman and Company

75

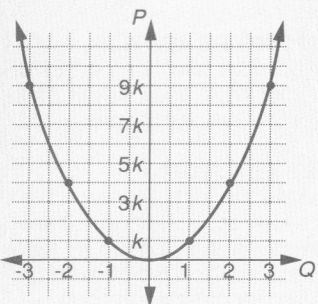
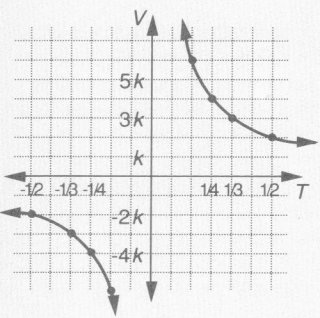
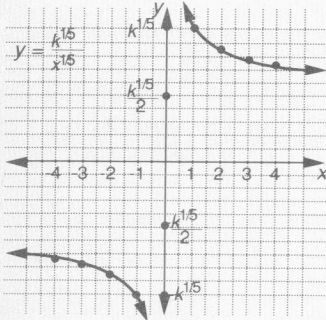
21. If $f(x) = \dfrac{9}{x^2}$, find:

    a. f(4) $\dfrac{9}{16}$
    b. f(x + 4) $\dfrac{9}{x^2 + 8x + 16}$

    c. f(4x) $\dfrac{9}{16x^2}$
    d. $f\left(\dfrac{4}{x}\right)$ $\dfrac{9x^2}{16}$

22. Find a formula $f(x) = \underline{\ ?\ }$ for the direct-variation function described below. $f(x) = 3x^2$

x	1	4	-1	6	10	...
$f(x)$	3	48	3	108	300	...

23. Use the equation $t = \dfrac{k}{w}$, where t = the time in hours an appliance can be run on 1 kilowatt-hour (kwh) of electricity. (1 kwh of electricity runs a 1000-watt appliance for one hour.) w = the wattage rating of the appliance.

    a. t varies $\underline{\ ?\ }$ as $\underline{\ ?\ }$.   inversely, w

    b. Rewrite the equation using Euler's notation. Let g be the name of the function. $g(w) = \dfrac{k}{w}$

24. Let $f(x) = 3x + 10$. Pick any two distinct numbers x_1 and x_2 and evaluate

$$\frac{f(x_2) - f(x_1)}{x_2 - x_1}.$$

What have you evaluated?
The slope of the line through $(x_1, f(x_1))$ and $(x_2, f(x_2))$

Review

25. Amy's will stipulates that $\frac{1}{4}$ of her estate goes to charity, $\frac{1}{8}$ goes to her nephew, and $\frac{1}{2}$ goes to her son. Her college gets the rest.
    a. If her college gets $50,000, write a sentence to find the value of the estate. $\$50,000 = \frac{1}{8}E$
    b. Find the value of the estate. *(Lesson 1-7)*   **$400,000**

In 26–28, translate each situation into a variation equation using k as a constant and graph the equation. *(Lessons 2-1, 2-2)*

26. P varies directly with the square of Q. $P = kQ^2$

27. V varies inversely with T. $V = \dfrac{k}{T}$

28. x is inversely proportional to the fifth power of y. $x = \dfrac{k}{y^5}$

Exploration

29. Euler was one of the greatest mathematicians of all time. Find out some of his contributions to mathematics.   **See margin.**

380

7-2

Graphs of Functions

Braking and stopping distances, graphed below and charted on page 376, also vary with road, terrain, and weather conditions.

There are three ways to describe functions: by listing their ordered pairs; by giving a rule or equation; and by graphing them. Below are the graphs of the three functions studied in the previous lesson. Notice how Euler's notation helps to distinguish the y-coordinate of the functions. One of the great advantages of Euler's $f(x)$ notation is apparent when more than one function is being studied.

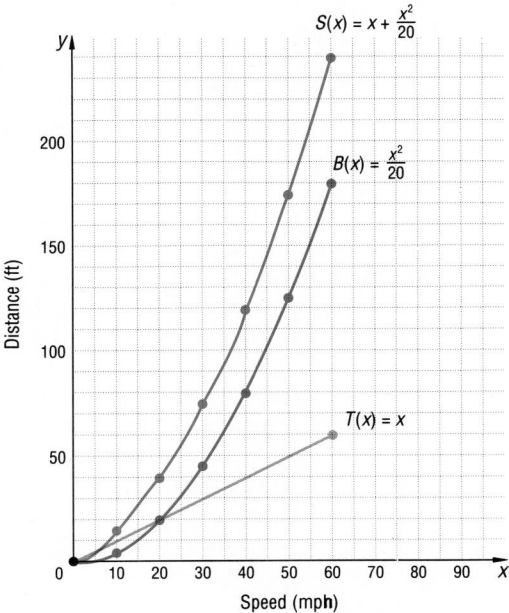

$S(x) = x + \frac{x^2}{20}$

$B(x) = \frac{x^2}{20}$

$T(x) = x$

RESOURCES
- Lesson Master 7-2
- Visual for Teaching Aid 39 displays the graphs of the three functions related to braking distances.
- Visual for Teaching Aid 40 provides the graph that is used for **Questions 19–22.**

OBJECTIVES

F Determine the domain and range of simple functions given the function rule.
I Graph a function, given its rule.
J Determine the domain and range of a relation from its graph.
K Apply the vertical-line test for a function.

TEACHING NOTES

Emphasize that when the graph of a function is given, the domain can be determined quickly by scanning along the horizontal axis, and the range can be determined by scanning along the vertical axis. The skill of scanning along one dimension is also useful for deciding whether or not a relation is a function and for work with inverses later in the chapter.

Point out that the domain and range of a function may be restricted to a subset of the real numbers either by the mathematical expressions in the function or by the use of the function. For instance, in **Example 1**, the application restricts x to a nonnegative real number with a maximum value of 60 in order to represent speed. In **Example 2**, the domain is restricted because of mathematical considerations.

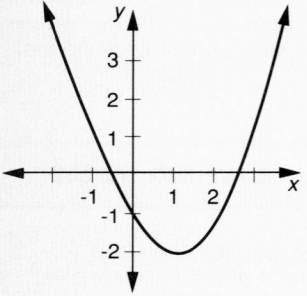
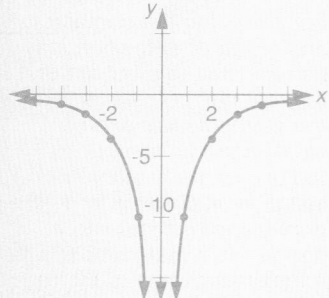
Each point on the graph of a function f has coordinates of the form
$(x, f(x))$. Below, to find the value of S(40) from the graph, start at
40 on the x-axis. Read up to the curve of the S function then across
to find the value on the y-axis.

$$S(40) = 120$$

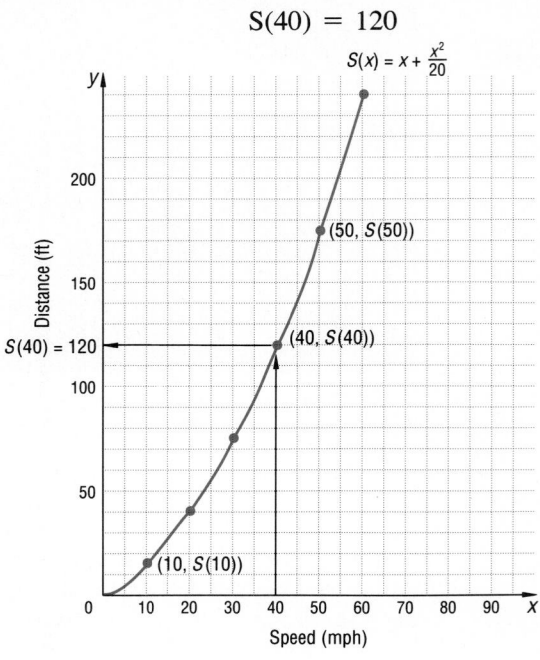

The **domain of a function** is the set of values that are allowable
substitutions for the independent variable. The **range of a function**
is the set of values that can result from the substitutions for the independent variable. The substitutions for the independent variable are
often called *input*, and the resulting values of the dependent variable
are often called *output*. For the graphs of functions T, B, and S on
page 381, the domain is the same set, $\{x: 0 \leq x \leq 60\}$, the allowable speeds in mph.

■ ■ ■ ■ ■ ■ ■ ■

Example 1 Refer to the graphs of the functions T and B on the previous page.
a. What is the range of T?
b. What is the range of B?

Solution The range is the set
of y-values of the function.
a. $T(x) = x$. The graph shows
that if x is between 0 and 60,
y is also between 0 and 60,
so the range of T is
$\{y: 0 \leq y \leq 60\}$.

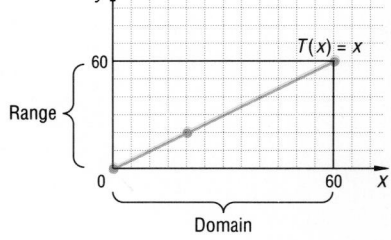

382

b. $B(x) = \dfrac{x^2}{20}$. From the graph you can see that when x is between 0 and 60, y is between 0 and 180. Thus the range of B is $\{y: 0 \le y \le 180\}$.

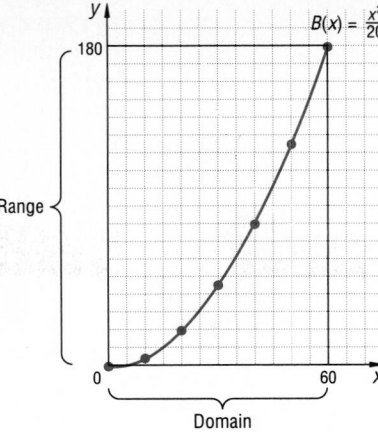

Check You can check by calculations. Look at the equation for each function.

a. $T(x) = x$ states that the y-values equal the x-values. Thus the domain $\{x: 0 \le x \le 60\}$ should equal the range $\{y: 0 \le y \le 60\}$.

b. $B(x) = \dfrac{x^2}{20}$ is an equation for a parabola which opens upward and has a vertex at $(0, 0)$. The range should extend from $B(0)$ to $B(60)$. $B(0) = \dfrac{0^2}{20} = 0$ and $B(60) = \dfrac{60^2}{20} = 180$, so it checks.

When you are not given the domain, assume that any real number possible can be substituted for the independent variable.

Example 2 For the function $f(x) = \dfrac{12}{x^2}$ state: (a) the domain; (b) the range.

Solution This is an inverse-square function.
a. Any real number except 0 can be substituted into $\dfrac{12}{x^2}$. Thus the domain of f is the set of nonzero real numbers.

b. When $x \ne 0$, x^2 is always positive; so $\dfrac{12}{x^2}$ is always positive. Thus the range of f is the set of positive real numbers.

Check Graph the function. Observe that the graph has points for all x-values except 0, and for all positive y-values.

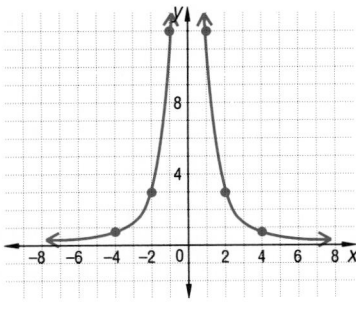

3. Is $y \le 2x + 1$ a sentence describing a function? Why or why not?
No. Each value of x has an infinite number of y-values. For instance, let $x = 0$. Then y could be any number less than one. Specifically, $(0, -4)$ and $(0, -5)$ are two ordered pairs that satisfy $y \le 2x + 1$. Alternatively, graph $y \le 2x + 1$.

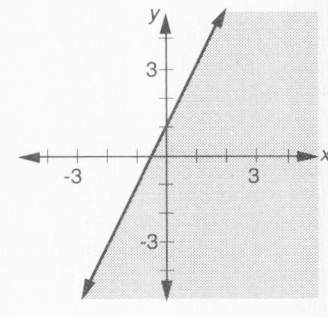

The graph does not pass the vertical-line test.

Question 12: Students should consider c the independent variable, and d the dependent variable. Customarily, if no variable is indicated as the domain variable, and the letters are consecutive in the alphabet, then the first letter is taken to be the independent variable.

Questions 16-18: Students may not realize why the graph "wiggles" up and down. The reason is that ovens do not have a constant temperature. An oven contains a thermostat that automatically turns it off when the temperature goes higher than the setting and turns it on when the temperature goes lower than the setting.

Questions 19-22: The purpose of these questions is to provide practice with the language of functions.

You have already seen examples of relations that are not functions. For example, consider the vertical line with equation $x = -3$, graphed below. Two different points on the graph have the same first coordinate, for instance: $(-3, -1)$ and $(-3, 3)$. By definition, in a function there cannot be two ordered pairs with the same first coordinate. This shows that $x = -3$ is not an equation for a function. Similarly, neither $y < 3x + 6$ nor $y^2 = x$ describes a function, because each contains two points with the same first coordinate.

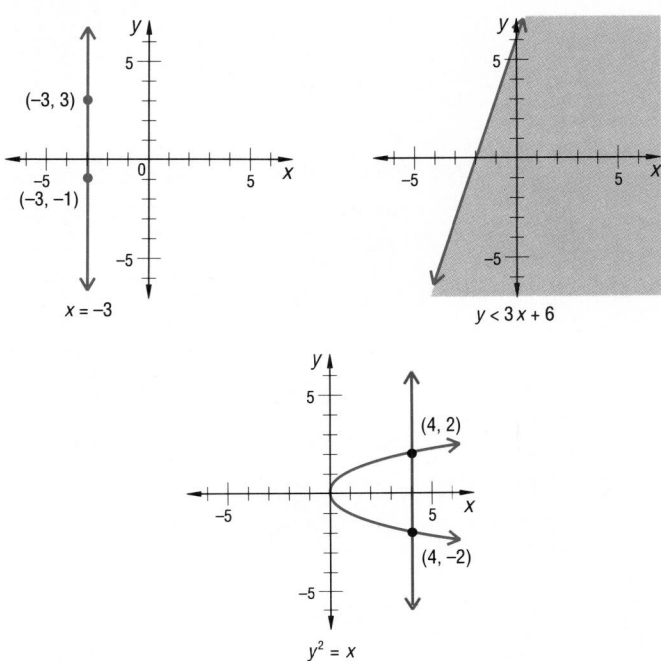

Relations that are not functions

When different points have the same first coordinate, they lie on the same vertical line. This simple idea shows how you can tell whether a relation is a function from its graph.

Theorem (Vertical-Line Test for Functions):

No vertical line intersects the graph of a function in more than one point.

However, a function can have two ordered pairs with the same second coordinate. For instance, the function $y = \dfrac{12}{x^2}$, graphed in Example 2, contains both $(2, 3)$ and $(-2, 3)$. This means that a horizontal line can intersect the graph of a function more than once.

384

Questions

Covering the Reading

In 1 and 2, define each term.

1. domain of a function
   the set of allowable substitutions for the independent variable
2. range of a function   **the set of possible values which result from the substitution for the independent variable**
3. *True or false* Every function has both a domain and a range.   **True**

In 4 and 5, refer to the graphs of functions T, B, and S at the beginning of this lesson.

4. Give their common domain.   **{x: 0 ≤ x ≤ 60}**

5. Give the range of S.   **{y: 0 ≤ y ≤ 240}**

6. In how many points does each line below intersect the graph of the parabola with equation $x = y^2$?
   a. $x = 4$ **two   b.** $x = 0$ **one   c.** $x = -1$ **zero**

7. Is $x = y^2$ an equation for a function? Why or why not?
   No: vertical lines for $x > 0$ intersect the graph twice.

In 8–10, a relation is graphed. Is the relation a function?

8. **yes**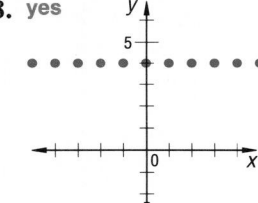

9. **yes**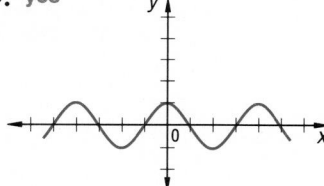

10. **yes**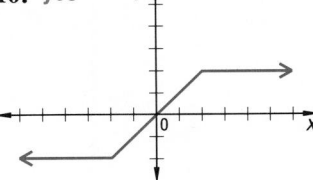

Applying the Mathematics

In 11–15, (a) graph the relation; (b) tell whether the relation is a function; (c) if it is a function, state its domain and range.

11. {(2, 4), (3, 4), (5, 4)}   **a) See margin; b) yes; c) D = {2,3,5}; R = {4}**

12. $5d + 3c > 30$, where c is the independent variable.
    a) See margin; b) no; c) Not a function

13. $y = 3x^2$ **a) See margin; b) yes; c) D = {all real numbers}, R = {y: y ≥ 0}**

14. $y = \dfrac{12}{x}$ **a) See margin; b) yes; c) D = {all real numbers except 0}, R = {all real numbers except 0}**

15. $x = -\frac{1}{2} y^2$, where $y \geq 0$
    a) See margin; b) yes c) D = {x : x ≤ 0}, R = {y : y ≥ 0}

LESSON 7-2   Graphs of Functions   **385**

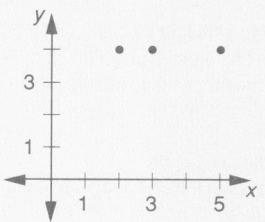
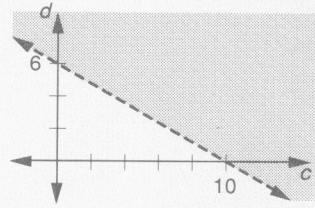
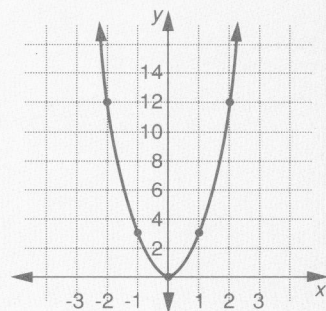
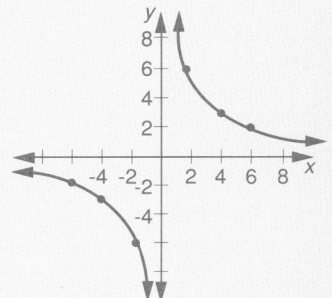
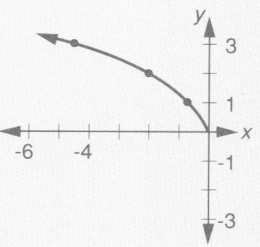

In 16–18, refer to the graph below. The oven was set for 350°, and the actual temperature T, was graphed as a function of time for 30 minutes.

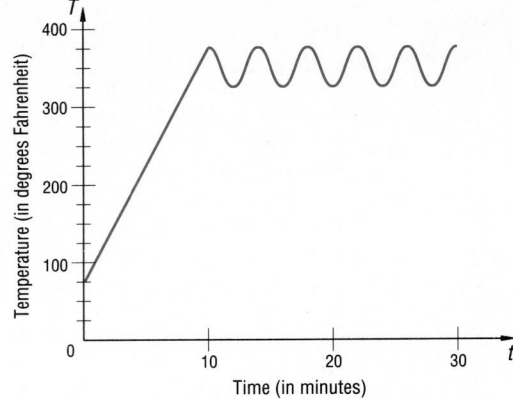

16. What was the temperature of the oven when it was turned on? **75° F**

17. If F is the name of this function, estimate F(20). **325° F**

18. What is the maximum value of the temperature function? **375°F**

In 19–22, refer to the graph below. Let A(*t*) be Alice's weight at age *t* and B(*t*) be Bill's weight at age *t*. The domain of both these functions is $\{t: 0 \leq t \leq 25\}$.

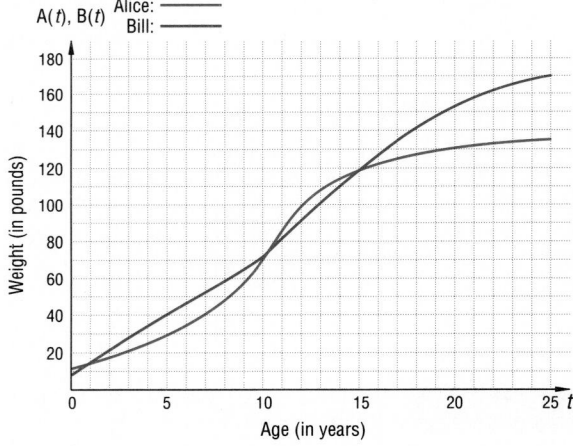

19. What is the range of A? **12 ≤ A(*t*) ≤ 138**

20. Estimate B(5) from the graph. **≈ 40lb**

21. For what two values of t is A(*t*) = B(*t*)? **t ≈ 9.8 and t ≈ 15**

22. During what age intervals did Bill weigh more than Alice?
{t:1 < t < 10} or {t: 15 < t ≤ 25}

386

23. Let f(x) = 1 + x^3. Find:
  a. f(2)   9   **b.** f(-2)   -7   **c.** f$\left(\dfrac{x}{2}\right)$ *(Lesson 7-1)* $1 + \dfrac{x^3}{8}$

24. Let g(x) = x^2. Find:
  a. g($x + h$) $x^2 + 2xh + h^2$
  b. g($x + h$) − g(x) $2xh + h^2$
  c. $\dfrac{g(x + h) - g(x)}{h}$ *(Lesson 7-1)* $2x + h$

25. The function CTOF converts degrees Celsius to degrees Fahrenheit. CTOF: $x \to 1.8x + 32$. Then CTOF: 100 → __?__. *(Lesson 7-1)*   212

26. A dress takes 4 yards of material, a skirt takes 2 yards, and a blouse takes 1.5 yards. Pearl Won wants to make 6 dresses, 3 skirts, and 7 blouses. *(Lesson 4-2)*
  a. Write a 1 x 3 matrix M for the materials needed for the various outfits.   M = [4 2 1.5]
  b. Write a 3 x 1 matrix P for the number of outfits wanted. $\begin{bmatrix} 6 \\ 3 \\ 7 \end{bmatrix}$
  c. Multiply the matrices in the correct order to find the total number of yards of material needed.   40.5

27. For what value(s) of c does $\begin{cases} 3x - 4y = 9 \\ 12x - 16y = c \end{cases}$ have infinitely many solutions? *(Lesson 5-6)*   36

28. Pick any one of the following statements and determine whether it is true or false. If it is false, give a counterexample. It may help to make several sketches.
  a. If the domain of a function equals its range, the function is symmetric to the line with equation $y = x$.   False; Sample: y = 2x
  b. The relation $y = \begin{cases} 1, \text{ for } x = \text{a terminating or repeating decimal} \\ 0, \text{ for } x = \text{a nonterminating, nonrepeating decimal} \end{cases}$ is a function.   True
  c. A function may have discrete domain and a continuous range.   True; sample: the probability function

---

LESSON 7-3

OBJECTIVE

B Find the composite of functions.

TEACHING NOTES

When writing the composition of functions, have students put them in the form f(g(x)). Remind students that when working with parentheses, the inner most pair is always calculated first. Explain to the students that this concept is also applied to the composition of functions. Tell them to evaluate the inner most function first, and then substitute the result for the variable in the outside function.

When discussing the material at the beginning of the lesson, you can show students that d(r(x)) is always greater than r(d(x)) by sketching the graphs of d(r(x)) = .85x − 850 and r(d(x)) = .85x − 1000:

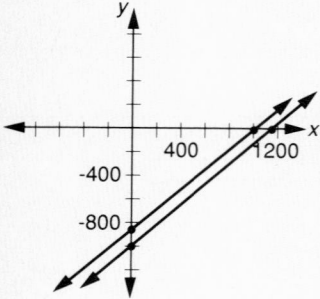

Since the slopes of the linear functions are equal, the graphs of the lines are parallel, and d(r(x)) is greater than r(d(x)) by the same amount for any value of x.

388

LESSON

7-3

Composition of Functions

A car dealer offers a $1000 rebate and 15% discount off the price of a new car. If the sticker price of the car is $12,000, how much will you pay?

The answer to this question depends on which is applied first, the rebate or the discount. If you take the rebate first and then the discount, the selling price in dollars is

$$.85(12,000 - 1000) = 9350.$$

(Recall that the price after a 15% discount is 85% of what it was before.) However, if you take the discount first, and then the rebate, the selling price in dollars is

$$.85(12,000) - 1000 = 9200.$$

For a $12,000 car, taking the 15% discount before the $1000 rebate results in a lower selling price. Should you always take the discount first? To answer this question it helps to know about the operation called **composition** of functions. As with transformations, the **composite** of two functions f and g, written **g ∘ f,** is the result of first applying f, then applying g to the result.

In mapping notation: g ∘ f: $x \rightarrow g(f(x))$ read "the composite of g and f maps x onto g of f of x."

In Euler's notation: $(g \circ f)(x) = g(f(x))$ read "the composite of g and f of x is g of f of x."

We call the rebate function r. This function subtracts 1000.

$$r(x) = x - 1000$$

The discount function is d. This function multiplies by .85.

$$d(x) = .85x$$

Doing the rebate first means calculating d(r(x)).

$$d(r(x)) = d(x - 1000) = .85(x - 1000) = .85x - 850$$

388

Doing the discount first means calculating r(d(x)).

$$r(d(x)) = r(.85x) = .85x - 1000$$

Thus r(d(x)) is always $150 less than d(r(x)). You should want the discount first.

■ ■ ■ ■ ■ ■ ■ ■

Example 1   Let p(x) = x + 5 and s(x) = x^2. Find (p ∘ s)(7).

Solution   The composite says to square 7, then add 5 to the result.

$$(p \circ s)(7) = p(s(7))$$
$$= p(49)$$
$$= 49 + 5$$
$$= 54$$

Notice (s ∘ p)(7) = s(p(7)) = s(12) = 144. So (s ∘ p)(7) ≠ p ∘ s(7). In general, *composition of functions is not commutative*.

■ ■ ■ ■ ■ ■ ■ ■

Example 2   Consider g(x) = x^2 − 4 and h(x) = $-\frac{x}{2}$. Find:
a. (h ∘ g)(x)   **b.** (g ∘ h)(x).

Solution
a. (h ∘ g)(x) = h(g(x))
First apply g to get h(x^2 − 4).

Now apply h to x^2 − 4 to get $\frac{-(x^2 - 4)}{2} = \frac{-x^2}{2} + 2$.

b. (g ∘ h)(x) = g(h(x))
First apply h to get g$\left(-\frac{x}{2}\right)$.

Now apply g to $-\frac{x}{2}$ to get $\left(-\frac{x}{2}\right)^2 - 4 = \frac{x^2}{4} - 4$.

Check
a. Does (h ∘ g)(x) = $-\frac{x^2}{2}$ + 2? One way to check is to evaluate the composite for a specific value of x, say 1. Does (h ∘ g)(1) = $-\frac{1^2}{2}$ + 2?

Does   h(g(1)) = $-\frac{1}{2}$ + 2   ?
          h(1^2 − 4) = 1.5   ?
          h(−3) = 1.5   ?
          $-\frac{(-3)}{2}$ = 1.5   ? Yes.

The answer checks for this particular case. This is not a fool-proof check.
b. This check is left for you to do.

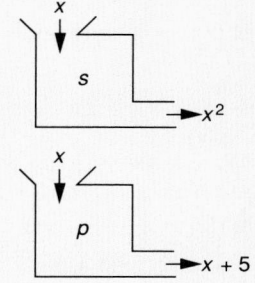
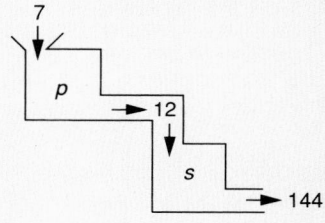

In function composition, you must be careful of the domain and range of each function. The domain of the composite cannot have values that are not in the domain of the function that is evaluated first, and the range of the first function must be in the domain of the function that is evaluated second. Occasionally, the domain of the first function must be *restricted* by excluding certain values so that its output is in the domain of the second.

Example 3   Suppose r is the reciprocal function, $r(x) = \frac{1}{x}$, and f is given by $f(x) = x^2 - 4$. Find a restriction on the domain of $r \circ f$.

Solution   There are no restrictions for function f while x cannot be 0 for $r(x)$. Now consider $r(f(x))$.

$$r(f(x)) = r(x^2 - 4) = \frac{1}{x^2 - 4}$$

Since the denominator cannot be zero, $x^2 - 4 \neq 0$ and $x^2 \neq 4$. So x cannot equal 2 or -2.

Questions

Covering the Reading

In 1–3, refer to the rebate and discount functions in this lesson.

1. If the sticker price is $13,500 and the rebate comes first, what is the cost of the car?   **$10,625**

2. If the sticker price is $13,500 and the discount comes first, what is the cost of the car?   **$10,475**

3. Explain why it is always better to take the discount first.
See margin.

4. If $f(x) = 3x^2$ and $g(x) = 4 - 5x$, calculate:
   a. $f(g(10))$ **6,348**   **b.** $(f \circ g)(10)$ **6,348**
   c. $(f \circ g)(0)$ **48**   **d.** $f(g(0))$ **48**

5. Let $f(x) = x^2 + x - 9$ and $g(x) = 7x$. Calculate:
   a. $f(g(5))$ **1251**   **b.** $g(f(5))$ **147**
   c. $g(f(x))$ $7x^2 + 7x - 63$ **d.** $f(g(x))$ $49x^2 + 7x - 9$

6. In Question 4, calculate $(f \circ f)(5)$.   **16,875**

7. *True or false* Composition of functions is commutative.   **False**

8. The domain for the composite must be in the __?__ of the function that is evaluated first, and the __?__ of the first function must be in the domain of the function that is evaluated second.   **domain; range**

390

In 9 and 10, let $r(x) = \dfrac{1}{x}$ and $n(x) = x^2 - 9$.

9. Find the restrictions on the domain of $r \circ n$.   **$x \neq 3$ and $x \neq -3$**

10. Find the restrictions on the domain of $n \circ r$.   **$x \neq 0$**

Applying the Mathematics

11. Let $d(x) = \sqrt{x}$ and $q(x) = x^3 - \pi$. Write a calculator key sequence to evaluate $d(q(1.9))$.   **1.9 $\boxed{y^x}$ 3 $\boxed{-}$ $\boxed{\pi}$ $\boxed{=}$ $\boxed{\sqrt{x}}$**

12. Let $f(x) = \sqrt{x}$ and $g(x) = x^2$.
    a. Calculate $f(g(-3))$.   **3**   b. Calculate $g(f(-3))$.   **Does not exist**

13. Consider $r(x) = \dfrac{1}{x}$.
    a. Simplify $r(r(x))$.   **x**
    b. When is $r(r(x))$ undefined?   **$x = 0$**

14. Composite functions can be used to describe relationships between functions of variation. Suppose w varies inversely as the square of z and z is proportional to the cube of x.
    a. Give an equation for the function mapping z onto w.   **$w = \dfrac{k_1}{z^2}$**
    b. Give an equation for the function mapping x onto z.   **$z = k_2 x^3$**
    c. Give an equation for the function mapping x onto w.   **See margin.**
    d. Use words to describe the function of part c.
    w is inversely proportional to the sixth power of x.

15. In the food chain, barracuda feed on bass and bass feed on shrimp. Suppose that the size of the barracuda population is estimated by the function $r(x) = 1000 + \sqrt{2x}$, where x is the size of the bass population. Also suppose that the size of the bass population is estimated by the function $s(x) = 2500 + \sqrt{x}$, where x is the size of the shrimp population.   **$(r \circ s)(x) = 1000 + \sqrt{2(2500 + \sqrt{x})}$**
    a. Find an equation of the composite which describes the size of the barracuda population in terms of the size of the shrimp population.
    b. About how many barracuda are there when the size of the shrimp population is 4,000,000?   **$\approx$1095 barracuda**

LESSON 7-3   Composition of Functions   391

NOTES ON QUESTIONS
Question 12: This question shows the noncommutativity of composition of functions. Notice that in part (b) students must use imaginary numbers.

Question 14: Since this question involves some abstract thinking, some students may have difficulty with part (c). Tell them that they must express w in terms of x. To do this, they should substitute $k_2 x^3$ for z in the equation for part (a).

Question 20: Have the students make at least one sketch before they answer this question. They will easily see that the slope must be -1.

Question 21: This exploration question allows for many extensions. For instance, $d_n(x)$ describes the nth daughter of x. Allowing subscripts like these (which really name new functions), any relative could be described.

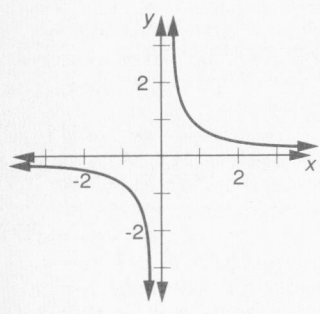
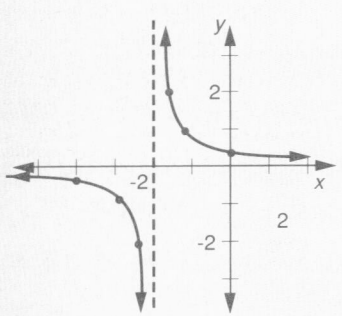
16. Let $w(x) = \sqrt{x^2 - 6}$. Find two functions f and g such that $w(x) = f(g(x))$.   **Sample: $f(x) = \sqrt{x}$, $g(x) = x^2 - 6$**

Review	**17.** A photograph is enlarged by a factor of K in each dimension. By what number is the area multiplied? *(Lesson 2-3, Previous course)* K^2

18. Graph each function and state its domain and range.

   a. $f(x) = \dfrac{1}{x}$ **See margin.**

   b. $g(x) = \dfrac{1}{x + 2}$. *(Lessons 2-7, 6-4, 7-1, 7-2)*   **See margin.**

19. Malone found the equation $h = -25(t - 2)^2 + 100$ gave the height h (in feet) of his model rocket t seconds after it was launched.
   a. How high did the rocket get?   **100 ft** $D = \{t: 0 \le t \le 4\}$
   b. What is the domain of the function mapping t onto h?
   c. What is the range of the function mapping t onto h? *(Lessons 6-4, 7-2)*
     $R = \{h: 0 \le h \le 100\}$

20. What is the slope of any line that has the same nonzero number for its x- and y-intercepts? *(Lessons 1-6, 2-4, 3-5)*   **-1**

Exploration	**21.** Let $f(x)$ = the father of x, let $m(x)$ = the mother of x, let $b(x)$ = the eldest brother of x, and let $h(x)$ = the husband of x. Then $(m \circ h)(x)$ is the mother-in-law of x. What relationship is defined by each of the following?

   a. $(h \circ m)(x)$ **the father of x**
   b. $(b \circ m)(x)$ **the uncle of x**

392

The daily charge to park a car at a city lot is 75¢ for the first half hour and 50¢ for each additional hour or portion of an hour. Thus the cost of parking is a function of time. The table below gives the cost if a car is parked at 7:00 P.M. and picked up before 1:30 A.M.

time	number of minutes since 7:00	cost (in dollars)
7:00– 7:30	$0 < n \leq 30$	.75
7:30– 8:30	$30 < n \leq 90$	$.75 + .50 = 1.25$
8:30– 9:30	$90 < n \leq 150$	$1.25 + .50 = 1.75$
9:30–10:30	$150 < n \leq 210$	$1.75 + .50 = 2.25$
10:30–11:30	$210 < n \leq 270$	$2.25 + .50 = 2.75$
11:30–12:30	$270 < n \leq 330$	$2.75 + .50 = 3.25$
12:30– 1:30	$330 < n \leq 390$	$3.25 + .50 = 3.75$

The graph below shows the cost of parking a car for up to and including 390 minutes. Notice that the graph represents a function. You can verify this with the vertical-line test. However, the function is discontinuous because you must lift your pencil to draw the graph.

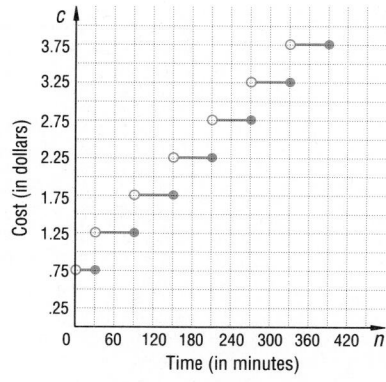

RESOURCES
- Lesson Master 7-4
- Quiz for Lessons 7-1 Through 7-4
- Visual for Teaching Aid 41 displays the data and graph for the cost of parking a car problem.
- Visual for Teaching Aid 42 provides a graph of the greatest integer function.
- Computer Master 14

OBJECTIVES

I Graph a function given its rule.
C Read simple BASIC programs involving the INT function.

TEACHING NOTES

There are many applications where step functions and the greatest integer function are used in students' lives. Begin by discussing sales tax tables, a step function with which almost all students are familiar. Mention a person's bowling average, which is usually defined as $\left[\frac{p}{g}\right]$, where p is the total score in g games bowled. (The average is rounded down, not to the nearest integer.)

Students are expected to evaluate and make graphs of functions whose formula is given in terms of the greatest integer function, whether written in algebra as $[x]$ or in BASIC as INT(X). Encourage students to *begin* tables with specific solutions, for example, $x = 1, 1.5, 2, 3.9, -2.1$, but to *extend* them to analyze the behavior of the function at all values between successive integers, for instance, $1 < x < 2$, $3 < x < 4, -3 < x < -2$.

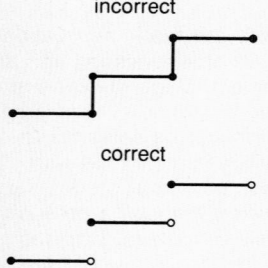
The domain consists of any positive real number of minutes less than or equal to the 1440 minutes in a day. The range is the discrete set of costs: {$.75, $1.25, $1.75, $2.25, $2.75, $3.25, $3.75, ...}.

The graph above looks like a series of steps and is called a **step function**. There is a special step function called the **greatest-integer** or **rounding-down function**, denoted [x].

Definition:

[x] = the greatest integer less than or equal to x.

Applying the definition gives $[4\frac{1}{2}] = 4$ because 4 is the largest integer that is less than or equal to $4\frac{1}{2}$. Likewise,

$$[\pi] = 3, [7] = 7, \text{ and } [-5.2] = -6.$$

The last instance may seem wrong, but recall that -6 < -5.2 < -5; so the largest integer less than or equal to -5.2 is -6. Notice that the domain of f: $x \rightarrow [x]$ is the set of real numbers; the range is the set of integers.

Here is how to graph the function f, where $f(x) = [x]$.

For all x greater than or equal to 0 but less than 1, the greatest integer is 0. For all x greater than or equal to 1 but less than 2, the greatest integer is 1. In a similar manner you can get the other values in the table below. The graph is at the right below.

x	$f(x) = [x]$
$-3 \leq x < -2$	-3
$-2 \leq x < -1$	-2
$-1 \leq x < 0$	-1
$0 \leq x < 1$	0
$1 \leq x < 2$	1
$2 \leq x < 3$	2
$3 \leq x < 4$	3

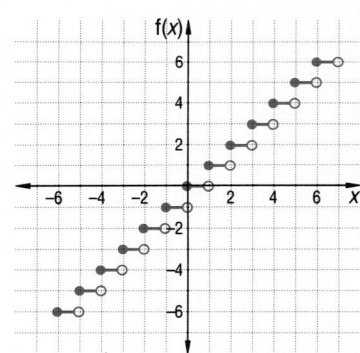

On the graph, there are open circles at (1, 0), (2, 1), (3, 2), and so forth to indicate that these values are not solutions to $f(x) = [x]$. At these points the function value is jumping to the next higher step.

394

The greatest-integer function has many applications in formulas, for instance, those for determining tax and postal rates. It is often used when function values must be integers but formulas would give noninteger values. On many computers, INT(X) denotes the greatest-integer function.

Example   Describe what the following computer program does for any number *N*.

```
10 INPUT "A REAL NUMBER"; N
20 PRINT INT(N + .5)
30 END
```

Solution   The PRINT statement computes [*N* + .5] for any value of *N* input into the program. We pick several values of *N* and evaluate this expression.

If N =	The computer calculates
4	[4 + .5] = 4
$33\frac{1}{2}$	$[33\frac{1}{2} + .5] = [34] = 34$
-78.8	[-78.8 + .5] = [-78.3] = -79
7.49	[7.49 + .5] = [7.99] = 7

You can see that this program takes any number, rounds it to the nearest integer, and prints the result.

To investigate how the function *N* → [*N* + .5] works, consider each step. Adding 0.5 keeps numbers whose tenths place has a 0 to 4 (and should be rounded down) without changing the integer portion of the number. For instance, 33.4 becomes 33.9, which is still between 33 and 34. Adding 0.5 moves numbers whose tenths place has a 5 to 9 (and should be rounded up) beyond the next integer. For instance, 7.6 is mapped onto 8.1. Then, taking the greatest integer, the result is that *N* is rounded up.

Questions

Covering the Reading

In 1 and 2, refer to the parking example at the beginning of this lesson.
1. What would be the cost to park a car for 408 minutes? $4.25
2. What is the domain of the function?   See margin.
3. **a.** f(*x*) = [*x*] is called the __?__ or __?__ function.   greatest integer; rounding down
   b. The range of f: *x* → [*x*] is __?__.   all integers
   c. Why are there open circles at (1, 0), (2, 1), (3, 2), and so forth in the graph of f?   Those values are not solutions of the function.

---

2. Graph f(x) = [x] − 1

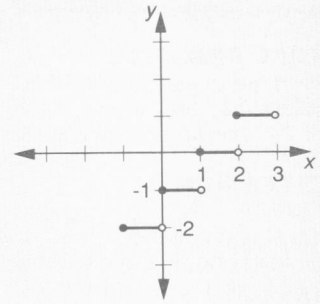

3. Describe what the following computer program accomplishes.

```
10 INPUT N
20 PRINT 100*INT((N+
   50)/100)
30 END
```

This program will round any positive number to the nearest hundred.

NOTES ON QUESTIONS
Question 25: This question is one of the more amazing applications of any function. Each part can be explained. The $\left[\frac{y}{4}\right]$ accounts for leap years. The $\left[\frac{y}{100}\right]$ is subtracted because the century years are not leap years except if they are divisible by 400, which is why the $\left[\frac{y}{400}\right]$ is added. (The years 1700, 1800, and 1900 were not leap years; 2000 will be a leap year.) The *d* at the beginning and the 2 at the end makes the formula begin at the right place. Only the terms involving *m* are not directly explainable; they are found by trial and error and account for the different numbers of days in the months.

Computer for Question 25: For the computer programmers in your class, suggest to them that by using the formula from this exploration question, a 12-month calendar can be printed for any year. The only real challenge of this program is formatting the output. Some students will also enjoy printing graphics at the top of their calendars.

MORE PRACTICE
For more questions on SPUR
Objectives, use *Lesson Mas-
ter 7-4*, shown on page 397.

EXTENSION
If INT(N) = N then we know
that N is an integer. Thus,
the following program can be
used to find all the factors of
a whole number N.

```
10 INPUT "A WHOLE
    NUMBER "; N
20 PRINT "THE FACTORS
    OF N ARE ";
30 FOR I=1 TO N
40   IF N/I=INT(N/I)
       THEN PRINT I", ";
50 NEXT I
60 END
```

Similarly, if INT(N/2) = N/2,
then N is even. Ask students:
How can the INT function be
used to determine whether a
number is divisible by *k*? (If
INT(N/K) = N/K, then N is
divisible by K.)

EVALUATION
A quiz covering Lessons 7-1
through 7-4 is provided in the
Teacher's Resource File.

ADDITIONAL ANSWERS
12.a.

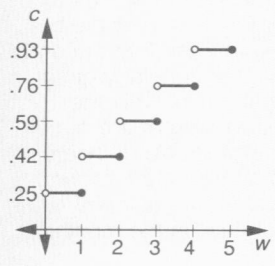

In 4–7, evaluate.

4. $[3\frac{1}{2}]$ 3   **5.** $[11.9]$ 11   **6.** $[-11.7]$ -12   **7.** $[8 + .5]$ 8

In 8–10, refer to the Example.

8. What will the computer print when $N = 64.39$?   64

9. When will the computer print 7? $6.5 \le N < 7.5$

Applying the Mathematics	**10.** If line 20 in the program is changed to

$$20 \text{ PRINT } 10*\text{INT}((N + 5)/10)$$

a different sort of rounding occurs. What kind of rounding is it?
The program would take any positive number and round it to the nearest ten.

11. Find a value of x for which $[x + .5] \neq [x] + .5$.   **any value of x**

12. At present to mail a letter first class in the U.S. costs 25¢ for the first
ounce or fraction thereof, and 17¢ for each additional ounce or fraction thereof. Let $w =$ the weight in ounces of a letter and $c =$ the cost
in dollars of mailing it first class.
  a. Draw a graph of c as a function of w for $0 < w \le 5$.   **See margin.**
  b. *True or false* The formula $c = .25 + .17[w - 1]$ describes this
      function.   **False. The formula is c = .25 + .17 ⌈w − 1⌉ (see problem 15).**

13. *Multiple choice* A stadium used for graduation has 25,000 seats.
There are s seniors graduating. Which of the following represents the
number of graduation tickets each senior may have?

  (a) $\dfrac{25000}{s}$ (b) $\left\lceil \dfrac{25000}{s} \right\rceil$ (c) $[25000 \cdot s]$ **b**

14. Tyrone is paid a weekly salary of \$175 plus an additional \$45 for each
\$300 in sales.
  a. Find his salary during a week when he has \$1000 in sales.   **\$310**
  b. *Multiple choice* When he has d dollars in sales, his weekly salary
      equals which of the following?   **ii**
      (i) $175 + \left\lceil \dfrac{45d}{300} \right\rceil$ (ii) $175 + 45\left\lceil \dfrac{d}{300} \right\rceil$ (iii) $175 + \left(\dfrac{45}{300}\right)d$

15. The **rounding-up function** is denoted $\lceil x \rceil$. This gives the smallest
integer *greater* than or equal to x. For example, $\lceil 4.7 \rceil = 5$.
  a. Find $\lceil 2.3 \rceil$.   3
  b. Find $\lceil -1.8 \rceil$.   -1
  c. For all $5 < x \le 6$, find $\lceil x \rceil$.   6
  d. Graph $r(x) = \lceil x \rceil$.   **See margin.**

Review	In 16–18, suppose f: $x \to 3x - 4$ and g: $x \to x^2$. *(Lesson 7-3)*

16. f ∘ g: 8 → _?_   188   **17.** f ∘ g: $x \to$ _?_. $3x^2 - 4$

18. f(g(x)) = _?_ $3x^2 - 4$

19. Graph the function with equation $x = y^2 + 1$, where $y \ge 0$.
(Lesson 7-2)   **See margin.**

20. Define: function. *(Lesson 7-1)* A function is a relation in which for each ordered pair, the first coordinate has exactly one second coordinate.

In 21 and 22, use the fact that a sequence is a special kind of function. It is a function whose domain is the set of positive integers. Find the range for the function determined by each formula. *(Lessons 1-3, 1-4, 7-1)*

21. $t_n = 2n$ range = {positive even integers}

22. $\begin{cases} t_1 = 1 \\ t_n = \dfrac{t_{n-1}}{2}, \text{ for } n \geq 2 \end{cases}$ range = {all nonnegative powers of $\frac{1}{2}$}.

23. Without using a calculator, simplify each root. *(Previous course)*
 a. $\sqrt{20}$ $2\sqrt{5}$ **b.** $\sqrt{147}$ $7\sqrt{3}$ **c.** $\sqrt{\sqrt{\sqrt{16}}}$ 2

24. Solve $2m^2 - 7 = 12m$. Round the solutions to the nearest hundredth. *(Lesson 6-6)* $m \approx -0.54$ or $m \approx 6.54$

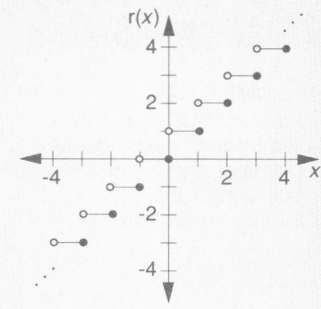

15.d.

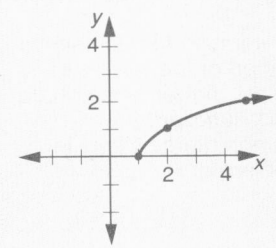

19.

| Exploration |

25. The formula $W = d + 2m + \left[\dfrac{3(m + 1)}{5}\right] + y + \left[\dfrac{y}{4}\right] - \left[\dfrac{y}{100}\right] + \left[\dfrac{y}{400}\right] + 2$ gives the day of the week based on our current calendar where

d = the day of the month of the given date

m = the number of the month in the year with January and February regarded as the 13th and 14th months of the previous year; that is, 2/22/90 is 14/22/89. The other months are numbered 3 to 12 as usual.

y = the year.

Once W is computed, divide by 7 and the remainder is the day of the week, with Saturday = 0, Sunday = 1, ..., Friday = 6.   Many answers are possible
 a. Find the day of the week on which you were born.
 b. On what day of the week was the Declaration of Independence adopted?   Thursday

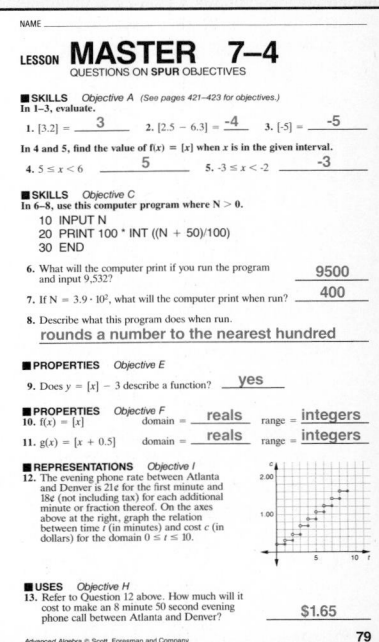

OBJECTIVES

F Determine the domain and
range of the absolute
value, power, and square
root functions.
I Graph the functions in
Objective F.

TEACHING NOTES

Most students conclude after
reading Lesson 7-5 that as
the positive integer n
increases, the values of
$f(x) = x^n$ increase more rapidly. This is true for values of
$x > 1$ and can be seen by
plotting various powering
functions on the same set
of axes or by reasoning
about powers. For $x > 1$,
$f(x) = x^5$ is steeper than
$f(x) = x^4$, which in turn is
steeper than $f(x) = x^3$, and
so on. However, not all students realize that for values
of x between -1 and 1 the
order of the steepness is
reversed.

This is a good lesson in
which to use a function plotter. To illustrate the property
mentioned in the preceding
paragraph, use your zoom or
scale change feature to focus
on the portion of the graphs
near the origin, say from
$x = -0.5$ to $x = 1.5$. Discuss
with students why it is that
for $0 < x < 1$, $f(x) = x^5$ is
"flatter" than $f(x) = x^4$, which
in turn is "flatter" than
$f(x) = x^3$, and so on.

LESSON

7-5

Other Special Functions

In addition to the greatest-integer function, other functions are important enough to have special names. One of these is the absolute-
value function and is denoted $|x|$. Recall the definition of absolute
value:

$$|x| = x \text{ if } x \geq 0 \text{ and } |x| = -x \text{ when } x < 0.$$

Because $-x$ is the opposite of x, $-x$ is positive when x is negative.
For this reason, $|x|$ is never negative. For example, $|24| = 24$ and
$|-24| = -(-24) = 24$. In general, $|x| = |-x|$. The function $f(x) = |x|$
is a function whose domain is the set of real numbers and whose
range is the nonnegative real numbers.

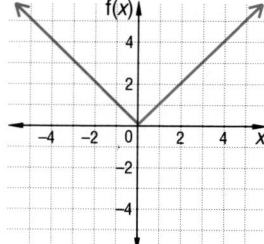

The graph of $f(x) = |x|$ consists of two rays. When $x \geq 0$,
the graph is a ray from $(0, 0)$ with slope 1. This is shown on
the graph in blue. When $x < 0$, the graph is a ray with
slope -1. This is shown in green. The graph of $f(x) = |x|$ is the
union of these two rays, and so the graph of $f(x) = |x|$ is an
angle. The minimum point $(0, 0)$ on the function is the
vertex of the angle.

In many computer programs, the absolute-value function is denoted
ABS. That is, $\text{ABS}(X) = |X|$.

■ ■ ■ ■ ■ ■ ■ ■

Example 1 Write a LET statement for each formula.
a. $d = |a - b|$
b. $y = |3x|$

Solution
a. LET D = ABS(A − B)
b. LET Y = ABS(3 * X)

Some special functions are the powering functions. The simplest
powering function is $f(x) = x^1$ which is called the **identity function**.

398

The simplest quadratic function is $f(x) = x^2$, which is called the **squaring function,** and the function $f(x) = x^3$ is called the **cubing function**. In general, the function $f(x) = x^n$, where n is a positive integer, is called the **nth power function**. The following BASIC program gives the coordinates of points graphed below and on the next page. Recall that X ^ N means x^n.

```
10 PRINT "VALUES FOR THE FUNCTION F(X) = X ^ N."
20 INPUT "FOR N = "; N
30 PRINT "F(X) = X ^ ";N
40 PRINT "X", "F(X)"
50 FOR X = -5 TO 5
60    PRINT X, X ^ N
70 NEXT X
80 END
```

If you have a function grapher, set the domain to $\{x: -5 \le x \le 5\}$ and verify these graphs.

x	f(x)
-5	-5
-4	-4
-3	-3
-2	-2
-1	-1
0	0
1	1
2	2
3	3
4	4
5	5

The Identity Function

x	f(x)
-5	25
-4	16
-3	9
-2	4
-1	1
0	0
1	1
2	4
3	9
4	16
5	25

The Squaring Function

x	f(x)
-5	-125
-4	-64
-3	-27
-2	-8
-1	-1
0	0
1	1
2	8
3	27
4	64
5	125

The Cubing Function

ADDITIONAL EXAMPLES
1. Graph $g(x) = |x| + 1$. State the domain and range.

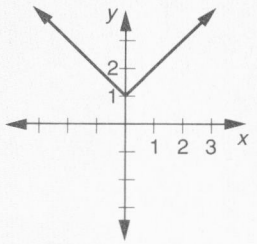

domain = set of real numbers; range = $\{y: y \ge 1\}$

2. The following functions are graphed below: $y = x^2$, $y = x^3$, $y = \sqrt{x}$, and $y = -|x|$. Label each graph with its proper equation.
a.

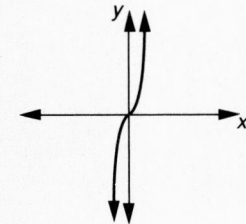

$y = x^3$

b.

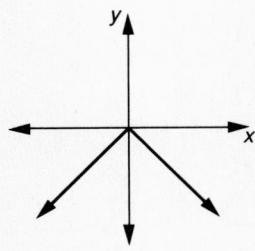

$y = -|x|$

c.

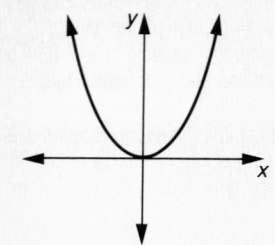

$y = x^2$

d.

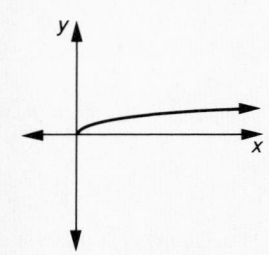

$y = \sqrt{x}$

x	$f(x)$
-5	625
-4	256
-3	81
-2	16
-1	1
0	0
1	1
2	16
3	81
4	256
5	625

The 4th-Power Function

x	$f(x)$
-5	-3125
-4	-1024
-3	-243
-2	-32
-1	-1
0	0
1	1
2	32
3	243
4	1024
5	3125

The 5th-Power Function

Several properties of the powering functions can be deduced.

1. The graph of every powering function $f(x) = x^n$ passes through the origin, because $0^n = 0$ for any positive integer value of n.

2. For all powering functions the domain is the set of real numbers, because you can raise any real number to a positive integer power. (Note: many calculators will give an error message when a negative number is raised to a power with the y^x key. This means the calculator cannot do the problem, not that it cannot be done.)

3. To find the range, two cases must be considered for n, a positive integer.
   (i) n is even:
      If $x \geq 0$, then $x^n \geq 0$ because any nonnegative number raised to a power is nonnegative. If $x < 0$, then raising x to an even power results in a positive number. Thus, when n is even, the range is $\{y: y \geq 0\}$, and the graph of $f(x) = x^n$ where n is even is in quadrants I and II. Check this by observing the graphs of $f(x) = x^2$ and $f(x) = x^4$.
   (ii) n is odd:
      If $x \geq 0$, then $x^n \geq 0$ because any nonnegative number raised to a power is nonnegative. If $x < 0$, then raising x to an odd power results in a negative number. Thus, the range is all real numbers, and the graph of $f(x) = x^n$ where n is odd is in quadrants I and III. Check this by observing the graphs of $f(x) = x$, $f(x) = x^3$, and $f(x) = x^5$.

4. The graph of every powering function has symmetry.
   (i) n is even:
      The even-powering functions have reflection symmetry. The graph of $f(x) = x^n$ is symmetric to the y-axis when n is an even positive number.

400

(ii) *n* is odd:

The odd-powering functions have rotation symmetry. The graph of f(x) = x^n can be mapped onto itself under a 180° rotation around the origin when *n* is an odd positive integer.

Example 2 Which of the following graphs could represent the function with equation $y = x^7$?

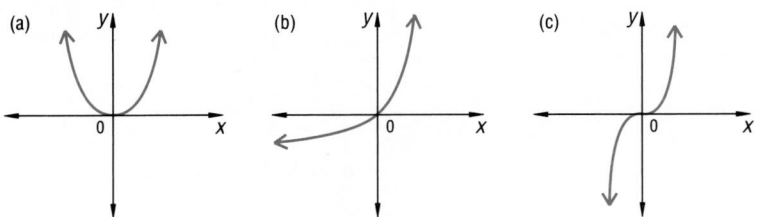

(a) (b) (c)

Solution This is an odd-powering function so the range is the set of all real numbers. Only (b) and (c) have the correct range. Also, the graph of $y = x^7$ must have rotation symmetry about the origin; only graph (c) does. Thus, (c) could be the correct graph.

Another special function is the **square-root function** f: $x \rightarrow \sqrt{x}$, where *x* is a nonnegative real number. In BASIC, $\sqrt{x}$ is represented by SQR(X). The square root function that is on your calculator, $\boxed{\sqrt{x}}$, always gives the nonnegative value for the square root. The square-root function on your calculator is the *upper* half of the parabola with equation $x = y^2$.

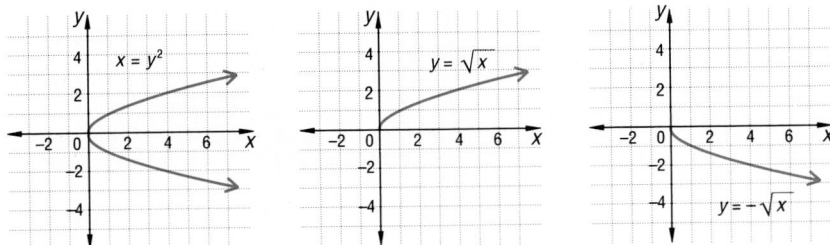

It would be possible to define a key on the calculator that would always give the nonpositive square root. This would be represented by the *lower* half of the parabola $x = y^2$, where $y \leq 0$. However, such a key is not needed. You can press $\boxed{\sqrt{x}}$ $\boxed{+/-}$ to get $-\sqrt{x}$. Few calculators deal with complex numbers, so the domain of SQR is the set of nonnegative real numbers.

Question 12: After seeing and sketching graphs over the domain of real numbers, students may have to be reminded that, when sketching the graph for this question, a negative value for *w* is not appropriate.

Questions 13 and 14: When discussing these questions, stress that an equation is expected. It is easy to see in **Question 14** that the equation must be of the form $y = x^n$, where *w* is odd. The specific point given, (2, 32), leads us to the equation $32 = 2^n$, from which $n = 5$.

Question 24: If students have difficulty with this question, have them sketch such a line first; the equation will then be easy to write.

Question 28: This question constitutes an important type of question, in which a function is arbitrarily defined. Ask students to invent other symbols for functions.

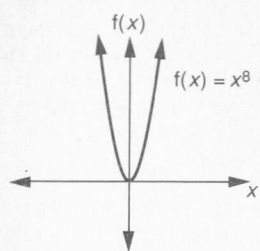
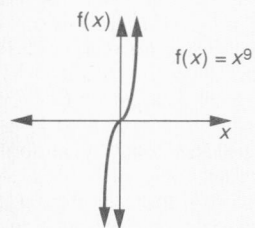
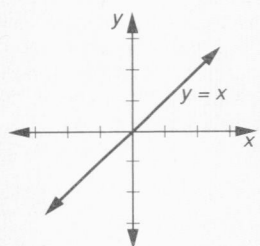
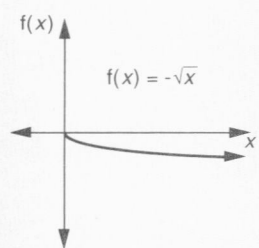
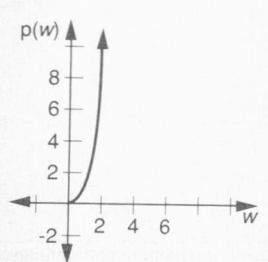
Covering the Reading

1. State the domain and range of the function f with $f(x) = |x|$.
   domain = {all real numbers}; range = {nonnegative real numbers}

2. **a.** $|17.8| = \underline{\ ?\ }$ 17.8   **b.** $|-11| = \underline{\ ?\ }$ 11

3. Fill in the blanks. The graph of $y = |x|$ can be thought of as the

   piecewise linear graph of $\begin{cases} y = \underline{(a)}\ \text{if } x < 0. \\ y = \underline{(b)}\ \text{if } x \geq 0 \end{cases}$ a) -x; b) x

4. **a.** $y = x^3$ is called the $\underline{\ ?\ }$ function.   cubing
   b. $y = x^n$ is called the $\underline{\ ?\ }$ function.   nth powering

5. Quickly sketch the graphs indicated without plotting points or doing
   any calculations.   See margin.
   a. $f(x) = x^8$ **b.** $f(x) = x^9$
   c. the identity function   **d.** $f(x) = -\sqrt{x}$

In 6–8, refer to the properties of the powering functions.

6. If n is even, the range of $y = x^n$ is $\underline{\ ?\ }$ and the graph is in quadrants
   $\underline{\ ?\ }$ and $\underline{\ ?\ }$.   {y: y ≥ 0}; I and II

7. If n is odd, the range of $y = x^n$ is $\underline{\ ?\ }$ and the graph is in quadrants
   $\underline{\ ?\ }$ and $\underline{\ ?\ }$.   {all real numbers}; I and III

8. What are acceptable values for n?   positive integers

9. *True or false* The graphs of the odd powering functions have no
   minimum or maximum values.   True

In 10 and 11, write a LET statement in BASIC for each formula.

10. $y = |x - 5|$
    LET Y = ABS(X−5)

11. $c = \sqrt{a^2 + b^2}$
    LET C = SQR(A^2 + B^2)

Applying the Mathematics

12. In Chapter 2 you read that the power generated by a windmill is
    proportional to the cube of the wind speed w. $P(w) = kw^3$
    a. Write an equation using Euler's notation to describe the variation.
    b. Sketch the graph over the appropriate domain.   See margin.

In 13 and 14, a powering function is graphed. Write an equation for each
function.

13.

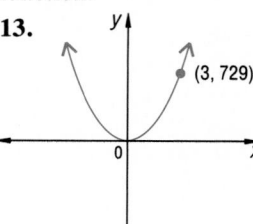

y

(3, 729)

0   x

14.

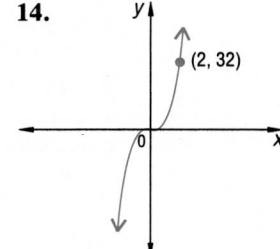

y

(2, 32)

0   x

15. **a.** Graph $d(x) = -|x|$.   See margin.
    b. State the domain and range.
       domain = {all real numbers}; range = {all nonpositive numbers}

16. **a.** Graph $f(x) = |2x|$, $g(x) = 2|x|$, $h(x) = |-2x|$, and $i(x) = -2|x|$.
    b. Make a generalization about the effect of the value of a on the
       graphs of $y = a|x|$ and $y = |ax|$.   See margin.

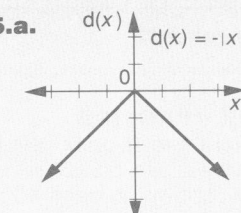
15.a.

16.a.,b., See Additional Answers in the back of this book.

17. The formula $e = |p - I|$ describes the allowable margin of error e for
    a given length of a product p where I stands for the ideal length.
    When constructing a swimming pool for international competitions the
    contractors aim for a length of 50.015 meters with an acceptable
    margin of error of .015 m.
    a. Write an equation satisfied by the possible lengths p of pools in
       this situation. $.015 = |p - 50.015|$
    b. What are the possible lengths? $50.000 \le p \le 50.030$

18. **a.** Complete the program below so it accepts as input any two real
       numbers and prints the distance between them on the number line.

    ```
    10 INPUT "TWO REAL NUMBERS"; X1; X2          (i) X1
    20 PRINT "THE DISTANCE BETWEEN"; (i);        (ii) X2
       "AND"; (ii); "IS"; (iii)                  (iii) ABS (X1−X2)
    30 END
    ```

    b. Modify the program above so it accepts as input the coordinates
       (x_1, y_1), (x_2, y_2) of any two points, and prints the distance between
       them.

    ```
    10  INPUT "TWO ORDERED PAIRS"; X1;Y1;X2;Y2
    20  PRINT "THE DISTANCE BETWEEN THE
        POINTS IS"; SQR((X1−X2)^2 + (Y1−Y2)^2)
    30  END
    ```

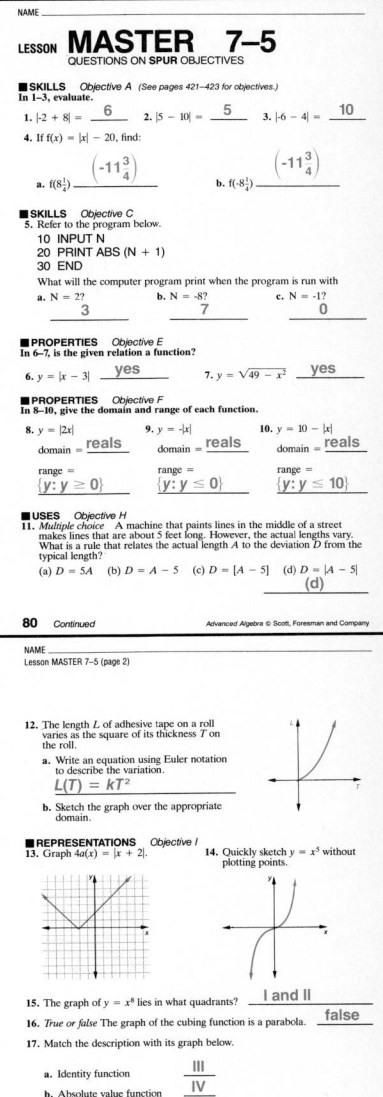

MORE PRACTICE
For more questions on SPUR
Objectives, use *Lesson Mas-
ter 7-5*, shown on page 403.

EXTENSION
Extend the idea of an even
and odd function using the
following definitions. An even
function f is a function such
that f(-x) = f(x) for all x. An
odd function f is a function
such that f(-x) = -f(x). Give
students functions such as
f(x) = |x|, f(x) = ∛x,
f(x) = x³ + x, f(x) = x² + 1
and have them characterize
them as even or odd. Have
students plot these graphs
on a function plotter and
make conjectures about the
symmetry of such functions.
They should realize that all
even functions are symmetric
with respect to the *y*-axis and
that all odd functions are rotation symmetric.

ADDITIONAL ANSWERS
19.

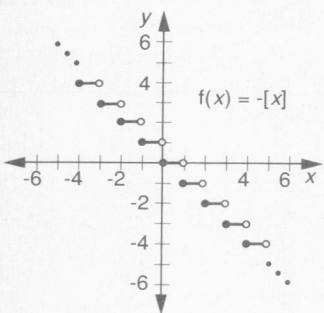

$f(x) = -[x]$

28.

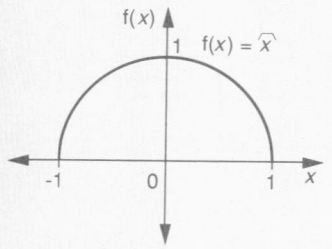

$f(x) = \hat{x}$

Semicircle
x-intercepts = -1 and 1
y-intercept = 1
symmetry about y-axis

---

19. Graph $f(x) = -[x]$. *(Lesson 7-4)*   **See margin.**

20. A school district has buses that hold 120
students each. Let *b* be the number of
buses needed to transport *s* students.
(Lesson 7-4)   **iii**

Multiple choice Which formula describes this situation? (Remember:
⌈ ⌉ indicates the rounding-up function.)

(i) $b = \left\lfloor \dfrac{s}{120} \right\rfloor$ (ii) $b = [120s]$ (iii) $b = \left\lceil \dfrac{s}{120} \right\rceil$

21. If $f(x) = 3x^2$ and $g(x) = 2x^3$, does $f(g(x)) = g(f(x))$ for all values of
x? *(Lesson 7-3)*   **No**

22. Give an equation for the line perpendicular to $3x + 2y = 5$ at the
point (1, 1). *(Lesson 4-7)* $y - 1 = \frac{2}{3}(x - 1)$

23. Solve for *t*: $y = m + xt$. *(Lesson 1-8)* $t = \frac{y - m}{x}$

24. Give an equation for a relation whose graph is a line but which is not
a function. *(Lesson 7-1)* $x = a$

25. What transformation changes

$\begin{bmatrix} 2 & -3 & 0 \\ 1 & 4 & 6 \end{bmatrix}$ to $\begin{bmatrix} 1 & 4 & 6 \\ -2 & 3 & 0 \end{bmatrix}$? *(Lesson 4-5)* $\begin{bmatrix} 0 & 1 \\ -1 & 0 \end{bmatrix}$

26. You are at the hair stylist looking in a mirror
at a clock. You see the figure at the right.
(Previous course)   **reflection across vertical axis**
a. In your mind, to tell the time, what
transformation do you need to apply?
b. What time is it?   **2:55**

27. In the last two chapters you have seen several functions, some of
which are listed below. Write an equation for the composite of two of
these, or two of your own choosing, and then graph your composite.
Try this with several pairs of functions. Some composites have surprising graphs.   **Sample:**
$f(x) = [x]$ $(k \circ f)(x) = \dfrac{6}{[x]}$ $g(x) = |x|$ $h(x) = x^2$
$i(x) = x^3$ $j(x) = \sqrt{x}$ $k(x) = \dfrac{6}{x}$

28. For this question, the symbol $\hat{x}$ means $\sqrt{1 - x^2}$, for $-1 \leq x \leq 1$.
Explore the graph of the function $f(x) = \hat{x}$. (That is, what is the
shape of the graph? What are its intercepts? Does the graph
have any symmetry?)   **See margin.**

404

7-6

Reflections and Inverses

Like a mathematical reflection, a physical reflection reverses the orientation (usually left-right) of the image. Unlike a mathematical reflection, a physical reflection often distorts that image.

LESSON 7-6

RESOURCES
■ Lesson 7-6
▯ Computer Master 16

OBJECTIVES

D Obtain rules for inverses of functions.
G Determine relationships between a function and its inverse.
K Apply the vertical and horizontal line tests for a function and its inverse.
L Graph the inverse of a function.

TEACHING NOTES

An important point to stress in this lesson is that if y is a function f of x, then x determines y. If, in addition, y also determines x, then the inverse of f is also a function.

Finding the inverse of a function that is given either as a list of ordered pairs or as a graph is usually not difficult for students. Since reflections preserve size and shape, when given the graph of a function, its inverse can be graphed by reversing some ordered pairs from the original graph and then connecting those points to form a graph which is the same size and shape of the original.

Some students will need to see additional examples which involve determining the inverse from the equation of a function. Point out that after finding an equation for the inverse, it may help to solve this equation for y before trying to graph it. Here is a simple example: If $y = -2x$, then its inverse is $x = -2y$. To graph the inverse, it is helpful to solve it for y.

Just as numbers and matrices can have inverses, so can functions. The **inverse of a function** has the following definition.

> **Definition:**
>
> The inverse of a function is the relation obtained by reversing the order of the coordinates of each ordered pair in the function.

That is, the inverse switches the x- and y-coordinates.

Example 1 Let f = {(1, 4), (2, 8), (4, 16), (-1, -4), (-2, -8), (-3, -12)}. Find the inverse of f.

Solution The inverse is found by switching the coordinates of each ordered pair. If we call the inverse g, then

g = {(4, 1), (8, 2), (16, 4), (-4, -1), (-8, -2), (-12, -3)}.

Check Notice that an equation for f is $y = 4x$. An equation for g is $x = 4y$. Thus x and y have been switched.

Recall that the domain of a function is the set of possible values for x and the range is the set of possible values for y. Because the inverse is found by switching the x- and y-coordinates, the domain and range of the inverse are found by switching the domain and range of the function. That is, in general, if f and g are inverses, then

domain of f = range of g
range of f = domain of g.

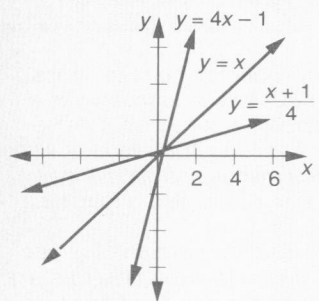
This relationship is illustrated in the graph below of a function f and its inverse g. From the graph you can see that:

$$\text{domain of } f = \{x\colon -2 \le x \le 2\}$$
$$\text{range of } g = \{y\colon -2 \le y \le 2\}$$

$$\text{domain of } g = \{x\colon 1 \le x \le 7\}$$
$$\text{range of } f = \{y\colon 1 \le x \le 7\}$$

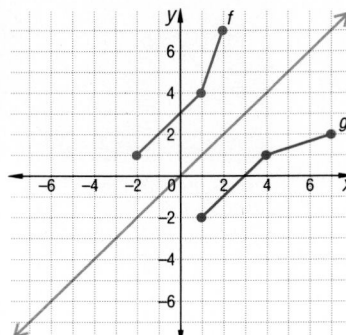

Recall that when the point (x, y) is reflected over the line with equation $y = x$, the image is (y, x). That is, the reflection over the identity line switches the coordinates of the ordered pairs. Thus, the graphs of a function and its inverse are reflection images of each other about the line $y = x$. This is easily seen in the above graph.

Caution: the word *inverse*, when used in the phrase *inverse of a function*, is different and unrelated to its use in the term *inverse variation*.

The inverse of a function is not always a function, as the next example shows.

⬛ ⬛ ⬛ ⬛ ⬛ ◼◼

Example 2 Consider the function with domain the set of all real numbers and equation $y = x^2$.
a. What is an equation for the inverse?
b. Graph the function and its inverse on the same coordinate axes.
c. Show that the inverse is not a function.

Solution
a. To find an equation for the inverse, switch the coordinates x and y. Given the function with equation $y = x^2$, its inverse has equation $x = y^2$.

b. The graphs of $y = x^2$ and $x = y^2$ are below. Notice again that the inverse is the reflection image of $y = x^2$ across the line with equation $y = x$.

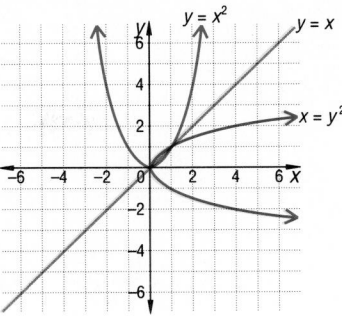

c. The inverse is not a function because both (4, 2) and (4, -2) are on the graph of $x = y^2$. The graph of $x = y^2$ fails the vertical-line test for a function.

In Example 1, each y value was paired with just one x value. There the inverse is a function. However, in Example 2 some y values are paired with two different x values; that is, (2, 4) and (-2, 4) are both on the graph of $y = x^2$. When the coordinates are switched, the new first coordinate is paired with two different second coordinates; that is, (4, 2) and (4, -2) are both on the graph of the inverse $x = y^2$. Thus the inverse cannot represent a function. We conclude that to have an inverse that is a function, the original function cannot map two distinct members of the domain onto the same member of the range. We say there must be a *one-to-one* (abbreviated *1-1*) *correspondence* between the domain and range of the function for its inverse to be a function.

You can also tell by looking at the graph of the original function whether or not its inverse represents a function. The horizontal-line test is useful in deciding if the situation of Example 2 exists.

Theorem (Horizontal-Line Test for Inverses):

The inverse of a function is itself a function if and only if no horizontal line intersects the graph of the function in more than one point.

To tell if an inverse is a function, you can either:
  a. apply the horizontal line test to the given function; or
  b. draw the graph of the inverse and apply the vertical-line test.

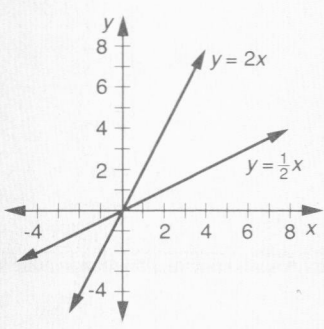
The graphs below show both strategies.

Function

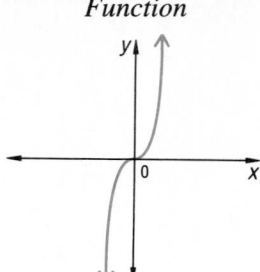

1-1 function.
Passes horizontal-line test.

Inverse

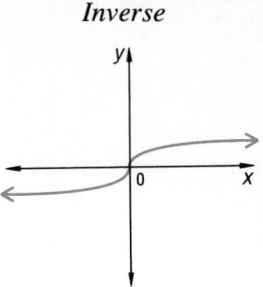

Inverse is a function.
Passes vertical-line test.

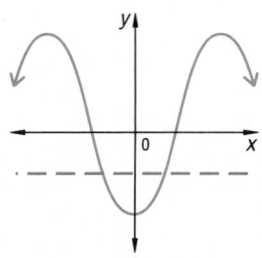

Not a 1-1 function.
Doesn't pass horizontal-line test.

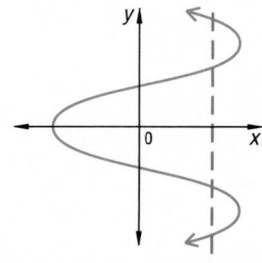

Inverse is not a function.
Doesn't pass vertical-line test.

In a function, the independent variable (usually x) determines the value of the dependent variable (usually y). In Example 2, because $y = x^2$ is a function, x determines y. When the function has an inverse, the process can be reversed. In Example 2, because the inverse is *not* a function, y does *not* determine x.

Questions

Covering the Reading

1. The inverse of a function can be found by __?__ the coordinates of the function.   **switching**

2. Let f = {(4, 8), (2, 4), (3, 6), (-1, -2), (-5, -10)}.
   a. Write an equation for the function and list the values of the domain. $y = 2x$, domain = {4,2,3,-1,-5}
   b. Write the coordinates of the inverse.   {(8, 4), (4, 2), (6, 3), (-2, -1), (-10, -5)}
   c. Write an equation for the inverse function. $y = \frac{1}{2}x$
   d. Graph the function f and the inverse on the same set of axes.
      See margin.
3. The graphs of any function f and its inverse are reflection images over the line __?__. $y = x$

408

408

4. Refer to Example 2.
   a. Is the function $y = x^2$ a 1-1 function?   No
   b. What is an equation for its inverse? $x = y^2$
   c. Find two points other than those in the lesson that show the inverse is not a function.   Sample: (9,3), (9,-3)

In 5 and 6, give an equation for the inverse of the function.

5. $y = 3x$ $x = 3y$

6. $y = 9x^2 + 12x - 6$ $x = 9y^2 + 12y - 6$

7. To tell if the inverse of a function is a function:
   a. apply the __?__ test if you have graphed the function.   horizontal line
   b. apply the __?__ test if you have graphed the inverse.   vertical line

In 8–10, (a) is the function 1-1? (b) Is the inverse a function?

8. No, No
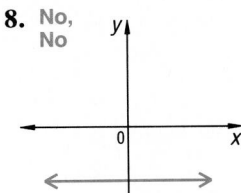

9. No, No
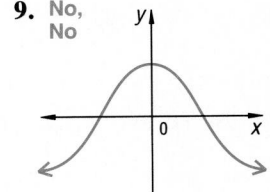

10. Yes, Yes
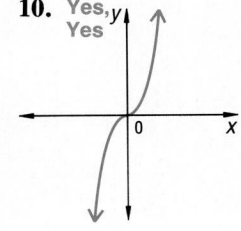

Applying the Mathematics

11. The graph of $y = 4x + 9$ is shown at the right.   See margin.
    a. Use the horizontal-line test to decide if the inverse is a function.
    b. Find an equation for the inverse.
    c. Graph the inverse.
    d. How are the slopes of the function and its inverse related?
       The slopes are reciprocals.

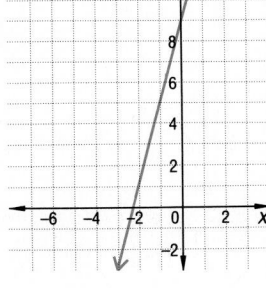

b) No; each positive value of x is mapped to two values of y.

12. a. Graph the inverse of the absolute-value function.   See margin.
    b. Is the inverse a function? Explain why or why not.
    c. What rule describes the inverse of the absolute value function?
       $x = |y|$

13. In 1987, a U.S. dollar was worth about 1.33 Canadian dollars. That means an item costing 1 U.S. dollar would cost about 1.33 Canadian dollars. Let x = cost in U.S. dollars and y = cost in Canadian dollars.
    a. Find an equation for f: $x \rightarrow y$. $f(x) = 1.3x$
    b. Find an equation for g: $y \rightarrow x$. $g(y) = .75y$

LESSON 7-6   Reflections and Inverses   **409**

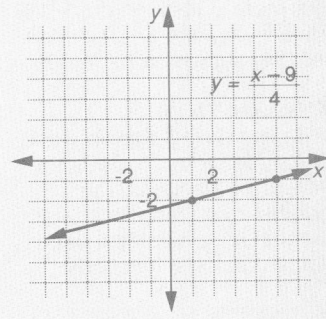

12.a.

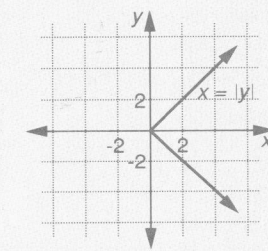

NAME _____

LESSON **MASTER   7–6**
QUESTIONS ON **SPUR** OBJECTIVES

■ SKILLS   Objective D   (See pages 421–423 for objectives.)
In 1–4, give an equation for the inverse of the function.

1. $f(x) = \dfrac{2}{x}$ 2. $g: x \rightarrow -\dfrac{3}{5}x - 8$

   $x = \dfrac{2}{y}$ $x = -\dfrac{3}{5}y - 8$

3. $y = x^2 - x - 12$ 4. $y = |3x|$

   $x = y^2 - y - 12$ $x = |3y|$

5. A function has equation $y = -\frac{1}{2}x + 3$. In slope-intercept form, what is an equation for its inverse? $y = -2x + 6$

■ PROPERTIES   Objective G
6. If f and g are inverses, then f ∘ g(x) = ____ x ____.

7. Let f = {(1, 2), (3, 4), (5, 6)}.
   a. What is the domain of f?   {1, 3, 5}
   b. What is the range of f?   {2, 4, 6}

8. Is the greatest integer function 1-1?   no

■ REPRESENTATIONS   Objective K
In 9 and 10, use the graphs below.

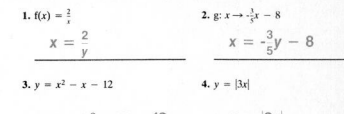

(a)   (b)   (c)   (d)

9. Multiple choice   Which of the above is a function whose inverse is not a function?   (b)

10. How can you restrict the domain of the function in your answer to Question 9 so that the inverse is a function?
    sample: restrict x to be positive

Review

14. This question examines the inverse of an inverse variation. Consider the function with equation $y = \dfrac{6}{x}$.
   a. Find an equation for the inverse. $x = \dfrac{6}{y}$
   b. Is the inverse a function? Why or why not? See margin.
   c. If *y* varies inversely as *x*, then *x* varies __?__ as *y*. inversely

15. The graph at the right shows the height of a flag on a pole as a function of time. This would be a difficult function to write as a formula. See margin.
   (Lessons 7-4, 3-8)
   a. What is happening to the flag?
   b. Why are there some horizontal segments on the graph?

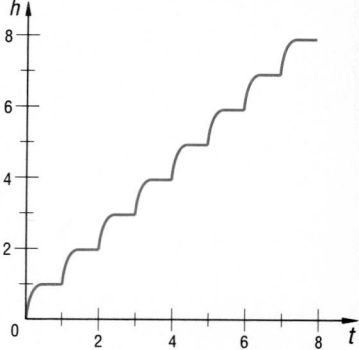

16. Given f(x) = x^2 + 1 and g(x) = x^2 − 1, find (f ∘ g)(x). *(Lesson 7-3)* $x^4 - 2x^2 + 2$

17. Let f(x) = 3x + 4 and g(x) = $\frac{1}{3}$(x − 4).
   a. Find (g ∘ f)(15). 15
   b. Find (g ∘ f)(x). x
   c. What is another name for the function f ∘ g? *(Lessons 7-3, 7-5)*
     identity function

18. Refer to the figure at the right. Lines ℓ and m are parallel. Find the measures of the numbered angles. *(Previous course E)*
   ∠1 = 30°, ∠2 = 50°, ∠3 = 80°

19. a. If f: x → $\frac{1}{2}$x + 5, calculate $\dfrac{f(10) - f(-10)}{10 - (-10)}$. $\frac{1}{2}$
   b. What have you calculated?
   (Lesson 7-1) the slope of y = f(x)

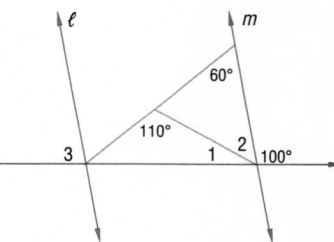

Exploration

20. Another way to think of an inverse is to do the opposite operations of the function in the reverse order.
   a. Pick an equation with 3 operations such as $y = \dfrac{2x - 3}{7}$. List the steps in the correct order that you would do to evaluate a value for *x*. Construct the inverse by doing the opposite operations in the reverse order to *x*. See margin.
   b. Pick a routine that you do every day and see if you also do its inverse. Try these or one of your own. See margin.

   Is your drive home the inverse of your drive to school?

   Is your routine for getting ready to go to sleep the inverse of getting up in the morning?

   Is parallel parking a car the inverse of getting out of a parking spot by the curb?

Inverse Functions

The image seen in your rear-view mirror is the reflection image of the lettering on the ambulance.

In the last lesson, you learned that the inverse of a function is not always a function. When the inverse is a function, the symbol f^{-1}, read "f inverse," is used to denote it. (Be careful: in this case the -1 is a symbol for inverse and is not an exponent.) Thus, for the function $f(x) = 4x$, the inverse, which is also a function, can be denoted by $f^{-1}(x) = \frac{1}{4} x$. This is read "the inverse of f of x is one fourth x."

Example 1 Use the function $f(x) = 4x + 1$.
a. Find a rule for the inverse and write the rule in Euler notation.
b. Find $(f \circ f^{-1})(x)$.
c. Find $(f^{-1} \circ f)(x)$.

Solution **a.** To find a rule for the inverse, replace $f(x)$ by y and then switch x and y.

$$f(x) = 4x + 1$$

The inverse of $\quad y = 4x + 1$

is $\quad\quad\quad x = 4y + 1$.

Now solve for y.

$$x - 1 = 4y \quad\quad \text{Subtract 1 from both sides.}$$

$$\frac{1}{4}(x - 1) = y \quad\quad \text{Multiply both sides by } \frac{1}{4}.$$

The inverse function can be written $f^{-1}(x) = \frac{1}{4}(x - 1) = \frac{x - 1}{4}$.

LESSON 7-7

RESOURCES
■ Lesson Master 7-7
▯ Computer Master 16

OBJECTIVES

D Obtain rules for inverses of functions.
G Determine relationships between a function and its inverse by applying the Inverse Function Theorem.

TEACHING NOTES

Ask students where they have seen inverses before.
  Addition: f and g are additive inverses if and only if $f + g = 0$. (0 is the identity element for multiplication.)
  Multiplication: f and g are multiplicative inverses if and only if $f \cdot g = 1$. (1 is the identity element for multiplication.)
  Matrix multiplication: A and B are inverses if and only if $AB = I$. (I is the identity for matrix multiplication.)
  Composition: f and g are inverse functions if and only if $f \circ g = I$. (I is the identity element for composition.)
Question 17 from the previous lesson is a good lead-in to Lesson 7-7. Students will have shown that
(a) $(g \circ f)(15) = 15$, and
(b) $(g \circ f)(x) = x$. It is natural for you to ask them to calculate $(f \circ g)(4)$ and $(f \circ g)(x)$. They will find that $(f \circ g)(4) = 4$ and $(f \circ g)(x) = x$. Now have students graph $y = f(x)$ and $y = g(x)$ on the same axes. They will observe that f and g are reflection images of each other over the line $y = x$. Thus, $f(x) = 3x + 4$ and $g(x) = \frac{1}{3}(x - 4)$ are inverses of each other.

411

Reading Because of the heavy use of symbolism in the lesson, you may want to spend part of the class period reading and discussing the first page. Point out that the Inverse Function Theorem provides an algebraic test for determining if two functions are inverses. A geometric test is that f and g are inverse functions if and only if each is 1-1 and they are reflection images of each other over the line $y = x$.

ADDITIONAL EXAMPLES

1. Use the function $f(x) = \frac{1}{2}x - 3$.

a. Find a rule for the inverse and write the rule in Euler notation.
$f^{-1}(x) = 2(x + 3)$

b. Find $(f \circ f^{-1})(x)$
x

c. Find $(f^{-1} \circ f)(x)$.
x

2. Are $f(x) = 3x + 2$ and $g(x) = \frac{1}{3}x - 2$ inverses of each other?
No. $(f \circ g)(x) = x - 4$ and $(g \circ f)(x) = x - \frac{4}{3}$. This could also be shown using a specific value of x.

3. Show that $f(x) = \frac{1}{4}x - 3$ and $g(x) = 4x + 12$ are inverses.
$(f \circ g)(x) = \frac{1}{4}(4x + 12) - 3 = x + 3 - 3 = x$
and
$(g \circ f)(x) = 4(\frac{1}{4}x - 3) + 12 = x - 12 + 12 = x$.

b.

$$\begin{aligned}(f \circ f^{-1})(x) &= f(f^{-1}(x)) \\ &= f\left(\frac{x-1}{4}\right) \\ &= 4\left(\frac{x-1}{4}\right) + 1 \\ &= x - 1 + 1 \\ &= x\end{aligned}$$

c.

$$\begin{aligned}(f^{-1} \circ f)(x) &= f^{-1}(f(x)) \\ &= f^{-1}(4x + 1) \\ &= \frac{(4x + 1) - 1}{4} \\ &= \frac{4x}{4} \\ &= x\end{aligned}$$

The results of parts b and c above make sense, since f^{-1} undoes what f did to x.

Inverse Function Theorem:

f and g are inverse functions if and only if

$$(f \circ g)(x) = (g \circ f)(x) = x.$$

This theorem states that if you input a value into either composite, it will output the same value. You can use the composite of two functions to check whether the functions are indeed inverses of each other.

Example 2 Are $f(x) \to \frac{2}{3}x + 8$ and $g(x) \to \frac{3}{2}x - 8$ inverses of each other?

Solution Find $f \circ g$.

$$\begin{aligned}(f \circ g)(x) &= f(g(x)) \\ &= f\left(\frac{3}{2}x - 8\right) \\ &= \frac{2}{3}\left(\frac{3}{2}x - 8\right) + 8 \\ &= x - \frac{16}{3} + 8 = x + \frac{8}{3}\end{aligned}$$

Since $(f \circ g)(x) \neq x$, f and g are *not* inverses of each other.

It is necessary to check both composites $f \circ g$ and $g \circ f$ to show that two functions are inverses of each other. In some situations one composite may lead to the conclusion that two functions are inverses, while the other shows that they are not.

■ ■ ■ ■ ■ ■ ■

Example 3   Show that $f(x) = x^2$ and $g(x) = \sqrt{x}$ are not inverses.

Solution   *Step 1:* Find $(f \circ g)(x)$.

$$
\begin{aligned}
(f \circ g)(x) &= f(g(x)) \\
&= f(\sqrt{x}) \\
&= (\sqrt{x})^2 \\
&= x
\end{aligned}
$$

It appears from this composite that f and g are inverses. However, notice that the domain is only the nonnegative real numbers, since the square-root function is done first.

Step 2: Find $(g \circ f)(x)$.

$$
\begin{aligned}
(g \circ f)(x) &= g(f(x)) \\
&= g(x^2) \\
&= \sqrt{x^2}
\end{aligned}
$$

The expression $\sqrt{x^2} \neq x$; rather, $\sqrt{x^2} = |x|$. You can see this by eval-uating a negative number, say -3.

$$
\sqrt{(-3)^2} = \sqrt{9} = 3
$$

The answer is not -3, but 3, which is |-3|. Thus, functions f and g are not inverses.

Example 3 shows that the squaring and square-root functions are not inverse functions. However, they can be inverses if the domain is restricted. Consider the graph of $f(x) = x^2$ at the right. It does not pass the horizontal-line test, so its inverse is not a function.

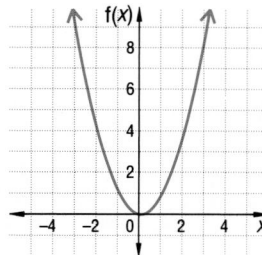

$f(x) = x^2$: x is any real number
not 1-1 function

However, at the right are shown graphs of $f(x) = x^2$ and $g(x) = \sqrt{x}$ for $x \geq 0$. Both f and g pass the vertical-line test so they are each functions.

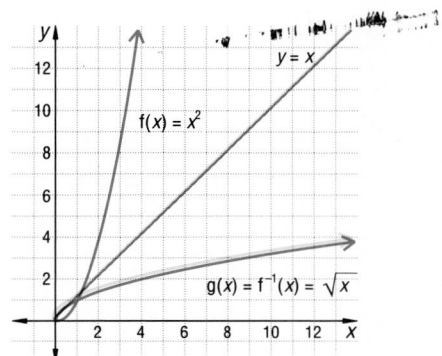

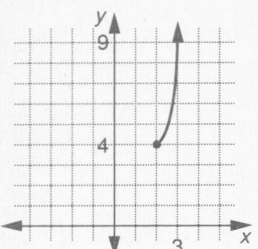
If $y = x^2$
then the inverse has equation $x = y^2$.
Solving for y gives $\sqrt{x} = \sqrt{y^2}$
$= |y|$.

Since $y > 0$, $\sqrt{y^2} = y$ and
we can write $y = \sqrt{x}$.
Thus the inverse of
$f(x) = x^2$ is $g(x) = \sqrt{x}$.

Since g is a function, we can write $g = f^{-1}$. That is, $f^{-1}(x) = \sqrt{x}$, where $x \geq 0$.

In general, the odd-powering functions have inverses that are functions, but the inverses of even-powering functions are not functions. However, by restricting the domain of the even-powering functions so that these functions are 1-1, it is possible to make the inverse a function.

Questions

1. If f is a function, then the symbol f^{-1} represents the __?__ of the function and is read __?__.   inverse; f inverse

   $h^{-1}(x) = \frac{1}{6}(x + 5)$

2. The function $h(x) = 6x - 5$ has an inverse which is a function.
   a. Find a rule for the inverse and write the rule in Euler notation.
   b. Check your answer to part a by finding $h \circ h^{-1}$.

   $(h \circ h^{-1})(x) = 6(\frac{1}{6}x + \frac{5}{6}) - 5 = x + 5 - 5 = x$

3. Refer to Example 1. Find $(f \circ f^{-1})(2)$.   2

4. For any function f that has an inverse, $(f \circ f^{-1})(x) = $ __?__.   x

5. Refer to Example 2. Find $(g \circ f)(x)$. $(g \circ f)(x) = x + 4$

In 6 and 7, refer to Example 3.

6. Why is it necessary to check both $f \circ f^{-1}$ and $f^{-1} \circ f$ to see if two functions are inverses?   See below.

7. True or false. The square root function is the inverse of the squaring function.   False

8. a. Graph $y = x^2$ where $x \geq 2$.   See margin.
   b. Is the relation in part (a) a function? Is its inverse a function?
   yes; yes

   6) In some situations one composite may lead to the conclusion that two functions are inverses while the other shows that they are not.

9. Refer to the graph at the right of the cubing function $y = x^3$.
   a. What are the domain and range of this function?
   domain = {all real numbers};
   range = {all real numbers}
   b. Graph the inverse function. (It is called the **cube-root function**.)
   See margin.
   c. Find the domain and range of the cube root function.
   domain = {all real numbers};
   range = {all real numbers}

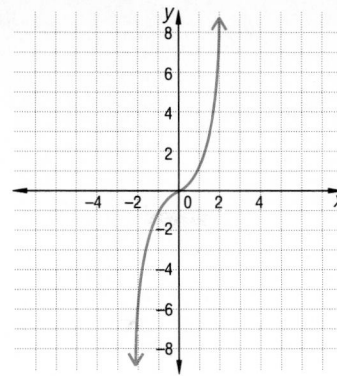

10. a. Find an equation for the inverse of the linear function $y = mx + b$.
    b. How are the slopes of a linear function and its inverse related?
    c. When is the inverse not a function?
    a) $y = \dfrac{x - b}{m}$; b) reciprocals; c) if $m = 0$

In 11–13, consider the absolute-value function graphed at the right. Which of the following ways of restricting the domain gives a function whose inverse is also a function?

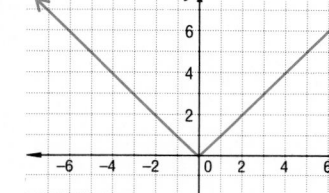

11. $-2 \le x \le 5$ No

12. $x \ge 1$ Yes

13. $x \ge -4.5$ No

14. Alexis makes a commission of 40% of her ticket sales to a health and nutrition seminar plus a salary of $25,000 per year. An equation for her total income y, in terms of ticket sales x, is

$$y = 25{,}000 + .4x.$$

a. Find the inverse. $y = \dfrac{x - 25000}{.4}$
b. What does the inverse find?   the number of tickets she has to sell to get a specific income

15. Let $g(x) = 6x$.
   a. Find an equation for g^{-1}. $g^{-1}(x) = \frac{1}{6}x$ $(g^{-1})^{-1}(x) = 6x$
   b. Find an equation for the inverse of g^{-1}. This is denoted by $(g^{-1})^{-1}$.
   c. If f is any function that has an inverse, what is $(f^{-1})^{-1}$?   f

Review

16. Consider the function f: $x \rightarrow x^2 + 8x + 16$. Graph f and its inverse on the same set of axes. *(Lessons 6-1, 7-6)*   See margin.

In 17–19, solve each equation. *(Lessons 1-7, 6-5, 6-8)*

17. $4x^2 = \dfrac{16}{289}$ $x = \pm\frac{2}{17}$ 18. $\dfrac{54}{y} = -144$ $y = -\frac{3}{8}$

19. $x^2 + 4 = 0$ $x = \pm 2i$

LESSON 7-7   Inverse Functions   **415**

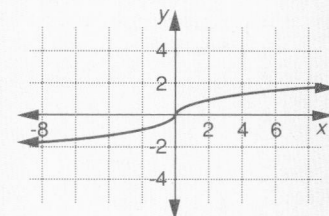
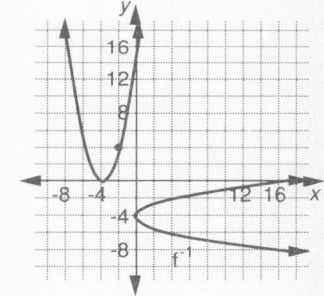

20. The Hidawa Family Acrobatic Troupe perform an act shown below. Suppose Hairnunda Hidawa leaves the teeter-totter at an initial velocity of 20 feet per second.

Before

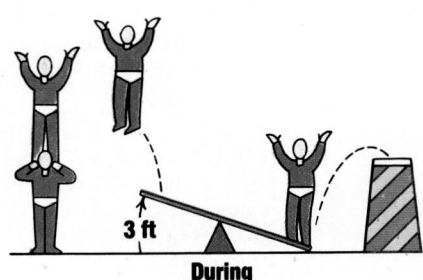

3 ft

During

$$h = -16t^2 + 20t + 3$$

a. Write an equation to describe Hairnunda's height after t seconds.
b. Assuming Hairnunda has good aim, will she be launched high enough to land atop her two brothers? *(Lesson 6-9)* **No**

In 21–24, match the graphs below to the correct function. *(Lessons 7-4, 7-5, 7-6)*

(a) y (b) y (c) y (d) y

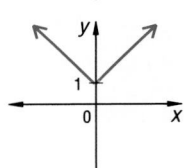
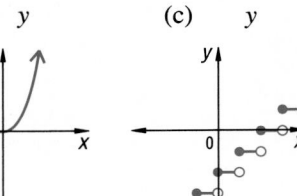

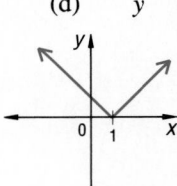

(e)   (f)   (g)

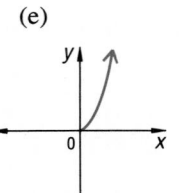
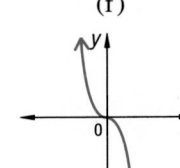
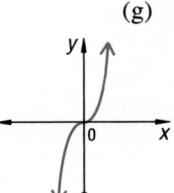

21. $f(x) = x^2$ for $x \geq 0$ **e**   **22.** $g(x) = |x| + 1$ **a**

23. $h(x) = x^3$ **g**   **24.** $k(x) = [x - 2]$ **c**

25. The graph below can be defined as:

$$f(x) = \begin{cases} x^2 & \text{if } -1 \le x \le 1 \\ 1 & \text{if } -3 \le x \le -1, \quad \text{or} \quad 1 \le x \le 3 \\ x-2 & \text{if } x \ge 3 \\ -x-2 & \text{if } x \le -3. \end{cases}$$

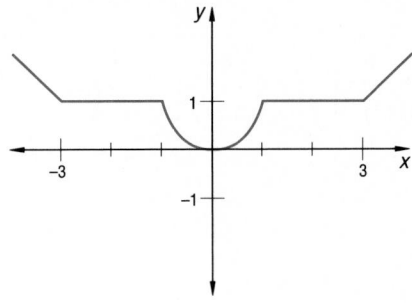

a. Make up a function of your own choosing that has a pleasing shape. Give a piecewise definition for it.   **Answers will vary.**

b. Draw its inverse.   **Answers will vary.**

LESSON 7-7   Inverse Functions   **417**

NAME _____

LESSON **MASTER 7–7**
QUESTIONS ON **SPUR** OBJECTIVES

■**SKILLS**   *Objective D* *(See pages 421–423 for objectives.)*
In 1–4, find $f^{-1}(x)$.

1. $f(x) = 3x + 12$

$\frac{1}{3}x - 4$

2. $f(x) = \frac{1}{5}x - 7$

$5x + 35$

3. $f(x) = -0.2x - 4.6$

$-5x - 23$

4. $f(x) = -\frac{8}{x}$

$-\frac{8}{x}$

■**PROPERTIES**   *Objective G*
In 5–8, determine whether the two functions are inverses of each other.
Write "yes" or "no."

5. $f(x) = 3x + 5, g(x) = \frac{1}{3}x - 5$

no

6. $m(x) = -\frac{1}{5}x + 2, n(x) = -5x + 10$

yes

7. $S(x) = 10x^2, M(x) = 10\sqrt{x}$

no

8. $D(x) = \frac{4}{x}$ and itself.

yes

■**REPRESENTATIONS**   *Objective L*
9. A function f and its inverse f^{-1} are graphed on the same coordinate axes. What transformation maps the graph of f onto the graph of f^{-1}?
a reflection over the line $y = x$

In 10 and 11, a function is graphed. Graph its inverse on the same axes.

10.

11.

Advanced Algebra © Scott, Foresman and Company

83

MORE PRACTICE
For more questions on SPUR Objectives, use *Lesson Master 7-7,* shown below.

Summary

A function is a correspondence that maps elements from one set (its domain) onto elements of the same or another set (its range). Functions are often named by the single letter f. The mapping notation f: $x \rightarrow 3x^2$, Euler's notation $f(x) = 3x^2$ and $y = 3x^2$ all describe the same quadratic function.

Some important functions have their own names.

Greatest-integer function

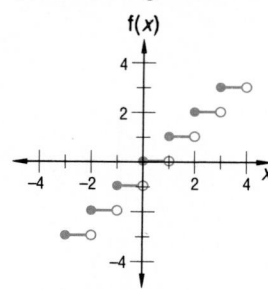

INT: $x \rightarrow [x]$

Absolute-value function

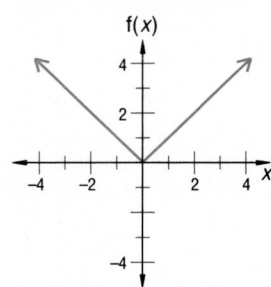

ABS: $x \rightarrow |x|$

Identity function

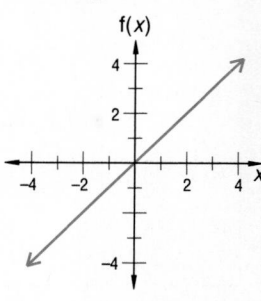

I: $x \rightarrow x$

Squaring function

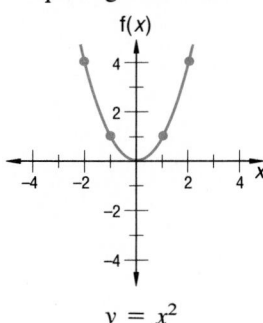

$y = x^2$

nth-Powering function, n even

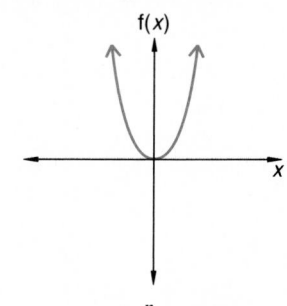

$y = x^n$, n even

nth-Powering function, n odd

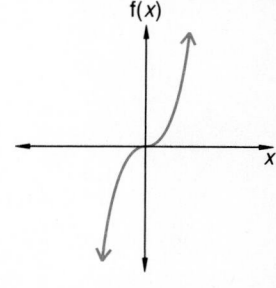

$y = x^n$, n odd

Every function has an inverse, found by switching components of its ordered pairs. Some inverses are functions. A relation is a function if no vertical line intersects its graph in two points. A function f has an inverse f^{-1} if no horizontal line intersects its graph in two points. The graphs of f and f^{-1} are reflection images of each other over the line $y = x$. At the right, the square-root function is graphed; its graph is the reflection image of part of the squaring function.

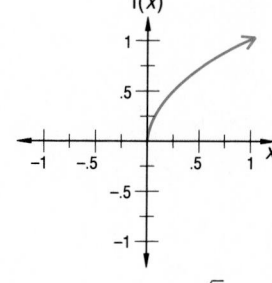

SQR: $x \rightarrow \sqrt{x}$

418

Vocabulary

Below are the most important terms and phrases for this chapter.
You should be able to give a definition for those terms marked with *.
For all other terms you should be able to give a general
description and a specific example.

Lesson 7-1
*relation
*function
 value of a function
 Euler's f(x) notation
 arrow or mapping notation

Lesson 7-2
*domain of a function
*range of a function
 Vertical-Line Test for Functions

Lesson 7-3
composition of functions
composite of f and g, g ∘ f

Lesson 7-4
 step function
*greatest-integer function, rounding-down function
 [x], INT (X)
 rounding-up function

Lesson 7-5
*absolute-value function
*identity function
*squaring, cubing, nth-powering function
*square-root function

Lesson 7-6
*inverse of a function f, f^{-1}
 one-to-one correspondence, 1-1 correspondence
 Horizontal-Line Test for Inverses

Lesson 7-7
 Inverse-Function Theorem
*cube-root function

Terms, symbols, and properties are listed by lesson to provide a checklist of things a student must know. Emphasize to students that they should read the vocabulary list carefully before starting the Progress Self-Test. If students do not understand the meaning of a term, they should refer back to the indicated lesson.

Definitions or descriptions of all terms in the vocabulary list may be found in the Glossary.

Progress Self-Test

Take this test as you would take a test in class. Use graph paper and a calculator. Then check your work with the solutions in the Selected Answers section in the back of the book.

1. If $f(x) = 9x^2 - 11x$, find f(3). **48**

2. Suppose T: $n \rightarrow \dfrac{n(n + 1)}{2}$. Then T(12) = __?__. **78**

3. If $f(n) = n^2$, find $f(n + 1)$. $n^2 + 2n + 1$

In 4 and 5, determine whether the relation is a function.

4. {(95, -5), (4, 4), (5, 5)} **Yes**

5.

x	1	2	3	-2	-1
y	2	5	10	5	2

Yes

In 6–8, consider the functions $f(x) = x^2$ and $g(x) = -8x$.

6. Find f(g(7)). **3136**

7. Determine g(f(x)). $-8x^2$

8. Are f and g inverses of each other? Justify your answer. **See margin.**

9. The graph of the powering function p: $x \rightarrow x^6$ lies in which quadrants? **quadrants I and II.**

In 10 and 11, a function contains only the points (1, 2), (3, 4), and (5, 6).

10. What is its domain? **{1, 3, 5}**

11. What is its inverse? **{(2, 1), (4, 3), (6, 5)}**

12. A function has equation $g(x) = 5x + 10$. Find an equation for g^{-1}. $y = \frac{1}{5}x - 2$

In 13 and 14, use the graphs below.

(a)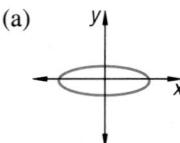

(b)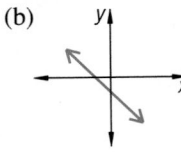

(c)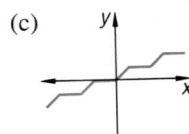

(d)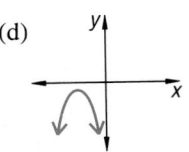

13. Which are graphs of functions? **b, c and d.**

14. Of those graphs that are functions, which have inverses that are also functions? **b**

15. The cost of making a phone call from an airplane is $7.50 for the first three minutes and $1.75 for each additional minute or portion of a minute.
    a. Graph the function for any call lasting up to 8 minutes. **See margin.**
    b. How much would it cost Isaiah Rich to make a call for $6\frac{1}{3}$ minutes? **See margin.**

In 16–19, refer to the function graphed below.

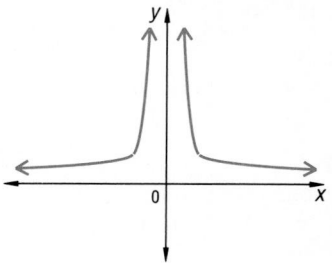

16. Is the function 1-1? **No**

17. What is the range of the function? **{y: y > 0}**

18. Graph the inverse of the function. **See margin.**

19. How can you restrict the domain of the original function so that the inverse is also a function? **See margin.**

20. For the function $f(x) = x^2 + 2$, determine
    a. the domain; **See margin.**
    b. the range. **See margin.**

21. Consider $g(x) = -[x + 1]$. Find g(-4.3). **4**

22. Graph f, where $f(x) = |x| - 3$. **See margin.**

23. In a computer program, ABS(X) denotes the absolute value function.

```
10 INPUT " TWO NUMBERS"; M,N
20 PRINT ABS(M−N)
30 END
```

a. If 3.2 is input for M and 7 for N, what will be printed when the program is run? **3.8**
b. In general, what will the output from this program represent? **See margin.**

Chapter Review

Questions on **SPUR** Objectives

SPUR stands for **S**kills, **P**roperties, **U**ses, and **R**epresentations.
The Chapter Review questions are grouped according to the
SPUR Objectives for this chapter.

SKILLS deal with the procedures used to get answers.

■ **Objective A:** *Find the value of a function. (Lessons 7-1, 7-4, 7-5)*

1. If $f(x) = 2x - 3$, what is f(4)?   **5**
2. Suppose t: $n \rightarrow 5 - 4n^2$. Then
t(-2) = __?__.   **-11**
3. Let h: $a \rightarrow a^5$. Find h(-3).   **-243**
4. If $g(x) = 4x^2$, find g(x + 2).   **$4x^2 + 16x + 16$**
5. If $h(x) = 8x - 20$, find h(x + 5) - h(x).   **40**
6. If M: $x \rightarrow 3x^2 + 4x$, then M(2k) = __?__.   **$12k^2 + 8k$**
7. $[-2.5] = $ __?__   **-3**
8. Find f(x) for $-2 \le x < -1$, if f(x) = [x].   **-2**
9. $|-5 - 9| = $ __?__   **14**
10. If $g(x) = |x| - 12$, find g(4.5).   **7.5**

■ **Objective B:** *Find the composite of functions. (Lesson 7-3)*

11. In the symbolism f ∘ g, which function is applied first?   **g**

In 12–15, let t(x) = x^2 + 1 and m(x) = x − 6.

12. Find t(m(5)).   **2**
13. Find t(m(x)).   **$x^2 - 12x + 37$**
14. What rule describes m ∘ t?   **(m ∘ t)(x) = $x^2 - 5$**
15. The function t ∘ m maps -10 onto what number?   **257**
16. If a: $x \rightarrow -\frac{2}{7}x$ and b: $x \rightarrow -\frac{7}{2}x$, what is (b ∘ a)(x)?   **x**

■ **Objective C:** *Read simple BASIC programs with special functions. (Lessons 7-4, 7-5)*

In 17–20, use this program where N > 0.

```
10 INPUT N
20 PRINT 1000 * INT((N + 500)/1000)
30 END
```

17. **a.** What will line 20 print if you run the program and input 25,962?   **26,000**
    b. If N = $1.2 \cdot 10^3$, what will line 20 print when the program is run?   **1000**
18. Describe what this program does when run.   **It rounds a number to the nearest thousand.**
19. Modify this program so it rounds positive numbers to the nearest hundred.   **See margin.**
20. If line 20 reads
    PRINT 3 + ABS(-8 * (N + 2))
    what will be printed when -4 is input for N?   **19**

■ **Objective D:** *Obtain rules for inverses of functions. (Lessons 7-6, 7-7)*

21. If f: $x \rightarrow 2x + 7$, then f^{-1}: $x \rightarrow$ __?__.   **$\frac{1}{2}(x - 7)$**
22. If $g(x) = -x^2$ for $x \le 0$, then $g^{-1}(x) = $ __?__.   **$-\sqrt{-x}$**
23. A function has equation y = 4x − 2. In slope-intercept form, what is an equation for its inverse?   **$y = \frac{1}{4}x + \frac{1}{2}$**
24. A function has equation y = |x|. What is an equation for its inverse?   **x = |y|**

RESOURCES
■ Chapter 7 Test, Form A
■ Chapter 7 Test, Form B
■ Chapter 7 Test, Cumulative Form

CHAPTER REVIEW

The main objectives for the chapter are organized here into sections corresponding to the four main types of understanding this book promotes: Skills, Properties, Uses, and Representations.

USING THE CHAPTER REVIEW
Whereas end-of-chapter material may be considered optional in some texts, in *Advanced Algebra* we have selected these objectives and questions with the expectation that they will be covered. Students should be able to answer these questions with about 85% accuracy after studying the chapter.

You may assign these questions over a single night to help students prepare for a test the next day, or you may assign the questions over a two-day period.

If you work the questions over two days, then we recommend assigning the *evens* for homework the first night so that students get feedback in class the next day, then assigning the *odds* the night before the test so students can use the answers provided in the book.

ADDITIONAL ANSWERS
18. This program will round any positive number to the nearest thousand.

19.
10 INPUT N
20 PRINT 100∗INT((N + 50)/100)
30 END

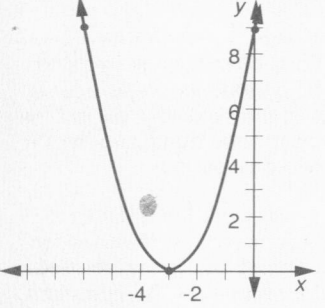
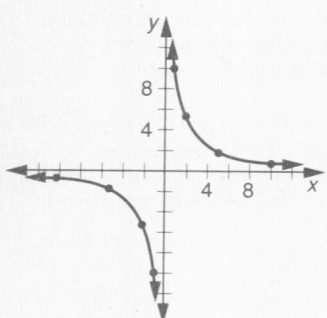
PROPERTIES deal with the principles behind the mathematics.

■ **Objective E:** *Determine whether a given relation is a function.* *(Lessons 7-1, 7-2, 7-4, 7-5)*

25. Is the relation described by the table below a function? If not, why not?

x	-1	-1	-4	0	-16
y	1	-1	2	0	-4

No, because -1 is mapped to both 1 and -1.

In 26–31, tell whether the set or rule describes a function.

26. $\{(1, 2), (2, 3), (3, 4), (4, 1)\}$ function

27. $x = y^2$ not a function

28. $y = [x + 1]$ function

29. $xy = 15$ function

30. $x = -5$ not a function

31. $x = |y|$ not a function

32. A relation has the points (1, 2), (2, 1), (1, 3), and (4, 1). Take out one point so that this relation is a function.
Take out either (1, 2) or (1, 3).

■ **Objective F:** *Determine the domain and range of simple functions given the function rule.* *(Lessons 7-2, 7-4, 7-5)*

33. What real number is not in the domain of f, where $f(x) = \frac{1}{x}$? $x = 0$

In 34–39, give the domain and range of the function described.   **See margin.**

34. $\{(2, -2), (3, -3), (-9, 9), (-\frac{1}{2}, \frac{1}{2})\}$

35. $y = x^4$

36. $f(x) = \sqrt{x}$

37. $f(x) = [x]$

38. $y = x^2 + 1$

39. $y + 5 = 3(x - 4)^2$

■ **Objective G:** *Determine relationships between a function and its inverse.* *(Lessons 7-6, 7-7)*

40. For what positive integer values of n does the function with equation $y = x^n$ have an inverse that is also a function?   All odd integers

41. Suppose the domain of a linear function is $\{x: x \geq 0\}$ and the range is $\{y: y = 6\}$. What are the domain and range of the inverse?   Domain: $\{x: x = 6\}$; Range: $\{y: y \geq 0\}$

In 42 and 43, *true or false.*

42. If a function is 1-1, then its inverse is also a function.   True

43. If functions f and g are inverses of each other, then $(f \circ g)(x) = (g \circ f)(x)$.   True

44. Show that f: $x \to 2x + 3$ and g: $x \to \frac{1}{2}x - 3$ are not inverses of each other.   See margin.

USES deal with applications of mathematics in real situations.

■ **Objective H:** *Find values of functions involving real data.* *(Lessons 7-1, 7-4, 7-5)*

In 45–47, let P(x) and B(x) be the populations of Philadelphia and Baltimore in year x.

	1900	1950	1980
Philadelphia	1,290,000	2,070,000	1,690,000
Baltimore	509,000	950,000	787,000

45. What does B(1950) represent?   the population of Baltimore in 1950

46. **a.** Calculate P(1980) − B(1980).   903,000
b. What does part a represent?   See below.

47. **a.** Calculate $\frac{P(1950) - P(1900)}{1950 - 1900}$.   15,600
b. What does the answer to part a represent?   the average yearly growth in Philadelphia from 1900 to 1950

48. The famous scientist Galileo found a relationship between the distance d(t) a dropped object falls (in feet) in the time t (in seconds). $d(t) = 32t^2$. (Of course, he used different units.) What was the approximate distance fallen when t = 1.5?   72 feet

49. *Multiple choice* You earn $5 per hour. The time you work is rounded down to the nearest hour. What is a rule for the function that relates time t in hours to wages w in dollars?   c
(a) $w = 5t$ (b) $w = 5|t|$
(c) $w = 5[t]$ (d) $w = 5(t - \frac{1}{2})$

46b) the amount by which the population of Philadelphia exceeded that of Baltimore in 1980

422

50. Evening phone rates (not including taxes) between Chicago and New York City are 47¢ for the first minute and 33¢ for each additional minute or portion of a minute. How much will it cost to make a 12 minute 10 second phone call between these cities? **$4.43**

REPRESENTATIONS deal with pictures, graphs, or objects that illustrate concepts.

■ **Objective I:** *Graph a function, given its rule. (Lessons 7-2, 7-4, 7-5)*

51. Graph f, where $f(x) = x^2 + 6x + 9$. **See margin.**

52. Graph g, if $g: x \rightarrow \dfrac{10}{x}$. **See margin.**

53. Graph $y = [x] + 4$. **See margin.**

54. If $h(x) = |x - 1|$, graph h. **See margin.**

55. Let $y = -2x^3$. Graph this function. **See margin.**

56. Refer to Question 50 above. Graph the relation between time t in minutes and cost c in dollars for the domain $0 \leq t \leq 10$. **See margin.**

57. The graph of $y = x^9$ lies in which quadrants? **I and III**

58. *True or false* The graph of the identity function lies in quadrants II and IV. **False**

■ **Objective J:** *Determine the domain and range of a relation from its graph. (Lesson 7-2)*

In 59–62, find the domain and range of the relation graphed below. **See margin.**

59.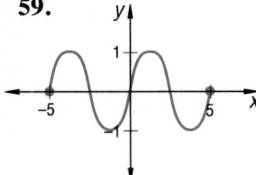

60.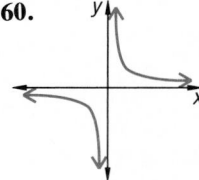

61.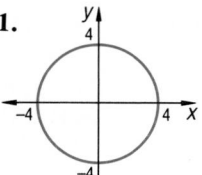

62.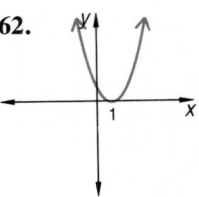

■ **Objective K:** *Apply the vertical and horizontal line tests for a function and its inverse. (Lessons 7-2, 7-6)*

In 63 and 64, use the graphs below.

(a)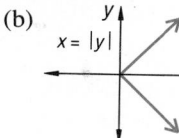
$y = -x^2$

(b)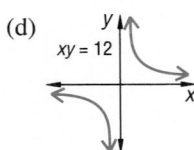
$x = |y|$

(c)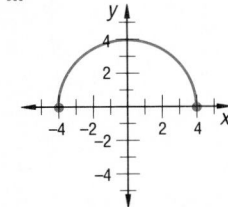
(−2, 3) • (1, 1) • (3, 0) • (5, −1)

(d)
$xy = 12$

63. *Multiple choice* Which of the above is not a graph of a function? **b**

64. a. *Multiple choice* Which of the above is a function whose inverse is not a function? **a**

   b. How can you restrict the domain of the function in your answer to part a so that the inverse is a function? $x \leq 0$ or $x \leq 0$

65. Draw a graph of a function with domain $\{-1 < x < 1\}$ that has an inverse which is not a function. **See margin.**

66. *True or false* The horizontal-line test fails if a function is not 1-1. **True**

■ **Objective L:** *Graph the inverse of a function. (Lessons 7-6, 7-7)*

67. Suppose f and f^{-1} are graphed on the same set of coordinate axes. How are the graphs related? **They are reflections about the line $y = x$.**

68. Graph the inverse of the function at the right. **See margin.**

69. Graph the inverse of the function with equation $y = |x|$. **See margin.**

CHAPTER 7 Chapter Review   **423**

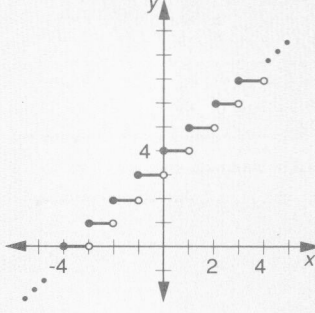
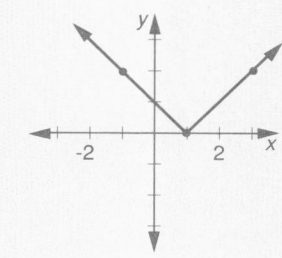

CHAPTER 8 ■ POWERS AND ROOTS

DAILY PACING CHART ■ CHAPTER 8

Students in the Full Course should complete all but one of the chapters by the end of the year. Students in the Minimal Course will spend more time on quizzes and the Chapter Review. As such, these students should complete about ten or eleven chapters.

DAY	MINIMAL COURSE	FULL COURSE
1	8-1	8-1
2	8-2	8-2
3	8-3	8-3
4	8-4	8-4
5	Quiz (TRF); Start 8-5.	Quiz (TRF); 8-5
6	Finish 8-5.	8-6
7	8-6	8-7
8	8-7	8-8
9	8-8	Quiz (TRF); 8-9
10	Quiz (TRF); Start 8-9.	8-10
11	Finish 8-9.	8-11
12	8-10	Progress Self-Test
13	8-11	Chapter Review
14	Progress Self-Test	Chapter Test (TRF)
15	Chapter Review	
16	Chapter Review	
17	Chapter Test (TRF)	

TESTING OPTIONS

■ Quiz for Lessons 8-1 Through 8-4　　■ Chapter 8 Test, Form A　　■ Chapter 8 Test, Cumulative Form
■ Quiz for Lessons 8-5 Through 8-8　　■ Chapter 8 Test, Form B

PROVIDING FOR INDIVIDUAL DIFFERENCES

The student text is written for the *average* student. The program, however, can be adapted for both less capable and for more capable students.

A blackline master (in the Teacher's Resource File) is provided for each lesson for those students who need more practice. The Teacher's Edition frequently provides Error Analysis and Alternate Approach features to provide additional instructional strategies.

For students who require additional challenge, Extension activities are regularly provided in the Teacher's Edition.

OBJECTIVES ■ CHAPTER 8

Students should master the chapter objectives by the time they complete the chapter. To ensure mastery, there is continual review built into each set of lesson questions. After students complete the chapter lessons, they assess their mastery on the Progress Self-Test. Then they do the Chapter Review and pay special attention to those questions that match the objectives missed on the Progress Self-Test. Students can get extra practice on these objectives by using the master for each lesson in the Teacher's Resource File.

OBJECTIVES FOR CHAPTER 8 (Organized into the SPUR categories—Skills, Properties, Uses, and Representations)	Progress Self-Test Questions	Chapter Review Questions	Lesson Master from Teacher's Resource File*
SKILLS			
A Evaluate x^n when n is an integer.	1	1 through 6	8-1, 8-4
B Evaluate x^b when b is a rational number.	2–4	7 through 17	8-5, 8-6, 8-7
C Simplify radicals.	5–6	18 through 29	8-8, 8-9, 8-10
D Solve equations of the form $ax^n = b$ or their equivalent radical forms.	7–8, 16	30 through 39	8-6, 8-10
E Solve equations of the form $a(x - h)^n = b$.	14–15	40 through 43	8-11
F Solve equations or simplify expressions using properties of exponents.	9, 17	44 through 51	8-1, 8-4, 8-6, 8-7
G Find terms or the rule for a geometric sequence.	19	52 through 59	8-3
PROPERTIES			
H Recognize properties of nth powers and nth roots.	20	60 through 67	8-1, 8-8
I Apply the definitions of $x^{1/n}$ and $\sqrt[n]{x}$ as they apply to nth roots of x.	21	68 through 74	8-5, 8-8, 8-9
USES			
J Apply the compound interest formulas.	11–13	75 through 79	8-2, 8-4, 8-11
K Solve real-world problems which can be modeled by powers and roots.	10, 18, 22	80 through 85	8-1, 8-4, 8-5, 8-6, 8-7, 8-10, 8-11
L Solve real-world problems by geometric sequences.	23	86 through 88	8-3
REPRESENTATIONS (There are no representation objectives in this chapter)			

* **The masters are numbered to match the lessons.**

OVERVIEW ■ CHAPTER 8

We assume students have studied the following topics in earlier courses: properties of positive integral powers, zero as an exponent, negative integral powers of ten, rewriting square roots, such as $\sqrt{75} = 5\sqrt{3}$, and the use of $\frac{1}{2}$ as an exponent. In this chapter, we extend the study of exponents to all rational powers and roots.

Chapter 8 emphasizes skills, properties, and the use of powers and roots. There are virtually no graphs in the chapter. Graphs of exponential functions are studied in Chapter 9, where they are related to the graphs of logarithmic functions.

Lesson 8-1 reviews the Properties of Powers with which students should be familiar. In Lesson 8-2, we introduce compound interest. This topic is interesting to students, and can be used later in the chapter to apply negative and fractional exponents.

Lesson 8-3 on geometric sequences builds on the study of sequences begun in Chapters 1 and 3. The next four lessons, 8-4 through 8-7, extend students' knowledge of negative integer exponents, nth roots, positive rational exponents, and negative rational exponents, respectively.

In Lessons 8-8 and 8-9, radical notation is used and nth roots are rewritten by applying properties of exponents.

The chapter ends with Lessons 8-10 and 8-11 on solving equations of the form $ax^n = k$ and $a(x - h)^n = k$, where n is any rational number.

PERSPECTIVES ■ CHAPTER 8

The Perspectives provide the rationale for the inclusion of topics or approaches, provide mathematical background, and make connections within UCSMP.

8-1

PROPERTIES OF POWERS

This lesson reviews the Properties of Powers and lays the groundwork for the development of the concepts that follow.

Four themes that appear throughout the chapter are introduced in this lesson. They are: (1) equivalent forms and notations, (2) using properties of real numbers to extend the concept of exponents, (3) using a calculator, and (4) doing mental arithmetic.

Students are not expected to memorize the names for properties. However, given a property name, they should be able to give the generalization. For instance, they should know that the Quotient of Powers Property deals with the expression $\frac{x^m}{x^n}$ and that the result is x^{m-n}.

Notice that the properties of powers are assumed for any nonnegative bases and real exponents. This enables us to *prove* such properties as $x^{-n} = \frac{1}{x^n}$.

We believe this is more intuitive and efficient than defining negative exponents and then using the definition to deduce the familiar properties.

8-2

COMPOUND INTEREST

Virtually everyone wants to know how to predict the value of his or her money in the future, or how to shop for the best buy. Thus, the content in this lesson is very interesting to most students.

A generation ago, compound interest could not be discussed until students studied logarithms because there was no other way to calculate large powers. The scientific calculator has changed that.

Many students believe the simple interest formula, $I = prt$, is the way that all interest is calculated. Actually, that formula is rather limited; it seldom applies except when $t = 1$.

8-3

GEOMETRIC SEQUENCES

Two types of sequences are of special interest in an advanced algebra course because their formulas are easily derived and because they model many real-world situations. One of these, the arithmetic (or linear) sequence, was studied in Chapter 3. The geometric (or exponential) sequence is introduced in this lesson.

The term *exponential sequence* is appropriate because every geometric sequence can be considered to be an exponential function whose domain is the set of natural numbers. Graphs of geometric sequences and exponential functions are studied in Chapter 9.

8-4

NEGATIVE INTEGER EXPONENTS

In many developments of exponents, one first *supposes* for a moment that the properties of powers are true for negative exponents. One deduces that x^{-n} would have to equal the reciprocal of x^n if the powers are still to be satisfied, and x^{-n} is defined to agree with that treatment. If one wishes to be rigorous, the properties of powers are deduced for these negative exponents.

The following approach, taken in this book, is simpler. We have already *assumed* that the properties of powers hold for all real exponents. Then, from these properties, we are able to prove that x^{-n} is the reciprocal of x^n.

8-5
NTH ROOTS
Every student needs to be able to evaluate nth roots on a calculator. Students are often surprised to find out that calculators (1) will not give both nth roots of a positive number x when n is even; and (2) will not generally calculate odd nth roots of negative numbers x. This provides added support for the restrictions we must impose on the base when the exponent is rational.

Just as there was a Negative Exponent Theorem, there is a $1/n$ Exponent Theorem. The fundamental property of $x^{1/n}$ as an nth root can be deduced from the properties of exponents.

A fundamental difference exists between negative integer exponents and rational exponents. If there is to be a unique power, both the power and the base have to be restricted to positive numbers.

8-6
POSITIVE RATIONAL EXPONENTS
This lesson illustrates skills, properties, and uses involving positive rational exponents. The examples and questions encourage students to do mental computation as well as calculator arithmetic.

Again, the relevant property of exponents, that $x^{m/n} = (x^{1/n})^m = (x^m)^{1/n}$ is deduced from the fundamental properties mentioned in Lesson 8-1, in this case, the Power of a Power Property.

The Rational Exponent Theorem has two major uses. First, it interprets rational powers in terms of integer powers and roots. Second, it states that if there are both a power and a root to be applied to the same base, the order in which they are calculated is irrelevant.

8-7
NEGATIVE RATIONAL EXPONENTS
In this lesson, students have to use what they learned about exponents to evaluate all rational powers of any given positive base. The base must be restricted to positive numbers in order to have a well-defined exponential function. In order to have a well-defined exponential function with negative bases, the complex plane must be involved. New terms or theorems are not introduced in this lesson.

8-8
RADICAL NOTATION FOR NTH ROOTS
In this lesson and the next, we practice the traditional skill of rewriting radicals by applying the Root of a Power and the Root of a Product Theorems. Here we restrict the base to being a positive number so that all the properties of powers learned in previous lessons can be employed.

Advanced algebra students have usually seen the Root of a Product Theorem in previous mathematics courses. That first exposure, however, is usually only to square roots. They may never have realized that the Root of a Product Theorem is just the special case of the Power of a Product Property when the exponent is $1/n$.

8-9
POWERS AND ROOTS OF NEGATIVE NUMBERS
This lesson extends the definitions and properties of Lesson 8-8 to nth roots with negative bases where n is odd. One source of error in

working with roots and powers results when a theorem is applied when its hypothesis is not satisfied. For this reason, the powers and roots which are not defined are carefully discussed, and the restrictions of bases and powers which must be made for the theorems to hold are emphasized.

8-10
SOLVING $ax^n = b$
Students may be surprised by the processes introduced here which cause them to get numbers that are not solutions to the original problem even though their work is correct. Stress that unlike the Addition and Multiplication Properties of Equality, which when applied produce an equation equivalent to the original, the procedure of taking the nth power of both sides of an equation produces an equation that has all the solutions of the original, but may also have some additional (extraneous) solutions. These extraneous results come from the fact that although $x = y$ implies $x^n = y^n$, the statement $x^n = y^n$ does not necessarily imply $x = y$. The statements $x = y$ and $x^n = y^n$ are not equivalent.

8-11
SOLVING $a(x - h)^n = b$
Determining the compound annual interest rate needed for an investment to double or the rate of growth needed for a population to reach a particular size are problems that can be modeled by equations of the form $a(x \pm h)^n = b$ which need to be solved for x. Examples 1 and 3, as well as the opening situation, illustrate an algorithm for solving such problems.

The Graph-Translation Theorem could be applied to all equations of this type. The solutions to $a(x - h)^n = b$ are h greater than the solutions to $ax^n = b$. Thus, this lesson rounds out this long chapter with many skills and interesting problems to be mastered.

CHAPTER 8

Powers and Roots

The ratio of F, the amount of food a mammal must eat per day, to m, its body mass, is not constant across species. For a mouse, $\frac{F}{m} \approx 0.6$; that is, it must eat three-fifths of its mass per day. At the other extreme, for the elephant $\frac{F}{m} \approx .02$, so an elephant needs to eat only .02, or $\frac{1}{50}$, of its mass per day.

It can be shown that the ratio of amount of food eaten daily to body mass varies as the negative one-third power of the mass. This can be written as

$$\frac{F}{m} = km^{-1/3}.$$

In this chapter you will learn how to interpret negative powers and fractional powers and how to solve equations involving powers and roots. You will also learn about other applications of powers and roots in the real world.

424

Mammal	Weight (lb)	Food per day (lb)	Food per day mass
elephant	14000	320	.023
moose	800	48	.060
raccoon	21	4	.20
guinea pig	1.5	.72	.48
mouse	.80	.48	.60

RESOURCES
■ Lesson Master 8-1
▣ Visual for Teaching Aid 45 displays the main ideas of the lesson.

OBJECTIVES

A Evaluate x^n when x is positive and n is an integer.
F Solve equations or simplify expressions using properties of exponents.
H Recognize properties of nth powers and nth roots.
K Solve real-world problems which can be modeled by powers and roots.

TEACHING NOTES

It is important to discuss the Properties of Powers even though most students are familiar with them. When dealing with positive bases and positive integral powers, the properties seem almost intuitive. However, when negative bases and rational exponents are introduced, the problems become less intuitive and therefore the properties become more important. Point out to students that the properties of powers and roots are listed in two places: in the Chapter 8 Summary on page 480 and in Appendix D.

Make sure that students can calculate powers with their calculators. Have them locate the power button. The most common key representations are $\boxed{y^x}$ or $\boxed{x^y}$. Emphasize that the order of input is : base, $\boxed{y^x}$, exponent, $\boxed{=}$.

Properties of Powers

Recall that the expression b^n, read "b to the nth power" or "the nth power of b," is the result of an operation called **powering** or **exponentiation**. The variable b is called the **base**, n is called the **exponent**, and the expression b^n is called a **power**. In your earlier study of algebra and on several occasions in this book you have worked with powers. You know, for example, that

$$10^2 = 10 \cdot 10,$$
$$\left(-\tfrac{5}{4}\right)^3 = \left(-\tfrac{5}{4}\right)\left(-\tfrac{5}{4}\right)\left(-\tfrac{5}{4}\right),$$
and $\quad x^7 = x \cdot x \cdot x \cdot x \cdot x \cdot x \cdot x$ for all numbers x.

These sentences are based on the following meaning of powering when the exponent is a positive integer.

Repeated Multiplication Model for Powering:

If b is a real number and n is a positive integer, then

$$b^n = \underbrace{b \cdot b \cdot b \cdot \ldots \cdot b}_{n \text{ factors}}.$$

In this chapter you will study powers with exponents that are not positive integers. The properties of the familiar powers will be used to determine the meaning of these new powers.

Recall how repeated multiplication can be used to work with powers.

Product of Powers:
$$10^2 \cdot 10^3 = (10 \cdot 10) \cdot (10 \cdot 10 \cdot 10) = 10 \cdot 10 \cdot 10 \cdot 10 \cdot 10 = 10^5$$
$$x^4 \cdot x^2 = (x \cdot x \cdot x \cdot x) \cdot (x \cdot x) = x \cdot x \cdot x \cdot x \cdot x \cdot x = x^6$$

Power of a Power:
$$(10^2)^3 = 10^2 \cdot 10^2 \cdot 10^2 = (10 \cdot 10) \cdot (10 \cdot 10) \cdot (10 \cdot 10) = 10^6$$
$$(x^4)^2 = x^4 \cdot x^4 = (x \cdot x \cdot x \cdot x) \cdot (x \cdot x \cdot x \cdot x) = x^8$$

Power of a Product:
$$(3 \cdot 10)^4 = (3 \cdot 10) \cdot (3 \cdot 10) \cdot (3 \cdot 10) \cdot (3 \cdot 10) = 3^4 \cdot 10^4$$
$$(8x^5)^2 = (8x^5) \cdot (8x^5) = (8 \cdot x \cdot x \cdot x \cdot x \cdot x) \cdot (8 \cdot x \cdot x \cdot x \cdot x \cdot x) = 8^2 x^{10} = 64x^{10}$$

Each situation above is an instance of a general pattern which we assume.

426

Postulate 4: Properties of Powers

For any nonnegative bases and real exponents, or any non-zero bases and integer exponents:

Product of Powers Property: $b^m \cdot b^n = b^{m+n}$

Power of a Power Property: $(b^m)^n = b^{mn}$

Power of a Product Property: $(ab)^m = a^m b^m$

Quotient of Powers Property: $\dfrac{b^m}{b^n} = b^{m-n}$

Power of a Quotient Property: $\left(\dfrac{a}{b}\right)^m = \dfrac{a^m}{b^m}$

Applying these postulates enables you to rewrite expressions and calculate with powers.

Example 1   Write $4^5 \cdot 4^8$ as a power of 4.

Solution   Apply the Product of Powers Postulate.

$$4^5 \cdot 4^8 = 4^{5+8} = 4^{13}$$

Check   Use your calculator.

$$4^5 = 1024; \ 4^8 = 65{,}536; \ 4^{13} = 67{,}108{,}864$$

Note that

$$(1024)(65{,}536) = 67{,}108{,}864.$$

Example 2   Simplify $(x^2)^5$.

Solution   Use the Power of a Power Postulate.

$$(x^2)^5 = x^{2 \cdot 5} = x^{10}$$

Check   Test a special case, say $x = 3$. Does $(3^2)^5 = 3^{10}$?

$$(3^2)^5 = 9^5 = 59{,}049$$
$$3^{10} = 59{,}049$$

This case checks.

This lesson deals only with nonnegative bases. When checking answers with their calculators, some students will likely try powers of negative bases. Please see notes on Lesson 8-9 for comments on calculator errors that sometimes result.

Alternate Approach
Another justification of the Zero Exponent Theorem is as follows: For any nonzero x and any m, consider $x^0 \cdot x^m$. Using the Product of Powers Property, $x^0 \cdot x^m = x^{0+m} = x^m$. Since $x^0 \cdot x^m = x^m$, x^0 must equal 1.

The Zero Exponent Theorem, $b^0 = 1$, is proved for any real $b \neq 0$. Some students may wonder what happens when $b = 0$. 0^0 is not defined because it cannot be done in a way consistent with the properties. Since $b^0 = 1$, the sequence $1^0, 0.1^0, 0.01^0, 0.001^0, \ldots$ suggests that $0^0 = 1$. However, now consider the sequence $0^1, 0^{0.1}, 0^{0.01}, 0^{0.001}, \ldots$. Since each of these equals 0, as the exponent approaches zero, it would appear that $0^0 = 0$. This ambiguity means that 0^0 cannot be defined in a way that $z = x^y$ is a continuous function in x and y. It is the reason for leaving 0^0 undefined.

ADDITIONAL EXAMPLES

1. Write $6^{10} \cdot 6^4$ as a power of 6.
6^{14}

2. Simplify $(y^4)^2$.
y^8

3. Verify that $\left(\frac{3}{2}\right)^3 = \frac{3^3}{2^3}$.
$\left(\frac{3}{2}\right)^3 = 1.5^3 = 3.375;$
$\frac{3^3}{2^3} = \frac{27}{8} = 3.375$

4. In 1984, the world population was approximately 4.7 billion ($4.7 \cdot 10^9$). The Earth's total water supply was $326 \cdot 10^{11}$ cubic miles, of which only about one-third of 1 percent is usable by humans. What was each person's share of usable water?
One-third of 1% of 326 is about 1.09. $\frac{1.09 \cdot 10^{11}}{4.7 \cdot 10^9} \approx$
$.232 \cdot 10^2 \approx 23$ **cubic miles**

Example 3 Verify that $\dfrac{2^{11}}{2^8} = 2^3$.

Solution 1 Rewrite the numerator and denominator using the repeated multiplication meaning of b^n.

$$\frac{2^{11}}{2^8} = \frac{2 \cdot 2 \cdot 2 \cdot 2 \cdot 2 \cdot 2 \cdot 2 \cdot 2 \cdot 2 \cdot 2 \cdot 2}{2 \cdot 2 \cdot 2 \cdot 2 \cdot 2 \cdot 2 \cdot 2 \cdot 2}$$
$$= \frac{2 \cdot 2 \cdot 2}{1} = 2^3$$

Solution 2 Use a calculator. A possible key sequence is

$2 \boxed{y^x} 11 \boxed{=} \boxed{\div} \boxed{(} 2 \boxed{y^x} 8 \boxed{=} \boxed{)} \boxed{=}$

The display shows that $2048 \div 256 = 8$, and $8 = 2^3$.

Properties of powers are often used when working with large numbers.

Example 4 The earth is about $93 \cdot 10^6$ miles from the sun. Light travels at about $1.86 \cdot 10^5 \frac{mi}{sec}$. About how long does it take light from the sun to reach the earth?

Solution Use the formula $d = rt$.

$$t \approx \frac{93 \cdot 10^6 \text{ mi}}{1.86 \cdot 10^5 \text{ mi/sec}}$$
$$\approx \frac{93}{1.86} \cdot 10^1 \text{ sec}$$
$$\approx 50 \cdot 10 \text{ sec}$$
$$\approx 500 \text{ sec}$$

It takes about 500 seconds, or 8.3 minutes, for light to travel from the sun to the earth.

When the Quotient of Powers Property is applied to equal powers of the same base, the result is surprising to some people. For instance,

$$\frac{2^8}{2^8} = 2^{8-8} = 2^0.$$

It is also true that

$$\frac{2^8}{2^8} = \frac{256}{256} = 1.$$

The above statements and the transitive property of equality prove that $2^0 = 1$.

In fact, whenever b is a nonzero real number,

$$\frac{b^n}{b^n} = b^{n-n} = b^0.$$

Also, $\frac{b^n}{b^n} = 1$ because any nonzero number divided by itself equals one. Thus we have proved the following theorem.

Zero Exponent Theorem:

If b is a nonzero real number,

$$b^0 = 1.$$

Properties of exponents are used to simplify many expressions.

Example 5

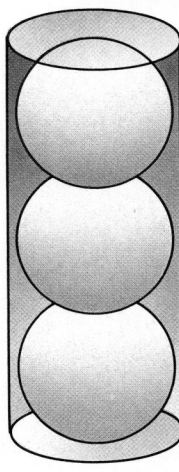

Three tennis balls stacked tightly as shown at the right just fill a cylindrical can. What is the ratio of the volume of the balls to the volume of the can?

Solution The balls may be considered as congruent spheres of radius r. The volume of each sphere is $\frac{4}{3}\pi r^3$. Let V_B equal the total volume of the three tennis balls. Then

$$V_B = 3(\tfrac{4}{3}\pi r^3) = 4\pi r^3.$$

The can is a cylinder with radius r and height $6r$. Let V_C equal the volume of the can. Then

$$V_C = \pi r^2 h = \pi r^2 (6r) = 6\pi r^3.$$

Therefore, $\quad \dfrac{V_B}{V_C} = \dfrac{4\pi r^3}{6\pi r^3} = \dfrac{2}{3}.$

Questions

Covering the Reading

In 1–3, (a) evaluate the expression using a postulate or theorem from this lesson. (b) Check your answer by applying the repeated multiplication model for powering.

1. $6^2 \cdot 6^3$
   6^5; See margin.

2. $\dfrac{10^8}{10^2}$
   10^6; See margin.

3. $(4^2)^5$ 4^{10}; See margin.

4. 2^3 raised to what power is 2^{12}? 4

5. Verify that $(2 \cdot 5)^4 = 2^4 \cdot 5^4$. See margin.

NOTES ON QUESTIONS
Questions 12-17: Ask students to indicate which property or properties should be used to simplify in each case. There are two ways to indicate the property, by name or by its description using variables.

Question 23: The integer solution to this question is $y = 0$. However, there are an infinite number of noninteger solutions described by the inequality $y < \log 2$.

Question 34: Students are expected to solve this question by graphing.

Making Connections for Question 35: The formula in this question generates a geometric sequence, the topic of Lesson 8-3.

ADDITIONAL ANSWERS
1.b. $(6 \cdot 6) \cdot (6 \cdot 6 \cdot 6) = 6^5$

2.b.
$$\frac{10 \cdot 10 \cdot 10 \cdot 10 \cdot 10 \cdot 10 \cdot \cancel{10} \cdot \cancel{10}}{\cancel{10} \cdot \cancel{10}}$$
$= 10^6$

3.b.
$(4 \cdot 4) \cdot (4 \cdot 4) \cdot (4 \cdot 4) \cdot (4 \cdot 4) \cdot$
$(4 \cdot 4) = 4^{10}$

5.
$(2 \cdot 5)^4 = (2 \cdot 5) \cdot (2 \cdot 5) \cdot$
$\qquad (2 \cdot 5) \cdot (2 \cdot 5)$
$= (2 \cdot 2 \cdot 2 \cdot 2) \cdot$
$\qquad (5 \cdot 5 \cdot 5 \cdot 5)$
$= 2^4 5^4$

In 6–11, name the property that justifies the statement.   See margin.

6. $x^2 \cdot x^7 = x^9$

7. $(3a)^5 = 3^5 a^5$

8. $\dfrac{y^{12}}{y^3} = y^9$

9. $\left(\dfrac{x}{2}\right)^{10} = \dfrac{x^{10}}{2^{10}}$

10. $(b^3)^{13} = b^{39}$

11. For $x \neq 0$, $x^0 = 1$.

In 12–17, simplify.

12. $(x^4)^3$ x^{12}

13. $(6x^7)^2$ $36x^{14}$

14. $10x^7 \cdot 3x$ $30x^8$

15. $\dfrac{n^{18}}{n^6}$ n^{12}

16. $\dfrac{n^{15}}{(n^3)^5}$ 1

17. $\dfrac{z^{100}}{z^0}$ z^{100}

18. Refer to Example 4. Pluto is about $4.6 \cdot 10^9$ mi from the sun. About how long does it take light to travel from the sun to Pluto?
$2.47 \cdot 10^4$ sec $\approx$ 6.86 hrs

In 19 and 20, refer to Example 5.

19. Which two properties of exponents are used in the solution?
See margin.

20. Suppose a tennis can could hold four balls stacked tightly on top of each other. What would be the ratio of the volume of the balls to the volume of the can? $\frac{2}{3}$

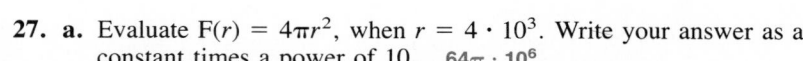
Applying the Mathematics

21. x^2 and x^6 are powers of x whose product is x^8. Find four more pairs of powers of x whose product is x^8.   See margin.

In 22 and 23, solve.

22. $(6 \cdot 10)^x = 216000$
$x = 3$

23. $0 < 10^y < 2$ if y is a nonnegative integer.
$y = 0$

In 24–26, simplify.

24. $\dfrac{w^5 \cdot w^6}{w^3 \cdot w^8}$ 1

25. $\dfrac{(-8x^2)^3}{2x^4}$ $-256x^2$

26. $\left(\dfrac{4}{x}\right)^2 \left(\dfrac{x}{2}\right)^4$ x^2

27. **a.** Evaluate $F(r) = 4\pi r^2$, when $r = 4 \cdot 10^3$. Write your answer as a constant times a power of 10. $64\pi \cdot 10^6$
b. If the value of r given in part a is the approximate radius of the earth in miles, what does $F(4 \cdot 10^3)$ represent?
surface area of the earth in square miles

28. **a.** For which figure is the ratio of volume to surface area greater: a sphere or a cube?   sphere
b. Justify your answer.   See margin.

In 29 and 30, the population of the U.S. in 1980 was about $227 \cdot 10^6$.

29. If the land of the U.S. was about $3.5 \cdot 10^6$ mi^2, what was the average number of people per square mile of land? $\approx$65 people per mi^2

30. In 1980 people in the U.S. consumed about 86.7 lbs of fresh fruit per person. What was the total weight of fresh fruit consumed in the U.S. that year? $\approx 1.97 \cdot 10^{10}$ lb

430

Review

31. What is a postulate? *(Lesson 1-5)* **See margin.**

32. What is a theorem? *(Lesson 1-6)* **See margin.**

In 33 and 34, solve the system. *(Lessons 5-2, 5-3, 6-6)*

33. $3A + B = 7$ $A = \frac{1}{6}$ **34.** $y = x^2$
  $B = 9A + 5$ $B = 6\frac{1}{2}$ $y = 3x + 4$ (-1, 1) or (4, 16)

35. Write the first four terms of the sequence generated by the formula

$$t_n = 500(1.1)^n. \text{ (Lesson 1-3)}$$
$$t_1 = 550; \ t_2 = 605; \ t_3 = 665.5; \ t_4 = 732.05$$

Exploration

36. a. Below is a table of some powers of 2.

$$2^0 = 1$$
$$2^1 = 2$$
$$2^2 = 4$$
$$2^3 = 8$$
$$2^4 = 16$$
$$2^5 = 32$$
$$2^6 = 64$$
$$2^7 = 128$$

Look carefully at the last (units) digit of each numeral. *Predict* the last digit of 2^{13}. *Check* your prediction by calculation.
b. What should be the last digit of 2^{20}? Justify your answer.
c. Explain how to find the last digit of any positive integral power of 2.
d. Explore powers of 3. Describe the patterns that occur in the last digits of these powers.

a. pattern 2, 4, 8, 6 of last digit repeats, suggests last digit is 2, 2^{13} = 8192
b. 6; sample justification: 2^{10} ends in 4, 2^{20} is the square of 2^{10}, so ends in same digit as 4^2.
c. Sample: The digits repeat periodically after every 4. If n is a multiple of 4, 2^n ends in 6. So use a multiple of 4 closest to the desired power.
d. Sample: The sequence of powers 1, 3, 9, 27, 81, ... ends in 1, 3, 9, 7, and these four numbers repeat.

31. A postulate is a statement assumed to be true.

32. A theorem is a statement which can be proved.

NAME _____

LESSON **MASTER 8–1**
QUESTIONS ON **SPUR** OBJECTIVES

■**SKILLS** *Objective A (See pages 482–485 for objectives.)*
In 1–6, write as a decimal or as a simple fraction.

1. $7^2 \cdot 7^3$ __16,807__   2. $8^3 \cdot 8^0$ __512__   3. $\frac{5^4}{5^2}$ __25__

4. $\frac{6^3}{6^9}$ __216__   5. $(0.5^2)^3$ __.015625__   6. $\left(\frac{1}{2}\right)^4$ __$\frac{1}{16}$__

■**SKILLS** *Objective F*
In 7–9, solve.

7. $\frac{12^3}{12^2} = 12^y$ 8. $(5 \cdot 6)^3 = x^3$ 9. $(8^6)^2 = 8^n$
  $y = 3$ $x = 30$ $n = 12$

In 10–18, simplify.

10. $(x^4)^7$ __x^{28}__   11. $(12p^8)^2$ __$144p^{16}$__   12. $8a^5 \cdot 6a^3$ __$48a^8$__

13. $\frac{r^{15}}{r^3}$ __r^{12}__   14. $\frac{t^{21}}{(t^7)^2}$ __t^7__   15. $\frac{m^0}{m^4}$ __m^{-4}__

16. $\frac{(-5c^3)^2}{10c^4}$ __$2.5c^2$__   17. $\frac{n^4 \cdot n^5}{n^6 \cdot n^3}$ __n^{-3}__   18. $\left(\frac{v}{3}\right)^4\left(\frac{3}{v}\right)^2$ __$\frac{25v^2}{81}$__

■**PROPERTIES** *Objective H*
In 19–21, give the general pattern that justifies the statement.

19. $(d^2)^8 = d^{16}$ __Power of a Power Prop.__
20. $(8k)^3 = 8^3k^3$ __Power of a Product Prop.__
21. $w^5 \cdot w^8 = w^{13}$ __Product of Powers Prop.__

■**USES** *Objective K*

22. In 1986, General Motors and Boeing had about $1.6 \cdot 10^{10}$ in sales to foreign countries. Excluding the U.S., the world population in 1986 was about $4.7 \cdot 10^9$. What were the average sales of these two companies to each person in the world?   __$3.40__

23. A baseball of radius r is packaged in a cube-shaped box as shown. Find the ratio of the volume of the box to the volume of the baseball.   __$\frac{6}{\pi}$__

84   *Advanced Algebra © Scott, Foresman and Company*

RESOURCES
■ Lesson Master 8-2
🖳 Computer Master 17

OBJECTIVE

J Apply the compound interest formulas.

TEACHING NOTES

You might introduce this lesson by bringing in ads from a local newspaper about current interest rates on savings accounts. Duplicate the development of the Compound Interest Formula shown in the text, using an annual rate of interest available in your area.

To emphasize how the number of compounded periods affects the return of an investment, set up expressions for the amount an investment is worth after several years under a fixed rate of interest. For instance, $1000 invested for 3 years at an annual interest rate of 8% when compounded

annually ⎫
semiannually ⎪
quarterly ⎬ is worth
monthly ⎪
daily ⎭

$$1000(1 + .08)^3 =$$
$$1000\left(1 + \frac{.08}{2}\right)^{2 \cdot 3} =$$
$$1000\left(1 + \frac{.08}{4}\right)^{4 \cdot 3} =$$
$$1000\left(1 + \frac{.08}{12}\right)^{12 \cdot 3} =$$
$$1000\left(1 + \frac{.08}{365}\right)^{365 \cdot 3} =$$

$1000(1.08)^3 = 1259.71$
$1000(1.04)^6 = 1265.32$
$1000(1.02)^{12} = 1268.24$
$1000(1.00667)^{36} = 1270.39$
$1000(1.00022)^{1095} = 1272.36$,
respectively.

Compound Interest

Suppose a person deposits $2000 in a bank that pays interest at an annual rate of 6%. If no money is added or withdrawn, after one year the bank account will have the original amount invested plus 6% interest.

Amount after 1 year: $2000 + .06(2000) = 2000(1 + .06)$
$= 2000(1.06)$
$= 2120$

Notice that to find the amount after 1 year, you do not have to add the interest; rather you just multiply the amount invested by 1.06. Similarly, at the end of the second year there will be 1.06 times the balance from the first year.

Amount after **2** years: $2000(1.06)(1.06) = 2000(1.06)^2$
$= 2247.20$
Amount after **3** years: $2000(1.06)^2(1.06) = 2000(1.06)^3$
≈ 2382.03

Because the *interest* earns interest each year, the process is called **compounding**. Notice the general pattern.

Amount after t years: $2000(1.06)^t$

For example, after 12 years there will be $2000(1.06)^{12}$
$\approx 4024.39.$

The amount of money will be more than double the original deposit.

There is a more general formula. Replace 6% by r, the annual interest rate, and 2000 by P, the **principal**, or original amount invested. Repeat the process shown above to find A, the amount the investment is worth after t years.

Compound Interest Formula:

Let P be the amount of money invested at an annual interest rate of r compounded annually. Let A be the total amount after t years. Then

$$A = P(1 + r)^t.$$

In the Compound Interest Formula, notice that A is directly proportional to P; for example, doubling the principal doubles the amount at the end. However, A is not directly proportional to r; doubling the rate does not necessarily double the amount earned.

432

Covering the Reading

In 1 and 2, Lucy invests $3000 in a CD (certificate of deposit) that pays interest at a rate of 8% compounded annually. The interest is left in the account and she makes no deposits or withdrawals.

1. To find next year's balance, you can multiply this year's balance by ___?___.   1.08

2. How much will be in the account after four years?   *A* = $4081.47

3. A person deposits $2000 in a bank account that pays interest at an annual rate of 6%. If no money is added or withdrawn, tell how much will be in the account after 1, 2, 3, 4, and 5 years.
$2120; $2247.20; $2382.03; $2524.95; $2676.45

In 4 and 5, refer to Examples 1 and 2.

4. *True or false* Emilio earned more than $500 interest in each of his accounts in the first four years.   false

5. In two ways find the interest earned in the fourth year in the account paying 6% compounded annually.   See margin.

6. In Example 2, why do the solutions show different answers?
See margin.

7. *True or false* Noel invests $1000 compounded annually at 4%. Chris invests $1000 compounded annually at 8%.   true
   a. In the first year, Chris's account will earn twice as much as Noel's.
   b. In the second year, Chris's account will earn twice as much as Noel's.   false

8. Refer to Example 3. Glenda's parents charged $600 worth of clothes and didn't pay for seven months. How much did they wind up paying for the clothes?   ≈$665.91

9. *Multiple choice* In a compound interest situation, the total amount *A* is directly proportional to: d
   (a) the rate *r*.
   (b) the time *t*.
   (c) the number *n* of compoundings in a year.
   (d) the initial amount *P*.

10. Write the compound interest formula for an account that compounds interest: (a) quarterly; (b) monthly; (c) daily.
$$A = P\left(1 + \frac{r}{4}\right)^{4t}; \quad A = P\left(1 + \frac{r}{12}\right)^{12t}; \quad A = P\left(1 + \frac{r}{365}\right)^{365t}$$

Applying the Mathematics

11. Katie puts $10,000 in a 6-year 8.625% savings certificate where interest is compounded daily. $6777.25
    a. How much will she earn during the entire six year period?
    b. How much will she earn in the sixth year? $1386.23

12. In 1987 the U.S. national debt was about $2.35 trillion. If none of this old debt is paid off and the interest on the debt is 9.5% compounded annually, what would the debt be eight years later in 1995?
≈4.86 trillion

LESSON 8-2   Compound Interest   **435**

435

In 13 and 14, recall that **simple interest** I is found by the formula $I = Prt$, where P is principal, r is the rate, and t is the time.

13. Suppose $1000 is invested at 6%.
    a. How much simple interest is earned in 5 years? $300
    b. How much interest would be earned in 5 years if the $1000 was compounded annually at 6% interest? $338.23
    c. How much more does compound interest yield than simple interest for the problems in parts a and b? $38.23

14. Jody's rich uncle sends her $2000 to help her meet expenses for college. She insists that he charge her interest, so he makes the following list of how much she needs to pay according to when she can pay it back.

After:	Pay:
3 years	$2360
4 years	$2480
5 years	$2600
6 years	$2720
7 years	$2840

    a. Is her uncle charging Jody simple or compound interest? Justify your answer.   See margin.
    b. What is the interest rate?   6%

15. Refer to the BASIC program below.

```
10 PRINT "A PROGRAM TO CALCULATE BANK BALANCE"
20 INPUT "PRINCIPAL, ANNUAL RATE, NO. OF YEARS"; P, R, Y
30 PRINT "YEAR", "AMOUNT"
40 FOR C = 1 TO Y
50    A = P * (1 + R)
60    PRINT C, A
70    P = A
80 NEXT C
90 END
```

    a. Lines 40 through 80 calculate A recursively. Modify the program so it calculates A explicitly from an interest formula.   See margin.
    b. Use the given program or your modification to print the amount that will be in an account at the end of each of the first 10 years, if $250 is invested at a rate of 6% compounded annually.   See margin.

16. Banks are required to advertise the *effective annual yield* on an account. This is the rate of interest earned after all the compoundings that take place within a year. Find the effective annual yield in a 6% account which is compounded monthly. (Hint: Use $P = \$1$.)   6.17%

In 17–22, simplify. *(Lesson 8-1)*

17. $3x^2 \cdot 2x^3$ $6x^5$ **18.** $y^5 \cdot y^0$ y^5 **19.** $(4z^2)^5$ $1024z^{10}$

20. $(ab)^2 \cdot a$ a^3b^2 **21.** $v^3 \cdot v^6 \cdot v^9$ v^{18} **22.** $\dfrac{b^{n+1}}{b^n}$ b

In 23–25, give all positive integer solutions. *(Lesson 8-1)*

23. $\dfrac{9^8}{9^2} = 9^x$ $x = 6$ **24.** $(7.3)^4 = x^4$ $\varnothing$ **25.** $0 < 2^n < 100$ $n = 1, 2, 3, 4, 5, 6$

26. Skill sequence. Solve for x. *(Lessons 1-7, 6-6)*
   a. $90 \quad\quad = \frac{1}{4}x + 20$ 280
   b. $90 - x = \frac{1}{4}x + 20$ 56
   c. $90 - x^2 = \frac{1}{4}x + 20$ $\dfrac{-1 \pm \sqrt{4481}}{8} \approx 8.24$ or -8.49

27. Gretta tied a ball to a string and twirled it around. She wanted to know how the tension T in the string is related to the speed s of her action. She started by twirling a 2 ft string and obtained the following data.

Speed (ft/sec)	1	2	3	4	5	6
Tension (lb)	300	1200	2700	4800	7500	10800

   a. Graph the above data points.   See margin.
   b. Write an equation relating T and s. (You do not have to find the constant of variation.) *(Lesson 2-6)* $T = ks^2$

28. a. Find out the interest rate on a passbook savings account at a local savings institution. Find out also how often the interest rate is compounded, and how the institution calculates the interest it pays.
   b. Conduct a survey of several local savings institutions. Which offers the highest rate of interest? Which institution do you recommend? Why?   Various student answers are possible.

29. a. Use either the computer program given in Question 15 or one of your modifications to find out how long it will take to double your money if it is invested annually at a rate of   See margin.
   (i) 4%   (ii) 6%   (iii) 8%   (iv) 10%
   b. Generalize your results from part a.   See margin.

NAME _____

LESSON 8-3

RESOURCES
■ Lesson Master 8-3
▣ Computer Master 18

OBJECTIVES

G Find terms or the rule for a geometric sequence.
L Solve real-world problems by geometric sequences.

TEACHING NOTES

To help students focus on the salient features of geometric sequences, compare and contrast geometric and arithmetic sequences with a table such as the following.

arithmetic

explicit formula $a_n = a_1 + (n - 1)d$

recursive formula $\begin{cases} a_1 \\ a_n = a_{n-1} + d \end{cases}$

constant $a_n - a_{n-1} = d$ (constant difference)

geometric

explicit formula $g_n = g_1 r^{(n-1)}$

recursive formula $\begin{cases} g_1 \\ g_n = g_{n-1} \cdot r \end{cases}$

constant $\dfrac{g_n}{g_{n-1}} = r$ (constant ratio)

Point out that the magnitude of the terms of a geometric sequence changes rapidly after the first few terms. The implications of this for compound interest are important; keeping money invested for twice as long generates more than twice the interest.

Geometric Sequences

Arithmetic or linear sequences are formed by beginning with some number and adding a constant to each term to get the next term. If, instead, each term is *multiplied* by a constant to get the next term, then a **geometric** or **exponential sequence** is formed.

Definition:

A geometric or exponential sequence is a sequence in which $g_n = r \cdot g_{n-1}$, and $r \neq 0$. The number r is the constant multiplier.

Notice that the definition above gives a recursive formula for the nth term of a geometric sequence whose first term is g_1.

Example 1 Write the first six terms of the geometric sequence in which $g_1 = 3$ and $r = 5$.

Solution The values for g_1 and r are given. Use the definition.

$$g_2 = 5 \cdot g_1 = 5 \cdot 3 \quad = 15$$
$$g_3 = 5 \cdot g_2 = 5 \cdot 15 \quad = 75$$
$$g_4 = 5 \cdot g_3 = 5 \cdot 75 \quad = 375$$
$$g_5 = 5 \cdot g_4 = 5 \cdot 375 \quad = 1875$$
$$g_6 = 5 \cdot g_5 = 5 \cdot 1875 = 9375$$

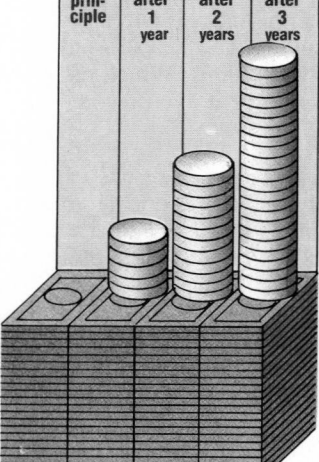

From the first term and the constant multiplier of a geometric sequence, you can find an explicit formula for the sequence. In Lesson 8-1 a $2000 investment in an account at 6% interest compounded annually was discussed. The amounts in the account after successive years exemplify a geometric sequence. The sequence begins with 2000. The constant multiplier is 1.06.

g_1	g_2	g_3	g_4
principal	*after 1 yr*	*after 2 yr*	*after 3 yr*
2000	$2000(1.06)^1$	$2000(1.06)^2$	$2000(1.06)^3$
2000	2120	2247.20	2382.03

An expression for the amount of money at the end of the nth year is $2000(1.06)^n$. However, a formula for g_n, which is the amount the investment is worth at the end of $n - 1$ years, is

$$g_n = 2000(1.06)^{n-1}.$$

This formula can be generalized to any geometric sequence.

438

Explicit Formula for a Geometric Sequence:

In the geometric sequence with first term g_1 and constant ratio r,

$$g_n = g_1 r^{n-1}.$$

Notice that in the explicit formula, the exponent is $n-1$. When you substitute 1 for n to find the first term, the constant multiplier has an exponent of zero.

$$g_1 = g_1 r^{1-1}$$
$$= g_1 r^0$$

This is consistent with the property that if $r \neq 0$, $r^0 = 1$.

Example 2 Write the first five terms of the sequence defined by $g_n = 8(-5)^{n-1}$.

Solution Substitute $n = 1, 2, 3, 4,$ and 5 into the formula.

$$g_1 = 8 \cdot (-5)^0 = 8 \cdot 1 \quad\;\; = \quad\;\; 8$$
$$g_2 = 8 \cdot (-5)^1 = 8 \cdot (-5) \quad = \quad -40$$
$$g_3 = 8 \cdot (-5)^2 = 8 \cdot 25 \quad\;\; = \quad\;\; 200$$
$$g_4 = 8 \cdot (-5)^3 = 8 \cdot (-125) = -1000$$
$$g_5 = 8 \cdot (-5)^4 = 8 \cdot 625 \quad = \quad 5000$$

Notice that in each case, the ratio of successive terms is the same. For instance

$$\frac{-40}{8} = \frac{200}{-40} = \frac{-1000}{200} = \frac{5000}{-1000} = -5.$$

For this reason the constant multiplier r is also called the *constant ratio* of successive terms.

Example 3 A ball is dropped from a height of 50 feet, and it bounces to 90% of its previous height after each bounce. Let h_n be the height after n bounces.
a. Find an explicit formula for h_n.
b. Find the height of the ball on the tenth bounce.

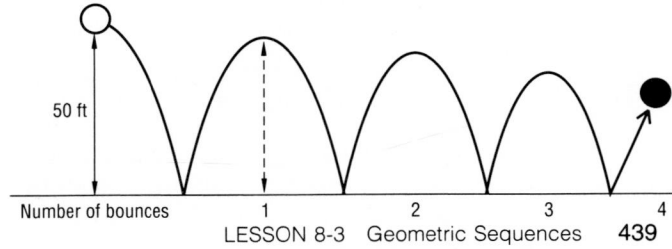

50 ft

Number of bounces   1   2   3   4

LESSON 8-3 Geometric Sequences **439**

1. Write the first six terms of the geometric sequence in which $g_1 = 6$ and $r = -2$.
6, –12, 24, –48, 96, –192

2. Write the first five terms of the sequence defined by $g_n = 4(3)^{n-1}$.
4, 12, 36, 108, 324

3. Write (a) a recursive formula and (b) an explicit formula for the geometric sequence $8, 4, 2, 1, \frac{1}{2}, \frac{1}{4} \dots$.
(a) $t_1 = 8, t_n = \frac{1}{2}t_{n-1}$;
(b) $t_n = 8\left(\frac{1}{2}\right)^{n-1}$

4. If the ball from **Example 3** on page 439 were dropped from a height of 100 feet and bounced up to 80% of its previous height after each bounce, find the height of the ball on the tenth bounce.
$h_1 = 100(.8) = 80$ **ft,** $r = .8$,
$h_n = 80(.8)^{n-1}$, $h_{10} \approx$ **10.74; the ball will rise between 10 and 11 feet on the tenth bounce.**

Error Analysis In Additional Example 4, students often incorrectly use the original height of 100 feet as the first term of the sequence. Point out that the first term occurs as the result of the first bounce. Therefore, the first term is 80% of 100 or 80 feet.

Solution

a. Because each term is the constant value .9 times the previous term, the sequence is geometric. On the first bounce, the ball will bounce to 50(.9) ft = 45 ft so $h_1 = 45$. Also, $r = .9$. Thus,

$$h_n = 45(.9)^{n-1}.$$

b. On the tenth bounce, $n = 10$ and

$$h_{10} = 45(.9)^{10-1} \approx 17.43.$$

So on the tenth bounce the ball will rise between 17 and 18 feet.

Questions

Covering the Reading

1. Arithmetic sequences are formed by beginning with some number and __?__ a constant to each term to get the next term; geometric sequences are formed by __?__ each term by a constant to get the next term.
   adding; multiplying

2. Could the sequence 5, 15, 45, 135, ... be an exponential sequence? Justify your answer.   **Yes, the constant ratio is 3.**

3. In a geometric sequence, the __?__ of successive terms is constant.
   ratio

In 4 and 5, give the first five terms of the sequence defined by the given formula.

4. $g_n = 2 \cdot 3^{n-1}$
   2; 6; 18; 54; 162

5. $t_1 = 6$, $t_n = \frac{2}{3}t_{n-1}$ **6; 4; $\frac{8}{3}$; $\frac{16}{9}$; $\frac{32}{27}$**

6. **a.** Write the first six terms of the geometric sequence whose first term is -3 and whose constant ratio is 4.   **-3; -12; -48; -192; -768; -3072**
   b. Give a recursive formula for the nth term. $g_n = 4 \cdot g_{n-1}$
   c. Give an explicit formula for the nth term. $g_n = -3 \cdot 4^{n-1}$

7. Refer to Example 3. If the ball bounces to 75% of its previous height each time, and the ball was dropped from a height of 50 ft, find the height of the tenth bounce.   **≈2.82ft**

In 8–10, find **a.** the next term, and **b.** an explicit formula for the nth term of the geometric sequence.

8. 2, 6, 18, 54, 162, ...
   486; $g_n = 2 \cdot 3^{n-1}$

9. 100, 20, 4, .8, ...
   .16; $g_n = 100 \cdot .2^{n-1}$

10. 40, -40, 40, -40, ...
   40; $g_n = 40(-1)^{n-1}$

Applying the Mathematics

11. The fifth term of a geometric sequence is 140. The constant multiplier is 2.
    a. What is the sixth term?   **280**   **b.** What is the first term?   **8.75**

12. Your little brother agreed to pay you some money because you helped him stay out of trouble. He agreed to show his gratitude by paying you 1¢ on July 1st, 2¢ on July 2nd, 4¢ on July 3rd, 8¢ on July 4th, and doubling the amount each day for the entire month. How much will he have to pay you on July 31?   **about $1.0737 \cdot 10^9$ cents = $10,737,000**

440

13. A diamond was purchased for \$2500. If its value increases 6% each year, give the value of the diamond after ten years.   ≈**\$4,223.70**

14. Use the formula for simple interest $I = Prt$ where
P = the principal sum invested
r = the annual interest rate
t = the time in years.
  a. If you invest \$1000 at 8% interest, write the sequence of your balances over the next 6 years.   **See margin.**
  b. Use your answer to part a. Does simple interest create a geometric sequence? If so, what is the common ratio? If not, what kind of sequence does it lead to?   **No, it leads to an arithmetic sequence.**

15. S_1 is a side of a square with length 8 cm. S_2 is the side of the square formed by joining the midpoints of the sides of S_1. S_2 is found using the Pythagorean theorem.

$$(S_2)^2 = (\tfrac{1}{2}S_1)^2 + (\tfrac{1}{2}S_1)^2$$
$$= 4^2 + 4^2$$
$$= 32$$
$$S_2 = 4\sqrt{2}$$

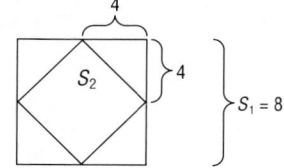

  a. Let S_n be a side of the square formed by joining the midpoints of the sides of S_{n-1}. Find the lengths of S_3, S_4, S_5.   **4; $2\sqrt{2}$; 2**
  b. Is the sequence S_n geometric? If so, what is the common ratio? If not, explain why not.   **yes; $r = \dfrac{1}{\sqrt{2}}$**
  c. Let A_n be the area of the square with side S_n. Find A_1 and A_2.   **64, 32**
  d. Is the sequence A_n, the areas of the squares with sides S_n, geometric? If so, what is the common ratio? If not, explain why not.   **yes; $r = .5$**

In 16–18, consider the BASIC program below.

```
10 REM GENERATING A GEOMETRIC SEQUENCE
20 INPUT "FIRST TERM, COMMON RATIO, NO. OF TERMS";
   G1, R, N
30 PRINT "POSITION","TERM"
40 FOR I = 1 TO N
50    GI = G1 * R ^ (I − 1)
60    PRINT I, GI
70 NEXT I
80 END
```

16. What is printed when this program is run and the user inputs 10 for G1, 2 for R, and 7 for N?   **See margin.**

17. What values should you input for G1, R, and N to print the table at the right.   **G1 = 16; R = .25; N = 5**

POSITION	TERM
1	16
2	4
3	1
4	.25
5	.0625

MORE PRACTICE
For more questions on SPUR
Objectives, use *Lesson Mas-
ter* 8-3, shown on page 441.

EXTENSION
You can extend this lesson
by showing that the recursive
and explicit definitions of
geometric sequences are
equivalent. According to the
definition, the recursive formula

g_1
$g_n = g_{n-1}r$ for $n > 1$

generates a geometric se-
quence. The first terms of
this sequence are:

g_1
$g_2 = g_{2-1}r = g_1 r$
$g_3 = g_{3-1}r = g_2 r =$
$\quad (g_1 r)r = g_1 r^2$
$g_4 = g_{4-1}r = g_3 r =$
$\quad (g_1 r^2)r = g_1 r^3$

From the above pattern, it
is not difficult to see that
$g_n = g_1 r^{n-1}$, which is the
explicit formula for the nth
term of a geometric se-
quence. Conversely, the
explicit formula implies the
recursive one. For $n > 1$,

$$\frac{g_{n+1}}{g_n} = \frac{gr^{(n+1)-1}}{gr^{n-1}} = \frac{gr^n}{gr^{n-1}} = r.$$

So $g_{n+1} = g_n r$, or $g_n = g_{n-1}r$.

EVALUATION
Alternative Assessment
Have students give the first
four terms of arithmetic or
geometric sequences. Then
ask other students to identify
the next term of each se-
quence and a formula for the
nth term of each sequence.

ADDITIONAL ANSWERS
27.a. and b.

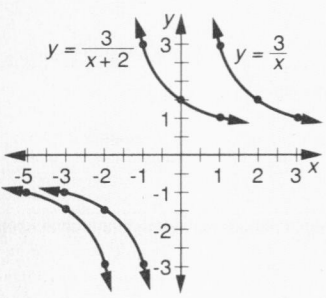

---

18. **a.** Use the program to print the first 50 terms of the geometric sequence that begins .001, .003, .009 ... .
    b. Write the last term of the sequence in part a without scientific no-
tation. ≈ **239,300,000,000,000,000,000**

19. An account pays 7.75% interest compounded quarterly. How much
would be in the account if $500 were left untouched for 10 years?
(Lesson 8-2) **$1077.28**

20. *Multiple choice* Which of these accounts will have twice as much in it
as an account where $1000 is compounded at an annual rate of 5% for
3 years?
(Lesson 8-2) **a**
    (a) an account where $2000 is compounded at 5% for 3 years
    (b) an account where $1000 is compounded at 10% for 3 years
    (c) an account where $1000 is compounded at 5% for 6 years

In 21–24, simplify. *(Previous course, Lesson 8-1)*

21. $4x \cdot 5x^2$ **20x³**
22. $(y^m)^n + (y^n)^m$ **2y^{mn}**

23. $\left(\frac{z}{3}\right)^4$ **$\frac{z^4}{81}$**
24. $\frac{a^5}{a^3}$ **a²**

In 25 and 26, rewrite using the Distributive Postulate. *(Lessons 1-5, 6-1)*

25. $2m^6 + m^3$ **$m^3(2m^3 + 1)$**   26. $4(\frac{1}{6} + t^3)^2$ **$\frac{1}{9} + \frac{4}{3}t^3 + 4t^6$**

27. **a.** Graph the function with equation $y = \frac{3}{x}$. **See margin.**
    b. On the same coordinate axes as part a, sketch the image of $y = \frac{3}{x}$
    translated 2 units to the left. **See margin.**
    c. Write an equation for the image. *(Lesson 6-4)* **$y = \frac{3}{x + 2}$**

In 28 and 29, find the slope:

28. of the line of symmetry of $f(x) = \frac{3}{x}$. *(Lessons 2-4, 2-7)*
    y = x: slope is 1; y = -x: slope is -1

29. of the line through $(8, 9)$ and $(-5, 9)$. **0**

30. If h: $x \rightarrow 2(x - 1)^2$, then $h(3) - h(0) = \underline{\ ?\ }$. *(Lesson 7-1)* **6**

31. In 1987 the world population passed 5 billion and was estimated to be
increasing at the rate of 1.7% per year. Using this model, in what
year would the world population be 10 billion?
in about 41 years, the year 2028

442

LESSON 8-4

Negative Integer Exponents

You have seen negative exponents when writing numbers in scientific notation. For example,

$$10^6 = 1,000,000 = \text{one million}$$
$$\text{and } 10^{-6} = .000001 = \text{one millionth.}$$

This suggests that, in general, x^n and x^{-n} are reciprocals. This is easily proved.

Negative Exponent Theorem:

If $x > 0$, then $x^{-n} = \dfrac{1}{x^n}$.

Proof:

By the Product of Powers Postulate, $x^n \cdot x^{-n} = x^{n+-n}$
$$= x^0$$
$$= 1$$

Dividing both sides by x^n (which can always be done because $x \neq 0$),

$$x^{-n} = \frac{1}{x^n}.$$

Thus the negative sign in an exponent means *reciprocal*. The Negative Exponent Theorem states that an expression with a negative exponent is the reciprocal of the expression without the negative sign.

In fact, x^{-1} equals $\dfrac{1}{x^1}$, so x^{-1} *is the reciprocal of* x.

■ ■ ■ ■ ■ ■ ■ ■ ■

Example 1   Write 5^{-3} as a decimal.

Solution 5^{-3} is the reciprocal of 5^3.

Thus $5^{-3} = \dfrac{1}{5^3} = \dfrac{1}{125} = .008$.

Check   Use a calculator to find 5^{-3}. Press

$5 \; \boxed{y^x} \; 3 \; \boxed{\pm} \; \boxed{=} \;$ or $5 \; \boxed{y^x} \; 3 \; \boxed{=} \; \boxed{1/x}$.

The Negative Exponent Theorem allows formulas to be rewritten without fractions. This may be desirable if the formula appears in a typed prose paragraph.

LESSON 8-4

RESOURCES
■ Lesson Master 8-4
■ Quiz for Lessons 8-1
   Through 8-4
▤ Visual for Teaching Aid 46
   displays the chart used for
   Question 33.

OBJECTIVES

A Evaluate x^n when n is a negative integer.
F Solve equations or simplify expressions with negative exponents.
H Recognize properties of negative integer powers.
J Apply a compound interest formula when the exponent is negative.
K Solve real-world problems which can be modeled by equations with negative exponents.

TEACHING NOTES

Point out that multiplying by 10^6 moves the decimal point of the other factor 6 places to the right because we are multiplying by 1,000,000. When we multiply by 10^{-6}, we are multiplying by .000001, or dividing by 1,000,000. Stress to students that multiplying by 10^{-6} is the same as dividing by 10^6.

Hence, $10^{-6} = \dfrac{1}{10^6}$.

Emphasize that the negative sign in an exponent does not have the same meaning as the negative sign before any other number. Tell students that the negative sign before an exponent indicates that the reciprocal of the number is to be used. Point out also that a negative sign in an exponent *never* affects the sign of the base.

■ ■ ■ ■ ■ ■ ■ ■

Example 2 Rewrite Newton's Law of Universal Gravitation

$$W = \frac{k}{r^2}$$

using negative exponents.

Solution $W = k \cdot \frac{1}{r^2}$ definition of division

$W = kr^{-2}$ Negative Exponent Theorem

Caution: a negative sign in an exponent does not make the expression negative. *All* the powers of a positive number are positive. Here are some powers of 9.

$$9^0 = 1$$

$$9^1 = 9 \qquad\qquad 9^{-1} = \frac{1}{9^1} = \frac{1}{9}$$

$$9^2 = 81 \qquad\qquad 9^{-2} = \frac{1}{9^2} = \frac{1}{81}$$

$$9^3 = 729 \qquad\qquad 9^{-3} = \frac{1}{9^3} = \frac{1}{729}$$

$$9^4 = 6561 \qquad\qquad 9^{-4} = \frac{1}{9^4} = \frac{1}{6561}$$

When a positive exponent signifies time in the future, the corresponding negative exponent stands for time in the past.

■ ■ ■ ■ ■ ■ ■ ■

Example 3 In an account with a rate of 7% compounded annually, how much money did Soren invest 5 years ago if he has $9817.86 now?

Solution Dividing both sides of the compound interest formula by $(1 + r)^t$, we get $\frac{A}{(1 + r)^t} = P$ or $P = A(1 + r)^{-t}$. Here $A = \$9817.86$ and $r = .07$. Soren wants to know how much was invested 5 years ago, so $t = -5$.

Then $P = 9817.86(1 + .07)^{-5}$
$P = 9817.86(1.07)^{-5}$
$P = \dfrac{9817.86}{1.07^5}$
$P = 6999.9985$

Soren originally invested $7000.

Check If $7000 is invested at 7% for five years, then

$A = 7000(1.07)^5$
$\quad = 9817.8621,$

which checks with the given information.

Negative exponents satisfy the postulates about powers stated in Lesson 8-1.

▪ ▪ ▪ ▪ ▪ ▪ ▪ ▪ ▪

Example 4   Simplify (a) $\dfrac{10^3}{10^7}$ and (b) $x^5 \cdot x^{-1}$. (Assume $x > 0$.)

Solution

(a) This is a quotient of powers of the same base.

$$\frac{10^3}{10^7} = 10^{3-7} = 10^{-4}$$

(b) Use the Product of Powers Postulate.

$$x^5 \cdot x^{-1} = x^{5+-1} = x^4$$

Check

(a) Use the repeated multiplication meaning of 10^n.

$$\frac{10^3}{10^7} = \frac{10 \cdot 10 \cdot 10}{10 \cdot 10 \cdot 10 \cdot 10 \cdot 10 \cdot 10 \cdot 10} = \frac{1}{10 \cdot 10 \cdot 10 \cdot 10} = \frac{1}{10^4}$$

(b) From the Negative Exponent Theorem you know that

$$x^{-1} = \frac{1}{x}.$$

Use the definition of b^p to rewrite $x^5 \cdot x^{-1} = x \cdot x \cdot x \cdot x \cdot x \cdot \dfrac{1}{x} = x^4$.

Questions

Covering the Reading

1. Simplify.
   a. $b^x \cdot b^y$ b^{x+y} **b.** $b^x \cdot b^0$ b^x **c.** $b^x \cdot b^{-x}$ 1

2. *Multiple choice* a^y and a^{-y} are: a
   (a) reciprocals
   (b) opposites
   (c) neither (a) nor (b).

3. Write without an exponent. Do not use a calculator.
   a. 8^0 1   **b.** 8^{-1} $\frac{1}{8}$ **c.** 8^{-2} $\frac{1}{64}$

4. Write 7^x without an exponent when x is:
   a. -3 $\frac{1}{343}$ **b.** -2 $\frac{1}{49}$ **c.** -1. $\frac{1}{7}$

5. *Multiple choice* Assume $b > 0$. For what values of n is $b^n < 0$?   d
   (a) $n < 0$ (b) $0 < n < 1$
   (c) all values of n (d) no values of n

6. Rewrite $\dfrac{k}{r^2}$ using negative exponents and without a fraction. kr^{-2}

LESSON 8-4   Negative Integer Exponents   445

NOTES ON QUESTIONS
Question 16: You may want to have students answer this question by looking at special cases and generalizing. Have them try $x = \frac{1}{2}, \frac{3}{4}, \frac{99}{100}$, or $\frac{1}{100}$.

Question 26: This question asks students to evaluate and graph an exponential function with a finite domain. Continuous functions with this equation will be encountered in Chapter 9. Part (c) previews the next lesson. For now, have students use their power key with .5 as the exponent. In the next lesson, they will study $\frac{1}{2}$ as a power in relation to square roots.

Question 29: The answers to parts (a), (b), and (c) of this question all seem to generate Pascal's triangle ($\times$ 1000, $\times$ 100, $\times$ 10) until the 5th year. You might ask students why the pattern does not continue. (Digits begin to carry over into the next place value when new interest is added.)

Question 31: This question provides a good opportunity to discuss the difference between -1 used as an exponent and -1 used to indicate the inverse of a function.

Question 33: The reasons for the occurrence of similar digits is that $5^{-n} = (1/5)^n = .2^n$, and similarly, $2^{-n} = (1/2)^n = .5^n$.

445

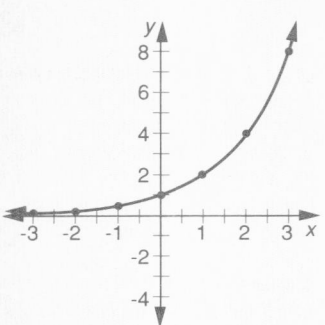
7. Interpret the formula $P = A(1 + r)^{-t}$ when $t = 2$.
   The principal invested two years ago

8. Alex has $20,000 now in an account. The interest rate compounded annually has been 8%. How much was in the account 4 years ago?
   $14,700.60

In 9–11, write without an exponent.

9. $10^7 \cdot 10^{-6}$ **10**
10. $2^{-3} \cdot 13^0$ $\frac{1}{8}$
11. $(10^{-3})^2$ **.000001**

In 12–14, simplify.

12. $\frac{8x^6}{6x^8}$ $\frac{4}{3}x^{-2}$
13. $\frac{4y^{-1}}{y^{-2}}$ **4y**
14. $\frac{z^5}{10z^{-6}}$ $\frac{z^{11}}{10}$

Applying the Mathematics

15. If $x^3 = 5$, what is the value of x^{-3}? $\frac{1}{5}$

16. Suppose $0 < x < 1$. Is x^{-2} smaller or larger than x?   **Larger**

In 17–22, write without an exponent.

17. $(3^{-2})^{-4}$ **6561**
18. $3.78 \cdot 10^{-4}$ **0.000378**
19. $\frac{1}{2^{-5}}$ **32**

20. $\frac{3^{-3}}{3^{-2}}$ $\frac{1}{3}$
21. $\left(\frac{1}{2}\right)^{-5}$ **32**
22. $\frac{1}{4^{-3}}$ **64**

23. Write $(2.5 \cdot 10^{-2})^3$ in scientific notation. $1.5625 \cdot 10^{-5}$

24. The intensity I of light varies inversely as the square of the distance d from the observer. Let k be the constant of variation. $I = \frac{k}{d^2}$
    a. Write this inverse variation formula with positive exponents.
    b. Rewrite this inverse variation formula with negative exponents.
    $I = kd^{-2}$

25. Benjamin Franklin was one of the most famous scientists of his day and conducted many science experiments. In one he noticed that a given amount of oil dropped on the surface of a lake would not spread out beyond a certain area. In units we use today, he found that 0.1 cm^3 of oil spread to cover about 40 m^2 of the lake. About how thick is such an oil layer? Express your answer in scientific notation. (Although in Franklin's time no one knew about molecules, Franklin's experiment resulted in the first estimate of a molecule's size. Nowadays we know that the layer of oil stops spreading when it is one molecule thick.) $2.5 \cdot 10^{-7}$ cm or $2.5 \cdot 10^{-9}$ m

26. Let $f(x) = 2^x$.
    a. Evaluate the function for integers between -3 and 3.   **See margin.**
    b. Graph $y = f(x)$ **See margin.**
    c. Use your graph to estimate the value of $2^{1/2}$. Check your estimate with a calculator.
    Calculator = 1.4142...; the graph estimate will depend on each student's gra

Review

27. Consider the sequence 6561, 2187, 729, ...
    a. Can it be geometric?   **yes**
    b. Find an explicit rule for the nth term. $g_n = 6561\left(\frac{1}{3}\right)^{n-1}$
    c. Find the 15th term. *(Lesson 8-3)* ≈ 0.0014

446

28. Suppose $g_n = g_1 r^{n-1}$ where $g_1 \neq 0$ and $r_1 \neq 0$. *(Lesson 8-3)*
   a. Write an explicit formula for g_{n+1}. $g_{n+1} = g_1 r^n$
   b. Prove that $\dfrac{g_{n+1}}{g_n} = r$. $\dfrac{g_{n+1}}{g_n} = \dfrac{g_1 r^n}{g_1 r^{n-1}} = r^{n-(n-1)} = r^1 = r$
   c. State in words the theorem you proved in part b.
      The ratio of consecutive terms of a geometric sequence is constant.

29. Bonnie invests $1000 for 5 years at 10% interest compounded annually. *(Lessons 2-6, 8-3)*   **See margin for a-c.**
   a. How much money will Bonnie have at the end of each year?
   b. How much interest does she earn each year?
   c. Calculate how much more interest Bonnie earned in the second year than in the first, and again in the third year than in the second, and so on.
   d. If the differences you found in part c are thought of as the values of a function, would it be increasing, decreasing, or neither?
      increasing

30. Find the matrix for R_{90} and R_{90}^{-1}. *(Lesson 4-5)* **See margin.**

31. If f: $x \to 3x + 6$, then f^{-1}: $x \to$ __?__. *(Lesson 7-7)* $\dfrac{x-6}{3}$

32. This question causes some students trouble: Simplify $\dfrac{1}{\frac{10}{9}}$. *(Previous course)* $\dfrac{9}{10}$

Exploration

33. Examine these columns closely. Describe two patterns relating the powers of 5 at the left to the powers of 2 at the right.

5^6	$=$	15,625		2^6	$=$	64
5^5	$=$	3,125		2^5	$=$	32
5^4	$=$	625		2^4	$=$	16
5^3	$=$	125		2^3	$=$	8
5^2	$=$	25		2^2	$=$	4
5^1	$=$	5		2^1	$=$	2
5^0	$=$	1		2^0	$=$	1
5^{-1}	$=$	0.2		2^{-1}	$=$	0.5
5^{-2}	$=$	0.04		2^{-2}	$=$	0.25
5^{-3}	$=$	0.008		2^{-3}	$=$	0.125
5^{-4}	$=$	0.0016		2^{-4}	$=$	0.0625
5^{-5}	$=$	0.00032		2^{-5}	$=$	0.03125
5^{-6}	$=$	0.000064		2^{-6}	$=$	0.015625

$5^n = 10^n \cdot 2^{-n}$ and $2^n \cdot 5^n = 10^n$

34. Make a chart similar to the one in Question 33 using the powers of 4 and 2.5. **See margin.**
   a. Describe how the patterns in these charts are similar to the patterns in Question 33. **The decimal pattern is the same as found here.**
   b. Find another pair of numbers with the same properties.
      Sample: powers of 8 and 1.25.

FOLLOW-UP

MORE PRACTICE
For more questions on SPUR Objectives, use *Lesson Master 8-4*, shown below.

EVALUATION
A quiz covering Lessons 8-1 through 8-4 is provided in the Teacher's Resource File.

34.

4^6	$=$	**4096**
4^5	$=$	**1024**
4^4	$=$	**256**
4^3	$=$	**64**
4^2	$=$	**16**
4^1	$=$	**4**
4^0	$=$	**1**
4^{-1}	$=$	**0.25**
4^{-2}	$=$	**0.0625**
4^{-3}	$=$	**0.015625**
4^{-4}	$=$	**0.00390625**
$(2.5)^6$	$=$	**244.140625**
$(2.5)^5$	$=$	**97.65625**
$(2.5)^4$	$=$	**39.0625**
$(2.5)^3$	$=$	**15.625**
$(2.5)^2$	$=$	**6.25**
$(2.5)^1$	$=$	**2.5**
$(2.5)^0$	$=$	**1**
$(2.5)^{-1}$	$=$	**0.4**
$(2.5)^{-2}$	$=$	**0.16**
$(2.5)^{-3}$	$=$	**0.064**
$(2.5)^{-4}$	$=$	**0.0256**

NAME _____

LESSON **MASTER 8–4**
QUESTIONS ON **SPUR** OBJECTIVES

■**SKILLS** *Objective A (See pages 482–485 for objectives.)*
In 1–12, write as a decimal or as a simple fraction.

1. $10^6 \cdot 10^{-4}$ ___**100**___   2. $2 \cdot 5^{-5} \cdot 4^1 \cdot 0$ ___$\frac{1}{32}$___

3. $(5^{-2})^2$ ___$\frac{1}{625}$___   4. $\left(\frac{2}{3}\right)^{-1}$ ___$\frac{7}{2}$___

5. $\left(\frac{3}{4}\right)^{-3}$ ___$\frac{64}{27}$___   6. 8^{-3} ___$\frac{1}{512}$___

7. $(3 \cdot 6)^{-5}$ ___$\frac{1}{1,889,568}$___   8. $(-7)^{-2}$ ___$\frac{1}{49}$___

9. $1.48 \cdot 10^{-3}$ ___**.00148**___   10. $36 \cdot 10^{-5}$ ___**.00036**___

11. $\frac{6^{-5}}{6^{7}}$ ___$\frac{1}{279,936}$___   12. $\frac{3^{7}}{3^{5}}$ ___$\frac{1}{9}$___

13. Write $(3.9 \cdot 10^{-5})^2$ in scientific notation. ___**1.521 · 10⁻⁹**___

■**SKILLS** *Objective F*
In 14 and 15, simplify.

14. $\frac{12x^5}{8x^7}$ ___$\frac{3}{2x^2}$___   15. $\frac{18d}{(10d^{-4})(9d^2)}$ ___$\frac{1}{5}d^3$___

■**USES** *Objective J*
In 16 and 17, Jaclyn now has $8000 in an account earning an annual interest rate of 8%, compounded monthly.

16. How much money was in the account 5 years ago? ___**$5369.68**___

17. How much interest will she earn in the next 10 years? ___**$9757.12**___

■**USES** *Objective K*

18. Find the surface area of the circular head of a pin with radius $5.6 \cdot 10^{-1}$ mm. ___**.31π mm²**___

Advanced Algebra © Scott, Foresman and Company

OBJECTIVES

B Evaluate $x^{1/n}$ when n is an integer.
I Apply the definition of $x^{1/n}$ as it applies to nth roots of x.
K Solve real-world problems which can be modeled by equations with nth roots.

TEACHING NOTES

Reading Have students read through the beginning paragraphs about the Delians. They will need this information for **Question 7.** Stress each highlighted sentence. Show examples for each.

Point out that the definition of nth roots requires n to be both positive and an integer greater than 1.

Discuss even and odd roots and their application to positive and negative numbers. Stress that the symbol $x^{1/n}$, when it stands for a real number, is the largest nth root of x.

The proof of the $\frac{1}{n}$ Exponent Theorem is similar to other proofs students have seen in this chapter. Begin by asking students what the symbol $9^{1/2}$ might mean. By showing $(9^{1/2})^2 = 9^{1/2 \cdot 2} = 9^1 = 9$, you prove that $9^{1/2}$ is a square root of 9. Similarly, you can show that $(9^{1/n})^n = 9$, so $9^{1/n}$ is an nth root of 9. Now, work through the general case for the proof of the $\frac{1}{n}$ Exponent Theorem.

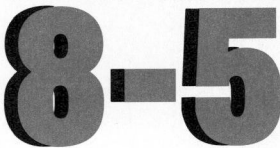

LESSON

8-5

nth Roots

The island of Delos today

According to Greek history, about 400 B.C., inhabitants of the island Delos (called Delians) were suffering from a serious epidemic. As was common in those times, the community leaders sought advice from an oracle, a wise person through whom a god was believed to speak. The Delians were told that if they *exactly* doubled the size of their cubical altar to Apollo, the epidemic would end. "Double the size" meant, in this case, "double the volume."

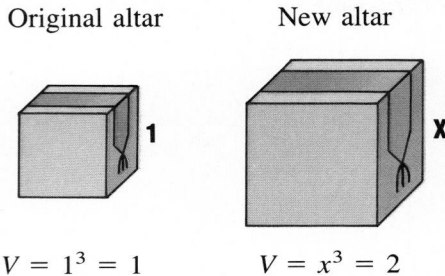

Original altar   New altar

$V = 1^3 = 1$ $V = x^3 = 2$

If each side of the original altar was one unit, the Delians knew that the length of the new altar had to be a number that when cubed gave 2; that is, they needed to solve $x^3 = 2$.

> Recall that x is a **square root** of t when $x^2 = t$.
> Similarly, x is a **cube root** of t when $x^3 = t$.

As examples:

> -12 is a square root of 144 because $(-12)^2 = 144$.
> 4 is a cube root of 64 because $4^3 = 64$.

In effect, the Delians were told by their oracle to construct a length equal to the cube root of 2. They could not do this, and the epidemic continued, so the story goes.

Square roots and cube roots are special cases of the following, more general, idea.

448

Definition:

Let n be an integer greater than 1. Then b is an ***nth root*** of x if and only if $b^n = x$.

There are no special names for nth roots other than *square* roots (when $n = 2$) and *cube* roots (when $n = 3$). We call them fourth roots, fifth roots, and so on. The nth roots of a real number may be real or complex.

■ ■ ■ ■ ■ ■ ■ ■ ■

Example 1   Show that 2, -2, 2i, and -2i are fourth roots of 16.

Solution   Each of 2, -2, 2i, and -2i is a fourth root of 16 because each satisfies $b^4 = 16$:

$$2^4 = 16$$
$$(-2)^4 = 16$$
$$(2i)^4 = 2^4 \cdot = 16 \cdot 1 = 16$$
$$(-2i)^4 = (-2i)(-2i)(-2i)(-2i) = (-2)^4 i^4 = 16 \cdot 1 = 16$$

It can be proved that every nonzero real number has n distinct nth roots. The real nth roots can be determined from a graph. For instance, the real nth roots of 16 are the first coordinates of the points where the horizontal line $y = 16$ intersects the curve $y = x^4$, as shown below at the left.

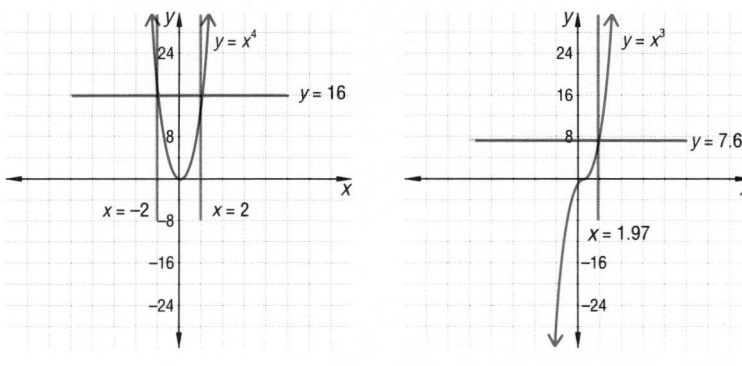

n even n odd

The number 7.6 has only one real cube root; it is the x-coordinate of the point where $y = 7.6$ intersects $y = x^3$ as shown above at the right. An accurate drawing might show $x \approx 2$; a calculator displays:

1.9660951

ADDITIONAL EXAMPLES

1. Show that $1 - i$ is a fourth root of -4. The number -4 has three more fourth roots. Can you guess what they are? Check to be sure you are right.
$-1 + i, 1 + i, -1 - i$

2. Calculate.
a. $27^{1/3}$
3
b. $.25^{1/2}$
.5
c. $\left[\dfrac{16}{625}\right]^{1/4}$
$\dfrac{2}{5}$
d. $115^{1/3}$
≈4.86

449

The graph of $y = x^n$, for n even, looks much like the graph of $y = x^4$. It verifies:

When n is even, a positive real number has 2 real nth roots.
When n is even, a negative real number has no real nth roots.

When n is odd, every horizontal line intersects $y = x^n$ in exactly one point. Thus:

When n is odd, every real number has exactly 1 real nth root.

Not until 2000 years after the Greeks was it recognized that nth roots could be represented as powers. However, to ensure that every power has exactly one value, it is necessary to restrict the domain of the base and the power to the positive reals.

$\frac{1}{n}$ Exponent Theorem:

When $x \geq 0$ and n is an integer greater than 1, $x^{1/n}$ is an nth root of x.

Proof:

By the definition of nth root, b is an nth root of x if and only if $b^n = x$. Suppose $b = x^{1/n}$.

Then
$$(x^{1/n})^n = x^{(\frac{1}{n} \cdot n)} \quad \text{Power of a Power Property}$$
$$= x^1$$
$$= x.$$

Thus $x^{1/n}$ is an nth root.

In order for the other properties of powers to hold for the $\frac{1}{n}$th power, $x^{1/n}$ must be the nonnegative root of x. Specifically, $x^{1/2}$ is the nonnegative square root of x and $2^{1/3}$ represents the positive cube root of 2.

In the $\frac{1}{n}$ Exponent Theorem, x is assumed to be nonnegative to avoid complex roots and multiple solutions. Thus,

$$81^{1/4} = 3 \text{ and } \left(\tfrac{64}{27}\right)^{1/3} = \tfrac{4}{3}.$$

450

Pay close attention to parentheses. While $(-4)^{1/2}$ and $(-8)^{1/3}$ are not defined,

$$-4^{1/2} = -(4^{1/2}) = -2.$$

Because roots can be written as powers, you can use a calculator's power key to evaluate $x^{1/n}$.

Example 2   Approximate $70^{1/7}$ to the nearest hundredth.

Solution 1   Key in 70 $\boxed{y^x}$ $\boxed{(}$ 1 $\boxed{\div}$ 7 $\boxed{)}$ $\boxed{=}$. The calculator will display 1.8347861 or something close. $70^{1/7} \approx 1.83$.

Solution 2   You can shorten the key sequence by using the reciprocal key $\boxed{1/x}$. Key in 70 $\boxed{y^x}$ 7 $\boxed{1/x}$ $\boxed{=}$.

Check   Calculate $(1.8347861)^7$. You should get 70 or very close to it.

Questions

Covering the Reading

1. Let n be an integer greater than 1. Then x is an nth root of t if and only if __?__. $x^n = t$

2. Which are 6th roots of 64: 2, -2, 2i, -2i?   2, -2

In 3 and 4, without using a calculator find the positive

3. 4th roots of 81   3   **4.** cube roots of 8.   2

In 5 and 6, state the real roots of the equation.

5. $x^3 = 125$ x = 5   **6.** $x^4 = 1000$ x = 10 or x = -10

7. a. Who were the Delians?   Inhabitants of the island Delos
   b. What length did the Delians have to construct to satisfy the oracle?
       the cube root of two
8. What is the meaning of $x^{1/n}$?
    the nth root of x, a number t such that $t^n = x$
9. a. Write a calculator key sequence to evaluate $80^{1/3}$.   See margin.
   b. Estimate $80^{1/3}$ to the nearest hundredth.   4.31

10. *True or false*
   a. Both 5 and -5 are 6th roots of 15,625.   true
   b. $15{,}625^{1/6} = 5$ true
   c. $15{,}625^{1/6} = -5$ false
   d. 5i is a 6th root of 15,625.   false

11. For what values of t and n is the symbol $t^{1/n}$ defined?
    $t \geq 0$ and n is an integer greater than 1.

LESSON 8-5   *n*th Roots   451

ADDITIONAL ANSWERS
9.a. 80 $\boxed{y^x}$ $\boxed{(}$ 1 $\boxed{\div}$ 3 $\boxed{)}$ =

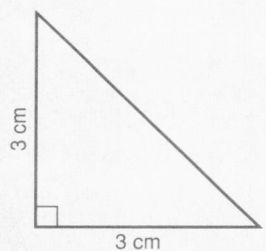
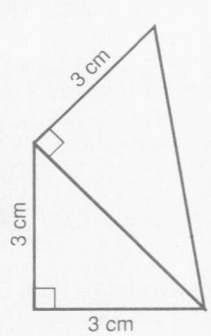
In 12–14, evaluate without a calculator.

12. $125^{1/3}$ 5   **13.** $144^{1/2}$ 12   **14.** $\left(\frac{16}{81}\right)^{1/4}$ $\frac{2}{3}$

In 15–17, use a calculator to approximate to the nearest thousandth.

15. $24^{1/24}$ 1.142   **16.** $(1{,}419{,}857)^{1/5}$ 17   **17.** $1000^{1/10}$ 1.995

18. *Multiple choice* Try the key sequence

t $\boxed{y^x}$ 3 $\boxed{1/x}$ $\boxed{=}$ $\boxed{y^x}$ 3 $\boxed{=}$

for some positive number t. Repeat for other positive numbers t until you see a pattern. What generalization about positive numbers does this illustrate?   b

(a) $\dfrac{3t}{3} = t$ (b) $(t^{1/3})^3 = t$

(c) $(3^t)^3 = t$ (d) $3(t^{1/3}) = t$

In 19–26, tell which symbol, $<$, $=$, or $>$, will give a true statement.

19. $100^{1/2}$ __?__ $100^{1/5}$ $>$ **20.** -7 __?__ $2401^{1/4}$ $<$

21. $-18^{1/3}$ __?__ $18^{1/3}$ $<$ **22.** $(8^{1/3})^3$ __?__ 8 $=$

23. $9^{1/2}$ __?__ $\left(\frac{1}{2}\right)^9$ $>$ **24.** $9^{1/2} \cdot 4^{1/2}$ __?__ $(9 \cdot 4)^{1/2}$ $=$

25. $(z^6)^{1/3}$ __?__ z^2 $=$ **26.** $64^{1/2} \cdot 64^{1/2}$ __?__ 64^1 $=$

27. Use $t = \frac{1}{2}$ in the compound interest formula $A = P(1 + r)^t$ to calculate the amount you would have after 6 months if you invested \$2000 at a yearly effective yield of 6%. Does the answer seem reasonable?
\$2059; yes

28. a. Verify that $i\sqrt{2}$ is a 4th root of 4.   See margin.
    b. Why then is $4^{1/4} \neq i\sqrt{2}$?
    $4^{1/4}$ is the positive real 4th root of 4, which is $\sqrt{2}$.

29. Let the frequency of the musical note A above middle C be F_1, which is often set to 440 vibrations per second. Let n be the number of notes above that A. Then the frequencies that determine the other notes found on a piano can be found by the recursive formula

$$F_1 = 440$$
$$F_n = F_{n-1} \cdot 2^{1/12}.$$

a. Rewrite the formula explicitly.
$F_n = 440(2^{1/12})^{n-1}$

b. What is the frequency of the note one octave above F_1 (one octave is 12 notes)?   831

452

In 30–32, write without negative exponents. *(Lesson 8-4)*

30. $\dfrac{3x^{-3}}{y^2}$ $\dfrac{3}{x^3y^2}$

31. $4m^{-1}$ $\dfrac{4}{m}$

32. $\dfrac{2x}{9x^{-2}} + \dfrac{-7}{9x^{-3}}$ $\dfrac{-5x^3}{9}$

In 33–35, evaluate. *(Lesson 8-4)*

33. $\left(\dfrac{5}{2}\right)^{-2}$ .16 or $\dfrac{4}{25}$

34. $3^{-1} + (-1)^3$ $-\dfrac{2}{3}$

35. $(((14^{-1})^0)^1)^2$ 1

In 36 and 37, (a) give the next term of the geometric sequence and (b) give an explicit expression for the *n*th term. *(Lesson 8-3)*

36. 10, 20, 40, 80, ...
160; $10 \cdot 2^{n-1}$

37. 6, 3, ... 1.5; $6(.5)^{n-1}$

38. State the Power of a Product Postulate. *(Lesson 8-1)*
See Below.

39. If the expenses of a $1000 vacation are charged for four months on a credit card with an annual rate of 16% with interest compounded monthly, how much will the vacation cost? *(Lesson 8-2)* $1054.41

40. If $\sqrt{32} = x\sqrt{2}$, what is *x*? *(Previous course, Lesson 6-8)*
4

41. **a.** Draw an isosceles triangle with legs 3 cm long.
   b. Find the length of the hypotenuse in part a without measuring. (Check your answer by measuring.) $3\sqrt{2} \approx 4.24$cm
   c. Draw a second triangle adjacent to the first as shown at the right. (One leg is 3 cm; the other is the hypotenuse of the first right triangle.) See margin.
   d. Find the length of the hypotenuse in part c without measuring. *(Previous course)* $3\sqrt{3} \approx 5.196$cm

42. Consider the sequence $2^{1/2}$, $2^{1/3}$, $2^{1/4}$, $2^{1/5}$, ... 1
   a. As the sequence keeps going, what number do the terms approach?
   b. Suppose 2 is replaced by 4 in the sequence. What happens then?
   c. Generalize parts a and b. still approaches 1

In the expression $t^{1/n}$, as *n* gets larger $\dfrac{1}{n}$ gets smaller or closer to 0, and $t^{1/n}$ approaches 1.

38. For $a \geq 0$, $b \geq 0$, and *m* a real number, or for $a \neq 0$, $b \neq 0$, and *m* an integer, $(ab)^m = a^m b^m$.

LESSON 8-5 *n*th Roots **453**

MORE PRACTICE
For more questions on SPUR Objectives, use *Lesson Master 8-5*, shown below.

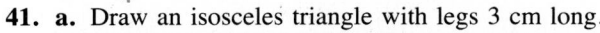
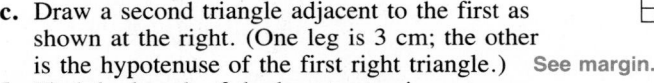
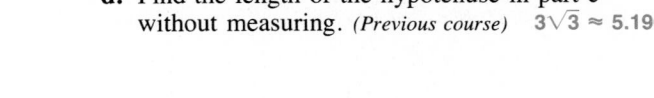

NAME _____

LESSON MASTER 8–5
QUESTIONS ON **SPUR** OBJECTIVES

■ SKILLS *Objective B (See pages 482–485 for objectives.)*
In 1–6, write as a decimal or as a simple fraction. Estimate decimals to the nearest hundredth.

1. $-27^{1/3}$ -3
2. $32^{1/5}$ 2
3. $64^{1/2}$ 8
4. $(.09)^{1/2}$ .3
5. $(16 + 81)^{1/4}$ 3.14
6. $\left(\frac{1000}{27}\right)^{1/3}$ $\frac{10}{3}$

In 7–12, write <, =, or > in the blank to make the statement true.

7. $900^{1/2}$ > $900^{1/3}$
8. -11 = $-1331^{1/3}$
9. $8^{1/3}$ > $\left(\frac{1}{3}\right)^0$
10. 42 > $42^{1/4}$
11. $(7^{1/3})^5$ = 7
12. $27^{1/3} \cdot 64^{1/3}$ = $(27 \cdot 64)^{1/3}$

■ PROPERTIES *Objective I*
13. Identify:
   a. all square roots of 169 13, -13
   b. $\sqrt{169}$ 13
   c. $169^{1/2}$ 13

14. Identify:
   a. all real cube roots of -64 -4
   b. $(-64)^{1/3}$ -4

15. Explain why -136 has no real 6th roots.
No real number raised to the sixth power is negative.

16. Explain why -136 has a real 7th root.
Any real number has a real odd *n*th root.

■ USES *Objective K*
In 17 and 18, Jill invested $3000 compounded daily at a yearly rate of 7%.

17. Use $t = \frac{1}{3}$ in the compound interest formula $A = P(1 + r)^t$ to calculate the amount Jill would have after 4 months. $3068.43

18. Use $t = \frac{3}{2}$ in the compound interest formula.
   a. Calculate the amount. $3320.44
   b. What have you calculated? the amount Jill would have after $1\frac{1}{2}$ years

88 Advanced Algebra © Scott, Foresman and Company

OBJECTIVES

B Evaluate x^b when b is a positive rational number.
D Solve equations of the form $ax^n = b$ or their equivalent forms.
F Simplify expressions with positive rational exponents.
H Recognize properties of positive rational powers.
K Solve real-world problems which can be modeled by equations with rational exponents.

TEACHING NOTES

After discussing **Example 1**, encourage students to use the idea of the solution and first check of **Example 1** on other powers. (See Additional Examples 1 and 2 below.)

Before you discuss the solution of equations containing rational exponents, you may want to have the class try to write the solutions to some simple equations such as $x^3 = 64$ and $y^5 = 32$.

Although all the examples of this lesson have fractions as exponents, tell students that the Rational Exponent Theorem can help to evaluate powers with decimal exponents. Rewrite the exponents in the examples as decimals to make this point.

Example 1 becomes:
  Simplify $25^{1.5}$.
Example 2 becomes:
  Simplify $12358^{.6}$, or $12358^{0.6}$.
Example 3 becomes:
  Solve $x^{1.25} = 243$.
The equation of Example 4 is: $V = .094A^{1.5}$.

Positive Rational Exponents

You know that $16^{1/4}$ is the positive 4th root of 16. What does $16^{3/4}$ signify? The answer depends on both the meaning of the fraction $\frac{3}{4}$ and on the Power of a Power Property.

Rewrite $\frac{3}{4}$ as $\frac{1}{4} \cdot 3$. $\qquad$ $16^{3/4} = 16^{1/4 \cdot 3}$
Use the Power of a Power Property. $\qquad = (16^{1/4})^3$

Thus $16^{3/4}$ is the 3rd power of the positive 4th root of 16. We can calculate this.

$$(16^{1/4})^3 = 2^3 = 8$$

Notice also that $16^{3/4} = 16^{3 \cdot 1/4} = (16^3)^{1/4}$. So $16^{3/4}$ is the 4th root of the 3rd power of 16. In general, with fraction exponents the numerator is the power and the denominator the root. This generalizes to the following theorem.

Rational Exponent Theorem:

For any positive real number x and positive integers m and n,

$x^{m/n} = (x^{1/n})^m$, the mth power of the positive nth root of x, and

$= (x^m)^{1/n}$, the positive nth root of the mth power of x.

Because $x^{1/n}$ is defined only when $x > 0$, *the Rational Exponent Theorem applies only to a positive base x.*

Proof:

The proof generalizes the special case considered above.

	$x^{m/n} = x^{(1/n)m}$	$m/n = \frac{1}{n} \cdot m$
	$= (x^{1/n})^m$	Power of a Power Property
Also,	$x^{m/n} = x^{m \cdot (1/n)}$	$m/n = m \cdot \frac{1}{n}$
	$= (x^m)^{1/n}$	Power of a Power Property

An expression with a rational exponent can be simplified by finding either powers first or roots first. Usually it is easier to find the root first, because you end up working with fewer digits.

■ ■ ■ ■ ■ ■ ■■

Example 1 Simplify $25^{3/2}$.

  Solution Find the square root of 25 first, then cube it.

$$25^{3/2} = (25^{1/2})^3 = 5^3 = 125$$

454

Check 1 Find the power first: $25^{3/2} = (25^3)^{1/2} = 15625^{1/2} = 125$.
As expected, the result is the same in both cases.

Check 2 Use your calculator. Many machines require parentheses for the fraction exponent. Here is a possible key sequence:

$$25 \; \boxed{y^x} \; \boxed{(} \; 3 \; \boxed{\div} \; 2 \; \boxed{)} \; \boxed{=}$$

With practice, you should be able to simplify many expressions with fraction exponents mentally. There is a property of fraction exponents that will help you do this. Notice in Example 1 that the exponent $\frac{3}{2}$ is greater than 1 and subsequently the answer 125 is larger than the base 25. In general:

when $x > 1$ and $\dfrac{m}{n} > 1$, $x^{m/n}$ will be *larger* than the base x, and

when $x > 1$ and $0 < \dfrac{m}{n} < 1$, $x^{m/n}$ will be *smaller* than the base x.

This can be verified with other rational powers of 25.

$$25^0 = 1$$
$$25^{1/4} = 2.236\ldots$$
$$25^{1/2} = 5$$
$$25^{3/4} = 11.180\ldots$$
$$25^1 = 25$$
$$25^{5/4} = 55.901\ldots$$
$$25^{3/2} = 125$$
$$25^{7/4} = 279.508\ldots$$

Example 2 Simplify $12358^{3/5}$.

Solution Use the following key sequence on your calculator. Use $\frac{3}{5} = .6$.

$$12358 \; \boxed{y^x} \; .6 \; \boxed{=}$$

The answer is approximately 285.21.

Check 1 Because $\frac{3}{5} < 1$ the answer should be smaller than the original base; it is. This is a rough check.

Check 2 If $12358^{3/5} \approx 285.21$, then 285.21 to the $\frac{5}{3}$ power should be about 12358. We find

$$285.21^{5/3} \approx 12357.8,$$

so it checks.

Error Analysis Most advanced algebra students will have little difficulty simplifying expressions in the form $x^{m/n}$. Problems may occur when they are asked to solve equations. Some students will attempt to solve the equation $x^{m/n} = b$ by calculating $b^{m/n}$. Stress that the exponent of x must be 1. Since $x^{m/n}$ must be raised to the reciprocal power of n/m, the right-hand member must also be raised to the n/m power. Remind students of the Multiplication Property of Equality.

ADDITIONAL EXAMPLES
1. Simplify $8^{5/3}$.
32

2. Simplify $42861^{5/6}$.
approximately 7245.23

3. Solve $y^{4/3} = 625$.
y = 125

4. Refer to **Example 4** in the textbook.
a. Find the volume of a soap bubble with surface area 20 cm².
approximately 8.4 cm³
b. Find the surface area of a bubble that has a volume of 25 cm³.
approximately 41.4 cm²

Question 19: This question is a good starting point for a discussion on the restriction of base values to positive numbers when using rational exponents.

Questions 23-25: Because of their rational exponents, these questions are not as easily done using algebraic intuition as the same problems with integral exponents. Remind the students of the Properties of Powers listed in Lesson 8-1.

Questions 27 and 28: Show how the formula in **Example 4** generalizes into the proportion in these questions.

If $V = .094A^{3/2}$ then $V_1 = .094A_1^{3/2}$ and $V_2 = .094A_2^{3/2}$

so $\dfrac{V_1}{A_1^{3/2}} = .094$

and $\dfrac{V_2}{A_2^{3/2}} = .094$.

Thus $\dfrac{V_1}{A_1^{3/2}} = \dfrac{V_2}{A_2^{3/2}}$,

so $\dfrac{V_1}{V_2} = \dfrac{A_1^{3/2}}{A_2^{3/2}}$,

and finally,

$\left(\dfrac{V_1}{V_2}\right)^{2/3} = \dfrac{A_1}{A_2}$.

Question 35: This is a multi-purpose conceptual question. It suggests the idea of limits of the value of an expression as n gets larger and larger. It also verifies the continuity of the exponential function, in that the values of the function are quite close to one another.

You can check that the Properties of Powers Postulate given in Lesson 8-1 holds with rational powers. For instance, $25^{1/2} \cdot 25^1 = 25^{3/2}$. The properties of powers can be used to solve equations with positive rational exponents. The strategy in solving equations of this kind is to raise both sides of the equation to a power. This can be done because any number can be substituted for its equal in an algebraic expression. Thus if $x = y$, then x^n and y^n must give the same value, so $x^n = y^n$.

Example 3 Solve $x^{5/4} = 243$.

Solution Recall that any number times its reciprocal equals 1. Thus to solve for x, raise both sides of the equation to the $\frac{4}{5}$ power.

$$(x^{5/4})^{4/5} = 243^{4/5}$$

Apply the Power of a Power Property. $\qquad x^1 = 243^{4/5}$
Simplify and calculate. $\qquad x = 81$

Check Does $81^{5/4} = 243$? Yes. It is reasonable that x should be less than 243 because $\frac{5}{4}$ is more than 1.

Rational exponents have many applications, including growth situations, investments, radioactive decay, and change-of-dimension situations (for example, area to volume and back). The following application involves a dimensional relation.

Example 4 The volume V of a soap bubble is related to its surface area by the formula $V = .094A^{3/2}$. What is the surface area of a bubble with volume 5 cm³?

Solution Here $V = 5$, so $\qquad\qquad\qquad\qquad .094A^{3/2} = 5.$
Divide both sides by .094. $\qquad\qquad\qquad\qquad\qquad A^{3/2} = 53.19$
Raise each side to the $\frac{2}{3}$ power. $\qquad\qquad (A^{3/2})^{2/3} = 53.19^{2/3}$

Finally, simplify and calculate. $\qquad\qquad\qquad\qquad\qquad A \approx 14.14$

A 5 cm³ bubble has a little more than 14 cm² of surface area.

Check This is left for you to do in the questions.

456

In 1 and 2, write as a power of x.

1. the 4th power of the 9th root of x $x^{4/9}$

2. the seventh root of the cube of x $x^{3/7}$

$(100,000^4)^{1/5}$ or $(100,000^{1/5})^4$

3. a. Rewrite $100,000^{4/5}$ in two ways as a power of a power of 100,000.
   b. Which way would be easier to calculate mentally?   **the second**
   c. Calculate $100,000^{4/5}$.   **10,000**

In 4–6, simplify without a calculator.

4. $27^{2/3}$ **9**   **5.** $32^{3/5}$ **8**   **6.** $36^{3/2}$ **216**

In 7–9, evaluate with a calculator.

7. $729^{3/2}$ **19,683**   **8.** $729^{2/3}$ **81**   **9.** $1331^{5/3}$ **161,051**

In 10–12, $x > 1$. Complete with $<$, $>$, or $=$.

10. $x^{7/8}$ __?__ x $<$ **11.** $x^{5/3}$ __?__ $x^{3/5}$ $>$ **12.** $x^{3/4}$ __?__ $x^{3/5}$ $>$

In 13–15, solve and check.

13. $V^{5/2} = 100$ **14.** $k^{2/3} = 64$ **512; $512^{2/3} = 64$**
   ≈ 6.31; $6.31^{5/2} \approx 100.01$
15. $x^{4/9} = 12$ **268.0142; $268.0142^{4/9} = 12$**

In 16 and 17, refer to Example 4.

16. Check the answer found. $.094(14.14)^{3/2} \approx 4.998$

17. A bubble with volume 10 cm^3 does not have twice the surface area as a bubble with volume 5 cm^3. How much surface area does a 10 cm^3 bubble have? ≈ 22.5cm^2

18. a. Calculate $16^{1/4}$, $16^{2/4}$, $16^{3/4}$, $16^{4/4}$, and $16^{5/4}$.   **2, 4, 8, 16, 32**
   b. Simplify $16^{n/4}$, where n is a positive integer. 2^n

19. This exercise shows why rational exponents are used only with positive bases.
   a. If $(-8)^{1/3}$ were to equal the real cube root of -8, then $(-8)^{1/3} = -2$
   __?__.
   b. If $(-8)^{2/6}$ follows the Rational Exponent Theorem, then
   $(-8)^{2/6} = ((-8)^2)^{1/6} = $ __?__.   **2**
   c. In this question, does $(-8)^{1/3} = (-8)^{2/6}$?   **no**

In 20–22, apply the property of exponents $\left(\dfrac{x}{y}\right)^n = \dfrac{x^n}{y^n}$ to calculate.

20. $\left(\dfrac{64}{27}\right)^{2/3}$ $\dfrac{16}{9}$ **21.** $\left(\dfrac{1000}{343}\right)^{4/3}$ $\dfrac{10,000}{2401}$ **22.** $\left(\dfrac{16}{625}\right)^{3/4}$ $\dfrac{8}{125}$

In 23–25, use properties of powers to simplify.

23. $(x^8)^{1/4}$ x^2 **24.** $B^{2/3} \cdot B$ $B^{5/3}$ **25.** $\dfrac{2}{3}y^{2/3} \cdot \dfrac{3}{2}y^{3/2}$ $y^{13/6}$

MORE PRACTICE
For more questions on SPUR
Objectives, use *Lesson Master 8-6*, shown on page 457.

EXTENSION
The coefficient in the formula of **Example 4** is an approximation. The exact value is found by solving the volume and surface area formulas for a sphere for r. The derivation below can be used to extend the lesson.

$V = \frac{4}{3}\pi r^3$, so $r = \left(\frac{3V}{4\pi}\right)^{1/3}$

$A = 4\pi r^2$, so $r = \left(\frac{A}{4\pi}\right)^{1/2}$

Thus, $\left(\frac{3V}{4\pi}\right)^{1/3} = \left(\frac{A}{4\pi}\right)^{1/2}$.

Now take the sixth power of each side. This gives

$\left(\frac{3V}{4\pi}\right)^2 = \left(\frac{A}{4\pi}\right)^2$.

Multiply both sides by $64\pi^3$.

$36\pi V^2 = A^3$

$V^2 = \frac{1}{36\pi}A^3$

Raise each side to the 1/2 power.

$V = \left(\frac{1}{36\pi}\right)^{1/2} A^{3/2}$

To three decimals,

$\left(\frac{1}{36\pi}\right)^{1/2} \approx 0.094$, which is the coefficient we have used.

26. The diameter D of the base of a tree of a given species roughly varies directly with the $\frac{3}{2}$ power of its height h.
    a. Suppose a young sequoia 500 cm tall has a base diameter of 14.5 cm. Find the constant of variation. $k = .001297$
    b. The largest known living tree is a California sequoia called "General Sherman." It has a base diameter of about 985 cm. Approximately how tall is General Sherman? ≈ 8324 cm
    c. One story on a modern office building is about 3 m high. General Sherman is about as tall as a __?__ story office building. 28 m

In 27 and 28, use this information about similar figures: If A_1 and A_2 are the areas of two similar figures and V_1 and V_2 are their volumes, then

$$\frac{A_1}{A_2} = \left(\frac{V_1}{V_2}\right)^{2/3}.$$

27. Two similar figurines have volumes 20 cm^3 and 25 cm^3. What is the ratio of the amounts of paint (surface area) they need? ≈ 0.862

28. Solve the formula for $\frac{V_1}{V_2}$. $\frac{V_1}{V_2} = \left(\frac{A_1}{A_2}\right)^{3/2}$

Review

29. If $a^b = c$ then __?__ is a __?__ root of __?__. *(Lesson 8-5)*   a; bth; c

30. If x^t is the reciprocal of x, what is the value of t? *(Lesson 8-4)*   -1

31. Simplify: $\frac{2^{-100}}{2^{-99}}$. *(Lesson 8-4)* $\frac{1}{2}$

32. State the Power of a Power Property. *(Lesson 8-1)*   See below.

33. Each year, the Bruised Beauties Car Lot marks down a certain model of car to 75% of its value in the preceding year. If the car is worth $7000 at the end of the first year, what will be its value at the end of the fifth year? *(Lesson 8-3)* $2214.84

34. Find the lateral area and surface area of the right circular cylinder shown at the right. *(Previous course)*

    L.A. = $1000\pi \approx 3142$ cm^2;
    S.A. = $1312.5\pi \approx 4123$ cm^2

    5.000, 8.550, 11.180,
    13.133, 14.620

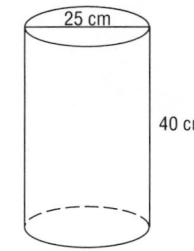
25 cm
40 cm

Exploration

35. a. Consider the numbers $25^{1/2}$, $25^{2/3}$, $25^{3/4}$, $25^{4/5}$, and $25^{5/6}$. Approximate these with decimals rounded to the nearest thousandth.
    b. Let $f(n) = 25^{n/(n+1)}$. Calculate $f(100)$ and $f(1000)$.   24.216, 24.920
    c. What is the approximate value of $25^{n/(n+1)}$ when n is a very large number, say 1 billion?   very close to 25

32. For $a \geq 0$ and m and n real numbers, or for $a \neq 0$ and m and n integers, $(a^m)^n = a^{mn}$.

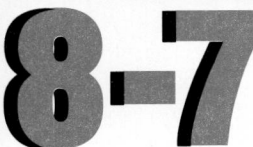
You have now learned meanings for many rational exponents. For any positive number x and any positive integer values of m and n (except $n = 0$):

$x^0 = 1$ (Zero Exponent Theorem, Lesson 8-1)

$x^{-n} = \dfrac{1}{x^n}$ (Negative Exponent Theorem, Lesson 8-4)

$x^{1/n} = $ positive nth root of x ($\frac{1}{n}$ Exponent Theorem, Lesson 8-5)

$x^{m/n} = (x^{1/n})^m = (x^m)^{1/n}$ (Rational Exponent Theorem, Lesson 8-6).

Now we apply these properties to evaluate expressions in which the exponent is a negative rational number. Since $x^{-m/n} = \left(\left(x^{-1}\right)^m\right)^{1/n} = \left(\left(x^m\right)^{1/n}\right)^{-1}$, and these exponents can be in any order, you have the choice of first taking the reciprocal, the mth power, or the nth root.

Example 1   Evaluate $81^{-1/4}$

Solution   Here we take the reciprocal and then the 4th root.

$$81^{-1/4} = \frac{1}{81^{1/4}} = \frac{1}{3}$$

Check   You can evaluate $81^{-1/4}$ on a calculator. One possible key sequence is

81 $\boxed{y^x}$ $\boxed{(}$ 1 $\boxed{\pm}$ $\boxed{\div}$ 4 $\boxed{)}$ $\boxed{=}$.

Your calculator should display 0.333333, or $\frac{1}{3}$, which checks.

Example 2   Simplify $\left(\dfrac{27}{1000}\right)^{-2/3}$.

Solution 1   Think $\left(\left(\left(\dfrac{27}{1000}\right)^{-1}\right)^{1/3}\right)^2$. This applies the reciprocal, cube root, and square in that order. Remember to work with the innermost parentheses first.

$$\left(\left(\left(\dfrac{27}{1000}\right)^{-1}\right)^{1/3}\right)^2 = \left(\left(\dfrac{1000}{27}\right)^{1/3}\right)^2 = \left(\dfrac{10}{3}\right)^2 = \dfrac{100}{9}$$

Solution 2   Think $\left(\left(\left(\dfrac{27}{1000}\right)^{1/3}\right)^2\right)^{-1}$. This does the cube root, square, and reciprocal in that order.

$$\left(\left(\left(\dfrac{27}{1000}\right)^{1/3}\right)^2\right)^{-1} = \left(\left(\dfrac{3}{10}\right)^2\right)^{-1} = \left(\dfrac{9}{100}\right)^{-1} = \dfrac{100}{9}$$

LESSON 8-7

RESOURCES
■ Lesson Master 8-7

OBJECTIVES

B Evaluate x^b when b is a negative rational number.
F Solve equations or simplify expressions using properties of negative rational exponents.
H Recognize properties of negative rational exponents.
K Solve real-world problems which can be modeled by equations with negative rational exponents.

TEACHING NOTES

You can introduce this lesson by making a table of powers of 8 with the exponent decreasing by $\frac{1}{3}$ each time.

$8^2 = 64$
$8^{5/3} = (\sqrt[3]{8})^5 = 32$
$8^{4/3} = (\sqrt[3]{8})^4 = 16$
$\vdots$
$8^0 = 1$
$8^{-1/3} = \dfrac{1}{8^{1/3}} = \dfrac{1}{2}$
$\vdots$
$8^{-5/3} = \dfrac{1}{8^{5/3}} = \dfrac{1}{32}$
$8^{-2} = \dfrac{1}{8^2} = \dfrac{1}{64}$

Have students observe that finding the ratio of any two terms in the left-hand column in the list above (for instance, $\dfrac{8^2}{8^{-1/3}} = 8^{2-(-1/3)} = 8^{7/3}$) provides practice in applying the Quotient of Powers Property.

Calculating the ratio of corresponding terms in the right-hand column (for instance, $\dfrac{64}{\frac{1}{2}} = 128$) provides practice in dividing fractions

459

Check Change everything to decimals. $\frac{27}{1000} = .027$ and $-\frac{2}{3} = -.\overline{6}$. Key in .027 $\boxed{y^x}$ .66666667 $\boxed{\pm}$ $\boxed{=}$ on a calculator. We get 11.11111124, which is very close to $11.\overline{1}$ or $\frac{100}{9}$.

The ideas used in Lesson 8-6 to solve equations with positive rational exponents can be employed with negative rational exponents as well.

Example 3 Solve $x^{-2/5} = 9$.

Solution The reciprocal of $-\frac{2}{5}$ is $-\frac{5}{2}$, so take each side to the $-\frac{5}{2}$ power.

$$\left(x^{-2/5}\right)^{-5/2} = 9^{-5/2}$$

$$x = 9^{-5/2} = \left(\left(9^{1/2}\right)^5\right)^{-1} = \left(3^5\right)^{-1} = 243^{-1} = \frac{1}{243}$$

Check Does $\left(\frac{1}{243}\right)^{-2/5} = 9$? $\left(\left(\left(\frac{1}{243}\right)^{-1}\right)^{1/5}\right)^2 = \left(243^{1/5}\right)^2 = 3^2 = 9$. Yes.

You should not need a calculator to evaluate many expressions involving simple fractional exponents, such as $\frac{1}{4}$ or $-\frac{2}{3}$, when the answer is a simple fraction. However, when the powers you must evaluate are not simple fractions, you will usually need a calculator.

Example 4 The number of hours h that milk stays fresh is a function of the surrounding temperature t. Use the formula

$$h(t) = 180 \cdot 10^{-.04t}$$

to predict how long newly pasteurized milk will stay fresh when stored at temperature 8° C.

Solution Substitute $t = 8$ in the formula.

$$h(8) = 180 \cdot 10^{-.04(8)}$$
$$h(8) = 180 \cdot 10^{-.32}$$

Use a calculator. $h(8) \approx 86$

When left at 8°C, newly pasteurized milk will stay fresh about 86 hours, or a little more than $3\frac{1}{2}$ days.

Covering the Reading

In 1–3, evaluate without using a calculator.

1. $125^{-1/3}$ $\frac{1}{5}$ **2.** $81^{-3/4}$ $\frac{1}{27}$ **3.** $(\frac{9}{4})^{-5/2}$ $\frac{32}{243}$

In 4–6, estimate to the nearest thousandth with a calculator.

4. $10^{-1/2}$ .316   **5.** $10^{-.004}$ 0.991   **6.** $50 \cdot 2.79^{-3/5}$ 27.015

In 7–9, solve.

7. $s^{-1/4} = 3$ $\frac{1}{81}$ **8.** $t^{-2/3} = 36.$ $\frac{1}{216}$ **9.** $x^{-3/2} = \frac{1}{8}$ 4

10. Refer to Example 4.
   a. How long will newly pasteurized milk stay fresh if it is left out at 24°C?   ≈**20 hours**
   b. When milk is stored at 8°C it stays fresh about __?__ times as long as it will at 24°C.   4

11. Tell whether or not the expression equals $b^{-3/4}$ for $b > 0$.

   a. $\frac{1}{b^{3/4}}$ yes   **b.** $\frac{1}{(b^3)^{1/4}}$ yes   **c.** $\left((b^{-1})^3\right)^{1/4}$ yes
   d. $-b^{3/4}$ no   **e.** $(b^{1/4})^{-3}$ yes   **f.** $\left(b^{-1/4}\right)^3$ yes

Applying the Mathematics

In 12–14, tell whether the number is positive, negative, or zero. Do *not* use a calculator.

12. $(.98956)^{-3/4}$ positive   **13.** $(1.0825)^0$ positive   **14.** $(-.07)(3)^{-.4}$ negative

15. Find n if $\left(\frac{99}{100}\right)^{-3/4} = \left(\frac{100}{99}\right)^{n}$. $\frac{3}{4}$

In 16 and 17, simplify each expression into the form ax^n. Check your answer by substituting values.

16. $\frac{x}{3x^{-2/3}} \cdot 6x^{1/2}$ $2x^{13/6}$ **17.** $\frac{-\frac{3}{4}x^{-3/4}}{\frac{1}{4}x^{1/4}}$ $-3x^{-1}$

18. **a.** Evaluate 64^x, where x increases by sixths from -1 to 1. (There are 13 values to evaluate: 64^{-1}, $64^{-5/6}$, $64^{-4/6} = 64^{-2/3}$, and so on until 64^1.)   **See margin.**
   b. Explain the pattern of answers to part a.   **See margin.**

19. Let F be the amount of food a mammal with body mass m must eat daily to maintain its mass. In the chapter opener you read that $\frac{F}{m} = km^{-1/3}$. Is F directly proportional to m? Justify your answer.   **No, F is directly proportional to $m^{2/3}$.**

Review

20. The product of x^2 and x^3 is x^5. Find six more pairs of integer powers of x whose product is x^5. *(Lessons 8-1, 8-4)*
   $(x^1)(x^4); (x^6)(x^{-1}); (x^7)(x^{-2}); (x^{12})(x^{-7}); (x^8)(x^{-3}); (x^{10})(x^{-5});$

Question 20: There are infinitely many possible responses to this question. All but $x^1 \cdot x^4$ and $x^0 \cdot x^5$ require one positive and one negative exponent.

ADDITIONAL ANSWERS
18.a.

64^{-1} =	.015625 =	$\frac{1}{64}$
$64^{-5/6}$ =	.03125 =	$\frac{1}{32}$
$64^{-4/6}$ =	.0625 =	$\frac{1}{16}$
$64^{-3/6}$ =	.125 =	$\frac{1}{8}$
$64^{-2/6}$ =	.25 =	$\frac{1}{4}$
$64^{-1/6}$ =	.50 =	$\frac{1}{2}$
64^0 =	1	
$64^{1/6}$ =	2	
$64^{2/6}$ =	4	
$64^{3/6}$ =	8	
$64^{4/6}$ =	16	
$64^{5/6}$ =	32	
64^1 =	64	

b. Every power of 64 can be rewritten as a power of 2, because $64 = 2^6$. Specifically, $64^x = (2^6)^x = 2^{6x}$. As x increases by $\frac{1}{6}$, the power of 2 increases by $6\left(\frac{1}{6}\right) = 1$.

461

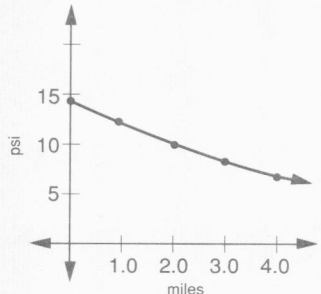
21. The Galapagos Islands are a chain of islands in the Pacific Ocean that belong to Ecuador. They are famous for their variety of plant and animal life. A biologist has shown that S, the number of different plant species on an island, varies with the area A of the island according to the formula:

$$S = 28.6A^{0.32}$$

Estimate S (round to the nearest whole number) for:
   a. the smallest island in the Galapagos chain, which has an area of about 2 square miles; and   36
   b. the largest island, Albemarle, which has an area of about 2250 square miles. *(Lesson 8-6)*   338

22. Solve $\left(\dfrac{16}{625}\right)^{n} = \dfrac{2}{5}$. *(Lesson 8-6)* $n = \frac{1}{4}$

23. Solve this system $\begin{cases} 3x^{-1} + 2y^{-1} = 27 \\ 2x^{-1} - y^{-1} = 4 \end{cases}$.
   (Hint: Let $a = x^{-1}$ and $b = y^{-1}$.) *(Lesson 5-3, 8-4)* $x = \frac{1}{5}; y = \frac{1}{6}$

Exploration

24. Use the formula $P = 14.7 \cdot 10^{-.09h}$, in which P is the atmospheric pressure in pounds per square inch at altitude h in miles above sea level. Find the atmospheric pressure:
   a. in Albuquerque, NM, where $h \approx .9$;   12.20psi
   b. in Miami, FL, which is approximately at sea level;   14.7psi
   c. on top of Mt. McKinley, AK, which is about 20,320 feet above sea level.   6.62psi
   d. Graph this relation, using the three points determined in parts a–c and two points of your choice.   See margin.
   e. As h increases, does P increase or decrease?   decrease

Mt. McKinley, Alaska

462

LESSON 8-8

Radical Notation for *n*th Roots

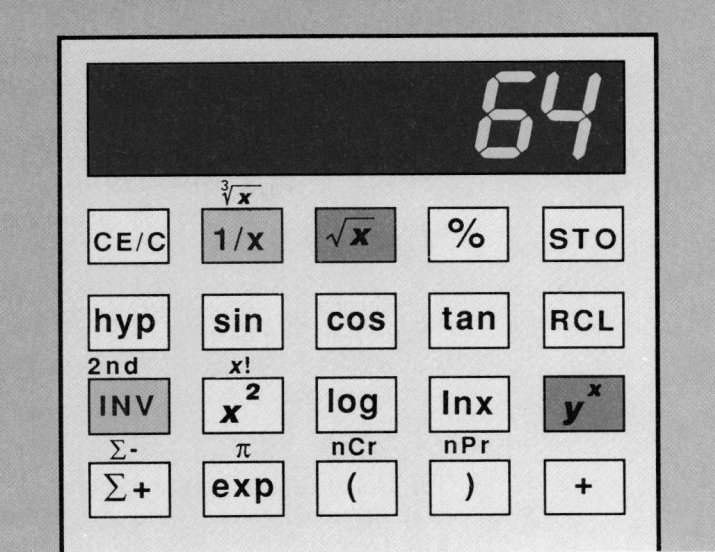

The symbol $\sqrt{}$ is called the **radical sign**, or just a **radical**. Its origin is the Latin word radix, which means root. When x is positive, $\sqrt{x}$ stands for the positive square root of x. Since $x^{1/2}$ also stands for this square root, $\sqrt{x} = x^{1/2}$. There is a natural generalization from square roots to nth roots of positive numbers.

Definition:

When x is positive and n is an integer ≥ 2, $\sqrt[n]{x} = x^{1/n}$.

Example 1 Evaluate $\sqrt[4]{81}$.

Solution $\sqrt[4]{81} = 81^{1/4}$, the *positive* number whose 4th power is 81. You probably know that $3^4 = 81$. If so, you have found $\sqrt[4]{81} = 3$ without a calculator.

The symbol $\sqrt[n]{}$ was first used by Albert Girard around 1633. Note that $\sqrt[n]{x}$, like $x^{1/n}$, does not represent all nth roots of x. When x is positive and n is even, x has two real nth roots, but only the *positive* real root is denoted by $\sqrt[n]{x}$. Thus 2, -2, 2*i*, and -2*i* are fourth roots of 16, but $\sqrt[4]{16} = 2$ only. The negative fourth root can be denoted by $-\sqrt[4]{16}$, or -2.

Scientific calculators sometimes have a key for nth roots, $\boxed{\sqrt[x]{y}}$ or $\boxed{\sqrt[x]{x}}$ or $\boxed{\sqrt[x]{}}$. You may also be able to find the nth root of a number by using the $\boxed{\text{INV}}$ or $\boxed{\text{2ndF}}$ key before the powering key $\boxed{y^x}$.

RESOURCES
- Lesson Master 8-8
- Quiz for Lessons 8-5 through 8-8
- Visual for Teaching Aid 47 provides the diagram for **Question 35**.

OBJECTIVES

C Simplify radicals.
H Recognize properties of nth powers and nth roots of positive numbers written in radical form.
I Apply the definitions of $x^{1/n}$ and $\sqrt[n]{x}$ as they apply to nth roots of x.

TEACHING NOTES

Stress the definition of radical notation for nth roots, $\sqrt[n]{x} = x^{1/n}$. Note that the definition in this lesson is for positive bases only. In Lesson 8-9, the nth root of a negative number is defined.

Make sure each student knows how to find nth roots on his or her calculator. Use **Examples 1 and 2** or the Additional Examples that follow as tests.

Encourage students to use the method of **Example 4** when rewriting roots. Students should move toward doing the second and third steps mentally, while continuing to work for accuracy.

You may wish to use a good portion of class time for guided practice during this lesson.

1. Evaluate.

a. $\sqrt[3]{27}$

3

b. $\sqrt[6]{64}$

2

c. $\sqrt[4]{2401}$

7

2. Estimate to the nearest hundredth.

a. $\sqrt{15}$

3.87

b. $\sqrt[5]{4829}$

5.45

3. Rewrite. Assume all variables are positive.

a. $\sqrt[4]{x^8}$

x^2

b. $\sqrt[3]{y^{18}}$

y^6

c. $\sqrt{4x^4y^5}$

$2x^2y^2\sqrt{y}$

d. $\sqrt[5]{32x^{10}y^2}$

$2x^2\sqrt[5]{y^2}$

■ ■ ■ ■ ■ ■ ■ ■

Example 2   Estimate $\sqrt[3]{2}$, the length of the altar the Delians (Lesson 8-5) were asked to make.

Solution 1   Use the following key sequence:

$$2 \;\boxed{\sqrt[x]{y}}\; 3 \;\boxed{=}$$

Our calculator displays 1.2599211, which is about 1.26. The Delians had to make an altar with an edge about 1.26 times as long as the edge of the original altar.

Solution 2   Key in $2 \boxed{\text{INV}} \boxed{y^x} 3 \boxed{=}$. You should get 1.259911, the same answer as in Solution 1.

Check   Key in $1.2599211 \boxed{y^x} 3 \boxed{=}$ to see whether $(1.2599211)^3 \approx 2$. It is.

The Delians did not have calculators, of course. They also did not have decimals, which were invented only in 1585. They could work with fractions, but no simple fraction cubed equals 2; that is, $\sqrt[3]{2}$ is irrational. The Delians did not have the mathematical tools to follow the oracle's advice.

Since $\sqrt[n]{x} = x^{1/n}$, the nth powers of these numbers are equal; that is, $(\sqrt[n]{x})^m = (x^{1/n})^m$, $x^{m/n}$. Also, if x is replaced by x^m in the definition, the result is $\sqrt[n]{x^m} = (x^m)^{1/n}$, which also equals $x^{m/n}$. Thus there are two radical expressions equal to $x^{m/n}$.

Root of a Power Theorem:

When $x > 0$, m and n are integers and $n \geq 2$, $\sqrt[n]{x^m} = (\sqrt[n]{x})^m = x^{mn}$.

■ ■ ■ ■ ■ ■ ■ ■

Example 3   Simplify $\sqrt[3]{x^{12}}$.

Solution 1   Use the definition of $\sqrt[3]{}$: $\sqrt[3]{x^{12}} = (x^{12})^{1/3} = x^4$.

Solution 2   Use the Root of a Power Theorem: $\sqrt[3]{x^{12}} = x^{12/3} = x^4$.

When products or quotients are under the radical sign, the Power of a Product Property can help to simplify them. You are familiar with this property. If $x \geq 0$ and $y \geq 0$, then for any value of m,

$$(xy)^m = x^m \cdot y^m.$$

If m is replaced by $\frac{1}{2}$, the result looks like a new property.

$$(xy)^{1/2} = x^{1/2} \cdot y^{1/2}$$

464

However, rewriting the $\frac{1}{2}$ powers as square roots, the property becomes familiar.

$$\sqrt{xy} = \sqrt{x} \cdot \sqrt{y}$$

You used this property to simplify radicals in Chapter 6.

If $m = \dfrac{1}{n}$ in the Power of a Product Property, then

$$(xy)^{1/n} = x^{1/n} \cdot y^{1/n}.$$

Rewriting these nth roots with radical signs results in the following theorem.

Root of a Product Theorem:

For any positive real numbers x and y, and any integer $n > 1$,

$$\sqrt[n]{xy} = \sqrt[n]{x} \cdot \sqrt[n]{y}.$$

The Root of a Product Theorem allows you to rewrite nth roots. The idea is to find perfect nth powers under the radical sign. For instance,

$$\sqrt[3]{80} = \sqrt[3]{8}\sqrt[3]{10} = 2\sqrt[3]{10}.$$

Example 4 Suppose $x > 0$. Rewrite $\sqrt[3]{875x^7}$.

Solution Factor the expression inside the root into as many perfect cubes as possible.

$$\sqrt[3]{875x^7} = \sqrt[3]{125 \cdot 7 \cdot x^6 \cdot x}$$

Use the Root of a Product Theorem.

$$= \sqrt[3]{125} \cdot \sqrt[3]{7} \cdot \sqrt[3]{x^6} \cdot \sqrt[3]{x}$$

Apply the definition of the nth root and the Root of a Power Theorem.

$$= 5 \cdot \sqrt[3]{7} \cdot x^2 \cdot \sqrt[3]{x}$$

Use the Root of a Product Theorem to multiply $\sqrt[3]{7}$ and $\sqrt[3]{x}$. Thus,

$$\sqrt[3]{875x^7} = 5x^2\sqrt[3]{7x}.$$

These questions are interesting for discussing equivalent forms of expressions. In **Question 22**, the students will probably have no difficulty seeing that $\sqrt{5} = 5^{0.5}$, but may need some help in realizing that $\sqrt[4]{25} = 25^{1/4} = (5^2)^{1/4} = 5^{1/2} = \sqrt{5}$.

Error Analysis for Question 23: Students will often *incorrectly* <u>assume</u> that $\sqrt[n]{a} + \sqrt[n]{b} = \sqrt[n]{a+b}$. They are generalizing the Root of a Product Theorem inappropriately. Stress that the two terms in $\sqrt[3]{2} + \sqrt[3]{3}$ cannot be combined algebraically and that the Root of a Product Theorem can only be used on a product of radicals, not on the sum or difference of radicals.

Question 24: Remind students that cubing both sides of the equation in this question is a good way (but not the only way) to start their solution.

Check 1 The inverse of taking the cube root is cubing. To check, cube the answer.

$$(5x^2\sqrt[3]{7x})^3 = 5^3(x^2)^3(\sqrt[3]{7x})^3$$
$$= 125x^6 \cdot 7x$$
$$= 875x^7$$

This checks with the original expression under the cube root symbol.

Check 2 Substitute some number for x and use a calculator. We let $x = 2$.

$$\text{Does } \sqrt[3]{875 \cdot 2^7} = 5 \cdot 2^2\sqrt[3]{7 \cdot 2}?$$
$$\text{Does } \sqrt[3]{112000} = 20\sqrt[3]{14}?$$

Yes, both equal approximately 48.20.

Questions

Covering the Reading

1. The radical expression $\sqrt[n]{x}$ equals what power of x? $\frac{1}{n}$th

In 2–4, evaluate without a calculator.

2. $\sqrt[4]{16}$ 2   3. $\sqrt[3]{216}$ 6   4. $\sqrt[5]{10^5}$ 10

5. State the Root of a Power Theorem.   When $x > 0$, $\sqrt[n]{x^m} = (\sqrt[n]{x})^m = x^{m/n}$.

In 6–8, simplify. Assume all variables are positive.

6. $\sqrt[3]{x^{15}}$ x^5 7. $\sqrt[4]{x^6}$ $x^{3/2}$ 8. $(\sqrt[7]{t})^{14}$ t^2

9. Who first used the "$\sqrt[n]{}$" symbol, and in what century?
   Albert Girard, 17th century

10. **a.** Write a calculator key sequence to evaluate $\sqrt[4]{38.720}$.   **See below.**
    b. Estimate $\sqrt[4]{38.720}$ to the nearest tenth.   2.5

In 11–13, use a calculator to approximate to the nearest hundredth.

11. $\sqrt[3]{10}$ 2.15   12. $\sqrt[4]{4}$ 1.41   13. $\sqrt[5]{314892}$ 12.58

14. State the Root of a Product Theorem.
    For any positive real numbers x and y and any integer $n > 1$,
    $$\sqrt[n]{xy} = \sqrt[n]{x} \cdot \sqrt[n]{y}$$

In 15–17, simplify. Assume $x > 0$.

15. $\sqrt{10} \cdot \sqrt{40}$ 20   16. $\sqrt[3]{900} \cdot \sqrt[3]{30}$ 30   17. $\sqrt[4]{x} \cdot \sqrt[4]{x^7}$ x^2

In 18–20, rewrite with a smaller number or exponent under the radical sign. Assume all variables are positive.

18. $\sqrt{121x^5}$ $11x^2\sqrt{x}$ 19. $\sqrt[3]{54}$ $3\sqrt[3]{2}$ 20. $\sqrt[3]{125p^9q^{12}}$ $5p^3q^4$

10a)   38.720 $\boxed{\sqrt[x]{y}}$ 4 $\boxed{=}$ or   38.720 $\boxed{\text{INV}}$ $\boxed{y^x}$ 4 $\boxed{=}$

466

Multiple choice. In 21 and 22, which of (a) to (c) is not equal to the others?

21. (a) $3^{1/2}$ (b) $\sqrt[6]{3}$ (c) $(\sqrt[6]{3})^3$ (d) All are equal.   **b**

22. (a) $\sqrt[4]{25}$ (b) $\sqrt{5}$ (c) $5^{0.5}$ (d) All are equal.   **d**

23. Which is greater, $\sqrt[3]{2} + \sqrt[3]{3}$ or $\sqrt[3]{5}$? $\sqrt[3]{2} + \sqrt[3]{3} > \sqrt[3]{5}$

24. Solve for x: $\sqrt[3]{432} = x\sqrt[3]{2}$. $x = 6$

13.5, 20.25, 30.375

25. a. Write the next three terms in this geometric sequence: 4, 6, 9, ...
    b. Write an explicit formula for the nth term. *(Lesson 8-2)*
    $t_n = 4 \cdot \left(\frac{3}{2}\right)^{n-1}$

26. Suppose that a copy machine can reduce to 74% of its original size in linear dimensions. If you made copies of copies, what would be the new dimensions of an $8\frac{1}{2} \times 11$ in. original which was copied
    a. two times?   **b.** four times?   **c.** n times? *(Lesson 8-3)*
    ≈4.65 × 6.02 in.   ≈2.55 × 3.30 in. $(8.5)(.74)^n \times (11)(.74)^n$ in.

In 27–29, write without exponents. *(Previous course, Lesson 8-7)*

27. 10^{-6} **28.** $4^{-5/2}$ $\frac{1}{32}$ **29.** $\left(\frac{1}{7}\right)^{-3}$ 343
    0.000001 or $\frac{1}{1000000}$

30. Simplify **a.** $\dfrac{\frac{7}{5}}{35}$ $\frac{1}{25}$ **b.** $\dfrac{\frac{x}{y}}{xy}$ $\frac{1}{y^2}$ *(Lesson 1-5)*

31. If $f(x) = \left(\dfrac{x+1}{x-2}\right) \Big/ \left(\dfrac{x+3}{x-4}\right)$, what values of x are not in the domain of f?
    (Lessons 1-5, 7-2)   2, -3, 4

In 32 and 33, solve. *(Lessons 8-6, 8-7)*

32. $m^{-3/2} = 27$ $m = \frac{1}{9}$ **33.** $157 = x^{-5/3}$ $x = \dfrac{1}{\sqrt[5]{157^3}} \approx \dfrac{1}{20.77} \approx .048$

34. If a savings bond is to grow to $10,000 after earning 6.5% interest compounded annually for 10 years, how much money should the bond cost originally? *(Lesson 8-4)* $x \approx 5,327.26$

33. Right triangles are built on each other as pictured at the right.
    a. Find h_1, h_2, h_3, and h_4.
    b. Make a conjecture about h_5 and h_6.
    c. What would happen if the outside legs were all of length 5?
    d. Suppose the outside legs are all of length x. Find a formula for h_n, the length of the nth hypotenuse.

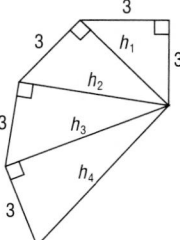

33a) $h_1 = 3\sqrt{2}$, $h_2 = 3\sqrt{3}$
    $h_3 = 3\sqrt{4}$, $h_4 = 3\sqrt{5}$
    b) $h_5 = 3\sqrt{6}$, $h_6 = 3\sqrt{7}$

c) The hypotenuse would be $5\sqrt{2}$, $5\sqrt{3}$, and so on.
    d) $h_n = x\sqrt{n+1}$

FOLLOW-UP

MORE PRACTICE
For more questions on SPUR Objectives, use *Lesson Master 8-8*, shown below.

EXTENSION
To extend **Question 35**, you might ask students: "What is the largest number n of triangles that can be drawn in this pattern without the nth triangle overlapping the first?" At this point, a student could answer the question by drawing.

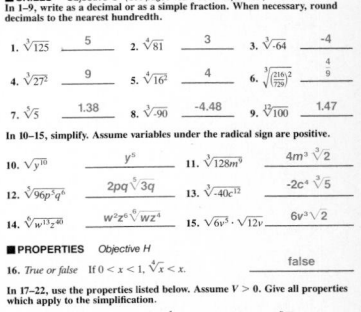

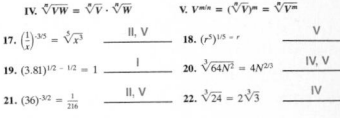

467

LESSON 8-9

RESOURCES
■ Lesson Master 8-9

OBJECTIVES

A Evaluate x^n when x is negative and n is an integer.

C Simplify radicals with negative bases.

H Recognize properties of powers and roots of negative numbers.

I Apply the definition of $\sqrt[n]{x}$ when x is negative.

TEACHING NOTES

Students are already familiar with square roots of negatives, so they should realize that there are some differences in the properties held by nth roots of positive and negative numbers. However, they may not be ready for the special interpretation of the notation $\sqrt[n]{x}$ when x is negative, a notation that only has meaning when n is an odd number.

Throughout the discussion, you must be careful to distinguish between an nth root of a number x (there may be n of these) and $\sqrt[n]{x}$. If x has a real nth root, then the *largest* of these can be denoted by $\sqrt[n]{x}$. However, x does not have a real nth root when x is negative and n is even. Then the radical notation is only used for square roots, which stand for imaginary numbers.

Students are sometimes confused by the use of the absolute value sign in the nth Root of nth Power Theorem. Some of this confusion can be avoided by thoroughly discussing the examples

Powers and Roots of Negative Numbers

Integer powers: You have for many years calculated positive integer powers of negative numbers using repeated multiplication. Here are the first few positive integer powers of -8.

$$(-8)^1 = -8$$
$$(-8)^2 = (-8)(-8) = 64$$
$$(-8)^3 = (-8)(-8)(-8) = -512$$
$$(-8)^4 = (-8)(-8)(-8)(-8) = 4096$$

Notice that these integer powers alternate between positive and negative. The same is true if zero and negative powers of -8 are considered. As you might expect, $(-8)^{-n}$ is the reciprocal of $(-8)^n$.

$$(-8)^0 = 1$$
$$(-8)^{-1} = -\frac{1}{8}$$
$$(-8)^{-2} = \frac{1}{64}$$
$$(-8)^{-3} = -\frac{1}{512}$$
$$(-8)^{-4} = \frac{1}{4096}$$

Again even powers are positive, odd powers are negative. All the power properties still work with integer powers. However, be aware of the order of operations. Whereas $(-8)^4 = 4096$, $-8^4 = -4096$ because the power is calculated before taking the opposite.

nth roots: Even the simplest roots of negative numbers cause problems. Recall what happens when square roots of negative numbers are multiplied. For example, the property $\sqrt{x} \cdot \sqrt{y} = \sqrt{xy}$ does not hold.

$$\sqrt{-2} \cdot \sqrt{-3} = i\sqrt{2} \cdot i\sqrt{3} = i^2 \cdot \sqrt{6} = -\sqrt{6}$$

In general, 4th roots, 6th roots, and other even roots present so much trouble that neither the symbol $\sqrt[n]{x}$ nor the symbol $x^{1/n}$ is defined when n is even and x is negative.

If a number is negative, then it has exactly one real odd root. For instance, -8 has one real cube root, namely -2. It is customary to write

$$\sqrt[3]{-8} = -2$$

just as you would for a positive base. Similarly,

$$\sqrt[3]{-27} = -3.$$

Now multiply these numbers by each other. The product is 6, which is the cube root of 216, so it is true that $\sqrt[3]{-8} \cdot \sqrt[3]{-27} = \sqrt[3]{216} = 6$. Fifth roots, seventh roots, and all other odd roots have the same property. Thus it is possible to use radical signs to represent these roots and have the Product of Roots property hold.

468

Definition:

When x is negative and n is an odd integer ≥ 3, $\sqrt[n]{x}$ stands for the real nth root of x.

For example, $\sqrt[5]{-32}$ = the real 5th root of -32, which is -2. However, -17 has no real 4th roots, so the symbol $\sqrt[4]{-17}$ is not defined.

Rational powers: The properties of rational exponents do not work even for cube roots of negative numbers. Again consider -2, the cube root of -8. If we would write $(-8)^{1/3} = -2$

then it would seem necessary that $(-8)^{2/6} = -2$.

But $(-8)^{2/6}$ would have to equal $((-8)^2)^{1/6} = (64)^{1/6} = 2$. Since we could not substitute even $\frac{2}{6}$ for $\frac{1}{3}$ when they are exponents with negative numbers, and keep the properties of powers, we do not define rational powers of negative numbers.

To summarize: When x is negative,

x^n is defined if and only if n is an integer.
$\sqrt[n]{x}$ is defined if and only if n is 2 (resulting in an imaginary number) or n is an odd integer greater than 2 (resulting in a negative number).

When n is even, x^n is positive, so $\sqrt[n]{x^n}$ is defined for all integers greater than 2. In Lesson 6-1 you learned that for all real numbers x, $\sqrt{x^2} = |x|$. Can $\sqrt[n]{x^n}$ be simplified in a similar way? Consider some specific cases:

$$\sqrt[3]{10^3} = \sqrt[3]{1000} = 10 \qquad \sqrt[4]{10^4} = \sqrt[4]{10000} = 10$$
$$\sqrt[3]{(-10)^3} = \sqrt[3]{-1000} = -10 \qquad \sqrt[4]{(-10)^4} = \sqrt[4]{10000} = 10$$
$$\sqrt[5]{2^5} = \sqrt[5]{32} = 2 \qquad \sqrt[6]{3^6} = \sqrt[6]{729} = 3$$
$$\sqrt[5]{(-2)^5} = \sqrt[5]{-32} = -2 \qquad \sqrt[6]{(-3)^6} = \sqrt[6]{729} = 3$$

The sentences above are instances of a general pattern for simplifying $\sqrt[n]{x^n}$.

nth Root of nth Power Theorem:

For all real numbers x, and integers $n \geq 2$:

if n is odd, $\quad \sqrt[n]{x^n} = x$;
if n is even $\quad \sqrt[n]{x^n} = |x|$.

(Note that the statement $\sqrt{x^2} = |x|$ is a special case of the Root of a Power Theorem when $n = 2$.)

preceding it. Stress that when taking an even root of an even power, absolute value is used unless the base is known to be positive. This theorem is applied extensively in the next two lessons.

Some calculators will not calculate powers with negative bases. To test for this capability, have students try to calculate $(-2.1)^5$. If an error message appears, that particular calculator will not allow the input of a negative base. These students will have to key in the base as a positive number, use the calculator for the absolute value of the power, and then calculate the sign mentally.

Alternate Approach In either the development portion of this lesson or as a summary, it might be helpful to make a chart such as the following which shows uses of these equivalent forms.

power form	words
$2^8 = 256$	2 is an 8th root of 256.
$(-2)^8 = 256$	-2 is an 8th root of 256.
$(-6)^3 = -216$	-6 is a cube root of -216.

root forms		
radical form	fractional exponent form
$2 = \sqrt[8]{256}$	$2 = (256)^{1/8}$
But $-2 \neq \sqrt[8]{256}$	$-2 \neq (256)^{1/8}$
$-6 = \sqrt[3]{-216}$	not defined

Emphasize that $-2 \neq \sqrt[8]{256}$ because we wish every symbol to stand for only one number. For the same reason, $(256)^{1/8} \neq -2$. Also, $(-216)^{1/3} \neq -6$ because the symbol $x^{1/n}$ is defined only for positive values of x.

1. Simplify.

a. $\sqrt[5]{(-2)^5}$

-2

b. $\sqrt[6]{a^6}$

$|a|$

c. $\sqrt[8]{(-2)^8}$

2

d. $\sqrt[8]{x^8}$

$|x|$

2. Rewrite.

a. $\sqrt[7]{z^8}$

$z\sqrt[7]{z}$

b. $\sqrt[6]{64x^9y^{18}}$

$2|xy^3|\sqrt[6]{x^3}$

c. $\sqrt{16a^2b^2}$

$4|ab|$

d. $\sqrt{72x^4z^7}$

$6x^2|z^3|\sqrt{2z}$

e. $\sqrt[3]{8x^4y^{11}}$

$2xy^3\sqrt[3]{xy^2}$

NOTES ON QUESTIONS

Questions 10–12: These questions are designed to show the difference in meaning of odd and even nth roots of negative numbers.

Question 20: A rewritten form of the root in this question may be illuminating.

$\sqrt[3]{\sqrt{2000}} = \sqrt[3]{2000^{1/2}} = (2000^{1/2})^{1/3} = 2000^{1/6} = \sqrt[6]{2000}$

Question 21: Part (c) sets up a simple situation that is extended in the following lesson.

Example 1: Simplify:

a. $\sqrt[11]{(-4)^{11}}$

b. $\sqrt[8]{c^8}$

Solution Apply the Root of a Power Theorem.

a. 11 is odd, so $\sqrt[11]{(-4)^{11}} = -4$.

b. 8 is even, so $\sqrt[8]{c^8} = |c|$.

Example 2 Simplify $\sqrt[4]{16x^{12}}$, (a) for $x \geq 0$; (b) for any real number x.

Solution (a) When $x \geq 0$, $\sqrt[4]{16x^{12}} = \sqrt[4]{16}\sqrt[4]{x^{12}}$

$= 2x^3$

(b) If x may be positive or negative, then the answer to (a) is incorrect because $\sqrt[4]{16x^{12}}$ is always positive and $2x^3$ could be negative. This can be rectified by using the $|\ |$ sign.

$$\sqrt[4]{16x^{12}} = 2|x^3| = 2|x|^3$$

Questions

Covering the Reading

1. Calculate $(-6)^n$ for all integer values of n from 3 to -3.
-216; 36; -6; 1; $-\frac{1}{6}$; $\frac{1}{36}$; $-\frac{1}{216}$

2. Tell whether the number is positive or negative.

a. $(-2)^3$ negative **b.** $(2)^{-3}$ positive **c.** $(-2)^{-3}$ negative

In 3–8, simplify.

3. $\sqrt[3]{-27} \cdot \sqrt[3]{-1}$ 3   **4.** $\sqrt[3]{-64} + \sqrt[3]{-8}$ -6   **5.** $\sqrt{-16} \cdot \sqrt{-1}$ -4

6. $5\sqrt[5]{32}$ 10   **7.** $\sqrt[7]{y^7}$ y **8.** $\sqrt[6]{x^6}$ $|x|$

9. *True or false* $\sqrt[3]{(-6)^3} = -6$ true

In 10–12, tell whether the symbol is defined or not. If defined, tell whether the number is real or complex. If real, tell whether the number is positive or negative.

10. $\sqrt[4]{-16}$ not defined   **11.** $\sqrt[5]{-16}$ defined, real, negative   **12.** $\sqrt{-16}$ defined, complex

In 13–15, simplify the expression (a) when $x \geq 0$; (b) for any real number x.   See margin.

13. $\sqrt[3]{-8x^3}$ **14.** $\sqrt[4]{x^{20}}$ **15.** $\sqrt[6]{x^3}$

In 16–19, rewrite each root. Assume variables may stand for any real numbers.

16. $\sqrt[4]{432x^{12}}$ $2|x|^3(\sqrt[4]{27})$ 17. $\sqrt[5]{-3125x^{10}y^{17}}$ $-5x^2y^3\sqrt[5]{y^2}$

18. $\sqrt[3]{-m^9p^{15}}$ $-m^3p^5$ 19. $\sqrt[8]{(-10)^8a^{11}b^{18}}$ $10|a|b^2\sqrt[8]{a^3b^2}$

See margin.

Review

20. a. Write a calculator key sequence to evaluate $\sqrt[3]{\sqrt{2000}}$.
    b. Use a calculator to evaluate the expression in part a. *(Lesson 8-8)* ≈ 3.55
21. a. If $\sqrt[5]{x} = 7$, then __?__ is a __?__ root of __?__.   7; 5th; x
    b. Rewrite the equation in part a using rational exponents. $x^{1/5} = 7$
    c. Solve this equation. *(Lesson 8-8)*   16,807

22. A fast ship's speed *s* (in knots) varies directly as the seventh root of the power *p* (in horsepower) being generated by the engine. *(Lessons 2-1, 8-5, 8-8)*
    a. Write an equation expressing this relation. $s = kp^{1/7}$
    b. By how much is the speed multiplied when the horsepower is tripled? $3^{1/7}$ or $\sqrt[7]{3}$

In 23 and 24, the maximum distance *d* you can see from a building of height h is given by the formula

$$d \approx k\sqrt{h}.$$

23. The CN Tower in Toronto is about 4 times as tall as the Los Angeles City Hall. About how many times farther can you see from the top of the CN Tower than from the top of L.A. City Hall? *(Lesson 8-8)*
    two times
24. About how many times farther can you see from the 108th floor of the World Trade Center than from the sixth floor? (Assume floors have the same height.) *(Lesson 8-8)*   about 4.25 times more

25. A ball is thrown upwards and its height *h* in feet after *t* seconds is described by the equation

$$h = -16t^2 + 48t + 6.$$

    a. From what height was the ball thrown upwards?   6 feet
    b. What is the maximum height the ball attains?   42 feet
    c. When will the ball hit the ground? *(Lessons 6-2, 6-5, 6-6)* ≈ 3.12 seconds

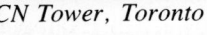
CN Tower, Toronto

Exploration

26. Many students memorize the approximations $\sqrt{2} \approx 1.414$ and $\sqrt{3} \approx 1.732$. If you know these, you can estimate $\sqrt{8}$ without a calculator because $\sqrt{8} = 2\sqrt{2} \approx 2 \cdot 1.414 = 2.828$. Name some other irrational square roots of integers between 1 and 100 that you could estimate from knowing approximate values of $\sqrt{2}$ or $\sqrt{3}$.
    See margin.

FOLLOW-UP

MORE PRACTICE
For more questions on SPUR Objectives, use *Lesson Master 8-9*, shown below.

ADDITIONAL ANSWERS
13.a. –2x
b. –2x

14.a. x^5
b. $|x|^5$

15.a. $x^{1/2}$
b. if $x \geq 0$, $x^{1/2}$;
if $x < 0$, undefined

20.a. 2000 $\boxed{\sqrt{}}$ $\boxed{y^x}$ $\boxed{(}$ 1 $\boxed{\div}$
3 $\boxed{)}$ =

26. sample:
$\sqrt{12} = (\sqrt{2} \cdot \sqrt{2} \cdot \sqrt{3}) = 2\sqrt{3}$
$\sqrt{18} = (\sqrt{2} \cdot \sqrt{3} \cdot \sqrt{3}) = 3\sqrt{2}$
$\sqrt{24} = (\sqrt{2} \cdot \sqrt{2} \cdot \sqrt{2} \cdot \sqrt{3}) =$
$2(\sqrt{2} \cdot \sqrt{3})$
$\sqrt{27} = (\sqrt{3} \cdot \sqrt{3} \cdot \sqrt{3}) = 3\sqrt{3}$

NAME _____

LESSON **MASTER 8–9**
QUESTIONS ON **SPUR** OBJECTIVES

■**SKILLS**   *Objective C   (See pages 482–485 for objectives.)*
1. Calculate $(-5)^n$ for all integer values from -3 to 3.
$-\frac{1}{125}, \frac{1}{25}, -\frac{1}{5}, 1, -5, 25, -125$

In 2–10, write as a decimal or as a simple fraction.
2. $\sqrt[3]{-27}$ –3   3. $\sqrt[5]{-32}$ –2   4. $\sqrt[3]{-64}$ –4
5. $\sqrt[3]{-8} \cdot \sqrt[3]{-1}$ 2   6. $\sqrt[5]{-243} + \sqrt[3]{-1}$ –4   7. $\sqrt{\frac{1}{4}} \cdot \sqrt{2}$ $\frac{1}{2}$
8. $7\sqrt[3]{125}$ 35   9. $2\sqrt[5]{-32}$ –4   10. $8\sqrt[5]{-1024}$ –32

In 11–13, simplify the expression (a) when $x \geq 0$; (b) for any real number x.
11. $\sqrt[3]{-27x^9}$ 12. $\sqrt[4]{x^{12}}$ 13. $\sqrt[5]{x^5}$
a. $-3x^3$ a. x^3 a. $x^{5/6}$
b. $-3x^3$ b. $|x^3|$ b. undefined

In 14–16, simplify.
14. $\sqrt[3]{-343x^{15}}$ 15. $\sqrt[5]{-7776x^{10}y^{12}}$ 16. $\sqrt[3]{-m^5n^2}$
$-7x^5$ $-6x^2y^2\sqrt[5]{y^2}$ $-m^2\sqrt[3]{m^2n^2}$

■**PROPERTIES**   *Objective I*
In 17–20, match each description with one of the following.
I. $\sqrt[n]{x^n}$, *n* even   II. $\sqrt[n]{x^n}$, *n* odd
17. Expression is always positive.   I   18. Expression is negative if *x* is negative.   II
19. Expression equals *x*.   II   20. Expression equals $|x|$.   I

92   *Advanced Algebra © Scott, Foresman and Company*

471

RESOURCES
■ Lesson Master 8-10

OBJECTIVES

D Solve equations of the form $ax^n = b$ or their equivalent radical forms.
K Solve real-world problems which can be modeled by powers and roots.

TEACHING NOTES

Note that in **Example 1**, students were asked to find *all* real solutions. Point out that $x = (15,625)^{1/6}$ has *only one solution*, $x = 5$. In contrast, the equation $(x^6)^{1/6} = (15,625)^{1/6}$ has *two solutions*, $x = 5$ or $x = -5$. This is because $(x^6)^{1/6} = \sqrt[6]{x^6} = |x|$ and $|x| = 5$ has two solutions, $x = \pm 5$.

In **Example 2**, note that we could have solved the equation $t = 2\pi\sqrt{\dfrac{L}{G}}$ for L $\left(L = \left(\dfrac{t^2 G}{4\pi^2}\right)\right)$, and then substituted $t = 2$. Explain to students that this might be a useful strategy for a clock manufacturer who wants to calculate the lengths of string needed to make pendulum clocks with different properties ($t = \frac{1}{2}$, $t = 1$, and so on).

Error Analysis If students are not careful, it is possible to lose solutions when taking the nth root of each side. To prevent errors, encourage students to refer to the nth Root of nth Power Theorem in Lesson 8-9. To catch errors, have students check answers by substitution into the original equation.

LESSON

8-10

Acrobats carefully time the pendulum swing of a trapeze. See Example 2.

The general strategy for solving an equation with nth powers or nth roots is to raise both sides to the reciprocal power as that will make the exponent of the variable one. For example, if an equation involves the 6th power, take the 6th root.

■ ■ ■ ■ ■ ■ ■ ■ ■

Example 1   Find all real solutions to $3x^6 = 46,875$.

Solution   Divide both sides by 3 to get $x^6 = 15,625$. By definition, x is a 6th root of 15,625. Take the 6th root of each side.

$$\sqrt[6]{(x^6)} = \sqrt[6]{15,625}$$
$$|x| = 5$$

Thus $x = 5$ or $x = -5$.

Check   Substitute each solution into the original equation.

$$3(5)^6 = 3(15,625) = 46,875$$
$$3(-5)^6 = 3(15,625) = 46,875$$

If an equation involves an nth root, take the nth power. In Example 2, the equation involves square roots, so square both sides.

■ ■ ■ ■ ■ ■ ■ ■ ■

Example 2   The time t (in seconds) that it takes a pendulum to complete one full swing is given by the formula

$$t = 2\pi\sqrt{\frac{L}{g}}$$

where L is the length of the arm of the pendulum (in cm) and g is a constant due to gravity. Suppose a ball on a string, swinging like a pendulum, takes 2 seconds to complete one swing back and forth. If $g = 980$ cm/sec^2, find the length of the string.

472

Solution Here $t = 2$ sec, $g = 980$ cm/sec^2, and we wish to find L.

$$2 = 2\pi\sqrt{\frac{L}{980}}$$

Divide both sides by 2π.

$$\frac{1}{\pi} = \sqrt{\frac{L}{980}}$$

Square both sides of the equation.

$$\left(\frac{1}{\pi}\right)^2 = \left(\sqrt{\frac{L}{980}}\right)^2$$

$$\frac{1}{\pi^2} = \frac{L}{980}$$

$$\frac{980}{\pi^2} = L$$

Use a calculator.

$$99.29 = L$$

The string is about 99 cm long, a little short of one meter.

Check

$2\pi\sqrt{\dfrac{99.29}{980}} \approx 1.99995 \approx 2$. The answer checks.

When you take the nth power or root of both sides of an equation, you may gain or lose solutions. Consequently, every answer that you find must be checked. If an answer does not check, it is called **extraneous** and is not a solution to the original equation. The following example shows this.

Example 3 Solve $3 - \sqrt[4]{y} = 10$.

Solution Add -3. $-\sqrt[4]{y} = 7$
Raise both sides to 4th power. $(-\sqrt[4]{y})^4 = 7^4$
Simplify. $y = 2401$

Check Does $3 - \sqrt[4]{2401} = 10$?
$3 - 7 = 10$?

No, so 2401 is not a solution. It is extraneous. The original sentence has no solution.

Notice that, in the solution of Example 3, as soon as you write the equation

$$-\sqrt[4]{y} = 7,$$

you might see there is no solution. The left side represents a negative number, so it cannot equal the positive number 7.

LESSON 8-10   Solving $ax^n = b$ 473

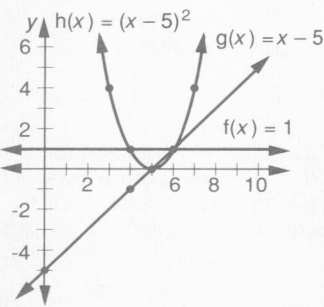
Covering the Reading

In 1–3, determine the number of real solutions.

1. $x^2 = -100$ **zero**   **2.** $x^3 = -100$ **one**   **3.** $x^4 = 16$ **two**

In 4–9, find all real solutions.

4. $\sqrt{v} = 9$ **v = 81**   **5.** $w^{1/3} = 4$ **w = 64**

6. $4\sqrt[5]{x} = 2$ **x = .03125**   **7.** $y^4 = 14641$ **y = 11 or -11**

8. $27 = z^3$ **z = 3**   **9.** $3x^5 = 96$ **x = 2**

10. In Example 2, if the pendulum takes 4 sec to complete one full swing, how long is the pendulum?   **about 397 cm**

11. What is an *extraneous* solution?   **See margin.**

12. Explain why you don't need to solve $\sqrt{m - 3} = -10$ in order to know that it has no solutions.
The left side, $\sqrt{m - 3}$, can have only nonnegative values.

Applying the Mathematics

In 13–16, find all real solutions.

13. $-3x^3 = 13824$ $x = -8\sqrt[3]{9}$ **14.** $\sqrt{3x - 4} = 10$ $x = \frac{104}{3}$

15. $s^{1/3} + 2.4 = 8$ **16.** $\sqrt[4]{z} + 9 = 10\sqrt[4]{z}$ **z = 1**
s = 175.616

17. Recall that when traveling at a fast rate, a ship's speed s (in knots) varies directly as the seventh root of the power p (in horsepower) being generated by the engine. The equation $s = 6.492p^{1/7}$ describes the situation. If a ship is traveling at a speed of 25 knots, about how much horsepower is the engine generating?   **12,558 horsepower**

18. In a geometric sequence $g_1 = 2000$ and $g_5 = 125$.
  a. Find all possible real values for r, the common multiplier. $r = \frac{1}{2}$ or $-\frac{1}{2}$
  b. List the possible values for g_2, g_3, and g_4.
  1000, 500, 250 or -1000, 500, -250

19. A formula that police use for finding the speed s (in mph) that a car was going from the length L (in feet) of its skid mark is $s = 2\sqrt{5L}$.
  a. The *Guinness Book of World Records* (1985 Edition) reports that in 1960, a Jaguar in England had the longest skid mark recorded, 950 feet. About how fast was the Jaguar going? $\approx$ **138 mph**
  b. About how far does an auto travel if it skids from 50 mph to a stop? $\approx$ **125 ft**

Review

20. Solve for m: $\sqrt[6]{m^6} = 64$. *(Lesson 8-9)*   **m = 64 or m = -64**

In 21–23, rewrite each root. Assume all variables are nonnegative. *(Lesson 8-9)*

21. $\sqrt[3]{-125x^6}$ **22.** $\sqrt[4]{32x^5y^{11}}$ **23.** $\sqrt{50a^3} \cdot \sqrt{8b^4}$
     $-5x^2$ $2xy^2\sqrt[4]{2xy^3}$ $20ab^2\sqrt{a}$

24. Let $f(x) = (x - 5)^0$, $g(x) = (x - 5)^1$, and $h(x) = (x - 5)^2$. *(Lessons 3-2, 6-4, 7-1)*

   a. Graph f, g, and h on the same axes.   **See margin.**

   b. For what value(s) of x does $f(x) = g(x)$?   **x = 6**

   c. For what value(s) of x does $g(x) = h(x)$?   **x = 6 or 5**

25. In 1980 the world was using petroleum at a rate of $1.35 \cdot 10^{20}$ J/yr, where J is a unit of energy called a joule. At that time the world's supply of petroleum was estimated to be about 10^{22} J. If the global rate of consumption remains constant, about how long will the world's supply of petroleum last? *(Lesson 8-1)*   **≈ 74.1 years**

26. Consider the function f described by $f(x) = 3x - 4$. *(Lesson 7-6)*

   a. Write an algebraic expression for $f^{-1}(x)$. $f^{-1}(x) = \frac{1}{3}x + \frac{4}{3}$

   b. Describe the relationship between the slopes of f and f^{-1}.
    The slopes are the reciprocals of each other, 3 and $\frac{1}{3}$.

Exploration

27. The length of the skid mark in Question 19 is the same as would be found by using the braking distance formula of Lesson 7-1.

   a. Explore other speeds, calculating skid mark lengths and braking distances. Are they the same for any other speeds?   **See margin.**

   b. Should they be the same?   **yes.**

MORE PRACTICE
For more questions on SPUR Objectives, use *Lesson Master 8-10*, shown below.

EVALUATION
Alternative Assessment
Without having students actually calculate roots, ask them to identify the number of roots, the sign of the roots, and whether the roots are real or imaginary for radicals such as the following:
$\sqrt[3]{-8}$; $\sqrt[4]{5}$; $\sqrt[5]{n}$, if $n < 0$; $\sqrt[6]{64}$

NAME _____

LESSON **MASTER** **8–10**
QUESTIONS ON **SPUR** OBJECTIVES

■**SKILLS** *Objective C* *(See pages 482–485 for objectives.)*
In 1–12, solve.

1. $5x^2 = 245$	2. $2t^4 = 1250$	3. $6h^7 = -768$
$x = \pm 7$	$t = \pm 5$	$h = -2$
4. $a^4 = \frac{1}{81}$	5. $3w^{4/7} = 48$	6. $-5r^{2/5} = -125$
$a = \pm \frac{1}{3}$	$w = 128$	$r = 312^{E}$
7. $9v^{-2/3} = 16$	8. $\sqrt[5]{n} = 3$	9. $3\sqrt[5]{v} = 6$
$v = \frac{27}{64}$	$n = 243$	$v = 32$
10. $-12\sqrt[4]{z} = -24$	11. $\sqrt[6]{x} + 12 = 15$	12. $4\sqrt[4]{q} - 1 = 2$
$z = 16$	$x = 6561$	$q = \frac{27}{64}$

■**USES** *Objective K*

13. Recall that the average distance d (in millions of miles) of a planet from the sun is $d = 1.82r^{2/3}$, where r is the number of days it takes the planet to revolve once around the sun.

  a. Suppose a planet is 200 million miles from the sun. Find its period of revolution.   **about 1152 days**

  b. How many earth years is this planet's period of revolution?   **3.16 earth yrs**

14. A rabbit population grew geometrically from a population of 16 the first year to 625 the fifth year.

  a. Find r, the factor by which the population was growing each year.   **2.5**

  b. Give the population in the intermediate years.   **40, 100, 250**

Advanced Algebra © Scott, Foresman and Company   **93**

RESOURCES
■ Lesson Master 8-11

E Solve equations of the form $a(x - h)^n = b$.
J Apply the compound interest formula.

Before you have students read the examples in this lesson, you might want to have them practice the solution algorithm at the beginning of the lesson. Have them use the three-step process on problems like these:
(a) $3(x - 2)^4 = 36$ (≈ 3.86)
(b) $-2(y + 3)^5 = 64$ ($= -5$)
(c) $-6(x - 5)^2 = -12$ (≈ 6.41)

In **Example 1**, ask students how the book can justify the statement that $1 + r$ is positive. (The context is the justification. Interest rates r must be positive.) Then note how the nth Root of an nth Power Theorem is used to conclude that because $1 + r$ is positive, $((1 + r)^4)^{1/4}$ equals $1 + r$.

Alternate Approach
Students might find **Example 1** easier if they replace $1 + r$ by x. Then the equation to solve becomes $1000 = 500x^4$, which seems less formidable than $1000 = 500(1 + r)^4$. Again, the context justifies that $x > 0$. If the student fails to notice this restriction at first, applying the nth Power of an nth Power Theorem gives $|x| = 2^{1/4}$ or $x \approx \pm 1.19$. Substituting into $1 + r = x$ gives $r \approx .19$ or $r \approx -2.19$. Note that checking in the original statement of **Example 1** will show that $r \approx -2.19$ is extraneous.

Solving $a(x-h)^n = b$

You have solved equations of the form $x^n = b$. Simply take the nth root of each side or raise each side to the $\frac{1}{n}$ power. It takes one step. Solving $ax^n = b$ takes two steps. First divide both sides by a; then take each side to the $\frac{1}{n}$ power. The equation $a(x - h)^n = b$ can be solved in three steps.

Step 1. Divide each side by a.

Step 2. Raise each side to the $\frac{1}{n}$ power. Remember that it is possible to gain or lose solutions.

Step 3. Add h to each side.

The solutions to $a(x - h)^n = b$ are h larger than the solutions to $ax^n = b$.

■ ■ ■ ■ ■ ■ ■ ■

Example 1 Michael has $500 he would like to save for college. His goal is to find an investment that would allow his money to double to $1000 in four years. What compound annual interest rate r would make this happen?

Solution Use the formula from Lesson 8-2.
$$A = P(1 + r)^t$$

Here P is the original principal, r the annual rate, t the number of years, and A is the total value of the investment after t years.

Substitute in the formula.
$$1000 = 500(1 + r)^4$$

Now use the steps. First divide both sides by 500.
$$2 = (1 + r)^4$$

Since $1 + r$ is positive, take the $\frac{1}{4}$ power of each side.
$$2^{1/4} = ((1 + r)^4)^{1/4}$$
$$2^{1/4} = 1 + r$$

A calculator shows that $2^{1/4} \approx 1.189207$. Rounding to the nearest hundredth gives $2^{1/4} \approx 1.19$. Thus
$$1.19 \approx 1 + r.$$
Add -1 to each side. $\quad 0.19 \approx r$

Thus, for $500 to double to $1000 in four years, Michael needs to find an investment yielding at least 19% interest. A savings account will not do the job. His goal is probably unrealistic.

Example 2 A piece of furniture loses a fixed part of its value each year. If in five years it is worth 60% of what it was originally, what percent of value is it losing each year?

Solution Think of its original value as 100%. Let r be the rate of loss. The value is multiplied by $1 - r$ five times. The result is 60% of its value.

The equation is $.60 = 1.00(1 - r)^5$
or $.60 = (1 - r)^5$.
Raise both sides to the $\frac{1}{5}$ power. $(.60)^{1/5} = ((1 - r)^5)^{1/5}$
                                                  $(.60)^{1/5} = 1 - r$
                                        $(.60)^{1/5} - 1 = -r$
                                               $-0.097 \approx -r$

The furniture is losing about 9.7% of its value each year.

Check If the furniture loses 9.7% of its value each year, then each year its value is 90.3% of the previous year. Is $(90.3\%)^5 \approx .60$? Yes, $(0.903)^5 = 0.600397...$ Since the furniture loses 40% of its original value after 5 years, it is reasonable that the yearly depreciation should be between 8% and 10%.

The algorithm for solving $a(x - h)^n = k$ applies to any real exponent n, including fractions.

Example 3 Given $x + 9 > 0$, solve for x: $3(x + 9)^{2/5} = 48$.

Solution Divide each side by 3. $(x + 9)^{2/5} = 16$
Raise each side to the $\frac{5}{2}$ power. $((x + 9)^{2/5})^{5/2} = 16^{5/2}$
                                                          $x + 9 = 1024$
                                                              $x = 1015$

Check Does $3(1015 + 9)^{2/5} = 48$?
                $3 \cdot (1024)^{2/5} = 48$?
                    $3 \cdot 16 = 48$? Yes.

Questions

Covering the Reading

1. You wish to solve $a(x - h)^n = k$, where a and k are positive.
   a. What is a reasonable first step? **Divide by a.**
   b. What is a second step? **Raise both sides to the $1/n$th power.**
   c. What is a third step? **Add h to both sides.**

2. *Multiple choice* The equation $y^2 = 17$ has solutions of $y = \sqrt{17}$ or $y = -\sqrt{17}$. Compared to these, the solutions to $(y - 3)^2 = 17$ are: c
   (a) 3 units smaller   (b) $\sqrt{-3}$ units smaller
   (c) 3 units larger   (d) $-\sqrt{3}$ units larger.

LESSON 8-11 Solving $a(x - h)^n = b$ **477**

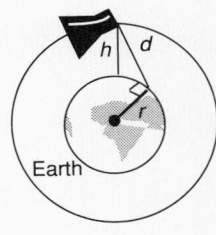

3. Solve for y. Assume
$y - 4 > 0$.
$9(y - 4)^{4/3} = 2304$
y = 68

NOTES ON QUESTIONS
Question 8: There are two ways to solve this question: (1) by using the algorithm taught in this lesson, or (2) by squaring the expression on the left side and solving the quadratic equation. In either case, there are two real solutions.

Question 10: If students are able to discern, after transforming the equation of this question into $\sqrt[4]{2x - 5} = -4$, that there are no solutions, they should immediately state that fact and stop the solution process.

Question 12: This question asks for a literal solution to $a(x - h)^n = b$, an abstract application of the algorithm.

Computer for Question 26: This question illustrates a common use of computers. Once an equation is solved for a desired variable, a program can easily be written which will allow the user to input different sets of data to quickly see the affect the input has on the desired output.

3. Refer to Example 1. Suppose that Michael could leave his $500 in an investment for 7 years instead of 4.
  a. What equation can be used to find the annual interest rate Michael must get to double his money? $1000 = 500(1+r)^7$
  b. What compound annual interest rate would allow his money to double in 7 years?   **10.4%**

4. Sherri wants to invest $200 for 6 years. What compound annual interest rate would allow her investment to triple in that time?
about 20.1%

In 5 and 6, solve and check.

5. $8(t - 5)^3 = 27$ $t = 6\frac{1}{2}$ **6.** $5(x + 2)^{1/4} = 405$ **x = 43,046,719**

7. Refer to Example 2. Suppose a piece of furniture is worth 70% of its original cost after 4 years. If its depreciation has been at a constant rate, find the percent of value it has been losing each year.   **8.6%**

a probate court

Applying the Mathematics

In 8–11, solve and check.

8. $\left(\dfrac{m - 3}{16}\right)^2 = 16$ **9.** $110(r + 1)^{1/2} = 1870$ **r = 288**
m = 67 or -61

10. $5 + \sqrt[4]{2x - 5} = 1$ **11.** $(3x + 5)^{2/3} = 4$ **x = 1**
no solution

12. *Multiple choice* Which of these is a solution to $a(x - h)^n = k$?   **b**
  (a) $\left(\dfrac{k}{a - h}\right)^{1/n}$ (b) $\left(\dfrac{k}{a}\right)^{1/n} + h$ (c) $\left(\dfrac{k - a}{n}\right)^{1/n}$ (d) $\dfrac{\sqrt[n]{k}}{a} + h$

13. Joyce was left $5000 by her great aunt. It took $4\frac{1}{2}$ years for the will to go through probate, and she was told the amount had grown to $6247.12 through annual compounding.
  a. At what rate was the amount growing?   **5.07%**
  b. Is this a fair return?   **yes**

14. A cube has sides of length s millimeters. Then 0.5 millimeter is shaved off each dimension, so the volume V of the shaved cube is $V = (s - 0.5)^3$. What was the original length of a side of a cube which ended up with a volume of 1000 cubic millimeters?
s = 10.5 mm

15. Refer to Michael's situation at the beginning of the lesson. Suppose Michael invested d dollars. What rate would it take to double in 4 years if the account were compounded
  a. monthly?   ≈ **17.45%**
  b. daily?   ≈ **17.33%**

16. *Multiple choice* A health spa installed a circular tub with a 3′ radius. A contractor was hired to build a circular deck of width w around the tub. The total surface area of the deck and the area under the tub should be 100 square feet. Which equation can be solved to find w in this situation?   **a**
  (a) $100 = \pi(w + 3)^2$
  (b) $100\pi = (w + 3)^2$
  (c) $100 = \pi(w - 3)^2$
  (d) $100\pi = (w - 3)^2$

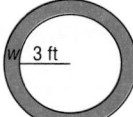

In 17–19, simplify each expression without a calculator. *(Lessons 8-6, 8-8)*

17. $(64)^{7/6}$ **128**   **18.** $(\frac{25}{9})^{3/2}$ $\frac{125}{27}$ **19.** $\sqrt[3]{125^2}$ **25**

20. Solve $2z^7 = \frac{1}{8192}$. *(Lesson 8-10)* $z = \frac{1}{4}$

21. a. Give a counterexample to the statement
"$\sqrt[4]{x^4} = x$ for all real numbers x."   **x = -1**
b. For what values of x is it true that $\sqrt[4]{x^4} = x$? *(Lesson 8-9)*   **x ≥ 0**

22. *Multiple choice* Which is not a 4th root of 625? *(Lesson 8-4)*   **d**
(a) 5   (b) -5   (c) 5i   (d) $\sqrt{5}$

23. Write the system of three inequalities whose solutions comprise the shaded region graphed at the right. *(Lesson 5-7)*
$x \geq 0$; $4x + 30 \geq y$; $4x \leq y$

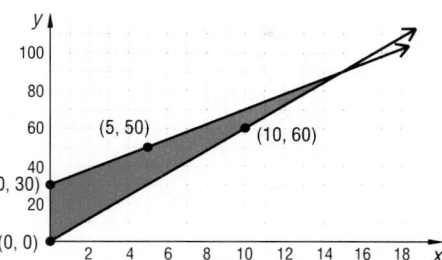
(5, 50)
(10, 60)
(0, 30)
(0, 0)

24. Write in scientific notation. *(Previous course)*
a. 30,000,000   **b.** 300   **c.** .03   **d.** .0000003
3.0×10^7 3.0×10^2 3.0×10^{-2} 3.0×10^{-7}
25. The square of the cube of the nth power of x is what power of x? *(Lesson 8-1)* x^{6n}

In 26–27, consider the BASIC program below.

```
10 REM T = NO. OF YRS TO DOUBLE MONEY
20 REM R = RATE OF INTEREST AS DECIMAL
30 PRINT "HOW LONG DOES IT TAKE TO DOUBLE YOUR MONEY?"
40 PRINT "TIME IN YRS.","ANNUAL RATE"
50 FOR T = 1 TO 15
60    LET R = 2^(1/T) − 1
70    PRINT T,R
80 NEXT T
90 END
```

26. a. Solve the formula $2 = 1(1 + R)^T$ for R to derive the formula in
line 60. $R = 2^{1/T} - 1$
b. Is R a linear function of T? Why or why not?
No, doubling the time does not reduce the interest rate by exactly $\frac{1}{2}$.
27. Run the program and study the output. At what rate of interest must
you invest to double your money in 5 years compounded annually? 10
years? 15 years?   **5 years ≈ 14.9%; 10 years ≈ 7.18%; 15 years ≈ 4.73%**

28. Given the interest rates at the banks in your neighborhood, what is a
reasonable range of doubling times for an investment?
**Answer(s) depend on the interest rates at the neighborhood banks. For
$.05 \leq R \leq .08$, doubling time ranges from 14 to 9 years.**

LESSON 8-11   Solving $a(x - h)^n = b$ **479**

Summary

When $x > 0$, the expression x^m is defined for any real number m. This chapter has covered the meanings of x^m when m is a positive or negative rational number.

In previous courses, you have learned basic properties of powers, which we assume as postulates:

Product of Powers Property $\qquad x^m \cdot x^n = x^{m+n}$

Power of a Power Property $\qquad (x^m)^n = x^{mn}$

Power of a Product Property $\qquad (xy)^n = x^n y^n$

Quotient of Powers Property $\qquad \dfrac{x^m}{x^n} = x^{m-n}$

Power of a Quotient Property $\qquad \left(\dfrac{x}{y}\right)^m = \dfrac{x^m}{y^m}$

These properties hold for all values of x when m and n are positive integers. If we restrict x to be positive, then they hold for all values of m and n. These values can be calculated using theorems:

Zero Exponent Theorem $\qquad x^0 = 1$

Negative Exponent Theorem $\qquad x^{-m} = \dfrac{1}{x^m}$

$\dfrac{1}{n}$ Exponent Theorem $\qquad x^{1/n} = $ positive solution to b^n

Root of a Power Theorem $\qquad x^{m/n} = \sqrt[n]{x^m} = (\sqrt[n]{x})^m$

When x is positive, $\sqrt[n]{x} = x^{1/n}$. When x is negative and n is odd, then $\sqrt[n]{x}$ is the real nth root of x. If $n = \frac{1}{m}$ in the Power of a Product Property, then a new property results:

Root of a Product Property $\qquad \sqrt[m]{xy} = \sqrt[m]{x} \cdot \sqrt[m]{y}$

These properties are of assistance in solving equations of the form $x^n = b$, $ax^n = b$ or $a(x - h)^n = b$. These equations can arise from compound interest situations, from relations between lengths, areas, and volumes, and a variety of situations leading to geometric sequences. Three formulas are:

Compound Interest Formula: $\qquad A = P(1 + r)^t$

Explicit Formula for a Geometric
Sequence: $\qquad g_n = g_1 r^{n-1}$

Recursive Formula for a Geometric
Sequence: $\qquad g_n = r g_{n-1}, \, n > 1.$

Vocabulary

Below are the most important terms and phrases for this chapter. You should be able to give a definition or statement for those terms marked with an *. For all other terms you should be able to give a general description and a specific example of each.

Lesson 8-1
powering, exponentiation
base, exponent, power
*Repeated Multiplication Model
  for Powering
Product of Powers Property
Power of a Power Property
Power of a Product Property
Quotient of Powers Property
Power of a Quotient Property
Zero Exponent Theorem

Lesson 8-2
principal
compounding
*Compound Interest Formula

General Compound Interest
  Formula
simple interest

Lesson 8-3
geometric sequence, exponential
  sequence
*explicit formula for a geometric
  sequence
*recursive formula for a geometric
  sequence

Lesson 8-4
Negative Exponent Theorem

Lesson 8-5
*square root, cube root, nth root
$\frac{1}{n}$ Exponent Theorem

Lesson 8-6
Rational Exponent Theorem

Lesson 8-8
$\sqrt[n]{x}$
Root of a Power Theorem
Root of a Product Theorem

Lesson 8-9
nth Root of nth Power Theorem

Lesson 8-10
extraneous solution

480

Progress Self-Test

Take this test as you would take a test in class. You will need a calculator. Then check your work with the solutions in the Selected Answers section in the back of the book.

1. Order from largest to smallest: 3^{-4}, -3^4, $(-3)^{-4}$, $(-3)^4$.   **-3^4; $(-3)^{-4}$ and 3^{-4}; $(-3)^4$**

In 2–4, write as a decimal or simple fraction.

2. $(625)^{1/2}$ **25**

3. $\sqrt[6]{11{,}390{,}625}$ **15**

4. $\left(\frac{1}{32}\right)^{-6/5}$ **64**

In 5 and 6, simplify. Assume $x > 0$ and $y > 0$.

5. $\sqrt[4]{625x^4y^8}$ **$25xy^2$**

6. $\sqrt[5]{-96x^{15}y^3}$ **$-2x^3y\sqrt[5]{3}$**

In 7–9, solve.

7. $9x^4 = 144$ **$x = 2$ or $x = -2$**

8. $c^{3/2} = 64$ **$c = 16$**

9. $5^n \cdot 5^{21} = 5^{29}$ **$n = 8$**

10. Recall the formula $T = 2\pi\sqrt{\dfrac{L}{g}}$ for the time T (in seconds) it takes a pendulum to complete one full swing, where L is length (in centimeters) and g is acceleration due to gravity. How long (to the nearest cm) is a pendulum that takes 1 second to swing? (Use 980 cm/sec² for g.)   **24.82cm**

11. An original set of architect's sketches is increasing in value at an annual rate of 17%. If it is valued at $13,500 now, what will it be worth (to the nearest hundred dollars) in three years?   **$21,600**

12. A bank account pays 5.75% compounded daily. If you deposit $200 in the account and leave it untouched for 5 years, how much will be in the account then?   **$266.61**

13. $400 is to be invested. What rate of interest should be paid to allow the money to double to $800 in 4 years if the account is compounded annually?   **18.92%**

In 14–16, solve.

14. $100(A - 5)^4 = 1600$ **$A = 7$**

15. $\frac{1}{6}(20 - P)^{1/2} = 5$ **$P = -880$**

16. $\sqrt[n]{\dfrac{125}{343}} = \dfrac{5}{7}$ **$n = 3$**

17. Write without an exponent: $\dfrac{2.1 \cdot 10^2}{10^{-3}}$.   **210,000**

18. Suppose each of a certain type of bacterium splits into two every half hour. If there are 5 bacteria initially, about how many will there be after 24 hours?   **$(5)2^{48}$**

19. Find an explicit formula for the nth term in the geometric sequence: 2, 8, 32, 128....   **$t_n = 2 \times 4^{n-1}$**

20. *Multiple choice*   Which expression equals $a^{-4/5}$ for all $a > 0$?   **b**
    (a) $\dfrac{1}{\sqrt[4]{a^5}}$ (b) $\dfrac{1}{\sqrt[5]{a^4}}$ (c) $a^{5/4}$ (d) $(-a)^{4/5}$

21. Evaluate without a calculator: $216^{1/3}$.   **6**

22. Recall the formula $h(t) = 180 \cdot 10^{-.04t}$ for the number of hours h that milk stays fresh in a surrounding temperature $t°C$. How long will milk stay fresh when stored at $15°C$?   **45.2 hours**

23. Identify all real 4th roots of 81.   **3, -3**

24. *True or false* $\sqrt[6]{64} = -2$.   **False**

25. Radioactive material will change (decay) to different material over a period of time. The time it takes half of the mass of the radioactive material to decay is called the **half-life.** Radioactive carbon₁₄ has a half-life of 5600 years. If one starts with 40 grams of carbon₁₄, how many grams are left after 3 half-lives?   **5 grams**

CHAPTER 8   Progress Self-Test   **481**

CHAPTER REVIEW

The main objectives for the chapter are organized here into sections corresponding to the four main types of understanding this book promotes: Skills, Properties, Uses, and Representations.

USING THE CHAPTER REVIEW

Whereas end-of-chapter material may be considered optional in some texts, in *Advanced Algebra* we have selected these objectives and questions with the expectation that they will be covered. Students should be able to answer these questions with about 85% accuracy after studying the chapter.

You may assign these questions over a single night to help students prepare for a test the next day, or you may assign the questions over a two-day period.

If you work the questions over two days, then we recommend assigning the *evens* for homework the first night so that students get feedback in class the next day, then assigning the *odds* the night before the test so students can use the answers provided in the book.

Chapter Review

Questions on **SPUR** Objectives

SPUR stands for **S**kills, **P**roperties, **U**ses, and **R**epresentations.
The Chapter Review questions are grouped according to the
SPUR Objectives for this chapter.

SKILLS deal with the procedures used to get answers.

■ **Objective A.** *Evaluate x^n when n is an integer.*
(*Lessons 8-1, 8-4, 8-9*)

In 1–6, write as a decimal or simple fraction.

1. $.2^6$ .000064
2. 12^{-5} $\frac{1}{248832}$
3. $3.4 \cdot 10^{-3}$ .0034
4. $\left(\frac{2}{3}\right)^{-1}$ $\frac{3}{2}$
5. $\left(\frac{1}{5}\right)^{-4}$ 625
6. $(-2)^{-2}$ $\frac{1}{4}$

■ **Objective B.** *Evaluate x^b when b is a rational number.* (*Lessons 8-5, 8-6, 8-7*)

In 7–12, write as a decimal or simple fraction. Estimate decimals to the nearest hundredth.

7. $1000^{1/3}$ 10
8. $\sqrt[3]{27 + 64}$ 4.50
9. $3 \cdot 27^{1/8}$ 4.53
10. $16^{3/4}$ 8
11. $16^{-1/2}$ $\frac{1}{4}$
12. $\left(\frac{27}{216}\right)^{-2/3}$ $\frac{36}{9} = 4$
13. $\left(\frac{1}{64}\right)^{-3/2}$ 512
14. $2^{1.5}$ 2.828
15. $80^{2/3}$ 18.566

In 16 and 17, *true or false*.

16. $-7 = \sqrt[6]{117,649}$ false
17. $3^{-6.4} < 3^{-6.5}$ false

■ **Objective C.** *Simplify radicals.* (*Lessons 8-8, 8-9*)

In 18–20, write as a decimal or simple fraction.

18. $\sqrt[4]{625}$ 5
19. $\sqrt[3]{-8}$ -2
20. $\sqrt[3]{\left(\frac{8}{125}\right)^2}$ $\frac{4}{25}$

In 21–23, estimate to the nearest hundredth.

21. $\sqrt[4]{4}$ 1.41
22. $\sqrt[3]{-80}$ -4.31
23. $\sqrt[10]{346}$ 1.79

In 24–29, simplify. Assume variables under the radical sign are positive.

24. $\sqrt{a^6}$ a^3
25. $\sqrt[3]{54x^3}$ $3x\sqrt[3]{2}$
26. $\sqrt[6]{128x^8y^7}$ $2xy\sqrt[6]{2x^2y}$
27. $\sqrt[3]{-80a^9}$ $-2a^3\sqrt[3]{10}$
28. $\sqrt[5]{-b^{14}c^{30}}$ $-b^2c^6\sqrt[5]{b^4}$
29. $\sqrt{7x^3} \cdot \sqrt{14x}$ $7x^2\sqrt{2}$

■ **Objective D.** *Solve equations of the form $ax^n = b$ or their equivalent radical forms.* (*Lessons 8-6, 8-7, 8-10*)

In 30–39, solve.

30. $3x^2 = 192$ x = 8 or -8
31. $-27 = a^4$ No real solution
32. $x^3 = 12$ $x = \sqrt[3]{12}$
33. $x^{-2} = 9$ $x = \frac{1}{3}$ or $-\frac{1}{3}$
34. $m^{3/2} = \frac{1}{27}$ $m = \frac{1}{9}$
35. $4q^{-2/5} = 9$ $\frac{32}{243}$
36. $\sqrt[3]{a} = 2$ $a = 8$
37. $4\sqrt[4]{b} = 3$ $b = \frac{81}{256}$
38. $\sqrt[6]{c} + 4 = 3$ no real solution
39. $\sqrt[6]{c} - 4 = 3$ c = 117,649

482

■ **Objective E.** *Solve equations of the form*
$a(x - h)^t = k$. *(Lesson 8-11)*

40. *Multiple choice* From the equation
$200(r + 1)^4 = 3200$, you can conclude that
$|r + 1| = 2$ if, to both sides, you: c
(a) divide by 200 and then take the fourth power;
(b) take the 4th power and then divide by 200;
(c) divide by 200 and then take the $\frac{1}{4}$ power;
(d) subtract 1, then divide by 200, and then take the $\frac{1}{4}$ power.

In 41–43, solve. Round answers to the nearest tenth.

41. $\sqrt[3]{x + 1} - 9 = 16$ x = 15624
42. $\frac{1}{4}(9 + y)^{1/2} = 14$ y = 3127
43. $.2(r - 1)^5 = 3.4$ r = 2.8

■ **Objective F.** *Solve equations or simplify expressions using properties of exponents. (Lessons 8-1, 8-4, 8-6, 8-7)*

In 44–47, solve.

44. $(9^5 \cdot 9^3) = 9^x$ x = 8
45. $\frac{2^5}{2^{-1}} = 2^x$ x = 6
46. $(7^{1/2})^3 = 7^n$ $n = \frac{3}{2}$
47. $(2 \cdot 5)^{-3} = y^{-3}$ y = 10

In 48–51, simplify.

48. $(-4x^2)^3$ $-64x^6$
49. $\dfrac{-8x^{10}y^{3/2}}{2xy^{1/2}}$ $-4x^9y$
50. $\left(\dfrac{a}{b}\right)^3\left(\dfrac{2b}{3a}\right)^4$ $\dfrac{16b}{81a}$
51. $\dfrac{15c}{(3c^{-6})(20c^6)}$ $\dfrac{c}{4}$

■ **Objective G.** *Find terms or the rule for a geometric sequence. (Lesson 8-3)*

In 52–54, give the first five terms of the geometric sequence described.

52. constant ratio 4, first term 5
  5, 20, 80, 320, 1280
53. first term $\frac{1}{2}$, second term $\frac{3}{4}$
  $\frac{1}{2}, \frac{3}{4}, \frac{9}{8}, \frac{27}{16}, \frac{81}{32}$
54. $a_1 = 10$, $a_n = -2a_{n-1}$ 10, -20, 40, -80, 160

55. *Multiple choice* Which of the following contains the first three terms of a geometric sequence? c
(a) 16, 4, -8, ...   (b) $\frac{4}{5}, \frac{9}{5}, \frac{14}{5}, ...$
(c) $3\frac{1}{3}, 33\frac{1}{3}, 333\frac{1}{3}, ...$ (d) -0.04, 0.16, 0.36, ...

56. *True or false* The first four terms of the geometric sequence described by the formula $a_n = \frac{3}{16}(-2)^{n-1}$ are $\frac{-3}{8}, \frac{3}{4}, \frac{-3}{2}, 3$. false

In 57 and 58, find an explicit rule for the nth term of the geometric sequence.

57. 2, 1, .5, ... $g_n = 2(.5)^{n-1}$
58. 10, 30, 90, ... $g_n = 10(3)^{n-1}$

59. Find the 50th term of a geometric sequence whose first term is 6 and whose constant multiplier is 1.05. ≈65.53

PROPERTIES deal with the principles behind the mathematics.

■ **Objective H.** *Recognize properties of nth powers and nth roots. (Lessons 8-1, 8-4, 8-6, 8-7, 8-8, 8-9)*

60. *True or false* If $0 < x < 1$, $\sqrt[3]{x} > x$.
  true

61. Suppose $x > 1$. Arrange from smallest to largest: x, $\sqrt{x}$, x^{-2}, $x^{5/4}$, $x^{-2/3}$
  $x^{-2}, x^{-2/3}, \sqrt{x}, x, x^{5/4}$

In 62–67, use the properties listed below. Assume $Q > 0$, $x \neq 0$, and n is an integer greater than 1. Identify all properties which apply to the simplification.

I. $Q^0 = 1$ II. $Q^{-x} = \left(\dfrac{1}{Q}\right)^x$

III. $Q^{1/n} = \sqrt[n]{Q}$ IV. $\sqrt[n]{PQ} = \sqrt[n]{P}\sqrt[n]{Q}$

V. $Q^{y/n} = (\sqrt[n]{Q})^y = \sqrt[n]{Q^y}$

62. $(6.789)^{5-5} = 1$ I

63. $(8Z)^{2/3} = 2\sqrt[3]{Z^2}$ IV, V

64. $(y^{1/7})^7 = y$ V

65. $(25)^{-1/2} = \frac{1}{5}$ II, III

66. $(\frac{1}{y})^{-3/4} = (\sqrt[4]{y})^3$ II, V

67. $\sqrt[4]{32} = 2\sqrt[4]{2}$ IV

■ **Objective I.** *Apply the definitions of $x^{1/n}$ and $\sqrt[n]{x}$ as they apply to nth roots of x. (Lessons 8-5, 8-8, 8-9)*

68. Identify: **a.** all square roots of 225; **b.** $\sqrt{225}$; and **c.** $225^{1/2}$. a) 15, -15; b) 15; c) 15

69. Identify: **a.** all real cube roots of -125; **b.** $\sqrt[3]{-125}$; and **c.** $(-125)^{1/3}$. a) -5; b) -5; c) undef

70. Identify: **a.** all real 4th roots of 16; **b.** $\sqrt[4]{16}$; and **c.** $16^{1/4}$. a) 2 and -2; b) 2; c) 2

71. Explain why -10 has no real 8th roots. See margin.

72. Explain why -10 has a real 5th root. See margin.

73. For what values of n does $\sqrt[n]{x^n} = x$ for all real numbers x? odd integers $n \geq 3$

74. For what values of n does $\sqrt[n]{x^n} = |x|$ for all real numbers x? even integers $n \geq 2$

USES deal with applications of mathematics in real situations.

■ **Objective J.** *Apply the compound interest formula. (Lessons 8-2, 8-4, 8-11)*

75. Sue invests $150 in a savings account which pays 5.75% interest, compounded annually. How much money will be in the account if the $150 is left untouched for 6 years? ≈$209.78

76. Investment A offers an annual interest rate of 8%, compounded daily. Investment B offers an annual interest rate of 6%, compounded daily. Leo is considering investing $200 in one of these accounts. Which will yield a higher amount: investment A for 3 years, or investment B for 4 years? investment B

In 77 and 78, Caryn now has $6000 in an account earning interest at a rate of 9%, compounded quarterly. ≈$4202.79

77. Assuming she made no deposits or withdrawals in the past four years, how much money did she have four years ago?

78. How much interest will she earn in the eighth year? ≈$729.43

79. Melvin has $4000 and wants to find an investment which will allow the amount to double in 10 years. What interest rate compounded annually will accomplish this? ≈7.2%

■ **Objective K.** *Solve real world problems which can be modeled by powers and roots. (Lessons 8-1, 8-4, 8-5, 8-6, 8-10)*

80. The Pentagon, one of the world's largest office buildings, occupies about $1.2 \cdot 10^5$ m². The Pentagon occupies what percent of the area $1.9 \cdot 10^6$ m² which is the area of Monaco, a small country in the Southcoast of France? ≈6.3%

81. The power P of a radio signal varies inversely as the square of the distance d, from the transmitter. Write a formula for P as a function of d using:
a. a positive exponent $P = k(\frac{1}{d})^2$
b. a negative exponent. $P = kd^{-2}$

In 82 and 83, use the following information: Meteorologists use the equation $D^3 = 216T^2$ as a model to describe the size and intensity of four types of violent storms: tornadoes, thunderstorms, hurricanes, and cyclones, where D is the diameter of the storm in miles and T is the number of hours the storm travels before dissipating.

82. The world's worst recorded hurricane took place on November 13-14, 1970, in the Ganges delta islands in Bangladesh. More than 1,000,000 people died. If this storm lasted 24 hours, what was its diameter? ≈49.92 miles

83. If a tornado's diameter is 1.5 miles, how long would it be expected to last? .125 hours

84. A sphere has a volume of 400 in³. Another sphere has a radius half as long. 2.29 in.
   a. What is the radius of the second sphere?
   b. What is the volume of the second sphere? 50.3 in³

85. A spherical raindrop has radius r millimeters. Through evaporation the radius decreases by .05 millimeters. If the volume of the condensed drop is 7.2 mm³, what was the original radius of the drop? 1.25 mm

■ **Objective L.** *Solve real world problems by geometric sequences. (Lesson 8-3)*

86. The height reached by a bouncing ball on successive bounces generates a geometric sequence. Suppose a ball reaches heights in cm of 120, 96, and 76.8 on its first three bounces. How high will the ball reach on:
   a. the next bounce? ≈61.4 cm
   b. the 10th bounce? ≈16.1 cm
   c. the nth bounce? $h_n = 120(.8)^{n-1}$

87. A copying machine is set to reduce linear dimensions by 95%. If an 8 in. by 10 in. original is reduced five times, what will be its dimensions? ≈6.2 in. × 7.7 in.

88. A vacuum pump removes 10% of the air from a chamber with each stroke.
   a. Find a formula for P_n, the percent of air that remains in the chamber after the nth stroke. $P_n = P(.90)^{n-1}$
   b. How many strokes must be taken to remove 75% of the air in the chamber? ≈14.16 strokes

REPRESENTATIONS deal with pictures, graphs, or objects that illustrate concepts.

There are no representation objectives in this chapter.

EVALUATION
Three tests are provided for this chapter in the Teacher's Resource File. Chapter 8 Test, Forms A and B cover just Chapter 8. The third test is Chapter 8 Test, Cumulative Form. About 50% of this test covers Chapter 8, 25% covers Chapter 7, and 25% covers previous chapters. For information on grading, see *General Teaching Suggestions: Grading* on page T44 in the Teacher's Edition.

ASSIGNMENT RECOMMENDATION
We strongly recommend that you assign Lesson 9-1, both reading and some questions, for homework the evening of the test.

CHAPTER 9 ■ EXPONENTS AND LOGARITHMS

DAILY PACING CHART ■ CHAPTER 9

Students in the Full Course should complete all but one of the chapters by the end of the year. Students in the Minimal Course will spend more time on quizzes and the Chapter Review. As such, these students should complete about ten or eleven chapters.

DAY	MINIMAL COURSE	FULL COURSE
1	9-1	9-1
2	9-2	9-2
3	9-3	9-3
4	Quiz (TRF); Start 9-4.	Quiz (TRF); 9-4
5	Finish 9-4.	9-5
6	9-5	9-6
7	9-6	9-7
8	9-7	Quiz (TRF); 9-8
9	Quiz (TRF); Start 9-8.	9-9
10	Finish 9-8.	Progress Self-Test
11	9-9	Chapter Review
12	Progress Self-Test	Chapter Test (TRF)
13	Chapter Review	Comprehensive Test (TRF)
14	Chapter Review	
15	Chapter Test (TRF)	
16	Comprehensive Test (TRF)	

TESTING OPTIONS

■ Quiz for Lessons 9-1 Through 9-3   ■ Chapter 9 Test, Form A   ■ Chapter 9 Test, Cumulative Form
■ Quiz for Lessons 9-4 Through 9-7   ■ Chapter 9 Test, Form B   ■ Comprehensive Test, Chapters 1-9

PROVIDING FOR INDIVIDUAL DIFFERENCES

The student text is written for the *average* student. The program, however, can be adapted for both less capable and for more capable students.

A blackline master (in the Teacher's Resource File) is provided for each lesson for those students who need more practice. The Teacher's Edition frequently provides Error Analysis and Alternate Approach features to provide additional instructional strategies.

For students who require additional challenge, Extension activities are regularly provided in the Teacher's Edition.

OBJECTIVES ■ CHAPTER 9

Students should master the chapter objectives by the time they complete the chapter. To ensure objective mastery, there is continual review built into each set of lesson questions. After students complete the chapter lessons, they assess their mastery on the Progress Self-Test. Then they do the Chapter Review and pay special attention to those questions that match the objectives missed on the Progress Self-Test. Students can get extra practice on these objectives by using the master for each lesson in the Teacher's Resource File.

OBJECTIVES FOR CHAPTER 9 (Organized into the SPUR categories—Skills, Properties, Uses, and Representations)	Progress Self-Test Questions	Chapter Review Questions	Lesson Master from Teacher's Resource File*
SKILLS			
A Determine values of logarithms.	1–6	1 through 14	9-4, 9-5, 9-6, 9-8
B Solve exponential equations.	7, 10	15 through 22	9-9
C Solve logarithmic equations.	8–9	23 through 30	9-4, 9-5, 9-6, 9-8
PROPERTIES			
D Apply the definition of logarithm.	11, 20d	31 through 38	9-4, 9-5, 9-8
E Identify properties of logarithms.	12–14	39 through 44	9-6, 9-8
F Recognize properties of exponential and logarithmic functions.	21	45 through 49	9-1, 9-2, 9-4, 9-5, 9-8
USES			
G Apply exponential models and formulas.	15–18	50 through 54	9-1, 9-2, 9-7, 9-9
H Apply logarithmic scales (Richter, pH, decibel), models, and formulas.	19	55 through 58	9-3, 9-4, 9-8
REPRESENTATIONS			
I Graph exponential functions.	24	59 through 62	9-1, 9-2, 9-7
J Graph logarithmic functions.	20, 22	63, 64	9-5, 9-8

* The masters are numbered to match the lessons.

OVERVIEW ■ CHAPTER 9

This chapter builds on students' knowledge of exponents and functions to develop competence in working with exponential and logarithmic functions. Unlike Chapter 8, which has virtually no work with graphs, this chapter has a strong representational strand.

The first two lessons of this chapter are devoted to exponential functions emphasizing both uses and representations.

The next three lessons develop the meanings for the word logarithm. Lesson 9-3 introduces logarithmic scales; Lesson 9-4 covers logarithms to base 10; and Lesson 9-5 presents logarithms to other bases.

In Lesson 9-6, some important properties about the logarithms of products, powers, and quotients are derived. Lesson 9-7 introduces the constant e, and Lesson 9-8 develops logarithms to the base e. In Lesson 9-9, students use both common and natural logarithms and the theorems from Lesson 9-6 to solve exponential equations.

This textbook does not use logarithms for computation, and there are no log tables in the book. With the widespread availability of scientific calculators, using logarithms to calculate complicated products, quotients, powers, or roots is now obsolete.

However, logarithms *per se* are not obsolete. As indicated in this chapter, they are used in many equations which model real-world phenomena, and they are used to solve exponential equations.

PERSPECTIVES ■ CHAPTER 9

The Perspectives provide the rationale for the inclusion of topics or approaches, provide mathematical background, and make connections within UCSMP.

9-1

EXPONENTIAL GROWTH

Students are familiar with some examples of exponential functions from their work in Chapter 8. The formulas $a_n = a_1 r^{n-1}$ for the nth term of a geometric sequence and $A = P(1 + r)^t$ for compound interest are each of the form $y = ab^x$.

The major ideas in this lesson are the graphing of exponential functions and their *monotonicity*, namely that if x is between m and n, then a^x is between a^m and a^n. This property enables values of a^x to be calculated between any two other values and insures that the exponential curve does not have waves.

9-2

EXPONENTIAL DECAY

This lesson deals with the exponential growth model $a \cdot b^x$ when $0 < b < 1$ (the result is decay). The goal of the lesson is to have students realize that the growth factor determines growth or decay just as the slope of a line determines increase or decrease.

Students who have studied UCSMP *Algebra* have seen this content before but have not been taught how to calculate powers for the noninteger exponents directly.

Linear increase or decrease and exponential growth or decay are mathematically *isomorphic*; that is, they have the same structure. The former is related to addition and the latter is related to multiplication. Zero is the pivot in linear increase or decrease; a slope greater than 0 means increase, whereas a slope less than 0 means decrease. Similarly, 1 is the pivot in exponential growth or decay; a growth factor greater than 1 means growth, whereas a growth factor less than 1 means decay. Note that b must be positive in order for us to apply properties of real exponents.

9-3

LOGARITHMIC SCALES

This is the first of three lessons that develop basic concepts about logarithms. As an introductory lesson, it is unusual, for it focuses on a topic that is not typically taught at this level.

The main objective of this lesson is that students be able to read and interpret logarithmic scales. The logarithmic scales (decibel, pH, Richter) which are part of this and subsequent lessons are so common that familiarity with these uses of mathematics is also an objective for the chapter. Students are generally quite interested in knowing about these scales.

9-4

COMMON LOGARITHMS

The content of this lesson is traditional, with the exception that calculators are used instead of tables. Common logarithms are introduced before a general definition is given, since students have more experience with powers of 10 than with other numbers.

Logarithms to the base 10 are used often; therefore, scientific calculators have a key for common logarithms but not for logarithms to other integer bases.

9-5

LOGARITHMS TO BASES OTHER THAN 10

In many ways, this lesson mirrors Lesson 9-4. The objectives are essentially the same, except that they have been extended to cover logarithms to any base.

Only integer bases are used, because the use of other bases is rare. Specifically, bases other than base 10, base 2, and base e are seldom used.

However, the properties of logarithms hold for any base, and it is just as easy to introduce all bases as it would be to focus on special cases. Also, introducing all bases provides an alternate approach to the solving of equations of the form $a^x = b$ in Lesson 9-9.

9-6

PROPERTIES OF LOGARITHMS

Five properties of logarithms are introduced and practiced in this lesson. The major objective is to use these properties to assist in obtaining values of logarithmic functions and in solving equations. Using these properties to do computation is illustrated to give historical perspective only; it is not an objective.

Since logarithmic functions are inverses of exponential functions, properties of powers lead to properties of exponents. The correspondence is shown in the Chapter Summary on page 534.

9-7

THE NUMBER e

This lesson introduces students to the number e. They are expected

to understand that the constant e arises from a realistic context, in this case, the Continuously Compounded Interest Formula. In the next lesson, they will learn that e is often used as a base of logarithms.

The number e is important in mathematics for many reasons. For one, the exponential function $y = e^x$ has the property that it equals its derivative. (That is, the slope of the tangent to a point on the curve of $y = e^x$ equals the second coordinate of the point.) This makes it a most valuable function in solving differential equations.

Although it will not be covered in this book, students may be interested to learn that it is possible to take complex powers of numbers. The pure imaginary powers of e are particularly interesting:

$$e^{ix} = \cos x + i\sin x.$$

By letting $x = \pi$,
$$e^{i\pi} = \cos \pi + i\sin \pi = -1 + i \cdot 0.$$
This leads to the famous equation (discovered by Euler) $e^{i\pi} + 1 = 0$, connecting perhaps the five most important numbers in all of mathematics.

9-8

NATURAL LOGARITHMS

This lesson introduces e as a base of logarithms and so defines natural logarithms.

There are many objectives in this lesson, but all parallel what students have seen with logarithms to other bases. Students should realize that natural logarithms are simply a specific kind of logarithm, and thus they can use what they have learned about logarithmic functions in general to solve problems involving natural logarithms.

Base e logarithms have many useful properties that are important in higher mathematics. For example, the area under the curve $y = \frac{1}{x}$ between $x = 1$ and $x = p$, where p is any positive number, equals $\ln p$.

9-9

SOLVING $b^x = a$

When logarithms were first defined by Napier, and even when common logarithms were first invented by Briggs, they were not connected with exponents. At that time, the concept of a general real exponent had not been defined.

Euler first attached logarithms to exponents by considering them as the solutions to equations of the form $b^x = a$. He was the first to give the definition of logarithm we use today, namely that $b^x = a$ if and only if $x = \log_b a$.

In this lesson, we wish to solve equations of the form $b^x = a$. By definition, $x = \log_b a$ is the solution; however, without knowing what $b^x = a$ is, we cannot evaluate $\log_b a$ using its definition alone. Thus, we use the general properties of logarithms to reduce the solution to a ratio of two logarithms with a base of our choice. Then, we need only to know the values of logarithms to one base. As both natural logarithms and common logarithms can usually be evaluated or estimated on a calculator, we reduce solutions of $b^x = a$ to logarithms with these bases.

Exponents and Logarithms

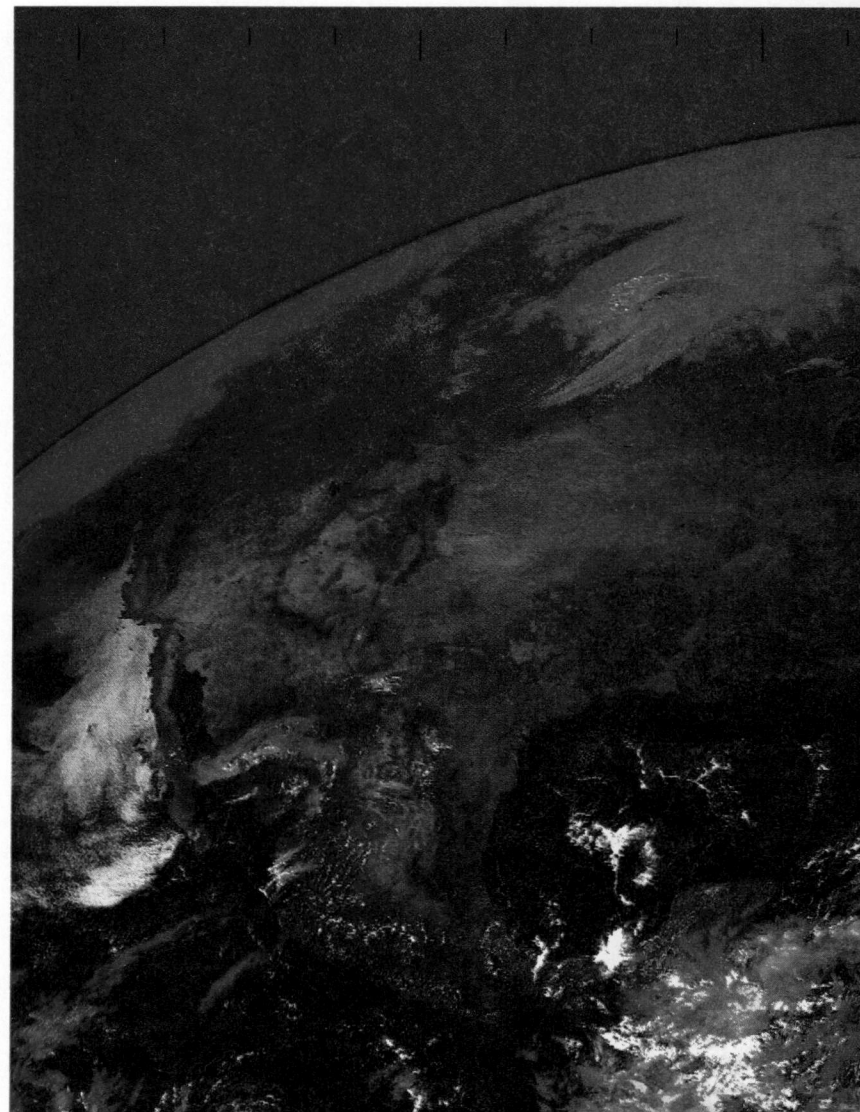

This weather-satellite picture was taken from an altitude of 35,800 km.

The bar graph below gives the U.S. population for each census from 1790 to 1980. The population P (in millions) is closely approximated by the equations

$$\begin{cases} P = 13(1.03)^{x-1830} & \text{for 1790–1860} \\ P = 63(1.02)^{x-1890} & \text{for 1870–1910} \\ P = 151(1.013)^{x-1950} & \text{for 1920–present,} \end{cases}$$

where x is the year of the census.

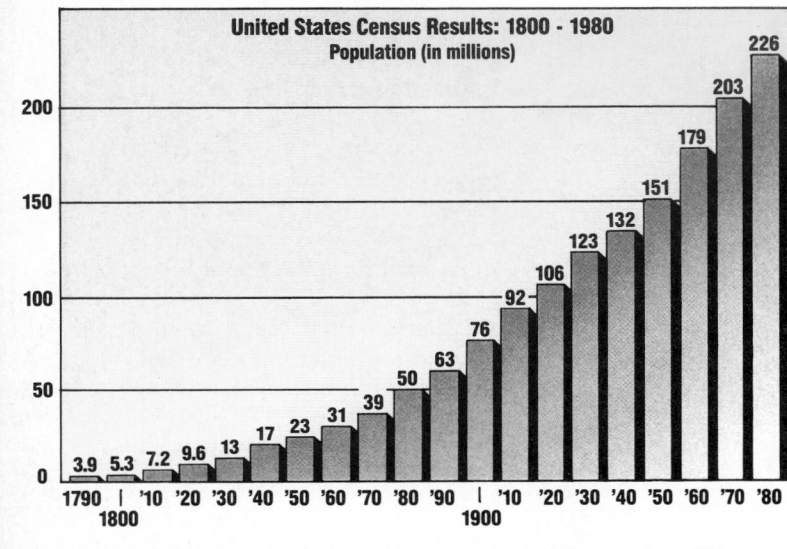

Each equation above represents an *exponential function*. We need several equations to estimate the population at different times because the yearly *growth factor* of the population of the United States has changed from about 1.03 to about 1.013 since 1790.

In this chapter you will learn about exponential functions and their inverses.

OBJECTIVES

F Recognize properties of exponential growth functions.
G Apply exponential models and formulas.
I Graph exponential functions with bases > 1.

TEACHING NOTES

Have students graph a simple exponential function such as $y = 3^x$. Students are likely to find ordered pairs by using positive integers for values of x. Remind them that they have also studied zero and nonpositive integral exponents and rational exponents in Chapter 8. Suggest using $x = 0, -1, -2, \frac{1}{2}, 2.5$. Then compare the graph of the exponential function with that of the U.S. population on page 487. The similarity is quite evident. The graph of the equation modeling the bacteria growth on page 489 provides still another example.

LESSON 9-1

Exponential Growth

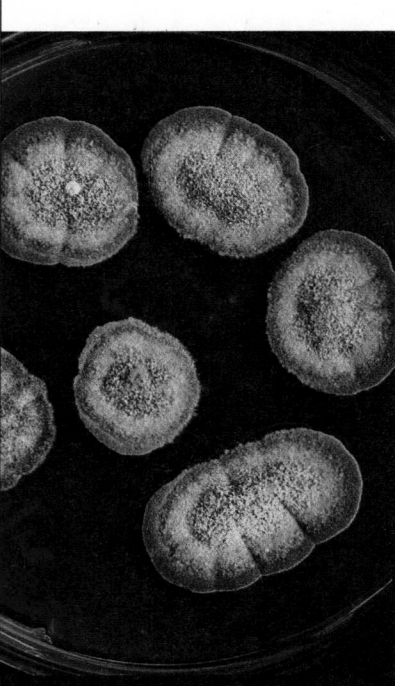

Growing on agar are colonies of fungus Aspergillus fumigatus.

488

Consider an experiment that begins with 300 bacteria. Bacteria can quickly increase in number. Let us suppose that the population doubles every hour.

Here is the population y after x hours for $x = 0, 1, 2,$ and 3.

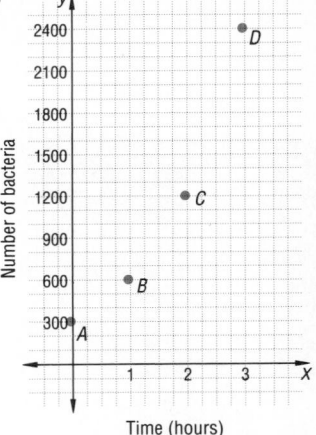

x	0	1	2	3
y	300	600	1200	2400
point	A	B	C	D

The points for these values are graphed at the right.

The table shows that as x takes on integer values increasing by 1, the values of y form a geometric sequence with constant ratio 2. A formula for this sequence is $y = 300 \cdot 2^x$.

Of course, the bacteria population does not double all at once. Using fractions as exponents, you can estimate the population at intermediate times. For instance, after half an hour $y = 300 \cdot 2^{1/2} \approx 424$. Here are other approximate values at some intermediate times.

x	.25	.5	.8	1.4	2.6
y	357	424	522	792	1819

Check these values on your calculator.

You can also find population values *before* the experiment started. For instance, an hour before the experiment began, $x = -1$, so $y = 300 \cdot 2^{-1} = 150$.

Here are other earlier values.

x	-1	-1.5	-2
y	150	106	75

At the right is the graph with values from all three tables of values included. The graph looks like it would be a continuous curve if you filled in all the gaps. Intermediate rational values of x produce intermediate values of y.

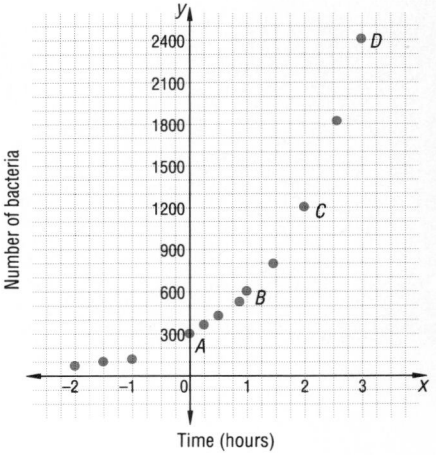

The same is true for irrational values of x. For instance, the value
$$x = \sqrt{5} \text{ yields } y = 300 \cdot 2^{\sqrt{5}}.$$

To approximate y, first approximate $\sqrt{5}$, which as a decimal is 2.236067977.... If you approximate $\sqrt{5}$ by 2.2, then
$$y = 300 \cdot 2^{2.2} \approx 1378.$$

This y-value is less than $300 \cdot 2^{\sqrt{5}}$. If you use 2.24 for $\sqrt{5}$,
$$y = 300 \cdot 2^{2.24} \approx 1417.$$

This y-value is more than $300 \cdot 2^{\sqrt{5}}$. If you use 2.236067 for x,
$$y = 300 \cdot 2^{2.236067} \approx 1413.3329\ldots .$$

If you use 2.236068 for x
$$y = 300 \cdot 2^{2.236068} \approx 1413.3339\ldots .$$

Thus $300 \cdot 2^{\sqrt{5}} \approx 1413.33\ldots .$

By extending this reasoning for other irrational values of x, you can think of the graph as having points for all real values of x.

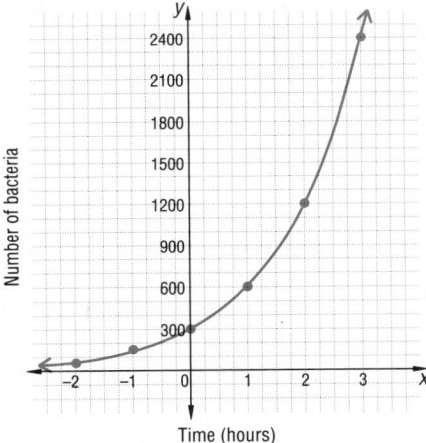

Time (hours)

The completed graph of $y = 300 \cdot 2^x$ is shown above. The graph is called an **exponential curve**. The shape of an exponential curve is different from the shape of a parabola or an arc of a circle.

In the discussion of the equation $y = ab^x$, point out the restrictions on the value of b. We need $b > 0$, so that we can apply the properties of real exponents. We need $b \neq 1$, so that exponential growth is just what the name implies. If b were allowed to equal 1, the equation $y = ab^x$ would be equivalent to $y = a \cdot 1^x = a$, which is a constant function.

Making Connections
You can use **Example 2** to lead into the problem of predicting when the population will reach a certain level. To find such an answer would involve solving the exponential equation $y = ab^x$ for x, which we cannot do at this point. Students *will* be able to solve this type of equation before the end of the chapter. Inform them that this is one of the major purposes of logarithms.

ADDITIONAL EXAMPLES

1. The Consumer Price Index (CPI) measures the cost of goods and services. Between 1967 and 1977, the CPI rose exponentially at an average rate of 6.3% per year.
a. Write an exponential function that models this data, starting with $100 in 1967. Let x = number of years after 1967, and let y = the CPI.
$y = 100(1.063)^x$
b. Estimate what the same goods and services cost in 1988.
$CPI = 100(1.063)^{21} \approx \$361$

2. The world population in 1985 was 4.9 billion. At the growth rate of the time, the population would double every 35 years.
a. Write an exponential equation modeling this situation. Let x equal the number of 35-year periods after 1985, and let p equal the population in billions.
$p = 4.9 \cdot 2^x$
b. With this model, what will be the world's population in the year 2000?
$p = 4.9 \cdot 2^{15/35} \approx 6.6$. The population will be about 6.6 billion.
c. What was the population in 1980, assuming the same growth factor?
$p = 4.9 \cdot 2^{-5/35} \approx 4.4$. The population was approximately 4.4 billion.

■ ■ ■ ■ ■ ■ ■ ■

Example 1 Use the exponential curve above to estimate:
  a. the number of bacteria after 20 minutes;
  b. the time when 1500 bacteria were present.

Solution **a.** 20 minutes = $\frac{1}{3}$ hour. On the graph, when $x = \frac{1}{3}$, y is a bit under 400. At 20 minutes there were a little less than 400 bacteria.
  b. When $y = 1500$, $x \approx 2\frac{1}{4}$, so there were 1500 bacteria after about 2 hours, 15 minutes.

Check **a.** Substitute $x = \frac{1}{3}$ into the equation $y = 300 \cdot 2^x$ to get $y \approx 378$.
  b. Substitute $x = 2.25$ into $y = 300 \cdot 2^x$. You get $y \approx 1427$, so it checks.

The equation $y = 300 \cdot 2^x$ is of the form $y = ab^x$ and defines a function in which the independent variable x is in the exponent. Such a function is called an **exponential function**. In the exponential function $f(x) = ab^x$, b is the **growth factor**, the amount by which y is multiplied for every unit increase in x. The y-intercept $f(0)$ is equal to a. When $b > 1$, the situation is one of **exponential growth**.

The compound-interest formula $A = P(1 + r)^t$ defines an exponential function when P and r are fixed. Then t is the independent variable, $A = f(t)$ is the dependent variable, and $1 + r$ is the growth factor. The explicit formula for any geometric sequence $a_n = a_1 r^{n-1}$ also defines an exponential function with n as the independent variable, a_n as the dependent variable, and r as the growth factor.

As we noted earlier, populations can grow exponentially over short periods of time. This relationship can be used to predict future populations, an important consideration in planning or building schools, roads, airports, and other public facilities. To predict what the U.S. population will be in the year 2000, we might first examine recent censuses.

Year	Population	Decade Growth Factor
1920	106,020,000	
1930	123,200,000	1.162
1940	132,160,000	1.073
1950	151,330,000	1.145
1960	179,320,000	1.185
1970	203,300,000	1.134
1980	226,540,000	1.114

The *decade* growth factor for 1930 is $\frac{123,200,000}{106,020,000}$ or approximately 1.162, indicating a 16.2% population increase from 1920 to 1930.

490

The *yearly* growth factor is the 10th root of the decade growth factor, $\sqrt[10]{1.162}$ or about 1.015, indicating a mean yearly population increase of about 1.5%. Over the sixty-year period the mean yearly increase was a little under 1.3%, corresponding to a growth factor of 1.013.

Let the exponent x be the year. We will start from 1950, the middle of this period. If we take 1.013 as the growth factor and 151 (in millions) as the population in 1950, a good approximation to the U.S. population y (in millions) since 1920 is

$$y = 151 \cdot (1.013)^{x-1950}$$

This is the equation given on the opening pages of the chapter.

Example 2   Use $y = 151 \cdot (1.013)^{x-1950}$ to predict the U.S. population (a) in 1990 and (b) in 2000.

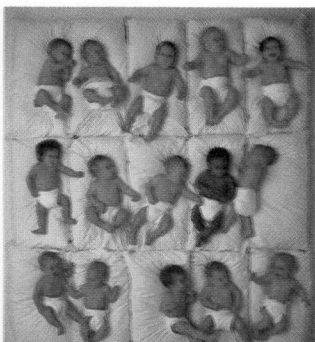

Solution   With a calculator, the computation is straightforward.
a. For 1990: $y = 151 \cdot (1.013)^{1990-1950} = 151 \cdot (1.013)^{40} \approx$ 253,000,000
b. For 2000: $y = 151 \cdot (1.013)^{2000-1950} = 151 \cdot (1.013)^{50} \approx$ 288,000,000
Because the growth factor has been declining, these figures are likely to be high, but probably not by much.

It is natural to wonder when the population will reach 400 million or some other number. If population grows exponentially, that problem requires solving the exponential equation $y = ab^x$ for x. We examine this equation in depth beginning in Lesson 9-3 after we have looked at examples of exponential functions in which the growth factor is less than one.

Questions

Covering the Reading

In 1–3, refer to the bacteria experiment at the beginning of the lesson.
1. How many bacteria are there after 4 hours?   **4800**

2. What does $x = -1.5$ mean in terms of the experiment?
   106 bacteria $1\frac{1}{2}$ hr before the experiment
3. Use the exponential curve to estimate:
   a. the number of bacteria after 1.75 hours;   **1000 bacteria**
   b. when 1700 bacteria were present.   **after about $2\frac{1}{2}$ hr**

4. *True or false* Because $\sqrt{7}$ is between 2.64 and 2.65, $2^{2.64} < 2^{\sqrt{7}} < 2^{2.65}$.   **true**

LESSON 9-1   Exponential Growth   **491**

NOTES ON QUESTIONS
Questions 10 and 11: Students with access to an automatic grapher can confirm their choices in these questions by graphing each equation.

Question 14: The question can be answered by using the result of **Question 13** and the decade growth factor on page 490, or equivalently by solving $203(1 + r)^{10} = 226$, using the technique studied in Lesson 8-11.

Questions 16, 24, and 25: For an excellent source of current data on population growth and an analysis of the effects of various growth rates on the standard of living in Kenya, China, Hungary, India, Brazil, and the U.S., see "Population, Plenty, and Poverty" by Paul and Anne Ehrlich (*National Geographic*, Vol. 174, No. 6, December 1988, pages 914–945).

Question 16: The equation in this question, $y = 18.5(1.041)^{x-1983}$, where x represents the year in question, could have been written as $y = 18.5(1.041)^a$, where a represents the number of years after 1983. If a is negative, it represents years before 1983. The advantage of the first equation is that the year itself is used in the equation, and another variable does not need to be defined.

Question 17: To answer part (c), students are expected to use trial and error or the zoom or rescale features on an automatic grapher. In Lesson 9-9, they will learn an algebraic algorithm for solving such equations.

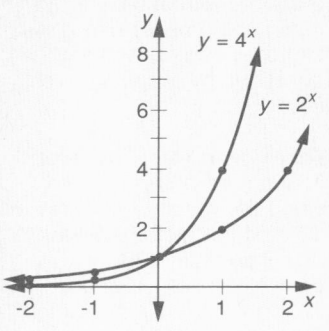

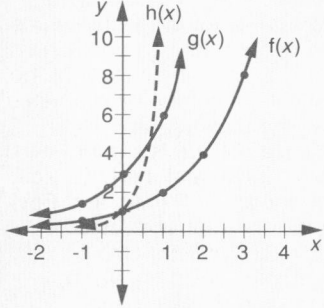

5. Use your calculator to evaluate each power.
   a. $2^{1.73}$ 3.317   b. $2^{1.74}$ 3.340   c. $2^{\sqrt{3}}$ 3.322

6. Define: exponential function.
   a function with the independent variable as exponent

7. In an exponential function, for each unit increase in the __?__ variable,
   the __?__ variable is __?__ by a constant growth factor.
   independent; dependent; multiplied

In 8 and 9, refer to the standard equation for an exponential model
$y = ab^x$.

8. The initial value of y is __?__.   **a**

9. The constant growth factor is __?__ for each unit of __?__.   **b; x**

In 10 and 11, *multiple choice*

10. Which equation has a graph that is an exponential curve?   **c**
    (a) $y = 2x + 5$ (b) $y = x^2 + 5$
    (c) $y = 2.5^x$ (d) $y = 2x^5$

11. Which of the following is an equation for an exponential function?   **c**
    (a) $y = 3x$ (b) $y = x^3$
    (c) $y = 3^x$ (d) $y = 3x^{1/3}$

Applying the Mathematics

12. a. Graph $y = 2^x$.   **See margin.**
    b. On the same axes, graph $y = 4^x$.   **See margin.**
    c. Where do the graphs in (a) and (b) intersect?

In 13–15, refer to the U.S. population data given in this lesson.

13. a. Suppose the yearly growth factor for all years in a decade is y.
       What is the decade growth factor?   **y^{10}**
    b. Suppose the decade growth factor is d. What is the yearly growth
       factor?   **$\sqrt[10]{d}$**

14. What was the yearly growth rate of the U.S. population from 1970 to
    1980?   **1.011**

15. a. Examine the formula for the years 1790–1860. By what percent
       was the population growing each year?   **3%**
    b. What would the 1980 population have been if the population had
       kept growing by the 1790–1860 rate?   **1.095 billion**

    16. a) $18.5(1.041)^{x-1983}$

16. In 1983 Kenya was the fastest growing nation on Earth. Its population
    was 18.5 million people and its yearly growth rate was about 4.1%.
    a. Write an equation expressing Kenya's population y in the year x.
    b. Project Kenya's population for the year 2015 if the growth rate
       remains the same.   **66.93 million**
    c. Under this model, what was Kenya's population in 1976?
       13.96 million

17. Let $f(x) = 2^x$, $g(x) = 3 \cdot 2^x$, and $h(x) = 10^x$.
    a. Graph f,g, and h on the same set of axes.   **See margin.**
    b. For what value(s) of x does $f(x) = h(x)$?   **0**
    c. For what value(s) of x does $g(x) = h(x)$?   **≈ .68**
    d. Write two or three sentences describing properties of all exponen-
       tial growth functions.   **See margin.**

492

18. Suppose you invest $400 in a bank that pays 6% interest compounded annually. Your money is left in the bank for 18 months. *(Lesson 8-4)*
a. Write the expression representing your final balance. $400(1.06)^{1.5}$
b. Calculate the balance. $436.53

In 19 and 20, (a) state whether the sequence is arithmetic, geometric, or neither; (b) write an explicit formula for the sequence; (c) write a recursive formula for the sequence. *(Lessons 3-6, 3-7, 8-3)*

19. 100, 90, 81, 72.9, 65.61, ...   See margin.

20. 100, 91, 82, 73, 64, ...   See margin.

21. Find an equation for H^{-1} when $H(x) = x^3$. *(Lesson 7-6)* $H^{-1}(x) = \sqrt[3]{x}$

22. This program calculates postage for first class mail (1988 prices). What will be printed if 4.5 ounces is input for W? *(Lesson 7-4)*
The postage for your letter is 1.05.

```
10 INPUT "WEIGHT OF A FIRST CLASS LETTER"; W
20 P = .25 − .20 ∗ INT(1 − W)
30 PRINT "THE POSTAGE FOR YOUR LETTER IS";P
40 END
```

23. A teacher finds that her grades are low and need to be rescaled. A 100 will remain a 100, but a 65 will become an 80. $y - 100 = \frac{4}{7}(x - 100)$
a. If the rescaling is linear, find a relationship between the new score y and the old score x. (Hint: write the scores as ordered pairs.)
b. What will an old score of 51 become? *(Lesson 3-5)*   72

24. For what reasons may a population's growth rate decrease? increase? Which of these factors were present in the United States between 1920 and 1980?   See margin.

25. China and India are the two most populous countries in the world. Find an estimate for the current population and growth rate in each country. Use these figures to estimate what their populations will be in the year 2000.   See margin.

26. Graph the population equations on the first page of this chapter using a function grapher or graphing calculator. For what year do these equations most poorly model the population?   See margin.

FOLLOW-UP

MORE PRACTICE
For more questions on SPUR Objectives, use *Lesson Master 9-1*, shown below.

24. sample: Rate of population decrease is associated with a country's industrialization and greater wealth. Population increase may be due to immigration, advances in medical and nutritional knowledge, better sanitary conditions, and so on. All of the changes listed were present in U.S. between 1800–1980.

25. sample: China: 1988 population ≈ 1,087,000,000; annual growth rate ≈ 1.4%. **India:** 1988 population ≈ 816,800,000; annual growth rate ≈ 1.9%.

26. The equations are good models in the middle of each of the three ranges, but not so good at the extremes of each range.

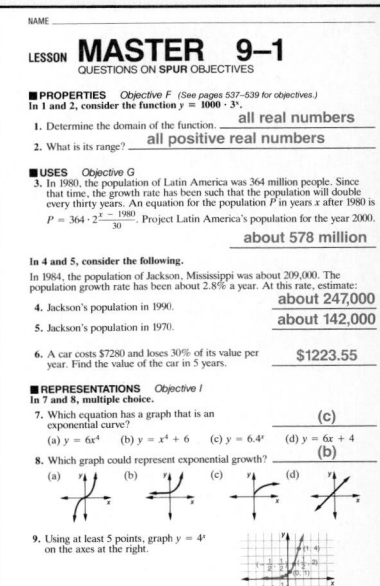

NAME

LESSON **MASTER 9–1**
QUESTIONS ON **SPUR** OBJECTIVES

■ **PROPERTIES**   *Objective F (See pages 537–539 for objectives.)*
In 1 and 2, consider the function $y = 1000 \cdot 3^x$.
1. Determine the domain of the function.   all real numbers
2. What is its range?   all positive real numbers

■ **USES**   *Objective G*
3. In 1980, the population of Latin America was 364 million people. Since that time, the growth rate has been such that the population will double every thirty years. An equation for the population P in years x after 1980 is $P = 364 \cdot 2^{\frac{x - 1980}{30}}$. Project Latin America's population for the year 2000.   about 578 million

In 4 and 5, consider the following.
In 1984, the population of Jackson, Mississippi was about 209,000. The population growth rate has been about 2.8% a year. At this rate, estimate:
4. Jackson's population in 1990.   about 247,000
5. Jackson's population in 1970.   about 142,000

6. A car costs $7280 and loses 30% of its value per year. Find the value of the car in 5 years. $1223.55

■ **REPRESENTATIONS**   *Objective I*
In 7 and 8, multiple choice.
7. Which equation has a graph that is an exponential curve?   (c)
(a) $y = 6x^4$ (b) $y = x^4 + 6$ (c) $y = 6 \cdot 4^x$ (d) $y = 6x + 4$
8. Which graph could represent exponential growth?   (b)
(a)   (b)   (c)   (d)

9. Using at least 5 points, graph $y = 4^x$ on the axes at the right.

Advanced Algebra © Scott, Foresman and Company   95

LESSON 9-2

Exponential Decay

1988 Trans Am Firebird

In Lesson 9-1, the populations studied were increasing, so the constant growth factor is greater than one. Sometimes a growth factor is less than one. When this is true, the value of the function decreases over time. These situations are sometimes called **exponential decay** or **depreciation**.

Example 1 A Trans Am Firebird cost $6490 new in 1978. Suppose its value decreased exponentially and that the car depreciated 44% during its first 7 years.
a. What equation models its value?
b. Find the car's value in 1988.

Solution **a.** Because the car is depreciating in value by a constant factor, the situation can be modeled by an exponential function with equation $y = ab^x$. Here y is the value of the car; a is the original value, 6490; $b = 0.56$ (depreciating by 44% means the growth factor is $1 - .44 = 0.56$); and x is the number of 7-year intervals after 1978. Thus an equation modeling the value is

$$y = 6490(0.56)^x.$$

b. The year 1988 is 10 years after 1978. This is $\frac{10}{7}$ of a 7-year interval.

$$x = \frac{10}{7}.$$
$$y = 6490(0.56)^x$$
$$y = 6490(0.56)^{10/7}$$
$$y \approx 2835.$$

In 1988 the Trans Am was worth approximately $2835.

Example 2 Radioactive carbon-14 (C_{14}) decays exponentially. In 5730 years, half of the original amount decays (5730 is called the **half-life** of C_{14}) and half remains. Suppose you start with a sample that has 100 g of C_{14}. For this situation determine:

a. an equation for the amount of C_{14} remaining in the original sample, and

b. the graph for the equation.

Solution **a.** Since half remains in a fixed time period, $b = \frac{1}{2}$ or 0.5. Here the initial amount is 100 g. Use the exponential equation $y = ab^x$, with $a = 100$ and $b = 0.5$. The equation is

$$y = 100(0.5)^x,$$

where x is the number of 5730-year intervals.

b. Evaluate y for various values of x, plot these points, and sketch the curve. The completed graph is shown below.

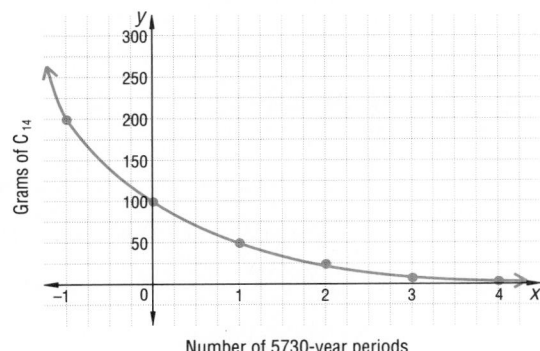

Number of 5730-year periods

x	-1	0	1	2	3	4
y	200	100	50	25	12.5	6.25

Notice that 5730 years before the time the amount of C_{14} was measured, there would have been 200 g of C_{14} in the sample. In 11,460 years after the measurement (when $x = 2$), only 25 g would be left.

These examples of growth and decay fit a general model called the **exponential growth model**.

Exponential growth model:

If a quantity a grows by a factor b in each unit period, then after a period of length x, there will be ab^x of the quantity.

LESSON 9-2 Exponential Decay **495**

ADDITIONAL EXAMPLES

2. Experimentation and theory have shown that at altitudes of less than 80 km, standard atmospheric pressure (1035 g/cm²) is halved for each 5.8 km of vertical ascent.

a. Describe the relationship between altitude x and pressure y.

$y = 1035(\frac{1}{2})^x$, **where x is the number of 5.8 km units above sea level.**

$y = 1035(2^{-1})^x = 1035 \cdot 2^{-x}$ **are alternate answers.**

If x is the altitude (in km), then $y \approx 1035(\frac{1}{2})^{x/5.8}$.

b. Find the atmospheric pressure at an altitude of 40 km.

$y \approx 1035(\frac{1}{2})^{40/5.8}$, **so** $y \approx 8.7$ **g/cm².**

NOTES ON QUESTIONS

Question 10: Note that the table in part (b) can be completed without using the equation by starting at $x = 0$, $y = 20$, and then successively doubling or halving y for each decrease or increase of one in the x value. Regardless of which of part (a) or (b) is done first, have students use the answer to the other part as a check. To increase the accuracy of the estimate in part (d), the graph also can be drawn with an automatic grapher.

Question 12: You might want to note that the value of the car will become zero in 10 years under the linear depreciation model. Theoretically, the car will always have some value using the exponential model. However, for tax reasons, linear depreciation is often used.

Question 13: This question is here for two reasons: (1) to give you an opportunity to point out that in exponential models, the coefficient a may equal one (contrast this with the restriction that $b \neq 1$); and (2) to review the exponential curve $y = 10^x$ that generates the common logarithm function introduced in the next lesson.

When the growth factor b is less than 1, the value of $y = ab^x$ decreases as x increases and so the graph of $y = ab^x$ goes down to the right. Decay curves have the same shape as in exponential growth; they are reflection images of growth curves over the y-axis.

By looking at the graphs of the exponential functions $y = ab^x$ in this and the previous lesson, you should observe several properties.

1. The domain of each function is the real numbers.
2. The graph never crosses the x-axis; exponential curves have no x-intercepts.
3. Each graph has a y-intercept a, where a is the value of the function.
4. The range of each function is the positive real numbers.
5. In one of its two quadrants, the graph gets closer and closer to the x-axis. The x-axis is an asymptote of the graph.
6. When the constant growth factor b is greater than one, as in Lesson 9-1, the graph is increasing. However, if $0 < b < 1$, as in Example 2 above, the graph is decreasing.

Questions

Covering the Reading

1. If $y = ab^x$ and $0 < b < 1$, then y _?_ as x increases. decreases

2. *Multiple choice* Which equation represents exponential decay? d

(a) $f(x) = \frac{1}{3}x$ (b) $f(x) = \sqrt[3]{x}$
(c) $f(x) = 3^x$ (d) $f(x) = (\frac{1}{3})^x$

3. Refer to Example 1. If you assume that the depreciation model continues to be valid, what would the Firebird be worth in 1992? $2035

4. If an item decreases in value by 10% each year, what is the yearly growth factor? 0.9

In 5–7, refer to Example 2.

5. What does the term "half-life" mean?
the period of time in which half the material decays

6. Find how much C_{14} remains after 17,190 years. 12.5 g

7. Find how much C_{14} existed 1910 years before the 100 g were measured. 126 g

8. *True or false*

a. Unless specifically stated, there are no restrictions on the domain of an exponential function. true

b. The y-axis is an asymptote for an exponential curve. false

496

9. *Multiple choice* Which graph could represent exponential decay? **a**

(a)

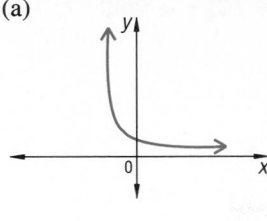

(b)

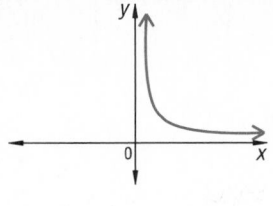

(c)

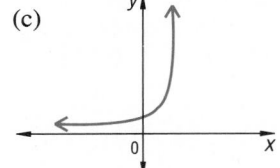

(d)

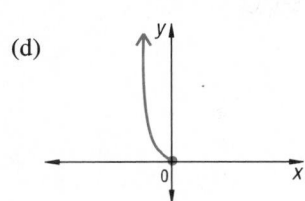

Nuclear-energy technician

10. The half-life of iodine-123 (I_{123}) is about 13 hours. Suppose you begin with a sample of 20 grams.
  a. Write an equation to model the decay. $y = 20(.5)^x$, where x represents 13-hour intervals
  b. Copy and complete the table below.
  (-2, 80); (-1, 40); (0, 20); (1, 10); (2, 5); (3, 2.5)

$x = $ number of 13-hour periods	-2	-1	0	1	2	3
$y = $ amount of I_{123}						

  c. Plot these points and graph the function. **See margin.**
  d. Use the graph to estimate the number of hours needed for 20 g to decay to 4 g. $\approx$ 2.3 13-hr intervals $\approx$ 30 hr

11. a. Graph $y = 3^x$ for values of x between -4 and 4. **See margin.**
  b. Graph $y = (\frac{1}{3})^x$ for values of x between -4 and 4, on the same axes. **See margin.**
  c. The graphs in parts a and b are related to each other. How are they related, and why are they so related? **See margin.**

12. Suppose a car costs $10,000 and loses value every year. Let N be its value after t years.
  a. Assume the depreciation is exponential, with 20% of the value lost per year. Then $N = 10,000(0.8)^t$.
  Complete a table like this one. (1, 8000); (2, 6400); (3, 5120)

t	1	2	3
N			

  b. Assume the depreciation is linear with $1000 lost per year. Then $N = 10,000 - 1000t$. Fill in a table. (1, 9000); (2, 8000); (3, 7000)

t	1	2	3
N			

  c. If this were your car and you were trading it in after 4 years, explain why you would probably prefer that the car dealer assumed the model of part b. **See margin.**
  d. Under what circumstances would you prefer that the dealer assume the model in part a? Justify your answer using tables or graphs. **See margin.**

LESSON 9-2 Exponential Decay   **497**

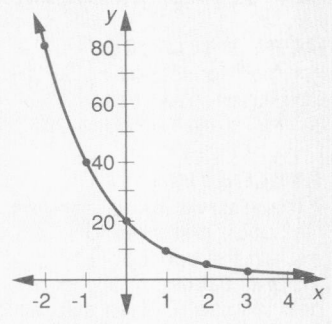
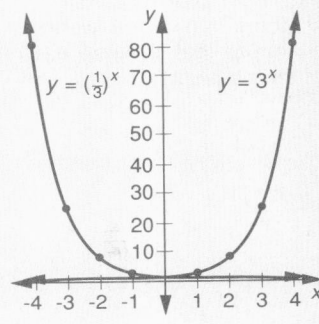
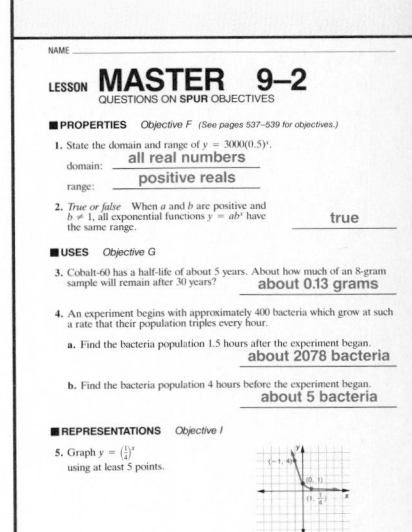

ADDITIONAL ANSWERS
20.a.

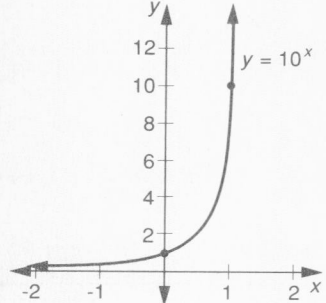

i. If $10^x = 3$, then $x \approx .478$.
$10^{-.478} \approx \frac{1}{3}$
ii. If $10^x = 2$, then $x \approx .301$.
$10^{-.301} \approx \frac{1}{2}$
b. $a^x = y$ implies $a^{-x} = \frac{1}{y}$.

Review

13. Use the graph at the right. *(Lesson 9-1)*

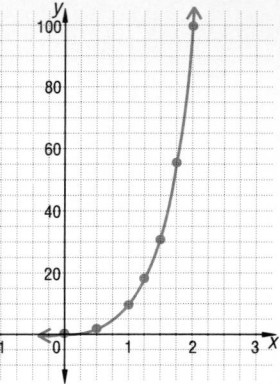

   a. When $x = \underline{\ ?\ }$, $y = 100$.   **2**
   b. *Multiple choice* An equation
      for the graph could be   **iii**
      (i) $y = 10x$.
      (ii) $y = 10 + x$.
      (iii) $y = 10^x$.
      (iv) $y = (\frac{1}{10})^x$.
   c. The domain of the function
      is $\underline{\ ?\ }$.   **all real numbers**
   d. The range of the function
      is $\underline{\ ?\ }$.   **all positive numbers**

14. Suppose an experiment begins with 120 bacteria which double every
hour.   **960**
   a. About how many bacteria will there be after 3 hours? *(Lesson 8-3)*
   b. What is an equation for the number y of bacteria after x hours?
      (Lesson 9-1) $y = 120 \cdot 2^x$

15. Use the equation on the first page of this chapter to estimate the
U.S. population in 1995. *(Lesson 9-1)*   **about 270 million**

16. Give a decimal approximation to the nearest hundredth. *(Lessons 8-6, 9-1)*
   a. 4^3 **64**   **b.** $4^{7/2}$ **128**   **c.** $4^{\sqrt{10}}$ **80.15**

17. Explain why the answer to Question 16(c) should be between the
answers to 16(a) and 16(b). *(Lesson 9-1)* $\sqrt{10}$ **is between 3 and 3.5**

18. Write as a decimal. *(Lesson 8-6)*
   a. $10^{10.8}$ **63,095,734,450**
   b. $10^{8.4}$ **251,886,431**
   c. $\frac{10^{10.8}}{10^{8.4}}$ **251.19**

19. The inflation rate is typically reported monthly. Suppose a monthly
rate of 0.5% is reported for January. Assume this rate continues for
1 year. *(Lesson 8-2)*
   a. What is the inflation rate for the year?   **6.17%**
   b. The value 0.5% has been rounded. The actual value could be any
      number equal to or greater than 0.45%, and less than 0.55%.
      Write an inequality for r, the annual inflation rate, based on those
      two extreme values. $5.54 \le x \le 6.80$

Exploration

20. a. Graph $y = 10^x$ using a function plotter. Use the graph to estimate
      solutions to the following pairs of equations: **See margin.**
      (i) $10^x = 3$ and $10^x = \frac{1}{3}$
      (ii) $10^x = 2$ and $10^x = \frac{1}{2}$.
   b. What generalization have you verified?   **See margin.**

21. Consult a car dealer or books or magazines about automobiles. Find
out how automobile depreciation is typically calculated. Is automobile
depreciation described better by linear (Question 12(b)) or exponential
(Question 12(a)) models?   **Many answers are possible.**

498

Logarithmic Scales

Mexico City earthquake, 1985

LESSON 9-3

RESOURCES
■ Lesson Master 9-3
■ Quiz for Lessons 9-1
Through 9-3
◉ Visual for Teaching Aid 52
provides the table that
describes the effect of an
earthquake for Richter
scale values.
◉ Visual for Teaching Aid 53
provides the decibel scale.
◉ Visual for Teaching Aid 54
provides the pH scale.

An earthquake is the sudden release of energy in the form of vibrations caused by rock suddenly moving along a fault, which is an edge of the earth's crust. Perhaps 100,000 earthquakes that can be felt occur each year, and about 1,000 cause damage. This release can be measured in *joules*; the intensity of a destructive earthquake may be a million times the intensity of a minor tremor. A million is too wide a range to fit on a normal number line. So, instead, a scale based on *exponents* is used. The scale most widely reported in the United States is the **Richter scale,** named after Charles F. Richter (1900–1985), a seismologist at the California Institute of Technology, its inventor. The table below describes the effect of an earthquake of a particular Richter scale value magnitude at the epicenter, the place on the earth's surface above the location of the release of energy.

Richter magnitude	Description
1	cannot be felt except by instruments
2	cannot be felt except by instruments
3	cannot be felt except by instruments
4	like vibrations from a passing train
5	strong enough to wake sleepers
6	very strong; walls crack, people injured
7	ruinous; ground cracks, houses collapse
8	very disastrous; few buildings survive, landslides

An increase of 1 on the Richter scale roughly corresponds to a multiplication of the energy released by a factor of 10. Thus the energy released by an earthquake with Richter magnitude 6.4 is ten times that of an earthquake with magnitude 5.4. An increase of 2 corresponds to a multiplication of the energy by a factor of 100. This pattern is easily described algebraically; a value of x on the Richter scale corresponds to an energy release of $k \cdot 10^x$, where the constant k depends on the units being used.

OBJECTIVE

H Apply logarithmic scales
(Richter, pH, decibel),
models, and formulas.

TEACHING NOTES

To introduce this lesson,
bring in a radio with a dial.
On the AM scale, compare
the distance between 600
and 800 with the distance
between 1200 and 1400.
(They are not equal.) The radio scale is not linear. Point
out, however, that the distance between 600 and 800,
and the distance between
1200 and 1600 are equal.
The radio scale is an example of a logarithmic scale. A
logarithmic scale is one in
which equal distances
correspond to equal ratios of
the numbers on the scale.

Stress the difference between a linear and a logarithmic scale. A linear scale has
a common *difference* between successive units;
these units form an arithmetic sequence. A logarithmic scale, however, has a
common *ratio* between successive units; these units
form a geometric sequence.

■ ■ ■ ■ ■ ■ ■■

Example   An earthquake in Alaska in 1964 had a Richter magnitude of 8.6. The famous San Francisco earthquake of 1906 is estimated to have had a Richter magnitude of 8.3. How many times more intense was the Alaskan earthquake?

Solution   Divide the larger energy release by the smaller.

$$\frac{\text{Alaska energy release}}{\text{San Francisco energy release}} = \frac{k \cdot 10^{8.6}}{k \cdot 10^{8.3}} = 10^{0.3} \approx 2.0$$

The Alaskan earthquake was twice as intense. However, its epicenter was in an unpopulated area, and so damage from it, though substantial, was quite a bit less than the damage from the San Francisco earthquake.

The Richter scale is called an **exponential scale** or a **logarithmic scale** because it is calculated using exponents of numbers with the same base. The word *logarithm* literally means "ratio of numbers."

Another logarithmic scale describes the intensity of sound. The quietest sound that a human can hear has an intensity of about 10^{-12} watts per square meter (w/m^2). The human ear can also hear sounds with an intensity as large as 10^2 w/m^2. Because the range from 10^{-12} to 10^2 is so large, it is convenient to use another unit, the **decibel** (dB), to measure sound intensity. The decibel is $\frac{1}{10}$ of a **bel**, a unit named after Alexander Graham Bell (1847–1922), the inventor of the telephone.

The chart below gives the decibel and the corresponding w/m^2 values for some common sounds.

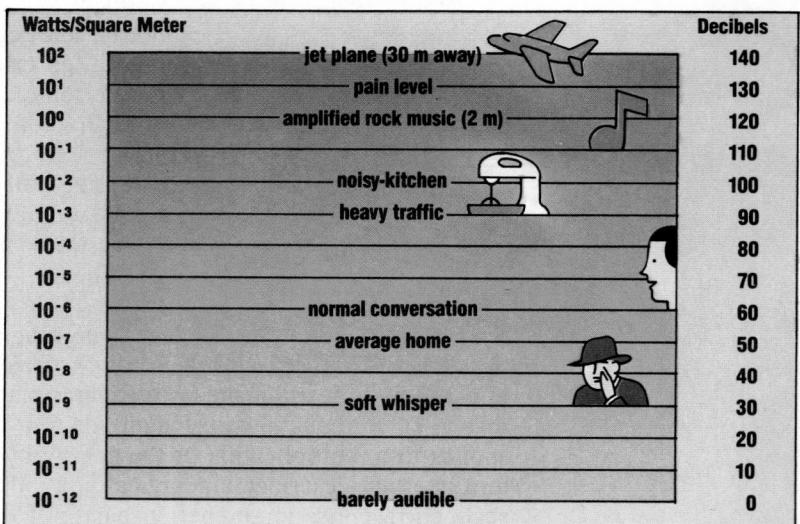

Watts/Square Meter		Decibels
10^2	jet plane (30 m away)	140
10^1	pain level	130
10^0	amplified rock music (2 m)	120
10^{-1}		110
10^{-2}	noisy-kitchen	100
10^{-3}	heavy traffic	90
10^{-4}		80
10^{-5}		70
10^{-6}	normal conversation	60
10^{-7}	average home	50
10^{-8}		40
10^{-9}	soft whisper	30
10^{-10}		20
10^{-11}		10
10^{-12}	barely audible	0

500

As the decibel values in the right column increase by 10, the corresponding intensities in the left column multiply by 10. Thus, if the number of decibels is increased by 20, the sound intensity is multiplied by 100. If you increase the sound intensity by 40 dB, you multiply the watts per square meter by 10,000. *In general, an increase of n dB multiplies the intensity by $10^{n/10}$.* The 120 dB intensity of loud rock music is $10^{60/10} = 10^6 = 1,000,000$ times the 60 dB intensity of normal conversation.

Logarithmic scales are different from linear scales. On a linear scale the units are spaced so that the difference between successive units is the same.

The w/m² scale is an example of a **logarithmic scale**. On a logarithmic scale the units are spaced so that the *ratio* between successive units is the same.

Logarithmic scales are often used to model data with a very wide range of values.

Some other examples of logarithmic scales include the pH scale for measuring the acidity of solutions and the scales used on radio dials.

Questions

Covering the Reading

In 1–3, refer to the chart of Richter scale values.
1. Why is a scale like the Richter scale used?
   to graph a large range from very small to very large values
2. A logarithmic scale is a scale calculated using what numbers?
   powers of numbers with the same base
3. On October 1, 1986, an earthquake measuring 6.1 on the Richter scale struck southern California. Was this a strong quake? yes

4. An increase of one unit on the Richter scale corresponds to multiplying the energy of a quake by what number? 10

5. To what factor does an increase of two units on the Richter scale correspond? 100

6. How many times more intense is an earthquake with a Richter magnitude of 6.3 than one with magnitude 4.7? about 40

NOTES ON QUESTIONS
Question 14: This question illustrates a noninteger pH value. The corresponding concentration of H_3O^+ is easy to calculate with a calculator. Note that $10^{-8.5}$ is midway between 10^{-8} and 10^{-9} on the logarithmic scale, but it is not the average of these two numbers.

Question 16: Note that $t/40$, the exponent of the correct formula in this question, expresses the number of 40-minute periods in t minutes.

Question 25: This question involves base 100 to illustrate that bases other than 10 can be used in logarithmic scales.

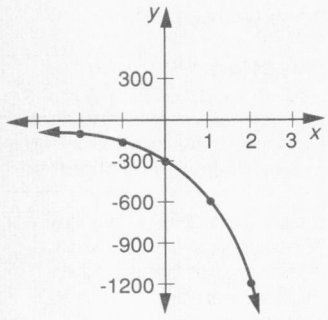

In 7–10, refer to the chart of sound intensity levels.

7. What is the intensity of sound which is barely audible to human beings? 10^{-12} w/m²

8. Give an example of a sound that is 100 times more intense than a noisy kitchen.   **amplified rock music**

9. How many times more intense is normal conversation than a soft whisper?   **1000 times**

10. The intensity level of a jet plane at 600 m is 20 dB more than that of a pneumatic drill at 15 m. How many times more intense is the sound of the jet?   **100**

11. What is the major difference between a linear scale and a logarithmic scale?   **See margin.**

12. Why is a logarithmic scale better than a linear scale for illustrating the data below?   **the range of values is large**
5×10^{-34} kg; 1.6726×10^{-27} kg; 10^{-21} kg; 3.15 kg; 1.38×10^5 kg

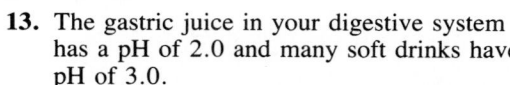

In 13–15, refer to the *pH* scale below. The pH scale is a logarithmic scale that is used to measure how acidic or alkaline a solution is. This is done by measuring the concentration of hydronium ions, H_3O^+, in the solution. The concentration is expressed as a power of 10 and is then converted to a pH value as shown in the graph at the right. Pure water has a pH of 7. Acidic solutions have pH values less than 7. Alkaline or basic solutions have pH values greater than 7.

13. The gastric juice in your digestive system has a pH of 2.0 and many soft drinks have pH of 3.0.
  a. Which is more acidic, gastric juice or soft drinks?   **gastric juice**
  b. What is the concentration of H_3O^+ ions in the more acidic solution?   **10 times**

14. Seawater has pH of 8.5.
  a. Is seawater acidic or basic?   **basic**
  b. What is the concentration of H_3O^+ ions in seawater? $10^{-8.5}$
  c. Rewrite your answer to part b in scientific notation. 3.16×10^{-9}

15. An acidic solution is increased in strength from pH 5 to pH 1. How many times more concentrated is the solution?   **10,000 times**

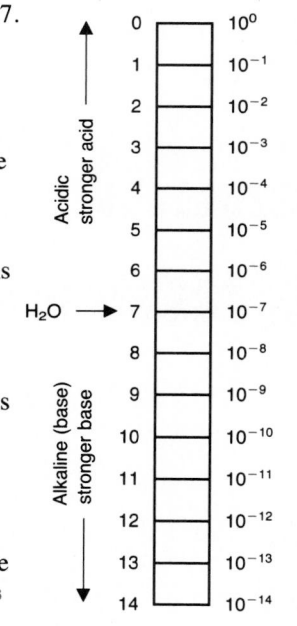

16. *Multiple choice* A culture of 8000 bacteria triples every 40 minutes. Let P = the population and t = the number of minutes after the start. Which equation models the population size? *(Lesson 9-1)*   **c**
(a) $P = 8000 + 40t$ (b) $P = 40t^2 + 8000$
(c) $P = 8000 \cdot 3^{t/40}$ (d) $P = 3 \cdot 8000^{t/40}$
(e) $P = 8000 + 3 \cdot 40t$

17. Plot points and then graph $y = -300(2)^x$. Is this an example of exponential decay? *(Lesson 9-2)*   **See margin.**

18. Suppose that the inverse of function f is also a function. If the domain of f is the set of all real numbers and the range is the set of positive real numbers, find the domain and range of f^{-1}. *(Lesson 7-6)*
domain of f^{-1}: positive reals; range of f^{-1}: all reals

In 19 and 20, write each expression as the square of a sum or difference. *(Lesson 6-3, Previous Course)*

19. $m^2 + 6mp + 9p^2$ **20.** $49y^2 - 14y + 1$ $(7y - 1)^2$
$(m + 3p)^2$

In 21–23, solve for x. *(Lessons 8-11, 6-6, 1-7)*

21. $3x + 6(x - 7) = 93$ **15**   **22.** $3x^2 + 6(x - 7)^2 = 93$ $x = \dfrac{14 \pm i\sqrt{5}}{3}$

23. $3 + 6(x - 7)^{1.25} = 93$ **15.73**

24. Acid rain is a serious environmental issue in many parts of the world. Find the pH level of acid rain and how acid rain affects the pH level of lakes. How are biologists trying to make lakes less acidic?
See margin.

25. Not all logarithmic scales are based on 10. Apparent magnitudes of stars are given on a logarithmic scale. A difference of 5 magnitudes means that the star with the *lower* magnitude is 100 times brighter than the star with the higher magnitude.   **See margin.**
a. How much brighter is the sun, magnitude -26.5, than Sirius (the brightest star in the sky), with magnitude -1.5?
b. Find out some other star magnitudes.

MORE PRACTICE
For more questions on SPUR Objectives, use *Lesson Master 9-3*, shown below.

EXTENSION
Humans do not grow proportionately. At birth, the arm is 1/3 as long as the body, and by adulthood it is about 2/5 as long. If we plot body height versus arm length on ordinary graph paper with linear scales, we get a curve. This is called *allometric growth*.

If we graph the data on log-log paper—on which each axis is marked off in orders of magnitude: 1, 10, 100, 1000, and so on—we find the data plot closely to a straight line. If the line had a slope of 1, it would show that arm length is increasing at the same rate as body height. What would the slope have to be to show that arm length is increasing relatively faster than height? (slope would be greater than 1)

OBJECTIVES

A Determine values of logarithms to the base 10.
C Solve equations involving common logarithms.
D Apply the definition of logarithm to the base 10.
H Apply models and formulas involving common logarithms.
J Graph the common logarithmic functions.

TEACHING NOTES

Begin this lesson by asking students to graph the exponential function $y = 10^x$. Have them apply the horizontal line test to determine whether its inverse is also a function.

Then ask students to try to derive an equation for its inverse. Explain that one way to do this is to interchange the roles of x and y to obtain $x = 10^y$ and to solve for y. If students are unable to solve for y, have them verbalize the solution. Lead them to say something similar to "y is the exponent of ten that gives the value of x."

Introduce the definition of logarithm and have students write $y = \log_{10} x$. Stress that $y = \log_{10} x$ and $10^y = x$ are equivalent forms of the inverse of $y = 10^x$.

LESSON

9-4

Common Logarithms

The Richter and decibel scales discussed in Lesson 9-3 are based on powers of 10. We say that 10 is the *base* of these logarithmic scales. Here is a number line with this kind of scale.

.0001	.001	.01	.1	1	$\sqrt{10}$	10	100	1000
10^{-4}	10^{-3}	10^{-2}	10^{-1}	10^0	$10^{0.5}$	10^1	10^2	10^3

To graph a number on this scale, you need to write it as a power of 10. For instance $\sqrt{10}$ is $10^{1/2}$ or $10^{0.5}$, so $\sqrt{10}$ is graphed between 10^0 and 10^1. Because $\sqrt{10} \approx 3.162$, the number 3.162 is plotted between $10^0 = 1$ and $10^1 = 10$ on a logarithmic scale.

The sentence $10^{0.5} \approx 3.162$ tells us how to write 3.162 as a power of 10. The exponent 0.5 is called the **logarithm** or **log** of 3.162 **to the base** 10.

Definition:

n is the logarithm of m to the base 10, written $n = \log_{10} m$, if and only if

$$10^n = m.$$

For instance $10^2 = 100$, so $2 = \log_{10} 100$. The logarithm of 100 to the base 10 is simply the power of 10 which gives 100. *Thus, a logarithm is an exponent.* Logarithms to the base 10 are called **common logarithms** and written without the 10. That is, $\log_{10} m = \log m$.

Scientific calculators contain a ⌊log⌋ key to calculate logarithms to the base 10. Use your calculator's ⌊log⌋ key by pressing 100 ⌊log⌋ to check that $\log_{10} 100 = 2$. Now press 3.162 ⌊log⌋ to show that $\log 3.162 \approx 0.5$.

Some common logarithms can be found without using a calculator.

■ ■ ■ ■ ■ ■ ■ ■

Example 1 Evaluate without a calculator.
a. $\log_{10} 1,000,000$　　**b.** $\log .1$　　**c.** $\log \sqrt[3]{10}$.

Solution First write each number as a power of ten. Then apply the definition of logarithm.
a. $1,000,000 = 10^6$. Since 1,000,000 is the 6th power of 10, $\log_{10} 1,000,000 = 6$.
b. You need to find n such that $10^n = .1$. Since $.1 = 10^{-1}$, $\log .1 = -1$.
c. $\sqrt[3]{10} = 10^{1/3}$. By definition, $\log \sqrt[3]{10} = \frac{1}{3}$.

504

Check Use your calculator.

a. Press 1000000 [log]. The number 6 is displayed.

b. Press .1 [log]. The number -1 is displayed.

c. Press 10 [y^x] [(] 1 [÷] 3 [)] [=] [log]. The calculator displays 0.3333333. Notice how much simpler it is to use the definition of logarithm to evaluate log $\sqrt[3]{10}$ than it is to use a calculator. All three answers check.

You can estimate the common logarithm of a number by putting it into scientific notation.

Example 2 Estimate log 4598.

Solution 1 Since 4598 is between 10^3 and 10^4, log 4598 is between 3 and 4.

Solution 2 $4598 = 4.598 \cdot 10^3$. This indicates that log 4598 will be slightly larger than 3.

Check A calculator shows that log 4598 ≈ 3.66... .

By using the definition of common logarithms you can solve *logarithmic equations*. In this chapter you may use either radical form or a decimal approximation for answers unless told otherwise.

Example 3 Solve for *x*: log $x = 1.5$.

Solution 1 log $x = 1.5$ if and only if $10^{1.5} = x$.
(radical form) $10^{1.5} = 10^{3/2} = (\sqrt{10})^3 = (\sqrt{10} \cdot \sqrt{10} \cdot \sqrt{10}) = 10\sqrt{10}$.
Thus $x = 10\sqrt{10}$.

Solution 2 Begin as in Solution 1, but evaluate $10^{1.5}$ with a calculator:
(decimal form) 10 [y^x] 1.5 [=]. Your calculator displays 31.622777... .
Thus, $x \approx 31.62$.

The table below shows some solutions to the equation $y = \log x$. The ordered pairs (.1, -1), and $\left(\sqrt[3]{10}, \frac{1}{3}\right)$ are derived from Example 2. The other pairs were obtained by evaluating the expression $\log_{10} x$ using the definition or a calculator.

x	.1	1	$\sqrt[3]{10}$ (≈ 2.15)	$\sqrt{10}$ (≈ 3.16)	5	8	10	31.6*	100
$y = \log_{10} x$	-1	0	$\frac{1}{3}$	.5	.7*	.9*	1	1.5	2

*These values have been rounded to the nearest tenth.

Have students graph $y = \log_{10} x$ on the same coordinate plane on which they graphed $y = 10^x$ and then sketch in the line $y = x$. Tell students that the easiest way to graph the logarithmic function is by reversing the ordered pairs of the exponential function, since the functions are inverses of each other.

ADDITIONAL EXAMPLES

1. Rewrite in logarithmic form.
a. $10^4 = 10{,}000$
$\log_{10} 10{,}000 = 4$
b. $10^{-2} = .01$
$\log_{10} .01 = -2$
c. $\sqrt{10} \approx 3.16$
$\log_{10} 3.16 \approx .5$

2. Rewrite in exponential form.
a. $\log_{10} 1000 = 3$
$10^3 = 1000$
b. $\log_{10} .001 = -3$
$10^{-3} = .001$
c. $\log_{10} 1.78 \approx \frac{1}{4}$
$10^{1/4} \approx 1.78$

3. Evaluate without a calculator.
a. $\log_{10} 100$
2
b. $\log_{10} .00001$
-5

4. Solve. log $x = 3.5$
$x = 10^{3.5} = 10^{7/2} = \sqrt{10^7} = 10^3\sqrt{10} = 1000\sqrt{10}$ or $10^{3.5} \approx 3162$; any of these is acceptable.

When these and other solutions to $y = \log x$ are plotted, the graph shown below is the result. This graph is called a *logarithmic curve*, and it has the shape of an exponential curve. In fact, the functions $y = 10^x$ and $y = \log x$ are inverses. Here is why.

The equation $y = \log_{10} x$ is equivalent to $x = 10^y$. When x and y are switched in $x = 10^y$, the resulting equation $y = 10^x$ is an equation for the inverse of the common log function. Thus, the exponential and logarithmic functions with base 10 are inverses of each other. The graphs below verify that each graph is the reflection image of the other over the line $y = x$.

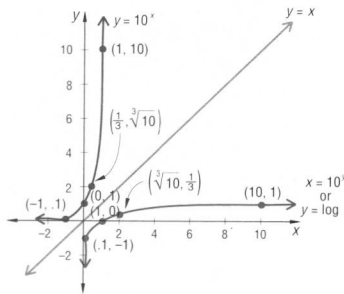

Notice several key features of the graph of $y = \log x$. Its x-intercept is 1 (the log of 1 is 0). It increases as you go to the right (the larger a number, the larger its logarithm). Because real powers of 10 are never negative, there are no real logarithms of negative numbers. Thus the domain of $y = \log x$ is the set of positive real numbers. Since any number can be an exponent of 10, the range of $y = \log x$ is the set of all real numbers.

Although the graph of $y = \log x$ gets very close to the y-axis, it has no y-intercept. If it did, there would be a value of y satisfying $y = \log_{10} 0$ or $10^y = 0$, which is impossible. By evaluating $\log x$ for small positive values you can check that the y-axis is an asymptote of the logarithmic curve. The closer x gets to zero, the smaller y gets.

Questions

Covering the Reading

1. What is a logarithm?   **an exponent**

2. $\log_{10} 6$ is read __?__ .   **logarithm of 6 to the base 10**

3. If $x = \log_{10} y$, what other relationship exists between x, 10, and y?
   $10^x = y$

506

In 4–9, evaluate without using a calculator.

4. log 1,000,000 6   **5.** log 10^8 8

6. log .00001 -5

7. log $\sqrt{10}$ 0.5   **8.** log 1 0   **9.** log -10 undefined

In 10–12 evaluate to the nearest thousandth with a calculator.

10. log 2 0.301   **11.** log 0.00046   **12.** log 4,600,000 6.663
                                   -3.337

13. *Multiple choice* The common logarithm of 1,000,529 is approximately b
   (a) 3   (b) 6   (c) 7   (d) 10.

In 14 and 15 solve for *x*.

14. log x = 4 x = 10,000   **15.** log x = 2.5 $x \approx$ 316.23

16. Consider the graph of $y = \log_{10} x$.
   a. Name its *x*- and *y*-intercepts. x-intercept: 1; no y-intercepts
   b. Name three points on the graph. samples: (.1,-1), (10,1), (100,2)
   c. Name three corresponding points on the graph of $y = 10^x$.
   d. What are the domain and range of the given logarithmic function?
   e. What are the domain and range of the exponential function in part
       c? domain: all real numbers; range: all positive real numbers
   f. The functions f and g with equations f(x) = $\log_{10} x$ and
       g(x) = __?__ are inverses of each other. 10^x
       d) domain: all positive real numbers; range: all real numbers

Applying the Mathematics

17. If a number is between 100 and 1000, its common logarithm is be-
    tween __?__ and __?__. 2, 3

18. The common logarithm of .0012 is closest to what integer? -3

19. *Multiple choice* If log $t \approx$ -0.3098, then *t* is close to b
   (a) -4.9   (b) 0.49   (c) 4.9   (d) 49   (e) 490.

20. The common logarithm of a number is -2. What is the number? .01

21. A formula which relates the intensity of sound in decibels *B* to its
    intensity *I* in w/m² is

$$B = 10 \log \left(\frac{I}{10^{-12}} \right).$$

Find *B* when $I = 10^8$. 200

22. The rate at which potassium-40 decays to argon-40 is known. This
    enables geologists to estimate the age of rocks by use of the formula

$$t = 1.26 \cdot 10^9 \left(\frac{\log(1 + 8.33 \; A/P)}{\log 2} \right)$$

where t is the age in years and $\frac{A}{P}$ is the ratio of argon atoms to potas-
sium atoms in the sample. If the $\frac{A}{P}$ ratio of a rock is 0.421, find the
age of the rock. $\approx 2.74 \times 10^9$ years old

LESSON 9-4 Common Logarithms **507**

FOLLOW-UP

MORE PRACTICE
For more questions on SPUR
Objectives, use *Lesson Mas-
ter 9-4,* shown below.

NAME _____

LESSON **MASTER 9–4**
QUESTIONS ON **SPUR** OBJECTIVES

■**SKILLS** *Objective A (See pages 537–539 for objectives.)*
In 1–6, write each number as a decimal. Do not use a calculator.

1. log 100 2   2. log(0.0001) -4   3. log 10 1
4. log -100 not defined   5. log 10^{-3} -3   6. log $\sqrt[4]{10}$ 0.25

In 7–9, find each logarithm to the nearest hundredth.

7. log(8.56) 0.93   8. log 35,182 4.55   9. log -20 not defined

■**SKILLS** *Objective C*
In 10–13, solve.

10. log x = 5 x = 100,000   11. log x = -2 x = 0.01
12. log x = 1.3 $x = 10^{1.3} \approx 19.95$ 13. log x = 0 x = 1

■**PROPERTIES** *Objective D*
In 14–16, write in exponential form.

14. log 100 = 2   15. log 0.5 ≈ -.3   16. log $\sqrt[5]{10} = \frac{1}{5}$
    $10^2 = 100$ $10^{-3} \approx 0.5$ $10^{1/5} = \sqrt[5]{10}$

In 17–19, write in logarithmic form.

17. $10^5 = 100,000$ 18. $10^{-2} = 0.01$ 19. $10^{1.5} \approx 31.6$
    log 100,000 = 5   log 0.01 = -2   log 31.6 = 1.5

■**PROPERTIES** *Objective F*
In 20 and 21, answer true or false.

20. The range of the common log function is the set false
    of positive numbers.
21. The logarithm of 0 is undefined. true

■**USES** *Objective H*
22. A formula which is used to compute the number
    of decibels *B* when given the sound intensity *I* in
    w/m² is $B = 10 \log(\frac{I}{10^{12}})$.
    a. Find *B* when $I = 10^{-8}$. 40dB
    b. If the sound intensity in part (a) doubles about 43 dB
       so that $I = 2 \cdot 10^{-8}$, find *B*.

98   Advanced Algebra © Scott, Foresman and Company

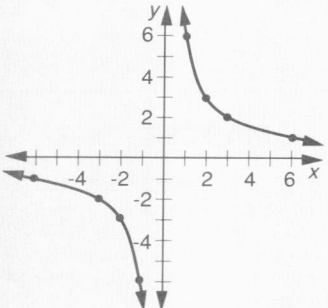
23. A foundation decided to hold the following contest. It made a test with ten very hard questions. It offered 2¢ to anyone correctly answering one question. It would give ten times that for two questions correctly answered, ten times that for 3 questions, and so on. Construct a logarithmic scale showing the number of questions and the amount of money offered. *(Lesson 9-3)* **See margin.**

In 24–29, simplify without a calculator. *(Lessons 8-1, 8-4, 8-5, 8-6, 8-7, 8-8)*

24. $(8^2 \cdot 8^{-4})^5$ $\frac{1}{8^{10}}$ **25.** $\sqrt[3]{10^{12}}$ 10^4

26. $27^{1/3} \cdot 64^{2/3}$ 48   **27.** $(\frac{1}{4})^{-1/2}$ 2

28. $(\frac{4}{5})^5 \cdot (\frac{1}{5})^{-5}$ 4^5 **29.** $\sqrt{x} \cdot \sqrt[3]{x} \cdot \sqrt[4]{x}$ $x^{13/12}$

30. Translucent materials allow light to pass through them but reduce the amount or intensity of the light. Suppose each 1 mm thickness of a translucent plastic reduces the intensity of light by 30% of the original amount. *(Previous course, Lesson 9-2)*
  a. What percent of light does pass through 1 mm? **70%**
  b. What percent of light passes through 2 mm? **49%**
  c. Complete a table like the one below. **See margin.**

$x =$ thickness	0 mm	1 mm	2 mm	3 mm	4 mm	5 mm
$y =$ % of light passing through						

  d. Write an equation to describe the data. $y = 100(.7)^x$
  e. Why is your equation not meaningful for $x < 0$?   **See margin.**

31. Graph $f(x) = \frac{6}{x}$ and refer to the graph to answer the questions.
  (Lessons 2-6, 4-6) **See margin.**
  a. State equations for both asymptotes.
  b. State equations for all lines of symmetry.
  c. Graph the image of $f(x)$ under R_{45}. What are equations for the lines of symmetry of the image?

32. An earthquake in December, 1988, in Armenia had a Richter magnitude of 6.9.   **almost ruinous**
  a. What kind of damage should you expect from this earthquake?
  b. How many times as strong would this quake be than one of magnitude 6.2? *(Lesson 9-3)* **about 5**

See margin.

33. Refer to the U.S. census bar graph at the beginning of this chapter.
  a. Determine log P for each population P.
  b. Graph x on the horizontal axis, and log P on the vertical axis.
  c. What do you notice about the points you plotted?

x	P	log P
1790		
1800		
1810		
:		
:		
1980		

508

Logarithms to Bases Other than 10

Any positive number except 1 can be the base of a logarithm.

Definition:

Let $b > 0$ and $b \neq 1$. Then n is the **logarithm of m to the base b**, written $n = \log_b m$, if and only if

$$b^n = m.$$

For example, because $2^6 = 64$ we say that "6 is the logarithm of 64 to the base 2" or "6 is log 64 to the base 2" and write $\log_2 64 = 6$.

Here are some other logs to the base 2.

Exponential Form		Logarithmic Form
$2^5 = 32$	means	$\log_2 32 = 5$
$2^4 = 16$	means	$\log_2 16 = 4$
$2^3 = 8$	means	$\log_2 8 = 3$
$2^2 = 4$	means	$\log_2 4 = 2$
$2^1 = 2$	means	$\log_2 2 = 1$
$2^0 = 1$	means	$\log_2 1 = 0$
$2^{-1} = \frac{1}{2}$	means	$\log_2 \left(\frac{1}{2}\right) = -1$
$2^{-2} = \frac{1}{4}$	means	$\log_2 \left(\frac{1}{4}\right) = -2$
$2^{-3} = \frac{1}{8}$	means	$\log_2 \left(\frac{1}{8}\right) = -3$

The domain of the exponential function $y = 2^x$ is the set of all real numbers. Its range is the set of positive real numbers. That means that any positive real number can be written as a power of 2. Just as in the case of common logs, the inverse of $y = 2^x$ is the function $y = \log_2 x$. The graphs of these functions are shown below. You are asked to find the domain and range of $y = \log_2 x$ in the questions. Notice that logarithms to the base 2 can be negative, but you cannot have the logarithm of a negative number. The methods of evaluating logs and solving equations of logs with bases other than 10 are very similar to the methods you used in the last lesson with common logs.

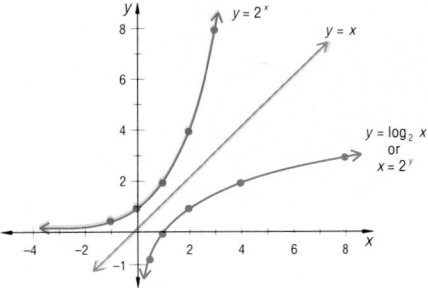

LESSON 9-5   Logarithms to Bases Other Than 10   **509**

RESOURCES
- Lesson Master 9-5
- Visual for Teaching Aid 56 provides some examples of base 2 logarithms.
- Computer Master 20
- Computer Master 21

OBJECTIVES

A Determine values of logarithms to any base.
C Solve logarithmic equations.
D Apply the definition of logarithm.
F Recognize properties of logarithmic functions.
J Graph logarithmic functions.

TEACHING NOTES

Point out that because powers of any positive base can be calculated, the logarithm to any positive base (except for $b = 1$) can be defined. In theory, students should be able to evaluate expressions of the form $\log_b m$ for any $b > 0$, $b \neq 1$. In practice, we use only whole numbers for b, and typically only small whole numbers. The problems tend to involve bases that are powers or products of 2, 3, or 5, because simple rational powers with these bases can be evaluated easily.

Stress that the argument of a logarithmic function must represent a positive number. Illustrate this by referring to the graph on the first page of this lesson. Another convincing demonstration is to have students use a calculator to try to find the logarithm of a negative number. Most calculators will respond with an ERROR message.

509

Reading It is useful to have students read aloud logarithmic expressions and equations to insure that they are using the correct terminology.

Computer You may also want to use a computer to generate a table such as the one on page 509 for either powers of 8 (from $8^{6/3}$ to $8^{-6/3}$) or for powers of 9 (from $9^{4/2}$ to $9^{-4/2}$). Then graph the exponential equation $y = 8^x$ or $y = 9^x$ and the logarithmic function $y = \log_8 x$ or $y = \log_9 x$ on the same set of coordinate axes. Discuss the domain, range, and intercepts of each function, and how the definition of logarithm ensures that the functions are inverses of each other.

ADDITIONAL EXAMPLES

1. Rewrite in logarithmic form.

a. $8^{-2} = \frac{1}{64}$

$\log_8 \frac{1}{64} = -2$

b. $8^{1/3} = 2$

$\log_8 2 = \frac{1}{3}$

2. Evaluate.

a. $\log_9 81$

2

b. $\log_9 27$

$\frac{3}{2}$

3. Solve. $\log_{64} x = \frac{2}{3}$

16

4. Find x if $\log_x 9 = \frac{2}{3}$.

27

NOTES ON QUESTIONS

Question 18: Note that the 2 in the exponent comes from the fact that the population was 4 billion in 1975. According to the growth model, an equation would be

$P = 4 \cdot 2^{(Y-1975)/35}$,

but we have taken advantage of the fact that 4 is an integer power of 2.

Question 24: Students need to refer to the chart in Lesson 9-3 to answer this question.

Example 1 Evaluate

a. $\log_2 16$;

b. $\log_6 \sqrt{6}$.

Solution You cannot simply use the [log] key on your calculator. The [log] key is for common logarithms only.

a. Let $x = \log_2 16$.

Apply the definition to rewrite the equation in exponential form.

$$2^x = 16$$
$$x = 4.$$

Therefore, $\log_2 16 = 4$.

b. Let $\log_6 \sqrt{6} = x$.

By definition, that means $6^x = \sqrt{6}$.

Since $\sqrt{6} = 6^{1/2}$, $x = \frac{1}{2}$.

Thus, $\log_6 \sqrt{6} = \frac{1}{2}$.

Notice that when you solve a problem about logarithms in base b, just as with base 10 logarithms, it often helps to write the equation in exponential form.

Example 2 Solve for x if $\log_{81} x = \frac{5}{4}$.

Solution Write an equivalent equation in exponential form.

$$81^{5/4} = x$$

Simplify the left side. $243 = x$

To solve some logarithmic equations, you need to apply the techniques of the last chapter for solving equations with n^{th} powers.

Example 3 Find x if $\log_x 8 = \frac{3}{4}$.

Solution Rewrite the equation in exponential form. $x^{3/4} = 8$

Take the $\frac{4}{3}$ power of each side. $(x^{3/4})^{4/3} = 8^{4/3}$

Simplify each side of the equation. The left side is equivalent to x^1, which is x. The solution is $x = 16$

Check Does $\log_{16} 8 = \frac{3}{4}$? It will if $16^{3/4} = 8$, which is the case.

Note also that in the definition of the logarithm of m to the base b, b cannot equal 1. We do not consider $b = 1$ because the inverse of $y = 1^x$ is not a function.

John Napier

Logarithms were invented by John Napier in the early 1600s. Henry Briggs first used common logarithms about 1620. In England even today logs to the base 10 are sometimes called Briggsian logarithms. Leonard Euler was the first person to realize that *any* real number could be an exponent. He was also the first to relate logarithms to exponents. Today most people study real exponents before logarithms, but that is not the order in which they developed historically.

Question 28: You might ask students to compare the data given in this question with that predicted by the formula of **Question 18.** (The prediction is 5.07 billion, which is quite close.) Note that the growth rate had slowed to where the 1987 rate would cause the population to double in 40 years, whereas the 1975 rate would cause doubling in 35 years.

ADDITIONAL ANSWERS
6.b. $\log_3 \frac{1}{9} = -2$, $\log_3 \frac{1}{3} = -1$, $\log_3 1 = 0$, $\log_3 3 = 1$, $\log_3 9 = 2$, $\log_3 27 = 3$

17.a.

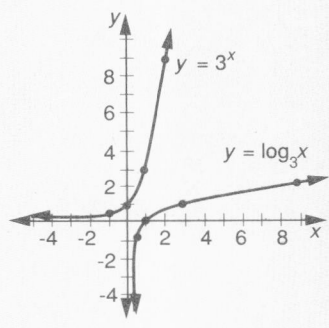

Questions

Covering the Reading

1. **a.** $\log_6 216$ is the logarithm of _?_ to the base _?_. 216, 6
   b. $\log_6 216 =$ _?_ because _?_ to the _?_ power equals 216.
   3, 6, 3rd

2. Suppose $b > 0$ and $b \neq 1$. When $b^n = m$, $n =$ _?_. $\log_b m$

3. Write the equivalent logarithmic form for $8^7 = 2{,}097{,}152$.
   $\log_8 2{,}097{,}152 = 7$

4. Write the equivalent exponential form for $\log_2 0.5 = -1$. $2^{-1} = 0.5$

5. Write the equivalent exponential form for $\log_b a = c$. $b^c = a$

6. **a.** Calculate 3^{-2}, 3^{-1}, 3^0, 3^1, 3^2, and 3^3. $\frac{1}{9}, \frac{1}{3}, 1, 3, 9, 27$
   b. Write six logarithmic equations that are suggested by the calculations. See margin.

In 7–9, simplify.

7. $\log_{1000} 100$ $\frac{2}{3}$

8. $\log_3 (\frac{1}{27})$ -3

9. $\log_5 \sqrt{5}$ 0.5

In 10–15, find x if:

10. $\log_x 3 = \frac{1}{2}$ $x = 9$

11. $\log_x 32 = 5$ $x = 2$

12. $\log_{100} x = -1.5$ $x = .001$

13. $\log_6 x = 3$ $x = 216$

14. $\log_{17} x = 0$ $x = 1$

15. $\log_x (\frac{1}{243}) = -\frac{5}{6}$. $x = 729$

Applying the Mathematics

16. For the function $y = \log_2 x$, state
   a. the domain; the set of positive real numbers
   b. the range. all real numbers

17. **a.** Graph $y = 3^x$ and $y = \log_3 x$ on the same set of axes. See margin.
   b. *True or false* The domain of $y = 3^x$ is the range of $y = \log_3 x$. True

18. The population (in billions) of the Earth in the year Y, using the year 1975 as a base, can be described by the equation
   $$P = 2^{(Y-1975)/35} + 2.$$
   a. Write this equation in logarithmic form. $\log_2(P) = \dfrac{Y - 1975}{35} + 2$
   b. When $P = 8$, what is Y? 2010
   c. What does your answer in part b mean?
   In the year 2010, there will be about 8 billion people on Earth.

LESSON 9-5   Logarithms to Bases Other Than 10   **511**

NAME _____

LESSON **MASTER** **9–5**
QUESTIONS ON **SPUR** OBJECTIVES

■SKILLS *Objective A (See pages 537–539 for objectives.)*
In 1–9, write each number as a decimal.
1. $\log_4 16$ 2   2. $\log_7 343$ 3   3. $\log_9 3$ $\frac{1}{2}$
4. $\log_8 2$ $\frac{1}{3}$ 5. $\log_{12} \frac{1}{144}$ -2   6. $\log_8 \frac{1}{2}$ $-\frac{1}{3}$
7. $\log_{21} 1$ 0   8. $\log_{21} 21^2$ 2   9. $\log_{17} 17$ 1

■SKILLS *Objective C*
In 10–13, solve. If necessary, round to the nearest hundredth.
10. $\log_x 51 = \log_{19} 51$ $x = 19$ 11. $\log_8 x = 6.2$ $x = 21558.28$
12. $\log_9 x = 1$ $x = 9$ 13. $\log_{81} x = 0.25$ $x = 3$

■PROPERTIES *Objective D*
In 14–16, write in exponential form.
14. $\log_{11} 121 = 2$ 15. $\log_3 \frac{1}{243} = -5$ 16. $\log_x x = y$
   $11^2 = 121$ $3^{-5} = \frac{1}{243}$ $c^y = x$

In 17–19, write in logarithmic form.
17. $5^6 = 15{,}625$ 18. $12^n = 87$ 19. $b^a = c, b > 0, b \neq 1$
   $\log_5 15{,}625 = 6$ $\log_{12} 87 = n$ $\log_b c = a$

■PROPERTIES *Objective F*
20. For what values of x is the expression $\log_8 x$ undefined? $x \leq 0$

■REPRESENTATIONS *Objective J*
21. Graph the equation $y = \log_3 x$.

22. The graph below has equation $y = \log_Q x$. Find Q.
   $Q = 5$

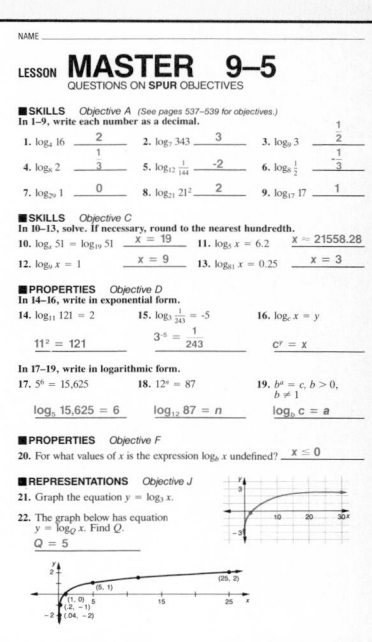

MORE PRACTICE
For more questions on SPUR
Objectives, use *Lesson Master 9-5*, shown on page 511.

19. **a.** Calculate $\log_5 125$ and $\log_{125} 5$ without a calculator. $3, \frac{1}{3}$
    b. Calculate $\log_4 16$ and $\log_{16} 4$ without a calculator. $2, \frac{1}{2}$
    c. Generalize the results of parts a and b. $\log_a b = \frac{1}{\log_b a}$

Review

20. When $\log \left(\frac{x}{y}\right)$ is rounded to the nearest whole number, the result is sometimes called the "number of orders of magnitude difference between x and y." (Each order of magnitude roughly means a substantial difference between the things being measured.) Find the number of orders of magnitude difference between the given numbers.
    a. 1 billion, the population of China, and 1 million, the population of Detroit.   3
    b. 4,000,000,000,000 km, the distance from Earth to the second nearest star, Alpha Centauri, and 149,000,000 km, the distance from Earth to the nearest star to the sun. *(Lesson 9-4)*   4

In 21 and 22, evaluate without a calculator. *(Lesson 9-4)*

21. $\log 10^5$ 5

22. $\log .00001$ -5

23. Solve $\log x = 9$. *(Lesson 9-4)* 10^9 or 1,000,000,000

24. Suppose one sound has an intensity of 80 decibels and a second sound has an intensity of 40 decibels. How many times more intense is the first sound? (The answer is *not* 2.) *(Lesson 9-3)* 10^4 or 10,000

In 25–27, simplify each expression. *(Lessons 8-1, 8-6, 8-7)*

25. $b^{1.6} \cdot b^{-3/4}$ $b^{.85}$

26. $53^a \cdot 53^b \cdot 53^{(a+b)}$ 53^{2a+2b}

27. $\frac{x^{3rt}}{x^{rt}}$ x^{2rt}

Open air market on Qingnian Street, Chongqing, in Sichuan province

28. The world population passed 5 billion in 1987 and was growing at a rate that would cause it to double in 40 years. With this assumption, what would the world population be in 2050? (Hint: Find the number of 40-year periods.) *(Lesson 9-1)*   14.9 billion

29. Mona invested $800 in a 6.7% account compounded daily for five years. What was her final balance? *(Lesson 8-2)* $1118.32

Exploration

30. **a.** Solve $\log_3 x = \log_5 x$ $x = 1$
    b. Generalize the idea of part a.
    If $\log_a x$ and $\log_b x$ are equal, then $x = 1$, because $\log_b 1 = 0$ for all bases b ($b > 0$, $b \neq 1$).

512

Properties of Logarithms

As you have seen, some logarithms can be found without a calculator. You know that $b^0 = 1$ for any nonzero b. If you rewrite this equation in logarithmic form, it becomes $\log_b 1 = 0$.

Logarithm Theorem 1:

For any nonzero base b, $\log_b 1 = 0$.

You know that the common log of $10^{7.2}$ is 7.2; that is, $\log_{10} 10^{7.2} = 7.2$. This property can be generalized. Start from the definition of logarithm: $b^n = m$ means $\log_b m = n$. Since $b^n = m$, substitute b^n for m in the left side of the equation $\log_b m = n$. Then you get $\log_b b^n = n$.

Logarithm Theorem 2:

For any nonzero base b, $\log_b b^n = n$.

In words, if a number can be written as a power of the base, the exponent of the number is its logarithm; so, for instance, $\log_4 4^5 = 5$. This means it is not necessary to calculate 4^5 in order to find its logarithm in base 4.

The other basic properties of logarithms come from properties of powers. The Product of Powers Property states that to multiply two powers, add their exponents. In particular, for any base b ($b > 0$, $b \neq 1$) and any real numbers m and n,

$$b^m \cdot b^n = b^{m+n}.$$

Now let $x = b^m$, $y = b^n$, and $z = b^{m+n}$. Then $z = xy$. However, from the definition of log,

$$\log_b x = m,$$
$$\log_b y = n,$$
and $\qquad \log_b z = m + n.$
By substitution, $\qquad \log_b z = \log_b x + \log_b y.$

Since $z = xy$, we have proved the following theorem.

Logarithm Theorem 3 (Product Property):

For any nonzero base b and positive real numbers x and y,

$$\log_b (xy) = \log_b x + \log_b y.$$

In words, the log of a product equals the sum of the logs of the factors.

RESOURCES
■ Lesson Master 9-6
▣ Visual for Teaching Aid 57 provides the five logarithm theorems.

OBJECTIVES

A Determine values of logarithms using the properties of logarithms.
C Solve logarithmic equations.
E Identify properties of logarithms.

TEACHING NOTES

To introduce this lesson, begin with properties of exponents with which students are familiar. Rewrite the properties using the definition of logarithm. When written as a logarithm, $b^0 = 1$ becomes Logarithm Theorem 1. Now let $b^n = x$. Then $\log_b x = n$ using the definition of logarithm. Have students substitute b^n for x and the result is Logarithm Theorem 2.

A proof of Theorem 3 is given in the lesson; proofs of Theorems 4 and 5 are found in **Questions 18 and 19**. Explain to students that the theorems can be remembered in words as corresponding to properties of powers. From Logarithm Theorem 3, when multiplying two powers of the same number, add exponents. With logarithms, we say that the logarithm of the product is found by adding logarithms of the numbers. Similar corresponding sentences can be said for the Quotient and Powering Properties.

ADDITIONAL EXAMPLES

1. Find $\log_{15}5 + \log_{15}45$.
$\log_{15}(5 \cdot 45) = \log_{15}225 = 2$

2. Use the Quotient Property to show that $\log_b\frac{1}{N} = -\log_b N$.
$\log_b\frac{1}{N} = \log_b 1 - \log_b N = 0 - \log_b N = -\log_b N$
This property corresponds to the theorem $b^{-n} = \frac{1}{b^n}$.

3. From a calculator, a person discovers that $\log_b 2 = .69$. How can this value be used to find $\log_b 8$?
Write $\log_b 8$ as $\log_b 2^3$. Then $\log_b 2^3 = 3\log_b 2 = 3(.69) = 2.07$.

4. Solve. $1 = \log_7\left(\frac{x}{49}\right)$
343

Example 1 Find $\log_6 2 + \log_6 108$.

Solution By the Product Property of Logarithms,

$$\begin{aligned}\log_6 2 + \log_6 108 &= \log_6 (2 \cdot 108)\\ &= \log_6 216\\ &= 3.\end{aligned}$$

There is also a Quotient Property of Logarithms, the proof of which is very similar to that of the Product Property. The Quotient Property follows from the related Quotient of Powers Property:

$$b^m \div b^n = b^{m-n}.$$

The proof is derived in Question 18.

Logarithm Theorem 4 (Quotient Property):

For any nonzero base b and for any positive real numbers x and y,

$$\log_b\left(\frac{x}{y}\right) = \log_b x - \log_b y.$$

Example 2 The formula $B = 10\log\left(\frac{I}{10^{-12}}\right)$ is used to compute the number of decibels B from the intensity I of sound when measured in watts/m^2. Use the theorem about the log of a quotient to find an equivalent formula.

Solution By Theorem 4 above:

$$\log\frac{I}{10^{-12}} = \log I - \log 10^{-12}$$
$$\log 10^{-12} = -12.$$
$$\begin{aligned}B &= 10\log\left(\frac{I}{10^{-12}}\right)\\ &= 10(\log I - (-12))\\ &= 10(\log I + 12).\end{aligned}$$

The last basic property of logarithms comes from the Power of a Power Property for exponents

$$(b^m)^n = b^{mn}.$$

Logarithm Theorem 5 (Powering Property):

For any nonzero base b and for any positive real number x,

$$\log_b(x^n) = n\log_b x.$$

Question 19 asks you to complete the proof of this theorem.

■ ■ ■ ■ ■ ■ ■ ■ ■

Example 3   Rewrite $\log x^7$ in terms of $\log x$.

Solution   By the Powering Property, $\log x^7 = 7 \cdot \log x$.

Check   Let $x = 2$. Does $\log 2^7 = 7 \cdot \log 2$? $2^7 = 128$, so
$\log 2^7 = \log 128 \approx 2.107$. $\log 2 \approx 0.30103$, so $7 \cdot \log 2 \approx 2.107$.
It checks.

Before calculators were invented, these properties of logarithms were applied to perform difficult multiplications, divisions, and powerings. For example, to compute

$$N = 507 \cdot 386^{1.4},$$

people would take the common logarithm of both sides:

$$\log N = \log (507 \cdot 386^{1.4}).$$

Then they would use the properties of logarithms.

$$= \log 507 + \log (386^{1.4})$$
$$= \log 507 + 1.4 \log 386$$

They would look up these logarithms in a table and then do the arithmetic.

$$\approx 2.7050 + 1.4(2.5866)$$
$$\log N \approx 6.3262.$$

Then they would find N from the tables: $N \approx 2,119,000$.

Even though this is a long, complicated procedure, it was the only reasonable way to calculate powers and it simplified some multiplications and divisions. Calculators have eliminated the need to do problems this way. It is interesting (and a little ironic) that calculators perform many of their arithmetic operations by using ideas of logarithms.

Questions

Covering the Reading

In 1–5, simplify without a calculator.
1. $\log_7 7^{26.8}$
2. $\log_m (m^n)$
3. $\log_\pi 1$
4. $\log_{12} 3 + \log_{12} 4$
5. $\log_5 40 - \log_5 8$

Questions 14, 15, and 17: These questions are excellent for classroom discussion on the most common errors that are made in the application of the logarithm theorems.

Question 19: An alternate proof for that of the Powering Property given in this question is as follows: When p is a positive integer,
$$\log_b x^p = \log_b(x \cdot x \cdot x \ldots \cdot x)$$
$$(p \text{ factors})$$
$$= \log_b x + \log_b x + \ldots + \log_b x$$
$$(p \text{ addends})$$
$$= p \log_b x$$

Question 20: The solution to the equation in this question involves an inference from the statement $\log x = \log 48$ to $x = 48$. The justification for this inference is as follows: Since $y = \log x$ is a one-to-one function, if two y-values, $\log x$ and $\log 48$, are equal, the x-values that produced them also must be equal.

ADDITIONAL ANSWERS
9. Using properties of logarithms; multiplying and dividing long complicated numbers became converted to easier addition and subtraction problems. Raising problems to a power became converted to simpler multiplication problems.

30. $\log 4 = \log 2^2 =$
2 log 2 = 0.6021

$\log 5 = \log \frac{10}{2} =$
log 10 − log 2 = 0.6990

$\log 6 = \log 2 + \log 3 =$
0.7782

$\log 8 = \log 2^3 = 3 \log 2 =$
0.9031

$\log 9 = \log 3^2 = 2 \log 3 =$
0.9542

In 6–8, express as the logarithm of a single number.

6. $\log_2 25 + \log_2 7$ **7.** $\log 85 - \log 17 + \frac{1}{2}\log 25$ **log 25**
$\log_2 175$

8. $\log_b x + \log_b y - \log_b z$ $\log_b\left(\frac{xy}{z}\right)$

9. How did people compute expressions like $(9.76)^{3.2} \cdot (16.8)$ before calculators? Why was this an efficient technique?   **See margin.**

10. How have calculators been programmed to do some of the more complicated calculations?   **using logarithms**

In 11–13, use $\log_2 5 = 2.3219$ and $\log_2 6 = 2.5850$ to evaluate.

11. $\log_2 30$ **4.9069**   **12.** $\log_2 1.2$ **.2631**   **13.** $\log_2 25$ **4.6438**

In 14–17, true or false; if false, correct it to make it true.

14. $\log (M + N) = \log M \cdot \log N$ **false; log(MN) = logM + logN**

15. $\frac{\log 4}{\log 3} = \log\left(\frac{4}{3}\right)$ **false; log 4 − log 3 = log $\frac{4}{3}$**

16. $\log x^{10} = 10 \log x$ **true**

17. $\log_b(3x) = 3 \log_b x$ **false, log$_b$(3x) = log$_b$ 3 + log$_b$ x**

18. Fill in the blanks in this proof of the Quotient Property of Logarithms. Let $x = b^m$, $y = b^n$, and $z = b^{m-n}$. Assume $b > 0$, $b \neq 1$.

Since $x = b^m$, _(a)_   definition of logarithm $\log_b x = m$
Since $y = b^n$, _(b)_   definition of logarithm $\log_b y = n$

$\frac{x}{y} = $ _(c)_   Quotient of Powers Property b^{m-n}

$\log_b\left(\frac{x}{y}\right) = $ _(d)_   definition of logarithm $m - n$

$\log_b\left(\frac{x}{y}\right) = \log_b x - \log_b y$ Substitution

19. Justify each step in the proof of the Powering Property of Logarithms given here. Let $\log_b x = m$.

Then	$x = b^m$	_(a)_	definition of logarithm
	$x^n = (b^m)^n$	_(b)_	Substitution
	$x^n = b^{mn}$	_(c)_	Power of a Power
Property	$x^n = b^{nm}$	_(d)_	Comm. Prop. of Mult.
	$\log_b x^n = nm$	_(e)_	Logarithm Theorem 2
	Therefore, $\log_b x^n = n \log_b x$.	_(f)_	Logarithm Theorem 5

20. Solve for x: $\log x = 4 \log 2 + \log 3$.   **48**

In 21 and 22 use the following information. The pH of a chemical solution is defined to be pH $= -\log x$, where x is the H_3O^+ ion concentration. Determine the pH of each of the following substances with the given H_3O^+ ion concentration.

21. black coffee: 1×10^{-5} **5**   **22.** hydrochloric acid (HCl): 6.3×10^{-3} **2.2**

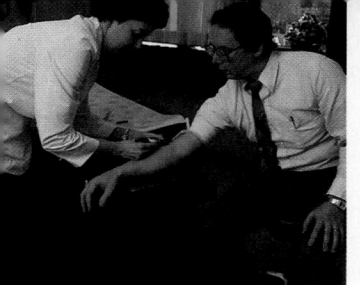

23. The Henderson-Hasselbach formula pH $= 6.1 + \log\left(\dfrac{B}{C}\right)$ gives
    the pH of a patient's blood as a function of the bicarbonate concentration B and the carbonic acid concentration C. The normal pH is about 7.4.   pH $= 6.1 + \log B - \log C$
    a. Rewrite this equation using the Quotient Property of Logarithms.
    b. A patient has a bicarbonate concentration of 24 and a pH reading of 7.2. Find the concentration of carbonic acid. (Hint: first solve the equation in part a for log C.) ≈ 1.9064

Review

24. Simplify these logs to the base 64 without a calculator. *(Lesson 9-5)*
    a. $\log_{64} 64$ 1
    b. $\log_{64} 8$ 0.5
    c. $\log_{64} 2$ $\frac{1}{6}$
    d. $\log_{64} 1$ 0
    e. $\log_{64} \frac{1}{64}$ -1
    f. $\log_{64} \frac{1}{8}$ -.5

25. Solve $\log_x 81 = 4$. *(Lesson 9-5)* $x = 3$

26. Solve $\log y = -1$. *(Lesson 9-4)* $y = 0.1$

27. Refer to the pH scale described in Lesson 9-3. Lemons have a pH of 2.3 and milk of magnesia has a pH of 10.5. Which of these has a higher concentration of H_3O^+ ions? *(Lesson 9-3)*   lemons

28. Newton's Law of Cooling states that the difference in the temperatures of a warm body and its cooler surroundings decreases exponentially. Suppose a bowl of soup is 100°C. In a room which is 20°C, its cooling is described by the equation
$$y = 80(.875)^t$$
    where y is the temperature difference in °C between the soup and the room at time t in minutes.
    a. What will be the temperature of the soup after 5 minutes?   61°
    b. According to this equation will the soup ever be 20°C? *(Lesson 9-1)*
       No

29. The charge to park a car at a city lot is 90¢ for the first hour and 75¢ for each additional hour or fraction thereof. Let $t =$ the number of hours parked. *(Lesson 7-4)*
    Multiple choice.   Which equation models this situation?   ii
    (i) $f(t) = 90 + 75t$
    (ii) $f(t) = 90 + 75[t]$
    (iii) $f(t) = 75 + 90[t]$
    (iv) $f(t) = [90 + 75(t \cdot 60)]$

Exploration

30. When asked why he memorized that log 2 is about 0.301 and log 3 is about 0.477, Leonhard answered, "Of course I know log 1 and log 10. Using log 2 and log 3, I can get the logs of all but one of the other integers from 1 to 10." Which logs between 4 and 9 can be found from the logs of 2 or 3, and what are they?   See margin.

FOLLOW-UP

MORE PRACTICE
For more questions on SPUR Objectives, use *Lesson Master 9-6*, shown below.

EXTENSION
The following exercises apply the theorems of logarithms, algebraic manipulation, restrictions on the domains of logarithmic functions, and their relation to extraneous roots.

1. Solve for x.
a. $\log_2 x + \log_2(x - 1) = 1$
$(x = 2)$
$(x = -1$ is extraneous.$)$
b. $\log(x + 3) - 1 =$
$\log(x - 6)$
$(x = 7)$

2. Show that the statement is true for all values in the domain of each logarithmic expression.

a. $\log\left(\dfrac{x^2 + 3x + 2}{2x^2 + 5x + 2}\right) =$
$\log(x + 1) - \log(2x + 1)$

b. $\dfrac{\log(a + b) - \log b}{c} =$
$\log\left(\dfrac{a}{b} + 1\right)^{1/c}$

RESOURCES
■ Lesson Master 9-7
■ Quiz for Lessons 9-4
Through 9-7
📄 Visual for Teaching Aid 58
provides two tables that
show a continuous com-
pounding of 100% interest
and 5% interest using different periods.

OBJECTIVE

G Apply exponential models
and formulas with e as a
base.

TEACHING NOTES

The lesson begins with a
natural compound interest
question: How much does
compounding gain the inves-
tor? While compounding
always increases the yield, it
is surprising that the increase
does not go to infinity but
rather to a fixed value related
to the number e. Stress that,
like π, e represents a constant, not a variable.

Some students may not have
an $\boxed{e^x}$ key on their calculators. An alternative to
keying in an approximation
for e is to use the key
sequence 1 $\boxed{\text{INV}}$ $\boxed{\ln x}$ to
display the calculator's value
for e.

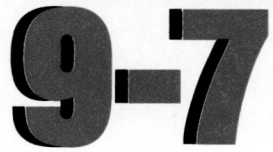

LESSON

9-7

The Number e

Recall the General Compound Interest Formula

$$A = P\left(1 + \frac{r}{n}\right)^{nt},$$

where an amount P is invested in an account paying an annual interest rate r and the interest is compounded n times per year for t
years. The number of compoundings can make quite a difference.
Suppose you begin with $P = \$1$ and a bank pays 100% interest
(don't we wish!). The following table shows the value of A at the
end of one year ($t = 1$) for successively shorter compounding periods. Check the values of A with your calculator.

$n = \left(\dfrac{\text{compoundings}}{\text{per year}}\right)$		$P\left(1 + \dfrac{r}{n}\right)^{nt}$	A
annually	1	$1\left(1 + \dfrac{1}{1}\right)^{1}$	$2.00
semi-annually	2	$1\left(1 + \dfrac{1}{2}\right)^{2}$	$2.25
quarterly	4	$1\left(1 + \dfrac{1}{4}\right)^{4}$	$2.44141
monthly	12	$1\left(1 + \dfrac{1}{12}\right)^{12}$	$2.61304
daily	365	$1\left(1 + \dfrac{1}{365}\right)^{365}$	$2.71457
hourly	8760	$1\left(1 + \dfrac{1}{8760}\right)^{8760}$	$2.71813
by the second	31,536,000	$1\left(1 + \dfrac{1}{31,536,000}\right)^{31,536,000}$	$2.71830

The sequence of values for the total amount gets closer and closer to
the number 2.71828.... Euler proved that this is indeed the case. We
call this situation **continuous** or **instantaneous compounding**. In his
honor this limiting number is called e. Like the number π, e looks
like a variable, but it is a particular irrational number which can be
expressed as an infinite, non-repeating decimal. Here are the first
fifty places.

2.71828182845904523536028747135266249775724709369995...

518

In a more realistic situation, suppose a bank pays 5% interest on $1 for one year. Here are some values of A for different compounding periods.

compounding method	$P\left(1+\frac{r}{n}\right)^{nt}$	A
annually	$1\left(1+\frac{.05}{1}\right)^{1}$	$1.05
semi-annually	$1\left(1+\frac{.05}{2}\right)^{2}$	$1.050625
quarterly 4	$1\left(1+\frac{.05}{4}\right)^{4}$	$1.050945
daily	$1\left(1+\frac{.05}{365}\right)^{365}$	$1.051267
hourly	$1\left(1+\frac{.05}{8760}\right)^{8760}$	$1.051271

Notice that the total amount seems to be getting closer to \$1.051271... This number is very close to the value of $e^{0.05} \approx 1.0512711...$ In fact, \$1 compounded continuously at 5% annual interest for one year will be worth exactly $\$e^{0.05}$. To evaluate $e^{0.05}$ on your calculator press .05 [eˣ]. (On some calculators you may need to press [INV], [2nd], or [f] before the [ln x] key.) If your calculator does not have an [eˣ] key you can approximate $e^{0.05}$ by calculating $(2.71828)^{0.05}$ using the powering key [yˣ].

Thus for situations where interest is compounded continuously, the general compound interest formula can be greatly simplified.

Continuously Compounded Interest Formula:

If an amount P is invested in an account paying an annual interest rate r compounded continuously, the amount A in the account after t years will be

$$A = Pe^{rt}.$$

Example 2 may seem contrived. Why have the base e? An alternate approach would be to calculate $e^{-0.0001}$, call that number k, and make the formula $L = Bk^t$. This shows that k (equivalently, $e^{-0.0001}$) is the growth (decay) factor. However, it is traditional in many fields to use e as a base. The tradition arose because of the ease with which powers of e can be calculated (see the Extension) and because there existed tables of those powers.

ADDITIONAL EXAMPLES

1. Suppose that the Native Americans who sold Manhattan Island to Peter Minuit in 1626 had put his $24 in an account that paid 8% compounded continuously. How much would have been in the account in 1988?

$A = 24e^{.08(362)}$. About \$90,652,000,000,000, enough to retire our national debt many times over.

2. The function

$$y = f(x) = \frac{1}{\sqrt{2\pi}} e^{-x^2/2}$$

is called the normal density function. Its graph is what we call "the standard normal curve." Estimate f(-1), f(0), and f(1).

$f(0) \approx .399$, $f(-1) = f(1) \approx .242$. You could graph this curve using an automatic grapher to see its bell shape.

3. A mail order company finds that the proportion P of small towns in which exactly n people place an order from their catalog is approximated by

$$P = \frac{e^{-.5}(.5)^n}{n!}.$$

From what proportion of small towns can the company expect: (a) exactly three people to order; (b) exactly two people to order? Recall that $n!$ is the product of all integers from 1 to n inclusive.

(a) $\approx .013$, (b) $\approx .076$ This approximation formula comes from a statistical topic known as the Poisson distribution.

■ ■ ■ ■ ■ ■ ■ ■

Example 1 If $850 is invested at an annual interest rate of 6% compounded continuously, what is the amount in the account after 10 years?

> **Solution 1** Use the formula $A = Pe^{rt}$, where $P = 850$, $r = 0.06$, and $t = 10$.
>
> $$A = 850e^{0.06(10)}$$
> $$A = 850e^{0.6}$$
>
> One calculator key sequence is : 850 $\boxed{\times}$ .6 $\boxed{e^x}$ $\boxed{=}$.
>
> $$A \approx \$1548.80$$
>
> **Solution 2** If your calculator does not have an $\boxed{e^x}$ key, use the approximation 2.71828 for e^x and substitute.
>
> $$A = 850e^{0.6} \approx 850(2.71828)^{0.6} \approx 1548.80$$
>
> The balance will be about $1548.80 after 10 years.

The exponential function $y = e^x$ has special properties that make it particularly suitable for applications. Some of these properties are studied in calculus. For now, you only need to know that many formulas for growth and decay are written using e as the base. This is why most scientific calculators have a key to find values of e^x.

■ ■ ■ ■ ■ ■ ■ ■

Example 2 The amount L of a certain radioactive substance remaining after t years decreases according to the formula $L = Be^{-0.0001t}$. When $t = 0$, $L = B$, so B is the original amount of the substance. If 2000 μ (micrograms) are left after 6000 years, how many micrograms were present initially?

> **Solution** When $t = 6000$, $L = 2000$. Substitute these values and solve for B.
>
> $$L = Be^{-0.0001t}$$
> $$2000 = Be^{-.0001(6000)}$$
> $$2000 \approx B(0.54881)$$
> $$3644 \approx B$$
>
> About 3600 μ were present initially.

Formulas such as those in Examples 1 and 2,

$$A = 850e^{0.06t}$$
$$\text{and } L = Be^{-0.0001t},$$

are instances of a general model for situations involving continuous change. The continuous-change model is often described using function notation. Let N_0 (read "N naught") be the initial amount, and let r be the rate of continuous growth or decay per unit of time t. Then N(t), the amount at time t, is given by the equation

$$\text{N}(t) = N_0e^{rt}.$$

This equation is an exponential equation of the form

$$y = ab^x$$

where $a = N_0$, $x = t$, and the growth factor $b = e^r$. If r is positive, then $e^r > 1$, so there is growth. If r is negative, then $0 < e^r < 1$ and there is decay.

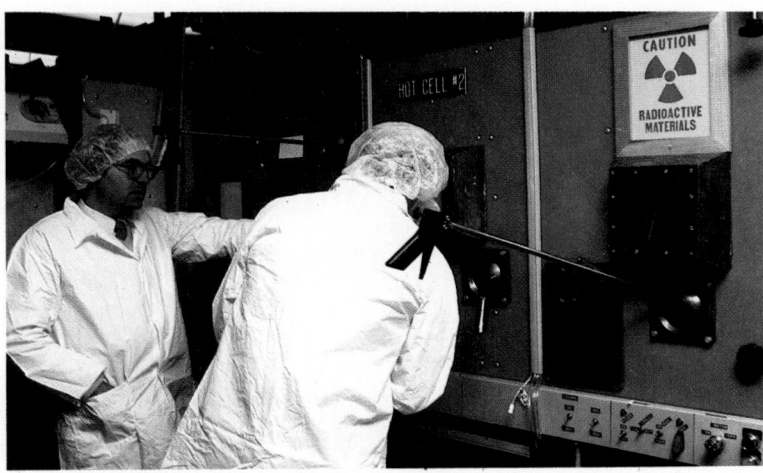

Technicians working with radioactive substance

Questions

Covering the Reading

In 1 and 2, $P = \$1$, $r = 100\%$, and $t = 1$ year. Use the table in the lesson.

1. As n increases, the value of A becomes closer and closer to what number?   e

2. Write the key sequence for your calculator to verify that $A \approx$ \$2.71457 when interest is compounded daily.
   Sample: (1 + 365 1/x) y^x 365 =

3. In whose honor did the number e get its name?   **Leonard Euler**

4. Approximate e to the nearest hundred-thousandth.   **2.71828**

LESSON 9-7   The Number e **521**

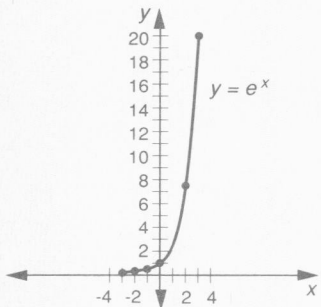
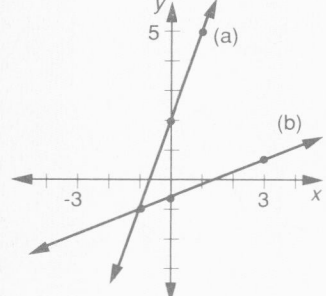
5. If \$1 is invested at 10% interest compounded continuously, find its value at the end of one year. **\$1.11**

6. The amount of \$700 is invested at an annual interest rate of 5% compounded continuously. How much is in the account after 10 years?
\$1154.10

7. Consider the function $N(t) = N_0 e^{rt}$.
  a. What does N_0 represent? **initial amount**
  b. What does r represent? **rate of continuous growth or decay**
  c. What is true about r when this function models exponential decay? **r is negative.**

8. Refer to Example 2. If at the end of 2000 years there are 1000 micrograms of the substance remaining, how many micrograms were present initially? **$\approx 1221\mu$**

9. Suppose \$3000 is invested at 7.5% interest compounded continuously for 8 years. **\$5466.35**
  a. How much is the investment worth at the end of that period?
  b. How much would the investment be worth if the 7.5% interest were compounded annually? **\$5350.43**

10. In 1985 the population of Nairobi, Kenya was 1 million. At that time the formula $N(t) = N_0 e^{0.08t}$ was being used to project the population t years later. **8% compounded continuously**
  a. What annual rate of population increase was assumed?
  b. Find N(2000), the projected population for the year 2000.
  3,320,000

Nairobi, Kenya

11. Graph $y = e^x$ for values of x between -3 and 3, inclusive.
See margin.

12. Complete with $>$, $<$, or $=$: π^e __?__ e^π. **<**

13. A machine used in an industry depreciates so that its value after t years is given by $N(t) = N_0 e^{-.25t}$. **25% compound continuously**
  a. What is the annual rate of depreciation of the machine?
  b. After 3 years the machine is worth \$12,000. What was its original value? **\$25,400**

14. Rumor spreads like an epidemic at a rate directly proportional to the number of people who have heard the rumor (and thus perpetuate it). Rumor spreading can be modeled by the equation

$$H = \frac{C}{1 + (C - S)e^{-0.4t}},$$

where C is the total number of people in the community, S is the number of people who initially spread the rumor, and H is the number of people who have heard the rumor after t minutes. In a school of 1800 students, one student going to lunch on Friday overhears the principal saying the following Monday there will be a surprise school holiday. About how many students will have heard the rumor after 45 minutes?   **all 1800 students**

Review

15. Solve for z: $\log z = \frac{2}{3} \log 8 + \log 3$. *(Lesson 9-6)*   **12**

16. Write $\log (pq^2)$ in terms of $\log p$ and $\log q$. *(Lesson 9-6)*   **log p + 2 log q**

In 17 and 18, suppose $f(x) = \log x$. Then find: *(Lesson 9-4)*

17. $f(.1)$ **-1**   **18.** $f^{-1}(3)$ **1000**

19. Find $\log_4 \left(\frac{1}{2}\right)$ without a calculator. *(Lesson 9-5)*   **-0.5**

In 20 and 21, solve for x. *(Lesson 1-7)*

20. $25 = \frac{-3}{x}$ $x = \left(\frac{-3}{25}\right)$ **21.** $\frac{x}{3} = 25$. $x = 75$

22. a. Graph: $g: x \rightarrow 3x + 2$.   **See margin.**
   b. Give a formula for $g^{-1}(x)$ and graph on the same axes. *(Lesson 7-7)*
   $g^{-1}(x) = \frac{x}{3} - \frac{2}{3}$

23. For what value of m does the equation $mx^2 + 12x + 9 = 0$ have exactly one solution for x? *(Lesson 6-7)*   **m = 4**

Exploration

24. Another way to get an approximate value of e is to evaluate the infinite sum

$$1 + \frac{1}{1!} + \frac{1}{2!} + \frac{1}{3!} + \cdots$$

(recall that $n!$ is the product of all integers from 1 to n inclusive). Use your calculator to calculate

$$1 + \frac{1}{1!} + \frac{1}{2!} + \frac{1}{3!}$$
$$1 + \frac{1}{1!} + \frac{1}{2!} + \frac{1}{3!} + \frac{1}{4!}$$
$$1 + \frac{1}{1!} + \frac{1}{2!} + \frac{1}{3!} + \frac{1}{4!} + \frac{1}{5!}$$
and so on

until you have approximated $e = 2.71828\ldots$ to the nearest thousandth. What is the last term you need to add to do this? $\frac{1}{7!}$

FOLLOW-UP

MORE PRACTICE
For more questions on SPUR Objectives, use *Lesson Master 9-7*, shown below.

EXTENSION
The formula for e in **Question 24** is a special case of a formula for e^x.

$$e^x = 1 + x + \frac{x^2}{2!} + \frac{x^3}{3!} + \frac{x^4}{4!} + \cdots$$

Ask students to use this formula to confirm that it gives values that agree with values given on their calculator for various powers of e. For instance, $\sqrt{e} \approx 1.649$ and $e^2 \approx 7.389$.

EVALUATION
A quiz covering Lessons 9-4 through 9-7 is provided in the Teacher's Resource File.

NAME _____

LESSON **MASTER   9–7**
QUESTIONS ON **SPUR** OBJECTIVES

■ **USES**   *Objective G (See pages 537–539 for objectives.)*

1. *Multiple choice* If $100 is invested at 8%, what period of compounding is most like continuous compounding?
   (a) monthly   (b) weekly   (c) yearly   **(b)**

2. Rachel has $3000 to invest. Investment A pays 7% compounded quarterly. Investment B pays 6.5%, compounded continuously.
   a. Which investment will be worth more at the end of 3 years?   **Investment A**
   b. How large is the difference?   **$48.39**

3. Under ideal conditions, a certain bacteria colony grows according to $N = N_0 e^{0.35t}$, where t is time in hours. At 8 a.m., there are 10,000 bacteria. How large is the colony by 12 noon of the same day?   **40,552**

4. Fast driving often requires more fuel per mile than driving at slower speeds. The Environmental Protection Agency has indicated that fuel efficiency is 10 to 15 percent less for every 10 mph above a speed of 50 mph. For a car that gets 30 miles/gallon at 50 mph, the mileage M at speed s is $M = 30e^{-.015(s - 50)}$. Find the car's mileage at 75 mph.   **20.62 mi/gal**

■ **REPRESENTATIONS**   *Objective I*

5. **a.** Graph $y = e^x$.
   b. State the domain of $y = e^x$.   **all real numbers**
   c. State the range of $y = e^x$. $\{y: y > 0\}$

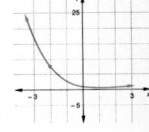

101

RESOURCES
- Lesson Master 9-8
- Visual for Teaching Aid 59 provides a graph showing that $y = \ln x$ is the inverse of $y = e^x$.

OBJECTIVES

A Determine values of natural logarithms.
C Solve equations involving natural logarithms.
D Apply the definition of natural logarithm.
E Identify properties of natural logarithms.
G Apply models and formulas involving natural logarithms.

TEACHING NOTES

You may want to introduce the topic of natural logarithms in a manner similar to that used for common logarithms, as students are familiar with the constant e from the previous lesson. Have students make a table of values and graph $y = e^x$, then graph its inverse by reversing the ordered pairs.

Students should recognize the graph of the inverse as a logarithmic curve. Introduce the definition of natural logarithm and show students how to use the $\boxed{\ln x}$ key on a calculator.

Remind students that the theorems proved in Lesson 9-6 apply to logs with any positive base $b \neq 1$. Nothing in the proofs restricts b to being a whole number. All properties proved in Lesson 9-6 apply to natural logs as well as to common logs. These properties are used to

---

Logarithms to the base e are called **natural logarithms**. Sometimes they are called *Napierian logarithms* after John Napier (1550–1617), the first person to use logarithms of any kind. Just as $\log x$ (without any base named) is a shorthand for $\log_{10} x$, so there is an abbreviation for $\log_e x$, namely **ln x**.

Definition: **ln $m = n$** if and only if $m = e^n$.

The symbol $\ln x$ is read "the natural log of x." Natural logarithms of powers of e can be determined mentally.

$$\ln 1 = 0 \text{ because } 1 = e^0.$$
$$\ln e = 1 \text{ because } e = e^1.$$

In general, $\ln(e^x) = x$ is a special case of the theorem $\log_b(b^x) = x$.

To determine natural logarithms of numbers not in e^x form, you need a calculator, computer, or table of values. On a scientific calculator use the key sequence $x \boxed{\ln x}$. For instance, to find $\ln 10$ press $10 \boxed{\ln x}$; you should get approximately 2.3026. This means that $e^{2.3026} \approx 10$. In some computer languages the natural logarithm function is denoted LOG. This can be confusing because log usually refers to base 10.

Natural logarithms are frequently used in formulas.

Example 1 Ignoring the force of gravity, the maximum velocity v of a rocket is given by the formula $v = c \ln R$, where c is the velocity of the exhaust and R is the ratio of the mass of the rocket with fuel to its mass without fuel. To achieve a stable orbit a spacecraft must attain a velocity of about 7.8 km/s.

a. With a small payload a solid-propellant rocket could have a mass ratio of about 19. A typical exhaust velocity for such a rocket might be about 2.4 kilometers per second. Could a spacecraft propelled by this rocket achieve a stable orbit?

b. Find R for a V-2 rocket if $c = 6440$ ft/sec and $v = 6630$ ft/sec.

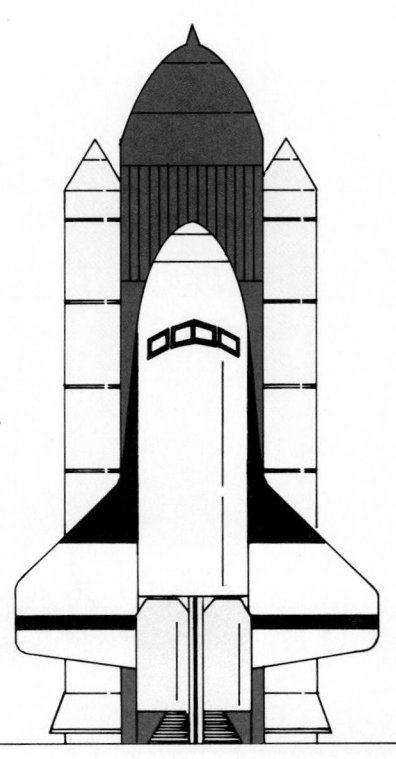

524

Solution **a.** For the solid propellant rocket, $R \approx 19$ and $c \approx 2.4$ km/s. Find v using the formula above.

$$\approx 2.4 \ln 19$$
$$v \approx 2.4 \,(2.944)$$
$$\approx 7.1$$

Notice that the maximum velocity of this rocket is *less than* the velocity needed for orbit. This rocket *could not* propel a spacecraft into orbit.

b. Substitute the given values for c and v, and solve for R.

$$v = c \ln R$$
$$6630 = 6440 \ln R$$

To solve for R, you must first solve for $\ln R$.
$$1.0295 \approx \ln R$$

Now, use the definition of natural logarithm to solve for R.

$$R \approx e^{1.0295}$$
$$\approx 2.7997$$

The mass of the rocket with fuel is about 2.8 times the mass of the rocket without fuel. (Thus the mass of the fuel is 1.8 times the rocket's mass.)

In previous lessons, you have seen that $y = \log x$ is the inverse function of $y = 10^x$, and that $y = \log_2 x$ is the inverse of $y = 2^x$. Similarly, $y = \ln x$ is the inverse of $y = e^x$, as can be seen in the graph below. Each is the reflection image of the other over the line with equation $y = x$.

$e^x = y$

x	y
-1	0.37
0	1.00
1	2.72
1.6	4.95
2	7.39

$\ln x = y$

x	y
0.37	-1
1.00	0
2.72	1
4.95	1.6
7.39	2

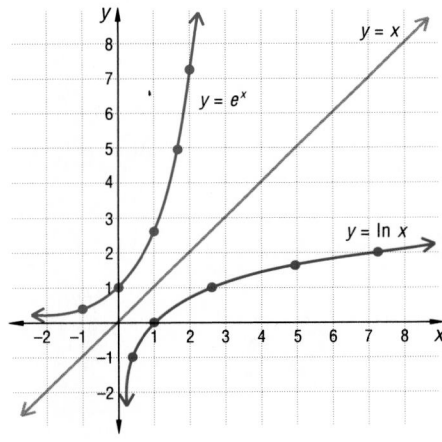

Because the functions above are inverses, formulas involving e^x can lead to finding natural logarithms.

evaluate and rewrite expressions in **Example 1** and to solve equations in **Example 2**.

Computer BASIC has a built-in function LOG(X) that calculates the natural logarithm of *x*. See *Computer Master 20* for related activities to be used in demonstration or laboratory mode.

ADDITIONAL EXAMPLES
1. Rewrite in logarithmic form.
a. $e^3 \approx 20.1$
ln 20.1 ≈ 3
b. $e^{-1} \approx .368$
ln .368 ≈ -1

2. Rewrite in exponential form.
a. ln 264 ≈ 5.58
$e^{5.58} \approx 264$
b. ln 1 = 0
$e^0 = 1$

3. Evaluate: ln e^{-6}.
-6

4. From the formula $A = Pe^{rt}$, one can deduce that money in a continuously compounded account will double when $rt = \ln 2$; that is, when the rate of interest times the number of years is equal to the natural logarithm of 2.
a. How long will it take money to double if it is invested at 8%?
.08t = ln 2. It will take approximately 8.7 years to double.
b. What interest rate would an investment have to earn in order to double in 5 years?
r(5) = ln 2; almost 14%
c. There is a banker's rule that money invested at *p* percent doubles in approximately $\frac{72}{p}$ years. Do your answers to parts (a) and (b) agree with this rule?
In (a), $\frac{72}{8} = 9 \approx 8.7$.
In (b), $\frac{72}{14} \approx 5$. Yes, the rule does seem to agree with the answers.

525

5. Under certain geographic conditions the wind velocity v at a height h centimeters above the ground is given by $v = k \ln \left(\frac{h}{h_0}\right)$, where k is a positive constant (depending on air density, average wind velocity, and so on), and h_0 is a "roughness value" (depending on the roughness of the vegetation on the ground.) Suppose that $h_0 = 0.7$ cm (a value that applies to a lawn 3 cm high) and $k = 300$ cm/sec.
a. At what height above the ground is the wind velocity zero?
0.7 cm
b. At what height is the wind velocity 1500 cm/sec?
$0.7e^5 = 104$ cm

■ ■ ■ ■ ■ ■ ■ ■

Example 2 Jamie has $600 to invest in an account which compounds interest continuously at a rate of 8%. How long should the money be in the account in order for it to double in value?

Solution   Use the formula for continuously compounded interest.

$$A = Pe^{rt}$$

Substitute $P = 600$, $r = .08$, and $A = 1200$.

$$1200 = 600e^{0.08t}$$
$$2 = e^{0.08t}$$

To solve for t, use the definition of natural log.

$$\ln 2 = 0.08t$$

Divide by 0.08.

$$t = \frac{\ln 2}{0.08} \approx \frac{0.6931}{0.08} \approx 8.7$$

Jamie should leave the money in the account for about 8.7 years.

All the properties of logarithms derived in Lesson 9-6 apply to natural logarithms. For all $x > 0$ and $y > 0$,

$$\ln (xy) = \ln x + \ln y,$$

$$\ln \left(\frac{x}{y}\right) = \ln x - \ln y,$$

and $\ln (x^n) = n \ln x.$

For instance, $\ln 64 = \ln 2^6$
$$= 6 \ln 2.$$

Because $\ln 2 \approx 0.6931$, $\ln 64 \approx 6(0.6931)$
$$\approx 4.159.$$

Questions

Covering the Reading

1. The base of natural logarithms is ___?___ **e.**

2. *Multiple choice* $y = \ln x$ is the same as: **c**
(a) $x = \log_e y$ (b) $x = \log_y e$
(c) $y = \log_e x$ (d) $y = \log_x e$

In 3 and 4, write the equivalent exponential form.
3. $\ln 1 = 0$ **$e^0 = 1$**   **4.** $\ln 300 \approx 5.70$ **$e^{5.70} \approx 300$**

In 5 and 6, write in logarithmic form.
5. $e^2 \approx 7.39$ **$\ln 7.39 \approx 2$**   **6.** $e^{0.06} \approx 1.06$ **$\ln 1.06 \approx 0.06$**

526

7. The graph of what function is the reflection image of the graph of $y = \ln x$ over the line $x = y$? **$y = e^x$**

8. Name a point on the graph of $y = \ln x$ whose coordinates are not given on the previous page. **sample: (2, 0.69)**

In 9 and 10, approximate each value to the nearest thousandth.

9. $\ln 400$ **5.991**

10. $\ln 1.6161$ **0.480**

In 11 and 12, refer to Example 1.

11. The space shuttle has an R value of about 3.5. Its main engines can produce an exhaust velocity of about 4.6 km/s. Can the space shuttle achieve a stable orbit with its main engines? **no**

12. The Viking rocket has an exhaust velocity of about 190 km/s and travels without fuel at a rate of 310 km/s. Find its mass ratio R.
$R \approx 5.11$

13. In Example 2, how long should Jamie leave the money in the account in order for it to triple in value? **about 13.7 years**

14. a. What happens when you try to find $\ln(-2)$ on your calculator? **You get an "error" message.**
    b. Justify your answer to part a. **The domain of the natural log function is the set of positive real numbers.**

15. At what point does the line with equation $x = \frac{1}{2}$ intersect the graph of $y = \ln x$? **at about $(\frac{1}{2}, -0.693)$**

16. Refer to Example 1. If the maximum velocity of a rocket is 7200 ft/sec and the mass ratio is 2.5, what is the maximum velocity of the exhaust? **≈ 7858 ft/sec**

In 17 and 18, suppose $\ln x = 8$ and $\ln y = 4$. Evaluate:

17. $\ln(3xy)$ **≈ 13.1**

18. $\ln\left(\sqrt[4]{\dfrac{x}{y}}\right)$ **1**

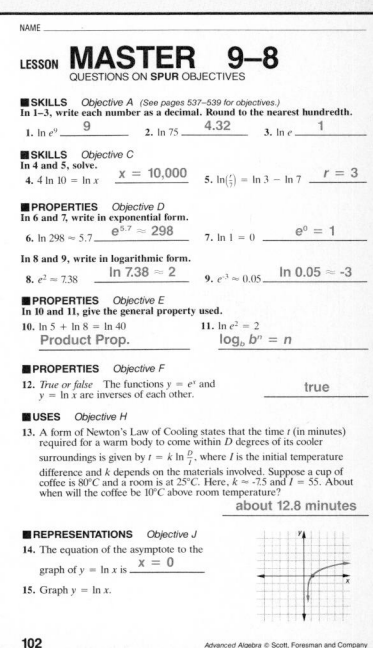

19. The percent risk R of an auto accident is exponentially related to the percent b of the alcohol blood level of the driver and is given by this formula
$$R = e^{21.4b}$$
    a. What is the relative risk of an auto accident if the blood alcohol level is 0.10%? **8.5%**
    b. At what percent alcohol blood level of the driver is the car considered certain to crash? **.22%**

20. In 1982, it was projected that t years later the population of the Phillipines would be given by $P(t) = 50e^{0.02t}$ million. According to this projection, what will the population be in the year 2012? *(Lesson 9-7)* **about 91.1 million**

21. Solve for x: $\log_x 7 = 2$. *(Lesson 9-5)* **$x = \sqrt{7}$**

22. Solve for A: $\log A = \log x + 2 \log y$. *(Lesson 9-6)* **$A = xy^2$**

Question 27: When discussing this question, you might review from geometry the Fundamental Theorem of Similarity: If the ratio of similitude of similar figures is r, then the ratio of any corresponding lengths is r, the ratio of any corresponding areas is r^2, and the ratio of any corresponding volumes is r^3.

Question 28: The series in this question allows logarithms to be calculated from scratch, but only works when $-1 < x < 1$.

NAME _____

LESSON **MASTER 9–8**
QUESTIONS ON **SPUR** OBJECTIVES

■**SKILLS** *Objective A (See pages 537–539 for objectives.)*
In 1–3, write each number as a decimal. Round to the nearest hundredth.
1. $\ln e^9$ __**9**__   2. $\ln 75$ __**4.32**__   3. $\ln e$ __**1**__

■**SKILLS** *Objective C*
In 4 and 5, solve.
4. $4 \ln 10 = \ln x$ __**x = 10,000**__   5. $\ln(\frac{3}{7}) = \ln 3 - \ln 7$ __**r = 3**__

■**PROPERTIES** *Objective D*
In 6 and 7, write in exponential form.
6. $\ln 298 \approx 5.7$ __**$e^{5.7} \approx 298$**__   7. $\ln 1 = 0$ __**$e^0 = 1$**__

In 8 and 9, write in logarithmic form.
8. $e^2 \approx 7.38$ __**$\ln 7.38 \approx 2$**__   9. $e^{-3} \approx 0.05$ __**$\ln 0.05 \approx -3$**__

■**PROPERTIES** *Objective E*
In 10 and 11, give the general property used.
10. $\ln 5 + \ln 8 = \ln 40$ 11. $\ln e^2 = 2$
__**Product Prop.**__   __**$\log_b b^n = n$**__

■**PROPERTIES** *Objective F*
12. *True or false* The functions $y = e^t$ and $y = \ln x$ are inverses of each other. __**true**__

■**USES** *Objective H*
13. A form of Newton's Law of Cooling states that the time t (in minutes) required for a warm body to come within D degrees of its cooler surroundings is given by $t = k \ln \frac{D}{I}$, where I is the initial temperature difference and k depends on the materials involved. Suppose a cup of coffee is 80°C and a room is at 25°C. Here, $k \approx -.75$ and $I = 55$. About when will the coffee be 10°C above room temperature?
__**about 12.8 minutes**__

■**REPRESENTATIONS** *Objective J*
14. The equation of the asymptote to the graph of $y = \ln x$ is __**$x = 0$**__
15. Graph $y = \ln x$.

102   *Advanced Algebra © Scott, Foresman and Company*

527

EXTENSION
Students will learn in calculus that the area under the curve $y = \frac{1}{x}$ and above the *x*-axis between 1 and any positive number *p* is ln *p* − ln 1 = ln *p* − 0 = ln *p*. Students will enjoy being able to solve such calculus problems. Have them draw the curve $y = \frac{1}{x}$ and shade in the region from 1 to 2. Have them estimate the area of this region by drawing a polygon under the curve that approximates this area, and then drawing a polygon above the curve and finding its area. The actual area ln 2 should be in between these two values.

23. *True or false* $\log(1.7 \times 10^3) = (\log 1.7)(\log 10^3)$. *(Lesson 9-6)*
    false

24. A lab assistant accidentally poisoned a bacteria culture. The bacteria died off approximately exponentially as shown in the graph below. *(Lesson 9-2)*   ≈ 900
    a. About how many bacteria were there at the time of the poisoning?
    b. About how many were there 6 minutes later?   ≈ 100
    c. Approximately what is the half-life of the poisoned culture?
       ≈ 2 minutes

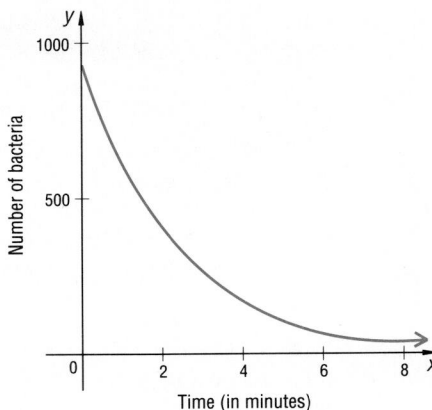

Time (in minutes)

In 25 and 26, solve for *w*.

25. $-3w < 3(1 - w)$ *(Lesson 1-9)*   **w is any real number**

26. $-3w^2 = 3(w - 1)$ *(Lesson 6-6)* $w = \frac{-1 \pm \sqrt{5}}{2}$

27. Solids A' and A are similar. The ratio of similitude is 5, with A' larger. If the volume of A is 400 cubic millimeters, what is the volume of A'? *(Previous Course)*   **50,000 mm³**

Exploration

28. Natural logarithms can be calculated using the series
    $$\ln(1 + x) = x - \frac{x^2}{2} + \frac{x^3}{3} - \frac{x^4}{4} + \frac{x^5}{5} - \dots .$$

    Substitute 0.5 for *x* to estimate ln 1.5 to the nearest hundredth.
    0.41 (need 8 terms)

29. When a single rocket engine cannot produce enough velocity to launch a spacecraft, NASA often uses "staging." Find out what staging means, and how many stages recent spacecraft have used.
    Many answers are possible.

9-9

Solving
$b^x = a$

Bikini Atoll nuclear test, 1946; see question 15, page 532.

In the previous lessons, you have learned about exponential and logarithmic functions: how to work with them, what they model, and how to use them in some applications. You now have the tools to solve equations of the form $b^x = a$.

The procedure is to:
1. take the logarithm of both sides, then
2. use the Powering Property of logarithms.

- - - - - ■ ■ ■

Example 1 Solve $5^x = 20$ for x, by
  a. taking common logarithms of each side.
  b. taking natural logarithms of each side.

Solution

a.
$$5^x = 20$$
$$\log 5^x = \log 20 \quad \text{Take the log of both sides.}$$
$$x \log 5 = \log 20 \quad \text{Powering Property of Logs}$$
$$x = \frac{\log 20}{\log 5} \quad \text{Division}$$
$$x = \frac{1.3010}{.6990} \quad \text{Use your calculator!}$$
$$x \approx 1.86$$

b.
$$5^x = 20$$
$$\ln 5^x = \ln 20$$
$$x \ln 5 = \ln 20$$
$$x = \frac{\ln 20}{\ln 5}$$
$$x = \frac{2.9957}{1.6094}$$
$$x \approx 1.86$$

Check Note that $5^1 = 5$ and $5^2 = 25$, so it makes sense that $5^{1.86} \approx 20$.

In these solutions, (a) and (b), $x = \frac{\log 20}{\log 5} = \frac{\ln 20}{\ln 5}$. In fact, any base t for the logs of 20 and 5 could be used. This result can be presented as a theorem.

LESSON 9-9   Solving $b^x = a$ **529**

LESSON 9-9

RESOURCES
■ Lesson Master 9-9
▢ Computer Master 22

┌─────────────────┐
│ **OBJECTIVES** │
└─────────────────┘

B Solve exponential equations.
G Apply exponential models and formulas.

┌─────────────────┐
│ **TEACHING NOTES** │
└─────────────────┘

You may want to introduce this lesson by asking students to solve (a) $x^2 = 144$, and (b) $2^x = 144$. The first equation is easy to solve. ($x = \pm 12$) The second equation can be approximated. Because $2^7 = 128$ and $2^8 = 256$ we know that in part (b) $7 < x < 8$, and x is probably closer to 7 than to 8. To find the exact value of x, have students pattern the solution to **Example 1**, and find that
$$x = \frac{\log 144}{\log 2} = \frac{\ln 144}{\ln 2}$$
(the exact answer) or $x \approx 7.17$ (an approximation to the nearest hundredth). If you have a computer available for demonstration, examine the graph of $y = 2^x$ near $x = 7$ and verify that $2^{7.17} \approx 144$.

Note that when solving $b^x = a$, if $b = e$ the equation can be solved easily by using the definition of natural logarithm. When $b = 10$, solve by using the definition of common logarithm. However, if b is neither e nor 10, then it becomes the solver's choice; the equation can be solved using either common or natural logs, or logs to any other base. We pick base 10 or base e because the needed values are on calculators.

529

ADDITIONAL EXAMPLES

1. Solve. $3^x = 57$

$x = \frac{\ln 57}{\ln 3} = \frac{\log 57}{\log 3} \approx 3.68$

2. At what rate of interest compounded continuously would you have to invest your money so that it would quadruple in 25 years?
$4P = Pe^{25r}$; about 5.5%

3. The number of milligrams of radium present at the end of t years is given by the formula $A = A_0 10^{-.000174t}$, where A_0 is the initial amount of radium. What is the half-life of radium; that is, how long will it take for an initial amount to reduce to half its size?
$\frac{1}{2}A_0 = A_0 10^{-.000174t}$; about 1730 years

4. Suppose the population of Ghana continues to grow continuously at a rate of 3.4% annually. If the population were 13.6 million in mid-1986, when will it reach 20 million?
$20 = 13.6e^{.034t}$; $t \approx 11.3$ years; so toward the end of 1997.

Theorem:

When $a > 0$ and $b > 0$, and $b \neq 1$, the unique real number x satisfying $b^x = a$ is $\frac{\log_t a}{\log_t b}$ for any base t, where $t > 0$, $t \neq 1$.

By the definition of logarithm $5^x = 20$ is equivalent to $x = \log_5 20$. So, in general, there are two distinct ways of solving $b^x = a$. Either use the definition of log to get $x = \log_b a$ or divide $\log_t a$ by $\log_t b$ in any base t.

Observe that in Example 1 you get the same answer using common logs as you do using natural logs. Because the same results are *always* obtained by using *either common or natural logarithms*, you may choose either one for a given situation. In some cases, one is more efficient or easier to use than the other. When the base of the exponential equation is 10, it is usually easier to use common logarithms; when the base is e, it is usually easier to use natural logs.

Example 2 At what rate of interest, compounded continuously, would you have to invest your money so that it would triple in 10 years?

Solution Use $A = Pe^{rt}$.

Since A, the total amount desired, is triple the starting amount P, $A = 3P$. Here $t = 10$. Substituting,

$$3P = Pe^{10r}.$$

Dividing by P, $3 = e^{10r}$.

Take the logarithm of each side to the base e. (This gives the same result as applying the definition of the natural logarithm.)

$$\ln 3 = 10r$$

$$r = \frac{\ln 3}{10} \approx \frac{1.0986}{10} = 0.10986$$

It takes an interest rate of about 11%, compounded continuously, to triple your money in 10 years.

Decay or depreciation problems are often modeled by exponential equations with negative powers. Such equations can also be solved by the above techniques.

530

Example 3   The intensity I_t of light through ordinary glass of thickness t (in centimeters) is modeled by the exponential equation

$$I_t = I_0 10^{-0.0434t}$$

where I_0 is the intensity before entering the glass. How thick must the glass be to block out 10% of the light?

Solution   Blocking out 10% of the light means that $I_t = .90\ I_0$.
Substitute into $I_t = I_0 10^{-0.0434t}$
to get $.90 I_0 = I_0 10^{-0.0434t}$
Divide by I_0. $.90 = 10^{-0.0434t}$
Take the log of both sides. $\log .90 = -0.0434t$

Divide by -0.0434. $t = \dfrac{\log .90}{-0.0434} \approx 1.05432$

To block out 10% of the light, ordinary glass should be a bit more than 1 cm thick.

Questions

Covering the Reading

1. Refer to Example 1. *True or false*

   $\dfrac{\log 20}{\log 5} = \dfrac{\ln 20}{\ln 5}$ **true**

2. Solve for $7^x = 15$ by
   a. taking common logarithms. $x \approx \frac{1.176}{0.845} \approx 1.39$
   b. taking natural logarithms. $x \approx \frac{2.708}{1.946} \approx 1.39$

   LESSON 9-9   Solving $b^x = a$ **531**

NOTES ON QUESTIONS
Question 3: The answer to this question is true only if we assume that both sides of the equation represent positive numbers.

Questions 11–13: It is useful to estimate the exponent between consecutive integers before solving these equations.

ADDITIONAL ANSWERS
14.a.

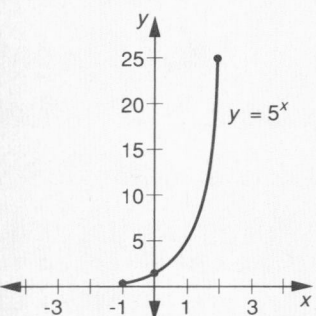

3. *True or false* If you can take the natural logarithm of both sides of an equation, then you do not change the solutions to that equation.
   true

In 4–6, solve to the nearest hundredth.

4. $2^x = 3$ $x \approx 1.59$
5. $3^y = 12$ $y \approx 2.26$
6. $25.6^z = 2.89$ $z \approx 0.33$

In 7 and 8, refer to Example 2.

7. Why is this problem more efficiently solved with natural logarithms than with common logarithms?   **the base of the equation is e**

8. What interest rate would it take to double your money in 7 years?
   about 10%

9. In Example 3, find the thickness of glass needed to block out 40% of the light.   **a little more than 5.1 cm thick**

Applying the Mathematics

10. Suppose you invested $200 in a savings account paying 6.25% interest compounded continuously. How long would it take for your account to be worth $300 if you assume that no other deposits or withdrawals are made?   **about $6\frac{1}{2}$ years**

In 11–13, solve.

11. $5^{2y} = 1986$
    $y \approx 2.36$
12. $8^{-4x} = 256$
    $x = -\frac{2}{3}$
13. $10^{r+1} = 2$ $r \approx -0.699$

14. **a.** Graph $y = 5^x$ for $-1 \le x \le 2$.   **See margin.**
    b. How does Example 1 relate to this graph?
    The graph could be used to estimate x for $5^x = 20$.

15. The amount A of radioactivity from a nuclear explosion is estimated to decrease exponentially by $A = A_0 e^{-2t}$, where t is measured in days. How long will it take for the radioactivity to reach $\frac{1}{1000}$ of its original intensity?   **about 3.5 days**

16. A colony of bacteria grows according to $N_t = N_0 e^{2t}$, where N_0 is the initial number of bacteria, t is the time in hours, and N_t is the number of bacteria after t hours. How long does it take the colony to quadruple in size?   **about 0.69 hours**

Review

17. Suppose $\ln a = 5$ and $\ln b = 10$. Find $\ln (ab)^2$. *(Lessons 9-8, 9-6)*   **30**

18. For a small 3-stage rocket, the formula

$$V = c_1 \ln R_1 + c_2 \ln R_2 + c_3 \ln R_3$$

is used to find the velocity of the rocket at the final burnout. If $R_1 = 1.46$, $R_2 = 1.28$, $R_3 = 1.41$, $c_1 = 7400$ ft/sec, and $c_2 = c_3 = 8100$ ft/sec, find V. *(Lesson 9-8)*   **$V \approx 7,583$ ft/sec**

19. Which equations model decay situations? *(Lessons 9-7, 9-2)*   **a, b, c, e**
    a. $y = ae^{-r}, r > 0$ **b.** $y = ae^{-7}$
    c. $y = 700(.69)^x$ **d.** $y = 1.66(1.08)^x$
    e. $y = 2\left(\frac{1}{e}\right)^3$

532

20. Where is the error in the following "proof" of the inequality $5 < 2$?
(Lessons 9-6, 9-4) $5 \log(\frac{1}{2}) < 2 \log(\frac{1}{2})$ gives $5 > 2$ since $\log \frac{1}{2}$ is negative.

Proof:
$$\frac{1}{32} < \frac{1}{4}$$
$$\log\left(\frac{1}{32}\right) < \log\left(\frac{1}{4}\right)$$
$$\log\left[\left(\frac{1}{2}\right)^5\right] < \log\left[\left(\frac{1}{2}\right)^2\right]$$
$$5 \log\left(\frac{1}{2}\right) < 2 \log\left(\frac{1}{2}\right)$$
$$5 < 2$$

21. In 1950 an earthquake with Richter value 8.7 hit Assam, India. How many times more intense was this earthquake than the one of intensity 8.3 that hit San Francisco in 1906? *(Lesson 9-3)*   **About 2.5**

22. The graph at the right shows a feasible region for a certain situation. Which vertex would minimize cost if the expression

$$15x + 14y$$

denotes the cost? *(Lesson 5-8)*   **(2, 3)**

In 23 and 24, solve.

23. $3f^{5/3} = 96$ *(Lesson 8-6)*
$f = 8$

24. $\log 64 = x \log 2$ *(Lesson 9-6)* $x = 6$

25. Let $N = \begin{bmatrix} 4 & 7 \\ 1 & 3 \end{bmatrix}$ and $R = \begin{bmatrix} 3 & -1 & 4 \\ 5 & 7 & -6 \end{bmatrix}$.

Find $N \cdot R$. *(Lesson 4-2)* $\begin{bmatrix} 47 & 45 & -26 \\ 18 & 20 & -14 \end{bmatrix}$

Exploration

26. Suppose $a^x = b$ and $b^y = a$. How are x and y related? (Hint: If you cannot figure this out in general, start by letting a and b have certain values and solving for x and y.)   Since $b^y = a^{xy} = a$, then $x = \frac{1}{y}$.

FOLLOW-UP

MORE PRACTICE
For more questions on SPUR Objectives, use *Lesson Master 9-9*, shown below.

EVALUATION
Alternative Assessment
Suggest that each student write the procedure to solve equations of the form $b^x = a$ on a piece of notebook paper. Then have them check their answers with the procedure stated in the textbook. Call upon a volunteer to explain the Powering Property of logarithms.

NAME

LESSON **MASTER   9–9**
QUESTIONS ON **SPUR** OBJECTIVES

■**SKILLS**   *Objective B* *(See pages 537–539 for objectives.)*
In 1–8, solve. If necessary, round to the nearest hundredth.

1. $5^x = 625$

$x = 4$

2. $18^w = 5832$

$w = 3$

3. $36^r = 216$

$r = 1.5$

4. $8^m = 4$

$m = \frac{\log 4}{\log 8} \approx .67$

5. $3e^t = 57$

$t = \ln 19 \approx 2.94$

6. $(3.1)^k = e$

$k = \frac{1}{\ln 3.1} \approx .88$

7. $6^{n-5} = 400$

$n = \frac{\log 400}{\log 6} + 5 \approx 8.34$

8. $11^{2d} = 0.5$

$d = \frac{\log 0.5}{2 \log 11} \approx -0.14$

■**USES**   *Objective G*

9. If $3000 is compounded continuously at 9.125% a year, in how many years will it triple?   **about 12 years**

10. The volume of a camphor moth ball decreases due to evaporation. If a ball has an initial volume of 4 cm³, its volume V after t weeks is given by $V = 4e^{-0.173t}$. How many weeks must pass for the ball to have a volume of 1 cm³?   **8 weeks**

Advanced Algebra © Scott, Foresman and Company

103

Summary

When $b > 0$ and $b \neq 1$, the function f: $x \to b^x$ is the exponential function with base b. We write $b^x = a$ if and only if $x = \log_b a$, so we can write f as f: $\log_b a \to a$. Its inverse f^{-1}: $b^x \to x$ is the logarithm function with base b. Because exponential and logarithmic functions are inverses, their graphs are reflection images of each other.

Exponential Curves

Growth: $y = ab^x$, $b > 1$
e.g., $y = 2^x$

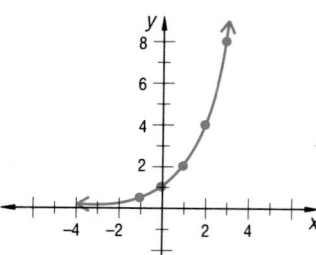

Decay: $y = ab^x$, $0 < b < 1$
e.g., $y = (\tfrac{1}{2})^x$

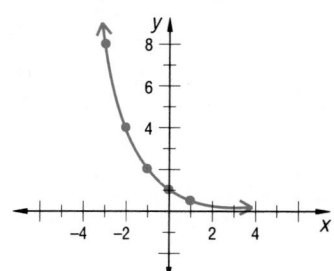

Logarithmic Curve

$y = \log_b x$, $b > 1$
e.g., $y = \log_2 x$

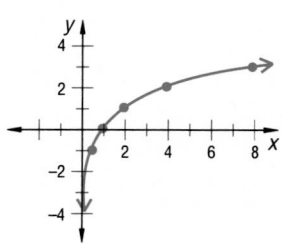

Exponential functions find their major uses in situations of growth (e.g., population growth or compound interest) or decay (e.g., depreciation or half-life). Logarithmic functions are used to scale data having a wide range (e.g., earthquake or sound intensities) and to solve equations of the form $b^x = a$, where b and a are positive. The solution to $b^x = a$ is $x = \dfrac{\log a}{\log b}$. Both kinds of functions appear in many formulas. The base of

a log function can be 10, in which case its values are called common logarithms, or the base can be $e \approx 2.71828$, in which case the values are called natural logarithms.

All the basic properties of logarithms correspond to properties of powers. Let b be any base $b > 0$, $b \neq 1$. Let $\log_b x = m$ and $\log_b y = n$. Then $b^m = x$ and $b^n = y$.

	Power property	Logarithm property
Zero exponent:	$b^0 = 1$	$\log_b 1 = 0$
To multiply powers, add exponents.	$b^m \cdot b^n = b^{m+n}$	$\log_b (xy) = \log_b x + \log_b y$
To divide powers, subtract exponents.	$\dfrac{b^m}{b^n} = b^{m-n}$	$\log_b \left(\dfrac{x}{y}\right) = \log_b x - \log_b y$
To take the power of a power, multiply the exponents.	$(b^m)^a = b^{ma}$	$\log_b (x^a) = a \log_b x$

534

Vocabulary

Below are the most important terms and phrases for this chapter. You should be able to give a definition for those terms marked with *. For all other terms you should be able to give a general description and a specific example.

Lesson 9-1
exponential function
exponential curve
exponential growth, growth factor

Lesson 9-2
exponential decay, depreciation
half-life

Lesson 9-3
logarithmic scale
Richter scale
decibel

Lesson 9-4
*common logarithm, logarithm of *m* to the base 10
logarithmic curve

Lesson 9-5
*logarithm of *m* to the base *b*

Lesson 9-6
Product Property of Logarithms
Quotient Property of Logarithms
Powering Property of Logarithms

Lesson 9-7
*The number *e*
continuous compounding
Continuously Compounded Interest Formula

Lesson 9-8
*natural logarithm, ln *x*

VOCABULARY

Terms, symbols, and properties are listed by lesson to provide a checklist of things a student must know. Emphasize to students that they should read the vocabulary list carefully before starting the Progress Self-Test. If students do not understand the meaning of a term, they should refer back to the indicated lesson.

Definitions or descriptions of all terms in the vocabulary list may be found in the Glossary.

Progress Self-Test

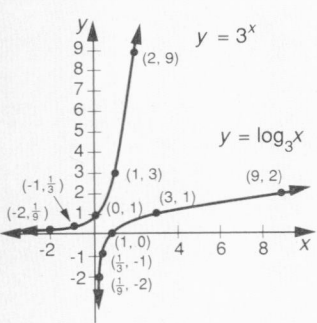

Take this test as you would take a test in class. Use graph paper and a calculator. Then check your work with the solutions in the Selected Answer section in the back of the book.

In 1–4, find each logarithm exactly.

1. $\log (1{,}000{,}000)$ **6**
2. $\log_4 \left(\frac{1}{16}\right)$ **-2**
3. $\ln e^{-6}$ **-6**
4. $\log_2 1$ **0**

In 5 and 6, find each logarithm to the nearest hundredth.

5. $\ln (42.7)$ **3.75**
6. $\log 25$ **1.40**

In 7–10, solve. If necessary, round to the nearest hundredth.

7. $e^y = 412$ **6.02**
8. $\log_x 8 = \frac{3}{4}$ **16**
9. $\log_{m+1} 30 = \log_{12} 30$ **$m = 11$**
10. $6^x = 32$ **$x \approx 1.93$**
11. Write in exponential form: $\log 45 \approx 1.65$.
    $10^{1.65} \approx 45$

In 12–14, true or false.

12. $\ln (23)^{-2} = -2 \ln 23$ **True**
13. $\log \left(\dfrac{M}{N^2}\right) = \log M - 2 \log N$ **True**
14. $\log_3 7 \cdot \log_3 13 = \log_3 91$ **False**

In 15–17, assume that bacteria decay according to the exponential model $y = A(.92)^x$, where A cells of bacteria would become y cells x hours later.

8% per hour

15. What is the rate at which the bacteria decay?
16. If you start with 12,000 bacteria, how many will remain after 8 hours?   **$y \approx 6200$ bacteria**
17. If at some time there are 1000 bacteria, how many were there two hours earlier?   **≈1200 bacteria**
18. Lana invested some money in an account in which interest is compounded continuously. If the rate is 7%, how long will it take her to double her money?   **about 10 years**
19. Suppose one sound measures 105 decibels while a second measures 125 decibels. How many times more intense is the second than the first?   **100 times**

In 20–24, consider the function $y = \log_3 x$.

20. Name five points on the graph.   **See margin.**
21. State the domain and range of the function.
    domain = positive real numbers; range = all real numbers
22. Graph the function.   **See margin.**
23. State an equation for its inverse.   **$y = 3^x$**
24. Graph the equation from Question 23 on the same axes you used in Question 22.
    See margin.

Chapter Review

Questions on **SPUR** Objectives

SPUR stands for **S**kills, **P**roperties, **U**ses, and **R**epresentations.
The Chapter Review questions are grouped according to the
SPUR Objectives for this chapter.

SKILLS deal with the procedures used to get answers

■ **Objective A:** *Determine values of logarithms. (Lessons 9-4, 9-5, 9-6, 9-8)*

In 1–8, write each number as a decimal. Do not use a calculator.

1. log 1000   3
2. log (.000001)   -6
3. ln e^9 9
4. $\log_3 243$ 5
5. $\log_{11} 11^{15}$ 15
6. ln 1   0
7. $\log_{1/2} 8$ -3
8. $\log_5 \sqrt[3]{5}$ $\frac{1}{3}$

In 9–14, find each logarithm to the nearest hundredth.

9. log 97,234   4.99
10. ln (100.95)   4.61
11. ln 87   4.47
12. log (.0003)   -3.52
13. ln (-4.1)   undefined
14. ln 10   2.30

■ **Objective B:** *Solve exponential equations. (Lesson 9-9)*

In 15–22, solve. If necessary, round to the nearest hundredth.

15. $7^x = 343$ 3
16. $9^y = 27$ $\frac{3}{2}$
17. $1000(1.05)^n = 2000$ 14.21
18. $3 \cdot 2^x = 1$ -1.59
19. $e^z = 22$ 3.09   20. $(0.4)^w = e$ -1.09
21. $12^{a+1} = 1000$ 1.78   22. $3^{-2b} = 51$ -1.79

■ **Objective C:** *Solve logarithmic equations. (Lessons 9-4, 9-5, 9-6, 9-8)*

In 23–30, solve. If necessary, round to the nearest hundredth.

23. $\log_x 37 = \log_{11} 37$ x = 11
24. ln (4y) = ln 9 + ln 12   y = 27
25. log z = 4   z = 10,000
26. log x = 2.91   x ≈ 812.83
27. 2 ln 15 = ln x   x = 225
28. $\log_8 x = \frac{3}{4}$ x ≈ 4.76
29. $\log_x 64 = 3$ x = 4
30. $\log_x 5 = 10$ x ≈ 1.17

PROPERTIES deal with the principles behind the mathematics.

■ **Objective D:** *Apply the definition of logarithm. (Lessons 9-4, 9-5, 9-8)*

In 31–34, write in exponential form.

31. $\log_6 (\frac{1}{216}) = -3$ $6^{-3} = \frac{1}{216}$
32. ln (6.28) ≈ 1.8 $e^{1.8} ≈ 6.28$
33. log a = b $10^b = a$
34. $\log_b m = n$ $b^n = m$

In 35–38, write in logarithmic form.

35. $10^{-1.2} ≈ 0.0631$ log 0.0631 ≈ -1.2
36. $e^4 ≈ 54.5982$ ln 54.5982 ≈ 4
37. $x^y = z, x > 0, x \neq 1$ $\log_x z = y$
38. $3^n = 12$ $\log_3 12 = n$

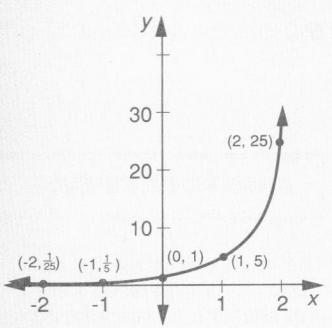
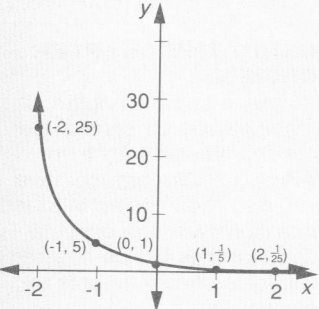
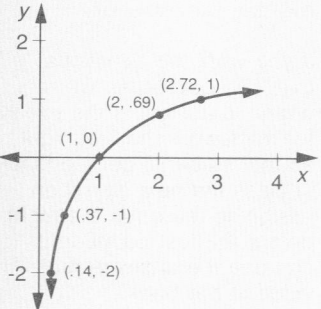
■ **Objective E:** *Identify properties of logarithms.*
(Lessons 9-6, 9-8)

In 39–44, state the general property used in simplifying the expression.

39. $\ln 3 + \ln 4 = \ln 12$ $\log_b xy = \log_b x + \log_b y$

40. $\log 40 - \log 4 = \log 10$ **See margin.**

41. $\log_{16}(13^{-2}) = -2\log_{16} 13$ $\log_b (x^n) = n \log_b x$

42. $\ln e = 1$ $\log_b b^n = n$

43. $\log_{92} 92^{81} = 81$ $\log_b b^n = n$

44. $\log_{2.1} 1 = 0$ $\log_b 1 = 0$

■ **Objective F:** *Recognize properties of exponential and logarithmic functions.* (*Lessons 9-1, 9-2, 9-4, 9-5, 9-8*)

45. What is the range of f where $f(x) = e^x$?   **all positive real numbers**

46. State the domain of the exponential function $y = 2^x$.   **all real numbers**

In 47–49, true or false.

47. The domain of the log function to the base 5 is the range of the exponential function to the base 5.   **True**

48. The logarithm of a negative number is not defined.   **True**

49. The common log function is increasing.   **True**

USES deal with the applications of mathematics in real situations.

■ **Objective G:** *Apply exponential models and formulas.* (*Lessons 9-1, 9-2, 9-7, 9-9*)

50. A certain strain of bacteria grows according to $N = N_0 e^{0.827t}$ where t is the time in hours. How long will it take for 30 bacteria to increase to 500 bacteria?   **about 3.4 hours**

51. Dennis invests $2500 at 12% interest for one year. How much more money would he have if the interest is compounded continuously than if it is compounded monthly?   **$1.68**

52. If $1000 is compounded continuously at 7.25% a year, in how many years will it triple?   **about 15.2 years**

53. The power output P (in watts) of a satellite is given by the equation $P = 50e^{-t/250}$ where t is the time in days. If the equipment aboard a satellite requires 15 watts of power, how long will the satellite be operating?   **about 301 days**

54. Strontium 90 (Sr^{90}) has a half-life of 25 years. How much will be left of 5 grams of Sr^{90} after 100 years?   **about .3125 g**

Objective H: *Apply logarithmic scales (Richter, pH, decibel), models, and formulas.* (*Lessons 9-3, 9-4, 9-8*)

about 31.6 times

55. Sea water has a pH of 8.5 while pure water has a pH of 7. How many times more acidic is pure water than sea water?

56. The formula $B = 10 \log \left(\dfrac{I}{10^{-12}} \right)$ converts sound intensity I in w/m² into decibels B. Find B when $I = 2.48 \cdot 10^9$. **about 213.9 dB**

57. How many times more intense is an earthquake with a Richter magnitude of 7.2 than one with a magnitude of 5.2? **100**

58. Under certain conditions, the height h in feet above sea level can be approximated by knowing the atmospheric pressure P in pounds per square inch (psi) using the model

$$\frac{\ln P - \ln 14.7}{-0.000039} = h.$$

If human blood at body temperature will boil at 0.9 psi, at what height would your blood boil in an unpressurized cabin? **at about 71,600 ft**

REPRESENTATIONS deal with pictures, graphs, or objects that illustrate concepts.

Objective I: *Graph exponential functions.* (*Lessons 9-1, 9-2, 9-7*)

See margin.

59. Graph $y = 5^x$ using at least 5 points.

See margin.

60. Graph $y = (\frac{1}{5})^x$ using at least 5 points.

61. Which graph, that of Question 59 or 60, represents decay? Why? **See margin.**

62. The equation of the asymptote to the graph of $y = e^x$ is ___?___. **y = 0**

Objective J: *Graph logarithmic functions.* (*Lessons 9-4, 9-5, 9-8*)

See margin.

63. **a.** Graph 5 points on $y = \ln x$.
    b. Name its inverse function.

64. The graph below has the equation $y = \log_Q x$. Find Q. **4**

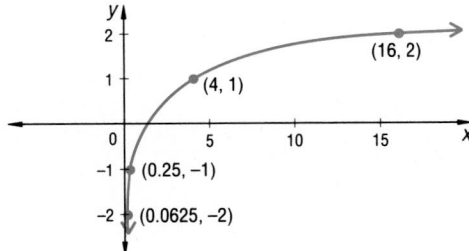

CHAPTER 9   Chapter Review   **539**

EVALUATION
Three forms of a Chapter Test are provided in the Teacher's Resource File. Chapter 9 Test, Forms A and B cover just Chapter 9. The third test is Chapter 9 Test, Cumulative Form. About 50% of this test covers Chapter 9, 25% covers Chapter 8, and 25% covers previous chapters. A fourth test, Comprehensive Test, Chapters 1–9, that is primarily multiple choice in format, is also provided. For information on grading, see *General Teaching Suggestions: Grading* on page T44 in the Teacher's Edition.

ASSIGNMENT RECOMMENDATION
We strongly recommend that you assign Lesson 10-1, both reading and some questions, for homework the evening of the test.

CHAPTER 10 ■ TRIGONOMETRY

DAILY PACING CHART ■ CHAPTER 10

Students in the Full Course should complete all but one of the chapters by the end of the year. Students in the Minimal Course spend more time on quizzes and the Chapter Review. As such, these students should complete about ten or eleven chapters.

DAY	MINIMAL COURSE	FULL COURSE
1	10-1	10-1
2	10-2	10-2
3	10-3	10-3
4	Quiz (TRF); Start 10-4.	Quiz (TRF); 10-4
5	Finish 10-4.	10-5
6	10-5	10-6
7	10-6	Quiz (TRF); 10-7
8	Quiz (TRF); Start 10-7.	10-8
9	Finish 10-7.	10-9
10	10-8	10-10
11	10-9	Progress Self-Test
12	10-10	Chapter Review
13	Progress Self-Test	Chapter Test (TRF)
14	Chapter Review	
15	Chapter Review	
16	Chapter Test (TRF)	

TESTING OPTIONS
■ Quiz for Lessons 10-1 Through 10-3   ■ Chapter 10 Test, Form A   ■ Chapter 10 Test, Cumulative Form
■ Quiz for Lessons 10-4 Through 10-6   ■ Chapter 10 Test, Form B

PROVIDING FOR INDIVIDUAL DIFFERENCES
The student text is written for the *average* student. The program, however, can be adapted for both less capable and for more capable students.

A blackline master (in the Teacher's Resource File) is provided for each lesson for those students who need more practice. The Teacher's Edition frequently provides Error Analysis and Alternate Approach features to provide additional instructional strategies.

For students who require additional challenge, Extension activities are regularly provided in the Teacher's Edition.

OBJECTIVES ■ CHAPTER 10

Students should master the chapter objectives by the time they complete the chapter. To ensure mastery, there is continual review built into each set of lesson questions. After students complete the chapter lessons, they assess their mastery on the Progress Self-Test. Then they do the Chapter Review and pay special attention to those questions that match the objectives missed on the Progress Self-Test. Students can get extra practice on these objectives by using the master for each lesson in the Teacher's Resource File.

OBJECTIVES FOR CHAPTER 10 (Organized into the SPUR categories—Skills, Properties, Uses, and Representations)	Progress Self-Test Questions	Chapter Review Questions	Lesson Master from Teacher's Resource File*
SKILLS			
A Approximate values of trigonometric functions using a calculator.	1–2	1 through 9	10-1, 10-5, 10-10
B Find exact values of trigonometric functions of certain angles.	8, 19	10 through 15	10-3, 10-4, 10-5, 10-10
C Determine the measure of an angle given its trigonometric values.	3	16 through 21	10-2, 10-8
D Convert angle measures from radians to degrees or degrees to radians.	18	22 through 29	10-10
E Find missing parts of a triangle using the Law of Sines or the Law of Cosines.	14–16	30 through 35	10-6, 10-7, 10-8
PROPERTIES			
F Identify and use definitions and theorems relating sines and cosines.	7, 20	36 through 43	10-3, 10-8
USES			
G Solve real-world problems using the trigonometry of right triangles.	5–6, 17	44 through 48	10-1, 10-2
H Solve real-world problems using the Law of Sines or Law of Cosines.	13	49 through 51	10-6, 10-7
REPRESENTATIONS			
I Use the properties of a unit circle to find trigonometric values.	4	52 through 55	10-4, 10-5
J Identify properties of the sine and cosine functions using their graphs.	9–12	56 through 60	10-9, 10-10

* The masters are numbered to match the lessons.

540B

OVERVIEW ■ CHAPTER 10

This chapter is an introduction to trigonometry. UCSMP *Advanced Algebra* covers only the sine, cosine, and tangent ratios. The reciprocal ratios are studied in *Functions, Statistics, and Trigonometry with Computers.*

Trigonometry is included because every student at this level should know something about this branch of mathematics. It is important, not only in engineering and the sciences, but also in the trades, such as carpentry, electronics, drafting, and metals.

Knowledge of the sine, cosine, and tangent ratios provides sufficient mathematical power to solve virtually all trigonometry problems.

Chapter 10 contains ten lessons. The first three are devoted to right triangle trigonometry. The content is traditional. It covers solving for the lengths of sides or measures of angles in right triangles and the proofs of some standard identities, such as $(\cos \theta)^2 + (\sin \theta)^2 = 1$. Calculators are used to find values of trigonometric ratios. Trigonometric tables are not provided in this text.

In Lessons 10-4 and 10-5, the definitions of the sine and cosine ratios are extended from acute angles to angles of any possible magnitude. In Lesson 10-6 through 10-8, this knowledge is employed to develop and apply the Law of

Cosines and the Law of Sines. By the end of Lesson 10-8, students will have had extensive experience with the classical meaning of *trigonometry*, that is, triangle measuring.

The last two lessons introduce two ideas which are central to the study of trigonometry in advanced mathematics courses: the trigonometric ratios as functions (Lesson 10-9), and radian measure (Lesson 10-10).

PERSPECTIVES ■ CHAPTER 10

The Perspectives provide the rationale for the inclusion of topics or approaches, provide mathematical background, and make connections within UCSMP.

10-1

THE TRIGONOMETRIC RATIOS

In this lesson, students learn to apply the definitions of sine, cosine, and tangent to find the lengths of sides in right triangles. Solving triangles for missing angle measures is introduced in the next lesson.

The definitions are justified by a customary argument based on properties of similar triangles. However, we incorporate two innovative methods: (1) the use of calculators rather than tables to determine values of trigonometric functions, and (2) the use of decimal notation to express fractions of a degree. These changes reflect corresponding changes in modern usage.

10-2

MORE RIGHT TRIANGLE TRIGONOMETRY

This lesson uses the sine, cosine, and tangent ratios to find angle measures in right triangles and provides practice in determining

sides of right triangles when auxiliary lines are needed. The applications involve angles of elevation, angles of depression, and diagonals of regular polygons.

10-3

PROPERTIES OF SINES AND COSINES

In this lesson, we prove three identities: $\sin \theta = \cos(90° - \theta)$, $\cos \theta = \sin(90° - \theta)$, and $(\cos \theta)^2 + (\sin \theta)^2 = 1$; and a theorem about exact values of the sine and cosine ratios for 30°, 45°, and 60°. In spite of the use of calculators, knowledge of exact values of various ratios is still very useful, especially with regard to regular polygons, for graphing the functions, and for providing benchmarks for comparison with other values.

10-4

THE UNIT CIRCLE

In this lesson, the concept of sine and cosine is extended to apply to rotations of any magnitude. The definitions are given in terms of the coordinates of the image of the point (1, 0) as it is rotated around the center of the unit circle. These definitions make the Pythagorean Identity $(\cos \theta)^2 + (\sin \theta)^2 = 1$ readily apparent and, because of the use of the unit circle, help to prepare the students for the concept of radian measure, introduced in Lesson 10-10.

10-5

COSINES AND SINES IN QUADRANTS II–IV

With the definition of $(\cos \theta, \sin \theta)$ based on rotations, it follows to use reflections and rotations to obtain exact values of sines and cosines for multiples of 30° and 45° that are not in the first quadrant. This method is also very efficient, because it uses reference points rather than reference angles.

Of course, a calculator will give approximations to these values regardless of the value of θ. The reason for this lesson is to give the student a way to check the calculator. This exemplifies our philosophy: students should have a way to check everything they do.

10-6
THE LAW OF COSINES
The existence of a possible Law of Cosines is predicted by the SAS Triangle Congruence proposition of geometry. SAS implies that the measures of the other side and other two angles are determined by two sides and the included angle. The Law of Cosines indicates how to find that third side and, if it is applied twice, how to find the other angles.

The text points out (at the end of Lesson 10-7) that an equivalent form of the Law of Cosines was known to Euclid. The form in which the Law of Cosines is stated in Euclid's *Elements* is quite different from today's form. The cosine of the angle is not used because cosines had not been identified. Instead, the equivalent right triangle ratio is found using projections of one side on another.

The historical importance of the Law of Cosines and the Law of Sines and the entire realm of triangle trigonometry should not be minimized. During the previous few centuries, explorers mapped new regions of Earth using the method of triangulation, which requires a knowledge of these theorems only. Not until the man-made satellites of the 1960s were significantly better methods available for mapping.

10-7
THE LAW OF SINES
This is the first of two lessons on the Law of Sines. We use the fact that a triangle has a unique area to develop the proof of the theorem. In this lesson, the Law of Sines is used to find lengths of sides in a triangle when either an ASA or AAS condition is given. The SSA condition is discussed in Lesson 10-8.

10-8
SOLVING SIN $\theta = k$
When solving a triangle given the SSA conditions, a unique triangle does not always exist.

When the Law of Sines is employed to find the other angle θ, an equation of the form $\sin \theta = k$ appears, and θ may be either obtuse or acute. This lesson examines this case and points out to students that they must always check both possibilities when solving such a triangle.

10-9
THE COSINE AND SINE FUNCTIONS
For the past three lessons, students have been working primarily with values of θ between 0° and 180°. In this lesson, θ can again be any real number, and we introduce the idea of functions mapping θ either to cos θ or to sin θ. The relationships between the unit circle and the graphs of these functions will be extended in later courses.

10-10
RADIAN MEASURE
Distances are measured in many different units (centimeters, meters, inches, feet) and so are angles. The two most commonly used angle measurements are the degree and the radian. This lesson relates these two systems of angle measurement.

Radians are important because the formulas for calculating the values of the trigonometric functions (the formulas used in calculators) are based on them, and because the trigonometric functions in terms of radians have nice properties. Also, the derivative and integral formulas for trigonometric functions students will use in calculus are based on radian measure.

CHAPTER 10

We recommend 13 to 16 days for this chapter: 10 to 12 on the lessons; 1 for the Progress Self-Test; 1 or 2 for the Chapter Review; and 1 for a Chapter test. (See the Daily Pacing Chart on page 540A.) If you spend more than 16 days on this chapter, you are moving too slowly. Keep in mind that each lesson includes Review questions to help students firm up content studied previously.

USING PAGES 540–541
Have students read the material on these pages the night after their test on Chapter 9. When discussing Lesson 10-1, note that the method used to find the height of the flag pole is the method used to measure the height of the Egyptian pyramids. The use of shadows to measure the angle of the sun is explained in Lesson 10-2.

Point out that trigonometry is one of the oldest branches of mathematics, but that it is still very useful in solving problems in today's modern world.

CHAPTER 10

Trigonometry

The word *trigonometry* is derived from Greek words meaning "triangle measure," and its study usually begins by examining relationships between sides and angles in right triangles. These ideas originated thousands of years ago. As early as 1500 B.C., the Egyptians had sun clocks. Using their ideas, the ancient Greeks created sundials by erecting a gnomon, or staff, in the ground. The shadows and the height of the gnomon created triangles that could be used to measure the angle of the sun. With these measurements, the Greeks could measure the duration of a year.

540

By measuring shadows and the angle of the sun, ancient people were also able to measure heights of natural or man-made objects. "Shadow reckoning" was used by the Greeks to measure heights of the Egyptian pyramids. In the 15th to 18th centuries, instruments were developed to aid in measuring the height of the sun and of various other objects. Today the shadows cast by the sun are employed to find the depths of craters on the moon or the heights of dust tornadoes on Mars.

Trigonometry is also used to describe the motion of radio and other waves, called *sinusoidal motion*. For instance, for a spacecraft launched from Cape Canaveral, trigonometry helps to describe its motion. The spacecraft's distance from the equator with respect to time is sinusoidal, and can be described with trigonometry.

This chapter proceeds as the history of trigonometry did; it starts with right triangle relationships, moves to the study of all triangles, and then considers the ideas needed to describe sinusoidal motion.

This modern sundial is decorated with the twelve signs of the zodiac.

RESOURCES
■ Lesson Master 10-1

A Approximate values of trigonometric functions using
a calculator.
G Solve real-world problems
using the trigonometry of
right triangles.

TEACHING NOTES

Most students will benefit
from actually measuring the
angles and sides of triangles
ABC and A'B'C'. Have stu-
dents calculate selected
ratios. Discuss how the AA
Similarity Theorem guarantees that whenever $m\angle A =$
$m\angle A'$ and $m\angle B = m\angle B'$,
the ratios $\frac{AC}{AB}$ and $\frac{A'C'}{A'B'}$ must
be equal.

Now have students use their
calculators to determine
cos 35°, sin 35°, and tan 35°,
and compare these to the
ratios $\frac{AC}{AB}$, $\frac{BC}{AB}$, and $\frac{BC}{AC}$,
respectively, from their
measurements.

Discuss **Examples 2 and
3** to illustrate how the trigonometric ratios are used to
solve problems. Note that in
Example 3 exact values for
cos 30° and sin 30° are not
used. These are introduced
in Lesson 10-3.

Encourage students to solve
their equations for the unknowns *before* using their
calculators.

The Trigonometric Ratios

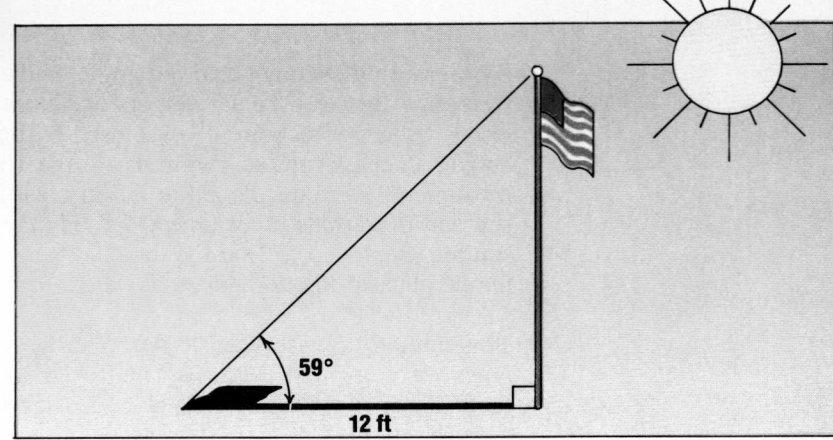

Suppose a flagpole casts a 12-ft shadow when the sun is at an angle
of 59° with the ground. What is the height of the pole?

Problems such as this one can be solved by using trigonometry.
Consider the two right triangles ABC and $A'B'C'$, with $\angle A \cong \angle A'$.

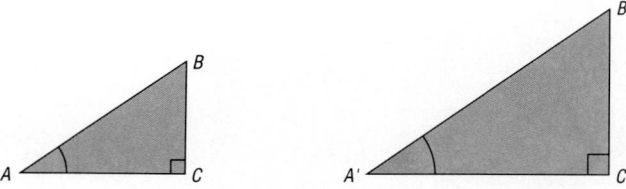

By the AA Similarity Theorem, these triangles are similar, so the
ratios of the lengths of corresponding sides are equal. In particular,

$$\frac{B'C'}{BC} = \frac{A'B'}{AB}.$$

Exchanging the means gives the equivalent proportion,

$$\frac{B'C'}{A'B'} = \frac{BC}{AB}.$$

Look more closely at these ratios:

$$\frac{B'C'}{A'B'} = \frac{\text{length of leg opposite } \angle A'}{\text{length of hypotenuse of } \triangle A'B'C'}$$

and

$$\frac{BC}{AB} = \frac{\text{length of leg opposite } \angle A}{\text{length of hypotenuse of } \triangle ABC}.$$

542

In all right triangles with an angle congruent to $\angle A$, the ratio of the length of the leg opposite that angle to the length of the hypotenuse of the triangle is the same. Likewise, in these triangles, any other ratio of sides is constant. These ratios are called **trigonometric ratios**. There are six possible ratios. All six have special names, but three of them are more important and are defined here. The Greek letter θ (theta) is customarily used to refer to either the angle or its measure.

Definitions:

In a right triangle with acute angle θ,

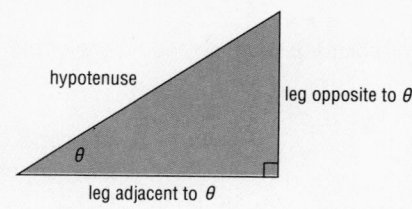

$$\text{sine of } \theta = \frac{\text{length of leg opposite } \theta}{\text{length of hypotenuse}};$$

$$\text{cosine of } \theta = \frac{\text{length of leg adjacent to } \theta}{\text{length of hypotenuse}};$$

$$\text{tangent of } \theta = \frac{\text{length of leg opposite } \theta}{\text{length of leg adjacent to } \theta}.$$

To follow a practice begun by Euler, we use the abbreviations **sin** θ, **cos** θ, and **tan** θ to stand for the above ratios. Also, the definitions can be abbreviated as follows:

$$\sin \theta = \frac{\text{opposite}}{\text{hypotenuse}} = \frac{\text{opp}}{\text{hyp}}$$

$$\cos \theta = \frac{\text{adjacent}}{\text{hypotenuse}} = \frac{\text{adj}}{\text{hyp}}$$

$$\tan \theta = \frac{\text{opposite}}{\text{adjacent}} = \frac{\text{opp}}{\text{adj}}$$

Most scientific calculators have a [DRG] key which allows you to enter angle measures in three different units: degrees, radians, or gradients. Small type on the display screen indicates what type of unit your calculator will display (DEG, RAD, GRAD). You should press the [DRG] key until the screen displays DEG. Then, to evaluate the sine of $n°$, enter n then press [sin]. Your calculator will display a 7- or 8-place decimal. In this book, we will round this value to 3 places. The other ratios are evaluated in the same way.

Alternate Approach
Some teachers like to use the mnemonic SOH-CAH-TOA (pronounced "sō-kă-tō-ah") to help the students remember the three ratios:

SOH: $\mathbf{s}$in $= \dfrac{\mathbf{o}\text{pp}}{\mathbf{h}\text{yp}}$;

CAH: $\mathbf{c}$os $= \dfrac{\mathbf{a}\text{dj}}{\mathbf{h}\text{yp}}$;

TOA: $\mathbf{t}$an $= \dfrac{\mathbf{o}\text{pp}}{\mathbf{a}\text{dj}}$.

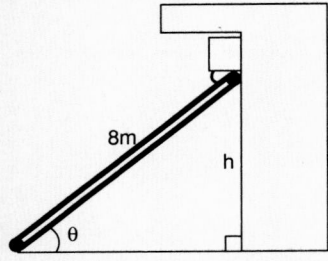
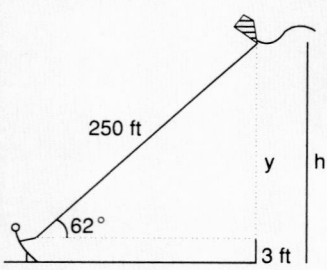
■ ■ ■ ■ ■ ■ ■ ■

Example 1   Find tan 49°.

Solution   The key sequence 49 [tan] shows that tan 49° ≈ 1.150 ... .

Check   Use the definition and draw a 49° angle in a right triangle. In right triangle *ABC*,

$$\tan A = \tan 49° = \frac{\text{leg opposite } \angle A}{\text{leg adjacent to } \angle A} = \frac{BC}{AB}.$$ We measure the sides and find *BC* ≈ 25 mm and *AB* ≈ 22 mm. Thus tan 49° ≈ $\frac{25}{22}$ ≈ 1.136.

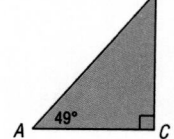

■ ■ ■ ■ ■ ■ ■ ■

Example 2   Find the height of the flagpole mentioned in the first paragraph of this lesson.

Solution   With respect to the 49° angle, the adjacent leg is known and the opposite leg is needed. Consequently, use the tangent ratio to set up an equation.

$$\tan 49° = \frac{\text{opposite}}{\text{adjacent}}$$

$$\tan 49° = \frac{x}{12}$$

Solve for *x*.   12 · tan 49° = *x*

From Example 1, we know tan 49° ≈ 1.150,

so   *x* ≈ 12(1.150) ≈ 13.8.

The flagpole is about 13.8 ft high.

Check   Recall from geometry that within a triangle, longer sides are opposite larger angles. We have found that the side opposite the 49° angle is about 13.8 feet long. The angle opposite the 12 foot side is 41°, which is smaller than 49°. So the answer makes sense.

Trigonometry is often used in navigation. By using the path of a ship or plane, and a map with north-south and east-west lines, you can calculate the distance traveled even without a ruler.

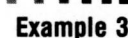

■ ■ ■ ■ ■ ■ ■

Example 3   A rocket with a range of 200 km is launched at sea with a bearing of 30°. (A bearing is the angle measured clockwise from due north.)
a. How far north of its original position will the rocket land?
b. How far east of its original position will the rocket land?

544

Solution   Call the original position Q and the landing position L. Construct right triangle QPL.

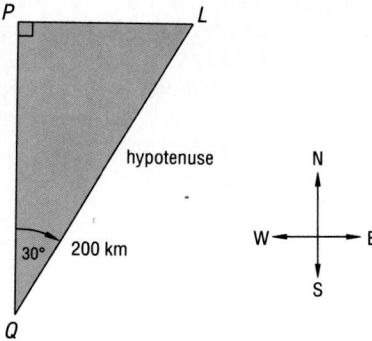

a. The leg adjacent to $\angle Q$, QP, is needed and the hypotenuse QL is known. Use the cosine ratio.

$$\cos Q = \frac{adj}{hyp} = \frac{QP}{QL}$$

$$\cos 30° = \frac{QP}{200}$$

$$QP = 200 \cdot \cos 30°$$

Use the calculator sequence 200 ⨯ 30 cos =.

$$QP \approx 173.21.$$

The rocket should land 173 km north of its original position.

b. The leg opposite $\angle Q$, PL, is needed. The hypotenuse QL is known. Use the sine of $\angle Q$.

$$\sin Q = \frac{opp}{hyp} = \frac{PL}{QL}$$

$$\sin 30° = \frac{PL}{200}$$

$$PL = 200 \sin 30°$$

Use the calculator sequence 200 ⨯ 30 sin =.

$$PL = 100$$

The rocket should land 100 km east of its original position.

Check 1 $\triangle PQR$ is a 30-60-90 right triangle. The leg opposite the 30° angle should be half the hypotenuse, which it is.

Check 2   The sides should agree with the Pythagorean Theorem.
Does $(173.21)^2 + 100^2 = 200^2$?
Does $30001.704 + 10000 = 40000$?
Yes. Slight differences are due to rounding.

NOTES ON QUESTIONS
Questions 6 and 7:
These questions provide drill on the definitions of the three trigonometric ratios. Stress that each acute angle in a right triangle has its own "personal" adjacent leg and opposite leg.

Question 13: Students may need to be directed to **Example 3** for the definition of bearing.

The first person to calculate values akin to today's sines was the Greek mathematician Ptolemy in the 2nd century A.D. The first elaborate tables of values for the sine ratio were due to Johannes Müller (1436–1476), who called himself Regiomontanus. Both Ptolemy and Regiomontanus dealt with lengths of chords in circles, not directly with right triangles. The idea of using ratios in right triangles to solve these problems is due to Georg Joachim Rhaeticus (1514–1576). Today's calculators have made tables almost entirely unnecessary.

Questions

Covering the Reading

1. What is the origin of the word "trigonometry"?
   Greek word meaning "triangle measure"
2. Name one current application where "shadow reckoning" is used.
   To find the depths of craters on the moon.
3. The motion of radio and other waves is called __?__.
   sinusoidal motion
4. In similar triangles the ratios of the lengths of corresponding sides are __?__. **equal**

5. *Multiple choice* Consider the ratios $\frac{QV}{PV}$, $\frac{RU}{PU}$, and $\frac{ST}{PT}$ in triangles PQV, PUR, and PTS at the right. Which ratio is largest? **d**
   (a) $\frac{QV}{PV}$ (b) $\frac{RU}{PU}$ (c) $\frac{ST}{PT}$
   (d) They are all equal.

6. Refer to the figure below. Copy and complete with the correct ratio.
   a. $\sin \theta = $ __?__. $\frac{x}{z}$
   b. $\cos \theta = $ __?__. $\frac{y}{z}$
   c. $\tan \theta = $ __?__. $\frac{x}{y}$

7. Refer to right $\triangle ABC$ at the right.
   a. $\overline{BC}$ is the __?__. **hypotenuse**
   b. The leg opposite $\angle B$ is __?__. $\overline{AC}$
   c. The leg adjacent to $\angle B$ is __?__. $\overline{AB}$
   d. $\overline{AB}$ is the leg opposite __?__. $\angle C$
   e. $\frac{AC}{AB} = $ __?__ $\angle B$. **the tangent of**
   f. $\frac{AC}{BC} = $ __?__ $\angle B$. **the sine of**
   g. $\frac{AB}{BC} = $ __?__ $\angle B$. **the cosine of**

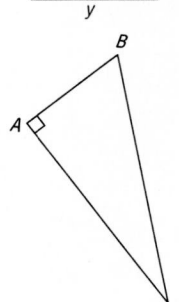

546

8. a. Measure the lengths of each side of
$\triangle DEF$ at the right to the nearest
millimeter, and then estimate sin D,
cos D, and tan D using ratios.   See margin.
b. m$\angle D \approx 25°$. Check your answers from
part a by finding sin D, cos D, and
tan D on a calculator.   See margin.

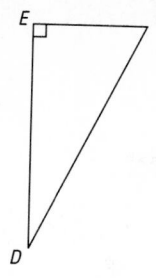

In 9–11, use your calculator to evaluate each of the following to three decimal places.

9. sin 22.5°   0.383   **10.** tan 45°   1.000   **11.** cos 87°   0.052

12. Refer to Example 2. If the shadow were 20 feet long, what would be the height of the flagpole? (Assume the angle of the sun is still 49°.)
about 23 feet

Applying the Mathematics

13. A ship sails 340 kilometers on a bearing of 75°.
a. How far north of its original position is the ship?   ≈88 km
b. How far east of its original position is the ship?   ≈328 km

14. Refer to the figure at the right.
Find the lengths of x and z.
$x \approx 7.3$, $z \approx 12.4$

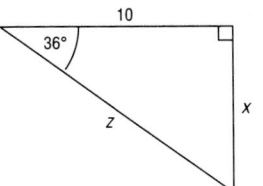

15. A 20-ft ladder is placed against a wall at an angle of 50° with the ground. How far from the base of the wall is the bottom of the ladder?   ≈12.9 ft

MORE PRACTICE
For more questions on SPUR
Objectives, use *Lesson Master 10-1*, shown below.

ADDITIONAL ANSWERS
8.a. *EF* ≈ 19 mm,
DF ≈ 42 mm, *DE* ≈ 38 mm;
sin *D* ≈ .452, cos *D* ≈ .905,
tan *D* ≈ .5
b. sin *D* ≈ .423, cos *D* ≈
.906, tan *D* ≈ .466

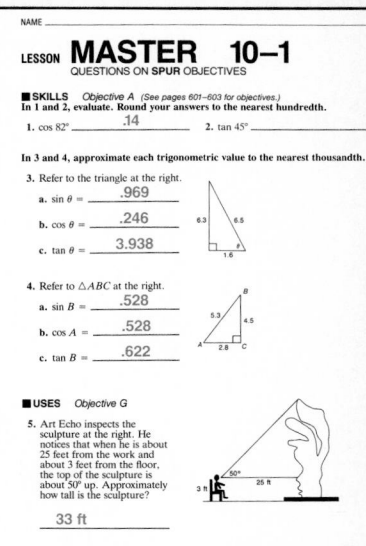

NAME _____

LESSON **MASTER   10–1**
QUESTIONS ON **SPUR** OBJECTIVES

■ **SKILLS**   *Objective A (See pages 601–603 for objectives.)*
In 1 and 2, evaluate. Round your answers to the nearest hundredth.

1. cos 82° _____ .14   2. tan 45° _____

In 3 and 4, approximate each trigonometric value to the nearest thousandth.

3. Refer to the triangle at the right.
a. sin θ = _____ .969
b. cos θ = _____ .246
c. tan θ = _____ 3.938

4. Refer to △*ABC* at the right.
a. sin *B* = _____ .528
b. cos *A* = _____ .528
c. tan *B* = _____ .622

■ **USES**   *Objective G*

5. Art Echo inspects the
sculpture at the right. He
notices that when he is about
25 feet from the work and
about 3 feet from the floor,
the top of the sculpture is
about 50° up. Approximately
how tall is the sculpture?

_____ 33 ft

6. A ship sails 230 kilometers on a bearing of 17°.   _____ 67.25 km
How far north of its original position is the ship?

104   *Advanced Algebra © Scott, Foresman and Company*

547

NOTES ON QUESTIONS
Questions 18 and 19:
These questions review material needed in Lesson 10-4.

Questions 20 and 21:
These questions review material needed in Lesson 10-2.

ADDITIONAL ANSWERS
16.a.

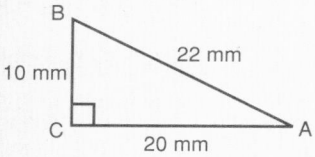

c. All triangles will be similar, so the ratios will be the same for all triangles.

16. In right triangle ABC, $\angle C$ is the right angle and $CA = 2CB$.
 a. Draw one such triangle. **See margin.**
 b. Measure each side to the nearest mm and calculate $\cos A$. $\cos A = .909$
 c. Why should your answer for part b be about the same as your classmates'? **See margin.**

Review

17. Give the measure of each angle in a regular polygon of n sides. *(Previous course)* $\frac{180(n - 2)}{n}$

18. Give the coordinates of the image of $(1, 0)$ under each transformation. *(Lessons 4-4, 4-5)*
 a. R_{90} $(0, 1)$ **b.** R_{-90} $(0, -1)$ **c.** R_{180} $(-1, 0)$ **d.** r_x $(1, 0)$

19. What is the image of (x, y) under r_y? *(Lesson 4-5)* $(-x, y)$

In 20 and 21, *true or false*.
Refer to the figure at the right where $j \parallel k$. *(Previous course)*

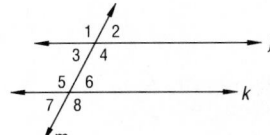

20. $\angle 3 \cong \angle 6$ true

21. $\angle 2 \cong \angle 5$ false

22. The number of prime numbers less than a positive integer p is given approximately by $\frac{p}{\ln p}$. About how many primes are there less than 1 billion? *(Lesson 9-8)* $\approx 4.83 \times 10^7$

23. The half-life of carbon-14 is about 5730 years. How many years does it take 1 kg of C^{14} to decay to 250 g? *(Lessons 9-2, 9-9)* $\approx 11,460$ years

Exploration

24. Find a book containing tables of sines and cosines.
 a. To how many decimal places are the values given?
 b. To how many decimal places does your calculator give values?
 Answers will vary.

548

LESSON

10-2

More Right Triangle Trigonometry

In the last lesson you learned how to find lengths of sides in right triangles using the trigonometric ratios. It is also possible to use the trigonometric ratios to find angle measures in right triangles.

The **angle of elevation** of the sun is the angle between the line of sight to the sun and the horizontal. From this angle the ancient Greeks, like present-day astronomers, could determine the time of day. Using other stars, they could also tell time at night.

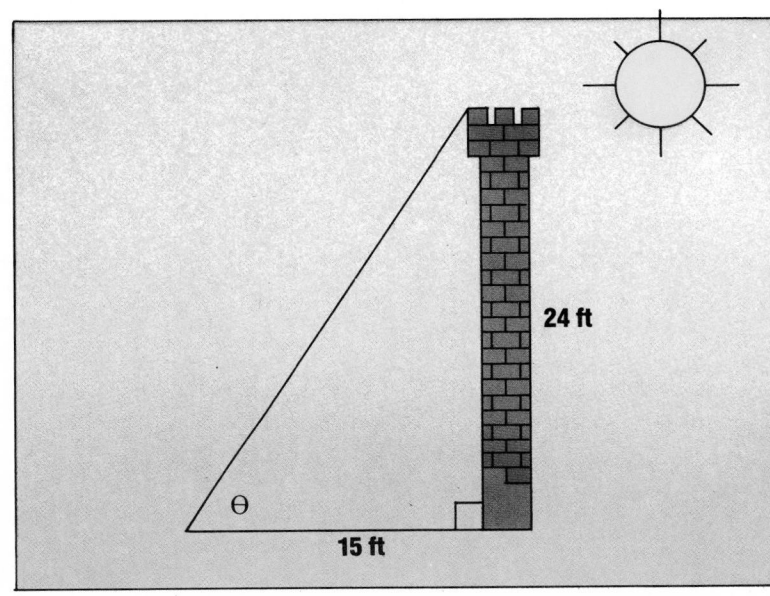

Example 1 A 24-foot high tower casts a 15-foot shadow. What is the angle of elevation of the sun?

Solution Let θ be the angle of elevation. You are given the lengths of the sides opposite and adjacent to θ so use the tangent ratio.

$$\tan \theta = \frac{\text{opposite}}{\text{adjacent}} = \frac{24}{15} = 1.6$$

Now find an angle θ whose tangent equals 1.6. To find that angle, use the $\boxed{\text{INV}}$ or $\boxed{\text{2nd}}$ key on your calculator. A possible key sequence is 1.6 $\boxed{\text{INV}}$ $\boxed{\text{tan}}$; the display should show 57.994617, which is the measure of θ in degrees. The angle of elevation is about 58°.

LESSON 10-2

RESOURCES
■ Lesson Master 10-2
▱ Visual for Teaching Aid 60 displays the problem of Additional Example 2.
▱ Visual for Teaching Aid 61 displays the problem of Additional Example 3.

OBJECTIVES

C Determine the measure of an acute angle given one of its trigonometric values.
G Solve real-world problems using the trigonometry of right triangles.

TEACHING NOTES

In this lesson, students are given (or can compute) the value of a trigonometric ratio for a particular acute angle and are asked to find the value of the angle. Make certain that each student is using the calculator correctly before proceeding with the lesson.

Explain that one side of an angle of elevation or an angle of depression is horizontal while the other side is directed toward the object being viewed.

In **Example 3**, it might be helpful to work through the geometry of the problem with the class. (The sum of the measures of the interior angles of a regular polygon is $180(n - 2)$. Divide by n and conclude that the measure of each angle is $180(n - 2)/n$.)

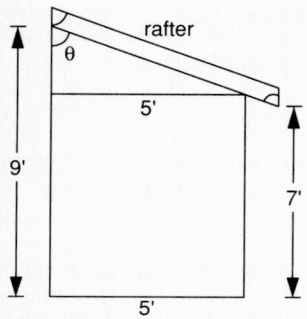
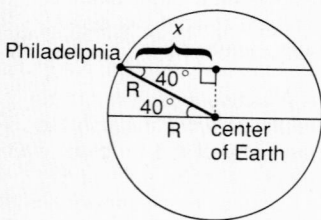
Related to the angle of elevation is another angle. In the figure at the right, if A looks up at B, then θ is the angle of elevation. B has to look down at A. The angle between B's line of sight and the horizontal is called the **angle of depression**. In the figure at the right, the angle of depression is labeled α (the Greek letter alpha). The line of sight between A and B is a transversal for the parallel horizontal lines. Thus θ and α are alternate interior angles and must be congruent. *So the angle of elevation is equal to the angle of depression.*

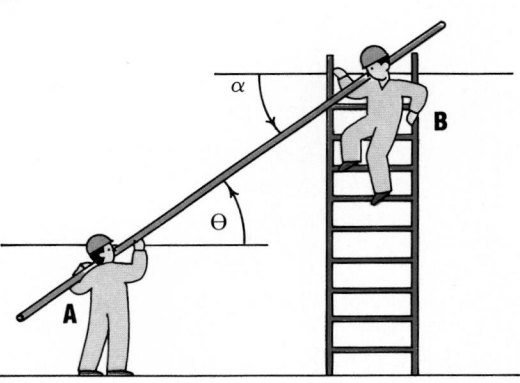

Example 2   A surveyor on top of a building finds that there is a 28° angle of depression to the head of the 6-ft tall assistant. If the assistant is 40 ft from the building, how tall is the building?

Solution   Draw a picture. The angle of depression, which is not inside the drawn triangle, is congruent to the angle of elevation, which is in the drawn triangle. The height of the building can be found by adding x to the 6-ft height of the assistant. To find x, use the tangent ratio because the adjacent side is known and the opposite side is needed.

$$\tan 28° = \frac{\text{opposite}}{\text{adjacent}} = \frac{x}{40}$$
$$(40)(\tan 28°) = x$$
$$(40)(.532) \approx x$$
$$21 \approx x$$

The height of the building is about 21 + 6 = 27 ft.

550

550

In some situations you may need to draw auxiliary lines to create right triangles.

■ ■ ■ ■ ■ ■ ■ ■ ■ ■

Example 3 Each edge in the regular pentagon *VIOLA* is 7.8 cm. Find the length of diagonal $\overline{VO}$.

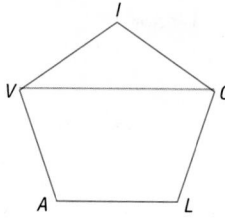

Solution Create a right triangle by drawing the perpendicular to $\overline{VO}$ from *I*. Call the intersection point *P*, as in the drawing at the right. Recall that each angle in a regular pentagon has measure

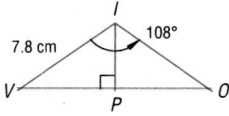

$$\frac{180(5 - 2)}{5} = 108°,$$

so m∠*VIO* = 108°. $\overline{IP}$ bisects ∠*VIO*. So m∠*VIP* = 54°. Since the hypotenuse of △*VIP* is known and the opposite leg, $\overline{VP}$, is needed, use the sine ratio.

$$\sin 54° = \frac{\text{opposite}}{\text{hypotenuse}}$$

$$\sin 54° = \frac{VP}{7.8}$$

$$7.8 \cdot \sin 54° \approx VP$$

$$6.3 \approx VP$$

The perpendicular $\overline{IP}$ bisects $\overline{VO}$, so the diagonal is about 2(6.3) or 12.6 cm long.

North Pole below. The length of the 40° circle of latitude is the circumference of the circle with radius *x* ≈ 4900. The circumference is 2π*x* ≈ 31,000 km. One degree is 1/360th of that, or about 86 km.

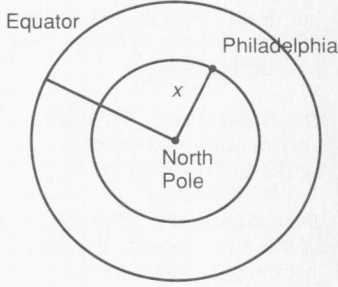

Questions

Covering the Reading

1. Write a key sequence to find θ if cos θ = .866.   .866 [INV] [COS]

In 2–4, find the value of θ to the nearest degree.

2. tan θ = .25   14°   **3.** sin θ = .61   38°   **4.** cos θ = .80   37°

5. The angle of elevation is the angle made between the line of sight of the object and the __?__.   **horizontal**

6. Refer to Example 1. If a 37-ft tower casts a 6.2-ft shadow, what is the angle of elevation of the sun?   **about 80°**

LESSON 10-2 More Right Triangle Trigonometry   **551**

NOTES ON QUESTIONS
Questions 11–15: To ease students into the study of trigonometry, we provide diagrams for these questions. Later in the chapter, students are expected to draw their own sketches.

Question 16: This question leads directly to Lesson 10-3 and should be discussed in detail.

Question 20: This question will be needed for Lessons 10-4 and 10-5.

Question 21: The results of this question will be used in Lessons 10-6 through 10-8.

Question 24: This question requires knowledge of latitude. You may need to refer students to a globe or atlas.

7. In the picture below, a person is standing on a cliff looking down at a boat. __?__ is the angle of depression.   θ

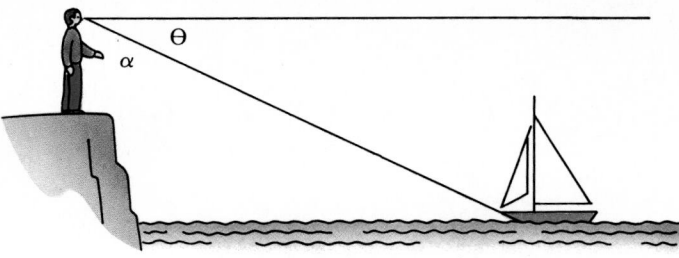

8. *True or false* The angle of elevation from a point *A* to a point *B* equals the angle of depression from *B* to *A*.   true

9. Refer to Example 2. Suppose the same assistant stands 50 ft from another building, and the angle of depression is 65°. How tall is this new building?   ≈113 ft

10. In Example 3, find *IP* to the nearest tenth of a centimeter.   4.6 cm

Applying the Mathematics

11. Refer to △*RFK* below. Find θ to the nearest degree.   ≈31°

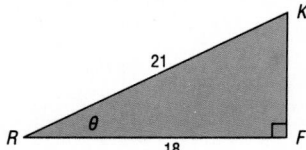

12. To avoid a steep descent, a plane flying at 35,000 ft starts its descent 150 miles from the airport. For the angle of descent θ to be constant, at what angle should the plane descend?   ≈2.5°

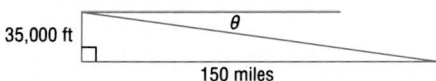

M10-2,12

13. A certain ski slope is 580 meters long with a vertical drop of 150 m. At what angle does the skier descend?   ≈15°

552

552

14. Suppose each side in regular octagon *ABCDEFGH* at the right has a length of 4 cm. Find the length of $\overline{AC}$.   ≈7.4 cm

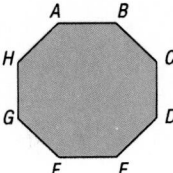

Review

15. To estimate the distance across a river Sir Vare marks point *A* near one bank, sights a tree *T* growing on the opposite bank, and measures off a distance *AB* of 100 ft. At *B* he sights *T* again. If m∠*A* = 90° and m∠*B* = 76°, how wide is the river? *(Lesson 10-1)*   ≈401 ft

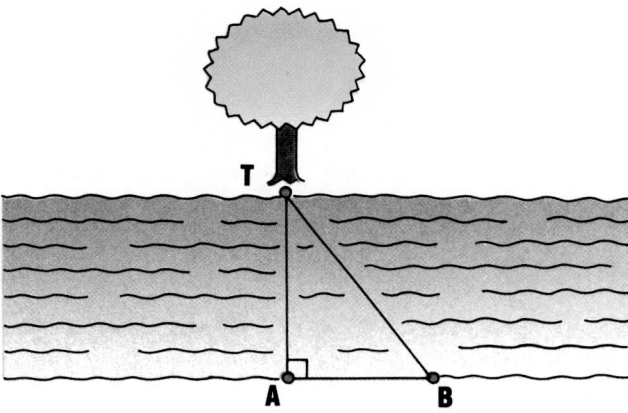

16. There is an interesting relationship between the sine and cosine that is illustrated below. *(Lesson 10-1)*

a. Copy and complete the chart with the aid of a calculator.

θ	10°	20°	30°	40°	50°	60°	70°	80°
sin θ	≈.174	≈.342	.5	≈.643	≈.766	≈.866	≈.940	≈.985
cos θ	≈.985	≈.940	≈.866	≈.766	≈.643	.5	≈.342	≈.174

b. Make a conjecture. For all θ between 0° and 90°, sin θ = __?__ . $\cos(90° - θ)$

c. Prove your conjecture. (You may wish to use the triangle below.)

See margin.

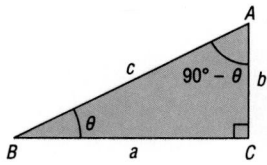

NAME _____

LESSON **MASTER   10–2**
QUESTIONS ON **SPUR** OBJECTIVES

■ **SKILLS**   *Objective C (See pages 601–603 for objectives.)*
In 1–4, find an acute value for θ to the nearest degree.

1. sin θ = 0.5   30°   ≈ 35°
2. cos θ = $\frac{\sqrt{3}}{2}$ 30°
3. tan θ ≈ .700
4. sin θ ≈ .996   ≈ 85°

■ **USES**   *Objective G*
In 5–7, answer with angles *A, B, C, D, E,* or *F* from the picture at the right.

5. Name all angles of depression.   B, E
6. Name all angles of elevation.   C, D
7. Name two pairs of congruent angles. (Assume $\overline{BE}$ is parallel to the water.)   B and C   E and D

8. A plane flying at 10,000 feet begins descending when the runway is 50,000 feet away. Find θ, its angle of descent.   ≈ 11.3°

9. An 800-meter mine shaft has a vertical drop of 215 meters. Find the angle of depression at which the shaft was dug.   ≈ 15.6°

10. An A-frame house is 30 ft high and 20 ft wide. Find θ, the slant of the roof.   ≈ 72°

Advanced Algebra © Scott, Foresman and Company

105

553

MORE PRACTICE
For more questions on SPUR Objectives, use *Lesson Master 10-2*, shown on page 553.

EXTENSION
A common way to express the measure of angles has been in degrees and subunits of a degree, called minutes and seconds. By definition, there are 60 minutes in one degree and 60 seconds in one minute. An angle which measures 38 degrees, 40 minutes and 24 seconds would be written 38°40′24″. For use with calculators, the measure of angles is often expressed in degrees and a decimal fraction of a degree.

An angle expressed in degrees and minutes can be converted to decimal notation by writing the number of minutes as a fraction over 60 and changing the fraction to a decimal.

$$29°45′ = 29\tfrac{45°}{60} = 29.75°$$

In 1–5, convert the following angle measures to decimal notation to the nearest hundredth of a degree.

1.	20°30′	(20.50°)
2.	40°27′	(40.45°)
3.	75°18′	(75.30°)
4.	00°10′	(0.17°)
5.	38°05′	(38.08°)

Have students propose an algorithm for changing from decimal notation to minutes.

In 6–10, convert the angle measure from decimals to minutes, to the nearest minute.

6.	60.70°	(60°42′)
7.	80.52°	(80°31′)
8.	13.25°	(13°15′)
9.	55.92°	(55°55′)
10.	1.33°	(01°20′)

In 17–19, use triangle *SKY* given below.

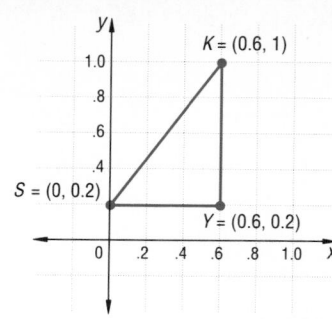

K = (0.6, 1)
S = (0, 0.2)
Y = (0.6, 0.2)

17. Find the coordinates of the vertices of the image triangle under the transformation R$_{270}$. *(Lesson 4-5)* **S = (.2, 0); K = (1, -.6); Y = (.2, -6)**

18. Find *SK*. *(Previous course)* **1**

19. Find m∠*SKY*. *(Lesson 10-1)* **≈37°**

20. State the quadrant (I, II, III, or IV) the point (x, y) is found in given the following conditions. Assume $x \neq 0$.
a. x is negative and y is positive. **II**
b. x is positive and y is negative. **IV**
c. $x = y$. *(Previous course)* **I or III**

21. Recall from your geometry course the SAS, SSS, and ASA triangle congruence theorems. Explain what each of these means. *(Previous course)* **See margin.**

22. Solve for x: $mx^2 + px + t = 0$. *(Lesson 6-6)* $x = \dfrac{-p \pm \sqrt{p^2 - 4mt}}{2m}$

23. If $\log 2 + \log 3 - \log 4 = \log x$, what is x? *(Lesson 9-6)* $x = \tfrac{3}{2}$

Exploration

24. A *British nautical mile* is defined as the length of a minute of arc of a meridian (a minute is $\tfrac{1}{60}$ of a degree). In feet, it is approximated by

$$6{,}077 - 31 \cos (2\theta)$$

where θ is the latitude in degrees. **Answer will depend on the latitude where you live.**
a. Find the length of a British nautical mile where you live. (You need to find your latitude.)
b. The *U.S. nautical mile* is defined to be 6080.2 feet. At what north latitude do the two definitions agree? **≈48°**

LESSON

10-3

Properties of Sines and Cosines

In this lesson we prove three important theorems relating sines and cosines. Consider triangle ABC with right angle C. Then $m\angle A + m\angle B = 90°$. So if $m\angle A = \theta$, then $m\angle B = 90° - \theta$.

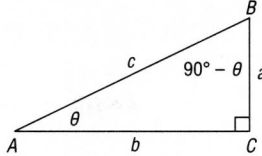

First, notice that $\sin \theta = \dfrac{\text{opp}}{\text{hyp}} = \dfrac{a}{c}$

and also $\cos (90° - \theta) = \dfrac{\text{adj}}{\text{hyp}} = \dfrac{a}{c}$.

Similarly, both $\cos \theta$ and $\sin (90° - \theta)$ equal $\dfrac{b}{c}$.

Thus we have proved the following theorem.

Complements Theorem:

For all θ between 0° and 90°,

$$\sin \theta = \cos (90° - \theta)$$

and $\qquad\qquad \cos \theta = \sin (90° - \theta)$.

In words, if two angles are complementary, the sine of one angle equals the cosine of the other. *Cosine* is short for *complement's sine*. For instance, $\cos 23° = \sin (90° - 23°) = \sin 67°$. You should check with your calculator that both $\cos 23°$ and $\sin 67°$ are approximately 0.921.

Second, notice that because $\sin \theta = \dfrac{a}{c}$ and $\cos \theta = \dfrac{b}{c}$,

$$(\sin \theta)^2 + (\cos \theta)^2 = \left(\dfrac{a}{c}\right)^2 + \left(\dfrac{b}{c}\right)^2$$

$$= \dfrac{a^2}{c^2} + \dfrac{b^2}{c^2}$$

$$= \dfrac{a^2 + b^2}{c^2}.$$

Triangle ABC is a right triangle, so by the Pythagorean Theorem, $a^2 + b^2 = c^2$. Thus,

$$(\sin \theta)^2 + (\cos \theta)^2 = \dfrac{c^2}{c^2} = 1.$$

RESOURCES
■ Lesson Master 10-3
■ Quiz for Lessons 10-1 Through 10-3
▯ Computer Master 23

OBJECTIVES

B Find exact values of trig-onometric functions of 30°, 60°, and 45° angles.
F Identify and use definitions and theorems relating sines and cosines.

TEACHING NOTES

The proofs of the three the-orems introduced in this lesson are not complicated, and you should expect stu-dents to follow them. The theorems can be proved here only for acute angles. They are extended to hold for an-gles of any magnitude in the next lesson.

You may wish to review the ratios of sides in 30°-60°-90° triangles and isosceles right triangles before discussing the Exact Value Theorem.

Although we encourage stu-dents to use calculators, the values of $\sin \theta$ and $\cos \theta$ for $\theta = 30°$, 45°, and 60° occur so often that they are worth memorizing. Students should know the exact values and how to derive them. Point out that they actually need to memorize (or derive) only two values: $\sin 30° = 0.5$ and $\sin 45° = \dfrac{\sqrt{2}}{2}$. The oth-ers are easily deduced from the Complements Theorem and the Pythagorean Identity.

Some books introduce the notation $\cos^2 \theta$ for $(\cos \theta)^2$. We do not, because we believe that for beginners the latter is clearer. It emphasizes that $\cos \theta$ is a number which is then squared.

Alternate Approach
The patterns in the chart below may help some students remember the exact values for $\cos \theta$ and $\sin \theta$.

	$\cos \theta$	$\sin \theta$
0°	$\frac{\sqrt{4}}{2}$	$\frac{\sqrt{0}}{2}$
30°	$\frac{\sqrt{3}}{2}$	$\frac{\sqrt{1}}{2}$
45°	$\frac{\sqrt{2}}{2}$	$\frac{\sqrt{2}}{2}$
60°	$\frac{\sqrt{1}}{2}$	$\frac{\sqrt{3}}{2}$
90°	$\frac{\sqrt{0}}{2}$	$\frac{\sqrt{4}}{2}$

This argument proves another theorem, called the Pythagorean Identity.

Theorem (Pythagorean Identity):

For all θ between 0° and 90°,

$$(\cos \theta)^2 + (\sin \theta)^2 = 1.$$

The Pythagorean Identity can be used to find the value of $\sin \theta$ if only $\cos \theta$ is known, or vice versa.

Example Suppose θ is an acute angle in a right triangle, and $\sin \theta = 0.6$. Find $\cos \theta$.

Solution From the Pythagorean Identity, you know that

$$(\cos \theta)^2 + (\sin \theta)^2 = 1.$$

Substitute 0.6 for $\sin \theta$ and solve for $\cos \theta$.

$$\begin{aligned} (\cos \theta)^2 + 0.6^2 &= 1 \\ (\cos \theta)^2 + 0.36 &= 1 \\ (\cos \theta)^2 &= 0.64 \\ \cos \theta &= \pm 0.8 \end{aligned}$$

For acute angles, $\cos \theta$ is always positive, so $\cos \theta = 0.8$.

Check Use your calculator to find θ, and then $\cos \theta$. Key in .6 [INV] [sin] [cos]. The calculator displays 0.8.

Generally, calculators give decimal approximations for values of sines and cosines. However, there are a few angles for which the sine and cosine have simple exact values. The angles and the values of their sines and cosines are given below.

Exact Value Theorem:

a. $\sin 30° = \cos 60° = \frac{1}{2}$

b. $\sin 45° = \cos 45° = \frac{\sqrt{2}}{2}$

c. $\sin 60° = \cos 30° = \frac{\sqrt{3}}{2}$

Proof:

a. In geometry you learned that the side opposite a 30° angle is half the hypotenuse h. Use the figure at the right:

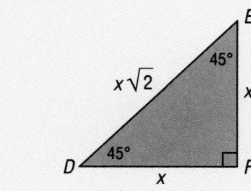

$$\sin 30° = \cos 60° = \frac{BC}{AB}$$

$$= \frac{\frac{1}{2}h}{h} = \frac{1}{2}$$

b. From geometry you also learned that the hypotenuse of a 45°-45°-90° triangle is $\sqrt{2}$ times the length of either leg. Therefore:

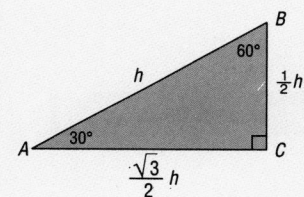

$$\sin 45° = \cos 45° = \frac{EF}{DE} = \frac{x}{x\sqrt{2}} = \frac{1}{\sqrt{2}} = \frac{1}{\sqrt{2}} \cdot \frac{\sqrt{2}}{\sqrt{2}} = \frac{\sqrt{2}}{2}.$$

c. Use the triangle in part a. Using the Pythagorean Theorem, you can express AC in terms of h.

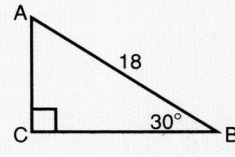

$$(AC)^2 + (\tfrac{1}{2}h)^2 = h^2$$

$$(AC)^2 + \tfrac{1}{4}h^2 = h^2$$

$$(AC)^2 = \tfrac{3}{4}h^2$$

$$AC = \frac{\sqrt{3}}{2}h$$

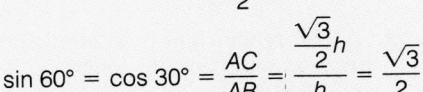

$$\sin 60° = \cos 30° = \frac{AC}{AB} = \frac{\frac{\sqrt{3}}{2}h}{h} = \frac{\sqrt{3}}{2}$$

Since $\sqrt{2} \approx 1.414$ and $\sqrt{3} \approx 1.732$, the Exact Value Theorem yields the following decimal approximations to the sine and cosine.

(a) $\sin 30° = \cos 60° = 0.5$ (exact value)
(b) $\sin 45° = \cos 45° \approx 0.707$
(c) $\sin 60° = \cos 30° \approx 0.866$.

For sine and cosine of these angles, the exact values occur often, as do the decimal approximations. You should memorize both.

1. Solve for θ given θ is acute.
a. $\sin θ = \cos 37°$
53°
b. $\sin 87° = \cos θ$
3°
c. $\cos 45° = \sin θ$
45°

2. If $\cos θ = .375$ and θ is acute, use the Pythagorean Identity to find $\sin θ$ correct to three decimal places.
.927

3.a. Find the exact values of AC and BC in the triangle below.

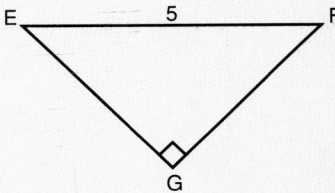

$AC = 9, BC = 9\sqrt{3}$
b. Find the exact values of EG and FG in the isosceles right triangles below.

$EG = \frac{5\sqrt{2}}{2}, FG = \frac{5\sqrt{2}}{2}$

Covering the Reading

1. *Multiple choice.* Which is the measure of the complement of an angle with measure θ? c
   (a) $\theta - 90°$ (b) $180° - \theta$ (c) $90° - \theta$ (d) $90° + \theta$

In 2 and 3, copy and complete with the measure of an acute angle.

2. $\cos 40° = \sin \underline{\ ?\ }$ 50°   3. $\sin 72° = \cos \underline{\ ?\ }$ 18°

4. State the Pythagorean Identity. See margin.

5. $(\cos 15°)^2 + (\sin 15°)^2 = \underline{\ ?\ }$. 1

In 6 and 7, assume that θ is an acute angle in a right triangle. Use the Pythagorean Identity to find $\cos \theta$ if:

6. $\sin \theta = .28$ 0.96   7. $\sin \theta = \dfrac{\sqrt{3}}{2}$. $\frac{1}{2}$

8. Name three acute angles whose sine and cosine can be found by using the Exact Value Theorem. 30°, 45°, 60°

In 9–11, copy and complete with an exact value.

9. $\sin 45° = \underline{\ ?\ }$ $\dfrac{\sqrt{2}}{2}$ 10. $\cos 60° = \underline{\ ?\ }$ $\dfrac{1}{2}$ 11. $\cos 30° = \underline{\ ?\ }$ $\dfrac{\sqrt{3}}{2}$

Applying the Mathematics

12. In $\triangle TIP$ at the right, $IP = 10$.
    Find exact values of:
    a. IT
    b. PT a) $\dfrac{10\sqrt{3}}{3}$; b) $\dfrac{20\sqrt{3}}{3}$

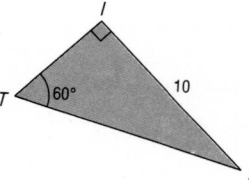

13. $\triangle QLE$ at the right is an equilateral triangle with sides 6″ long.
    a. Find the exact height h. $3\sqrt{3}$ inches
    b. Find the exact area of $\triangle QLE$.
       $9\sqrt{3}$ sq inches

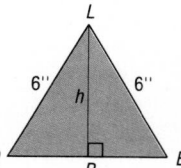

In 14–16, use the figures below and the definition of $\tan \theta$ to find exact values.

14. $\tan 30°$ $\dfrac{\sqrt{3}}{3}$

15. $\tan 60°$ $\sqrt{3}$

16. $\tan 45°$ 1

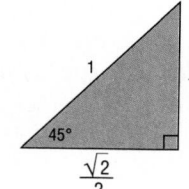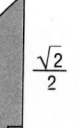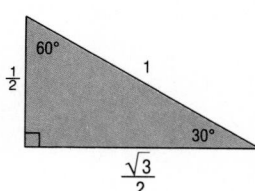

558

17. The angle of elevation of a pipeline up the side of a mountain is 45°.
    a. What is the exact vertical rise of a length of pipe 20 meters long? **10√2m**
    b. Approximate your answer to part a to the nearest tenth of a meter.
    14.1m
18. Refer to the triangle at the right.
    a. Express in terms of x, y, or z, and
       simplify: $\dfrac{\sin \theta}{\cos \theta}$. $\dfrac{y}{x}$
    b. *True or false.* For all θ between 0°
       and 90°, $\dfrac{\sin \theta}{\cos \theta} = \tan \theta$. **true**

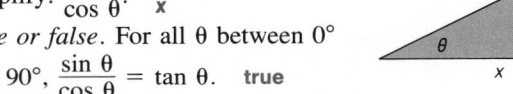

Review

19. A private plane begins its descent to an airport when it is a ground distance of 6 miles away and 1 mile high. At what constant angle of depression would it need to descend? *(Lesson 10-2)* **≈9.5°**

20. Find the value of θ to the nearest degree if $\sin \theta = .67$. *(Lesson 10-2)*
    42°
21. Given that $c^2 = a^2 + b^2 - 1.88ab$, solve for a if $b = 5$ and $c = -1.78$. *(Lesson 6-5)* **a ≈ 4.2 or a ≈ 5.2**

22. Find the distance from $(-3, 5)$ to $(1, 9)$. *(Previous course)*
    ≈5.7
23. Find the image of $(1, 0)$ under the given transformation.
    a. R_{360} **(1, 0)**   **b.** R_{270} **(0, -1)**   **c.** R_{-90} **(0, -1)**

Exploration

24. **a.** Verify that:
    (i) $\sin 60° = 2 \cdot \sin 30° \cdot \cos 30°$ **See margin.**
    (ii) $\sin 84° = 2 \cdot \sin 42° \cdot \cos 42°$.   **See margin.**
    b. Generalize the result of part a and verify your generalization with some other values.   **See margin.**

LESSON 10-3   Properties of Sines and Cosines   **559**

FOLLOW-UP

MORE PRACTICE
For more questions on SPUR Objectives, use *Lesson Master 10-3*, shown below.

EVALUATION
A quiz covering Lessons 10-1 through 10-3 is provided in the Teacher's Resource File.

24.a. (i) sin 60° = $\dfrac{\sqrt{3}}{2}$
2 sin 30° · cos 30° =
$2 \cdot \dfrac{1}{2} \cdot \dfrac{\sqrt{3}}{2} = \dfrac{\sqrt{3}}{2}$
(ii) sin 84° ≈ .995
2 sin 42° · cos 42 ≈
(2)(.669)(.743) ≈ .994
b. sin (2θ) = 2 sin θ cos θ

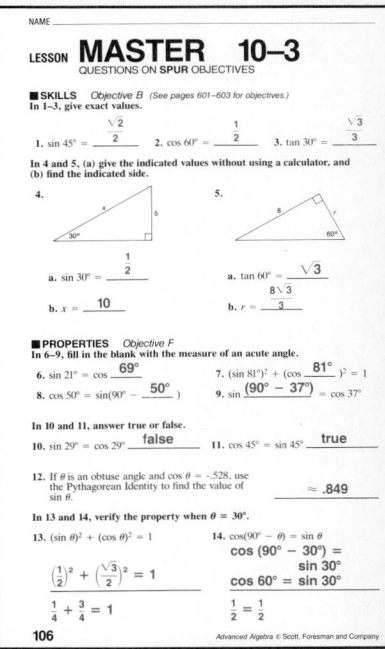

LESSON

10-4

The Unit Circle

In right triangles the acute angles measure between 0° and 90°. So the definitions of cosine and sine given in Lesson 10-1 cannot apply to measures greater than 90°. However, rotations may have any magnitude, positive or negative. So rotations can be used for defining cosines and sines in general.

The **unit circle** is the circle with center at the origin and radius 1. If the point (1, 0) on the circle is rotated around the origin with a magnitude θ, then the image point (x, y) is also on the circle. The coordinates of the image point can be found using sines and cosines.

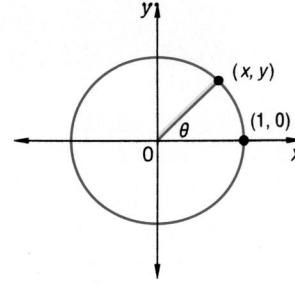

Example 1 What are the coordinates of the image of (1, 0) under R_{70}?

Solution Let $A = (x, y)$ be the image of (1, 0) under R_{70}. Using the figure at the right, $OA = 1$, since the radius of the unit circle is 1. Draw a vertical line from A to form a right triangle with $\overline{OA}$ and the x-axis. Then $\triangle ABO$ is a right triangle with legs of length x and y and hypotenuse of length 1. Now use the definitions of sine and cosine.

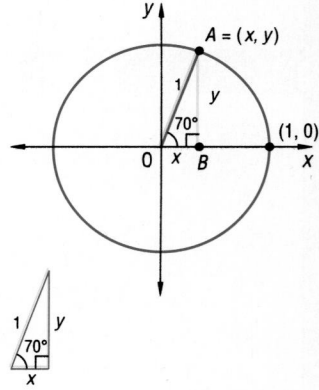

$$\cos 70° = \frac{adj}{hyp} = \frac{x}{1} = x$$

$$\sin 70° = \frac{opp}{hyp} = \frac{y}{1} = y$$

The first coordinate is cos 70° and the second coordinate is sin 70°. Thus $(x, y) = (\cos 70°, \sin 70°) \approx$ (.342, .940); that is, the image of (1, 0) under R_{70} is (.342, .940).

Check Use the Pythagorean Identity.

Does $(.342)^2 + (.940)^2 = 1^2$?
$$.117 + .884 = 1.001 \approx 1, \text{ so it checks.}$$

560

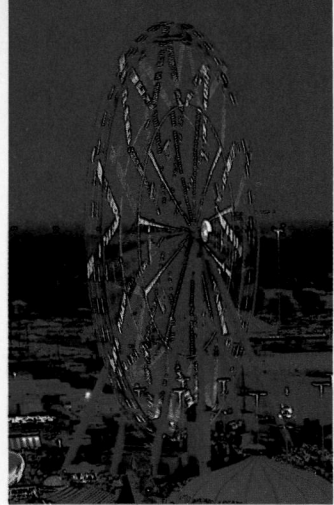

Rotating Ferris wheel at the State Fair in Dallas

In Example 1, the image of (1, 0) under R_{70} is (cos 70°, sin 70°). We generalize this idea to define the sine and cosine for a rotation of any magnitude θ.

Definition:

Let θ be the magnitude of a rotation. Then for any θ, the point (cos θ, sin θ) is the image of (1, 0) under $R_θ$.

Stated another way, cos θ is the *x*-coordinate of the image of (1, 0) under a rotation of θ; sin θ is the *y*-coordinate of the image.

The sines and cosines of angles which are multiples of 90° can be found without using a calculator.

Example 2 Find:
a. sin 90°
b. cos (-180°).

Solution
a. The image of (1, 0) under R_{90} is (0, 1). Because sin 90° is the *y*-coordinate of this image point, sin 90° = 1.

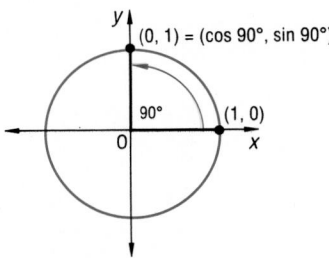

b. The image of (1, 0) under R_{-180} is (-1, 0). Since cos (-180°) is the *x*-coordinate of this point, cos (-180°) = -1.

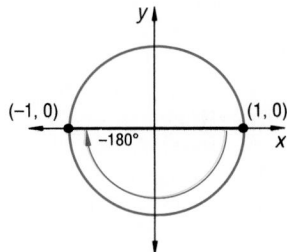

Check You can check each of these on your calculator. For instance, for part b use the key sequence 180 ⌊+/-⌋ ⌊cos⌋. You should get -1 on the display.

LESSON 10-4   The Unit Circle   **561**

Recall that rotations of magnitude greater than 360° refer to more than one complete revolution.

■ ■ ■ ■ ■ ■ ■■

Example 3 Find:
  a. sin 630°
  b. cos 385°.

Solution
  a. R_{630} equals one complete revolution R_{360} around the circle, followed by R_{270}. Because the image of (1, 0) under R_{630} is (0, -1), sin 630° = -1.

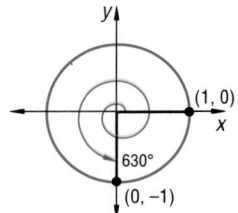

  b. R_{385} equals one complete revolution followed by a rotation of 25°, thus, cos 385° = cos 25° ≈ .906.

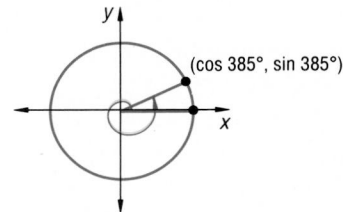

Generally, the unit circle is a good tool to use *along with* your calculator to help solve problems involving angles. The definitions of sine and cosine in terms of rotations on the unit circle determine the trigonometric values of *any angle*. They can also be used to prove that both the Complements Theorem and the Pythagorean Identity proved in the previous lesson apply to all real numbers θ.

Questions

Covering the Reading

1. If (1, 0) is rotated θ around the origin:
   a. cos θ is the __?__-coordinate of its image.   **x**
   b. sin θ is the __?__-coordinate of its image.   **y**

2. *True or false.* The image of (1, 0) under R_{23} is (sin 23°, cos 23°).
   false

3. $R_0(1, 0) = $__?__, so cos 0° = __?__ and sin 0° = __?__.   **(1, 0); 1; 0**

562

562

In 4–7, use the unit circle without your calculator to find:

4. cos 90° 0

5. sin 180° 0

6. cos 270° 0

7. sin (-90°). -1

a rotation of 180°

8. a. A rotation of 540° equals a rotation of 360° followed by __?__.
   b. The image of (1, 0) under R_{540} is __?__. (-1, 0)
   c. Evaluate sin 540°. 0

In 9–12, Evaluate without using a calculator.

9. cos 450° 0

10. sin 450° 1

11. cos (-630)° 0

12. sin (-720°) 0

In 13 and 14, use a calculator to approximate to the nearest thousandth.

13. cos 392° ≈0.848

14. sin 440° ≈0.985

In 15–17, suppose $A = (1, 0)$, $B = (0, 1)$, $C = (-1, 0)$, and $D = (0, -1)$. Which point is the image of (1, 0) under each rotation?

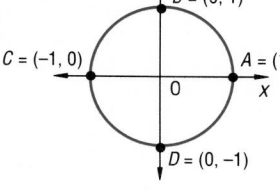

15. R_{450} B

16. R_{540} C

17. $R_{(-720)}$ A

In 18–23, which letter in the figure at the right could stand for each of the following?

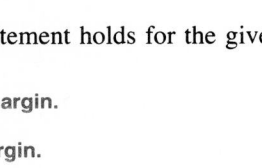

18. cos 80° c

19. sin 80° d

20. cos (-280°) c

21. sin 800° d

22. cos 380° a

23. sin (-340°) b

24. If $0° \le \theta \le 360°$,
   a. What is the largest possible value of cos θ? 1
   b. What is the smallest possible value of sin θ? -1

In 25 and 26, verify by substitution that the statement holds for the given value of θ.

25. $(\cos \theta)^2 + (\sin \theta)^2 = 1$; θ = 630° See margin.

26. $\sin \theta = \cos (90° - \theta)$; θ = -90° See margin.

In 27 and 28, find the exact value without using a calculator.

27. cos 420° $\frac{1}{2}$

28. $(\sin 405°)^2 + (\cos 405°)^2$ 1

MORE PRACTICE
For more questions on SPUR
Objectives, use *Lesson Mas-
ter 10-4*, shown on page 563.

EXTENSION
Let $T = (-3, 4)$. Let θ be the
angle formed by T, the origin,
and a point on the negative
x-axis. Find sin θ, cos θ, and
tan θ.

Solution:
Draw the figure.

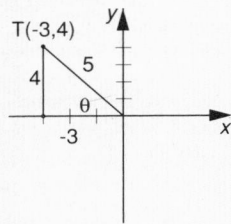

Find the hypotenuse.
$c^2 = a^2 + b^2$
$c^2 = 9 + 16$
$c^2 = 25$
$c = 5$

Apply the definitions of the
trig functions.
$\sin θ = \frac{4}{5}$, $\cos θ = \frac{-3}{5}$,
$\tan θ = \frac{-4}{3}$

Have students find θ using
the method above and the
given point T.

1. $T = (12, 5)$
$\left(c = 13; \sin θ = \frac{5}{13},\right.$
$\left.\cos θ = \frac{12}{13}, \tan θ = \frac{5}{12}\right)$

2. $T = (-6, -8)$
$\left(c = 10; \sin θ = \frac{-4}{5}, \cos θ = \right.$
$\left.\frac{-3}{5}, \tan θ = \frac{4}{3}\right)$

3. $T = (3, -5)$
$\left(c = \sqrt{34}; \sin θ = \frac{-5\sqrt{34}}{34},\right.$
$\left.\cos θ = \frac{3\sqrt{34}}{34}, \tan θ = \frac{-5}{3}\right)$

ADDITIONAL ANSWERS
32. See Additional
Answers in the back of this
book.

564

Review		

29. At 65 feet up in a lookout tower, a ranger sights a fire. The angle of depression to the fire measures 4°. How far from the base of the tower is the fire? *(Lesson 10-2)* **about 930 ft.**

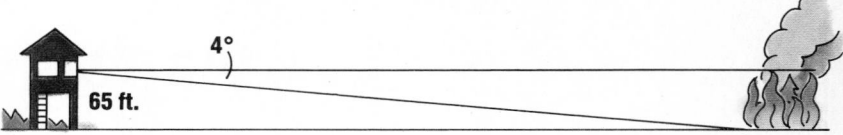

30. Refer to the diagram below. A roof has a pitch of $\frac{1}{12}$. What angle θ does it make with the horizontal? *(Lesson 10-2)* **≈4.8°**

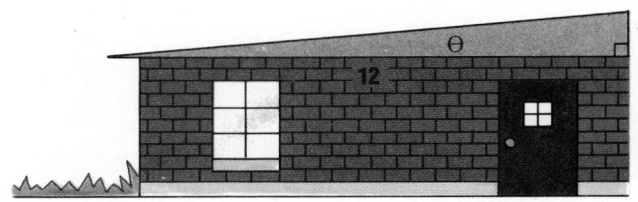

31. Use the equation $y = 5x^2 - 7x + 4$. Determine the number of x-intercepts of the graph of this parabola. *(Lesson 6-7)* **none**

Exploration	

32. a. Draw a set of coordinate axes on graph paper.
b. With the origin as the center, use a compass to draw a unit circle with radius 1 inch.
c. Label $A = (1, 0)$.
d. With a protractor, locate the image of A under R_{150}.
e. Use your drawing to estimate cos 150° and sin 150°.
f. Compare your estimated value from part e to those displayed by your calculator. **See margin.**

564

Every value of cos θ or sin θ is a coordinate of a point on the unit circle. With a calculator, it is easy to determine these values. If $0° < θ < 90°$, you can check calculator values by drawing a right triangle. In this lesson, we show how to find and check other values.

Think of the image of (1, 0) under $R_θ$. Unless θ is a multiple of 90°, the image is in one of the four quadrants. As the diagram below at the left shows, each quadrant is associated with a range of values of θ.

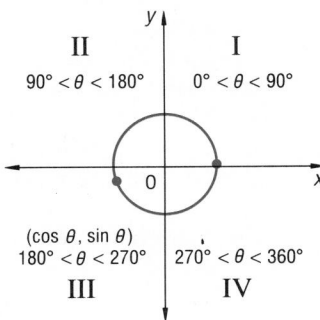

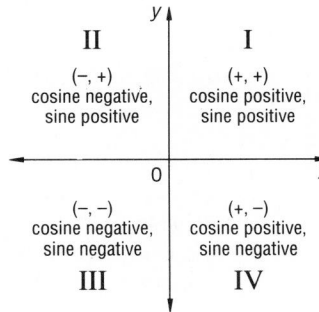

The quadrants enable you to determine quickly whether cos θ and sin θ are positive or negative. Refer to the graph above at the right. Because cos θ is the first or x-coordinate of the image, it is positive in Quadrants I and IV and negative in Quadrants II and III. The sine, which is the y-coordinate of the image, is positive in Quadrants I and II and negative in Quadrants III and IV.

You do *not* need to memorize these ideas. You can always visualize them on the unit circle.

RESOURCES
■ Lesson Master 10-5
▨ Visual for Teaching Aid 62 displays the values of the cosines and sines in Quadrants I–IV.
▨ Teaching Aid 63 provides the pointer and unit circle with the images of (1, 0) under $R_θ$.

OBJECTIVES

A Approximate values of trig-onometric functions in all four quadrants by using a calculator.
B Find exact values of trig-onometric functions of multiples of 30° and 45° in all quadrants using the unit circle.

TEACHING NOTES

A useful teaching tool for this lesson is illustrated at the top of the next page. It consists of a "unit circle" drawn on a piece of cardboard or tag board with a pointer fixed at the origin that can rotate either clockwise or counter-clockwise. In order for the unit circle to be visible throughout your classroom, make the circle with radius at least 10 cm. Use a scale of tenths for the axes. The length of the pointer should be equal to or slightly larger than the radius of the circle. Another possibility is to make such a device on a trans-parency. Show students that when you rotate the pointer a fixed amount in either direc-tion from (1, 0), a unique point P on the circle is deter-mined. That point P has unique coordinates.

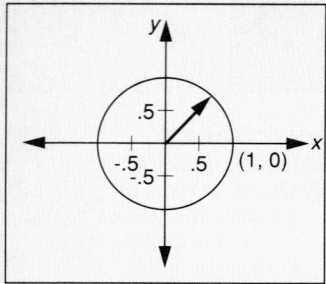

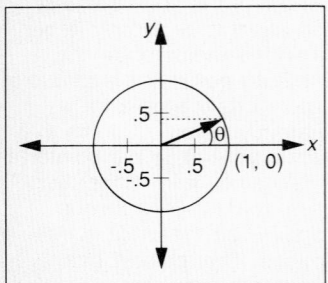

Example 1 Is sin 150° positive or negative?

Solution 150° is between 90° and 180°, so it refers to a point in Quadrant II. The sine is the second coordinate. In this quadrant the second coordinate is positive, so sin 150° is positive.

Once you know the *sign* of the cosine or sine, find its value by referring to points in the first quadrant. For instance, you know sin 150° is the second coordinate of a point in the second quadrant. By reflecting this point over the *y*-axis, you get a reference or image point in the first quadrant, namely (cos 30°, sin 30°). Notice that the angles formed with the *x*-axis are congruent.

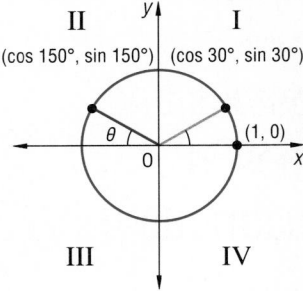

The first coordinates of these points are opposites, so

$$\cos 150° = -\cos 30° = -\frac{\sqrt{3}}{2}.$$

The second coordinates are equal, so $\sin 150° = \sin 30° = \frac{1}{2}$.

When the image is in Quadrant III, rotating the point 180° gives a corresponding point in the first quadrant.

Example 2 Show that sin (-125°) = -sin 55°.

Solution Make a sketch. The point *P* = (cos (-125°), sin (-125°)) is in the third quadrant, so the sine is negative. Rotate *P* 180° to get a first quadrant point *P'*. This image point has coordinates (cos 55°, sin 55°) because 180° - 125° = 55°. Because the image of (*x*, *y*) under a rotation of 180° is (-*x*, -*y*), *P'* also has coordinates (-cos (-125°), -sin (-125°)). Thus sin (-125°) = -sin 55°.

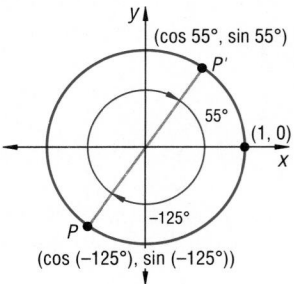

Check Using a calculator, sin (-125°) ≈ -0.819 and sin 55° ≈ 0.819, so it checks.

Points in Quadrant IV are reflection images, over the *x*-axis, of points in the first quadrant.

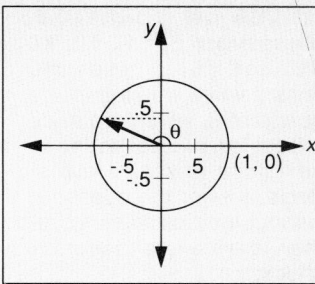

Example 3 Find an exact value for cos 315°.

Solution Cos 315° is the first coordinate of a point in Quadrant IV, so the cosine is positive. Reflect (cos 315°, sin 315°) over the *x*-axis. The image forms an angle of 360° − 315° = 45°, so the image point is (cos 45°, sin 45°). Since the first coordinates of these points are equal,

$$\cos 315° = \cos 45°$$
$$= \frac{\sqrt{2}}{2}.$$

Check A calculator shows cos 315° ≈ 0.707. Recall that 0.707 is an approximation to $\frac{\sqrt{2}}{2}$, so it checks.

If you add or subtract multiples of 360° to 315°, you will get the same value for the cosine. This is because $R_{315°} = R_{675°} = R_{1035°}$, and so on. Thus cos 315° = cos 675° = cos 1035°. Similarly, sin 315° = sin 675° = sin 1035°. The fact that values of sines and cosines repeat is a very important property. You will learn more about this later in this chapter.

Questions

Covering the Reading

In 1 and 2, *multiple choice*. Select from the following choices.
  (a) is always positive
  (b) is always negative
  (c) may be positive or negative

1. If $R_θ(1, 0)$ is in quadrants II or III then cos θ ? .   b

2. If 180° < θ < 360°, sin θ ? .   b

In 3 and 4, (a) draw the corresponding point on the unit circle; (b) without using a calculator, state whether the value is positive or negative.

3. sin 343°   a) See margin.;   **4.** cos 217°   a) See margin. b) negative
                    b) negative

LESSON 10-5   Cosines and Sines in Quadrants II–IV   567

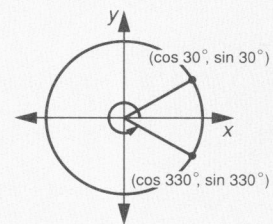

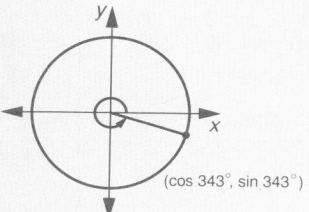
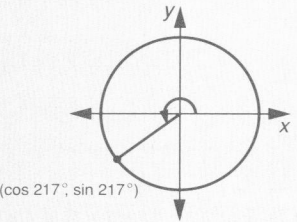
5. Evaluate (a) cos 118° and (b) sin 118° with a calculator.
   a) ≈ -0.469; b) ≈ 0.883

In 6 and 7, find θ if 0° < θ < 90°.

6. sin 182° = -sin θ   θ = 2°   7. cos 295° = cos θ   θ = 65°

In 8–11, find the exact value.

8. sin 315°   9. cos 240°   10. cos (-150°)   11. sin 135°
   $\frac{-\sqrt{2}}{2}$ -.5 $\frac{-\sqrt{3}}{2}$ $\frac{\sqrt{2}}{2}$

Applying the Mathematics

12. Copy and complete with "positive" or "negative." If ∠B is obtuse, then cos B is _?_ and sin B is _?_.   negative, positive

13. Refer to the graph at the right. Find θ to the nearest degree.   127°

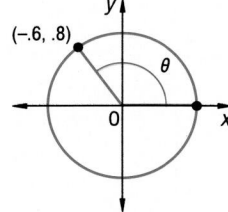

14. Find θ such that cos θ = $-\frac{1}{2}$ and sin θ = $-\frac{\sqrt{3}}{2}$, for 0° < θ < 360°.   240°

15. Suppose sin θ = $-\frac{\sqrt{2}}{2}$. Find two possible values for cos θ. $\frac{-\sqrt{2}}{2}$ or $\frac{\sqrt{2}}{2}$

16. Find C such that 0° < C < 180° and cos C = -0.251.   ≈ 104.5°

17. Find two values of θ such that sin θ = cos θ. (Hint: sketch the unit circle.)   sample: 45°, 225°

18. Refer to the figure at the right.
    a. Find the area of △ABC. $\frac{1}{2}hc$
    b. Find sin B. $\frac{h}{a}$

    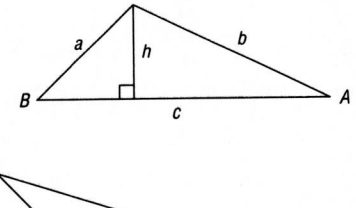

    c. By substituting your answer to part b for sin B, prove that the area of △ABC equals $\frac{1}{2}ac \sin B$.   See margin.

    d. Use the result of part c to estimate the area of △DEF at the right.   ≈ 26.8

    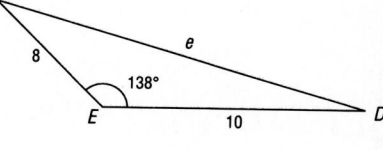

Review

19. Give exact coordinates of the image of (1, 0) under $R_{135°}$. (Lesson 10-4) $\left(\frac{-\sqrt{2}}{2}, \frac{\sqrt{2}}{2}\right)$

20. Evaluate cos 270° without a calculator. (Lesson 10-4)   0

21. If 0° < θ < 90° and sin 83.5° = cos θ, find θ. (Lesson 10-3)   6.5°

22. Refer to the triangle at the right (m∠OFX = 63°).
    OX ≈ 56 mm, FX ≈ 63 mm; sin 63° ≈ .889
    a. Measure OX and FX, then calculate sin 63°.
    b. Check your answer to part a by finding sin 63° on a calculator. (Lesson 10-1)   ≈ 0.891

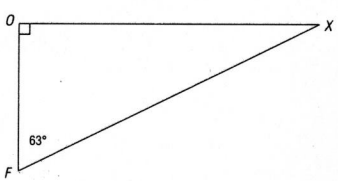

23. Solve $3(x - 4)^5 = 215$ for x. *(Lesson 8-11)* $x \approx 6.35$

24. Which of the following are congruent due to ASA triangle congruence? *(Previous course)*   b

(a)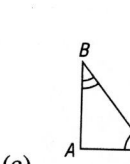

(b)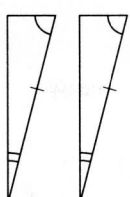

(c)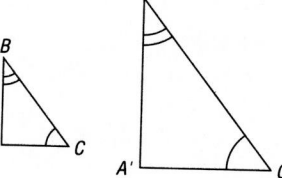

(d)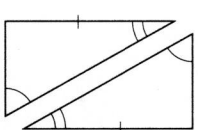

Exploration

25. Copy and complete the following chart using your calculator to estimate each value to the nearest thousandth.

θ	sin θ	tan θ
10°	.174	.176
5°	.087	.087
2°	.035	.035
1°	.017	.017
0.5°	.009	.009
0.1°	.002	.002

  a. Generalize what the table shows.   For small θ, tan θ ≈ sin θ.
  b. Explain your generalization. (You may wish to draw a series of triangles with these angles.)   In a right triangle, as one of the acute angles gets small, the length of the opposite leg becomes close to the length of the hypotenuse.

MORE PRACTICE
For more questions on SPUR Objectives, use *Lesson Master 10-5*, shown below.

EXTENSION
In **Question 25,** have students put their calculators in radian mode and then calculate sines and tangents. They will find that when x is close to 0, $x \approx \sin x \approx \tan x$. Use this idea as motivation for the discussion of radians to occur in Lesson 10-10.

NAME _____

LESSON **MASTER   10–5**
QUESTIONS ON **SPUR** OBJECTIVES

■**SKILLS**   *Objective A (See pages 601–603 for objectives.)*
In 1–6, evaluate. Round your answer to the nearest hundredth.
1. cos 192°   −.98
2. sin(-280°)   .98
3. sin 577°   −.60
4. cos 345°   .97
5. sin 337.5°   −.38
6. cos(-601°)   −.48

■**SKILLS**   *Objective B*
In 7–12, give the exact value.
7. sin 225° = $-\frac{\sqrt{2}}{2}$
8. cos 270° = 0
9. sin 150° = $\frac{1}{2}$
10. sin(-180°) = 0
11. cos 660° = $\frac{1}{2}$
12. cos(-315°) = $\frac{\sqrt{2}}{2}$

■**REPRESENTATIONS**   *Objective I*
In 13–16, use your calculator to find:
13. x-coordinate of P = −.985
14. y-coordinate of P = .174
15. x-coordinate of Q = −.174
16. y-coordinate of Q = −.985

In 17–20, give the letter which could stand for:
17. cos 160°   (c)
18. sin(-60°)   (f)
19. cos 405°   (a)
20. cos 300°   (e)

In 21–24, use the sketch at the right to find each value.
21. sin θ = −.174
22. cos α = .940
23. θ = ≈ 190°
24. α = ≈ 340°

569

RESOURCES
■ Lesson Master 10-6
■ Quiz for Lessons 10-4
  Through 10-6
🖳 Visual for Teaching Aid 64
  provides the proof of the
  Law of Cosines.
🖳 Visual for Teaching Aid 65
  provides the problem of
  the Extension.

OBJECTIVES

E Find missing parts of a triangle using the Law of
Cosines.
H Solve real-world problems
using the Law of Cosines.

TEACHING NOTES

Although the concepts in this
lesson are not difficult for
most *Advanced Algebra* students, the equation in the
Law of Cosines is long and
potentially intimidating. Either
read this lesson with students in class, or preview it
with a problem such as the
one in **Example 1**. It is also
helpful to prove the theorem
in class.

Alternate Approach
Stress to students that it is
important to know the three
equations for the Law of
Cosines. For students having
difficulty remembering the
equations, explain that if
using cos *A*, then the side *a*
is on the opposite side of the
equation. The order of the
other two sides is irrelevant.
For example, $a^2 =$
$b^2 + c^2 - 2bc \cos A$.
  To reinforce algebraic
skills, have students solve for
the cos θ in each of the three
equations.

In the previous lessons you have learned to use the trigonometric ratios to find unknown sides or angles of *right* triangles. This lesson
will give you the means to determine some unknown sides or angles
in *any* triangle.

The captain of a clipper ship C spots two other ships on the ocean.
Ship A is about 5 miles away and ship B is about 5.2 miles away.
The angle between the two sightings is 20°. How far apart are ships
A and B? The problem is illustrated below, and *c* is the required
distance.

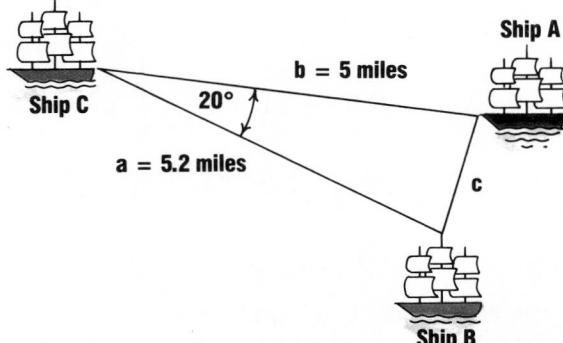

The captain knows the measures of two sides and the included angle. This is the *SAS condition* and all other sides and angles can be
determined. Because △*ABC* is not a right triangle, the solution cannot be found using only what you have already learned. However,
the unique measure of the third side can be found using the **Law of
Cosines**.

In this theorem and throughout the rest of this chapter, we follow a
standard convention that in triangle *ABC*, *a* is the length of the side
opposite ∠*A*, *b* is the length of the side opposite ∠*B*, and *c* is the
length of the side opposite ∠*C*. That is, lower-case letters stand for
sides opposite the points named by the corresponding capital letters.

Theorem (Law of Cosines)

In any triangle *ABC*,

$$c^2 = a^2 + b^2 - 2ab \cos C.$$

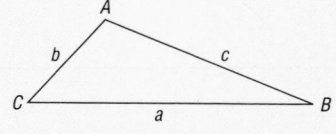

This theorem works for *any* two sides and the included angle of a
triangle. Thus it is also true that

$$a^2 = b^2 + c^2 - 2bc \cos A$$
$$b^2 = a^2 + c^2 - 2ac \cos B.$$

Before proving this theorem, we provide an example.

Example 1 Use the Law of Cosines to find the distance between ships A and B above.

Solution The unknown side is c and the two known sides are $a = 5.2$ miles and $b = 5$ miles. The included angle is 20°. Substituting into the Law of Cosines gives

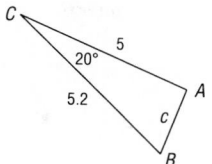

$$c^2 = (5.2)^2 + 5^2 - 2(5.2)(5) \cos 20°$$
$$c^2 \approx 27.04 + 25 - 52(.940)$$
$$c^2 \approx 3.16$$
$$c \approx \pm\sqrt{3.16}$$
$$c \approx \pm 1.78.$$

Because c is a distance, $c > 0$ and only the positive solution is acceptable. The two ships are about 1.8 miles apart.

Though the Law of Cosines is called a "law," it is also a theorem. That means it can be proved from definitions, other theorems, and postulates. Here is a proof that, in any $\triangle ABC$,

$$c^2 = a^2 + b^2 - 2ab \cos C.$$

Proof

Set up $\triangle ABC$ on a coordinate plane so that $C = (0, 0)$ and $A = (b, 0)$. To find the coordinates of B, notice that B is a times farther from the origin than the intersection of the unit circle and $\overline{CB}$. Since that intersection has coordinates $(\cos C, \sin C)$, $B = (a \cos C, a \sin C)$. All that remains is to find c^2 by using the distance formula. In general,

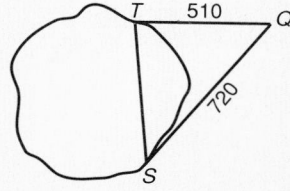

$c = \sqrt{(x_2 - x_1)^2 + (y_2 - y_1)^2}$	Distance Formula
$c^2 = (x_2 - x_1)^2 + (y_2 - y_1)^2$	squaring both sides
$c^2 = (a \cos C - b)^2 + (a \sin C - 0)^2$	substitution
$c^2 = a^2 (\cos C)^2 - 2ab \cos C + b^2 + a^2(\sin C)^2$	expansion
$c^2 = a^2 (\cos C)^2 + a^2(\sin C)^2 + b^2 - 2ab \cos C$	Commutative Property of +
$c^2 = a^2 ((\cos C)^2 + (\sin C)^2) + b^2 - 2ab \cos C$	Distributive Postulate
$c^2 = a^2 + b^2 - 2ab \cos C$	Pythagorean Identity

When finding the unknown side, emphasize that the side is the square root of the answer obtained. Once the solution is found, have students determine if the answer is feasible. Students may discover a calculation or substitution error.

When working real-world problems, stress to the students the importance of drawing a picture. This must be done as the first step in solving each problem.

ADDITIONAL EXAMPLES
1. Points S and T are the endpoints of a tunnel to be built through a mountain. From a point Q, away from the mountain, it is possible for a surveyor to see both points S and T. The surveyor finds that $QS = 720$ meters, $QT = 510$ meters, and $\angle SQT = 84.5°$. Find the length of the tunnel to the nearest meter.

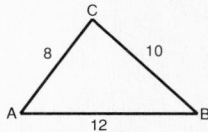

841 meters

2. Find the measure of the smallest angle in the triangle with sides 8, 10, and 12.

A triangle with vertices labeled C (top), A (bottom left), B (bottom right). Side from A to C is 8, side from C to B is 10, side from A to B is 12.

Since AC is the shortest side, $\angle B$ is the smallest angle. Using the Law of Cosines $m\angle B \approx 41°$.

Example 1 shows how the Law of Cosines can be used to solve problems where two sides and their included angle are known (SAS). If the lengths of all three sides are known (SSS), the Law of Cosines can be used to find the measure of any angle of the triangle.

Example 2 A triangle has sides of length 4, 5, and 8.5. What is the measure of its largest angle?

Solution Draw a figure. The largest angle is opposite the longest side. We call that angle A. Then $a = 8.5$. Let $b = 5$ and $c = 4$.

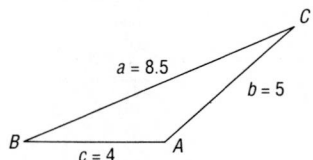

By the Law of Cosines,

$$a^2 = b^2 + c^2 - 2bc \cos A$$
$$(8.5)^2 = 5^2 + 4^2 - 2(4)(5) \cos A$$
$$72.25 = 25 + 16 - 40 \cos A$$
$$31.25 = -40 \cos A$$
$$-.781 \approx \cos A.$$

To find $m \angle A$, press .781 $\boxed{\pm}$ $\boxed{\text{INV}}$ $\boxed{\text{cos}}$.

Your display should read 141.352 ... . Thus $m \angle A \approx 141°$.

Check Draw such a triangle. The largest angle seems to be about 141°.

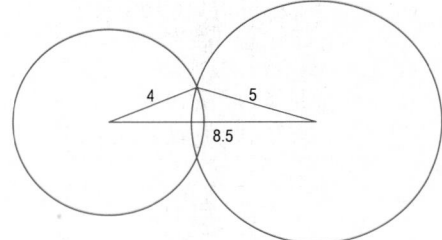

Questions

Covering the Reading

1. *True or false* In $\triangle ABC$,
   $a^2 = b^2 + c^2 - 2ab \cos A$.   false

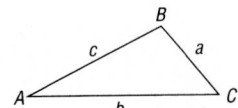

2. According to the Law of Cosines, in $\triangle WXY$, $y^2 = \underline{\ ?\ }$.
   $x^2 + w^2 - 2xw \cos Y$

572

572

3. *Multiple choice.* Which of the following verbally describes the Law of Cosines? c

(a) The third side of a triangle equals the sum of the squares of the other two sides minus the product of the two sides and the included angle.

(b) The square of the third side of a triangle equals the sum of the squares of the other two sides minus the product of the two sides and the cosine of the included angle.

(c) The square of the third side of a triangle equals the sum of the squares of the other two sides minus twice the product of the two sides and the cosine of the included angle.

(d) none of these

4. In the proof of the Law of Cosines, why does
$$a^2 ((\cos C)^2 + (\sin C)^2) = a^2?$$ See margin.

5. Refer to the ships in the lesson. Suppose the clipper ship is 1.1 miles from ship A and 2.4 miles from ship B and the angle between the two sightings is 135°. How far apart are ships A and B?   ≈ 3.3 miles

6. Refer to the figure of Example 2. Find the measure of $\angle B$.   ≈ 21.5°

Applying the Mathematics

7. The water molecule H_2O can be modeled by the figure below. The angle between the oxygen-hydrogen bonds is 105°. If the average distance between the oxygen and hydrogen nuclei is p units, how far apart (on average) are the two hydrogen nuclei?   about 2.52 p^2 units

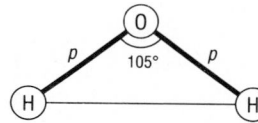

8. Refer to the diagram below. Two planes leave from Dallas, one toward Bismar k, and the other toward Chicago. By approximately what angle do their headings differ?   about 46°

Chicago O'Hare Airport

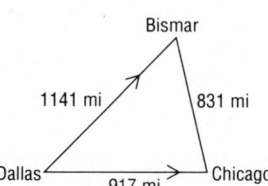

9. Refer to the triangle below.
a. Find the value of b.   ≈ 49 mm
b. Use your answer from part a to find the measure of θ.   ≈ 29°

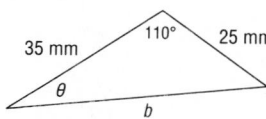

LESSON 10-6   The Law of Cosines   **573**

NOTES ON QUESTIONS
Question 10: The Law of Cosines can be used to determine a distance which is truly impossible (at least in our lifetimes) to measure directly. This power of mathematics is often overlooked. Some problems can only be solved by using some advanced mathematics.

Question 12: This question illustrates a situation that violates the Triangle Inequality. Demonstrate the unconstructability of a triangle with these sides.

Question 23: The Law of Cosines is also a generalization of the Pythagorean Theorem. The special case of the Pythagorean Theorem occurs when the included angle is a right angle.

ADDITIONAL ANSWERS
4. $(\cos C)^2 + (\sin C)^2 = 1$ by the Pythagorean Identity, and $a^2 \cdot 1 = a^2$.

12.a., b., 19.c., 23. See Additional Answers in the back of this book.

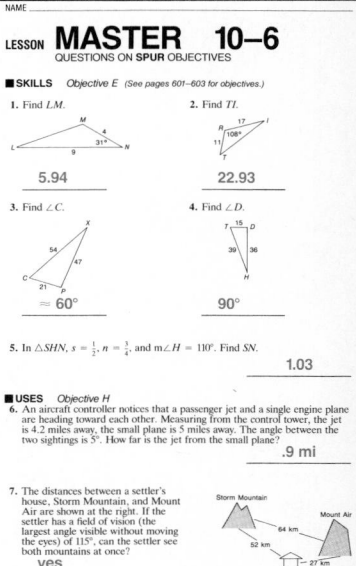

MORE PRACTICE
For more questions on SPUR Objectives, see *Lesson Master 10-6*, shown on page 573.

EXTENSION
The following application is taken from the *Sourcebook of Applications of School Mathematics*, published by NCTM.

The *tracking-angle error* of a record player is the ratio

$\frac{\alpha}{CB}$, where α is the measure in degrees of the angle between the center line and the tangent to the record groove at the stylus, and CB is the distance in inches from the stylus to the center of the record.

Suppose that the tone arm ($\overline{BD}$) is straight and supported at a point 8″ from the center of a record and 8.25″ from the stylus. Find the tracking-angle error when the stylus is at the end of a 12″ (diameter) record.

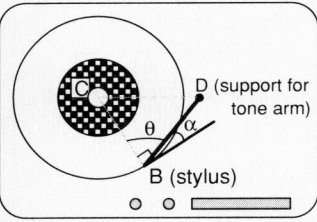

(In the figure above, we are given $CD = 8$, $BD = 8.25$, and $CB = 6$. We must first find θ and then the ratio α/CB. Using the Law of Cosines, $8^2 = 6^2 + (8.25)^2 - 2 \cdot 6 \cdot 8.25 \cos \theta \Leftrightarrow \cos \theta \approx .405 \Leftrightarrow \theta \approx 66.1°$. Now $\alpha = 90 - \theta \approx 23.9°$, and $\alpha/CB \approx 23.9°/6$ in. $\approx 4°$/in. Note that most modern record players use crooked arms to reduce the distortion. Stereo engineers try to keep the tracking-angle below 0.5°/in.)

EVALUATION
A quiz covering Lessons 10-4 through 10-6 is provided in the Teacher's Resource File.

10. The distance from Earth to the star Sirius is about 8.8 light years. The distance from Earth to Alpha Centauri is about 4.3 light years (a light year is the distance light travels in one year). The angle between these stars, with Earth as a vertex, is about 44°. What is the approximate distance (in light years) between Sirius and Alpha Centauri?

11. Solve the Law of Cosines to get a formula for cos C in terms of a, b, and c. $\cos C = \dfrac{a^2 + b^2 - c^2}{2ab}$

12. At a criminal trial, the witness gave the following testimony: "The defendant was 20 ft from the victim. I was 50 ft from the defendant and 75 ft from the victim when the shooting occurred. I saw the whole thing."
  a. Use the Law of Cosines to show that the testimony has errors. See margin
  b. How else could you know that the testimony has errors? See margin.

Review

In 13–16, give an exact value. Do not use a calculator. *(Lessons 10-3, 10-4, 10-5)*

13. cos 30° $\dfrac{\sqrt{3}}{2}$

14. $3(\sin 17°)^2 + 3(\cos 17°)^2$ 3

15. sin 150° 0.5

16. cos (-45°) $\dfrac{\sqrt{2}}{2}$

17. If sin 160° = sin θ and 0° < θ < 90°, what is θ? *(Lesson 10-5)* 20°

18. Solve sin α = sin 18° if 90° < α < 180°. *(Lesson 10-5)* $\alpha = 162°$

19. Use the function f(x) = $x^2 - 1225$. *(Lessons 6-2, 6-3, 6-4)*
  a. How many x-intercepts does the function have? 2
  b. Find the x-intercepts. ±35
  c. Graph the function. See margin.
  d. Name the curve of part c. parabola

20. To the nearest tenth, find the real number b such that $3.2(2 - b)^3 = 8$. *(Lesson 8-11)* $b \approx 0.64$

21. During the investigation of a shooting, the police found a bullet imbedded in the wall 7 ft above the floor. Investigation revealed that the bullet was fired from a height of 4 ft at a distance of 3 ft from the wall. At what angle of elevation was the bullet fired? *(Lesson 10-2)* 45°

22. If log x = 3.5, find x to the nearest tenth. *(Lesson 9-4)* $x \approx 3162.3$

Exploration

23. The Law of Cosines is sometimes described as "the Pythagorean Theorem with a correction term." Explain why this is an appropriate description. See margin.

574

The Law of Sines

Two forest rangers are in stations 25 miles apart at locations S and T. On a certain day, the ranger at S sees a fire F at an angle of 40° with the line connecting the stations. The ranger at T sees the fire at an angle of 60°. How far is the fire from each ranger's station?

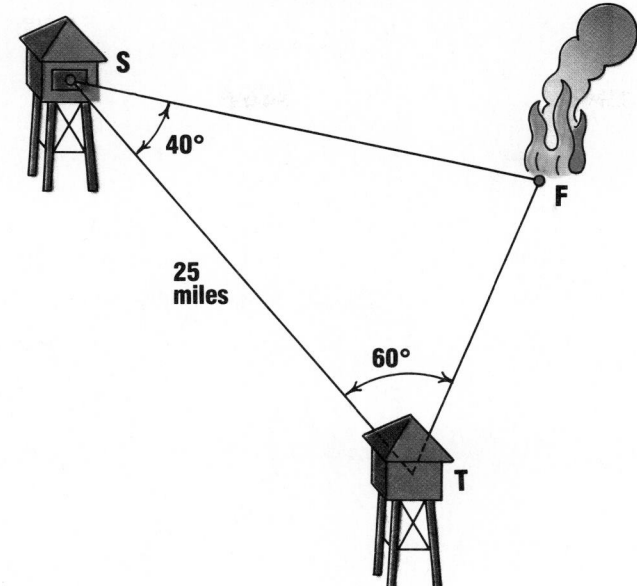

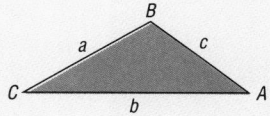

The given information here is the ASA condition; only one side is known. As a result, if you try to use the Law of Cosines to solve this problem, you will find that there are two unknowns. Since the Law of Cosines involves the three sides and only one angle of a triangle, it is not useful when only one side is known.

However, the missing distance can be found using an extraordinarily beautiful, simple theorem called the Law of Sines. In a triangle, the ratios of the sine of an angle to the length of its opposite side are equal. Here is a symbolic statement and proof.

Law of Sines Theorem:

In any triangle ABC,

$$\frac{\sin A}{a} = \frac{\sin B}{b} = \frac{\sin C}{c}.$$

LESSON 10-7

RESOURCES
■ Lesson Master 10-7
◳ Visual for Teaching Aid 66 provides the triangle to use with **Question 24**.
◳ Visual for Teaching Aid 67 provides the problem of Additional Example 3.

OBJECTIVES

E Find missing parts of a triangle using the Law of Sines.
H Solve real-world problems using the Law of Sines.

TEACHING NOTES

For most students, both the statement of the Law of Sines and its proof are easier than the statement and proof of the law of Cosines. Consequently, you could assign this reading without a lot of preliminary development.

Emphasize to students the connection between the Law of Sines with the AAS and ASA triangle congruence propositions. This is the most important mathematical application of those propositions.

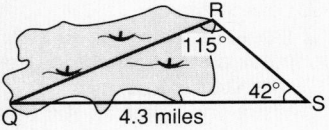
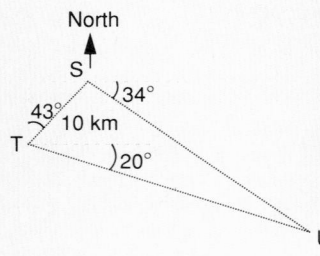
Proof:

Draw the altitude h to side $\overline{AC}$. Because $\sin C = \dfrac{h}{a}$, $h = a \sin C$.

So the area of $\triangle ABC$ is $\frac{1}{2}bh = \frac{1}{2}ba\sin C$. Similarly, by drawing the altitudes to the other sides, the area can be shown to equal $\frac{1}{2}ac\sin B$ and $\frac{1}{2}bc\sin A$.

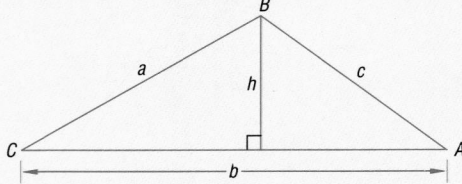

Because the area of the triangle is a constant,

$$\tfrac{1}{2}ab\sin C = \tfrac{1}{2}ac\sin B = \tfrac{1}{2}bc\sin A$$

So $\quad ab\sin C = ac\sin B = bc\sin A$.

Now divide all three expressions by abc.

$$\dfrac{ab\sin C}{abc} = \dfrac{ac\sin B}{abc} = \dfrac{bc\sin A}{abc}$$

Simplify. $\qquad \dfrac{\sin C}{c} = \dfrac{\sin B}{b} = \dfrac{\sin A}{a}$

The Law of Sines is useful whenever two angles and a side of a triangle are known and you wish to find a second side.

ush fire in Napa, California

Example 1 In the situation described at the beginning of this lesson, find the distance from the ranger at station T to the fire.

Solution The desired length is s. The angle opposite s is $\angle S$, with measure 40°. To use the Law of Sines you need the values of another angle and its opposite side. Because the sum of the measures of the angles in a triangle is 180°, $\angle F$ has measure 80°. Since you know $m\angle A = 40°$, $m\angle F = 80°$, and $f = 25$ miles, use the two ratios for S and F

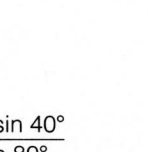

$$\dfrac{\sin S}{s} = \dfrac{\sin F}{f} \qquad\qquad s = \dfrac{25\sin 40°}{\sin 80°}$$

$$\dfrac{\sin 40°}{s} = \dfrac{\sin 80°}{25} \qquad\qquad s \approx \dfrac{25(.643)}{.985} \approx 16.3$$

The fire is about 16 miles from the ranger at T.

Example 1 illustrates how to use the Law of Sines when you are given two angles and the included side (ASA) and want to find the length of another side. The Law of Sines can also be used in an AAS situation: that is, in a triangle in which two angles and a non-included side are given.

Example 2   In $\triangle XYZ$, $m\angle X = 25°$, $m\angle Y = 75°$, and $x = 4$. Find y.

Solution

$$\frac{\sin X}{x} = \frac{\sin Y}{y}$$

$$\frac{\sin 25°}{4} = \frac{\sin 75°}{y}$$

$$y = \frac{4 \sin 75°}{\sin 25°}$$

$$y \approx \frac{4(.966)}{.423} \approx 9.1$$

The Law of Sines was known to Ptolemy in the 2nd century A.D. A theorem equivalent to the Law of Cosines is in Euclid's *Elements* written four centuries earlier. The Greeks used these theorems as the forest ranger used them in Example 1, to locate landmarks. This made it possible for reasonably accurate maps of parts of the Earth to be drawn well before the days of man-made satellites.

Questions

Covering the Reading

1. State the Law of Sines.   See margin.

2. With information satisfying the given condition, which theorem is more useful for finding other parts of a triangle, the Law of Cosines or the Law of Sines?   See margin.
   a. SAS   b. ASA   c. AAS   d. SSS

3. What does the expression $\frac{1}{2}ab \sin C$ represent for triangle ABC?   area

4. *Multiple choice* Which of the following verbally describes the Law of Sines? In a triangle: c
   (a) the ratio of an angle to the length of a side is a constant.
   (b) the ratio of the sine of an angle to the length of the adjacent side is a constant.
   (c) the ratio of the sine of an angle to the length of the opposite side is a constant.
   (d) None of (a) to (c) describes the Law of Sines.

5. Refer to the forest fire in the lesson. Find the distance of the fire from the ranger at S.   about 22 miles

LESSON 10-7   The Law of Sines   **577**

a. How far is each ship from U?
$m\angle STU = 67°$; $m\angle TSU = 90°$; $m\angle U = 14°$
$$\frac{\sin 14°}{10} = \frac{\sin 67°}{SU} = \frac{\sin 99°}{TU}$$
$SU \approx 38$ km; $TU \approx 40.8$ km
b. If S can travel at 27 km/hr and T at 30 km/hr, which ship can get to U first?
$\frac{38}{27} \approx 1.41$ hr; $\frac{40.8}{30} \approx 1.36$ hr
T can get there faster.

NOTES ON QUESTIONS
Question 9: This question illustrates that in some situations either the Law of Sines *or* the Law of Cosines may be used. In this situation, most people use the Law of Sines because it is computationally easier.

Question 12: The intent of this question is to show that the right triangle definition of $\sin \theta$ is a special case of the Law of Sines. After you discuss this question, you may want to examine the Law of Cosines for the same triangle. Specifically, $f^2 = a^2 + t^2 - 2at \cos 90°$, which is equivalent to $f^2 = a^2 + t^2$. Again, this shows that the Pythagorean Theorem is a special case of the Law of Cosines.

Question 24: The Law of Sines is always derived algebraically. This question provides the opportunity for students to validate the law geometrically. You might want to use it as a classroom activity.

ADDITIONAL ANSWERS
1. For any triangle ABC,
$\frac{\sin A}{a} = \frac{\sin B}{b} = \frac{\sin C}{c}$.

2a. Law of Cosines
b. Law of Sines
c. Law of Sines
d. Law of Cosines

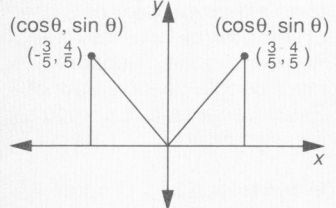
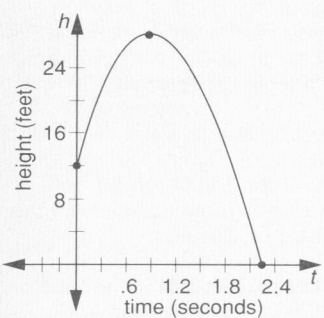
In 6 and 7, find *y*.

6. ≈12.2

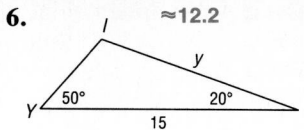

7. ≈35.9

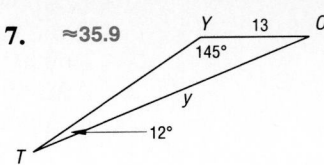

8. In △*ABC*, suppose you are given m∠*A* = 45°, m∠*B* = 60°, and *a* = 24. Find the exact value of *b*.   12√6

9. Refer to △*PQR* at the right.
   a. Find *RQ*.   ≈42 mm
   b. Use your answer to part a and the Law of Sines to find m∠*R*.   ≈55°
   c. Use the Law of Cosines and your answer to part a to find m∠*R*.   ≈55°
   d. *True or false*. In an SAS situation, once you find the third side, you can use either the Law of Sines or the Law of Cosines to find a second angle.   True

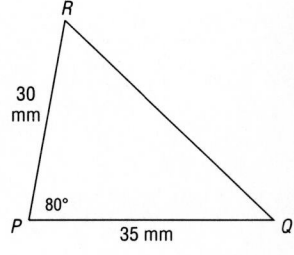

10. When a beam of light in air strikes the surface of water, it is refracted or bent as shown at the right. The relationship between α and θ is given by Snell's Law,

$$\frac{\sin \alpha}{\text{speed of light in air}} = \frac{\sin \theta}{\text{speed of light in water}}.$$

The speed of light in air is about 3.00×10^8 km/sec. If α = 45° and θ = 32°, find the speed of light in water.   ≈2 × 10⁸ km/sec

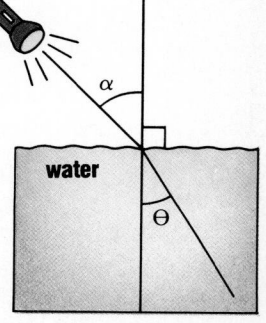

11. Because surveyors cannot get to the inside center of a mountain, its height must be measured in a more indirect way as shown in this problem. Refer to the diagram below.

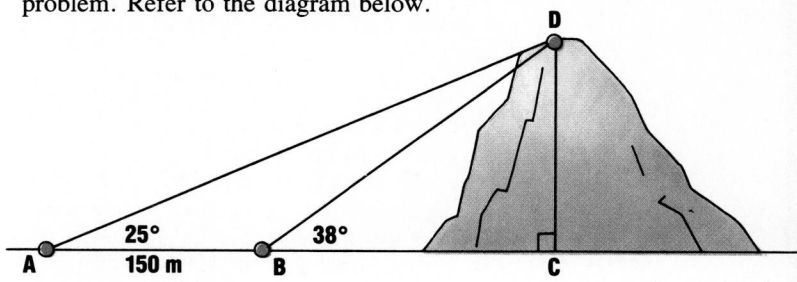

   a. Find the measures of ∠*ABD* and ∠*ADB*. (Hint: you only need to use your basic knowledge from geometry.)
   b. Find *BD*.   ≈282m   m∠*ABD* = 142°, m∠*ADB* = 13°
   c. Find *DC*, the height of the mountain.   ≈174m

578

12. a. Write the Law of Sines for the triangle at the right when m∠F = 90°. **See margin.**
b. How do the ratios from your answer to part a compare to the trigonometric ratios? *They are the same.*

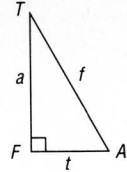

13. In using the Law of Sines, Katrina came up with sin A = 1.234. What can you tell Katrina about her solution? **See margin.**

Review

14. Kate has $800 to invest in an account which compounds interest continuously at a rate of $7\frac{1}{2}\%$.
a. How long will it take until the account doubles in value? *about $9\frac{1}{4}$ yrs*
b. How long will it take until the account doubles a second time? *(Lesson 9-7)* *another $9\frac{1}{4}$ yrs*

15. *Multiple choice.* Which of the following is the Law of Cosines?
(Lesson 10-6) **d**
(a) $a^2 = b^2 + c^2 + 2bc \cos A$
(b) $a^2 = b^2 + c^2 - bc \cos A$
(c) $a^2 = b^2 + c^2 - 2 \cos A$
(d) $a^2 = b^2 + c^2 - 2bc \cos A$

16. Give the coordinates of $R_{60}(1, 0)$ (a) exactly; (b) to the nearest thousandth. *(Lesson 10-4)* a) $\left(\frac{1}{2}, \frac{\sqrt{3}}{2}\right)$; b) (.500, .866)

17. If sin θ = $\frac{4}{5}$: (a) find the two possible values of cos θ and (b) graph the two points (cos θ, sin θ). *(Lesson 10-5)* a) cos θ = $\frac{3}{5}$ or cos θ = $-\frac{3}{5}$
b) See margin.

In 18 and 19, *true or false*. *(Lessons 10-4, 10-5)*

18. cos 180° = -1 **True**   **19.** sin 225° = $\frac{\sqrt{2}}{2}$ **False**

20. To the nearest tenth of a degree, find the measure of an acute angle and an obtuse angle whose sine is 0.921. *(Lessons 10-2, 10-5)*
67.1°, 112.9°

In 21 and 22, consider $A = \begin{bmatrix} -100 & 5 \\ -80 & 4 \end{bmatrix}$.

21. a. Find det A. **0**
b. Does A^{-1} exist? If so, find it. *(Lesson 5-5)* **no**

22. a. Find an equation for the line through the two points in matrix A. *(Lessons 3-5, 4-1)* **y = 0.8x**
b. What kind of variation is described by part a? *(Lesson 2-1)* **direct**

23. A rock is thrown upward with an initial velocity of 30 $\frac{ft}{sec}$ from a height of 12 ft. *(Lessons 6-1, 6-5, 6-6)*
a. Write an equation to describe the rock's height h (in feet) with respect to time t (in seconds). **h = -16t² + 30t + 12**
b. Graph the equation. **See margin.**
c. What is the maximum height of the rock? **≈26 feet**
d. When does the rock hit the ground?
≈2.2 seconds after being thrown

LESSON 10-7 The Law of Sines **579**

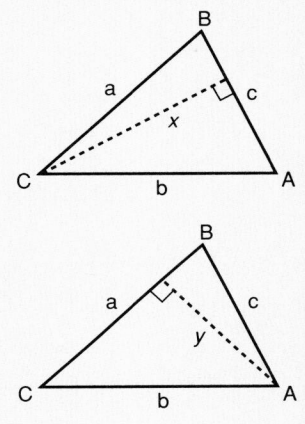
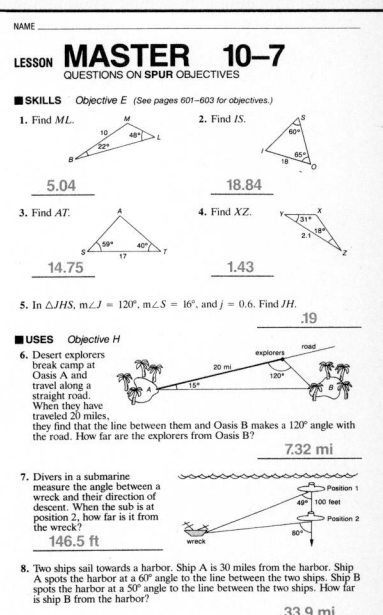

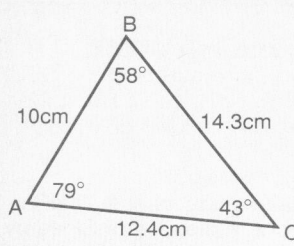

Exploration

24. Refer to the triangle shown below.
   a. Measure the sides of this triangle in centimeters and the angles in degrees.
   b. Find the sines of the angles.
   c. Substitute the values you get into the Law of Sines.
   d. How nearly equal are the fractions?   **a.–d. See margin.**

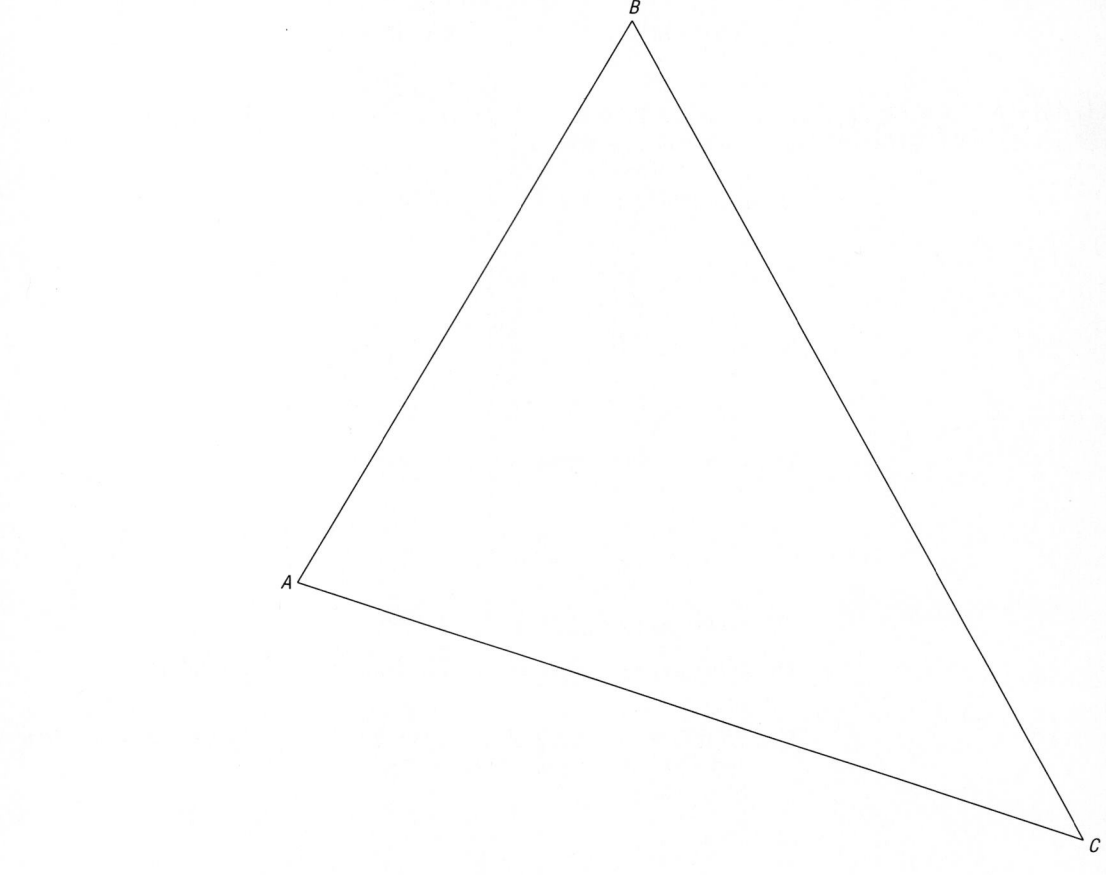

580

LESSON 10-8

Solving Sin θ = k

Every angle θ in a triangle has a measure between 0° and 180°. Each value of cos θ corresponds to a vertical line $x = \cos \theta$ intersecting the unit circle, and there is only one intersection point for $0° < \theta < 180°$. Thus if you know cos θ is positive, then $0° < \theta < 90°$ and the angle must be acute. If cos θ is negative, then $90° < \theta < 180°$ and the angle is obtuse.

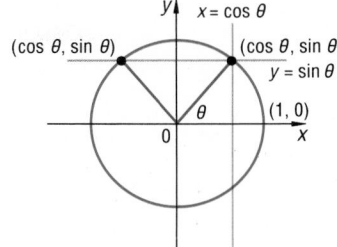

The situation is different for sin θ. Each value of sin θ between 0 and 1 corresponds to a horizontal line $y = \sin \theta$, which intersects the unit circle in two points. One point is in the first quadrant; one is in the second quadrant. Consequently, the equation $\sin \theta = k$ has two solutions between 0° and 180°, one where θ is acute and one where θ is obtuse.

Example 1 If sin θ = .624, find θ.

Solution For one solution, use a calculator.

The key sequence .624 [INV] [sin] yields θ ≈ 38.6°. In the drawing below, sin ∠POA = .624 and sin ∠QOA = .624, where Q is the reflection image of P over the y-axis. We have found m∠POA ≈ 38.6°. Since m∠QOB = m∠POA ≈ 38.6°, m∠QOA ≈ 180° − 38.6° ≈ 141.4°. Thus θ ≈ 141.4°.

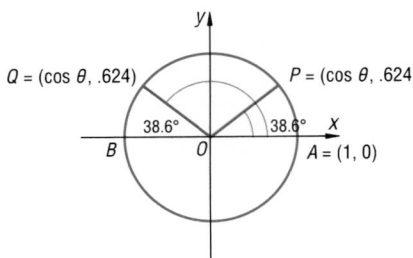

Notice that ∠QOB and ∠QOA are supplementary. Thus ∠POA and ∠QOA are also supplementary. In general, when $0° < \theta < 180°$, the two solutions to sin θ = k are supplementary angles. This result follows from the following theorem.

RESOURCES
■ Lesson Master 10-8

OBJECTIVES

C Determine the measure of an angle given its sine.
E Find missing parts of a triangle using the Law of Sines.
F Use the Supplements Theorem.
H Solve real-world problems using the Law of Sines.

TEACHING NOTES

Emphasize that the SSS, SAS, and AAS triangle congruence theorems *guarantee* a unique solution to a triangle when the given data conform to one of these three cases. It is only in the case where the given information fits the SSA pattern that we must consider whether there is more than one, if any, solution to the triangle. You may wish to point out that the proof in **Question 11** shows that SsA (the first S is longer, the A is opposite the first S) does guarantee a unique solution.

Alternate Approach
Encourage students to be particularly careful in making a scale drawing of the given information. Often a good drawing is enough to determine whether there are one, two, or no solutions to a particular triangle, as is illustrated in **Example 3**.

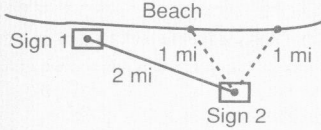

Supplements Theorem:

> For all θ in degrees
>
> $$\sin \theta = \sin (180° - \theta).$$

The Supplements Theorem is critical when using the Law of Sines to find measures of angles.

■ ■ ■ ■ ■ ■ ■ ■

Example 2 In a triangle ABC, $a = 13$, $c = 20$, and $m\angle A = 35°$. Find the measure of $\angle C$.

[M10-8, E2a]

Solution Sketch a picture. It is natural to use the Law of Sines.

$$\frac{\sin A}{a} = \frac{\sin C}{c}$$

$$\frac{\sin 35°}{13} = \frac{\sin C}{20}$$

$$\frac{20 \sin 35°}{13} = \sin C$$

$$.882 \approx \sin C$$

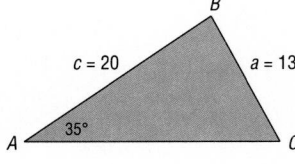

Because values of the sine are positive in both the first and second quadrants, there are two possible values for $m\angle C$ in $\triangle ABC$. One angle is acute (in the first quadrant) and the other is obtuse (in the second quadrant).

A calculator shows $m\angle C \approx 61.9°$. Thus triangle ABC can look like the one at the right.

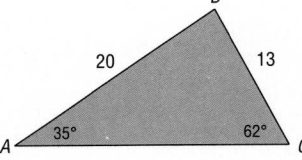

The obtuse angle whose sine equals .882 is $180° - 62° = 118°$. The triangle at the right represents a second solution to the problem.

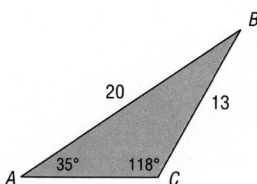

The situation in Example 2 illustrates the SSA condition, when two sides and a nonincluded angle are given. With SSA, there may be more than one solution. As the next example shows, it is not true that there is always more than one solution.

582

Example 3 In triangle SPX, $m\angle S = 75°$, $s = 11$, and $x = 9$. Find the measure of $\angle X$.

Solution Since you have the SSA situation, use the Law of Sines.

$$\frac{\sin S}{s} = \frac{\sin X}{p}$$

$$\frac{\sin 75°}{11} = \frac{\sin X}{9}$$

$$\frac{9 \sin 75°}{11} = \sin X$$

$$.790 \approx \sin X$$

A calculator shows $m\angle X \approx 52°$.
The triangle is pictured at the right.

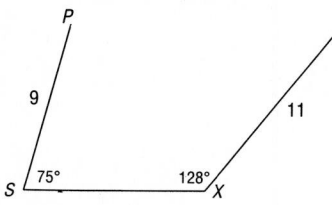

A second angle with sine equal to
.790 is the supplement of the first,
with measure $180° - 52° = 128°$.
However, $75° + 128° > 180°$, so
these two angles cannot be parts
of a triangle.

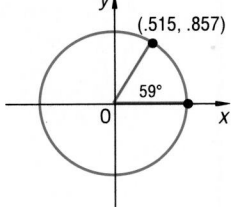

Thus, in this case, there is only one solution to the problem.

The use of trigonometry to find all the missing measures of sides and angles of a triangle is called **solving the triangle**. When enough information is given, the Law of Cosines and the Law of Sines are all that is needed to solve any triangle.

Questions

1. **a.** According to the figure at the right, $\cos 59° \approx$ __?__. **.515**
   b. Give a value of θ different from $59°$ with $\cos \theta = \cos 59°$. **301°**
   c. According to the figure, $\sin 59° \approx$ __?__. **.857**
   d. Give a value of θ different from $59°$ with $\sin \theta = \sin 59°$. **121°**

NOTES ON QUESTIONS
Questions 4–10: Students should decide whether the use of the Law of Sines or the Law of Cosines is more appropriate for each problem.

Question 11: Students will most likely need a class discussion of the proof in this question. Be sure to emphasize the application of the Law of Sines.

Questions 19 and 20: These questions preview the concept of periodic function introduced in Lesson 10-9.

Question 21a: The circle in this question is called the *circumcircle* of the triangle. This question provides the opportunity to mention still another amazing theorem: the area of a triangle with sides a, b, and c equals $\frac{abc}{4R}$, where R is the radius of the circumcircle.

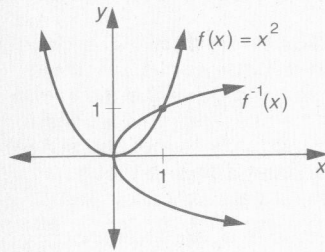
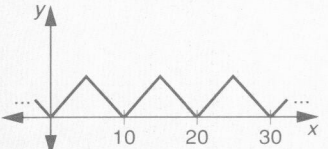
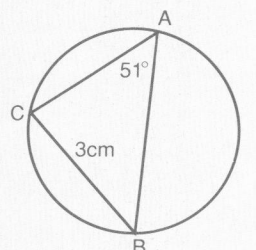
2. Solve for θ, where $0° < \theta < 180°$: $\sin\theta = \frac{1}{5}$.
   11.5°, 168.5°
3. In a triangle ABC, $m\angle B = 42°$, $c = 13$, and $b = 18$.
   a. Use the Law of Sines to find the measure of angle C. $\approx 29°$
   b. Explain why there is only one solution to part a.   **See margin.**

In 4–7, use the Law of Sines or the Law of Cosines to find x.

4. $x \approx 13.9$

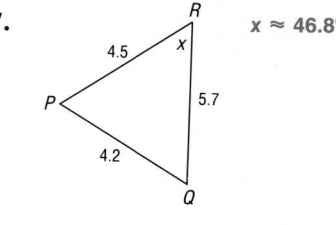

5. $x \approx 14.4$

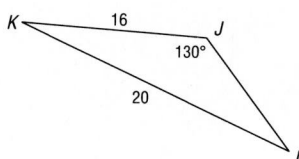

6. $x \approx 51.4°$ **7.** $x \approx 46.8°$

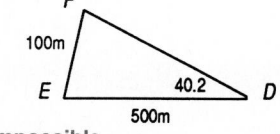

8. Solve $\triangle JKL$ at the right.
   (Approximate each value to the
   nearest tenth.)
   $m\angle L \approx 37.8°$, $m\angle K \approx 12.2°$, $k \approx 5.5$

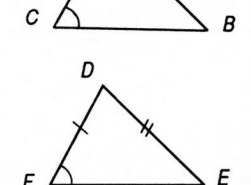

9. Consider the triangle RST, where $\angle R = 52.8°$, $r = 20.1$, and
   $s = 23.1$.
   a. Find all possible values of the measure of $\angle S$. $\approx 66.3°$, $\approx 113.7°$
   b. For each solution in part a find the length of the third side.
      ≈ 22.0, ≈ 5.9
10. A surveyor marks off points D, E, and
   F and records that $m\angle D = 40.2°$,
   $d = 100$ m, and $f = 500$ m. Show that
   there is a problem with the surveyor's
   measurements by trying to find $m\angle F$.
   By the Law of Sines, $\sin F = 3.23$, which is impossible.
11. There is the SSA Triangle Congruence
   Theorem: If, in two triangles, two sides
   and the angle opposite the larger side of
   one are congruent respectively to two
   sides and the angle opposite the larger
   side of the other, then the triangles are
   congruent.

   Take as given: $AB = DE$, $AC = DF$,
   $\angle C \cong \angle F$, and $AB > AC$. Use the
   Law of Sines to show that $\angle B \cong \angle E$
   and thus that the triangles are congruent.   **See margin.**

584

12. To design a map, a cartographer needs to find the distances between city C on one side of a river and cities A and B on the other side. He measured AB to be 130 mi, $m\angle A = 110°$, and $m\angle B = 40°$. Find AC and BC. *(Lesson 10-7)* $AC \approx 167mi, BC \approx 244mi$

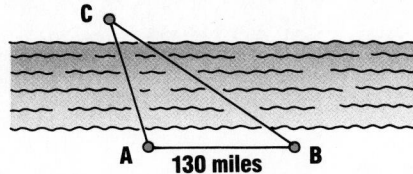

In 13–16, give the exact values without using a calculator. *(Lessons 10-3, 10-4, 10-5)*

13. $\sin (-90°)$ -1

14. $\cos (-60°)$ $\frac{1}{2}$

15. $\sin (390°)$ $\frac{1}{2}$

16. $\cos (720°)$ 1

17. **a.** Graph $f(x) = x^2$.   See margin.
 b. On the same set of axes, graph the reflection image of f about $y = x$.   See margin.
 c. Is f^{-1} a function? *(Lessons 7-6, 2-6)*   No

18. Solve $-12 + \sqrt{3A + 10} = -10$. *(Lesson 8-10)* $A = -2$

In 19 and 20 refer to the relation graphed below.

19. Is the relation graphed below a function? Why or why not? *(Lesson 7-2)*
 Yes; the vertical-line test holds

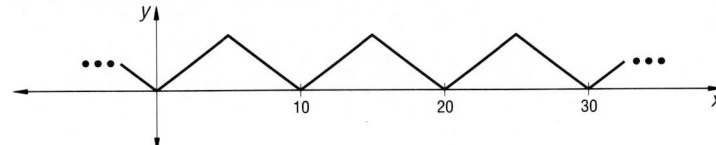

20. Graph the image of the relation above under the translation $T_{10, 0}$.
 (Lesson 4-9)   See margin.

21. Draw a circle and a triangle ABC with vertices on that circle.
 a. Measure $\angle A$ and side a. Verify that the ratio $\dfrac{a}{\sin A}$ equals the diameter of the circle.   See margin.
 b. What does $\dfrac{b}{\sin B}$ equal?   the diameter of the circle

---

FOLLOW-UP

MORE PRACTICE
For more questions on SPUR Objectives, use *Lesson Master 10-8*, shown below.

EXTENSION
Point out to students that there is a Law of Sines for triangles drawn on the surface of a sphere. If a, b, and c are the sides of the spherical triangle (the sides are arcs of great circles) and A, B, and C are the angles,
then $\dfrac{\sin A}{\sin a} = \dfrac{\sin B}{\sin b} = \dfrac{\sin C}{\sin c}$.
As a research project, ask students to determine how the angles of a spherical triangle are defined and how such a theorem can be used.

NAME _____

LESSON **MASTER 10-8**
QUESTIONS ON **SPUR** OBJECTIVES

■ **SKILLS** *Objective C (See pages 601–603 for objectives.)*
In 1–3, solve for θ where 0 < θ < 180°. Round your answers to the nearest tenth of a degree.

1. $\sin \theta = \frac{1}{3}$	2. $\sin \theta = .4$	3. $\sin \theta \approx .908$
19.5°	23.6°	65.2°
160.5°	156.4°	114.8°

■ **SKILLS** *Objective E*
4. In △GNP, $m\angle G = 22°$, $p = 8$, and $g = 6$.
 Find $m\angle P$. $\approx 30°$

5. In △RHT, $m\angle R = 45°$, $r = 0.71$, and $t = 1$.
 Find $m\angle T$. $\approx 85°$

6. Find all missing parts of the triangle below. Approximate each value to the nearest tenth.

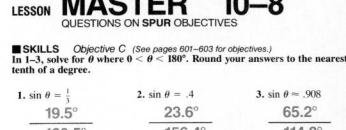

 $m\angle E =$ $\approx 22.5°$
 $m\angle P =$ $\approx 57.5°$
 $NE =$ ≈ 15.4

■ **PROPERTIES** *Objective F*
In 7 and 8, answer true or false. If false, change it so that it is true.

7. $\sin(180° - \theta) = \sin \theta$
 true

8. $\cos(180° - \theta) = \cos \theta$
 false; sample:
 $\cos(180° - \theta) = -\cos \theta$

9. Give an acute value of θ such that $\sin \theta = \sin 127°$.
 53°

LESSON 10-9

RESOURCES
■ Lesson Master 10-9
▣ Computer Master 24

OBJECTIVE

J Identify the domain, range, *x*-intercepts, *y*-intercepts, and period of the sine and cosine functions from their graphs.

TEACHING NOTES

This is a lesson for which a class discussion can be particularly illuminating. If you made a unit circle on tag board or a transparency of *Teaching Aid 63*, we recommend you use it here. Again, note that the rotation of magnitude θ from (1, 0) determines a point P(θ) on the circle with unique coordinates (cos θ, sin θ). In this lesson, we consider the mappings θ → cos θ and θ → sin θ separately.

You may wish to graph the function f(θ) = sin θ with students and then use a portion of the class period for guided practice while the students draw the graph of f(θ) = cos θ.

Be sure to discuss the properties of these functions, given on pages 586 and 587.

LESSON

10-9

The Cosine and Sine Functions

The changing height of each swinging seat can be described as a sine or cosine function.

When (1, 0) is rotated θ degrees around the origin its image is the point (cos θ, sin θ). We can set up a correspondence θ → cos θ, associating the magnitude of this rotation with the *x*-coordinate of the image of (1, 0). This correspondence is a function, because for each θ there is only one value for cos θ. Similarly, the correspondence θ → sin θ is a function that associates θ with the *y*-coordinate of the image of (1, 0) under R_θ.

> f: θ → cos θ is called the **cosine function**.
> g: θ → sin θ is called the **sine function**.

Some ordered pairs of the function g(θ) = sin θ are given and graphed below. The exact values that you have learned are shown in the table. For instance, since sin 30° = $\frac{1}{2}$, the point (30°, $\frac{1}{2}$) is graphed.

θ	0	15	30	45	60	75	90	105	120	135	150	165
sin θ*	0	.26	.50	.71	.87	.97	1	.97	.87	.71	.50	.26
sin θ**	0		$\frac{1}{2}$	$\frac{\sqrt{2}}{2}$	$\frac{\sqrt{3}}{2}$		1		$\frac{\sqrt{3}}{2}$	$\frac{\sqrt{2}}{2}$	$\frac{1}{2}$	

θ	180	195	210	225	240	255	270	285	300	315	330	345	360
sin θ*	0	-.26	-.5	-.71	-.87	-.97	-1	-.97	-.87	-.71	-.5	-.26	0
sin θ**	0		$\frac{-1}{2}$	$\frac{-\sqrt{2}}{2}$	$\frac{-\sqrt{3}}{2}$		-1		$\frac{-\sqrt{3}}{2}$	$\frac{-\sqrt{2}}{2}$	$\frac{-1}{2}$		0

*decimal approximation
**exact value

586

As θ continues to increase beyond 360°, the rotation images of (1, 0) coincide with previous ones. The value of the y-coordinate, sin θ, repeats itself every 360°. As a result, the ordered pairs of the function g(θ) = sin θ repeat every 360°. A more complete graph is below.

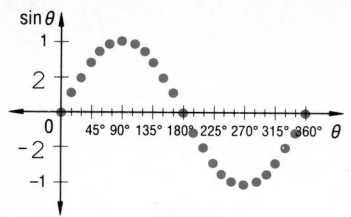

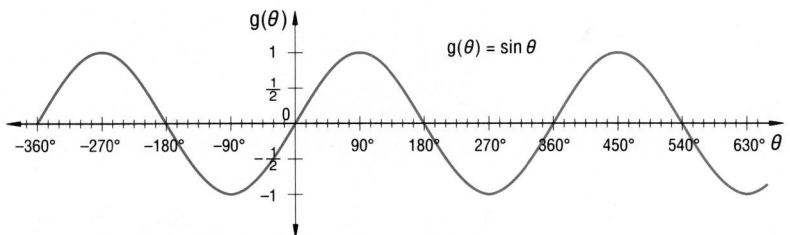

The graph of f(θ) = cos θ shown below was constructed by doing a similar analysis of the first coordinate of the rotation image of (1, 0). For instance, because cos 30° = $\frac{\sqrt{3}}{2}$ ≈ .87, the point (30°, .87) is graphed.

θ	0	15	30	45	60	75	90	105	120	135	150	165
cos θ*	1	.97	.87	.71	.50	.26	0	-.26	-.5	-.71	-.87	-.97
cos θ**	1		$\frac{\sqrt{3}}{2}$	$\frac{\sqrt{2}}{2}$	$\frac{1}{2}$		0		$\frac{-1}{2}$	$\frac{-\sqrt{2}}{2}$	$\frac{-\sqrt{3}}{2}$	

θ	180	195	210	225	240	255	270	285	300	315	330	345	360
cos θ*	-1	-.97	-.87	-.71	-.5	-.26	0	.26	.50	.71	.87	.97	1
cos θ**	-1		$\frac{-\sqrt{3}}{2}$	$\frac{-\sqrt{2}}{2}$	$\frac{-1}{2}$		0		$\frac{1}{2}$	$\frac{\sqrt{2}}{2}$	$\frac{\sqrt{3}}{2}$		1

*decimal approximation
**exact value

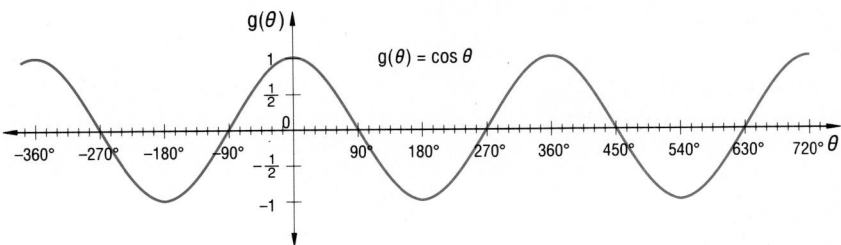

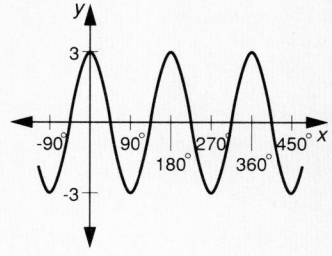

ADDITIONAL EXAMPLE
Below is a graph of
f(θ) = 3 cos (2θ).

a. What is the domain of f?
the set of real numbers
b. What is the range of f?
the set of real numbers
between 3 and –3 inclusive
c. What is the y-intercept?
3
d. What are the x-intercepts
between 0° and 360°?
45°, 135°, 225°, 315°
e. What is the period of f?
180°

The graphs of the sine and cosine functions have several properties.

1. Because the measure of the angle of rotation, θ, may be any real number, the domain of both the sine and cosine functions is the set of real numbers. Because $\cos \theta$ and $\sin \theta$ are coordinates of points on the unit circle, the range of these functions is the set of real numbers between -1 and 1, inclusive.

2. The sine graph has a y-intercept of 0 and x-intercepts of the even multiples of 90°; that is, ... , -180°, 0, 180°, 360°, 540°, ... The cosine graph has a y-intercept of 1 and x-intercepts of the odd multiples of 90°, that is, ... , -270°, -90°, 90°, 270°, 450°, ...

3. A function is **periodic** if its graph can be mapped to itself under a horizontal translation. Both the sine and cosine functions are periodic. For each function the period is 360°. This means that $\sin (\theta \pm 360n°) = \sin \theta$ and $\cos (\theta \pm 360n°) = \cos \theta$ where n is any integer.

4. The graphs of $f(\theta) = \cos \theta$ and $g(\theta) = \sin \theta$ are congruent. Each can be mapped to the other with a horizontal translation of 90°. For this reason both are often called **sine waves.** They are said to be **sinusoidal.**

Definition:

A sine wave is a graph which can be mapped onto the graph of $g(\theta) = \sin \theta$ by any composite of reflections, translations, and scale changes.

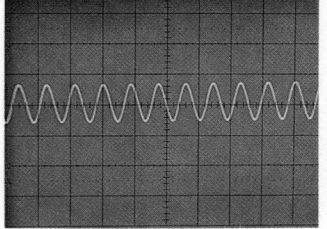

Sound waves on an oscilloscope

Sine waves have many applications. Pure sound tones travel in sine waves; these can be pictured on an oscilloscope, as shown at the left. The path of a satellite as it travels around the earth is an approximate sine wave, and the time of sunrise for a given location over the year also shows sinusoidal behavior.

Questions

Covering the Reading

1. The function f: $\theta \rightarrow \cos \theta$ maps θ onto the __?__-coordinate of the image of (1, 0) under R_θ.   x

2. The function g: $\theta \rightarrow \sin \theta$ maps θ onto the __?__-coordinate of the image of (1, 0) under R_θ.   y

In 3 and 4, for each function: (a) name two points on the function; (b) give its domain; (c) give its range.

3. $f(\theta) = \cos \theta$ See margin.   4. $g(\theta) = \sin \theta$ See margin.

588

5. As θ increases from 0° to 90°, sin θ increases from __?__ to __?__.   **0; 1**

6. As θ increases from 90° to 180°, sin θ decreases from __?__ to __?__.
1; 0

7. As θ increases from 180° to 270°, does the value of g(θ) = sin θ increase or decrease?   **decrease**

8. As θ increases from 270° to 360°, how do the values of sin θ change?
They increase from -1 to 0.

9. Define: periodic function.   **See margin.**

In 10–12, *true or false*.

10. The function f(θ) = cos θ is periodic.   **true**

11. The cosine function intersects the *x*-axis at -720°.   **false**

12. cos θ = cos (360° + θ) for all θ.   **true**

Applying the Mathematics

13. a. On the same set of axes, graph f(θ) = cos θ and g(θ) = sin θ over the interval -360° ≤ θ ≤ 360°.   **See margin.**
   b. Find all values of θ between -360° and 360° such that cos θ = sin θ.   **-315°, -135°, 45°, 225°**

14. Let h(θ) = 2 + sin θ.
   a. Use the Graph Translation Theorem to predict where the graph of *h* will lie on the coordinate plane, and what its maximum and minimum values will be.   **1 ≤ h(θ) ≤ 3 for any θ; minimum = 1, maximum = 3**
   b. Graph this function.   **See margin.**
   c. Is this function a sine wave? Justify your answer.
   Yes, sin θ can be mapped onto h with a vertical translation of 2 units.

15. *Multiple choice* Which choice completes a symbolic definition of "periodic function"?   **a**
   f is periodic if and only if there is a number *p* such that for all *x*:
   (a) f(x + p) = f(x)   (c) f(x) + f(p) = f(x + p)
   (b) p · f(x) = f(px)   (d) f(x) + p = f(x)

In 16–19, part of a function is graphed. (a) Is the function periodic? (b) If so, what is the period?

16.   **No**
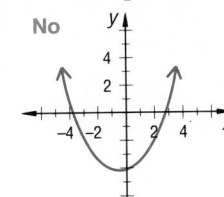

17.   **No**
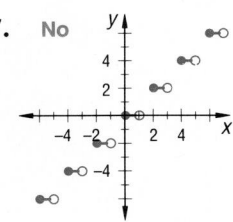

18.
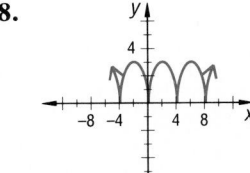
a) Yes   b) 4

19.
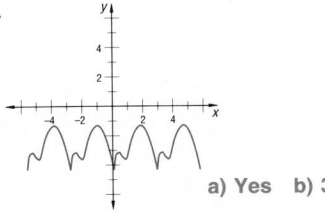
a) Yes   b) 3

LESSON 10-9   The Cosine and Sine Functions   **589**

NOTES ON QUESTIONS
Question 13a: This question asks students to draw graphs of functions. Students could use an automatic grapher to do this.

Question 22: Students may need a hint for this question. Point out that if the total span of the bridge is 200 ft, each half measures 100 ft. By drawing an appropriate perpendicular segment they will be able to use the cosine ratio to solve for θ. Even more quickly, if they recognize that the ratio of the hypotenuse to the short leg in the triangle formed by the perpendicular is 2:1, θ may be immediately seen to measure 60°.

Question 27: Before students draw the graph, remind them to represent the dates on the horizontal axis and the times on the vertical axis.

9. Periodic function: one that can be mapped onto itself under a horizontal translation.

13.a.
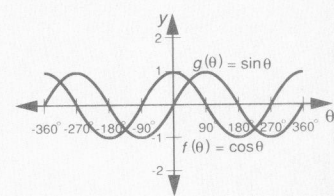

14.b.
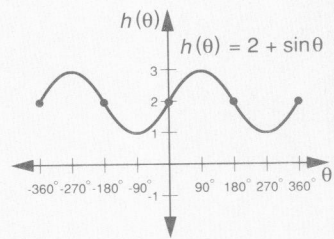

MORE PRACTICE
For more questions on SPUR
Objectives, use *Lesson Mas-
ter 10-9,* shown on page 591.

EXTENSION
Have students graph other
equations of the form $y = a \sin (b\theta + c) + k$ on an
automatic grapher. Ask them
to determine the composition
of reflections, translations,
and scale changes needed to
map these graphs onto the
graph of $y = \sin \theta$.

Review

In 20 and 21, complete each statement with a trigonometric expression to make the equation true.

20. $(\sin \theta)^2 + (\underline{\ ?\ })^2 = 1$ *(Lesson 10-3)*   cos θ

21. $\sin (90° - \theta) = \underline{\ ?\ }$ *(Lesson 10-3)*   cos θ

22. At what angle θ must each side of a 200-foot drawbridge be raised to create a 100-foot gap? *(Lesson 10-2)*   60°

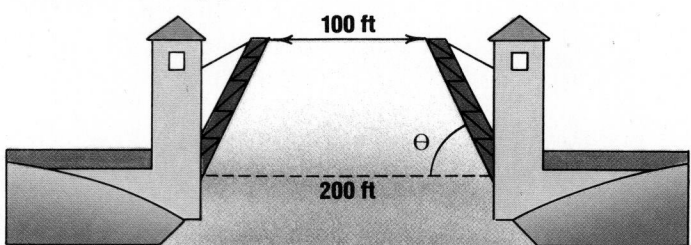

23. In a triangle *GHI*, $g = 15$, $i = 21$, and $m\angle G = 42°$. Find the measure of $\angle I$. *(Lesson 10-8)*   ≈69.5° or ≈110.5°

24. In a triangle *JKL*, $m\angle L = 81°$, $l = 20$, $k = 21$. Find the measure of $\angle K$. *(Lesson 10-8)*   no solution

25. The circle at the right is tangent to the axes at (8, 0) and (0, 8). Find its area and circumference. *(Previous course)*
area: 64π; circumference: 16π

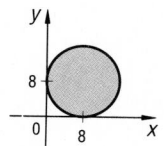

26. An observer in a lighthouse on the shore sees a ship in distress. The ship is 15 miles away at an angle of 20° to the shoreline. A Coast Guard station is on the shoreline 30 miles away from the lighthouse.

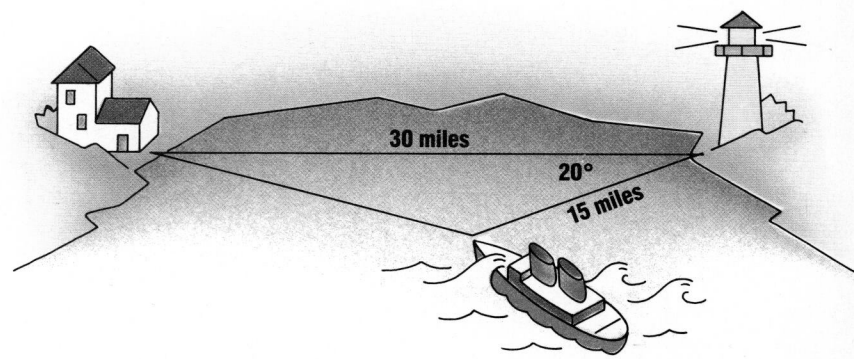

a. How far will a Coast Guard rescue ship have to travel from the station to reach the ship? *(Lesson 10-6)*   ≈16.7 miles

b. The path of the rescue vessel should be at what angle to the shoreline? (Hint: use your answer from part a.) *(Lesson 10-7)*   ≈17.9°

590

27. The following table lists the time of sunset each Sunday of 1966 for Denver, Colorado. (Daylight savings time has been ignored.)

a. Accurately graph an appropriate function.   **See below.**

b. Is the graph of sunset times periodic? If so, what is its period?
The graph appears to have a period of one year.

1/2	4:46	4/3	6:26	7/3	7:32	10/2	5:42
1/9	4:53	4/10	6:33	7/10	7:31	10/9	5:31
1/16	5:00	4/17	6:40	7/17	7:27	10/16	5:20
1/23	5:08	4/24	6:47	7/24	7:22	10/23	5:10
1/30	5:16	5/1	6:54	7/31	7:15	10/30	5:01
2/6	5:24	5/8	7:01	8/7	7:07	11/6	4:53
2/13	5:33	5/15	7:08	8/14	6:59	11/13	4:46
2/20	5:41	5/22	7:14	8/21	6:49	11/20	4:41
2/27	5:49	5/29	7:20	8/28	6:39	11/27	4:37
3/6	5:57	6/5	7:25	9/5	6:28	12/4	4:35
3/13	6:04	6/12	7:29	9/12	6:17	12/11	4:35
3/20	6:12	6/19	7:32	9/19	6:03	12/18	4:36
3/27	6:19	6/26	7:33	9/26	5:53	12/25	4:40

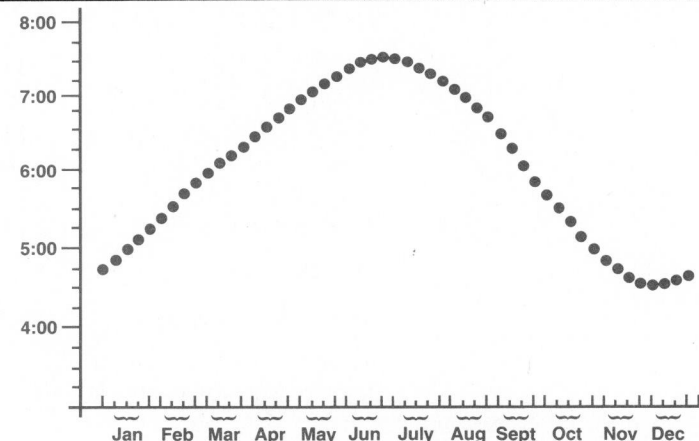

OBJECTIVES

A Approximate values of trigonometric functions using
a calculator.
D Convert angle measures
from radians to degrees or
degrees to radians.
J Identify properties of the
sine and cosine functions
using their graphs.

TEACHING NOTES

To introduce this lesson, we
suggest you again use the
unit circle. This time calculate
its circumference (2π). Ask
students to find the length of
the arc determined by rotations of various amounts
(90° → π/2; 180° → π;
45° → π/4, 270° → 3π/2).
Then state the definition of
radian given in the text.

Have students practice converting from degrees to
radians and from radians to
degrees. We suggest you
use examples that are multiples of 30° or 45°, that is,
$\frac{\pi}{6}$ or $\frac{\pi}{4}$ radians. For the benefit of those whose fractions
skills are weak, point out to
students that the fraction
$\frac{a\pi}{b} = \frac{a}{b}\pi$. Record your result
on a circle with equivalent
measures like the one pictured on page 593.

Virtually every student wants
to know "how big" one ra-
dian is. As a class, have
students convert 1 radian to
degrees.

Radian
Measure

592

So far in this chapter you have learned to evaluate sin x, cos x, and
tan x when x has been given in degrees. Another unit, called the
radian, is widely used when measuring angles or magnitudes of
rotation. In fact, in some later mathematics courses radians are used
more than degrees. Here is the idea behind the radian.

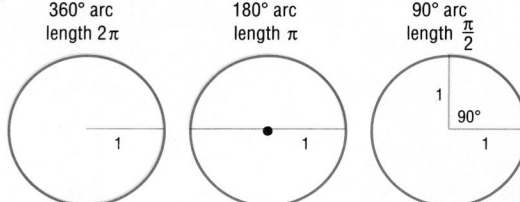

Since the radius of a unit circle is the number 1, the circumference
of the unit circle is 2π. Thus, on a unit circle, a 360° arc has a
length of 2π. Similarly, a 180° arc has a length of π, and a 90° arc
has a length of

$$\tfrac{1}{4}(2\pi) \text{ or } \frac{\pi}{2}.$$

The radian is a unit created so that the arc measure and the arc
length use the same number.

Definition:

> The radian is a unit of angle, arc, or rotation measure such
> that
>
> $$\pi \text{ radians} = 180 \text{ degrees}.$$

The definition indicates that a 180° angle has measure π radians,
and its arc has length π. Thus a 90° angle has measure $\frac{\pi}{2}$ radians,
and its arc has length $\frac{\pi}{2}$. To repeat, *the measure of an angle in
radians equals the length of its arc on the unit circle*. This is one
major reason for using radians.

The definition can be transformed to give the two conversion factors
for changing degrees into radians and vice versa, without a calculator. Begin with

$$\pi \text{ radians} = 180°.$$

Divide both sides by π radians.   Divide both sides by 180 degre

$$1 = \frac{180 \text{ degrees}}{\pi \text{ radians}}$$ $$\frac{\pi \text{ radians}}{180 \text{ degrees}} = 1$$

So to convert radians to degrees, multiply by $\dfrac{180 \text{ degrees}}{\pi \text{ radians}}$; to convert degrees to radians, multiply by $\dfrac{\pi \text{ radians}}{180 \text{ degrees}}$.

Example 1   Convert 45° to radians.

Solution 1   Multiply by one of the conversion factors. Because you want radians, choose the ratio with radians in the numerator.

$$45° \cdot \dfrac{\pi \text{ radians}}{180°} = \dfrac{45°}{180°}\pi \text{ radians}$$

$$= \dfrac{\pi}{4} \text{ radians}$$

Solution 2   A scientific calculator usually has a [DRG] key to convert from one unit to another. Key in 45 [INV] [DRG]. You should see RAD on your display along with 0.7853981... . This approximates $\dfrac{\pi}{4}$.

The answer to Example 1 should make sense to you. If 180° equals π radians, then $\dfrac{\pi}{4}$ is $\frac{1}{4}$ of π, and $\frac{1}{4}$ of 180° is 45°. The diagram below shows other common equivalences.

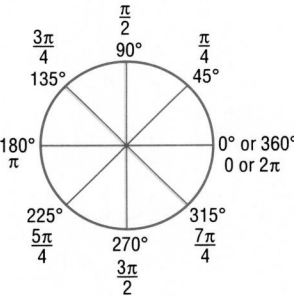

Radian expressions are usually left in terms of π because this form gives an exact value. Since magnitudes of rotation and angle measures are often given in radians, the word radian or abbreviation *rad* is usually omitted.

Many calculators will not easily convert radians to degrees, so you may need to do the conversion by hand.

LESSON 10-10   Radian Measure   **593**

ADDITIONAL EXAMPLES
1. Convert each degree measure to radians.
a. 120°
$\dfrac{2\pi}{3}$
b. 270°
$\dfrac{3\pi}{2}$
c. 135°
$\dfrac{3\pi}{4}$
d. 330°
$\dfrac{11\pi}{6}$

2. Convert each radian measure to degrees.
a. $\dfrac{7\pi}{6}$
210°
b. $\dfrac{5\pi}{4}$
225°
c. 4π
720°
d. $\dfrac{4\pi}{3}$
240°

3. Evaluate on your calculator.
a. $\cos \dfrac{\pi}{6}$
$\approx .866$
b. $\sin \dfrac{2\pi}{3}$
$\approx .866$
c. $\sin \dfrac{7\pi}{4}$
$\approx -.707$

Example 2   Convert 2 radians to degrees.

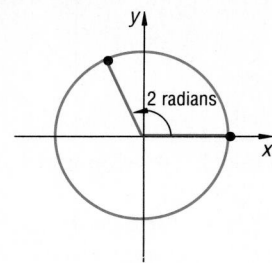

Solution 1   2 radians = 2 radians $\cdot \dfrac{180°}{\pi \text{ radians}}$.

$$= \dfrac{360°}{\pi}$$

$$\approx 114.6°$$

Notice that one radian is much larger than one degree. (1 rad ≈ 57°)

Solution 2   Use a calculator.
Press ⌊DRG⌋ until the screen of your calculator displays RAD. Then key in 2 ⌊INV⌋ ⌊DRG⌋, repeating ⌊INV⌋ ⌊DRG⌋ until the screen displays DEG. You should see 114.591... .

The multiples of π and the simplest divisors of π (e.g., $\dfrac{\pi}{2}$, $\dfrac{\pi}{3}$, and $\dfrac{\pi}{4}$) correspond to those angle measures which give exact values of cosines and sines.

Example 3   Evaluate $\sin\left(\dfrac{\pi}{4}\right)$ on your calculator.

Solution   Since there is no degree symbol, we assume $\dfrac{\pi}{4}$ means $\dfrac{\pi}{4}$ radians. Put your calculator in radian mode by pressing ⌊DRG⌋ until RAD appears on the screen. Now press ⌊(⌋ ⌊π⌋ ⌊÷⌋ 4 ⌊)⌋ ⌊sin⌋. The result is about .707.

Check 1   From Example 1, $\dfrac{\pi}{4} = 45°$. You know $\sin 45° = \dfrac{\sqrt{2}}{2}$, so $\sin \dfrac{\pi}{4} = \dfrac{\sqrt{2}}{2}$ which is about .707.

Check 2   Return the calculator to the DEG setting. Press 45 ⌊sin⌋. You should get approximately .707 again.

594

The cosine and sine functions are graphed below with radians instead of degrees. Notice that the scales on the *x*-axis and *y*-axis can be equal and the periods are 2π, a simpler number (in some ways) than 360°.

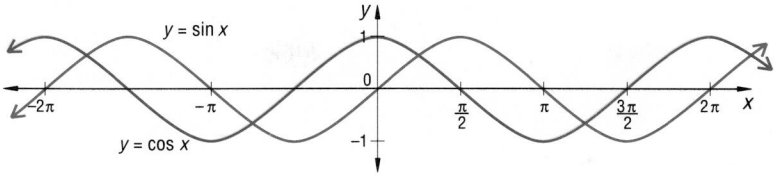

Questions

1. A circle has a radius of 1 unit. Give the length of an arc whose measure is:
   a. 360° 2π b. 180° π c. 90°. $\frac{\pi}{2}$

2. On a circle of radius 1 meter, find the length of a 45° arc. $\frac{\pi}{4}$ meter

3. State how radians and degrees are related. π radians = 180°

In 4–7, convert to radians. Give your answer as a number times π.

4. 90° $\frac{1}{2}\pi$

5. 60° $\frac{1}{3}\pi$

6. 225° $\frac{5}{4}\pi$

7. 30° $\frac{1}{6}\pi$

In 8 and 9, convert the radian measure to degrees.

8. $\frac{\pi}{6}$ 30°

9. $\frac{-5\pi}{4}$ -225°

In 10–12, evaluate.

10. a. Evaluate $\sin\left(\frac{3\pi}{2}\right)$ on your calculator.   -1
    b. Check your answer to part a, using degrees. $\frac{3\pi}{2} = 270°$; $\sin 270° = -1$

11. $\cos\frac{\pi}{3}$ .5

12. $\tan\frac{\pi}{6}$ $\frac{\sqrt{3}}{3} \approx .577$

13. In radians, what is the period of the sine function? 2π

NOTES ON QUESTIONS
Question 20: Gradients are briefly discussed here. It is interesting to students to encounter this third unit of angle measure. Scientific calculators usually have a DRG key. This is a toggle key that tells the calculator whether you will input in degrees, radians, or gradients. A modification of the technique illustrated in Solution 2 of **Example 2** can be used to convert from gradients to other units and vice versa.

Question 26: This question gives the first few terms of the infinite series for sin *x*. You might ask students to find the series for cos *x* and tan *x*.

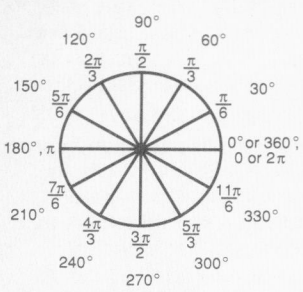
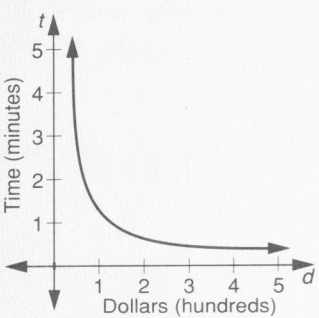
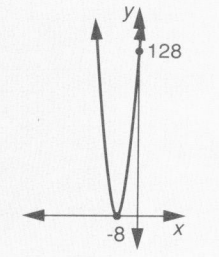
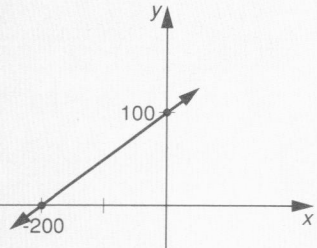
14. How far apart are the hands of a clock at 2:00,
 a. in degrees? **60°**
 b. in radians? $\frac{\pi}{3}$

15. Copy and complete this unit circle for equivalent degrees and radians. (All lines which appear to be straight are diameters.) **See margin.**

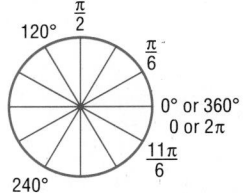

In 16 and 17, find the exact values.

16. $\sin\left(\frac{7\pi}{6}\right)$ $\frac{1}{2}$

17. $\cos\left(\frac{15\pi}{4}\right)$ $\frac{\sqrt{2}}{2}$

In 18 and 19, use this relationship between radian measure and arc length. In a circle of radius r, an angle of x radians has an arc of length rx.

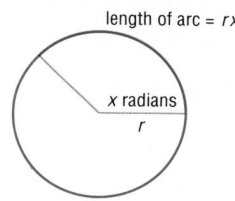

length of arc = rx

x radians

r

18. a. How long is the arc of a $\frac{\pi}{4}$ radian angle in a circle of radius 20? 5π

    b. How long is a 45° arc in a circle of radius 20?   **5π**

19. How long is the arc of a $\frac{2\pi}{3}$ radian angle in a circle of radius 6 feet?   **4π feet**

20. The *gradient* (abbreviated grad) is another unit for measuring angles. It is based on one quarter of a circle having 100 grads.
 a. How many grads are in a full circle?   **400**
 b. How many grads equal 45°?   **50**
 c. Sin 45° ≈ .707. Use your answer to part b and the ⃞DRG key to verify this value for grads.   **sin (50 grad) ≈ .707**

21. State (a) the domain and (b) the range of the function $y = \sin x$.
 (Lesson 10-9)   **a) all real numbers   b) all numbers between -1 and 1, inclusive**

22. The newspaper article at the right is from the Detroit Free Press, January 29, 1985. Explain why the construction technique leads to an angle of 26.5° using the drawing below at the right. *(Lesson 10-2)* **See margin.**

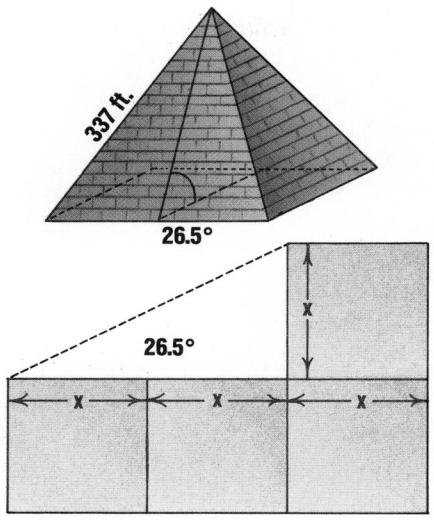

23. One of Murphy's Laws states that the time a committee spends debating a budget item is inversely proportional to the number of dollars involved. Suppose the function is $t = \dfrac{1}{d}$, where t is measured in minutes and d is in hundreds of dollars.

   a. How much time is spent on a $300 item?   **20 seconds or $\frac{1}{3}$ minute**

   b. Graph the equation with d as the independent variable. *(Lesson 2-2)* **See margin.**

In 24 and 25 sketch a graph. *(Lessons 6-1, 3-2)*   **See margin.**

24. $y = 2x^2 + 32x + 128$ **25.** $y = \dfrac{x}{2} + 100$

Exploration

26. When x is measured in radians, $\sin x$ can be estimated by the expression $\sin x \approx x - \dfrac{x^3}{6} + \dfrac{x^5}{120} - \dfrac{x^7}{5040}$.   **See margin.**

   a. How close is the value of this expression to $\sin x$ when $x = \dfrac{\pi}{4}$?

   b. To get greater accuracy, you can add $\dfrac{x^9}{362880}$ to the value you got in part a. Where does the denominator come from?   **See margin.**

FOLLOW-UP

MORE PRACTICE
For more questions on SPUR Objectives, use *Lesson Master 10-10*, shown below.

EXTENSION
Questions 18 and 19 relate arc length in a circle to the radius of the circle and the measure in radians of the angle which intercepts the arc. For your more capable students, you might want to discuss the formula for the area of a sector of a circle in terms of radius and arc length, $A = \frac{1}{2}rs$, and point out its similarity to the triangle area formula.

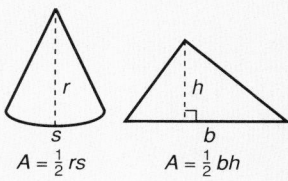

$A = \frac{1}{2}rs$ $A = \frac{1}{2}bh$

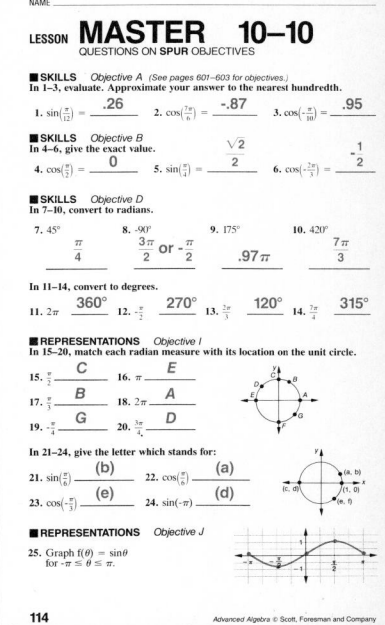

Summary

Trigonometry is the study of relations between sides and angles in triangles. In a right triangle, three important trigonometric ratios are the following:

$$\sin \theta = \frac{\text{opp}}{\text{hyp}}$$

$$\cos \theta = \frac{\text{adj}}{\text{hyp}}$$

$$\tan \theta = \frac{\text{opp}}{\text{adj}}$$

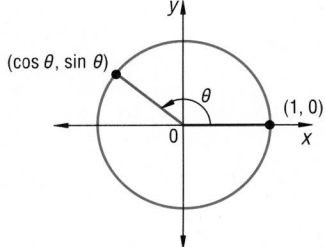

The sine, cosine, and tangent ratios are frequently used to find lengths or angle measures in situations that are modeled by right triangles.

Some of the trigonometric ratios may be calculated exactly.

$$\sin 30° = \cos 60° = \frac{1}{2}$$

$$\sin 45° = \cos 45° = \frac{\sqrt{2}}{2}$$

$$\sin 60° = \cos 30° = \frac{\sqrt{3}}{2}$$

Others are given as decimal approximations by a calculator or computer.

Lengths of sides or angle measures in nonright triangles may be determined using either the Law of Cosines or the Law of Sines. In any triangle *ABC*,

$$c^2 = a^2 + b^2 - 2ab \cos C \quad \text{(Law of Cosines)}$$

$$\frac{\sin A}{a} = \frac{\sin B}{b} = \frac{\sin C}{c} \quad \text{(Law of Sines)}.$$

The Law of Cosines is most useful when an SAS or SSS condition is given; the Law of Sines is used in all other situations that determine triangles. When the Law of Sines is used to find an angle in an SSA condition, two solutions may be possible.

By considering rotations of magnitude θ of the point (1, 0) around the origin, the trigonometric ratios can be generalized to find sines and cosines for any real number θ. On the unit circle,

$$\cos \theta = \text{the } x\text{-coordinate of the image of (1, 0) under } R_\theta$$

$$\sin \theta = \text{the } y\text{-coordinate of the image of (1, 0) under } R_\theta.$$

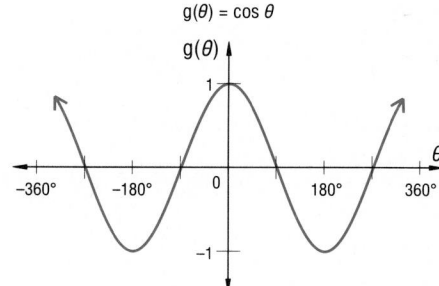

The correspondences

$$f: \theta \rightarrow \sin \theta$$
$$g: \theta \rightarrow \cos \theta$$

are functions whose domains are the set of real numbers and whose ranges are {y: $-1 \leq y \leq 1$}.

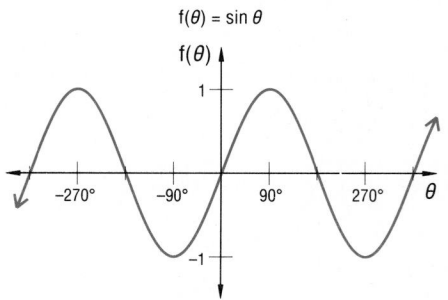

598

Whether considered as ratios in right triangles, co-ordinates on a unit circle, or values of functions, $\cos \theta$ and $\sin \theta$ satisfy several properties for all θ.

$$\sin \theta = \cos (90° - \theta) \qquad \text{(Complements Theorem)}$$
$$\cos \theta = \sin (90° - \theta)$$

$$\sin \theta = \sin (180° - \theta) \qquad \text{(Supplements Theorem)}$$

$$(\cos \theta)^2 + (\sin \theta)^2 = 1 \qquad \text{(Pythagorean Identity)}$$

$$\sin \theta = \sin (\theta \pm 360n°) \qquad \text{(Periodicity)}$$
$$\cos \theta = \cos (\theta \pm 360n°)$$

For all these properties, θ may be in radians; if so, the degree measure should be replaced by its radian equivalent. For example, the Supplements Theorem would be $\sin \theta = \sin (\pi - \theta)$.

Vocabulary

Below are the most important terms and phrases for this chapter. You should be able to give a definition for those terms marked with an *. For all other terms you should be able to give a general description and a specific example of each.

Lesson 10-1
trigonometric ratios
*sine of θ, sin θ
*cosine of θ, cos θ
*tangent of θ, tan θ

Lesson 10-2
angle of elevation
angle of depression

Lesson 10-3
Complements Theorem
Exact Value Theorem
Pythagorean Identity

Lesson 10-4
unit circle

Lesson 10-6
Law of Cosines Theorem

Lesson 10-7
Law of Sines Theorem

Lesson 10-8
Supplements Theorem
solving a triangle

Lesson 10-9
*cosine function
*sine function
periodic
sine wave
sinusoidal function

Lesson 10-10
radian, rad

Terms, symbols, and properties are listed by lesson to provide a checklist of things a student must know. Emphasize to students that they should read the vocabulary list carefully before starting the Progress Self-Test. If students do not understand the meaning of a term, they should refer back to the indicated lesson.

Definitions or descriptions of all terms in the vocabulary list may be found in the Glossary.

Progress Self-Test

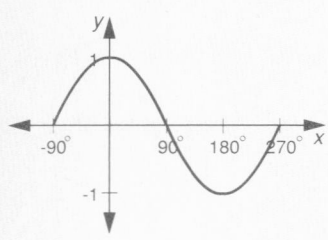
Take this test as you would take a test in class. You will need a calculator. Then check your work with the solutions in the Selected Answers section in the back of the book.

In 1 and 2, use the triangle at the right. Round answers to the nearest thousandth. Find:

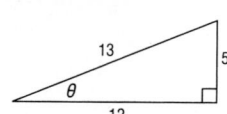

1. $\cos \theta$ ≈0.923   **2.** $\sin \theta$ ≈0.385

3. If $\tan \theta = 1$ and $0 \le \theta \le 90°$, what is θ? 45°

4. Name all points which are images of $(1, 0)$ under R_{120}. **a, b, c**
(a) $(\cos 120°, \sin 120°)$
(b) $(-.5, .866...)$ (c) $\left(-\frac{1}{2}, \frac{\sqrt{3}}{2}\right)$

In 5 and 6, a 14-foot ladder is leaning against a wall. The base of the ladder is 7 feet from the wall.

5. Find the angle of elevation of the ladder. $\theta = 60°$

6. To the nearest inch, how high up the wall does the ladder reach? ≈145 inches

7. For what value of x such that $0° < x \le 360°$ and $x \ne 57$ does $\cos 57° = \cos x°$? $x = 303°$

8. Find an exact value for $\cos 210°$. $-\frac{\sqrt{3}}{2}$

In 9–11, use the graph below.

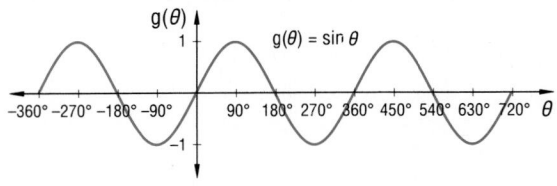

9. The period of the function is ___?___. 360°

10. As θ increases from 90° to 180°, the value of $\sin \theta$ decreases from ___?___ to ___?___. 1; 0

11. What is the range of the sine function? $-1 \le g(\theta) \le$

12. Graph $y = \cos x$ for $-90° \le x \le 270°$. **See margin.**

13. An observer of a road race estimates that runner A is 110 meters away and runner B is 85 meters away from the observation post. The angle between the sightings is 40°. How far apart are the runners from each other?
The runners are about 71 m apart.

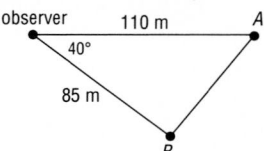

In 14 and 15, find x.

14. 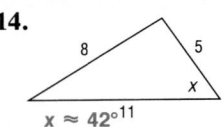   **15.**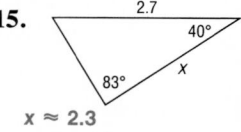

$x \approx 42°11$ $x \approx 2.3$

16. In $\triangle SLR$, $m\angle S = 110°$, $s = 525$, and $l = 421$. Find $m\angle L$. $m\angle L \approx 49°$

17. A 2-foot tall eagle is perched on a 6-foot high road sign. It flies 130 feet directly to its nest on the side of a cliff. The angle of elevation of the flight path (from the eagle's beak) is about 70°. About how high off the ground is the nest? ≈130 feet

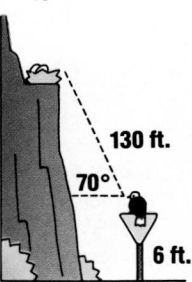

18. Convert $\frac{\pi}{3}$ radians to degrees. 60°

19. Find the exact value of $\sin \frac{7\pi}{6}$. $-\frac{1}{2}$

20. *Multiple choice*. Which of the following statements is *not* true? **b**
(a) $\sin (90° - \theta) = \cos \theta$ (b) $\cos 690° = .5$
(c) $(\sin \theta)^2 + (\cos \theta)^2 = 1$ (d) $\sin \frac{-\pi}{2} = -1$

600

Chapter Review

Questions on SPUR Objectives

SPUR stands for **S**kills, **P**roperties, **U**ses, and **R**epresentations. The Chapter Review questions are grouped according to the SPUR Objectives for this chapter.

SKILLS deal with the procedures used to get answers.

Objective A. *Approximate values of trigonometric functions using a calculator.* *(Lessons 10-1, 10-5, 10-10)*

In 1–6, evaluate. Round your answer to the nearest hundredth.

1. sin 17° 0.29
2. cos 143° -0.80
3. sin (-50°) -0.77
4. $\cos \frac{\pi}{3}$ 0.50
5. $\sin \frac{11\pi}{6}$ -0.50
6. $\tan \frac{\pi}{12}$ 0.27

In 7–9, use the triangle at the right. Approximate each trigonometric value to the nearest thousandth.

7. sin θ 0.923
8. cos θ 0.385
9. tan θ 2.400

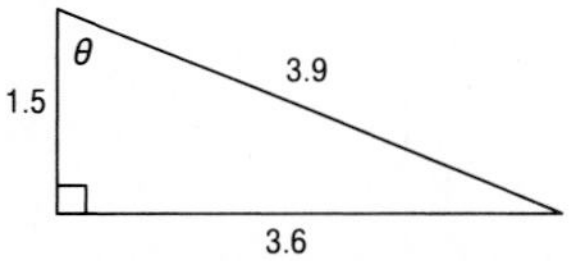

Objective B. *Find exact values of trigonometric functions of certain angles.* *(Lessons 10-3, 10-4, 10-5, 10-10)*

In 10–15, give exact values.

10. cos 45° $\frac{\sqrt{2}}{2}$
11. sin 405° $\frac{\sqrt{2}}{2}$
12. tan 30° $\frac{\sqrt{3}}{3}$
13. $\cos\left(\frac{-\pi}{6}\right)$ $\frac{\sqrt{3}}{2}$
14. $\sin \frac{3\pi}{2}$ -1
15. $\tan \frac{\pi}{4}$ 1

Objective C. *Determine the measure of an angle given its trigonometric values.* *(Lessons 10-2, 10-8)*

In 16–18, find all θ between 0° and 180° with the given trigonometric value.

16. cos θ = .5 60°
17. $\sin \theta = \frac{\sqrt{2}}{2}$ 45° or 135°
18. sin θ = 1 90°

In 19–21, solve for all θ between 0 and $\frac{\pi}{2}$.

19. tan θ ≈ .466 ≈ 0.436 rad
20. cos θ ≈ .309 ≈1.257 rad
21. $\sin \theta = \frac{2}{3}$ ≈.730 rad

Objective D. *Convert angle measures from radians to degrees or degrees to radians.* *(Lesson 10-10)*

In 22–25, convert to radians.

22. 30° $\frac{\pi}{6}$
23. 105° $\frac{7\pi}{12}$
24. 360° 2π
25. 540° 3π

In 26–29, convert to degrees.

26. π 180°
27. $\frac{9\pi}{4}$ 405°
28. $\frac{5\pi}{3}$ 300°
29. $-\frac{\pi}{8}$ -22.5°

Objective E. *Find missing parts of a triangle using the Law of Sines or the Law of Cosines.* *(Lessons 10-6, 10-7, 10-8)*

30. Find *BC*. ≈8.9

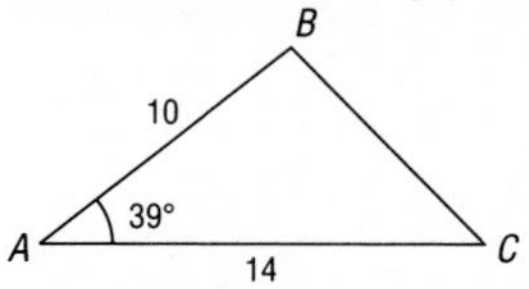

31. Find m∠*E*. ≈139.7°

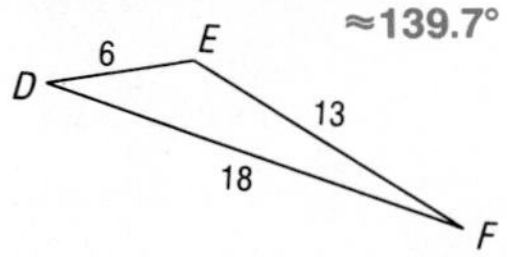

32. Find *GH*. ≈19.9

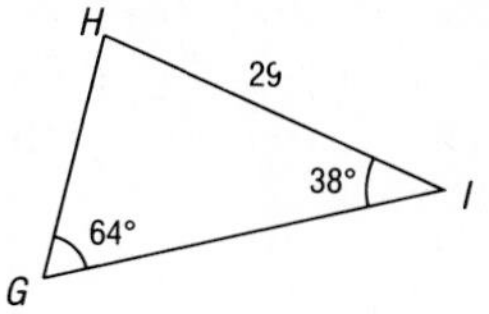

33. Find *JK*. ≈25.4

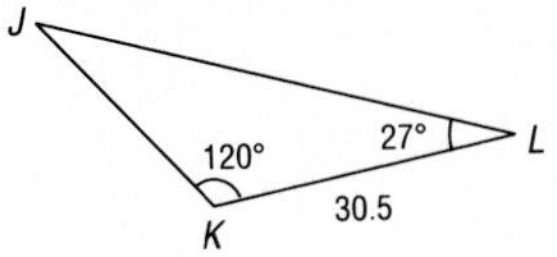

RESOURCES
- Chapter 10 Test, Form A
- Chapter 10 Test, Form B
- Chapter 10 Test, Cumulative Form

CHAPTER REVIEW

The main objectives for the chapter are organized here into sections corresponding to the four main types of understanding this book promotes: Skills, Properties, Uses, and Representations.

USING THE CHAPTER REVIEW

Whereas end-of-chapter material may be considered optional in some texts, in *Advanced Algebra* we have selected these objectives and questions with the expectation that they will be covered. Students should be able to answer these questions with about 85% accuracy after studying the chapter.

You may assign these questions over a single night to help students prepare for a test the next day, or you may assign the questions over a two-day period.

If you work the questions over two days, then we recommend assigning the *evens* for homework the first night so that students get feedback in class the next day, then assigning the *odds* the night before the test so students can use the answers provided in the book.

34. In △WET, m∠W = 112°, w = 9, and
e = 7. Find the measure of ∠E.
m∠E ≈ 46.1°

35. In △JHS, j = 2, s = 3, and m∠J = 25°.
Find m∠S.   m∠S ≈ 39.3° or ≈ 140.7°

PROPERTIES deal with the principles behind the mathematics.

■ **Objective F.** *Identify and use definitions and theorems relating sines and cosines.* (Lesson 10-8)

In 36–39, *true or false*. If false, change it so that it is true.

36. $(\sin \theta)^2 + (\cos \theta)^2 = 1$ true

37. $\cos (90° - \theta) = \sin \theta$ true

38. $\sin (180° - \theta) = \cos \theta$ false; sin (180° − θ)

39. $\cos \theta = \sin (90° - \theta)$ true   = sin θ

0.93 and -0.93
40. Find two values of cos θ if sin θ = .36

41. If sin θ = .8 and θ is obtuse, find cos θ.
-.6

In 42 and 43, copy and complete with the measure of an acute angle.

42. $\sin 73° = \cos$ __?__   17°

43. $\cos (90° -$ __?__$) = \sin 41°$ 41°

USES deal with applications of mathematics in real situations.

■ **Objective G.** *Solve real-world problems using the trigonometry of right triangles.* (Lessons 10-1, 10-2)

44. How tall is the building pictured at the right if a person 6 feet tall sights the top of the building at 49° while standing 53 feet away?   ≈67 ft

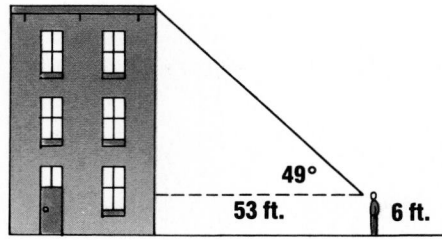

45. A ship sails 695 kilometers on a bearing of 75°. How far east of its original position is the ship?   ≈671 km

46. A wheelchair ramp must be built so that it has a slope of $\frac{1}{12}$. What angle will the ramp make with the horizontal?   ≈4.8°

47. An airplane begins a smooth final descent to the runway from an altitude of 5,000 feet when it is 30,000 horizontal feet away. At what angle of depression will the plane descend?   ≈9.5°

48. The ancient Greeks carved amphitheaters out of the sides of hills. Suppose one amphitheater went 200 feet vertically down while covering 300 feet horizontally. At what angle of depression did they dig?
≈33.7°

Theater at Epidaurus, Greece, from about 325 B.C.

■ **Objective H.** *Solve real-world problems using the Law of Sines or Law of Cosines. (Lessons 10-6, 10-7)*

49. An ocean liner pilot spots a freighter and a schooner on the horizon. The freighter is 7.5 miles away and the schooner is 8 miles away. The angle between the two sightings is 16°. How far from the schooner is the freighter? **≈2.2 miles**

50. The observers in the lookout towers of two ships 8 miles apart spot land ahead. The observer in ship A spots land at an angle of 44° to the line between the two ships, while the observer in ship B spots land at an angle of 105° to the same line. How far is the land from ship A? **about 15 miles**

51. Two observers are in lighthouses 75 miles apart, as shown at the right. The observer in the northern lighthouse spots a ship in distress at an angle of 15° to the line between the lighthouses. The other observer spots the ship at an angle of 35°. How far is the ship from each lighthouse?

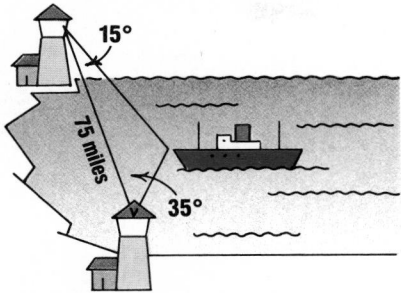

about 56 miles from the northern lighthouse and about 25 miles from the southern lighthouse.

REPRESENTATIONS deal with pictures, graphs, or objects that illustrate concepts.

■ **Objective I.** *Use the properties of a unit circle to find trigonometric values. (Lessons 10-4, 10-5, 10-10)*

In 52 and 53, use the sketch below.

52. What is the value of sin θ? **0.191**

53. Find θ to the nearest degree. **≈169°**

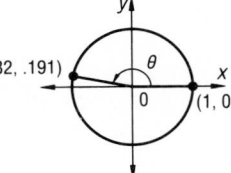

In 54 and 55, use the unit circle below. Give the letter that stands for:

54. sin 220° **f**

55. $\cos \dfrac{2\pi}{3}$. **c**

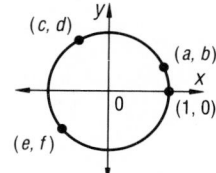

■ **Objective J.** *Identify properties of the sine and cosine functions using their graphs. (Lessons 10-9, 10-10)*

56. a. Graph f: θ → sin θ, for 0° ≤ θ ≤ 360°.
b. State the domain and range of the sine function. **Domain is all real numbers; range is 1 ≤ f(θ) ≤ -1 See margin.**

See margin.

57. a. Graph g: θ → cos θ, with the *x*-axis given in radians, for 0 ≤ θ ≤ 2π.
b. What is the period of the cosine function? **2π**
c. At what points does the graph of y = cos x intersect the *x*-axis? $\dfrac{\pi}{2}, \dfrac{3\pi}{2}$

58. As θ increases from 0° to 180°, cos θ decreases from __?__ to __?__. **1 to -1**

59. The graph of y = cos x is an image of the graph of y = sin x under what translation? **sample: T₋₉₀°,₀**

60. What is the period of the function graphed below? (Assume the graph continues in both directions.) **180°**

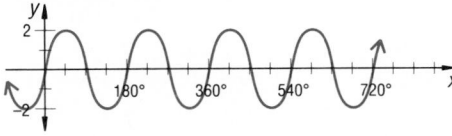

56.a.

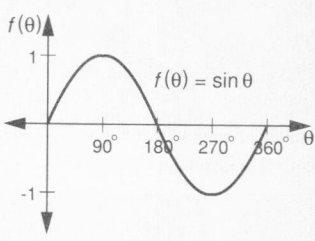

57.a.

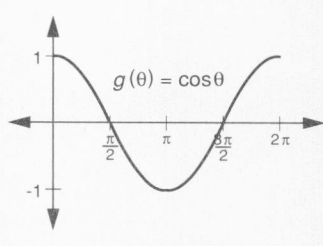

EVALUATION
Three tests are provided for this chapter in the Teacher's Resource File. Chapter 10 Test, Forms A and B cover just Chapter 10. The third test is Chapter 10 Test, Cumulative Form. About 50% of this test covers Chapter 10, 25% covers Chapter 9, and 25% covers previous chapters. For information on grading, see *General Teaching Suggestions: Grading* on page T44 in the Teacher's Edition.

ASSIGNMENT RECOMMENDATION
We strongly recommend that you assign Lesson 11-1, both reading and some questions, for homework the evening of the test.

CHAPTER 11 ■ POLYNOMIALS

DAILY PACING CHART ■ CHAPTER 11

Students in the Full Course should complete all but one of the chapters by the end of the year. Students in the Minimal Course will spend more time on quizzes and the Chapter Review. As such, these students should complete about ten or eleven chapters.

DAY	MINIMAL COURSE	FULL COURSE
1	11-1	11-1
2	11-2	11-2
3	11-3	11-3
4	11-4	11-4
5	Quiz (TRF); Start 11-5.	Quiz (TRF); 11-5
6	Finish 11-5.	11-6
7	11-6	11-7
8	11-7	11-8
9	11-8	Progress Self-Test
10	Progress Self-Test	Chapter Review
11	Chapter Review	Chapter Test (TRF)
12	Chapter Review	
13	Chapter Test (TRF)	

TESTING OPTIONS
■ Quiz for Lessons 11-1 Through 11-4   ■ Chapter 11 Test, Form A   ■ Chapter 11 Test, Cumulative Form
■ Chapter 11 Test, Form B

PROVIDING FOR INDIVIDUAL DIFFERENCES
The student text is written for the *average* student. The program, however, can be adapted for both less capable and for more capable students.

A blackline master (in the Teacher's Resource File) is provided for each lesson for those students who need more practice. The Teacher's Edition frequently provides Error Analysis and Alternate Approach features to provide additional instructional strategies.

For students who require additional challenge, Extension activities are regularly provided in the Teacher's Edition.

OBJECTIVES ■ CHAPTER 11

Students should master the chapter objectives by the time they complete the chapter. To ensure mastery, there is continual review built into each set of lesson questions. After students complete the chapter lessons, they assess their mastery on the Progress Self-Test. Then they do the Chapter Review and pay special attention to those questions that match the objectives missed on the Progress Self-Test. Students can get extra practice on these objectives by using the master for each lesson in the Teacher's Resource File.

OBJECTIVES FOR CHAPTER 11 (Organized into the SPUR categories—Skills, Properties, Uses, and Representations)	Progress Self-Test Questions	Chapter Review Questions	Lesson Master from Teacher's Resource File*
SKILLS			
A Multiply polynomials.	6	1 through 6	11-2
B Factor polynomials using common monomial factoring, perfect square patterns, trial and error with trinomials, or patterns for the sum or difference of cubes.	16–18	7 through 16	11-3
C Calculate or estimate zeros of polynomial functions.	7–8, 12	17 through 24	11-4, 11-5, 11-6
D Determine an equation for a polynomial function from data points using the Polynomial Difference Theorem.	19–20	25 through 27	11-7, 11-8
PROPERTIES			
E Use technical vocabulary to describe polynomials.	4–5	28 through 33	11-1, 11-2
F Apply the Zero Product Theorem, Factor Theorem, and Fundamental Theorem of Algebra.	13–14	34 through 42	11-4, 11-6
USES			
G Use polynomials to model real-world situations.	1–3	43 through 49	11-1, 11-2, 11-8
REPRESENTATIONS			
H Determine properties of a polynomial function from its graph.	15	50 through 53	11-4, 11-5
I Read or generate computer output to graph or find zeros of polynomials.	9–11	54 through 57	11-5, 11-6

* **The masters are numbered to match the lessons.**

OVERVIEW ■ CHAPTER 11

Students have already studied special cases of polynomial expressions and functions: linear in Chapters 2 and 3, quadratic in Chapters 2 and 6, and powering in Chapter 7. In this chapter, we extend students' previous experiences to *general* polynomial expressions and functions. Although the definitions and theorems apply to any polynomial of degree *n*, the examples and questions usually involve polynomials of degree 3 or 4.

This chapter has eight lessons. The first six develop the concepts, notation, and properties associated with polynomials. These lessons, however, depart from traditional materials in two significant ways. First, polynomials are presented in many realistic contexts. Second, the work with graphs emphasizes the use of computers and general properties of functions rather than relying solely on plotting points.

The last two lessons, Finite Differences and Modeling Data with Polynomials, cover material that is only occasionally found in algebra texts at this level. We include these lessons because (1) they teach a technique that is useful for generating formulas for certain common

sequences; (2) the ability to obtain formulas for patterns is highly motivating to students and (3) they are important in modeling (continuing a theme that was introduced in Chapter 2). Modeling is emphasized also in the UCSMP course following this one: *Functions, Statistics, and Trigonometry with Computers*.

If you do not have access to a computer on a daily basis, we suggest you reserve one or more for demonstration or laboratory work when you are teaching Lessons 11-4, 11-5, and 11-6.

PERSPECTIVES ■ CHAPTER 11

The Perspectives provide the rationale for the inclusion of topics or approaches, provide mathematical background, and make connections within UCSMP.

11-1

POLYNOMIAL MODELS

This lesson introduces technical vocabulary and uses polynomial functions to model data representing two fundamentally different applications.

In the first population example in the opening page of the chapter, the data exist and a polynomial is found which fits. This polynomial does not necessarily predict population other than for the data points which gave rise to it.

In the annuity example, the mathematics exists before the data. That is, the formula provides the basis from which the amounts are calculated.

An analogy can be made to lines. Some situations are inherently linear; a formula can be derived for them. A common example is the Fahrenheit-Celsius conversion formula. In other situations, points seem to lie close to a line and we describe the points with a line of best fit.

11-2

POLYNOMIALS AND GEOMETRY

This lesson discusses the use of polynomials in modeling geometric applications of area and volume. The Extended Distributive Property is introduced to handle the resulting polynomial products of degrees 2 (for area) or 3 (for volume).

Example 3 contains the construction of a box from a rectangular piece of cardboard, a classic maximization situation treated in calculus. The solution is estimated by examining the graph and substituting values.

11-3

FACTORING POLYNOMIALS

This is entirely a skill lesson. Except for the Sum and Difference of Cubes Patterns, most of the concepts introduced are considered review. The material in this and the following lesson will be combined in Lesson 11-5 to find zeros of polynomial functions.

11-4

THE FACTOR THEOREM

The method of solving a quadratic by factoring and applying the Zero Product Theorem dates back at least to the Englishman Thomas Harriott (1560–1621), who as a young man had been a member of Sir Walter Raleigh's expedition to Virginia. (Remember that modern algebraic notation dates only from the last part of the 16th century.) Later, Harriott's method was applied to polynomials of higher degree, so that by Gauss's time (1777–1855), the theorems and examples in this lesson were well known by mathematicians.

However, the existence of function graphers has changed the way the idea can be developed. Polynomial functions are now easy to graph, and thus a graphical representation of zeros to go along with the factoring view can be presented.

11-5

This lesson deals with the iterative process of finding zeros of functions more accurately. Although the examples are polynomial functions, the ideas extend to any continuous function.

This lesson could not be developed with students ten years ago. Although students did learn that the zeros of polynomial functions are x-intercepts of the graph, they could not be expected to draw accurate graphs and calculate coordinates to so many decimal places.

The chapter opener and the previous lesson show that graphs of polynomial functions can have many different shapes. Therefore, students should not draw graphs of polynomials of degree 3 or higher simply by plotting points whose x-values are consecutive integers. Instead, emphasize using properties of polynomials to sketch graphs of polynomial functions, and to use a function plotter or a computer-generated table of non-integer values to draw more detailed graphs.

11-6

This lesson extends the study of quadratics in a previous chapter to all polynomials. The theorems discussed guarantee the existence of roots for any polynomial equation. Students should be able to find the roots of any equation of the forms
$x^n(ax^2 + bx + c) = 0$,
$x^n(x^3 - a) = 0$,
or $x^n(x^3 + a) = 0$.

The theorems in this lesson are very powerful and are of great importance in the history of mathematics. Prior to 1797, algorithms for finding solutions to polynomial equations of the first four degrees had been developed, but no one had been able to find an algorithm for solving quintics. Perhaps it was because new numbers had to be invented just as the complex numbers were invented to solve quadratics. Gauss was only eighteen when he solved this problem that had been around for two hundred years.

The Fundamental Theorem of Algebra is generally proved in college courses in complex variables, not before.

11-7

This is the first of two lessons devoted to the topic of finite differences. In this lesson, students learn to determine the degree of a polynomial that models a given set of data. In Lesson 11-8, they will learn how to find the equation for the polynomial.

11-8

This lesson is a continuation of the previous one. Here, students, having determined that a polynomial of a certain degree models given data, use algebraic techniques to find the coefficients of the polynomial.

Students sometimes need to solve a large system of equations to find the coefficients. The system may seem difficult, but if the domain values have been taken in an arithmetic sequence order, the system can be solved by repeatedly subtracting equations from each other. In Chapter 14, students will learn to solve such large systems using extended matrices.

Polynomials

The twin towers of the World Trade district of Manhattan Island.

604

The population of Manhattan Island (part of New York City) has gone up and down over the past 100 years.

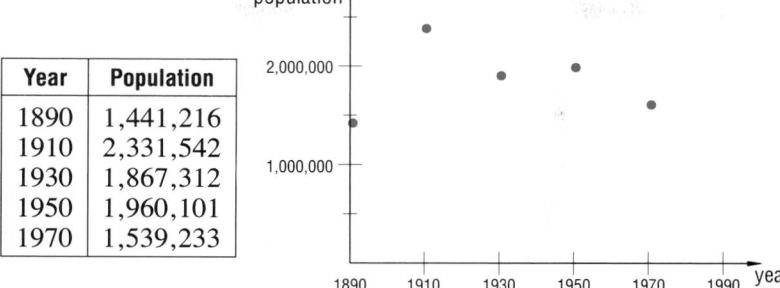

Year	Population
1890	1,441,216
1910	2,331,542
1930	1,867,312
1950	1,960,101
1970	1,539,233

None of the kinds of functions you have studied fits these points very well. However, if x = the number of 20-year periods since 1890, then the population P(x) of Manhattan (in ten thousands) is closely approximated by the equation

$$P(x) = \tfrac{-37}{3}x^4 + \tfrac{317}{3}x^3 - \tfrac{1789}{6}x^2 + \tfrac{1763}{6}x + 144.$$

The above equation is a *polynomial equation*, and the function P is a *polynomial function*. Although the formula for P(x) is quite complicated, mathematicians would not be surprised by it. For any finite set of points, no two of which are on the same vertical line, there is a polynomial function whose graph contains those points. A graph of $y = P(x)$ on the domain $-1 \le x < 5$ is shown below.

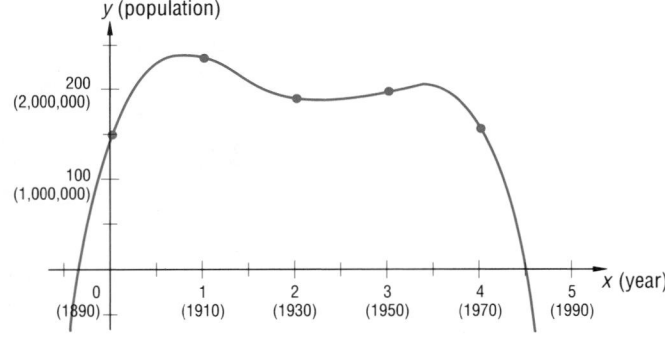

In this chapter, you will study situations that lead to polynomial functions. You will see how to graph and analyze such functions, learn when data can be described by a *polynomial model*, and learn how to find the model for specific data points. Along the way, you will encounter various properties of polynomials, some of which you have studied before.

...ter visually dominate the financial

CHAPTER 11 Polynomials **605**

OBJECTIVES

E Use technical vocabulary to describe polynomials.
G Use polynomials to model real-world situations.

TEACHING NOTES

Setting up polynomials to model situations may be difficult for students. We suggest you spend a few minutes discussing problems such as those in the examples.

When referring to **Example 2**, you might ask:
(a) How much would Yolanda have at the end of her fourth year in college if the summer after her senior year in high school she earned $1000, and if each summer thereafter she saved $100 more than she did the previous summer?
$(1000(1.06)^4 + 1100(1.06)^3 + 1200(1.06)^2 + 1300(1.06) + 1400 = 6698.91. In general, the formula is $1000x^4 + 1100x^3 + 1200x^2 + 1300x + 1400$, where $x = 1 + r$, and r is the annual rate of interest.)
(b) In the above problem, how much would Yolanda have saved if she had been able to obtain an interest rate of 7%?
(Substituting 1.07 for x in the formula she would have $6823.22.)

LESSON

Polynomial Models

The expression $\frac{-37}{3}x^4 + \frac{317}{3}x^3 - \frac{1789}{6}x^2 + \frac{1763}{6}x + 144$ from the previous page is a **polynomial in the variable** x. When the polynomial is in only one variable, the largest exponent is the *degree* of the polynomial. This polynomial has degree 4. The expressions $\frac{-37}{3}x^4$, $\frac{317}{3}x^3$, $\frac{-1789}{6}x^2$, $\frac{1763}{6}x$, and 144 are *terms* of the polynomial. We have written the terms in decreasing order of the exponents. Polynomials are commonly written in this order to make them easier to read.

Definition:

A polynomial in x is an expression of the form
$$a_nx^n + a_{n-1}x^{n-1} + a_{n-2}x^{n-2} + \ldots + a_1x^1 + a_0,$$
where n is a positive integer and $a_n \neq 0$.

The definition displays the **general form** of a polynomial. The number n is the **degree** of the polynomial and the numbers a_n, a_{n-1}, a_{n-2}, ... , a_0 are its **coefficients**. The number a_n is called the **leading coefficient** of the polynomial. For instance, when $n = 4$, the degree is 4 and the subscript for the leading variable is also 4.

$$a_nx^n + a_{n-1}x^{n-1} + a_{n-2}x^{n-2} + \ldots + a_1x^1 + a_0$$
$$\downarrow \qquad \downarrow \qquad \downarrow \qquad \qquad \downarrow \qquad \downarrow$$
$$a_4x^4 + a_3x^3 \qquad + a_2x^2 \qquad \qquad + a_1x^1 + a_0$$

We can say that on page 605, the population of Manhattan for twenty-year periods from 1890 to 1970 has been modeled by a 4th degree polynomial. The leading coefficient of this polynomial is $\frac{-37}{3}$. Polynomials of the first degree, such as $mx + b$, are called **linear polynomials**. Those of the second degree, such as $ax^2 + bx + c$, are called **quadratic polynomials,** and those of the third degree, such as $ax^3 + bx^2 + cx + d$, are **cubic polynomials**.

A **polynomial function** is a function whose rule can be written as a polynomial. You can evaluate polynomial functions in the same way that you evaluate other functions. For instance, consider the function $P(x) = 6x^5 - 3x^4 + 4x^2 - 2x - 7$. The value of this function when $x = 2$ is represented by P(2), and $P(2) = 6(2)^5 - 3(2)^4 + 4(2)^2 - 2(2) - 7 = 149$.

■ ■ ■ ■ ■ ■ ■ ■

Example 1 Consider the polynomial function P modeling the population of Manhattan.
a. Find P(1).
b. P(1) approximates the population for which year?

Solution **a.** $P(1) = \frac{-37}{3}(1)^4 + \frac{317}{3}(1)^3 - \frac{1789}{6}(1)^2 + \frac{1763}{6}(1) + 144$
$= 233$

606

b. P(1) gives the population in ten thousands in one 20-year period after 1890, that is, the population in 1910.

Check 233 · 10,000 = 2,330,000, which is close to the 1910 population listed in the table.

The calculation of compound interest can involve polynomial functions of any degree. You have learned that the compound interest formula $A = P(1 + r)^t$ gives you the value of P dollars invested at an annual interest rate r after t years. If amounts of money are deposited for different periods of time, then this formula must be applied to each amount separately. Example 2 illustrates such a situation.

■ ■ ■ ■ ■ ■ ■ ■ ■ ■

Example 2 Starting with the summer after her senior year in high school, Yolanda Fish worked to earn money for medical school. At the end of each summer she put her money in a savings account with an annual yield of 6%. How much will be in her account when she goes to medical school, if no other money is added or withdrawn? (Assume Yolanda goes to medical school in the fall following her 4th year in college.)

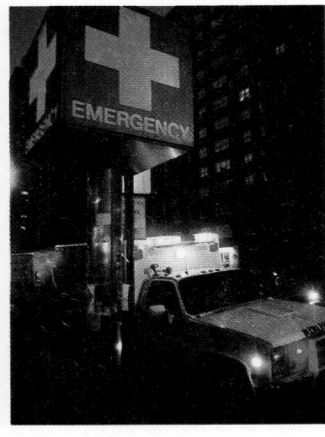

summer	earned
after senior year	$1000
after 1st year of college	1500
after 2nd year of college	1400
after 3rd year of college	2000
after 4th year of college	2200

Solution The money put in the bank after her senior year earns interest for 4 years. It is worth $1000(1.06)^4$ when Yolanda goes to medical school. Similarly, the amount saved at the end of her first year of college is worth $1500(1.06)^3$. When the values from each summer are added together, we find the total amount that will be in Yolanda's account.

$$1000(1.06)^4 + 1500(1.06)^3 + 1400(1.06)^2 + 2000(1.06) + 2200$$

| from summer after senior year in high school | from summer after 1st year college | from summer after 2nd year college | from summer after 3rd year college | from summer after 4th year college |

Evaluating this expression shows that Yolanda will have about $8942 in her account.

Note that in **Example 2** each coefficient and each exponent has a meaning which comes directly from the data in the situation. The general situation is known as an annuity, an investment in which money is deposited periodically rather than all at one time. The largest money matters we deal with in our lifetimes can be considered to be annuities: retirement accounts, home or car loans, insurance, and even salaries.

Stress that, no matter what order the terms of a polynomial are generated, the accepted practice is to write those terms in descending order of degree, as is illustrated in the example. There are applications, however, in which the reverse, ascending order, is more appropriate.

ADDITIONAL EXAMPLES
1. This example is based on a study by D.G. Embree reported in the *Memoirs of the Entomological Society of Canada*, no. 46, 1965. A study of the winter moth of Nova Scotia found that the average number y of eggs in a female moth with abdominal width x (in millimeters) was given by $y \approx 14x^3 - 17x^2 - 16x + 34$, where $1.5 \le x \le 3.5$.
a. Is this a polynomial model?
Yes
b. What is its degree?
3
c. What is the domain of the function?
$1.5 \le x \le 3.5$, x in mm
d. About how many eggs should you expect a female winter moth whose abdomen measures 2 mm to produce?
$f(2) \approx 46$

In Example 2, if you don't know the interest rate, it's reasonable to replace 1.06 with x. Then when she goes to medical school Yolanda will have

$$1000x^4 + 1500x^3 + 1400x^2 + 2000x + 2200.$$

This expression gives the amount in the account for any interest rate compounded annually. If the interest rate is r, just substitute $1 + r$ for x and find the new total. Be careful when constructing an expression in a situation like this. Check whether or not the last amount saved earns interest. You can see that if the first deposit has earned interest for n years, the result is a polynomial of degree n.

Questions

Covering the Reading

In 1–3, tell whether or not the expression is a polynomial. If it is, state its degree and leading coefficient.

1. $4x + 7$ yes; 1, 4   **2.** $7x^4 - 12x^2 + 100$ **3.** $x^{-2} + x^{-1} + 1$ no
    yes; 4, 7

In 4–6, write the general form of:

4. a cubic polynomial in the variable x $a_3x^3 + a_2x^2 + a_1x + a_0$

5. a fifth degree polynomial in the variable y
    $a_5y^5 + a_4y^4 + a_3y^3 + a_2y^2 + a_1y + a_0$
6. an nth degree polynomial in the variable x
    $a_nx^n + a_{n-1}x^{n-1} + ... + a_2x^2 + a_1x + a_0$
7. Refer to the definition of an nth degree polynomial and the polynomial
$$5x^7 + 4x^6 - 8x^3 + 1.3x^2 - x.$$

State the value of each of the following.
a. n **b.** a_n **c.** a_{n-1} **d.** a_0 **e.** a_1 **f.** a_2 **g.** a_5
$n = 7$ $a_n = 5$ $a_{n-1} = 4$ $a_0 = 0$ $a_1 = -1$ $a_2 = 1.3$ $a_5 = 0$

In 8 and 9, refer to the population function P for Manhattan Island.

8. What is the leading coefficient of P? $\frac{-37}{3}$

9. a. Evaluate P(3).   P(3) = 196
    b. How close is P(3) to the 1950 population?   differs by 101

10. Refer to Example 2. Suppose that in successive summers beginning after eighth grade, Yolanda saved $200, $500, $1475, $1600, and $1300.
    a. If the bank pays 6% interest compounded yearly and no other money is added or withdrawn, how much is in her account when she goes to college? (Assume Yolanda goes to college in the fall immediately after finishing high school.) $5501.31
    b. Let $x = 1.06$. Write a polynomial in x to give the amount in Yolanda's account. $200x^4 + 500x^3 + 1475x^2 + 1600x + 1300$
    c. What is the degree of the polynomial in part b?   4

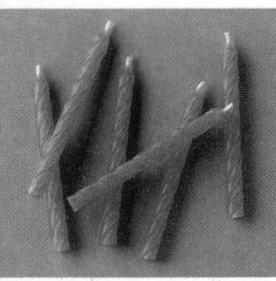

11. On her first birthday, Jennifer got $25. On each successive birthday she got twice as much money. The money was put into a bank paying 7% interest, compounded annually. No additional money was added or withdrawn.
  a. Write a polynomial expression to give the total amount in Jennifer's account on her sixth birthday. (The money from her sixth birthday earns no interest.) Do not calculate the total.   **See margin.**
  b. Replace 1.07 by x and write a polynomial in x that gives the total amount in the account. $25x^5 + 50x^4 + 100x^3 + 200x^2 + 400x + 800$
  c. What is the degree of the polynomial in part b?   **5**

In 12 and 13, recall the formula for the height of an object thrown upward:

$$h(t) = -\frac{1}{2} gt^2 + v_0 t + h_0$$

where t is the number of seconds after being thrown, h_0 the initial height, v_0 the initial velocity and g the acceleration due to gravity (32 ft/sec^2). This formula describes a polynomial function in t.

12. What is the degree of this polynomial?   **2**

13. Suppose a ball is thrown upward from the ground with initial velocity 45 ft/sec. Find its height after .9 seconds.   **27.54 ft**

14. Consider the sequences A and B below. *(Lessons 8-5, 3-7, 3-6)*

A: 16, 4, 1, $\frac{1}{4}$, ...   B: 53, 41, 29, 17, ...

  a. Write the next two terms of each sequence.   A: $\frac{1}{16}$, $\frac{1}{64}$; B: 5, -7
  b. Write an explicit formula for the geometric sequence. $g_n = 16(\frac{1}{4})^{n-1}$
  c. Write a recursive formula for the arithmetic sequence.   **See margin.**
  d. Which sequence might model the consecutive heights of a bouncing ball?   **sequence A**

15. A cheetah trots along at 5 mph for a minute, then spies a small deer and speeds up to 60 mph in just 6 seconds. After chasing the deer at this speed for 30 seconds, the cheetah gives up and, over the next 20 seconds, slows to a stop. Graph this situation, plotting time on the horizontal axis and speed on the vertical axis. *(Lesson 3-8)*   **See margin.**

16. Graph $y = 2x^2 - 4x + 1$. *(Lesson 6-5)*   **See margin.**

17. Multiply $5(7x + 2)(3x - 1)$. *(Lesson 1-5)*
$105x^2 - 5x - 10$
18. Find an expression for the volume of the rectangular solid below. *(Previous course)* $2x^2$

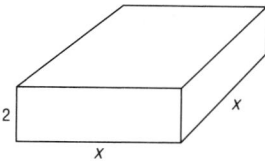

ADDITIONAL ANSWERS
11.a. $25(1.07)^5 + 50(1.07)^4 + 100(1.07)^3 + 200(1.07)^2 + 400(1.07) + 800$

15.

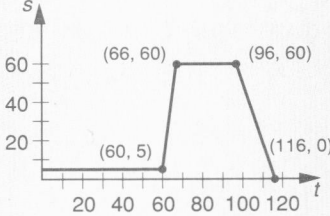

16.

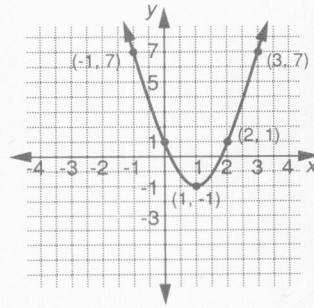

NAME _____

LESSON **MASTER   11–1**
QUESTIONS ON **SPUR** OBJECTIVES

■ **SKILLS**   *Objective E (See pages 662–665 for objectives.)*

1. Is $3x^2 - \frac{1}{x} + 2$ a polynomial? ____ **no**

In 2 and 3, state (a) the degree and (b) the leading coefficient of each polynomial.

2. $3x^6 - 2x$ a. ___ **6**   b. ___ **3**   3. $4 - 3x^2 - x^9$ a. ___ **9**   b. ___ **-1**

In 4 and 5, refer to the polynomial function $P(x) = -7x^5 - 3x^2 - 2x + 9$.

4. Use the definition of an nth degree polynomial to identify the following.
  a. $a_5 =$ ___ **-7**   b. $a_2 =$ ___ **-3**   c. $a_0 =$ ___ **9**

5. Find:
  a. $P(3)$ ___ **-1725**   b. $P(-5)$ ___ **21,819**   c. $P(0)$ ___ **9**
  d. State a relationship between $P(0)$ and a_0.   ___ $P(0) = a_0$

■ **USES**   *Objective G*

6. Carrie Danoos had a paper route for five years. At the end of each year, she deposited a portion of her earnings into a savings account at interest rate r, compounded annually. Below are the amounts she deposited. She made no withdrawals.

year	deposits
1	$50
2	$125
3	$300
4	$550
5	$400

  a. Write a polynomial in x, where $x = 1 + r$, that represents the amount of money she would have at the end of her fifth year.
  $50x^4 + 125x^3 + 300x^2 + 550x + 400$

  b. If the bank pays 5.5% annually, calculate Carrie's account balance at the end of the fifth year.   **$1522.88**

Advanced Algebra © Scott, Foresman and Company

MORE PRACTICE
For more questions on SPUR
Objectives, use *Lesson Master 11-1*, shown on page 609.

ADDITIONAL ANSWERS
22.a.

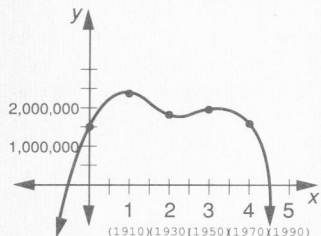

In 19 and 20, refer to the population of Manhattan given on the opening page of the chapter. *(Lesson 2-4)*

19. Find the rate of change in population per year for the period 1890 to 1910.   ≈ **44,500 increase per year**

20. What was the average yearly change in population between 1950 and 1970   ≈ **21,000 decrease per year**

Exploration

21. What did the keeper say to the parrot who needed to go on a diet?
Polly-No-meal.

22. Use the Manhattan Island population function given on page 605.
  a. Graph P using a function plotter.   **See margin.**
  b. Use the graph to estimate the population in 1900, 1920, 1940, and 1960.   **b.–f. See below.**
  c. Find the actual population of Manhattan Island in 1900, 1920, 1940, and 1960.
  d. How close are the estimates in part b to the actual values?
  e. According to the function P, when did Manhattan's population peak?
  f. How good is P(x) in approximating the population of Manhattan for other dates?

(b) 1900: 2,250,000; 1920: 2,100,000; 1940: 1,900,000; 1960: 2,100,000 (c) 1900: 1,850,093; 1920: 2,252,804; 1940: 1,889,924; 1960: 1,698,281 (d) The estimates are close for 1920 and 1940, not close for other years. (e) about 1905 (f) P(x) is useful for years from 1890 to 1970, but not useful for earlier or later years. (For example, the actual 1980 population was 1,428,285, while the estimate from the graph is zero.)

11-2

Polynomials and Geometry

Polynomials are sometimes classified according to the number of terms they have. For instance, a **monomial** is a polynomial with one term; a **binomial** is a polynomial with two terms; and a **trinomial** is a polynomial with three terms. Below are some examples.

monomial $-7, x^2, 3y^4$
binomial $x^2 - 11, 3y^4 + y, 12a^5 + 4a^3$
trinomial $x^2 - 5x + 6, 10y^6 - 9y^5 + 17y^2$

Notice that monomials, binomials, and trinomials can be of any degree.

When a polynomial in one variable is added to or multiplied by a polynomial in another variable, the result is called a polynomial in several variables. The degree is the largest sum of the exponents of the variables in any term. For instance, $x^3 + 8x^2y^3 + y^4$ is a trinomial of degree 5 in two variables, x and y.

Some applications of polynomials arise from geometry, particularly from the study of area.

Example 1 The widths of the town houses at the right are x, y, and z. Each has height $f + s$. Find a polynomial for A, the surface area of the fronts of the three town houses.

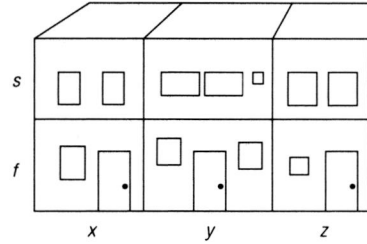

Solution 1 Think of the surface area of the front of the town houses as the sum of the areas of the six smaller rectangles (three first floors, three second floors).

$$A = fx + fy + fz + sx + sy + sz$$

Solution 2 Think of the surface area of the front of the town houses as the area of one large rectangle with base $x + y + z$ and height $f + s$. Thus,

$$A = (x + y + z)(f + s).$$

Use the Distributive Property, considering $x + y + z$ as a chunk, to rewrite this as

$$A = (x + y + z)f + (x + y + z)s.$$

Further applications of the Distributive Property lead to the same results obtained in Solution 1.

$$A = xf + yf + zf + xs + ys + zs$$

LESSON 11-2 Polynomials and Geometry   **611**

LESSON 11-2

RESOURCES
■ Lesson Master 11-2
▣ Visual for Teaching Aid 70 displays the solution for **Example 3**.

OBJECTIVES

A Multiply polynomials.
E Use technical vocabulary to describe different types of polynomials.
G Use polynomials to model geometric situations.

TEACHING NOTES

Most students are familiar with the prefixes mono- (one), bi- (two), and tri- (three) from previous mathematics courses and are adept at using the FOIL Theorem to multiply two binomials.

Stress that *all* products of polynomials, including those using the FOIL Theorem, may be found using one or more applications of the Distributive Property.

Since most of the concepts in this lesson are extensions of those previously learned, and since the examples are clearly presented, you might wish to assign the reading for this lesson without further discussion. The questions outline the major ideas of the lesson in order.

Making Connections
Beginning with this lesson, many questions ask students to relate the geometry of perimeter, area, and volume to the algebra of polynomials. Refer students to Appendix B for a list of important geometry formulas.

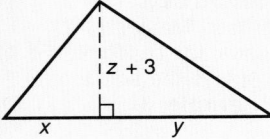
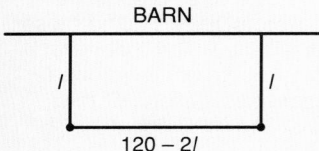
Because of the multiple use of the Distributive Property, we call this an instance of the *Extended Distributive Property*.

The Extended Distributive Property:

To multiply two polynomials, multiply each term in the first polynomial by each term in the second.

If one polynomial has m terms and the second n terms, there will at first be mn terms in their product. When possible, you should simplify the product by adding like terms.

Example 2   Multiply $(5x^2 - 4x + 3)(x - 7)$.

Solution   Multiply each term in the first polynomial by each in the second. There will be six terms in the product.

$$= \mathbf{5x^2} \cdot x + \mathbf{5x^2} \cdot (-7) + (\mathbf{-4x}) \cdot x + (\mathbf{-4x}) \cdot (-7) + \mathbf{3} \cdot x + \mathbf{3} \cdot (-7)$$
$$= 5x^3 - 35x^2 - 4x^2 + 28x + 3x - 21$$

Now simplify by adding or subtracting like terms.

$$= 5x^3 - 39x^2 + 31x - 21$$

Other applications of polynomials arise from volume. Consider a piece of metal 20″ by 24″ which is to be folded into a box after cutting out a square from each corner. What will be the volume of the box?

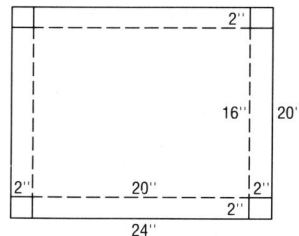

The volume depends on the length x of the side of the square cut out. Suppose $x = 2″$. Then the box will be 2″ high and its other dimensions will be 20″ and 16″. Its volume is then $2″ \cdot 20″ \cdot 16″$, or 640 cubic inches.

Is this the largest possible volume? To answer that question, we need the volume in terms of x.

612

Example 3 A piece of metal 20 inches by 24 inches is made into a box by cutting out squares of side x from each corner. Let $V(x)$ be the volume of the box. Find a polynomial formula for $V(x)$.

Solution The volume of a rectangular box is the product of the dimensions, that is, $V = lwh$. When the metal is folded up, the dimensions of the box will be $(24 - 2x)$ in. by $(20 - 2x)$ in. by x in. high.

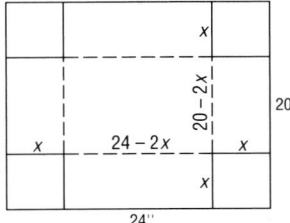
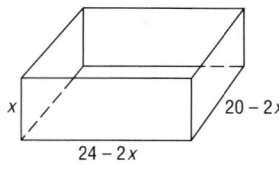

So $V(x) = (24 - 2x)x(20 - 2x)$

$V(x) = (24x - 2x^2)(20 - 2x)$	Distribute the x.
$V(x) = 480x - 48x^2 - 40x^2 + 4x^3$	FOIL Theorem
$V(x) = 4x^3 - 88x^2 + 480x$	Collect like terms; write with decreasing exponents.

Check Because volume is 3-dimensional, you should expect a volume formula to involve a third power. Choose a particular value of x, and calculate the volume using the formula.

When $x = 2''$, $V(x) = 4 \cdot 2^3 - 88 \cdot 2^2 + 480 \cdot 2$
$$= 32 - 352 + 960 = 640 \text{ cubic inches.}$$

This agrees with the value found using dimensions 2″, 20″, and 16″ on page 612.

With a formula known for $V(x)$, the function V can be graphed. The graph below shows that $x = 2$ does not give the largest volume. A slightly larger volume occurs when $x = 3$, and the largest volume occurs when x is a little less than 4. You are asked to estimate this value in Question 11.

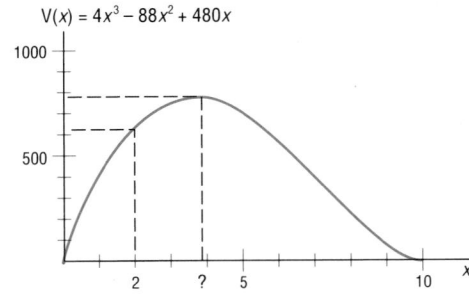

NOTES ON QUESTIONS
Question 11: If a function grapher is not available, have students make their estimates from the graph on page 613.

Question 12a: Two solution methods are:
(i) Subtract the areas of the four small squares from the area of the original sheet metal, $S_1(x) = 20 \cdot 24 - 4x^2 = 480 - 4x^2$.
(ii) Add the areas of the five faces of the box:
$S_2(x) = 2x(24 - 2x) + 2x(20 - 2x) + (20 - 2x)(24 - 2x)$.
Ask the question, "Does $S_1(x) = S_2(x)$?" to illustrate the need to know how to rewrite polynomials in expanded form. Point out that each expression is quadratic, a result consistent with the fact that area is two-dimensional. Then expand the formulas for $S_2(x)$ to prove that $S_2x = 480 - 4x^2$.

Question 13: In part (a), accept answers in either factored or expanded (general) form. In part (b), have students evaluate $V(2)$ using both factored and general form. As a natural extension of part (c), ask for the x-value such that $V(x)$ is as large as possible. Use an automatic grapher to estimate the x-coordinate of the highest point on the graph of $y = V(x)$ on the interval $0 < x < 5$.

Question 17: Students may need to be reminded of the formula $V = \frac{1}{3}\pi r^2 h$ for the volume of a cone.

Questions

In 1–6, *multiple choice*. State whether the polynomial is (a) a monomial, (b) a binomial, or (c) a trinomial, and give its degree.

1. $x^9 - x$ b, degree 9
2. $3x^5 + x^2$ b, degree 5
3. $a^3 - b^3$ b, degree 3
4. $5x + x$ a, degree 1
5. $x^2 + 7xy - 8$ c, degree 2
6. $173x^2y^3z$ a, degree 6

7. Find the area A of the largest rectangle below:

   a. summing the areas of the six small rectangles.   See margin.

   b. using the formula $A = lw$ directly and applying the Extended Distributive Property.
   $A = (b + t)(a + b + c) = ba + b^2 + bc + at + bt + ct$

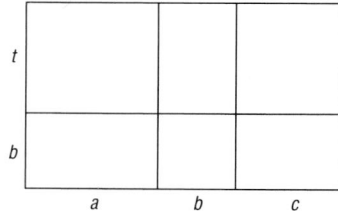

In 8 and 9, multiply and simplify.

8. $(3x^2 + x - 5)(x + 2)$
   $3x^3 + 7x^2 - 3x - 10$

9. $(4a^2 + 2a + 1)(2a - 1)$ $8a^3 - 1$

In 10–12, refer to Example 3.

10. a. Use the equation $V(x) = 4x^3 - 88x^2 + 480x$ to complete the table below for $x = 1$ to 5.

x	1	2	3	4	5	6	7	8	9	10	11
$V(x)$	396	640	756	768	700	576	420	256	108	0	-44

   b. Use the factored form $V(x) = x(24 - 2x)(20 - 2x)$ to check the value of the polynomial for $x = 9$. $V(x) = (9)(6)(2) = 108$

   c. Use the factored form to calculate the value of the polynomial for the other integer values of x from $x = 6$ to 11.   See 10a. above.

   d. For what integer value of x between 1 and 11 is $V(x)$ greatest? Least?   greatest for $x = 4$; least for $x = 11$

   e. Interpret your results for $x = 10$ in terms of the box.   when $x = 10$, width $= 0$ so area $= 0$

   f. What is a reasonable domain for the function V? $0 < x < 10$

614

11. a. Use a function grapher to estimate to the nearest tenth the value of x at which V achieves its maximum value.   **3.6**
   b. Use this value to find the dimensions of the box with the largest possible volume.   **(16.8)(12.8)(2) ≈ 430**

12. a. Find a polynomial formula in terms of x for the surface area $S(x)$ of the open box. (Hint: There are five sides.)   **$S(x) = -4x^2 + 480$**
   b. Calculate $S(3)$.   **$S(3) = 444$**
   c. Explain why you can tell that $S(5) < S(4)$ without calculating these values.   **$S(5) < S(4)$ because the leading coefficient is negative and the other term is a constant.**

13. Suppose a piece of metal is 18 inches by 10 inches and squares of side x are cut out of the corners. An open box is formed from the remaining metal.
   a. Find a polynomial formula in terms of x for the volume $V(x)$ of the box.   **$V(x) = 4x^3 - 56x^2 + 180x$**
   b. Calculate $V(2)$.   **$V(2) = 168$**
   c. Find a value of x such that $V(x) > V(2)$.   **Sample: $V(2.01) = 168.03$**

In 14–16, multiply and simplify.

14. $(x^2 - 2x + 2)(x^2 + 2x + 2)$ **$x^4 + 4$**

15. $(a + b - c)(a - b + c)$ **$a^2 - b^2 - c^2 + 2bc$**

16. $(2a - 1)^3$ **$8a^3 - 12a^2 + 6a - 1$**

17. The slant height of a right circular cone is 15 cm. Show that the volume of the cone can be expressed as a polynomial in h by following the steps below.

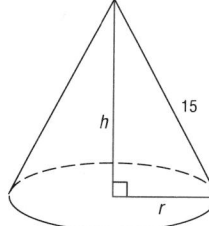

   a. Write the volume in terms of r and h.   **$V = \frac{\pi}{3} r^2 h$**
   b. Use the Pythagorean Theorem to express r in terms of h.   **$r = \sqrt{225 - h^2}$**
   c. Substitute the result of part b into the formula in part a.   **$V = -\frac{\pi}{3} h^3 + 75\pi h$**

18. For 6 years, after each birthday Devin invested his money in an account which compounded interest annually at rate r. He saved

$$56x^5 + 32x^4 + 40x^3 + 47x^2 + 61x + 59 \text{ dollars,}$$

where $x = 1 + r$.
   a. What is the degree of this polynomial?   **5**
   b. How much money would Devin have if the money were invested at a rate of 7.25%? *(Lesson 11-1)*   **$349.63**

MORE PRACTICE
For more questions on SPUR Objectives, use *Lesson Master 11-2,* shown on page 615.

EXTENSION
Use the figures below to prove the identities:

1. $(a + b)^2 = a^2 + 2ab + b^2$

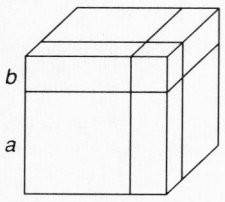

Solution: The area of the large square = $(a + b)^2$. The areas of the inner parts are a^2, b^2, ab and ab. Since the whole is equal to the sum of the parts,
$(a + b)^2 = a^2 + ab + ab$
$\qquad\qquad + b^2$
$\qquad\quad = a^2 + 2ab + b^2$.

2. $(a + b)^3 = a^3 + 3a^2b + 3ab^2 + b^3$

Solution: The volume of the big cube is $(a + b)^3$. It consists of the sum of the volumes of 8 rectangular solids: 2 cubes of volumes a^3 and b^3, 3 blocks each with volume a^2b, and 3 blocks each with volume ab^2. So the volume of the big cube also equals $a^3 + 3a^2b + 3ab^2 + b^3$. Use a solid model to help students see the eight components of the big cube.

In 19–21, consider that during the early part of the twentieth century, the deer population of the Kaibab Plateau in Arizona grew rapidly, because hunters had reduced the number of natural predators. Later, the increase in population depleted the food supply and the deer population declined quickly. From 1905 to 1930 the number $N(t)$ of deer was approximated by

$$N(t) = -.125t^5 + 3.125t^4 + 4000$$

where t is the time in years after 1905. This function is graphed below. *(Lesson 11-1)*

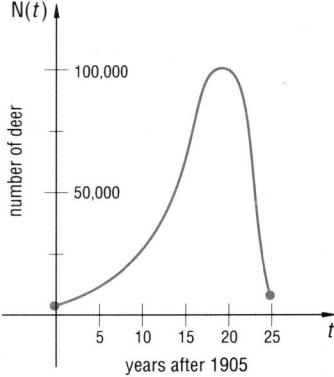

19. To the nearest thousand, what was the deer population in 1905?   **4000**

20. To the nearest thousand, what was the deer population in 1930?   **4000**

21. a. Over what time period (between 1905 and 1930) was the deer population increasing?   **1905 to 1925**
   b. In about what year did the deer population start to decline?   **1925**

In 22 and 23, consider that the price of a diamond tends to vary directly as the square of its weight. Suppose a half-carat diamond costs $640. *(Lessons 2-1, 2-3)*

22. Estimate the cost of a $1\frac{1}{2}$ carat diamond of similar quality.   **$5760**

23. How many times more will a 2-carat diamond cost than a half-carat diamond of similar quality?   **16 times**

Exploration

24. In Question 14, the product of two trinomials simplifies to be a binomial. Find another two trinomials whose product is a binomial.
sample: $(5x^2 - 10x + 10)(5x^2 + 10x + 10) = 25x^4 + 100$

11-3

Polynomials are usually written in the general form as a sum:

$$P(x) = a_nx^n + a_{n-1}x^{n-1} + a_{n-2}x^{n-2} + \ldots + a_2x^2 + a_1x^1 + a_0$$

When evaluating or graphing a polynomial, it may help to rewrite the polynomial as a product of factors. For instance, the polynomial $4x^3 - 88x^2 + 480x$ in the last lesson was originally in the factored form $x(24 - 2x)(20 - 2x)$. This can be further factored into $4x(12 - x)(10 - x)$.

There are four common ways of factoring:
1. factoring the largest common monomial factor
2. factoring following a pattern
3. quadratic trinomial factoring
4. using the Factor Theorem

You may have seen these in earlier courses. We review three types here and one type in the next lesson.

Example 1   Factor $6x^5 - 18x^3 + 42x^2$.

Solution   First we look for the largest common monomial factor of the terms. The greatest common factor of 6, -18, and 42 is 6. The highest power of x that divides each term is x^2. So $6x^2$ is the largest common monomial factor of $6x^5$, $-18x^3$, and $42x^2$.
Now apply the Distributive Property.

$$6x^5 - 18x^3 + 42x^2 = 6x^2 (\underline{\;?\;} - \underline{\;?\;} + \underline{\;?\;})$$
$$= 6x^2(x^3 - 3x + 7)$$

This cannot be factored further.

Check: Test a special case. Let $x = 2$. Do the first and last expressions have the same values?

$$6x^5 - 18x^3 + 42x^2 = 6 \cdot 32 - 18 \cdot 8 + 42 \cdot 4 = 216$$
$$6x^2(x^3 - 3x + 7) = 6 \cdot 4(8 - 6 + 7) = 216$$

Yes.

RESOURCES
■ Lesson Master 11-3
▣ Visual for Teaching Aid 71 provides for five polynomial factoring patterns.

OBJECTIVE

B Factor polynomials using common monomial factoring, perfect square patterns, trial and error with trinomials, or patterns for the sum or difference of two cubes.

TEACHING NOTES

Most students will need only a brief review of the factoring techniques for a common monomial, perfect square trinomial, difference of two squares, and general trinomial factoring.

More time needs to be spent on the sum or difference of two cubes, since most students will be encountering these two factoring patterns for the first time.

Emphasize that each of the *quadratic* expressions $a^2 + 2ab + b^2$, $a^2 - 2ab + b^2$, $a^2 - b^2$ can be written as the product of *two linear* factors. In contrast, each of the *cubic* expressions $a^3 + b^3$ and $a^3 - b^3$ can be rewritten as the product of *one linear* and *one quadratic* factor. As a memory aid, point out that the operation in the linear factor of the *sum* of two cubes is $+$, and the operation in the linear factor of the *difference* of two cubes is $-$.

Thus,
$a^3 + b^3 = (a + b)(a^2 - ab + b^2)$,
$a^3 - b^3 = (a - b)(a^2 + ab + b^2)$.
The signs in the quadratic factors can be figured out by working backwards. Students should multiply these out to verify the patterns.

Alternate Approach
$a^3 \pm b^3$ may be rewritten as $(a)^3 \pm (b)^3$; for example, $27x^3 - 125y^6 = (3x)^3 - (5y^2)^3$. This will allow students to more readily identify the quantities to be substituted into the factoring pattern.

ADDITIONAL EXAMPLES

1. Factor the largest common monomial factor.
a. $12x^2 - 4x$
$4x(3x - 1)$
b. $15x^3y + 5x^2y^2 - 35xy^2$
$5xy(3x^2 + xy - 7y)$

2. Factor using the Difference of Two Squares Pattern.
a. $y^2 - 36$
$(y + 6)(y - 6)$
b. $64x^2 - 81y^2$
$(8x + 9y)(8x - 9y)$
c. $x^4 - 16$
$(x + 2)(x - 2)(x^2 + 4)$

3. Factor using the Sum or Difference of Two Cubes Pattern.
a. $x^3 + 64$
$(x + 4)(x^2 - 4x + 16)$
b. $27 - 125x^3y^3$
$(3 - 5xy)(9 + 15xy + 25x^2y^2)$

4. Factor.
a. $x^2 - x - 6$
$(x - 3)(x + 2)$
b. $6x^2 - 7x - 20$
$(2x - 5)(3x + 4)$
c. $25x^2 + 10x + 1$
$(5x + 1)^2$

There are five factoring patterns you should memorize. You learned two of them in Chapter 6.

Perfect Square Trinomial Patterns:

For all a and b,

$$a^2 + 2ab + b^2 = (a + b)^2$$
and
$$a^2 - 2ab + b^2 = (a - b)^2.$$

The sum of two squares, $a^2 + b^2$, cannot be factored without using complex numbers. However, the difference of two squares, $a^2 - b^2$, has a well-known factorization.

Difference of Squares Pattern:

For all a and b,

$$a^2 - b^2 = (a + b)(a - b).$$

Example 2 shows the use of this pattern to factor a polynomial of the form $a^2 - b^2$.

Example 2 Factor $9m^2n^2 - 49$.

Solution Both terms of the polynomial are perfect squares.

$$9m^2n^2 = (3mn)^2$$
$$49 = 7^2$$

Thus the difference of squares pattern can be applied using $a = 3mn$ and $b = 7$.

$$9m^2n^2 - 49 = (3mn)^2 - (7)^2$$
$$= (3mn + 7)(3mn - 7)$$

Check: Use the FOIL Theorem.

$$(3mn + 7)(3mn - 7) = 9m^2n^2 - 21mn + 21mn - 49$$
$$= 9m^2n^2 - 49$$

618

The final two patterns involve cubes. They are easily proved using the Distributive Property. The proof of the sum of cubes pattern is below. You are asked to complete the proof of the difference of cubes pattern in Question 26.

For all a and b,
Sum of Cubes Pattern: $a^3 + b^3 = (a + b)(a^2 - ab + b^2)$
Difference of Cubes Pattern: $a^3 - b^3 = (a - b)(a^2 + ab + b^2)$

Proof

$(a + b)(a^2 - ab + b^2)$

$= a(a^2 - ab + b^2) + b(a^2 - ab + b^2)$	Distributive Property
$= a(a^2) - a(ab) + a(b^2) + b(a^2) - b(ab) + b(b^2)$	Distributive Property
$= a^3 \quad - a^2b \quad + ab^2 \quad + a^2b \quad - ab^2 \quad + b^3$	Product of Powers Property
$= a^3 - a^2b + a^2b + ab^2 - ab^2 + b^3$	Commutative Property
$= a^3 + b^3$	Adding Like Terms; Additive Identity

Example 3   Factor $x^3 + 125$.

Solution   This polynomial is the sum of two cubes, so use that pattern with $a = x$ and $b = 5$.

$$x^3 + 5^3 = (x + 5)(x^2 - x \cdot 5 + 5^2)$$
$$= (x + 5)(x^2 - 5x + 25)$$

Example 4   Factor $8 - s^3p^6$.

Solution   Notice that 8 is the cube of 2, and s^3p^6 is the cube of sp^2. So the pattern for the difference of two cubes can be used.

Thus, $8 - s^3p^6 = (2)^3 - (sp^2)^3 = (2 - sp^2)(4 - 2(sp^2) + (sp^2)^2)$
$$= (2 - sp^2)(4 - 2sp^2 + s^2p^4).$$

Usually we consider only polynomials with integer coefficients. Then the quadratic trinomial $ax^2 + bx + c$ can be factored into linear factors if and only if $b^2 - 4ac$ is a perfect square. Once you know a trinomial can be factored, the usual method for finding the factors is trial and error.

■ ■ ■ ■ ■ ■ ■■

Example 5 Factor $6y^2 - 7y - 5$ if possible.

Solution Here $a = 6$, $b = -7$, and $c = -5$. Since $b^2 - 4ac = (-7)^2 - 4(6)(-5) = 169$, a perfect square, this quadratic polynomial is factorable. First write the form of two linear polynomials in y.

$$6y^2 - 7y - 5 = (\underline{} y + \underline{})(\underline{} y + \underline{})$$

The coefficients of y will multiply to 6. Thus either they are $3y$ and $2y$, or y and $6y$. The constant terms will multiply to -5, so they are either 1 and -5, or -1 and 5.

Here are all the possibilities with $3y$ and $2y$.

$$(3y + 1)(2y - 5)$$
$$(3y - 1)(2y + 5)$$
$$(3y - 5)(2y + 1)$$
$$(3y + 5)(2y - 1)$$

Here are all the possibilities with y and $6y$.

$$(y + 1)(6y - 5)$$
$$(y - 1)(6y + 5)$$
$$(y - 5)(6y + 1)$$
$$(y + 5)(6y - 1)$$

At most, you need to do these eight multiplications. If one of them gives $6y^2 - 7y - 5$, then that is the correct factoring.

We show all eight products. You can see that the desired one is third.

$$(3y + 1)(2y - 5) = 6y^2 - 13y - 5$$
$$(3y - 1)(2y + 5) = 6y^2 + 13y - 5$$
$$(3y - 5)(2y + 1) = 6y^2 - 7y - 5$$
$$(3y + 5)(2y - 1) = 6y^2 + 7y - 5$$
$$(y + 1)(6y - 5) = 6y^2 + y - 5$$
$$(y - 1)(6y + 5) = 6y^2 - y - 5$$
$$(y - 5)(6y + 1) = 6y^2 - 29y - 5$$
$$(y + 5)(6y - 1) = 6y^2 + 29y - 5$$

So $6y^2 - 7y - 5 = (3y - 5)(2y + 1)$.

In the lessons that follow you will learn how factoring a polynomial can help you graph and analyze polynomial functions.

620

Questions

Covering the Reading

1. Copy and complete: $9d^2 + 3ed - 6d^3 = 3d(\underline{\ ?\ } + \underline{\ ?\ } - \underline{\ ?\ })$.
$3d + e - 2d^2$

In 2 and 3, factor.

2. $-62x^5y^2 + 124x^4y^3$ **3.** $21x^3 - 28x + 35x^4$ $7x(3x^2 - 4 + 5x^3)$
$62x^4y^2(-x + 2y)$

In 4 and 5, choose from the following:
$$a^2 - b^2 \qquad a^2 + b^2$$
$$a^3 - b^3 \qquad a^3 + b^3$$

4. List all expressions that have $a - b$ as a factor. $a^2 - b^2, a^3 - b^3$

5. List all expressions that have $a + b$ as a factor. $a^2 - b^2, a^3 + b^3$

In 6–14, (a) describe the polynomial as a perfect square, difference of squares or cubes, or sum of squares or cubes, and (b) factor.   **See margin.**

6. $x^2 - y^2$ **7.** $a^2 - 2ab + b^2$ **8.** $m^3 + n^3$

9. $x^2 - 256$ **10.** $25a^2 - 36b^2$ **11.** $64 - 27c^3$

12. $64 + 27c^3$ **13.** $49a^2 - 42ab + 9b^2$ **14.** $x^3 + 27$

15. If a, b, and c are integers, when is $ax^2 + bx + c$ factorable into factors with integer coefficients?   **when $b^2 - 4ac$ is a perfect square**

16. One factor of $6x^2 + 7x - 10$ is $(x + 2)$. Find the other factor. $6x - 5$

In 17–19, (a) determine whether the trinomial is factorable, and (b) if so, factor.   **See margin.**

17. $5x^2 + 8x - 4$ **18.** $y^2 + 3y + 4$ **19.** $7z^2 - z - 8$

Applying the Mathematics

20. *Multiple choice*   Which of the following is a perfect square trinomial?   **c**
(a) $9x^2 + 60x + 25$ (b) $a^4 + 24a^3 + 144$ (c) $4q^2 + r^2 - 4qr$

21. a. Write $16x^4 - 81$ as the product of two binomials. $(4x^2 + 9)(4x^2 - 9)$
    b. Write $16x^4 - 81$ as the product of three binomials.
    $(4x^2 + 9)(2x + 3)(2x - 3)$

In 22 and 23, first factor out the common monomial factor. Then complete the factorization.

22. $4x^3 - 88x^2 + 480x$ **23.** $1000x^3 + 216x^3y^3$
$4x(x - 12)(x - 10)$ $8x^3(5 + 3y)(25 - 15y + 9y^2)$

24. a. Multiply $(x - \sqrt{7})(x + \sqrt{7})$. $x^2 - 7$
    b. Use your answer to part a to help factor $x^2 - 19$ over the set of real numbers. $(x + \sqrt{19})(x - \sqrt{19})$

25. *Multiple choice*   Which is a factorization of $x^2 + y^2$ over the complex numbers?   **d**
(a) $(x + y)(x + y)$ (b) $(x + iy)(x + iy)$
(c) $(x - iy)(x - iy)$ (d) $(x + iy)(x - iy)$

26. Prove that for all numbers a and b, $(a - b)(a^2 + ab + b^2) = a^3 - b^3$.
    See margin.

NOTES ON QUESTIONS

Questions 6-14: In each question, encourage students to identify a factoring pattern before they begin to factor each expression.

Question 15: This question suggests that the choice of domain in factoring may be optional. Point out that, for the most part, factoring is done over the set of integers.

Questions 22 and 23: Stress that looking for a common monomial factor should almost *always* be the first step in a factoring problem.

Questions 30 and 31: These set up key ideas used in the next two lessons. Do not skip them.

Question 32: This is a special case of a Difference of Two nth Powers Theorem:
$a^n - b^n = (a - b)(a^{n-1} + a^{n-2}b + a^{n-3}b^2 + \ldots + ab^{n-2} + b^{n-1})$.

NAME _____

LESSON **MASTER**   **11–3**
QUESTIONS ON SPUR OBJECTIVES

■**SKILLS**   *Objective B*   *(See pages 662–665 for objectives.)*
In 1 and 2, fill in the blanks.

1. $6a^2b - 3ab^2 = 3ab(\underline{\quad 2a \quad} + \underline{\quad -b \quad})$

2. $16x^2 - 2x = 2x(\underline{\quad 8x \quad} - \underline{\quad 1 \quad})$

In 3 and 4, fill in the blank with the value(s) which make a perfect square trinomial.

3. $r^2 + \underline{\quad 20r \quad} + 100$ 4. $9n^2 + \underline{\quad 24mn \quad} + 16m^2$

In 5–13, factor.

5. $x^2 - 6x + 9$ 6. $64 - 4t^2$ 7. $2y^3 - 4y^2 - 48y$
                                          $2y(y - 6)$
  $(x - 3)^2$ $(8 + 2t)(8 - 2t)$ $(y + 4)$

8. $x^4 - 9x^2$ 9. $a^4 - 16$ 10. $49c^2 + 70c + 25$
                          $(a^2 + 4)$
  $x^2(x + 3)(x - 3)$ $(a - 2)(a + 2)$ $(7c + 5)^2$

11. $r^3 + 125$ 12. $27p^6 - 8q^3$ 13. $132a^6b^3 - 66a^5b^4$
  $(r + 5)$ $(3p^2 - 2q)(9p^4$
  $(r^2 - 5r + 25)$ $+ 6p^2q + 4q^2)$ $66a^5b^3(2a - b)$

In 14–16, factor.

14. $3a^2 + a - 2$ 15. $x^2 - 10x + 24$ 16. $n^2 + 5n + 7$
  $(a + 1)(3a - 2)$ $(x - 6)(x - 4)$ not possible

17. **a.** Multiply $(x + \sqrt{2})(x - \sqrt{2})$. $x^2 - 2$
    b. Use your answer in part (a) to help factor $(x - \sqrt{23})(x + \sqrt{23})$
    $x^2 - 23$ over the set of real numbers.

Advanced Algebra © Scott, Foresman and Company   **117**

EXTENSION
You may wish to introduce a short method for finding squares. Since $a^2 - b^2 = (a + b)(a - b)$, then $a^2 = (a + b)(a - b) + b^2$. Example: Find $(96)^2$. Let $a = 96$ and choose a value of b such that $a + b$ or $a - b$ becomes a number whose square is known and easy to multiply mentally. In this case, we choose $b = 4$. Applying the Difference of Squares Theorem,

$$(96)^2 = (96 + 4)(96 - 4) + 4^2$$
$$= (100)(92) + 16$$
$$= 9216$$

Have students find $(97)^2$, $(53)^2$, and $(48)^2$ by this method.

EVALUATION
Alternative Assessment
Ask each of four students to state one of the four common ways of factoring.

ADDITIONAL ANSWERS
30.a.

x	f(x)
-5	-90
-4	-32
-3	0
-2	12
-1	10
0	0
1	-12
2	-20
3	-18
4	0
5	40

b. and c.

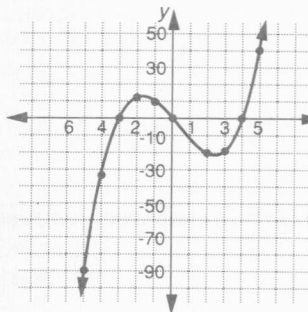

Review

In 27 and 28, consider a closed rectangular box with dimensions h, $h + 2$, and $h + 5$. Write a polynomial in standard form for

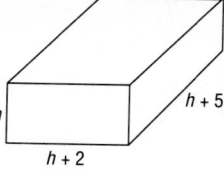

27. $S(h)$, the surface area of the box;
$S(h) = 6h^2 + 28h + 20$

28. $V(h)$, the volume of the box.
(Lesson 11-2) $V(h) = h^3 + 7h^2 + 10h$

29. A graphic designer works with sheets of paper 11 in. by 17 in. Suppose the designer lays out a rectangular design in the center of the sheet with a border of x in. on each side. *(Lesson 11-2)*
   a. Find the area of the design in the center if $x = 3$.   55 in²
   b. Write an expression for $A(x)$, the area of the design in the center.
   $A(x) = 4x^2 - 56x + 187$

30. **a.** Let $f(x) = x^3 - x^2 - 12x$. Construct a table using integer values of x on the domain $-5 \le x \le 5$.   See margin.   See margin.
   b. Plot the eleven points in part a. Estimate what the graph of $y = f(x)$ looks like by drawing a smooth curve through the points.
   c. Check your work in part a by using a function grapher. *(Lesson 11-1)*
   See margin.

31. A function $P(x)$ is graphed at the right.
   (Lessons 6-3, 6-4, 6-8)   See margin.
   a. Which word best describes the function: constant, linear, quadratic, or exponential? Explain how you know.
   quadratic; the shape is a parabola
   b. For what value(s) of x does $P(x) = 0$?
   $x = 1, x = 5$

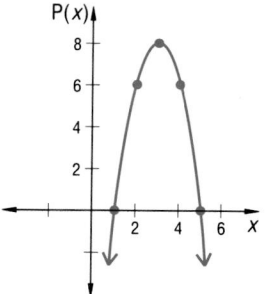

Exploration

32. **a.** $x^2 - 1$ is the product of $x - 1$ and __?__. $x + 1$
   b. $x^3 - 1$ is the product of $x - 1$ and __?__. $x^2 + x + 1$
   c. $x^4 - 1$ is the product of $x - 1$ and __?__. $x^3 + x^2 + x + 1$
   d. Generalize the above pattern.
   $x^n - 1 = (x - 1)(x^{n-1} + x^{n-2} + \ldots + x^2 + x + 1)$

The Factor Theorem

A product equals 0 if and only if one of the factors equals 0. This result is called the *Zero Product Theorem*.

Zero Product Theorem:

For all a and b, $ab = 0$ if and only if $a = 0$ or $b = 0$.

This theorem is true for any expressions a and b, so it holds for polynomials. Example 1 uses a polynomial from Lesson 11-2.

■ ■ ■ ■ ■ ■ ■ ■ ■

Example 1 Let $V(x) = 4x^3 - 88x^2 + 480x$. Solve $V(x) = 0$ for x.

Solution We want to know when $4x^3 - 88x^2 + 480x = 0$. The Zero Product Theorem can be applied if the polynomial is factored. Factoring $V(x)$ we have

$$4x(x - 12)(x - 10) = 0.$$

Now, applying the Theorem,

$$4x = 0 \quad \text{or} \quad x - 12 = 0 \quad \text{or} \quad x - 10 = 0.$$
$$\text{Thus} \quad x = 0 \quad \text{or} \quad x = 12 \quad \text{or} \quad x = 10.$$

Solution 2 Graph the function V. $V(x) = 0$ at the x-intercepts of V, that is, when the function intersects the x-axis. A graph verifies that these intersections are at 0, 10, and 12.

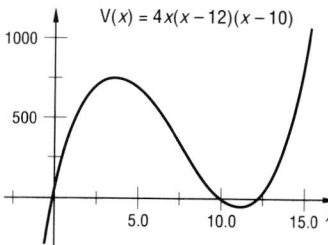

$V(x) = 4x(x-12)(x-10)$

Solution 3 The equation $V(x) = 4x^3 - 88x^2 + 480x$ gives the volume of a box with sides of dimensions x, $24 - 2x$, and $20 - 2x$. The volume of the box will be 0 exactly when any one side has length 0, leading to the same values as in the other two solutions.

RESOURCES
■ Lesson Master 11-4
■ Quiz for Lessons 11-1 Through 11-4
▨ Visual for Teaching Aid 72 provides the graphs of the functions for **Example 4**.
▣ Computer Master 26

OBJECTIVES

C Calculate or estimate zeros of polynomial functions.
F Apply the Zero Product Theorem and the Factor Theorem.
H Determine properties of a polynomial function from its graph.

TEACHING NOTES

Explain to students that function plotting software or graphing calculators can generate many instances of the Factor Theorem quickly and easily. When using this software, first graph the function in **Example 2**. Use the zoom or rescale features of the grapher to illustrate that P has zeros at 0, $-\frac{2}{3}$, and 10.

Then, graph the three functions given at the bottom of page 626, following **Example 4**. Have students give other examples of polynomials in the form $P(x) = k(x + 4)(x - 4)(x - 0.5)$, where k is a nonzero constant or any polynomial in x. Graph each polynomial function, and observe that in every case the graph has x-intercepts at -4, 4, and 0.5.

When k is a nonzero constant, all graphs have exactly three x-intercepts: -4, 4, 0.5; and are stretch images of each other, the magnitude of the stretch being equal to k.

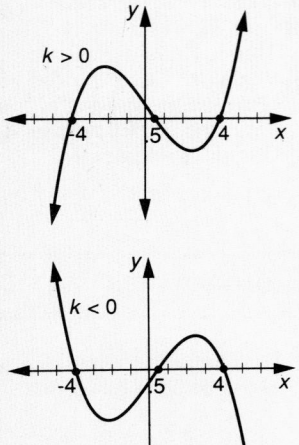

When k is a nonconstant polynomial, for example, x^2, $(x - 7)$, or $(2x^3 + 8)$, the graph still has the three x-intercepts, -4, 4, and 0.5, but may have others, and no other generalization about shape can be made.

The x-intercepts of the graph of a function are called the **zeros** of the function. The function V has zeros at 0, 10, and 12. It has factors x, $x - 10$, and $x - 12$. The general relationship, which holds for any polynomial function, is surprisingly simple.

Factor Theorem:

$x - r$ is a factor of a polynomial P(x) if and only if P(r) = 0.

Proof

The general polynomial is P(x) = $a_nx^n + a_{n-1}x^{n-1} + ... + a_1x + a_0$. If x is a factor of P(x), then $a_0 = 0$ and so P(0) = 0. And, if P(0) = 0, then $a_0 = 0$, so x is a factor. This means x is a factor of P(x) if and only if P(0) = 0. The graph will then go through the origin.

Now apply the Graph Translation Theorem. Replace x by $x - r$. This translates the graph r units to the right. The graph will contain (r, 0). Then r is a zero of the function and $x - r$ is a factor of the polynomial.

The words "if and only if" in the Factor Theorem mean that the theorem has two parts. If P(r) = 0, then $x - r$ is a factor of P(x). And, if $x - r$ is a factor of P(x), then P(r) = 0. So zeros determine factors and vice-versa.

Example 2   Find the zeros of P(x) = $3x^4 - 28x^3 - 20x^2$ by factoring.

Solution $P(x) = x^2(3x^2 - 28x - 20)$
$= x^2(3x + 2)(x - 10)$
$= 3x^2(x + \frac{2}{3})(x - 10)$

The factors are x, x, $x + \frac{2}{3}$, and $x - 10$, so the zeros are 0, 0, $-\frac{2}{3}$, and 10.

Check   Graph P using a function plotter. The graph shows zeros at approximately 10, 0, and $-\frac{2}{3}$. You might wish to zoom in on the origin to verify the last two values and show that P(x) crosses the x-axis at $x = -\frac{2}{3}$.

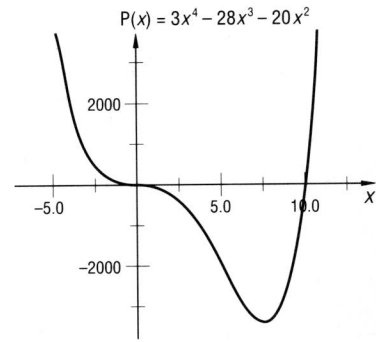

624

624

Example 3 reverses the process of Example 2.

Example 3   Factor $f(x) = 2x^3 - 5x^2 - 28x + 15$ by graphing.

Solution   The graph below was drawn with a function plotter. It shows two zeros at approximately 5 and -3 and a third zero between 0 and 1.

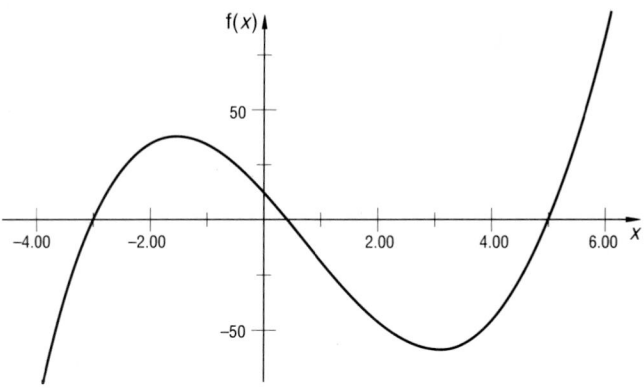

We check 5 by calculation: $f(5) = 2 \cdot 5^3 - 5 \cdot 5^2 - 28 \cdot 5 + 15 = 0$.
Thus $x - 5$ is a factor. Similarly, $f(-3) = 2(-3)^3 - 5(-3)^2 - 28(-3) + 15 = 0$, and $x + 3$ is a factor. Thus

$$f(x) = 2x^3 - 5x^2 - 28x + 15 = (x - 5)(x + 3)(?)$$
$$= (x^2 - 2x - 15)(?)$$

The third factor must be linear of the form $ax + b$ because $f(x)$ has degree 3. To find a, we know $2x^3 = x^2(ax)$, so $a = 2$. To find b, $15 = (-15)b$, so $b = -1$. Thus the third factor is $2x - 1$ and

$$2x^3 - 5x^2 - 28x + 15 = (x^2 - 2x - 15)(2x - 1).$$

If $2x - 1 = 0$, then $x = \frac{1}{2}$.
Check by calculation: $f(\frac{1}{2}) = 2(\frac{1}{2})^3 - 5(\frac{1}{2})^2 - 28(\frac{1}{2}) + 15 = 0$.

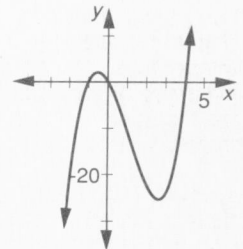

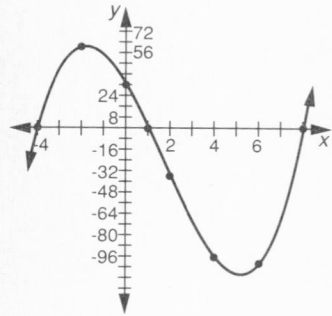
The Factor Theorem can be used to find equations of polynomials given their zeros.

Example 4 Find an equation for a polynomial function with zeros -4, $\frac{7}{2}$, and $\frac{5}{3}$.

Solution Call the polynomial p(x). It is given that $p(-4) = 0$, $p(\frac{7}{2}) = 0$, and $p(\frac{5}{3}) = 0$. So the zeros of p are -4, $\frac{7}{2}$, and $\frac{5}{3}$. By the Factor Theorem, $(x - -4)$, $(x - \frac{7}{2})$, and $(x - \frac{5}{3})$ must be factors of p(x). Thus

$$p(x) = k(x + 4)(x - \tfrac{7}{2})(x - \tfrac{5}{3})$$

where k is any nonzero constant or polynomial in x.

Check Substitute -4 for x. Is $p(-4) = 0$?

$$p(-4) = k(-4 + 4)(-4 - \tfrac{7}{2})(-4 - \tfrac{5}{3})$$
$$= k(0)(-\tfrac{15}{2})(-\tfrac{17}{3})$$

So, $p(-4) = 0$.
Similarly, $p(\frac{7}{2}) = 0$ and $p(\frac{5}{3}) = 0$.

Notice that the degree of p(x) in Example 4 is at least 3. However, from the given information we cannot conclude the value of k, nor even whether k is a constant or a variable. Thus, we cannot be sure of the degree of p(x). Many polynomials go through the points $(-4, 0)$, $(\frac{7}{2}, 0)$, and $(\frac{5}{3}, 0)$. Three examples are

$$f(x) = 6(x + 4)(x - \tfrac{7}{2})(x - \tfrac{5}{3}) = 6x^3 - 7x^2 - 89x + 140,$$
$$g(x) = (x + 4)(x - \tfrac{7}{2})(x - \tfrac{5}{3}),$$
$$\text{and } h(x) = x^2(x + 4)(x - \tfrac{7}{2})(x - \tfrac{5}{3}).$$

Graphs of these three functions are shown below.

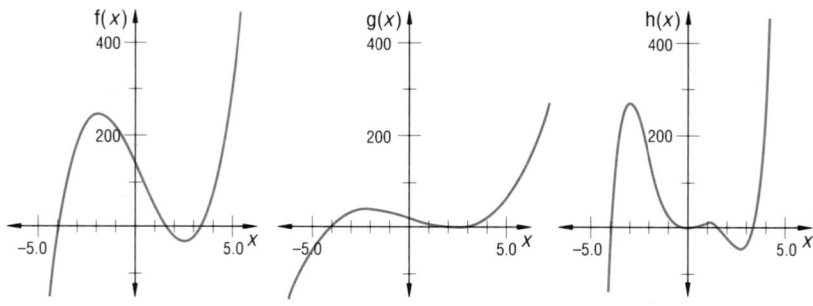

$f(x) = 6(x + 4)(x - \tfrac{7}{2})(x - \tfrac{5}{3})$ $g(x) = (x + 4)(x - \tfrac{7}{2})(x - \tfrac{5}{3})$ $h(x) = x^2(x + 4)(x - \tfrac{7}{2})(x - \tfrac{5}{3})$

626

Questions

10.

n	$P(n)$
-2	0
-1	3
0	-20
1	-33
2	0

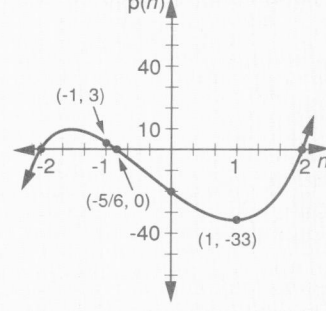

$P(n) =$
$(n + 2)(n - 2)(6n + 5)$

12. sample:
$P_1(x) = x^3 - .5x^2 - 16x + 8,$
$P_2(x) = x^4 - .5x^3 - 16x^2 + 8x$
$P_3(x) = 5x^4 - 2.5x^3 - 80x^2 + 40x$

15.a. $g(x) = x(2x - 5)(4x^2 + 10x + 25)$
b. $x = 0, x = \frac{5}{2}$
c.

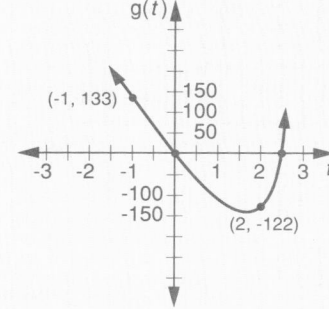

16.a. $f(x) = 3x^2(x + 6)(x - 6)$
b. $x = 0, x = -6, x = 6$
c.

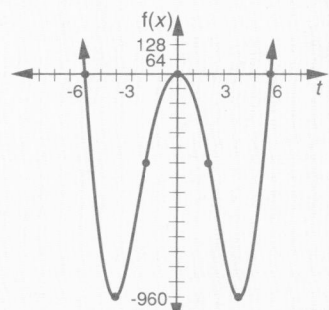

Covering the Reading

1. State the Zero Product Theorem. $ab = 0$ if and only if $a = 0$ or $b = 0$

In 2 and 3, solve.

2. $(x + 9)(3x + 4) = 0$
$x = -9$ or $x = -\frac{4}{3}$

3. $(-\frac{5}{7}k + 2)(k - 2)(k - .9) = 0$
$k = \frac{14}{5}, k = 2,$ or $k = .9$

4. If $f(x) = x(x + 7)(x - 3)$, solve $f(x) = 0$. $x = 0, x = -7,$ or $x = 3$

5. Suppose that $P(x)$ is a polynomial and $x - 4$ is a factor of $P(x)$. According to the Factor Theorem, what can you conclude? $P(4) = 0$

In 6 and 7, factor each polynomial and find its zeros.   See margin.

6. $j(x) = x^2 - 10x - 24$

7. $k(x) = 2x^3 - 17x^2 + 8x$

8. *True or false*   If the graph of a polynomial function crosses the x-axis at $(3, 0)$ and $(-4, 0)$, then $(x + 3)$ and $(x - 4)$ are factors of the polynomial.   **False**

In 9 and 10, find the zeros of the polynomial function by graphing. Use this information to factor the polynomial.   **9 and 10, See margin.**

9. $y = x^3 - 5x^2 - 28x + 32$ **10.** $P(n) = 6n^3 + 5n^2 - 24n - 20$

In 11 and 12, refer to Example 4.

11. What is the form of the equation for a polynomial function with zeros equal to -4, $\frac{7}{2}$, and $\frac{5}{3}$? $P(x) = k(x + 4)(x - \frac{7}{2})(x - \frac{5}{3})$, where k is a non-zero constant or a polynomial in x.

12. Name three specific polynomial functions whose zeros are -4, 4, and .5.   **See margin.**

13. Find a general equation for a polynomial function whose zeros are 8, -10, and 2.4. $P(x) = k(x^3 - .4x^2 - 84.8x + 192)$

14. At the right is the graph of a third degree polynomial function with zeros at 0, 3, and 6 and leading coefficient 1. What is an equation for this function?
$P(x) = x^3 - 9x^2 + 18x$

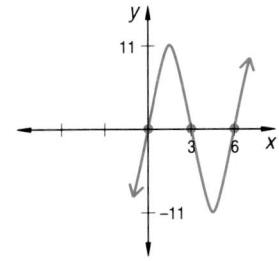

Applying the Mathematics

In 15 and 16: (a) factor each polynomial; (b) find the zeros of each function; and (c) check your answers by drawing a graph using a function plotter.   **See margin.**

15. $g(x) = 8x^4 - 125x$ **16.** $f(x) = 3x^4 - 108x^2$

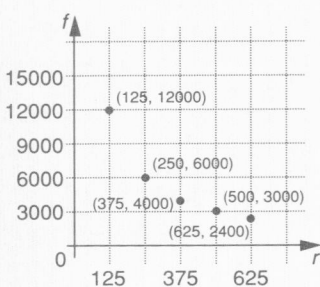
17. A horizontal beam has its left end built into a wall and its right end rests on a support, as shown in the figure below. The weight of the beam is distributed uniformly along its length. As a result, the beam sags downward according to the equation

$$y = -x^4 + 24x^3 - 135x^2$$

where x is the distance (in meters) from the wall to a point on the beam, and y is the distance (in hundredths of a millimeter) from the x-axis to the beam caused by the sag.

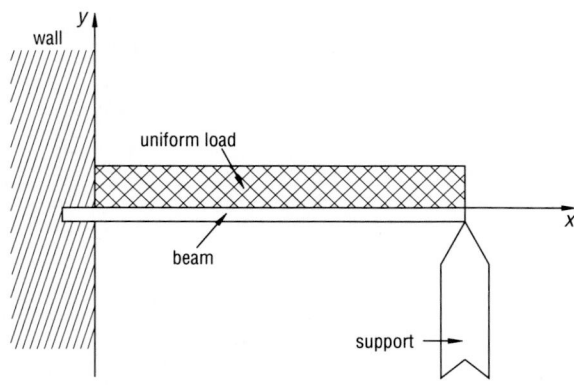

a. What is an appropriate domain for x if the beam is 9 meters long?
$0 \le x \le 9$
b. Find the zeros of this function and tell what they represent in the real world.   See margin.

Review

18. Cassandra has a piece of construction paper 9 in. by 12 in. Suppose she cuts squares with side x inches from each corner, and folds the paper as in Lesson 11-2 to make a box. Let V(x) = the volume of the box and S(x) = the surface area of the open box. Find polynomial formulas for **a.** V(x) and **b.** S(x). *(Lesson 11-2)*
a. V(x) = 4x³ - 42x² + 108x; b. S(x) = -4x² + 108

In 19–21, factor if possible. *(Lesson 11-3)*

19. $27x^3 - 1$ **20.** $a^2 + 14ab + 49b^2$ (a + 7b)²
(3x - 1) (9x² + 3x +1)
21. $3x^2 - 3y^2$ 3(x + y)(x - y)

In 22–24, complete the expression to form a perfect square. *(Lessons 11-3, 6-5)*

22. $x^2 + \underline{\;?\;} + 100$ 20x   **23.** $n^2 - 18n + \underline{\;?\;}$ 81

24. $y^2 + 5y + \underline{\;?\;}$ $\frac{25}{4}$

25. Multiply and simplify: $(x + 2)(x + 3)(x + 4)$. *(Lesson 11-2)*
x³ + 9x² + 26x + 24

628

26. Brianna, a traffic engineer, wanted to know how much force F would be needed to keep a car of weight w traveling at S mph from skidding on a curve of radius r. She determined that the force varied jointly as the weight and the square of the speed. But she still needed to find the relationship between the force and the radius. *(Lessons 2-7, 2-8)*

a. With a 2000 lb car traveling at 30 mph, she obtained the following data.

radius of curve (ft)	125	250	375	500	625
force (lb)	12000	6000	4000	3000	2400

Graph these data points.   **See margin.**

b. How does F vary with r?   **F varies inversely with r.**

c. Write an equation relating F, r, S, and w. Do not find the constant of variation k. $F = \dfrac{kwS^2}{r}$

Exploration

27. Graphs of cubic functions may have any one of the four kinds of shapes below.   **See margin.**

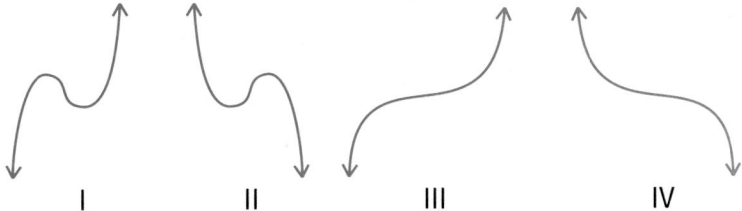

I   II   III   IV

a. Using your function plotter or the Factor Theorem, find an equation for a cubic function other than those given in this chapter
  (i) with 3 x-intercepts whose graph looks like I.
  (ii) with 3 x-intercepts whose graph looks like II.
  (iii) with 1 x-intercept whose graph looks like III.
  (iv) with 1 x-intercept whose graph looks like IV.

b. Can the graph of a cubic polynomial function ever have 2 x-intercepts? If so, give an equation for such a function. If not, explain why not.

LESSON 11-4   The Factor Theorem   **629**

MORE PRACTICE
For more questions on SPUR Objectives, use *Lesson Master 11-4*, shown below.

EVALUATION
A quiz covering Lessons 11-1 through 11-4 is provided in the TRF.

NAME _____

LESSON **MASTER 11-4**
QUESTIONS ON **SPUR** OBJECTIVES

■**SKILLS** *Objective C (See pages 662–665 for objectives.)*
In 1 and 2, find the exact zeros of the given polynomial function.

1. $y = x(x - 7)(x + 2)(3x - 5)$ **2.** $P(x) = x^2 - 49$

$0, 7, -2, \frac{5}{3}$ $7, -7$

■**PROPERTIES** *Objective F*
In 3–5, multiple choice.

3. If $(x - a)(x - b)(x - c) = 0$, then which of the following must be true?   (c)
  (a) $x = a$ (b) $x = 0$
  (c) $x = a$ or $x = b$ or $x = c$ (d) none of these

4. Suppose $P(x)$ is a polynomial where $P(r) = 0$ and $P(s) = 0$. Which of the following is not necessarily true?   (a)
  (a) P has degree two.   (b) $P(x) = k(x - r)(x - s)$.
  (c) P has degree at least two.   (d) r and s are solutions of the equation $P(x) = 0$.

5. Suppose $p(x)$ is a polynomial with factors $x - 1$ and $x - 2$. Which of the following is not necessarily true?   (b)
  (a) $p(x) = k(x - 1)(x - 2)$ (b) $p(x) = x^2 - 3x - 2$
  (c) $p(2) = 0$ (d) 1 and 2 are zeros of the graph of $y = p(x)$

6. Is the following statement always true, sometimes true, or never true? If $x - 5$ is a factor of some polynomial function P, then $P(-5) = 0$.   **sometimes true**

7. Find an equation of a quadratic function whose graph crosses the x-axis at $(3.2, 0)$ and $(-5, 0)$. $f(x) = k(x - 3.2)(x + 5)$

8. a. Find a general equation for a polynomial function whose zeros are $-5, -1, -\frac{1}{2},$ and 7. $p(x) = k(x + 5)(x + 1)(x + \frac{1}{2})(x - 7)$

  b. Name two specific polynomial functions which satisfy the conditions in part (a).
  sample: k can be any constant, $p(x) = 3(x + 5)$ $(x + 1)(x + \frac{1}{2})(x - 7)$ $p(x) = \frac{1}{10}(x + 5)(x + 1)$ $(x + \frac{1}{2})(x - 7)$

118 *Continued*   *Advanced Algebra © Scott, Foresman and Company*

NAME _____
Lesson MASTER 11-4 (page 2)

■**REPRESENTATIONS** *Objective H*

9. At the right is the graph of a second degree polynomial function with zeros at -2.5 and 3.7 and leading coefficient -1. What is an equation for the function?
$y = -1(x + 2.5)(x - 3.7)$

10. Factor $P(x) = x^4 - x^3 - 9x^2 + 9x$ by using a function grapher. $x(x - 1)(x + 3)(x - 3)$

11. Use a function grapher to find the zeros of each polynomial function.
  a. $y = x^2 - 7x + 6$ **1, 6**
  b. $y = 3x^2 - 21x + 18$ **1, 6**
  c. $y = -2x^3 + 14x^2 - 12x$ **0, 1, 6**

Advanced Algebra © Scott, Foresman and Company   **119**

LESSON 11-5

RESOURCES
■ Lesson Master 11-5
▨ Visual for Teaching Aid 73
provides the graphs for
Example 1.
▨ Visual for Teaching Aid 74
displays the BASIC pro-
gram and output for
Example 2.
▣ Computer Master 27

OBJECTIVES

C Estimate zeros of polynomial functions.
H Determine properties of a
polynomial function from
its graph.
I Read or generate computer output to graph or
find properties of poly-
nomials.

TEACHING NOTES

To be most effective, this
lesson should be studied with
access to a computer
equipped with a function
grapher that also makes tables of values. Such software
enables you to appeal to
both visual and numerical
abilities when trying to explain how to estimate zeros.
Because not all function
graphers make tables, we
provide a simple table-
making program in BASIC.
Novice computer users are
advised to use only one
piece of software during a
class period.

If you do not have access to
either a computer or cal-
culator, you should still do
this lesson. It covers important objectives, and many
questions can be done without access to technology.

LESSON

Estimating Zeros of Polynomial Functions

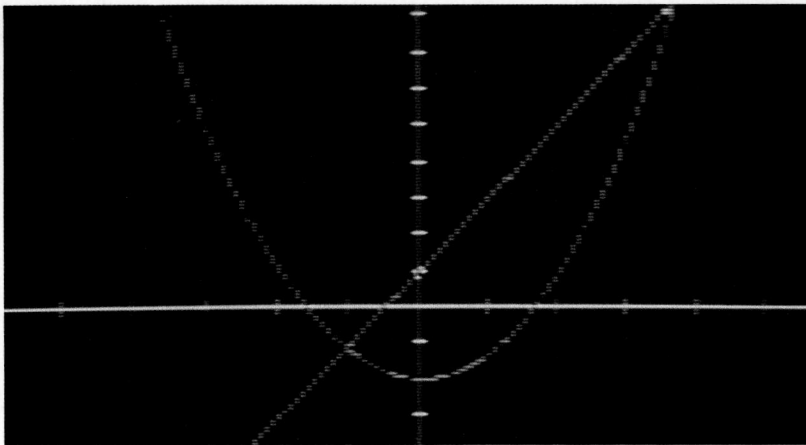

The two equations shown above (and on page 374) are $y = (3/4) x^2 - 2$ and $y = 2x + 1$.

You already know how to find exact zeros of any linear or quadratic polynomial function. You can find zeros of any higher degree poly-nomial function if it can be factored. You may also be fortunate and find zeros by substitution. But for higher degree polynomial func-tions which cannot be factored or are difficult to factor, the best that can be done is estimate the zeros.

There are two basic ways to estimate zeros.
1. Draw a graph.
2. Make a table of values.

Either way can be done by hand, but today's function plotters and computer programs allow graphs and tables to be made quickly.

■ ■ ■ ■ ■ ■ ■

Example 1   At the right is a graph of $P(x) = 10x^4 + 15x^3 + 14x^2 + 20x - 78$ for the interval $-3 \le x \le 3$. From it you can see that P has a zero between -3 and -2 and another zero between 1 and 2. Using a function plotter, esti-mate to the nearest hundredth the x-intercept between -3 and -2.

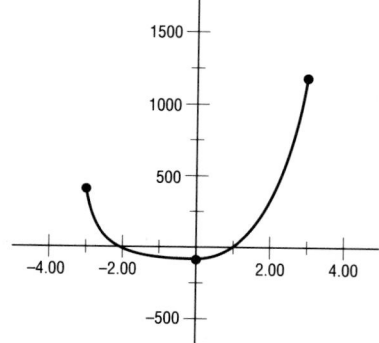

630

Solution Use the zoom or rescale feature on your function plotter to examine the graph on a smaller domain. Here is a graph of P when x is between -3.1 and -1.9.

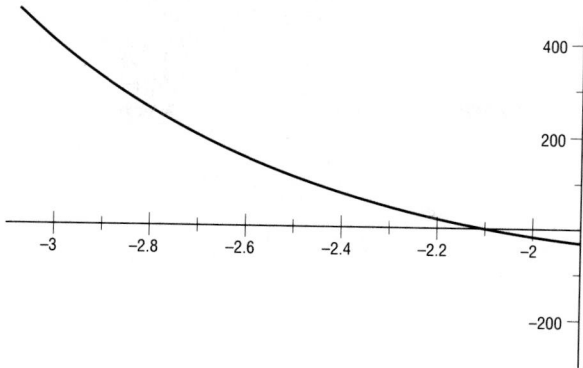

A zero of P looks to be between -2.2 and -2.1. Zoom or rescale again to examine the graph between these two values. If possible, adjust the y-values on the window. Our function plotter shows the following with a viewing window of $-2.2 \le x \le -2.09$ and $-5 \le y \le 7$.

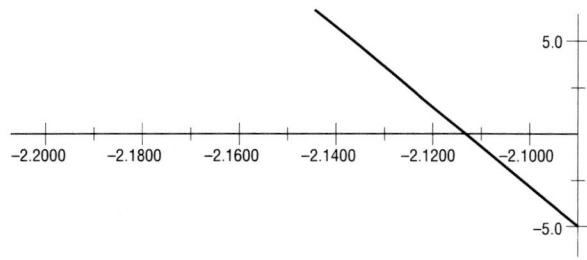

From this graph you can see that one x-intercept of $y = P(x)$ occurs closer to -2.11 than it does to -2.12. Thus, to the nearest hundredth, $x = -2.11$ is a zero of $P(x) = 10x^4 + 15x^3 + 14x^2 + 20x - 78$.

Check
$P(-2.11) = 10(-2.11)^4 + 15(-2.11)^3 + 14(-2.11)^2 + 20(-2.11) - 78$
≈ -0.57
$P(-2.12) = 10(-2.12)^4 + 15(-2.12)^3 + 14(-2.12)^2 + 20(-2.12) - 78$
≈ 1.60
$P(-2.11)$ is close to 0.

Many function graphers also make tables of values. If your function plotter does not make tables, you can use a computer program to do so.

LESSON 11-5 *Estimating Zeros of Polynomial Functions* **631**

If you are going to use the program on page 632, type and save it on your computer before class.

Introduce this lesson by reading and discussing **Example 1** with students. Explain how to use the technology in your school to find the zeros both graphically and numerically. If you have BASIC but no function grapher, run the program inputting -4 and 4 for A and B, respectively, and step size 0.5. Plot these values to show a more detailed graph. Then read and discuss **Examples 2 and 3.**

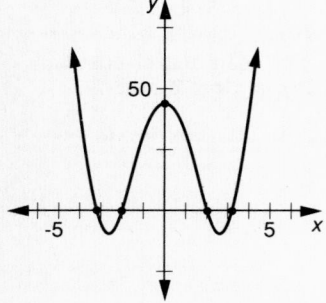
Here is a BASIC program that lists values of any function $y = f(x)$ for $x = A$ to $x = B$ in increments of C.

```
10 REM PROGRAM TO PRINT TABLE OF FUNCTIONAL VALUES
20 INPUT "ENDPOINTS A AND B OF DOMAIN", A, B
30 INPUT "STEP SIZE"; C
40 PRINT "X", "Y"
50 FOR X = A TO B STEP C
60      REM TYPE IN YOUR OWN FUNCTION AT LINE 70
70      Y =
80      PRINT X, Y
90 NEXT X
100 END
```

To use this program, first type the formula for y as a function of x in line 70. Then each time you run the program, enter values for A, B, and C when prompted.

Example 2 From the graph in Example 1 you know that the polynomial

$$P(x) = 10x^4 + 15x^3 + 14x^2 + 20x - 78$$

has a zero between $x = 1$ and $x = 2$. Use the program above to estimate this zero to the nearest hundredth.

Solution Load the program above, and for line 70 type

$$Y = 10*X^4 + 15*X^3 + 14*X^2 + 20*X - 78$$

Run the program using $A = 1$ and $B = 2$. A step size of 0.1 will locate the zero to the tenths place. Our output is as follows:

```
ENDPOINTS A AND B OF DOMAIN? 1, 2
STEP SIZE? 0.1
    X          Y
    1         -19
    1.1        -4.454
    1.2        12.816
    1.3        33.176
    1.4        57.016
    1.5        84.75
    1.6       116.816
    1.7       153.676
    1.8       195.816
    1.9       243.746
    2.0       298
```

632

Note that the output shows that the *y*-values change from negative to positive as *x* changes from 1.1 to 1.2. This means that there is a zero of P between $x = 1.1$ and 1.2. Run the program again using these as the values of *A* and *B*. Make the step size 0.01. The output is as follows:

ENDPOINTS A AND B OF DOMAIN? 1.1, 1.2
STEP SIZE? 0.01

X	Y
1.1	-4.454
1.11	-2.85543
1.12	-1.22929
1.13	.424791
1.14	2.10716
1.15	3.81819
1.16	5.55823
1.17	7.32767
1.18	9.12686
1.19	10.9562
1.20	12.816

The output shows that the function has a zero between 1.12 (where the value of *y* is negative) and 1.13 (where *y* is positive). It appears to be closer to 1.13 than to 1.12. To achieve more accuracy, enter 1.12 for *A*, 1.13 for *B*, and .001 for *C*. The output is

ENDPOINTS A AND B OF DOMAIN? 1.12, 1.13
STEP SIZE? 0.001

X	Y
1.12	-1.22929
1.121	-1.06514
1.122	-.900717
1.123	-.736012
1.124	-.571027
1.125	-.405762
1.126	-.240215
1.127	-.074386
1.128	.091724
1.129	.258116
1.13	.424791

This shows there is a zero between 1.127 and 1.128. Thus, to the nearest hundredth, $x = 1.13$ is a zero of $P(x) = 10x^4 + 15x^3 + 14x^2 + 20x - 78$.

The techniques illustrated in Examples 1 and 2 for estimating zeros of functions apply to all polynomial functions. In fact they can be used with any function that is continuous on the domain $A \leq x \leq B$.

ADDITIONAL EXAMPLES

1.a. Use a function plotter to graph $f(x) = 2x^3 - x + 2$.

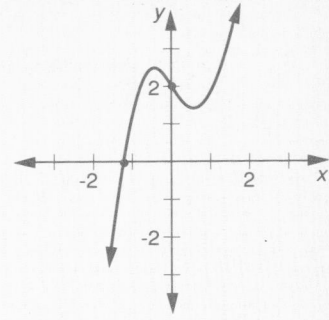

b. From the graph above, there is a zero between -2 and -1. Estimate this zero to the nearest hundredth.
-1.17.

2.a. A graph of $g(x) = 8x^3 - 20x^2 - 2x + 5$ is drawn below.

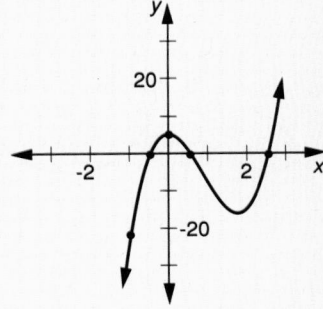

Use an automatic grapher or computer program to estimate the zeros to the nearest tenth.
zeros: ±0.5, 2.5
b. The polynomial $8x^3 - 20x^2 - 2x - 5$ is factorable over the integers. Use the result of part (a) to factor this polynomial.
g(x) =
(2x − 1)(2x + 1)(2x − 5)

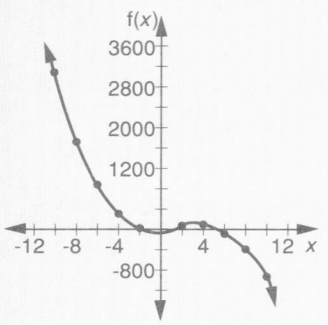
Estimating zeros of polynomials has many applications. Recall Yolanda Fish's savings (Example 2 of Lesson 11-1). With a 6% annual rate she was able to save $8942 for medical school. Suppose you wondered: What rate would Yolanda need to save $10,000? Then you would have to solve

$$1000x^4 + 1500x^3 + 1400x^2 + 2000x + 2200 = 10{,}000.$$

Here $x = 1 + r$, where r is the annual rate of interest.

■ ■ ■ ■ ■ ■ ■ ■ ■

Example 3 **a.** Solve the equation above for x.
b. Use the solution(s) to find a rate r at which Yolanda would have to invest in order to save $10,000.

Solution
a. Rewrite the equation so it is in the form $f(x) = 0$. That is, subtract 10,000 from each side.

$$1000x^4 + 1500x^3 + 1400x^2 + 2000x - 7800 = 0$$

Divide each side by 100 to simplify.

$$10x^4 + 15x^3 + 14x^2 + 20x - 78 = 0$$

Now consider the equation $y = f(x) = 10x^4 + 15x^3 + 14x^2 + 20x - 78$. This is the polynomial of Examples 1 and 2. In Example 1 we found that one zero is about -2.11; in Example 2 we found that another zero is about 1.13. Thus, $x \approx -2.11$ or $x \approx 1.13$ are solutions to Yolanda's equation

$$1000x^4 + 1500x^3 + 1400x^2 + 2000x + 2200 = 10{,}000.$$

b. $x = 1 + r$, so solve

$$1 + r \approx -2.11 \qquad \text{or} \qquad 1 + r \approx 1.13.$$
$$r \approx -3.11 \qquad \text{or} \qquad r \approx 0.13$$

Only $r \approx 0.13 = 13\%$ makes sense for an interest rate. Yolanda would need a yield of almost 13% compounded annually to save $10,000. (From the last part of Example 2 you can conclude even more specifically that $0.127 < r < 0.128$.)

In a similar way, any polynomial equation can be written in a form which asks for the zeros of a polynomial function. This is why finding zeros is so important.

634

Covering the Reading

1. Refer to the polynomial function from Examples 1–3:
$P(x) = 10x^4 + 15x^3 + 14x^2 + 20x - 78$
   a. How many zeros does the function have?   2
   b. Estimate them to the nearest hundredth. $x = -2.11, x = 1.13$

2. Describe how to estimate a zero of a function from a graph.
   The zero is the x-value where the graph crosses the x-axis.
3. Describe how to estimate a zero of a function from a table of values.
   The zero is the x-value where the y-value changes sign.
4. A graph of a polynomial function f is shown below.
   a. What is the minimum number of zeros f has?   3
   b. Between which pairs of consecutive integers must they occur?
   $-1 < x < 0; 1 < x < 2; 4 < x < 5$

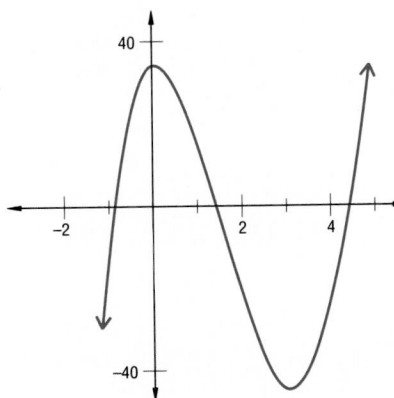

Question 6: This question stresses the fact that a sign change in consecutive y-values indicates that the graph of the function has crossed the x-axis, verifying the existence of a zero.

Question 11: Point out to students that this question asks for the value(s) of x when y = 5. Graphically, the solution is just like asking for the zeros of a function, only looking at a different horizontal line. Stress that the factor theorem cannot be applied unless one side is zero.

In 5–8, Vernon used a BASIC program like that in the lesson to obtain values of the function $f(x) = -2x^3 + 11x^2 - x - 8$ from $x = -10$ to 10, and got the output at the right.

X	Y
-10	3102
-8	1728
-6	826
-4	300
-2	54
0	-8
2	18
4	36
6	-50
8	-336
10	-918

5. Sketch a graph of f.   See margin.

6. Between which pairs of consecutive even integers must the zeros of f occur?
   $-2 < x < 0; 0 < x < 2; 4 < x < 6$
7. Estimate the largest zero to the nearest tenth.   5.3

8. Estimate the smallest zero to the nearest tenth.   -.8

9. The solutions to the equation $-2x^3 + 4x^2 = 1$ are equal to the zeros of which function?
   $f(x) = -2x^3 + 4x^2 - 1$
10. Refer to Example 3. Using either a graph or a table of values, determine r, the rate of interest Yolanda Fish would need to save $9500. Give your answer to the nearest whole percent.   10%

Question 22: Point out that to describe the end behavior of a function, the student must write *two* sentences—one stating what happens to y when x is very large, another stating the effect on y when x is very small. In part (d), students may need to be convinced as to the behavior of the function in this question. They should realize that as x gets very large m(x) gets very large, but they may need to try examples of x getting very small to determine the behavior of m(x).

LESSON 11-5   *Estimating Zeros of Polynomial Functions*   **635**

11. $x \approx -.8$ and $x \approx 2.3$

12.a.

x	A(x)
1	1.043
2	1.996
3	2.769
4	3.272
5	3.415
6	3.108
7	2.261
8	0.784

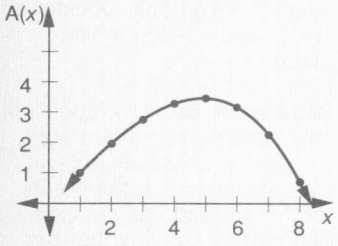

18.a.

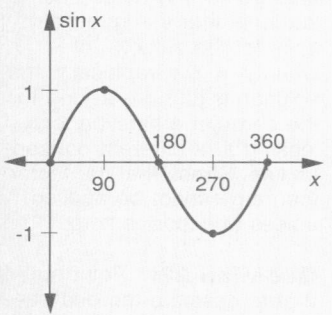

11. As shown below, there are two values of x between -2 and 4 at which the graphs of $y = 5$ and $y = -x^4 + 3x^3 - 3x^2 + x + 10$ intersect. Use a function plotter to estimate these values to the nearest tenth.   **See margin.**

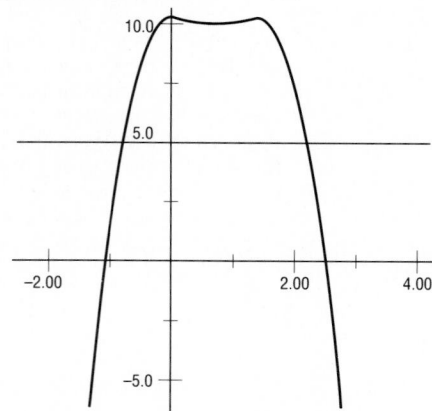

12. The polynomial function A defined by

$$A(x) = -.015x^3 + 1.058x$$

gives the approximate alcohol concentration (in tenths of a percent) in an average person's bloodstream x hr after drinking about 8 oz of 100 proof whiskey.

a. Graph $y = A(x)$.   **See margin.**
b. From the graph estimate the number of hours necessary for the alcohol concentration to revert back to 0.   **between 8 and 9 hours**
c. Check your answer to part b by solving $A(x) = 0$. (The function A is approximately valid for x between 0 and 8, so be careful how you interpret this answer.) $x \approx 8.4$ **hours**
d. Using the graph, estimate the time at which the alcohol concentration was the greatest. $x = 5$ **hours**
e. In some countries a person is legally drunk if the blood alcohol concentration exceeds 0.07%. Use your graph to estimate the length of time in which this average person is legally drunk.
8 hours

In 13 and 14, multiply and simplify. *(Lesson 11-2)*

13. $(x^2 - y^2)(x^2 + y^2)$ $x^4 - y^4$ **14.** $(a + b + c)(a - b)$ $a^2 - b^2 + ac - bc$

In 15–17, factor. *(Lesson 11-3)*

15. $4x^2 - 12x + 9$ $(2x - 3)^2$ **16.** $x^3 + 8y^6$ $(x + 2y^2)(x^2 - 2xy^2 + 4y^4)$

17. $100n^4 - 100$ $100(n^2 + 1)(n + 1)(n - 1)$

636

18. a. Graph f(x) = sin x, 0° ≤ x ≤ 360°.   **See margin.**
   b. For what value(s) of x in this domain does f(x) = 0?   *(Lesson 10-9)*
   x = 0, x = 180, x =360

19. Consider square MATH shown at the right. Show using slope that the diagonals of MATH are perpendicular to each other. *(Lesson 4-7)*
   slope of $\overline{MT}$ = -1, slope of $\overline{AH}$ = 1; (-1)(1) = -1

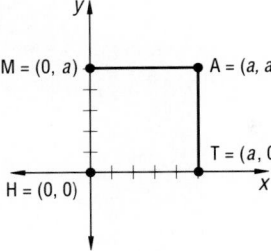

20. Suppose that the lateral height of a cone is 6 cm and its height is *h*.

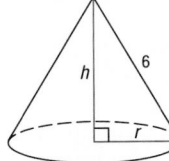

$$r = \sqrt{36 - h^2}$$

   a. Express the radius *r* of the cone in terms of *h*. *(Previous course)*
   b. Write a formula for V(*h*), the volume of the cone as a function of *h*. *(Lesson 11-2)*   **$V(h) = 12\pi h - \frac{1}{3}h^3$**

Exploration

21. Which is largest, $\dfrac{\frac{1}{2}}{\frac{3}{4}}$, $\dfrac{1}{\frac{2}{\frac{3}{4}}}$, $\dfrac{\frac{\frac{1}{2}}{3}}{4}$, or $\dfrac{1}{\frac{2}{\frac{\frac{1}{2}}{3}}}$?

22. The *end behavior* of a function refers to the values of a function f: x → y when |x| is very large. The values get larger and larger, that is, more and more positive, or get smaller and smaller, that is, more and more negative. (For instance, in Example 2, when x is very large, h(x) gets larger and larger. When x is very small, h(x) gets smaller and smaller.) Describe the end behavior of each function.   **See below.**
   a. the function f of Questions 5–8
   b. g(x) = 3x⁴ − 100x + 600
   c. y = 2x⁷
   d. m(x) = x⁶ − x⁵ + x⁴ − x³ + x² − x + 1

21. The end behavior is determined by the leading coefficient. (a) As x gets small, f(x) gets large; as x gets large, f(x) gets small. (b) As x gets small, g(x) gets large; as x gets large, g(x) gets large. (c) As x gets small, y gets small, as x gets large, y gets large. (d) As x gets small, m(x) gets large; as x gets large, m(x) gets large.

LESSON 11-5   Estimating Zeros of Polynomial Functions   **637**

FOLLOW-UP

MORE PRACTICE
For more questions on SPUR Objectives, use *Lesson Master 11-5*, shown below.

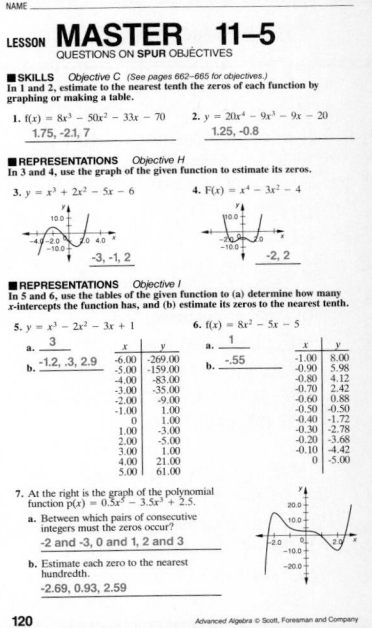

OBJECTIVES

C Calculate or estimate roots of polynomial functions.
F Apply the Fundamental Theorem of Algebra and the Number of Roots of a Polynomial Equation Theorem to analyze polynomial equations.
I Read and generate computer output to graph or find zeros of polynomials.

TEACHING NOTES

You may want to start the lesson by having students solve a linear equation ($2x + 5 = 18$), a quadratic ($3x^2 + x - 5 = 0$), a cubic ($x^3 + 27 = 0$), and perhaps a quartic ($x^4 - 1 = 0$). A discussion of the solutions to these equations can easily lead to a discussion of the two theorems in this lesson, which are easy to conjecture but difficult to prove.

Point out that although The Number of Roots of a Polynomial Equation Theorem tells us *how many* roots a polynomial equation has, it does not explain how to find them. It is an existence theorem.

Cardano   *Tartaglia*

You know a way to find an exact solution to any linear equation with real coefficients. To solve any quadratic equation exactly, there is the Quadratic Formula. But that formula requires new numbers, the complex numbers. The formula works even with those quadratic equations having complex coefficients. In the last lesson you learned that all polynomial equations can be solved using either graphs or tables of values. It is natural to wonder whether all polynomial equations can be solved *exactly* and whether any new types of numbers are needed to solve them.

These questions occupied mathematicians even before today's notation for polynomials was invented. In the sixteenth century a number of Italian mathematicians began to answer these questions. Scipione del Ferro (1465–1526) discovered how to solve all cubic equations exactly. (His method is too complicated to be discussed in this book.) Perhaps independently, by about 1541 Niccolo Tartaglia (1500–1557) learned to solve cubic equations by the same method. Girolamo Cardano, whom we have mentioned in Lessons 6–8 and 6–10, published del Ferro's method in 1545 in his book *Ars magna*. About the same time, Cardano's secretary, Ludovico Ferrari (1522–1565), discovered how to solve any *quartic* (fourth degree polynomial) equation. Cardano also published this result in *Ars magna*. The amazing thing was that you didn't need to learn any new types of numbers to solve cubic or quartic equations. Then, for the next 250 years mathematicians tried unsuccessfully to find a formula for solving any *quintic* (fifth degree polynomial) equation. Perhaps new numbers were needed.

638

However, new numbers are not needed. In 1797, at the age of 18, the great German mathematician Karl Gauss proved the following theorem.

The Fundamental Theorem of Algebra:

Every polynomial equation P(x) = 0 of any degree with complex number coefficients has at least one complex number solution.

(Remember that complex numbers include the reals.) From the Fundamental Theorem of Algebra, and the Factor Theorem, it is possible to prove that *every solution* to a polynomial equation is a complex number. Thus, no new type of number is needed to solve higher degree polynomials. So, for instance, the solutions to $x^5 + 3x^3 - ix^2 + 4 - 3i = 0$ are complex numbers.

How many complex solutions does a given polynomial have? Recall that the linear equation $ax + b = 0$ has one root: $x = -\frac{b}{a}$. The quadratic equation $ax^2 + bx + c = 0$ generally has two roots: $x = \frac{-b \pm \sqrt{b^2 - 4ac}}{2a}$. However, when the discriminant is 0, the two roots are equal. When this happens this root is considered to be a *double root* or a *root of multiplicity 2*. For instance, when $x^2 - 8x + 16 = 0$, then $x = \frac{-(-8) \pm \sqrt{(-8)^2 - 4(1)(16)}}{2(1)} = \frac{8 \pm \sqrt{0}}{2} = 4$. So $x = 4$ is the only root of $x^2 - 8x + 16 = 0$, but the number 4 is said to be a double root.

Notice that $x^2 - 8x + 16 = (x - 4)^2$; that is, $x - 4$ appears twice as a factor. The **multiplicity of a root** r is the highest power of $x - r$ that appears as a factor of the polynomial. For instance, the equation $(x - 3)^{10} = 0$ is an equation with only one root, 3, but the root has multiplicity 10.

Recall the Factor Theorem: if r is a root of a polynomial equation P(x) = 0, then $(x - r)$ is a factor of P(x). Another way to state this is to say that if r is a root of the polynomial equation P(x) = 0, there is some polynomial Q(x) such that P(x) = $(x - r) \cdot$ Q(x) and the degree of Q(x) is one less than the degree of P(x). For instance, when P(x) is cubic, then Q(x) is quadratic. This implies that when P(x) is cubic, P(x) = 0 has three roots: one from the linear factor $(x - r)$, and two from the quadratic factor Q(x). Of course, one of these might be a multiple root.

1. Find all the solutions of
$x^4 + 10x^3 + 25x^2 = 0$.
0 and -5 are each double roots.

2. How many roots does each of the following equations have?
a. $x^{15} + 1 = 0$
15
b. $\sqrt{2}x^4 - 3x^2 + \pi = 0$
4

3. Refer to Lesson 11-5, Example 1. How many real solutions are there to $P(x) = 0$?
2

Similarly, 4th degree polynomials can be rewritten as the product of a linear and a cubic polynomial, or of two quadratic polynomials. Thus, 4th degree polynomial equations have 4 complex roots. By extending this pattern we know we can express any higher degree polynomial equation as a product of lower degree polynomials.

■ ■ ■ ■ ■ ■ ■ ■ ■

Example 1   **a.** Find all solutions of $x^5 - 8x^2 = 0$.
b. Are any multiple roots? If so, which?

Solution   **a.** Factor out the common factor x^2.

$$x^5 - 8x^2 = x^2(x^3 - 8)$$

Now factor the cubic into a linear and quadratic factor.

$$x^5 - 8x^2 = x^2(x - 2)(x^2 + 2x + 4)$$

Thus, $x^5 - 8x^2 = 0$ if and only if $x = 0$, $x = 2$, or $x^2 + 2x + 4 = 0$. The solutions to $x^2 + 2x + 4 = 0$ can be found by the Quadratic Formula. They are $-1 \pm i\sqrt{3}$. Thus, $x^5 - 8x^2 = 0$ has five roots— three real and two nonreal: $0, 0, 2, -1 + i\sqrt{3}, -1 - i\sqrt{3}$.

b. The number 0 is a double root.

These instances can be summarized in the following theorem.

The Number of Roots of a Polynomial Equation Theorem:

Every polynomial equation of degree n has exactly n roots, provided that multiple roots are counted as separate roots.

■ ■ ■ ■ ■ ■ ■ ■

Example 2   How many roots does each of the following equations have?
a. $x^5 - 7x^3 + 15x^2 + 3 = 10$
b. $-2ix^4 - ex^2 + \pi x - 12 = 0$

Solution
a. The degree is 5, so the equation has 5 roots.
b. The degree is 4, so the equation has 4 roots.

The question of whether a formula exists for solving all quintic equations was finally settled in 1799 by an Italian mathematician, Paolo Ruffini (1767–1822). He proved that the general quintic equation cannot be solved by formulas. A Norwegian mathematician, Niels Henrik Abel (1802–1829), made the same discovery independently in 1824.

Perhaps the most important discovery about solving polynomial equations was made by a Frenchman, Évariste Galois (1811–1832). The night before he was killed in a duel, Galois wrote a letter which

640

Évariste Galois

included some important mathematical discoveries. In it, Galois showed a method to determine which polynomial equations of degree five or more can be solved exactly using formulas. We now know that there are no methods for finding exact solutions of all polynomials of degree higher than four.

The two theorems of this Lesson tell you how many roots a polynomial equation $P(x) = k$ has, and that all roots can be expressed as complex numbers. They do not tell you how to find the roots, nor do they tell you how many of the roots are real. To answer these questions, you can apply the methods studied in the last two lessons for finding zeros of polynomial functions.

■ ■ ■ ■ ■ ■ ■ ■ ■

Example 3 Consider the equation from Example 2(a),

$$x^5 - 7x^3 + 15x^2 + 3 = 10.$$

How many of its solutions are real?

Solution Set one side of the equation equal to zero, by subtracting 10 from each side.

$$x^5 - 7x^3 + 15x^2 - 7 = 0$$

The solutions to this equation are the zeros of the function $f(x) = x^5 - 7x^3 + 15x^2 - 7$. Use approximation methods from Lesson 11-5. First, look at the behavior of the function over a large domain. We show both a table and a graph below.

x	y
-50	-311587507
-40	-101928007
-30	-24097507
-20	-3138007
-10	-91507
0	-7
10	94493
20	3149993
30	24124493
40	101975993
50	311662493

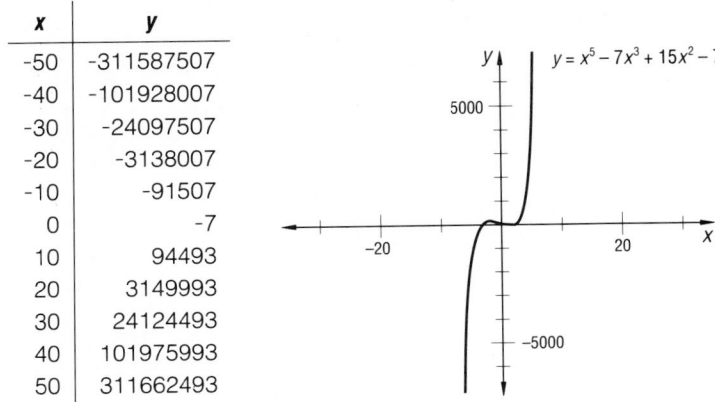

Observe the sign changes in y-values. The graph and table together show that a zero or zeros occur between $x = -10$ and $x = 10$. Also, when $x < -10$ or $x > 10$, the value of x^5 dominates the value of $f(x)$, so there are no zeros outside $-10 < x < 10$. Another search shows that zeros occur on the intervals $-4 \le x \le -3$, $-1 \le x \le 0$, and $0 \le x \le 1$.

Question 11: Ask students why this equation cannot have a positive root. (The left side would be positive and not equal zero.) Then ask if the equation can have a negative root. (No, because the left side would be negative and not equal to zero.) Thus, the roots of this polynomial are 0 or nonreal.

Question 12: Ask students why this equation cannot have a real root. (The left side would be a nonreal complex number and could not equal 12.)

Question 17: Students may need to be reminded that $x^3 + 1$ can be factored as the sum of two cubes.

ADDITIONAL ANSWERS
2. every polynomial equation of any degree with complex coefficients has at least one complex number solution

14.b. $x \approx -1.3$, $x \approx -.6$, $x \approx 1.4$

21.b. $n \approx .75$

22. $y - 4 = 3(x + 3)^2$

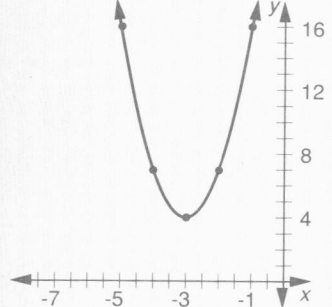

x	y
-5	-1882
-4	-343
-3	74
-2	77
-1	14
0	-7
1	2
2	29
3	182

$y = x^5 - 7x^3 + 15x^2 - 7$

Thus, there are three real roots. The other two roots are nonreal and are not indicated on this graph.

Further use of tables or graphs shows that, to the nearest tenth, $f(x) = x^5 - 7x^3 + 15x^2 - 7$ has zeros at -3.4, -0.6, and 0.8.

Questions

Covering the Reading

1. Name three 16th-century mathematicians who worked on solving cubic or quartic equations.
   Scipione del Ferrro, Niccolo Tartaglia, Ludovico Ferrari

2. The Fundamental Theorem of Algebra states that __?__.   See margin.

3. Who proved the Fundamental Theorem of Algebra?   Karl Gauss

In 4 and 5, a ≠ 0. Solve for x.

4. $ax + b = 0$ $x = -\dfrac{b}{a}$

5. $ax^2 + bx + c = 0$ $x = \dfrac{-b \pm \sqrt{b^2 - 4ac}}{2a}$

In 6–8: **a.** solve for x by factoring the polynomial; and **b.** identify any multiple roots.

6. $x^2 - 10x + 25 = 0$
   a. x = 5; b. x = 5

7. $x^3 - 25x = 0$
   See margin.

8. $x^3 - 8 = 0$
   See margin.

9. Every polynomial equation of degree n has exactly __?__ roots, provided that __?__.   n, multiple roots are counted as separate roots

10. *True or false* All solutions to polynomial equations are complex numbers.   true

In 11 and 12, state the number of roots each equation has. Do not solve.

11. $x^5 + x^3 + x = 0$ 5

12. $17y^2 + \pi y^7 + iy^3 = 12$ 7

13. State one result about polynomials discovered by Galois.
    How to determine which polynomials of degree ≥ 5 can be solved exactly using formulas.

14. Consider the equation $2x^5 - 3x^3 - x = 1$.
    a. How many solutions does it have?   5
    b. Approximate the real solutions to the nearest tenth by using tables or graphs.   See margin.

642

In 15 and 16, solve.

15. $-3x + 7i = 0$ $x = \frac{7}{3}i$ **16.** $2ix^2 + 8x + 5i = 0$ $\frac{-4 \pm \sqrt{26}}{2i}$

17. The equation $x^3 + 1 = 0$ is equivalent to $x^3 = -1$. Thus, the roots of $x^3 + 1 = 0$ can be considered cube roots of -1.
  a. Find all cube roots of 1. $1, \frac{-1 + i\sqrt{3}}{2}, \frac{-1 - i\sqrt{3}}{2}$
  b. In Question 8, you are finding the cube roots of __?__.   8

18. One root of $x^3 - 8x^2 + 22x - 20 = 0$ is 2. Find all the other roots.
  $3 + i, 3 - i$
19. Find all the roots of $z^4 - 1 = 0$ by factoring and solving the resulting equations. $(z^2 + 1)(z + 1)(z - 1) = 0; z = i, -i, 1, -1$

20. A table of values for a polynomial function g is given at the right.
  a. What is the minimum number of zeros g may have?   4
  b. Between which pairs of consecutive integers must they occur? *(Lesson 11-5)*
  $-3 < x < -2; -1 < x < 0; 1 < x < 2; 3 < x < 4$

x	y
-5	544
-4	164
-3	4
-2	-32
-1	-16
0	4
1	4
2	-16
3	-32
4	4
5	164

21. The sum of the cube and the square of a number is 1.
  a. Let n equal this number. Write a polynomial equation that can be used to find n.
  (Lesson 11-1) $p(n) = n^3 + n^2 - 1$
  b. To the nearest hundredth, what is that number? (Hint: Draw a graph or make a table.) *(Lesson 11-5)* $n \approx .75$

22. Graph and state an equation of the image of $y = 3x^2$ under $T_{-3,4}$.
  (Lessons 2-5, 4-9, 6-1)   See margin.

23. A person sights a pier directly across a river, then walks 100′ and sights the pier at an angle of 70°. How wide is the river at the pier?
  (Lesson 10-1)   about 275 ft

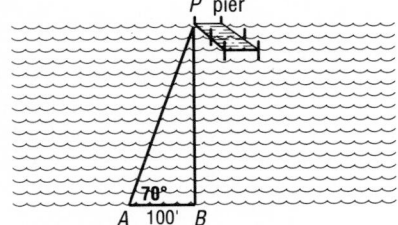

In 24–27, solve.

24. $\log x = 5$ *(Lesson 9-4)* $x = 100{,}000$
25. $e^x = 5$ *(Lessons 9-7, 9-8)* $x \approx 1.609$
26. $\sin x = 5$ *(Lesson 10-2)*   no solution
27. $\sqrt{x} = 5$ *(Lesson 6-1)* $x = 25$

28. A theorem called the "Fundamental Theorem of Algebra" is discussed in this lesson. There is also a theorem called the "Fundamental Theorem of Arithmetic." Look in a dictionary to find out what theorem this is. (You probably know it but didn't know it has this name.)   Any positive integer other than 1 can be written as a unique product of prime numbers.

MORE PRACTICE
For more questions on SPUR Objectives, use *Lesson Master 11-6*, shown below.

EXTENSION
Let $F(x) = 2x^3 - 3x^2 - 11x + 6$. A theorem known as the Rational Root Theorem states that any possible rational roots of F must be of the form $\pm \frac{a}{b}$ where b is a factor of 2 and a is a factor of 6. So the possible rational roots are $\pm 6, \pm 3, \pm 2, \pm \frac{3}{2}, \pm \frac{1}{2}, \pm 1$. Have students check to see if any are roots of F. ($\frac{1}{2}$, 3, -2 are roots.)

Graphing this polynomial on an automatic grapher reduces the number of checks. The grapher shows that $\frac{1}{2}$, 3, -2 are the only possible rational intercepts. These are verified by substituting into the equation.

NAME _____

LESSON **MASTER 11-6**
QUESTIONS ON **SPUR** OBJECTIVES

■ **SKILLS** *Objective C (See pages 662–665 for objectives.)*
In 1 and 2, (a) solve for x by factoring the polynomial, and (b) identify any multiple roots.

1. $x^2 + 20x + 100 = 0$
  $(x + 10)(x + 10);$
  a. $x = -10$
  b. -10

2. $x^4 - 25x^2 = 0$
  $x^2(x^2 - 25) = 0;$
  a. $x = 0, 5, -5$
  b. 0

■ **PROPERTIES** *Objective F*
In 3–6, state the number of roots each equation has. Do not solve.

3. $-3x^6 - 2x^2 + x - 1 = 0$ 6
4. $\pi^2 - x^5 + i^6 = 0$ 5
5. $(x - 8)(5 - x)(2 - 5x) = 0$ 3
6. $(3 - x) + 7(x - 2) = 0$ 1

7. State the Fundamental Theorem of Algebra.
  Every polynomial equation $P(x) = 0$ of any degree with complex coefficients has at least one complex solution.

■ **REPRESENTATIONS** *Objective I*
8. Refer to the graph of $f(x) = x^4 - 1$ at the right.

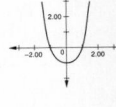

  a. How many zeros does the function have?   4
  b. Name the real zeros of this function.   1, -1
  c. How many nonreal zeros does this function have?   2

OBJECTIVE

D Determine an equation for a polynomial function from data points using the Polynomial Difference Theorem.

TEACHING NOTES

Point out that the Polynomial Difference Theorem does not give a method for finding a specific formula, but it does let us know which type of polynomial, if any, will model the data.

Stress to students that the fact that a polynomial equation does not exist for certain data does not mean that no equation exists. The data could be described by a logarithmic, an exponential, a trigonometric, or any number of other functions.

ADDITIONAL EXAMPLES
In addition to the real-world applications studied earlier in the chapter, polynomials arise in a number of games or puzzles. Discuss some of these and ask students to predict if a polynomial models the situation. (The actual equations are also provided; these can be used when doing Lesson 11-8.) You may want to organize students into **small groups** and provide a type of laboratory structure for the class period. Stress to students that these puzzles can be solved more easily by first *considering a simpler problem*.

LESSON 11-7

Finite Differences

You have seen many instances in this book where mathematics is used to model real life situations. In some cases it helps to graph data points. Graphs can often be used to find an equation to describe the situation.

In Chapter 2 you used this idea in the context of variation models. Consider the following data points:

W	0	10	20	30	40
N	0	50	200	450	800

If you graphed them as below, you might say that N varies directly as the square of W because the graph looks like a parabola through the origin. This would give the equation $N = kW^2$, which is a quadratic polynomial function.

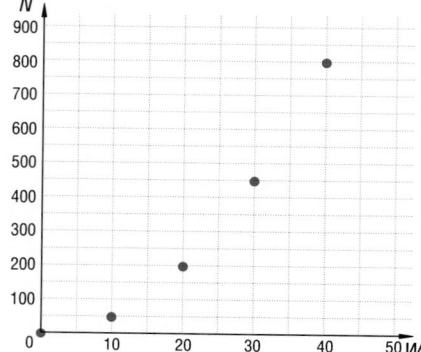

As you have seen, other equations may have graphs which resemble the one above. Is it possible to determine in a conclusive way which equation fits? When the function is a polynomial function, the answer is yes.

To see why this is true, we need to look at some polynomial functions. First, consider a linear polynomial function like $y = 4x + 5$. Choose consecutive integer values of x, such as 1, 2, 3, 4, 5, ... Find the corresponding values of the polynomial.

x	1	2	3	4	5	...
$y = 4x + 5$	9	13	17	21	25	...

Now take the differences of the consecutive y-values (right minus left).

$$9 \quad\quad 13 \quad\quad 17 \quad\quad 21 \quad\quad 25 \ldots$$
$$4 \quad\quad 4 \quad\quad 4 \quad\quad 4 \quad\quad \ldots$$

Note that the differences are all equal or constant.

644

Next consider a quadratic polynomial function like $y = 5x^2$. For x use the consecutive integer values 1, 2, 3, 4, 5, 6, ... As before, find the values of the polynomial and find the differences of consecutive terms.

x	1	2	3	4	5	6	...
$y = 5x^2$	5	20	45	80	125	180	...

1st differences   15   25   35   45   55   ...

The differences are not all equal, but notice what happens if differences are taken a second time.

        15   25   35   45   55   ...

2nd differences   10   10   10   10   ...

The 2nd differences are all equal.

Consider the cubic polynomial function $h(x) = x^3 - 5x^2 + 10x + 50$. Let us try the method of differences again, using -1, 0, 1, 2, 3, 4, and 5 for x and the corresponding values of $h(x)$.

x	-1	0	1	2	3	4	5	...
$h(x)$	34	50	56	58	62	74	100	...

1st differences   16   6   2   4   12   26   ...

2nd differences   -10   -4   2   8   14   ...

3rd differences   6   6   6   6   ...

In this case the 3rd differences are equal.

Do all polynomial functions eventually lead to constant differences? The answer is yes, if the x-values form an arithmetic sequence. Consider again the linear function of $y = 4x + 5$ from the previous page. For x-values, use the arithmetic sequence -2, 1, 4, 7, 10, ...

x	-2	1	4	7	10	...
$y = 4x + 5$	-3	9	21	33	45	...

1st differences   12   12   12   12   ...

Again the 1st differences are all equal.

---

1. *Squares on a Checkerboard.*
a. How many squares are on an 8 × 8 checkerboard?
Count the number of 1 × 1 squares, 2 × 2 squares, 3 × 3 squares, and so on.

n = dimension of side of board	f(n) = number of squares
1	1
2	5
3	14
4	30
5	55
6	91
7	140
8	204

b. Let f(n) = the number of squares on an $n \times n$ checkerboard. Is f(n) a polynomial function? Justify your answer.
Yes. Third differences are constant. A cubic polynomial predicts the number of squares. It can be shown that
$$f(n) = \tfrac{1}{3}n^3 + \tfrac{1}{2}n^2 + \tfrac{1}{6}n.$$

2. *Tower of Hanoi.* In this game, three pegs are perpendicular to a base board. On one of the pegs are five to seven graduated disks. The object is to move all the disks to another peg. You are allowed to move only one disk at a time, and you may never put a large disk on top of a smaller one.

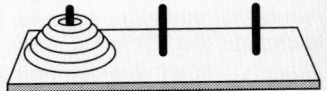

a. What is the minimum number of moves required to move five disks?
31
b. Let t(n) = the minimum number of moves for n disks. Is t(n) a polynomial function? Justify your answer.

n	1	2	3	4	5	6	7
t(n)	1	3	7	15	31	63	127

No. There are no constant differences. Each set of differences is 2, 4, 8, 16, ... It can be shown that t(n) = $2^n - 1$.

3. *Oxbow Puzzle.* This puzzle usually consists of a wooden board in the shape of an oxbow, on which there are nine shallow indentations. You are given eight marbles, four of one color and four of another. You align the marbles separated by color on either side of the center depression. The object is to reverse the order of the colors by moving only one marble at a time. The only allowable moves are forward to the adjoining empty space or forward jumping over one marble of another color to the empty space.

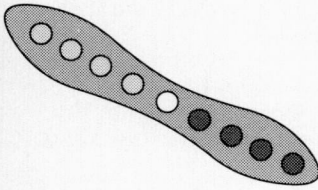

a. What is the minimum number of moves needed to exchange the four marbles of each color?
24

n	1	2	3	4
f(n)	3	8	15	24

b. Suppose you were to use *n* marbles of each color. What kind of equation models the relation between *n* and f(*n*), the minimum number of moves needed to exchange the colors?
The second differences are constant, so a quadratic model fits. In the next lesson, students will learn how to find the equation $f(n) = n^2 + 2n$ which describes the number of moves.

Each of these examples is an instance of the following theorem. Its proof requires ideas from calculus beyond the scope of this book, and so is omitted.

Polynomial Difference Theorem:

$y = f(x)$ is a polynomial function of degree *n* if and only if, for any set of *x*-values that forms an arithmetic sequence, the *n*th differences of corresponding *y*-values are equal and non-zero.

The Polynomial Difference Theorem is important for at least two reasons. First, it indicates that functions known to be polynomial eventually yield differences which are all equal. Second, it provides a technique to determine whether a function expressed as data points is a polynomial. The technique suggested by this theorem is called **finite differences.** That is, from a table of *y*-values corresponding to an arithmetic sequence of *x*-values, take differences of consecutive *y*-values. Only if those differences are eventually constant is the function polynomial.

Example 1 Consider the data points at the beginning of the lesson. Use the method of finite differences to show that N is a polynomial function of *W* with degree 2.

Solution Notice that the values of the independent variable *W* form an arithmetic sequence, so the Polynomial Difference Theorem applies.

W	0	10	20	30	40	...
N	0	50	200	450	800	...

1st differences	50	150	250	350	...
2nd differences		100	100	100	...

N is a polynomial function of *W* because the differences eventually are all equal. Because the 2nd differences are equal, the degree of the polynomial is 2. Notice that all differences after the second differences will be zero.

Calculating differences can also be used to tell when a sequence cannot be described with an explicit polynomial formula.

646

■ ■ ■ ■ ■ ■ ■ ■ ■

Example 2 The recursive formula

$$a_1 = 4$$
$$a_{n+1} = 2a_n - 1, n > 1$$

generates the sequence

4, 7, 13, 25, 49, 97, 193, ...

Is there an explicit polynomial formula for this sequence?

Solution Take differences between consecutive terms.

n	1	2	3	4	5	6	7	...
a_n	4	7	13	25	49	97	193	...

1st differences   3   6   12   24   48   96   ...
2nd differences   3   6   12   24   48   ...

The pattern will continue to repeat and will never yield constant differences. So there is no polynomial formula.

In the next lesson you will learn how to find the equation for a function given as data points once you determine it to be polynomial.

Questions

Covering the Reading

In 1–3, refer to the Polynomial Difference Theorem.

1. If the y-values are all equal and nonzero for the 10th set of differences of consecutive x-values, what is the degree of the polynomial?   10

2. *True or false*   The technique of finite differences takes only the differences of consecutive x-values.
False; any arithmetic progression will serve.

3. State two reasons why this theorem is important.   **See margin.**

In 4 and 5, refer to Example 1.

4. How do we know that N is a polynomial function of W?
The second differences are equal.

5. Why must the degree of the polynomial be 2?
The second differences are equal.

6. Refer to Example 2. Write the values of the 3rd differences.
3, 6, 12, 24, 48, ...

NOTES ON QUESTIONS
Questions 11 and 12: These questions review recursive sequences.

Question 14: Be sure to work through this question with students as it previews Lesson 11-8.

Question 24: This reviews solving a simple 3 × 3 system in preparation for Lesson 11-8. Do not skip it.

Question 27: Let students know that there is an infinite number of answers to this question. They should start with differences of 30 and work backwards to find a sequence.

ADDITIONAL ANSWERS
3. The theorem proves that polynomial functions eventually yield equal differences, and provides a test to show whether a sequence can be modeled by a polynomial function.

LESSON 11-7 *Finite Differences*   **647**

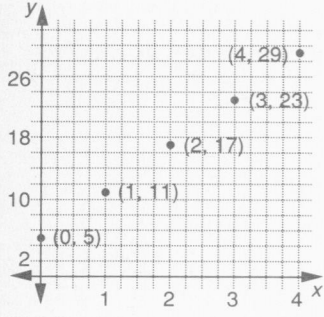
In 7–9, use the data points listed in each table below.
  a. Determine if y is a polynomial function of x of degree less than 6.
  b. Find the degree, if the function is a polynomial.

7.

x	1	2	3	4	5	6	7	8	9
y	3	11	31	69	131	223	351	521	739

a. yes, $y = p(x)$;
b. 3

8.

x	0	1	2	3	4	5	6	7	8	9
y	1	1	3	7	15	31	63	127	255	511

a. no, $y \neq p(x)$;
b. does not apply

9.

x	1	4	9	16	25	36	49	64	81	100
y	1	2	3	4	5	6	7	8	9	10

a. no, $y \neq p(x)$; b. does not apply

10. a. How many times will it take to get equal differences for the polynomial function $y = x^4 + x^2$? The fourth differences will be equal.
  b. Construct a table of x and y values for the above function for integer values of x between -3 and 4. See margin.
  c. Use the technique of finite differences to justify your response to part a. See margin.

In 11 and 12, (a) generate the first seven terms of the sequence. (b) Tell whether the sequence can be described explicitly by a polynomial function. (c) If it can, state its degree. See margin.

11. $a_1 = 7$;
  $a_{n+1} = a_n + 3$ for $n \geq 1$

12. $a_1 = 4$;
  $a_{n+1} = 2a_n + 1$ for $n \geq 1$

13. a. Find the values of the first differences of the function represented by the data points below. 6, 6, 6, ...

x	0	1	2	3	4
y	5	11	17	23	29

  b. Find the degree of the function. 1
  c. Plot the data points. See margin. $y = 6x + 5$
  d. Find an equation for the line passing through these points.
  e. Make a generalization about what first differences represent on this graph. Does your generalization apply to other linear functions? See margin.

14. a. If $f(x) = ax^2 + bx + c$, find f(1), f(2), f(3), f(4), and f(5). See margin.
  b. Prove that the 2nd differences of these values are constant. See margin.

15. Consider the following pattern:

$f(1) = 1^2 = 1$
$f(2) = 1^2 + 2^2 = 5$
$f(3) = 1^2 + 2^2 + 3^2 = 14$
$f(4) = 1^2 + 2^2 + 3^2 + 4^2 = 30$
and so on.

  a. Find f(5) and f(6). F(5) = 55; F(6) = 91
  b. Using the Polynomial Difference Theorem, what is the degree of the polynomial $f(n)$? 3

648

16. Consider the polynomial sequence
$$4, 15, 38, 79, 144, 239, \ldots .$$
By using finite differences, predict the next term.
The third differences are all 6. Working from that, the next term is 370.

Review

In 17–20, consider the function $y = x^3 + x^2 - 144x - 144$. Computer-generated coordinate values for it are shown at the right.
(Lessons 11-5, 11-4, 11-3)

X	Y
-10	396
-8	560
-6	540
-4	384
-2	140
0	-144
2	-420
4	-640
6	-756
8	-720
10	-484

17. According to the Fundamental Theorem of Algebra, how many zeros does the function have? Justify your answer.   *3, since the degree is 3*

18. According to the table, between which two even numbers must a zero occur?
-2 < x < 0

19. Sketch a graph of this function. Number the x-axis by ones and the y-axis by hundreds.
See margin.

20. Find a zero of this function to the nearest tenth.   *-1, 12, or -12*

21. Consider the equation $x^4 - x^3 + 5x^2 = 200\pi$.
  a. How many solutions does it have?   *4*
  b. Approximate its real solutions to the nearest tenth. *(Lesson 11-5)*
  5.0, -4.6

22. Find all roots of $z^3 + 125 = 0$. *(Lessons 11-3, 11-6)*
$z = -5, \dfrac{5 + 5i\sqrt{3}}{2}, \dfrac{5 - 5i\sqrt{3}}{2}$

23. Below is the graph of the polynomial function $y = (x - 1)(-x^2 + 2x + 2)$.

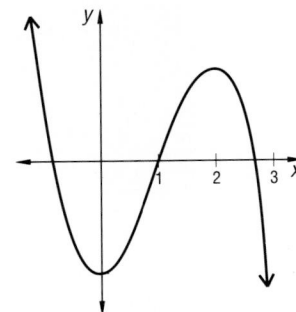

$y = p(x) = -x^3 + 3x^2 - 2$

  a. Rewrite the function in the standard form of a polynomial.
  b. How many x-intercepts does the function have? Find all of them.
  (Lessons 11-4, 11-1)
  $3; 1, 1 - \sqrt{3}, 1 + \sqrt{3}$

MORE PRACTICE
For more questions on SPUR Objectives, use *Lesson Master 11-7*, shown below.

19.

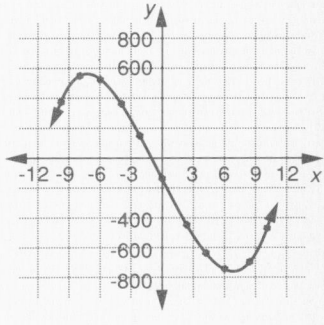

NAME _____

LESSON **MASTER** **11–7**
QUESTIONS ON **SPUR** OBJECTIVES

■ **SKILLS** *Objective D (See pages 662–665 for objectives.)*
In 1–4, (a) determine whether the given values can be described by a polynomial function of degree ≤ 5. (b) If so, give its degree.

1. The function (n, a_n) where $a_1 = -3$ and $a_{n+1} = a_n + 2$.   **a.** _yes_ **b.** _1_

2.
x	1	2	3	4	5	6	7
y	11	12	15	20	27	36	47

a. _yes_ **b.** _2_

3.
x	1	2	3	4	5	6	7
y	2	4	10	28	82	244	730

a. _no_ **b.** _____

4.
x	1	2	3	4	5	6	7
y	-1	5	11	11	-1	-31	-85

a. _yes_ **b.** _3_

5. a. How many times will it take to get equal differences of the function $y = x^3 + x^2$?   _3_

  b. Complete the table below.
x	1	2	3	4	5	6	7
y	2	12	36	80	150	252	392

  c. Use this table and finite differences to justify your answer to part (a).

  2   12   36   80   150   252   392
    10   24   44   70   102   140
      14   20   26   32   38
        6   6   6   6

6. Consider the polynomial sequence
3, 10, 43, 132, 307, ...
Use the method of finite differences to predict the next term.   _598_

24. Solve the system. *(Lesson 5-3)*

$$\begin{cases} x + 4y - 3z = 6 \\ \quad\;\; 2y + \;\; z = 9 \\ \qquad\qquad\; z = 8 \end{cases}$$

$(x, y, z) = (28, 1/2, 8)$

25. *Multiple choice*

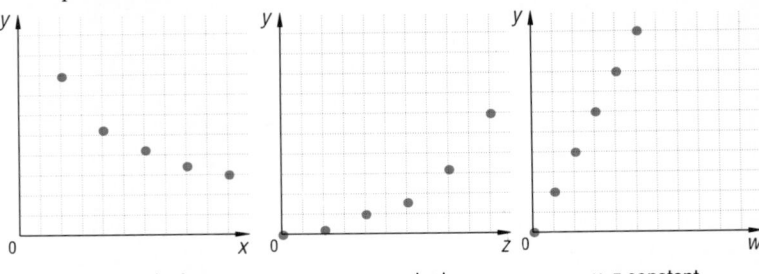

z, w constant   x, w constant   x, z constant

Which of the following equations could describe the relationships graphed above, where k is a constant? *(Lesson 2-8)*   c

(a) $y = \dfrac{kwz}{x^2}$ (b) $y = kwzx$

(c) $y = \dfrac{kwz^2}{x}$ (d) $y = \dfrac{kwx^2}{z}$

26. A window sill of a building is twelve feet above the ground. How long must a ladder be if it is to reach from the sill to the ground and form less than an 80° angle with the ground? *(Lesson 10-1)*
at least 12.19 ft

27. Find a sequence of at least 6 terms in which the 3rd differences are all 30.   sample; 1, 31, 121, 301, 601, 1051, ...

650

11-8

Modeling Data with Polynomials

LESSON 11-8

RESOURCES
- Lesson Master 11-8
- Visual for Teaching Aid 78 provides the solution for **Example 2**.

The employees at Primo's Pizzeria liked to cut pizza into odd shaped pieces. In so doing they noticed that there is a maximum number of pieces that can be formed from a given number of cuts.

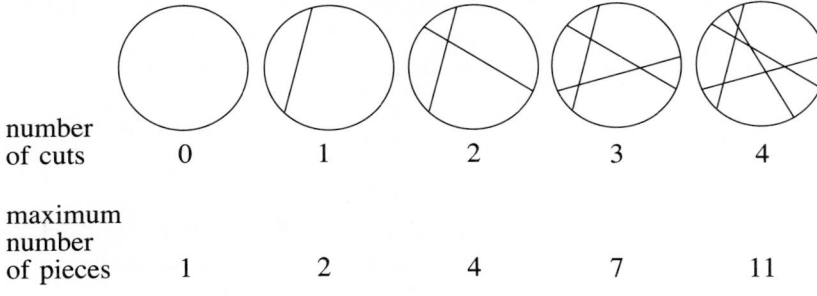

number of cuts	0	1	2	3	4
maximum number of pieces	1	2	4	7	11

Primo's employees wondered if there was a formula relating p, the maximum number of pieces that could be obtained, from x, a given number of cuts. As in the last lesson, they found differences between consecutive terms.

x	0	1	2	3	4
p	1	2	4	7	11
1st differences		1	2	3	4
2nd differences			1	1	1

Because it took two times to get equal differences, they knew that a quadratic polynomial could be used to model these points. That is, they knew that

$$p = ax^2 + bx + c$$

but they did not know a, b, or c.

OBJECTIVES

D Determine an equation for a polynomial function from data points using the Polynomial Difference Theorem.
G Use polynomials to model real-world situations.

TEACHING NOTES

Encourage students to organize their work for solving a system of three equations with three variables by using the method shown on page 652. They will be surprised to find the computations are less difficult than they appear.

Example 2 can be difficult for students to follow without help, since it involves a third degree polynomial. You may want to discuss this example with them, guiding them through the solution.

Point out that it is always advisable to check additional data points in the formula, and once it is obtained, to be certain that it is correct.

Alternate Approach If your students had trouble solving systems of equations in the past and also struggled with Question 24 in Lesson 11-7, you may want to have them solve one more simple 3 × 3 system before introducing this topic. Give them an example which is as easily done as the ones in this lesson.

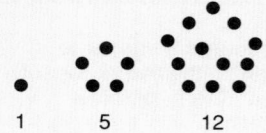
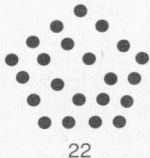
It is possible to find the values of a, b, and c by solving a system of equations. Because there are three variables, you need three equations. Solutions of the equation

$$p = ax^2 + bx + c$$

are ordered pairs of the form (x, p). Thus, to determine a system of equations substitute any data point into the equation to get a true statement. It is usually easiest to use three small values of x in an arithmetic sequence.

$$\text{When} \quad \begin{array}{ll} x = 0, \, p = 1: & 1 = a(0)^2 + b(0) + c = \quad c \\ x = 1, \, p = 2: & 2 = a(1)^2 + b(1) + c = \quad a + \, b + c \\ x = 2, \, p = 4: & 4 = a(2)^2 + b(2) + c = 4a + 2b + c \end{array}$$

This system of three equations with three variables may look hard to solve. However, the systems encountered using the technique of this lesson can be solved easily using subtraction and substitution. Here's how you can organize the work. Reorder the equations so that the largest coefficients are on the top line. You will always subtract an equation from the one above it.

$$\begin{cases} 4a + 2b + c = 4 \\ \quad a + b + c = 2 \\ \qquad\qquad c = 1 \end{cases} \rightarrow \begin{cases} 3a + b = 2 \\ \, a + b = 1 \end{cases} \rightarrow 2a = 1$$

From the equation $2a = 1$, $a = \frac{1}{2}$. Now substitute $a = \frac{1}{2}$ and $c = 1$ into $a + b + c = 2$ to get $\frac{1}{2} + b + 1 = 2$. Thus, $b = \frac{1}{2}$. Therefore, the equation

$$p = \frac{1}{2}x^2 + \frac{1}{2}x + 1$$

models the data from Primo's Pizzeria.

■ ■ ■ ■ ■ ■ ■ ■

Example 1   **a.** Show that the formula $p = \frac{1}{2}x^2 + \frac{1}{2}x + 1$ correctly describes the relation between number of cuts and maximum number of pieces for $x = 3$.

     b. Predict the maximum number of pieces that can result from 5 cuts to a pizza. Check your answer with a drawing.

Solution

a. Substitute $x = 3$ into the formula. Verify that $p = 7$, the value in the table on the previous page.

$$p = \frac{1}{2}(3)^2 + \frac{1}{2}(3) + 1$$

$$= \frac{9}{2} + \frac{3}{2} + 1$$

$$= \frac{12}{2} + 1$$

$$p = 7$$

652

b. Substitute $x = 5$.

$$p = \frac{1}{2}(5)^2 + \frac{1}{2}(5) + 1$$

$$= \frac{25}{2} + \frac{5}{2} + 1$$

$$p = 16$$

The figure below shows how to get 16 pieces of pizza with 5 cuts.

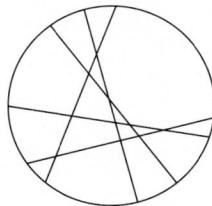

The following example shows how to use finite differences and systems of equations to handle a polynomial of higher degree.

■ ■ ■ ■ ■ ■ ■ ■ ■ ■

Example 2 A display of oranges can be stacked in a square-based pyramid in the following way: 1 orange is in the top level, 4 oranges in the second level, 9 in the third level, 16 in the fourth level, etc. How many oranges are needed for a display with n rows?

Solution First, list some values showing how the number of oranges depends on the number of rows. The total number of oranges in the display is the following:

top row	1
top two rows	$1 + 4 = 5$
top three rows	$1 + 4 + 9 = 14$
top four rows	$1 + 4 + 9 + 16 = 30$
top five rows	$1 + 4 + 9 + 16 + 25 = 55$

Second, use the method of finite differences to determine whether a polynomial model fits.

Number of Rows	1	2	3	4	5	6 ...
Number of Oranges	1	5	14	30	55	91 ...
1st Differences		4	9	16	25	36 ...
2nd Differences			5	7	9	11 ...
3rd Differences				2	2	2 ...

The 3rd differences are constant. Thus the situation can be represented by a polynomial function of degree three.

Third, use a system of equations to find a polynomial model. Let n be the number of rows and $f(n)$ the total number of oranges in n rows. We know the polynomial is of the form

$$f(n) = an^3 + bn^2 + cn + d.$$

Substitute $n = 4, 3, 2,$ and 1 into the equation and solve the system as before. That is, subtract pairs of equations to eliminate, in this order, d, c, and b.

$$\begin{cases} f(4) = 64a + 16b + 4c + d = 30 \\ f(3) = 27a + 9b + 3c + d = 14 \\ f(2) = 8a + 4b + 2c + d = 5 \\ f(1) = a + b + c + d = 1 \end{cases}$$

$$\begin{cases} 37a + 7b + c = 16 \\ 19a + 5b + c = 9 \\ 7a + 3b + c = 4 \end{cases}$$

$$\begin{cases} 18a + 2b = 7 \\ 12a + 2b = 5 \end{cases}$$

$$6a = 2$$

From the equation $6a = 2$, $a = \frac{1}{3}$. By substitution into $12a + 2b = 5$, $b = \frac{1}{2}$. Then another substitution gives $c = \frac{1}{6}$. Finally, using $a + b + c + d = 1$, $d = 0$. Thus,

$$f(n) = \frac{1}{3}n^3 + \frac{1}{2}n^2 + \frac{1}{6}n.$$

Check You should check that this equation fits the data points. For instance, if $n = 5$, then

$$f(n) = \frac{1}{3}(5)^3 + \frac{1}{2}(5)^2 + \frac{1}{6}(5) = \frac{125}{3} + \frac{25}{2} + \frac{5}{6} = 55,$$

which checks.

When using finite differences, you must have a sufficient number of data points to check the formula you get. For instance, suppose you are given only the data

x	1	2	3 ...
y	1	2	4 ...

The 1st differences are 1 and 2 and you only have one 2nd difference. So you cannot tell whether the second differences are constant. If the next y-values are 7 and 11, then the 2nd differences are equal and the polynomial model is

$$y = \frac{x^2 - x + 2}{2}.$$

654

However, if 8 and 15 are the next y-values, then the 3rd differences are equal and the polynomial equation modeling the data would be

$$y = \frac{x^3 - 3x^2 + 8x}{6}.$$

These are only two of many polynomial equations fitting the data points $(1, 1)$, $(2, 2)$, $(3, 4)$.

Questions

Covering the Reading

In 1–3, refer to Primo's data at the beginning of this lesson.

1. What is the general quadratic polynomial equation which models these data? $p = ax^2 + bx + c$

2. Primo employees had three variables to find, so they needed to solve a system of ___?___ equations.   3

3. Show that the formula $p = \frac{1}{2}x^2 + \frac{1}{2}x + 1$ is correct for $x = 4$.
$\frac{1}{2}(4)^2 + \frac{1}{2}(4) + 1 = 11$

In 4–6, refer to Example 2.

4. In which equation could you substitute $a = \frac{1}{3}$ and $b = \frac{1}{2}$ to find $c = \frac{1}{6}$?   Sample: any equation without d can be used to find c if a and b are known.

5. **a.** Predict the number of oranges in a display with 6 rows.   See margin.
   b. Justify your answer with a drawing.   The six layers contain, respectively, 1, 4, 9, 16, 25, and 36 oranges; the total is 91.

6. Predict the number of oranges in a display with 15 rows.
   $f(15) = 1240$

7. Consider the table below.

x	1	2	3	4	5	6
y	3	16	39	72	115	168

   a. Determine the degree of a polynomial function that models these data.   2
   b. Find a formula for the polynomial model. $p(x) = 5x^2 - 2x$

8. Suppose that the data in the table below have a formula of the form $y = ax^3 + bx^2 + cx + d$. What four equations are satisfied by a, b, c, and d?

x	2	4	6	8	...
y	0	40	168	432	...

See margin.

In 9 and 10, solve each system.

9. $x + y + z = -2$
    $4x + 2y + z = 7$
    $9x + 3y + z = 5$
    $(x, y, z) = (\frac{-11}{2}, \frac{51}{2}, -22)$

10. $p + q + r + s = 4$
    $8p + 4q + 2r + s = 15$
    $27p + 9q + 3r + s = 40$
    $64p + 16q + 4r + s = 85$
    $(p, q, r, s) = (1, 1, 1, 1)$

NOTES ON QUESTIONS
Questions 13 and 14:
These questions ask students to use all of the skills they have learned in this lesson and in Lesson 11-7. They must organize data, use patterns, and find formulas. Both of the questions should be assigned.

Question 19: For this question, students may need to be reminded that $77x^5$ represents the total amount of deposit and interest on the $77 that has been in the account for five years.

ADDITIONAL ANSWERS
11.a. $f(1) = 1^2 - 1 + 2 = 2$;
$f(2) = 2^2 - 2 + 2 = 4$;
$f(3) = 3^3 - 3 + 2 = 8$

18.

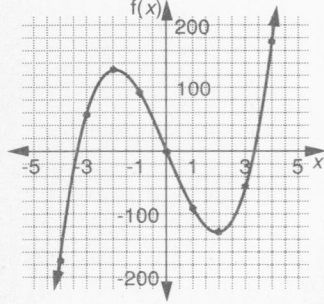

11. Suppose Norma, using the technique of finite differences, determined $y = n^2 - n + 2$ to be the formula for the data below.

n	1	2	3
y	2	4	8

 a. Check that these data satisfy Norma's equation.   **See margin.**
 b. Can Norma be assured that her equation is the correct one? If so, why? If not, find another formula which Norma's data also satisfy.
  No; another formula is $y = 2^n$

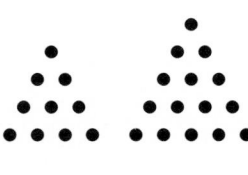
Applying the Mathematics

12. a. Complete the table below which describes the number of diagonals d for a polygon with n sides.   **0, 2, 5, 9, 14, 20, ...**

n	3	4	5	6	7	...
d						...

  12b. $f(n) = \frac{1}{2}n^2 - \frac{3}{2}n$

 b. Use the technique of finite differences to determine the polynomial function which models the number of diagonals in an n-gon.

13. When objects are arranged in equilateral triangles, the numbers of objects determine a sequence called *triangular numbers*.

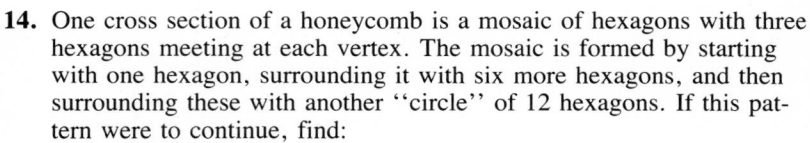

n: 1   2   3   4   5

t_n: 1   3   6   10   15

Above are the first five triangular numbers. Find a formula which will generate any triangular number t_n in terms of n, its position in the sequence. $t_n = f(n) = \frac{1}{2}n^2 + \frac{1}{2}n$

14. One cross section of a honeycomb is a mosaic of hexagons with three hexagons meeting at each vertex. The mosaic is formed by starting with one hexagon, surrounding it with six more hexagons, and then surrounding these with another "circle" of 12 hexagons. If this pattern were to continue, find:
 a. the number of hexagons in the 4th circle   **18**
 b. the total number of hexagons in the first four circles   **37**
 c. a polynomial equation which expresses the *total* number of hexagons h as a function of the number of circles n
  $h(n) = 3n^2 - 3n + 1$
 d. the total number of hexagons in a honeycomb with 10 circles.   **271**

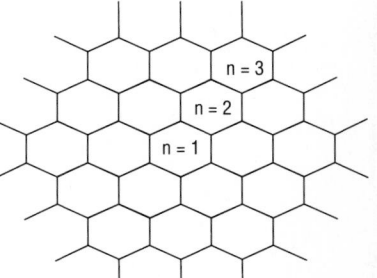

656

15. Consider the data below.

m	1	2	3	4	5	6	7	...
n	10	5	2	1	2	5	10	...

  a. Can the data be modeled by a polynomial function?   **yes**
  b. If so, what is the degree of the polynomial? *(Lesson 11-7)*   **2**

16. Consider the graph below of a polynomial. *(Lessons 11-5, 11-4, 7-2)*

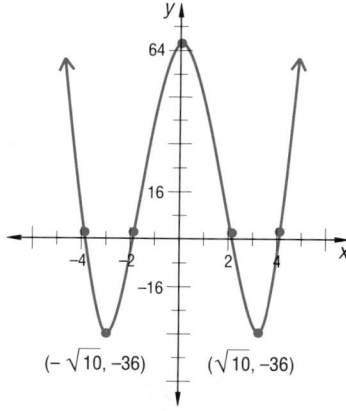

$(-\sqrt{10}, -36)$ $(\sqrt{10}, -36)$

  a. What are the zeros of the polynomial? $x = -4, -2, 2, 4$
  b. Suppose the polynomial has degree 4. Find a polynomial function which fits this graph. $f(x) = x^4 - 20x^2 + 64$
  c. What is the range of this function? $y \geq -36$

In 17 and 18, consider the function $f(x) = 9x^3 - 100x$. *(Lessons 11-5, 11-4)*

17. a. How many zeros does f have?   **3**
  b. Find the zero(s) of the function f. $x = 0, \frac{-10}{3}, \frac{10}{3}$

18. Graph the function over the domain $x = -5$ to 5.   **See margin.**

19. Sergei earns 1% interest a month on every dollar he saves from working. He receives interest on the interest, paid at the end of each month. His deposits, made on the first of each month, were $77 in March, $51 in April, $37 in May, $86 in June, $39 in July, and $35 in August. On August 1st how much will he have altogether, including the interest? [Hint: $77x^5 + 51x^4 + 37x^3 + 86x^2 + 39x + 35$]
(Lesson 11-1)   **$334.24**

20. Ben Spender recently had his credit limit reduced by 25%. What percent increase would he need to return to his original amount?
(Previous course) $33\frac{1}{3}\%$

MORE PRACTICE
For more questions on SPUR Objectives, use *Lesson Master 11-8*, shown below.

EXTENSION
In many of the examples of Lessons 11-7 and 11-8 which modeled real-world situations, the derived function $f(n)$ was zero when n was zero. Ask students to discuss the consequences of this fact when determining the coefficients of the modeling polynomial when that polynomial is third degree. ($c = 0$). Ask students to develop a shorter procedure to solve these type of problems. (Use $p = ax^2 + bx$; now only two equations need to be solved simultaneously.) Point out to students that the pizza problem, however, does not fit this model; here $f(0) = 1$.

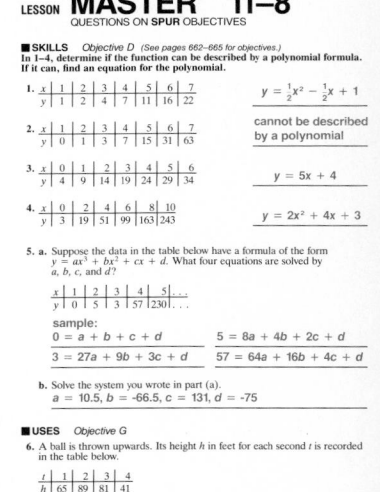

NAME _____

LESSON **MASTER 11–8**
QUESTIONS ON **SPUR** OBJECTIVES

■**SKILLS** *Objective D (See pages 662–665 for objectives.)*
In 1–4, determine if the function can be described by a polynomial formula. If it can, find an equation for the polynomial.

1.
x	1	2	3	4	5	6	7
y	1	2	4	7	11	16	22

$y = \frac{1}{2}x^2 - \frac{1}{2}x + 1$

2.
x	1	2	3	4	5	6	7
y	0	1	3	7	15	31	63

cannot be described by a polynomial

3.
x	0	1	2	3	4	5	6
y	4	9	14	19	24	29	34

$y = 5x + 4$

4.
x	0	2	4	6	8	10
y	3	19	51	99	163	243

$y = 2x^2 + 4x + 3$

5. a. Suppose the data in the table below have a formula of the form $y = ax^3 + bx^2 + cx + d$. What four equations are solved by a, b, c, and d?

x	1	2	3	4	5	...
y	0	5	3	57	230	...

sample:
$0 = a + b + c + d$ $5 = 8a + 4b + 2c + d$
$3 = 27a + 9b + 3c + d$ $57 = 64a + 16b + 4c + d$

b. Solve the system you wrote in part (a).
$a = 10.5, b = -66.5, c = 131, d = -75$

■**USES** *Objective G*
6. A ball is thrown upwards. Its height h in feet for each second t is recorded in the table below.

t	1	2	3	4
h	65	89	81	41

a. Find a polynomial function which describes the height h of the ball at time t. $-16t^2 + 72t + 9$

b. What was the initial velocity of the ball?   72 ft/sec

c. From what height was it initially thrown?   9 ft

Advanced Algebra © Scott, Foresman and Company   **123**

21. Factor $4x^4y^2 - 16x^2y^4$. *(Lesson 11-3)* $4x^2y^2(x + 2y)(x - 2y)$

In 22–24, solve for z. *(Lessons 10-2, 9-9, 8-6)*

22. $8^z = 16$ $z = \frac{4}{3}$

23. $5z^{-1/6} = 5^7$
$z = 5^{-36}$

24. $\cos z = -.57$
$z \approx 125°$ or $\approx 235°$

[M 11-8, 25]

25. The strength S of a wooden beam of rectangular cross section is directly proportional to the width w of the beam and the square of its depth d.
   a. Express the above statement with a variation formula. *(Lesson 2-9)* $S = kwd^2$
   b. Suppose a beam is to be sawed from a round log of diameter 2 ft. Express d in terms of w. *(Previous course)* $d = \sqrt{4 - w^2}$
   c. Use the results of part a and part b to express S as a polynomial function of w. *(Lesson 11-1)* $S = -kw^3 + 4kw$
   d. What is the degree of the polynomial in part c? *(Lesson 11-1)*   3

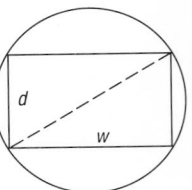

26. In Example 1b, explore how to cut the pizza so that the 16 pieces are closer to the same size.
It is not possible to get all 16 pieces exactly the same size.

658

658

Summary

A polynomial in x is an expression of the form $a_nx^n + a_{n-1}x^{n-1} + \ldots + a_2x^2 + a_1x + a_0$. Polynomials arise directly from compound interest situations and questions of surface area and volume. They also can be modeled to fit points on a graph of a function. By solving a system of equations, any n points can be fit by a polynomial whose degree is at most n. The degree of the polynomial can be found by the method of finite differences. Polynomial functions include the linear and quadratic functions and the direct variation and power functions you studied in previous chapters.

The polynomial above has degree n; when set equal to zero, the equation has n roots. The roots of a polynomial equation $P(x) = 0$ are the zeros of the function P. Sometimes they can be found exactly by factoring, by substitution of a (lucky?) value for $x,$ or by the Factor Theorem. They can be approximated by making a table or drawing a graph. The most efficient tables and graphs are created with the help of a calculator or computer.

Vocabulary

Below are the most important terms and phrases for this chapter. You should be able to give a definition for those terms marked with *. For all other terms you should be able to give a general description and a specific example of each.

Lesson 11-1
*polynomial in x
*degree of a polynomial
*coefficients of a polynomial
leading coefficient
*general form of a polynomial
*linear, quadratic, cubic polynomials

Lesson 11-2
monomial
binomial
trinomial
Extended Distributive Property

Lesson 11-3
Perfect Square Trinomial Patterns
Difference of Squares Pattern
Sum of Cubes Pattern
Difference of Cubes Pattern

Lesson 11-4
Zero Product Theorem
*zero of a function
Factor Theorem

Lesson 11-5
end behavior of a function

Lesson 11-6
quartic, quintic equations
Fundamental Theorem of Algebra
multiplicity of a root
Number of Roots of a Polynomial Equation Theorem

Lesson 11-7
method of finite differences
Polynomial Difference Theorem

Progress Self-Test

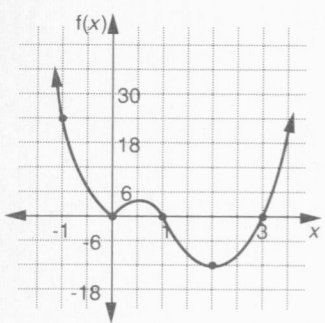

Take this test as you would take a test in class. You will need a calculator. Then check your work with the solutions in the Selected Answers section in the back of the book.

In 1 and 2, use this information. The summer after Beth turned 16, she began saving money from her summer jobs. After the first summer she put away $750. Following the summer after her 17th birthday she saved $600. After the next summer she saved $925 and after the following two summers she put away $1075 and $800, respectively. Beth invested all this money at an interest rate of r, compounded annually, and did not add or withdraw any other money.

1. If $x = 1 + r$, write a polynomial in terms of x which models the final amount of money in her account the summer after her 21st birthday. $750x^5 + 600x^4 + 925x^3 + 1075x^2 + 800x$

2. How much money would she have the summer after her 21st birthday if she had been able to invest at 7% interest? $5058.32

3. Elysa needs to make a box from cardboard with dimensions 40 in. by 60 in. Find a polynomial formula for the volume $V(x)$ of the box if she forms the box by cutting out squares of length x from each corner and folding up the sides. $V(x) = 4x^3 - 200x^2 + 2400x$

In 4 and 5, consider the polynomial function P where $P(x) = x^4 + 9x^2 - 3 - 8x^5$.

4. What is the degree of the polynomial?   5

5. Is $P(x)$ a monomial, binomial, trinomial, or none of these?   none of these   See margin.

6. Multiply and simplify $(a^2 + 3a - 7)(5a + 2)$.

7. Find the zeros of the polynomial function with equation
$$p(x) = 4x^3(5x - 11)(x + \sqrt{7}).$$
$x = 0$ (triple root), $\frac{11}{5}$, $-\sqrt{7}$

In 8 and 9, use the function f, where $f(x) = 3x^4 - 12x^3 + 9x^2$.

8. Find its zeros. $x = 0$ (double root), 3, 1

9. Graph the function on the domain $-1 \le x \le 4$.
See margin.

In 10 and 11, consider the table of values below for the polynomial function with equation
$$y = x^3 - 3x^2 - 3x + 9.$$

x	y
-3	-36
-2	-5
-1	8
0	9
1	4
2	-1
3	0
4	13

See below.

10. How many zeros does this polynomial have?

11. a. Between what pairs of consecutive integers must the zeros of the polynomial be located?   See below.
    b. Estimate the non-integer zeros to the nearest tenth.   See below.

10. 3 zeros
11a. between: $x = -2$ and -1; $x = 1$ and 2; and $x = 2$ and 3
    b. $x \approx 1.7$; $x \approx -1.7$

660

12. Find all solutions: $z^3 - 216 = 0$.
$z = 6, -3 + 3i\sqrt{3}, -3 - 3i\sqrt{3}$

13 and 14, *Multiple choice*.

13. A polynomial equation of degree 11 has 12 complex roots.   **c**
(a) always   (b) sometimes (c) never

14. When $f(x) = x^4 + 3x - 22$, $f(2) = 0$. Which is a factor of $x^4 + 3x - 22$?   **d**
(a) 0   (b) 2   (c) $x + 2$ (d) $x - 2$

15. Write a possible equation for the 4th degree polynomial function with the integer zeros graphed below.

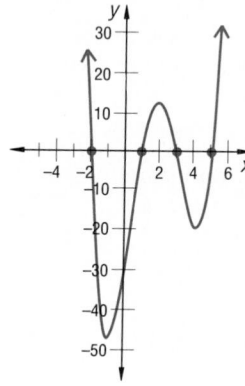

$f(x) = k(x^4 - 7x^3 + 5x^2 + 31x - 30)$

In 16–18, factor.

16. $10s^7t^2 + 15s^3t^4$ $5s^3t^2(2s^4 + 3t^2)$

17. $9z^2 - 196$ $(3z + 14)(3z - 14)$

18. $25y^2 + 60y + 36$ $(5y + 6)^2$

19. Refer to the table below.

n	1	2	3	4	5	6	7	8	...
t	2	5	9	14	20	27	35	44	...

a. Can the data points be modeled by a polynomial function of degree ≤ 5?   **Yes**
b. If so, what is the smallest possible degree of the polynomial? If not, why not?   **2**

20. Find an equation for a polynomial function which is described by the data points below.

x	-2	-1	0	1	2	3	4	...
z	12	4	0	0	4	12	24	...

$z = f(x) = 2x^2 - 2x$

Chapter Review

Questions on **SPUR** Objectives

CHAPTER REVIEW

The main objectives for the chapter are organized here into sections corresponding to the four main types of understanding this book promotes: Skills, Properties, Uses, and Representations.

USING THE CHAPTER REVIEW

Whereas end-of-chapter material may be considered optional in some texts, in *Advanced Algebra* we have selected these objectives and questions with the expectation that they will be covered. Students should be able to answer these questions with about 85% accuracy after studying the chapter.

You may assign these questions over a single night to help students prepare for a test the next day, or you may assign the questions over a two-day period.

If you work the questions over two days, then we recommend assigning the *evens* for homework the first night so that students get feedback in class the next day, then assigning the *odds* the night before the test so students can use the answers provided in the book.

SPUR stands for **S**kills, **P**roperties, **U**ses, and **R**epresentations. The Chapter Review questions are grouped according to the SPUR Objectives for this chapter.

SKILLS deal with the procedures used to get answers.

■ **Objective A.** *Multiply polynomials.* *(Lesson 11-2)*

In 1–4, multiply and write in the general form of a polynomial.   2. $a^3 + 21a^2 + 146a + 336$

1. $(x^2 + x + 3)(x - 1)$ $x^3 + 2x - 3$

2. $(a + 6)(a + 7)(a + 8)$ See above.

3. $(2y + 5)^3$ $8y^3 + 60y^2 + 150y + 125$

4. $(2x^2 - x + 4)(3x - 10)$ $6x^3 - 23x^2 +$

In 5 and 6, multiply and simplify. $22x - 40$

5. $(2x^2 - y)(3x + y)$ $6x^3 + 2x^2y - 3xy - y^2$

6. $(p + q + r)(p + q - r)$
$p^2 + 2pq + q^2 - r^2$

■ **Objective B.** *Factor polynomials using common monomial factoring, perfect square patterns, trial and error with trinomials, or patterns for the sum or difference of cubes.* *(Lesson 11-3)*

7. Copy and complete:
$7a^5b^2 - 63a^2b^4 = 7a^2b^2(\underline{\ ?\ } + \underline{\ ?\ })$.
a^3; $-9b^2$

8. Copy and complete with the value(s) which will make a perfect square trinomial:
$w^2 + \underline{\ ?\ } + 25$. $10w$

In 9–16, factor.

9. $x^2 - 14x + 49$ $(x - 7)^2$

10. $a^2 - b^2$ $(a + b)(a - b)$

11. $4x^3 - 12x^2 - 28x$ $4x(x^2 - 3x - 7)$

12. $16m^2 - 88m + 121$ $(4m - 11)^2$

13. $r^4s^4 - 81$ $(r^2s^2 + 9)(rs + 3)(rs - 3)$

14. $6x^2 + 26x + 8$ $2(3x + 1)(x + 4)$

15. $z^3 - 27$ $(z - 3)(z^2 + 3z + 9)$

16. $8g^3 + 125h^6$
$(2g + 5h^2)(4g^2 - 10gh^2 + 25h^4)$

■ **Objective C.** *Calculate or estimate zeros of polynomial functions.* *(Lessons 11-4, 11-5, 11-6)*

In 17 and 18, find the exact zeros of the polynomial function with the given equation.

17. $f(x) = x^2(x - .5)(3x + 1)$ $x = .5, -\frac{1}{3}, 0$

18. $P(x) = x^2 - 36$ $x = 6, -6$

In 19 and 20, estimate to the nearest tenth the zeros of the function by graphing or making a table.   See margin.

19. $f(x) = -9x^3 + 5x^2 - 7$

20. $y = x^4 + 3x^3 - 20$

In 21–24, (a) solve. (b) Identify any multiple roots. $x = 0, -4, -\frac{7}{9}$;

21. $0 = 5x(x + 4)(9x + 7)$ no multiple roots

22. $0 = (x - 1)^3(x - 2)^2$ See below.

23. $n^3 + 64 = 0$ $n = -4, 2 + 2i\sqrt{3}, 2 - 2i\sqrt{3}$;
no multiple roots

24. $n^4 - 81 = 0$
$n = 3, -3, 3i, -3i$; no multiple roots

■ **Objective D.** *Determine an equation for a polynomial function from data points using the Polynomial Difference Theorem.* *(Lessons 11-7, 11-8)*

In 25 and 26, is the function defined below a polynomial? If so, find an equation for the polynomial. If not, why not?

25. The function (n, a_n) where $a_1 = 5$ and
$a_{n+1} = a_n - 6$ for $n \geq 1$.   See below.

26.

x	1	2	3	4	5	6
y	1	3	7	15	31	63

no, because the differences never become constant

22. $x = 2$(double root), 1(triple root)

25. yes; $a_n = f(n) = -6n + 11$

ADDITIONAL ANSWERS
19. $x = -.8$

20. $x \approx 1.6$ or $x \approx -3.5$

39. $p(x) =$
$x^2 + 73.5x + 310.5$

40. $p(x) = 24x^4 + 278x^3 - 119x^2 + 12x$
$q(x) = 48x^4 + 556x^3 - 238x^2 + 24x$

27. Consider the polynomial function described by the data points below.

x	y
1	5
2	19
3	43
4	77
5	121
6	175

a. What is the degree of the polynomial function?   **2**

b. *Multiple choice*   Which system of equations could be solved to find the coefficients of the polynomial?   **i**

(i) $\begin{cases} 9a + 3b + c = 43 \\ 4a + 2b + c = 19 \\ a + b + c = 5 \end{cases}$

(ii) $\begin{cases} 3x^2 + 3x + 3 = 43 \\ 2x^2 + 2x + 2 = 19 \\ x^2 + x + 1 = 5 \end{cases}$

(iii) $\begin{cases} 2a + b = 19 \\ a + b = 5 \end{cases}$

(iv) none of these

c. Determine an equation for the polynomial function. $f(x) = 5x^2 - x + 1$

PROPERTIES deal with principles behind the mathematics.

■ **Objective E.** *Use technical vocabulary to describe polynomials. (Lessons 11-1, 11-2)*

In 28 and 29, state (a) the degree and (b) the leading coefficient of the polynomial.

28. $7x^5 + 3x^2 - 15$ a. 5; b. 7

29. $1 + x - 12x^2 - 8x^9$ a. 9; b. -8

In 30–33, *multiple choice*. State whether the polynomial is (a) a monomial, (b) a binomial, (c) a trinomial, or (d) none of (a)–(c).

30. $x^5 - 6$ b

31. $32x^2y^3$ a

32. $\dfrac{6}{x^2}$ d

33. $x^2 + x + 7$ c

■ **Objective F.** *Apply the Zero Product Theorem, Factor Theorem, and Fundamental Theorem of Algebra. (Lessons 11-4, 11-6)*

In 34–36, *multiple choice*.

34. If $xyz = 0$, then which of the following is true?   b
(a) $x = 0$
(b) $x = 0$ or $y = 0$ or $z = 0$
(c) $x = 0$ and $y = 0$ and $z = 0$
(d) none of these

35. Every polynomial equation of degree n has exactly __?__ roots, provided that __?__ roots are counted separately.   **n; multiple**

36. Suppose $p(x)$ is a polynomial, $p(r) = 0$, $p(s) = 0$, and $p(t) = 7$. Which of the following is *not* true?   b
(a) $p(r) \cdot p(s) = 0$
(b) $k(x - r)(x - s)(x - t) = p(x)$
(c) r and s are x-intercepts of $p(x)$
(d) r and s are roots of the equation $p(x) = 0$

37. *True or false*   If $(x - 7)$ is a factor of some polynomial function P, then $P(7) = 0$.   **37. true**

38. Suppose $x - r$ and $x - s$ are factors of a quadratic polynomial $p(x)$. Which of the following is *not* true for all x?   d
(a) $p(r) = 0$
(b) $p(s) = 0$
(c) $k(x - r)(x - s) = p(x)$
(d) $(x - r)(x - s) = 0$

39. Find an equation for a quadratic polynomial function whose graph crosses the x-axis at $(-69, 0)$ and $(-4.5, 0)$.   **39. & 40. See margin.**

40. Find equations for two polynomial functions whose zeros are -12, 0, $\frac{1}{4}$, and $\frac{1}{6}$.

In 41 and 42, explain why the Zero Product Theorem cannot be used directly on the given equation.

41. $(x - 8)(x + 11) = 10$ **The product is not equal to zero.**

42. $2(x + 2) - (x + \frac{2}{3}) = 0$ **The left-hand expression is not a product.**

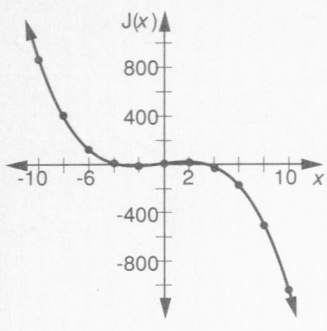
EVALUATION
Three tests are provided for this chapter in the Teacher's Resource File. Chapter 11 Test, Forms A and B cover just Chapter 11. The third test is Chapter 11 Test, Cumulative Form. About 50% of this test covers Chapter 11, 25% covers Chapter 10, and 25% covers previous chapters. For information on grading, see *General Teaching Suggestions: Grading* on page T44 in the Teacher's Edition.

ASSIGNMENT RECOMMENDATION
We strongly recommend that you assign Lesson 12-1, both reading and some questions, for homework the evening of the test.

USES deal with applications of mathematics in real situations.

◼ **Objective G.** *Use polynomials to model real world situations. (Lessons 11-1, 11-2, 11-8)* See below.

43. Each birthday from age 9 on, Charles decided to save $150 of his gifts. He put the money in a savings account at an interest rate of r, compounded annually, without withdrawing or adding any other money.
  a. Write a polynomial in x, where $x = 1 + r$, that represents the amount of money he would have after his 16th birthday.
  b. If the bank pays 6% interest annually, calculate how much money Charles would have after his 16th birthday?
  c. At about what rate of interest would Charles have to invest in order to have $2000 on his 16th birthday?

In 44 and 45, suppose that a manufacturer determines that n employees on a certain production line will produce f(n) units per month, where $f(n) = 80n^2 - 0.1n^4$.

44. How many units will be produced monthly by
  a. 3 employees? ≈ 712
  b. 10 employees? 7000

45. Use an automatic grapher to sketch a graph of f, and determine a reasonable domain for f in this model. See below.

In 46 and 47, consider that a worker cuts a square out of each corner of a piece of sheet metal which measures 1 m × 1.5 m. If the length of the side of the square is x meters long, find a polynomial for each quantity: See below.

46. V(x), the volume of the box when folded.

47. S(x), the surface area of the open box.
  $S(x) = -4x^2 + 1.5$

48. Recall that when a beam of light in air strikes the surface of water it is refracted or bent (see page 578, question 10). Below at the right are the earliest known data on the relation between i, the angle of incidence in degrees, and r, the angle of reflection in degrees. The measurements are recorded in the *Optics* of Ptolemy, a Greek scientist who lived in the 2nd century A.D.
  a. Can these data be modeled by a polynomial function? yes
  b. If so, what is the degree of the polynomial function? If not, explain why a polynomial function is not a good model. Degree is 2 (2nd difference is $\frac{1}{2}$)

i	r
10	8
20	15.5
30	22.5
40	29
50	35
60	40.5
70	45.5
80	50

49. Suppose that Theresa stacks soccer balls in a triangular pyramid display.
  a. Complete the table below where n is the number of rows and T is the *total* number of soccer balls.

n	1	2	3	4	5	6
T	1	4				

T: 1, 4, 10, 20, 35, 56, 84, ...

  b. How many soccer balls are needed for a display with n rows?
  $f(n) = \frac{1}{6}n^3 + \frac{1}{2}n^2 + \frac{1}{3}n$

43a. $150x^7 + 150x^6 + 150x^5 + 150x^4 + 150x^3 + 150x^2 + 150x + 150$
  b. $1484.62
  c. $\approx 14\%$

45. The graph is an inverted "W" with critical points at (-20, 16000), (0, 0), and (20, 16000) and zeros at $n \approx$ -28, 0, and 28. A reasonable domain for n is $0 \leq n \leq 28$

46. $V(x) = 4x^3 - 5x^2 + 1.5x$

664

■ **Objective H.** *Determine properties of a polynomial function from its graph. (Lessons 11-4, 11-5)*

In 50–52, refer to the graph below for the general polynomial function
$$y = P(x) = a_3x^3 + a_2x^2 + a_1x + a_0.$$

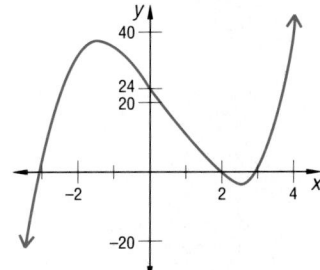

50. *Multiple choice* $a_0 = \underline{\ ?\ }$ **a**
(a) 24   (b) 2
(c) 0   (d) -3

51. *True or false* $P(2) = P(-2)$ **false**

52. Find an equation for the polynomial.   **See below.**

53. Refer to the graph of the polynomial function $y = f(x)$ below.

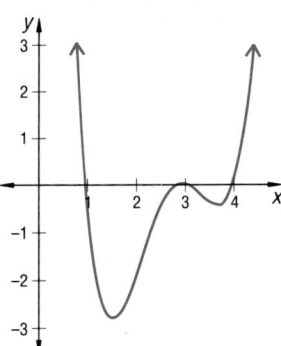

x = 1, 3, 3, 4

a. What are the zeros of this function?
b. What does your answer to part a imply about the degree of f?   **at least 4**
c. Find an equation for this polynomial function.
$f(x) = (x^4 - 11x^3 + 43x^2 - 69x + 36)$

52. $p(x) = k(x^3 - 2x^2 - 9x + 18)$

■ **Objective I.** *Read or generate computer output to graph or find zeros of polynomials. (Lessons 11-5, 11-6)*

In 54–56, use the computer output below for the function
$$J(x) = -x^3 - x^2 + 7x + 18.$$

54. Sketch a graph of $y = J(x)$. **See margin.**

55. How many x-intercepts does this polynomial function have? **1**

56. Use a computer program or a function grapher to estimate each x-intercept to the nearest tenth. **3.1**

DOMAIN FOR A TO B?
-10, 10

X	Y
-10	848
-8	410
-6	156
-4	38
-2	8
0	18
2	20
4	-34
6	-192
8	-502
10	-1012

57. Refer to the graph of the function $f(x) = x^4 + 10x^3 + 5x^2 + 200$ below.
a. Name two pairs of consecutive integers between which a zero of f must occur.
-10 < x < -9, -4 < x < -3
b. Estimate each real zero of f to the nearest hundredth.
-9.20, -3.39

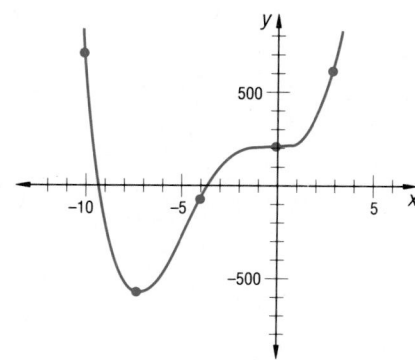

c. How many roots of the equation $x^4 + 10x^3 + 5x^2 + 200 = 0$ are not real? **two**

DAILY PACING CHART ■ CHAPTER 12

Students in the Full Course should complete all but one of the chapters by the end of the year. Students in the Minimal Course will spend more time on quizzes and the Chapter Review. As such, these students should complete about ten or eleven chapters.

DAY	MINIMAL COURSE	FULL COURSE
1	12-1	12-1
2	12-2	12-2
3	12-3	12-3
4	Quiz (TRF); Start 12-4.	Quiz (TRF); 12-4
5	Finish 12-4.	12-5
6	12-5	12-6
7	12-6	12-7
8	12-7	Quiz (TRF); 12-8
9	Quiz (TRF); Start 12-8.	12-9
10	Finish 12-8.	12-10
11	12-9	Progress Self-Test
12	12-10	Chapter Review
13	Progress Self-Test	Chapter Test (TRF)
14	Chapter Review	
15	Chapter Review	
16	Chapter Test (TRF)	

TESTING OPTIONS

■ Quiz for Lessons 12-1 Through 12-3   ■ Chapter 12 Test, Form A   ■ Chapter 12 Test, Cumulative Form
■ Quiz for Lessons 12-4 Through 12-7   ■ Chapter 12 Test, Form B

PROVIDING FOR INDIVIDUAL DIFFERENCES

The student text is written for the *average* student. The program, however, can be adapted for both less capable and for more capable students.

A blackline master (in the Teacher's Resource File) is provided for each lesson for those students who need more practice. The Teacher's Edition frequently provides Error Analysis and Alternate Approach features to provide additional instructional strategies.

For students who require additional challenge, Extension activities are regularly provided in the Teacher's Edition.

666A

OBJECTIVES ■ CHAPTER 12

Students should master the chapter objectives by the time they complete the chapter. To ensure mastery, there is continual review built into each set of lesson questions. After students complete the chapter lessons, they assess their mastery on the Progress Self-Test. Then they do the Chapter Review and pay special attention to those questions that match the objectives missed on the Progress Self-Test. Students can get extra practice on these objectives by using the master for each lesson in the Teacher's Resource File.

OBJECTIVES FOR CHAPTER 12 (Organized into the SPUR categories—Skills, Properties, Uses, and Representations)	Progress Self-Test Questions	Chapter Review Questions	Lesson Master from Teacher's Resource File*
SKILLS			
A Convert from the general form of a quadratic equation in two variables to standard form for a particular curve, and vice versa.	2	1 through 6	12-8
B Write equations or inequalities for quadratic relations given sufficient conditions.	3, 6	7 through 14	12-1, 12-2, 12-4, 12-6, 12-7
C Find the area of an ellipse.	7	15 through 18	12-5
D Solve systems of one linear and one quadratic equation or two quadratic equations by substitution or linear combination.	9	19 through 25	12-9, 12-10
PROPERTIES			
E Identify characteristics of circles, ellipses, and hyperbolas.	5, 15	26 through 32	12-1, 12-4, 12-6, 12-7
F Classify curves as circles, ellipses, parabolas, or hyperbolas using algebraic or geometric properties.	1	33 through 39	12-1, 12-3, 12-8
G Describe relations between conics.	4	40 through 45	12-3, 12-5
USES			
H Use circles, ellipses, and hyperbolas to solve real-world problems.	10, 13	46 through 50	12-1, 12-2, 12-4, 12-5
I Use systems of quadratic equations to solve real-world problems.	14	51 through 55	12-9, 12-10
REPRESENTATIONS			
J Graph circles, ellipses, and hyperbolas.	11–12, 16	56 through 65	12-1, 12-2, 12-3, 12-4, 12-6, 12-7
K Solve systems of quadratic equations geometrically.	2, 8	66 through 70	12-9, 12-10

* The masters are numbered to match the lessons.

OVERVIEW ■ CHAPTER 12

Quadratic Relations, which might also be termed Conic Sections, are loved by some teachers and ignored by others. The systematic study of the conic sections dates back to Apollonius in about 225 B.C. In the 17th century, Fermat and Descartes first studied them analytically. Traditionally, they are covered either in a second-year course in algebra or in a pre-calculus course.

There are many interesting applications of conic sections. The applications of conics to orbits of planets are of historical importance and should be studied by every educated person. Conics are also important in understanding orbits of satellites and comets. The reflection properties of the conics, as used in headlights and radio antennas, are more common applications.

Conceptually, quadratic relations complete an area of study, including the nonfunctions and inequalities, and provide a picture of all quadratic sentences in two variables. This is the same role played by linear relations of the form $Ax + By \ \Box \ C$, where the box is filled by an equality or inequality sign.

At this point in the year, quadratic relations also provide a second look at quadratic equations and systems of equations. Thus, they provide appropriate skill enhancement by practicing and extending previous knowledge without introducing new concepts.

The chapter begins with two lessons on circles, continues with five lessons on ellipses and hyperbolas, puts all the quadratic relations together in Lesson 12-8, and closes with two lessons on quadratic systems.

PERSPECTIVES ■ CHAPTER 12

The Perspectives provide the rationale for the inclusion of topics or approaches, provide mathematical background, and make connections within UCSMP.

12-1

CIRCLES

The chapter opener is an organizer for the chapter, showing the kinds of curves to be studied. Since parabolas were covered in Chapters 2 and 6, the focus in this chapter is on circles, ellipses, and hyperbolas.

We use the term *double cone* in place of two-napped cone, as it is sometimes called, since the latter is rarely used outside this context.

Quadratic relations are defined in three ways: (1) geometrically as intersections of a plane with a double cone; (2) as the locus of points satisfying certain conditions; and (3) by equations. This chapter uses the first definition to show the broad geometric relationship between the curves and then makes the connection between the other two definitions.

The purpose of Lesson 12-1 is to derive and apply the center-radius equation for any circle. First, the customary locus definition of a circle as the set of points at a given distance from a fixed point is given. The equation follows in one step from the Distance Formula.

12-2

SEMICIRCLES, INTERIORS, AND EXTERIORS OF CIRCLES

There are two parts to this lesson. The first is the derivation of an equation for a semicircle. This derivation characterizes the circle as the union of two functions. Thus, it enables a circle to be drawn on any function grapher that allows two graphs on the same screen. Some function graphers make allowances and graph them directly without needing to be split into two parts.

The second part is the discussion of sentences for the interior and exterior of a circle. Students have seen this idea before in connection with lines. A line splits the plane into two half-planes. Sentences describing the half-planes can be found by replacing the $=$ sign in the equation by $<$ or $>$. Similarly, a circle splits the plane into its interior and exterior, and sentences describing those two parts can be found in the same way.

12-3

DRAWING ELLIPSES AND HYPERBOLAS

This lesson describes ellipses and hyperbolas using locus definitions and concentrates on their graphs. Students have seen ellipses and hyperbolas before, the former as ovals and drawings of cross-sections of three-dimensional figures in geometry, the latter in graphing $xy = k$ in Chapter 2. They are likely to know the terms as well. The definitions, however, are new for most. Because the definitions are so similar, we discuss them together.

We believe it is important that students draw so they can see the shapes of the conics appear a little at a time rather than viewing them as finished products. The conic graph paper is provided in *Teaching Aid 81* for this purpose.

12-4

EQUATIONS FOR SOME ELLIPSES

The derivation of an equation for an ellipse from its locus definition is among the most difficult algebraic manipulation in this entire book. We do not expect students to be able to reconstruct it. The goal is that students realize that the equation comes from the definition using only properties they have had. It is also important that students see some examples of complicated manipulation, so that they understand the rationale for occasionally being subjected to that kind of problem themselves.

In Lesson 12-7, a similar derivation is used to obtain equations for some hyperbolas.

12-5

RELATIONS BETWEEN ELLIPSES AND CIRCLES

There are many relations between ellipses and circles, among them the following: (1) Until Kepler, it was thought that the orbits of heavenly bodies revolving around another object were circular; now we know that the ellipse is the basic orbit. (2) When a circle is seen from an angle, it is an ellipse. (3) When a circle is stretched uniformly, the result is an ellipse. (4) An ellipse in which the two foci are the same point is a circle.

This lesson emphasizes the relation in (3) because it provides an explanation for the equation of an ellipse and enables us to obtain the area of an ellipse.

Students first encountered scale changes in Lesson 4-4, in conjunction with matrices, where it was shown that the matrix for $S_{a, b}$ is $\begin{bmatrix} a & 0 \\ 0 & b \end{bmatrix}$. The area property of scale changes is a special case of the following theorem: Under a transformation with matrix M, the area of a figure is multiplied by the determinant of M. If the determinant is negative, the orientation of the figure is reversed; however, if the determinant is positive, the ori-

entation of the figure is the same. Since the determinant of the above matrix is ab, $S_{a, b}$ multiplies area by ab.

Without transformations, it would take calculus to obtain the area of an ellipse. It still takes calculus to obtain the circumference of an ellipse, because scale changes do not affect length uniformly.

12-6

EQUATIONS FOR SOME HYPERBOLAS

Just as ellipses were related to circles, equations with which students are familiar, hyperbolas will be related to equations of the form $xy = k$, which students first encountered in Chapter 2.

There are three reasons for beginning with these hyperbolas. First, the derivation of the equation of a hyperbola with foci on the line $y = x$ uses less formidable algebra than if the foci are on one of the axes. Second, the motivation is natural; students have seen this equation before. The graph even has been called a hyperbola; now it can be proved. Third, it is easier to discuss the asymptotes when they are the axes than when they are other lines.

12-7

MORE HYPERBOLAS

Until this lesson, all the equations for a given conic section have looked somewhat alike. The equations $xy = k$ and $\frac{x^2}{a^2} - \frac{y^2}{b^2} = 1$, however, would seem to have quite different graphs. Thus, one reason for having this lesson is to show that quite different equations may lead to quite similar curves.

A second more obvious reason for the lesson is to complete the hyperbola-ellipse analogy. Just as the locus definitions are similar, so are certain equations.

12-8

CLASSIFYING QUADRATIC RELATIONS

This chapter contains examples of the unity of mathematics. It comes as a pleasant and unexpected surprise to many students to learn that all the conic sections have equations of the same general form, the quadratic relation. In fact, not only do all conics have the same general formula, but also the discriminant can be used to determine which conic is given by any general form equation. These two facts are summarized in the Discriminant Theorem for Conics.

12-9

QUADRATIC-LINEAR SYSTEMS

The content here is standard and provides an opportunity to increase knowledge of conic sections, and also of system solving.

Graphing helps to obtain the number of solutions; algebraic procedures then can be used to find them. Without the graphing, it is easy to lose track of one or more solutions.

The Examples involve all three conics. Examples 1 and 2 ask for intersections of a line and a hyperbola. Example 3 asks for the intersection of a line and an ellipse, and Example 4 searches for intersections of a parabola and a line. Example 4 illustrates how algebraic procedures can signal that there are no points of intersection.

12-10

QUADRATIC-QUADRATIC SYSTEMS

When a linear-quadratic system cannot be solved by graphing or by sight, substitution is almost the only method available. In contrast, any of the methods used in solving linear systems can be appropriate for solving quadratic-quadratic systems: substitution, graphing, or linear combination.

CHAPTER 12

We recommend 13 to 16 days for this chapter: 10 to 12 on the lessons; 1 for the Progress Self-Test; 1 or 2 for the Chapter Review; and 1 for a Chapter test. (See the Daily Pacing Chart on page 666A.) If you spend more than 16 days on this chapter, you are moving too slowly. Keep in mind that each lesson includes Review questions to help students firm up content studied previously.

USING PAGES 666–667

Use a cone, if available, to illustrate how the conic sections can be viewed geometrically. Discuss the connection between the conic sections and quadratic relations. Ask students to give a few examples of quadratic equations that describe parabolas and hyperbolas. Show how these equations are special cases of the general quadratic equation given at the top of this page.

Quadratic Relations

A quadratic equation in two variables x and y is an equation which can be written in the form

$$Ax^2 + Bxy + Cy^2 + Dx + Ey + F = 0,$$

where A, B, C, D, E, and F are real numbers, and at least one of A, B, or C is not zero. If the relation symbol in the sentence above is the equal symbol $=$ or one of the inequality symbols $>$, $<$, $\geq$, or $\leq$, the resulting sentence is called a **quadratic relation in two variables.**

The parabolas you studied in Chapters 2 and 6 and the hyperbolas studied in Chapter 2 are examples of curves that can be described by quadratic relations. Circles, which you have studied since elementary school, can also be described by quadratic equations in two variables.

Quadratic relations have connections with a wide variety of ideas you already know. They describe the paths of thrown objects, the orbits of comets and planets, and the shapes of communication receivers and mirrors used in car headlights.

Quadratic relations may also be interpreted geometrically. Surprisingly, all quadratic equations in two variables can be derived from the intersection of a *double cone,* shown at the left, and a plane. Such cross-sections of a double cone are usually called *conic sections,* or simply *conics*.

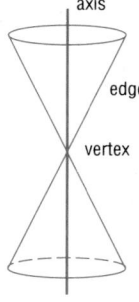

axis

edge

vertex

666

The four most important conic sections are hyperbolas, parabolas, ellipses, and circles.

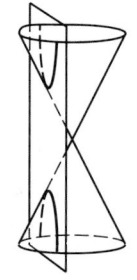

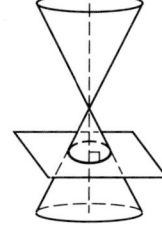

plane intersecting
both cones

hyperbola

plane ‖ to edge
of cone

parabola

plane intersecting
one cone not ‖ to edge

ellipse

plane intersecting
one cone ⊥ to axis

circle

In this chapter you will study quadratic relations algebraically and geometrically; that is, as equations or inequalities and as figures with certain properties. You will also learn how to solve systems of quadratic equations.

RESOURCES
- Lesson Master 12-1
- Visual for Teaching Aid 79 displays the four conic sections: hyperbola, parabola, ellipse, and circle.

OBJECTIVES

B Write an equation for a circle given its center and radius.
E Identify the center and radius of a circle with a given equation.
H Use circles to solve real-world situations.
J Graph a circle from its equation, and vice versa.

TEACHING NOTES

Begin the lesson by asking students to find the distance from the point (3, 4) to the origin. Then ask for coordinates of other points at the same distance from the origin.

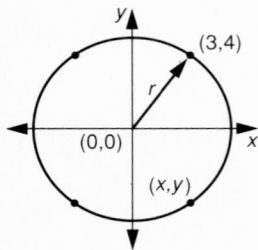

You can then point out the pattern: The sum of the squares of the coordinates of these points is 25. In symbols, $x^2 + y^2 = 25$. This is easily generalized to obtain the equation $x^2 + y^2 = r^2$ for the circle with center (0, 0) and radius r.

LESSON

12-1

Circles

Circles occur in many situations. You have probably noticed that when you throw a pebble into a calm body of water, concentric circles soon form around the point where the pebble hit the water. Similarly, when an earthquake occurs, energy waves radiate in concentric circles from the *epicenter,* the point on the earth's surface above the point where the earthquake began. Using an instrument called a *seismograph,* scientists can calculate the distance from a recording station to the epicenter. In Lesson 12-10 you will see how seismographs at three stations can determine the exact location of an earthquake's epicenter.

In this lesson you will learn how to find an equation for any circle. Recall the definition of a circle.

Definition:

A **circle** is the set of all points in a plane at a given distance (its **radius**) from a fixed point (its **center**).

From its definition and the Distance Formula, you can find an equation for any circle.

Example 1 Suppose a seismograph shows the epicenter to be about 60 miles away from Station 1. Find an equation for the set of points satisfying this condition.

Solution The given information means that the epicenter is located somewhere on a circle with center at Station 1 and radius 60. Set up a coordinate system with (0, 0) at Station 1. Let (x, y) be any point on the circle. The distance between (x, y) and (0, 0) is 60.

The Distance Formula gives

$$\sqrt{(x - 0)^2 + (y - 0)^2} = 60.$$

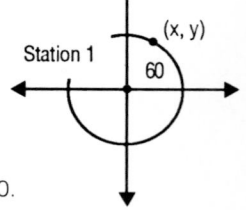

By squaring both sides,

$$(x - 0)^2 + (y - 0)^2 = 60^2$$
or
$$x^2 + y^2 = 3600.$$

668

Notice that the equation determined in Example 1 is a quadratic equation in x and y.

Example 2 Suppose Station 2 is 150 miles east and 100 miles north of Station 1; that is, at the point (150, 100). If the seismograph at this station shows the epicenter to be 130 miles away, find an equation for the circle 130 miles from Station 2.

Solution The epicenter is on a circle with center (150, 100) and radius 130.

Let (x, y) be any point on the circle. Using the Distance Formula,

$$\sqrt{(x - 150)^2 + (y - 100)^2} = 130.$$

Squaring gives

$$(x - 150)^2 + (y - 100)^2 = 16900.$$

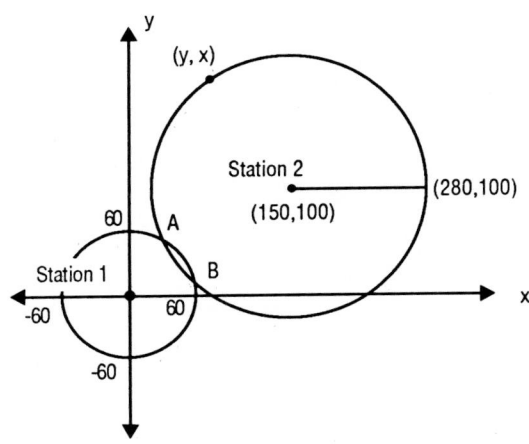

Check The point (280, 100) is 130 units from (150, 100) and its coordinates should satisfy the equation.

Does

$$(280 - 150)^2 + (100 - 100)^2 = 16900?$$

Does

$$130^2 + 0^2 = 16900? \text{ Yes.}$$

Notice that Examples 1 and 2 together determine that the epicenter is at one of two points, A or B. A third circle is needed to determine which is really the epicenter.

Following the pattern established in **Example 2**, use the Distance Formula to generalize an equation for any circle with center at (h, k).

Alternate Approach
You can translate the circle at the origin to have its center at (h, k). Applying the Graph Translation Theorem, replace x by $x - h$ and y by $y - k$. This yields the Center-Radius Equation. After discussing several instances of the Center-Radius Equation for a Circle, ask students to generalize what is true about circles whose equations have:
(a) equal values of r?
(They are congruent.)
(b) equal values of h and k?
(They are concentric.)

Error Analysis Some students have difficulty distinguishing the variables x and y from the constants h and k. Stress that the point (h, k) represents the center of the circle, while (x, y) represents a point on the circle, and the set of all (x, y) satisfying the equation $(x - h)^2 + (y - k)^2 = r^2$ is the set of all points on the circle.

ADDITIONAL EXAMPLES

1. Suppose a building demolition explosion can be heard as far away as 6 miles. Considering the origin of the explosion as (0, 0), give an equation satisfied by all points 6 miles away from it.
$x^2 + y^2 = 36$

2. A disaster team is located 20 miles south and 14 miles east of a chemical spill. Instructions are to evacuate everyone within 1/2 mile of the spill. From the standpoint of the disaster team, within what circle will everyone be evacuated?
The center is at (-14, 20). An equation is $(x + 14)^2 + (y - 20)^2 = .25$.

3. Find the center and radius of the circle with equation $(x + 5)^2 + (y + 10)^2 = 7$.
(-5, -10), $\sqrt{7}$

4. Find the coordinates of two points on the circle of Example 3 above.
Convenient points to find are the endpoints of the horizontal and vertical diameters:
$(-5 + \sqrt{7}, -10)$,
$(-5 - \sqrt{7}, -10)$, and
$(-5, -10 + \sqrt{7})$,
$(-5, -10 - \sqrt{7})$.
Other points can be found by substituting for one variable and solving for the other.

Example 2 can be generalized to determine an equation for *any* circle. Let (h, k) be the center of a circle with radius r, and let (x, y) be any point on the circle. Then from the definition of a circle, the distance between (x, y) and (h, k) equals r.

From the Distance Formula,

$$\sqrt{(x - h)^2 + (y - k)^2} = r.$$

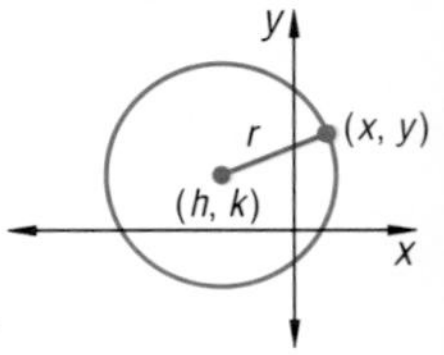

Squaring gives

$$(x - h)^2 + (y - k)^2 = r^2.$$

This argument proves the following theorem.

Theorem (Center-Radius Equation for a Circle):

The circle with center (h, k) and radius r is the set of points (x, y) that satisfies

$$(x - h)^2 + (y - k)^2 = r^2.$$

For a circle centered at the origin, $(h, k) = (0, 0)$. The equation

$$(x - h)^2 + (y - k)^2 = r^2$$

becomes

$$(x - 0)^2 + (y - 0)^2 = r^2$$

or

$$x^2 + y^2 = r^2.$$

This proves the following special case of the Center-Radius Equation for a Circle.

Theorem:

The circle with center at the origin and radius r is the set of points (x, y) that satisfies the equation $x^2 + y^2 = r^2$.

The following example illustrates how to graph a circle given an equation for it.

Example 3 **a.** Find the center and radius of the circle with equation $(x - 1)^2 + (y + 2)^2 = 9$.
b. Graph this circle.

Solution

a. The equation is in the center-radius form for a circle with $(h, k) = (1, -2)$ and $r = 3$.

b. You can sketch this circle by locating the center and then four points whose distance from the center is 3, as illustrated at the right.

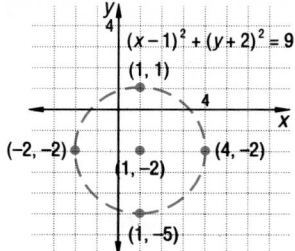

$(x-1)^2 + (y+2)^2 = 9$

$(1, 1)$

$(-2, -2)$

$(1, -2)$

$(4, -2)$

$(1, -5)$

If you know an equation for a circle and one coordinate of a point on the circle, you can determine the other coordinate of that point.

Example 4 Refer to the circle in Example 3. There are two points at which $x = 3$. Find the y-coordinate of each point.

Solution Substitute $x = 3$ into the equation for the circle, and solve for y.

$$(3 - 1)^2 + (y + 2)^2 = 9$$
$$4 + (y + 2)^2 = 9$$
$$(y + 2)^2 = 5$$
$$y + 2 = \pm\sqrt{5}$$
$$y = -2 \pm \sqrt{5}$$

So $y \approx 0.236$ or $y \approx -4.236$.

Check Refer to the graph above. Both $(3, 0.236)$ and $(3, -4.236)$ seem to be on the circle.

Questions

Covering the Reading

1. State the general form of a quadratic equation in x and y.
   $Ax^2 + Bxy + Cy^2 + Dx + Ey + F = 0$

2. A conic section is the intersection of a(n) __?__ and a(n) __?__.
   Double cone, plane

3. Name four types of conic sections.   **hyperbola, parabola, ellipse, circle**

4. As conic sections, how do parabolas and hyperbolas differ?
   See margin.

5. What is the epicenter of an earthquake?
   The point on the earth's surface above the point where the earthquake began.

NOTES ON QUESTIONS
Question 17: This question helps to set up the standard form for a quadratic equation to be studied in Lesson 12-8.

Questions 18-20: These questions relate to the geometric conception of conics on the opening page of the chapter.

Question 21: Point out that the parabola is a conic section.

Question 27: One or more parts of this question may be difficult for some students. You might wish to give them a number of days to think about it.

ADDITIONAL ANSWERS
4. A parabola is a "single branched" curve while a hyperbola is a "double branched" curve. Both are determined by the intersection of a plane and a double cone. If the plane is parallel to an edge of the cone, the intersection is a parabola; if it intersects both cones, the intersection is a hyperbola.

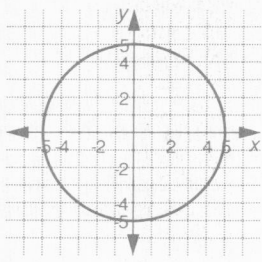
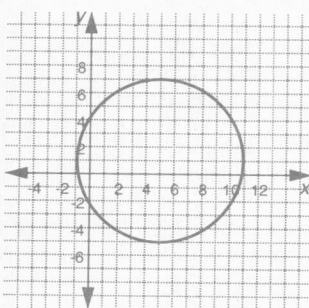
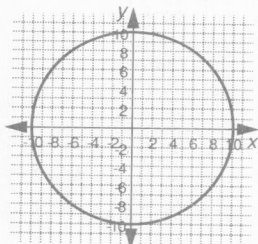
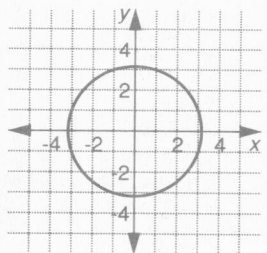
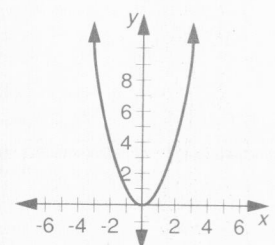
In 6 and 7, consider the circle with equation $x^2 + y^2 = 60^2$.

6. *Multiple choice*   Find the radius of this circle.   **c**
   (a) 30   (b) $\sqrt{60}$ (c) 60   (d) 3600

7. *Multiple choice*   Tell which point(s) is (are) on the circle.   **b, c**
   (a) (0, 0)   (b) (0, 60)   (c) (-60, 0)   (d) (30, 30)   (e) (60, 60)

8. The circle with equation $(x - h)^2 + (y - k)^2 = r^2$ has center __?__
   and radius __?__.   **(h, k), r**

In 9 and 10, for each circle (a) state its center; (b) state its radius; and (c) sketch it.

9. $x^2 + y^2 = 25$
   a. (0, 0); b. 5; c. See margin.
10. $(x - 5)^2 + (y - 1)^2 = 36$
    a. (5, 1); b. 6; c. See margin.
11. Consider the circle $x^2 + y^2 = 100$.
    a. Find the y-coordinates of all points where $x = -6$.   **$y = \pm 8$**
    b. Sketch the circle.   **See margin.**

In 12 and 13, find an equation for the circle with the given center C and radius r.

12. $C = (0, 0); r = 9$
    $x^2 + y^2 = 81$
13. $C = (-3, -2); r = 8$
    $(x + 3)^2 + (y + 2)^2 = 64$

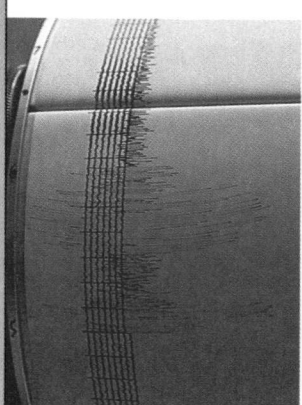

Seismograph record

In 14 and 15, use the coordinates of the earthquake recording stations in Example 2.

14. Suppose Station 3 is 40 miles west and 125 miles north of Station 1. If the epicenter of an earthquake is 100 miles from Station 3, give an equation for the circle on which it must lie.
    $(x + 40)^2 + (y - 125)^2 = 10,000$
15. Suppose the epicenter is known to be 30 miles east of Station 1, and 60 miles away. Then how far north or south of the station is it?
    $30\sqrt{3} \approx 52$ mi
16. A circle has center at the origin and radius $\sqrt{10}$.
    a. Find an equation for this circle.   **$x^2 + y^2 = 10$**
    b. Give the coordinates of eight points on the circle with integer coordinates.   **(1, 3), (-1, 3), (1, -3), (-1, -3), (3, 1), (3, -1), (-3, 1), (-3, -1)**
    c. Graph the circle.   **See margin.**

17. **a.** Expand the binomials in the equation for the circle of Example 2. Then simplify to get an equation of the form $Ax^2 + Bxy + Cy^2 + Dx + Ey + F = 0$.   **$x^2 + y^2 - 300x - 200y + 15,600 = 0$**
    b. What are the values of A, B, C, D, E, and F?
    $A = 1, B = 0, C = 1, D = -300, E = -200, F = 15,600$

In 18–20, the shape of the light beam from a flashlight is a cone. When that cone of light hits a flat surface, the outline is a conic section. Use an actual flashlight and a wall in a darkened room to tell which conic section is formed when the flashlight is held:

18. perpendicular to the wall
circle

19. at an angle of 75° to the wall
ellipse

20. touching the wall, parallel to it.
one branch of a hyperbola

Review

21. a. Graph $\{(x, y): y = x^2\}$.   See margin.
b. Name the line of symmetry. *(Lesson 2-5)*   **y-axis**

22. *Skill sequence* Expand and simplify. *(Lessons 6-1, 11-2)*
a. $(x + 3)^2 + y^2$ **b.** $(x + y)^2 + 3^2$ **c.** $(x + y + 3)^2$
$x^2 + y^2 + 6x + 9$ $x^2 + 2xy + y^2 + 9$ $x^2 + 2xy + y^2 + 6x + 6y + 9$

23. *Skill sequence* Solve for *y*. *(Lesson 6-1)*
a. $y^2 = 100$ $y = \pm 10$
b. $25 + y^2 = 100$ $y = \pm 5\sqrt{3}$
c. $x^2 + y^2 = 100$ $y = \pm\sqrt{100 - x^2}$

24. Find an equation for the line containing the origin and (5, -4).
(Lesson 3-5) $y = -\frac{4}{5}x$

25. Let $A = \begin{bmatrix} 3 & 4 \\ -1 & 2 \end{bmatrix}$ and $B = \begin{bmatrix} 0.2 & -0.4 \\ 0.1 & 0.3 \end{bmatrix}$. $\begin{bmatrix} 1 & 0 \\ 0 & 1 \end{bmatrix}$
a. Find AB.
b. How are *A* and *B* related? *(Lessons 4-5, 5-5)*   **They are inverses.**

26. What are the zeros of the polynomial function graphed at the right? *(Lesson 11-4)*
-4, -1, 1, 4

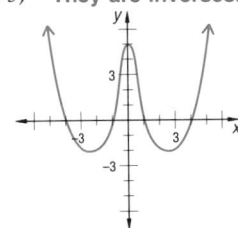

Exploration

27. A **lattice point** is a point with integer coordinates. If possible, find an equation for a circle that passes through
a. no lattice points   sample: $x^2 + y^2 = \sqrt{2}$, $(x - 1)^2 + (y - 3)^2 = \sqrt{2}$

b. exactly one lattice point   sample: $(x - \sqrt{3})^2 + y^2 = 3$; (0, 0)

c. exactly two lattice points   sample: $x^2 + (y - \sqrt{3})^2 = 12$; (3, 0) and (-3, 0)

d. exactly three lattice points   sample: $(x - \frac{2}{3})^2 + y^2 = \frac{4}{9}$; (0, 0), (1, 1), (1, -1)

e. more than ten lattice points.
sample: $x^2 + y^2 = 100$;
($\pm$10, 0), ($\pm$6, $\pm$8), ($\pm$8, $\pm$6), (0, $\pm$10)

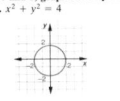 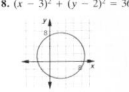

FOLLOW-UP

MORE PRACTICE
For more questions on SPUR Objectives, use *Lesson Master 12-1*, shown below.

LESSON 12-2

RESOURCES
■ Lesson Master 12-2

OBJECTIVES

B Write an inequality describing the interior or exterior of a circle.
H Use interiors or exteriors of circles to analyze real-world situations.
J Graph interiors or exteriors of circles given their sentences, and vice versa.

TEACHING NOTES

The inequalities tend to present few problems for students; discussion should center around the equations for semicircles. Use either the first paragraph of the lesson or **Question 1** to initiate the discussion.

Computer Demonstrate how to graph circles on your automatic grapher. Even if your grapher can handle directly equations in the form $x^2 + y^2 = r^2$, it is useful to illustrate how the union of the two semicircles $y = \sqrt{r^2 - x^2}$ and $y = -\sqrt{r^2 - x^2}$ gives the same graph.
  Note that some automatic graphers choose a default window with different scales on the x- and y-axes, thus distorting the graphs of circles. On such graphers, you will need to adjust manually the window for each graph. On other graphers, even when the x- and y-axes have the same scale, there is still some distortion. Generally, you can minimize the distortion on computer screens by adjusting the aspect ratio.

LESSON 12-2

Semicircles, Interiors and Exteriors of Circles

Many vertical lines intersect a circle in two points. Consequently, the Vertical-Line Test shows that a circle is a relation but not a function. Thus many automatic function graphers cannot graph a circle directly. With these graphers, you need to think of the circle as the union of two semicircles, each of which is a function. To graph the circle $x^2 + y^2 = 100$ with center $(0, 0)$ and radius 10, solve the equation for y and graph each part separately.

$$x^2 + y^2 = 100$$
$$y^2 = 100 - x^2$$
$$y = \sqrt{100 - x^2} \text{ or } y = -\sqrt{100 - x^2}$$

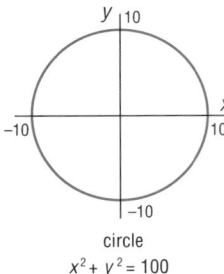

circle
$x^2 + y^2 = 100$

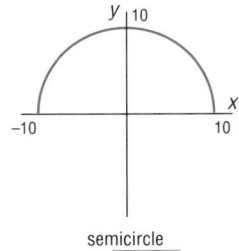

semicircle
$y = \sqrt{100 - x^2}$

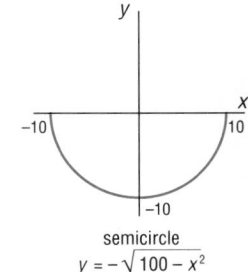

semicircle
$y = -\sqrt{100 - x^2}$

Semicircles occur often in architecture. The following example shows how to use graphs and equations to determine the height of a semicircular arch at points on the arch.

Example 1   A semicircular arch over a street has radius 10 feet. How high is it at a point whose ground distance is 4 feet from the center?

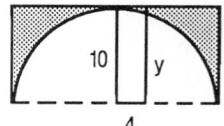

Solution   Make a mathematical model of the situation. Imagine that the arch is on a coordinate system with the x-axis representing the street and the origin at the center of the arch. Then the circle determined by the arch has center $(0, 0)$ and radius 10, so its equation is $x^2 + y^2 = 10^2$. The height of the circle 4 feet from the center equals the y-coordinate of the point on the graph where $x = 4$. Thus, you should evaluate $x^2 + y^2 = 100$ at $x = 4$.

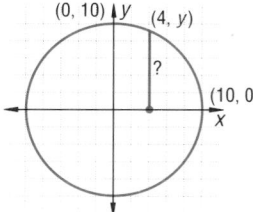

674

Substitute 4 for x in the equation and solve for y.

$$16 + y^2 = 100$$
$$y^2 = 84$$
$$y = \sqrt{84} \text{ or } -\sqrt{84}$$

It is necessary to reject $-\sqrt{84}$ because y, the height above the ground, cannot be negative. Thus, $y = \sqrt{84} \approx 9.17$. The bridge is about 9.17 ft (about 9 ft 2 in.) high at a point whose ground distance is 4 ft from its center.

Check 1 Examine the graph. This value looks about right.

Check 2 Substitute (4, 9.17) into $x^2 + y^2 = 100$.
Does $4^2 + (9.17)^2 \approx 100$? Yes.

Every circle separates the plane into three regions. The region inside the circle is called the **interior** of the circle. The region outside the circle is called the **exterior** of the circle. The circle itself is the **boundary** between these two regions.

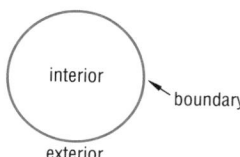

Concentric circles are often used in target practice. The object can hit the target only in the shaded regions and not on the boundaries. To describe the regions mathematically, place the target on a coordinate system with the center at (0, 0). The region worth 50 points is the interior of the circle with radius 3. All points in this region are less than 3 units from the origin. Thus if (x, y) is a point in this region, from the distance formula you can conclude that $\sqrt{x^2 + y^2} < 3$. In the inequality, the expressions on both sides are positive. Whenever a and b are positive and $a < b$, then $a^2 < b^2$. Thus, when both sides of the inequality $\sqrt{x^2 + y^2} < 3$ are squared, the sentence becomes $x^2 + y^2 < 9$. So $x^2 + y^2 < 9$ describes the region worth 50 points.

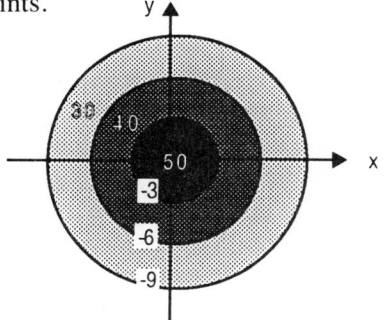

LESSON 12-2   Semicircles, Interiors and Exteriors of Circles   **675**

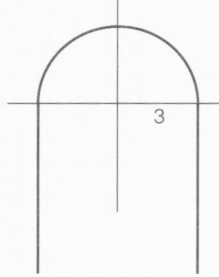
Example 2 Write a sentence to describe all points in those regions of the target worth less than 40 points.

Solution All (x, y) in the region worth less than 40 points are in the exterior of the circle with radius 6. The distance formula gives $\sqrt{x^2 + y^2} > 6$ or, squaring both sides, $x^2 + y^2 > 36$.

The two instances above can be generalized in the following theorem.

Theorem (Interior and Exterior of a Circle):

Given a circle with center (h, k) and radius r.

The interior of the circle is described by
$$(x - h)^2 + (y - k)^2 < r^2.$$

The exterior of the circle is described by
$$(x - h)^2 + (y - k)^2 > r^2.$$

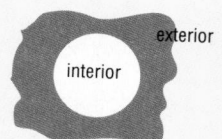

If $\geq$ or $\leq$ is used, the boundary is included.

Example 3 Graph the points satisfying $(x - 3)^2 + (y + 5)^2 \geq 16$.

Solution The sentence represents the union of a circle, with center at (3, -5) and radius 4, and its exterior.

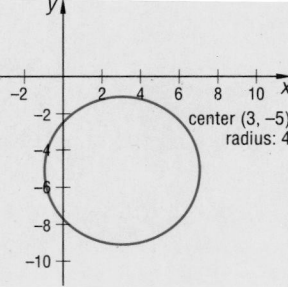
center (3, –5)
radius: 4

Example 4 Consider the target on page 675. Write a sentence to describe all points in the region worth 30 points.

Solution This region is the intersection of the interior of the circle with radius 9 and the exterior of the circle with radius 6.

The interior of the circle with radius 9 is the set $\{(x, y): x^2 + y^2 < 81\}$, and the exterior of the circle with radius 6 is the set $\{(x, y): x^2 + y^2 > 36\}$.

So $\{(x, y): 36 < x^2 + y^2 < 81\}$ describes the 30-point region.

676

Questions

Covering the Reading

1. Sketch by hand on separate sets of axes. **See margin.**
   a. $x^2 + y^2 = 49$ **b.** $y = \sqrt{49 - x^2}$ **c.** $y = -\sqrt{49 - x^2}$

2. Refer to Example 1. How high is the arch at a point whose ground distance is 2 feet from the center?   ≈**9.8 ft**

3. The region outside a circle is called its __?__.   **exterior**

4. *Multiple choice*   On the target shown in the lesson, all (x, y) in the region worth 50 points lie   **a**
   (a) in the interior of the circle with radius 3.
   (b) on the circle with radius 3.
   (c) in the exterior of the circle with radius 3.

5. Write a sentence to describe the set of points (x, y) in the 40-point region of the target.   **{(x, y): 9 < x² + y² < 36}**

6. Graph the points satisfying $(x - 3)^2 + (y + 5)^2 < 16$.   **See margin.**

In 7 and 8, *multiple choice*. Given a circle with center (h, k) and radius r, state which of the following the given sentence describes:
   (a) the interior of the circle   (b) the exterior of the circle
   (c) the union of the circle   (d) the union of the circle
       and its interior   and its exterior

7. $(x - h)^2 + (y - k)^2 \geq r$ **8.** $(x - h)^2 + (y - k)^2 < r$ **a**
   d

Applying the Mathematics

In 9 and 10, use your automatic grapher to graph each entire circle.
9. $x^2 + y^2 = 8$ **See margin. 10.** $(x + 3)^2 + (y + 4)^2 = 25$
   See margin.

11. The BASIC program at the left printed the output at the right.

```
10 INPUT "RADIUS"; R
20 PRINT "X" "Y"
30 FOR X = -R TO R STEP 0.5
40 Y1 = SQR(R^2 - X^2)
50 PRINT X, Y1
60 NEXT X
70 FOR X = -R TO R STEP 0.5
80 Y2 = -1 * SQR(R^2 - X^2)
90 PRINT X, Y2
100 NEXT X
110 END
```

X	Y
-2	0
-1.5	1.322876
-1	1.732051
-0.5	1.936492
0	2
0.5	1.936492
1	1.732051
1.5	1.322876
2	0

See margin.

   a. Plot the coordinates given in the output.
   b. Find the value of R input by the user.   **2**
   c. Find an equation for the circle you graphed in part a.   **x² + y² = 4**
   d. To print a table of solutions to $x^2 + y^2 = 169$, what number should be input for R?   **13**
   e. What lines in the program generate the points on the semicircle above the x-axis?
   30 through 60

Questions 9 and 10:
Note that on some automatic graphers, the graph of a circle will appear to be an ellipse. This phenomenon can be used as motivation for the study of ellipses in the next two lessons.

Question 11: The program in this question can be used to print a table of solutions to an equation of any circle with radius greater than .25. Practically, if $r \leq 1$, you may want to reduce the step size so you get enough values to graph.

Question 12: This question can initiate discussion of what happens when a truck driver misjudges the ability of his or her truck to fit under a bridge.

Question 23: Books on the history of art, Morris Kline's *Mathematics in Western Culture*, books on architecture, even encyclopedias often have discussions of various kinds of arches. Circles and semicircles are used as outlines of windows, forms of buildings, and even plazas and gardens.

ADDITIONAL ANSWERS
1.a.

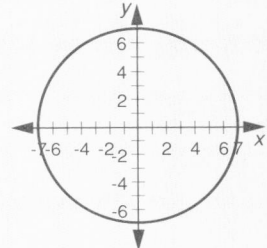

1.b. and c. See Additional Answers on page 679.

6., 9., 10., 11.a. See Additional Answers in the back of this book.

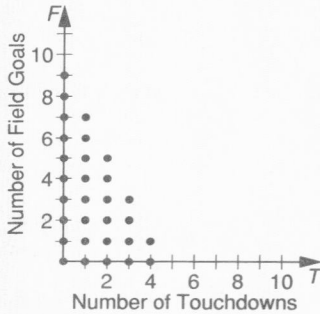
12. A moving van 6 ft wide and 12 ft high is
approaching a semicircular tunnel with radius 13 ft.
   a. Explain why the truck cannot pass through the
      tunnel if it goes on only one side of the median
      strip.   **See margin.**
   b. Can the truck fit through the tunnel if it is
      allowed to drive anywhere on the roadway?
      Justify your answer.   **See margin.**

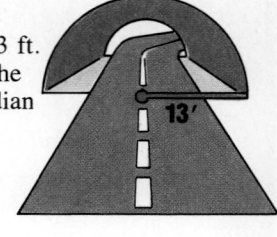

13. In sumo wrestling, the participants wrestle in the interior of a circle.
A wrestler wins by pushing his opponent out of the circle. Suppose
the circle has radius r and its center is $(0, 0)$. $x^2 + y^2 \leq r^2$
   a. What sentence describes positions where a wrestler is in bounds?
   b. What sentence describes losing positions? $x^2 + y^2 > r^2$

In 14–16, refer to the graph at the right.

14. What inequality describes the points
in the checked region? $x^2 + y^2 < 4$

15. What inequality describes all (x, y)
in the striped region?
   $16 < x^2 + y^2 < 36$

16. *Multiple choice*   The region described by
$\{(x, y): 4 < x^2 + y^2 \leq 16\}$ is   c
   (a) the gray region.
   (b) the union of the gray region and
       its inner boundary.
   (c) the union of the gray region and its outer boundary.
   (d) the union of the gray region and both its boundaries.

| Review |

In 17 and 18, define the term. *(Lessons 6-3, 12-1)*   **See margin.**

17. circle   18. parabola

19. a. Find an equation for the circle with center at $(0, 0)$ and radius 1.
       (Lesson 12-1) $x^2 + y^2 = 1$
    b. What is this circle called? *(Lesson 10-4)*   the unit circle

20. A circle has center at the origin and passes through the point $(3, -4)$.
    a. Find the radius of the circle.   5
    b. Find an equation for the circle. *(Lesson 12-1, Previous course)*
       $x^2 + y^2 = 25$

In 21 and 22, recall that in football a touchdown is worth 6 points, a field
goal 3 points, a safety 2 points, and a point-after-touchdown 1 point.

21. If a team gets T touchdowns, F field goals, S safeties, and P points-
after-touchdown, how many total points does it have? *(Lesson 3-3)*
    $6T + 3F + 2S + P$

22. A team has no safeties and no points-after-touchdown and a total of at
most 27 points. Graph the set of possible ways this could happen.
    (Lesson 3-9)   **See margin.**

678

23. Semicircular arches were popular with the early Romans. Below is an example. Prepare a brief report on the use of circles and semicircles in architecture. Consider Roman, Renaissance, and modern uses of this form. **many possible answers**

The Basilica of Constantine

24. Can you draw a circle with a ruler? "Of course not," you may think. "A circle is round and a ruler is straight." **See margin.**
   a. Try this. Mark a point P on a sheet of plain paper. Take a ruler and put one edge so that it goes through the point. Then draw a line along the other edge.
   b. Repeat this twice using the same point and the same ruler. Perhaps you have something like this:
   c. Draw more lines in the same way. You will begin to see something like the following:

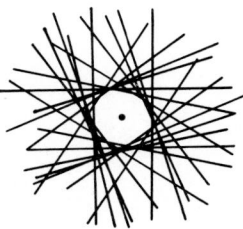

   d. The lines are said to form an *envelope* of a circle. No line drawn as suggested above will intersect the interior of this circle. Where is the center of the circle you've formed? What is its radius?
   e. If you were to repeat this process using a ruler of a different width, how would the outcome be affected?

MORE PRACTICE
For more questions on SPUR Objectives, use *Lesson Master 12-2*, shown below.

1.b.

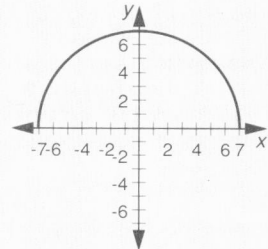

c.

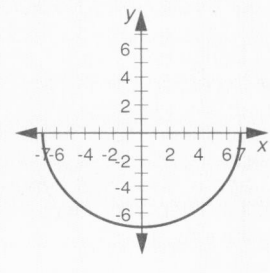

NAME _____

LESSON **MASTER 12–2**
QUESTIONS ON **SPUR** OBJECTIVES

■**SKILLS** *Objective B (See pages 735–739 for objectives.)*
1. a. Solve the equation $x^2 + y^2 = 5$ for y. $y = \pm \sqrt{5 - x^2}$

   b. Is your answer to part (a) a function? Explain.
   No, for each x there are two y values.

2. a. Write a sentence describing all points in the interior of the circle $(x + 4)^2 + (y - 5)^2 = 18$. $(x + 4)^2 + (y - 5)^2 < 18$

   b. Use your answer to part (a) to show that the point (-2, 6) is inside the circle.
   $(-2 + 4)^2 + (6 - 5)^2 = 2^2 + 1^2 = 5 < 18$

■**USES** *Objective H*
3. A truck 7 ft high and 5 ft wide approaches a semicircle tunnel with a diameter 16 ft.
   a. Will the truck fit through the tunnel? Justify your answer.
   Yes, at 2.5 ft from the center the tunnel ≈ 7.6 ft.

   b. Find the diameter of the smallest tunnel the truck could enter.   ≈ 14.8 ft

4. A small plane pilot tells an air traffic controller he is within a 10-mile radius of a town that is 20 miles north of the airport.
   a. Sketch the situation.
   b. Write a sentence that describes his possible locations (x, y) from the point of view of the controller. $x^2 + (y - 20)^2 = 100$

■**REPRESENTATIONS** *Objective J*
In 5 and 6, graph.
5. $(x + 1)^2 + (y + 7)^2 \geq 9$ **6.** $4 \leq x^2 + y^2 \leq 25$

Advanced Algebra © Scott, Foresman and Company

125

OBJECTIVES

F Classify curves as ellipses
   or hyperbolas from their
   locus definition.
G Describe relations between
   ellipses and circles.
J Graph ellipses and hyperbolas given their locus
   definition.

TEACHING NOTES

Distribute sufficient conic
graph paper provided as
Teaching Aid 81 for students
to use for the examples in
class and for the assignment.

Use the text's vocabulary
and correct students if they
misuse terms. Students will
gradually realize that they
need words for key points on
these curves.

The conic graph paper we
provide has foci 10 and 12
units apart. You might ask
what should be done if the
foci are 8 units apart. Two
possible answers: use the
12-unit graph paper but think
of the foci as being 8 units
apart which would mean that
the circles labelled 3, 6, 9,
12, . . . would actually be 2,
4, 6, 8, . . . in the new system; or draw new graph
paper in which each focus

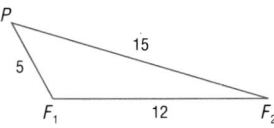
Drawing
Ellipses and
Hyperbolas

The first pages of this chapter used 3-dimensional ideas to describe
ellipses and hyperbolas as conic sections. It is also possible to give
definitions for the curves using only 2 dimensions.

Recall from Lesson 6-3 that a parabola is determined by a point
(its focus) and a line (its directrix). Both ellipses and hyperbolas—
although they look totally unlike each other—are determined by two
points (their *foci*, pronounced "foe sigh," plural of focus) and a
number (the *focal constant*). Consider first an ellipse.

Let the foci be the points F_1 and F_2 with the distance between them
$F_1F_2 = 12$. The focal constant can be any number larger than this
distance. Suppose it is 20. A point P is on this ellipse if and only if
the sum of its distances from the foci equals 20.

In the drawing below, think of F_1 and F_2 as the foci. The
Triangle Inequality guarantees that the sum of distances from P to
the foci must be greater than 12. Here $PF_1 + PF_2 = 20$, which is
greater than 12.

Now we look for all points P such that $PF_1 + PF_2 = 20$. These
points are on a curve. The drawing below shows the curve and six
points on it, P_1, P_2, P_3, P_4, P_5, and P_6. You should verify that
$P_nF_1 + P_nF_2 = 20$ for each n. By definition, the curve is said to be
an *ellipse*, with *foci* F_1 and F_2 and *focal constant* 20.

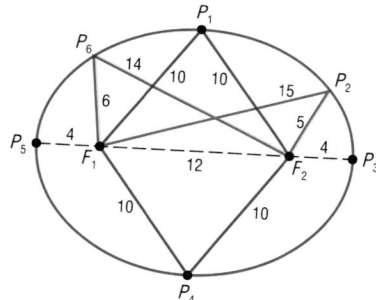

Definition:

Let F_1 and F_2 be any two points and d be a constant
with $d > F_1F_2$. Then the **ellipse with foci F_1 and F_2 and
focal constant d** is the set of points P in a plane which
satisfy $PF_1 + PF_2 = d$.

We need $d > F_1F_2$ because of the Triangle Inequality. The **vertices** of the ellipse are the points of intersection of the ellipse and the line containing its foci. So in the diagram above, points P_3 and P_5 are the vertices of the ellipse. Note that the distance $P_3P_5 = 20$, the focal constant.

Graph paper consisting of two intersecting sets of concentric circles makes it easy to draw ellipses. Such graph paper is sometimes called *conic graph paper*. In the conic graph paper below the centers of the two sets of circles are 12 units apart.

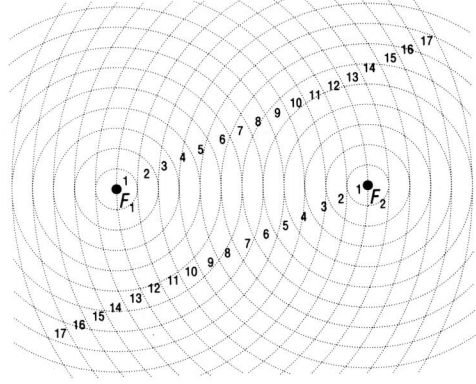

Example 1   Draw the ellipse with $F_1F_2 = 12$ and $PF_1 + PF_2 = 20$.

Solution   Use conic graph paper for which $F_1F_2 = 12$. Now consider two numbers whose sum is 20, say 14 and 6. Mark the four points that are 14 units from one focus and 6 units from the other. On the figure below we have labeled such points P_1, P_2, P_3, and P_4. Find two other numbers whose sum is 20, say 15 and 5. Mark the four points that are 15 units from one focus and 5 from the other. Continue for other pairs of whole numbers whose sum is 20. Draw a smooth curve through the points you have marked. Note that V_1 and V_2, which were found using the pair of numbers 4 and 16, are the vertices of the ellipse.

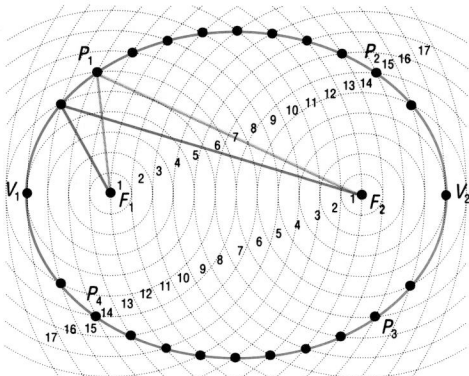

goes through the 8th smallest circle centered at the other focus.

In **Example 2**, note that one branch of the hyperbola is where $PF_1 - PF_2 = 10$ and the other branch is where $PF_2 - PF_1 = 10$. The use of absolute value to combine these two equations into one is a beautiful illustration of the utility of that concept.

ADDITIONAL EXAMPLES
1. Use conic graph paper to draw an ellipse in which the foci are 12 units apart and the focal constant is 19.
Points on the ellipse are the intersection points of circles with radii that add to 19.

2. Use conic graph paper to draw an hyperbola in which the foci are 12 units apart and the focal constant is 5.
Points on the hyperbola are the intersection points of circles with radii whose difference is 5.

If, in the definition of an ellipse, the distances from P to the foci are subtracted instead of added, then the curve that results is a hyperbola.

Definition:

Let F_1 and F_2 be any two points and d be a constant with $0 < d < F_1F_2$. Then the **hyperbola with foci F_1 and F_2 and focal constant d** is the set of points P in a plane which satisfy $|PF_1 - PF_2| = d$.

Consider again points F_1 and F_2 with $F_1F_2 = 12$, and the set of points P such that $|PF_1 - PF_2| = 10$. Below are three points, P_1, P_2, and P_3, which lie on the resulting hyperbola.

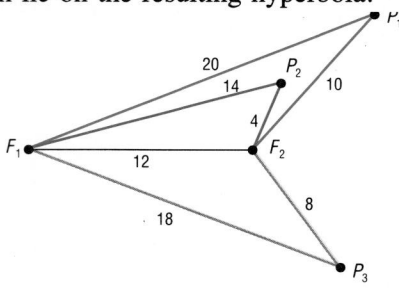

■ ■ ■ ■ ■ ■ ■

Example 2 Use conic graph paper to draw a hyperbola in which the distance between foci is $F_1F_2 = 12$ and the focal constant is $|PF_1 - PF_2| = 10$.

Solution Use graph paper in which the centers of the two sets of circles are 12 units apart. Find a pair of numbers whose difference is 10, say 16 and 6. Mark a point P such that $PF_1 = 16$ and $PF_2 = 6$. (Notice that there are two such points, labeled P_1 and P_2 in our drawing below.) Now mark points such that $PF_2 = 16$ and $PF_1 = 6$. (We have labeled these P_3 and P_4.) Continue marking points determined by other pairs of numbers whose difference is 10. Connect these points with two smooth curves.

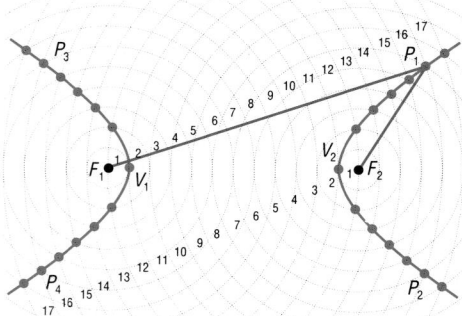

682

The two unconnected parts of a hyperbola are called its **branches**. One branch results from $PF_1 - PF_2 = d$; the other from $PF_1 - PF_2 = -d$. The segment joining the foci intersects the branches in the **vertices** of the hyperbola. In the hyperbola in Example 2, the vertices V_1 and V_2 can be found using the pair of numbers 11 and 1.

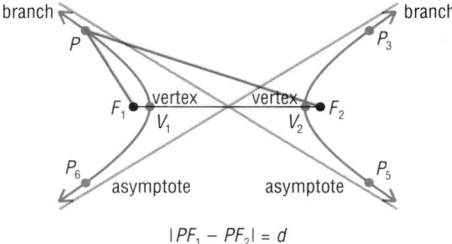

$$|PF_1 - PF_2| = d$$

At first glance, each branch may seem to be a parabola, but the shape of the curve is different. In particular, as points on a branch get farther from the foci, they approach but do not meet one of the two dashed lines. These lines are the *asymptotes* of the hyperbola.

Every ellipse and hyperbola has two symmetry lines, the line through the foci and the perpendicular bisector of the segment joining the foci. So once you have found a point on one of these curves, you can use that point to find three others.

Ellipses and hyperbolas have many applications. In 1609 Johannes Kepler discovered that each planet orbits the sun in an ellipse in which the sun is at one focus. This is known as Kepler's first law of planetary motion. About 60 years later, Sir Isaac Newton used this idea to formulate his theory of universal gravitation. Besides planets, moons and artificial satellites around planets have elliptical orbits. Comets either have elliptical or hyperbolic orbits.

LESSON 12-3 *Drawing Ellipses and Hyperbolas* **683**

NOTES ON QUESTIONS
Questions 9 and 10: The graphs could still be drawn using a ruler and compass without the conic paper, but it would take much more time.

Question 14: This question extends a reflection property that some students (particularly UCSMP students) will have seen in their geometry course. The ball or sound reflects off the curve at a point as it would off the tangent to the curve at that point. Consider point P on an ellipse with foci F and G. Because the tangent to the ellipse at P makes equal angles with $\overline{PF}$ and $\overline{PG}$, the ball or sound reflects off the ellipse from one focus to the other. This can be proved— the proof requires no advanced mathematics but is not trivial.

Question 29: This question can be demonstrated in class on a chalkboard. Have two students hold the ends of a piece of string while you or a third student draws the curve.

9.

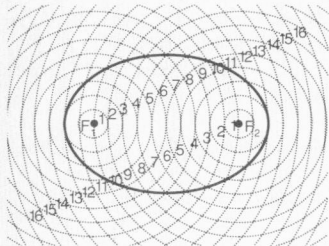

10.

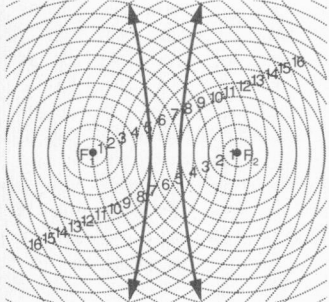

12.

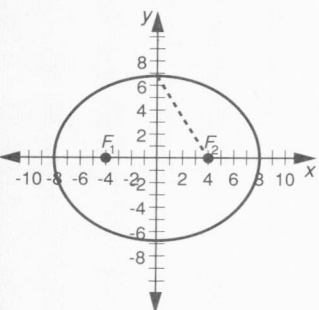

14.

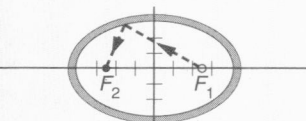

15.b.

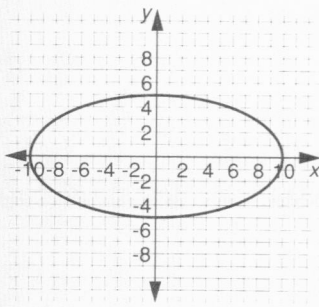

Questions

In 1–3, refer to Example 1.

1. The distance between the foci is ___?___.   **12**

2. The focal constant is ___?___.   **20**

3. $F_1V_2 + F_2V_2 = $ ___?___.   **20**

In 4 and 5, give the singular form of each word.

4. foci   **focus**   **5.** vertices   **vertex**

In 6 and 7, *true or false*.

6. The focal constant of a hyperbola equals the distance between the foci.   **False**

7. If F_1 and F_2 are the foci of a hyperbola, then $\overleftrightarrow{F_1F_2}$ is a line of symmetry for the curve.   **True**

8. The orbit of a comet is either ___?___ or ___?___.   **elliptical, hyperbolic**

In 9 and 10, use conic graph paper with concentric circles with radii from 1 to 16 units, and with centers 10 units apart.

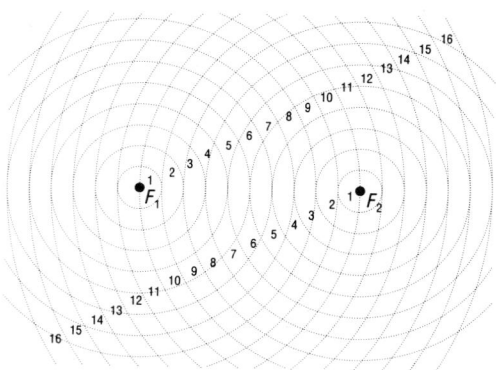

9. Draw an ellipse with foci F_1 and F_2, where $F_1F_2 = 10$, and with focal distance 14.   **See margin.**

10. Draw a hyperbola with $F_1F_2 = 10$ and $|PF_1 - PF_2| = 2$.
See margin

In 11–13, use this definition. The **eccentricity** of an ellipse or hyperbola is the ratio of the distance between its foci to its focal constant.

11. What is the eccentricity of the ellipse in Example 1? $\frac{12}{20} = \frac{3}{5}$

12. Sketch an ellipse with eccentricity $\frac{1}{2}$.   **See margin.**

13. Why must the eccentricity of an ellipse be a number between 0 and 1?
Focal constant > distance between foci

684

14. An elliptical surface has a special reflecting property. When sound, light, or some other object originating at one focus reaches the ellipse, it is reflected in such a way that it passes through the other focus. Suppose you are playing pool at an elliptical table which has only one pocket located at one focus. If the cue ball is placed at the other focus, trace a path the ball would follow if it strikes the cushion.
See margin.

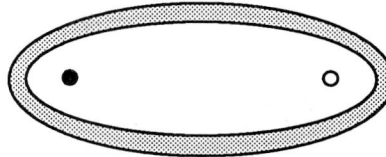

15. The points $(10, 0)$, $(0, 5)$, $(8, 3)$, and $(6, 4)$ satisfy $x^2 + 4y^2 = 100$.
  a. Use this information to find 8 other points with integer coordinates which satisfy the equation. $(-10, 0)$, $(0, -5)$, $(-8, 3)$, $(8, -3)$, $(-8, -3)$, $(-6, 4)$,
  $(6, -4)$, $(-6, -4)$
  b. Graph these 12 solutions. **See margin.**
  c. Name the conic section being graphed. **ellipse**
  d. Give equations for the symmetry lines. $x = 0, y = 0$

16. Consider the equation $x^2 - y^2 = 144$.
  a. Find 14 points with integer coordinates between -20 and 20 which satisfy this equation. $(\pm12, 0)$, $(\pm13, \pm5)$, $(\pm15, \pm9)$, $(\pm20, \pm16)$
  b. Graph these points. **See margin.**
  c. Name the vertices. $(-12, 0)$, $(12, 0)$
  d. Conjecture which lines might be the asymptotes for this hyperbola. $y = x, y = -x$

17. Use a ruler and compass. **See margin.**
  a. Draw two points, F_1 and F_2, 3 cm apart as shown at the right. Now find five points P_n, $n = 1, 2, 3, 4,$ and 5, such that $P_nF_1 + P_nF_2 = 5$ cm.

F_1 •————————• F_2
3 cm

  b. The points P_n in part a lie on a(n) __?__ with foci __?__ and __?__ and focal constant __?__.
  c. Sketch the rest of the curve satisfying conditions in parts a and b.

Review

18. The figure below shows a cross-section of a semicircular tunnel with diameter 40 feet. A sign [Entering Tunnel—Do Not Pass] must be hung 16 feet above the roadway. Find the length BE of the beam that will support the bottom of the sign. *(Lesson 12-2)* **24 ft**

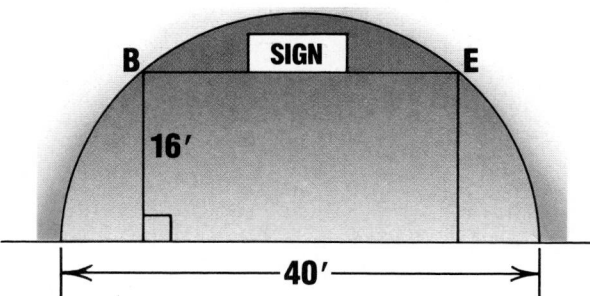

16.b.

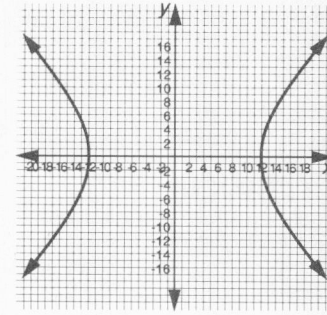

17.a. and c.

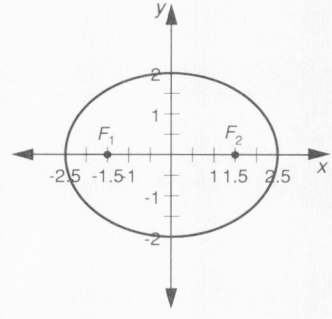

b. ellipse; F_1; F_2; 5

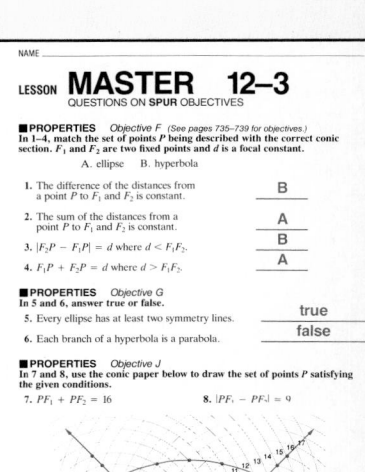

MORE PRACTICE
For more questions on SPUR
Objectives, use *Lesson Mas-
ter 12-3*, shown on page 685.

EXTENSION
The French mathematician
Germinal Pierre Dandelin
(1794–1847) provided an ele-
gant way of connecting the
locus definitions to the cross-
section description of the
conics. The *Dandelin
spheres* are two spheres inscribed inside a cone that
are tangent to the plane of
the conic section.

The points of tangency of the
spheres with the plane are
the foci of the ellipse (drawn
above) or the hyperbola.
Each edge of the cone intersects each sphere in one
point. Because tangents to a
sphere from an external point
are of equal length, it can be
shown (for the ellipse) that
the sum of the distances
from any point on the ellipse
to the foci equals the distance between those points,
which is constant.

EVALUATION
A quiz covering Lessons
12-1 through 12-3 is provided
in the Teacher's Resource
File.

ADDITIONAL ANSWERS
29.a. The curve should
look like the example in
the text.
b. If the tacks are called
F_1 and F_2, for any point
P on the curve, $PF_1 +
PF_2 = l$, the length of the
string. This satisfies the
definition of an ellipse.

19. Write a sentence describing the set of all
points (x, y) in the shaded region at the
right. *(Lesson 12-2)* $9 < x^2 + y^2 < 49$

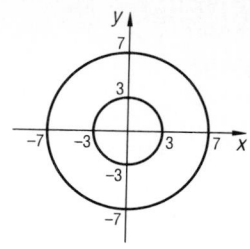

In 20 and 21, find (a) the center and (b) the radius of the circle with the
given equation. *(Lesson 12-1)*

20. $x^2 + y^2 = 2$
   a) (0, 0); b) $\sqrt{2}$

21. $(x + 5)^2 + (y - \frac{1}{2})^2 = 9$
   a) $(-5, \frac{1}{2})$; b) 3

22. The circle at the right is tangent to
the axes at (2, 0) and (0, 2).
   a. Write an equation for this
      circle. $(x - 2)^2 + (y - 2)^2 = 4$
   b. Find two values of y such
      that $(1, y)$ is on this circle.
      (Lesson 12-1)
      $y = 2 + \sqrt{3}$ or $y = 2 - \sqrt{3}$

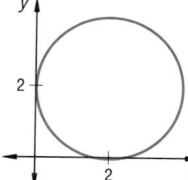

23. Give the distance between (x, y)
and $(c, 0)$. *(Previous course)*
$\sqrt{(x - c)^2 + y^2}$

In 24–27, simplify. *(Lessons 6-1, 8-5)*

24. $(\sqrt{x})^2$ x

25. $(\sqrt{x + 3})^2$ $x + 3$

26. $(\sqrt{x}) + 3)^2$
   $x + 6\sqrt{x} + 9$

27. $(2a - \sqrt{p})^2$ $4a^2 - 4a\sqrt{p} + p$

28. a. Find the vertices of the image of
      the square at the right under $S_{5, 1/2}$.
   b. Describe what S does to the
      preimage.
   c. Find the area of the square and the
      area of the image. *(Lesson 4-4)*   2, 5
      a) (5, 0), (0, $\frac{1}{2}$), (-5, 0), (0, -$\frac{1}{2}$)
      b) horizontal stretch, vertical shrink

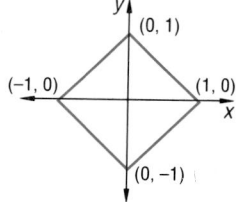

Exploration

29. a. Using two thumbtacks and a piece of string, draw a curve as
      shown below.   See margin.
   b. Explain why the curve is an ellipse.   See margin.

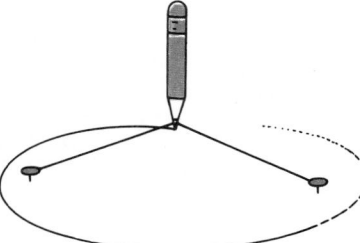

Equations of Some Ellipses

A boat company operates a sightseeing tour and shuttle between two small islands 12 miles apart. Because of fuel restrictions boats cannot travel more than 20 miles in going from one island to the other.

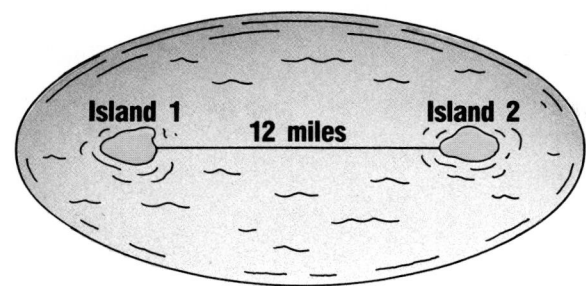

This situation is like that found in the previous lesson. A boat can go no farther than the ellipse determined by the islands as foci and focal constant 20 miles.

To find an equation for this ellipse, consider a coordinate system that locates the origin midway between the islands with the islands on an axis. Then the islands are located at (-6, 0) and (6, 0). This is called the *standard position* for the ellipse.

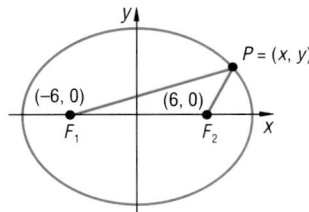

If $P = (x, y)$ is on the ellipse, then by the definition of an ellipse,

$$PF_1 + PF_2 = 20.$$

So by the Distance Formula,

$$\sqrt{(x + 6)^2 + (y - 0)^2} + \sqrt{(x - 6)^2 + (y - 0)^2} = 20$$

or $\qquad \sqrt{(x + 6)^2 + y^2} + \sqrt{(x - 6)^2 + y^2} \qquad = 20.$

This is an equation for the ellipse and it is quite complicated. Surprisingly, it is easier to begin with a more general case. The resulting simplified equation is well worth the effort it takes to get it.

RESOURCES
■ Lesson Master 12-4
▯ Visual for Teaching Aid 82 provides the theorem and proof of the equation for an ellipse.

OBJECTIVES

B Write an equation for an ellipse satisfying given conditions.
E Identify characteristics of ellipses.
H Use ellipses to analyze real-world situations.
J Graph ellipses given their equations, and vice versa.

TEACHING NOTES

Go through the proof of the Equation for an Ellipse Theorem with students. Next, work through the questions in order.

Alternate Approach
You can begin by finding the equation for an ellipse given specific foci and the focal constant, for example, (-5, 0), (5, 0) and 14 from Question 9 of Lesson 12-3. Explain the terms major axis, minor axis, and center of an ellipse. Then ask students to identify these using your example.
   Show how to graph an ellipse knowing its equation by using your example from before. Now, go through the proof of the theorem with students.
   Work through **Questions 3-9** orally with students. Then assign the reading and the rest of the questions for homework.

In the following theorem, the focal constant is called $2a$, rather than d, because that simplifies equations in the proof starting with step 6:

Theorem (Equation for an Ellipse):

The ellipse with foci $(c, 0)$ and $(-c, 0)$ and focal constant $2a$ has equation

$$\frac{x^2}{a^2} + \frac{y^2}{b^2} = 1, \text{ where } b^2 = a^2 - c^2.$$

Proof

Let $F_1 = (-c, 0)$, $F_2 = (c, 0)$, and $P = (x, y)$. We number the steps for reference.

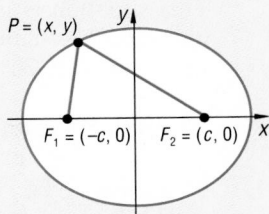

1. By the definition of an ellipse,
$$PF_1 + PF_2 = 2a.$$

Using the Distance Formula, this becomes
$$\sqrt{(x + c)^2 + y^2} + \sqrt{(x - c)^2 + y^2} = 2a.$$

2. Subtracting one of the square roots from both sides,
$$\sqrt{(x - c)^2 + y^2} = 2a - \sqrt{(x + c)^2 + y^2}.$$

3. Squaring both sides (the right side is like a binomial),
$$(x - c)^2 + y^2 = 4a^2 - 4a\sqrt{(x + c)^2 + y^2} + (x + c)^2 + y^2.$$

4. Expanding binomials and doing appropriate subtractions,
$$-2cx = 4a^2 - 4a\sqrt{(x + c)^2 + y^2} + 2cx.$$

5. Using the Addition Property of Equality and rearranging terms,
$$4a\sqrt{(x + c)^2 + y^2} = 4a^2 + 4cx.$$

6. Multiplying by $\frac{1}{4}$,
$$a\sqrt{(x + c)^2 + y^2} = a^2 + cx.$$

7. Squaring a second time,
$$a^2[(x + c)^2 + y^2] = a^4 + 2a^2cx + c^2x^2.$$

688

8. Expanding the binomial and subtracting $2a^2cx$ from both sides,

$$a^2x^2 + a^2c^2 + a^2y^2 = a^4 + c^2x^2.$$

9. Subtracting a^2c^2 and c^2x^2 from both sides, then factoring,

$$(a^2 - c^2)x^2 + a^2y^2 = a^2(a^2 - c^2).$$

10. Since $c > 0$, $F_1F_2 = 2c$, and $2a > F_1F_2$, we have $2a > 2c > 0$. So $a > c > 0$. Thus $a^2 > c^2$ and $a^2 - c^2$ is not negative. So $a^2 - c^2$ can be considered as the square of some real number, say b. Now let $a^2 - c^2 = b^2$ and substitute.

$$b^2x^2 + a^2y^2 = a^2b^2$$

11. Dividing both sides by a^2b^2, $\dfrac{x^2}{a^2} + \dfrac{y^2}{b^2} = 1$.

The equation $\dfrac{x^2}{a^2} + \dfrac{y^2}{b^2} = 1$ is in the *standard form* for an equation of this ellipse. By substitution, it is easy to check that $(a, 0)$, $(-a, 0)$, $(0, b)$, and $(0, -b)$ are on this ellipse. This helps graph it. Note that $(-a, 0)$ and $(a, 0)$ are the vertices of the ellipse.

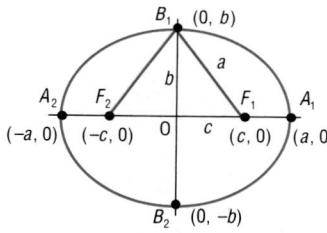

Since $2a$ is the focal constant, $B_1F_1 = a$. By the Pythagorean theorem, $b^2 + c^2 = a^2$. This confirms step 10 of the proof that $b^2 = a^2 - c^2$.

The segments $\overline{A_1A_2}$ and $\overline{B_1B_2}$ are, respectively, the **major** and **minor axes** of the ellipse. (The major axis contains the foci and is always longer.) The two axes lie on the symmetry lines and intersect at the **center O** of the ellipse. The previous diagram illustrates the following theorem which applies to all ellipses centered at the origin with foci on one of the coordinate axes.

Theorem:

In the ellipse with equation $\dfrac{x^2}{a^2} + \dfrac{y^2}{b^2} = 1$, $2a$ is the length of the horizontal axis, and $2b$ is the length of the vertical axis.

LESSON 12-4 Equations of Some Ellipses **689**

The longer axis, on which the foci lie, is the major axis. Its length is the focal constant. Specifically, if $a > b$, then $(c, 0)$ and $(-c, 0)$ are the foci, the focal constant is $2a$, and $b^2 = a^2 - c^2$ as in the ellipse on page 688. If $b > a$, then the major axis is vertical. So the foci are $(0, c)$ and $(0, -c)$, the focal constant $2b$, and $a^2 = b^2 - c^2$.

■ ■ ■ ■ ■ ■ ■ ■
Example 1 Graph the ellipse with equation $\dfrac{x^2}{4} + \dfrac{y^2}{9} = 1$.

Solution Since $a^2 = 4$ and $b^2 = 9$, then $a = 2$ and $b = 3$. Since $b > a$, the foci of the ellipse are on the y-axis. The length of the major axis is 6; the minor axis has length 4. Four points on this ellipse are easy to find: $(2, 0)$, $(-2, 0)$, $(0, 3)$, and $(0, -3)$. They are the endpoints of the minor and major axes, respectively.

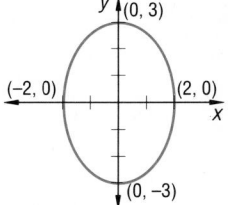

With these two theorems, the possible locations of the shuttle boat can be described algebraically.

■ ■ ■ ■ ■ ■ ■ ■
Example 2 Find an equation in standard form for the ellipse with foci $(6, 0)$ and $(-6, 0)$ and focal constant 20.

Solution This ellipse is in standard position, so it has an equation of the form

$$\frac{x^2}{a^2} + \frac{y^2}{b^2} = 1.$$

Only the values of a^2 and b^2 are needed. From the given information, $c = 6$ and $2a = 20$. So $a = 10$, and $a^2 = 100$. Now $b^2 = a^2 - c^2 = 100 - 6^2 = 64$. Thus an equation is

$$\frac{x^2}{100} + \frac{y^2}{64} = 1.$$

A graph is shown at the right. The boats can reach anywhere on or in the interior of this ellipse, which is described by the inequality

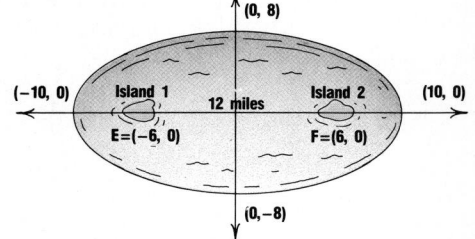

$$\frac{x^2}{100} + \frac{y^2}{64} \leq 1.$$

690

In general, if the equal sign in the equation for an ellipse is replaced by $<$ or $>$, the resulting inequality represents either the interior or exterior of the ellipse, respectively.

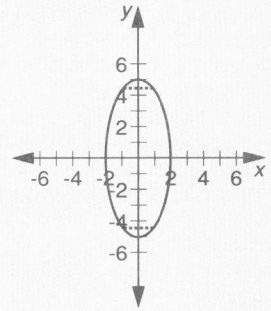

Questions

Covering the Reading

1. **a.** An equation for the ellipse with foci $(6, 0)$ and $(-6, 0)$ and focal constant 20 is $\sqrt{(x-6)^2 + y^2} + \underline{\ ?\ } = \underline{\ ?\ }$. $\sqrt{(x+6)^2 + y^2}$; 20
   b. The equation of part a can be simplified to what equation in standard form? $\dfrac{x^2}{100} + \dfrac{y^2}{64} = 1$

2. The boat company's shuttle can reach anywhere in the region described by what inequality? $\dfrac{x^2}{100} + \dfrac{y^2}{64} \leq 1$

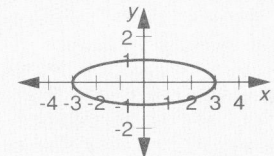

In 3–6, use the ellipse at the right. The foci are F and G. Name:

3. the major axis $\overline{AC}$

4. the minor axis $\overline{BD}$

5. the center E

6. the vertices. A, C

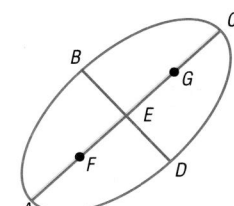

In 7–9, for the ellipse with equation $\dfrac{x^2}{a^2} + \dfrac{y^2}{b^2} = 1$, identify:

7. its center $(0,0)$

8. the length of the major and minor axes $2a$ (if $a > b$); $2b$

9. the endpoints of the major and minor axes. $(-a, 0), (a, 0)$; $(0, b), (0, -b)$

In 10 and 11, graph the ellipse with the given equation.

10. $\dfrac{x^2}{4} + \dfrac{y^2}{25} = 1$ See margin.   **11.** $\dfrac{x^2}{9} + y^2 = 1$ See margin.

12. Find an equation in standard form for the ellipse with focal constant 25 and foci $(10, 0)$ and $(-10, 0)$. $\dfrac{x^2}{156.25} + \dfrac{y^2}{56.25} = 1$

13. If the company's boat in this lesson has the fuel to travel 30 miles in going from one island to another, give a sentence in standard form for the possible positions of the boat. $\dfrac{x^2}{225} + \dfrac{y^2}{189} \leq 1$

Applying the Mathematics

14. Refer to the ellipse graphed at the right.
   a. Find an equation for the ellipse. $\dfrac{x^2}{49} + \dfrac{y^2}{36} = 1$
   b. What is a sentence to describe the interior of this ellipse? $\dfrac{x^2}{49} + \dfrac{y^2}{36} < 1$

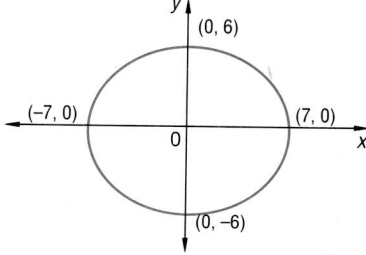

LESSON 12-4   Equations of Some Ellipses   **691**

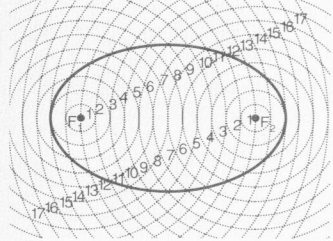
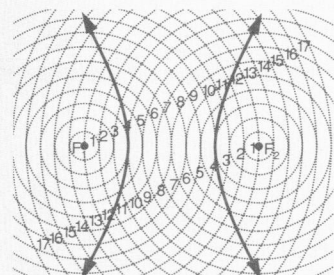
15. *Multiple choice* Which of the following describes the set of points P whose distances from $(7, 2)$ and $(3, 4)$ add up to 12? **c**
    (a) $(x - 7)^2 + (y - 2)^2 + (x - 3)^2 + (y - 4)^2 = 12$
    (b) $(x + 7)^2 + (y + 2)^2 + (x + 3)^2 + (y + 4)^2 = 12$
    (c) $\sqrt{(x - 7)^2 + (y - 2)^2} + \sqrt{(x - 3)^2 + (y - 4)^2} = 12$
    (d) $\sqrt{(x + 7)^2 + (y + 2)^2} + \sqrt{(x + 3)^2 + (y + 4)^2} = 12$

16. In the United States Capitol there is an elliptical chamber in which a person whispering while standing at one focus can be easily heard by another person standing at the other focus. The whispering gallery in the Capitol's Statuary Hall is 46 ft wide and 96 ft long.

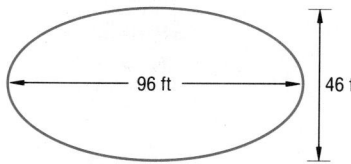

96 ft   46 ft

   a. A politician noted this feature of the chamber because the desk of the opposing party's floor leader was at one focus. How far from that desk should the politician stand to overhear the floor leader's whispered conversations?   ≈84 ft
   b. How far from either end of the gallery would they be?   ≈6 ft
   c. Find an equation which could describe the ellipse of the whispering gallery. $\dfrac{x^2}{2304} + \dfrac{y^2}{529} = 1$

17. The orbits of the planets are elliptical with the sun at one focus. Venus's orbit can be described by the equation

$$\frac{x^2}{5013} + \frac{y^2}{4970} = 1,$$

   where x and y are in millions of miles.
   a. What is the farthest Venus gets from the sun?   ≈77.4 million mi
   b. What is the closest Venus gets to the sun?   ≈64.2 million mi

692

18. Consider $6x^2 + 3y^2 = 36$.

 a. Show that this is the equation for an ellipse by rewriting it in the form

$$\frac{x^2}{a^2} + \frac{y^2}{b^2} = 1. \quad \frac{x^2}{6} + \frac{y^2}{12} = 1$$

 b. What is the length of the major axis? $4\sqrt{3}$

Review

In 19 and 20, use conic graph paper with centers 12 units apart. Draw the set of points P satisfying each equation.

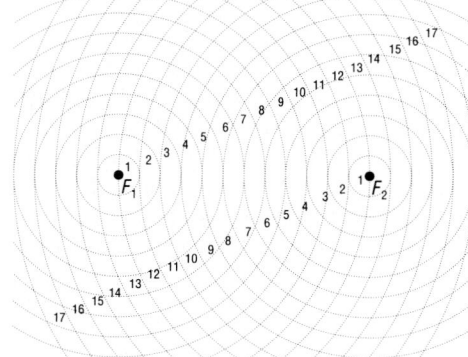

19. $PF_1 + PF_2 = 16$ **See margin.**

20. $|PF_1 - PF_2| = 6$ *(Lesson 12-3)*   **See margin.**

In 21–24, each circle drawn below has radius 4 and its center is on either the x- or y-axis. *(Lessons 12-1, 12-2, Previous course)*

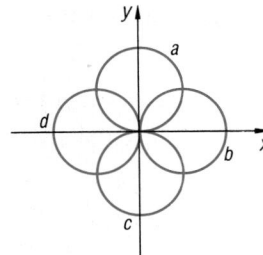

21. Write an equation for circle a.
$x^2 + (y - 4)^2 = 16$

22. Find an inequality describing the interior of circle b.
$(x - 4)^2 + y^2 < 16$

23. Find the circumference of each circle.
8π

24. *True or false*   The area of each circle is 4π.
False

MORE PRACTICE
For more questions on SPUR
Objectives, use *Lesson Master 12-4*, shown on page 693.

EXTENSION
Here are some famous whispering galleries: Statuary Hall (see **Question 16** note); the dome of St. Paul's Cathedral in London, England; the vases in the Salle des Cariatides in the Louvre museum in Paris, France; St. John Lateran in Rome, Italy; and the Ear of Dionysius, in Syracuse, Italy. Several museums in the United States also have whispering galleries. A student might write a report about such galleries, describing their size and why they were built, for example.

ADDITIONAL ANSWERS
26.a. and b.

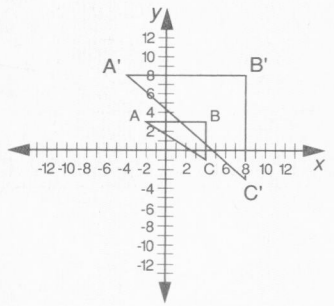

c. No. The corresponding sides of the two triangles are not proportional.

29.a., b., c., d. See Additional Answers in the back of the book.

---

25. Solve for h: $2\pi r^2 + 2\pi rh = 132$. *(Lesson 1-9)* $h = \dfrac{66}{\pi r} - r$

26. a. Draw the triangle *ABC* with vertices $A = (-2, 3)$, $B = (4, 3)$, and $C = (4, -1)$. **See margin.**
   b. Draw its image $\triangle A'B'C'$ under the scale change $S_{2,3}$. **See margin.**
   c. Is $\triangle ABC \sim \triangle A'B'C'$? Why or why not? **See margin.**
   d. Find the area of $\triangle ABC$. **12**
   e. Find the area of $\triangle A'B'C'$. **72**
   f. The area of $\triangle A'B'C'$ is how many times larger than the area of $\triangle ABC$? *(Lesson 4-4, Previous course)* **6**

27. Use the triangle at the right.
   a. Find the length of $\overline{BC}$ to the nearest tenth. ≈ 19.5
   b. Find the measures of $\angle B$ and $\angle C$ to the nearest degree.
   (Lessons 10-6, 10-7)
   $\angle B \approx 59.7°$, $\angle C \approx 70.3°$

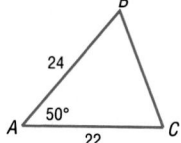

Exploration

28. Look up each word in a dictionary. Explain how each is connected with ellipses. (The last word is relatively new, having first been used in the 1960s.)
   a. aphelion — the point farthest from the sun in the orbit of a planet or comet
   b. perihelion — the point closest to the sun in the orbit of a planet or comet
   c. apogee — the point farthest from the earth in the orbit of the moon or any other earth satellite
   d. apses — vaulted or arched semicircular or many-sided recesses in churches, usually at the east end
   e. perilune — the point closest to the moon in the orbit of a satellite

29. a. Use the Graph Translation Theorem to predict what the graph of $\dfrac{(x-2)^2}{9} + \dfrac{(y+6)^2}{25} = 1$ will look like. **See margin for a–d.**
   b. Check your conjecture with an automatic grapher.
   c. Graph some other equations of the form $\dfrac{(x-h)^2}{a^2} + \dfrac{(y-k)^2}{b^2} = 1$.
   d. Write a paragraph summarizing your work.

694

12-5

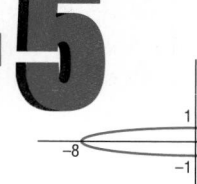

Relations Between Ellipses and Circles

As you know, in some ellipses the major axis is much longer than the minor axis. In others, the two axes are almost equal. Consider the three cases below.

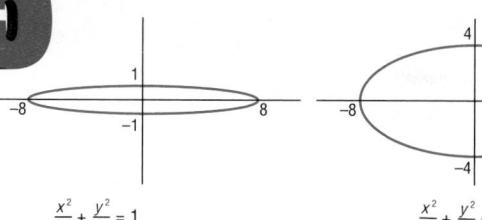

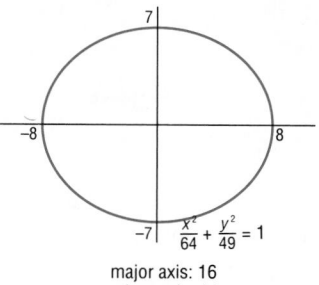

$\frac{x^2}{64} + \frac{y^2}{1} = 1$
major axis: 16
minor axis: 2

$\frac{x^2}{64} + \frac{y^2}{16} = 1$
major axis: 16
minor axis: 8

$\frac{x^2}{64} + \frac{y^2}{49} = 1$
major axis: 16
minor axis: 14

If the major and minor axes are equal, as in the case below, the ellipse is a circle.

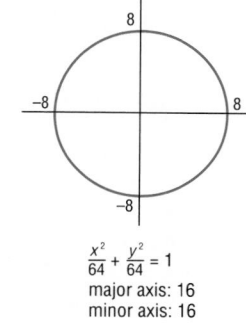

$\frac{x^2}{64} + \frac{y^2}{64} = 1$
major axis: 16
minor axis: 16

This can be verified in general by looking at the equations for circles and ellipses. Consider the standard form of an equation for an ellipse, $\frac{x^2}{a^2} + \frac{y^2}{b^2} = 1$. Suppose the major and minor axes are equal and each of length $2r$. Then we may substitute r for a and r for b. The equation becomes $\frac{x^2}{r^2} + \frac{y^2}{r^2} = 1$. Now, multiplying both sides of the equation by r^2, the result is $x^2 + y^2 = r^2$. This is an equation for a circle with center at the origin and radius r. Thus a circle is a special kind of ellipse whose major and minor axes are equal.

Ellipses and circles are related in other ways. If you look at a circle on an angle, then it appears to be a non-circular ellipse. Notice how the circular hoop at the left appears to be taller than it is wide. Artists who want to draw circles in perspective must actually draw non-circular ellipses.

RESOURCES
■ Lesson Master 12-5

OBJECTIVES

C Find the area of an ellipse.
G Relate ellipses and circles.
H Use ellipses to analyze real-world situations.

TEACHING NOTES

A stretched circle looks like an ellipse, but how can we be sure? Explain to students that some curves, like parabolas and hyperbolas, look alike until examined more closely. For instance, an egg is oval-shaped—consider the origin of the word "oval"—but is not shaped like an ellipse. One side is wider than the other.

This lesson is neither very difficult nor very long. Thus, we suggest you assign the reading and questions without preliminary discussion. Then work through the questions in order. **Example 1** of the lesson can be covered while going over **Questions 6 and 7**.

From Lesson 12-4, graphs of certain equations are known to be ellipses. Since a stretch can be described algebraically, the image of a circle can be obtained algebraically. Stress to students not only can we explain that a stretched circle is an ellipse, but also the relation between the equations $\frac{x^2}{a^2} + \frac{y^2}{b^2} = 1$ and $x^2 + y^2 = 1$ can be explained. This is done in **Question 10**.

695

An ellipse can also be thought of as a stretched circle. The basic transformation which causes stretches and shrinks is the scale change which you studied in Lesson 4-4.

Consider the circle with equation $x^2 + y^2 = 1$ under the scale change $S_{2,3}$. The scale change $S_{2,3}$ has a horizontal magnitude of 2 and a vertical magnitude of 3. The images of several points on the circle are graphed below at the right.

$$(1,0) \rightarrow (2, 0)$$
$$(0, 1) \rightarrow (0, 3)$$
$$(-1, 0) \rightarrow (-2, 0)$$
$$(0, -1) \rightarrow (0, -3)$$
$$(-0.8, 0.6) \rightarrow (-1.6, 1.8)$$
$$(0.6, -0.8) \rightarrow (1.2, -2.4)$$

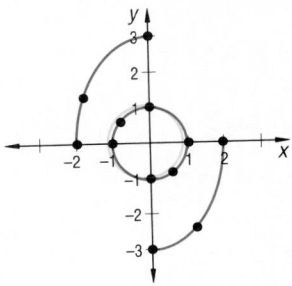

From these six points you can see that the image of the unit circle under this scale change is not another circle.

▪ ▪ ▪ ▪ ▪ ▪ ▪ ▪

Example 1   Find an equation for the image of the circle $x^2 + y^2 = 1$ under $S_{2,3}$.

Solution   To find an equation of the image of the circle, let (x', y') be the image of (x, y).

Since $S_{2,3}$: $(x, y) \rightarrow (2x, 3y)$
$$2x = x' \quad \text{and} \quad 3y = y'.$$
So $x = \frac{x'}{2} \quad \text{and} \quad y = \frac{y'}{3}.$

We know that $x^2 + y^2 = 1$. Substituting for x and y in that equation, an equation for the image is

$$\left(\frac{x'}{2}\right)^2 + \left(\frac{y'}{3}\right)^2 = 1.$$

Because equations are usually written with x and y, the primes are dropped. So an equation of the image is

$$\frac{x^2}{4} + \frac{y^2}{9} = 1.$$

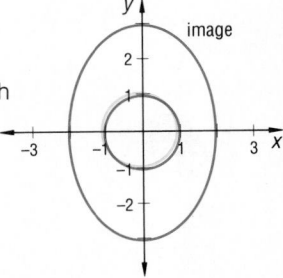

This is an equation for an ellipse with a minor axis of length 4 and a major axis of length 6.

696

Check Substitute some points known to be on the image. Do their coordinates satisfy this equation?

Try (2, 0). $\qquad\dfrac{2^2}{4} + \dfrac{0^2}{9} = 1 + 0 = 1$ $\qquad$ It checks.

Try (-1.6, 1.8). $\quad\dfrac{(-1.6)^2}{4} + \dfrac{(1.8)^2}{9} = \dfrac{2.56}{4} + \dfrac{3.24}{9}$

$\qquad\qquad\qquad\qquad = 0.64 + 0.36 = 1$ $\quad$ It checks.

The argument in Example 1 can be repeated with a in place of 2 and b in place of 3. It shows that any ellipse in standard form can be thought of as a stretched circle.

Theorem

The image of the unit circle with equation $x^2 + y^2 = 1$ under $S_{a,b}$ is the ellipse with equation $\left(\dfrac{x}{a}\right)^2 + \left(\dfrac{y}{b}\right)^2 = 1$.

Because the ellipse is related in so many ways to the circle it should not surprise you that the area of an ellipse is related to the area of a circle. In general for any figure, the scale change $S_{a,b}$ multiplies the area of the preimage by ab. Since the area of a unit circle, which has radius 1, is $\pi(1)^2 = \pi$, the area of the ellipse that is its image under $S_{a,b}$ has area $\pi \cdot (ab) = \pi ab$.

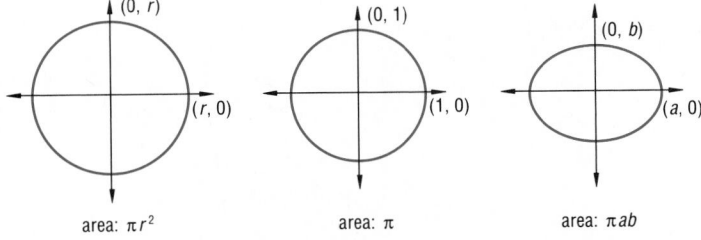

area: πr^2 $\qquad\qquad\qquad$ area: π $\qquad\qquad\qquad$ area: πab

---

Theorem:

An ellipse with axes of lengths $2a$ and $2b$ has area $A = \pi ab$.

Example 2 Find the area of the ellipse in Example 1.

Solution The length of the major axis is 6 and the length of the minor axis is 4. So $a = 3$ and $b = 2$ and the area of the ellipse is $\pi \cdot 3 \cdot 2 = 6\pi$.

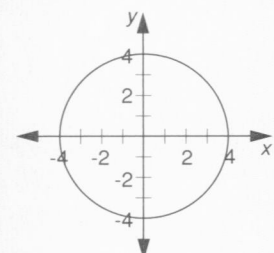
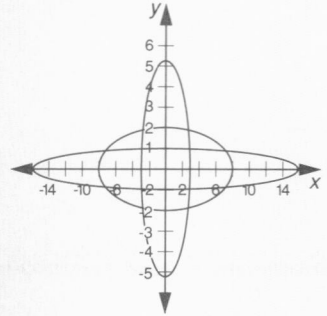
Questions

1. An ellipse in which the major and minor axes are equal in length is called a(n) __?__.   circle

In 2 and 3, *true* or *false*.

2. Every circle is an ellipse.   True

3. All ellipses are circles.   False

In 4 and 5, consider the circle $x^2 + y^2 = 1$ and the scale change $S_{4,3}$.

4. What is an equation for the image of the circle under $S_{4,3}$?
$\left(\frac{x}{4}\right)^2 + \left(\frac{y}{3}\right)^2 = 1$

5. a. What is the area of the circle? π
   b. What is the area of its image? 12π

In 6 and 7, consider the ellipse drawn at the right.

6. a. What scale change maps the unit circle to this ellipse? $S_{5,10}$
   b. Find an equation for this ellipse. $\left(\frac{x}{5}\right)^2 + \left(\frac{y}{10}\right)^2 = 1$

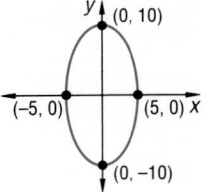

7. Find its area. 50π

8. a. Below are equations of the ellipses shown at the start of this lesson. Find their foci.   See margin.
   (i) $\dfrac{x^2}{64} + \dfrac{y^2}{1} = 1$ (ii) $\dfrac{x^2}{64} + \dfrac{y^2}{16} = 1$ (iii) $\dfrac{x^2}{64} + \dfrac{y^2}{49} = 1$
   b. As the distance between the foci decreases, what happens to the shape of an ellipse?   It becomes more and more circular.
   c. Use the relationship $a^2 - c^2 = b^2$ to find the distance between the foci for the circle $\dfrac{x^2}{64} + \dfrac{y^2}{64} = 1$.   0
   d. Are your answers to parts b and c consistent?   yes

9. a. *True* or *false*   Under a scale change, a figure is similar to its image.   False
   b. Justify your answer to part a by using an example from this lesson.   See Example 1.

10. Prove that the image of the unit circle under the scale change $S_{a,b}$ is the ellipse $\dfrac{x^2}{a^2} + \dfrac{y^2}{b^2} = 1$. (Hint: Follow the idea of Example 1.)   See margin.

11. a. Sketch a circle that has area 16π.   See margin.
    b. Sketch three noncongruent ellipses whose areas are also 16π.   See margin.

698

12. In Australia, a type of football is played on elliptical regions called Aussie Rules fields. One such field has a major axis of length 185 m and minor axis of length 155 m. A 1-meter track surrounding the field is to be covered with turf. Find the area of the track. **$171\pi \approx 537$ sq. m**

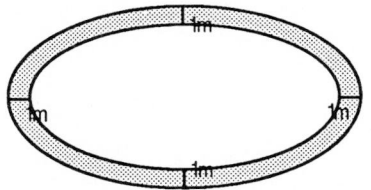

Review

In 13–17, match each equation with the best description. A letter may be used more than once. Do not graph. *(Lessons 12-1, 12-2, 12-4)*

13. $x^2 + y^2 = 25$ a

14. $\dfrac{x^2}{25} + \dfrac{y^2}{81} = 1$ b

15. $4x^2 + y^2 = 100$ b

16. $x^2 + y^2 < 25$ c

17. $\dfrac{x^2}{81} + \dfrac{y^2}{25} > 1$ f

(a) circle

(b) ellipse

(c) interior of circle

(d) interior of ellipse

(e) exterior of circle

(f) exterior of ellipse

18. The ellipse at the right has x-intercepts of 5 and -5 and foci at $(0, 12)$ and $(0, -12)$. Find:
a. F_1V_1 13
b. the focal constant   26
c. an equation for this ellipse.
   (Lesson 12-4) $\dfrac{x^2}{25} + \dfrac{y^2}{169} = 1$

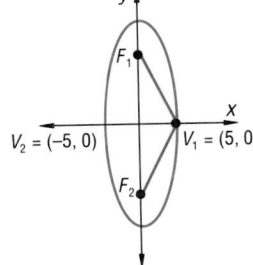

$V_2 = (-5, 0)$ $V_1 = (5, 0)$

19. In Chicago, elliptical flower beds have been planted over the Monroe Street parking garage. A landscape architect in a botanical garden decides to copy this idea. The elliptical gardens will have a major axis with length 18 ft and a minor axis with length 14 ft. Assuming the center is at $(0, 0)$ and foci are on the x-axis, find an equation for the ellipse. *(Lesson 12-4)* $\dfrac{x^2}{81} + \dfrac{y^2}{49} = 1$

LESSON 12-5   Relations Between Ellipses and Circles   **699**

 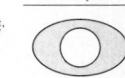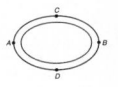

EXTENSION
Explain to students that by cutting a cylinder at certain angles, an ellipse is obtained. For example, if a tree is cut perpendicular to its axis of symmetry, the cross-section is circular; but if it is cut at another angle, the cut will result in an ellipse.

(1) Have students try this exercise at home using other tubular objects.

(2) Ask students what four shapes can be obtained from the intersection of an infinitely long cylinder and a plane. (Circle, from a plane perpendicular to the cylinder's axis of symmetry; ellipse, from a plane intersecting the axis of symmetry at some acute angle; a line, from a plane tangent to the cylinder; two lines, from a plane parallel to the axis of symmetry of the cylinder, but not tangent to the cylinder.)

(3) Have students investigate the relation between the size of the angle θ between the cylinder's axis of symmetry and the intersecting plane, and the shape of the ellipse. (As θ increases from 0° to 90°, the ellipse becomes more circular.)

ADDITIONAL ANSWERS
25.a., b. See Additional Answers in the back of this book.

20. Below is the top view of a castle surrounded by a circular moat 15 feet wide. The distance from the center of the castle to the outside of the moat is 500 feet. If the center of the castle is considered the origin, write a system of inequalities to describe the set of points on the surface of the moat. *(Lesson 12-2)* $235,225 < x^2 + y^2 < 250,000$

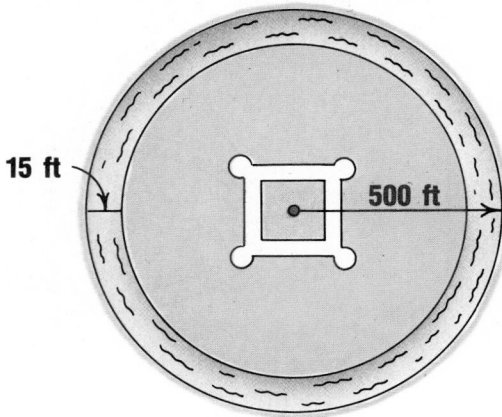

21. *Multiple choice*   In a hyperbola the focal constant is less than the distance between the foci.   a
    (a) always
    (b) sometimes
    (c) never *(Lesson 12-3)*

In 22 and 23, consider the line *l* with equation $y = -\frac{1}{2}x + 4$ and the point $P = (3, -1)$.

22. Find an equation for the line through P parallel to l. *(Lesson 3-5)*
    $y+1 = -\frac{1}{2}(x - 3)$

23. Find an equation for the line through P perpendicular to l. *(Lesson 4-8)*
    $y+1 = 2(x - 3)$

24. A vacuum pump is designed so that each stroke leaves only 97% of the gas in the chamber.
    a. What percent of the gas remains after 2 strokes?   94.09%
    b. Write an equation to model the percent P of the gas left after s strokes. $p = (.97)^s$
    c. How many strokes are necessary so that no more than 5% of the gas remains? *(Lessons 8-3, 8-10)*   99

Exploration

25. a. Modify the BASIC program in Question 11 of Lesson 12-2 so that it prints points on an ellipse in standard form.   See margin.
    b. Run your program for the ellipse $\frac{x^2}{4} + \frac{y^2}{9} = 1$.   See margin.

700

12-6

Equations for Some Hyperbolas

You have seen hyperbolas generated in two ways. First, in Chapter 2 you studied hyperbolas that arise from situations modeled by inverse variation of the form $y = \frac{k}{x}$. For instance, the formula $r = \frac{d}{t}$ can be used by a person traveling on a highway with mileage markers to check a speedometer by driving at a constant speed for one mile and timing how long it takes.

$$\text{rate in } \frac{\text{miles}}{\text{hour}} = \frac{\text{distance in miles}}{\text{time in hours}}$$

If the distance between markers is 1 mile, the above equation becomes

$$\text{rate in } \frac{\text{miles}}{\text{hour}} = \frac{1}{\text{time in hours}}.$$

There are 3600 seconds in an hour, so when time is measured in seconds this relationship is equivalent to

$$\text{rate in } \frac{\text{miles}}{\text{hour}} = 3600 \cdot \frac{1}{\text{time in seconds}} = \frac{3600}{\text{time in seconds}}.$$

Here are some pairs of values (rounded to the nearest tenth) that satisfy the equation $r = \frac{3600}{t}$.

time (sec)	40	45	50	55	60	65	70	75	80	85	90	100
rate (mph)	90	80	72	65.5	60	55.4	51.4	48	45	42.4	40	36

RESOURCES
- Lesson Master 12-6
- Visual for Teaching Aid 83 provides the proof of the equation for a hyperbola with foci $F_1 = (6, 6)$ and $F_2 = (-6, 6)$ and focal constant 12.

OBJECTIVES

B Write an equation for a rectangular hyperbola satisfying given conditions.
E Identify characteristics of rectangular hyperbolas.
J Graph rectangular hyperbolas given their equations, and vice versa.

TEACHING NOTES

Since the graph of $y = \frac{18}{x}$ is a hyperbola with foci at (6, 6) and (-6, -6) and focal constant 12, have students begin by picking a point on that curve and show that it verifies the definition. For instance, pick (2, 9). Its distance from (6, 6) is 5. Its distance from (-6, -6) is 17. The difference is 12.

Next, outline how to derive the equation $y = \frac{18}{x}$. Finally, you might wish to outline (or with more capable students, detail) how to prove the general theorem stated in the lesson. The proof follows the steps of the proof for the specific case when $k = 18$, but with the following replacements:
  replace each 6 by $\sqrt{2k}$
  replace each 12 by $2\sqrt{2k}$
  replace each 24 by $4\sqrt{2k}$
  replace each 36 by $2k$
  replace each 144 by $8k$.
You should not expect students to memorize the general theorem.

701

Since r is inversely proportional to t, the graph of $tr = 3600$ for $t > 0$ and $r > 0$ is one branch of a hyperbola.

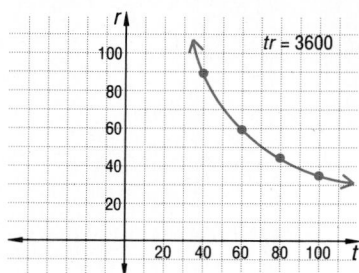

You learned a second situation in Lesson 12-3. A hyperbola can be defined geometrically as the set of points P in a plane such that $|PF_1 - PF_2| = d$, where F_1 and F_2 are two fixed points and d is a constant with $0 < d < F_1F_2$. For instance, below is a sketch of the set of points where $F_1F_2 = 12$ and $|PF_1 - PF_2| = 10$.

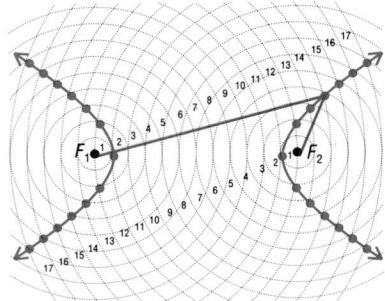

To show that the algebraic view of hyperbolas studied in Chapter 2 is consistent with the geometric view of hyperbolas, we begin with simple numbers.

Consider the hyperbola with foci $F_1 = (6, 6)$ and $F_2 = (-6, -6)$ and focal constant 12. We now prove that this hyperbola has an equation of the form $y = \dfrac{k}{x}$. Specifically, its equation is $y = \dfrac{18}{x}$.

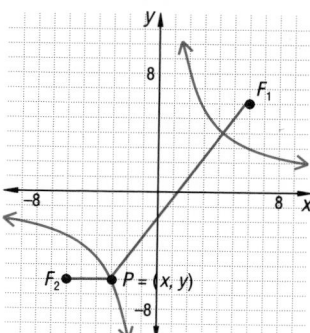

Theorem:

The hyperbola with foci (6, 6) and (-6, -6) and focal constant 12 has equation $y = \dfrac{18}{x}$.

Proof

1. Let $P = (x, y)$ be a point on the hyperbola. One branch of the curve is given by

$$PF_1 - PF_2 = d.$$

2. Here $F_1 = (6, 6)$, $F_2 = (-6, -6)$, and $d = 12$. From the distance formula,

$$\sqrt{(x - 6)^2 + (y - 6)^2} - \sqrt{(x + 6)^2 + (y + 6)^2} = 12.$$

3. Adding one of the square roots to both sides,

$$\sqrt{(x - 6)^2 + (y - 6)^2} = 12 + \sqrt{(x + 6)^2 + (y + 6)^2}.$$

4. Squaring both sides (the right side is like a binomial),

$$(x - 6)^2 + (y - 6)^2 = 144 + 24\sqrt{(x + 6)^2 + (y + 6)^2} + (x+6)^2 + (y+6)^2.$$

5. Expanding the binomials,

$$x^2 - 12x + 36 + y^2 - 12y + 36 = 144 + 24\sqrt{(x+6)^2 + (y+6)^2} + x^2 + 12x + 36 + y^2 + 12y + 36.$$

6. Adding $-x^2 - y^2 - 72 - 12x - 12y - 144$ to each side,

$$-24x - 24y - 144 = 24\sqrt{(x + 6)^2 + (y + 6)^2}.$$

7. Dividing each side by -24 and then squaring,

$$(x + y + 6)^2 = (x + 6)^2 + (y + 6)^2.$$

8. Expanding the trinomial and the two binomials,

$$x^2 + y^2 + 12x + 12y + 2xy + 36 = x^2 + 12x + 36 + y^2 + 12y + 36.$$

9. (The next steps are easy — can you see what was done?)

$$2xy = 36$$

10. $$y = \dfrac{18}{x}$$

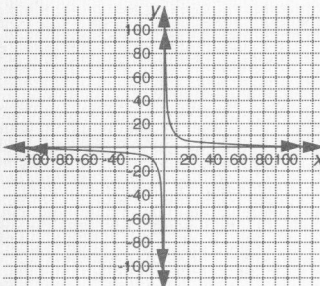
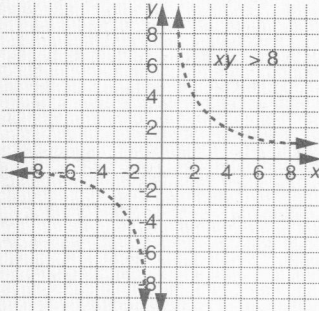
By a long process just like that used in the preceding proof, the general theorem stated below can be proved.

Theorem:

The graph of $xy = k$ is a hyperbola. (When $k > 0$, this is the hyperbola with foci ($\sqrt{2k}$, $\sqrt{2k}$) and ($-\sqrt{2k}$, $-\sqrt{2k}$) and focal constant $2\sqrt{2k}$.)

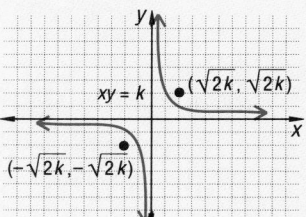

The foci are labeled ($\sqrt{2k}$, $\sqrt{2k}$) and ($-\sqrt{2k}$, $-\sqrt{2k}$) so no radicals appear in the final equation $xy = k$. In the following example you are given the foci and asked to find k.

Example Find an equation for the hyperbola with foci at (4, 4) and (-4, -4) and focal constant 8.

Solution In the theorem above $\sqrt{2k} = 4$. Then $2k = 16$ and $k = 8$. Thus, an equation for this hyperbola is $y = \dfrac{8}{x}$ or $xy = 8$.

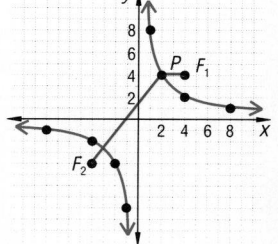

Check Sketch a graph. Verify that for points P on the graph, $|PF_1 - PF_2| = 8$. We use the point (2, 4).

$$|\sqrt{(2-4)^2 + (4-4)^2} - \sqrt{(2+4)^2 + (4+4)^2}|$$
$$= |\sqrt{4} - \sqrt{36 + 64}|$$
$$= |2 - 10|$$
$$= |-8| = 8$$

It checks.

By reversing the process used above you can conclude that the graph of $y = \dfrac{3600}{x}$ is a hyperbola. Since $k = 3600$, the foci are at ($\sqrt{7200}$, $\sqrt{7200}$) and ($-\sqrt{7200}$, $-\sqrt{7200}$) and the focal constant is $2\sqrt{7200}$.

704

Recall that the x- and y-axes are asymptotes of all equations of the form $y = \dfrac{k}{x}$, where $k \neq 0$. A hyperbola with perpendicular asymptotes is called a **rectangular hyperbola.** Thus, graphs of equations of the form $y = \dfrac{k}{x}$ are rectangular hyperbolas.

In the next lesson you will learn to find equations for other hyperbolas, both rectangular and nonrectangular.

Questions

Covering the Reading

1. If it takes 75 seconds to drive a mile, what is the average speed in miles per hour? **48 mph**

2. If it takes t seconds to drive a mile, what is the average speed in miles per hour? $\frac{3600}{t}$ **mph**

3. Consider the hyperbola with equation $xy = 18$. Name its
   a. foci **b.** asymptotes **c.** focal constant.
   (6,6), (-6,-6) x-axis, y-axis 12

4. Consider the hyperbola with equation $xy = k$. Name its
   a. foci **b.** asymptotes **c.** focal constant.
   ($\sqrt{2k}$, $\sqrt{2k}$), (-$\sqrt{2k}$, -$\sqrt{2k}$) x-axis, y-axis $2\sqrt{2k}$

5. Verify that the point $(8, 1)$ is on the hyperbola of the Example.
   See margin.

6. **a.** Find an equation for the hyperbola with foci at $(10, 10)$ and $(-10, -10)$ and focal constant 20. **xy = 50**
   b. Verify that the point $(-2, -25)$ is on this hyperbola. **See margin.**

Applying the Mathematics

7. A car travels the 2.5 miles around the Indianapolis Speedway in t seconds at an average rate of r mph. Racing fans with stopwatches can calculate how fast a car is traveling if they know the value of the constant rt. What is that value? **9000**

8. The product of two real numbers is 100. **See margin.**
   a. Graph all possible pairs of numbers.
   b. Identify the foci and focal constant for this hyperbola.

In 9 and 10, sketch a graph. **See margin.**

9. $xy > 8$

10. $xy \leq 8$

In 11 and 12, give an equation for the conic or region.

11. the rectangular hyperbola with vertices $(8, 8)$ and $(-8, -8)$ **xy = 64**

12. the interior of the rectangular hyperbola with vertices $(1.5, 1.5)$ and $(-1.5, -1.5)$ **xy ≤ 2.25**

MORE PRACTICE
For more questions on SPUR Objectives, use *Lesson Master 12-6*, shown below.

10.

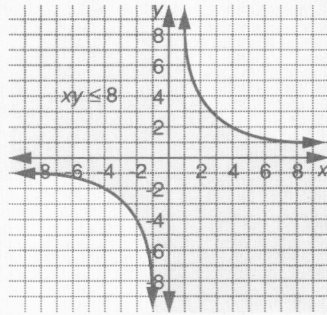

NAME _____

LESSON **MASTER   12–6**
QUESTIONS ON **SPUR** OBJECTIVES

■ SKILLS   *Objective B*   (See pages 735–739 for objectives.)
1. **a.** Find an equation for the hyperbola with foci at (3, 3) and (-3, -3), and focal constant 6.   xy = 4.5

   b. Verify that the point (-.5, -9) is on the hyperbola.   (-.5)(-.9) = 4.5

   c. Verify that the point (3, 3) is not on the hyperbola.   3 · 3 = 9 ≠ 4.5

2. Find an equation for the hyperbola whose vertices are (-5, 5) and (5, -5) and which has the x- and y-axes as asymptotes.   xy = -25

■ PROPERTIES   *Objective E*
3. Consider the hyperbola with equation xy = 32. Name its

   a. foci   (8, 8), (-8, -8)
   b. asymptotes   y = 0, x = 0
   c. focal constant   16

■ REPRESENTATIONS   *Objective J*
4. Use the conic paper below to draw the set of points P satisfying |PF₁ - PF₂| = 6.

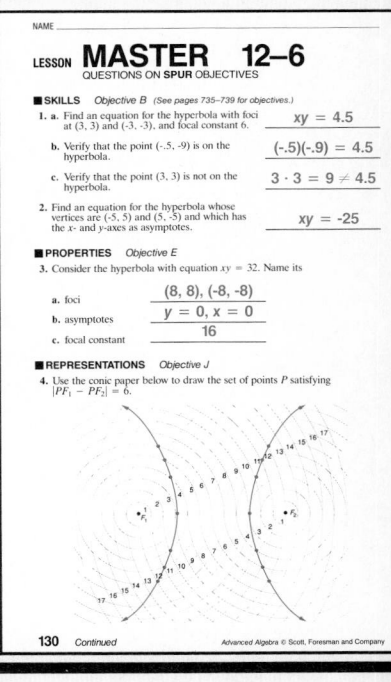

130   *Continued*   *Advanced Algebra © Scott, Foresman and Company*

705

NOTES ON QUESTIONS
Question 18: This question reviews a skill which is needed for Lesson 12-8.

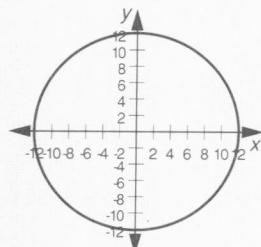
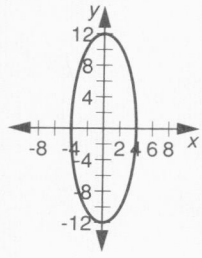
Review

13. An ellipse has foci F_1 and F_2 on the x-axis, and $F_1F_2 = 4$. Also $PF_1 + PF_2 = 7$. Find
   a. the length of the major axis   7
   b. an equation in standard form for the ellipse $\frac{x^2}{12.25} + \frac{y^2}{8.25} = 1$
   c. the area of the ellipse. *(Lessons 12-4, 12-5)* $\approx 10\pi$

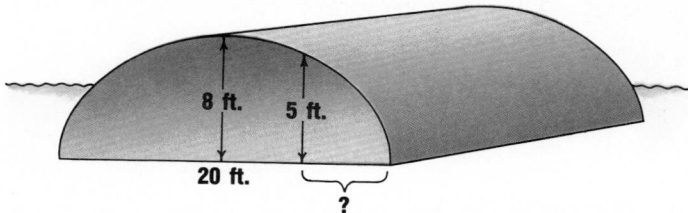

14. An exhibition tent is in the form of half a cylinder with each cross-section a semiellipse (half an ellipse) having base 20 ft and height 8 ft. How close to either end can a person 5 ft tall stand straight up? *(Lessons 12-2, 12-4)* $\approx$ **2.2 ft**

In 15 and 16, sketch a graph. *(Lessons 12-1, 12-4)*   **See margin.**

15. $\{(x, y): x^2 + y^2 = 144\}$ **16.** $\{(x, y): 9x^2 + y^2 = 144\}$

17. Find two nonreal numbers whose product is 100. *(Lessons 6-8, 6-9)*
   Sample: 100i, $\frac{1}{i}$
18. What number must be put into the blank to make the expression $y^2 - 13y +$ __?__ a perfect square? *(Lessons 6-5, 11-3)*   **42.25**

19. Solve $x^5 - 81x = 0$. *(Lesson 11-4)*   **x = 0, x = 3, x = -3, x = 3i, x = -3i**

20. Are ellipses functions? Why or why not? *(Lessons 7-1, 12-3, 12-4)*
   No, they do not pass the vertical line test.
21. A tank has a slow leak. Suppose the water level starts at 100 inches and falls $\frac{1}{2}$ inch per day. *(Lesson 3-1)*
   a. Write an equation relating the number N of days the tank has been leaking and the water level L.   **L = 100 $- \frac{1}{2}N$**
   b. After how many days will the tank be empty?   **N = 200**

Exploration

22. The words *ellipsis* and *hyperbole* have meanings in grammar. What are these meanings?

   ellips :   marks used to show an omission in writing or printing, usually shown as ...
   hyperbole: an exaggerated statement used specifically as a figure of speech for rhetorical effect

706

The hyperbolas studied in Lesson 12-6 are special. Each has foci on the line $y = x$ and has the x- and y-axes for asymptotes. The resulting equations of the form $xy = k$ do not look like those of any of the other conic sections you have studied. We can generate an equation for a hyperbola which resembles an equation of an ellipse by choosing foci $(c, 0)$ and $(-c, 0)$ and a general focal constant.

Theorem: (Equation for a Hyperbola):

The hyperbola with foci $(c, 0)$ and $(-c, 0)$ and focal constant $2a$ has equation $\dfrac{x^2}{a^2} - \dfrac{y^2}{b^2} = 1$, where $b^2 = c^2 - a^2$.

Proof

The proof is almost identical to the proof of the equation for an ellipse in Lesson 12-4. Let $P = (x, y)$ be any point on the hyperbola. By the definition of a hyperbola,

$|PF_1 - PF_2| = 2a.$

This equation is equivalent to

$PF_1 - PF_2 = \pm 2a.$

That is, with $P = (x, y)$, $F_1 = (-c, 0)$, and $F_2 = (c, 0)$,

$\sqrt{(x+c)^2 + (y-0)^2} - \sqrt{(x-c)^2 + (y-0)^2} = \pm 2a.$

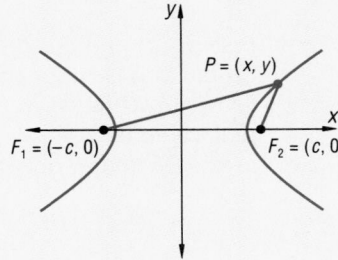

Doing manipulations similar to those in steps 2-8 of that proof, the same equation in step 9 results.

$$(a^2 - c^2)x^2 + a^2y^2 = a^2(a^2 - c^2)$$

Then in step 10, for hyperbolas, $c > a > 0$, so $c^2 > a^2$. Thus we can let $b^2 = c^2 - a^2$. So $-b^2 = a^2 - c^2$. This accounts for the minus sign in the equation:

$$\frac{x^2}{a^2} - \frac{y^2}{b^2} = 1$$

OBJECTIVES

B Write an equation in standard form for a hyperbola satisfying given conditions.
E Identify characteristics of hyperbolas.
J Graph hyperbolas given their equations in standard form, and vice versa.

TEACHING NOTES

You might begin with *Teaching Aid 82* for Lesson 12-4 that contains the derivation of the standard equation for an ellipse. Make the substitutions suggested in the proof of the Equation for a Hyperbola Theorem directly on that transparency. This brings home the analogy between ellipses and hyperbolas and shortens the time needed for an explanation.

Continually emphasize to students what these proofs utilize. This one begins with the definition of the hyperbola and uses only the Distance Formula and algebraic manipulation. Thus, just as in geometry, justifications in the proof are either definitions, previously proved theorems (the Distance Formula being an example), or postulates (the postulates of real numbers providing justifications for the algebra).

You might wish to offer the following observation. The asymptotes of $xy = k$ can be found by solving $xy = 0$; they are always $x = 0$ or $y = 0$. The asymptotes for

$\frac{x^2}{a^2} - \frac{y^2}{b^2} = 1$ can always be found by solving $\frac{x^2}{a^2} - \frac{y^2}{b^2} = 0$.

From that equation, $\frac{x^2}{a^2} = \frac{y^2}{b^2}$, so $\frac{x}{a} = \pm\frac{y}{b}$.

Example 1 Consider the hyperbola with distance between foci $F_1F_2 = 12$ and focal constant $|PF_1 - PF_2| = 10$. (It was drawn with conic graph paper in Example 2, Lesson 12-3.) Suppose a rectangular coordinate system is placed so that the x-axis coincides with $\overline{F_1F_2}$ and the y-axis bisects it. Find an equation for this hyperbola.

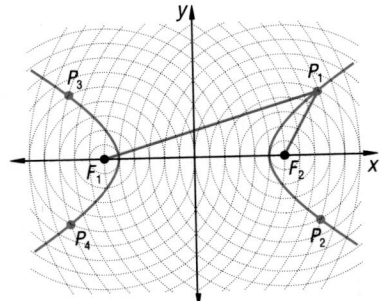

Solution $F_1F_2 = 12$, so $2c = 12$, and $c = 6$. The focal constant $2a = 10$, so $a = 5$. Thus $b^2 = 6^2 - 5^2 = 11$. An equation for this hyperbola is

$$\frac{x^2}{25} - \frac{y^2}{11} = 1.$$

We say that the equation $\frac{x^2}{a^2} - \frac{y^2}{b^2} = 1$ is **standard form** for the equation of a hyperbola. To graph $\frac{x^2}{a^2} - \frac{y^2}{b^2} = 1$, notice that $(a, 0)$ and $(-a, 0)$ satisfy the equation. Since the foci are on the x-axis, the hyperbola is symmetric about that axis. Thus, $(a, 0)$ and $(-a, 0)$ are the vertices. When $x = 0$, no real value of y works, so the hyperbola does not intersect the y-axis. A rough drawing using this information is given below.

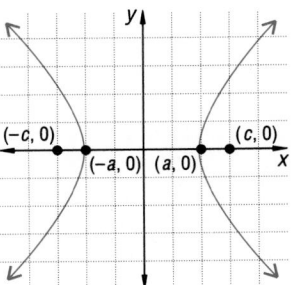

But this drawing is a little too rough. More points or asymptotes are needed to do a better job. To find general equations for the asymptotes, it is helpful to examine the simplest hyperbola of this kind, that is, the hyperbola with equation $x^2 - y^2 = 1$.

Some points on the graph of $x^2 - y^2 = 1$ are given below at the left. Because of the hyperbola's symmetry, these points in the first quadrant have reflection images on the hyperbola in the other three quadrants.

$(1, 0)$
$(2, \sqrt{3}) \approx (2, 1.73)$
$(3, \sqrt{8}) \approx (3, 2.83)$
$(4, \sqrt{15}) \approx (4, 3.87)$
$(5, \sqrt{24}) \approx (5, 4.90)$

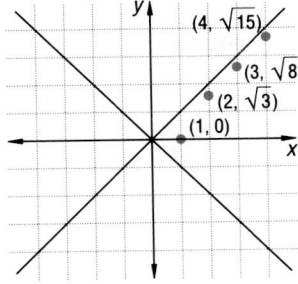

As x gets larger, the points get closer to the line with equation $y = x$. For instance, the point $(100, \sqrt{9999}) \approx (100, 99.995)$ is on the hyperbola. The line whose equation is $y = x$ appears to be an asymptote.

Every hyperbola is symmetric to the line through its foci, in this case the x-axis. So the union of both asymptotes is also symmetric to that line. Thus we reflect $y = x$ over the x-axis to get the other asymptote $y = -x$. This can be verified algebraically. When $x^2 - y^2 = 1$,

$$y^2 = x^2 - 1.$$

So
$$y = \pm \sqrt{x^2 - 1}.$$

As x gets larger, $\sqrt{x^2 - 1}$ becomes closer to $\sqrt{x^2}$, which is $|x|$. So y gets closer to x or $-x$.

The scale change $S_{a,b}$ transforms $x^2 - y^2 = 1$ onto $\dfrac{x^2}{a^2} - \dfrac{y^2}{b^2} = 1$.

The asymptotes $y = \pm x$ are mapped onto the lines $\dfrac{y}{b} = \pm \dfrac{x}{a}$. These lines become the asymptotes of $\dfrac{x^2}{a^2} - \dfrac{y^2}{b^2} = 1$.

Theorem:

The asymptotes of the hyperbola with equation $\dfrac{x^2}{a^2} - \dfrac{y^2}{b^2} = 1$ are $\dfrac{y}{b} = \pm \dfrac{x}{a}$.

ADDITIONAL EXAMPLES
1. Find an equation for the hyperbola in which $F_1 = (-6, 0)$, $F_2 = (6, 0)$, and $|PF_1 - PF_2| = 6$.
$$\frac{x^2}{9} - \frac{y^2}{27} = 1$$
(This is the hyperbola of Lesson 12-4, Question 20.)

2. Graph $\frac{x^2}{25} - y^2 = 1$ and give equations for its asymptotes.
The graph is a hyperbola with vertices at (5, 0) and (-5, 0) and asymptotes $y = \frac{x}{5}$ and $y = -\frac{x}{5}$.

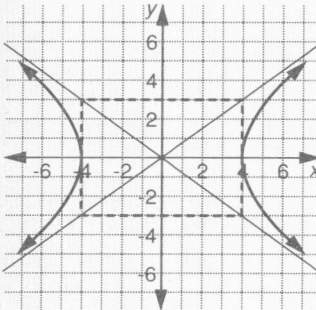
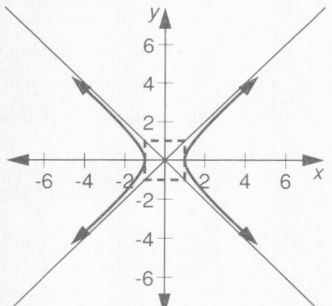
■ ■ ■ ■ ■ ■ ■■■

Example 2   Sketch a graph of $\dfrac{x^2}{9} - \dfrac{y^2}{16} = 1$.

Solution $a^2 = 9$, so $a = 3$. Thus the vertices are (3, 0) and (-3, 0). The asymptotes are $\dfrac{y}{4} = \pm\dfrac{x}{3}$. Carefully graph the vertices and asymptotes. Then sketch the hyperbola.

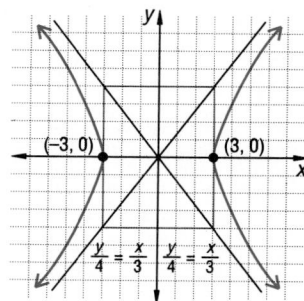

Check   Find coordinates of a point on the hyperbola. If $x = 5$, then $\dfrac{25}{9} - \dfrac{y^2}{16} = 1$, from which $y = \pm\dfrac{16}{3}$. The points $(5, \frac{16}{3})$ and $(5, -\frac{16}{3})$ do seem to be on the hyperbola. It checks.

Questions

Covering the Reading

1. A hyperbola with foci $(c, 0)$ and $(-c, 0)$ and focal constant $2a$ has an equation of the form ___?___. $\dfrac{x^2}{a^2} - \dfrac{y^2}{b^2} = 1$

2. Why is the hyperbola with equation $x^2 - y^2 = 1$ so useful?
   It is the simplest hyperbola in standard form.

In 3 and 4, give (a) the vertices and (b) the asymptotes of each hyperbola.

3. $1 = x^2 - y^2$
   a) (-1,0),(1,0); b) $y = \pm x$

4. $\dfrac{x^2}{a^2} - \dfrac{y^2}{b^2} = 1$
   a) (-a,0),(a,0); b) $\dfrac{y}{b} = \pm\dfrac{x}{a}$

5. Consider the hyperbola with equation $\dfrac{x^2}{25} - \dfrac{y^2}{11} = 1$ from Example 1.

   a. Name its vertices.   (-5,0), (5,0)

   b. State equations for its asymptotes. $\dfrac{y}{\sqrt{11}} = \pm\dfrac{x}{5}$

In 6 and 7, consider the hyperbola with equation $\dfrac{x^2}{16} - \dfrac{y^2}{9} = 1$.

6. Graph this hyperbola.   See margin.

7. Find two points on the curve with x-coordinate equal to 6.
   $\approx$(6, 3.35), (6, -3.35)

8. *True or false*   A single equation for *both* asymptotes of $x^2 - y^2 = 1$ is $y = |x|$.   **False**

710

9. Solve $x^2 - y^2 = 1$ for y. Use your solution to graph $x^2 - y^2 = 1$ using an automatic grapher.   **See margin.**

10. By making a table of values and analyzing properties, graph the set of points satisfying $y^2 - x^2 = 1$. (Hint: The graph is like a graph in this lesson with x and y switched.)   **See margin.**

11. The point $(-7, 4)$ is on a hyperbola with foci $(5, 0)$ and $(-5, 0)$.

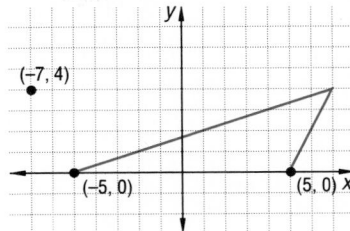

   a. Find the focal constant. $\sqrt{160} - \sqrt{20}$
   b. Give an equation for that hyperbola in standard form. (Hint: Find b using $b^2 = c^2 - a^2$.) $\dfrac{x^2}{16.716} - \dfrac{y^2}{8.284} = 1$
   c. Graph the hyperbola using either a rectangular grid or conic graph paper.   **See margin.**

In 12 and 13, (a) sketch a graph; (b) state the eccentricity of the hyperbola. (The *eccentricity* of a hyperbola is defined to be the ratio of the distance between its foci and its focal constant; that is, $\dfrac{2c}{2a}$ or $\dfrac{c}{a}$.)

12. $\dfrac{x^2}{25} - \dfrac{y^2}{9} = 1$ **See margin.**

13. $\dfrac{x^2}{25} - \dfrac{y^2}{4} = 1$ **See margin.**

14. Refer to the graphs in Questions 12 and 13. Make a conjecture about the shape of the hyperbola in relation to its eccentricity.   **See margin.**

15. What hyperbola in this lesson is a rectangular hyperbola? $x^2 - y^2 = 1$

In 16–18, *multiple choice.*   Choose the best term from the following:
(a) circle   (b) ellipse
(c) parabola   (d) hyperbola
(Lessons 6-3, 12-1, 12-3, 12-4, 12-6)

16. What is the set of points satisfying the equation
   $|\sqrt{(x - 3)^2 + (y - 3)^2} - \sqrt{(x + 3)^2 + (y + 3)^2}| = 6$?   d

17. What is the set of points equidistant from a given focus and directrix?
   c

18. What is the set of points satisfying the equation $4x^2 + 5y^2 = 100$?   b

LESSON 12-7   More Hyperbolas   **711**

FOLLOW-UP

MORE PRACTICE
For more questions on SPUR Objectives, use *Lesson Master 12-7*, shown below.

EXTENSION
Discuss with students hyperbolas whose standard form equations are $\dfrac{y^2}{a^2} - \dfrac{x^2}{b^2} = 1$.
Explain that these hyperbolas have branches that open up and down. They have y-intercepts $\pm a$ and asymptotes $\dfrac{y}{a} = \pm\dfrac{x}{b}$. If students think of the hyperbola as the union of the graphs of two functions, then the hyperbola whose standard form equation is $\dfrac{y^2}{a^2} - \dfrac{x^2}{b^2} = 1$ is the union of the graphs of the inverses of the functions whose union is the graph $\dfrac{x^2}{a^2} - \dfrac{y^2}{b^2} = 1$.

EVALUATION
A quiz covering Lessons 12-4 through 12-7 is provided in the Teacher's Resource File.

 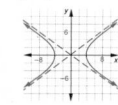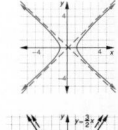

10.

x	y
0	±1
±$\sqrt{3}$	±2
±$\sqrt{8}$	±3
±$\sqrt{15}$	±4
±$\sqrt{24}$	±5
⋮	⋮

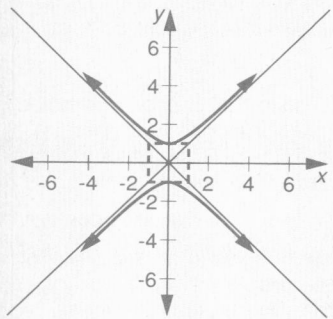

11.c.

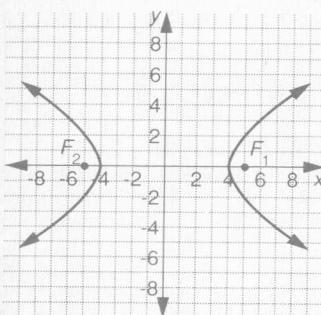

24.b. The points P traced by the pencil are such that PA − PC = 2a, where 2a is the difference between the length of the ruler and the piece of string, and A and C are the foci of the hyperbola. This, the construction obeys the definition of a hyperbola.

In 19 and 20, consider that the compulsory circles made by a figure skater must have radius 1.5 times the height of the skater.

Assuming a coordinate system shown in the figure at the right, write a sentence to describe, for a skater 5 ft 4 in. tall, the points

19. on the upper circle;
$x^2 + (y - 8)^2 = 64$

20. in the interior of the lower circle. *(Lessons 12-1, 12-2)*
$x^2 + (y + 8)^2 < 64$

21. Find the vertex of the parabola with equation $y = 3x^2 - 18x + 7$.
(Lesson 6-5)   **(3, -20)**

22. If $2000 is compounded continuously at 6.25%, in how many years will it quadruple? *(Lesson 9-9)*   **≈ 22.2**

Exploration

23. How close does a hyperbola get to its asymptotes? In particular, how large does x have to be in order for a point (x, y) on $x^2 - y^2 = 1$ to be within .001 of the line $y = x$?   **|x| > 500**

24. a. Refer to the diagram below. To do the following you will need 3 tacks, a ruler, a piece of string of length shorter than that of the ruler, a pencil, and a piece of board.

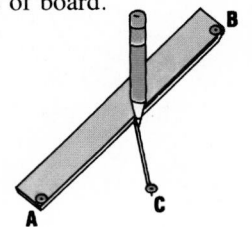

  (i)   Tack the ruler to a piece of board so that it pivots at point A.
  (ii) Tack one end of the piece of string to the other end of the ruler (point B).
  (iii) Take the other end of the string and tack it to the board at point C. (The distance between tacks A and C must be larger than the difference between the length of the ruler and the length of the string.)
  (iv) Holding the string taut against the ruler with a pencil, rotate the ruler about point A.

  b. Explain why the resulting curve must be one branch of a hyperbola.   **See margin.**

712

12-8

Classifying Quadratic Relations

You have now seen equations for all the different types of conics. Here are some of these equations in standard form.

$$y = ax^2 + bx + c$$
parabola

$$\frac{x^2}{a^2} + \frac{y^2}{b^2} = 1$$
ellipse

$$(x - h)^2 + (y - k)^2 = r^2$$
circle

$$\frac{x^2}{a^2} - \frac{y^2}{b^2} = 1 \text{ or } xy = k$$
hyperbola

Although the equations for the hyperbola and ellipse look similar, the others look different. However, all these equations only contain terms with x^2, xy, y^2, x, or y and constants. All the conic sections are special types of quadratic relations, and their equations can be written in the *general form*

$$Ax^2 + Bxy + Cy^2 + Dx + Ey + F = 0,$$

where A, B, C, D, E, and F are real numbers, and at least one of A, B, or C is nonzero.

Example 1 Show that the circle with equation $(x - 3)^2 + y^2 = 14$ is a quadratic relation.

Solution To do this, the equation for this circle must be put into the general form of a quadratic relation. So first expand the binomial.

$$x^2 - 6x + 9 + y^2 = 14$$

Now add -14 to both sides. Then use the Commutative Property of Addition to reorder the terms so that they are in the order x^2, xy, y^2, x, y, and constants.

$$x^2 + 0xy + y^2 - 6x + 0y - 14 = 0$$

This is in the desired form with $A = 1$, $B = 0$, $C = 1$, $D = -6$, $E = 0$, and $F = -14$.

By expanding the standard-form equation of a circle, $(x - h)^2 + (y - k)^2 = r^2$, you can show that it has no xy term. So $B = 0$ and $A = C$. Given an equation for a circle in general form, you can complete the square to determine the center and radius of the circle.

RESOURCES
- Lesson Master 12-8
- Visual for Teaching Aid 84 displays the graph for **Question 24**.
- Computer Master 28

OBJECTIVES

A Convert from the general form of a quadratic equation in two variables to standard form for a particular curve, and vice versa.

F Classify conics using the Discriminant Theorem for Conics.

TEACHING NOTES

An important aspect of this lesson is that the type of conic can be determined easily from its equation by putting that equation into standard form. **Examples 1 and 2** show how to get an equation for a circle into and out of standard form.

Stress to students that the only restriction for the Discriminant Theorem for Conics is that the coefficients be real numbers. Point out that **Question 2** has rational and irrational coefficients.

Explain that the Discriminant Theorem for Conics shows again why it helps to think of the parabola as being between the hyperbola and ellipse. If you discussed the Exploration question in Lesson 12-6, your students will know that hyperbola comes from a Greek word meaning "excess" and ellipse comes from a Greek word meaning "deficit." This is precisely mirrored in the hyperbola having a positive discriminant and the ellipse having a negative one.

713

ADDITIONAL EXAMPLES

1. Show that the curve with equation $y = 3(x - 5)^2 + \sqrt{2}$ is a quadratic relation by rewriting the equation in standard form.
$3x^2 - 30x - y + 75 + \sqrt{2} = 0$, which is in standard form with $A = 3$, $B = 0$, $C = 0$, $D = -30$, $E = -1$, and $F = 75 + \sqrt{2}$.

2. Find the center and radius of the circle with equation $x^2 + y^2 + 26x + 8y + 12 = 0$.
center (-13, -4), radius $\sqrt{173}$

3. Classify the conic section with equation $x^2 + xy + y^2 = 0$.
ellipse

Example 2 Find the center and radius of the circle with equation $x^2 + 10x + y^2 - 8y - 20 = 0$.

Solution Complete the square on $x^2 + 10x$ and on $y^2 - 8y$, and add the same numbers to both sides of the equation.

$$x^2 + 10x + \mathbf{25} + y^2 - 8y + \mathbf{16} - 20 = \mathbf{25} + \mathbf{16}$$

Factor the perfect square trinomials.

$$(x + 5)^2 + (y - 4)^2 - 20 = 41$$

Add 20 to each side.

$$(x + 5)^2 + (y - 4)^2 = 61$$

The center is (-5, 4) and the radius is $\sqrt{61}$.

The values of A, B, and C in a quadratic relation tell quite a bit about that relation. For instance, when $B = 0$, then the equation has no xy term. As a result, the relation is symmetric to either a horizontal line or a vertical line. The only relation with an xy term that you have studied is $xy = k$, and that relation is symmetric to the lines $y = x$ and $y = -x$.

There is an amazing theorem that tells whether a quadratic relation is a hyperbola, parabola, or ellipse. The proof is beyond the scope of this book.

Discriminant Theorem for Conics:

If A, B, C, D, E, and F are real numbers and at least one of A, B, or C is nonzero, then the graph of

$$Ax^2 + Bxy + Cy^2 + Dx + Ey + F = 0$$

is an ellipse if $B^2 - 4AC$ is negative,
a parabola if $B^2 - 4AC = 0$,
and a hyperbola if $B^2 - 4AC$ is positive.

Example 3 Identify the conic section with equation $3x^2 - 5xy + 4y^2 - 2x + 9y - 6 = 0$.

Solution Here $A = 3$, $B = -5$, and $C = 4$. The other coefficients can be ignored. Since $B^2 - 4AC = (-5)^2 - 4 \cdot 3 \cdot 4 = 25 - 48 < 0$, the conic section is an ellipse.

714

Check If your automatic grapher allows you to plot quadratic relations in general form, enter the coefficients and draw the graph. The output below from our grapher shows an ellipse with major and minor axes not parallel to the coordinate axes.

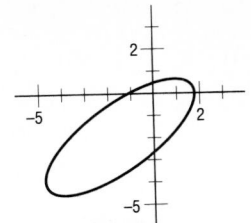

You may wonder how there ever could be such a theorem. Recall that the conic sections are intersections of a plane with a double cone. The value of $B^2 - 4AC$ determines the angle of the plane that intersects the cone. Let k be the measure of the acute angle between the axis and an edge of the cone. Let θ be the measure of the smallest angle between the axis and the plane.

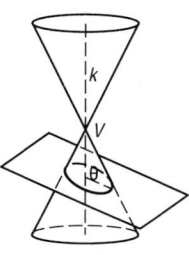

$k < \theta < 90°$
ellipse

$\theta = k$
parabola

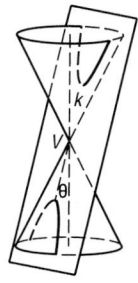

$\theta < k$
hyperbola

There are special cases of the Discriminant Theorem in which the graph does not resemble an ellipse, a parabola, or a hyperbola. Geometrically, these occur when the intersecting plane contains the vertex V of the cone. Then the ellipse *degenerates* to a single point (V), the parabola to a single line (an edge through V), and the hyperbola to two lines (intersecting edges through V).

plane not ‖ to any edge
cutting only vertex

plane ‖ to edge
through vertex

plane cutting both
nappes through vertex

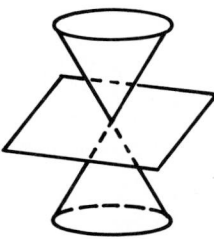

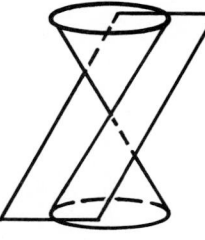

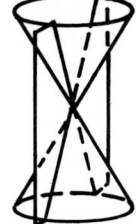

point
(degenerate ellipse)

line
(degenerate parabola)

two lines
(degenerate hyperbola)

LESSON 12-8 *Classifying Quadratic Relations* **715**

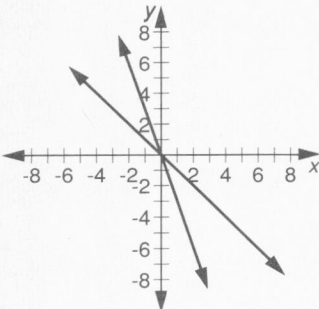
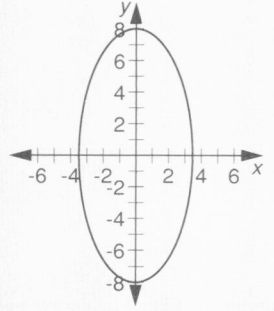
For instance, the graph of the equation $x^2 + y^2 = 0$ is the single point $(0, 0)$. Using the Discriminant Theorem with $A = 1$, $B = 0$, $C = 1$, and $D = E = F = 0$, $B^2 - 4AC = -4$, which is negative. The point is a degenerate ellipse.

Questions

Covering the Reading

In 1–4, (a) tell whether or not the sentence is an equation for a quadratic relation. (b) If so, put the equation in general form. If not, tell why not.

1. $x^2 + 4xy^2 = 6$
a) no; b) It has an xy^2 term.

2. $\frac{1}{2}y - 13x^2 = \sqrt{5}\, x$
a) yes; b) $-13x^2 + 0xy + 0y^2 - \sqrt{5}x + \frac{1}{2}y + 0 = 0$

3. $x^2 + 2xy + 3y^2 + 4x + 5y = 6$
a) yes; b) $1x^2 + 2xy + 3y^2 + 4x + 5y - 6 = 0$

4. $xy - 8 = 2xy$
a) yes; b) See margin.

In 5–8, tell whether the graph is a hyperbola, parabola, or ellipse.

5. $3x^2 + 9x + 3y^2 + 12y = 0$ ellipse

6. $25x^2 - 10xy + y^2 + 3x + 6y + 11 = 0$ parabola

7. $x^2 - xy = 2$ hyperbola

8. $0 = x^2 + 5xy + 7y^2 - 32$ ellipse

In 9–12, consider the equation $Ax^2 + Bxy + Cy^2 + Dx + Ey + F = 0$. What conic results from the given situation?

9. $A = C$ and $B = 0$ circle   **10.** $B = 0$ See margin.

11. $B^2 - 4AC = 0$ parabola   **12.** $B^2 - 4AC > 0$ hyperbola

In 13 and 14, find the center and radius of the circle.

13. $x^2 + 4x + y^2 + 4y + 2 = 0$ $(-2, -2), r = \sqrt{6}$ **14.** $x^2 - 8x + y^2 + 10y - 6 = 0$ $(4, -5), r = \sqrt{47}$

15. A degenerate parabola is a(n) __?__.   line

Applying the Mathematics

In 16 and 17, show that the equation describes a quadratic relation by putting it in general form. Give the values of $A, B, C, D, E,$ and F.

16. $\frac{x^2}{4} - \frac{y^2}{9} = 1$ See margin.   **17.** $y = 3(x + 1)^2 - 8$ See margin.

18. If $3x^2 + 4xy + y^2 = 0$, then $(3x + y)(x + y) = 0$, so $3x + y = 0$ or $x + y = 0$. Thus the original equation is equivalent to the union of two lines.
a. Graph all points satisfying $3x^2 + 4xy + y^2 = 0$.   See margin.
b. The graph is a degenerate form of what conic?   hyperbola

19. Consider the equation $64x^2 + 12y^2 = 768$.
a. Identify the conic.   ellipse
b. Solve the equation for y. $y = \pm\sqrt{64 - \frac{16}{3}x^2}$
c. Use the result of part b to graph the conic on an automatic grapher.   See margin.

716

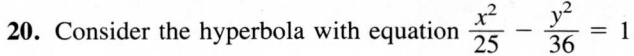

Review

20. Consider the hyperbola with equation $\dfrac{x^2}{25} - \dfrac{y^2}{36} = 1$.
  a. What are its foci?   **b.** Name its vertices.
  c. State equations for its asymptotes. *(Lesson 12-7)*
    a. $(-\sqrt{61}, 0)$, $(\sqrt{61}, 0)$ **b.** (-5, 0) (5, 0)   **c.** $\frac{y}{6} = \pm\frac{x}{5}$

21. In the hyperbola with equation $xy = 148$, what is the focal constant?
  (Lesson 12-6) $4\sqrt{74} \approx 34.4$

22. The picture at the left shows the entrances to an amphitheater in Yugoslavia. It is typical of early Roman construction in which a semicircular arch is built over a square opening. Suppose the gate is 10 ft wide.
  a. How high is it?   **15 ft**
  b. Can a truck 6 ft wide and 12 ft high fit through the gate? *(Lesson 12-2, Previous course)*   **yes**

23. Consider the following system: $\begin{cases} y = 4x \\ 2x - 3y = -15 \end{cases}$

  (Lessons 5-2, 5-3, 5-4)   **See margin.**
  a. Name three methods you can use to solve this system.
  b. Solve the system using any method.   **(1.5, 6)**

24. Refer to the graph below which shows the number of calories of heat needed to raise the temperature so that ice will turn to water and eventually to steam. *(Lesson 3-8)*

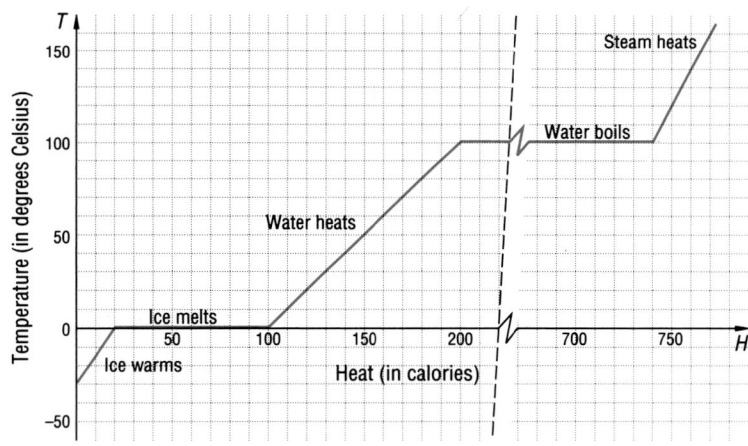

  a. At what temperature in °C does ice melt?   **0 °C**
  b. *True or false*   Water boils at a constant temperature.   **True**
  c. Find the slope of the line between the points (100, 0) and (200, 100).   **1**
  d. What does your answer to part c mean?   **The rate of calories per temperature rise is 1, or it takes 1 calorie to raise the temperature 1 degree C.**

LESSON 12-8   Classifying Quadratic Relations   **717**

FOLLOW-UP

MORE PRACTICE
For more questions on SPUR Objectives, use *Lesson Master 12-8*, shown below.

EXTENSION
Discuss conics in the context of function. Explain that the parabola with equation $y = ax^2 + bx + c$ and the hyperbola with equation $xy = k$ are functions. Ask students to identify their domain and range. The other conics are the union of two functions. For example, have students solve the standard form equation of the hyperbola studied in Lesson 12-7 for y. They will get two equations:

$$y = \sqrt{b^2\left(\dfrac{x^2}{a^2} - 1\right)} \text{ and}$$

$$y = -\sqrt{b^2\left(\dfrac{x^2}{a^2} - 1\right)},$$

each being the equation of a function. Ask students to discuss the domain and range of these functions and to identify which portions of the graph of the hyperbola correspond to the graph of these functions.

NAME _____

LESSON **MASTER   12–8**
QUESTIONS ON **SPUR** OBJECTIVES

■ **SKILLS**   *Objective A   (See pages 735–739 for objectives.)*
In 1–3, rewrite in the form $Ax^2 + Bxy + Cy^2 + Dx + Ey + F = 0$.

1. $x^2 + (y - 8)^2 = 9$ $x^2 + y^2 - 16y + 55 = 0$

2. $\frac{x^2}{100} + \frac{y^2}{81} = 1$ $81x^2 + 100y^2 - 8100 = 0$

3. $y = \frac{10}{x}$ $xy - 10 = 0$

In 4–7, rewrite the equation in standard form.

4. circle: $x^2 + y^2 + 6x + 18y - 5 = 0$
   $(x + 3)^2 + (y + 9)^2 = 95$

5. ellipse: $30x^2 + 45y^2 = 90$
   $\frac{x^2}{3} + \frac{y^2}{2} = 1$

6. hyperbola: $5x^2 - 7y^2 = 35$
   $\frac{x^2}{7} - \frac{y^2}{5} = 1$

7. parabola: $y - x = x^2 + 10$
   $y^2 = x^2 + x + 10$

■ **PROPERTIES**   *Objective F*
In 8 and 9, consider the equation $Ax^2 + Bxy + Cy^2 + Dx + Ey + F = 0$. What conic results from the given conditions?

8. $C = 0$
   for $B \ne 0$, hyperbola;
   for $B = 0$, parabola

9. $A \cdot C = 5$ and $B = 20$
   hyperbola

In 10 and 11, tell whether the graph of the equation is a hyperbola, parabola, or an ellipse.

10. $2y^2 - 10x + 4x^2 - 2y = 0$
    ellipse

11. $4y^2 - x^2 + 8xy - 10 = x$
    hyperbola

Advanced Algebra © Scott, Foresman and Company   **133**

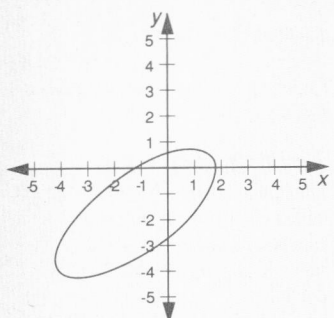
25. If your automatic grapher cannot plot conics in the form $Ax^2 + Bxy + Cy^2 + Dx + Ey + F = 0$ directly, you can plot the general conic by first solving for y. Rewrite the equation as

$$Cy^2 + (Bx + E)y + (Ax^2 + Dx + F) = 0.$$

Applying the quadratic formula to solve for y gives

$$y = \frac{-(Bx + E) \pm \sqrt{(Bx + E)^2 - 4(C)(Ax^2 + Dx + F)}}{2C}$$

Separate this into two equations, one using the $+$ sign, the other the $-$ sign, and input the constants A, B, C, D, E, and F. See margin.
a. Use these equations to plot the curve in Example 3.
b. Plot some other general second degree equations with xy terms. Do the results agree with the Discriminant Theorem?

26. The polynomial $ax^4 + bx^3 + cx^2 + dx + e$ can be written as $(((ax + b)x + c)x + d)x + e$. This latter expression can be easier to evaluate, particularly by computers, since it does not involve exponents and it can be described by an iterative, or repeating, algorithm. For any particular value for x, multiply the first coefficient by x, then add the next coefficient. Multiply that sum by x, then add the next coefficient. Again, multiply that sum by x, then add the next coefficient. And so on, until the last coefficient has been added. The process can be done without a computer, and is then called *synthetic substitution*. First write down the coefficients a, b, c, d, and e. Then follow the arrows.

$$
\begin{array}{ccccc}
a & b & c & d & \\
\downarrow \searrow ax & \nearrow (ax+b)x & \nearrow (ax^2+bx+c)x & \nearrow (ax^3+bx^2+cx+d) & \\
a & ax+b & ax^2+bx+c & ax^3+bx^2+cx+d & ax^4+bx^3+cx^2+dx+
\end{array}
$$

For instance, to find P(5) for $P(x) = 2x^4 - 9x^3 + 4x - 7$, you would write the following:

$$
\begin{array}{ccccc}
2 & -9 & 0 & 4 & -7 \\
\downarrow \nearrow 10 & \nearrow 5 & \nearrow 25 & \nearrow 145 & \\
2 & 1 & 5 & 29 & 138
\end{array}
$$

and find that P(5) = 138.
a. Verify that P(5) = 138 by substituting in the formula for P(x). **138**
b. Use synthetic substitution to evaluate Q(7) when $Q(x) = 3x^4 + 2x^3 - 20x^2 - 3x + 12$. **6900**
c. Use synthetic substitution to evaluate Q(x) in part b when $x = -3$ **30**

718

12-9

Quadratic-Linear Systems

A **quadratic system** is a system that involves at least one quadratic sentence. As with linear systems, you may solve quadratic systems by

    (1) graphing,
    (2) substitution,
 or (3) linear combinations.

No new properties are needed. In this lesson, the systems consist of a quadratic and a linear equation.

From geometry you know that a line can intersect a circle in 2, 1, or 0 points.

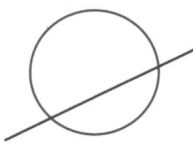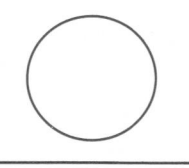

Similarly, a system of one linear and one quadratic equation may have 2, 1, or 0 solutions.

Example 1   By graphing, approximate solutions to the following system:

$$\begin{cases} y - 3x = 1 \\ xy = 10 \end{cases}$$

Solution   Graph both curves on the same set of axes. From the graph you can see that there are two solutions, one in the first quadrant, the other in the third. Zoom or rescale to estimate the coordinates. One point appears to be (-2, -5); the other about (1.7, 6).

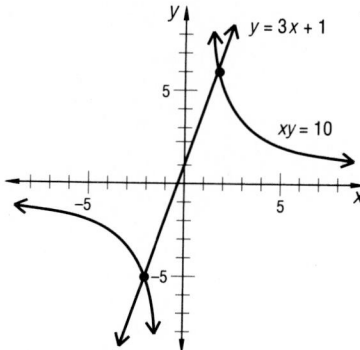

Check   Substitute into the first equation.
-5 − 3(-2) = 1 and (-2)(-5) = 10.
So (-2, -5) is an exact solution.
6 − 3(1.7) = 0.9 ≈ 1 and (1.7)(6) = 10.2 ≈ 10.
So (1.7, 6) is an approximate solution.

LESSON 12-9

RESOURCES
■ Lesson Master 12-9
✏ Computer Master 29

OBJECTIVES

D Solve quadratic-linear systems by substitution.
I Use quadratic-linear systems to solve real-world problems.
K Solve quadratic-linear systems by graphing.

TEACHING NOTES

The lesson can be covered rather easily in two ways, either by going through the four Additional Examples in order in some detail and then assigning the lesson to be read, or by assigning the lesson to be read without preliminary discussion and then going through the questions in order the next day.

Note how technology, graphical solutions, and algebraic manipulation support each other. For instance, in some cases we first estimate solutions graphically and then confirm them or get exact values algebraically. In others, we find an exact solution first and then check it graphically.

Quadratic systems take some time for most students to solve. Eight systems are given in the Questions to solve exactly; that is quite enough for almost all students. You may wish to use a couple of these for class discussion and not assign them.

With an automatic grapher, the solutions can be found to as much accuracy as you wish. Still, it is sometimes nice to get exact solutions. These can be found by substitution.

■ ■ ■ ■ ■ ■

Example 2 Find exact solutions to the system $\begin{cases} y - 3x = 1 \\ xy = 10. \end{cases}$

Solution Solve the first sentence for y.

$$y = 3x + 1.$$

Substitute the expression $3x + 1$ for y in the second sentence.

$$x(3x + 1) = 10$$

This is a quadratic equation that you can solve by the Quadratic Formula or by factoring.

$$3x^2 + x = 10$$
$$3x^2 + x - 10 = 0$$
$$x = \frac{-1 \pm \sqrt{1 - 4 \cdot 3(-10)}}{2 \cdot 3} = \frac{-1 \pm \sqrt{121}}{6}$$
$$x = \frac{-1 - 11}{6} \text{ or } x = \frac{-1 + 11}{6}$$
$$x = -2 \text{ or } x = \frac{5}{3}$$

Now remember that $y = 3x + 1$.
When $x = -2$, $y = 3(-2) + 1 = -5$.
When $x = \frac{5}{3}$, $y = 3(\frac{5}{3}) + 1 = 6$.

Check The solutions (-2, -5) and ($\frac{5}{3}$, 6) agree with the graph in Example 1.

In the above example, the substitution of the linear quantity into the quadratic relation resulted in a quadratic equation in one variable. Because quadratic equations may have 2, 1, or 0 solutions, a *quadratic-linear system* may also have 2, 1, or 0 solutions.

■ ■ ■ ■ ■ ■

Example 3 At the right are graphs of the equations $6x^2 + y^2 = 100$ and $y = -12x + 50$. It appears that they intersect in only one point. Is this so? Justify your answer.

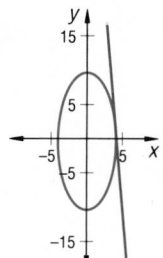

720

Solution Solve the system $\begin{cases} 6x^2 + y^2 = 100 \\ y = -12x + 50. \end{cases}$

The second sentence is already solved for y. Substitute for y in the first sentence.

$$6x^2 + (-12x + 50)^2 = 100$$

Expand and rewrite in the general form of a quadratic equation.

$$6x^2 + 144x^2 - 1200x + 2500 = 100$$
$$150x^2 - 1200x + 2400 = 0$$

Divide each side by 150 to simplify.

$$x^2 - 8x + 16 = 0$$

The left side is a perfect square.

$$(x - 4)^2 = 0$$

So $x = 4$ is the only solution. When $x = 4$ in the first sentence,

$$6(4)^2 + y^2 = 100$$
$$y^2 = 4$$
$$y = \pm 2.$$

Thus, there are two possible solutions: $(4, 2)$ and $(4, -2)$. The point $(4, 2)$ satisfies the equation $y = -12x + 50$, but the point $(4, -2)$ does not. Therefore, there is only one solution to this system.

Quadratic systems, just as linear systems, can be inconsistent. The signal for inconsistency is that the solutions to the quadratic system are not real.

Example 4 Find the points of intersection of the line $y = x - 1$ and the parabola $y = x^2$.

Solution 1 Graphs of the line and parabola, shown at the right, show there is no solution.

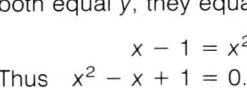

Solution 2 Solve the system $\begin{cases} y = x - 1 \\ y = x^2 \end{cases}$ algebraically. Since $x - 1$ and x^2 both equal y, they equal each other.

$$x - 1 = x^2$$
Thus $x^2 - x + 1 = 0$.

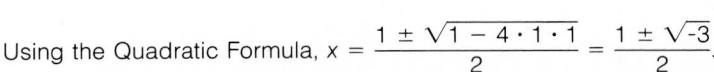

Using the Quadratic Formula, $x = \dfrac{1 \pm \sqrt{1 - 4 \cdot 1 \cdot 1}}{2} = \dfrac{1 \pm \sqrt{-3}}{2}$.

The nonreal solutions indicate there are no points of intersection.

LESSON 12-9 Quadratic-Linear Systems   **721**

721

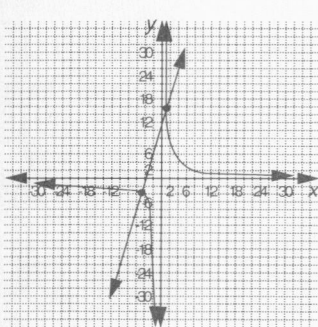
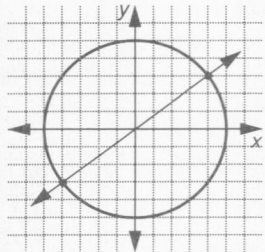
Questions

1. Which of the three strategies for solving systems is not found in this lesson? **Linear combinations**

2. How many solutions may a system of one linear and one quadratic equation have? **0, 1, or 2**

In 3 and 4, solve by (a) graphing and (b) substitution. **See margin.**

3. $\begin{cases} xy = 18 \\ y = 3x + 12 \end{cases}$

4. $\begin{cases} x^2 + y^2 = 25 \\ y = \frac{3}{4}x \end{cases}$

5. Find the points of intersection of the line $y = x + 2$ and the parabola $y = x^2$. **(-1,1), (2,4)**

6. Find the points of intersection of the line $y = x - 1$ and the parabola $y = 2x^2$. **No points of intersection.**

7. **a.** What name is given to a system which has no solutions? **inconsistent**
   b. Give an example of such a system. **Sample: $y = x - 1$ and $y = 2x^2$**

8. Refer to the equation $3x^2 + x - 10 = 0$ in the solution of Example 2.
   a. Solve this equation by factoring. **See margin.**
   b. Compare your answers to those in the lesson.

9. A graph of the system

   $$\begin{cases} y = x^2 - 2x - 15 \\ x + y = -3 \end{cases}$$

   is shown at the right.
   a. How many solutions are there? **2**
   b. Approximate the solutions. **(-3, 0), (4, -7)**
   c. Check that your estimates are close.
   See margin.

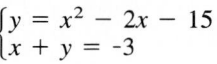

In 10 and 11, consider the figure at the right which suggests that the parabola $y = x^2 - 8x + 18$ and the line $y = 2x - 7$ intersect near the point (5, 3).

10. Check by substitution that this point is on both curves. **See margin.**

11. Solve the system algebraically and verify that this is the only solution. **See margin.**

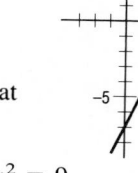

In 12 and 13, use the following system: $\begin{cases} x^2 + y^2 = 9 \\ 2x + y = 2 \end{cases}$

12. Estimate the solutions to this system by graphing. **See margin.**

13. Solve the system algebraically. $\left(\dfrac{4 + \sqrt{41}}{5}, \dfrac{2 - 2\sqrt{41}}{5}\right)$
    $\left(\dfrac{4 - \sqrt{41}}{5}, \dfrac{2 + 2\sqrt{41}}{5}\right)$

722

14. Phillip has 150 m of fencing material and wants to form a rectangle whose area is 1300 square meters. $2x + 2y = 150; xy = 1300$
    a. Let x = the width of the field and y = its length. Write a system of equations that models this situation.
    b. Use graphing to estimate the dimensions of this region. **See margin.**
    c. Solve this system. $x \approx 27.2, y \approx 47.8$ or $x \approx 47.8, y \approx 27.2$

15. The sum of two real numbers is to be 10 and their product 30. Use graphs to show that this is impossible. **See margin.**

16. What conic section is described by the equation $3x^2 + 4y^2 - 6x + 16y - 19 = 0$? *(Lesson 12-8)* **ellipse**

17. Find an equation for a hyperbola with foci at (2, 2) and (-2, -2) and focal constant 4. *(Lesson 12-6)* $xy = 2$

18. Give an equation for a hyperbola that
    a. is a function. **Sample:** $xy = 2$
    b. is not a function. *(Lessons 7-1, 12-6, 12-7)* **Sample:** $x^2 - y^2 = 1$

19. Halley's comet has an elliptical orbit with the sun at one focus. Its closest distance to the sun is about $9 \cdot 10^7$ km, while its farthest distance is about $5.34 \cdot 10^9$ km.

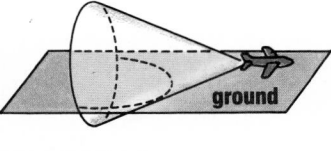

9 • 10⁷ km Sun Halley's comet 5.34 • 10⁹ km

   a. Find the length of the major axis of Halley's comet's orbit. $5.43 \cdot 10^9$
   b. What is the length of its minor axis? $1.387 \cdot 10^9$ km
   c. How long does it take Halley's comet to complete each orbit? *(Lesson 12-4)* **76 years**

20. A supersonic jet traveling parallel to the ground has a shock wave in the shape of a cone. The sonic boom is felt on all the points located on the intersection of the cone and the ground. What kind of conic section is that intersection? *(Lesson 12-1)* **one branch of a hyperbola**

ground

21. Factor completely: $x^4 - 8xy^3$ *(Lesson 11-3)* $x(x - 2y)(x^2 + 2xy + 4y^2)$

22. A lemonade stand reports the following monthly profit P (in hundreds of dollars) in relation to the average monthly temperature T (in degrees Celsius).

T	-10	0	10	20
P	-125	-50	25	100

   a. Does a linear function fit these data? **yes**
   b. If so, write P as a function of T, and tell what quantity the slope represents. If not, tell why not. *(Lessons 2-4, 3-1, 11-7)* $P = 7.5T - 50$; the slope represents the profit per degree.

23. Draw an example of a system involving a hyperbola and an oblique line that has exactly one solution. **See margin.**

MORE PRACTICE
For more questions on SPUR Objectives, use *Lesson Master 12-9*, shown below.

9.c. Does $0 = (-3)^2 - 2(-3) - 15$, and $-3 + 0 = -3$? **Yes.**
Does $-7 = 4^2 - 2(4) - 15$, and $4 + -7 = -3$? **Yes.**

10. Does $3 = 5^2 - 8 \cdot 5 + 18$, and $3 = 2 \cdot 5 - 7$? **Yes.**

11. $2x - 7 = x^2 - 8x + 18$, $x^2 - 10x + 250$, $(x - 5)^2 = 0$
So, $x = 5$ is the only solution. Substituting $x = 5$ in either equation yields $y = 3$. Thus, (5, 3) is the only solution.

12., 14.b., 15., 23. See Additional Answers in the back of this book.

RESOURCES
- Lesson Master 12-10
- Computer Master 29

OBJECTIVES

D Solve quadratic-quadratic systems by substitution.
I Use quadratic-quadratic systems to solve real-world problems.
K Solve quadratic-quadratic systems by graphing.

TEACHING NOTES

As **Examples 3 and 4** suggest, the algebraic manipulation required to obtain exact solutions can be considerable. In practice, automatic graphers can get solutions to any desired accuracy, so algebraic solutions have lost some of their importance. Most of the questions have been designed so that the manipulation is not tedious.

Notice that the Questions refer again and again to the Examples. By going through the Questions in order, you will cover the entire lesson.

LESSON

12-10

Quadratic-Quadratic Systems

Systems of hyperbolas are used to locate ships at sea. See page 728.

Quadratic-quadratic systems involve the intersection of curves represented by quadratic relations: circles, ellipses, hyperbolas, and parabolas. They are a bit more complicated than linear systems; there may be 0, 1, 2, 3, 4, or infinitely many solutions. The first two examples illustrate systems with 4 solutions each.

To find exact solutions, the first goal is always the same: *work to get an equation in one variable*. In Example 1 we use substitution to solve the system.

■ ■ ■ ■ ■ ■ ■ ■

Example 1 At the right is pictured the following system:

$$\begin{cases} x^2 + y^2 = 25 \\ y = x^2 - 13 \end{cases}$$
circle with center (0, 0), radius 5
parabola with vertex (0, -13)
congruent to $y = x^2$

Find the four solutions shown in the graph.

Solution Substitute $x^2 - 13$ for y in the first equation. The result is what is desired—an equation in one variable.

$$x^2 + (x^2 - 13)^2 = 25$$
$$x^2 + x^4 - 26x^2 + 169 = 25$$
$$x^4 - 25x^2 + 144 = 0$$

It looks difficult! A fourth-degree equation! But let $m = x^2$, and the resulting equation is quadratic.

$$m^2 - 25m + 144 = 0$$

Using the quadratic formula,

$$m = \frac{25 \pm \sqrt{625 - 576}}{2} = \frac{25 \pm \sqrt{49}}{2} = \frac{25 \pm 7}{2}.$$

So $m = 16$ or $m = 9$.
Thus $x^2 = 16$ or $x^2 = 9$.
Therefore, $x = 4, -4, 3,$ or -3.

724

For each value of x, there is a corresponding value of y. Substitute in the equation $y = x^2 - 13$ to find that value. When $x = 4$ or -4, $y = 3$. When $x = 3$ or -3, $y = -4$.

The four solutions are (4, 3), (-4, 3), (3, -4), and (-3, -4).

In the next example, because both relations are symmetric to the x- and y-axes, so is the set of solutions. Note how the Linear Combination method studied in Lesson 5-3 is applied.

Example 2 Find all points of intersection of the ellipse $\frac{x^2}{16} + \frac{y^2}{9} = 1$ and the hyperbola $x^2 - y^2 = 4$.

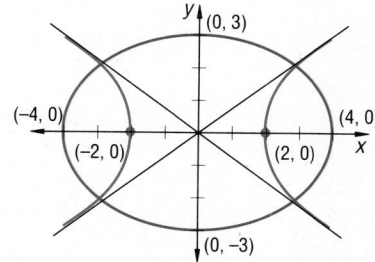

Solution Multiply the first equation by $16 \cdot 9 = 144$ to remove fractions.

$$9x^2 + 16y^2 = 144$$
$$x^2 - y^2 = 4$$

Now the system can be solved using the linear combination method. Multiply the second equation by -9 and add the equations.

$$9x^2 + 16y^2 = 144$$
$$\underline{-9x^2 + 9y^2 = -36}$$
$$25y^2 = 108$$

Solve for y. $y^2 = \frac{108}{25}$ $y = \pm\frac{\sqrt{108}}{5} = \pm\frac{6\sqrt{3}}{5}$

Use $x^2 - y^2 = 4$ to find x^2. Since $y^2 = \frac{108}{25}$, $x^2 - \frac{108}{25} = 4$, and so $x^2 = \frac{208}{25}$.

Thus for each value of y, $x = \pm\sqrt{\frac{208}{25}} = \pm\frac{4\sqrt{13}}{5}$.

The points of intersection are $\left(\frac{4\sqrt{13}}{5}, \frac{6\sqrt{3}}{5}\right)$, $\left(\frac{-4\sqrt{13}}{5}, \frac{6\sqrt{3}}{5}\right)$, $\left(\frac{4\sqrt{13}}{5}, \frac{-6\sqrt{3}}{5}\right)$, and $\left(\frac{-4\sqrt{13}}{5}, \frac{-6\sqrt{3}}{5}\right)$, or approximately (2.88, 2.08), (-2.88, 2.08), (2.88, -2.08), and (-2.88, -2.08).

Check The graph shows these solutions to be quite reasonable.

LESSON 12-10 Quadratic-Quadratic Systems   **725**

Recall from Lesson 12-1 that with a seismograph, a tracking station can determine its distance from the center of an earthquake. Two such tracking stations can determine that the center is at one of two locations.

■ ■ ■ ■ ■ ■ ■ ■ ■

Example 3   One station determines that the center of the quake is 30 miles away. A second station 40 miles east and 10 miles north of the first finds that it is 20 miles from the center. Where is the center of the earthquake?

Solution   First draw a rough picture. It seems there may be two points. We call them P and Q. Locate a coordinate system at the center of the first station. Now find the equations of the circles.

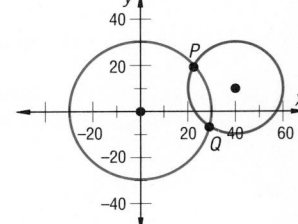

Earthquake damage, Mexico City

Circle (1) has center (0, 0) and radius 30: $\qquad x^2 + y^2 = 900$
Circle (2) has center (40, 10)
and radius 20: $\qquad\qquad\qquad (x - 40)^2 + (y - 10)^2 = 400$

The system has been determined. Now it must be solved.
Expand the squares of the binomials in the equation for circle (2):

Now subtract $\qquad x^2 - 80x + 1600 + y^2 - 20y + 100 = 400$
equation (1). $\qquad\quad x^2 \qquad\qquad\quad + y^2 \qquad\qquad\quad = 900$
A linear equation results. $\quad\overline{\quad - 80x + 1600 \qquad - 20y + 100 = -500}$

Solve for one of the variables in the linear equation. We solve for y.

$$2200 - 80x = 20y$$
$$110 - 4x = y$$

Now substitute for y in the equation of one of the circles. We use $x^2 + y^2 = 900$, because it is simpler.

$$x^2 + (110 - 4x)^2 = 900$$

This is finally an equation in one variable.

$$x^2 + (12100 - 880x + 16x^2) = 900$$
$$17x^2 - 880x + 11200 = 0$$

Using the quadratic formula,

$$x = \frac{880 \pm \sqrt{880^2 - 4 \cdot 17 \cdot 11200}}{34} = \frac{880 \pm \sqrt{12800}}{34}$$

$$\approx \frac{880 \pm 113.1}{34}. \qquad \text{So} \qquad x \approx 29.2 \quad \text{or} \quad x \approx 22.6.$$

726

726

Corresponding estimates of y can be found by substituting into $y = 110 - 4x$.

When $x \approx 29.2$, $y \approx$ -6.8.
When $x \approx 22.6$, $y \approx 19.6$.

The points are near (29.2, -6.8) and (22.6, 19.6).

Check 1   Examine the graph. The points seem correct. That is, from the given information the center of the quake is either about 29.2 miles east and 6.8 miles south of the first station, or about 22.6 miles east and 19.6 miles north of it.

Check 2   Substitute into the original equations. Try each point in each equation. Does $(29.2)^2 + (-6.8)^2 = 900$? We get about 899, which is close enough. The three other substitutions are left to you.

Other situations can lead to systems of quadratic equations which require multiple substitutions to solve.

■ ■ ■ ■ ■ ■ ■ ■ ■

Example 4   One month, Wanda's Western Wear took in $12,000 from boot sales. The next month, although Wanda sold 40 fewer pairs of boots, the store took in $12,800 from boot sales because they had raised the price by $20. Find the price of a pair of boots in each month.

Solution   Let n = the number of pairs of boots sold in the first month.
c = the cost of a pair of boots in the first month.
The equations for total sales in the first and second months respectively are:

(1) $nc = 12000$
(2) $(n - 40)(c + 20) = 12800$

From (1), you know $c = \dfrac{12000}{n}$.

From (2), $nc + 20n - 40c - 13600 = 0$. The two forms of equation (1) allow you to make two substitutions into the expanded form of equation (2), namely 12000 for nc and $\dfrac{12000}{n}$ for c, to get:

$$12000 + 20n - 40\left(\frac{12000}{n}\right) - 13600 = 0$$

Simplify. $20n - 1600 - \dfrac{480000}{n} = 0$

Multiply by n. $20n^2 - 1600n - 480000 = 0$
Divide by 20. $n^2 - 80n - 24000 = 0$
Solve by factoring. $(n - 200)(n + 120) = 0$
                                  $n = 200$ or $n = $ -120

The number of pairs of boots can only be positive, so use the positive answer and substitute in equation (1) to find the price.

$$200c = 12000$$
$$c = 60$$

The boots cost $60 the first month, and $c + 20 = \$80$ the second month.

Check First month: $(200)(60) = 12000$ Yes, it checks.
Second month: $(200 - 40)(60 + 20) = (160)(80)$
$$= 12800 \qquad \text{Yes, it checks.}$$

Intersections of hyperbolas are the basis for the LORAN system. In this system, three LOng RAnge Navigational stations simultaneously send electronic signals to a ship at sea. The ship receives these signals at slightly different times. If A and B are two stations, then by measuring the time differential and by knowing the speed of the radio waves, the ship P can be located on a hyperbola with foci at A and B. A similar process locates the ship on a hyperbola with foci at stations B and C. The intersection of the two hyperbolas gives the ship's location.

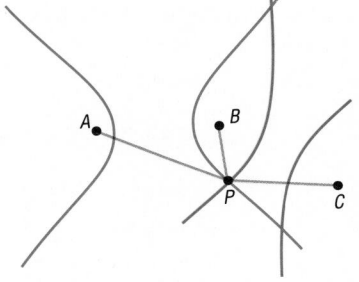

ADDITIONAL ANSWERS
11. sample: (2.5, 1.9), (2.5, –1.9), (–2.5, 1.9), (–2.5, –1.9)

Covering the Reading

1. **a.** How many solutions may a system of two quadratic equations in x and y have?   0, 1, 2, 3, 4, or infinitely many
   b. Which of these possibilities is illustrated in Examples 1-4?
   Ex. 1: 4; Ex. 2: 4; Ex. 3: 2; Ex. 4: 1

In 2–4, refer to Example 1.

2. What technique was used in obtaining the equation

$$x^2 + (x^2 - 13)^2 = 25?   \text{substitution}$$

3. What substitution changed $x^4 - 25x^2 + 144 = 0$ into a quadratic equation? $m = x^2$

4. Explain how the step $m = 16$ leads to $x = 4$ or $x = $ -4.
   If $m = 16$, then $x^2 = 16$ and $x = \pm 4$.

In 5 and 6, refer to Example 2.

5. What in the original equations signifies that the solutions will be symmetric to the axes?   Both x and y only appear with the exponent 2.

6. The four solutions are vertices of what figure?   rectangle

7. Refer to Example 3. *True or false*   The solution to this system used both a linear combination and substitution.   True

8. Refer to Example 2 of Lesson 12-1. Find the coordinates of the two possible epicenters A and B of the earthquake.
   $\approx$ (59.64, 6.54), (28.97, 52.54)

In 9 and 10, refer to Example 4.

9. What were the two substitutions that transformed the second equation into an equation with only one variable? $nc = 12{,}000$ and $c = \dfrac{12000}{n}$

10. If in the second month Wanda had instead raised prices by $30 and earned $10,800 from 80 fewer sales than the previous month, what would be the second equation? $(n - 80)(c + 30) = 10{,}800$

Applying the Mathematics

In 11 and 12, refer to the relations $x^2 + y^2 = 9$ and $2x^2 + 3y^2 = 22$ graphed at the right.

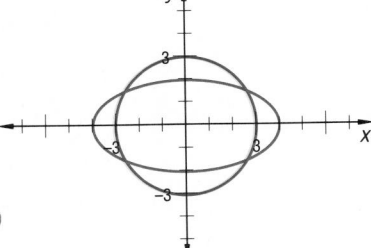

11. Estimate the solutions from the graph.
    See margin.

12. Find the exact solutions algebraically.
    $(\sqrt{5},2), (-\sqrt{5},2), (\sqrt{5},-2), (-\sqrt{5},-2)$

13. Solve the following system:

$$\begin{cases} y = x^2 - 4x + 3 \\ y = x^2 - 9 \end{cases}$$

   (3, 0)

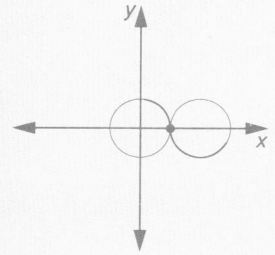
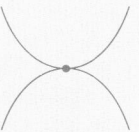
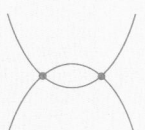

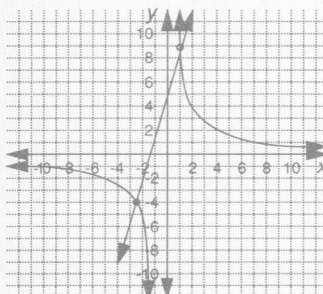
14. Refer to Example 3. A third station 50 miles west and 20 miles south of the first station determines that the center of the quake is about 80 miles away. $(x + 50)^2 + (y + 20)^2 = 6400$
  a. Find an equation to describe this information.
  b. Using the points found in Example 3, determine which point was really the location of the epicenter.   near (29.2, −6.8)

In 15 and 16, consider this situation. The product of two numbers is 1073. If one number is increased by 3 and the other is decreased by 7, the new product is 960.

15. *Multiple choice*   Which of the following systems represents this situation?   c

(a) $\begin{cases} xy = 960 \\ (x + 3)(y - 7) = 1073 \end{cases}$ (b) $\begin{cases} xy = 1073 \\ (x - 3)(y + 7) = 960 \end{cases}$

(c) $\begin{cases} xy = 1073 \\ (x + 3)(y - 7) = 960 \end{cases}$ (d) $\begin{cases} xy = 1073 \\ (x + 3)(y - 7) = 960 \end{cases}$

16. Find the numbers.   (29,37) or $\left(-\dfrac{111}{7}, -\dfrac{203}{3}\right)$

17. Without doing any calculations, solve the following system:

$$\begin{cases} (x - 3)^2 + y^2 = 4 \\ (x + 3)^2 + y^2 = 4 \end{cases}$$

Explain how you found your answer.   See margin.

18. One circle has a center at the origin, the other at (4, 0). Each has a radius of 2. Where do they intersect? Check by graphing.
See margin.

19. Draw two parabolas which intersect in: See margin.
  a. exactly one point   **b.** exactly two points   **c.** exactly three points

In 20 and 21, how many possible solutions could there be to the following systems?

20. a circle and a parabola   **21.** two circles
0, 1, 2, 3, or 4   0, 1, 2, or infinitely many

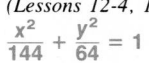

22. By graphing the system $\begin{cases} xy = 10 \\ y = 4x + 5 \end{cases}$
  a. determine the number of real solutions, and
  b. estimate them. *(Lesson 12-9)*   See margin.

In 23 and 24, for the ellipse pictured at the right, find

23. the area 96π

24. an equation in standard form.
(Lessons 12-4, 12-5)
$\dfrac{x^2}{144} + \dfrac{y^2}{64} = 1$

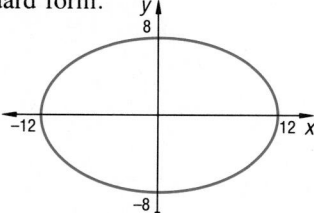

730

MORE PRACTICE
For more questions on SPUR
Objectives, use *Lesson Mas-
ter 12-10*, shown below.

27.a. sample: $x^2 + y^2 = \frac{1}{4}$
b. sample: $(x - 2)^2 + y^2 = 1$
c. sample: $(x - 2)^2 + y^2 = 4$
d. sample: $y = x^2 - 1$
e. sample: $y = 4x^2 - 2$

25. A skydiver jumping from a plane falls about 16 ft the first second, 48 ft the next second, and 80 ft the third second, if air resistance is ignored. How many feet will the diver fall in the thirtieth second? *(Lesson 3-6)* **944 ft**

26. Consider the geometric sequence 8, -12, 18, -27, ... Find
a. the next term $\frac{81}{2}$
b. an explicit formula for the nth term. *(Lesson 8-3)* $a_n = 8(\frac{-3}{2})^{n-1}$

Exploration

27. Give an equation for a quadratic relation that intersects the unit circle $x^2 + y^2 = 1$: (a) in no points; (b) in exactly one point; (c) in exactly two points; (d) in exactly three points; (e) in exactly four points.
See margin.

28. Consider the ellipse with equation $\dfrac{x^2}{a^2} + \dfrac{y^2}{b^2} = 1$, and the circle whose diameter has endpoints at the foci $(c, 0)$ and $(-c, 0)$. The area of the ellipse is πab; the area of the circle is πc^2. Are these two areas ever equal? If so what relation exists between a, b, and c?

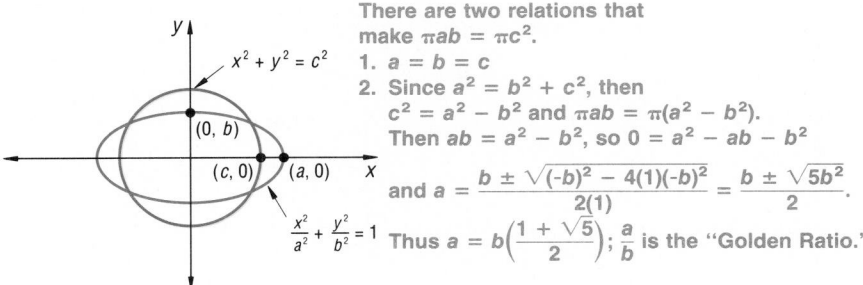

There are two relations that make $\pi ab = \pi c^2$.
1. $a = b = c$
2. Since $a^2 = b^2 + c^2$, then $c^2 = a^2 - b^2$ and $\pi ab = \pi(a^2 - b^2)$. Then $ab = a^2 - b^2$, so $0 = a^2 - ab - b^2$
and $a = \dfrac{b \pm \sqrt{(-b)^2 - 4(1)(-b^2)}}{2(1)} = \dfrac{b \pm \sqrt{5b^2}}{2}$. Thus $a = b\left(\dfrac{1 + \sqrt{5}}{2}\right)$; $\dfrac{a}{b}$ is the "Golden Ratio."

Summary

In this chapter you studied quadratic relations in two variables, their graphs, and geometric properties of these figures. A quadratic equation in two variables is of the form

$$Ax^2 + Bxy + Cy^2 + Dx + Ey + F = 0,$$

where not all of A, B, and C are zero.

The Discriminant Theorem states that
if $B^2 - 4AC < 0$, the curve is an ellipse,
if $B^2 - 4AC = 0$, the curve is a parabola,
and if $B^2 - 4AC > 0$, the curve is a hyperbola.
Additionally, you can identify the curve by knowing the standard-form equations as given below.

Conic	Equation in Standard form	Graph
circle center: (h, k) radius: r	$(x - h)^2 + (y - k)^2 = r^2$	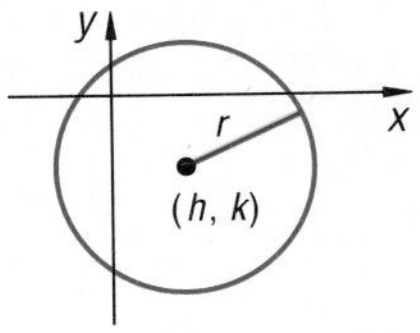
ellipse center: $(0, 0)$	$\dfrac{x^2}{a^2} + \dfrac{y^2}{b^2} = 1$	
hyperbola center: $(0, 0)$	$xy = k$	
	$\dfrac{x^2}{a^2} - \dfrac{y^2}{b^2} = 1,$ where $b^2 = c^2 - a^2$	

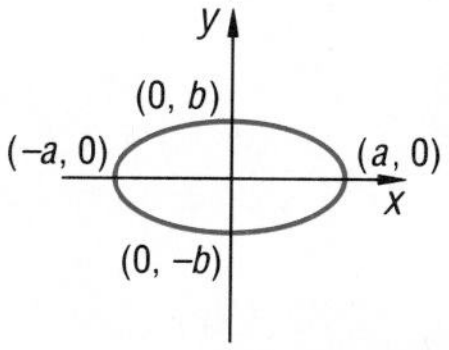

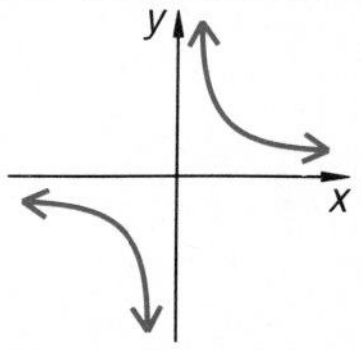

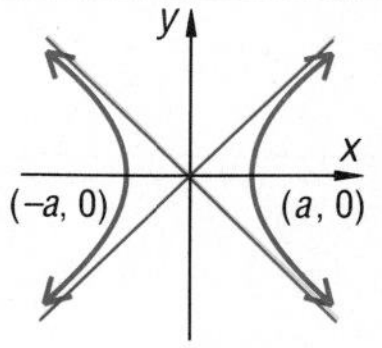

Ellipse ($a > b$):
foci: $(-c, 0)$, $(c, 0)$
Length of major axis (focal constant): $2a$
Length of minor axis: $2b$
$b^2 = a^2 - c^2$

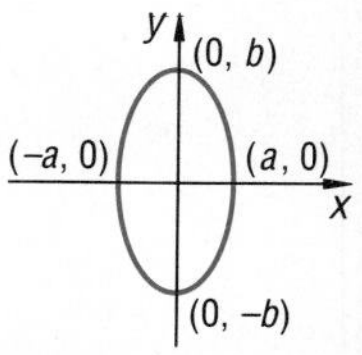

Ellipse ($b > a$):
foci: $(0, -c)$, $(0, c)$
Length of major axis (focal constant): $2b$
Length of minor axis: $2a$
$a^2 = b^2 - c^2$

Hyperbola $xy = k$:
foci: $(\sqrt{2k}, \sqrt{2k})$, $(-\sqrt{2k}, -\sqrt{2k})$
focal constant: $2\sqrt{2k}$
asymptotes: $x = 0$, $y = 0$

Hyperbola:
foci: $(-c, 0)$, $(c, 0)$
focal constant: $2a$
asymptotes: $\dfrac{y}{b} = \pm \dfrac{x}{a}$

732

The graph of every quadratic equation in two variables is a conic section. That is, it can be formed by the intersection of a plane and a double cone. If the plane does not contain the vertex of the cone, the intersection may be an ellipse (of which the circle is a special case), a hyperbola, or a parabola. If the plane contains the vertex of the cone, degenerate conic sections—a point, line, or two lines—are formed.

These curves may also be generated geometrically in two dimensions. In a plane a circle is the set of points at a given distance (its radius) from a fixed point (its center); an ellipse is the set of points such that the sum of its distances to two fixed points (its foci) is constant; and a hyperbola is the set of points such that the difference of its distances from two fixed points (its foci) is constant.

Conic sections appear naturally as orbits of planets and comets, in paths of objects thrown in the air, as energy waves radiating from the epicenter of an earthquake, and in many manufactured objects such as tunnels, windows, and satellite receiver dishes.

Systems of equations with quadratic sentences are solved much the same as linear systems, that is, by graphing, by substitution, or by using linear combinations. A system of one linear and one quadratic equation may have 0, 1, or 2 solutions; a system of two quadratics may have 0, 1, 2, 3, 4, or infinitely many solutions.

Below are the most important terms and phrases for this chapter. You should be able to give a definition for those terms marked with a *. For all other terms you should be able to give both a general description and a specific example.

VOCABULARY

Terms, symbols, and properties are listed by lesson to provide a checklist of things a student must know. Emphasize to students that they should read the vocabulary list carefully before starting the Progress Self-Test. If students do not understand the meaning of a term, they should refer back to the indicated lesson.

Definitions or descriptions of all terms in the vocabulary list may be found in the Glossary.

Vocabulary

Lesson 12-1
*quadratic equation in two variables
*quadratic relation in two variables
conic section, conic
*circle, radius, center
Center-Radius Equation for a Circle Theorem
*lattice point

Lesson 12-2
*interior, exterior of a circle
Interior and Exterior of a Circle Theorem

Lesson 12-3
foci, focal constant of an ellipse or hyperbola
*ellipse
vertices of an ellipse or hyperbola
*hyperbola
asymptotes of a hyperbola
eccentricity

Lesson 12-4
standard position for an ellipse
standard form of equation for an ellipse
Equation for an Ellipse Theorem
*major axis, minor axis, center of an ellipse

Lesson 12-5
area of an ellipse

Lesson 12-6
*rectangular hyperbola

Lesson 12-7
*standard form for an equation of a hyperbola

Lesson 12-8
*general form of a quadratic relation
Discriminant Theorem for Conics
degenerate form of a conic

Lesson 12-9
quadratic system
quadratic-linear system

Lesson 12-10
quadratic-quadratic system

CHAPTER 12 Summary and Vocabulary 733

Progress Self-Test

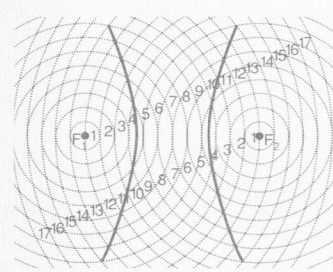
Take this test as you would take a test in class. Use graph paper and a ruler. Then check your work with the solutions in the Selected Answer section in the back of the book.

In 1 and 2, consider the equation $x^2 + 9x + y^2 - 26y - 163 = 0$.

1. Determine which conic section the equation represents. **ellipse (circle)**

2. Rewrite the equation in standard form for that conic. $(x + \frac{9}{2})^2 + (y - 13)^2 = 352.25$

In 3–5, consider the image of $x^2 + y^2 = 1$ under the scale change $S_{3,4}$.

3. State an equation for the image.
$\left(\frac{x}{3}\right)^2 + \left(\frac{y}{4}\right)^2 = 1$

4. *Multiple choice* The image is a(n) **b**
(a) circle (b) ellipse (c) parabola
(d) hyperbola.

5. Find the coordinates of the vertices of the image. **(-3, 0), (3, 0), (0, -4), (0, 4)**

In 6 and 7, refer to the ellipse drawn below.

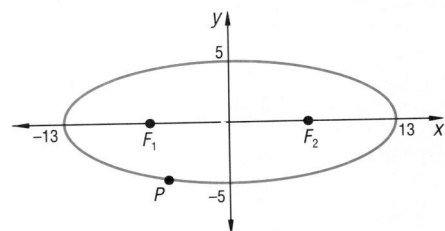

6. Determine an equation for this ellipse.

7. Find its area. $65\pi \approx 204$ $\frac{x^2}{169} + \frac{y^2}{25} = 1$

In 8 and 9, consider the following system:
$\begin{cases} y = x - 2 \\ y = 4x - x^2 \end{cases}$
near (3.5, 1.5) and (-.5, -2.5)

8. Estimate the solutions by graphing the system.

9. Find the exact solutions algebraically.
$\left(\frac{3 + \sqrt{17}}{2}, \frac{-1 + \sqrt{17}}{2}\right)$ and $\left(\frac{3 - \sqrt{17}}{2}, \frac{-1 - \sqrt{17}}{2}\right)$

10. Pluto has an elliptical orbit with the Sun at one focus. Its closest distance to the Sun is about 2.8 billion miles, while its farthest distance is about 4.6 billion miles. What is the length of the major axis of Pluto's orbit?
7.4 billon miles

11. Use conic graph paper with centers 12 units apart to sketch the set of points P such that $|PF_1 - PF_2| = 5$. **See margin.**

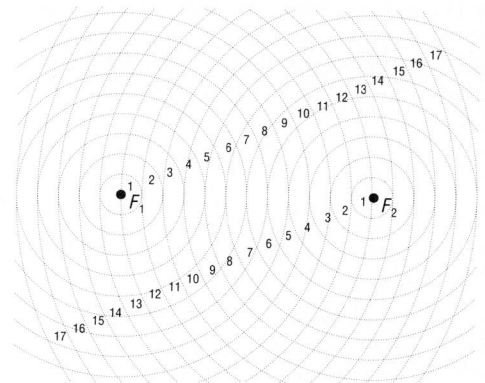

12. Graph the set of points (x, y) such that $9 < x^2 + y^2 < 25$. **See margin.**

In 13 and 14, one earthquake station determines that the center of a quake is 40 miles away. A second station 25 miles west and 60 miles north of the first station finds that it is 30 miles from the center.

13. Write an equation to describe each situation. $x^2 + y^2 = 1600, (x + 25)^2 + (y - 60)^2 = 900$

14. Where is the epicenter of the quake (to the nearest tenth of a mile)? **near (-2.7, 40) or (-26, 30)**

15. The graph of $xy = 2$ is a hyperbola. What are the asymptotes of this hyperbola? $x = 0, y = 0$

16. Graph the set of points (x, y) satisfying $\frac{x^2}{9} - \frac{y^2}{4} = 1$. **See margin.**

Chapter Review

Questions on **SPUR** Objectives

SPUR stands for **S**kills, **P**roperties, **U**ses, and **R**epresentations.
The Chapter Review questions are grouped according to the
SPUR Objectives for this chapter.

SKILLS deal with the procedures used to get answers.

■ Objective A: *Convert from the general form of a quadratic equation in two variables to standard form for a particular curve, and vice versa.*
(Lesson 12-8)

In 1 and 2, rewrite in the form $Ax^2 + Bxy + Cy^2 + Dx + Ey + F = 0$. $x^2 + 0xy + y^2 - 6x +$

1. $(x - 3)^2 + (y + 7)^2 = 100$ $14y - 42 = 0$

2. $\frac{x^2}{25} - \frac{y^2}{9} = 1$ $9x^2 + 0xy - 25y^2 + 0x + 0y - 225 = 0$

In 3–6, rewrite the equation in standard form.

3. ellipse: $25x^2 + 75y^2 = 150$ $\frac{x^2}{6} + \frac{y^2}{2} = 1$

4. parabola: $y + 3x = x^2 - 5$ $y = x^2 - 3x - 5$

5. hyperbola: $2x^2 - 4y^2 = 8$ $\frac{x^2}{4} - \frac{y^2}{2} = 1$

6. circle: $x^2 + y^2 + 6x - 9y - 12 = 0$
$(x + 3)^2 + (y - \frac{9}{2})^2 = 41.25$

■ Objective B: *Write equations or inequalities for quadratic relations given sufficient conditions.*
(Lessons 12-1, 12-2, 12-4, 12-6, 12-7)

In 7 and 8, find an equation for the circle satisfying the conditions.

7. center at origin, radius 6 $x^2 + y^2 = 6$

8. center is $(-7, 5)$, radius 12
$(x + 7)^2 + (y - 5)^2 = 144$

9. a. Solve the equation $x^2 + y^2 = 20$ for y.
$y = \pm\sqrt{20 - x^2}$

b. Explain how the graph of the equation $x^2 + y^2 = 20$ is related to the graph of your response to part a.
The graph of $x^2 + y^2 = 20$ is the union of the graphs of $y = \sqrt{20 - x^2}$ and $y = -\sqrt{20 - x^2}$.

10. Determine a quadratic relation describing the interior of the ellipse with equation $x^2 + 3y^2 = 75$. $\frac{x^2}{75} + \frac{y^2}{25} < 1$

In 11 and 12, write an equation for the ellipse satisfying the given conditions.

11. foci are $(0, 5)$ and $(0, -5)$; focal constant is 26 $\frac{x^2}{144} + \frac{y^2}{169} = 1$

12. foci are $(9, 0)$ and $(-9, 0)$; minor axis has length 6 $\frac{x^2}{90} + \frac{y^2}{9} = 1$

In 13 and 14, find an equation for the hyperbola satisfying the given conditions.

13. foci at $(7, 0)$ and $(-7, 0)$; focal constant 8 $\frac{x^2}{16} - \frac{y^2}{33} = 1$

14. vertices are $(1, 1)$ and $(-1, -1)$; asymptotes are the x- and y-axes $xy = 1$

■ Objective C. *Find the area of an ellipse.* *(Lesson 12-5)*

In 15 and 16, find the area of the ellipse satisfying the given conditions.

15. Its equation is $\frac{x^2}{121} + \frac{y^2}{9} = 1$. $33\pi \approx 104$

16. The endpoints of its major and minor axes are $(0, 10)$, $(0, -10)$, $(5, 0)$, and $(-5, 0)$.
$50\pi \approx 157$

17. Which has a larger area: a circle of radius 5 or an ellipse with major and minor axes of lengths 12 and 8, respectively? Justify your answer. See below.

18. Find the area of the shaded region below, which is between an ellipse with major axis of length 10 and minor axis of length 8, and a circle with diameter 8.
$4\pi \approx 12.6$

17) The circle has an area of 25π, ellipse has an area of 24π; circle has greater area.

RESOURCES
■ Chapter 12 Test, Form A
■ Chapter 12 Test, Form B
■ Chapter 12 Test, Cumulative Form

CHAPTER REVIEW

The main objectives for the chapter are organized here into sections corresponding to the four main types of understanding this book promotes: Skills, Properties, Uses, and Representations.

USING THE CHAPTER REVIEW
Whereas end-of-chapter material may be considered optional in some texts, in *Advanced Algebra* we have selected these objectives and questions with the expectation that they will be covered. Students should be able to answer these questions with about 85% accuracy after studying the chapter.

You may assign these questions over a single night to help students prepare for a test the next day, or you may assign the questions over a two-day period.

If you work the questions over two days, then we recommend assigning the *evens* for homework the first night so that students get feedback in class the next day, then assigning the *odds* the night before the test so students can use the answers provided in the book.

■ **Objective D.** *Solve systems of one linear and one quadratic equation or two quadratic equations by substitution or linear combination. (Lessons 12-9, 12-10)*

In 19–26, solve.

19. $\begin{cases} y = x^2 + 5 \\ y = -x^2 + 5x + 8 \end{cases}$ (-.5, 5.25), (3, 14)

20. $\begin{cases} 2x + y = 23 \\ y = 2x^2 - 7x + 5 \end{cases}$ (4.5, 14), (-2, 27)

21. $\begin{cases} y = x^2 + 3x - 4 \\ y = 2x^2 + 5x - 3 \end{cases}$ (-1, -6)

22. $\begin{cases} x^2 + y^2 = 1 \\ x^2 + y^2 = 9 \end{cases}$ no solution

23. $\begin{cases} (x - 3)^2 + y^2 = 25 \\ x^2 + (y - 1)^2 = 25 \end{cases}$ (0, -4), (3, 5)

24. $\begin{cases} x^2 - y^2 = 9 \\ \dfrac{x^2}{50} + \dfrac{y^2}{32} = 1 \end{cases}$ (±5, ±4)

25. $\begin{cases} xy = 12 \\ y = 3x - 1 \end{cases}$

$\left(\dfrac{1 \pm \sqrt{145}}{6}, \dfrac{-1 \pm \sqrt{145}}{2} \right)$

PROPERTIES deal with the principles behind the mathematics.

■ **Objective E:** *Identify characteristics of circles, ellipses, and hyperbolas. (Lessons 12-1, 12-4, 12-6, 12-7)*

In 26 and 27, identify the center and radius of the circle with the given equation.

26. $(x + 8)^2 + y^2 = 196$ center (-8,0), radius 14

27. $x^2 + y^2 = 5$ center (0,0), radius $\sqrt{5}$

In 28 and 29, consider the ellipse with equation
$$\frac{x^2}{169} + \frac{y^2}{400} = 1.$$

28. Name its vertices.   (0,20), (0,-20)

29. State the length of its minor axis.   26

■ **Objective F:** *Classify curves as circles, ellipses, parabolas, or hyperbolas using algebraic or geometric properties. (Lessons 12-1, 12-3, 12-8)*

In 33 and 34, consider two fixed points F_1 and F_2 and a focal constant d. Identify the set of points P satisfying the given conditions.

33. $F_1P + F_2P = d$, where $d > F_1F_2$ ellipse

34. $|F_1P - F_2P| = d$, where $d < F_1F_2$

In 35 and 36, consider the equation   hyperbola
$Ax^2 + Bxy + Cy^2 + Dx + Ey + F = 0$.
What conic results from the given conditions?

35. $A = C$ and $B = 0$ ellipse (circle)

36. $B^2 - 4AC = 0$ parabola

In 37 and 38, tell whether the graph is a hyperbola, a parabola, or an ellipse.

37. $5x^2 + 10x - y^2 + 3y = 0$ hyperbola

38. $x^2 - 3x + y^2 + 4y = xy$ ellipse

30. Consider the ellipse with equation
$$\frac{x^2}{100} + \frac{y^2}{36} = 1.$$
 a. Find the foci F_1 and F_2.   (-8, 0), (8, 0)
 b. Suppose P is on this ellipse. Find the value of $PF_1 + PF_2$.   20

31. Consider the hyperbola with equation
$$\frac{x^2}{16} - \frac{y^2}{4} = 1.$$
 a. Name its vertices.   (-4, 0), (4, 0)
 b. State equations for its asymptotes. $\dfrac{y}{2} = \pm \dfrac{x}{4}$

32. Identify the asymptotes of the hyperbola $xy = 5$.   x = 0, y = 0

39. The figure below shows a double cone intersected by four planes *A*, *B*, *C*, and *D*. Identify the curve produced by each intersection.   A: hyperbola; B: parabola; C: ellip D: circl

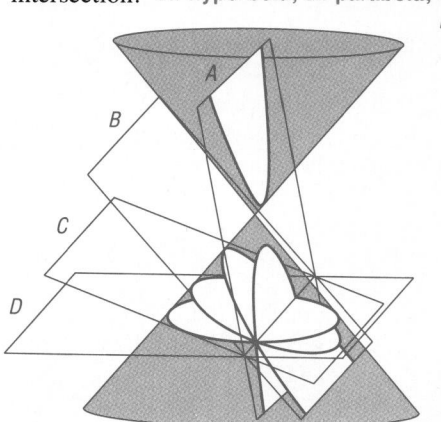

■ **Objective G:** *Describe relations between conics.*
(Lessons 12-3, 12-5)

In 40–43, *true or false*.

40. Every circle is an ellipse.   **True**

41. The image of the unit circle under a scale change is an ellipse.   **True**

42. A hyperbola can be considered as the union of two parabolas.   **False**

43. All quadratic relations in two variables can be determined from the intersection of a plane and a double cone.   **True**

USES deal with applications of mathematics in real situations.

■ **Objective H:** *Use circles, ellipses, and hyperbolas to solve real world problems. (Lessons 12-1, 12-2, 12-4, 12-5)*

44. A truck 10 ft high and 5 ft wide approaches a semicircular tunnel with a radius of 12 ft. Will the truck fit through the tunnel? Justify your answer.

At 2.5 feet from the center line, the tunnel has a height of 11.7 ft. so the truck will fit.

45. The elliptically shaped pool below is to be surrounded by tile so that the outer boundary of the tile is also an ellipse. The tiler needs to know the area of the shaded region to determine how much tile to buy. The major axis of the pool is 15 m and the minor axis of the pool is 8 m. The major axis AB is 18 m and the minor axis DC is 11 m. What is the area of the shaded region?
19.5π ≈ 61.3 sq m

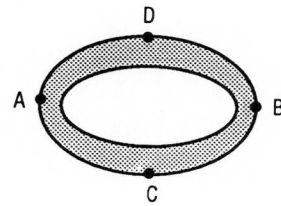

46. The orbit of the Earth around the Sun is elliptical with the Sun as one focus. The closest and farthest distances of the Earth from the Sun are 91.4 and 94.5 million miles, respectively.
  a. How far is F_2, the second focus, from the Sun?   **3.1 million miles**
  b. What is the length of the minor axis of the Earth's orbit?   **92.9 million miles**

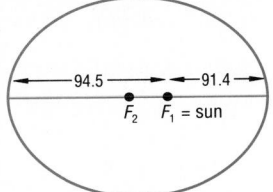 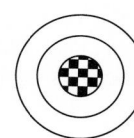

In 47–50, a computer programmer needs to write instructions to draw a figure, such as the one above at the right, with concentric circles with radii of 10, 30, and 50 pixels. The center of the circles is at the point (200, 100).

47. What sentence does the checkerboard region satisfy? $(x - 200)^2 + (y - 100)^2 < 100$

48. What sentence does the light-shaded ring satisfy? $100 < (x - 200)^2 + (y - 100)^2 < 900$

49. What sentence lets the programmer describe points (x, y) in the exterior of the circle with equation $(x + 8)^2 + y^2 = 5?$ $(x + 8)^2 + y^2 > 5$

50. a. For the circle $x^2 + y^2 = 1$, what sentence is the image of the circle under the scale change S: $(x, y) \rightarrow (6x, 9y)$? $\left(\frac{x}{6}\right)^2 + \left(\frac{y}{9}\right)^2 = 1$
  b. What kind of curve is the image in part a?   **ellipse**

56.

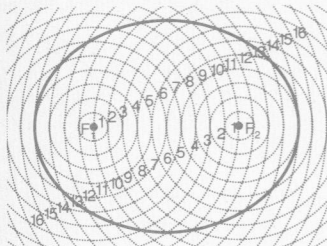

57.

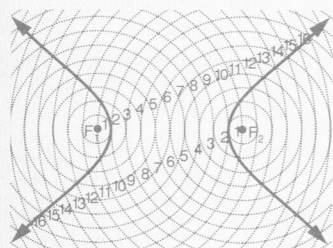

58.

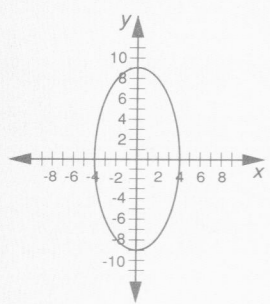

59.

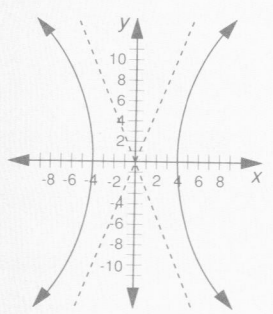

60.

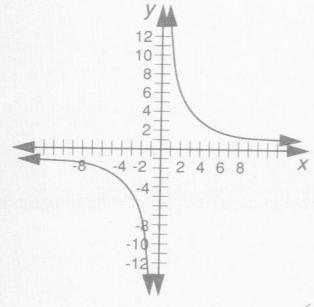

■ **Objective I:** *Use systems of quadratic equations to solve real problems.* *(Lessons 12-9, 12-10)*

51. A rectangular Oriental rug has an area of 216 square feet and a perimeter of 60 feet. Find the dimensions of the rug.   **12 by 18**

In 52 and 53, suppose a seismograph shows the epicenter of an earthquake to be about 50 miles away from station 1. Another station, which is 60 miles east and 40 miles south of station 1, finds that the quake is also 50 miles away.

52. Find the possible locations for the epicenter.
If station 1 is (0, 0), then at (49.2, 8.8) or (10.8, -48.8)

53. Station 3, 70 miles west and 20 miles north of station 1, finds that the same quake is about 106 miles away. Where is the actual epicenter of the earthquake?
(10.8, -48.8)

54. The demand function for Peewee's Sports Company is $xp = 250$, where x is the number of baseballs in hundreds, and p is the unit price of a baseball. The supply function for the Giant Baseball Manufacturer is $p = 2x^2$. Find the equilibrium point, that is, the point where supply and demand are the same. $x = 5, p = 50$

55. Eileen's Eye Extravaganza took in $5600 in sunglass sales for last year. This year Eileen lowered the price by two dollars, sold seventy more pairs of sunglasses, and made $5880.
  a. How much is she selling her sunglasses for now? $14
  b. How many pairs did she sell this year?
  420

REPRESENTATIONS deal with pictures, graphs, or objects that illustrate concepts.

■ **Objective J:** *Graph quadratic relations given sentences for them, and vice-versa.* *(Lessons 12-1, 12-2, 12-3, 12-4, 12-6, 12-7)*

In 56 and 57, use conic graph paper with centers 10 units apart to draw the set of points P satisfying the given condition.

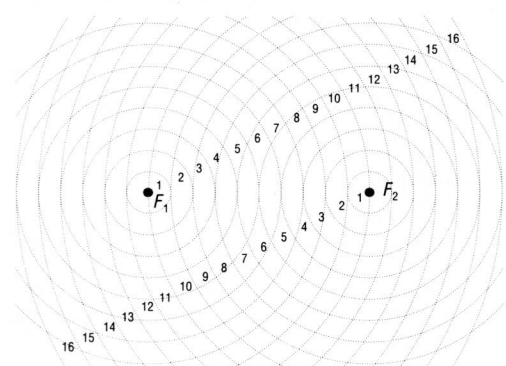

See margin.

56. $PF_1 + PF_2 = 18$, $F_1F_2 = 10$
57. $|PF_1 - PF_2| = 8$, $F_1F_2 = 10$
See margin.

In 58–61, sketch a graph.

58. $\dfrac{x^2}{16} + \dfrac{y^2}{81} = 1$ See margin.

59. $\dfrac{x^2}{16} - \dfrac{y^2}{81} = 1$ See margin.

60. $xy = 12$ See margin.

61. $x^2 + y^2 \geq 9$ See margin.

In 62 and 63, state an equation for the curve.

62. a circle tangent to the coordinate axes at (0, -1) and (1, 0) $(x-1)^2 + (y+1)^2 = 1$

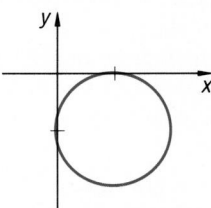

63. an ellipse with x-intercepts ± 7 and y-intercepts ± 4 $\quad \dfrac{x^2}{49} + \dfrac{y^2}{16} = 1$

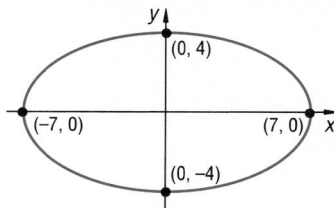

In 64 and 65, *multiple choice*. Select the equation that best describes each graph.

(a) $\dfrac{x^2}{a^2} + \dfrac{y^2}{b^2} = 1$ (b) $\dfrac{x^2}{a^2} - \dfrac{y^2}{b^2} = 1$

(c) $\dfrac{y^2}{a^2} - \dfrac{x^2}{b^2} = 1$ (d) $xy = a; a > 0$

64.   d

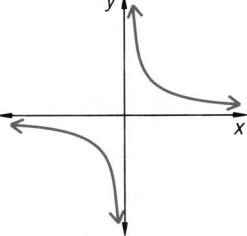

65.   b

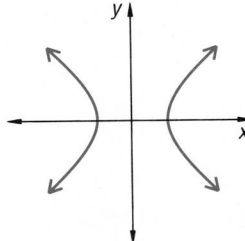

■ **Objective K:** *Solve systems of quadratic equations geometrically.* *(Lessons 12-9, 12-10)*

In 66 and 67, solve by graphing.

66. $\begin{cases} y = x^2 - 10 \\ y = 11 - x \end{cases}$ See margin.

67. $\begin{cases} x^2 + y^2 = 81 \\ x^2 + (y + 18)^2 = 81 \end{cases}$ See margin.

In 68 and 69, draw an example showing how the situation can occur.

68. a circle and a hyperbola that intersect in 4 points   See margin.

69. two parabolas that do not intersect   See margin.

70. Refer to the graphs below of the curves $\dfrac{x^2}{40} + \dfrac{y^2}{10} = 1$ and $x + y = 1$.

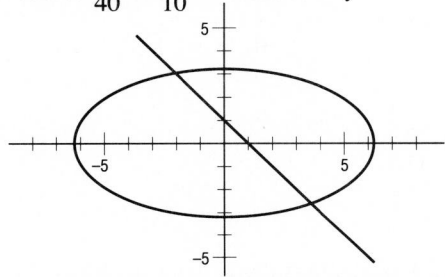

a. Estimate the points of intersection from this sketch.   (-2, 3), (3.5, -2.5)

b. Use an automatic grapher to estimate the solutions to the nearest tenth.   (-2, 3), (3.6, -2.6)

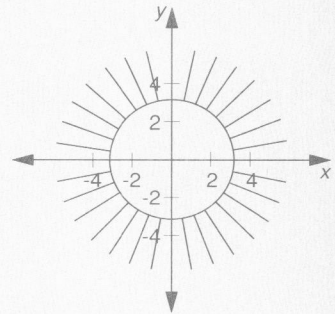
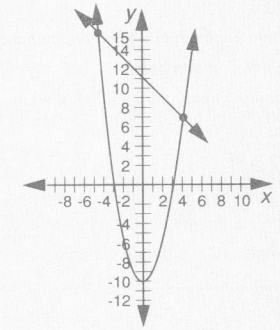

DAILY PACING CHART ■ CHAPTER 13

Students in the Full Course should complete all but one of the chapters by the end of the year. Students in the Minimal Course will spend more time on quizzes and the Chapter Review. As such, these students should complete about ten or eleven chapters. Students who will be taking *Functions, Statistics, and Trigonometry with Computers,* the next course in the UCSMP curriculum, should consider this chapter optional. (See Overview on page 740C.)

DAY	MINIMAL COURSE	FULL COURSE
1	13-1	13-1
2	13-2	13-2
3	13-3	13-3
4	13-4	13-4
5	Quiz (TRF); Start 13-5.	Quiz (TRF); 13-5
6	Finish 13-5.	13-6
7	13-6	13-7
8	13-7	13-8
9	13-8	Quiz (TRF); 13-9
10	Quiz (TRF); Start 13-9.	13-10
11	Finish 13-9.	13-11
12	13-10	Progress Self-Test
13	13-11	Chapter Review
14	Progress Self-Test	Chapter Test (TRF)
15	Chapter Review	
16	Chapter Review	
17	Chapter Test (TRF)	

TESTING OPTIONS

■ Quiz for Lessons 13-1 Through 13-4   ■ Chapter 13 Test, Form A   ■ Chapter 13 Test, Cumulative Form
■ Quiz for Lessons 13-5 Through 13-8   ■ Chapter 13 Test, Form B

PROVIDING FOR INDIVIDUAL DIFFERENCES

The student text is written for the *average* student. The program, however, can be adapted for both less capable and for more capable students.

A blackline master (in the Teacher's Resource File) is provided for each lesson for those students who need more practice. The Teacher's Edition frequently provides Error Analysis and Alternate Approach features to provide additional instructional strategies.

For students who require additional challenge, Extension activities are regularly provided in the Teacher's Edition.

OBJECTIVES ■ CHAPTER 13

Students should master the chapter objectives by the time they complete the chapter. To ensure mastery, there is continual review built into each set of lesson questions. After students complete the chapter lessons, they assess their mastery on the Progress Self-Test. Then they do the Chapter Review and pay special attention to those questions that match the objectives missed on the Progress Self-Test. Students can get extra practice on these objectives by using the master for each lesson in the Teacher's Resource File.

OBJECTIVES FOR CHAPTER 13 (Organized into the SPUR categories—Skills, Properties, Uses, and Representations)	Progress Self-Test Questions	Chapter Review Questions	Lesson Master from Teacher's Resource File*
SKILLS			
A Calculate values of finite arithmetic series, and both finite and infinite geometric series.	1, 12	1 through 8	13-1, 13-2, 13-4
B Use summation (Σ) and factorial (!) notations.	3, 13, 21	9 through 16	13-3, 13-9
C Calculate entries in Pascal's Triangle, binomial coefficients, and the number of subsets of a given set.	6, 7, 18a	17 through 25	13-5, 13-7
D Expand binomials.	4, 20	26 through 32	13-6
E Calculate descriptive statistics for a data set.	9–11	33 through 36	13-9
PROPERTIES			
F State whether or not an infinite geometric series has a limit.	17	37 through 40	13-4
G State properties of Pascal's Triangle.	19, 18b	41 through 45	13-5, 13-7
USES			
H Solve applied problems using arithmetic or geometric series.	2	46 through 51	13-1, 13-2, 13-4
I Use combinations, permutations, or probability to solve problems.	5, 8	52 through 61	13-7, 13-8
J Use measures of central tendency or dispersion to describe data or distributions.	14, 15	62 through 71	13-9, 13-10
K Give reasons for sampling.	22	72, 73	13-11
REPRESENTATIONS			
L Graph and analyze binomial and normal distributions.	16	74, 75	13-10

* The masters are numbered to match the lessons.

740B

OVERVIEW ■ CHAPTER 13

The title of this chapter conveys the three main themes: series, namely the sums of various sequences to which students have already been introduced; combinations, including Pascal's Triangle and the binomial theorem; and a brief introduction to the ways in which these ideas are used in statistics.

Each part of the chapter provides only an introduction to each topic, and in this sense, Chapter 13 should not be viewed as one in which mastery is expected of all of its ideas. In the USCMP series, the ideas presented in this chapter are discussed twice more, once in *Functions, Statistics, and Trigonometry with Computers*, and once again in *Precalculus and Discrete Mathematics*. The treatments in those courses are more in depth

than the treatment in this book. If your students will be taking *Functions, Statistics, and Trigonometry with Computers,* you should consider this chapter to be optional and you should do Chapter 14 first.

Lessons 13-1 to 13-4 cover arithmetic and geometric series, including sigma (Σ) notation. Sigma notation is one of the unifying ideas of the chapter. Lesson 13-3 also introduces factorial (!) notation and permutations, so the idea is in hand before combinations are encountered in Lesson 13-6.

Another unifying idea is the idea of a sequence. In Lesson 13-5, Pascal's Triangle is introduced as a two-dimensional sequence whose elements can be described with $\binom{n}{r}$ notation, and the familiar factorial formula for $\binom{n}{r}$ is given. In Lesson 13-6, the geometric se-

quence of powers of $(x + y)$ gives rise to polynomials whose coefficients are found in Pascal's triangle.

The application of Pascal's Triangle to combinations is discussed in Lesson 13-7. A second lesson (13-8) on this topic relates it to probability.

Lesson 13-9 uses summation notation to describe the most common statistics: mean, median, mode, and standard deviation. These ideas are needed to discuss the binomial and normal probability distributions in Lesson 13-10. The distributions of college entrance exam scores and IQ scores are of great interest to students. These distributions are applied to sampling and the Central Limit Theorem in Lesson 13-11.

PERSPECTIVES ■ CHAPTER 13

The Perspectives provide the rationale for the inclusion of topics or approaches, provide mathematical background, and make connections within UCSMP.

13-1

ARITHMETIC SERIES

This first of three lessons on series (13-1, 13-2, and 13-4), is devoted to arithmetic (or linear) series. Formulas are given specifically for the sum of the integers from 1 to n, and then more generally for the sum of any arithmetic sequence given the number of terms in the sequence and either (1) the first and last terms, or (2) the first term and constant difference.

The distinction between a sequence and a series is simple: a series is a sum of terms of a sequence. If a sequence is a_1, a_2, a_3, . . . ,a_n, then the corresponding series is $a_1 + a_2 + a_3 + \ldots + a_n$. We follow the common practice of thinking of a series as an *indicated* sum, as shown above. The number which is the sum of the series is called the *value* of the series.

13-2

GEOMETRIC SERIES

This lesson covers finite geometric series; infinite geometric series are delayed until Lesson 13-4.

Geometric series have a number of important applications. For finite series, the most common application is annuities, illustrated in Example 3. In general, if an amount A is deposited (or paid) periodically, and the periodic yield is r, let $x = 1 + r$. Suppose this continues for n payments. Then the amount one has (or the amount one has effectively spent) is $Ax^{n-1} + Ax^{n-2} + \ldots + Ax + A$. This is a finite geometric series with first term A and constant ratio x. Its sum is given by

$$S_n = \frac{A(x^n - 1)}{x - 1}.$$

Now, recall that $x = 1 + r$, so that $r = x - 1$. Substituting these values into the formula above yields the following formula which is found in some finance books and books of tables:

$$S_n = \frac{A[(1 + r)^n - 1]}{r}$$

13-3

THE Σ AND ! SYMBOLS

Σ-notation, called *sigma* or *summation* notation, is one of those symbols that looks difficult, but after it is understood, is found to be a natural abbreviation. It is fundamental notation for both calculus and statistics.

Purposely, we have done two lessons without this notation so that students can see how useful it is. The formulas for arithmetic and finite geometric series are quite a bit shorter using this notation. This lesson provides an opportunity for additional work with arithmetic and geometric series.

Factorial notation is quite a bit simpler and is also natural from consideration of the possible permutations of n different objects.

13-4
INFINITE GEOMETRIC SERIES
Any finite series can be extended to an infinite series. With nonzero arithmetic series, the resulting sum is always infinite, so there is no need to attempt to evaluate them. With geometric series, the sum is finite if and only if the constant ratio r satisfies $|r| < 1$, a beautiful result by itself.

This lesson tries to explain these ideas using informal notions of limits. The examples and problems extend the applications of Lesson 13-2 and introduce one new application: the infinite repeating decimal.

13-5
PASCAL'S TRIANGLE
The array of numbers known as Pascal's Triangle is two-dimensional, both geometrically and algebraically. As a triangle, it goes in two directions. As a sequence, it requires two variables to be described.

Pascal's triangle has three basic applications: it can be applied to powers of binomials, to combinations, and to probability. These applications are discussed in the next three lessons. The purpose of this lesson is to present the triangle and the two ways in which it is generated, namely by a recursive pattern in which two elements from one row are added to get an element in the next; and by an explicit formula involving factorials.

13-6
THE BINOMIAL THEOREM
The purpose of this lesson is to show that powers of binomials can be expanded by using Pascal's Triangle.

If the factorials in the Binomial Theorem are expanded, for instance, $\binom{n}{2} = \dfrac{n(n-1)}{2}$, then it is possible to interpret the Binomial Theorem when n is not an integer. This was first done by Newton, who is credited with the first proof of the Binomial Theorem.

13-7
SUBSETS AND COMBINATIONS
The goal of this lesson is to show that Pascal's Triangle displays the answer to the problem of finding the number of combinations of n things taken r at a time. Some students find it easier to conceptualize this problem as counting the number of subsets of n objects from a set of r objects.

Finally, the total number of subsets of a set is found. This gives the sum of the elements in a row of Pascal's Triangle.

13-8
PROBABILITIES AND COMBINATIONS
One of the most powerful theorems of elementary mathematics is the theorem of this lesson, which gives the probability of throwing r heads in n tosses of a fair coin, or the probability of guessing r questions correct on a true-false test of n questions.

In general, if a coin has a probability p of heads, then the probability of r heads in n tosses is $\dfrac{\binom{n}{r}p^r(1-p)^{n-r}}{2^n}$. This lesson covers only the simplest cases of probabilities with combinations, when $p = \frac{1}{2}$.

13-9
DESCRIPTIVE STATISTICS
The lesson covers four basic statistics: mean, median, mode, and standard deviation. The mean and standard deviation are written both with and without Σ-notation to reinforce understanding of the notation.

Some statistics books have $n - 1$ in the denominator of the formula for the standard deviation. Some will distinguish the population standard deviation from a sample standard deviation. We make no such distinction because the idea is more important than the detail.

13-10
BINOMIAL AND NORMAL DISTRIBUTIONS
The binomial distribution is the probability function that arises from the binomial coefficients. It is a natural extension of Lesson 13-8. The normal distribution is the limit of the binomial.

The shape of a binomial distribution, which comes from graphing binomial probabilities is discussed first. That shape is then extended to the normal distribution. The distribution of probabilities in the normal curve is given and related to IQ scores and SAT scores.

13-11
POLLS AND SAMPLING
There are two major ideas in this lesson. The first idea is that of sampling and randomness. Random sampling, stratified sampling, and random stratified sampling are defined.

The second major idea is the Central Limit Theorem, which states that responses from samples of a particular size from a population are normally distributed about the mean response of the population. Furthermore, it is possible to predict the standard deviation of that distribution.

CHAPTER 13

We recommend 14 to 17 days for this chapter: 11 to 13 on the lessons; 1 for the Progress Self-Test; 1 or 2 for the Chapter Review; and 1 for a Chapter test. (See the Daily Pacing Chart on page 740A.) If you spend more than 17 days on this chapter, you are moving too slowly. Keep in mind that each lesson includes Review questions to help students firm up content studied previously.

USING PAGES 740–741
You might read page 741 together with students. Then explain the addition pattern shown with Pascal's Triangle. Go over the titles of the chapter and the lessons to give students an overview of the contents of the chapter.

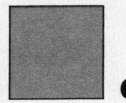

CHAPTER 13

Series, Combinations, and Statistics

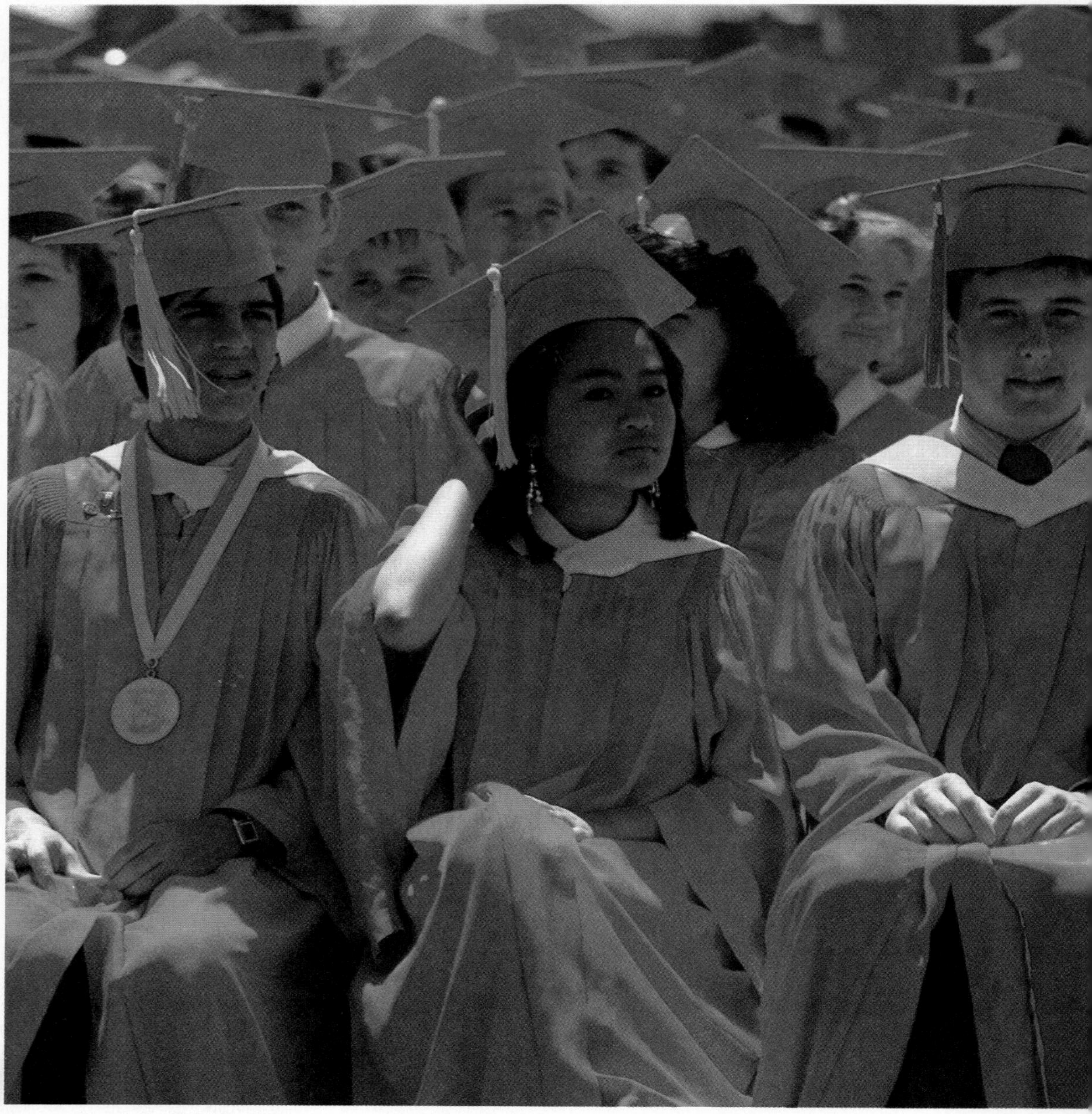

Addition is as fundamental in advanced mathematics as it is in arithmetic. In this chapter, you will study sums of terms of various sequences, learn a special notation for sums, and see

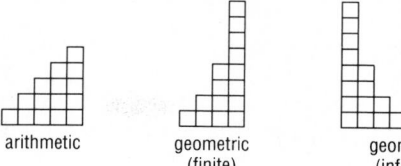

arithmetic   geometric   geometric
              (finite)   (infinite)

many applications of Pascal's Triangle, a triangular array which is formed by adding.

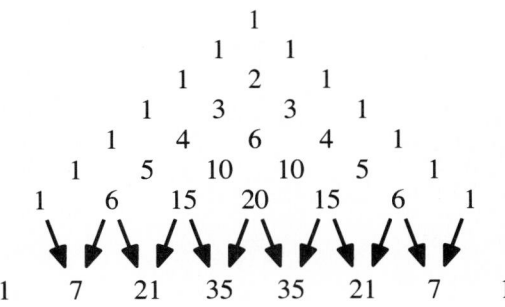

The applications of these ideas are diverse: to counting committees, to powers of binomials, to probability, to statistics, and even to IQ scores, scores on standardized tests, and bell-shaped distribution curves.

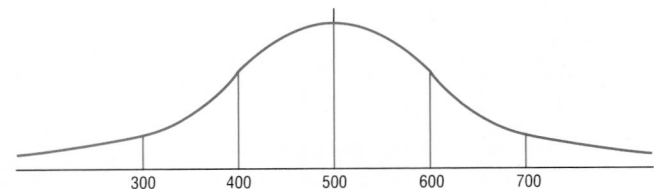

Standardized tests are familiar to students entering or graduating from academic, technical, or professional training.

OBJECTIVES

A Calculate values of finite arithmetic series.
H Solve applied problems using arithmetic series.

TEACHING NOTES

The story about Gauss seems to be true. The moral is not that Gauss was brilliant (though he was), but that there is a way of looking at the sum of the integers from 1 to *n* which even a third grade student can understand.

This is a lesson which you may wish to go over very carefully. In the examples and derivations of the formulas, students need to understand how each sentence follows from the previous one. Then they should have a relatively easy time with the questions.

LESSON 13-1

Arithmetic Series

Gauss as a child

There is a story often told about Karl Friedrich Gauss. (At age 18, he proved The Fundamental Theorem of Algebra; see page 639.) When he was in third grade, his class misbehaved and the teacher gave the following problem as punishment.

"Add the integers from 1 to 100."

It is said that Gauss solved the problem in almost no time at all. His method was something like the following. Let S be the desired sum.

$$S = 1 + 2 + 3 + \ldots + 98 + 99 + 100$$

Using the Commutative and Associative Properties, the sum can be rewritten in reverse order.

$$S = 100 + 99 + 98 + \ldots + 3 + 2 + 1$$

Now add corresponding terms. The sums are the same!

$$2S = \underbrace{101 + 101 + 101 + \ldots + 101 + 101 + 101}_{100 \text{ terms}}$$

$$2S = 100 \cdot 101$$
$$S = 5050$$

The story is that Gauss wrote only the number 5050 on his slate, having done all the figuring in his head. The teacher (who had hoped the problem would keep the students working for a long time) was quite disturbed. However, the teacher did recognize that Gauss was extraordinary and gave him some advanced books to read. Gauss' method of solution is the basis for the proof of the next theorem.

Theorem:

    The sum of the integers from 1 to *n* is $\frac{1}{2}n(n + 1)$.

Proof:

  1. Let $S = 1 + 2 + \ldots + (n - 1) + n$
  2. Reversing the order of the terms.
        $S = n + (n - 1) + \ldots + 2 + 1$
  3. Add corresponding terms.
        $2S = (1 + n) + (2 + n - 1) + \ldots + (n - 1 + 2) + (n + 1)$
  4. $= \underbrace{(n + 1) + (n + 1) \quad + \ldots + (n + 1) \quad + (n + 1)}_{n \text{ terms}}$
  5. $2S = n(n + 1)$
  6. So, $S = \frac{1}{2}n(n + 1)$.

742

Using the formula, the sum of the integers from 1 to 100 is $\frac{1}{2}(100)(101) = 5050$, the answer Gauss gave. Similarly, the sum of the integers from 1 to 4 is $\frac{1}{2}(4)(5) = 10$, a result easy to check.

Recall that an arithmetic or linear sequence is one in which the difference between consecutive terms is constant. An arithmetic sequence has the form $a_1, a_1 + d, a_1 + 2d, \ldots, a_1 + (n-1)d$. The integers from 1 to 100 form a finite arithmetic sequence with $a_1 = 1$, $n = 100$, and $d = 1$. Reasoning similar to that of Gauss can be used to find the sum of the consecutive terms of any finite arithmetic sequence.

Example 1   Find the sum of the first 30 terms of the arithmetic sequence

$$4, 11, 18, 25, \ldots .$$

> **Solution**   First, calculate the 30th term. The common difference is 7. The 30th term is $4 + 29 \cdot 7$, or 207.
>
> Thus, $S = 4 + 11 + \ldots + 200 + 207$.
> Also, $S = 207 + 200 + \ldots + 11 + 4$.
> So, $2S = \underbrace{211 + 211 + \ldots + 211 + 211}_{30 \text{ terms}}$
>
> $= 30 \cdot 211$.
> Thus, $S = \frac{1}{2}(30)(211) = 3165$.

In general, an indicated sum of terms is called a **series.** If the terms form an arithmetic sequence with first term a_1 and common difference d, the indicated sum of the terms is called an **arithmetic series**. The sum of the first n terms, represented S_n, is

$$S_n = a_1 + a_2 + a_3 + \ldots + a_{n-2} + a_{n-1} + a_n.$$

You can find a formula for S_n by noticing that the series can be written in two ways:
   (i)   Start with the first term a_1 and successively add the common difference d.
   (ii) Start with the last term a_n and successively subtract the common difference d.

$$S_n = a_1 + (a_1 + d) + (a_1 + 2d) + \ldots + [a_1 + (n-1)d]$$
$$S_n = a_n + (a_n - d) + (a_n - 2d) + \ldots + [a_n - (n-1)d]$$

Alternate Approach A formula for the sum of any arithmetic series can be derived from the sum of the integers from 1 to n in the following way.
   Suppose the series is
$S_n = a + (a + d) + (a + 2d) + a + (n-1)d$.
Now, let $T = 1 + 2 + \ldots + n - 1$. So, $dT = d + 2d + \ldots + (n-1)d$. If we add a to each term of the series dT, there are $(n-1)$ a's added, and if we add one more a, we get S. Thus,
$$S = na + dT$$
However, by the sum of integers formula,
$$T = \frac{n(n-1)}{2}.$$
Consequently,
$$S = na + d\frac{n(n-1)}{2}$$
$$= \frac{n}{2}[2a + (n-1)d].$$
   For a specific example of this kind of thinking, consider the series $3 + 5 + \ldots + 201$. There are 100 terms. Since the sum of the integers from 1 to 100 is 5050, the sum of the even integers from 2 to 200 is twice as great, or 10,100, and the sum of the odd integers from 3 to 201 is 100 greater than that, or 10,200.

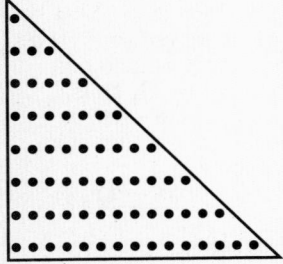
When you add corresponding pairs of terms of these two formulas, as Gauss did, each of the n pairs adds to the same amount, $a_1 + a_n$:

$$S_n + S_n = (a_1 + a_n) + (a_1 + a_n) + (a_1 + a_n) + \ldots + (a_1 + a_n)$$

n terms

So
$$2S_n = n(a_1 + a_n)$$

and, multiplying both sides by $\frac{1}{2}$, $S_n = \frac{n}{2}(a_1 + a_n)$.

This formula is convenient if the first and nth terms are known. If the nth term is not known, an alternative formula can be found using the formula for the nth term of an arithmetic sequence,

$$a_n = a_1 + (n - 1)d.$$

Substituting for a_n in the right side of the expression for S_n,

$$S_n = \frac{n}{2}[a_1 + a_1 + (n - 1)d].$$

That is, $S_n = \frac{n}{2}[2a_1 + (n - 1)d].$

This argument proves the following theorem.

Theorem:

Let $S_n = a_1 + a_2 + \ldots + a_n$ be an arithmetic series with constant difference d. Then the value S_n of that series is

$$S_n = \frac{n}{2}(a_1 + a_n)$$

or $S_n = \frac{n}{2}[2a_1 + (n - 1)d].$

Example 2 An auditorium has 15 rows, with 20 seats in the front row and 2 more seats in each row thereafter.
   a. How many seats are there in the last row?
   b. How many seats are there in all?

Solution

a. The sequence of seats is 20, 22, 24, ... The 15th row has 20 + 14 · 2 seats, or 48 seats.

b. Use the formula

$$S_n = \frac{n}{2}(a_1 + a_n).$$

In this case, $n = 15$, $a_1 = 20$, and $a_n = a_{15} = 48$.

$$S_{15} = \frac{15}{2}(20 + 48) = \frac{15}{2} \cdot 68 = 510$$

There are 510 seats in the auditorium.

Check Use the formula $S_n = \frac{n}{2}(2a_1 + (n-1)d)$.

Then
$$S_{15} = \frac{15}{2}(2 \cdot 20 + (15 - 1) \cdot 2)$$
$$= \frac{15}{2}(40 + 28) = 510. \text{ It checks.}$$

Questions

Covering the Reading

1. If Gauss was 8 years old when in third grade, what year was that?
1785

2. What properties ensure that
$1 + 2 + ... + (n - 1) + n = n + (n - 1) + ... + 2 + 1$?
Commutative and Associative Properties of Addition.

3. Consider $20 + 18 + 16 + 14$ and 20, 18, 16, 14.
a. Which is an arithmetic sequence?   20, 18, 16, 14
b. Which is an arithmetic series?   20 + 18 + 16 + 14

4. What is the nth term of the arithmetic sequence with first term a_1 and constant difference d? $a_n = a_1 + (n - 1)d$

5. Find the sum of the integers from 1 to 1000.   500,500

6. **a.** Write out all the terms in the arithmetic series
$5 + 9 + 13 + ... + 37$.
b. How many terms are there?
c. What is the sum of all the terms?   a) See margin.   b) 9;   c) 189

7. Suppose a theater has 26 seats in the first row and that each row has 4 more seats than the previous row. If there are 30 rows in the theater,
a. how many seats are in the last row?   142
b. how many seats are there in all?   2520

Applying the Mathematics

8. Find the sum of the odd integers from 25 to 75.   1300

9. Finish this sentence: The sum of the n terms of an arithmetic sequence equals the average of the first and last terms multiplied by ? .
the number of terms.

10. Find the sum of all the positive even integers with 3 digits.   247,050

11. Let S_n be the sum of the first n terms of the sequence defined by $a_n = 11n - 3$. Find:
    a. S_2 27
    b. S_3 57
    c. S_{25} 3500

12. An organization has new officers for the year and is ordering new stationery. In January, a mailing is sent to the 325 current members. If the membership increases each month by 5 members, how many envelopes will be needed for one year's monthly mailings?   4230

In 13 and 14, two salaries are compared.

13. Suppose a firefighter earns $24,000 the first year on the job. The second year and each year thereafter, the firefighter earns $1200 more than the previous year.
    a. Write the first and last terms of the series whose sum gives the total amount earned in 8 years. $24,000; $32,400
    b. Find the total amount earned in 8 years. $225,600

14. After 6 months on the job, and every 6 months thereafter, another firefighter gets a raise of $600. If that firefighter earns

    $$12,000 \text{ the 1st half-year,}$$
    $$12,600 \text{ the 2nd half-year,}$$
    and $$13,200 \text{ the 3rd half-year,}$$

    find the total amount earned by this firefighter in 8 years. $264,000

15. The following BASIC program generates recursively the terms of an arithmetic sequence and the sum of the terms of that sequence.

```
10 REM PROGRAM TO PRINT TERMS OF ARITHMETIC
       SEQUENCE AND SUM OF SERIES
15 LET N = 1
20 LET TERM = 10
25 LET SUM = 0
30 LET SUM = SUM + TERM
35 PRINT "N", "TERM", "SUM"
40 PRINT N, TERM, SUM
45 FOR N = 2 TO 15
50      TERM = TERM + 3
55      SUM = SUM + TERM
60      PRINT N, TERM, SUM
65 NEXT N
70 END
```

    a. Run this program and list the last line of output.   15, 52, 465
    b. What explicit formulas could have been used to calculate the last term and sum directly? $T = 10 + 3(n - 1)$; $S = \frac{3}{2}n^2 + \frac{17}{2}n$
    c. Modify the program so it generates the sequence and series determined by Question 13.   See margin.

16. In the triangle at the right, find:
   a. $m\angle Q$ to the nearest degree   **56°**
   b. $\sin Q$ to the nearest thousandth. *(Lesson 10-2)*
       .832

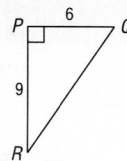

17. To estimate the height of a tall building you walk 100 meters from it and look up. Taking your protractor from your notebook, you estimate that you need to turn your head up 60° to see the top of the building. How tall is the building? *(Lesson 10-2)*   **≈173 m**

In 18 and 19, factor as much as possible. *(Lesson 11-3)*

18. $9x^4 - 9y^2$ **19.** $x - ax$ **x(1 − a)**
   9(x² + y)(x² − y)

20. *Multiple choice*   What is the 20th term of the geometric sequence that begins 3, 6, ... ? *(Lesson 8-3)*   **c**
   (a) $3 \cdot 20$ (b) $3 \cdot 2 \cdot 20$
   (c) $3 \cdot 2^{19}$ (d) $3 \cdot 2^{20}$

In 21–24, write as a power of 5. *(Lessons 8-1, 8-4, 8-6)*

21. $5^{10} \cdot 5^4$ **5¹⁴**   **22.** $5^6 \cdot 5$ **5⁷**

23. $5^9 \div 5^3$ **5⁶**   **24.** $\sqrt{5}$ **5^½**

25. The polynomial function $y = 3(x - 4)^2 + k$ contains the point $(2, -1)$.
   a. What is the value of k?   **-13**
   b. Describe the graph of this function. *(Lesson 6-4)*
       parabola congruent to y = 3x², with vertex at (4, -13)

26. The number 9 can be written as the sum of an arithmetic sequence $9 = 1 + 3 + 5$. What other numbers from 1 to 100 can be written as the sum of an arithmetic sequence whose terms are positive integers? (Assume the sequence must have at least three distinct terms.)
   all numbers except 1–5, 7, 8, and the prime numbers from 11 to 97

FOLLOW-UP

MORE PRACTICE
For more questions on SPUR Objectives, use *Lesson Master 13-1*, shown below.

EXTENSION
Ask students to find the sum of the integers from 1 to 100 that are not divisible by 3. (3367)

NAME _____

LESSON **MASTER 13–1**
QUESTIONS ON **SPUR** OBJECTIVES

■**SKILLS**   *Objective A (See pages 808–811 for objectives.)*
In 1–4, evaluate the arithmetic series.

1. $10 + 15 + 20 + ... + 100$ 2. $-8 - 2 + 4 + ... + 22$
   1045   42

3. the sum of the first 70 positive   4. the sum of the first 10 odd
   integers   positive integers
   2485   100

5. The sum of the integers $1 + 2 + 3 + ... + k$ is 378. Find k.   27

■**USES**   *Objective H*

6. A runner begins training by running 5 miles one week. The second week, she runs a total of 6.5 miles. The third week, she runs 8 miles. Each week thereafter, she runs 1.5 miles farther than the previous week.

   a. How far will she run in the 10th week?   18.5 mi

   b. At the end of the 10th week, what will be the total distance she ran since she began training?   117.5 mi

7. Congruent boxes are used to make a staircase as pictured at the right. If there are 12 steps, how many boxes are needed?   156

LESSON 13-2

RESOURCES
■ Lesson Master 13-2
♟ Computer Master 30

OBJECTIVES

A Calculate values of finite geometric series.
H Solve applied problems using geometric series.

TEACHING NOTES

The story which begins this lesson has many variants; the only common ingredients seem to be the chessboard, the grains, and the sum $1 + 2 + 4 + \ldots$. Work through the problems with students to arrive at the theorem for the sum of a geometric series.

Complex fractions are difficult for many students. You should go through **Example 1** carefully. Include both checks.

The questions included in this lesson are difficult for most students. Do not expect students to do all of them correctly. You may wish to save some questions in Applying the Mathematics to be discussed with Lesson 13-3 to allow students an extra day to work on this material.

13-2

Geometric Series

Legend has it that, when he first learned to play chess, the king of Persia was so impressed that he summoned the game's inventor to offer a reward. The inventor pointed to the chessboard, and said that a satisfactory reward would be one grain of wheat on the first square, two on the second, four on the third, eight on the fourth, and so on for all sixty-four squares. The king protested that this was surely not enough reward, but the inventor insisted. What do you think? Is this a large or small reward?

Recall that a geometric sequence is a sequence in which the ratio of consecutive terms is constant. The number of grains on the squares form a geometric sequence with first term 1 and constant ratio 2. The nth term of this sequence is 2^{n-1}. The total number of grains of wheat on the chessboard is the sum of the first 64 terms of this sequence. Call this total S_{64}.

$$S_{64} = 1 + 2 + 4 + 8 + \ldots + 2^{63}$$

An indicated sum like this of successive terms of a geometric sequence is called a **geometric series**.

To evaluate S_{64}, first write the series in reverse order:

$$S_{64} = 2^{63} + 2^{62} + \ldots + 8 + 4 + 2 + 1$$

Notice that if each term of S_{64} is doubled, many values identical to those in the first series are generated:

$$2S_{64} = 2^{64} + 2^{63} + 2^{62} + \ldots + 16 + 8 + 4 + 2$$

Subtracting the first equation from the second gives

$$2S_{64} - S_{64} = 2^{64} + (2^{63} - 2^{63}) + (2^{62} - 2^{62}) + \ldots + (8 - 8) + (4 - 4) + (2 - 2) - 1;$$

i.e., $\qquad S_{64} = 2^{64} - 1.$

748

This is about 1.84×10^{19} grains of wheat. If you assume that each grain can be approximated by a tiny rectangular box, 4 mm × 1 mm × 1 mm, the total volume of wheat would be about 74 cubic kilometers, quite a bit more than all the wheat in the world. We do not know what happened to the inventor after the king found out he had been tricked.

The above procedure can be generalized to find the value S_n of the geometric series with first term g, constant ratio r, and n terms.

$$S_n = g + gr + gr^2 + \ldots + gr^{n-1}$$

Multiply by r. $\quad rS_n = gr + gr^2 + \ldots + gr^{n-1} + gr^n$

Subtract. $\quad S_n - rS_n = g - gr^n$

Factor. $\quad (1 - r)S_n = g(1 - r^n)$

Divide both sides by $1 - r$. $\quad S_n = \dfrac{g(1 - r^n)}{1 - r}$

The constant ratio r cannot be 1 in this formula, but that is not a problem. If $r = 1$, the series is $g + g + g + \ldots + g$, with n terms, and its sum is ng.

This argument proves the following theorem.

Theorem:

Let $g + gr + gr^2 + \ldots + gr^{n-1}$ be a geometric series with $r \neq 1$. Then the value S_n of that series is

$$S_n = \frac{g(1 - r^n)}{1 - r}.$$

Example 1 Evaluate $18 + 6 + 2 + \frac{2}{3} + \frac{2}{9} + \frac{2}{27} + \frac{2}{81}$.

Solution This is a geometric series with $g = 18$, $r = \frac{1}{3}$, and $n = 7$.

$$S_n = \frac{g(1 - r^n)}{1 - r}$$

So $\quad S_7 = \dfrac{18(1 - (\frac{1}{3})^7)}{1 - \frac{1}{3}} = \dfrac{18(1 - \frac{1}{2187})}{\frac{2}{3}}$

$\quad\quad\quad = \dfrac{18 \cdot \frac{2186}{2187}}{\frac{2}{3}} = 18 \cdot \frac{2186}{2187} \cdot \frac{3}{2}$

$\quad\quad\quad = \dfrac{2186}{81}$

$\quad\quad\quad = 26\frac{80}{81}$.

Check 1 Because each of the fractions $\frac{2}{3}, \frac{2}{9}, \frac{2}{27}$, and $\frac{2}{81}$ is less than 1, the sum is between $18 + 6 + 2 = 26$ and $18 + 6 + 2 + 1 + 1 + 1 + 1 = 30$. That is a rough check.

LESSON 13-2 *Geometric Series* **749**

Error Analysis for Questions 2 and 5: A common error is to think that the number of terms is the same as the last power of r. Note that there are 10 terms in **Question 2** and 17 terms in **Question 5**.

Question 8: This kind of question will be extended to an infinite number of bounces in Lesson 13-4.

Questions 11-13: The general theorem is due to a French mathematician, Pierre Varignon (1654–1722): If the midpoints of the sides of any quadrilateral (even one in space) are connected, the figure formed is a parallelogram.

Question 22b: Although we think of people waiting longer to have children now than in previous generations, data suggest that the average mother's age at the birth of a child was greater years ago than now, primarily because families were larger. The length of a generation is most easily taken to be either 25 or $33\frac{1}{3}$ years. In either case, a person has had many more duplicate ancestors than one might at first realize. This increases the probability of recessive genes appearing in the population.

Check 2 Use a calculator. Add the decimal approximations for the fractions.

The formula for a geometric series works even when the ratio is negative.

Example 2 Find the sum of the first 100 terms of the geometric series $5 - 10 + 20 - 40 + 80 - \dots$.

Solution $S_n = \dfrac{g(1 - r^n)}{1 - r}$. In this case $g = 5$, $r = -2$, and $n = 100$.

$$S_{100} = \frac{5(1 - (-2)^{100})}{1 - (-2)} = \frac{5 - 5 \cdot 2^{100}}{3} \approx -2.11 \times 10^{30}$$

Check The sum is negative. This is what you would expect after an even number of terms.

When the constant ratio $r > 1$, it is often more convenient to use the formula $S_n = \dfrac{g(r^n - 1)}{r - 1}$, derived by multiplying the numerator and denominator of $\dfrac{g(1 - r^n)}{1 - r}$ by -1. This is the case when evaluating polynomials that arise from compound interest situations. They can be evaluated using this formula more quickly than by adding each deposit's yield.

Example 3 If $100 is deposited on January 1st of the years 2000, 2001, 2002, and so on to 2009, with an annual yield of 7%, how much will there be on January 1st, 2010?

Solution The scale factor in this situation is 1.07. On January 1st, 2010, there will be

$$100(1.07)^{10} + 100(1.07)^9 + \dots + 100(1.07)^2 + 100(1.07).$$

Think of this as a geometric series with the term at the right, $g = 100(1.07)$, as the first term, and ratio $r = 1.07$. There are 10 terms, so $n = 10$. Use the formula for the value of a geometric series.

$$S_{10} = \frac{g(r^{10} - 1)}{r - 1} = \frac{100(1.07)(1.07^{10} - 1)}{1.07 - 1} = \frac{107(1.07^{10} - 1)}{0.07}$$
$$\approx \$1478.36$$

Check From the middle of the year 2005, the value accrued would be $100(1.07)^5$, which is about $140.26. Multiplying that middle value by 10, an estimate is $1402.60. The answer $1478.36 seems reasonable.

Questions

Covering the Reading

1. According to the story about the king of Persia, how many grains of wheat were on the first two rows of the chess board?   65,535

In 2–5, give the value of the series.   5) $\dfrac{1 - b^{17}}{1 - b}$

2. $3 + 12 + 48 + \ldots + 3 \cdot 4^9$
   1,048,575

3. $50 + 10 + 2 + \frac{2}{5} + \frac{2}{25} + \frac{2}{125}$
   62.496

4. $50 - 10 + 2 - \frac{2}{5} + \frac{2}{25} - \frac{2}{125}$
   41.664

5. $1 + b + b^2 + \ldots + b^{16}$
   See above.

6. **a.** In the formula for the value of a geometric series, what value can r *not* have?   1
   b. Why can it not have this value?   The denominator would be zero.

7. If $200 is deposited on January 1st of five consecutive years and earns an annual yield of 8%, how much will there be on January 1st of the sixth year? $1584.56

Applying the Mathematics

8. A superball is dropped from a height of 2 meters and bounces to 90% of its height on each bounce. When it hits the ground for the eighth time, how far has it traveled?   ≈20.78 m

9. **a.** Write the first 8 terms of the geometric series from the sequence

$$\begin{cases} g_1 = 6 \\ g_n = -\frac{2}{3}g_{n-1} \text{ for } n > 1. \end{cases}$$

   6, -4, $\frac{8}{3}$, $-\frac{16}{9}$, $\frac{32}{27}$, $-\frac{64}{81}$, $\frac{128}{243}$, $-\frac{256}{729}$

   b. Find the sum of these terms.   ≈3.46

10. On the first day of each month Mollie pays $100 on a car loan. Suppose she had no loan and could earn 1% per month on this money. How much would she have at the end of the year? $1280.93

In 11–13, as shown at the right, midpoints of a 12 by 16 rectangle have been connected to form a rhombus. Then midpoints of the rhombus are connected to form a rectangle, and so on.

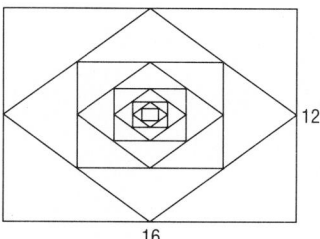
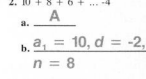

11. **a.** List the perimeters of the first 10 rectangles formed (including the largest rectangle).
    b. What is the sum of the perimeters of the first 10 rectangles formed?
    a. 56, 28, 14, 7, 3.5, 1.75, .875, .4375, .21875, .109375   b. ≈111.9
12. What is the sum of the perimeters of the first 10 rhombi formed?
    ≈79.9
13. If the figure contains 10 rectangles and 10 rhombi, into how many regions has the original rectangle been divided?   77

MORE PRACTICE
For more questions on SPUR Objectives, use *Lesson Master 13-2*, shown below.

EXTENSION
Have students find the sum of the first n terms of
(a) $1 + x^3 + x^6 + x^9 + \ldots$
(b) $1 - x^3 + x^6 - x^9 + \ldots$

NAME _____

LESSON **MASTER   13–2**
QUESTIONS ON **SPUR** OBJECTIVES

■ **SKILLS**   *Objective A (See pages 808–811 for objectives.)*
In 1–4, (a) write A by the series if it is arithmetic, G if it is geometric, and N by the series if it is neither arithmetic nor geometric. (b) For each arithmetic series, give a_1, d, and n as defined in the text. For each geometric series, give g_1, r, and n. DO NOT EVALUATE THE SERIES.

1. $1 + 3 + 9 + 81 + 729$
   a. __N__
   b. _____

2. $10 + 8 + 6 + \ldots -4$
   a. __A__
   b. $a_1 = 10, d = -2,$
      $n = 8$

3. $20 + 10 + 5 + \frac{5}{2} + \frac{5}{4} + \frac{5}{8}$
   a. __G__
   b. $g_1 = 20, r = \frac{1}{2},$
      $n = 6$

4. $-6 + 4 + 14 + \ldots + 54$
   a. __A__
   b. $a_1 = -6, d = 10,$
      $n = 7$

In 5–8, evaluate each geometric series.

5. $\frac{1}{2} + \frac{1}{4} + \frac{1}{8} + \ldots + \frac{1}{64}$
   $\frac{63}{64}$

6. $27 + 9 + 3 + \ldots + \frac{1}{9}$
   $\frac{364}{9}$ or $40\frac{4}{9}$

7. $9 + 18 + 36 + \ldots + 9 \cdot 2^8$
   4599

8. $1 - 2 + 4 - 8 + 16 - 32 + 64$
   43

■ **USES**   *Objective H*

9. A superball is dropped from a height of 10 feet and bounces up to 70% of its previous height on each bounce. When it hits the ground for the twelfth time, how far has it traveled in a vertical direction?   33 ft

10. Suppose that beginning in January, Sam Saver begins saving $100 per month into an account that has a monthly yield of .75%. How much will be in his account at the end of December of that year? $1980.87

Advanced Algebra © Scott, Foresman and Company   137

751

14. If the chessboard inventor had wanted 1 grain on the first square, 2 on the second, 3 on the third, and so on in arithmetic sequence, how many grains would have been the reward? *(Lesson 13-1)*   2080

15. Find the sum of all integers between 100 and 1000 that are divisible by 3. *(Lesson 13-1)*   165,150

16. Give the coordinates of the points of intersection of the line $y = 2x + 5$ and the parabola $x = y^2$. *(Lesson 12-9)*   no solution

17. Give an equation for the line parallel to $3x + 2y = 10$ and containing (8, 4). *(Lesson 3-5)* $y = -\frac{3}{2}x + 16$

18. a. Identify the quadrilateral graphed at the right.   Trapezoid
 b. Prove or disprove: The diagonals of this quadrilateral have the same length. *(Previous course)*
  See margin.

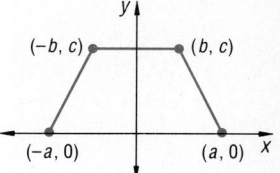

19. Use the formula $h = h_0 + v_0t - 4.9t^2$ to estimate the amount of time a skydiver is in free fall if the skydiver leaves a plane at an altitude of 2500 meters and opens the parachute at 500 meters. *(Lesson 6-2)*
  ≈20.2 sec

20. An ellipse is inscribed in a rectangle 20 cm long and 12 cm wide. The area of the ellipse is what percent of the area of the rectangle? *(Lesson 12-5, Previous course)* $\frac{60\pi}{240} \approx$ 79%

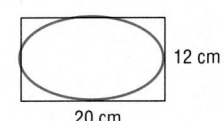

21. Refer to Lesson 13-1. Modify the program in Question 15 so it generates terms in the geometric series in the story about chess and the king of Persia. Write a short paragraph about some interesting aspect of your computer output.   See margin.

22. Your ancestors consist of 2 parents, 4 grandparents, 8 great-grandparents, 16 great-great-grandparents, and so on. Pick some estimate for the number of years in a generation.
 a. Use that estimate to help calculate the total number of ancestors you have had in the past 2000 years.
 b. Must there have been some duplicates (people from whom you descended in two different ways)? Explain your answer.
  a) Sample: If a generation is 20 years, then $n = \frac{2000}{20} = 100$; $S_{100} \approx 2.5 \times 10^{30}$;   b) Yes; 2.5×10^{30} is more people than ever were on the planet.

752

Mathematicians use symbols to shorten writing. Consider the arithmetic sequence 8, 11, 14, ... Any term of this sequence can be calculated from the formula $a_n = 3n + 5$. For example, the 1000th term is 3005.

The sum of the first 1000 terms of this sequence is

$$8 + 11 + 14 + ... + 3005.$$

A shorthand notation for such sums uses the Greek capital letter Σ (sigma).

"The sum of the numbers of the form
$3n + 5$ for integer values of n from
$n = 1$ to $n = 1000$"   is written $\sum_{n=1}^{1000} (3n + 5)$.

This is called **Σ-notation**, which is read as **sigma notation** or **summation notation.** In Σ-notation:

$$8 + 11 + 14 + ... + 3005 = \sum_{n=1}^{1000} (3n + 5).$$

In summation notation, the variable n under the Σ sign is the **index variable** or **index.** In this book, index variables have only integer values. It is common to use letters i, j, k, or n as index variables. (In summation notation, i is *not* the complex number $\sqrt{-1}$ unless it is so specified.) To evaluate an expression written in sigma notation, substitute into the expression following the sigma sign each integer from the lower value of the index variable to the upper value, and add the results.

■ ■ ■ ■ ■ ■ ■ ■ ■ ■

Example 1 **a.** Read and **b.** write $\sum_{i=5}^{11} 2^i$ without using Σ.

Solution
a. "The sum of the numbers of the form 2 to the ith power for integer values of i from 5 to 11."

b. $\sum_{i=5}^{11} 2^i = 2^5 + 2^6 + 2^7 + 2^8 + 2^9 + 2^{10} + 2^{11}$
or $32 + 64 + 128 + 256 + 512 + 1024 + 2048$

The expression in Example 1 can be evaluated using the formula for a geometric series with $g = 2^5$, $r = 2$, and $n = 7$.

$$\sum_{i=5}^{11} 2^i = \frac{2^5(2^7 - 1)}{2 - 1} = 32 \cdot 127 = 4064$$

RESOURCES
■ Lesson Master 13-3

OBJECTIVE

B Use summation (Σ) and factorial (!) notations.

TEACHING NOTES

The important broad point to make to students is that they should try not to be psyched out by strange notations. They should ask themselves why the notation is used. In the two notations introduced here, the reason is the same: the notation provides a very useful shorthand.

Students often think strange notations are just made up and not used, because they have not used them before. Have each student find the factorial key [!] on a calculator. Also have them look to see if the calculator has some second functions which automatically do sums. These will have a Σ by them.

We suggest you go over the first page of the lesson with the class, through **Example 1**. **Example 2** evaluates the series which opens the lesson. Then take **Questions 1–11** in order. Next, look at the last part of the lesson, which most students should be able to read on their own. Now go through the other questions.

Each of the theorems of the last two lessons can be restated using Σ-notation. Notice that i is used as the index variable to avoid confusion with the variable n. Compare these restatements with the original statements.

Sum of integers from 1 to n:

$$\sum_{i=1}^{n} i = \tfrac{1}{2}n(n + 1)$$

In an arithmetic sequence $a_1, a_2, a_3, \ldots, a_n$ with constant difference d:

$$\sum_{i=1}^{n} a_i = \tfrac{1}{2}n(a_1 + a_n) = \frac{n}{2}[2a_1 + (n - 1)d]$$

In a geometric sequence $g_1, g_2, g_3, \ldots, g_n$ with constant ratio r:

$$\sum_{i=1}^{n} g_i = g_1 \frac{(1 - r^n)}{1 - r}$$

Example 2   Evaluate $\sum\limits_{n=1}^{1000} (3n + 5)$.

Solution   This is the arithmetic series mentioned at the start of this lesson. Its first term is $3 \cdot 1 + 5$, or 8, and the constant difference is 3. There are 1000 terms. Using the formula

$$S_n = \frac{n}{2}(2a_1 + (n - 1)d),$$

$$S_{1000} = \tfrac{1000}{2}(2 \cdot 8 + (1000 - 1)3)$$
$$= 500(16 + 2997)$$
$$= 1,506,500$$

A number in base 10, our familiar decimal system, is a sum of powers of 10.

$$834.57 = 8 \cdot 10^2 + 3 \cdot 10^1 + 4 \cdot 10^0 + 5 \cdot 10^{-1} + 7 \cdot 10^{-2}$$

If all the digits are alike, then the number can be represented in Σ-notation.

$$9999.9 = 9 \cdot 10^3 + 9 \cdot 10^2 + 9 \cdot 10^1 + 9 \cdot 10^0 + 9 \cdot 10^{-1}$$

Each term has the form $9 \cdot 10^i$ where i goes from 3 to -1. When using Σ-notation, the smallest and largest values of the index variable are written below and above the sigma, respectively.

754

Using Σ-notation, 9999.9 can be written as

$$\sum_{i=-1}^{3} (9 \cdot 10^i).$$

Notice that the index variable may have negative values.

Another symbol with immediate application is the *factorial* symbol, an exclamation point. The symbol $n!$ is read "*n* factorial".

Definition:

$n!$ = product of the integers from n to 1.

The **factorial function** is defined by the equation $f(n) = n!$. For now, we take the domain of the factorial function to be the set of positive integers. In Lesson 13-5, the domain is extended to include 0. Small values of the factorial function can be calculated by hand or in your head.

$f(1) = 1! = 1$ $\qquad\qquad$ $f(4) = 4! = 4 \cdot 3 \cdot 2 \cdot 1 = 24$
$f(2) = 2! = 2 \cdot 1 = 2$ $\qquad$ $f(5) = 5! = 5 \cdot 4 \cdot 3 \cdot 2 \cdot 1 = 120$
$f(3) = 3! = 3 \cdot 2 \cdot 1 = 6$ $\qquad$ $f(6) = 6! = 6 \cdot 5 \cdot 4 \cdot 3 \cdot 2 \cdot 1 = 720$

Larger values require a calculator or computer. Many scientific calculators have a **factorial key** $\boxed{x!}$. For instance, to calculate 20!, key in 20 $\boxed{x!}$. The display indicates that $20! \approx 2.4329 \cdot 10^{18}$, or about 2,432,900,000,000,000,000.

The factorial function gives the number of possible arrangements of n different objects in a row. These different arrangements are called **permutations.** For instance, with three objects, A, B, and C, there are six possible permutations: ABC, ACB, BAC, BCA, CAB, and CBA, and $3! = 6$.

■ ■ ■ ■ ■ ■ ■ ■

Example 3 Find the number of possible orders in which four runners, Alan, Bob, Carl, and David, might finish a race.

Solution The number of possible orders is the number of permutations of the four runners. List the possible orders. We use only the runners' initials.

ABCD	BACD	CABD	DABC
ABDC	BADC	CADB	DACB
ACBD	BCAD	CBAD	DBAC
ACDB	BCDA	CBDA	DBCA
ADBC	BDAC	CDAB	DCAB
ADCB	BDCA	CDBA	DCBA

There are 24 permutations. This equals 4!.

Question 1: Sigma is the first letter of the Greek word for sum, so it was natural to use it. Western European mathematicians were forced to use letters from other alphabets because they ran out of letters from the Latin alphabet.

Question 18a: This is one of the more amazing theorems about sums of series. Note that these series are neither arithmetic or geometric. Another similar property is: The cube of the sum of the numbers from 1 to n is the mean of the sum of the 5th powers from 1 to n and the sum of the 7th powers from 1 to n.

Question 19: This question previews Lesson 13-9 by writing the mean of a set of numbers $x_1, x_2, \ldots x_n$.

$$\text{Mean} = \frac{\sum_{i=1}^{n} x_n}{n}$$

This points out that you do not need a formula for the nth term to use summation notation. You merely need to be able to denote the term.

Questions 21 and 22: These are important for work with combinations later in the chapter.

Question 31: The infinite series of reciprocals of the positive integers is called the *harmonic series* and is divergent. It has an infinite sum.

If you wished to list the possible ways in which five people could finish a race, you could begin with the list in Example 3. Call the 5th racer E. In each permutation in the list, you can insert the E at the beginning, in three middle spots, or at the end. For instance, inserting E into *ABCD* yields *EABCD, AEBCD, ABECD, ABCED,* or *ABCDE*. This means that the number of permutations of 5 objects is 5 times the number of permutations of 4 objects. So the number of permutations of 5 objects is $5 \cdot 4!$, which equals $5!$. Similarly the number of permutations of 6 objects is $6 \cdot 5!$, which equals $6!$. Extending this argument proves the following theorem.

Theorem:

There are $n!$ permutations of n distinct objects.

Numbers of permutations grow quickly. With 20 objects, there are 20! permutations, the large number estimated on the previous page.

Questions

Covering the Reading

1. The symbol Σ is the Greek letter __?__.   **sigma**

2. In Σ-notation, the variable under the Σ sign is the __?__ variable.
   index

In 3–6, *multiple choice*.

3. $\sum_{i=1}^{3} i^2 =$ **b**
   (a) 3^2 (b) $1 + 4 + 9$ (c) $1 + 2 + \ldots + 9$ (d) none of these

4. $\sum_{k=1}^{4} 3k =$ **b**
   (a) 16   (b) 30   (c) 82   (d) 94

5. $\sum_{n=1}^{5} (2n + 1) =$ **a**
   (a) $3 + 5 + 7 + 9 + 11$ (b) $3 + 11$
   (c) $1 + 5 + 11$ (d) $2 + 4 + 6 + 8 + 10 + 1$

6. $3 + 6 + 9 + 12 + 15 + 18 + 21 =$ **b**
   (a) $\sum_{i=3}^{21} i$ (b) $\sum_{i=1}^{7} (3i)$ (c) $\sum_{i=3}^{21} (3i)$ (d) none of these

In 7–10, give the value of the sum.

7. $\sum_{i=1}^{36} i$ **666**   8. $\sum_{i=1}^{100} (2i - 1)$ **10,000**

9. $\sum_{k=1}^{6} (2 \cdot 3^k)$ **2184**   10. $\sum_{n=-2}^{3} (4 \cdot 10^n)$ **4444.44**

756

11. In $\sum_{i=100}^{200} (4i)$, how many terms are added? **101**

12. The symbol $n!$ is read __?__. **n factorial**

13. Evaluate (a) 4! (b) 6! (c) 21!
          24   **720**   **$\approx 5.109 \times 10^{19}$**

14. a. Write out all permutations of the 4 letters P, E, R, M.

PERM	EPRM	RPEM	MPER
PEMR	EPMR	RPME	MPRE
PREM	ERPM	REPM	MEPR
PRME	ERMP	REMP	MERP
PMER	EMPR	RMPE	MRPE
PMRE	EMRP	RMEP	MREP

   b. How many permutations are there?
   24

Applying the Mathematics

In 15–17, write the series using Σ-notation.

15. $2 + 4 + 6 + 8 + 10 + 12 + 14$ $\sum_{i=1}^{7} 2i$

16. $9 + 18 + 36 + 72 + 144 + 288 + 576 + 1152$ $\sum_{i=1}^{8} 9 \cdot 2^{i-1}$

17. the sum of the squares of the integers from 1 to 100 $\sum_{i=1}^{100} i^2$

18. a. Translate this statement into an algebraic formula using Σ-notation: The sum of the cubes of the integers from 1 to n is the square of the sum of the integers from 1 to n. $\sum_{i=1}^{n} i^3 = \left(\sum_{i=1}^{n} i\right)^2$
   b. Verify part a when $n = 4$.
   Each value is 100.

19. Write the average (mean) of the n numbers $a_1, a_2, \dots, a_n$ using Σ-notation. $\frac{1}{n}\sum_{i=1}^{n} a_i$

20. Consider the sequence with the recursive definition
$$\begin{cases} a_1 = 1 \\ a_n = n \cdot a_{n-1} \text{ for } n > 1. \end{cases}$$ **1, 2, 6, 24, 120, 720, 5040**
   a. Give the first 7 terms of the sequence.
   b. What is an appropriate name for this sequence?
   the factorial sequence

21. Simplify (a) $\frac{15!}{14!}$ and (b) $\frac{(n+1)!}{n!}$.   **a) 15; b) n**

22. Show, by listing, that the number of different permutations of the letters of the word *DEEDED* is $\frac{6!}{3!3!}$.
   See margin.

Review

In 23 and 24, refer to the array of dots at the right.

23. If the array continued until there were 100 dots in the bottom row, how many dots would there be in all? *(Lesson 13-1)*   **5050**

24. If the total number of dots is 496, how many rows are there?   **31**

25. Graph $\{(x, y): x^2 + y^2 = 1\}$ and $\{(x, y): x^2 - y^2 = 1\}$ on the same axes. *(Lessons 12-1, 12-7)*   **See margin.**

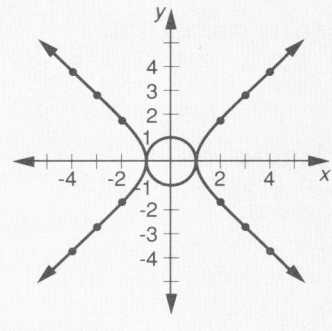

MORE PRACTICE
For more questions on SPUR
Objectives, use *Lesson Mas-
ter 13-3*, shown on page 757.

EXTENSION
Ask students to find the
value of:

a. $\sum_{k=1}^{7}\left(\sum_{j=1}^{k}1\right).$ (28)

b. $\sum_{k=1}^{7}\left(\sum_{j=1}^{k}j\right).$ (84)

Computer The program
below calculates N! for any
whole number N ≥ 1.

```
10 INPUT "A WHOLE
     NUMBER N"; N
20 LET A=1
30 FOR C=1 TO N
40     LET A=A * C
50 NEXT C
60 PRINT N; "! = "; C
70 END
```

Have students use the program to compute N! for both
large and small values of N,
and to compare their results
to those obtained with their
calculators. For large N, the
results may vary due to differences in algorithms used
and memory available on the
machines. Have students
check reference books or
with a computer science
teacher to learn more about
algorithms used to evaluate
functions on calculators and
computers. Many involve use
of infinite series, which are
introduced in the next lesson.

26. Consider the following investment. Ima Saver deposits $50 on the first
day of every month and earns 6% compounded monthly.
   a. How much interest will the first $50 deposit earn after 12 months?
   b. How much will there be in Ima's account just before she makes
   the 12th deposit? (Assume the account starts with $0, and that
   there are no withdrawals.) *(Lessons 8-2, 11-1, 13-2)* **a. $3.08**
   b. $566.78

27. A snail is crawling straight up a wall. The 1st hour it climbs 16
inches; the 2nd hour it climbs 12 inches; each succeeding hour it
climbs only $\frac{3}{4}$ the distance it climbed the previous hour. Assume this
pattern holds indefinitely.
   a. How far does the snail climb during the 7th hour?
   b. What is the total distance climbed in 7 hours? *(Lessons 8-3, 13-2)*
   a) ≈ 2.85 in.; b) ≈ 55.46 in.

28. If 3 blobs and 4 globs weigh 170 kg and 7 blobs and 6 globs weigh
330 kg, what will 4 blobs and 2 globs weigh? *(Lesson 5-3)* **160 kg**

29. How much louder is a sound of 100 decibels than one of 80 decibels?
(Lesson 9-3) **100 times as loud**

30. Arrange from smallest to largest without using a calculator.
(Lessons 9-4, 9-6)

   2 log 3, 3 log 2, log 3 + log 2 **log 3 + log 2, 3 log 2, 2 log 3**

Exploration

31. Consider the series of reciprocals of integers:

$$\sum_{i=1}^{n}\frac{1}{i} = 1 + \frac{1}{2} + \frac{1}{3} + \frac{1}{4} + \ldots + \frac{1}{n}$$

   a. How many terms of the series are needed before the sum exceeds
   2?
   b. How many terms of the series are needed before the sum exceeds
   3? **11**
   c. How many terms of the series are needed before the sum exceeds
   10? **about 2^{18}**
   d. Do you think the sum ever gets larger than 100? Why or why not?
   See below.

Notice that each indicated sum is greater than $\frac{1}{2}$:

$$1 + \frac{1}{2} + \underbrace{\frac{1}{3} + \frac{1}{4}}_{>\frac{1}{2}} + \underbrace{\frac{1}{5} + \frac{1}{6} + \frac{1}{7} + \frac{1}{8}}_{>\frac{1}{2}} + \underbrace{\ldots + \frac{1}{16}}_{>\frac{1}{2}} + \underbrace{\ldots + \frac{1}{32}}_{>\frac{1}{2}} + \underbrace{\ldots + \frac{1}{64}}_{>\frac{1}{2}} + \ldots$$

Thus the sum of the terms through $\frac{1}{8}$ is greater than $\frac{5}{2}$, through $\frac{1}{64}$ is greater
than 4, and so on. A general result for the sum of the terms through $\frac{1}{2^n}$ can
be illustrated in a table:

terms through:	$\frac{1}{2^0}$	$\frac{1}{2^2}=\frac{1}{4}$	$\frac{1}{2^4}=\frac{1}{16}$	$\frac{1}{2^6}$	$\frac{1}{2^8}$	$\frac{1}{2^{14}}$	$\frac{1}{2^{18}}$	$\frac{1}{2^{2n-2}}$	$\frac{1}{2^{198}}$
sum is ≥:	1	2	3	4	5	8	10	n	100

Since the sum can always be made greater than any given value, the sum is
infinite.

758

LESSON 13-4

Infinite Geometric Series

Suppose a ball is dropped from a height of 6 feet and on each bounce rebounds to $\frac{2}{3}$ of its previous height. Here is a diagram of the distance it travels.

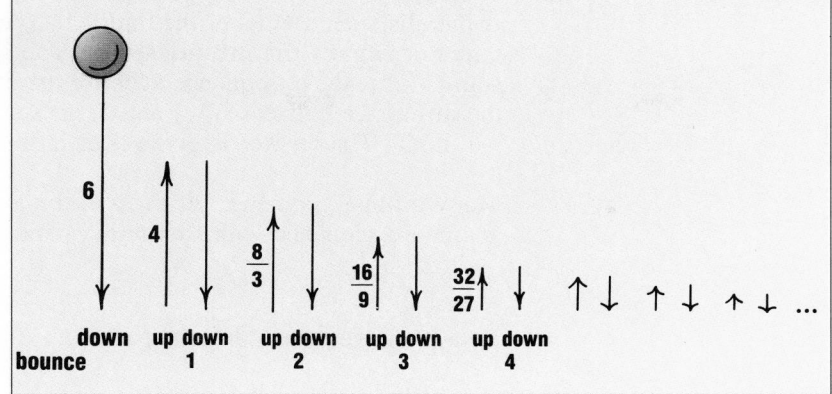

The lengths of the downward paths form a geometric sequence with first term 6 and constant ratio $\frac{2}{3}$. The lengths of the upward paths form a geometric sequence with first term 4 and constant ratio $\frac{2}{3}$. In Lesson 13-2, you learned how to calculate the total lengths for finite sequences. But in theory, this ball will bounce forever. (In reality, friction causes the ball to stop.)

$$\text{Distance down} = 6 + 4 + \tfrac{8}{3} + \tfrac{16}{9} + \tfrac{32}{27} + \ldots$$
$$\text{Distance up} \quad = \quad \ \ 4 + \tfrac{8}{3} + \tfrac{16}{9} + \tfrac{32}{27} + \ldots$$

These sums have infinitely many terms. They are **infinite geometric series.**

Do these "infinite sums" represent particular numbers? To answer this question, form a sequence S_n of **partial sums.** Let S_n be the sum of the first n terms of the sequence of distances down.

$$
\begin{aligned}
S_1 &= 6 & &= 6 \\
S_2 &= 6 + 4 & &= 10 \\
S_3 &= 6 + 4 + \tfrac{8}{3} & &= 12\tfrac{2}{3} \\
S_4 &= 6 + 4 + \tfrac{8}{3} + \tfrac{16}{9} & &= 14\tfrac{4}{9} \\
S_5 &= 6 + 4 + \tfrac{8}{3} + \tfrac{16}{9} + \tfrac{32}{27} & &= 15\tfrac{17}{27} \\
S_6 &= 6 + 4 + \tfrac{8}{3} + \tfrac{16}{9} + \tfrac{32}{27} + \tfrac{64}{81} & &= 16\tfrac{34}{81}
\end{aligned}
$$

As n gets larger, if S_n gets closer and closer to some number L, then we say "as n increases without bound, S_n approaches L as a limit." We write

$$S_n \to L$$
or
$$\lim_{n \to \infty} S_n = L.$$

RESOURCES
■ Lesson Master 13-4
■ Quiz for Lessons 13-1 Through 13-4

OBJECTIVE

A Calculate values of infinite geometric series.
F State whether or not an infinite geometric series has a limit.
H Solve applied problems using infinite geometric series.

TEACHING NOTES

Students are probably familiar with limits. They have seen the circle as a limit of regular polygons. They may have seen a tangent as a limit of secants. They may also have discussed an infinite repeating decimal, such as .2424242424242424 . . . , as being the limit of the sequence .24, .2424, .242424, and so on.

Still, students may not realize that the sum of an infinite number of terms can be a finite number. If the ball example does not convince students of this fact, use the sequence .6,
.6 + .06,
.6 + .06 + .006,
.6 + .06 + .006 + .0006,
and so on. If this example does not work, try the series $1 + \frac{1}{2} + \frac{1}{4} + \frac{1}{8} + \frac{1}{16} + \frac{1}{32} + \ldots$.

The expression "$n \rightarrow \infty$" is read "n approaches infinity" or "n gets larger and larger without bound". The last line is read "the limit as n goes toward infinity of S_n is L."

If there is such a number (or limit), that number L is called the **value** or **sum of the infinite series.** You can see that the partial sums of the above sequence keep on increasing. But as n increases, the difference between S_{n+1} and S_n gets smaller. Do you think there is a limit? The answer is given later in this lesson.

Many infinite geometric series have limits. Consider the infinite geometric sequence with first term $\frac{6}{10}$ and constant ratio $\frac{1}{10}$.

$$\frac{6}{10}, \frac{6}{100}, \frac{6}{1000}, \frac{6}{10,000}, \cdots$$

Here is the sequence of partial sums.

$$S_1 = \frac{6}{10} \qquad\qquad\qquad\qquad = 0.6$$

$$S_2 = \frac{6}{10} + \frac{6}{100} \qquad\qquad\qquad = 0.66$$

$$S_3 = \frac{6}{10} + \frac{6}{100} + \frac{6}{1000} \qquad\qquad = 0.666$$

$$S_4 = \frac{6}{10} + \frac{6}{100} + \frac{6}{1000} + \frac{6}{10,000} = 0.6666$$
$$\vdots \qquad\qquad\qquad \vdots \qquad\qquad \vdots$$

As n gets larger, S_n approaches the infinite repeating decimal $0.\overline{6}$ as a limit. Since $0.\overline{6} = \frac{2}{3}$,

$$S_n \rightarrow \frac{2}{3}.$$

Even though you have seen many infinite decimals before, you may not have thought of them as infinite sums.

$$\sum_{n=1}^{\infty} .6 \cdot \left(\frac{1}{10}\right)^{n-1} = \frac{2}{3}$$

We say that the sum of numbers of the form $6 \cdot \left(\frac{1}{10}\right)^n$, as n goes from 1 to infinity, is $\frac{2}{3}$.

Some infinite geometric series definitely have no limit. Consider the sequence of integer powers of 2: 1, 2, 4, 8, 16, 32, ... The infinite geometric series $1 + 2 + 4 + 8 + 16 + 32 + \ldots$ has the following partial sums.

$$S_1 = 1 \qquad\qquad\quad = 1$$
$$S_2 = 1 + 2 \qquad\qquad = 3$$
$$S_3 = 1 + 2 + 4 \qquad\quad = 7$$
$$S_4 = 1 + 2 + 4 + 8 = 15$$
$$\vdots \qquad\qquad \vdots \qquad\qquad \vdots$$

760

Clearly the sums increase and ultimately get larger than any given number. There is no limit. Some people write

$$S_n \to \infty$$
$$\text{or} \qquad \lim_{n\to\infty} S_n = \infty$$

read "S_n goes to infinity," or "S_n becomes infinitely large."

The geometric series $\frac{6}{10} + \frac{6}{100} + \frac{6}{1000} + \dots$ has a limit. In $1 + 2 + 4 + \dots$, there is *no* limit. When does a geometric series have a limit? Remember that the sum of the first n terms of the infinite geometric series with first term g and ratio r is

$$g \cdot \frac{1 - r^n}{1 - r}.$$

When $|r| < 1$, r^n gets nearer and nearer to zero as n gets larger. That is, if r is between -1 and 1, then as n gets larger,

$$r^n \to 0$$
$$\text{So,} \qquad (1 - r^n) \to 1.$$
$$\text{Multiplying,} \qquad \frac{g}{1 - r}(1 - r^n) \to \frac{g}{1 - r}.$$

This informally demonstrates the next theorem. A formal proof would require more advanced mathematics.

Theorem:

If $|r| < 1$, the infinite geometric series with first term g and ratio r has the value $S = \dfrac{g}{1 - r}$.

Using Σ-notation, this theorem can be stated more succinctly. If

$$|r| < 1, \ \sum_{n=1}^{\infty} gr^{n-1} = \frac{g}{1 - r}.$$

For instance, in the sequence 0.6, 0.06, 0.006, ... , where the ratio is $\frac{1}{10}$ and the first term g is $\frac{6}{10}$, the sum of all terms is

$$\frac{g}{1 - r} = \frac{\frac{6}{10}}{1 - \frac{1}{10}} = \frac{\frac{6}{10}}{\frac{9}{10}} = \frac{2}{3}.$$

This agrees with the result on the previous page. By this method, a simple fraction for any infinite repeating decimal can be found.

ADDITIONAL EXAMPLES

1. Give the value of the infinite geometric series

$7 + \frac{7}{3} + \frac{7}{9} + \dots$.

10.5

2. Give the value of the infinite geometric series

$1 - \frac{1}{2} + \frac{1}{4} - \frac{1}{8} + \frac{1}{16} - \dots$.

$\frac{2}{3}$

3. A ball is dropped from a height of 1.5 meters and each time rebounds to 2/3 of its former height. How far will it travel vertically if you let it bounce until it stops?
4.5 meters down and 3 meters up, for a total of 7.5 meters

Question 11: Zeno's problem was that he did not feel that time should be infinitely divisible. Though almost all mathematicians are comfortable with the theoretical notion of infinitely divisible time, there are some physicists who believe that time is discrete.

Questions 12 and 13: The snowflake curve is an example of a fractal and is examined again in Lesson 14-8.

ADDITIONAL ANSWERS

1.a. No
b. $|r| = 2 > 1$

2.a. Yes
b. 20

5. As n increases without bound, S_n approaches L as a limit.

7.a. $\sum_{n=1}^{\infty} .4 \cdot \left(\frac{1}{10}\right)^{n-1} = \frac{4}{10} + \frac{4}{100} + \frac{4}{1000} \cdots = .4 + .04 + .004 + \ldots$
b. $\frac{4}{9}$

8.a. $9 + \sum_{n=1}^{\infty} .25 \left(\frac{1}{100}\right)^{n-1} = 9 + \frac{25}{100} + \frac{25}{10000} + \frac{25}{1000000} + \ldots = 9 + .25 + .0025 + .000025 + \ldots$
b. $\frac{916}{99}$

9.a. $2.46 + \sum_{n=1}^{\infty} .008 \left(\frac{1}{10}\right)^{n-1} = 2.46 + .008 + .0008 + .00008 + \ldots$
b. $\frac{1111}{450}$

Example 1 Find a simple fraction equal to 8.521212121 … .

Solution $8.5\overline{21} = 8.5 + 0.021212121 \ldots$
$$= 8.5 + 0.021 + 0.00021 + 0.0000021 + \ldots$$

The terms beginning with 0.021 form an infinite geometric sequence with first term 0.021 and constant ratio 0.01. Using the theorem,

$$S = 8.5 + \frac{0.021}{1 - 0.01}$$
$$= 8.5 + \frac{0.021}{0.99} = \frac{85}{10} + \frac{21}{990}$$

Thus, $$S = \frac{1406}{165}.$$

Now let us return to the bouncing ball. Because the ratio $\frac{2}{3}$ is between -1 and 1, the series has a limit.

Example 2 Find the total distance traveled by the ball discussed at the beginning of this lesson.

Solution

Distance falling $= 6 + 4 + \frac{8}{3} + \ldots$ $= \frac{6}{1 - \frac{2}{3}} = 18$ feet

Distance rising $= 4 + \frac{8}{3} + \frac{16}{9} + \ldots$ $= \frac{4}{1 - \frac{2}{3}} = 12$ feet

Total distance $= 18 + 12 = 30$ feet.

Questions

Covering the Reading

In 1–4, (a) does the infinite geometric series have a value? (b) If so, what is this value? If not, why not?

1. $1 + 2 + 4 + 8 + \ldots$ See margin.

2. $10 + 5 + 2.5 + 1.25 + \ldots$ See margin.

3. $1 - 2 + 4 - 8 + \ldots$ a) no; b) $|r| > 1$

4. $g + gr + gr^2 + gr^3 + \ldots$ a) yes if $|r| < 1$; b) $\frac{g}{1 - r}$

5. Write in words: $\lim_{n \to \infty} S_n = L$. See margin.

6. If $S_1 = 0.6$, $S_2 = -.66$, $S_3 = 0.666$, $S_4 = -.6666$, and so on, what is $\lim_{n \to \infty} S_n$? $\frac{6}{11}$

In 7–9, an infinite repeating decimal is given. See margin.
a. Write the decimal as an infinite geometric series.
b. Find a fraction equal to the value of the series.

7. 0.4444 … **8.** 9.252525 … **9.** $2.46\overline{8}$

10. A ball is dropped from a height of 2 meters and on each bounce rebounds to $\frac{1}{4}$ of its previous height.
   a. What is the total length of the downward paths? $\frac{8}{3}$ m
   b. What is the total length of the upward paths? $\frac{2}{3}$ m
   c. How far does the ball travel before it stops bouncing? $\frac{10}{3}$ m

MORE PRACTICE
For more questions on SPUR Objectives, use *Lesson Master 13-4*, shown below.

EVALUATION
A quiz covering Lessons 13-1 through 13-4 is provided in the Teacher's Resource File.

Applying the Mathematics

11. The Greek philosopher Zeno was bothered by the idea of the infinite. He did not feel that time could be split into infinitely many parts. (This kind of split is done when one assumes that a dropped ball bounces infinitely often before stopping.) So he invented situations to make his point. One of these is the race between Achilles and the tortoise. (Achilles was a legendary fast Greek runner; a tortoise is a land turtle.)

Achilles, being faster than the tortoise, gives the tortoise a 10-meter head start. Achilles runs 10 times as fast. By the time Achilles runs 10 meters, the tortoise has gone 1 meter. When Achilles runs that 1 meter, the tortoise has gone 0.1 meter farther. When Achilles runs that 0.1 meter, the tortoise has gone 0.01 meter farther. This continues forever.

Zeno argued that Achilles never catches up to the tortoise. What do you think? Justify your answer.
They meet when the tortoise has traveled $1 + .1 + .01 + \ldots = 1.\overline{1}$ m.

In 12 and 13, a *snowflake curve* is the limit of a sequence of polygons formed in the following manner. F_1 is an equilateral triangle. F_n is formed by drawing an equilateral triangle outward on the middle third of each side of F_{n-1} and then deleting that middle third.

12. Suppose the perimeter of F_1 is 3.
   a. Find the perimeter of F_2.   4
   b. Find the perimeter of F_3. $\frac{16}{3}$
   c. What is the perimeter P_n of F_n? $3 \cdot \left(\frac{4}{3}\right)^{n-1}$
   d. Does the perimeter of F_3 have a limit as n gets larger and larger? If so, what is that limit? If not, why not?
   No, because $r = \frac{4}{3} > 1$

13. Suppose the area of F_1 is $\dfrac{\sqrt{3}}{4}$.   a) $\dfrac{4\sqrt{3}}{12}$; b) $\dfrac{10\sqrt{3}}{27}$;
   a. Find the area of F_2.
   b. Find the area of F_3.   c) $\dfrac{\sqrt{3}}{4} + \dfrac{\dfrac{\sqrt{3}}{12}\left(1 - \left(\dfrac{4}{9}\right)^{n-1}\right)}{1 - \dfrac{4}{9}}$;   d) $\dfrac{\sqrt{3}}{4} + \dfrac{\dfrac{\sqrt{3}}{12}}{\dfrac{5}{9}}$
   c. What is the area A_n of F_n?
   d. Does the area of F_n have a limit as n gets larger and larger? If so, what is that limit? If not, why not?

763

NAME _____

LESSON **MASTER 13–4**
QUESTIONS ON **SPUR** OBJECTIVES

■**SKILLS** *Objective A (See pages 808–811 for objectives.)*
In 1–4, find the value of each infinite, geometric series.

1. $3 + 1 + \frac{1}{3} + \frac{1}{9} + \ldots$ 2. $10 - 5 + \frac{5}{2} - \frac{5}{4} + \ldots$
   $\frac{9}{2}$ $\frac{20}{3}$

3. $1 - 2 + 4 - 8 + 16 - \ldots$ 4. $12 + .12 + .0012 + \ldots$
   no limit, $|r| > 1$ $12.\overline{12}$

5. **a.** Write the repeating decimal 4.967967... as an infinite geometric series.
   $4 + .967 + .000967 + .000000967 + \ldots$
   b. Find a simple fraction in lowest terms to equal this decimal. $\frac{4963}{999}$

■**PROPERTIES** *Objective F*
6. Under what condition(s) is it true that
   $a + ar + ar^2 + ar^3 + \ldots = \frac{1}{1-r}$? $a = 1$

In 7 and 8, (a) does the infinite geometric series have a value? (b) If so, what is this value? If not, why not?

7. $1 - 2 + 4 - 8 + 16 - \ldots$ 8. $\frac{3}{4} + \frac{3}{16} + \frac{3}{64} + \frac{3}{256} + \ldots$
   a. no   **a.** yes
   b. $|r| = |-2| = 2 > 1$ **b.** 1

■**USES** *Objective H*
9. A little boy decides to walk 20 feet, stop, walk 10 feet, stop, and continue to walk half of his previous distance until he can go no farther.
   a. Will he ever stop walking?   yes
   b. What is the longest distance he could cover in this way?   40 ft

Advanced Algebra © Scott, Foresman and Company   **139**

NOTES ON QUESTIONS
Question 15: This result may still bother some students at this level. If they think that 0.99999 . . . should be less than 1, ask for a number in between 0.9999 . . . and 1. Since there is none, they must be the same number.

Question 22: Arithmetic with factorials is needed in the next lesson, so be certain to discuss this question.

14. The ball in Question 10 is dropped from three times the height.
    a. Without calculating, how many times farther do you think the ball would travel before it stops bouncing? **3 times**
    b. Calculate how far the ball would travel, using the formula. **10 m**

15. a. Use the formula for an infinite geometric series to find the value of the infinite repeating decimal 0.9999999 . . . . **1**
    b. Use part a to give two different decimals equal to $\frac{1}{2}$. **.5, .4\overline{9}**

16. a. Write out the first five terms of the series $\sum_{n=1}^{\infty} 3 \cdot \left(\frac{2}{3}\right)^{n-1}$.
    b. What is the value of this series? **a. $3 + 2 + \frac{4}{3} + \frac{8}{9} + \frac{16}{27}$; b. 9**

Review

17. a. Expand $\sum_{n=1}^{10} (5n + 1)$. That is, write down the terms of the sum.
    b. Find its value. *(Lessons 13-1, 13-3)*
    a. 6 + 11 + 16 + 21 + 26 + 31 + 36 + 41 + 46 + 51; b. 285
18. Find the value of $100 + 100x + 100x^2 + 100x^3 + 100x^4$ when $x = 1.06$ using: (a) direct substitution and (b) a formula for geometric series. *(Lesson 13-2)* **≈563.71**

19. Find the points of intersection of the circle $x^2 + y^2 = 25$ and the ellipse $\frac{x^2}{64} + \frac{y^2}{16} = 1$ graphed at the right.
    (Lesson 12-10) **($\pm\sqrt{12}$, $\pm\sqrt{13}$)**

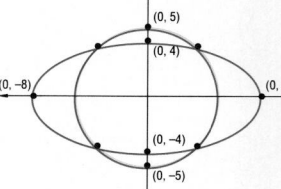

20. A line is perpendicular to $y = 3x$.
    a. What is its slope? **$-\frac{1}{3}$**   b. What is its y-intercept? *(Lesson 4-8)*
    any real number

21. *Multiple choice* Which does not equal the others?
    (Lessons 10-3, 10-4, 10-5, 10-8) **c**
    (a) sin 30°   (b) sin 150°   (c) sin 330°   (d) sin 390°

22. Let f(n) = n! Evaluate. *(Lesson 13-3)*
    a. f(3) **6**   **b.** $\frac{f(5)}{f(4)}$ **5**   **c.** $\frac{f(n+1)}{f(n)}$ **n + 1**

23. Which is larger, 100! or 100^{100}? *(Lesson 13-3)* **100^{100}**

24. Five candidates, Jerry, Kerry, Larry, Mary, and Perry, are to give speeches at an election assembly. In how many different orders could the candidates speak? *(Lesson 13-3)* **5! = 120**

In 25–27, find an equal expression of the form ax^n. *(Lessons 8-1, 8-4)*
25. $(2x)^3$ **$8x^3$**   26. $x^5(x^2)^4$ **$1x^{13}$**   27. $9x^{-2} \cdot (9x)^{-2}$ **$\frac{1}{9}x^{-4}$**

Exploration

28. Zeno (see Question 11) is also known for a paradox called the "arrow paradox." Using other books, find out what this paradox is.
    An arrow never reaches its target because it travels half the distance, then half the remaining distance, then half the remaining distance, and so on.

764

764

13-5

Pascal's Triangle

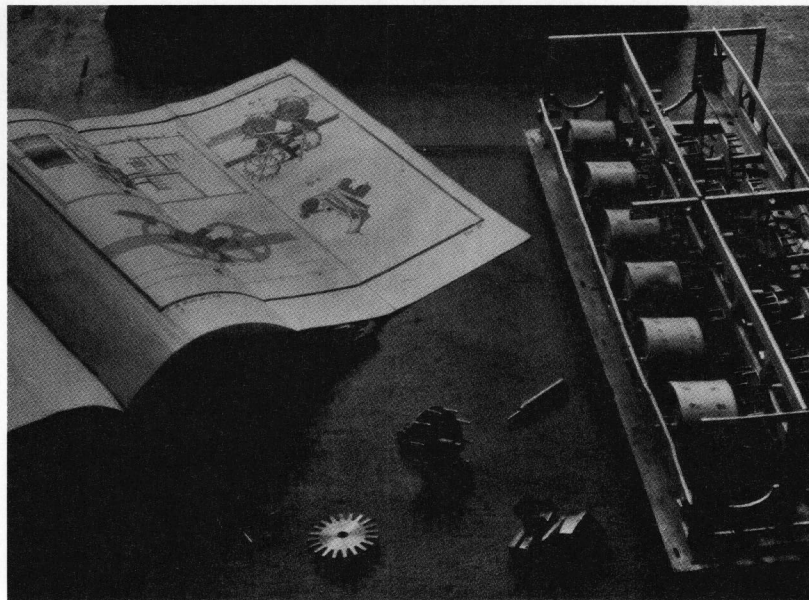

Pascal's adding machine

RESOURCES
■ Lesson Master 13-5
▯ Visual for Teaching Aid 86
provides the first ten rows
of Pascal's Triangle. Use
with **Questions 1–3**.

OBJECTIVE

C Calculate entries in
Pascal's Triangle.

TEACHING NOTES

Pascal's Triangle can be
generated by anyone who
knows addition of whole
numbers. The point of this
lesson is to use algebra to
generalize the process.
Thinking of the Triangle as a
two-dimensional sequence, it
is natural to ask if there is a
simple recursive definition or
a simple explicit definition.

It is common to define $\binom{n}{r}$ as
combinations. We find this
approach difficult because
very often students are learning the idea of combinations
on the same day. Thus, we
define $\binom{n}{r}$ to be an element
of the Triangle.

The recursive definition
comes directly from the arithmetic way in which the
Triangle is generated. It is
often difficult for students to
understand because it in-
volves two variables. The
explicit definition
$\binom{n}{r} = \dfrac{n!}{(n - r)!r!}$ is often
easier for students to under-
stand.

The theorem of this lesson
provides the explicit definition
of the sequence. Its proof is
subtle. We show that the sequence generated by the

Very often an idea from one part of mathematics has applications
to another part of mathematics. The triangular array below is such
an idea. (The top row of the array is called row 0 because this is
convenient in applications of the array.)

The triangular array below was known in ancient India. It was
rediscovered and discussed in 1544 by Michael Stifel, a German
mathematician. But the array is known as Pascal's triangle, named
after Blaise Pascal (1623–1662), the French mathematician and
philosopher who discovered many properties relating the elements
(numbers) in the array. Pascal himself called it the Triangle
Arithmetique, literally the "arithmetical triangle."

Pascal's Triangle

```
                    1                    ← row 0
                  1   1                  ← row 1
                1   2   1                ← row 2
              1   3   3   1              ← row 3
            1   4   6   4   1            ← row 4
          1   5  10  10   5   1          ← row 5
        1   6  15  20  15   6   1        ← row 6
      1   7  21  35  35  21   7   1      ← row 7
      ⋮   ⋮   ⋮   ⋮   ⋮   ⋮   ⋮   ⋮
```

The dots indicate
that the array goes
on without end.

formula is the same as the sequence defined by the recursive relation involving $\binom{n}{r}$. The second part is not in the text because of its complexity. We need to show that the desired formula for $\binom{n}{r}$ satisfies

$$\binom{n}{r} + \binom{n}{r+1} = \binom{n+1}{r+1}.$$

$$\binom{n}{r} + \binom{n}{r+1} =$$

$$\frac{n!}{(n-r)!r!} + \frac{n!}{(r+1)!(n-r-1)!}$$

$$= \frac{n!}{(n-r)!r!} + \frac{n!(n-r)}{(r+1)!(n-r)!}$$

$$= \frac{n!(r+1)}{(n-r)!(r+1)!} + \frac{n!(n-r)}{(r+1)!(n-r)!}$$

$$= \frac{n![(r+1) + (n-r)]}{(r+1)!(n-r)!}$$

$$= \frac{n!(n+1)}{(r+1)!(n-r)!}$$

$$= \frac{(n+1)!}{(r+1)!(n-r)!}$$

$$= \binom{n+1}{r+1}.$$

Pascal's triangle is formed in a very simple way. You can think of Pascal's triangle as a two-dimensional sequence. Each element is determined by a row and its position in that row. The only element in the top row (row 0) is 1. The first and last elements of every other row are also 1. If x and y are located next to each other on a row, the element just below and directly between them is $x + y$, as illustrated below.

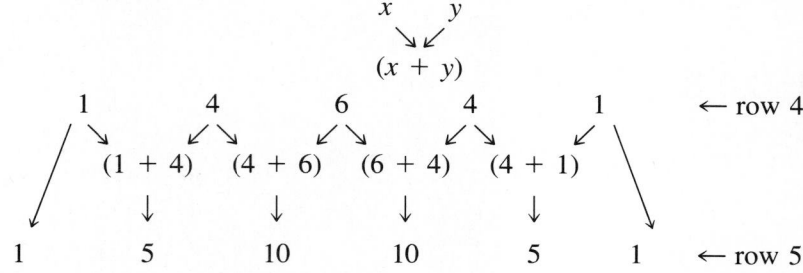

This is also shown by the arrows between rows 4 and 5. All other elements in the array follow the same patterns.

There is a standard symbol used to represent elements in Pascal's triangle.

Definition:

The $(r + 1)$st element in row n of Pascal's triangle is denoted by $\binom{n}{r}$.

For instance, the 1st element in the 7th row is $\binom{7}{0}$. The entire 7th row consists of the following elements.

$$\binom{7}{0} \quad \binom{7}{1} \quad \binom{7}{2} \quad \binom{7}{3} \quad \binom{7}{4} \quad \binom{7}{5} \quad \binom{7}{6} \quad \binom{7}{7}$$

That is, $\binom{7}{0} = 1$, $\binom{7}{1} = 7$, $\binom{7}{2} = 21$, and so forth. We found these values by referring to row 7 as it was given on the previous page. The top row has one element, $\binom{0}{0} = 1$.

The method of construction of Pascal's triangle lends itself to a recursive definition of the triangle using the above symbol. Since the triangle is a sequence in two directions—down and across—the recursive rule involves two variables.

766

Definition:

Pascal's triangle is the sequence satisfying

$$(1) \quad \binom{n}{0} = \binom{n}{n} = 1$$

and $$(2) \quad \binom{n+1}{r+1} = \binom{n}{r} + \binom{n}{r+1},$$

where n and r are any integers with $0 \le r \le n$.

Part (1) of the definition gives the "sides" of the triangle. Part (2) is a symbolic way of stating that adding two adjacent elements in one row gives the element below them in the next row.

In order to determine the elements in the 14th row of the triangle from the definition, you would have to construct the first 13 rows. The next theorem was first proved by Isaac Newton and shows how to calculate $\binom{n}{r}$ without constructing the triangle. The theorem is a surprising application of factorials and requires that 0! be defined to equal 1.

Theorem:

$$\binom{n}{r} = \frac{n!}{r!(n-r)!}$$

Before proving this theorem, here are some instances of it.

Example 1 Calculate $\binom{4}{2}$.

Solution Here $n = 4$ and $r = 2$. So $n - r = 2$ also.

$$\binom{4}{2} = \frac{4!}{2!(4-2)!} = \frac{4 \cdot 3 \cdot 2 \cdot 1}{2 \cdot 1(2 \cdot 1)} = 6$$

Check This agrees with $\binom{4}{2}$ being the 3rd element in the 4th row of Pascal's triangle.

ADDITIONAL EXAMPLES

In 1–3, give the value.

1. $\binom{3}{1}$
3

2. $\binom{9}{4}$
126

3. $\binom{n}{1}$
n

4. $\binom{11}{7} + \binom{11}{8}$ gives what element in Pascal's Triangle?
$\binom{12}{8}$

NOTES ON QUESTIONS

Questions 1-3: *Teaching Aid 86* displays the first ten rows of Pascal's Triangle. You may want to duplicate and distribute this teaching aid for students' reference after completing the questions.

Questions 19-21: You can connect Pascal's Triangle with series. The triangular numbers are the sums of the integers from 1 to n. This can be seen in the Triangle by going down the diagonal that has these integers in order. Suppose you go from 1 to 6 (going down to the left). Then the sum, 21, is found just to the right and below the 6. This pattern holds regardless of the diagonal being used. Thus, the sum of the first six triangular numbers (1 + 3 + 6 + 10 + 15 + 21) is found by going down their diagonal until you reach 21 and then move to the right and below (in the 8th row) to read 56. This property has been called the "hockey stick" property because if the numbers and their sum are surrounded by a simple closed curve, the figure resembles such a stick.

ADDITIONAL ANSWERS

1.

1
1 1
1 2 1
1 3 3 1
1 4 6 4 1
1 5 10 10 5 1
1 6 15 20 15 6 1
1 7 21 35 35 21 7 1

3. See Additional Answers in the back of this book.

Example 2 Calculate $\binom{11}{3}$.

Solution $\binom{11}{3} = \dfrac{11!}{3!(11-3)!}$

$$= \frac{11 \cdot 10 \cdot 9 \cdot 8 \cdot 7 \cdot 6 \cdot 5 \cdot 4 \cdot 3 \cdot 2 \cdot 1}{3 \cdot 2 \cdot 1 \cdot 8 \cdot 7 \cdot 6 \cdot 5 \cdot 4 \cdot 3 \cdot 2 \cdot 1} = 165$$

Check Use a calculator. 11 [!] [÷] [(] 3 [!] [×] 8 [!] [)] [=] yields 165.

Notice how easily the fraction of Example 2 can be simplified because of the common factors.

In Example 3, the equality $0! = 1$ must be used.

Example 3 Calculate $\binom{7}{0}$.

Solution $\binom{7}{0} = \dfrac{7!}{0!(7-0)!} = \dfrac{7!}{1 \cdot 7!} = 1$

Check This agrees with $\binom{7}{0}$ being the 1st element in the 7th row.

For a proof of the theorem, $\binom{n}{r} = \dfrac{n!}{r!(n-r)!}$, it is enough to show that the factorial formula $\dfrac{n!}{r!(n-r)!}$ satisfies the relationships involving $\binom{n}{r}$ which define Pascal's triangle. Does the formula for $\binom{n}{0}$ equal the formula for $\binom{n}{n}$ and equal 1?

$$\binom{n}{0} = 1 \text{ and } \frac{n!}{0!(n-0)!} = \frac{n!}{0!n!} = \frac{n!}{1 \cdot n!} = 1, \text{ so } \binom{n}{0} = \frac{n!}{0!(n-0)!}.$$

$$\binom{n}{n} = 1 \text{ and } \frac{n!}{n!(n-n)!} = \frac{n!}{n!0!} = \frac{n!}{n!(1)} = 1, \text{ so } \binom{n}{n} = \frac{n!}{n!(n-n)!}.$$

Thus the formula works for the "sides" of Pascal's triangle.

To prove that the formula for $\binom{n+1}{r+1}$ is the sum of the formulas for $\binom{n}{r}$ and $\binom{n}{r+1}$ requires substantial algebraic manipulation; it is omitted here.

Important applications of Pascal's triangle are given in the remaining lessons of this chapter.

Covering the Reading

1. Write down rows 0 through 7 of Pascal's triangle from memory.
   See margin.
2. What are the rules by which Pascal's triangle is defined? $\binom{n}{0} = \binom{n}{n} = 1; \binom{n+1}{r+1} = \binom{n}{r} + \binom{n}{r+1}$

3. Write down rows 8 through 10 of Pascal's triangle. (It is a good idea to keep rows 0 through 10 handy for reference.)   **See margin.**

4. **a.** The symbol $\binom{n}{r}$ denotes what element in which row of Pascal's triangle?   **(r + 1)st element in row n**
   b. In terms of factorials, $\binom{n}{r} = \underline{\ ?\ }$. $\dfrac{n!}{r!(n-r)!}$

In 5–12, calculate.

5. $\binom{8}{2}$ 28
6. $\binom{3}{2}$ 3
7. $\binom{10}{5}$ 252
8. $0!$ 1

9. $\binom{6}{6}$ 1
10. $\binom{15}{0}$ 1
11. $\binom{15}{14}$ 15
12. $\binom{20}{2}$ 190

Applying the Mathematics

13. If $10 \cdot 9! = x!$, then $x = \underline{\ ?\ }$.   10

14. If $(n - r)(n - r - 1)! = y!$, then $y = \underline{\ ?\ }$.   n − r

In 15 and 16, *true or false*.

15. $\binom{99}{17}$ is an integer.   **true**

16. $\dfrac{n!}{(n-2)!}$ is always an integer when $n \geq 2$.   **true**

17. If $\binom{10}{5} + \binom{10}{6} = \binom{x}{y}$, then $x = \underline{\ ?\ }$ and $y = \underline{\ ?\ }$.   **x = 11, y = 6**

18. If $\binom{9}{2} + \binom{a}{b} = \binom{10}{2}$, then $a = \underline{\ ?\ }$ and $b = \underline{\ ?\ }$.   **a = 9, b = 1**

In 19–21, tell where in Pascal's triangle the following sequence can be found.

19. the positive integers   **the 2nd elements in each row**

20. the triangular numbers: 1, 3, 6, 10, 15, …
    the 3rd elements in each row
21. the sequence of partial sums of triangular numbers:
    $1, 1 + 3, 1 + 3 + 6, 1 + 3 + 6 + 10, \ldots$
    the 4th elements in each row

Review

22. **a.** Write the repeating decimal 0.297297297297 … as an infinite geometric series. $\dfrac{297}{10^3} + \dfrac{297}{10^6} + \dfrac{297}{10^9} + \ldots$
    b. Find the fraction in lowest terms equal to this decimal. *(Lesson 13-4)* $\dfrac{297}{999} = \dfrac{11}{37}$

LESSON 13-5 Pascal's Triangle   **769**

MORE PRACTICE
For more questions on SPUR Objectives, use *Lesson Master 13-5*, shown below.

EXTENSION
Pascal was a remarkable individual. Students in your class who are studying French will almost surely have read some of his *Pensées* (Thoughts), among the most famous writing in the French language. The *Pensées* were published eight years after his death at the early age of 39. He tended to do mathematics in spurts of incredible creativity. Some students might be interested in doing some research into the life of Pascal.

NAME _____

LESSON **MASTER   13–5**
QUESTIONS ON **SPUR** OBJECTIVES

■ **SKILLS** *Objective C (See pages 808–811 for objectives.)*

1. Rows 0 to 2 of Pascal's Triangle are given below. Write the next four rows.

```
            1
          1   1
        1   2   1
      1   3   3   1
    1   4   6   4   1
  1   5  10  10   5   1
1   6  15  20  15   6   1
```

2. Use your work in Question 1 to find

   a. $\binom{5}{2}$ 10   **b.** $\binom{3}{2}$ 3   **c.** $\binom{4}{1}$ 4

In 3–8, evaluate.

3. $\dfrac{7!}{3!4!}$ 35   4. $\dfrac{12!}{6!6!}$ 924   5. $\dfrac{52!}{13!39!}$ 6.35×10^{11}

6. $\binom{11}{6}$ 462   7. $\binom{32}{1}$ 32   8. $\binom{99}{99}$ 1

■ **PROPERTIES** *Objective G*
In 9–13, answer true or false.

9. $\binom{n}{1} = n$, where *n* is a nonnegative integer.   **true**

10. $\binom{89}{10}$ is an integer.   **true**

11. $6 \cdot 5! = 30!$ **false**

12. $\binom{n}{r} = \dfrac{n!}{r!(n-r)!}$, where $0 \leq r \leq n$.   **true**

13. $\dfrac{n!}{0!}$ is undefined.   **false**

140   Advanced Algebra © Scott, Foresman and Company

NOTES ON QUESTIONS
Question 30: This property is known as the "Star of David Property" of the triangle, since it is explained by noting that the product of the two sets of alternating vertices is equal, and when these alternating vertices are connected, the result looks like the Star of David. Since every mathematician for the past 300 years was very familiar with Pascal's Triangle, the recent discovery by Hoggatt and Hansell of this property is dramatic proof that there are still simple properties to be discovered in familiar areas of mathematics.

ADDITIONAL ANSWERS
27.a. one real root
b. no real roots
c. two rational roots

30.a.
row 2: product surrounding 2 is 9.
row 3: product surrounding 3 is 144.
row 4: product surrounding 4 is 900, surrounding 6 is 14400.
row 5: product surrounding 5 is 3600, surrounding 10 is 360000.
b. The product is the square of the product of every other term surrounding the center number. For instance, surrounding the 10 in row 5 are the numbers 4, 6, 10, 20, 15, and 5. Then $360000 = (4 \cdot 10 \cdot 15)^2 = (6 \cdot 20 \cdot 5)^2$
c. sample: around the 15 in row 6 are the elements 5, 10, 20, 35, 21, and 6.
$5 \cdot 10 \cdot 20 \cdot 35 \cdot 21 \cdot 6 = 4410000$ and $(5 \cdot 20 \cdot 21)^2 = (10 \cdot 35 \cdot 6)^2 = 4410000$

23. Consider the squares below whose sides form a geometric sequence.

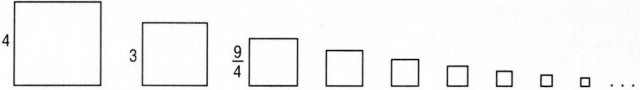

a. What is the sum of the areas of the nine squares pictured?   ≈35.9
b. What is the sum of the areas of this infinite geometric sequence of squares? *(Lessons 13-2, 13-4)* $\frac{256}{7}$

24. Very young children often play with rods whose lengths form the arithmetic sequence x, $2x$, $3x$, ... , $10x$.   **55x units**
a. What is the sum of the lengths of these rods? *(Lesson 13-1)*
b. If you wanted to make a set of such rods for a young relative out of a piece of wood 6 feet long, how long could you make the shortest rod? *(Lesson 1-7)*   ≈1.3 in.

25. Evaluate $\sum_{n=1}^{4} (n^2 + 3n)$. *(Lesson 13-3)*   60

26. The sum of the first n terms of the arithmetic sequence 1, 5, 9, 13, ... is 2415. What is n? *(Lesson 13-1)*   35

27. In the quadratic equation $ax^2 + bx + c = 0$, when a, b, and c are integers, state what you can conclude from the following.
a. $b^2 - 4ac = 0$ b. $b^2 - 4ac = -8$ c. $b^2 - 4ac = 16$
(Lesson 6-7)   **See margin.**

28. Multiply the complex numbers $2i$ and $2 - 2i$. *(Lesson 6-9)*   4 + 4i

29. In how many possible orders might six girls in a diving event finish? *(Lesson 13-3)*   6! = 720

Exploration

30. There are six elements surrounding each element not on a side of Pascal's triangle. For instance, around 15 in row 6 are the elements 5, 10, 20, 35, 21, and 6. In 1969, an amazing property about the product of these elements was discovered by Verner Hoggatt and W. Hansell of San Jose State University.   **See margin.**
a. Find this product for all the elements not on the sides of the first five rows of the triangle.
b. What is true of these products?
c. Verify your answer to part b by calculating the product for other elements in the triangle.

770

The Binomial Theorem

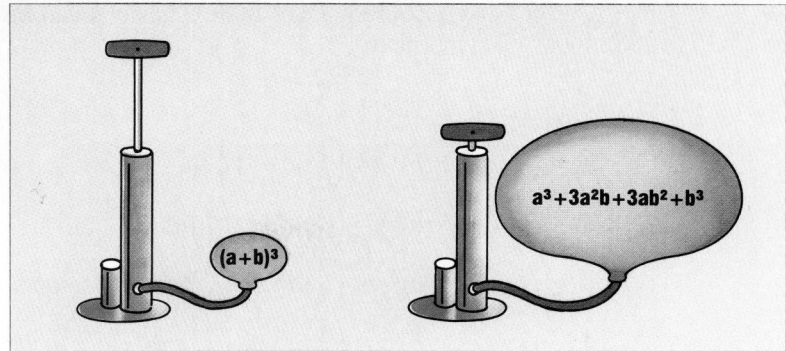

$(a+b)^3$

$a^3+3a^2b+3ab^2+b^3$

LESSON 13-6

RESOURCES
■ Lesson Master 13-6
▢ Visual for Teaching Aid 87
  displays the Binomial Theorem and the first four
  expansions of $(a + b)^n$.

You have seen powers of binomials in many places in this book. Here are a few examples, with the binomials identified in bold type.

$$A = P(\mathbf{1 + r})^t$$
Compound Interest Formula (Lesson 8-2)

$$y - k = a(\mathbf{x - h})^2$$
vertex form of the equation of a parabola (Lesson 6-4)

$$e = \left(\mathbf{1 + \frac{1}{n}}\right)^n$$
definition of e (Lesson 9-7)

The geometric sequence with first term 1 and the binomial $a + b$ as its constant ratio generates all the positive integer powers of binomials.

$$1, a + b, (a + b)^2, (a + b)^3, (a + b)^4, \ldots$$

You know the binomial $(a + b)^2 = a^2 + 2ab + b^2$. It is natural to try to expand the other powers of binomials. The results are known as *binomial expansions*.

$$(a + b)^0 = 1$$
$$(a + b)^1 = a + b$$
$$(a + b)^2 = a^2 + 2ab + b^2$$
$$(a + b)^3 = a^3 + 3a^2b + 3ab^2 + b^3$$
$$(a + b)^4 = a^4 + 4a^3b + 6a^2b^2 + 4ab^3 + b^4$$
$$\vdots \qquad\qquad\qquad \vdots$$

Looking at the expansions, it may seem that there is no pattern. But if the as and bs are ignored, and only the coefficients are written, then Pascal's triangle appears!

Powers of $(a + b)$	Coefficients of the expansion	Row of Pascal's triangle
$(a + b)^0$	1	0
$(a + b)^1$	1 1	1
$(a + b)^2$	1 2 1	2
$(a + b)^3$	1 3 3 1	3
$(a + b)^4$	1 4 6 4 1	4
$\vdots$	$\vdots$	$\vdots$

LESSON 13-6   The Binomial Theorem   **771**

The lesson first expands the binomials without using Pascal's triangle. Otherwise, students might not realize what is happening and view the exponent as simply another new notation, not similar to anything they have studied previously.

Having expanded the binomials, we see that Pascal's Triangle is hidden among the exponents.

The remainder of the lesson is devoted to examples. It takes practice and a lot of concentration to do these problems without error.

Note that the words "expand" or "expansion" arise from the written expanded form being an expression with more terms than the binomial. Emphasize that both $(a + b)^n$ and its expansion have equal value for all a, b, and n. (In this sense, the cartoon at the beginning of the lesson may be misleading.)

Emphasize to students that they should always check first by letting the variable equal a simple number, even 1. Then they should check with a second value of the variable.

ADDITIONAL EXAMPLES
In 1–3, expand.
1. $(a + b)^5$
$a^5 + 5a^4b + 10a^3b^2 + 10a^2b^3 + 5ab^4 + b^5$

2. $(t^2 - 2)^4$
$t^8 - 8t^6 + 24t^4 - 32t^2 + 16$

3. $(4x + 3y)^3$
$64x^3 + 144x^2y + 108xy^2 + 27y^3$

As a consequence, the expansions can be written using the $\binom{n}{r}$ symbolism.

$$(a + b)^0 = \binom{0}{0}$$
$$(a + b)^1 = \binom{1}{0}a + \binom{1}{1}b$$
$$(a + b)^2 = \binom{2}{0}a^2 + \binom{2}{1}ab + \binom{2}{2}b^2$$
$$(a + b)^3 = \binom{3}{0}a^3 + \binom{3}{1}a^2b + \binom{3}{2}ab^2 + \binom{3}{3}b^3$$
$$(a + b)^4 = \binom{4}{0}a^4 + \binom{4}{1}a^3b + \binom{4}{2}a^2b^2 + \binom{4}{3}ab^3 + \binom{4}{4}b^4$$
$$\vdots \qquad \qquad \vdots$$

Notice how easy Pascal's Triangle makes the expansion of $(a + b)^n$:

(1) All the powers of a from a^n to a^0 occur in order.
(2) In each term, the exponents of a and b add to n.
(3) If the power of b is r, then the coefficient of the term is $\binom{n}{r}$.

This information is summarized in a famous theorem, which was known to Omar Khayyam, the famous Persian poet, mathematician, and astronomer who died around the year 1123. Of course, he did not have our modern notation.

Binomial Theorem:

$$(a + b)^n = \sum_{r=0}^{n} \binom{n}{r} a^{n-r} b^r.$$

A formal proof of the Binomial Theorem requires a knowledge of mathematical induction, a powerful proof technique not discussed in this book, and first used by Pascal when he discussed the array.

Example 1 Expand $(a + b)^7$.

Solution First, fill in powers of a and b.

$(a + b)^7 = ___a^7 + ___a^6b + ___a^5b^2 + ___a^4b^3 + ___a^3b^4 + ___a^2b^5 + ___ab^6 + ___b^7$

Second, put in the coefficients.

$$(a + b)^7 = \binom{7}{0}a^7 + \binom{7}{1}a^6b + \binom{7}{2}a^5b^2 + \binom{7}{3}a^4b^3 + \binom{7}{4}a^3b^4 +$$
$$\binom{7}{5}a^2b^5 + \binom{7}{6}ab^6 + \binom{7}{7}b^7$$

Finally, evaluate the coefficients, either by referring to row 7 of Pascal's Triangle or by using the formula $\binom{n}{r} = \dfrac{n!}{r!(n - r)!}$.

$$(a + b)^7 = a^7 + 7a^6b + 21a^5b^2 + 35a^4b^3 + 35a^3b^4 +$$
$$21a^2b^5 + 7ab^6 + b^7$$

The Binomial Theorem can be used to expand powers of *any* binomial by substituting for *a* and *b*.

Example 2   Expand $(5x - 2y)^3$.

Solution   Use $(a + b)^3$ with $5x$ as a and $-2y$ as b.

$$(a + b)^3 = \binom{3}{0}a^3 + \binom{3}{1}a^2b + \binom{3}{2}ab^2 + \binom{3}{3}b^3$$

Substituting,

$$(5x - 2y)^3 = 1(5x)^3 + 3(5x)^2(-2y) + 3(5x)(-2y)^2 + 1(-2y)^3$$
$$= 125x^3 - 150x^2y + 60xy^2 - 8y^3$$

Check   Substitute specific values for x and y. Let $x = 2$ and $y = 3$. Then the given expression $(5x - 2y)^3 = (10 - 6)^3 = 64$. The value of the expanded form is:

$$125x^3 - 150x^2y + 60xy^2 - 8y^3 = 125\cdot8 - 150\cdot4\cdot3 + 60\cdot2\cdot9 - 8\cdot27$$
$$= 1000 - 1800 + 1080 - 216$$
$$= 64. \text{ It checks.}$$

Example 3   Expand $(x^2 + 1)^4$.

Solution   Think of x^2 as a and 1 as b and follow the form of $(a + b)^4$.

$$(x^2 + 1)^4 = \binom{4}{0}(x^2)^4 + \binom{4}{1}(x^2)^3\cdot1 + \binom{4}{2}(x^2)^2\cdot1^2 + \binom{4}{3}(x^2)^1\cdot1^3 + \binom{4}{4}\cdot1^4$$
$$= x^8 + 4x^6 + 6x^4 + 4x^2 + 1$$

Check   Let $x = 2$. Then $(x^2 + 1)^4 = (4 + 1)^4 = 5^4 = 625$. You should verify that the value of the polynomial when $x = 2$ is also 625. Also note as a check that the exponents of each variable in each expansion form an arithmetic sequence.

Due to their use in the binomial theorem, the numbers in Pascal's triangle are known as **binomial coefficients.** The binomial theorem has a surprising number of applications in estimations, counting problems, probability, and statistics.

Questions

Covering the Reading

In 1–4, expand each binomial power. **See margin.**
1. $(a + b)^2$ 2. $(a + b)^3$ 3. $(a + b)^4$ 4. $(a + b)^5$

5. State the Binomial Theorem. $(a + b)^n = \sum_{r=0}^{n} \binom{n}{r} a^{n-r} b^r$

In 6–11, expand each binomial power. **See margin.**
6. $(x + 1)^5$ 7. $(a - b)^3$ 8. $(2 - m)^4$ 9. $(x + y)^6$

10. $(8x + y)^3$ 11. $(a + 2b)^4$

Applying the Mathematics

12. Multiply the binomial expansion for $(a + b)^4$ by $a + b$ to check the expansion for $(a + b)^5$. $a^5 + 5a^4b + 10a^3b^2 + 10a^2b^3 + 5ab^4 + b^5$

In 13 and 14, convert to an expression in the form $(a + b)^n$.

13. $\sum_{r=0}^{n} \binom{n}{r} x^{n-r} 3^r$
$(x + 3)^n$

14. $\sum_{i=0}^{n} \binom{n}{i} y^{n-i} (2a)^i$
$(y + 2a)^n$

15. **a.** Multiply and simplify:
$(a^2 + 2ab + b^2)(a^2 + 2ab + b^2)$ $a^4 + 4a^3b + 6a^2b^2 + 4ab^3 + b^4$
b. Your answer to part a should be a power of $a + b$. Which one? Why? $(a + b)^4$ because $a^2 + 2ab + b^2 = (a + b)^2$

In 16 and 17, use the Binomial Theorem to approximate some powers quickly. Here is an example.

$$(1.002)^3 = (1 + .002)^3$$
$$= 1^3 + 3 \cdot 1^2 \cdot (.002) + 3 \cdot 1 \cdot (.002)^2 + (.002)^3$$
$$= 1 + .006 + .000012 + .000000008$$
$$= 1.006012008$$

Since the last two terms in the expansion are so small, they might be ignored in an estimate. $(1.002)^3 \approx 1.006$ to the nearest thousandth.

16. Estimate $(1.004)^3$ to the nearest thousandth. Check your answer with a calculator.   **1.012**

17. Estimate $(1.001)^{10}$ correct to fifteen decimal places.
1.010045120210252

Review

18. Write row 9 of Pascal's Triangle. *(Lesson 13-5)*
1 9 36 84 126 126 84 36 9 1

774

19. Consider the infinite geometric sequence
$$64, 48, 36, 27, \dots .$$

  a. Find the sum of the first six terms of the sequence.   **210.4375**

  b. Find the sum of all terms of the sequence.   **256**

  c. *Multiple choice* Which represents the sum in part b?
   (Lessons 13-2, 13-3, 13-4)   **iv**

  (i) $\displaystyle\sum_{i=1}^{\infty} 64 \cdot \left(\frac{3}{4}\right)^{i}$ (ii) $\displaystyle\sum_{i=0}^{\infty} \left(\frac{3}{4}\right)^{i-1}$ (iii) $\displaystyle\sum_{i=1}^{\infty} \left(\frac{3}{4}\right)^{i-1}$ (iv) $\displaystyle\sum_{i=1}^{\infty} 64\left(\frac{3}{4}\right)^{i-1}$

In 20–22, suppose you are offered two jobs. The first pays $10,000 the first year, with an annual increase of $1,500 each year thereafter. The second pays $6,000 the first year, with a 25% increase (compounded annually) each year thereafter.

20. List your projected annual salary for the first three years for each of the jobs.   **See margin.**

21. Find the first year in which the salary for the second job exceeds that of the first job.   **the sixth year**

22. If you plan to stay in one of these jobs for 10 years, which will give the largest total salary? Justify your answer. *(Lessons 3-6, 8-3, 13-1, 13-2)*
Job 1: $167,500; Job 2: $199,517

23. If the sum of the first n terms of the geometric sequence $-2, 4, -8, 16, \dots$ is -86, what is n?   **7**

24. If the measurements of a single brick are $3\frac{1}{2}'' \times 7\frac{3}{4}'' \times 2\frac{1}{4}''$, what is its volume, to the nearest cubic inch? *(Previous course)*   **61 in.³**

25. A pile of bricks is 10 bricks high, 6 bricks deep, and 15 bricks wide. If a single brick weighs between 4 and $4\frac{1}{4}$ lb, what is the largest possible weight of the pile? *(Previous course)*   **3825 lb**

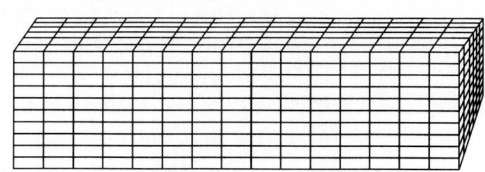

26. *Multiple choice* Which polynomial equals $\dfrac{(n + 2)!}{n!}$? *(Lesson 13-3)*   **c**

  (a) $n + 1$ (b) $n + 2$ (c) $(n + 1)(n + 2)$ (d) none of these

27. **a.** How many permutations of the letters of the word MOUSE are possible?   **5! = 120**

  b. List the first and last in dictionary order. *(Lesson 13-3)*
   EMOSU, USOME

Exploration

28. Calculate 11^n for $n = 0, 1, 2, 3, 4, 5,$ and 6. Explain how you can obtain *all* these powers from the binomial coefficients.

                                11   121
1; 11; 121; 1331; 14641; 161051 (= 150051); 1771561 (= 1650561); write the binomial coefficients in a string, "carrying" to the left if the coefficient has more than 1 digit.

LESSON 13-6 The Binomial Theorem   **775**

RESOURCES
■ Lesson Master 13-7

OBJECTIVES

C Calculate the number of subsets of a given set.
G Know the sum of elements in the *n*th row of Pascal's Triangle.
I Use combinations to solve problems.

TEACHING NOTES

Reading While most lessons in this chapter only contain one new major idea, the ideas are different enough that students may get overwhelmed. Help them by reading through this lesson carefully.

Whenever possible, enumerate the combinations. This not only checks answers, but it makes the idea more understandable for students. In this lesson, we enumerate the combinations of **Example 1** but obviously cannot enumerate the 142,506 combinations of **Example 2**. Still, you might number the items from 1 to 30, or call them *A, B, . . . , Z, AA, AB, AC, AD,* and ask students to give some examples of 5 items from these 30.

LESSON

13-7

Subsets and Combinations

A subcommittee of 3 people is to be chosen from the 10-person committee pictured below. In how many ways can this be done?

To answer this question, represent the full committee by the set {*A, B, C, D, E, F, G, H, I, J*}. Each set of three members from this committee is a subset of the original set. For instance, two possible subcommittees are Alan, Barbara, and Carlos, and Frank, Delphine, and Joe. These subcommittees can be represented as the subsets {*A, B, C*} and {*F, D, J*}. Order in sets makes no difference; {*F, D, J*} and {*D, F, J*} are the same subset. Thus the question can be viewed as a problem in counting subsets: How many subsets of 3 elements are possible from a set of 10 elements?

Think of forming the subsets one element at a time. There are 10 possibilities for the first element. Once the first element has been selected, there are 9 possibilities for the second element. Once the first two elements have been chosen, there are 8 possibilities for the third element. So it seems there are $10 \cdot 9 \cdot 8$ possibilities. This assumes that the order in which the elements are chosen makes a difference. But {*F, D, J*} and {*D, F, J*} are the same subset, and in fact there are 3! or 6 different orders which give rise to the same subset {*F, D, J*}. This is true of all 3-element subsets, so the answer $10 \cdot 9 \cdot 8$ is 3! times what we need. The number of subsets is thus

$$\frac{10 \cdot 9 \cdot 8}{3!}.$$

Now multiply the fraction by $\frac{7!}{7!}$. This multiplier equals 1, so it does not change the fraction's value. But it does change the way the fraction looks.

$$\frac{10 \cdot 9 \cdot 8}{3!} = \frac{10 \cdot 9 \cdot 8 \cdot 7!}{3! \cdot 7!}$$
$$= \frac{10!}{3! \, 7!}$$

776

The answer is a binomial coefficient! Evaluating directly, or looking for the 4th element in the 10th row of Pascal's triangle, the answer is seen to be 120.

The following theorem and its proof generalize the above argument.

Theorem:

The number of subsets of r elements which can be formed from a set of n elements is $\dfrac{n!}{r!(n-r)!}$, the binomial coefficient $\dbinom{n}{r}$.

Proof

There are n choices for the first element in a subset. Once that element has been picked, there are $n-1$ choices for the second element. This continues until all r elements have been picked. There are $(n-r+1)$ choices for the rth element. So, if different orders are considered different, there are

$$\underbrace{n(n-1)(n-2) \dots (n-r+1)}_{r \text{ factors}}$$

ways to pick them. But each subset is one of $r!$ subsets with the same elements. So the number of different subsets is

$$\frac{n(n-1)(n-2) \dots (n-r+1)}{r!}.$$

Multiplying both numerator and denominator by $(n-r)!$, the theorem results.

Here are several applications.

■ ■ ■ ■ ■ ■ ■ ■

Example 1 Five points are labeled in a plane, with no three collinear. How many triangles have these points as vertices?

Solution 1 Draw a picture. Label the points A, B, C, D, and E. Form triangles with the points as vertices.
The possible triangles are (in alphabetical order) ABC, ABD, ABE, ACD, ACE, ADE, BCD, BCE, BDE, and CDE. So 10 triangles can be formed.

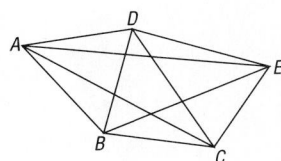

ADDITIONAL EXAMPLES

1. How many subcommittees of 6 people can be selected from a larger committee of 20?
$\binom{20}{6} = 38,760$

2. Suppose 10 points are in space, no four are coplanar, and no three are collinear. How many tetrahedra can be formed with them?
$\binom{10}{4} = 210$

3.a. How many subsets does the set {a,b,c,d,e} have?
32

b. List them.
abbreviated form: { }, a, b, c, d, e, ab, ac, ad, ae, bc, bd, be, cd, ce, de, abc, abd, abe, acd, ace, ade, bcd, bce, bde, cde, abcd, abce, abde, acde, bcde, abcde.

Solution 2 Any choice of 3 points from the 5 points determines a triangle. So use the theorem with $n = 5$ and $r = 3$. The number of possible triangles is $\binom{5}{3} = \dfrac{5!}{3!(5-3)!} = \dfrac{5!}{3!2!} = \dfrac{5 \cdot 4 \cdot 3 \cdot 2 \cdot 1}{3 \cdot 2 \cdot 1 \cdot 2 \cdot 1} = 10.$

Solution 3 Use the idea of the proof of the theorem. The first vertex of the triangle can be chosen in 5 ways. The second vertex can then be chosen in 4 ways. And the third vertex then can be chosen in 3 ways. So, if order made a difference, there would be $5 \cdot 4 \cdot 3$, or 60 different triangles. But order doesn't make a difference and each triangle is determined 3! or 6 times. So divide 60 by 6, yielding 10.

Any choice of r objects from n objects is called a **combination**. The theorem of this lesson can be restated: The number of combinations of r objects from n objects is $\binom{n}{r}$. Example 1 shows that the number of combinations of 3 objects from 5 objects is 10; in some books, you may see the symbol $_nC_r$. Like $\binom{n}{r}$, it stands for the number of combinations of r objects from n objects; $_5C_3 = \binom{5}{3} = 10$. The subcommittee situation at the beginning of this lesson shows that $_{10}C_3 = \binom{10}{3} = 120.$

Example 2 There are 30 items on a menu in a Vietnamese restaurant. A group of friends plans to order 5 items. In how many ways can this be done?

Solution Choosing 5 items from 30 items on a menu is equivalent to choosing subsets from a whole.

$_{30}C_5 = \binom{30}{5} = \dfrac{30!}{5!25!}$. To evaluate $\dfrac{30!}{5!25!}$ with a calculator, press 30 $\boxed{n!}$ $\boxed{\div}$ $\boxed{(}$ 25 $\boxed{n!}$ $\boxed{\times}$ 5 $\boxed{n!}$ $\boxed{)}$ $\boxed{=}$. Without a calculator, work as follows: $\dfrac{30!}{5!25!} = \dfrac{\overset{6}{\cancel{30}} \cdot 29 \cdot \overset{7}{\cancel{28}} \cdot \overset{9}{\cancel{27}} \cdot \overset{13}{\cancel{26}} \cdot 25!}{5 \cdot 4 \cdot 3 \cdot 2 \cdot 1 \cdot 25!}$. Either way, you should get 142,506.

There are 142,506 ways to select 5 items from 30.

Combinations enable you to determine the number of subsets of a particular size. You may wonder how many subsets there are in all. The answer is simple and surprising. For instance, consider the subsets of $\{A, B, C, D\}$.

$\{\ \}$	1 subset has 0 elements.
$\{A\}, \{B\}, \{C\}, \{D\}$	4 subsets have 1 element.
$\{A, B\}, \{A, C\}, \{A, D\}, \{B, C\},$	
$\{B, D\}, \{C, D\}$	6 subsets have 2 elements.
$\{A, B, C\}, \{A, B, D\}, \{A, C, D\},$	
$\{B, C, D\}$	4 subsets have 3 elements.
$\{A, B, C, D\}$	1 subset has 4 elements.

The numbers from Pascal's Triangle appear again! The total number of subsets is $1 + 4 + 6 + 4 + 1$, or 16. In general, the total number of subsets of a set with n elements is the sum of the elements in the nth row of Pascal's Triangle.

$$\binom{n}{0} + \binom{n}{1} + \binom{n}{2} + \ldots + \binom{n}{n} = \sum_{i=0}^{n} \binom{n}{i}$$

Multiply by powers of 1 to make the sum look like the Binomial Theorem.

$$\binom{n}{0} + \binom{n}{1} + \binom{n}{2} + \ldots + \binom{n}{n} = \sum_{i=0}^{n} \binom{n}{i} 1^{n-i} 1^{i}$$
$$= (1 + 1)^n$$
$$= 2^n$$

Theorem:

A set with n elements has 2^n subsets.

When $n = 4$, $2^n = 16$. This agrees with the number of subsets found above for a set with 4 elements.

Questions

Covering the Reading

1. *Multiple choice* Which is not a subset of $\{T, E, A, M\}$? d
   (a) $\{M, E, A, T\}$ (b) $\{\ \}$ (c) $\{A, M\}$ (d) $\{T, E, A, M, S\}$

2. **a.** How many subsets of $\{T, E, A, M\}$ have 3 elements? 4
   b. List them. $\{T, E, A\}, \{T, E, M\}, \{T, A, M\}, \{E, A, M\}$

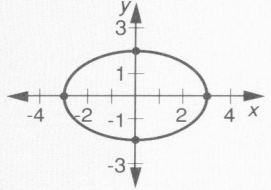
In 3–5, consider the set $\{p, q, r\}$.

3. List all the subsets of $\{p, q, r\}$.
   $\{ \}, \{p\}, \{q\}, \{r\}, \{p, q\}, \{p, r\}, \{q, r\}, \{p, q, r\}$

4. How many subsets are there with the indicated number of elements?
   a. 0 1   **b.** 1 3   **c.** 2 3   **d.** 3 1

5. How many subsets does $\{p, q, r\}$ have? 8

6. Any choice of r objects from n objects is called a(n) __?__.
   combination

7. The symbol $_nC_r$ is another way of writing __?__. $\binom{n}{r}$

8. How many subcommittees of 4 people can be formed from a committee of 10? 210

9. Ten points are in a plane, with no three collinear. How many triangles have these points as vertices? 120

10. **a.** How many triangles have three given points as vertices? 1
    b. Does this agree with the formula for $\binom{n}{r}$? Yes, $\binom{3}{3} = 1$

11. In how many ways can 6 dishes be chosen from a menu with 25 options? 177,100

12. **a.** What is the sum of the entries in row 7 of Pascal's Triangle? 128
    b. What does that have to do with this lesson?
       $128 = 2^7$, the number of subsets for a 7-element set
13. A set with 8 elements has how many subsets? $2^8 = 256$

Applying the Mathematics

14. Simplify: 512
    $_9C_0 + {_9C_1} + {_9C_2} + {_9C_3} + {_9C_4} + {_9C_5} + {_9C_6} + {_9C_7} + {_9C_8} + {_9C_9}$.

15. Copy and complete this pattern.

    | 1 | n |
    | 2 | $n - 1$ |
    | 3 | $n - 2$ |
    | 4 | __?__ $n - 3$ |
    | $\vdots$ | $\vdots$ |
    | r | __?__ $n - r + 1$ |

16. Simplify: $n \cdot (n - 1) \cdot \ldots \cdot (n - r + 1) \cdot ((n - r)!)$. $n!$

17. **a.** Suppose you pick one card from a 52-card playing deck. In how many ways can this be done? 52
    b. Suppose you pick two cards from a 52-card playing deck. In how many ways can this be done? 1326
    c. If you pick 4 cards from the deck, what are the chances of selecting the 4 aces? $\frac{1}{270,725}$

In 18–20, recall that the U.S. Congress consists of 100 senators and 435 representatives.

18. How many five-person Senatorial Committees are possible?
    $\binom{100}{5} = 75,287,520$

19. In how many ways can a "committee of the whole" be chosen in the House of Representatives? **1**

20. What is the total number of committees of any size (except the empty set) which can be formed in the Congress? $2^{535} - 1$

Review

In 21 and 22, expand. *(Lesson 13-6)* **See margin.**

21. $(a + b)^8$

22. $(2x - 3y)^3$

In 23 and 24, use the sequence of rectangles below. The largest rectangle has base 8 and height 6. Each subsequent rectangle is a size change image of the next larger with a magnitude of $\frac{1}{2}$.

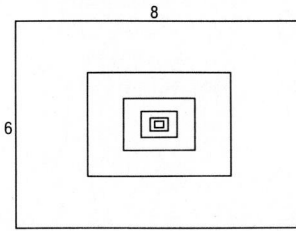

23. What is the sum of the perimeters of the five largest rectangles? *(Lesson 13-2)* **54.25**

24. What is the sum of the perimeters of all the rectangles (assuming the rectangles could be shrunk forever)? *(Lesson 13-4)* **56**

25. A runner, training for a marathon, runs 10 miles one day and then one more mile each day until 20 miles are run in a day. What is the total number of miles run? *(Lesson 13-1)* **165**

26. *Multiple choice* Which symbol does not stand for the sum in Question 25? *(Lesson 13-3)* **a**

(a) $\sum_{n=1}^{10} (n + 9)$ (b) $\sum_{n=10}^{20} n$ (c) $\sum_{n=1}^{11} (n + 9)$ (d) $\sum_{n=0}^{10} (10 + n)$

27. *Multiple choice* Which does not equal the number 2? *(Lesson 9-5)* **c**

(a) $\log 100$ (b) $\log_2 4$ (c) $\log_3 6$ (d) $\log_4 16$

28. **a.** Graph the ellipse with equation $\frac{x^2}{9} + \frac{y^2}{4} = 1$. **See margin.**

b. Where are its foci? *(Lesson 12-4)* $(-\sqrt{5}, 0), (\sqrt{5}, 0)$

See margin.

Exploration

29. In this lesson, the sum of the elements in the *n*th row of Pascal's Triangle was found to be 2^n. Find one or more of these expressions:
a. the sum of the squares of all the elements in the *n*th row of the triangle
b. the total in the *n*th row when alternate minus and plus signs are put between the elements of the row
c. the third element from the end of the *n*th row (i.e., $1 + 3 + 6 + 10 + \ldots$).

MORE PRACTICE
For more questions on SPUR Objectives, use *Lesson Master 13-7*, shown below.

NAME _____

LESSON **MASTER 13–7**
QUESTIONS ON **SPUR** OBJECTIVES

■**SKILLS** *Objective C (See pages 808–811 for objectives.)*
In 1–4, evaluate.
1. $_7C_1$ _____ **7**   2. $_6C_3$ _____ **20**
3. $_{15}C_{15}$ _____ **1**   4. $_9C_0$ _____ **1**

In 5 and 6, consider the set {0, 1, 2, ... , 9}.
5. How many subsets have
a. 1 element? **10**   b. 4 elements? **210**
c. 9 elements? **10**   d. 10 elements? **1**
6. What is the total number of subsets that can be found? **$2^{10} = 1024$**

■**PROPERTIES** *Objective G*
In 7 and 8, consider the top row of Pascal's Triangle to be the 0th row.

7. What is the sum of the numbers in the 6th row? **64**
8. What is the sum of the numbers in the *r*th row? **2^r**

■**USES** *Objective I*
In 9–12, the Mudville student council has 14 members, 6 of whom are sophomores.
9. How many 8-person committees could be formed from all students on the council? **3003**
10. How many 3-person teams could be formed that are made up entirely of sophomores? **20**
11. How many possible committees can be made up entirely of sophomores? (Do not include the empty set.) **63**
12. The entire student council decides to shake hands with everyone else exactly once. How many handshakes will take place? **91**

142 *Advanced Algebra © Scott, Foresman and Company*

781

RESOURCES
■ Lesson Master 13-8
■ Quiz for Lessons 13-5
  Through 13-8
▣ Visual for Teaching Aid 88
  displays the solution to
  Example 1.

OBJECTIVE

I Use combinations or probability to solve problems.

TEACHING NOTES

This lesson can be taught by having students read and do the questions before they come to class. Then go over the questions slowly so that students are able to follow the concepts involved. One situation carefully explained, such as that in **Questions 5 and 6**, will take a good deal of time.

ADDITIONAL EXAMPLES
1. If you guess on a 10-question, true-false exam, what is the probability of getting none of the questions correct?
$\frac{1}{1024}$

2. Imagine that a fair coin is tossed 10 times. If all heads occur, what is the probability of getting heads on the 11th toss?
$\frac{1}{2}$, as it is a fair coin.

3. Suppose the probability of a boy being born in a single birth is 0.5. What is the probability that in a random family with three children, all three children are boys?
$\frac{1}{8}$

LESSON

13-8

Probabilities and Combinations

You have seen applications of Pascal's Triangle to powers of binomials where the elements are called *binomial coefficients*, and to counting subsets where the elements are called *combinations*. Still another important application is to probability, and the elements are called **events.**

Suppose a hat contains 25 slips of paper numbered 1 through 25. As an experiment, you pick a slip blindfolded. The probability of getting the slip numbered 17 is $\frac{1}{25}$. This means that if the experiment is repeated many times, over the long run you could expect the event "getting the 17" to occur about $\frac{1}{25}$ of the time. The probability of getting an even-numbered slip is $\frac{12}{25}$ because there are 12 even-numbered slips.

Definition:

If a situation has a total of t equally likely possibilities and e of these possibilities satisfy conditions for a particular event, then the

$$\text{probability of the event} = \frac{e}{t}.$$

Some probabilities are calculated using combinations.

Example 1   You take a 5-question true-false test on a subject you know nothing about, so you guess. If a question is as likely to be true as false, and you need 75% correct to pass, what is your probability of passing?

782

Solution The equally likely possibilities are the ways you could answer the questions, R (for right) and W (for wrong). For instance, *RRRRW* would mean that you had the first 4 questions right and the last one wrong. There are 32 such possibilities, written here in alphabetical order.

RRRRR	*RWRRR*	*WRRRR*	*WWRRR*
RRRRW	*RWRRW*	*WRRRW*	*WWRRW*
RRRWR	*RWRWR*	*WRRWR*	*WWRWR*
RRRWW	*RWRWW*	*WRRWW*	*WWRWW*
RRWRR	*RWWRR*	*WRWRR*	*WWWRR*
RRWRW	*RWWRW*	*WRWRW*	*WWWRW*
RRWWR	*RWWWR*	*WRWWR*	*WWWWR*
RRWWW	*RWWWW*	*WRWWW*	*WWWWW*

Counting gives the following information.

	Number correct	Probability
1 possibility has 0 *R*s	0	$\frac{1}{32}$
5 possibilities have 1 *R*	1	$\frac{5}{32}$
10 possibilities have 2 *R*s	2	$\frac{10}{32}$
10 possibilities have 3 *R*s	3	$\frac{10}{32}$
5 possibilities have 4 *R*s	4	$\frac{5}{32}$
1 possibility has 5 *R*s	5	$\frac{1}{32}$

In order to pass you must get either 4 or 5 questions right. There are 6 possibilities with either 4 *R*s or 5 *R*s. Since there are 32 possibilities in all, the probability of passing is $\frac{6}{32}$, which is about 0.19 or 19%.

In a True-False test, the same situation—choosing *T* or *F*—occurs again and again. Each such choosing is called a *trial*. The numbers in Pascal's triangle always occur when calculating probabilities involving repeated trials.

Theorem:

If a situation consists of *n* trials with the same two equally likely outcomes for each trial, then the probability of one of these outcomes occurring exactly *r* times is

$$\frac{\binom{n}{r}}{2^n}.$$

Proof

Think of the n trials as slots into which a T or F can be put.

$$\underbrace{\begin{array}{cccccccc} T & T & T & T & & T & T \\ \underline{F} & \underline{F} & \underline{F} & \underline{F} & \cdots & \underline{F} & \underline{F} \end{array}}_{n \text{ trials}}$$

Selecting the r slots where a T is placed is selecting a combination of r elements from n. It can be done in $\binom{n}{r}$ ways. The total number of possible selections equals the total number of subsets, or 2^n. From the definition of probability, the theorem follows.

A **fair** or **unbiased** coin is one with an equal probability of landing on either side. When each trial is the tossing of a fair coin, $\dfrac{\binom{n}{r}}{2^n}$ is the probability of getting r heads in n tosses.

■ ■ ■ ■ ■ ■ ■ ■

Example 2   What is the probability of getting 2 heads in 4 tosses of a fair coin?

Solution 1   If the coin is tossed 4 times, there are 16 possible ways of getting H (heads) and T (tails).

HHHH	HTHH	THHH	(TTHH)
HHHT	(HTHT)	(THHT)	TTHT
HHTH	(HTTH)	(THTH)	TTTH
(HHTT)	HTTT	THTT	TTTT

Of these, $\binom{4}{2}$, or 6, have exactly 2 Hs. They are circled. So $\frac{6}{16}$ is the probability of obtaining 2 heads in 4 tosses of a fair coin.

Solution 2   Use the theorem. The probability of getting exactly 2 heads in 4 tosses of a fair coin is $\dfrac{\binom{4}{2}}{2^4} = \frac{6}{16} = \frac{3}{8}$, or 37.5%.

Many people think the answer to Example 2 is $\frac{1}{2}$. Until the beginnings of the theory of probability were put forth by Pascal and Pierre Fermat in the 17th century, these questions were quite difficult to answer.

Questions

Covering the Reading

In 1–4, slips of paper numbered 1 to 20 are tossed in a hat. One slip is picked out of the hat at random. Give the probability that its number is:

1. 15 $\frac{1}{20}$

2. even $\frac{1}{2}$

3. odd $\frac{1}{2}$

4. prime. $\frac{8}{20} = \frac{2}{5}$

In 5 and 6, a student is given the following test.

Question 1: In 1950, which city had the larger population, Boston or Washington D.C.?
Question 2: Was Joan of Arc born before or after 1400?
Question 3: Which city is farther north, Havana, Cuba, or Mexico City?
Question 4: Who died first, Pascal or Fermat?

5. List all possible ways the test might be corrected. (Assume that all questions are answered.) See margin.

6. Assuming that the student guesses on each item, calculate each probability.
  a. The student gets all 4 correct. $\frac{1}{16}$
  b. The student gets exactly 3 correct. $\frac{4}{16}$
  c. The student gets exactly 2 correct. $\frac{6}{16}$
  d. The student gets exactly 1 correct. $\frac{4}{16}$
  e. The student gets none correct. $\frac{1}{16}$

In 7–9, a fair coin is tossed 6 times. Give the probability of each event.

7. exactly 3 heads $\frac{20}{64}$

8. exactly 2 heads $\frac{15}{64}$

9. 6 heads $\frac{1}{64}$

10. A fair coin is tossed n times. State
  a. the number of ways r tails may occur. a) $\binom{n}{r}$;
  b. the total number of ways the coin may fall. b) 2^n;
  c. the probability of r tails. c) $\dfrac{\binom{n}{r}}{2^n}$

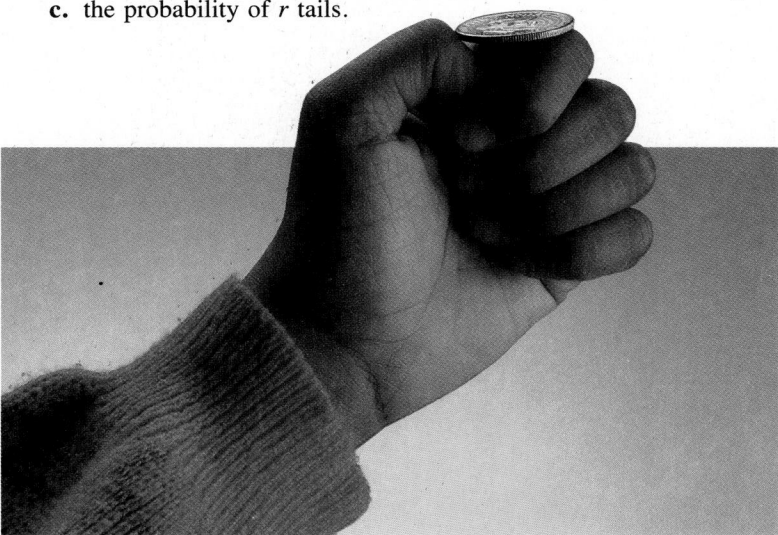

LESSON 13-8 *Probabilities and Combinations* **785**

NOTES ON QUESTIONS
Small Group Work for Questions 5 and 6: We chose these questions assuming that no one in a typical class would know the answers to any of them (though they might have a hunch). Try an experiment. Have students work together in small groups to come up with better guesses. Then have each group go to reference materials to find out the right answers. Conclude the activity by comparing the guesses of groups with the actual results. Does group work increase the number of correct answers?

Questions 13 and 14: Some biology courses study genetics and use probability in more detail than we do here. Ask your students what they have studied about Mendel.

ADDITIONAL ANSWERS
5.
RRRR WRRR RWWR WRWW
RRRW RRWW WWRR WWRW
RRWR RWRW WRWR WWWR
RWRR WRRW RWWW WWWW

11. Give the probabilities of getting 0, 1, 2, ... , 8 heads in 8 tosses of a fair coin. $\frac{1}{256}, \frac{8}{256}, \frac{28}{256}, \frac{56}{256}, \frac{70}{256}, \frac{56}{256}, \frac{28}{256}, \frac{8}{256}, \frac{1}{256}$

12. On a 10 question *true-false* test, what is the probability you will get 8 or more correct
   a. if you guess on all 10 questions? $\frac{56}{1024}$
   b. if you know 4 items and guess on 6 others? $\frac{22}{64} = \frac{11}{32}$

In 13 and 14, Gregor Mendel founded the field of *genetics* in the 19th century by studying the crossbreeding of peas and other plants. Mendel noted that some peas were smooth and others wrinkled. To explain the occurrence of this characteristic, Mendel assumed that each parent pea contributes one *gene* to its offspring and that determines the type of pea produced. The gene determining smoothness is represented as S, and the one for wrinkled is W.

Genes	both S	1S, 1W	both W
Type of pea	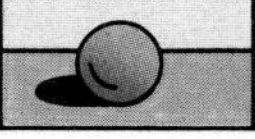	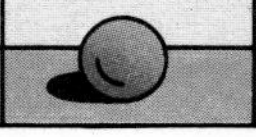	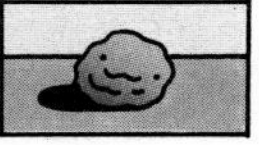

13. The crossbreeding of plants of pure stock in the first generation is shown below.

		gene from 2nd plant	
		W	W
gene from 1st plant	S	SW	SW
	S	SW	SW

The entries in the body of the table show that all peas in the second generation have one S gene and one W gene. In a second-generation cross of pure smooth and pure wrinkled peas, state the probability that the offspring will appear
   a. smooth   1
   b. wrinkled   0

14. Suppose two second generation peas are crossed.

   a. Complete the table below showing the possible genetic makeup of the third generation.

		gene from 2nd plant	
		S	W
gene from 1st plant	S	SS	SW
	W	SW	WW

   b. State the probability that plants in the third-generation will appear
   (i)   smooth $\frac{3}{4}$
   (ii)   wrinkled. $\frac{1}{4}$

786

15. Expand $(p + q)^9$. *(Lesson 13-6)* $p^9 + 9p^8q + 36p^7q^2 + 84p^6q^3 + 126p^5q^4 + 126p^4q^5 + 84p^3q^6 + 36p^2q^7 + 9pq^8 + q^9$

16. How many bridge foursomes can be formed from eight people? *(Lesson 13-7)* **70**

17. Evaluate $\dfrac{\displaystyle\sum_{i=1}^{5} a_i}{5}$ if $a_1 = 3$, $a_2 = 8$, $a_3 = 9$, $a_4 = -7$, and $a_5 = 2$.

(Lesson 13-3) **3**

18. Four positive even integers form an increasing arithmetic sequence. The sum of the integers is 100.
  a. Give the mean of the numbers. **25**
  b. *True or false* The four numbers can be determined exactly. *(Lesson 13-1)* **False**

19. A geometric series has 5 terms, the constant ratio is $\frac{3}{5}$, and the sum is 1441. What is its first term? *(Lesson 13-2)* **625**

20. If $\log n = 5$, what is the value of $\log(n^2)$? *(Lesson 9-6)* **10**

In 21–23, as shown below, three tennis balls with diameter 2.5″ fill a cylindrical can with the same diameter.

21. Find the surface area of one ball. **6.25π in.^{2}**

22. Find the internal surface area of the can. (Include the top and bottom.) **21.875π in.^{2}**

23. What percent of the volume of the can is occupied by the balls? *(Previous course, Lesson 8-1)* **66.$\overline{6}$%**

24. Toss 4 coins and record how many heads appear. Repeat this at least 25 times. How closely do your results agree with what would be predicted by the theorem of this lesson?
Answers will vary. The experimental data should average close to the predicted value of 2.

LESSON 13-8 Probabilities and Combinations **787**

FOLLOW-UP

MORE PRACTICE
For more questions on SPUR Objectives, use *Lesson Master 13-8*, shown below.

EXTENSION
Have students write or present an oral report about the use of probability in genetics.

NAME _____

LESSON **MASTER 13–8**
QUESTIONS ON **SPUR** OBJECTIVES

■USES *Objective I (See pages 808–811 for objectives.)*
In 1–5, suppose a fair coin is tossed 7 times. Calculate the probability of each event.

1. exactly 1 head $\frac{7}{128} = .055$

2. exactly 4 heads $\frac{35}{128} = .273$

3. exactly 3 tails $\frac{35}{128} = .273$

4. 7 heads $\frac{1}{128} = .008$

5. at least 6 tails $\frac{8}{128} = .063$

6. at least 1 head $\frac{127}{128} = .992$

In 7–10, suppose you took a true-false test with the given number of questions and answered each item by guessing. Find the probability of the given event.

7. 5 questions; 3 correct $\frac{5}{16} = .313$

8. 5 questions; none correct $\frac{1}{32} = .031$

9. 12 questions; 1 correct $\frac{12}{4096} = .003$

10. 12 questions; 11 correct $\frac{12}{4096} = .003$

11. On a 10-question, true-false test, what is the probability you will get 7 or more correct

  a. if you guess on all 10 items? $\frac{176}{1024} = .172$

  b. if you know 3 items and guess on the 7 others? $\frac{64}{128} = .5$

Advanced Algebra © Scott, Foresman and Company

143

OBJECTIVES

B Use summation notation to describe statistics.
E Calculate descriptive statistics for a data set.
J Use measures of central tendency or dispersion to describe data.

TEACHING NOTES

Two types of examples are used in this lesson: (1) those that arise from real situations and (2) those that are sets of numbers without a context. We use the latter for quick examples, as in **Question 2**. We use the former to gain information about the data.

Some calculators can keep sums of squares in memory. For these, an alternate form of the s.d. formula is useful.

$$\text{s.d.} = \sqrt{\dfrac{\Sigma S_i^2 - \dfrac{(\Sigma S_i)^2}{n}}{n}}$$

LESSON

13-9

Descriptive Statistics

Ten top students in a school take a college entrance exam and receive the scores shown at the right. These scores make up a *data set*. A **data set** is a set in which an element may be listed more than once.

Suppose you wished to describe these scores quickly. One way is to calculate a single number which in some way describes the entire set of scores. Three common numbers used for this purpose are the *mean*, the *median*, and the *mode*.

College Entrance Scores for Ten Students

750
742
736
725
725
690
662
660
650
640

Data Set I

Definitions:

Let S be a data set of n numbers $\{S_1, S_2, S_3, \ldots, S_n\}$.

mean of S = the *average* of all terms of $S = \dfrac{\sum\limits_{i=1}^{n} S_i}{n}$.

median of S = the *middle* term of S when the terms are placed in increasing order.

mode of S = the number which occurs most often in the sequence.

For the given college entrance test scores, the *mean* score is $\frac{6980}{10} = 698$. The *median* is considered to be the mean of the two middle scores, 690 and 725. So it is 707.5. The *mode* is the most common score, 725.

The mean, median, and mode are called *measures of central tendency* because they are intended to give a number which in some sense is at the "center" of the set. Geometrically, here is how these numbers and measures look on a number line.

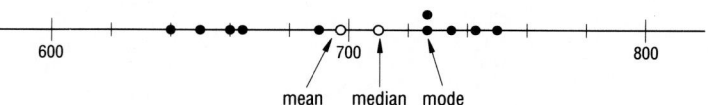

The *mean* is most often used when the terms of the sequence are fairly closely grouped, as in finding bowling averages.

The *median* is used when there are a few low or high terms which could greatly affect the mean, as with personal incomes.

788

The *mode* is particularly useful when the terms are the results of rounding, as often occurs when recording the ages of people.

These three measures of central tendency are examples of *statistical measures*. A **statistical measure** is a single number which is used to describe an entire set of numbers.

Here is a second set of numbers which might be college entrance scores of ten students in a different school.

Compare this set to the previous set of scores. Is this set of scores better?

Actually, the mean, median, and mode are identical to those in the first set. But these scores are more widely *dispersed*, or spread out, than the scores given earlier. One measure of dispersion is *standard deviation*.

College Entrance Scores for Ten Students

| 800 |
| 792 |
| 786 |
| 725 |
| 725 |
| 690 |
| 662 |
| 610 |
| 600 |
| 590 |

725 = mode
707.5 = median
698 = mean

Data Set II

Definition:

Let S be a data set of n numbers $\{S_1, S_2, \ldots, S_n\}$. Let m be the mean of S. Then the **standard deviation** s.d. of S is

$$\text{s.d.} = \sqrt{\frac{\sum_{i=1}^{n}(S_i - m)^2}{n}}.$$

Example Calculate the standard deviation s.d. of the college entrance scores of set II.

Solution Use the formula. The mean m was previously calculated to be 698. The number n of scores is 10.

$$\text{s.d.} = \sqrt{\frac{\sum_{i=1}^{n}(S_i - m)^2}{n}} = \sqrt{\frac{\sum_{i=1}^{10}(S_i - 698)^2}{10}}$$

Question 3: Mean low and mean high temperatures are reported by weather services; they are useful for describing the climate.

Question 5: You could ask students to name other sports in which averages are used. There are many examples: a batting average could be considered as the mean of a set of data in which 1 is recorded for a hit and 0 for an out; there is a golfing average; means of scores are calculated in rating diving events and gymnastics.

Question 10: You might ask: If the store wanted to look good to a prospective employee, which statistic of central tendency should they report for their salaries? (the mean)

ADDITIONAL ANSWERS

6.

S_i	$S_i - 698$	$(S_i - 698)^2$
750	52	2704
742	44	1936
736	38	1444
725	27	729
725	27	729
690	-8	64
662	-36	1296
660	-38	1444
650	-48	2304
640	-58	3364
		Sum = 16014

$$\text{s.d.} = \sqrt{\frac{16014}{10}} =$$

$$\sqrt{1601.4} \approx 40$$

To calculate the sum under the radical, organize your work.

S_i	$S_i - 698$	$(S_i - 698)^2$
800	102	10404
792	94	8836
786	88	7744
725	27	729
725	27	729
690	-8	64
662	-36	1296
610	-88	7744
600	-98	9604
590	-108	11664
		Sum = 58814

$$\text{Thus s.d.} = \sqrt{\frac{\sum_{i=1}^{10}(S_i - 698)^2}{10}} = \sqrt{\frac{58814}{10}} = \sqrt{5881.4} \approx 76.7$$

The steps in finding the standard deviation of a data set are as follows:

Step 1   Calculate the mean of S.
Step 2   Subtract the mean from each term of S.
Step 3   Square these differences.
Step 4   Add up the squares.
Step 5   Divide the sum by n (the number of terms).
Step 6   Find the square root of this quotient.

When this is done for Data Set I,

$$\text{s.d.} = \sqrt{\frac{16014}{10}} = \sqrt{1601.4} \approx 40.0.$$

Note that the standard deviation for Data Set II is larger than the standard deviation for Data Set I. Also, Data Set II is more widely dispersed. In general, the larger the standard deviation, the more widely dispersed are the scores. Although hard to calculate by hand, standard deviations are easily calculated by computers and are very widely used. Some calculators have special keys to calculate standard deviations.

The four measures mentioned in this section—mean, median, mode, and standard deviation—are by no means the only statistical measures in common use. There are many others.

790

Statistics is a large and relatively new branch of mathematics. It has many applications in the social, biological, and physical sciences. In fact, statistical methods have even been used to determine authorship of unsigned writings and to analyze languages. Although you probably know that statistics can be, and have been, used to distort information and mislead people, the wide use of statistical methods indicates the confidence which people have in statistics which are properly used and interpreted.

FOLLOW-UP

MORE PRACTICE
For more questions on SPUR Objectives, use *Lesson Master 13-9,* shown below.

EXTENSION
Have students collect data for the past 10-20 years about some topic of interest, for example, the weather (annual rainfall or snowfall, high or low temperatures for your city); sports (highest batting average, lowest ERA in professional baseball); and so on. Describe the data using the measures of central tendency and dispersion discussed here. Represent the data using bar graphs or some other displays. Write or present orally a brief report on the conclusions that can be made from the data.

Questions

Covering the Reading

1. How does a data set differ from ordinary sets?
   In a data set, an element may be listed more than once.
2. Give the mean, median, and mode of $\{1, 2, 2, 3, 3, 3, 4, 4, 4, 4\}$.
   mean: 3; median: 3; mode: 4
3. Here is a set of low temperatures for an Alaskan city for a week in January: $\{-14, -14, -9, 2, 3, -4, 0\}$. mean: -5.14; median: -4; mode: -14
   a. Give the mean, median, and mode of the data.
   b. Which of these numbers seems most representative of the set?
   median or mean
4. Name a statistic which is not a measure of central tendency.
   standard deviation
5. A person bowls games of 182, 127, 161, and 155.
   a. Which measure of central tendency is usually used to describe bowling scores? mean
   b. Give that measure for this data set. 156.25

6. In the lesson, the standard deviation of Data Set I is reported to be about 40.0. Do the calculations to verify this value, organizing your work as in the example. See margin.

In 7 and 8, calculate the mean and standard deviation of the data set.

7. $\{10, 20, 30, 40, 50\}$
   mean = 30; s.d. ≈ 14.14
8. $\{88, 90, 90, 90, 92\}$
   mean = 90, s.d. ≈ 1.26

9. *Copy and complete* The larger the standard deviation of a data set, the __?__ the numbers in the set are. more spread out

Applying the Mathematics

10. A store has two managers who each earn $35,000 a year, six employees who earn $20,000 a year, and three employees who earn $15,000 a year. Give the mean, median, and mode of the salaries paid by the store. mean ≈ $21,363.64; median = $20,000; mode = $20,000

11. a. Why is *median income* often considered a better indicator of the wealth of a community than *mean income*?
    A few extreme values can affect the mean, but not the median.
    b. Why is the mode income not used at all?
    The most common income will not reflect the wealth of the community.

12. The mean of 2 scores is x and of 3 scores is y. Find the mean if all the scores are considered together. $\dfrac{2x + 3y}{5}$

LESSON 13-9 Descriptive Statistics **791**

13. Calculate the mean and standard deviation of the elements in row 6 of Pascal's Triangle.   mean ≈ 9.14; s.d. ≈ 6.96

14. The mean of three numbers in a geometric sequence is 28. The first number is 12. What might the other numbers be?
24 and 48 or -36 and 108

15. Give an example, different from the one in the lesson, of two different data sets that have the same mean but different standard deviations.
Sample: {10, 10, 10, 10} and {0, 0, 0, 40}

Review

16. Suppose a fair coin is tossed 2 times. What are the probabilities of 0, 1, and 2 heads? *(Lesson 13-8)* $\frac{1}{4}, \frac{1}{2}, \frac{1}{4}$

17. You and two friends in your math class hope to be selected from the 20 students in your class to represent the school. What is the probability that if 3 students are selected from your class at random, it will be you and your friends? *(Lesson 13-8)* $\frac{1}{1140} \approx .000877$

18. How many subsets of $\{V, I, O, L, E, T\}$ contain 4 elements? *(Lesson 13-7)*   15

19. Expand $(x - 2y)^4$. *(Lesson 13-6)* $x^4 - 8x^3y + 24x^2y^2 - 32xy^3 + 16y^4$

20. Suppose y varies as x^4. If x is multiplied by 3, what is the effect on y? *(Lesson 2-3)*   y is multiplied by 3^4 or 81

In 21 and 22, use the graph below.

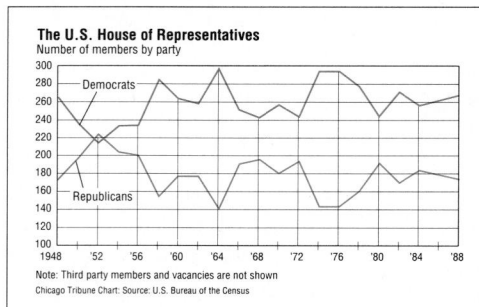

The U.S. House of Representatives
Number of members by party

Note: Third party members and vacancies are not shown
Chicago Tribune Chart: Source: U.S. Bureau of the Census

21. The graph has an approximate line of symmetry. What is an equation for that line of symmetry and why does the graph have this property?
x = 220; the total number in the House is 435.

22. In what year did the Republicans gain the most members in the House?   1966

Exploration

23. a. The graph in Questions 21 and 22 is called misleading by some people because the y-axis begins at 100, not 0. How would beginning at 0 affect the graph?   See margin.
b. Find an example of a misleading graph and tell why it seems to be misleading.   Many possible answers
c. Find an example of an interesting effective graph in a newspaper or other source, and tell what makes it interesting and effective.
Many possible answers

Binomial and Normal Distributions

If a fair coin is tossed 5 times, the probabilities of getting 0, 1, 2, 3, 4, or 5 heads can be graphed. These values are given in the table in Example 1 of Lesson 13-8.

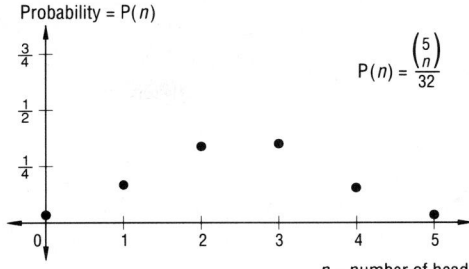

Let P(n) = the probability of n heads in 5 tosses of a fair coin. Then $P(n) = \frac{1}{32}\binom{5}{n}$. We call P a *probability function*. A **probability function** or **probability distribution** is a function which maps a set of events onto their probabilities.

If a fair coin is tossed 10 times, the possible numbers of heads are 0, 1, 2, ... , 10, so there are 11 points in the graph of the corresponding probability function. P(x), the probability of x heads, is

$$\frac{\binom{10}{x}}{1024},$$

as given by the theorem of Lesson 13-8. The 11 probabilities are easy to calculate because the numerators in the fractions are the numbers in the 10th row of Pascal's triangle. That is, they are binomial coefficients.

Number of heads	0	1	2	3	4	5
Probability	$\frac{1}{1024}$	$\frac{10}{1024}$	$\frac{45}{1024}$	$\frac{120}{1024}$	$\frac{210}{1024}$	$\frac{252}{1024}$

Number of heads	6	7	8	9	10
Probability	$\frac{210}{1024}$	$\frac{120}{1024}$	$\frac{45}{1024}$	$\frac{10}{1024}$	$\frac{1}{1024}$

For this reason, the function graphed at the top of the next page is called a **binomial probability distribution,** or simply, a **binomial distribution.**

LESSON 13-10 Binomial and Normal Distributions   **793**

LESSON 13-10

RESOURCES
■ Lesson Master 13-10
▣ Visual for Teaching Aid 90 displays the binomial and normal distributions for 10 tosses of a fair coin.
▣ Visual for Teaching Aid 91 displays the standardized SAT and IQ scores.

OBJECTIVES

J Use measures of central tendency or dispersion to describe distributions.
L Graph and analyze binomial and normal distributions.

TEACHING NOTES

Reading This is a lesson in which questions and reading might be discussed together. You might read the first paragraph and then ask **Question 1**. Read the second and third paragraphs, and then ask **Questions 2 and 3**. Next, read through the graph of test scores and ask **Questions 4 and 5**. Finally, read the rest of the lesson and ask the other questions covering the reading.

Point out to students that IQ scores are rather unreliable. They seem to test a particular kind of knowledge and certainly do not measure all forms of ability or intelligence. They are certainly influenced by education and they can be raised by special training. Despite these shortcomings, there are still many people who put much credence into these scores.

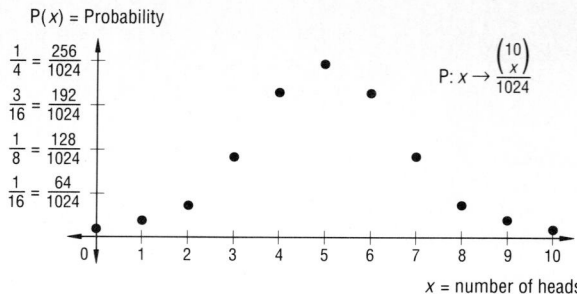

Examine this 11-point graph closely. The individual probabilities are all less than $\frac{1}{4}$. Notice how unlikely it is to get no heads or 10 heads in a row (the probability for each is less than $\frac{1}{1000}$). Even for 9 heads in 10 tosses the probability is less than $\frac{1}{100}$.

There are not enough points in the first (6-point) graph to see any pattern emerging. But the points of the 11-point binomial distribution could be connected by a fairly smooth curve. As the number of tosses is increased, lower rows in Pascal's triangle will give the probabilities, and the points more closely outline a curve shaped like a bell.

Below is the bell-shaped curve in the position where its equation is simplest—symmetric to the y-axis with y-intercept $\frac{1}{\sqrt{2\pi}}$.

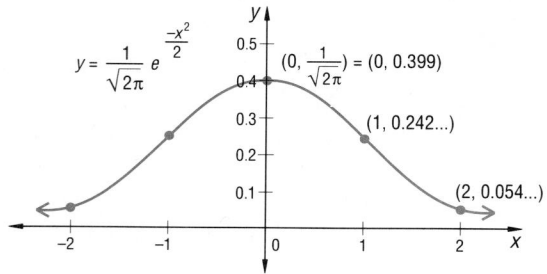

The function which determines this graph is called a **normal distribution**, and the curve is called a **normal curve**. Notice that its equation, shown on the graph, involves the constants $e \approx 2.718$ and $\pi \approx 3.14$. Every normal curve is the image of the above graph under a composite of translations or scale transformations.

Normal curves are models for many natural phenomena. The graph of the correspondence below would be very close to a normal curve.

$$\text{height to the nearest inch} \rightarrow \text{number of men in the U.S. with that height}$$

The curve would have its highest point around 5′ 10″ or 5′ 11″.

794

Normal curves are often good mathematical models for the distribution of scores on an exam. The graph below shows an actual distribution of scores on a 40-question test given by one of the authors to 209 geometry students. (It was a hard test!) A possible corresponding normal curve is shown in black dashes.

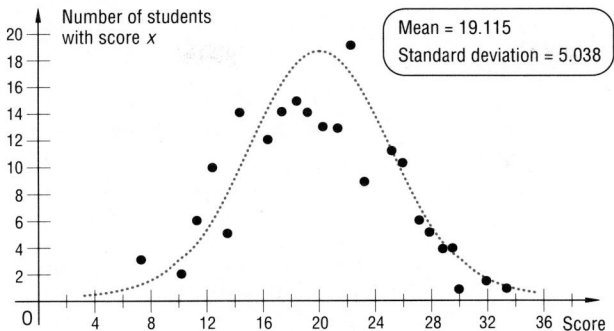

For other tests, the scores are *standardized* or *normalized*. This means that a person's score is not the number of correct answers, but some score chosen so that the distribution of scores is a normal curve.

SAT scores were standardized so that the original mean was 500 and the standard deviation was 100. Many IQ tests are normalized so that the mean IQ is 100 and the standard deviation is 15. One advantage of normalizing scores is that you need to know no other scores to know how a person's score compares with the scores of others.

The next graph shows percentages of scores in certain intervals of a normal distribution with mean *m* and standard deviation *s*. (An equation is also given.) Each percentage gives the probability of scoring in a particular interval. Actual values for endpoints of these intervals are given below the graph for particular applications.

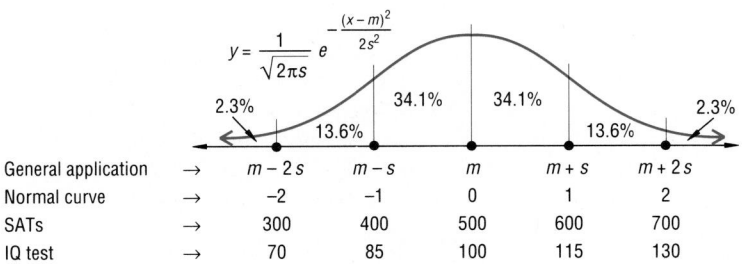

		$m-2s$	$m-s$	m	$m+s$	$m+2s$
General application	→	$m-2s$	$m-s$	m	$m+s$	$m+2s$
Normal curve	→	−2	−1	0	1	2
SATs	→	300	400	500	600	700
IQ test	→	70	85	100	115	130

The graph indicates that about 34.1% of IQ's are between 100 and 115. Thus, about 68.2% of the IQ scores are within one standard deviation of the mean. Other information may be similarly read from the graph.

Question 12: Because of the ways in which grade level tests are standardized, they do not usually give an accurate reading. For instance, a 7th grader who is scoring at the 11th grade level in mathematics would likely do very poorly on a test of 11th grade mathematics. The score means that this 7th grader is in a high percentile of all 7th graders.

Question 13: Certain states in the U.S. are "SAT (Scholastic Aptitude Test) states." Others are "ACT (American College Testing) states." Often people in these states are surprised that the test most of their students take is not taken by more students in all states. Generally, the center of the country is more ACT, while the coasts are more SAT.

Small Group Work for Question 25: The exploration could be done by arranging the class into groups of four or five students. The results of all groups can be combined to answer the questions. It also could be simulated on computer.

ADDITIONAL ANSWERS
10.

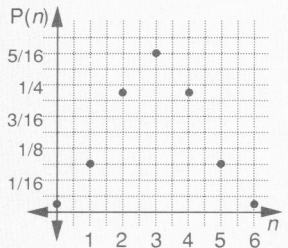

Questions

Covering the Reading

1. Let $P(n) = \dfrac{\binom{5}{n}}{32}$. $\frac{5}{16}$ It could represent the probability of getting 3 heads in 5 tosses of a fair coin.
   a. Calculate P(3) and indicate what it could represent.
   b. What kind of function is P?   a probability function

2. a. What is the domain of the function P: $x \to \dfrac{\binom{10}{x}}{1024}$ graphed in this lesson?   whole numbers 0 through 10, inclusive
   b. What is the range of this function?
      rational numbers $\frac{1}{1024}, \frac{10}{1024}, \frac{45}{1024}, \frac{120}{1024}, \frac{210}{1024},$ and $\frac{252}{1024}$

3. If a fair coin is tossed 10 times, what is the probability of getting exactly 5 heads? $\frac{252}{1024}$

4. Give the simplest equation for a normal curve. $y = \dfrac{1}{\sqrt{2\pi}} e^{-x^2/2}$

5. Give one application of normal curves.   analyzing scores on an exam

6. a. What does it mean for scores to be standardized?
      The distribution of scores is a normal curve.
   b. What is one advantage of doing this?   You do not need to know other scores to compare the individual's score to the population.

7. Approximately what percent of people score above 700 on SAT tests?   2.3%

8. Approximately what percent of people have IQs below 85?   15.9%

9. Approximately what percent of scores on a normal curve are within one standard deviation of the mean?   68.2%

Applying the Mathematics

10. Let P(n) = the probability of n heads in 6 tosses of a fair coin. Graph P.   See margin.

11. If you tossed a fair coin 10 times, about what percent of the time would you expect to get from 4 heads to 6 heads?   ≈66%

12. Some tests are standardized so that the mean is the grade level at which the test is taken and the standard deviation is 1 grade level. So, for students who take a test at the beginning of 10th grade, the mean is 10.0 and the standard deviation is 1.0.
    a. On such a test taken at the beginning of grade 10, what percent of students would be expected to score below 8.0 grade level?   2.3%
    b. If a test is taken in the middle of 8th grade (grade level 8.5), what percent of students score between 7.5 and 10.5?   81.8%

13. ACT scores range from 1 to 35 with a mean near 19 and a standard deviation near 6. What percent of students have an ACT score above 25?   15.9%

14. Let $y = \dfrac{1}{\sqrt{2\pi}} e^{-x^2/2}$. Estimate y to the nearest thousandth when x = 1.5.   .130

796

15. *Copy and complete* In a normal distribution, 0.13% of the scores lie more than 3 standard deviations away from the mean (in each direction). This implies that 1 out of __?__ people has an IQ over __?__.
769; 145

16. Find the mean, median, mode, and standard deviation of these scores. *(Lesson 13-9)*

$$83, 85, 88, 92, 92$$

mean = 88; median = 88; mode = 92; s.d. ≈ 3.6

17. Beginning with an equilateral triangle with sides of length 1 unit, new triangles are formed by connecting the midpoints of the sides of previous triangles. What is the sum of the perimeters of all triangles formed? *(Lesson 13-4)*   6

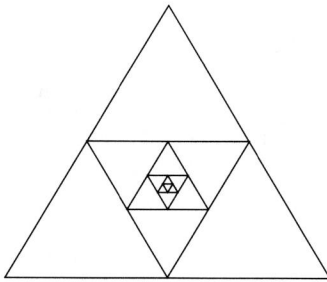

In 18 and 19, evaluate. *(Lesson 13-5)*

18. $\binom{15}{12}$ 455

19. $_nC_0$ 1

20. Expand $(1 - x^2)^3$. *(Lesson 13-6)* $1 - 3x^2 + 3x^4 - x^6$

21. *True or false* The probability of getting exactly 25 heads in 50 tosses of a fair coin is less than $\frac{1}{10}$. *(Lesson 13-8)*   True

In 22 and 23, solve (a) exactly; (b) to the nearest hundredth. *(Lessons 6-6, 9-9)*

22. $3^x = 10$ a) $\dfrac{\log 10}{\log 3}$; b) 2.10

23. $5x^2 + 3x = 10$ a) $\dfrac{-3 \pm \sqrt{209}}{10}$ b) 1.15 or -1.75

24. a. Graph $\{(x, y): x^2 + (y - 5)^2 = 1\}$.   See margin.
   b. Describe in words the graph of $\{(x, y): x^2 + (y - 5)^2 < 1\}$.
   (Lessons 12-1, 12-2)   Interior of a circle with center (0, 5) and radius 1.

25. Together with some other students, toss 25 coins and count the number of heads, but do this at least 200 times. Let $P(h)$ = the number of times h heads appear.   Answers will vary.
   a. How close is $P(h)$ to a normal distribution?
   b. What is the mean of the distribution (the mean number of heads)?
   c. Estimate the standard deviation of the distribution.

LESSON 13-10 Binomial and Normal Distributions   **797**

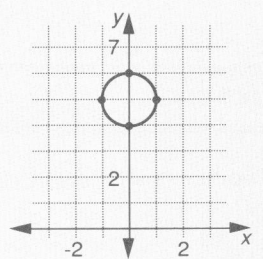
NAME _____

MASTER   13–10
QUESTIONS ON **SPUR** OBJECTIVES

■ **USES**   *Objective J (See pages 808–811 for objectives.)*
In 1–4, ACT scores range from 1 to 35 with a mean near 19 and a standard deviation near 6. Assume the scores are normally distributed.

1. About what percent of students have a score above 19?   50%
2. About what percent of students have a score below 13?   16%
3. What percent of students have a score above 31?   2.3%
4. Within what interval would you expect the middle 68% of the scores to occur?   from 13 to 25

■ **REPRESENTATIONS**   *Objective L*
In 5 and 6, consider the probability function $P(n) = \dfrac{\binom{7}{n}}{2^7}$.
5. Complete the table of values below and graph the function.

n	0	1	2	3	4	5	6	7
P(n)	.01	.05	.16	.27	.27	.16	.05	.01

6. What is the name given to this function?   normal dist.

In 7–9, consider the normal distribution with mean 10 and standard deviation 2 pictured at the right.

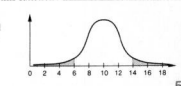

7. What percent of the data are greater than 10?   50%
8. About what percent of the data are between 8 and 12?   68.2%
9. **a.** Shade the portion(s) of the graph representing data more than two standard deviations away from 10.
   b. About what percent of the data should you have shaded?   5%

145

RESOURCES
■ Lesson Master 13-11
▣ Visual for Teaching Aid 92 provides a random number table.

OBJECTIVE

K Give reasons for sampling.

TEACHING NOTES

This is a reading and discussion lesson. You might ask if any student's household has been contacted for some sort of poll. Many households have at one time or another been contacted, either by political parties, manufacturers of consumer goods, or by TV ratings firms.

You might have students act as pollsters on an issue of concern to them. Some typical neighborhood issues are whether people want stoplights at a particular intersection or whether some old building should be torn down.

LESSON

13-11

Polls and Sampling

In a large school with 510 seniors, the administration wanted to know the percent of seniors who owned cars. The principal walked into a senior homeroom and polled the 25 seniors there. Four of the students said they owned cars. Since $\frac{4}{25} = 16\%$, the principal concluded that about 16% of the seniors in the school owned cars. The principal made an inference based on *sampling*.

In sampling the **population** is the set of all people or events or items that could be sampled. The **sample** is the subset of the population actually studied. Above, the population is the set of 510 seniors. The sample is the set of 25 seniors polled by the principal.

■ ■ ■ ■ ■ ■ ■ ■

Example 1   A company is testing light bulbs to see how long they shine before burning out. What is the sample and what is the population?

Solution   The population is the set of all light bulbs that could be tested, perhaps all the light bulbs that have been or will be made by this company. The sample is the set of light bulbs actually tested.

The principal could have polled all seniors, but perhaps there was no time. Sampling is often used to save time. However, in Example 1, sampling is absolutely necessary because testing destroys the light bulbs. Hence the manufacturer cannot sample all light bulbs.

Sampling is also necessary when the population is infinite. For instance, suppose a coin is tossed 100 times to determine whether or not it is fair. The population is the infinite set of all tosses that could be made. The sample is the set of 100 tosses actually used.

A use of sampling familiar to you is in getting ratings of television programs. Ratings are percents of households tuned to the program. The higher the rating for a program, the more a television station

798

can charge for advertising, so the more money the station earns. Because there are so many people who watch television, polling everyone would be too costly. So ratings companies use a sample of households, usually from 1000 to 3000 in number. The population for TV ratings is the set of all households with televisions. If 23.1% of all households sampled are tuned to a particular show, then the rating is 23.1.

The reliability of a sample depends on its being representative of the population. The only sure way to make it representative is for each element of the population to have the same probability of being selected for the sample. We then call the sample a **random sample.** If seniors in the school described above are assigned to homerooms according to extracurricular interests, the principal's sample may not have been a random sample. Coin tossing is closer to random.

TV stations often want to split the ratings sample to determine whether teenagers or senior citizens or other groups are watching. (Advertisers may be aiming their products at these groups.) Random sampling may not give them enough people in each of these smaller samples. So they *stratify* the sample, often by age. A **stratified sample** is a sample in which the population has first been split into subpopulations and then, from each subpopulation, a sample is selected. A **stratified random sample** occurs when the smaller samples are chosen randomly from the subpopulations.

How many ways can a sample be chosen? What is the probability that a sample will have particular characteristics? How large must a sample be in order to give accurate results? The answers involve Pascal's triangle and the normal distribution.

To see this, examine the table on page 801. This table is part of a larger **table of random numbers,** so called because it was constructed so that each digit from 0 to 9 has the same probability of being selected, each pair of digits from 00 to 99 has the same probability of being there, each triple of digits from 000 to 999 has the same probability of being there, and so on.

You can use this table of random numbers to *simulate* what the principal might find if 20% of the seniors actually owned cars. Think of each senior as being represented by a digit. To simulate the 20%, a 0 or 1 will mean that the senior owns a car. A digit of 2 through 9 means the senior does not.

To use such a table, you must start randomly as well. With your eyes closed, point to a pair of digits on the page; use that pair as the row. Then point again to a pair of digits; use that pair as the column. For instance if you point to 32 and then to 07, start at the 32nd row, 7th column. If you point to a pair of digits whose number does not refer to a row or column, ignore that and point again.

ADDITIONAL EXAMPLES
In 1–3, explain why a sample is needed.

1. A survey is taken to determine whether residents of a city want a new waste disposal plant.
sample: It is too time-consuming to ask every resident.

2. A cook samples the hors d'oeuvres before they are placed out for the guests at a party.
sample: If the cook ate every hors d'oeuvres, there would be none left for the guests!

3. A coin is tossed 100 times to determine whether it is fair enough to be used in a game.
sample: It is impossible to toss a coin infinitely many times.

4. Give a situation in which stratified sampling might be used.
sample: when you think the views of people might differ by age, sex, race, income group, etc.

Now suppose you begin at the digit in the 32nd row, 7th column. It is a 7. Examining the next 25 numbers is like going into a homeroom and asking 25 seniors whether they own a car. Now choose a direction to go in—up, down, left or right—perhaps by rolling a die. We go right. The next 25 numbers are 6, 2, 2, 2, 3, 6, 0, 8, 6, 8, 4, 6, 3, 7, 9, 3, 1, 6, 1, 7, 6, 0, 3, 8, 6. Since 4 of the digits are either 0 or 1, in this sample 4 seniors own a car. If there are 510 digits (seniors) to choose from, there are $\binom{510}{25}$ potential samples, a *very* large number (over 10^{42}). These samples would have from 0 to 25 seniors who own cars, but more of them will have 5 seniors than any other any number of seniors. Slightly fewer samples will have 4 or 6 seniors. Again slightly fewer will have 3 or 7 seniors. A small percentage of the 10^{42} possible samples will have 0 seniors and a very, very tiny percentage near 25 seniors.

Let P(x) be the probability that a sample of 25 from 510 random digits contains x digits that are 0s or 1s. That is, P(x) = the probability that a sample contains x seniors with cars. A famous theorem from statistics, called the *Central Limit Theorem,* states that the function P is very closely approximated by a normal distribution whose mean is 20% (the mean of the population) and whose standard deviation is $\sqrt{25 \cdot 20\% \cdot 80\%}$, which in this case is 2.

Central Limit Theorem:

> Suppose random samples of size *n* are chosen from a population of events in which the probability of an event having a certain characteristic is *p*. Let P(x) equal the number of elements in that sample with the characteristic. Then P is approximated by a normal distribution with mean *np* and standard deviation $\sqrt{np(1 - p)}$.

That function is graphed here.

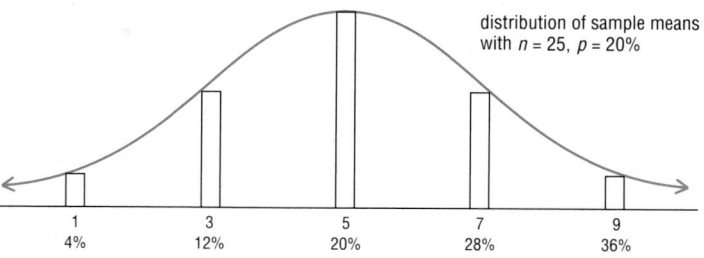

distribution of sample means
with *n* = 25, *p* = 20%

1	3	5	7	9
4%	12%	20%	28%	36%

Random Number Table

col. row	1	2	3	4	5	6	7	8	9	10	11	12	13	14
1	10480	15011	01536	02011	81647	91646	69719	14194	62590	36207	20969	99570	91291	90700
2	22368	46573	25595	85393	30995	89198	27982	53402	93965	34095	52666	19174	39615	99505
3	24130	48360	22527	97265	76393	64809	15179	24830	49340	32081	30680	19655	63348	58629
4	42167	93093	06423	61680	17856	16376	39440	53537	71341	57004	00849	74917	97758	16379
5	37570	39975	81837	16656	06121	91782	60468	81305	49684	60672	14110	06927	01263	54613
6	77921	06907	11008	42751	27756	53498	18602	70659	90655	15053	21916	81825	44394	42880
7	99562	72905	56420	69994	98872	31016	71194	18738	44013	48840	63213	21069	10634	12952
8	96301	91977	05463	07972	18876	20922	94595	56869	69014	60045	18425	84903	42508	32307
9	89579	14342	63661	10281	17453	18103	57740	84378	25331	12566	58678	44947	05585	56941
10	85475	36857	43342	53988	53060	59533	38867	62300	08158	17983	16439	11458	18593	64952
11	28918	69578	88231	33276	70997	79936	56865	05859	90106	31595	01547	85590	91610	78188
12	63553	40961	48235	03427	49626	69445	18663	72695	52180	20847	12234	90511	33703	90322
13	09429	93969	52636	92737	88974	33488	36320	17617	30015	08272	84115	27156	30613	74952
14	10365	61129	87529	85689	48237	52267	67689	93394	01511	26358	85104	20285	29975	89868
15	07119	97336	71048	08178	77233	13916	47564	81056	97735	85977	29372	74461	28551	90707
16	51085	12765	51821	51259	77452	16308	60756	92144	49442	53900	70960	63990	75601	40719
17	02368	21382	52404	60268	89368	19885	55322	44819	01188	65255	64835	44919	05944	55157
18	01011	54092	33362	94904	31272	04146	18594	29852	71585	85030	51132	01915	92747	64951
19	52162	53916	46369	58586	23216	14513	83149	98736	23495	64350	94738	17752	35156	35749
20	07056	97628	33787	09998	42698	06691	76988	13602	51851	46104	88916	19509	25625	58104
21	48663	91245	85828	14346	09172	30168	90229	04734	59193	22178	30421	61666	99904	32812
22	54164	58492	22421	74103	47070	25306	76468	26384	58151	06646	21524	15227	96909	44592
23	32639	32363	05597	24200	13363	38005	94342	28728	35806	06912	17012	64161	18296	22851
24	29334	27001	87637	87308	58731	00256	45834	15398	46557	41135	10367	07684	36188	18510
25	02488	33062	28834	07351	19731	92420	60952	61280	50001	67658	32586	86679	50720	94953
26	81525	72295	04839	96423	24878	82651	66566	14778	76797	14780	13300	87074	79666	95725
27	29676	20591	68086	26432	46901	20849	89768	81536	86645	12659	92259	57102	80428	25280
28	00742	57392	39064	66432	84673	40027	32832	61362	98947	96067	64760	64584	96096	98253
29	05366	04213	25669	26422	44407	44048	37937	63904	45766	66134	75470	66520	34693	90449
30	91921	26418	64117	94305	26766	25940	39972	22209	71500	64568	91402	42416	07844	69618
31	00582	04711	87917	77341	42206	35126	74087	99547	81817	42607	43808	76655	62028	76630
32	00725	69884	62797	56170	86324	88072	76222	36086	84637	93161	76038	65855	77919	88006
33	69011	65797	95876	55293	18988	27354	26575	08625	40801	59920	29841	80150	12777	48501
34	25976	57948	29888	88604	67917	48708	18912	82271	65424	69774	33611	54262	85963	03547
35	09763	83473	73577	12908	30883	18317	28290	35797	05998	41688	34952	37888	38917	88050
36	91567	42595	27958	30134	04024	86385	29880	99730	55536	84855	29080	09250	79656	73211
37	17955	56349	90999	49127	20044	59931	06115	20542	18059	02008	73708	83517	36103	42791
38	46503	18584	18845	49618	02304	51038	20655	58727	28168	15475	56942	53389	20562	87338
39	92157	89634	94824	78171	84610	82834	09922	25417	44137	48413	25555	21246	35509	20468
40	14577	62665	35605	81263	39667	47358	56873	56307	61607	49518	89656	20103	77490	18062

Recall the percents within given standard deviations for a normal distribution. If 20% of the seniors own cars and this principal polled 25 seniors at random, about 68% of the time the principal would find that from 3 to 7 seniors in the sample owned cars. That is what happened here. In these cases, the principal would infer that 12% to 28% of the seniors owned cars. That isn't too far off even with a sample of 25. About 95% of the time the principal would infer that from 1 to 9 seniors in the sample (between 4% and 36% of the sample) owned cars. That's a wider interval, but the principal could be 95% confident of the results.

Now let us turn to the TV polling example. Suppose that in reality 20% of households are tuned in to a particular show. Consider all the random samples of 1600 people. These samples will have a mean of 320 people (20%) tuned to the show. The standard deviation of these samples is $\sqrt{1600 \cdot 20\% \cdot 80\%}$, or 16. That means that 68% of the time the samples will have between 304 and 336 people (between 19% and 21%) watching the show. The sample percentage will be within 1% of the actual. Also, 95% of the time the sample will have between 288 and 352 watching the show; that is, between 18% and 22%. So 95% of the time, the sample is within 2% of the actual amount. This accuracy is probably good enough for the networks.

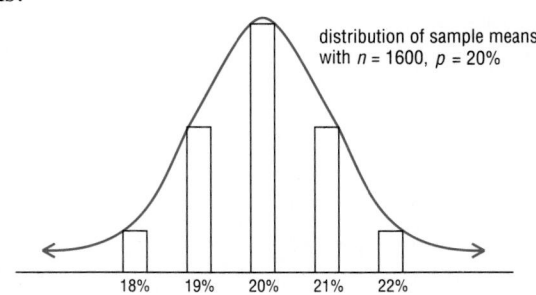

distribution of sample means
with $n = 1600$, $p = 20\%$

18% 19% 20% 21% 22%

Questions

Covering the Reading

1. Give two reasons for sampling.   the population may be infinite; sampling may destroy the element; polling everyone may be too expensive.

In 2 and 3, identify the population and the sample in the sampling situation.

2. sampling to obtain TV ratings
all TV watchers; the people who report what they watch

3. polling potential voters to see which candidate is favored
all potential voters; the people who are asked questions

4. What is the size of the samples often used in TV ratings?
usually from 1000 to 3000 households

5. What is the difference between a random sample and one that is not random?   In a random sample, every element of the population has an equal chance of being selected for the sample.

6. Why are stratified samples often used to obtain TV ratings?
Advertisers want information based on specific age groups.

7. What does a TV rating of 18.6 mean?
18.6% of all households with TVs are tuned in to a particular show.

8. *Copy and complete*   If 1600 people are polled randomly for TV ratings, 68% of the time the rating will be within _?_% of the actual percent of people watching the program.   1

802

9. *Multiple choice* In this lesson, 20% of a senior class of 510 owned cars. The principal walked into a class and found that 4 of 25, or 16% of the seniors he polled, owned cars. What is the *best* reason that the percents are not equal? **b**
   a. The sample was not random.
   b. Sample percents vary.
   c. Students may not have been telling the truth.

10. Means of samples of size n, from a distribution in which the probability of a characteristic is p, approximate a normal distribution with what mean and what standard deviation?
    mean = np; s.d. = $\sqrt{np(1-p)}$

Applying the Mathematics

In 11 and 12, a fair coin is tossed 1000 times.

11. The mean number of heads in such samples is __?__ and the standard deviation is __?__.   **500; 15.8**

12. This implies that 68% of the time, from __?__ to __?__ heads are expected.   **484; 516**

In 13 and 14, consider that in BASIC a function named RND generates random numbers with decimal values between 0 and 1. RND always has the argument 1 so in programs you must use RND(1) to generate such a number.   **See margin.**

13. **a.** Run this program and describe its output.

```
10   FOR N = 1 TO 10
20       PRINT RND(1)
30   NEXT N
40   END
```

   b. Run the program again and write a sentence or two comparing its output to that in part a.

14. The following program simulates tossing a coin.

```
10   REM COIN TOSS SIMULATION
20   REM NMTOS = NUMBER OF TOSSES
30   REM X = A RANDOM NUMBER
40   REM H = NUMBER OF HEADS, T = NUMBER OF TAILS
50   INPUT "HOW MANY TOSSES"; NMTOS
60   FOR I = 1 TO NMTOS
70       LET X = RND(1)
80       IF X < .5 THEN H = H+1 ELSE T = T+1
90   NEXT I
100  PRINT H; "HEADS AND"; T; "TAILS"
110  END
```

   a. Run the program for 50 tosses, and record the output.
   b. Run the program for 500 tosses, and record the output.
   c. Calculate the percent heads and percent tails for each run above. Which run more closely approximates the probability of getting a head on a toss of one coin?

FOLLOW-UP

MORE PRACTICE
For more questions on SPUR Objectives, use *Lesson Master 13-11*, shown below.

ADDITIONAL ANSWERS
13.a. Answers will vary; lists of 10 random numbers.
b. Each output should be different.

14.a. Program will state how many heads and tails there were; example: 27 heads, 23 tails.
b. Same as part (a), except the total will be 500 tosses, not 50 tosses.
c. the second run

NAME _____

LESSON **MASTER   13–11**
QUESTIONS ON **SPUR** OBJECTIVES

■ **USES**   *Objective K   (See pages 808–811 for objectives.)*
In 1 and 2, consider a school election in which each of the freshmen, sophomore, junior, and senior classes elect a class president. Suppose Darrell, a sophomore, had a poll taken to find out how his campaign was going.

1. What is the population in this situation? __sophomores__

2. Describe two different ways the poll could be conducted?
   (a) poll a random sample
   (b) poll entire sophomore class

In 3–7, complete.

3. Give at least one reason why using a random sample might be preferred over studying an entire population.
   __population may be infinite__

4. Give at least one situation when using a random sample is not advantageous.
   __when population is very small__

5. If 800 people are selected at random and asked if they would vote for a candidate, 68% of the time the rating will be within __1__ % of the actual percent of the candidates' supporters.

6. In numerous samples, a coin that is thought to be fair is tossed 500 times. The mean number of heads in such samples is __250__ and the standard deviation is __85__. This implies that 68% of the time, from __165__ to __335__ heads are expected.

7. In Question 6 above, 95% of the time from __80__ to __420__ heads are expected.

146   *Advanced Algebra © Scott, Foresman and Company*

803

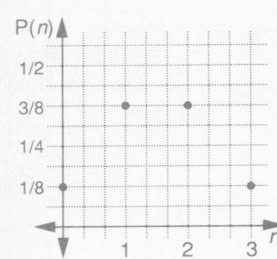

15. You call a classmate to find out if he or she thinks there will be a test on Chapter 13 next Friday. What is the population and what is the sample? **the class; the classmate you called**

Review

16. Construct a data set whose mean is 10, whose median is 9, and whose mode is 8. *(Lesson 13-9)* **Sample: 8, 8, 9, 10, 15**

17. Give the standard deviation of the data set $\{2, 4, 6, 8, 10, 12, 14, 16, 18\}$. *(Lesson 13-9)* **≈4.9**

18. Graph the binomial distribution for tossing a fair coin 3 times. *(Lesson 13-10)* **See margin.**

19. What is the probability of answering exactly 5 questions correctly on a 6-question test in which you have a 50% chance of getting each question correct? *(Lesson 13-8)* $\frac{6}{2^6} = \frac{3}{32}$

20. *True or false* Justify your answer. $3\left(\sum_{n=1}^{4} n^2\right) = \sum_{n=1}^{4} (3n^2)$. *(Lesson 13-3)*
True; 3(1 + 4 + 9 + 16) = 3(1) + 3(4) + 3(9) + 3(16)

21. If $2x = 45$, what is x? *(Lesson 9-9)* **22.5**

22. Solve: $t^{-1/2} = 81$. *(Lesson 8-10)* $\frac{1}{9}$

23. Find equations for two parabolas congruent to $y = x^2$ and having vertex $(6, 5)$. *(Lesson 6-4)* $y - 5 = (x - 6)^2, y - 5 = -(x - 6)^2$

24. Simplify $\sqrt{4} \cdot \sqrt{9} + \sqrt{-4} \cdot \sqrt{9} + \sqrt{-4} \cdot \sqrt{-9} + \sqrt{4} \cdot \sqrt{-9}$. *(Lessons 6-1, 6-8)* **12i**

25. Give an equation for the right angle graphed here. *(Lesson 7-5)* $x = |y|$

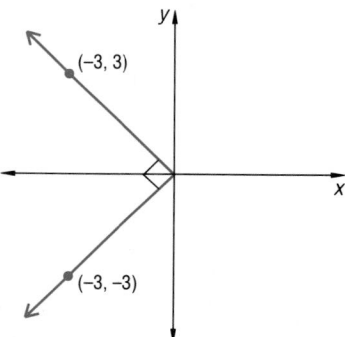

Exploration

26. Sample at least 25 people on controversial issues of concern to you. From the size of your sample and the results you find, make reasonable inferences using the Central Limit Theorem. **Answers will vary.**

804

Summary

A series is an indicated sum of terms of a sequence. The sum $x_1 + x_2 + \ldots + x_n$ can be represented by $\sum_{i=1}^{n} x_i$. Values of finite arithmetic (linear) sequences and of finite and infinite geometric (exponential) sequences may be calculated from the following formulas.

In an arithmetic sequence $a_1, a_2, \ldots, a_n$ with common difference d:

$$S_n = \sum_{i=1}^{n} a_i = \tfrac{1}{2}n(a_1 + a_n) = \frac{n}{2}[2a_1 + (n-1)d]$$

In a geometric sequence $g_1, g_2, \ldots, g_n$ with common ratio r:

$$S_n = \sum_{i=1}^{n} g_1 = g_1 \frac{(1 - r^n)}{1 - r}$$

If $|r| < 1$ then the infinite geometric series with first term g_1 and common ratio r has the value

$$S = \sum_{n=1}^{\infty} g_1 r^{n-1} = \frac{g_1}{1 - r}.$$

Pascal's Triangle is a 2-dimensional sequence. The $(r + 1)$st element in the nth row is denoted by $\binom{n}{r} = \frac{n!}{r!(n-r)!}$. The expression $\binom{n}{r}$, also denoted $_nC_r$, appears in several other important applications. It is the coefficient of $a^{n-r}b^r$ in the binomial expansion of $(a + b)^n$. It is the number of subsets, or combinations, with r elements taken from a set with n elements. And if a situation consists of n trials with two equally likely outcomes (say heads/tails on the toss of a coin), then the probability of getting exactly one of these outcomes r times is $\dfrac{\binom{n}{r}}{2^n}$.

A statistical measure is a number which is used to describe a data set. Measures of central tendency include the mean, median, and mode. The standard deviation of a data set is a measure of spread or dispersion.

Distributions of numbers such as test scores often resemble the graphs of probability values related to Pascal's Triangle. As the number of the row of Pascal's Triangle increases, the distribution takes on a shape more and more like a normal curve. Some tests are standardized so that their scores fit that shape. In a normal distribution, 68% of the data are within one standard deviation of the mean, and 95% within two standard deviations.

Sampling is a procedure by which one tries to describe a larger set (the population) by looking at a smaller set. Statistics calculated from samples are used as estimates of a population statistic. If the sample is random its mean can be compared to other possible means because the distribution of means is close to a normal distribution. This information can be used to obtain the accuracy of a sample of a particular size.

On the next page are the most important terms and phrases for this chapter. You should be able to give a definition for those terms marked with a *. For all other terms you should be able to give a general description or a specific example.

SUMMARY

The Summary gives an overview of the entire chapter and provides an opportunity for students to consider the material as a whole. Thus, the Summary can be used to help students relate the concepts presented in the chapter.

Teaching Aid 93 provides the theorems of this chapter.

Terms, symbols, and properties are listed by lesson to provide a checklist of things a student must know. Emphasize to students that they should read the vocabulary list carefully before starting the Progress Self-Test. If students do not understand the meaning of a term, they should refer back to the indicated lesson.

Definitions or descriptions of all terms in the vocabulary list may be found in the Glossary.

ADDITIONAL ANSWERS

16.a.

n	$P(n)$
0	$\frac{1}{64}$
1	$\frac{3}{32}$
2	$\frac{15}{64}$
3	$\frac{5}{16}$
4	$\frac{15}{64}$
5	$\frac{3}{32}$
6	$\frac{1}{64}$

b.

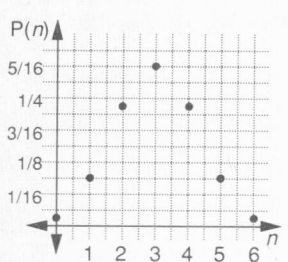

c. the probability of n heads in 6 tosses of a fair coin

18.a.

Vocabulary

Lesson 13-1
*series
*arithmetic series

Lesson 13-2
*geometric series

Lesson 13-3
Σ, sigma
Σ-notation, summation notation
index variable
!, factorial addition

Lesson 13-4
*infinite geometric series
limit
partial sums
sum of a series
snowflake curve

Lesson 13-5
Pascal's Triangle

Lesson 13-6
Binomial Theorem
binomial expansion

Lesson 13-7
subset
*combination

Lesson 13-8
*probability (of an event)
trial
fair coin, unbiased coin

Lesson 13-9
data set
*mean
*median
*mode
measure of central tendency
standard deviation
statistical measure
measure of dispersion

Lesson 13-10
binomial distribution
probability distribution
probability function
normal curve
normal distribution
standardized scores, normalized scores

Lesson 13-11
*population
*sample
random sample
stratified sample
random numbers
simulation
Central Limit Theorem

806

Progress Self-Test

Take this test as you would take a test in class. Then check your work with the solutions in the Selected Answers section in the back of the book.

1. Consider the sequence defined as follows.

$$\begin{cases} g_1 = 12 \\ g_{n+1} = \frac{1}{2}g_n \text{ for } n > 1. \end{cases}$$

a. Write the first four terms of the sequence.
   12, 6, 3, 1.5
b. Find the sum of the first 12 terms.
   $\frac{12,285}{512} \approx 23.99$

2. A concert hall has 30 rows. The first row has 12 seats. Each row has two more seats than the preceding row. How many seats are in the concert hall?   **1230**

3. Evaluate and write as a decimal. $\sum_{i=-2}^{3} 4(10)^i$
   4444.44

4. Expand. $(x^2 - 3)^4$
   $x^8 - 12x^6 + 54x^4 - 108x^2 + 81$

5. A pizza restaurant menu contains 15 possible ingredients for pizza. You order 3 of them. How many such combinations are possible?
   455

In 6 and 7, evaluate.

6. $_8C_0$ **1**

7. $\binom{40}{38}$ **780**

8. Consider a fair coin tossed 10 times.
a. State the total number of ways the coin may fall.   **1024**
b. What is the probability of getting exactly 5 heads and 5 tails? $\frac{252}{1024} \approx 25\%$

In 9–11, consider Sheila's scores on math quizzes this term: 80, 80, 88, 90, 93. Find the

9. mode   **80**   **10.** mean   **86.2**

11. score needed on the next quiz to bring her average up to 88.   **97**

12. If the sum of the first n integers is 300, what is the value of n?   **24**

13. Write using summation notation:
   $1^3 + 2^3 + 3^3 + \ldots + 20^3$
   $\sum_{i=1}^{20} i^3$

In 14 and 15, consider that on a recent administration of the ACT, composite scores had a mean of 18.8 and a standard deviation of 5.9. Assume that these scores are normally distributed.

14. About what percent of scores are within two standard deviations of the mean?   **95%**

15. About what percent of scores are at or above 24.7?   **16%**

16. Let $P(n) = \dfrac{\binom{6}{n}}{2^n}$.   **See margin.**

a. Make a table of values for this function for integers n from 0 to 6.
b. Graph the function.
c. Describe in words what $P(n)$ represents in the context of tossing a coin.

17. a. For what value(s) of x does the following infinite geometric series have a value?
   $$1 - x + x^2 - x^3 + \ldots \quad |x| < 1$$
b. What is that sum? $\frac{1}{1 + x}$

18. a. Write rows zero through five of Pascal's Triangle.   **See margin**
b. If the top row is considered the 0th row, what is the sum of the numbers in the nth row? 2^n

19. A poll of 1000 registered voters shows that 60% favor a school referendum. What is the population and what is the sample?   **all registered voters; the 1000 voters polled**

20. *True or false*   The second term in the binomial expansion of $(x - y)^7$ is $\binom{7}{2}x^6(-y)^1$.   **False**

21. *Multiple choice*   In how many ways can 8 different letters be ordered?   **a**
   (a) 8!   (b) 2^8 (c) 8^2 (d) $\binom{8}{1}$

22. Why is sampling necessary to test the fairness of a coin?   **the population (all possible tosses) is infinite.**

We cannot overemphasize the importance of these end-of-chapter materials. It is at this point that the material "gels" for many students, allowing them to solidify skills and understanding. In general, student performance should be markedly improved after these pages.

USING THE PROGRESS SELF-TEST
Assign the Progress Self-Test as a one-night assignment. Worked-out *solutions* for all questions are in the Selected Answers Section of the student book. Encourage students to take the Progress Self-Test honestly, grade themselves, and then be prepared to discuss the test in class.

Advise students to pay special attention to those Chapter Review questions (pages 808–811) which correspond to questions missed on the Progress Self-Test. A chart provided with the Selected Answers keys the Progress Self-Test questions to the lettered SPUR Objectives in the Chapter Review or to the Vocabulary. It also keys the question to the corresponding lessons where the material is covered.

CHAPTER 13   Progress Self-Test   **807**

CHAPTER 13

Chapter Review

Questions on **SPUR** Objectives

SPUR stands for **S**kills, **P**roperties, **U**ses, and **R**epresentations.
The Chapter Review questions are grouped according to the SPUR Objectives for this chapter.

SKILLS deals with the procedures used to get answers.

■ **Objective A:** *Calculate values of finite arithmetic series, and both finite and infinite geometric series.* (Lessons 13-1, 13-2, 13-4)

In 1–6, evaluate the series.

1. $3 + 7 + 11 + \ldots + 87$ 990
2. $2^0 + 2^1 + 2^2 + \ldots + 2^{19}$ $2^{20} - 1 = 1{,}048{,}575$
3. $2 + 1 + \frac{1}{2} + \frac{1}{4} + \ldots$ 4
4. $50 - 10 + 2 - \frac{2}{5} + \ldots$ $\frac{250}{6} = 41.\overline{6}$
5. the sum of the first 60 positive integers   1830
6. the sum of the first 10 terms of the sequence defined by the following:
$$\begin{cases} t_1 = 100 \\ t_{n+1} = t_n - 5 \quad \text{for } n \geq 1 \end{cases}$$ 775

7. **a.** Write the repeating decimal $0.354354\ldots$ as an infinite series.
   $.354 + .000354 + .000000354 + \ldots$
  b. Find a simple fraction in lowest terms equal to this decimal. $\frac{118}{333}$

8. The sum of the integers   35
$1 + 2 + 3 + \ldots + k$ is 630. What is k?

■ **Objective B:** *Use summation* (Σ) *or factorial* (!) *notation.* (Lessons 13-3, 13-9)

In 9 and 10, (a) write the terms of the series; and (b) evaluate.

9. $\displaystyle\sum_{n=1}^{6} (2n - 5)$ a) $(-3) + (-1) + 1 + 3 + 5 + 7$ b) 12

10. $\displaystyle\sum_{i=-2}^{3} (7 \cdot 10^i)$ a) $.07 + .7 + 7 + 70 + 700 + 7000$ b) 7777.77

11. *Multiple choice* Which equals the sum of squares $1 + 4 + 9 + 16 + \ldots + 100$?   c
(a) $\displaystyle\sum_{n=1}^{10} n$ (b) $\displaystyle\sum_{n=1}^{10} 2^n$ (c) $\displaystyle\sum_{n=1}^{10} n^2$ (d) $\displaystyle\sum_{n=1}^{100} n^2$

12. Suppose $a_1 = 15$, $a_2 = 16$, $a_3 = 16$, $a_4 = 17$, $a_5 = 18$. Evaluate $\displaystyle\sum_{i=1}^{5} a_i$. $\frac{82}{5} = 16.4$

In 13 and 14, rewrite using Σ-notation.

13. $2 + 4 + 6 + \ldots + 144$ $\displaystyle\sum_{n=1}^{72} 2n$

14. $M = \dfrac{x_1 + x_2 + \ldots + x_n}{n}$ $\dfrac{1}{n}\displaystyle\sum_{i=1}^{n} x_i$

15. If $f(n) = n!$, calculate $f(2) + f(6)$.   722

16. *Multiple choice* $\dfrac{(n + 1)!}{n!} =$ c
(a) 1   (b) n (c) $n + 1$ (d) $n - 1$

■ **Objective C:** *Calculate entries in Pascal's Triangle and the number of subsets of a given set.* (Lessons 13-5, 13-7)

17. Rows 0 to 2 of Pascal's Triangle are given at the right. Write the next three rows. **See margin.**
    1
   1 1
  1 2 1

18. *Copy and complete* The symbol $\binom{n}{r}$ represents the __?__ element in the __?__ row of Pascal's Triangle. $(r + 1)$th; nth

In 19–22, evaluate.

19. $\binom{10}{5}$ 252
20. $\binom{4}{4}$ 1
21. $_7C_0$ 1
22. $_{100}C_{99}$ 100

23. *Multiple choice* The quantity $\dfrac{12!}{9!3!}$ equals all but which of the following?   d
(a) $_{12}C_3$ (b) $\binom{12}{3}$
(c) $\binom{12}{9}$ (d) $12 \cdot 11 \cdot 10$

In 24 and 25, consider the set of letters in the English alphabet, {A, B, C, ... , Y, Z}.

24. How many subsets have   **2600**
   (a) 1 element **26**   (b) 3 elements
   (c) 20 elements? **230230**

25. What is the total number of subsets that can be formed? $2^{26} = 67,108,864$

▣ **Objective D:** *Expand binomials. (Lesson 13-6)*

In 26–29, expand. **See margin.**

26. $(x + y)^4$ 27. $(p - 8)^7$

28. $(3n^2 - 4)^3$ 29. $\left(\dfrac{a}{2} + 2b\right)^5$

In 30 and 31, *true or false*.

30. The first term of the binomial expansion of $(8x + y)^{17}$ is $(8x)^{17}$. **True**

31. The second term of the binomial expansion of $(4n - p)^{10}$ is $\dbinom{10}{2}(4n)^8(-p)^2$. **False**

32. *Multiple choice* The expression

$$\sum_{r=0}^{n}\binom{n}{r}x^{n-r}6^r \text{ equals }\quad \textbf{d}$$

   (a) $(x + n)^6$ (b) $(x + r)^n$
   (c) $(x + 6)^r$ (d) $(x + 6)^n$

▣ **Objective E:** *Calculate descriptive statistics for a data set. (Lesson 13-9)*

In 33–35, consider the test scores:
90, 68, 75, 80, 90, 68, 99, 87. Find the:

33. mean, median and mode
   82.125; 83.5; 90 or 68

34. possible values for the mean, median, and mode if one more score (ranging from 0 to 100) is added to the data set **See below.**

35. standard deviation. ≈ 10.53

36. Repeat Questions 33–35 for the scores:
   88, 90, 90, 90, 80. **See margin.**
   **34) $73 \leq$ mean $\leq 84.\overline{1}$;
   median = 87, 83.5, or 80;
   mode is any of the current scores.**

PROPERTIES deal with the principles behind the mathematics.

▣ **Objective F:** *State whether or not an infinite geometric series has a limit. (Lesson 13-4)*

37. Under what condition(s) is it true that
   $$|r| < 1$$
   $$g_1 + g_1r + g_1r^2 + g_1r^3 + \ldots = \frac{g_1}{1 - r}?$$

38. **a.** Does the infinite geometric series **No**
   $1 - 3 + 9 - 27 + \ldots$ have a value?
   b. If so, what is it? If not, why not?
   $r = -3$ so $|r| > 1$

In 39 and 40, (a) give the next 3 terms for each geometric series or (b) tell whether the infinite series has a limit.

39. $100 + 75 + \ldots$ **a) 56.25, 42, 1875,
   31.640625; b) yes**

40. $1 - 2 + 4 \ldots$ **a) -8, 16, -32; b) no**

▣ **Objective G:** *State properties of Pascal's Triangle. (Lesson 13-5)*

In 41 and 42, *true or false*.

41. The first and last number in each row of Pascal's Triangle is 1. **True**

42. For all positive integers n, $\dbinom{n}{1} = \dbinom{n}{n - 1}$. **True**

In 43–45, consider the top row in Pascal's Triangle to be the 0th row.

				row
	1			0th
	1	1		1st
1	2	1		2nd
		⋮		

43. What is the sum of the numbers in the 5th row? $2^5 = 32$

44. What is the sum in the nth row? 2^n

45. Which entry of row n in Pascal's Triangle is the coefficient of $a^{n-r}b^r$ in the binomial expansion of $(a + b)^n$? $(r + 1)$th

(margin answers)

26. $x^4 + 4x^3y + 6x^2y^2 + 4xy^3 + y^4$

27. $p^7 - 56p^6 + 1344p^5 - 17,920p^4 + 143,360p^3 - 688,128p^2 + 1,835,008p - 2,097,152$

28. $27n^6 - 108n^4 + 144n^2 - 64$

29. $\frac{1}{32}a^5 + \frac{5}{8}a^4b + 5a^3b^2 + 20a^2b^3 + 40ab^4 + 32b^5$

36. (33.) 87.6, 90, 90
   (34.) $73 \leq$ mean ≤ 89.7
   median: 89, 89.5, or 90
   mode: 90
   (35.) 3.878

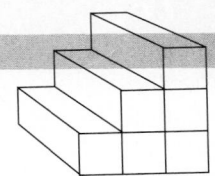

USES deal with applications of mathematics in real situations.

■ **Objective H:** *Solve applied problems using arithmetic or geometric series. (Lessons 13-1, 13-2, 13-4)*

46. Suppose on January 1 you deposit $1.00 in an empty Piggy Bank. On January 8 you deposit $1.50. On January 15, you deposit $2.00; on each week thereafter you deposit $.50 more than the previous week.
  a. What kind of sequence do the individual deposits generate? **arithmetic**
  b. What amount should you deposit in the 52nd week? **$26.50**
  c. What is the total at the end of 52 weeks? (Assume no withdrawals and no interest payments.) **$715**

In 47 and 48, a hiker walks 12 mi the first day and 0.6 mi less each succeeding day.

47. How far will the hiker walk in 5 days? **53 mi**

48. After how many days will the hiker have completed 99 miles? **11**

49. Carla's Clothing Shop opened 8 years ago. The first year she made $3000 profit. Each year thereafter her profits were about 50% greater than the previous year.
  a. How much profit did Carla earn during her 8th year in business? **$51,257**
  b. What is the total amount earned in the 8 years? **$147,773**

50. A ball on a pendulum moves 50 cm on its first swing. Each succeeding swing it moves .9 the distance of the previous swing.

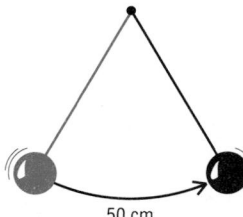

50 cm

  a. Write the first four terms of the series generated. **50, 45, 40.5, 36.45**
  b. Assuming this pattern continues indefinitely, how far will the ball travel before coming to a rest? **500 cm**

51. Congruent boxes are used to make a staircase as pictured above. If there are n steps, how many boxes are needed? $\frac{n}{2}(1 + n)$

■ **Objective I:** *Use permutations, combinations, or probability to solve problems. (Lessons 13-7, 13-8)*

52. There are 12 notes in a musical octave: A, A#, B, C, C#, D, D#, E, F, F#, G, and G#.
  In some twelve-tone music, a theme uses each of these notes exactly once. Ignoring rhythm, how many themes are possible? **12!**

53. In how many ways can the letters of the word *NICELY* be arranged? **6! = 720**

In 54–56, consider that in the 100th Congress there were 54 Democratic and 46 Republican senators.

$$\binom{100}{7} \approx 1.6 \times 10^{10}$$

54. How many seven person committees could be formed with members from either party?

55. How many four member committees could be formed entirely Democratic? **316,251**

56. What is the total number of possible committees that are entirely Republican? (Do not include the empty set.) $2^{46} - 1$

57. Ten people are in a room. Each decides to shake hands with everyone else exactly once. How many handshakes will take place? **45**

In 58–60, consider that a fair coin is tossed 5 times. Calculate the probability of each event.

58. exactly 1 head $\frac{5}{32}$ **59.** exactly 3 heads $\frac{10}{32}$

60. exactly 5 tails $\frac{1}{32}$

61. Assume a student takes a true-false test with 10 questions and that the student guesses on each question. Find the probability of getting:
  a. exactly 7 items correct $\frac{120}{1024}$
  b. 7 or more items correct. $\frac{176}{1024}$

Objective J: *Use measures of central tendency or dispersion to describe data or distributions.* (*Lessons 13-9, 13-10*)

In 62–64, consider the populations of the ten largest cities in the world. (Source: 1988 World Almanac; data rounded to the nearest 100,000).

Tokyo-Yokohama	25,400,000
Mexico City	16,900,000
Sao Paulo	14,900,000
New York	14,600,000
Seoul	13,700,000
Osaka-Kobe-Kyoto	13,600,000
Buenos Aires	10,800,000
Calcutta	10,500,000
Bombay	10,100,000
Rio de Janeiro	10,100,000

For this data set find the:

62. mean   14,060,000   **63.** median   13,650,000

64. mode.   10,100,000

In 65–67, consider the following heights of the starting five on a basketball team: 6'8", 6'10", 6'4", 6'8", 6'1". For this data set find the:

65. mode   6'8"   **66.** mean   6'6.2"

67. standard deviation.   3.25"

68. John played one round of golf each day during his vacation. If the first six days his average was 90, what would he need to score on the seventh day to bring his average to 88?   76

In 69–70, use the following data reported by the College Entrance Examination Board.

	n	mean	standard deviation
juniors	580,981	484	111
seniors	799,861	457	115

69. Which group, juniors or seniors, shows a greater dispersion of scores?   seniors

70. The mean score of all students taking this test was 467, which is not the average of the means of the juniors and seniors. Why not?   There were more seniors, which "weighted" the mean.

71. Assume mathematics aptitude is normally distributed among juniors. Within what interval would you expect the middle 68% of scores of juniors to occur?   373 to 595

Objective K: *Give reasons for sampling.* (*Lesson 13-11*)

72. What is an advantage of using a sample that is random?
You can apply the results of the Central Limit Theorem.

73. To find the ratings of a television show in a small town, a network uses a sample rather than the population.
  a. What is the population in this situation?
  All households in town with at least one TV.
  b. Why might a sample be preferred over the population?
  It may be difficult or too expensive to poll the entire population.

REPRESENTATIONS deal with pictures, graphs, or objects that illustrate concepts.

Objective L: *Graph and analyze binomial and normal distributions.* (*Lesson 13-10*)

74. Below is pictured a normal distribution with mean m and standard deviation s.

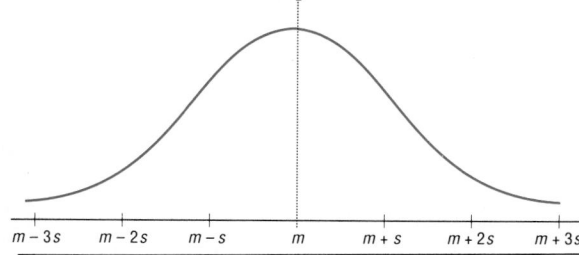

  a. What percent of the data are $\leq m$?   50%
  b. About what percent of the data are between $m - s$ and $m + s$?   68.2%
  c. About what percent of the data are more than two standard deviations away from m?   4.6%

75. Consider the probability function $P(n) = \dfrac{\binom{8}{n}}{2^8}$.
  See margin.
  a. Evaluate $P(n)$ for integers 0, 1, ..., 8.
  b. Graph this function.
  c. What name is given to this function?

EVALUATION
Three tests are provided for this chapter in the Teacher's Resource File. Chapter 13 Test, Forms A and B cover just Chapter 13. The third test is Chapter 13 Test, Cumulative Form. About 50% of this test covers Chapter 13, 25% covers Chapter 12, and 25% covers previous chapters. For information on grading, see *General Teaching Suggestions: Grading* on page T44 in the Teacher's Edition.

ASSIGNMENT RECOMMENDATION
We strongly recommend that you assign Lesson 14-1, both reading and some questions, for homework the evening of the test.

ADDITIONAL ANSWERS
75.a.

n	$P(n)$
0	$\frac{1}{256}$
1	$\frac{1}{32}$
2	$\frac{7}{64}$
3	$\frac{7}{32}$
4	$\frac{35}{128}$
5	$\frac{7}{32}$
6	$\frac{7}{64}$
7	$\frac{1}{32}$
8	$\frac{1}{256}$

b.

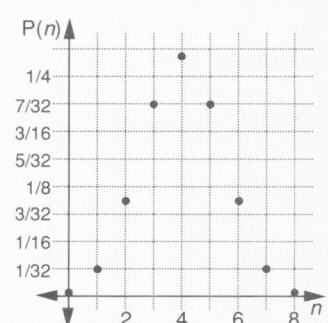

c. binomial probability distribution

CHAPTER 14 ■ DIMENSIONS AND SPACE

DAILY PACING CHART ■ CHAPTER 14

Students in the Full Course should complete all but one of the chapters by the end of the year. Students in the Minimal Course will spend more time on quizzes and the Chapter Review. As such, these students should complete about ten or eleven chapters.

DAY	MINIMAL COURSE	FULL COURSE
1	14-1	14-1
2	14-2	14-2
3	14-3	14-3
4	14-4	14-4
5	Quiz (TRF); Start 14-5.	Quiz (TRF); 14-5
6	Finish 14-5.	14-6
7	14-6	14-7
8	14-7	14-8
9	14-8	Progress Self-Test
10	Progress Self-Test	Chapter Review
11	Chapter Review	Chapter Test (TRF)
12	Chapter Review	Comprehensive Test (TRF)
13	Chapter Test (TRF)	
14	Comprehensive Test (TRF)	

TESTING OPTIONS

■ Quiz for Lessons 14-1 Through 14-4   ■ Chapter 14 Test, Form A   ■ Chapter 14 Test, Cumulative Form
■ Chapter 14 Test, Form B   ■ Comprehensive Test, Chapters 1–14

PROVIDING FOR INDIVIDUAL DIFFERENCES

The student text is written for the *average* student. The program, however, can be adapted for both less capable and for more capable students.

A blackline master (in the Teacher's Resource File) is provided for each lesson for those students who need more practice. The Teacher's Edition frequently provides Error Analysis and Alternate Approach features to provide additional instructional strategies.

For students who require additional challenge, Extension activities are regularly provided in the Teacher's Edition.

OBJECTIVES ■ CHAPTER 14

Students should master the chapter objectives by the time they complete the chapter.
To ensure mastery, there is continual review built into each set of lesson questions.
After students complete the chapter lessons, they assess their mastery on the Progress
Self-Test. Then they do the Chapter Review and pay special attention to those questions
that match the objectives missed on the Progress Self-Test. Students can get extra
practice on these objectives by using the master for each lesson in the Teacher's
Resource File.

OBJECTIVES FOR CHAPTER 14 (Organized into the SPUR categories—Skills, Properties, Uses, and Representations)	Progress Self-Test Questions	Chapter Review Questions	Lesson Master from Teacher's Resource File*
SKILLS			
A Solve 3 × 3 and 4 × 4 systems of equations.	8, 9	1 through 5	14-3, 14-7
B Find distances between points in 3- and 4-space.	3, 5	6 through 11	14-4, 14-6
C Write and analyze equations for spheres and hyperspheres.	7, 14	12 through 15	14-4, 14-6
PROPERTIES			
D Identify properties of planes in 3-space.	6, 10, 12, 15	16 through 21	14-2, 14-3
E Extend 2- and 3-dimensional ideas to higher or fractional dimensions.	17, 18	22 through 28	14-6, 14-8
USES			
F Use 3 × 3 or 4 × 4 linear systems to solve real-world problems.	19	29 through 31	14-3, 14-7
REPRESENTATIONS			
G Graph sets of points in 3-space.	1, 2, 4, 13	32 through 36	14-1, 14-2, 14-4
H Describe the surface of revolution generated by rotating a set of points.	11, 16	37 through 45	14-5

* The masters are numbered to match the lessons.

OVERVIEW ■ CHAPTER 14

Most students have poor skills in visualizing, drawing, or analyzing 3-dimensional figures. UCSMP addresses this problem by including work on 3-dimensional figures in every course. This chapter in *Advanced Algebra* provides opportunities for students to work analytically and synthetically with figures in 3-space. It also expands the horizons and imagination of students by introducing fractional dimensions and dimensions higher than 3.

In Lessons 14-1 and 14-2, the standard 3-dimensional rectangular coordinate system is introduced and students draw and interpret points, lines, planes, and rectangular solids. In Lesson 14-3, students learn a general linear combination technique to solve 3 × 3 systems, and the solution of systems is related to the intersection of planes in space.

In the next two lessons, students learn that curves in space can also be described by equations. Spheres are studied in Lesson 14-4 and cones and cylinders are studied in Lesson 14-5. Lesson 14-5 is unusual at this level because it emphasizes drawing and visualization as much as skill in generating equations for solids of revolution.

The last three lessons show that for both theoretical and practical reasons it makes sense to consider dimensions other than one, two, or three. Lesson 14-6 introduces integral dimensions greater than 3;

Lesson 14-7 considers systems with dimensions higher than 3; and Lesson 14-8 describes fractals. These lessons are meant to show students that mathematics continues to evolve, and that it is capable of describing sets of points that are considered by many people to be strange and mysterious but interesting. We suggest you read the notes to accompany Lessons 14-6 and 14-8 now, because you may want to order the film mentioned there, or to assign a project based on the book *Flatland* before you start this chapter.

The Review questions in this chapter, like those of Chapter 13, attempt to pull together many ideas from earlier chapters in preparation for the final exam.

PERSPECTIVES ■ CHAPTER 14

The Perspectives provide the rationale for the inclusion of topics or approaches, provide mathematical background, and make connections within UCSMP.

14-1

THREE-DIMENSIONAL COORDINATES

The purpose of this lesson is to introduce the student to the standard 3-dimensional rectangular coordinate system. Specific objectives are that students should be able to (1) plot points and rectangular solids in 3-space, and (2) identify and name the x-, y-, and z-axes and the xy-, xz-, and yz-planes.

There are two ways in which people customarily label the axes; in both, the xy-plane is the nearest to horizontal and the z-axis is vertical. The way we label the axes in this book (figure (a) below) is more popular because it enables the xy-plane to look like the familiar coordinate plane as seen from above. The alternative way (figure (b) below) switches x and y. Its one advantage is that the x-axis is horizontal.

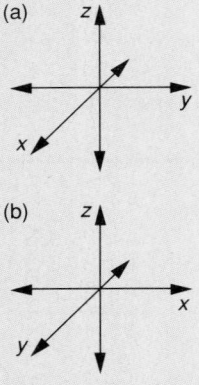

There are other coordinate systems used in three dimensions that generalize the idea of polar coordinates. They are not discussed in this book.

14-2

EQUATIONS OF PLANES

The purpose of this lesson is to develop further skill in working within

a 3-dimensional coordinate system. Specifically, the objectives are that the student will be able to: (1) sketch the graph in 3-space of any equation of the form $Ax + By + Cz = D$ where not all A, B, C, and D are zero; and (2) state an equation for any plane parallel to a coordinate plane.

This lesson provides many opportunities to relate concepts in 2-space to concepts in 3-space through equations and graphs. Lines parallel to axes correspond to planes parallel to axes. The equation $Ax + By = C$ for a line in a plane corresponds to the equation $Ax + By + Cz = D$ for a plane in space.

Students may ask about equations of lines in 3-space. These are more complicated because a line cannot easily be described by a single equation. There are two common forms:

(a) the parametric form
$x = a + bt$, $y = c + dt$,
$z = e + ft$;
(b) the proportion form (for the same line as in (a) above)
$$\frac{x - a}{b} = \frac{y - c}{d} = \frac{z - e}{f}.$$

14-3
SOLVING SYSTEMS IN 3-SPACE
Students solved some 3×3 linear systems in each of Lessons 5-4 and 11-6. Those in Lesson 5-4 were solved by substitution; those in Lesson 11-6 were solved by subtracting pairs of equations. In this lesson, we present a generalized technique using linear combinations to solve a 3×3 linear system, and then relate the idea of solving 3×3 systems to finding points of intersection of planes. In Lesson 14-7, still another method is given.

14-4
DISTANCE AND SPHERES
In this lesson, students learn to (1) find the distance between any two points in 3-space, and (2) determine an equation for a sphere centered at the origin in 3-space.

As in previous lessons, there are ample opportunities to compare and contrast concepts and formulas in 3-space with corresponding concepts and formulas in lower dimensions.

For instance, the distance formulas in 1-space, 2-space, and 3-space can be written using radical signs and exponents.

1-space: $d = \sqrt{(x_1 - x_2)^2} = |x_1 - x_2|$

2-space: $d = \sqrt{(x_1 - x_2)^2 + (y_1 - y_2)^2}$

3-space: $d = \sqrt{(x_1 - x_2)^2 + (y_1 - y_2)^2 + (z_1 - z_2)^2}$

It is customary to write the formula for 1-space with absolute value signs because evaluation of this form requires fewer computations than the radical form.

14-5
SOLIDS AND SURFACES OF REVOLUTION
Lesson 14-5 follows immediately from the previous one by showing another way to think about the sphere. Instead of viewing a sphere statically as the set of points in 3-space at a fixed distance from the center, we can think of it as the figure in 3-space generated by rotating a circle or semicircle about its diameter.

For the sake of simplicity, we assume that the circle is centered at the origin of the coordinate system and the axis of rotation is a coordinate axis.

The objectives of the lesson are that students will be able to (1) describe in words, and (2) draw the surface of revolution that results from rotating a line, semicircle or circle centered at (0, 0), or parabola with vertex at (0, 0), around a coordinate axis.

Additionally, we would like students to be able to describe cross sections of such surfaces. With the exception of the sphere, the analytic description of surfaces of revolutions is not an objective that requires mastery at this time.

14-6
HIGHER DIMENSIONS
The purpose of this lesson is to build meaning for the concept of the fourth dimension. Most students have heard of the fourth dimension, but generally they perceive it to be "time."

Our approach in this lesson is consistent with the first few lessons of the chapter. We compare and contrast work in one, two, and three dimensions, whether synthetic or analytic, and generalize patterns to give meaning to the fourth dimension (other than time) that is easily generalizable to even higher dimensions.

In contrast to the previous lesson, which presents mathematics that is very old and well known

by teachers, this lesson presents newer and less well-known content. Ordered n-tuples were first studied by Reimann in the 1850's and became the basis for much work on non-Euclidean geometry and topology.

The International Film Bureau (322 S. Michigan Ave; Chicago, IL 60604; (312) 427-4545) rents a film *The Hypercube: Projections and Slicing*, that we highly recommend.

14-7
SOLVING HIGHER DIMENSIONAL SYSTEMS
Students have been taught a variety of procedures for solving systems. With computers, a single procedure which works in all cases is often preferred to a multitude of procedures. The *row reduction* process discussed in this lesson is very commonly used to solve large systems.

14-8
FRACTALS
This last lesson in *Advanced Algebra* contains the "newest" mathematics in the book. Research on fractals is literally at the cutting edge of pure mathematics. Fractals are currently of great interest to many physicists, computer scientists, biologists, artists, and others.

In this lesson, we concentrate on the concept of dimension of a fractal curve, and show how the dimensions of many fractals are not whole numbers. In general, to determine the dimension of D of a fractal curve, we need to look at successive approximations to its length with units whose lengths are related by a scale factor S, $S > 1$. If N is the number of the smaller units needed to approximate the length of the curve, then

$$S^D = N \text{ and so } D = \frac{\log N}{\log S}.$$

**CHAPTER 14**

We recommend 12 to 14 days for this chapter: 8 to 9 on the lessons; 1 for the Progress Self-Test; 1 or 2 for the Chapter Review; 1 for a Chapter test; and 1 for the Comprehensive Test. (See the Daily Pacing Chart on page 812A.)

USING PAGES 812–813
Use the material on these pages to initiate a discussion of the concept of space. Ask students to express their ideas about space. If necessary, lead them to the mathematical definitions given on page 813. Point out that a new way of looking at the concept of dimension is a very recent development in mathematics that will be studied in the last lesson of the chapter.

Dimensions and Space

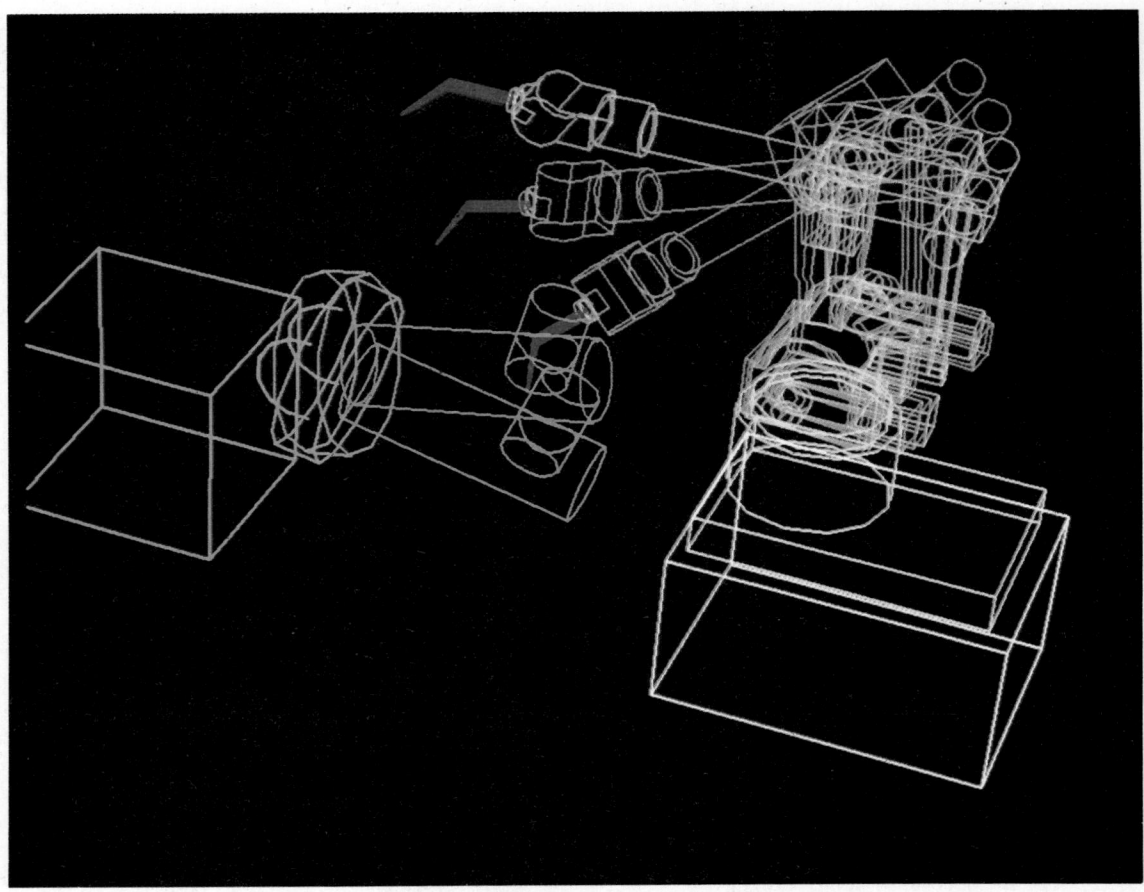

Computer screen representation of arcwelding 5-axis robot moving to varied welding positions

A line has one dimension. Each point on it can be located with a unique real number x. For this reason the real number line is often called *1-space*.

A plane has two dimensions. Each point on it can be located with a unique pair of real numbers (x, y). Thus, the coordinate plane is often called *2-space*.

What is called space in most geometry texts has three dimensions and is often called *3-space*. In this chapter, you will see how every point in 3-space can be located with an *ordered triple* of real numbers (x, y, z).

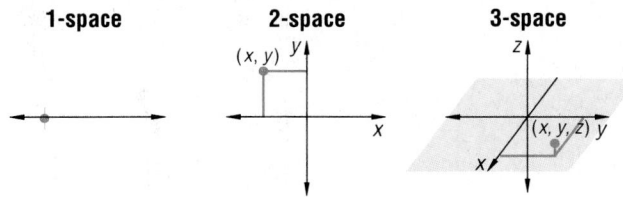

Many real-world situations can be described by the mathematics of lines (1-space), planes (2-space), or solids (3-space). However, some real situations are best described by mathematical models with four or more dimensions, and others by models with dimensions that are not whole numbers. For instance, Einstein's theory of special relativity requires a 4-dimensional model, and in Lesson 14-8 you will see why a coastline such as that of Britain (shown at the left) has a fractional dimension between 1 and 2.

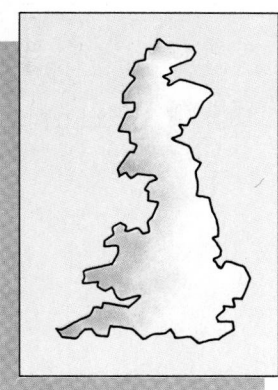

In this chapter you will learn to draw and analyze graphs and to solve equations in 3-space. You will also learn about uses of the mathematics of fractional dimensions and of dimensions greater than 3.

OBJECTIVE

G Graph sets of points in 3-
space.

TEACHING NOTES

The text introduces 3-
dimensional coordinates by
using the three lines meeting
in the corner of a classroom
as a model of the x-, y-, and
z-axes meeting at the origin.
Point out how each point in
the classroom can be located
by a unique order triple of
numbers. Have students
name what you are describing when you give a particular triple.

Show students how to represent the 3-dimensional coordinate system on a plane.
Initially, this is a difficult task
for many students, particularly those whose work in
geometry did not include
drawing figures in 3-space.

Note that, as in the coordinate plane, order makes a
difference. Suppose the unit
in the coordinate system is
feet. Then, for example,
(8, 4, 5) might locate the tip
of a student's nose; whereas
(4, 8, 5) might locate the top
button on a shirt. Ask students to estimate the coordi-
ates of the doorknob or some
other object. Have them
name the coordinates of
three points on the floor. (All
will have $z = 0$.)

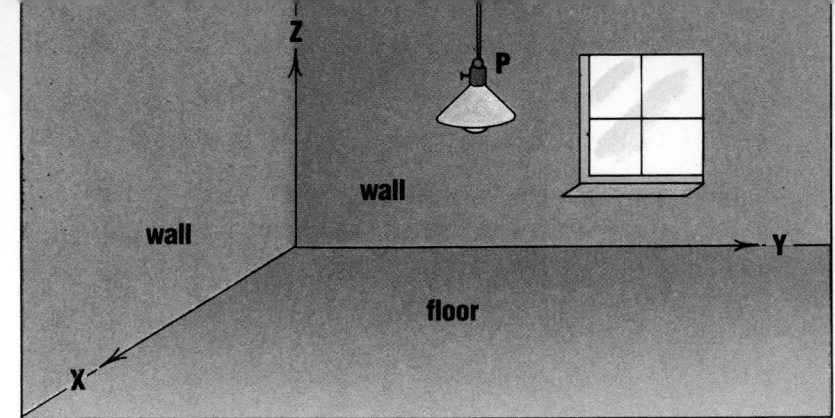

Points in a room can be located with a three-dimensional coordinate
system. It is convenient to let the origin be a corner of the room
where two walls and the floor intersect. Then with two coordinates x
and y you can describe the location of an object on the floor. However, to locate an object in the room which is not on the floor (such
as a point on a light hanging from the ceiling), you need a number
to indicate the height from the floor. This is the z-direction. Thus, if
the point P on the light is 6 ft from the origin in the x-direction, 8 ft
in the y-direction, and 9 ft in the z-direction (up), you could specify
the position of the point uniquely by the **ordered triple** (6, 8, 9).
The x-coordinate is 6, the y-coordinate is 8, and the **z-coordinate**
is 9.

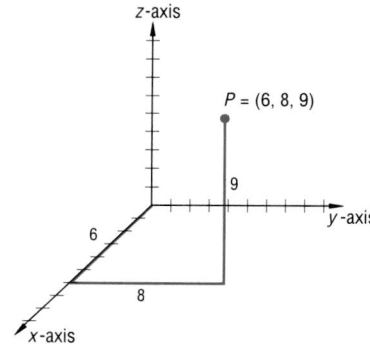

The lines where the walls and floor meet are the axes of this
3-dimensional coordinate system.

The three axes are called the
x-axis, the **y-axis,** and the
z-axis. The positive direction is
shown on each axis by a single
arrowhead. By extending each axis,
as shown in the figure at the right,
any point can be described by the
ordered triple (x, y, z).

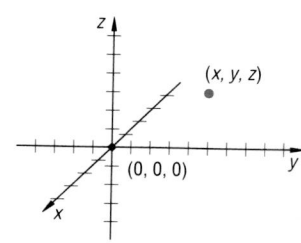

814

■ ■ ■ ■ ■ ■ ■ ■

Example 1 Plot the point $R = (-2, 4, 6)$ on a three-dimensional coordinate system.

Solution
1. Since the x-coordinate is -2, slide 2 units back (in a negative direction) on the x-axis.
2. Since the y-coordinate is 4, move 4 units in a positive direction parallel to the y-axis.
3. Since the z-coordinate is 6, go 6 units up parallel to the z-axis.

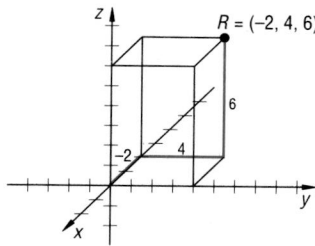

It helps to think of the point as the back, upper right vertex of a box with base dimensions 2 and 4 and height 6.

Recall from geometry that there is exactly one plane through two intersecting lines. The x-axis and the y-axis determine the *xy-plane*. Similarly, the x-axis and the z-axis determine the *xz-plane*, and the y-axis and z-axis determine the *yz-plane*. The *xy-*, *xz-*, and *yz-*planes are called **coordinate planes.** The three coordinate planes separate 3-space into eight regions called **octants.**

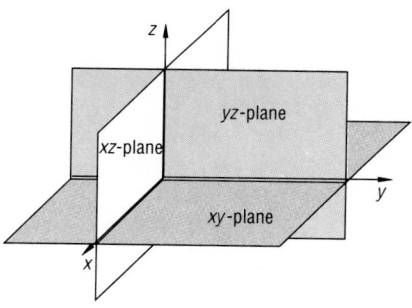

In the classroom coordinate system that opened the lesson, the entire classroom is in the upper right front octant, the one where all the coordinates are positive.

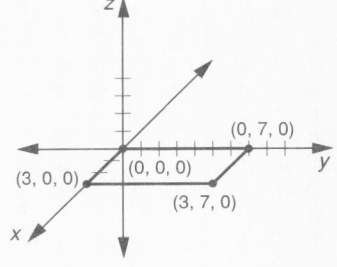

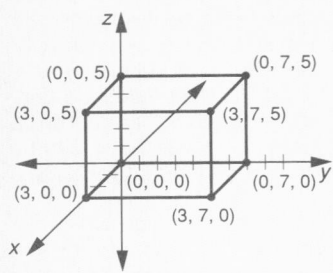
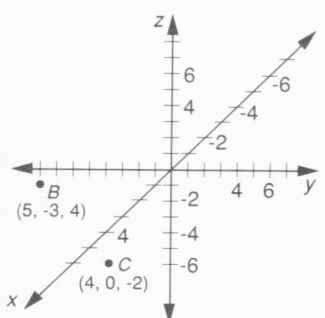
Example 2 What are the signs of the coordinates of a point in the lower right front octant?

Solution Examine the adjectives "lower right front". Lower means a negative z-value. Right means a positive y-value. Front means a positive x-value. If the coordinates of the point in this octant are (a, b, c), then a and b are positive and c is negative. Below are two representations of the point in 3-space.

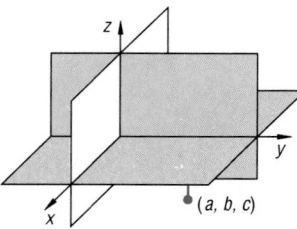
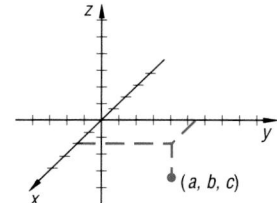

The point (2, -4, 0), shown at the right, is on the xy-plane. For any point on a coordinate plane, one of the coordinates is zero. This is similar to what happens in two dimensions: for any point on an axis, one of the coordinates is 0.

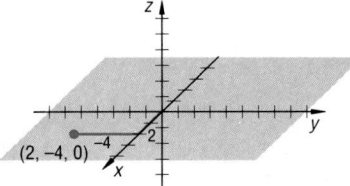

Questions

1. Any point in 3-space can be located with an ordered __?__.   **triple**

In 2–4, *true or false*.
2. The number line can be called 1-space.   **True**

3. Only integers can be coordinates of points in 3-space.   **False**

4. The intersection of two walls and the floor of a room can represent the origin of a coordinate system in 3-space.   **True**

5. Refer to the picture of the room in the lesson. Which coordinate plane represents the wall with the window?   **the yz–plane**

In 6–8, match the axis to its direction as pictured in this lesson.

6. x-axis   **b**   (a) up-down

7. y-axis   **c**   (b) forward-backward

8. z-axis   **a**   (c) left-right

816

9. Draw a coordinate system and plot the points $B = (5, -3, 4)$ and $C = (4, 0, -2)$. **See margin.**

10. The coordinate planes divide 3-space into eight regions called __?__.
octants

11. Point (a, b, c) is in the upper left back octant. What are the signs of $a, b,$ and c? **a, b are negative; c is positive**

12. *Multiple choice* For any point (a, b, c) on the xz-plane: **b**
(a) $a = 0$ (b) $b = 0$
(c) $c = 0$ (d) none of these

Applying the Mathematics

13. Suppose the point $(6, 8, 9)$ locates the bottom of the wire connecting the lamp to the ceiling in the classroom mentioned in this lesson. If the wire is one foot long, what are the coordinates of the top point of the wire? **(6, 8, 10)**

14. A point whose x- and y-coordinates are both zero must lie on the __?__-axis. **z**

15. A box has the following vertices: the origin, $(0, 8, 0)$, $(2, 0, 0)$, $(2, 8, 0)$, $(2, 8, 5)$, $(2, 0, 5)$, $(0, 0, 5)$, and $(0, 8, 5)$.
a. Draw the box on a 3-dimensional coordinate system. **See margin.**
b. Determine its volume. **80 cubic units**
c. Determine its surface area. **132 square units**

16. A cube which has sides of length 1 has one vertex at the origin. None of the coordinates of any vertex is negative. Find the coordinates of the other vertices of the cube.
(1, 0, 0), (1, 1, 0), (0, 1, 0), (0, 1, 1), (1, 1, 1), (1, 0, 1), (0, 0, 1)

17. In the rectangular box at the right, $D = (13, 2, 5)$ and F is the origin.
a. Find the coordinates of the **See margin.** points $A, B, C, E, G,$ and H.
b. Determine the volume of the box.
c. Determine its surface area.
b) 130 cubic units; c) 202 square units

Review

18. p varies directly as the square of t. If $t = -2$, then $p = -12$. Find p when $t = 4$. *(Lesson 2-1)* **-48**

In 19–21, suppose y is a function of x. Describe what happens in each function below when x is tripled. *(Lesson 2-3)*

19. $y = \dfrac{k}{x}$ **y is divided by 3**

20. $y = kx^2$ **y is multiplied by 9**

21. $y = 5x^3$ **y is multiplied by 27**

LESSON 14-1   Three-Dimensional Coordinates   **817**

MORE PRACTICE
For more questions on SPUR Objectives, use *Lesson Master 14-1*, shown below.

15.a.

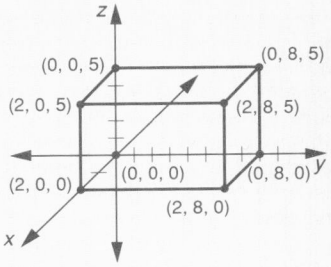

17.a. A = (13, 0, 5),
B = (0, 0, 5), C = (0, 2, 5),
E = (13, 0, 0), G = (0, 2, 0),
H = (13, 2, 0)

NAME _____

LESSON **MASTER 14–1**
QUESTIONS ON **SPUR** OBJECTIVES

■ **REPRESENTATIONS** *Objective G (See pages 867–869 for objectives.)*
In 1 and 2, use the coordinate system at the right to plot the following points.

1. $A = (1, 4, -2)$ 2. $B = (0, -3, 5)$

3. Point (a, b, c) is in the lower right back octant. Tell whether $a, b,$ and c are positive or negative.
a: _negative_
b: _positive_
c: _negative_

4. *Multiple choice* If a point (t, u, v) is on the yz-plane, which coordinate must be zero?   (a)
(a) t (b) u
(c) v (d) none of these

5. A point whose y-coordinate is zero must lie in the ___xz___-plane.

6. A box has the following vertices: the origin, $(4, 0, 0)$, $(4, 5, 0)$, $(0, 5, 0)$, $(0, 5, 6)$, $(0, 0, 6)$, $(4, 0, 6)$, and $(4, 5, 6)$.

a. Draw the box on the axes at the right.

b. Determine the volume of the box.
120 cubic units

c. Determine its surface area.
148 square units

7. In the rectangular box at the right, $S = (-3, -18, 16.5)$ and V is the origin. Find the coordinates of

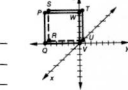

P: _(0, -18, 16.5)_   T: _(-3, 0, 16.5)_
Q: _(0, -18, 0)_   U: _(-3, 0, 0)_
R: _(-3, -18, 0)_   W: _(0, 0, 16.5)_

147

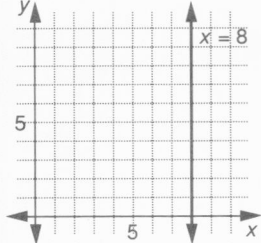
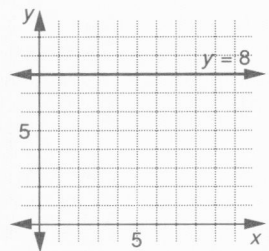
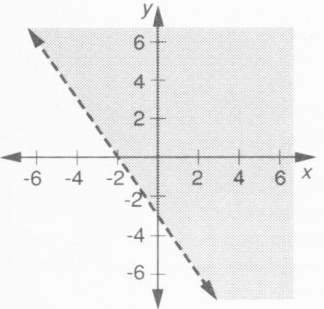
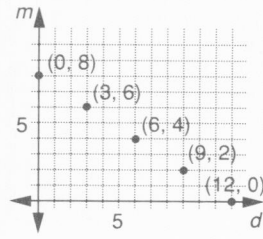
22. Graph: (a) $\{(x, y): x = 8\}$; (b) $\{(x, y): y = 8\}$. *(Lesson 3-4)* See margin.

In 23–26, match each graph with an appropriate equation. *(Lessons 10-9, 9-7, 2-7, 2-4)*

a. $y = \sin x$ b. $y = \frac{x}{4}$ c. $y = \frac{4}{x^2}$

d. $y = \frac{4}{x}$ e. $y = e^x$ f. $y = (.7)^x$

23. c

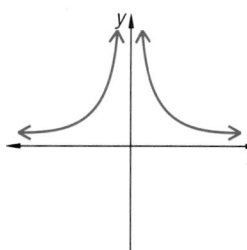

24. b

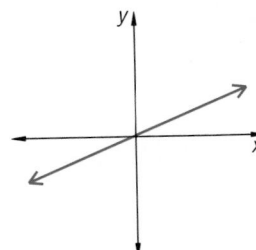

25. e

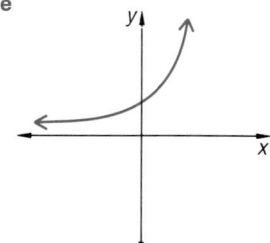

26. a

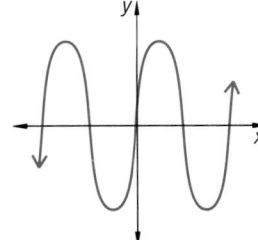

27. Graph $-2y < 3x + 6$. *(Lesson 3-9)* See margin.

28. Suppose one donut costs $.50 and one muffin costs $.75. .50d + .75m
   a. Write an expression for the cost of d donuts and m muffins.
   b. State three ways in which you might spend exactly $6.00 on donuts and muffins. samples: (d, m) = (12, 0) (6, 4), (9, 2), (0, 8), (3, 6)
   c. Graph all points (d, m) that represent ways to spend exactly $6.00 on donuts and muffins. *(Lessons 1-1, 3-3, 3-4)* See margin.

Exploration

29. Air traffic controllers must locate planes in the air. Explain how they can locate the position with three numbers. See below.

30. Imagine your classroom with a three-dimensional coordinate system.
   a. What point would you pick as the origin?
   b. Estimate the coordinates of a point in the middle of your desk.
   c. Estimate the coordinates of other key points in the room.
Many answers are possible.

29) Air controllers locate planes in the air by using a coordinate system in 3-space with the control tower at ground level as the origin and directional axes north-south, east-west, and up-down.

818

14-2

Equations of Planes

Consider the plane graphed at the right. It is four units to the right of the xz-plane and parallel to it. Every point on the plane has the same y-coordinate, 4. Thus $y = 4$ is an equation for this plane.

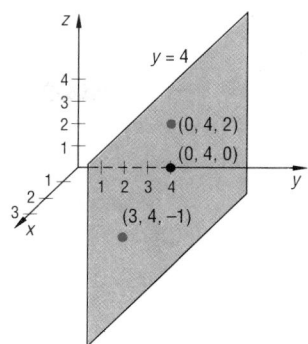

LESSON 14-2

RESOURCES
■ Lesson Master 14-2
▣ Visual for Teaching Aid 96 shows the diagram for **Example 2**.
▣ Visual for Teaching Aid 97 shows 3 planes intersecting in a point.

OBJECTIVES

D Identify properties of planes in 3-space.
G Graph planes in 3-space.

TEACHING NOTES

In 3-space every plane parallel to a coordinate plane has an equation similar to the one shown above. These equations and their graphs are analogous to the equations of lines parallel to the coordinate axes in 2-space. This is summarized below.

2-space	3-space
Line parallel to y-axis: $x = a$	Plane parallel to yz-plane: $x = a$
Line parallel to x-axis: $y = b$	Plane parallel to xz-plane: $y = b$
	Plane parallel to xy-plane: $z = c$

Example 1 shows how you can use this idea to describe points in 3-space.

■ ■ ■ ■ ■ ■ ■ ■

Example 1 Describe the set of all points 4 units away from the xy-coordinate plane.

Solution These points consist of two parallel planes P and Q where plane P is 4 units above the xy-coordinate plane and plane Q is 4 units below the xy-coordinate plane. An equation for plane P is $z = 4$. An equation for plane Q is $z = -4$.

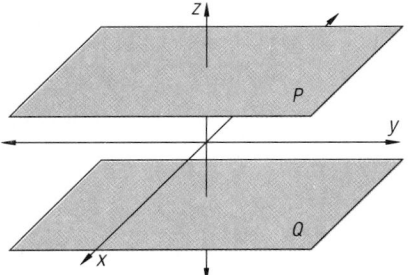

As some students may still be struggling with naming points in 3-space, introduce the lesson by referring to the coordinate system set up in your classroom or the models developed for the previous lesson. For instance, have students locate four points with a z-coordinate of zero. These will all be on the floor, the plane described by $z = 0$. Next, have them identify and name some points on the ceiling. If the ceiling is 9 ft high, all will have a z-coordinate of 9 and an equation for the plane of the ceiling will be $z = 9$. Stress that planes parallel to coordinate planes have equations of the form x (or y or z) $= k$.

Point out that the techniques for graphing planes in 3-space are similar to the techniques for graphing lines in 2-space. Specifically, students should plot the intercepts and analyze the form of the equation to tell whether the graph is parallel to an axis.

LESSON 14-2 Equations of Planes **819**

The description of these points in 3-space is analogous to a situation in 2-space.

2-space
The locus of points r units from a line l is two lines parallel to l a distance r from it.

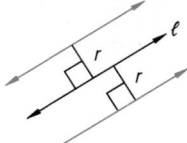

3-space
The locus of points r units from a plane P is two planes parallel to P at a distance r.

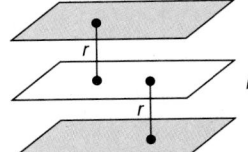

You have learned that in 2-space all lines have an equation equivalent to the form $Ax + By = C$. There is a similar equation for all planes in 3-space. It can be deduced using methods that are not difficult, but are beyond the scope of this book.

Theorem:

The set of points (x, y, z) satisfying
$Ax + By + Cz = D$,
where not all of A, B, and C are zero, is a plane.

The equation $Ax + By + Cz = D$ is called the **standard form of the equation of a plane.**

Planes parallel to coordinate planes are special cases of this theorem. For the plane $y = 4$ mentioned at the start of the lesson, $A = 0$, $C = 0$, and $D = 4$. In general, when two of the constants A, B, and C are zero, the plane is parallel to a coordinate plane.

Recall that in 2-space the x-intercept is the x-value of the point (or points) where the graph crosses the x-axis. The same definition applies in 3-space. Because three noncollinear points determine a plane, the three intercepts can be used to graph planes. Example 2 shows how to graph a triangular part of a plane when there are three intercepts.

820

Example 2   Graph the triangular region determined by the intercepts of the plane with equation $2x + 3y + 6z = 6$.

Solution   First find the intercepts. To find the x-intercept, let $y = 0$ and $z = 0$. Then $x = 3$, so $(3, 0, 0)$ is on the plane. To find the y-intercept, let $x = 0$ and $z = 0$. Then $y = 2$ and so $(0, 2, 0)$ is on the plane. To find the z-intercept, let $x = 0$ and $y = 0$. Then $z = 1$, and so $(0, 0, 1)$ is on the plane. Plot these points. Draw the triangle formed by these points. This triangular region is part of the plane determined by $2x + 3y + 6z = 6$.

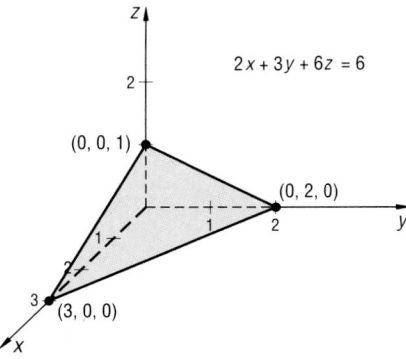

Not all planes have three intercepts. If exactly one of the constants A, B, and C is zero in the standard form of the equation of a plane, the plane is parallel to a coordinate axis. Example 3 illustrates this.

Example 3   In 3-space, graph $4x + 3z = 12$.

Solution   As in Example 2 find the intercepts. The x-intercept is 3 and the z-intercept is 4. However, there is no y-intercept because when substituting $x = 0$ and $z = 0$, you get
$$4(0) + 3(0) = 12, \text{ or } 0 = 12.$$

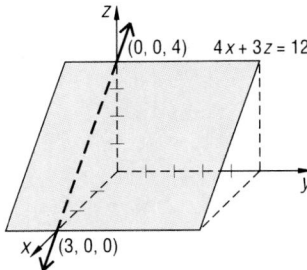

So, the plane does not intersect the y-axis and is therefore parallel to it. The rectangular region graphed at the right is part of the plane determined by $4x + 3z = 12$.

LESSON 14-2   Equations of Planes   **821**

NOTES ON QUESTIONS

Question 13: Note that the set of solutions to the equation $2x + 4y + 5z = 100$ is finite and discrete. All variables must be non-negative integers.

Question 14: This question follows up on ideas from the previous lesson. If students had difficulty with the questions on surface area or volume in that lesson, you might want to have them find both for this rectangular solid.

Making Connections for Questions 19–21: These questions are similar to Questions 23–26 in the last review set. However, while in Lesson 14-1 the equations considered had known constants, the equations here are in general form.

Making Connections for Questions 19 and 20: These questions are not only good review, but they also preview the content of Lesson 14-3.

ADDITIONAL ANSWERS

2.a.

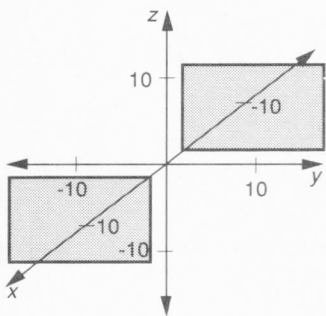

7.

Just as the intersection of two lines in 2-space represents the solution to a 2×2 linear system, the intersection of three planes in 3-space represents the solution to a 3×3 linear system. Each of the equations $\begin{cases} x = 3 \\ y = 8 \\ z = -1 \end{cases}$ represents a plane parallel to a coordinate plane.

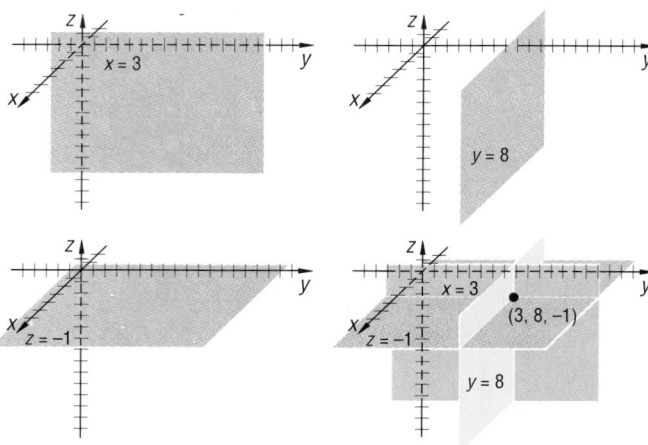

If these three graphs are placed on the same coordinate system, the lower right graph is obtained. There is a single point of intersection, $(3, 8, -1)$. The coordinates of this point satisfy all three equations.

Because graphing planes in 3-space is time consuming and may be difficult, most people do not solve systems of three linear equations by graphing. However, computers can easily graph even more complicated equations and are increasingly being used to study complex systems.

Questions

Covering the Reading

1. *True or false* The plane with equation $x = 5$ is parallel to the xz-plane. **False**

2. **a.** Graph the set of points 10 units away from the yz-plane. **See margin.**
   b. Write an equation for the set of points in part a. $x = 10$ or $x = -10$

822

In 3 and 4, consider the plane determined by the equation
$Ax + By + Cz = D$.

3. If exactly one of the constants A, B, and C is zero, the plane is parallel to a coordinate __?__.   **axis**

4. If exactly two of the constants A, B, and C are zero, the plane is parallel to a coordinate __?__.   **plane**

5. Define: z-intercept of a plane.
It is the z-value of the point where a plane intersects the z-axis.

6. Plane P, shown at the right, is parallel to the yz-plane and contains $(4, 0, 0)$. Give an equation for P.   **$x = 4$**

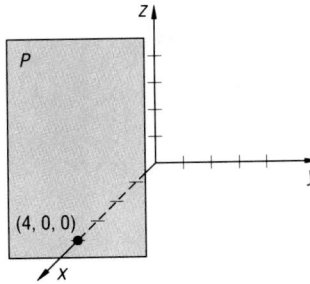

(4, 0, 0)

7. Graph the triangular region determined by the intercepts of the plane with equation $4x - 2y + 3z = 6$.   **See margin.**

8. The solution to the system $\begin{cases} x = 4 \\ y = 2 \\ z = 7 \end{cases}$ is the point of intersection of the three planes __?__, __?__, and __?__.   **$x = 4$, $y = 2$, $z = 7$**

9. Refer to the graph at the right.

   a. What system is graphed? $\begin{cases} z = 2 \\ x = -3 \\ y = 1 \end{cases}$

   b. Find the solution to the system.
   (-3,1,2)

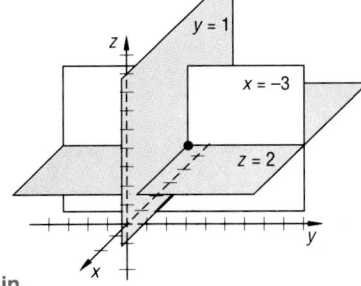

y = 1
x = -3
z = 2

Applying the Mathematics

10. Graph the plane $x - 3y = 6$.   **See margin.**

11. Give an equation for the plane containing the point $(0, 5, 0)$ and parallel to the xz-coordinate plane.   **$y = 5$**

12. Graph the triangular region determined by the intercepts of the plane with equation $12x - 3y + 8z = 24$.   **See margin.**

13. A 100-point test has x questions worth 2 points each, y questions worth 4 points each, and z questions worth 5 points each.
    a. Write an equation that describes all possible numbers of questions.
    $2x + 4y + 5z = 100$
    b. What is a suitable domain for x, y, and z?
    $0 \le x \le 50, 0 \le y \le 25, 0 \le z \le 20$
    c. Graph the triangular region determined by the intercepts of this equation.   **See margin.**
    d. Name 3 ordered triples (x, y, z) that satisfy the equation from part a. Are they in the region?
    Samples: (50, 0, 0), (0, 25, 0), (0, 0, 20); yes

LESSON 14-2 Equations of Planes   823

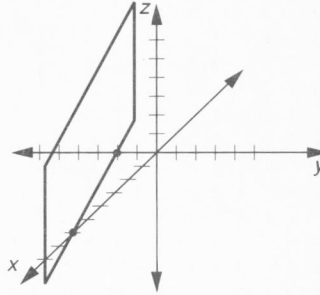

12.

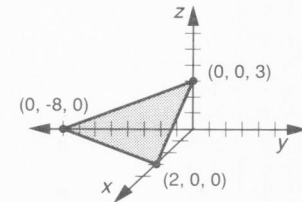

(0, 0, 3)
(0, -8, 0)
(2, 0, 0)

13.c.

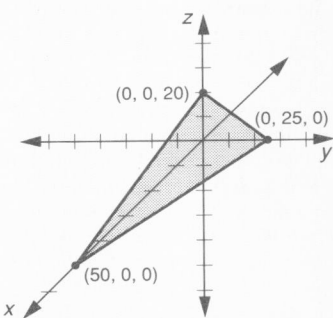

(0, 0, 20)
(0, 25, 0)
(50, 0, 0)

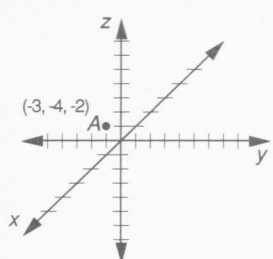
14. Give equations for the six planes which contain the faces of the box drawn at the right.
x = 4, x = 0, y = 6, y = 0, z = 9, z = 0

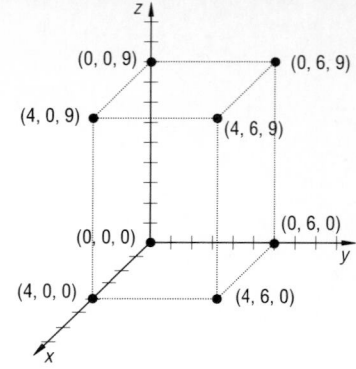

Review

15. Draw a coordinate system and plot the point $A = (-3, -4, -2)$. *(Lesson 14-1)* See margin.

16. *True or false* If point (a, b, c) lies in the lower right front octant, then a is negative and b and c are positive. *(Lesson 14-1)* **False**

17. In electricity, impedance for an alternating current is similar to resistance in a direct current. The rule for combining impedances z_1 and z_2 in series is simply $z_1 + z_2$. Find the impedance of z_1 and z_2 in series given that $z_1 = 2 + 3i$ and $z_2 = 1 - 5i$. *(Lesson 6-9)* **3 − 2i**

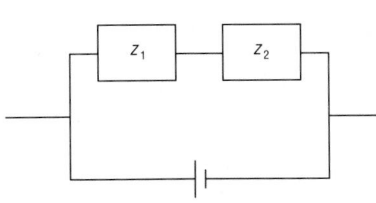

18. The pressure of a liquid on a submerged object varies jointly as the depth of the object and the density of the liquid. When an object is 50 in. below the surface of a liquid with density 1.5 lb/in.³ the pressure on it is 93.4 psi. Find the pressure on an object 125 in. below the surface of a liquid with density 2.3 lb/in³. *(Lesson 2-10)* about 358 psi

824

In 19–21, consider the following equations describing relations in (x, y) or (t, A). *(Lessons 9-7, 8-2, 6-5, 6-4, 3-4, 3-2, 2-7, 2-6, 2-4)*

$$y = kx \qquad\qquad y = mx + b \qquad\qquad Ax + By = C$$

$$y = kx^2 \qquad\qquad y = ax^2 + bx + c \qquad A = P\left(1 + \frac{r}{n}\right)^{nt}$$

$$y = \frac{k}{x} \qquad\qquad A = Pe^{rt} \qquad\qquad y = a(x - h)^2 + k$$

19. Which equations represent lines when graphed?
$y = kx, y = mx + b, Ax + By = C$

20. Which equations represent parabolas when graphed?
$y = kx^2, y = ax^2 + bx + c, y = a(x - h)^2 + k$

21. Which equation would you use to calculate interest earned in a bank account compounded daily? $A = P(1 + \frac{r}{n})^{nt}$

22. Solve $\begin{cases} 3x + 4y = 29 \\ 2x - 5y = -42 \end{cases}$ *(Lesson 5-3)* $x = -1, y = 8$

23. a. What is the probability of getting exactly 2 heads in 8 tosses of a fair coin? $\frac{8}{256} = \frac{1}{32}$
  b. *Multiple choice*   To which binomial expansion is part a related?   i
    (i) $(x + y)^8$ (ii) $(x + y)^6$ (iii) $(x + y)^4$ (iv) $(x + y)^2$
  c. To which combination is part a related? $\binom{8}{1}$
  d. To which row of Pascal's Triangle is part a related?   **eighth row**
    (Lessons 13-5, 13-6, 13-7, 13-9)

Exploration

24. The three-dimensional coordinate system used in this book is an example of a right-handed system. Find out what is meant by a left-handed coordinate system. Draw the coordinate axes of a left-handed system.

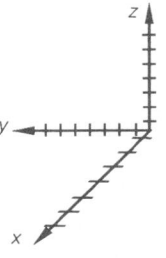

FOLLOW-UP

MORE PRACTICE
For more questions on SPUR Objectives, use *Lesson Master 14-2*, shown below.

EXTENSION
You might want to give extra credit to students who can tell you how many solutions there are to the equation in **Question 13** and who can list them systematically.

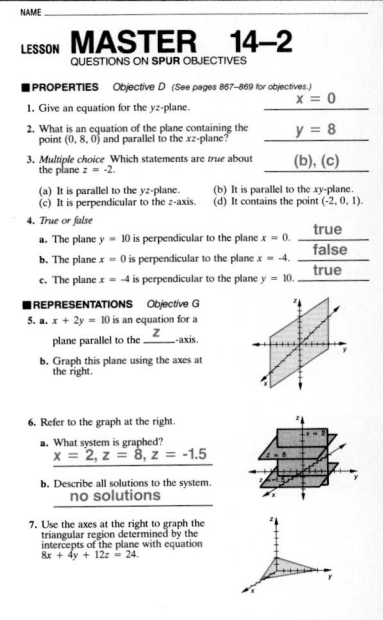

LESSON

14-3

Solving Systems in 3-Space

In a plane, two lines may intersect in 0 points, exactly 1 point, or in a line (if they are the same line). Any point of intersection is a solution to the system of equations of the lines. In space, two planes either are parallel or they intersect in a line. Therefore, a system of 2 equations in 3 variables cannot have exactly one solution. At least three equations are needed to solve for 3 variables. With 3 equations in 3 variables, there are four possible situations. They correspond to the possible relative positions of the 3 planes.

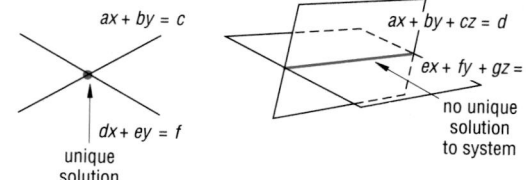

$ax + by = c$
$dx + ey = f$
unique solution to system

$ax + by + cz = d$
$ex + fy + gz = h$
no unique solution to system

Possible intersections of 3 planes	Instance	
no points	planes containing the floor, ceiling, and one wall of a room	
exactly 1 point	planes containing the floor and two intersecting walls intersect at a corner	
a line	planes containing three pages of an open book	
a plane	three identical (coincident) planes	

Any point of intersection is a solution to the system of equations of the planes.

Such systems arise in many settings.

Example 1 In looking back over its records, a publishing company noted the following costs for publishing books.
Job 1: 60 hr design, 100 hr writing, 200 hr production
Total cost: $23,000
Job 2: 30 hr design, 300 hr writing, 400 hr production
Total cost: $49,500
Job 3: 40 hr design, 80 hr writing, 150 hr production
Total cost: $17,400
Write a system that could be solved to find how much the company charged per hour for design, writing, and production.

826

Solution There are three variables. Let

d = the hourly charge for design,
w = the hourly charge for writing,
p = the hourly charge for production.

Note that each job represents a linear combination of d, w, and p. So, the system is as follows:

$$\begin{cases} 60d + 100w + 200p = 23000 \\ 30d + 300w + 400p = 49500 \\ 40d + 80w + 150p = 17400 \end{cases}$$

In Chapter 5 you learned how to solve 3 equations with 3 variables by using matrices. However, when the inverse of a 3 by 3 matrix is not given, there is another algebraic method to solve such systems. This method is an extension of the linear combination method you have used to solve a 2×2 system.

■ ■ ■ ■ ■ ■ ■ ■ ■

Example 2 Solve the system of Example 1. That is, find the hourly charge for design, writing, and production.

Solution
Step 1: First simplify each equation, if possible. The first equation can be divided by 20, all others by 10. Then number them for reference.

(1): $3d + 5w + 10p = 1150$
(2): $3d + 30w + 40p = 4950$
(3): $4d + 8w + 15p = 1740$

Step 2: Find a variable to eliminate. Two coefficients of d are the same, so d is a good candidate for elimination.
Step 3: Subtract (1) from (2).

(2) − (1): $25w + 30p = 3800$

Divide by 5 to simplify . We call this (4).

(4): $5w + 6p = 760$

Another equation in w and p is needed. We use (1) and (3) and again eliminate d.

$4 \cdot (1)$: $12d + 20w + 40p = 4600$
$3 \cdot (3)$: $\underline{12d + 24w + 45p = 5220}$
Subtract to get $-4w - 5p = -620$

Multiply by -1 to simplify. Call it (5).

(5): $4w + 5p = 620$

Step 4: Use (4) and (5) to solve for w and p as you normally would.

(4): $\qquad\qquad\qquad\qquad\qquad 5w + 6p = 760$
(5): $\qquad\qquad\qquad\qquad\qquad 4w + 5p = 620$

$4 \cdot$ (4): $\qquad\qquad\qquad\qquad 20w + 24p = 3040$
$5 \cdot$ (5): $\qquad\qquad\qquad\qquad \underline{20w + 25p = 3100}$
$\qquad\qquad\qquad\qquad\qquad\qquad\quad -p = -60$

So $p = 60$.

Step 5: Substitute in (4) or (5) to find $w = 80$. Then substitute in (1), (2), or (3) to find that $d = 50$.

The company seems to have charged \$50/hr for design, \$80/hr for writing, and \$60/hr for production.

Check Substitute $d = 50$, $w = 80$, and $p = 60$ into each equation of the original system.

Does $\quad 60(50) + 100(80) + 200(60) = 23000$?
$\qquad$ Yes, $3000 + 8000 + 12000 = 23000$.

Does $\quad 30(50) + 300(80) + 400(60) = 49500$?
$\qquad$ Yes, $1500 + 24000 + 24000 = 49500$.

Does $\quad 40(50) + 80(80) + 150(60) = 17400$?
$\qquad$ Yes, $2000 + 6400 + 9000 = 17400$.

The solution is correct.

Here is the general strategy for the method of *linear combinations*.

1. Simplify the equations, if possible.

2. Choose a variable to eliminate.

3. Take any two equations and eliminate the chosen variable. Then take another two equations and eliminate the same variable.

4. Solve the resulting system of two equations in two variables using techniques which you already know.

5. Substitute your solution from Step 4 into one of the three original equations to solve for the third variable.

6. Check that your solution works in *all* equations of the system.

In the second step of the solution, any of the three variables can be chosen for elimination. Sometimes a specific choice will allow you to eliminate two variables at once.

Example 3 Use the method of linear combinations to solve the following system:

$$\begin{cases} x + 2y + z = 11 \\ 5x + y + 4z = 73 \\ 3x + 2y + z = 31 \end{cases}$$

Solution

Step 1: Again we number the equations for easy reference. The equations are already simplified.

(1): $\qquad\qquad x + 2y + z = 11$
(2): $\qquad\qquad 5x + y + 4z = 73$
(3): $\qquad\qquad 3x + 2y + z = 31$

Step 2: Notice that in the first and third equations, the coefficients of y and z are equal. This means that if we subtract the equations we eliminate two variables at once.

Step 3: (3) − (1): $\qquad\qquad\qquad 2x = 20$

Thus, $x = 10$. Call this equation (4).

Step 4: Determine an equation with x and one other variable. That is, eliminate either y or z. We eliminate z, by multiplying the first equation by 4 and subtracting the second.

4 · (1): $\qquad\quad 4x + 8y + 4z = 44$
(2): $\qquad\qquad\; \underline{5x + y + 4z = 73}$
(5): $\qquad\qquad\; {-}x + 7y = {-}29$

Now solve the 2 × 2 system

(4): $\qquad\qquad\qquad x = 10$
(5): $\qquad\qquad\qquad {-}x + 7y = {-}29$

by adding (4) and (5).

$$7y = {-}19$$
$$y = {-}\tfrac{19}{7}$$

Step 5: Substitute $x = 10$ and $y = {-}\tfrac{19}{7}$ into one of the original equations and solve for z. We use (1) because it has the smallest coefficients.

$$10 + 2(\tfrac{-19}{7}) + z = 11$$
$$\tfrac{32}{7} + z = 11$$
$$z = \tfrac{45}{7}$$

The solution to the system is $x = 10$, $y = {-}\tfrac{19}{7}$, $z = \tfrac{45}{7}$. You should check this.

NOTES ON QUESTIONS
Question 4: Advise students that the first step in solving a large system is to look for two equations whose sum or difference eliminates variables.

Making Connections for Question 10: This question reviews material from Lesson 11-6 that led to systems solvable by the techniques of this lesson. But then, only subtraction was needed.

Remember that not all 3×3 systems have unique solutions. For instance, in the system

(1):	$3x + y - 2z = 6$
(2):	$x + 2y + z = 7$
(3):	$6x + 2y - 4z = 12$

notice that the third equation is a multiple of the first. Suppose we choose to eliminate x by using these equations. We would multiply the first equation by 2 and subtract the third equation from the result.

$2 \cdot (1):$	$6x + 2y - 4z = 12$
(3):	$6x + 2y - 4z = 12$
	$0 = 0$

As with 2×2 systems, a result such as $0 = 0$, which is always true, means that there are infinitely many solutions. In two-space this means that the two equations represent the same line. In three space there can be one of three possible interpretations: all three equations may represent the same plane; two equations represent the same plane which intersects the third plane in a line; or all three planes intersect in the same line. In the system above, equations (1) and (3) name the same plane. This plane intersects the plane named by the second equation in a line. This line yields an infinite number of solutions to the system.

Questions

Covering the Reading

In 1 and 2, *true or false*. Refer to the general linear combination strategy for solving a system of three equations in three variables.

1. The goal at first is to obtain a system with fewer variables. **True**

2. It is sufficient to check a solution in two of the three equations of a 3×3 system. **False**

3. Suppose a competitor to the publishing company discussed in Examples 1 and 2 quotes the following prices for the same number of hours.

Job 1:	$21,200
Job 2:	$46,850
Job 3:	$16,100

a. Write a system of equations that could be used to determine the hourly charge for design, writing, and production. **See below.**
b. Solve the system in part a. $d = $45/hr, $w = $85/hr, $p = $50/hr

a) $60d + 100w + 200p = 21200$
$30d + 300w + 400p = 46850$
$40d + 80w + 150p = 16100$

4. Consider the system
$$\begin{cases} 5x + y + 6z = 3 \\ x - y + 10z = 9 \\ 5x + y - 2z = -9 \end{cases}$$

a. Which equations can be added or subtracted to eliminate two variables at once?   **the first and the third**

b. Solve this system, and check your solution. $x = -2, y = 4, z = \frac{3}{2}$

c. What does the solution mean geometrically?
The three planes intersect in a single point, $(-2, 4, \frac{3}{2})$.

5. Refer to the following system.
$$\begin{cases} 5x + 4y + 8z = 170 \\ 4x + 3y + 6z = 132 \\ 3x + 5y + 4z = 130 \end{cases}$$

a. You decide to eliminate x by adding two equations. By what numbers should you multiply both sides of the first two equations?   **-4; 5**
$5x + 4y + 8z = 170$ multiply by __?__   **or 4; -5**
$4x + 3y + 6z = 132$ multiply by __?__

b. Use the second and third equations to eliminate x.   **See margin.**

c. Solve the original system using your results from parts a and b.
$x = 18, y = 12, z = 4.$

6. a. If you obtain a statement such as $0 = 0$ while solving a 3 × 3 system, then the system has how many solutions?   **infinitely many**

b. What does the solution to the system mean geometrically?
The three planes meet in a line or all three planes are identical.

Applying the Mathematics

7. Solve and check: $\begin{cases} 2x - 3y + 4z = -16 \\ 5x + 2y - 2z = 15 \\ x + y - z = 6 \end{cases}$ $x = 1, y = 2, z = -3$

8. If, while solving a system, you get a false statement such as $5 = 0$, what can you conclude about the solution to the system?
There is no solution.

9. A bicycle, three tricycles, and a unicycle cost $208. Seven bicycles and a tricycle cost $399. Five unicycles, two bicycles and seven tricycles cost $657. What is the cost of one bicycle?   **$53**

10. An experiment was conducted to find the height above ground, y, of an object t seconds after being dropped from a tall building. The following results were obtained.

t	0	1	2	3	4	5
y	800	784	736	656	544	400

a. It was expected that a polynomial model would describe the relationship between y and t. Use the method of finite differences to test this hypothesis. If the hypothesis is correct, determine the degree of the polynomial.   **The degree of the polynomial is 2.**

b. Write a system of equations to find the polynomial. Solve the system using the methods of this lesson and write the polynomial model for the data.   **See margin.**

FOLLOW-UP

MORE PRACTICE
For more questions on SPUR Objectives, use *Lesson Master 14-3*, shown below.

ADDITIONAL ANSWERS
5.b.
$\begin{cases} 4x + 3y + 6z = 132 \\ 3x + 5y + 4z = 130 \end{cases}$
$\begin{cases} -12x - 9y - 18z = -396 \\ 12x + 20y + 16z = 520 \end{cases}$
so $11y - 2z = 124$.

10.b.
$\begin{cases} 9a + 3b + c = 656 \\ 4a + 2b + c = 736 \\ a + b + c = 784 \end{cases}$
$a = -16, b = 0, c = 800$
$y = -16t^2 + 800$

NAME _____

LESSON **MASTER   14-3**
QUESTIONS ON **SPUR** OBJECTIVES

■ **SKILLS**   *Objective A (See pages 867–869 for objectives.)*

1. Describe how to go from the first system to the second.
$\begin{cases} -2x - y + z = -3 \\ x + 3y - z = 3 \\ x - 5y - z = -5 \end{cases}$ to $\begin{cases} -x + 2y = 0 \\ 8y = 8 \end{cases}$
Add the first equation to the second, and subtract the
third equation from the second.

In 2–4, solve each system using linear combinations.

2. $\begin{cases} p + 2q + r = 5 \\ 2p - q + r = 4 \\ 3p + q + 4r = 1 \end{cases}$ **3.** $\begin{cases} a - 2b + 3c = 3 \\ 2a + b + 5c = 8 \\ 3a - b - 3c = -22 \end{cases}$ **4.** $\begin{cases} 3x + 2y - z = 4 \\ 5x - 3y + 2z = 1 \\ 9x - 13y + 8z = -5 \end{cases}$

   (5, 2, -4)   (-4, 1, 3)   no solution

■ **PROPERTIES**   *Objective D*

5. a. How many solutions does the system in Question 4 have?   **none**

   b. Interpret part (a) geometrically.
   The three planes do not intersect at one point.

■ **USES**   *Objective F*

6. An electronics manufacturer makes three models of portable stereos, the Boomer, the Blaster, and the Super Blaster. The time in hours it takes each unit to be assembled, tested, and packaged is listed in the table below.

	Boomer	Blaster	Super Blaster
Assembly Department	0.2	0.3	0.4
Testing Department	0.1	0.2	0.2
Packaging Department	0.1	0.1	0.1

The assembly, testing, and packaging departments have available a maximum of 3170, 1770, and 1110 work-hours per month, respectively. How many of each model should be produced so the manufacturer operates at full capacity?
4500 Boomers; 3700 Blasters; 2900 Super Blasters

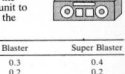

Advanced Algebra © Scott, Foresman and Company

149

831

NOTES ON QUESTIONS
Question 13: This question is necessary for the discussion of spheres in the next lesson.

Question 18: This question is deceptively difficult for many students.

ADDITIONAL ANSWERS
12.a.

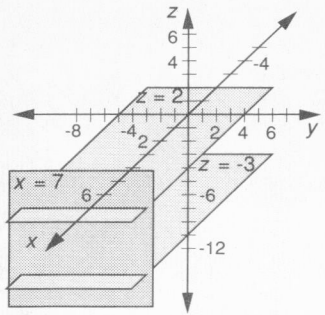

13.

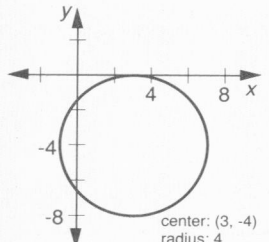

center: (3, -4)
radius: 4

11. Write the equation of the plane parallel to the xz-plane which contains (5, -6, -15). *(Lesson 14-2)* $y = -6$

12. a. Graph the system in 3-space: $x = 7$, $z = 2$, $z = -3$.   **See margin.**
   b. *Multiple choice* The solution to the system in part a is
   (a) a point   (b) a line   (c) a plane   (d) none of (a)–(c).
   (Lesson 14-2)   **d**

13. Graph $(x - 3)^2 + (y + 4)^2 = 16$ on a coordinate plane. *(Lesson 12-1)*
   See margin.

14. *Multiple choice* Which situation(s) below can be modeled by $y = mx + b$, $b \neq 0$? *(Lessons 3-1, 2-4)*   **b**
   (a) The depreciation of a car which retains 97% of its value each year.
   (b) The weight of a man on a diet who loses 2 pounds per week for six weeks.
   (c) The height of a rock thrown into the air after x seconds.
   (d) The perimeter of a square varies directly as the length of the side.

15. A ball is dropped to the ground from a height of 10 meters and bounces up to 60% of its height each time it bounces. Answer all parts to the nearest tenth of a meter.
   a. How far does it travel before hitting the ground the second time?   **22.0 m**
   b. How far does it travel before hitting the ground the eighth time?   **39.2 m**
   c. How far does it travel before stopping? *(Lessons 13-2, 13-4)*   **40 m**

16. Consider the functions: $f(x) = \cos x$, $g(x) = \log x$, and $h(x) = |x|$.
   (Lessons 10-9, 9-4, 7-5, 7-3)
   a. Which function has an inverse which is also a function?   **$g(x) = \log x$**
   b. How can you tell from the graph?   **It passes the horizontal line test.**

17. Consider the equation $\dfrac{x^2}{121} + \dfrac{y^2}{100} = 1$.
   a. Which conic does it describe?   **ellipse**
   b. Name its vertices. *(Lesson 12-4)*   **(-11, 0), (11, 0)**

18. a. Find equations for three different planes that contain both the points (1, 2, 3) and (4, 6, 8).   **See below.**
   b. Solve the system of three equations you found in part a to determine the intersection of these planes.   **The result is 0 = 0.**
   c. Interpret your solution.   **The planes intersect in a line.**
   18a) Using the two given points and the variable t,
   $x = 1 + 3t$, $y = 2 + 4t$, and $z = 3 + 5t$.
   Then $t = \dfrac{x - 1}{3} = \dfrac{y - 2}{4} = \dfrac{z - 5}{3}$.
   $\quad\;$ (A)$\quad\quad$ (B)$\quad\quad$ (C)
   Using A = B and A = C, 3x − y − z = 2.
   Using A = B and B = C, x − 2y + z = 0.
   Using B = C and A = C, 5x + 5y − 7z = -6.

Distance and Spheres

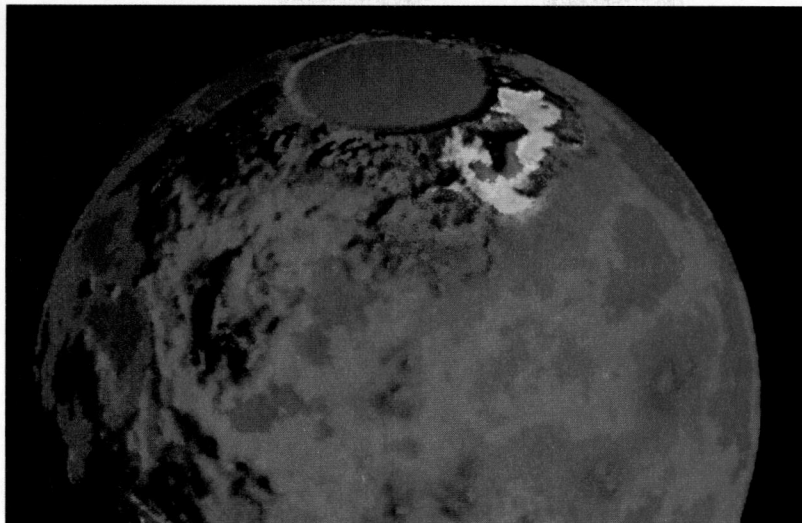

Computer-enhanced topography of planet Venus. Lower elevations are blue, medium elevations are green, high elevations are yellow.

In 1-space, on a number line, the distance between two points x_1 and x_2 is $|x_1 - x_2|$.

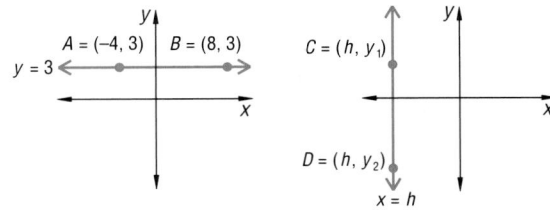

In 2-space, to determine the distance between two points which lie on a line parallel to the x-axis, you find the absolute value of the difference of the x-coordinates. For instance, if $A = (-4, 3)$ and $B = (8, 3)$,

$$AB = |-4 - 8| = 12.$$

In general, if A and B are the points (x_1, y_1) and (x_2, y_2) on a line parallel to the x-axis,

$$AB = |x_1 - x_2|.$$

Similarly, if C and D are two points on a line parallel to the y-axis (as pictured above),

$$CD = |y_1 - y_2|.$$

Thus, in both 1-space and 2-space the distance between two points on a line parallel to a coordinate axis is the absolute value of the difference of the *unequal* coordinates. This is true also in 3-space.

LESSON 14-4 Distance and Spheres **833**

LESSON 14-4

RESOURCES
■ Lesson Master 14-4
■ Quiz for Lessons 14-1
  Through 14-4
▣ Visual for Teaching Aid 98
  shows the Distance For-
  mula for 3-space.
▣ Visual for Teaching Aid 99
  shows the drawing of the
  sphere for **Example 3.**

OBJECTIVES

B Find distances between
  points in 3-space.
C Write equations for
  spheres.
G Graph spheres.

TEACHING NOTES

You may want to preview the distance formula in 3-space with a discussion of how to find distances in a noncoordinatized 3-dimensional world. Specifically, suppose a rectangular solid has dimensions 6″ × 8″ × 5″, as shown below. What is the length of the diagonal $\overline{AB}$?

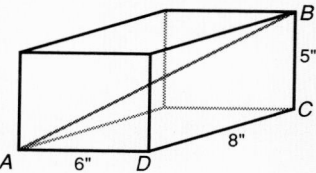

Use a skeleton model of a solid to make the situation concrete. Some students may "work forward" to find AC(10) first, and then use the Pythagorean Theorem again to get $AB(\sqrt{125})$. Others will "work backward" and see that in order to find AB they must find AC.

As a second example, give the coordinates of two points in 3-space, for instance, $A = (-5, 3, 6)$ and $B = (2, 4, 11)$, and have students calculate AB again by using the Pythagorean Theorem twice.

The proof of the distance formula is worth going over, whether or not you have done examples such as the one above. Some students will need help visualizing the two right triangles ($\triangle ABC$ and $\triangle ACD$).

ADDITIONAL EXAMPLES
1. If $A = (2, 3, 4)$, $B = (-7, 3, 4)$, and $C = (-7, 3, 10)$, find AB and BC.
$AB = 9$; $BC = 6$

2. Find the distance between A and C in Additional Example 1. Are A, B, and C on the same line with B between A and C?
$\sqrt{117}$; no, $AB + BC \neq AC$.

3. Give an equation for the unit sphere.
$x^2 + y^2 + z^2 = 1$

■ ■ ■ ■ ■ ■ ■ ■ ■

Example 1   If $R = (-5, 3, 2)$, $S = (-5, 1, 2)$, and $T = (-5, 3, -4)$, find
a. RS;
b. RT.

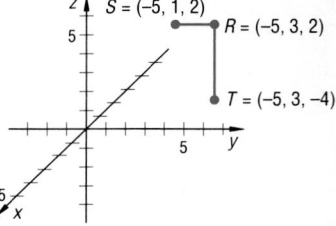

Solution
a. R and S lie on a line parallel to the y-axis. The y-coordinates are unequal. So
$RS = |y_1 - y_2| = |3 - 1| = 2$.
b. The line through R and T is parallel to the z-axis. Since the z-coordinates are not equal,
$RT = |z_1 - z_2| = |2 - -4| = 6$.

For distances in 2-space, when two points lie on an oblique line it is necessary to use the Distance Formula. Let E and F be points in 2-space with coordinates (x_1, y_1) and (x_2, y_2), respectively.

Then, $EF = \sqrt{(x_1 - x_2)^2 + (y_1 - y_2)^2}$.

You can think of EF as the length of a diagonal of a rectangle.

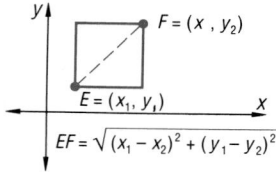

Similarly, to find AB if $A = (x_1, y_1, z_1)$ and $B = (x_2, y_2, z_2)$, we first draw the rectangular box with base parallel to the xy-plane. Then $\overline{AB}$ is the longest diagonal of the box, and is also the hypotenuse of right triangle ABC. By the Pythagorean Theorem,

$$AB^2 = AC^2 + BC^2.$$

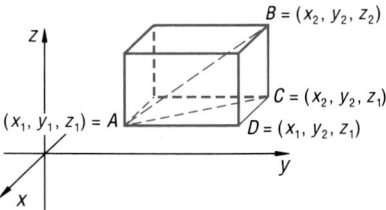

834

Since $\overline{AC}$ is the hypotenuse of right triangle ACD, by substitution we have

$$AB^2 = CD^2 + AD^2 + BC^2.$$

Now $CD = |x_1 - x_2|$, $AD = |y_1 - y_2|$, and $BC = |z_1 - z_2|$. So by substitution,

$$AB^2 = |x_1 - x_2|^2 + |y_1 - y_2|^2 + |z_1 - z_2|^2$$
$$= (x_1 - x_2)^2 + (y_1 - y_2)^2 + (z_1 - z_2)^2.$$

Take the square root of both sides:

$$AB = \sqrt{(x_1 - x_2)^2 + (y_1 - y_2)^2 + (z_1 - z_2)^2}$$

This proves the following theorem.

The Distance Formula in 3-Space

The distance d between the points (x_1, y_1, z_1) and (x_2, y_2, z_2) is

$$d = \sqrt{(x_1 - x_2)^2 + (y_1 - y_2)^2 + (z_1 - z_2)^2}.$$

■ ■ ■ ■ ■ ■ ■ ■

Example 2   Find the distance d between points $P = (-2, 4, 6)$ and $Q = (0, 3, -5)$.

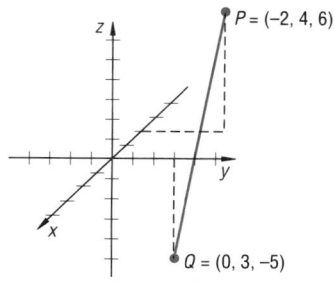

Solution $d = \sqrt{(0 - -2)^2 + (3 - 4)^2 + (-5 - 6)^2}$
$= \sqrt{4 + 1 + 121}$
$= \sqrt{126}$
≈ 11.2

In 2-space the set of points at a given distance from a fixed point is a circle with the fixed point as center and the given distance as the radius. In 3-space the set of points at a given distance from a fixed point is a **sphere.** Like a circle, a sphere is determined by its center (the fixed point) and its radius (the given distance).

In 2-space the circle with center (0, 0) and radius r has equation $x^2 + y^2 = r^2$. Now consider the sphere on a three-dimensional graph with center at the origin (0, 0, 0) and a radius r. If (x, y, z) is any point on the sphere, then using the Distance Formula:

$$r = \sqrt{(x - 0)^2 + (y - 0)^2 + (z - 0)^2}$$

$$r = \sqrt{x^2 + y^2 + z^2}$$

So $\quad r^2 = x^2 + y^2 + z^2$.

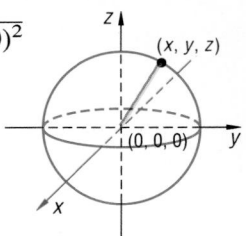

This proves the following theorem.

Theorem

The sphere with center (0, 0, 0) and radius r has equation

$$x^2 + y^2 + z^2 = r^2.$$

Example 3 Find an equation for the sphere with center at the origin and a radius of 8.

Solution Here $r = 8$. So an equation is

$$x^2 + y^2 + z^2 = 8^2$$

or $\quad x^2 + y^2 + z^2 = 64.$

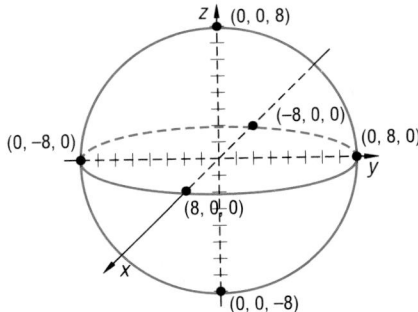

Check Graph the sphere by locating the points eight units on each axis in either direction from (0, 0, 0). There are six such points: (8, 0, 0), (-8, 0, 0), (0, 8, 0), (0, -8, 0), (0, 0, 8), and (0, 0, -8). All of these triples should satisfy the equation

$$x^2 + y^2 + z^2 = 64.$$

836

Equations for spheres whose centers are not at the origin are also possible. You might even be able to guess what they are. Question 15 asks you to think about this idea.

ADDITIONAL ANSWERS
11.

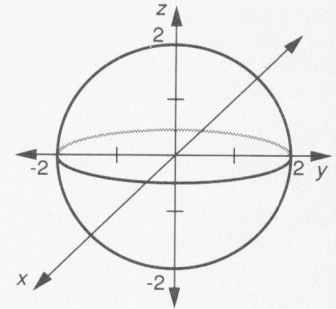

Questions

Covering the Reading

1. In 2-space, if points $C = (x_1, y_1)$ and $D = (x_2, y_2)$ lie on a line parallel to the x-axis, then $CD = \underline{\ ?\ }$.
   the absolute value of the difference of their x-coordinates

2. Let $P = (3, 4, 5)$ and $Q = (3, -2, 5)$.
   a. To which axis is $\overline{PQ}$ parallel? **y-axis**
   b. Find PQ. **6**

3. In words, explain how to find the length of a segment parallel to the z-axis. **Take the absolute value of the difference of the z-coordinates of the endpoints.**

4. Refer to the proof of the Distance Formula for 3-space.
   a. Why is $AB^2 = AC^2 + BC^2$? **The Pythagorean Theorem; $\overline{AB}$ is the hypotenuse of the right $\triangle ABC$.**
   b. Which is the right angle in $\triangle ACD$? **$\angle ADC$**
   c. Which is the right angle in $\triangle ABC$? **$\angle ACB$**

In 5–8, find the distance between the points to the nearest tenth.

5. $M = (1, 2, 11)$ and $N = (7, 2, 9)$ **6.3**

6. $O = (0, 0, 0)$ and $T = (-1, 2, 2)$ **3.0**

7. $P = (0, -16, 4.3)$ and $Q = (-1.2, 6, -3.1)$ **23.2**

8. $(-2, -2, -2)$ and $(3, 3, 3)$ **8.7**

9. Finish this definition. A sphere is the set of points $\underline{\ ?\ }$.
   equidistant from a given point

10. Give an equation for the sphere with radius 7 and center at the origin.
    $x^2 + y^2 + z^2 = 49$

11. Graph: $x^2 + y^2 + z^2 = 4$. **See margin.**

Applying the Mathematics

12. Triangle ABC has vertices $A = (2, -1, 7)$, $B = (4, 0, -5)$, and $C = (-11, 8, 2)$. Find the perimeter of $\triangle ABC$. **$\approx$ 47.2 units**

13. Use the drawing at the right.
    a. Find an equation for the sphere with center $(0, 0, 0)$ and radius 5. **$x^2 + y^2 + z^2 = 25$**
    b. Give the coordinates of a point on the sphere that is not on any of the axes.
    Samples: (3,4,0), (4,3,0), (4,0,3), etc.

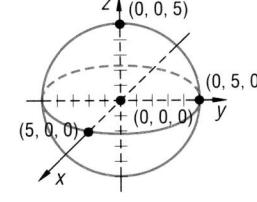

14. Describe the set of points that satisfy the sentence
$$x^2 + y^2 + z^2 \le 144.$$
It is the surface and interior of a sphere with radius 12 and center (0,0,0).

15. The set of points satisfying the equation
$$(x - 3)^2 + (y - 2)^2 + (z + 5)^2 = 36$$
is a sphere whose center is not at the origin.
   a. Where is the center of the sphere?   **(3, 2, -5)**
   b. What is the radius of the sphere?   **6**   **Sample: (9, 0, 0)**
   c. Give the coordinates of two points on the sphere.   **and (0, 8, 0)**
   d. Find an equation for the sphere with center (a, b, c) and radius r.
   $(x - a)^2 + (y - b)^2 + (z - c)^2 = r^2$

16. Question 15 suggests a 3-space analogue to the Graph Translation Theorem. State a Graph Translation Theorem for 3-space.
   See margin.

17. A daredevil is going to propel a motorized bike down a tightrope. The rope extends from a platform 30 meters high, 150 meters east and 40 meters north of its end, which is another platform 10 meters high. How long a rope is needed?
   $\approx$ 157 m (must be longer than $\sqrt{24500}$ m)

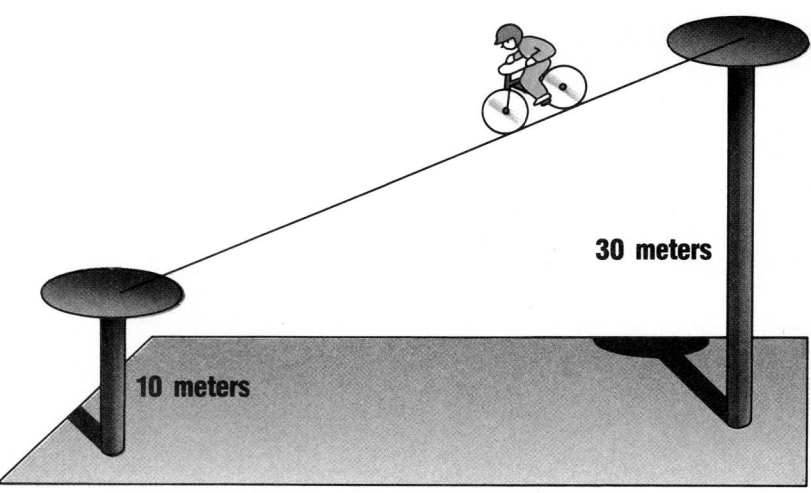

30 meters

10 meters

Review

18. An office furniture company has a sale on file cabinets. Luke's company bought 3 two-drawer, 3 three-drawer, and 6 four-drawer cabinets for $704.88. Obie's company bought 4 two-drawer, 1 three-drawer, and 8 four-drawer cabinets for $774.87. Ben's company bought 1 two-drawer, 1 three-drawer, and 12 four-drawer cabinets for $934.86.
   a. What is the cost of each type of cabinet? *(Lesson 14-3)*
   2-drawer: $39.99; 3-drawer: $54.99; 4-drawer: $69.99
   b. Use your answers to part a to find an equation which relates the price P to the number of drawers n. *(Lesson 3-5)*   **$P = \$9.99 + 15n$**
   c. According to your equation in part b, how much would a five-drawer cabinet cost? *(Lesson 1-1)*   **$84.99**

838

19. Refer to the appendix of geometry formulas if necessary.
  a. Find the area of the base of a right circular cylinder whose volume is 108π cm^3 if the height is 9 cm.   **12π cm^2**
  b. Find the radius of the base of the cylinder in part a.   **$2\sqrt{3}$ cm**
  c. Find the radius of a sphere with the same volume as the cylinder in part a.   **$3\sqrt[3]{3}$ cm**
  d. Which has more surface area, the cylinder in part a or the sphere in part c? *(Lessons 8-1, 1-2, Previous Course)*   **cylinder**

20. a. Solve using the linear combination method. *(Lessons 5-3, 12-10)*
$$\begin{cases} 9x^2 - 6y^2 = 291 \\ 6x^2 - 4y^2 = 394 \end{cases} \quad \textbf{no solution}$$
  b. Part a finds the points of intersection of what curves?
  (Lessons 12-7, 12-8)   **2 hyperbolas**

Exploration
21. A **lattice point in 3-space** is a point (x, y, z) in which x, y, and z are integers. Find ten lattice points on the sphere with equation $x^2 + y^2 + z^2 = 66$.   **See below.**

22. In 2-space, the midpoint of the segment with endpoints (x_1, y_1) and (x_2, y_2) is $\left(\dfrac{x_1 + x_2}{2}, \dfrac{y_1 + y_2}{2}\right)$. $\left(\dfrac{x_1 + x_2}{2}, \dfrac{y_1 + y_2}{2}, \dfrac{z_1 + z_2}{2}\right)$
  a. Conjecture a formula for the midpoint of the segment with end points (x_1, y_1, z_1) and (x_2, y_2, z_2).
  b. Test your conjecture by finding the midpoint of the segment with endpoints $(5, -1, 6)$ and $(3, 5, -10)$.   **(4, 2, -2)**
  c. Is the point you got in part b equidistant from these endpoints? If not, revise your conjecture.   **Yes, each distance is $\sqrt{74}$.**

21. Samples: (4, 5, 5), (-4, 5, 5), (4, -5, 5), (4, 5, -5), (-4, -5, 5), (4, -5, -5), (-4, 5, -5), (-4, -5, -5). Also (±5, ±4, ±5), (±5, ±5, ±4). Also similar permutations of (1, 4, 7).

LESSON 14-4 Distance and Spheres   **839**

FOLLOW-UP

MORE PRACTICE
For more questions on SPUR Objectives, use *Lesson Master 14-4*, shown below.

NAME _____

LESSON **MASTER 14-4**
QUESTIONS ON **SPUR** OBJECTIVES

■**SKILLS** *Objective B (See pages 867–869 for objectives.)*
In 1 and 2, find the distance between the points to the nearest integer.

1. (4, -1, 8) and (-7, 0, 3)   12
2. (.8, 6.2, 1.3) and (-4.8, -6.3, 2)   14

3. Rectangle *RECT* has vertices $R = (3.5, 4, 0)$, $E = (-4, 10.2, -2)$, $C = (2, 8.2, -30.7)$, and $T = (9.5, 2, -28.7)$.
  a. Find the perimeter of *RECT*.   78.6
  b. Find the length of any diagonal of *RECT*.   31.02

■**SKILLS** *Objective C*

4. Write an equation for the sphere with center at (0, 0, 0), and radius 6.5. $x^2 + y^2 + z^2 = 42.25$

5. Describe the graph of the equation $x^2 + y^2 + z^2 = 30$ in 3-space.
  a sphere with center at (0, 0, 0), radius 5.5

■**REPRESENTATIONS** *Objective G*

6. Use the coordinate axes at the right to graph the set of points satisfying $x^2 + y^2 + z^2 = 16$.

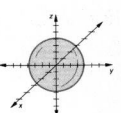

150   *Advanced Algebra © Scott, Foresman and Company*

OBJECTIVE

H Describe the surface or
  solid of revolution generated by rotating a set of
  points about a line in 3-
  space.

TEACHING NOTES

Note how the language of
transformations appears in
this lesson. **Example 1** and
the text following point out
how a cylinder can be generated either by rotating a line
segment that is parallel to a
coordinate axis around that
axis, or by translating a circle
in a plane perpendicular to
that coordinate axis. You can
illustrate this easily by rotating one of two parallel
pencils around the other, or
by sliding a circular ring up
and down a pencil. Have
some cylindrical surfaces
such as tin cans or paper
towel rolls to illustrate the result of such motions in
space.

LESSON
14-5

Solids and Surfaces of Revolution

A *lathe* is a machine which holds a solid piece of wood or metal and
spins it around at high speeds. By having a tool dig into the piece
while it spins, circular cuts can be made in the piece. The result is a
solid of revolution.

Some common figures are solids or surfaces of revolution. Begin
with the circle in the xy-plane with radius r centered at the origin.
Imagine rotating the circle about the x-axis. Each point on the circle,
except those on the x-axis, moves about the x-axis in a circular path.
The entire circle traces, or *generates*, a sphere. An equation for the
sphere is $x^2 + y^2 + z^2 = r^2$.

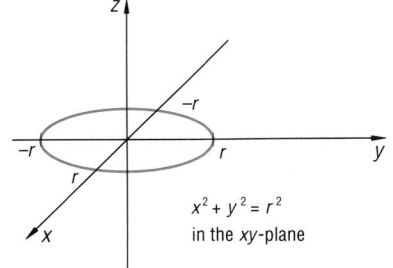

$x^2 + y^2 = r^2$
in the xy-plane

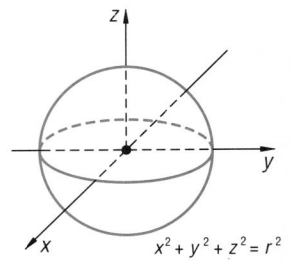

$x^2 + y^2 + z^2 = r^2$

840

The surface which is generated by rotating a curve in a plane about a line is called a **surface of revolution**. The line about which the curve is rotated is the **axis of rotation**. In the previous diagram, the *x*-axis is the axis of rotation. Each cross section perpendicular to the axis of rotation is a circle. When a lamp base or leg of a chair is made with a lathe, the axis of rotation is vertical and the horizontal cross-sections are **disks** (unions of circles and their interiors).

The sphere could have been generated by rotating only a semicircle. The semicircle defined by $x^2 + y^2 = r^2$ for $y \geq 0$ (in the first and second quadrants of the *xy*-plane) could generate the whole sphere. The half-disk shaded would generate a solid ball.

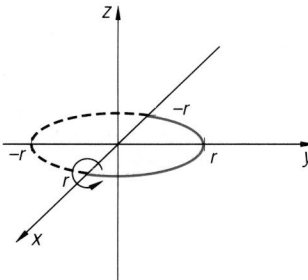

There are many other surfaces of revolution.

Example 1 The line segment $\overline{AB}$, with $A = (0, 4, 6)$ and $B = (0, 4, 1)$, is rotated about the *z*-axis. Describe the surface which is generated.

Solution Plot $\overline{AB}$. Make a sketch of its path as it rotates about the *z*-axis. Each point on $\overline{AB}$ moves in a circular path about the *z*-axis. So the cross section parallel to the *xy*-plane is a circle. Because $\overline{AB}$ is parallel to the *z*-axis, each circle has the same radius, 4. Also, $AB = |6 - 1| = 5$. So, the surface of revolution is a cylinder with radius 4 and height 5.

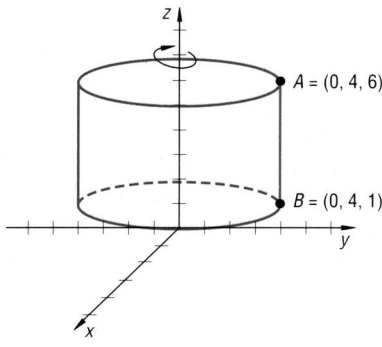

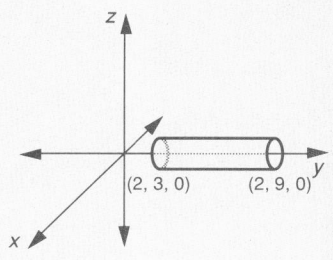
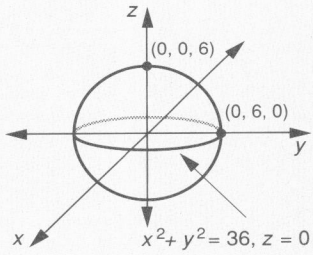
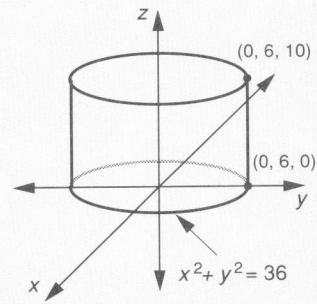

In Example 1, when we identified the surface of revolution as a cylinder we described it geometrically. We can also describe the surface algebraically. Choose any cross section of the cylinder, such as the one at the right, with C in the yz-plane. Then C has coordinates $(0, 4, z)$, where $1 \leq z \leq 6$. If D is the center of this cross section, its coordinates are $(0, 0, z)$. Let E be any other point on the same cross section. Then E has coordinates (x, y, z). Thus,

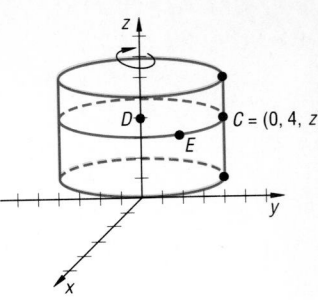

$$DE = \sqrt{(x - 0)^2 + (y - 0)^2 + (z - z)^2}$$
$$= \sqrt{x^2 + y^2}.$$

Because the cross section of the cylinder is a circle, radii $\overline{DE}$ and $\overline{DC}$ have the same length; i.e.,

$$DE = DC.$$

Since $DC = 4$, substituting into both sides we have

$$\sqrt{x^2 + y^2} = 4.$$

Square both sides of this equation to get

$$x^2 + y^2 = 16.$$

So, an *analytic description* of this cylinder is

$$x^2 + y^2 = 16, \ 1 \leq z \leq 6.$$

In the xy-plane, $x^2 + y^2 = 16$ is a circle. Any cross section of the cylinder of Example 1 is the circle $x^2 + y^2 = 16$ in the plane $z = c$ where $1 \leq c \leq 6$. The cylinder also can be considered as the surface traced by sliding $x^2 + y^2 = 16$ in the plane $z = 1$ to $x^2 + y^2 = 16$ in the plane $z = 6$.

In Example 1, a vertical line in the yz-plane was rotated about the z-axis. Example 2 shows what results when an oblique line through the origin is rotated about this axis.

■ ■ ■ ■ ■ ■ ■ ■

Example 2 Let $P = (0, 0, 0)$ and $Q = (0, 5, 8)$. Suppose $\overline{PQ}$ is rotated about the z-axis. Geometrically describe the surface which is generated.

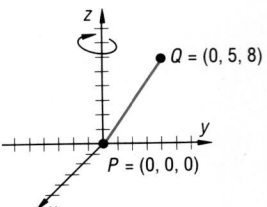

842

Solution If you spin $\overline{PQ}$ around the z-axis, you get a cone. Call C the center of the base of the cone. Then $C = (0, 0, 8)$, $CQ = 5$ and $CP = 8$. So the surface of revolution is a cone of radius 5 and height 8.

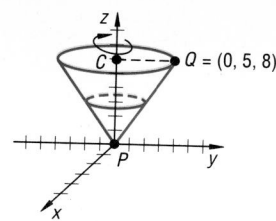

Notice that each cross section of the cone perpendicular to its axis is a circle. You would expect this both from the properties of conic sections and from the properties of surfaces of revolution.

You can rotate other curves to generate surfaces of revolution. Recall that in 2-space a parabola is the set of points equidistant from a point F (the focus) and a line l (the directrix). In 3-space a **paraboloid** is the set of points equidistant from a point F (the focus) and a plane P. If a parabola is rotated about its axis of symmetry, the paraboloid generated has the same focus as the parabola.

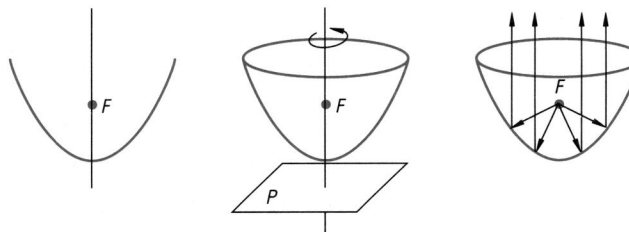

The paraboloid possesses an incredible reflection property. Any ray parallel to the axis of symmetry of a paraboloid (or parabolic) mirror is reflected into the focus. For this reason, paraboloids are the shape of radio telescope receivers and solar collectors to concentrate faint incoming parallel waves. This reflection property is used in reverse to make automobile headlights and search lights. A light is placed at the focus and reflects off the parabolic mirror to form a cylindrical beam of light. Paraboloids are sometimes used in both ways; the focus of a radar transmitter can alternately receive or send waves.

Questions

Covering the Reading

1. **a.** What is a lathe? a machine that spins a solid piece of wood or metal
   b. Give an example of an object made with a lathe.
      Samples: lamp bases, staircase ballisters, chair legs
2. A curve in a plane is rotated about a coordinate axis. What path does each point follow? a circle

3. **a.** Define: surface of revolution. See margin.
   b. Give an example of a surface of revolution. cylinder

LESSON 14-5 Solids and Surfaces of Revolution 843

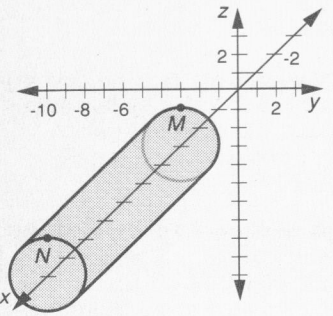
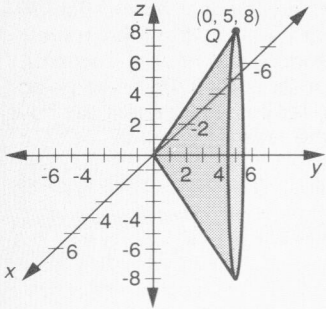
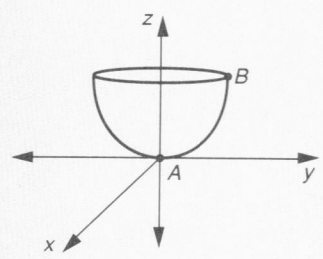
4. a. What does it mean to describe a surface algebraically or analytically?   See margin.
   b. What does it mean to describe a surface geometrically?
      See margin.
5. The graph of $y^2 + z^2 = 50$, $z \geq 0$, is a semicircle in the yz-plane. The curve is rotated about the y-axis.
   a. What geometric figure is generated?   a sphere
   b. Find an equation for the surface of revolution. $x^2 + y^2 + z^2 = 50$

6. Let $M = (3, 0, 2)$ and $N = (10, 0, 2)$. $\overline{MN}$ is rotated about the x-axis.
   a. Sketch the surface generated.   See margin.
   b. Describe it geometrically.   It is a cylinder of height 7 and radius 2.

7. The cylinder in Example 1 can be traced by sliding $x^2 + y^2 = 16$ from the plane $z = 1$ to the plane __?__. $z = 6$

8. In Example 2, suppose $\overline{PQ}$ were rotated about the y-axis.
   a. Draw the surface of revolution.   See margin.
   b. Describe the surface of revolution in as much detail as you can.
      a cone of radius 8 and height 5
9. Define: paraboloid.   The set of points equidistant from a point F (the focus) and a plane P.
10. a. Where can you find paraboloids in the world?
   b. What property causes them to have so many uses?
      a) in radio telescopes, headlights, parabolic microphones, solar collectors, etc.; b) See margin.

11. The circle $x^2 + y^2 = 36$ is rotated around the y-axis.
   a. What figure is generated?   a sphere
   b. What is its volume? 288π cubic units
   c. What is its surface area? 144π square units

12. The line $y = x$ in the xy-plane is rotated about the x-axis. Describe geometrically the surface generated.
   It is an infinite double cone with the x-axis as its axis.
In 13–15, refer to the diagram at the right. Sketch the graph of the surface generated by rotating the curve from A to B, where $B = (1,2,3)$, around the   See margin.
13. z-axis

14. y-axis

15. x-axis.

16. Consider the cylinder defined by $x^2 + y^2 = 36$ for $0 \leq z \leq 8$.
   a. Sketch its graph.   See margin.
   b. Find its volume. 288π cubic units

17. The curve $(x - 3)^2 + (y - 2)^2 = 1$ is rotated about the x-axis. What figure is traced?   a doughnut or torus

18. Find the distance between $(-3, 4, 8)$ and $(5, 2, 8)$. *(Lesson 14-4)*
  ≈ 8.25

19. *True or false*   The sphere $(x - 3)^2 + (y - 3)^2 + (z - 3)^2 = 4$ is contained entirely within the octant where all three coordinates are positive. *(Lesson 14-4)*   True

20. Solve the following system: $\begin{cases} x = y + z + 100 \\ y = x + z + 100 \\ z = x + y + 100 \end{cases}$ *(Lesson 14-3)*
  $x = y = z = -100$

21. The discriminant of a quadratic equation $ax^2 + bx + c = 0$ is -900. What does this tell you about the graph of $y = ax^2 + bx + c$? *(Lesson 6-7)*   It does not intersect the x-axis.

22. Some students make earrings and pendants in their spare time and sell all that they make. Every week they have available 10 kg of metal and 20 hours to work. It takes 48 g of metal to make an earring and 210 g to make a pendant. Each earring takes 30 minutes to make and each pendant takes 20 minutes. The profit on each earring is $3.00, and the profit on each pendant is $2.25. The students want to earn as much money as possible. Because you are taking this course, they ask you to give them advice. What numbers of earrings and pendants should they make each week? *(Lesson 5-8)*   10 earrings, 45 pendants

23. *True or false*   If matrix A has dimensions 3×4, then it has 3 columns and 4 rows. *(Lesson 4-1)*   False

24. A tennis ball is thrown upwards at 35 ft/sec from a height of 6.5 feet. When will it hit the ground? (Remember: $h = -16t^2 + v_0 t + h_0$.) *(Lesson 6-2)*   about 2.36 seconds later

25. *Multiple choice*   What kind of sampling is usually used in obtaining TV ratings? *(Lesson 13-12)*   c
  (a) normal sampling   (b) random sampling
  (c) stratified sampling   (d) Sampling is not used.

26. The Earth is (more or less) a solid of revolution called an *oblate spheriod*. What exactly is an "oblate spheroid"?
  a slightly flattened sphere

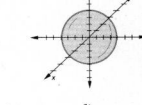
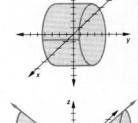
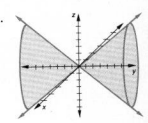

LESSON

14-6

Higher Dimensions

You know that a line segment is a one-dimensional figure, a square has two dimensions, and a cube has three. You may be surprised to learn that there is a four-dimensional figure analogous to these others. Such a figure is called a *hypercube*.

Reasoning by analogy from the figures in lower dimensions enables us to visualize a hypercube and to study some of its properties. Note that a square can be formed by first translating a line segment of length *s* a distance of *s* units in a direction perpendicular to the segment, and then connecting corresponding vertices. Because the segment has two vertices, the square has four: two from the preimage segment and two from the image segment. The square also has four edges: two are the preimage and image segments, and two connect the corresponding vertices.

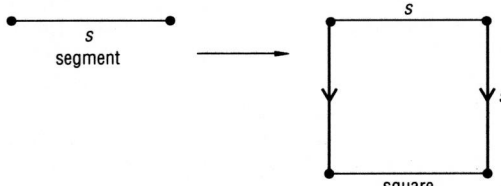

Similarly, the edges of a cube of side *s* can be formed by translating a square of side *s* a distance of *s* units in a direction perpendicular to the plane of the square, and then connecting corresponding vertices. The number of vertices and edges of a cube can be found from the number of vertices and edges of a square. The cube has 8 vertices: 4 from the preimage and 4 from the image. It has 12 edges: 8 are sides of the preimage and image squares and 4 join the corresponding vertices. Notice that to draw a cube on a page, many of the right angles on its faces must be distorted.

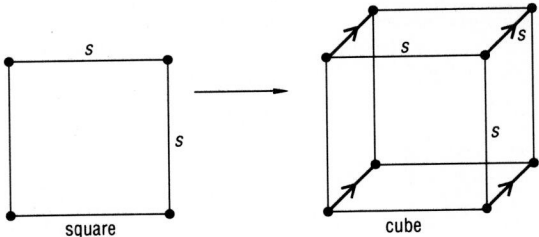

The four-dimensional **hypercube** is formed by generalizing the above process. Imagine a cube of side *s* being translated *s* units in a direction *perpendicular to its space*, and connecting corresponding vertices. Unfortunately, as in the case of picturing 3-dimensional

846

objects on a 2-dimensional page, a picture of a hypercube distorts perpendicular lines and planes. Although it may be difficult to visualize a hypercube, we know many of its properties. For instance, it has 16 vertices: 8 from each of the preimage and image cubes. The hypercube has 32 edges: 24 from the preimage and image cubes, and 8 formed by joining the corresponding vertices of the cube.

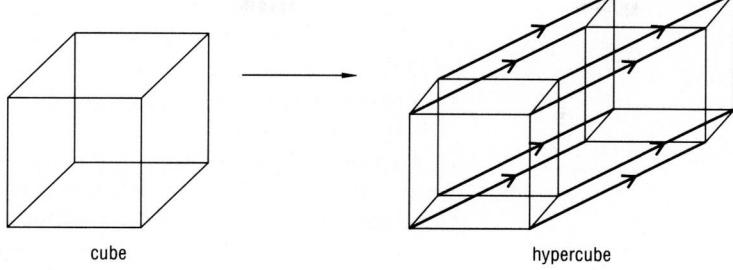

cube

hypercube

Four-dimensional figures can also be studied through coordinates. A single real number x locates a point on a number line (1-space). An ordered pair (x, y) of real numbers locates a point in 2-space; and an ordered triple (x, y, z) of real numbers locates a point in 3-space. We define **4-space** as the set of **ordered 4-tuples** (x, y, z, w) of real numbers. The point $(0, 0, 0, 0)$ is the origin of this four-dimensional coordinate system; the point $(0, -4, 0, 0)$ is on the y-axis. It may seem strange that the coordinates are not written in alphabetical order, but the order x, y, z, w maintains x as first, y as second, and z as third.

The distance between points in 4-space can be determined in ways similar to distance in 2- or 3-space. In any space, the distance between two points on a line parallel to one of the coordinate axes is the absolute value of the difference of the unequal coordinates. This can be generalized to find the distance between any two points in 4-space.

The Distance Formula in 4-Space

The distance d between the points (x_1, y_1, z_1, w_1) and (x_2, y_2, z_2, w_2) is given by

$$d = \sqrt{(x_1 - x_2)^2 + (y_1 - y_2)^2 + (z_1 - z_2)^2 + (w_1 - w_2)^2}.$$

■ ■ ■ ■ ■ ■ ■■

Example 1   Find the distance between the points in 4-space with coordinates (1, 10, 4, 3) and (1, 7, -2, 5).

Solution   Apply the distance formula for 4-space.

$$d = \sqrt{(1 - 1)^2 + (10 - 7)^2 + (4 - -2)^2 + (3 - 5)^2}$$
$$= \sqrt{0 + 9 + 36 + 4}$$
$$= \sqrt{49}$$
$$= 7$$

The distance between the points (1, 10, 4, 3) and (1, 7, -2, 5) is 7.

In 4-space, a **hypersphere** is the set of all points at a given distance from a fixed point. Thus, the set of points (x, y, z, w) at a distance r from the origin satisfies the equation

$$r = \sqrt{(x - 0)^2 + (y - 0)^2 + (z - 0)^2 + (w - 0)^2}.$$

Theorem

In 4-space, an equation for a hypersphere with center at (0, 0, 0, 0) and radius r is

$$x^2 + y^2 + z^2 + w^2 = r^2.$$

■ ■ ■ ■ ■ ■ ■■

Example 2   Find an equation for the hypersphere in 4-space with center at the origin and radius 10.

Solution   Apply the theorem above. Here $r = 10$.
An equation for this hypersphere is

$$x^2 + y^2 + z^2 + w^2 = 100.$$

One point on this sphere is (7, 1, 7, -1). Can you find others?

In the Questions you will see how a hypercube can be coordinatized. Besides ordered 4-tuples, points in 4-space can be represented as matrices. Just as the matrix $\begin{bmatrix} x \\ y \end{bmatrix}$ can be used to represent the point (x, y) in 2-space and the matrix $\begin{bmatrix} x \\ y \\ z \end{bmatrix}$ to represent (x, y, z) in 3-space, the matrix $\begin{bmatrix} x \\ y \\ z \\ w \end{bmatrix}$ represents the point (x, y, z, w) in 4-space.

848

Other figures in 4-space can then be represented by matrices with four rows. By applying matrix operations, computers are able to generate images of four-dimensional objects on two-dimensional computer screens.

Four-dimensional coordinate systems have many applications. For instance, a school that keeps records of a student's social security number S, year of graduation Y, grade point or grade average G, and rank in class R can store these data as an ordered 4-tuple (S, Y, G, R). Then the records of many students can be stored in a matrix with four rows. In fact, any system of equations or inequalities with four variables can be considered as an algebraic problem in 4-space.

In Einstein's theory of special relativity, x, y, and z represent the ordinary rectangular coordinates of 3-space and t represents a time coordinate. Each 4-tuple (x, y, z, t) represents the position of an object in space and time. Time is thus the fourth dimension in Einstein's coordinate system.

The concept of point as an ordered n-tuple generalizes to more than four dimensions. For instance, 6-space is a world in which each point is located by an ordered 6-tuple

$$(x_1, x_2, x_3, x_4, x_5, x_6).$$

Geometric models for such higher dimensional spaces are hard to visualize but through the use of coordinates and computers, problems in such spaces can be solved and figures we cannot visualize can be analyzed.

Questions

Covering the Reading

1. Name two four-dimensional figures described in the lesson.
   hypercube, hypersphere
2. State the number of vertices and edges for each figure.
   a. segment   2, 1
   b. square   4, 4
   c. cube   8, 12
   d. hypercube   16, 32

3. In 4-space, the distance d between the points (x_1, y_1, z_1, w_1) and (x_2, y_2, z_2, w_2) is given by the formula $d = \underline{\ ?\ }$.
   $\sqrt{(x_1 - x_2)^2 + (y_1 - y_2)^2 + (z_1 - z_2)^2 + (w_1 - w_2)^2}$

In 4 and 5, find the distance between P and Q.

4. $P = (3, -2, 2, 0)$ $Q = (3, 5, 2, 0)$ 7

5. $P = (1, 2, 3, 4)$ $Q = (0, 3, 2, 3)$ 2

6. Find an equation for a four-dimensional hypersphere with center at the origin and radius 8.5. $x^2 + y^2 + z^2 + w^2 = 72.25$

LESSON 14-6 Higher Dimensions   **849**

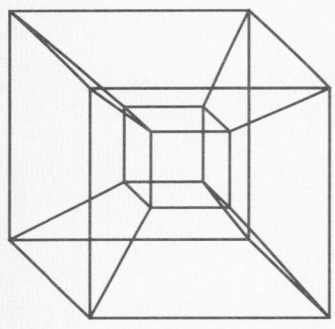
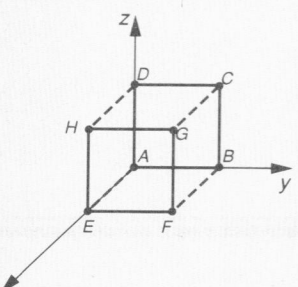
7. What is the radius of the hypersphere whose equation is
$x^2 + y^2 + z^2 + w^2 = 16$?   **4**

8. What do the four coordinates (x, y, z, t) in Einstein's theory of special relativity represent?   **x, y, z represent the ordinary coordinates of 3-space; t represents a time coordinate.**

9. *True or false*   The point $(x_1, x_2, x_3, x_4, x_5, x_6, x_7, x_8, x_9, x_{10})$ represents a point in 10-space.   **True**

10. In 2-space the midpoint of the line segment whose endpoints have coordinates (x_1, y_1) and (x_2, y_2) has coordinates $\left(\dfrac{x_1 + x_2}{2}, \dfrac{y_1 + y_2}{2}\right)$.

   a. State a conjecture about the coordinates of the midpoint of a segment in 4-space whose endpoints have coordinates (x_1, y_1, z_1, w_1) and (x_2, y_2, z_2, w_2).
$\left(\dfrac{x_1 + x_2}{2}, \dfrac{y_1 + y_2}{2}, \dfrac{z_1 + z_2}{2}, \dfrac{w_1 + w_2}{2}\right)$

   b. Using your conjecture in part a calculate the coordinates of the midpoint M of $\overline{PQ}$ where $P = (1, 10, 4, 3)$ and $Q = (1, 7, -2, 5)$.
$(1, 8\frac{1}{2}, 1, 4)$

   c. Using your answer to part b, find PM and MQ. Does each distance equal $\frac{1}{2} PQ$?   **PM = 3.5, MQ = 3.5; yes, PQ = 7**

In 11 and 12, use the sixteen points given here. They are vertices of a hypercube.

$P_1 = (0, 0, 0, 0)$	$P_9 = (0, 1, 1, 0)$
$P_2 = (1, 0, 0, 1)$	$P_{10} = (0, 1, 0, 1)$
$P_3 = (0, 1, 0, 0)$	$P_{11} = (0, 0, 1, 1)$
$P_4 = (0, 0, 1, 0)$	$P_{12} = (1, 1, 1, 0)$
$P_5 = (0, 0, 0, 1)$	$P_{13} = (1, 1, 0, 1)$
$P_6 = (1, 1, 0, 0)$	$P_{14} = (1, 0, 1, 1)$
$P_7 = (1, 0, 1, 0)$	$P_{15} = (0, 1, 1, 1)$
$P_8 = (1, 0, 0, 1)$	$P_{16} = (1, 1, 1, 1)$

11. *True or false*   The points P_1, P_2, P_3, P_4 are the vertices of a square. If true, justify your answer. If false, find four points from the list which are the vertices of a square with side 1.
False; Example: P_1, P_2, P_3, and P_6

12. A diagonal of a hypercube is the longest line segment connecting its vertices. Find the length of a diagonal of this hypercube. $P_1P_{16} = 2$

13. Use your answers to Question 2 to make a conjecture relating the dimension n of the figure and the number of vertices v of an n-dimensional cube. $v = 2^n$

14. Refer to the figure at the right, which shows another way to draw a hypercube by drawing a cube within a cube and connecting corresponding vertices with line segments.

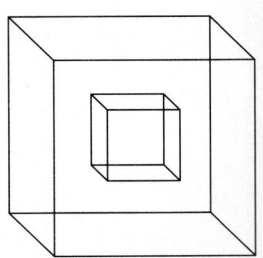

   a. How many line segments must be drawn to make the hypercube?   **8**

   b. Copy the figure and join corresponding vertices.   **See margin.**

   c. Explain how a 3-dimensional cube can be accurately drawn in a similar manner.   **See margin.**

15. a. Describe the intersection of the *xy*-plane and the sphere with center at the origin and radius 8.
a circle in the xy-plane with radius 8 and center at the origin
  b. Give an equation in the *xy*-plane for the cross section of part a. *(Lesson 14-5)* $x^2 + y^2 = 64$

16. The line segment from (2, 5, 3) to the origin is rotated around the *y*-axis.   **a cone with radius**
  a. Describe the surface generated. $\sqrt{13}$ **and height 5**
  b. Find the volume of the surface. *(Lesson 14-5)* $\frac{65}{3}\pi$ **cubic units**

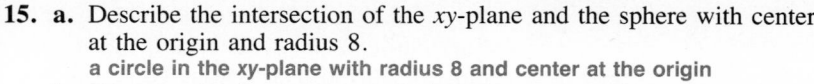

17. Three ounces of cheddar cheese, ten seedless grapes, and one large carrot were eaten by Vivian at a party, and she recorded 181 calories. Jan had one ounce of cheese, two grapes, and two carrots for a total of 94 calories. Bob had twenty grapes, three carrots, and a half ounce of cheese and a total of 211 calories. What can be deduced from this information? *(Lesson 14-3)*
oz of cheese is 32 cal., grape is 6 cal., carrot is 25 cal.

18. If a test is standardized with a mean of 500 and a standard deviation of 100, about what percent of test-takers would be expected to score between 100 and 600? *(Lesson 13-10)*   ≈ **84%**

19. Give an example of normalized scores whose mean is 500 and whose standard deviation is 100. *(Lesson 13-10)*   **SAT scores**

In 20–25, describe the graph in one word. Do not actually draw the graph. *(Lessons 2-7, 3-4, 6-2, 12-6, 14-2)*

20. $\{(x, y): y = 4x^2 - 4x - 4\}$ **parabola**

21. $\{(x, y): x = \frac{7}{y}\}$ **hyperbola**

22. $\{(x, y): x + y = 0\}$ **line**   **23.** $\{(x, y): x^2 + y^2 = 0\}$ **point**

24. $\{(x, y, z): y = 4\}$ **plane**   **25.** $\{(x, y): y = 4\}$ **line**

26. Solve for *x*: $3^x = 21$ *(Lesson 9-9)*   x ≈ **2.77**

27. Find an equation of a polynomial with zeros at (0, 0), (-2, 0), and (4, 0). *(Lesson 11-5)*   **Example: P(x) = kx(x + 2)(x - 4)**

28. a. Solve the system $\begin{cases} 2x - 7y = 15 \\ -5x + y = 1 \end{cases}$ using matrices. $(-\frac{2}{3}, -\frac{7}{3})$
  b. Check by solving using some other method.
    (Lessons 5-2, 5-3, 5-4, 5-6) $(-\frac{2}{3}, -\frac{7}{3})$

29. The book *Flatland* by Edwin Abbott Abbott (his real name) describes a world inhabited by two-dimensional beings who have the misfortune of being visited by a sphere from the third dimension. Read this book and describe how we as inhabitants of a three-dimensional world might perceive a visit by a four-dimensional hypersphere.
We would see a circle growing to a sphere, shrinking back to a circle, and vanishing.

FOLLOW-UP

MORE PRACTICE
For more questions on SPUR Objectives, use *Lesson Master 14-6*, shown below.

EXTENSION
The book *Flatland*, mentioned in the Exploration, can be used as the basis for many projects. Students can read the book and give individual written or oral reports on it. Individuals or groups of students can represent parts of the book artistically (posters, models, dramatizations). We heard of one class that developed a play based on the book which was performed for other classes.

NAME _____

LESSON **MASTER** **14–6**
QUESTIONS ON SPUR OBJECTIVES

■**SKILLS** *Objective B (See pages 867–869 for objectives.)*
In 1 and 2, find the distance between the points. Round your answers to the nearest integer.

1. (6, 2, -4, -7) and (0, 2, -4, -7)   ____6____

2. $(5\frac{1}{4}, 1, -7, 2)$ and (-1, 4, 30, -12)   ____40____

■**SKILLS** *Objective C*

3. What is an equation for the hypersphere with center at the origin and radius 0.5? $x^2 + y^2 + z^2 + w^2 = 0.25$

4. Consider the hypersphere with equation $x^2 + y^2 + z^2 + w^2 = 2304$. Name its center and radius.   **(0, 0, 0, 0), 48**

■**PROPERTIES** *Objective E*

5. In 1-space, a number line, the graph of x = 5 is a point which has dimension 0.
  a. In 2-space, the coordinate plane, the graph of x = 5 is a ___line___ which has dimension 1.
  b. In 3-space, the graph of x = 5 is a ___plane___ which has dimension ___2___.
  c. In 4-space, the graph of x = 5 is a hyperplane which has dimension ___3___.

6. A point in 6-space would have ___6___ coordinates.

   Advanced Algebra © Scott, Foresman and Company

OBJECTIVES

A Solve 4 × 4 systems of
linear equations by using
augmented matrices.
F Use 4 × 4 linear systems
to solve real-world prob-
lems.

TEACHING NOTES

One advantage of using matrices is that the variables do
not have to be written over
again. However, there is a
price to be paid for this convenience; the solver must be
very careful that the variables
are in a consistent order.

The idea of row reduction, as
used by computers, is very
similar, if not identical to the
method in the **Example**.
Sometimes the first step will
be to make the leading coefficient in the first row equal
to 1.

LESSON

14-7

Solving Higher Dimensional Systems

A system with m equations and n variables is said to have
dimensions $m \times n$. The numbers m and n may be any positive
integers. In the last lesson, you read that 4-tuples can represent
figures in space and time or four-category records of students. In
earlier lessons, you learned about linear programming applications
with hundreds or thousands of variables. The linear combination and
substitution methods useful with systems containing 2 or 3 variables
can be used to solve systems where m and n are greater than 3. But
there is a great deal of writing; a more efficient means is needed.

Consider this system.

$$
\begin{aligned}
(1) \quad & 4x - 2y + 3z + 7w = 1 \\
(2) \quad & \qquad -5y + 2z - w = -32 \\
(3) \quad & \qquad\qquad z + w = 5 \\
(4) \quad & \qquad\qquad\qquad 6w = -6
\end{aligned}
$$

It is easy to solve if you begin with equation (4). From $w = -1$,
substituting in equation (3) yields $z = 6$. Then substitute for z and w
in equation (2) to get $y = 9$. Finally, substitute for y, z, and w in
equation (1) to find $x = 2$.

The coefficient matrix is 4×4, the same as
the dimensions of the system. It is called a
triangular matrix because there are all zeros
in the lower left corner below the diagonal. If
a coefficient matrix is in triangular form, the
system is easy to solve. So to solve a system
easily we wish to convert it into one whose
coefficients form a triangular matrix.

$$
\begin{bmatrix}
4 & -2 & 3 & 7 \\
0 & -5 & 2 & -1 \\
0 & 0 & 1 & 1 \\
0 & 0 & 0 & 6
\end{bmatrix}
$$

To do this, rewrite the system as an **augmented matrix** consisting
of the coefficients and the constants. For instance,

$$
\begin{cases}
5a + 4b + 8c - 2d = 28 \\
-3a - 4b + 2c + 3d = 16 \\
a + b + c \qquad = 4 \\
2a + 3b - 2c + 5d = 1
\end{cases}
\text{ becomes }
\begin{bmatrix}
5 & 4 & 8 & -2 & 28 \\
-3 & -4 & 2 & 3 & 16 \\
1 & 1 & 1 & 0 & 4 \\
2 & 3 & -2 & 5 & 1
\end{bmatrix}
$$

Everything that can be done with the system can be done with the
matrix; and it is less work not to have to write the as, bs, cs, and
ds. Multiplying both sides of an equation by k means multiplying a
row by k. Adding or subtracting equations corresponds to adding or
subtracting rows. Switching the order of equations means switching
rows. These are the legal **row operations** for matrices representing
systems:

a. Any row can be multiplied by any non-zero number.
b. Any two rows may be added and one of the rows replaced
with the sum.
c. Any two rows may be switched.

852

Using the row operations wisely, any system can be converted into an augmented triangular matrix. Here is how that is done with the above matrix. Notice how we systematically convert the matrix into one in which the lower left hand corner is a triangular array of 0s.

Step 1: Switch rows (R1) and (R3) to get the number 1 in the upper left corner.

(R1):
(R2):
(R3):
(R4):

$$\begin{bmatrix} 1 & 1 & 1 & 0 & 4 \\ -3 & -4 & 2 & 3 & 16 \\ 5 & 4 & 8 & -2 & 28 \\ 2 & 3 & -2 & 5 & 1 \end{bmatrix}$$

Step 2: Multiply row (R1) by 3 and add the result to row (R2). This makes the first element in row (R2) equal to 0.

$3 \cdot$ (R1) + (R2):

$$\begin{bmatrix} 1 & 1 & 1 & 0 & 4 \\ 0 & -1 & 5 & 3 & 28 \\ 5 & 4 & 8 & -2 & 28 \\ 2 & 3 & -2 & 5 & 1 \end{bmatrix}$$

Step 3: Repeat the idea of Step 2 with rows (R3) and (R4). That is, multiply row (R1) by -5 and add it to row (R3). Then multiply row (R1) by -2 and add it to row (R4).

$-5 \cdot$ (R1) + (R3):
$-2 \cdot$ (R1) + (R4):

$$\begin{bmatrix} 1 & 1 & 1 & 0 & 4 \\ 0 & -1 & 5 & 3 & 28 \\ 0 & -1 & 3 & -2 & 8 \\ 0 & 1 & -4 & 5 & -7 \end{bmatrix}$$

Step 4: Switch rows (R2) and (R4). This gets a 1 in the second element of row (R2).

(R1):
(R2):
(R3):
(R4):

$$\begin{bmatrix} 1 & 1 & 1 & 0 & 4 \\ 0 & 1 & -4 & 5 & -7 \\ 0 & -1 & 3 & -2 & 8 \\ 0 & -1 & 5 & 3 & 28 \end{bmatrix}$$

Step 5: Now add row (R2) to row (R3) for the new row (R3). Then add row (R2) to row (R4) for the new (R4).

(R2) + (R3):
(R2) + (R4):

$$\begin{bmatrix} 1 & 1 & 1 & 0 & 4 \\ 0 & 1 & -4 & 5 & -7 \\ 0 & 0 & -1 & 3 & 1 \\ 0 & 0 & 1 & 8 & 21 \end{bmatrix}$$

Step 6: Switch rows (R3) and (R4).

(R1):
(R2):
(R3):
(R4):

$$\begin{bmatrix} 1 & 1 & 1 & 0 & 4 \\ 0 & 1 & -4 & 5 & -7 \\ 0 & 0 & 1 & 8 & 21 \\ 0 & 0 & -1 & 3 & 1 \end{bmatrix}$$

Step 7: Add row (R3) to row (R4). The result is a matrix in augmented triangular form.

(R3) + (R4):

$$\begin{bmatrix} 1 & 1 & 1 & 0 & 4 \\ 0 & 1 & -4 & 5 & -7 \\ 0 & 0 & 1 & 8 & 21 \\ 0 & 0 & 0 & 11 & 22 \end{bmatrix}$$

The matrix from step 7 corresponds to the following system:

$$\begin{cases} a + b + c & = 4 \\ b - 4c + 5d & = -7 \\ c + 8d & = 21 \\ 11d & = 22 \end{cases}$$

From the bottom, $d = 2$, then $c = 5$, $b = 3$, and $a = -4$.

Geometrically, an equation of the form $Ax + By + Cz + Dw = E$ is a **hyperplane.** Solving the above system obtains the unique point of intersection of four hyperplanes.

Although it takes a lot of work to solve a system using augmented matrices, the advantages of this method are that it is easily done by computer and that it can be used with any linear system.

■ ■ ■ ■ ■ ■

Example Use augmented matrices to solve this system: $\begin{cases} 3u + 3v - w = 1 \\ 4u - 2v + 4w = 3 \\ 5u + 8v - 2w = 2 \end{cases}$

Solution

1. Write the system as an augmented matrix.

   (R1):
   (R2):
   (R3):

   $$\begin{bmatrix} 3 & 3 & -1 & 1 \\ 4 & -2 & 4 & 3 \\ 5 & 8 & -2 & 2 \end{bmatrix}$$

2. In order to make the first entry in the second row a 0, multiply the first row by $-\frac{4}{3}$ and add it to the second row.

   $-\frac{4}{3} \cdot$ (R1) + (R2):

   $$\begin{bmatrix} 3 & 3 & -1 & 1 \\ 0 & -6 & \frac{16}{3} & \frac{5}{3} \\ 5 & 8 & -2 & 2 \end{bmatrix}$$

3. In order to make the first entry in the 3rd row 0, multiply the first row by $-\frac{5}{3}$ and add it to the third row.

   $-\frac{5}{3} \cdot$ (R1) + (R3):

   $$\begin{bmatrix} 3 & 3 & -1 & 1 \\ 0 & -6 & \frac{16}{3} & \frac{5}{3} \\ 0 & 3 & \frac{-1}{3} & \frac{1}{3} \end{bmatrix}$$

4. To make the second entry in the 3rd row 0, multiply the second row by $\frac{1}{2}$ and add it to the third row.

   $\frac{1}{2} \cdot$ (R2) + (R3):

   $$\begin{bmatrix} 3 & 3 & -1 & 1 \\ 0 & -6 & \frac{16}{3} & \frac{5}{3} \\ 0 & 0 & \frac{7}{3} & \frac{7}{6} \end{bmatrix}$$

The matrix is triangular but has fractions.

5. To clear the fractions, multiply the second row by 3 and the third row by 6.

   $3 \cdot$ (R2):
   $6 \cdot$ (R3):

   $$\begin{bmatrix} 3 & 3 & -1 & 1 \\ 0 & -18 & 16 & 5 \\ 0 & 0 & 14 & 7 \end{bmatrix}$$

The last matrix corresponds to the system:

$$\begin{cases} 3u + 3v - w = 1 \\ -18v + 16w = 5 \\ 14w = 7 \end{cases}$$

From the last equation, $w = \frac{1}{2}$. Substituting in the second equation, $v = \frac{1}{6}$. Then, substituting in the first equation, $u = \frac{1}{3}$.

854

It is very difficult to solve a large system by hand without making an error. To help locate an error, remember that each row of an augmented matrix corresponds to an equation the solution must satisfy. For instance, in step 3 of the Example, the bottom row corresponds to $3v - \frac{1}{3}w = \frac{1}{3}$. This is satisfied by $v = \frac{1}{6}$ and $w = \frac{1}{2}$. If there were an error in the solution, somewhere there would be rows not satisfied by it. By locating where the errors begin, you can find where the arithmetic is faulty.

Questions

Covering the Reading

1. Solve the following system:
   $w = 1, z = 8, y = 8.8, x = -7.4$
   $$\begin{cases} -x + 2y + 3z + w = 50 \\ 5y - 4z - 6w = 6 \\ 2z + 3w = 19 \\ 4w = 4 \end{cases}$$

2. Geometrically, the system of Question 1 can be interpreted as finding the point of intersection of four __?__.   hyperplanes

3. If the matrix at the right is a triangular matrix, which elements equal 0? d, g, h
   $$\begin{bmatrix} a & b & c \\ d & e & f \\ g & h & i \end{bmatrix}$$

4. *Multiple choice* Which is *not* a legal row operation?   b
   (a) Multiply each element of a row by 2.
   (b) Add 3 to each element of a row.
   (c) Add two rows and replace the first row with the sum.
   (d) Switch two rows.

5. a. Write the augmented matrix for the system at the right.
      $$\begin{cases} x - 4y + z = 1 \\ 3x - 2y - 3z = 15 \\ 2x + y - z = 8 \end{cases}$$
      $$\begin{bmatrix} 1 & -4 & 1 & 1 \\ 3 & -2 & -3 & 15 \\ 2 & 1 & -1 & 8 \end{bmatrix}$$
   b. Solve the system using augmented matrices.   (3, 0, -2)

6. Name an advantage of the use of augmented matrices.
   Computers can use augmented matrices to solve any linear system.

Applying the Mathematics

7. The sequence 1, 4, 10, 20, 35, 56, ... , has the recursive formula
   $$\begin{cases} a_1 = 1 \\ a_n = a_{n-1} + \dfrac{n(n+1)}{2} \text{ for } n > 1. \end{cases}$$

   An explicit formula for this sequence is of the form
   $a_n = an^3 + bn^2 + cn + d$,
   where a, b, c, d are the solutions to the system at the right:
   $$\begin{cases} a + b + c + d = 1 \\ 8a + 4b + 2c + d = 4 \\ 27a + 9b + 3c + d = 10 \\ 64a + 16b + 4c + d = 20 \end{cases}$$

   Solve this system using augmented matrices. $a = \frac{1}{6}, b = \frac{1}{2}, c = \frac{1}{3}, d = 0$

LESSON 14-7 Solving Higher Dimensional Systems   **855**

855

NAME _____

LESSON **MASTER**   **14–7**
QUESTIONS ON **SPUR** OBJECTIVES

■ **SKILLS**   *Objective A (See pages 867–869 for objectives.)*
In 1–4, solve each system using augmented matrices.

1. $\begin{cases} x + y + z = 5 \\ -3x + y - 2z = -5 \\ 2x + 5y + z = 7 \end{cases}$

2. $\begin{cases} 2x - 7 + z = -4 \\ x - \frac{1}{2}y + 2z = -\frac{13}{2} \\ 8x + 3y - z = 13 \end{cases}$

(-2, 1, 6) $(\frac{1}{2}, 2, -3)$

3. $\begin{cases} x + y + 3z - 2w = 0 \\ 4x - y - z + 5w = 12 \\ 2x - y - 10z - w = 16 \\ 3x - 6y - z - w = -8 \end{cases}$

4. $\begin{cases} x - 5y + 4z + 3w = 1 \\ -x + 8y - 2z + 7w = 0 \\ 2x - 4y - z - 2w = 17 \\ \frac{1}{2}x + y + 3y - w = 3 \end{cases}$

$\left(-\frac{44}{191}, \frac{72}{191}, \frac{380}{191}, \frac{584}{191}\right)$ (10, 1, -1, 0)

■ **USES**   *Objective F*
5. Listed below is some nutritional information about some lunch foods.

	Bread	Cottage Cheese	Tomato Soup	Salted Crackers
Calories (per serving)	80	120	100	120
Protein (grams/serving)	3	14	2	3
Carbohydrates (grams/serving)	16	4	16	20
Fat (grams/serving)	0	5	2	4

How many servings of each are needed to make a lunch with 600 calories, 32.5 grams of protein, 80 grams of carbohydrates, and 13.5 grams of fat?
2 bread, $1\frac{1}{2}$ cottage cheese, 2 soup, $\frac{1}{2}$ crackers

Advanced Algebra © Scott, Foresman and Company   153

8. Here are some quantities of foods and the total protein (in grams) in them.

Milk (ounces)	Whole-wheat bread (slices)	Roast beef (ounces)	Total
8	1	4	43
12	2	6	66
8	2	8	78

Solve a system using augmented matrices to find the amount of protein in 1 ounce of milk.   **See margin.**

Review

9. Find the distance between the points in 4-space with coordinates $(2, 5, -7, -2)$ and $(3, 5, 7, -1)$. *(Lesson 14-6)* $\sqrt{198} \approx 14.1$

10. State the number of vertices of a 4-dimensional hypercube. *(Lesson 14-6)*   **16**

11. How long a walking stick can fit diagonally into a box with dimensions 80 cm by 10 cm by 20 cm? *(Lesson 14-4)* $\sqrt{6900} \approx 83$ cm

12. What simple fraction equals the repeating decimal $2.5\overline{3}$? *(Lesson 13-4)*
$\frac{228}{90} = \frac{38}{15}$

13. Expand $(x + 2y)^5$. *(Lesson 13-6)* $x^5 + 10x^4y + 40x^3y^2 + 80x^2y^3 + 80xy^4 + 32y^5$

14. Here are mean temperatures for Fairbanks, Alaska and Minneapolis, Minnesota by month.

	J	F	M	A	M	J	J	A	S	O	N	D
Fairbanks	-13	-4	9	30	48	59	62	57	45	25	4	-10
Minneapolis	11	18	29	46	59	68	73	71	61	50	33	19

a. What is the yearly mean temperature for each city?   **F: 26; M: 44.8 ≈ 45**
b. Which city has the greater variation in temperature, as measured by standard deviation?   **Fairbanks (s.d. = 26.9 vs 21.3 for Minneapolis)**
c. Over a period of many years, what function might best approximate those mean temperatures, a sine wave, an absolute value function, or a parabola? *(Lessons 6-2, 7-5, 10-9)*   **sine wave**

In 15–18, find all real solutions.

15. $x^{3/4} = 64$ *(Lesson 8-6)*   **256**

16. $\sin t = 0$ *(Lesson 10-9)*   **$t = 180n$ for all integers n**

17. $3 \log m = 6$ *(Lesson 9-4)*   **100**

18. $12x^3 + 6x^2 - 3x = 0$ *(Lessons 6-6, 6-7, 11-4, 11-6)* $0, \frac{-1 + \sqrt{5}}{4}, \frac{-1 - \sqrt{5}}{4}$

19. Factor $4p^5 - 108p^2$ completely. *(Lesson 11-3)* $4p^2(p - 3)(p^2 + 3p + 9)$

Many answers are possible.

Exploration

20. Make up a 5×5 system for which you know the solution. Show that the system can be solved using augmented matrices.

856

14-8

Fractals

Below is a curve called the Mandelbrot set, named after Benoit Mandelbrot, a French-born American mathematician who works for IBM. It was brought to the attention of the world in the 1970s, and is created using ideas related to powers of complex numbers beyond the scope of this book.

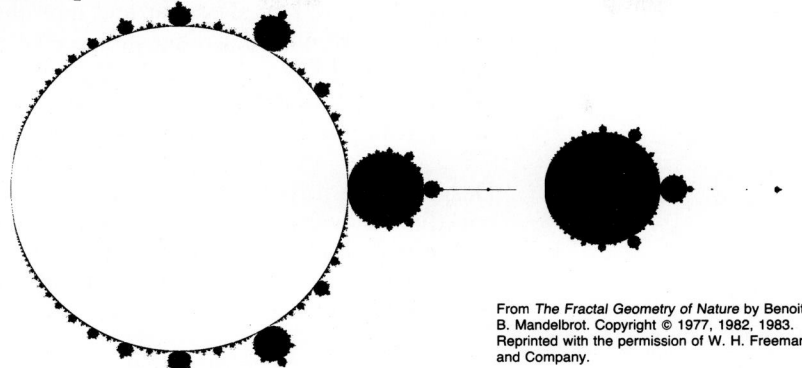

From *The Fractal Geometry of Nature* by Benoit B. Mandelbrot. Copyright © 1977, 1982, 1983. Reprinted with the permission of W. H. Freeman and Company.

The Mandelbrot set is an example of a *fractal*. Fractal objects are *self-similar*, that is, they do not change their appearance significantly when viewed under a microscope of arbitrary magnifying power. The word fractal is derived from the Latin word *fractus*, which means fragmented, broken, or irregular. Fractals often have very irregular, infinitely long boundaries.

Fractals may be abstract mathematical objects such as the Mandelbrot set or the pyramid shown below; or they may occur naturally as in the bark of a tree or the irregular coastline of Great Britain shown on the first page of the chapter.

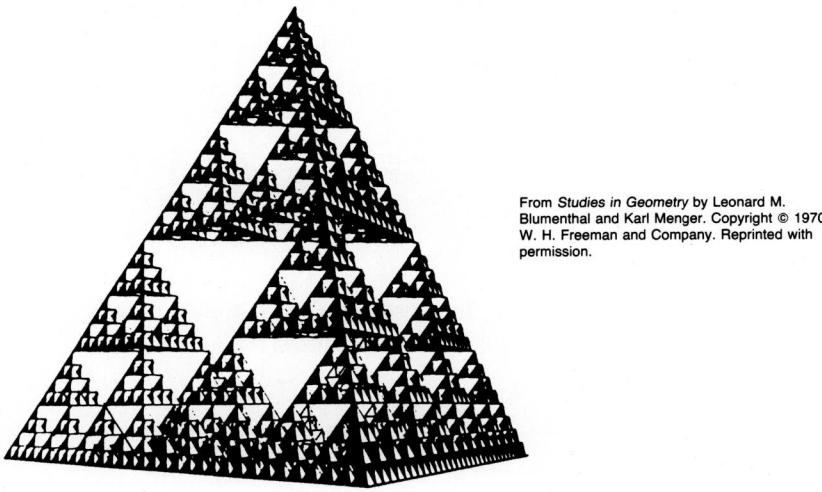

From *Studies in Geometry* by Leonard M. Blumenthal and Karl Menger. Copyright © 1970 W. H. Freeman and Company. Reprinted with permission.

RESOURCES
■ Lesson Master 14-8
▨ Visual for Teaching Aid 104 shows the drawings used in the **Example** of the lesson.

OBJECTIVE

E Extend 2- and 3-dimensional ideas to fractional dimensions.

TEACHING NOTES

Some students will be bothered by the idea of fractional dimension. You might mention that in elementary school, they might have been bothered by fractions. And then, thinking of powers only as repeated multiplication, they might have been bothered by rational exponents. It is a natural phenomenon in mathematics to extend ideas from integers to the numbers between integers.

Whereas Euler developed the idea of rational exponents in the 1700s, it was in 1976 that Mandelbrot's book *Fractals: Form, Chance, and Dimension* was published. It created immediate interest because the concept seems to have so many applications.

The **Example** provides one of these applications. Before Mandelbrot, the snowflake curve of the **Example** was called "pathological" because it was calculated to have infinite perimeter but finite area. Now this property can be interpreted differently; the

Both theoretical and natural fractals may have whole number dimensions. The fractal pyramid at the bottom of the previous page has dimension 2. But many fractals have dimensions that are not whole numbers.

To explain how fractals occur and how their dimensions are calculated, we consider a question asked by Mandelbrot: How long is the coast of Great Britain? There is no obvious way to answer this question. Coastlines move in and out. If a river goes to the sea, how far do you go in before you are inland and not on the coast?

Despite these difficulties, there is a reasonable way to measure a coastline. Consider the curve below which represents a coast. First, pick a unit (a mile or a kilometer, perhaps). Then put a stake in the ground at some point A along the coast. Now imagine drawing a circle with center at the stake and radius equal to the unit.

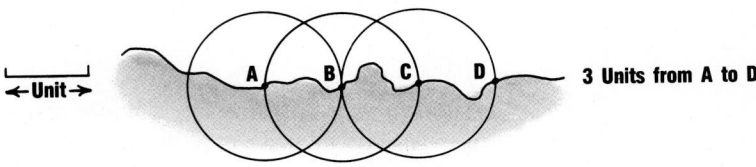

Go along the coast to B, where the imaginary circle intersects the coastline, and put another stake at B. Repeat this process to find C, D, and other points along the coastline. Count the stakes and you get the length of the coastline *in that unit*.

If you pick a smaller unit, the circles will be smaller. Then the points where the stakes are placed take the ins and outs of the coastline more into account. For instance, here is a unit $\frac{1}{3}$ the size of the previous unit, but on the same coastline.

In this case, you get 4 times as many stakes even though the unit is only $\frac{1}{3}$ the length.

For instance, suppose the first unit was *yards,* and the size of the coastline is y yards. Then the unit $\frac{1}{3}$ as long would be *feet,* and the size of the coastline is $4y$ feet.

858

Now let us bring in the idea of dimension: length is 1-dimensional; area is 2-dimensional; volume is 3-dimensional. Of what dimension is the above coastline? We make a table comparing units with yards to units with feet in different dimensions.

Measure	Dimension	Relationship between yards and feet in that dimension
Length	1	1 yard = 3 feet = 3^1 feet
Area	2	1 square yard = 9 square feet = 3^2 square feet
Volume	3	1 cubic yard = 27 cubic feet = 3^3 cubic feet

The general pattern implies that in dimension D, to convert yards to feet, multiply by 3^D. The base of 3 is due to the original unit being 3 times the smaller unit. In the unknown dimension of this coastline, to convert yards to feet, we multiplied by 4.

Measure	Dimension	Relationship between yards and feet in that dimension
Coastline	D	1 coastline yard = 4 coastline feet = 3^D coastline feet

So by solving $3^D = 4$ we can get the dimension of this coastline.

$$3^D = 4 \qquad D = \frac{\log 4}{\log 3} \qquad D \approx 1.26$$

The piece of the coastline drawn on the previous page has a dimension of about 1.26.

For a perfectly smooth coastline, there would be 3 coastline feet for each coastline yard. Solving $3^D = 3$ gives $D = 1$; the dimension is 1 as you would expect for a smooth coastline. Rougher coastlines, those that go in and out more, have dimensions nearer 2. The dimension of Great Britain's coastline is about 1.25.

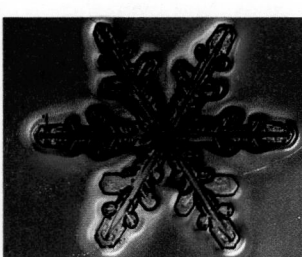

Example Consider a figure generated recursively as follows. Begin with an equilateral △ABC. Split each side of the triangle into five congruent parts. On two of those parts draw equilateral triangles as shown below. Then repeat this process on the smaller segments again and again. That is, each time replace ‾‾‾ by ‿ʌ‿ʌ‿ . The result is called a *snowflake curve*. What is the dimension of the "infinite-sided" boundary that arises?

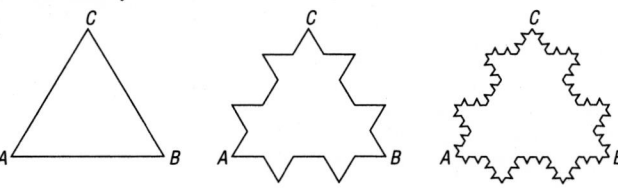

LESSON 14-8 Fractals   859

ADDITIONAL EXAMPLE
Here are the first two polygons in an infinite sequence of right-angled polygons in which all sides are the same length.

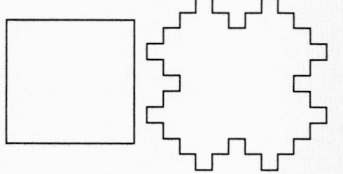

What is the dimension of the infinite-sided boundary of the limit curve?
$\frac{\log 8}{\log 4} = 1.5$

859

Solution Think of measuring the boundary first with a unit equal to the length of $\overline{AB}$. The boundary is 3 of these units. Now move to a smaller unit $\frac{1}{5}$ the length. Along the boundary, the distance from A to B, B to C, or A to C is now 7 of these smaller units in size. So the total boundary is 21 of the smaller units. At each stage, the boundary is multiplied by 7 when the unit is $\frac{1}{5}$ the size. Let D be the dimension of the boundary. Then, because the original segment is 5 times the next smaller segment,

$$5^D = 7.$$

Solving yields $\qquad D = \dfrac{\log 7}{\log 5} \approx 1.21.$

Thus, this snowflake fractal has dimension about 1.21.

In general, given a self-similar object of N parts scaled by a ratio r from the whole, its **fractal dimension D** is the solution to the equation $\left(\dfrac{1}{r}\right)^D = N$ or $D = \dfrac{\log N}{\log (1/r)}$. In the previous Example, $N = 7$ and $r = \dfrac{1}{5}$.

Mandelbrot and others have shown that cloud formations, holes in Swiss cheese, radio static, the motion of molecules, and even the shape of galaxies can be modeled by fractals. The concept of fractal dimensions, like the concept of dimensions higher than 3, is now seriously used by applied mathematicians. Fractals provide a striking example of how mathematical ideas continue to be invented, and on the next page, show the beauty of mathematics. It is a fitting way to end this book.

860

Picture of a Discretized Boundary Value Problem using
$f(\mu) = \mu - \mu^3$ *in 6-space and represented on the window*
$-4 \leq x \leq 4$, $-3 \leq y \leq 3$ *in 2-space.*

Question 14: Encourage students to divide both sides of the equation by 4 before beginning to work this question.

Question 16: This question can be done without a formula if it is recognized that the 51st term is 0. Thus, terms 52 through 100 are the opposites of terms 2 through 50, and the sum must equal the first term.

ADDITIONAL ANSWERS

8.

10.

Questions

Covering the Reading

1. What is a fractal?   **A fractal is a set of points that is self-similar.**

2. Who first introduced the idea of fractals, and when?
   Benoit Mandelbrot, in the 1970s

3. *True or false*   There are some curves which have a non-integral dimension.   **True**

4. *Multiple choice*   There are about 1.6 km in a mile. A coastline that is measured in miles to be 10 miles long will therefore be measured in km to be: **c**
   (a) less than 16 km long   (b) exactly 16 km long
   (c) at least 16 km long   (d) cannot be determined.

5. **a.** To change yards to feet, multiply by _?_.   **3**
   b. To change square yards to square feet, multiply by _?_.   **9**
   c. To change cubic yards to cubic feet, multiply by _?_.   **27**
   d. To change "dimension-D" yards to "dimension-D" feet, multiply by _?_.   **3^D**

6. If one coastline yard equals 4.5 coastline feet, what is the dimension of the coastline? $\approx$ **1.37**

7. State two phenomena that can be modeled by fractals.   **Examples: any two of: shapes of galaxies, cloud formation, holes in Swiss cheese, radio static**

Applying the Mathematics

In 8 and 9, consider the figures defined as follows.
Begin with a line segment.

Figure 1   ———————————————

To produce figure n divide each segment of figure $n - 1$ in four parts and replace the middle two by congruent segments placed as shown below.

Figure 2   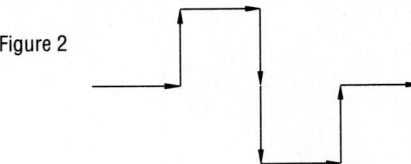

8. Draw Figure 3.   **See margin.**

9. Here is a sketch of the result of several more iterations of the above procedure. Find the fractal dimension of the figure that results if this procedure is applied indefinitely.   **1.5**

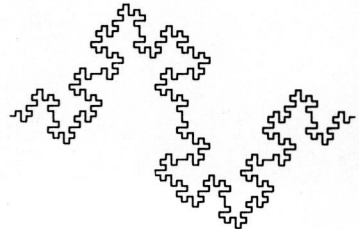

In 10 and 11, a figure is formed recursively so that at each stage

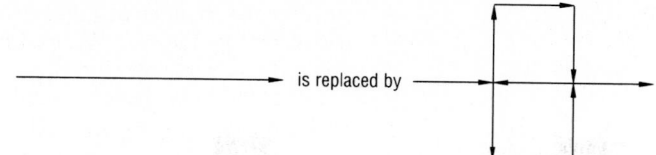

is replaced by

10. Draw the next figure in this pattern.   **See margin.**

11. Prove that when this pattern is repeated over and over again, the figure generated has dimension 2. $3^D = 9, D = 2$

12. At the right is an equilateral triangle. Each side has been split into three parts and on the middle part an equilateral triangle has been drawn. This is then repeated again and again. What is the dimension of the final boundary? ≈ 1.26

Review

13. Use augmented matrices to solve the following system:
$$\begin{cases} 2a + b + c = 3 \\ -5a - b + c = -9 \\ 8a + 2b - c = 14 \end{cases}$$
(Lesson 14-7)   **a = 2, b = -1, c = 0**

14. Graph the triangular region determined by the intercepts of the plane with equation $4x + 4y + 20z = 20$. *(Lesson 14-2)*   **See margin.**

15. In a lottery, you must match 6 numbers chosen from 50. $\binom{50}{6} = 15{,}890{,}700$
  a. How many different combinations of such numbers are there?
  b. What are your chances of winning? *(Lesson 13-7)*
     about 1 in 16 million

16. Find the sum of the first 100 terms of the arithmetic sequence that begins 1000, 980, ... *(Lesson 13-1)*   **1000**

17. What conic section is generated by intersecting a cone with a plane which is parallel to one edge of the cone? *(Lesson 12-1)*   **a parabola**

In 18 and 19, solve for θ. *(Lessons 10-2, 10-6)*

18. $\theta \approx 8.5°$

19.
$\theta \approx 104.5°$

20. Rewrite $\sqrt[5]{-161051a^{11}b^{19}}$. *(Lesson 8-8)* $-11a^2b^3\sqrt[5]{ab^4}$

21. Find an explicit formula for t_n, the nth term of the geometric sequence 12, 6, 3, 1.5, .75, ... *(Lesson 8-3)* $t_n = 12\left(\frac{1}{2}\right)^{n-1}$

MORE PRACTICE
For more questions on SPUR Objectives, use *Lesson Master 14-8*, shown below.

EXTENSION
You can extend **Question 12** by asking for the area and perimeter of each of the figures drawn. This provides a good (but challenging) application of the formulas for geometric sequences.

14.

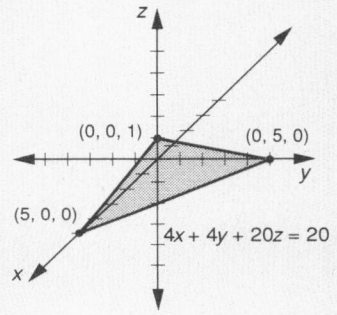

NAME _____

LESSON **MASTER   14–8**
QUESTIONS ON **SPUR** OBJECTIVES

■ **PROPERTIES**   *Objective E (See pages 867–869 for objectives.)*

1. If one coastline foot equals 20 coastline inches, what is the dimension of the coastline?   **1.206**

2. Suppose a fractal has dimension $\frac{7}{8}$. If measured in yards, the boundary of the figure is 10 yards. How long will the coastline be if measured in feet?   **46.5 ft**

In 3 and 4, consider the figures generated by the following recursive procedure. Begin with a line segment.

Figure 1 ————————

To construct Figure n, divide each segment of Figure $n - 1$ into 3 congruent parts and on the 2nd construct squares extending out.

That is, replace ———— with

Figure 2

3. Draw Figure 3.

4. Find the dimensions of the figure that results if this process is continued indefinitely.   **1.47**

154   Advanced Algebra © Scott, Foresman and Company

863

22. A rental car company charges $39 for a weekend rental plus $.15/mi. Suppose these are the only charges.
   a. Let m = the number of miles driven in one weekend, and C = the cost of renting the car. Write a formula that gives C as a function of m. $C = .15m + 39$
   b. If the cost of a weekend's rental is $96, how many miles was the car driven? *(Lessons 3-1, 1-7)*   380 mi

In 23 and 24, refer to the quadratic function graphed below.
(Lessons 6-3, 6-4, 11-3, 11-6)

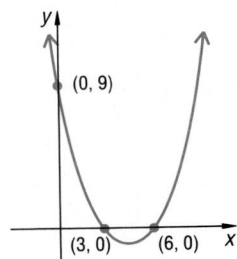

23. State an equation for its axis of symmetry. $x = 4.5$

24. Find an equation for the curve.
$y = \frac{1}{2}x^2 - \frac{9}{2}x + 9$

Exploration

25. Some reference books about fractals are *Fractals: Form, Chance and Dimension* and *The Fractal Geometry of Nature* by Benoit Mandelbrot, and *The Beauty of Fractals: Images of Complex Dynamical Systems* by H. O. Peitgen and P. H. Richter. Find examples of fractals different from those mentioned in this lesson with both whole-number and fractional dimensions.
Many answers are possible.

Summary

We think of the physical world we live in as 3-dimensional. With ordered 3-tuples, points can be located in that space, and equations for common figures such as planes, spheres, and cylinders can be derived.

However, the world can be viewed as 4-dimensional, with time as the fourth dimension. And many phenomena can be modeled by fractals, figures which may have fractional dimension.

To work in these dimensions, we use analogies from 2-space. The Distance Formula, equations for lines and circles, and the solving of 2×2 systems can all be extended to 3-space; the result is another Distance Formula, equations for planes and spheres, and the solving of 3×3 systems. Further extensions to 4-space yield still another Distance Formula, equations for hyperplanes and hyperspheres, and ways to solve higher dimensional systems.

Vocabulary

Below are the most important terms and phrases for this chapter. You should be able to give a definition for those terms marked with a *. For all other terms you should be able to give a general description or a specific example.

Lesson 14-1
ordered triple
3-dimensional coordinate system
z-coordinate, *z*-axis
coordinate plane, *xy*-plane, *yz*-plane, *xz*-plane
octant

Lesson 14-2
standard form of the equation of a plane

Lesson 14-3
extended linear combination method

Lesson 14-4
Distance Formula in 3-Space
* sphere
lattice point in 3-space

Lesson 14-5
analytic description
axis of rotation
disk
* surface of revolution
solid of revolution
* paraboloid

Lesson 14-6
hypercube
hypersphere
4-space
* ordered 4-tuple
Distance Formula in 4-Space
equation for a hypersphere

Lesson 14-7
dimensions of a system
triangular matrix
augmented matrix
row operations
hyperplane

Lesson 14-8
fractal, fractional dimension
self-similar
snowflake curve

SUMMARY

The Summary gives an overview of the entire chapter and provides an opportunity for students to consider the material as a whole. Thus, the Summary can be used to help students relate the concepts presented in the chapter.

VOCABULARY

Terms, symbols, and properties are listed by lesson to provide a checklist of things a student must know. Emphasize to students that they should read the vocabulary list carefully before starting the Progress Self-Test. If students do not understand the meaning of a term, they should refer back to the indicated lesson.

Definitions or descriptions of all terms in the vocabulary list may be found in the Glossary.

Progress Self-Test

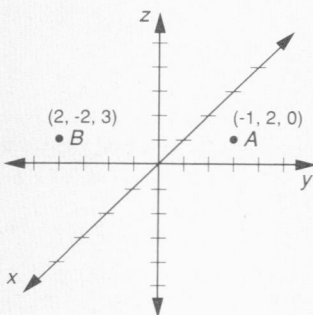
Directions: Take this test as you would take a test in class. Use graph paper and a calculator. Then check your work with the solutions in the Selected Answer section in the back of the book.

1. Draw one 3-dimensional coordinate system and plot these points on it. **See margin.**
   a. $(-1, 2, 0)$
   b. $(2, -2, 3)$

In 2 and 3, use the rectangular box at the right. Each tick mark is 1 unit.

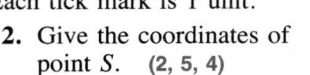

2. Give the coordinates of point S. **(2, 5, 4)**

3. Find UH. $\sqrt{45} \approx 6.7$

4. Give the coordinates of a point in the upper left front octant of a 3-dimensional coordinate system. **Sample: (2, -1, 4)**

5. A box has the following vertices: $(2, 0, 0)$, $(2, 0, 3)$, $(2, 4, 3)$, $(2, 4, 0)$, $(0, 0, 3)$, $(0, 4, 0)$, $(0, 4, 3)$, and $(0, 0, 0)$. Find the volume of the box. **24 cubic units**

6. a. Write an algebraic description of the points 3.5 units from the yz-plane. $x = \pm 3.5$
   b. Either sketch a graph of your response to part a or describe it in words. **See margin.**

7. A sphere has a radius of 13 units and center at the origin. Give an equation for the sphere.
   $x^2 + y^2 + z^2 = 169$

In 8 and 9, consider the system at the right:
$$\begin{cases} x + y - z = 2 \\ 6x + y + z = 4 \\ 4x - y + 3z = 0 \end{cases}$$
See margin.

8. Give the augmented matrix for the system.

9. Solve the system using any method. $(\frac{6}{7}, 0, -\frac{8}{7})$

In 10 and 11, *multiple choice*.

10. Which plane is ∥ to the z-axis in 3-space? **d**
    (a) $y = 7$ (b) $3z - x - y = 5$
    (c) $12y - 60z = 1$ (d) $x - y = 0$

11. The surface generated when a segment, parallel to the x-axis in the xy-plane, is rotated around the x-axis is a **b**
    (a) circle (b) cylinder (c) cone (d) paraboloid.

866

In 12 and 13, consider the plane with equation $4x + y + 2z = 4$.

12. *True or false* This plane is parallel to one of the coordinate planes. **False**

13. Graph the triangular region determined by the intercepts of the given plane. **See margin.**

14. Find an equation for a four-dimensional hypersphere with center at $(0, 0, 0, 0)$ and radius 12. $x^2 + y^2 + z^2 + w^2 = 144$

15. State the possible numbers of points in which 3 planes can intersect. **0, 1, or infinitely many**

16. Describe the intersection of a sphere with equation $x^2 + y^2 + z^2 = 49$ and the yz-plane. **circle with center $(y, z) = (0, 0)$ and $r = 7$ in yz-plane**

In 17 and 18, consider the figures generated by the following recursive procedure. Begin with a square.

To construct Figure n, trisect each segment of Figure $n - 1$ and on the middle segment construct a square extending out. That is, replace ——— with ⌐L

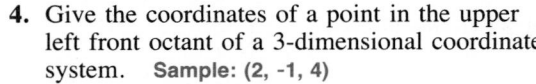

Figure 1   Figure 2

17. Draw Figure 3. **See margin.**

18. If this process is continued indefinitely, what is the dimension of the figure produced? ≈ 1.37

19. Tickets for a circus are priced differently for children, adults, and senior citizens. Marsha buys tickets for 3 adults, 2 children, and 1 senior citizen and pays $52.50. Nelson buys tickets for 4 adults and 4 children and pays $66. Olivia pays $47 for 1 adult, 5 children, and 1 senior citizen. **See margin.**
    a. Let a = the number of adults' tickets bought, c = the number of children's tickets bought, and s = the number of senior citizens' tickets bought. Write a system of equations that can be used to determine the cost of each type of ticket.
    b. How much should Pablo pay for one of each type of ticket? **adult: $11.00; child: $5.50; senior: $8.50**

Chapter Review

Questions on **SPUR** Objectives

SPUR stands for **S**kills, **P**roperties, **U**ses, and **R**epresentations.
The Chapter Review questions are grouped according to the
SPUR Objectives for this chapter.

SKILLS deal with the procedures used to get answers.

■ **Objective A:** *Solve 3 × 3 and 4 × 4 systems of equations. (Lessons 14-3, 14-7)*

1. *Multiple choice* Which step gives you $13y + 5z = -21$ from the following system:
$$\begin{cases} 2x + 3y - z = -1 \\ -x + 5y + 3z = -10 \\ 3x - y - 6z = 5 \end{cases}$$
c
   (a) Multiply the first equation by 3 and add it to the second equation.
   (b) Multiply the third equation by 5 and add it to the second equation.
   (c) Multiply the second equation by 2 and add it to the first equation.
   (d) Multiply the first equation by -6 and add it to the third equation.

In 2 and 3, solve each system using linear combinations.

2. $\begin{cases} 5x - y + z = 5 \\ 3x + y - z = 3 \\ x + 2y - z = 3 \end{cases}$ $x = 1, y = 2, z = 2$

3. $\begin{cases} r + 2s + t = 5 \\ 2r - s + t = 4 \\ 3r + s + 4t = 1 \end{cases}$ $r = 5, s = 2, t = -4$

In 4 and 5, solve each system using augmented matrices.

4. $\begin{cases} a - b + 2c = 2 \\ a + 2b - c = 1 \\ 2a + b + c = 4 \end{cases}$ no solution

5. $\begin{cases} 8x - 13y - z + w = 2 \\ 3x + 2y + 4z + w = 12 \\ x - y + 5z - 5w = -3 \\ 2x + 5y + 2z + 3w = 18 \end{cases}$
$(5, 3, -2, -1)$

■ **Objective B:** *Find distances between points in 3- and 4-space. (Lessons 14-4, 14-6)*

In 6–9, find the distance between the points. Round your answer to the nearest integer.

6. $(2, -8, 6)$ and $(-3, 9, 11)$ 18

7. $(.3, 1.2, .4)$ and $(-1.7, -.1, 4)$ 4

8. $(1, -1, 2, 3)$ and $(1, -1, 5, 3)$ 3

9. $(7\frac{1}{3}, 10, -6, 4)$ and $(8, 22, -6, -15)$ 22

In 10 and 11, refer to the cube shown at the right. Find:

10. *FA;* $6\sqrt{2} \approx 8.5$

11. the length of any diagonal of the cube.
$6\sqrt{3} \approx 10.4$

E $(0, -2, 7)$ *D* $(0, 4, 7)$
F $(6, -2, 7)$ *B* $(0, 4, 1)$
H $(0, -2, 1)$
G $(6, -2, 1)$ *C* $(6, 4, 7)$
A $(6, 4, 1)$

■ **Objective C:** *Write and analyze equations for spheres and hyperspheres. (Lessons 14-4, 14-6)*

12. Write an equation for the sphere with center at $(0, 0, 0)$ and radius 9. $x^2 + y^2 + z^2 = 81$

13. Describe the graph of the equation $x^2 + y^2 + z^2 = 50$ in 3-space.   See margin.

14. What is an equation for a hypersphere with center at the origin and radius 7?
$x^2 + y^2 + z^2 + w^2 = 49$

15. Consider the equation $x^2 + y^2 + z^2 + w^2 = 729$ of a hypersphere. Name its center and radius.   center $(0, 0, 0, 0)$; radius $= 27$

CHAPTER REVIEW

The main objectives for the chapter are organized here into sections corresponding to the four main types of understanding this book promotes: Skills, Properties, Uses, and Representations.

USING THE CHAPTER REVIEW
Whereas end-of-chapter material may be considered optional in some texts, in *Advanced Algebra* we have selected these objectives and questions with the expectation that they will be covered. Students should be able to answer these questions with about 85% accuracy after studying the chapter.

You may assign these questions over a single night to help students prepare for a test the next day, or you may assign the questions over a two-day period.

If you work the questions over two days, then we recommend assigning the *evens* for homework the first night so that students get feedback in class the next day, then assigning the *odds* the night before the test so students can use the answers provided in the book.

ADDITIONAL ANSWERS
13. a sphere with center $(0, 0, 0)$ and radius $5\sqrt{2}$

CHAPTER 14   Chapter Review   **867**

32.

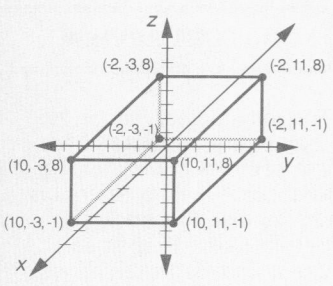

33.

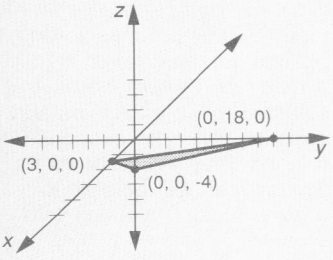

34.

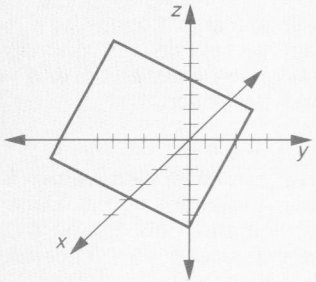

35.

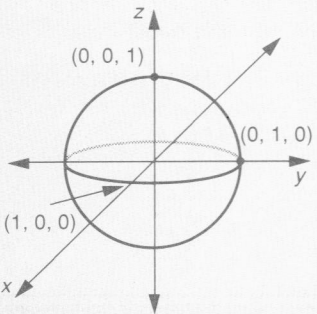

PROPERTIES deal with the principles behind the mathematics.

■ **Objective D:** *Identify properties of planes in 3-space.* (*Lesson 14-2*)

16. Give an equation for the *xz*-coordinate plane. **y = 0**

17. What is an equation of the plane containing the point (0, 0, -7) and parallel to the *xy*-plane? **z = -7**

18. *Multiple choice* The plane *x* = 7 is **c**
(a) parallel to the *x*-axis
(b) contained in the *yz*-plane
(c) perpendicular to the plane *y* = 10
(d) none of these.

19. The standard form of the equation of a plane is ___?___.
Ax + By + Cz = D where not all of A, B, C = 0

20. $7y - 2z = 4$ is an equation for a plane parallel to the ___?___-axis. **x**

21. a. How many solutions has the following system: **infinitely many**
$$\begin{cases} -x + y - 5z = 6 \\ x - 2y + 7z = 14 \\ 2x - 2y + 10z = -12 \end{cases}$$
b. Interpret part a geometrically.
The planes for equations 1 and 3 coincide.

■ **Objective E:** *Extend 2- and 3-dimensional ideas to higher or fractional dimensions.* (*Lessons 14-7, 14-8*)

22. A point in 5-space would have coordinates ___?___. **(x, y, z, w, v)**

23. What is the distance between (a, b, c, d) and (e, f, g, h)?
$$\sqrt{(a - e)^2 + (b - f)^2 + (c - g)^2 + (d - h)^2}$$

24. Give an equation for the hypersphere with center (0, 0, 0, 0) and radius 10.
$$x^2 + y^2 + z^2 + w^2 = 100$$

25. What is a fractal?
A fractal is a set of points that is self-similar.

26. If 1 coastline yd equals 5 coastline ft, what is the dimension of the coastline? **≈ 1.46**

In 27 and 28, consider figures generated by the following recursive procedure. Begin with a line segment.

Figure 1
_____

To construct Figure *n* divide each segment of Figure *n* − 1 into 5 congruent parts and on the 2nd and 4th construct squares extending out.

Figure 2

27. Draw Figure 3. **See margin.**

28. Suppose this process is continued indefinitely. Find the dimension of the figure that results. **≈ 1.365**

USES deal with applications of mathematics in real situations.

■ **Objective F:** *Use 3 × 3 or 4 × 4 linear systems to solve real world problems.* (*Lessons 14-3, 14-7*)

29. A test contains multiple-choice, fill-in-the-blank, short answer, and essay questions. All questions of a given type are worth the same number of points. Here are the number of questions correct for 4 students, and each student's total score.

mc = 2; fi = 2; sa = 9; es = 8
How much was each type of question worth?

Student	m.c.	fill-in	s.a.	essay	total
Neil	3	3	2	2	46
Ida	5	4	2	4	68
Carol	4	4	0	3	40
Evan	2	4	3	1	47

30. After two tests, Gordon's average in math was 76. After three tests, it was 83. If his teacher dropped the lowest test grade, Gordon's average would be 88. What were Gordon's three test scores?   **73, 79, 97**

31. A travel agent books three charter groups to go on a weekend cruise. A group of surgeons reserves 9 1st class, 22 2nd class, and 15 3rd class rooms for $15,380. A group of journalists has 4 1st class, 13 2nd class, and 8 3rd class rooms for $8,330. And finally an association of teachers books 5 1st class, 7 2nd class, and 25 3rd class rooms for $11,300. What is the charge for a room in 1st, 2nd, and 3rd class?
1st class: $395; 2nd class: $350; 3rd class: $275

REPRESENTATIONS deal with pictures, graphs, or objects that illustrate concepts.

■ **Objective G:** *Graph sets of points in 3-space.*
(Lessons 14-1, 14-2, 14-4)

32. Plot these vertices of a box: (10, -3, 8), (-2, -3, 8), (-2, 11, 8), (-2, 11, -1), (10, 11, -1), (10, 11, 8), (-2, -3, -1), and (10, -3, -1).   **See margin.**

33. Graph the triangular region determined by the intercepts of the plane with equation $12x + 2y - 9z = 36$.   **See margin.**

34. Graph the plane with equation $x + z = 8$.   **See margin.**

35. Graph the set of points satisfying $x^2 + y^2 + z^2 = 1$.   **See margin.**

36. Give an equation for plane P at the right which is parallel to the xz-plane.   **y = 4**

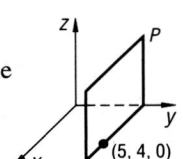
(5, 4, 0)

■ **Objective H:** *Describe cross-sections or the surface of revolution generated by rotating a set of points. (Lesson 14-5)*

In 37–39, (a) sketch and (b) describe in words the surface of revolution which is generated by rotating: **See margin for part a.**

37. a circle with radius 3 centered at the origin in the yz-plane around the y-axis.
b) a sphere of radius 3

38. the segment with endpoints $A = (0, -8, 7)$ and $B = (0, -8, 12)$ around the z-axis.
b) cylinder of radius 8 and height 5

39. the line with equation $y = x$ around the x-axis.   **b) an infinite double cone with the x-axis as its axis**

40. How is a paraboloid generated?
by rotating a parabola about its axis of symmetry

41. Triangle ABO is revolved in space around the x-axis.

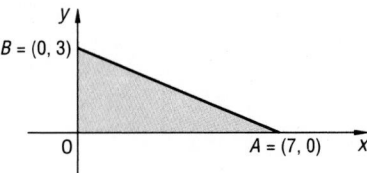
$B = (0, 3)$
$A = (7, 0)$

a. What solid figure is formed?   **a cone**
b. What is the volume of that figure?
21π cubic units

In 42–45, describe the cross-section when the cylinder below is intersected by a plane:

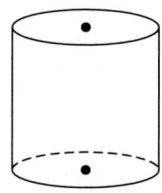

42. parallel to the bases and between them.
a circle congruent to the bases

43. not parallel to the bases but between them.
a non-circular ellipse

44. perpendicular to the bases and containing the center of one of them.
a rectangle with width equal to the diameter of the cylinder and height equal to the height of the cylinder

45. perpendicular to the bases and not containing the center of either of them.
a rectangle with width less than the diameter of the cylinder and height equal to the height of the cylinder

EVALUATION
Three forms of a Chapter Test are provided in the Teacher's Resource File. Chapter 14 Test, Forms A and B cover just Chapter 14. The third test is Chapter 14 Test, Cumulative Form. About 50% of this test covers Chapter 14, 25% covers Chapter 13, and 25% covers previous chapters. A fourth test, Comprehensive Test, Chapters 1–14, that is multiple choice in format, is also provided. For information on grading, see *General Teaching Suggestions: Grading* on page T44 in the Teacher's Edition.

37.a.

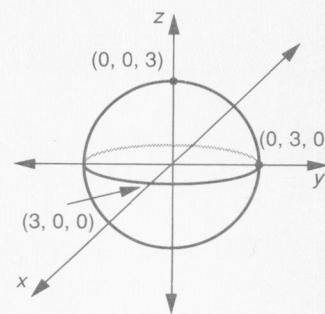
(0, 0, 3)
(0, 3, 0)
(3, 0, 0)

38.a.

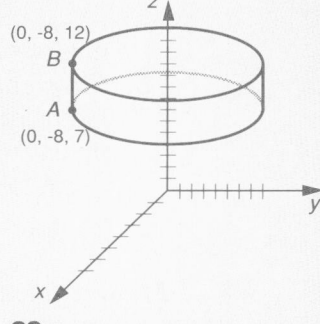
(0, -8, 12)
B
A
(0, -8, 7)

39.a.

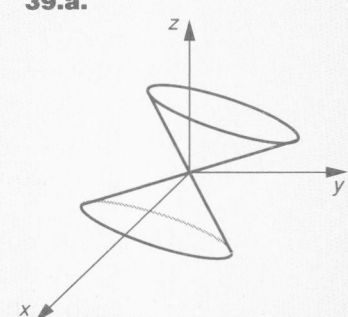

Models for Operations

A model for an operation is a pattern that describes many of the uses of that operation.

Models for addition: $x + y$ can stand for:

1. (Putting together model) the result of putting together quantities x and y when there is no overlap. Example: If you have $2m$ dollars and I have n dollars, our total is $2m + n$ dollars.
2. (Slide model) the result of a slide x followed by a slide y. Example: If the temperature changes $5°$ and then changes $c°$, the total change is $5 + c$ degrees.

Models for subtraction: $x - y$ can stand for:

3. (Take-away model) the result when a quantity y is taken away from a quantity x. Example: The measure of $\angle ABC$ pictured below is $90 - x°$. (An angle with measure $x°$ is taken away from an angle of measure $90°$.)

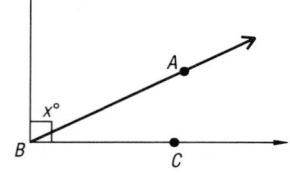

4. (Comparison model) how much more x is than y, or the difference between x and y. Example: Millie is 16 years old. Mel is Y years old. Millie is $16 - Y$ years older than Mel.

Models for multiplication: xy can stand for:

5. (Area model) the area of a rectangle with length x and width y. Example: A rectangular array of dots with m rows and n columns has mn dots in all.
6. (Size change model) the result of taking a quantity y and enlarging or contracting it by a scale factor of x. Example: If an insect leg has length L and the leg is magnified 50 times, then the image will have length $50L$.
7. (Rate factor model) the total when a rate x is applied to a quantity y. Example: A person walks $2\frac{1}{2}$ miles an hour for $3\frac{1}{2}$ hours. Then the total distance is $2\frac{1}{2} \frac{\text{miles}}{\text{hour}} \cdot 3\frac{1}{2}$ hours, or $8\frac{3}{4}$ miles.

Models for division: $\frac{x}{y}$ can stand for:

8. (Splitting-up model) the result of splitting up x things into y parts, or x things into parts with y per part. Example: If there are x muffins with 2 muffins per guest, then $\frac{x}{2}$ people can be served.
9. (Rate model) the rate x per y. Example: If there are 1500 students in a 4-year high school, then on the average there are $\frac{1500}{4}$ or 375 students per year.
10. (Ratio comparison model) how many times x is bigger than y. Example: In similar triangles, if the ratio of similitude is $\frac{3}{2}$, the first triangle is 1.5 times the second in linear dimensions.

Model for powering: xy can stand for:

11. (Growth model) the amount by which a quantity is multiplied in a time y if it is multiplied by x in each unit time. Example: If the population is growing at a rate by which it doubles every 35 years, then in 10 years it will be multiplied by $2^{10/35}$.

Geometry Formulas

In this book, we use many measurement formulas. The following symbols are used.

A = area
a = length of apothem
a, b, and c are lengths of sides
  (when they appear together)
b_1 and b_2 are lengths of bases
B = area of base
C = circumference
d = diameter
d_1 and d_2 are lengths of diagonals
h = height
L = lateral area

l = length or slant height
n = number of sides
p = perimeter
P = perimeter of base
r = radius
S = total surface area
s = side
θ = measure of angle
T = sum of measures of angles
V = volume
w = width

Two-Dimensional Figures	Perimeter, Length, and Angle Measure	Area
n-gon	$T = 180(n - 2)$	
regular n-gon	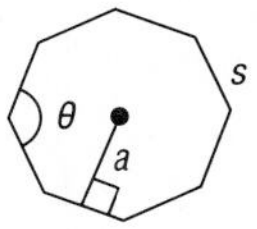 $p = ns$ $\theta = \dfrac{180(n - 2)}{n}$	$A = \frac{1}{2}ap$
triangle	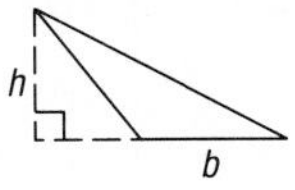 $p = a + b + c$	$A = \frac{1}{2}bh$ $A = \sqrt{\dfrac{p}{2}\left(\dfrac{p}{2} - a\right)\left(\dfrac{p}{2} - b\right)\left(\dfrac{p}{2} - c\right)}$ (Hero's formula)
right triangle	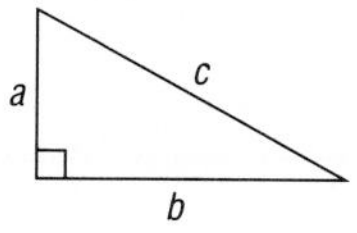 $c^2 = a^2 + b^2$ (Pythagorean theorem)	$A = \frac{1}{2}ab$
equilateral triangle	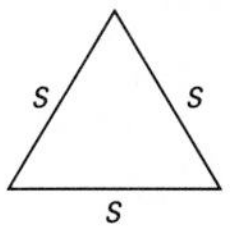 $p = 3s$	$A = \dfrac{\sqrt{3}}{4}s^2$
trapezoid	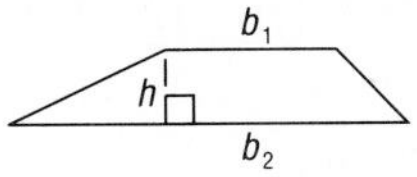	$A = \frac{1}{2}h(b_1 + b_2)$
parallelogram	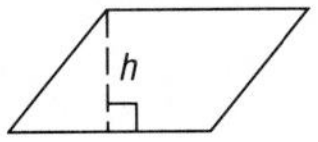	$A = bh$
rhombus	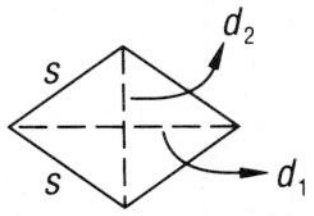 $p = 4s$	$A = \frac{1}{2}d_1 d_2$
rectangle	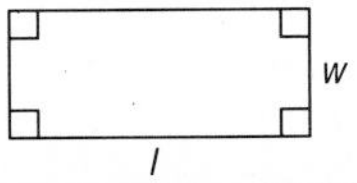 $p = 2l + 2w$	$A = lw$

Two-Dimensional Figures		Perimeter, Length, and Angle Measure	Area
square		$p = 4s$	$A = s^2$circle
$C = \pi d = 2\pi r$		$A = \pi r^2$	

Three-Dimensional Figures		Lateral and Total Surface Area	Volume
prism			$V = Bh$
right prism		$L = Ph$ $S = Ph + 2B$	$V = Bh$
box		$S = 2(lw + lh + hw)$	$V = lwh$
cube		$S = 6s^2$	$V = s^3$
pyramid			$V = \frac{1}{3}Bh$
regular pyramid		$L = \dfrac{Pl}{2}$ $S = \dfrac{Pl}{2} + B$	$V = \frac{1}{3}Bh$
cylinder			$V = Bh$
right circular cylinder		$L = 2\pi rh$ $S = 2\pi rh + \pi r^2$	$V = \pi r^2 h$
cone			$V = \frac{1}{3}Bh$
right circular cone		$L = \pi rl$ $S = \pi rl + \pi r^2$	$V = \frac{1}{3}\pi r^2 h$
sphere		$S = 4\pi r^2$	$V = \frac{4}{3}\pi r^3$

BASIC

Commands

The BASIC commands used in this course and examples of their uses are given below.

LET ...

A value is assigned to a given variable. Some versions of BASIC allow you to omit the word LET in the assignment statement.

LET X = 5   The number 5 is stored in a memory location called X.

LET N = N + 2   The value in the memory location called N is increased by 2 and then restored in the location called N.

PRINT ...

The computer prints on the screen what follows the PRINT command. If what follows is a constant or variable, the computer prints the value of that constant or variable. If what follows is in quotes, the computer prints exactly that quote.

PRINT X   The computer prints the number stored in memory location X.

PRINT "X-VALUES"   The computer prints the phrase X-VALUES.

INPUT ...

The computer asks for a value of the variable named, and stores that value.

INPUT X   When the program is run, the computer will prompt you to give it a value by printing a question mark, and then store that value in memory location X.

INPUT "HOW OLD?"; AGE   The computer prints HOW OLD? and stores your response in memory location AGE.

REM ...

This command allows remarks to be inserted in a program. These may describe what the variables represent, what the program does or how it works. REM statements are often used in long complex programs or programs others will use.

REM PYTHAGOREAN THEOREM   The statement appears when the LIST command is given, but it has no effect on the program.

FOR ...
NEXT ...
STEP ...

The FOR command assigns a beginning and ending value to a variable. The first time through the loop, the variable has the beginning value in the FOR command. When the computer hits the line reading NEXT, the value of the variable is increased by the amount indicated by STEP. The commands between FOR and NEXT are then repeated.

10 FOR N = 3 TO 6 STEP 2   The computer assigns 3 to N and then prints the
20   PRINT N   value of N. On reaching NEXT, the computer
30 NEXT N   increases N by 2 (the STEP amount), and prints 5.
40 END   The next N would be 7 which is too large. The computer executes the command after NEXT, ending the program.

IF ... THEN ...   The computer performs the consequent (the THEN part) only if the antecedent (the IF part) is true. When the antecedent is false, the computer *ignores* the consequent and goes directly to the next line of the program.

IF X > 100 THEN END
PRINT X

If the X value is less than or equal to 100, the computer ignores "END," goes to the next line, and prints the value stored in X. If the X value is greater than 100, the program goes to the END statement.

GO TO ...   The computer goes to whatever line of the program is indicated. GOTO statements are generally avoided because they interrupt program flow and make programs hard to interpret.

GOTO 70   The computer goes to line 70 and executes that command.

END ...   The computer stops running the program. No program should have more than one END statement.

Functions

The following built-in functions are available in most versions of BASIC. Each function name must be followed by a variable or constant enclosed in parentheses.

ABS   The absolute value of the number that follows is calculated.

LET X = ABS (-10)   The computer calculates $|-10| = 10$ and assigns the value 10 to memory location X.

INT   The greatest integer less than or equal to the number that follows is calculated.

X = INT (N + .5)   The computer adds .5 to the value of N, calculates [N + .5], and stores the result in X.

LOG   The natural logarithm, i.e., the log to base *e,* of the number that follows is calculated.

LET J = LOG(6)   The computer calculates *ln* 6 and assigns that value 1.791759 to memory location J.

SQR   The square root of the number or expression that follows is calculated.

C = SQR (A * A + B * B)   The computer calculates $\sqrt{A^2 + B^2}$ using the values stored in A and B and stores the result in C.

Algebra Properties

*For any real numbers **a, b,** and **c:***

	Addition	*Multiplication*
Closure properties	$a + b$ is a real number.	ab is a real number.
Commutative properties	$a + b = b + a$	$ab = ba$
Associative properties	$(a + b) + c = a + (b + c)$	$(ab)c = a(bc)$
Identity properties	There is a real number 0 with $0 + a = a + 0$.	There is a real number 1 with $1 \cdot a = a \cdot 1 = a$.
Inverse properties	There is a real number -a with $a + {-a} = {-a} + a = 0$.	If $a \neq 0$, there is a real number $\frac{1}{a}$ with $a \cdot \frac{1}{a} = \frac{1}{a} \cdot a = 1$.
Distributive property	$a(b + c) = ab + ac$	

Equality: *For any real numbers **a, b,** and **c:***

Reflexive property	$a = a$
Symmetric property	If $a = b$, then $b = a$.
Transitive property	If $a = b$ and $b = c$, then $a = c$.
Substitution property	If $a = b$, then a may be substituted for b in any arithmetic or algebraic expression.
Addition property	If $a = b$, then $a + c = b + c$.
Multiplication property	If $a = b$, then $ac = bc$.

Inequality: *For any real numbers **a, b,** and **c:***

Trichotomy property	Either $a < b$, $a = b$, or $a > b$.
Transitive property	If $a < b$ and $b < c$, then $a < c$.
Addition property	If $a < b$, then $a + c < b + c$.
Multiplication property	If $a < b$ and $c > 0$, then $ac < bc$. If $a < b$ and $c < 0$, then $ac > bc$.

Powers: *For any nonnegative bases and real exponents, or any nonzero bases and integer exponents:*

Product of Powers property	$b^m \cdot b^n = b^{m+n}$
Power of a Power property	$(b^m)^n = b^{mn}$
Power of a Product property	$(ab)^m = a^m b^m$
Quotient of Powers property	$\dfrac{b^m}{b^n} = b^{m-n}$, for $b \neq 0$
Power of a Quotient property	$\left(\dfrac{a}{b}\right)^m = \dfrac{a^m}{b^m}$, for $b \neq 0$

Selected Theorems

Addition and Multiplication: *For all real numbers **a, b,** and **c:***

Multiplication Property of 0	$0 \cdot a = 0$
Multiplication Property of -1	$-1 \cdot a = -a$
Opposite of an Opposite property	$-(-a) = a$
Opposite of a Sum	$-(b + c) = -b + -c$
Distributive Property of Multiplication over Subtraction	$a(b - c) = ab - ac$
Addition of Like Terms	$ac + bc = (a + b)c$
Addition of Fractions	$\dfrac{a}{c} + \dfrac{b}{c} = \dfrac{a + b}{c}$, for $c \neq 0$

Powers and Roots:

Zero Exponent If b is a nonzero real number, $b^0 = 1$.

Negative Exponent If $x > 0$, then $x^{-n} = \dfrac{1}{x^n}$.

$\dfrac{1}{n}$ **Exponent** When $x \geq 0$, $x^{1/n}$ is the nth root of x.

Rational Exponent For any positive real number x and positive integers m and n, $x^{m/n} = (x^{1/n})^m$, the mth power of the positive nth root of x, and $= (x^m)^{1/n}$, the positive nth root of the mth power of x.

nth Root of nth Power For all real numbers x, and integers $n \geq 2$: if n is odd, $\sqrt[n]{x^n} = x$, and if n is even, $\sqrt[n]{x^n} = |x|$.

Logarithm: *For any positive real number base **b** ≠ 1, and any positive real numbers **x** and **y:***

$\log_b 1 = 0$
$\log_b b^n = n$

Log of a Product property	$\log_b(xy) = \log_b x + \log_b y$
Log of a Quotient property	$\log_b\left(\dfrac{x}{y}\right) = \log_b x - \log_b y$
Log of a Power property	$\log_b(x^n) = n\log_b x$

Trigonometry:
In any triangle ABC:

Law of Sines $\dfrac{\sin A}{a} = \dfrac{\sin B}{b} = \dfrac{\sin C}{c}$

Law of Cosines $c^2 = a^2 + b^2 - 2ab\cos C$

For all real numbers θ:

Complements property $\sin \theta = \cos(90° - \theta)$ and $\cos \theta = \sin(90° - \theta)$
Supplements property $\sin \theta = \sin(180° - \theta)$
Pythagorean property $(\cos \theta)^2 + (\sin \theta)^2 = 1$
Periodicity property $\sin \theta = \sin(\theta + 360n°)$, for all integers n
$\cos \theta = \cos(\theta + 360n°)$, for all integers n

LESSON 1-1 (pp. 2–8)

3. expression **7.** $p < y$ **9.** $25 + 3w$ **13. a.** $10c¢$ **b.** $mc¢$
15. is not equal to **17.** sample: $7x - 8 \geq 3x + 2$ **19.** $x + y$
21. $xy¢$ **23.** $S - T$ liters **25.** $E + F$ eggs **27. a.** $1150 - 2x$
b. $(1150 - 2x)x$ **c.** $x(1150 - 2x) \geq 60,000$ **29.** quadrilateral
31. hexagon

LESSON 1-2 (pp. 9–13)

3. $d = 20$ **See below. 5. a.** samples: π, 5.8, $3\frac{1}{2}$ **b.** samples: π, $\sqrt{2}$, $0.101001000100001000001 \ldots$ **7.** c, b, a
9. 42.4 ft **11. a.** no **b.** no **13.** $n = 3, 4, 5, \ldots$
15. a. $s > 0$ **b.** 43.3 cm² **17.** -13 **19.** $-\frac{15}{11}$ **21.** $a + b$ **23.** ab
25. $b - a$ **27.** $n + 6 < 60$

3.

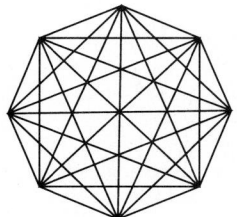

LESSON 1-3 (pp. 14–20)

3. See below. 5. 3, 6, 10, 15, 21, 28, 36, 45 **9.** the sequence of cubes of natural numbers **11. a.** fourth **b.** 262,144
13. a. See below. b. $S_n = n^2$ **15.** 1, 5, 12, 22
17. \$74,090.44 **19.** c **21.** sample: 10 FOR N = 1 TO 200
```
20 PRINT N
30 NEXT N
40 END
```
23. 727 **25.** S is undefined for $N = 88$; S is negative for $N > 88$. **27. See below.**

3.

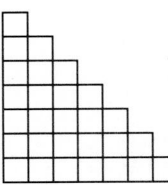

27.

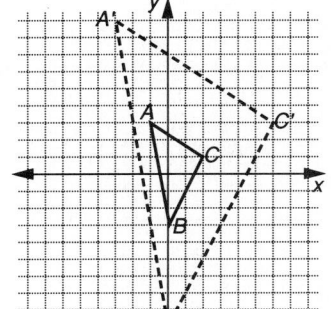

13. a.

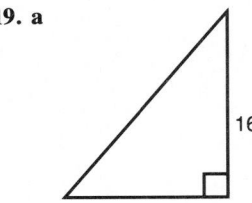

LESSON 1-4 (pp. 21–25)

1. 24, 36, 54, 81, 121.5 **3.** 40 ⊠ .5 ⊟ ⊠ .5 ⊟ ⊠ .5 ⊟
5. a. 11 **b.** T/2 or T ∗ .5 **7.** 7, 17, 27, 37, 47 **9.** 21, 34

11. a. 100 **b.** 6 less than **c.** $a_1 = 100$; $a_n = a_{n-1} - 6$, $n > 1$ **13.** 1, 4, 9, 16, 25, 36, 49, 64, 81, 100, 121, 144
15. {1, 2, 3, . . .} **17.** 2.8

LESSON 1-5 (pp. 26–31)

3. sample: $6(5 - 4) = 6(5) - 6(4)$ **5.** sample: $-10 \cdot -1 = 10$
7. Distributive Property **9. a.** Assoc. Prop. of Mult.
b. Comm. Prop. of Mult. **c.** def. of division **11. (i)** Dist. Prop. **(ii)** Dist. Prop. **(iii)** Assoc. Prop. of Add. **(iv)** Comm. Prop. of Add. **(v)** Assoc. Prop. of Add. **13.** $24x^2 + 60x - 36$ **15.** $P = 2(L + W)$ **17.** $a_n = 2.4n - 8.4$ **19.** $\frac{2x}{y}$
21. $5x - 13$ **23.** $\frac{3}{5}$ **25.** a **28.** $\frac{y}{x}$ **29.** $.055d$ dollars

LESSON 1-6 (pp. 32–36)

7. a, c **11.** "if $12 = 20 - 3t$, then $t = \frac{8}{3}$" and "if $t = \frac{8}{3}$, then $12 = 20 - 3t$." **13.** $z = -33\frac{1}{3}$ **15.** Add. Prop. of
Equality **17.** $2.6(3a - 4) = 9.1 \Rightarrow 7.8a - 10.4 = 9.1 \Rightarrow$
$7.8a = 19.5 \Rightarrow a = 2.5$; $a = 2.5 \Rightarrow 3a - 4 = 3.5 \Rightarrow$
$2.6(3a - 4) = 2.6(3.5) = 9.1$ **19.** sample: $(3 + 2)^2 \neq 3^2 + 2^2$ **21. a.** -3, 2, 5.7 **b.** The result is the original number.
c. $n, n - 4, 3(n - 4), 3(n - 4) + 9, \frac{3(n - 4) + 9}{3},$
$\frac{3(n - 4) + 9}{3} + 1; \frac{3(n - 4) + 9}{3} + 1 = \frac{3}{3} \cdot \frac{[(n - 4) + 3]}{1} =$
$\frac{(n - 4) + 3}{1} + 1 = n - 4 + 3 + 1 = n$ **23.** 3, 1, 3, 1, 3

LESSON 1-7 (pp. 37–41)

1. $33.\overline{3}$ m **3.** to clear fractions **5.** $.06s + .08(20,000 - s) = 1500$; $.06s + 1600 - .08s = 1500$; $-.0.2s = -100$; $s = 5000$
7. a. $2x - 9$ **b.** $x = \frac{5}{2}$ **9.** $m = \frac{21}{10}$ **11.** $x = 10$ **13.** $z = 0$
15. a. $x = 75,000$ **b.** A company invests \$100,000, some at 7% and some at 5%. If the annual total return is \$6,500, how much is invested at 7%? **17.** the 97th **19. a. See below.**
b. 5, 10, 15, 20 **c.** iv **21.** a, b

19. a

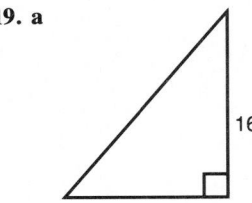

LESSON 1-8 (pp. 42–46)

1. 266 mi **3.** $r = \frac{d}{t}$ **5.** 48 cm **7.** b **9.** $\frac{C}{r} = 2\pi$ **11. a.** $S = \frac{R}{P}$ **b.** 30 ft **13.** $\frac{a_n - a_1}{d} + 1 = n$ **15.** 12 **17. a.** $0.6d$

b. .94d **19.** Each triangle with vertex V has area $\dfrac{\frac{1}{2}d_1 \cdot \frac{1}{2}d_2}{2}$, so

the total area of the 4 triangles is $\dfrac{4\left(\frac{1}{2}d_1 \cdot \frac{1}{2}d_2\right)}{2} = \frac{1}{2}d_1 d_2$.

LESSON 1-9 (pp. 47–50)
1. d **5.** the set of all x less than -3 **7.** $m < 7$; **See below.**
9. a. If C is the circumference, then $0 < C < 28$.
b. See below. 11. a. Dist. Prop., **b.** Add. of like terms,
c. Add. Prop. of Ineq., **d.** Add. Prop. of Ineq., **e.** Mult.

Prop. of Ineq. **13.** $x \geq \frac{1}{14}$ **See below. 15. a.** $T = 5000 + 50s$

b. 60 sacks or fewer **17.** $b = \dfrac{2A}{h}$ **21.** $x = 15.5°$,

$x + 5 = 20.5°, 4x = 62°$

7.
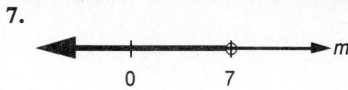

9. b.

13. b
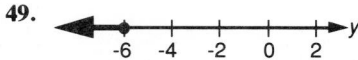

CHAPTER 1 PROGRESS SELF-TEST (pp. 51–52)

1. If $t_n = 5 + 7_n$, then $t_1 = 5 + 7(1) = 12$, $t_2 = 5 + 7(2) = 19$, $t_3 = 5 + 7(3) = 26$, $t_4 = 5 + 7(4) = 33$.
2. If $s_1 = 5$ and $s_n = s_{n-1} + 7$, $n > 1$, then $s_1 = 5$, $s_2 = s_1 + 7 = 5 + 7 = 12$, $s_3 = s_2 + 7 = 12 + 7 = 19$, $s_4 = s_3 + 5 = 19 + 7 = 26$. **3.** $t_8 = 5 + 7(t) = 5 + 56 = 61$ **4.** Since $s_5 = s_4 + 7 = 26 + 7 = 33$, $s_6 = s_5 + 7 = 33 + 7 = 40$, and $s_7 = s_6 + 7 = 40 + 7 = 47$, then $s_8 = s_7 + 7 = 47 + 7 = 54$. **5.** If $t_n = 5 + 7n$, then $t_n - 5 = 7n$ and $n = (t_n - 5)/7$. **6.** Since $t_n = n + 40$, $t_1 = 3(1) + 40 = 43$, $t_2 = 3(2) + 40 = 46$, $t_3 = 3(3) + 40 = 49$, and $t_4 = 3(4) + 40 = 52$. The program will print 43, 46, 49, 52. **7.** $(2x - 3)(6x - 5) = (2x - 3)6x - (2x - 3)5 = 12x^2 - 18x - 10x + 15 = 12x^2 - 28x + 15$ **8.** $3(4 + a) - (25 - a) = 12 + 3a - 25$; $ta = 4a - 13$ **9.** If $d = \frac{1}{2}gt^2$, then $d = \left(\frac{1}{2}\right)(32)(3)^2 = (16)(9) = 144$. **10.** If $1.7y = 0.9 + .5y$, then $10(1.7y) = 10(0.9 + .5y)$, $17y = 9 + 5y$, $12y = 9$, and $y = \frac{9}{12} = .75$.
11. If $\dfrac{.7}{x} = 3$, then $3x = .7$ and $x = \frac{.7}{3} = 0.2\overline{3}$. **12.** If $.12x +$

$.08(15,000 - x) = 1480$, then $100[.12x + .08(15,000 - x)] = 100(1480)$, $12x + 8(15,000 - x) = 148,000$, $12x + 120,000 - 8x = 148,000$, $4x + 120,000 = 148,000$, $4x = 28,000$, and $x = 7000$. **13.** If $\frac{1}{2}p \geq 1 + p$, then $-\frac{1}{2}p \geq 1$ and $p \leq -2$; **See below. 14.** Choices (b) and (c) are not formulas. **15.** Choice (b) is solved for d. **16.** A counterexample is $t = -3$: $t^2 = 9$ but $t \neq 3$. **17.** Commutative Property of Addition **18.** Distributive Property **19.** Definition of division **20.** If $V = \frac{1}{3}\pi r^2 h$, then $V \approx \left(\frac{1}{3}\right)(3.1416)(4)^2(6) \approx 100.53$; the volume is about 101 cm³. **21.** A reasonable domain for r is the positive real numbers. **22.** 12 miles in t hours is $\dfrac{12}{t}$ mph. **23.** Jane is J-3 years old. **24.** $t_1 = 20$, $t_n = t_{n-1} + 10$ for $n > 1$. **25.** Since $p = 2l + 2w$, the problem translates to $21.7 > 2(8.3) + 2w$. Thus $21.7 > 16.6 + 2w$, $5.1 > 2w$, and $w < 2.55$ m. **26.** An example of a real number that is not an integer is π.

13.

The chart below keys the **Progress Self-Test** questions to the objectives in the **Chapter Review** on pages 53–55 or to the **Vocabulary** (Voc.) on page 51. This will enable you to locate those **Chapter Review** questions that correspond to questions you missed on the **Progress Self-Test.** The lesson where the material is covered is also indicated in the chart.

Question	1	2	3	4	5	6	7–8	9	10–12	13
Objective	A	A	A	A	E	B	C	A	D	K
Lesson	1-3	1-4	1-3	1-4	1-8	1-3	1-5	1-2	1-7	1-9

Question	14	15	16	17–19	20	21	22–23	24	25	26
Objective	Voc.	E	F	G	A	H	J	I	H	Voc.
Lesson	1-2	1-8	1-6	1-5	1-2	1-2	1-1	1-4	1-2	1-2

CHAPTER 1 REVIEW (pp. 53–55)

1. 119 **3.** 6973.57 **5.** 10, 3, -4, -11, -18 **7.** .3, .03, .003, .0003, .00003 **9. a.** 100 **b.** 30 **c.** NEXT N **11.** $y + x + 11$ **13.** $20 - 5a - 5b$ **15.** $ab + ad + bc + cd$ **17.** 6

19. $\frac{3}{4}$ **21.** $w \geq .5$ **23.** 32,500 **25.** $n = \frac{360}{\theta}$ **27.** 3 **29.** sample:

$(12 \div 6) \div 2 \neq 12 \div (6 \div 2)$ **31.** $m = -2$ **33.** Add. Prop. of Eq. **35.** Mult. Prop. of Eq. **37. a.** def. of subt. **b.** Opp. of

a Sum **c.** Op-Op **d.** Comm. Prop. of Add. **e.** def. of subt. **39.** $n > 0$; n an integer **41. a.** $26,000; $27,560; $29,213.60; $30,966.42; $32,824.40 **b.** $78,665.59
43. $T - I$ **45.** sb **47. a.** $4000 + 200d \geq 14,000$ **b.** $d \geq 50$

49.

LESSON 2-1 (pp. 58–62)

3. b **5.** sample: Let n = the number of cans and r = the refund on n cans at 5¢ per can **7.** -120 **9.** 100 ft **11. a.** 3 **b.** 300,000 **13.** $d = kt$ **15. a.** sample: if $s = 10$, then $d =$ 6.25 ft **b.** 25 ft **c.** 4 (no matter what values were chosen in a. and b.) **17.** 1985 **19. See below. 21.** 3^6

19.

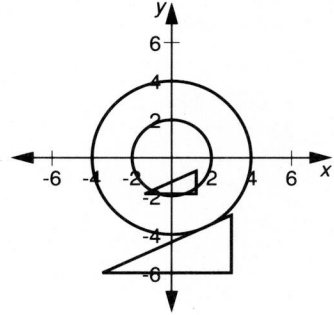

LESSON 2-2 (pp. 63–67)

3. a **5.** $\frac{40}{9}$ ft ≈ 4.4 ft **9.** 80 **11.** $I = k/D^2$ **13.** directly **15.** inversely **17.** 94 lb **19.** $y \le -\frac{2}{5}$ **21.** $8x^3$

LESSON 2-3 (pp. 68–72)

3. multiplied by c^n **5.** Nathan is $\frac{1}{3}$ as far from the pivot as Oprah. **7.** y is divided by 81 **9.** y is divided by 4. **11.** In a direct variation, doubling x multiplies y by 2^n, whereas in an inverse variation, y is divided by 2^n. **13.** $\frac{4}{1}$ **15.** $y_2 = \frac{k}{(cx)^n} = \frac{k}{c^n x^n} = \frac{1}{c^n} \cdot \frac{k}{x^n} = \frac{1}{c^n} \cdot y_1 = \frac{y_1}{c^n}$ **17.** about 5.86 **19. a.** $x = \pm 7$ **b.** $x = \pm \frac{7}{\sqrt{3}}$ **c.** $x = \pm \frac{7}{2}$

LESSON 2-4 (pp. 73–78)

3. $\frac{1}{5}$ **5.** a line; k; (0, 0) **7.** 0.06 **9.** $-\frac{1}{4}$ **11.** positive, negative **13. a.** k **b.** The slope of the line whose equation is the form $y = kx$ is k. **15. a.** W is divided by 3. **b.** W is multiplied by 2. **17. a.** $x = \frac{2}{3}$ **b.** $x = \frac{2y}{3}$ **c.** $x = \frac{2y}{3} + 2$ **d.** $x = \frac{2}{3}y - 1$

LESSON 2-5 (pp. 79–85)

3. False **5.** If the parabola is folded about the y-axis, the halves of the parabola coincide. **7. a. See below. b. See below. 9.** $a \cdot y = 3x^2$ **b.** $y = \frac{1}{2}x^2$ **c.** $y = -2x$ **d.** $y = -x^2$ **11. a.** 11 **b.** -5, 25k **c.** 5, 25k **d.** 21 pairs of the form x, kx^2 where x goes from -5 to 5 by increments of $\frac{1}{2}$. **13. a.** $I = k/d^2$ **b.** $\frac{1}{16}$th **15. See below. 17. a.** $\triangle DEF$; $\triangle KLM$ **b.** ASA, SSS

7. a.,b.

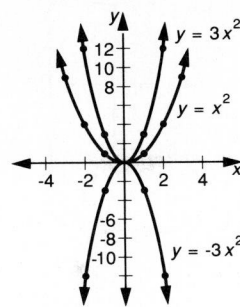

15.

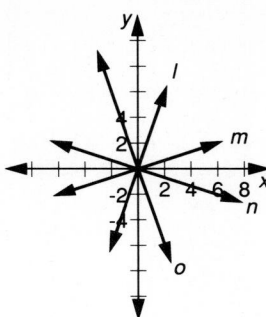

LESSON 2-6 (pp. 86–91)

3. the graph in the interval $-50 \le x \le 30$ and $-10 \le y \le 4$ **5.** yes **7. a.** the first **b.** the first **9. a. See below. b.** -6 **11. a. See below. b. See below. c. See below. 13. See below. 15. a.** 1.5 **b.** 216 **c.** 1.5 **d.** -108 **17. a.** $6x + 8$ **b.** $-2x - 2$ **c.** $8x^2 + 22x + 15$ **19. a. See below. b. See below. c.** Many answers are possible. The smallest value of b on our grapher is .370.

9. a.

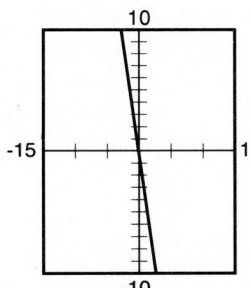

11. a.,b.

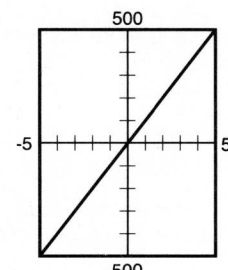

11. c.

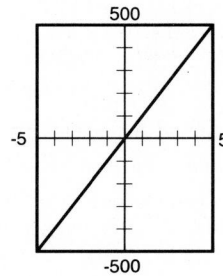

13.

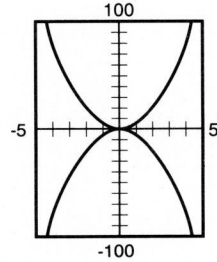

19. a.

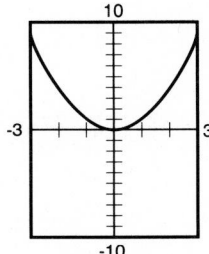

19. b.

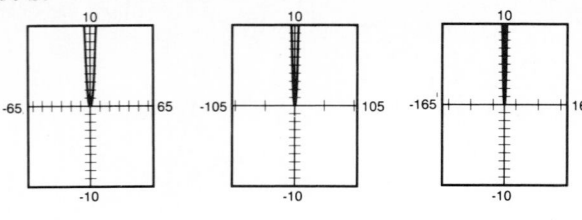

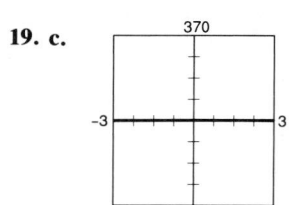

19. c.

3. The points appeared to lie on a line through the origin. **5.** a hyperbola **7.** Using $MAXWT = \frac{K}{d^2}$, with $K = 800$. Using this value of K when $d = 4$, $\frac{K}{d^2} = 800/16 = 50$. Yet $MAXWT = 200$ when $d = 4$. So this is not a good model. Using $MAXWT = \frac{K}{d}$, with $K = 800$. When $d = 4$, this model predicts $MAXWT = \frac{800}{4} = 200$, which is correct.
9. a. See below. b. directly **c. See below. d.** inversely **e.** $V = kT/P$ **11. a.** 0 **b.** iii **13. a.** 64.6 m **b.** 1.22 **15.** $0 \le w < 3.0$ m

9. a.

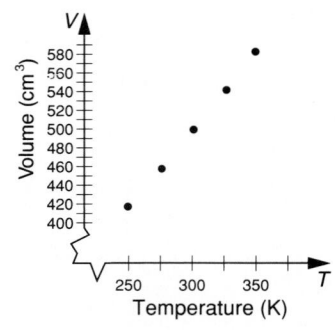

9. c.

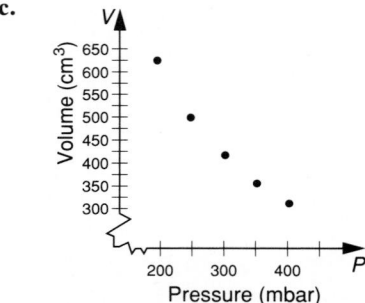

3. a. $-\frac{3}{4}$ **b.** $-\frac{3}{4}$ **5.** $\frac{3}{16}$ **7.** II and IV **9.** b **11. a. See below.**
b. -2 **c. See below. d.** $-\frac{4}{3}$ **e.** the graph of $y = \frac{24}{x}$ **13. a.** 2
b. $y = x$, $y = -x$ **c.** Yes **15.** $y = -16x^2$ **17.** Multiplication Property of Equality, Distributive Property **19. a.** Yes **b.** by SAS or SSS (use Pythagorean Theorem) to show $\overline{EC} \cong \overline{CA}$)

11. a.

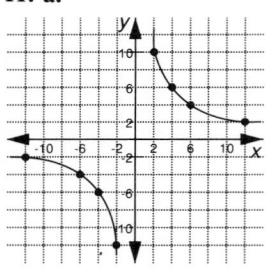

11. c.

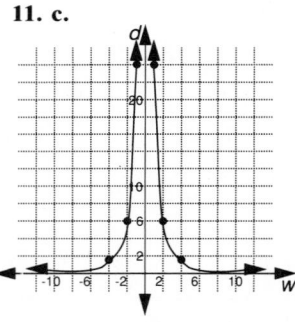

5. substitute 40 for P. $\frac{33,200}{40^2} = 20.75$, not 42, so the formula is not a good model. **7.** 92 psi **9. a. See below. b.** Quadrant III is part of "all solutions" but not part of real-world applications. **11.** d **13.** -1.36 **15.** c **17.** a **19.** k/r

9. a.

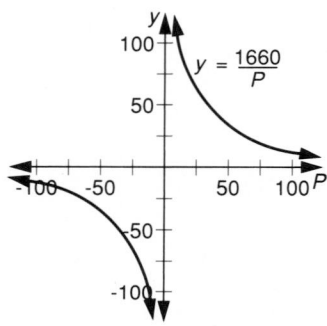

3. 66.7 ft-lb/in³ **5.** $R = kL/d^2$ **7.** About 430 BTU **9.** $k = wy/xz$ **11.** about 63 min **13.** It stays the same. **15. a. See below. b.** parabola **c.** 30 **d.** No **17.** False **19.** if $a < b$, then $a + c < b + c$ **21.** $x \ge -27$

15. a.

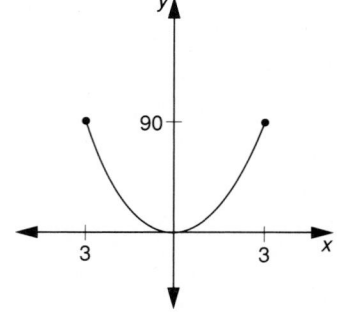

CHAPTER 2 PROGRESS SELF-TEST (pp. 117–118)

1. $y = \dfrac{k}{x}$ **2.** $n = \dfrac{k}{d^2}$ **3.** The two formulas are $w = k_1d^4$

and $w = \dfrac{k_2}{L^2}$, so the formula for all 3 variables is $w = \dfrac{kd^4}{L^2}$

4. Using $s = kp^2$ with $s = 10$ and $p = 3$, find k:

$10 = k(3)^2$, so $k = \dfrac{10}{9} = 1.\overline{1}$. Then use the formula $s =$

$1.\overline{1}p^2$ for $p = 8$: $s = 1.\overline{1}(8)^2 = 71.\overline{1}$. **5.** For $y = 3x^2$, when

x is doubled, y is multiplied by 2^2 or 4. **6.** For $y = \dfrac{6}{x}$, when

the x-value is multiplied by c, the y-value is divided by c.
7. For (12, 18) and (20, 30), $(y_2 - y_1)/(x_2 - x_1) =$

$(30 - 18)/(20 - 12) = \dfrac{12}{8} = \dfrac{3}{2}$. **8.** False (counterexamples

are $y = \dfrac{k}{x}$ or $y = \dfrac{k}{x^2}$, where x cannot be zero). **9.** para-

bola, k is positive **10.** The graph is not continuous.
11. a. neither inversely nor directly (Since $SA = 4\pi r^2$, the
surface area of a sphere varies directly as the <u>square</u> of the
radius.) **b.** inversely **12.** See below. **13.** See below.
14. Since the graph is symmetric to the y-axis, and is in

quadrants III and IV, the form is $y = \dfrac{-k}{x^2}$, which is option

c. $\left(y = \dfrac{-3}{x^2}\right)$. **15.** d **16. a. See below. b.** Use (3,620) to find

a value for K in $F = \dfrac{K}{L}$: $620 = \dfrac{k}{3}$, so $k = 620 \cdot 3 = 1860$.

Test this model $F = \dfrac{1860}{t}$ with other points: for (5, 372),

the model predicts $F = \dfrac{1860}{5} = 372$, which checks. The other

ordered pairs also check, so the model is $F = \dfrac{K}{L}$ or $F = \dfrac{1860}{L}$.

c. Use $F = \dfrac{1860}{L}$ for $L = 12$: $F = \dfrac{1860}{12} = 155$ lb. **17.** The

formula for V and g is $V = k_1g^2$ and the formula for V and h
is $V = k_2h$. The formula for all 3 variables is $V =$
khg^2. **18.** The model is $s = kPr^4$. Use the values $s =$
$.09604$, $r = .07$ (since $d = .14$), and $P = 100$ to calculate
k: $.09604 = k(100)(.07)^4$ so $k = \dfrac{.09604}{(100)(.07)^4} = \dfrac{.09604}{.002401} = 40$.

Then use the formula $s = 40Pr^4$ to calculate P for $r = .05$

(since $d = .1$) and $s = .09604$: $.09604 = 40P(.05)^4$, so $P =$

$\dfrac{.09604}{(40)(.05)^4} = \dfrac{.09604}{.00025} = 384.16 \approx 384$ units.

12.

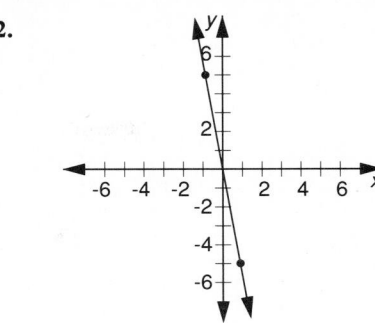

13.

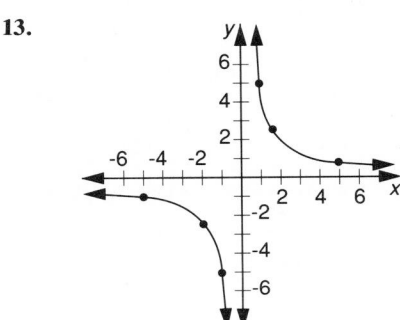

16. a.

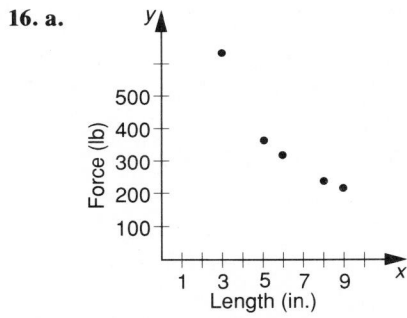

The chart below keys the **Progress Self-Test** questions to the objectives in the **Chapter Review** on pages 119–123 or to the **Vocabulary** (Voc.) on page 117. This will enable you to locate those **Chapter Review** questions that correspond to questions you missed on the **Progress Self-Test.** The lesson where the material is covered is also indicated in the chart.

Question	1–3	4	5–6	7	8	9	10	11	12	13	14	15	16–17	18
Objective	A	B	D	C	E	E	E	F	I	I	K	J	G	H
Lesson	2-10	2-1	2-3	2-4	2-5, 2-7	2-5	2-7	2-1, 2-2	2-4	2-7	2-9	2-6	2-9	2-10

CHAPTER 2 REVIEW (pp. 119–123)

1. $y = kx^2$ **3.** $n = k/r^3$ **5.** $U = \dfrac{k\sqrt{T}}{Ld}$ **7.** $P = km/d^2$

9. jointly; s, t, and u **11.** 21 **13.** -32 **15.** 1.8 **17.** -25

19. $-\dfrac{7}{16} = -.4375$ **21.** y is tripled. **23.** p is divided by 4.

25. divided by c^n **27.** not affected **29.** (0, 0) **31.** b

33. True **35.** inversely **37.** directly **39. a. See below.**
b. $L = Ks^2$ **c.** $L = .0455^2$ **d.** 220.5 ft **41. a. See below.**
b. P varies directly as R^2. **c. See below.** **d.** P varies directly
as C. **e.** $P = kR^2C$ **43.** \$13.50 **45.** 3 minutes **47.** about
15,188 lb **49. See below. 53. See below.**
55. c **57.** b **59. See below. 61.** d

39. a.

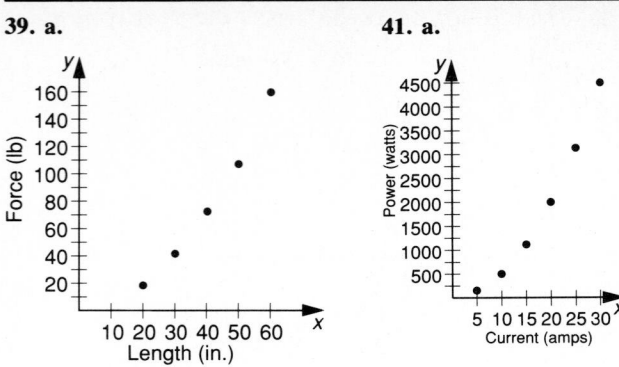

41. a.

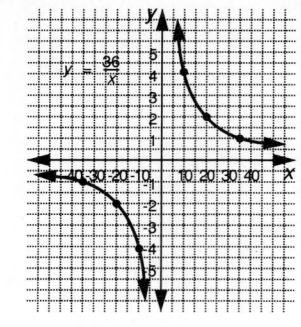

53.

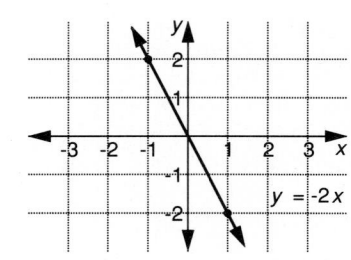

41. c.

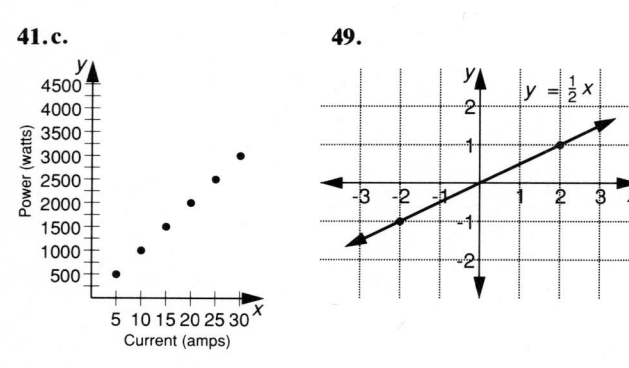

49.

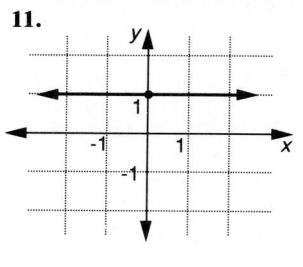

59.

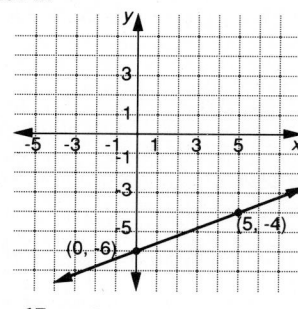

LESSON 3-1 (pp. 124–131)

5. True **7.** the initial condition **9.** 53 days **11. a.** 6 **b.** -5
13. a. 1 **b.** 3 **15. a.** (4, 10) is on the graph because it satisfies $y = \frac{3}{4}x + 7$: $y = \frac{3}{4}(4) + 7 = 3 + 7 = 10$. **b.** $\frac{3}{4}$
c. $\frac{10 - 7}{4 - 0} = \frac{3}{4}$ **d.** 7 **17. a.** $y = \frac{7}{2}x$ **b.** See below.
c. $m = \frac{7}{2}$, $b = 0$ **d.** constant increase **19.** $y = -\frac{1}{2}x + \frac{5}{2}$
21. a. 9π cm² **b.** $\frac{1}{4}\pi x^2$ cm² **23.** a

17. b.

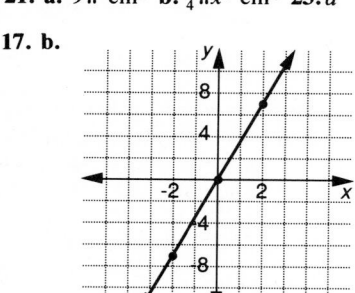

LESSON 3-2 (pp. 132–137)

1. slope-intercept **3.** b **5.** Does 2(-1) = -3(4) + 10? Yes,
-2 = -12 + 10. **7.** $\frac{1}{3}$ **9.** $\angle HGI \cong \angle KJL$; $\angle GHI \cong \angle JKL$;
$\overline{GH} \cong \overline{JK}$ **11.** See below. **13. a.** See below. **b.** $y = \frac{2}{5}x - 6$
c. $x = 22\frac{1}{2}$; yes **15. a.** $y = -\frac{5}{2}x + 12$ **b.** slope: $-\frac{5}{2}$; y-
intercept: 12 **c.** See below. **17. a.** See below. **b.** See below.
19. negative **21.** neither (zero) **23.** 5360.3825 **25.** $x < 22.5$

11.

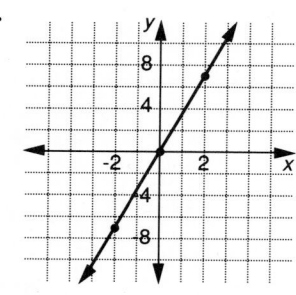

13. a.

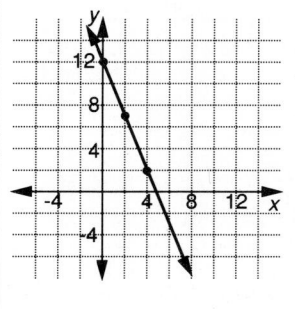

(0, -6) (5, -4)

15. c.

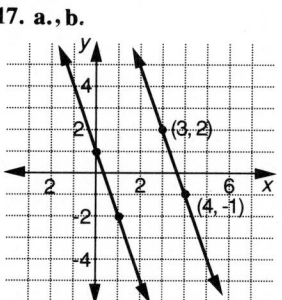

17. a., b.

(3, 2)

(4, -1)

Lesson 3-3 (pp. 138–142)

3. $2W + T$ **5.** linear combination **7. a.** .6S **b.** .9N **c.** .6S +
.9N **d.** .6S + .9N = 18 **e.** N = 20 − .67S **See below.**
f. 14 oz **9. a.** nonnegative integers **b.** 5S + 10L = 70
c. See below. d. 7 and 0, 6 and 2, 5 and 4, 4 and 6, 3 and
8, 2 and 10, 1 and 12, 0 and 14. **11. a.** $\frac{2}{3}$ **b.** 4 **c.** $y =$
$\frac{2}{3}x - 4$ **13.** 13 **15.** 18 **17.** $\sqrt{(a - c)^2 + (b - d)^2}$ **19.** See

882

below. 21. a. $R = 100 - \frac{2}{3}d$ **b.** 135 days

7. e.

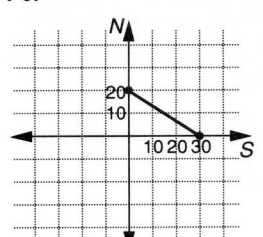

9. c.

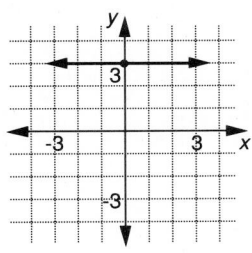

19.

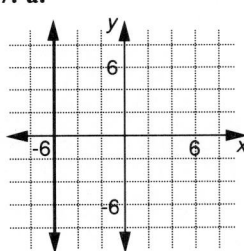

LESSON 3-4 (pp. 143–144)
1. a **3.** b **5.** 2 **7. a. See below. b.** The slope is undefined.
9. horizontal; 0 **11.** y **13. a.** horizontal **b.** x-intercept: none;
y-intercept: 4 **c. See below. 15. a.** vertical **b.** x-intercept: 8;
y intercept: none **15. c. See below. 17.** $10x - 5y = 1$
19. a. $08S + .06R = 84$ **b.** samples: (1000, 300);
(600, 600); (200, 900) **21.** b

7. a.

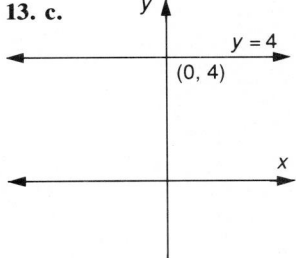

13. c.

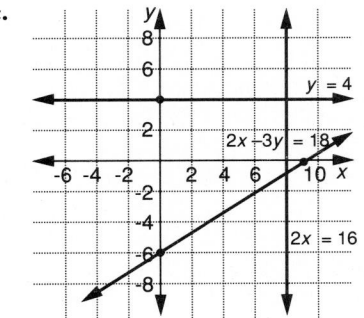

15. c.

LESSON 3-5 (pp. 148–153)
3. The y-intercept is given. **5.** True **7. a.** point-slope
b. slope-intercept **c.** point-slope **9.** $y - 1 = \frac{2}{3}(x - 7)$

11. The point-slope form is $y - 16 = -2(x - 5)$. This is
equivalent to the standard form $2x + y = 26$. **13.** $K -$
$273.15 = \frac{5}{9}(F - 32)$ **15. a. See below. b.** $\overline{PQ}$: $x = 3$; $\overline{GR}$:
$y = -5$; $\overline{RS}$: $x = -2$; $\overline{SP}$: $y = 4$ **c.** 45 sq. units
17. $L = 18 - g$ **19.** $A + 2B + 3C > 370$

15. a.

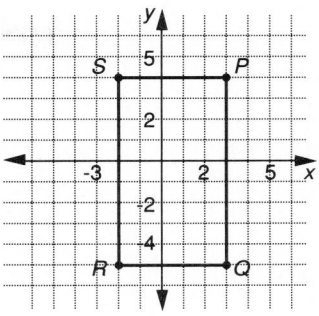

LESSON 3-6 (pp. 154–159)
1. b. See below. 3. a. $-6\frac{1}{2}$, -6, $-5\frac{1}{2}$ **b.** $\frac{1}{2}$ **c. See below.**
7. a. $a_n = 6 + (n - 1)9$ **b.** 897 **9.** 16 rows **11. a.** no
b. The domain is the set of natural numbers. **13.** $\frac{1}{2}$ mi
15. 49th **17.** $y = \frac{2}{3}x - 4$ **19.** $y = \frac{3}{5}x + \frac{61}{5}$ **21.** c

1. b.

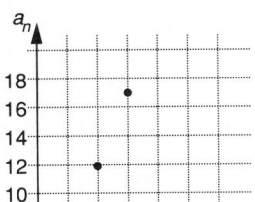

3. c.

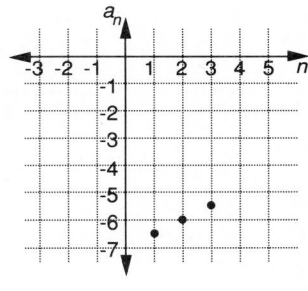

LESSON 3-7 (pp. 160–163)
3. a. 1, 7, 13, 19 **b.**
```
10 LET A=1
20 FOR N=1 TO 25
30 PRINT A
40 LET A=A+6
50 NEXT N
60 END
```
5. a. $\begin{cases} a_1 = 13 \\ a_n = a_{n-1} + 6 \text{ for } n > 1. \end{cases}$
b. $a_n = 13 + (n - 1)6$ **7.** $a_1 = 10.8$; $a_n = a_{n-1} + 2.4$ for
$n > 1$ **9.** $a_n = -x + (n - 1)3x = 3xn - 4x$
11.
```
10 FOR N=1 TO 1000
20 PRINT 2-N-1
30 NEXT N
40 END
```
13.
```
10 FOR N=1 TO 13
20 PRINT
30 NEXT N
40 END
```
15. 626 **17.** $2x + y = 0$ **19.** Use $y = 3 - x$; (3-2, 1-1, E)
a. See below. b. $0 \le x \le 3$ **c.** (1.5, 1.5)

19. a.

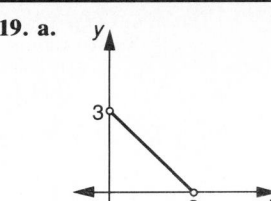

LESSON 3-8 (pp. 164–168)

3. $2\frac{1}{2}$ hr **5.** 14 mph **7.** \$42 **9.** 1.2 mi **11.** $\frac{1}{2}$ hr **13. See below. 15. a. See below. b.** $c = 10.15$ for $0 \le m \le 120$; $c = 10.15 + .035m$ for $120 < m$. **17. a.** $a_n = 7 - 5n$ **b.** $a_1 = 2$; $a_n = a_{n-1} - 5$ for $n > 1$ **19.** 13 rows **21.** $y > \frac{5}{8}x + \frac{9}{4}$ **23.** translation **25.** rotation **27.** rotation

13.   **15. a.**

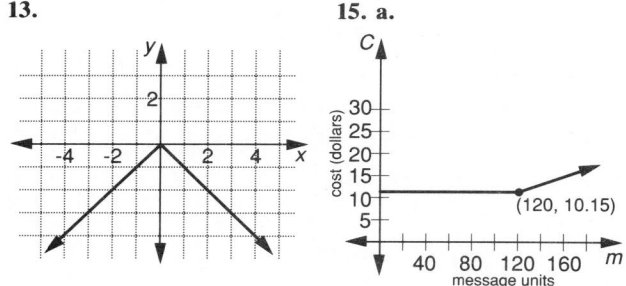

LESSON 3-9 (pp. 169–173)

3. left **5.** True; $3 > -1$ **7.** The other half-plane would be shaded. **9. a.** 5 **b.** (0, 4); (3, 3); (6, 2); (9, 1); (12, 0) **c.** on the boundary line, $x + 3y = 12$ **11. See below.**
13. a. $10x + 15y < 90$ **b. See below. c.** 33
15. $y < -\frac{3}{4}x - 4$ **17. See below. 19. a.** $y = x + 250$
b. $y = -50$

11.   **13. b.**

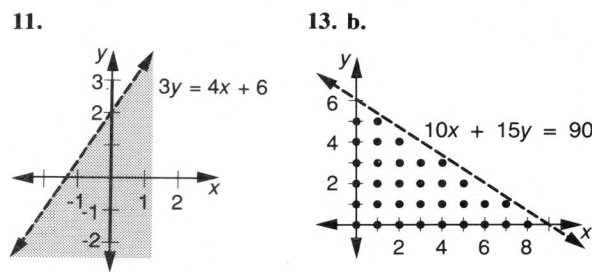

17.

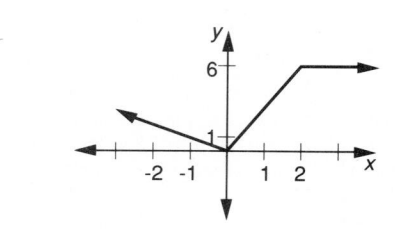

CHAPTER 3 PROGRESS SELF-TEST (pg. 175)

1. See below. 2. See below. 3. See below. 4. a. $m = \frac{-A}{B} = \frac{-4}{5}$ **b.** x-intercept: $\frac{C}{A} = \frac{12}{4} = 3$; y-intercept: $\frac{C}{B} = \frac{12}{-5} = \frac{-12}{5}$

5. $y = mx + b$; $y = 11x + 7$ **6.** $m = \frac{2 - 3}{4 - (-5)} = \frac{-1}{9}$; $y - 2 = \frac{-1}{9}(x - 4)$; $y - 2 = \frac{-1}{9}x + \frac{4}{9}$ **7.** $m = \frac{5}{3}$; $y - (-1) = \frac{5}{3}(x - 5)$; $y + 1 = \frac{5}{3}x - \frac{25}{3}$; $3y + 3 = 5x - 25$; $5x - 3y = 28$ **8. a.** vertical lines **b.** horizontal lines **9.** 36S + 48L in. **10.** 3000 = 36(50) + 48L; 3000 = 1800 + 48L; 1200 = 48L; L = 25; 25 long laces **11.** $-40 + 0.8t$ meters **12.** $-10 = -40 + 0.8t$; $30 = 0.8t$; $t = 37.5$ sec. **13. a.** The program represents the recursive formula of a sequence. The formula is $\begin{cases} a_1 = 1 \\ a_n = a_{n-1} - 3, \end{cases}$ for $n > 1$ and the first twelve terms of the sequence are: 1, 6, 11, 16, 21, 26, 31, 36, 41, 46, 51, 56 **b.** Yes **14.** $3y = x + 6$; $x - 3y = -6$ **15.** a **16.** $a_1 = -7$, $d = -3$; $a_n = -7 - (n - 1)3$; $a_n = -7 - 3n + 3$; $a_n = -3n - 4$ **17.** $a_1 = -7$, $d = -3$; $\begin{cases} a_1 = -7 \\ a_n = a_{n-1} - 3, \text{ for } n > 1 \end{cases}$ **18. a.** $0 \not> 0$; No **b.** $3(2) - 5(-1) \overset{?}{<} 8$; $6 - (-5) \overset{?}{<} 8$; $11 \not< 8$; No **19.** $a_1 = 20$, $d = 15$, $a_n = 110$; therefore $110 = 20 + (n - 1)15$; $110 = 20 + 15n - 15$; $105 = 15n$; $n = 7$; 7 weeks **20. a.** $m = \frac{800 - 400}{900 - 600} = \frac{400}{300} = \frac{4}{3}$ **b.** during the first 200 feet of horizontal distance

1.   **2.**

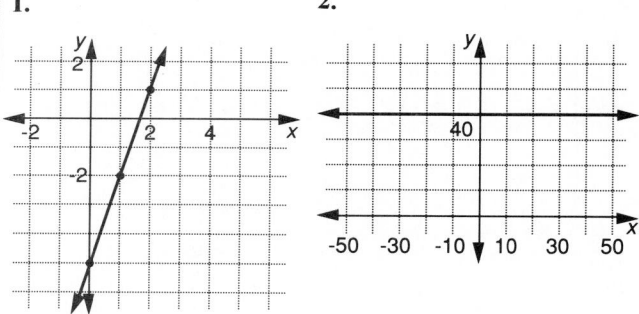

3.

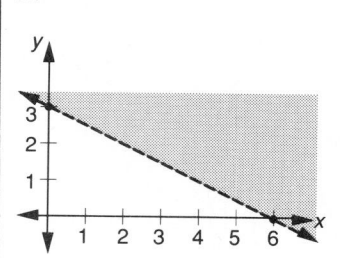

The chart below keys the **Progress Self-Test** questions to the objectives in the **Chapter Review** on pages 176–179 or to the **Vocabulary** (Voc.) on page 174. This will enable you to locate those **Chapter Review** questions that correspond to questions you missed on the **Progress Self-Test.** The lesson where the material is covered is also indicated in the chart.

Question	1–2	3	4	5	6–7	8	9–10	11–12	13
Objective	L	L	A	F	B	Voc.	J	K	G
Lesson	3-2	3-9	3-2	3-1	3-5	3-4	3-10	3-6	3-7

Question	14	15	16	17	18	19	20a	20b
Objective	C	M	D	D	E	H	M	I
Lesson	3-4	3-8	3-6	3-7	3-7	3-1	3-8	3-8

CHAPTER 3 REVIEW (pp. 176–179)

1. a. 7 **b.** -2 **3. a.** 0 **b.** 4 **5. a.** $x = -4.7$ **b.** none **7.** $y = 8x - 245$ **9.** $y - 4 = -\frac{2}{3}(x - 2)$ **11.** $3x + 2y = 1$ or $y - 2 = -\frac{3}{2}(x + 1)$ **13.** $y = -\frac{1}{3}x + 2$ **15.** $2x - 3y = 5$
17. a. $a_n = 7 + 5(n - 1)$ **b.** $a_1 = 7; a_n = a_{n-1} + 5$ for $n > 1.$ **c.** 377 **19.** $a_1 = 9; a_n = a_{n-1} + 2$ for $n > 1$
21. a. 1000 **b.** 100, 101, 102, 103, 104 **23.** horizontal
25. vertical **29.** The graph of $y > 2x - 7$ is the half-plane to the left and above the line $y = 2x - 7.$ **31.** no **33.** positive **35.** slope-intercept **37.** horizontal **39.** adding; constant difference **41.** yes **43.** yes **45.** yes **47.** no **49.** $w = 3 + .2n$ **51.** $500 - 30w$ **53.** $124,000 **55. a.** $C = 3p + 1000$ **b.** $2500 **57. a.** $(A + B)$ gal **b.** $(.06A + .08B)$ gal **c.** $.06A + .08B \geq 2$ **59.** 5 years **61.** See below. **63.** See below. **65.** See below. **67.** zero **69.** $x + 2y = 4$ **71.** 45 mph **73.** See below.

61.

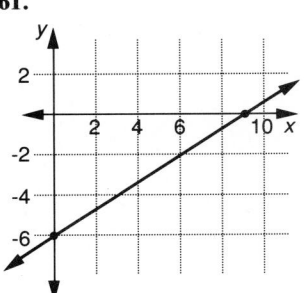

63.

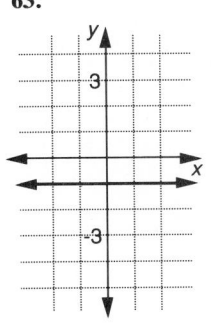

65.

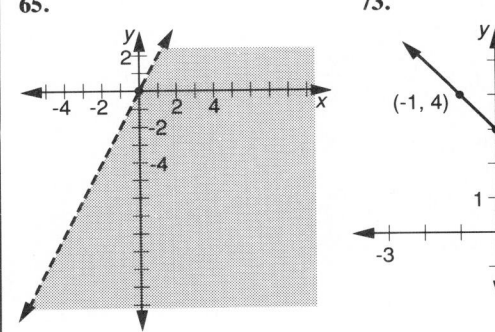

73.

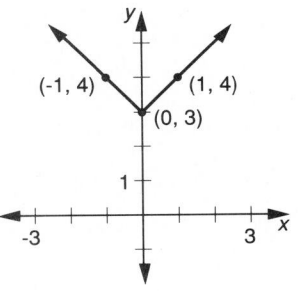

LESSON 4-1 (pp. 182–186)
3. a. 5 **b.** 4 **c.** 5 × 4 **7.** total number of shorts
9. $\begin{bmatrix} a \\ b \end{bmatrix}$; point **11. a.** $\begin{bmatrix} -1 & -4 & 3 & 6 & 4 \\ 6 & 1 & -2 & 2 & 7 \end{bmatrix}$ **b.** No; corresponding elements are not equal. **13. a.** 4 × 2 **b.** the total number of enlisted Navy personnel **c.** the total number of commissioned officers **15.** 2,0 **17.** See below. **19.** b, c, e, f

17.

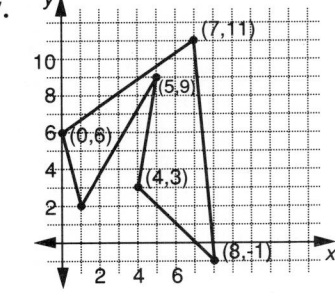

LESSON 4-2 (pp. 187–191)
1. [-11] **3. a.** 2 × 3, 2 × 2 **b.** No **c.** The number of columns in the first matrix does not equal the number of rows in the second matrix. **5.** $\begin{bmatrix} 22 & 50 & -12 \\ -12 & 3 & 0 \end{bmatrix}$ **7.** when $n = p$
9. Matrix multiplication is associative. **11.** $\begin{bmatrix} 8 & -8 & 6 \\ -1 & 4 & 2 \\ -13 & 16 & -7 \end{bmatrix}$
13. a. $\begin{bmatrix} a & b \\ c & d \end{bmatrix}$ **b.** $\begin{bmatrix} a & b \\ c & d \end{bmatrix}$ **c.** True **15.** $921.50
17. $\begin{bmatrix} 50 & 40 & 17 \\ 100 & 80 & 3 \\ 42 & 58 & 5 \end{bmatrix}, \begin{bmatrix} 50 & 100 & 42 \\ 40 & 80 & 58 \\ 17 & 3 & 5 \end{bmatrix}$ **19.** The distance between (1, 5) and (7, 6) is $\sqrt{37}$; between (1, 5) and (- 5, 4) is $\sqrt{37}$; between (7, 6) and (-5, 4) is $2\sqrt{37}$. The triangle is isosceles.

LESSON 4-3 (pp. 193–198)
1. A size change of magnitude 3 maps (3, 1) onto (9, 3).
7. True **9.** True **11. a.** $P' = (7.5, 10)$ **b.** $y = \frac{4}{3}x$ **13. a.** $\frac{7}{2}$

b. $\frac{7}{2}$ **c.** Yes, because the slopes are equal. **d.** Yes, because slopes are $\frac{-1}{6}$. **15. a.** $\begin{bmatrix} 2 & 0 \\ 0 & 2 \end{bmatrix}$ **b.** $\begin{bmatrix} 2 & 3 & 4 \\ 7 & 6.2 & 8.2 \end{bmatrix}$

c. twice as long **17. a.** 3×4 **b.** $\begin{bmatrix} 25 \\ 70 \\ 30 \\ 30 \end{bmatrix}$ **c.** Chicago:

$\$2,105,000$, Minneapolis: $\$1,125,000$, Syracuse: $\$465,000$

19. $a = \frac{-1}{2}b = \frac{-7}{6}$ **21.** See below.

21.

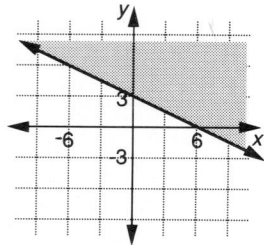

LESSON 4-4 (pp. 199–203)

3. $a = 1$, $b = \frac{1}{3}$ **5.** shrink, stretch **7. a.** $\frac{7}{2}$ **b.** $\frac{35}{4}$ **c.** No; the slopes are different. **d.** No **9.** size change, $\begin{bmatrix} 2 & 0 \\ 0 & 2 \end{bmatrix}$

11. a. rectangle **b.** $\begin{bmatrix} 0 & 12 & 12 & 0 \\ 0 & 0 & 12 & 12 \end{bmatrix}$ **c.** square **d.** See

below. **13. a.** See below. **b.** 45° **15.** $\begin{bmatrix} 9 & 3 & -12 \\ 5 & 3 & -2 \\ -6 & 1 & 12 \end{bmatrix}$

17. a. $x = 225$ **b.** $y = 25$

11. d.   **13. a.**

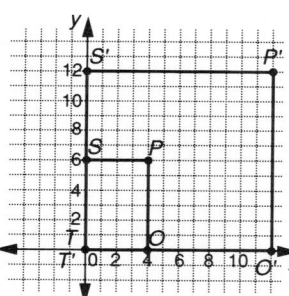   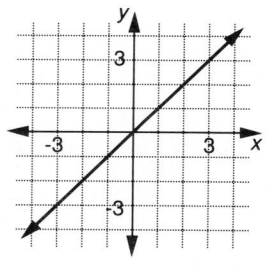

LESSON 4-5 (pp. 204–209)

3. $\begin{bmatrix} 2 & 4 & 4 \\ 1 & 1 & 2 \end{bmatrix}$ or $A^1 = (2, 1)$, $B^1 = (4, 1)$, $C^1 = (4, 2)$;

11. a. $F' = (a, c)$, $S' = (b, d)$ **b.** column **c.** column
d. The first column is the image of $(1, 0)$ and the second

column is the image of $(0, 1)$. **13.** $\begin{bmatrix} 0 & 1 \\ 1 & 0 \end{bmatrix}\begin{bmatrix} x \\ y \end{bmatrix} =$

$\begin{bmatrix} 0x + 1y \\ 1x + 0y \end{bmatrix} = \begin{bmatrix} y \\ x \end{bmatrix}$. Since $r_{y=x} (x, y) = (y, x)$, $\begin{bmatrix} 0 & 1 \\ 1 & 0 \end{bmatrix}$

is the matrix for $r_{y=x}$. **15.** The area is multiplied by 9. If
$A = bh$, and $b^1 = 3b$ and $h^1 = 3h$, then $A^1 = b^1h^1 = (3b)(3h) = 9bh = 9A$. **17.** 110° **19.** See below.

19.

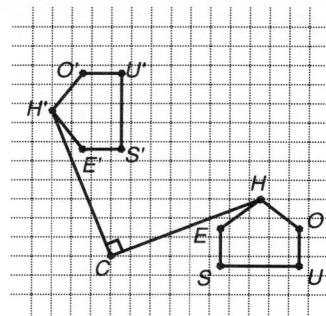

LESSON 4-6 (pp. 210–215)

3. sample: $\begin{bmatrix} 1 & 0 \\ 2 & 1 \end{bmatrix}\begin{bmatrix} 2 & 2 \\ 0 & 3 \end{bmatrix} = \begin{bmatrix} 2 & 2 \\ 4 & 7 \end{bmatrix}$;

$\begin{bmatrix} 2 & 2 \\ 0 & 3 \end{bmatrix}\begin{bmatrix} 1 & 0 \\ 2 & 1 \end{bmatrix} = \begin{bmatrix} 6 & 2 \\ 6 & 3 \end{bmatrix}$

5. a. $(AB)C = \left(\begin{bmatrix} a & b \\ c & d \end{bmatrix}\begin{bmatrix} e & f \\ g & h \end{bmatrix}\right)\begin{bmatrix} i & j \\ k & l \end{bmatrix}$

$= \begin{bmatrix} ae + bg & af + bh \\ ce + dg & cf + dh \end{bmatrix}\begin{bmatrix} i & j \\ k & l \end{bmatrix}$

$= \begin{bmatrix} aei + bgi + afk + bhk & aej + bgj + afl + bhl \\ cei + dgi + cfk + dhk & cej + dgj + cfl + dhl \end{bmatrix}$

b. $A(BC) = \begin{bmatrix} a & b \\ c & d \end{bmatrix}\left(\begin{bmatrix} e & f \\ g & h \end{bmatrix}\begin{bmatrix} i & j \\ k & l \end{bmatrix}\right)$

$= \begin{bmatrix} a & b \\ c & d \end{bmatrix}\begin{bmatrix} ei + fk & ej + fl \\ gi + hk & gj + hl \end{bmatrix}$

$= \begin{bmatrix} aei + afk + bgi + bhk & aej + afl + bgj + bhl \\ cei + cfk + dei + dfk & cej + cfl + dgj + dhl \end{bmatrix}$

11. Associative property of matrix multiplication

13. $\begin{bmatrix} 0 & 1 \\ -1 & 0 \end{bmatrix}$ **b.** R_{270} **c.** Not the same; $r_{y=x} \circ r_x = R_{90}$

15. a. $S_k \cdot C = \begin{bmatrix} K & O \\ O & K \end{bmatrix}\begin{bmatrix} m & n \\ p & q \end{bmatrix} = \begin{bmatrix} km & kn \\ kp & kq \end{bmatrix}$

$C \cdot S_k = \begin{bmatrix} m & n \\ p & q \end{bmatrix}\begin{bmatrix} K & O \\ O & K \end{bmatrix} = \begin{bmatrix} km & kn \\ kp & kq \end{bmatrix}$

b. Size change transformations are commutative.

17. isosceles right triangle **b.** $\begin{bmatrix} -28 & 28 & 0 \\ 0 & 0 & 7 \end{bmatrix}$ **c.** isosceles

d. 49 units², 196 units² **19.** a

LESSON 4-7 (pp. 217–221)

1. 135° **9.** (-5, 3) **11.** (5, -3) **13.** $\begin{bmatrix} 1 & 0 \\ 0 & 1 \end{bmatrix}$ **15. a.** $\begin{bmatrix} 1 & 0 \\ 0 & -1 \end{bmatrix}$

b. r_x **17. a.** See below. **b.** See below. **c.** R_{180}

19. $\begin{bmatrix} 1 & 0 \\ 0 & 1 \end{bmatrix}$ **21.** $\begin{bmatrix} 1 & 0 \\ 0 & 3 \end{bmatrix}$ **23.** $6.9\overline{4}$ **25.** Perpendicular lines
are lines that meet to form equal adjacent angles; lines that
meet to form 90° angles; lines that meet to form right angles.

27. a. The reflection over the y-axis

b. $\begin{bmatrix} -1 & 0 \\ 0 & 1 \end{bmatrix}\begin{bmatrix} 0 & -4 & -6 & -4 & 0 \\ 3 & 3 & 2.5 & 2 & 2 \end{bmatrix} = \begin{bmatrix} 0 & 4 & 6 & 4 & 0 \\ 3 & 3 & 2.5 & 2 & 2 \end{bmatrix}$

c. $R(x, y) = (-x, y)$

17. a. b.

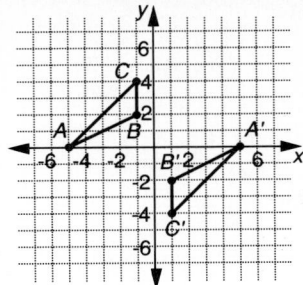

LESSON 4-8 (pp. 222–227)

5. a. 3 **b.** $y + 2 = 3(x - 7)$ **7.** $y - 3 = \frac{2}{7}(x + 1)$ **9. a**

11. $x = 6$ **13. a.** ∥ **b.** ⊥ **c.** ⊥ **d.** ∥ **15. a.** $\begin{bmatrix} 1 & 0 \\ 0 & -1 \end{bmatrix}$ **b.** r_x

17. 1, 9, 36, 100, 725 **19.** 2307.7

LESSON 4-9 (pp. 228–233)

3. $\begin{bmatrix} 13 & 11 & 13 & 13 & 13 \\ 8 & 7 & 10 & 7 & 6 \\ 23 & 32 & 26 & 36 & 17 \\ 20 & 23 & 24 & 39 & 29 \end{bmatrix}$ **5.** $\begin{bmatrix} 6 & -6 \\ -36 & 18 \end{bmatrix}$ **7.** $\begin{bmatrix} 1 & -10 \\ -2 & 4 \end{bmatrix}$

9. a. $\begin{bmatrix} 8 & -1 \\ -1 & 1 \end{bmatrix}$ **b.** $\begin{bmatrix} 8 & -1 \\ -8 & 1 \end{bmatrix}$ **c.** Addition of matrices is asso-

ciative. **11.** $a = 8$, $b = -\frac{3}{5}$; $c = 21$, $d = 24.5$

13. a. $\begin{bmatrix} -1 & 5 & -4 & -6 \\ -7 & 16 & -9 & -23 \\ 10 & -4 & -6 & 14 \\ 8 & -6 & -2 & 14 \\ 9 & -12 & 3 & 21 \end{bmatrix}$ **b.** How many more points each

team had in 1983–84 than in 1982–83. **c.** How many more
wins each team had in 1983–84 than in 1982–83. **15. a.** $y -$

$0 = \frac{1}{2}(x - 3)$ **b.** $y - 0 = -2(x - 3)$ **17.** $\begin{bmatrix} 1 & 0 \\ 0 & -1 \end{bmatrix}$

19. $\begin{bmatrix} 3 & 0 \\ 0 & 4 \end{bmatrix}$ **21.** on $y - 21 = \frac{17}{13}(x - 5)$

LESSON 4-10 (pp. 234–237)

5. See below. 7. (98, -92) **9.** $\begin{bmatrix} 7 & 2 \\ 11 & 3 \end{bmatrix}$

11. a. $\begin{bmatrix} 11 & 6 & 5 & 3 & 8 \\ -8 & 3 & -2 & -6 & -15 \end{bmatrix}$ **b. See below. 13. a. See**

below. b. Western Hemisphere **15.** $\begin{bmatrix} -2 & 0 \\ 0 & \frac{1}{2} \end{bmatrix}$

17. a. $\begin{bmatrix} 0 & 1 \\ -1 & 0 \end{bmatrix}$ **b.** $(b, -a)$ **19. a.** $\begin{bmatrix} 4 & 0 \\ 0 & 4 \end{bmatrix}$ **b.** $(4a, 4b)$

21. a. $\begin{bmatrix} -1 & 0 \\ 0 & -1 \end{bmatrix}$ **b.** (b, a)

5.

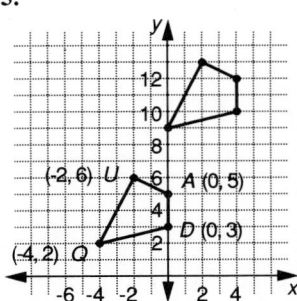

11. b.

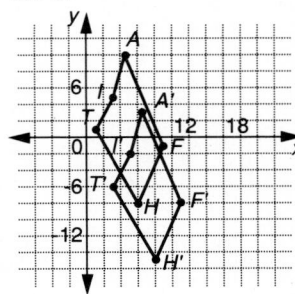

13. a.

	Exports	Imports
WH	-3342	-9406
Europe	-4074	1830
Asia	-1009	6294
Africa	7499	5657
Oceania	-2569	-1783

CHAPTER 4 PROGRESS SELF-TEST (p. 240)

1. See below. 2. $\begin{bmatrix} 14 & 3 & 8 \\ 120 & 190 & 250 \end{bmatrix}$ **3.** Two matrices with

dimensions $m \times n$ and $n \times p$ can be multiplied—the number
of columns in the left matrix must match the number of rows
in the right matrix. AB would be a 3×2 times a 2×2 matrix; the product would exist. BA would be a 2×2 times a
3×2 matrix; the product would not exist.

4. $BC = \begin{bmatrix} 2 & 0 \\ 1 & 5 \end{bmatrix} \begin{bmatrix} 8 & 6 \\ -2 & 2 \end{bmatrix} =$

$\begin{bmatrix} 16 + 0 & 12 + 0 \\ 8 - 10 & 6 + 10 \end{bmatrix} = \begin{bmatrix} 16 & 12 \\ -2 & 16 \end{bmatrix}$

5. $B - C = \begin{bmatrix} 2 & 0 \\ 1 & 5 \end{bmatrix} - \begin{bmatrix} 8 & 6 \\ -2 & 2 \end{bmatrix} =$

$\begin{bmatrix} 2 - 8 & 0 - 6 \\ 1 - (-2) & 5 - 2 \end{bmatrix} = \begin{bmatrix} -6 & -6 \\ 3 & 3 \end{bmatrix}$

6. $\begin{bmatrix} -1 & 0 \\ 0 & 1 \end{bmatrix} \begin{bmatrix} 2 & 0 \\ 1 & 5 \end{bmatrix} = \begin{bmatrix} -2 + 0 & 0 + 0 \\ 0 + 1 & 0 + 5 \end{bmatrix} =$

$\begin{bmatrix} -2 & 0 \\ 1 & 5 \end{bmatrix}$ **7.** $\begin{bmatrix} 0 & -1 \\ 1 & 0 \end{bmatrix} \begin{bmatrix} 8 & 6 \\ -2 & 2 \end{bmatrix} =$

$\begin{bmatrix} 0 + 2 & 0 - 2 \\ 8 + 0 & 6 + 0 \end{bmatrix} = \begin{bmatrix} 2 & -2 \\ 8 & 6 \end{bmatrix}$

8. $7B = 7\begin{bmatrix} 2 & 0 \\ 1 & 5 \end{bmatrix} = \begin{bmatrix} 14 & 0 \\ 7 & 35 \end{bmatrix}$

9. Since $\begin{bmatrix} 1 & 0 \\ 0 & 1 \end{bmatrix} \begin{bmatrix} a & b \\ c & d \end{bmatrix} =$

$\begin{bmatrix} 1a + 0c & 1b + 0d \\ 0a + 1c & 0b + 1d \end{bmatrix} = \begin{bmatrix} a & b \\ c & d \end{bmatrix}$ and $\begin{bmatrix} a & b \\ c & d \end{bmatrix}$

$\begin{bmatrix} 1 & 0 \\ 0 & 1 \end{bmatrix} = \begin{bmatrix} a \cdot 1 + b \cdot 0 & a \cdot 0 + b \cdot 1 \\ c \cdot 1 + d \cdot 0 & c \cdot 0 + d \cdot 1 \end{bmatrix} = \begin{bmatrix} a & b \\ c & d \end{bmatrix}$,

the result of multiplying any 2×2 matrix by $\begin{bmatrix} 1 & 0 \\ 0 & 1 \end{bmatrix}$ is the

original matrix. Another way to express that is the image of
any point under that transformation is the same as the preimage. **10.** The slope of the line $y = 5x - 3$ is 5, so the

slope of the line perpendicular to $y = 5x - 3$ is $-\frac{1}{5}$. Using

the point (3, -2.5) and $y - y_1 = m(x - x_1)$, the desired

equation is $y - (-2.5) = -\frac{1}{5}(x - 3)$ or $y + 2.5 = -\frac{1}{5}$

$(x - 3)$. **11.** $r_x \cdot R_{270} = \begin{bmatrix} 1 & 0 \\ 0 & -1 \end{bmatrix} \begin{bmatrix} 0 & 1 \\ -1 & 0 \end{bmatrix} =$

$\begin{bmatrix} 0 + 0 & 1 + 0 \\ 0 + 1 & 0 + 0 \end{bmatrix} = \begin{bmatrix} 0 & 1 \\ 1 & 0 \end{bmatrix}$ **12.** Each point is moved 8

units to the right and 8 units down, so the transformation is
$T_{8, -8}$. **13.** The product can be written as

$$\begin{bmatrix} 23 & 8 & 10 & 5 \\ 11 & 5 & 10 & 15 \\ 2 & 3 & 15 & 15 \end{bmatrix} \begin{bmatrix} 18 \\ 58 \\ 12 \\ 76 \end{bmatrix} =$$

$$\begin{bmatrix} 23 \cdot 18 + 8 \cdot 58 + 10 \cdot 12 + 5 \cdot 76 \\ 11 \cdot 18 + 5 \cdot 58 + 10 \cdot 12 + 15 \cdot 76 \\ 2 \cdot 18 + 3 \cdot 58 + 15 \cdot 12 + 15 \cdot 76 \end{bmatrix} =$$

$$\begin{bmatrix} 414 + 464 + 120 + 380 \\ 198 + 290 + 120 + 1140 \\ 36 + 174 + 180 + 1140 \end{bmatrix} = \begin{bmatrix} 1378 \\ 1748 \\ 1530 \end{bmatrix}$$; The revenues are:

Los Angeles, \$1,378,000; Tucson, \$1,748,000; Santa Fe, \$1,530,000. **14.** The sum of the two matrices is

$$\begin{bmatrix} 8 & 11 \\ 5 & 4 \\ 15 & 16 \\ 2 & 0 \end{bmatrix} + \begin{bmatrix} 10 & 14 \\ 11 & 13 \\ 7 & 9 \\ 0 & 3 \end{bmatrix} = \begin{bmatrix} 18 & 25 \\ 16 & 17 \\ 22 & 25 \\ 2 & 3 \end{bmatrix}.$$

15. If $\begin{bmatrix} a & 0 \\ 0 & b \end{bmatrix} \begin{bmatrix} -9 \\ -7 \end{bmatrix} = \begin{bmatrix} -3 \\ 14 \end{bmatrix}$, then

$\begin{bmatrix} -9a \\ -7b \end{bmatrix} = \begin{bmatrix} -3 \\ 14 \end{bmatrix}$. Thus $-9a = -3$, so $a = \frac{1}{3}$, and $-7b = 14$, so $b = -2$. **16.** The matrix for a horizontal stretch of 2

and vertical shrink of $\frac{1}{2}$ is $\begin{bmatrix} 2 & 0 \\ 0 & \frac{1}{2} \end{bmatrix}$. **17.** $r_{y=x} = \begin{bmatrix} 0 & 1 \\ 1 & 1 \end{bmatrix}$

18. A translation of 4 units left and 12 units up is $T_{-4, 12}$; or $T_{-4, 12}(x, y) = (x - 4, y + 12)$. **19.** To find R_{90} ($\triangle ABC$),

$\begin{bmatrix} 0 & -1 \\ 1 & 0 \end{bmatrix} \begin{bmatrix} 7 & -1 & 3 \\ 6 & 2 & -4 \end{bmatrix} = \begin{bmatrix} -6 & -2 & 4 \\ 7 & -1 & 3 \end{bmatrix}$, so $A^1 = (-6, 7)$, $B^1 = (-2, -1)$, $C^1 = (4, 3)$. **See below.** **20.** Two points on $x + 2y = 5$ are (5, 0) and (1, 2). Applying the transformation to these points gives $\begin{bmatrix} 3 & 0 \\ 0 & 3 \end{bmatrix} \begin{bmatrix} 5 & 1 \\ 0 & 2 \end{bmatrix} = \begin{bmatrix} 15 & 3 \\ 0 & 6 \end{bmatrix}$,

or the two points (15, 0) and (3, 6). The slope of the line through these two points is $\frac{(y_2 - y_1)}{(x_2 - x_1)} = \frac{(6 - 0)}{(3 - 15)} = \frac{6}{-12} = -\frac{1}{2}$.

Using that slope and (3, 6), an equation is $y - 6 = -\frac{1}{2}(x - 3)$.

1.

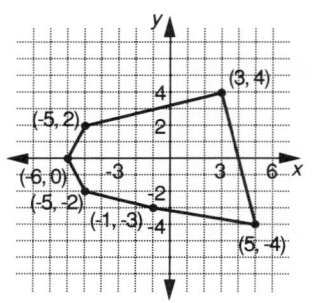

19.

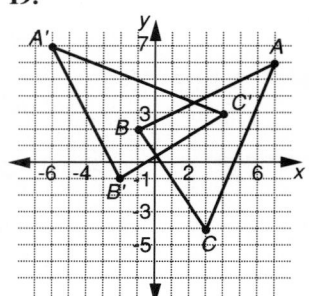

The chart below keys the **Progress Self-Test** questions to the objectives in the **Chapter Review** on pages 241–243 or to the **Vocabulary** (Voc.) on page 239. This will enable you to locate those **Chapter Review** questions that correspond to questions you missed on the **Progress Self-Test.** The lesson where the material is covered is also indicated in the chart.

Question	1	2	3	4	5	6	7	8	9	10
Objective	H	D	C	A	A	G	G	G	C	B
Lesson	4-1	4-1	4-2	4-2	4-9	4-5	4-7	4-9	4-6	4-8

Question	11	12	13	14	15	16	17	18	19	20
Objective	F	F	E	E	A	F	F	F	H	G
Lesson	4-7	4-5	4-2	4-8	4-2	4-4	4-7	4-10	4-7	4-3, 4-5

CHAPTER 4 REVIEW (pp. 241–243)

1. [59] **3.** [512 200] **5.** $\begin{bmatrix} 11 & 6 \\ 4 & -8 \\ 8 & 2 \end{bmatrix}$

7. $\begin{bmatrix} 2 & 33 & 12 \\ 13 & 3 & -7 \\ -13 & -30 & -8 \end{bmatrix}$ **9.** $a = -8; b = 5$ **11.** $a = 8; b = 5$

13. $y - 8 = \frac{1}{4}(x - 7)$ **15.** $y - 2 = 4(x - 2)$ **17. a.** Yes

b. See Question 5, Lesson 4-6. **19. a.** *TN* **b.** $q \times p$

21. $\begin{bmatrix} 5 & 3 & 1 \\ 10 & 12 & 6 \end{bmatrix}$ **23.** element in 2nd row and 1st column

25. Factory 1: \$7,670,000; Factory 2: \$4,390,000

27. $\begin{bmatrix} 249 & 403.20 & 154.80 \\ 118.80 & 236.40 & 65.40 \end{bmatrix}$ **29.** $\begin{bmatrix} 1 & 0 \\ 0 & 1 \end{bmatrix}$;

it is the identity transformation. **31. a.** $\begin{bmatrix} -1 & 0 \\ 0 & 1 \end{bmatrix}$ **b.** r_y **33.** c

35. e **37.** $\begin{bmatrix} 0 & 1 & 5 & 4 \\ 0 & -4 & -3 & 1 \end{bmatrix}$ **39.** $T_{2, -1}$ **41.** $\begin{bmatrix} 1 & 3 & 9 & 6 \\ 1 & 7 & 1 & -6 \end{bmatrix}$

43. See below.

43.

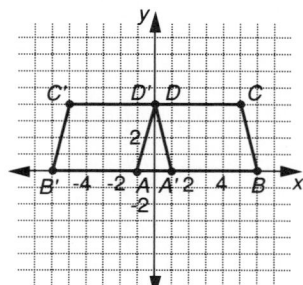

LESSON 5-1 (pp. 546–550)
3. See below. 7. $\{x: 0 < x < 10\} = \{x: x > 0\} \cap \{x: x < 10\}$
9. a. See below. b. See below. 13. a. ii **b.** iv **c.** i **d.** v
15. The conjunction should be "or." **17. a. See below.**
b. a rectangle with dimensions 3×5 and its interior
19. a. 67, 68, 69, . . . , 83 **b.** 1, 2, 3, . . . , 100 **21. a.** y is
divided by 4. **b.** y is multiplied by 8. **23.** $\begin{bmatrix} -1 & -4 & 3 \\ 2 & 0 & -3 \end{bmatrix}$;

See below.

3.
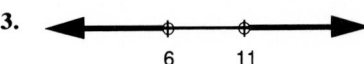
6   11

9. a.
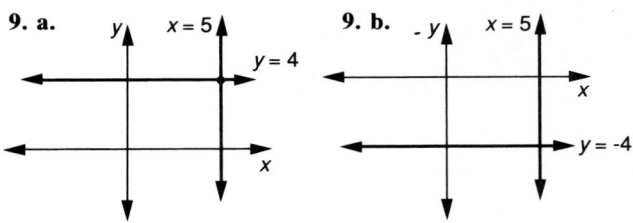

9. b.

17. a.
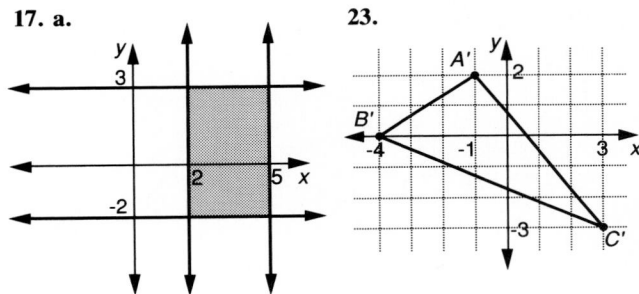

23.

LESSON 5-2 (pp. 251–257)
3. a. (6, 20) **b.** (6, 20) satisfies both equations.

7. sample: $\begin{cases} x - y = 5 \\ -2x + 2y = -10 \end{cases}$ **13. a.** two **b.** consistent

c. (2, 1), $\left(-\frac{1}{2}, -4\right)$ **d.** substitute both points into both sentences of the system: $(2)(1) = 2, 2(2) - 1 = 3$;
$\left(-\frac{1}{2}\right)(-4) = 2, 2\left(-\frac{1}{2}\right) - (-4) = 3.$ **15. a. See below. b.** 2
c. about (2.5, 2.5) & (-4.25, 9.25) **17. a.** $y = 9x$ **b.** father:
9 m; daughter: 45 m **c.** 10 sec **d.** 90 m **19. See below.**
21. See below. 23. $5.99x + 6.25y + 7.99z = T$

15. a.
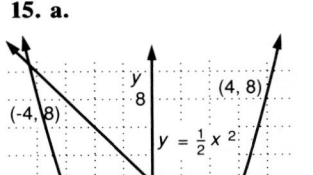

19.
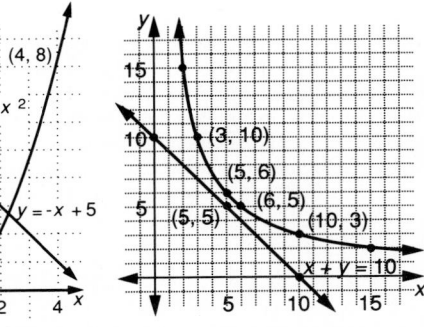

21.

-.5   4   6

LESSON 5-3 (pp. 258–261)
3. We would like to have techniques for solving systems
that always provide exact solutions. **5.** $1\frac{1}{2}$ servings of stew;
1 slice of bread **7.** (1.5, .75) **9.** infinitely many
11. $\left(\frac{7}{24}, \frac{1}{24}\right)$ **13.** consistent **15.** inconsistent **17. a.** $N + S = $
35 **b.** $N(.60) + S(.80) = 25.2$ **c.** $S = 21, N = 14$
19. See below. 21. a. one **b.** consistent

19.
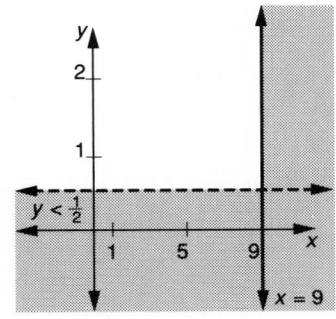

LESSON 5-4 (pp. 264–268)
3. one **5.** (15, -14, 7) **9.** b, d **11. a.** iii **b.** $H = 48,000$;
$V = 12,000$ **13.** juice: .4 C; vinegar: 1.2 C; oil: 5.4 C
15. $\left(\frac{-7}{3}, \frac{-31}{9}\right)$ **17.** $\begin{bmatrix} 2 & \sqrt{3} & -1 \\ 0 & 5.1 & 0 \\ -4 & 11 & -2 \end{bmatrix}$ **19.** $\angle ROC = 70°$,
$\angle CKR = 60°, \angle KRO = 80°, \angle OCK = 150°$

LESSON 5-5 (pp. 269–274)
9. a. 2 **b.** $\begin{bmatrix} 1 & -2 \\ -1 & \frac{5}{2} \end{bmatrix}$ **c.** $\begin{bmatrix} 1 & -2 \\ -1 & \frac{5}{2} \end{bmatrix}\begin{bmatrix} 5 & 4 \\ 2 & 2 \end{bmatrix} = \begin{bmatrix} 1 & 0 \\ 0 & 1 \end{bmatrix}$
11. a. ab **b.** $\begin{bmatrix} \frac{1}{a} & 0 \\ 0 & \frac{1}{b} \end{bmatrix}$ **c.** $\begin{bmatrix} a & 0 \\ 0 & b \end{bmatrix}\begin{bmatrix} \frac{1}{a} & 0 \\ 0 & \frac{1}{b} \end{bmatrix} = \begin{bmatrix} 1 & 0 \\ 0 & 1 \end{bmatrix}$

13. a. 64 **b.** 9 **c.** 576 **15. a.** $e = \frac{1}{6}, f = \frac{1}{3}, g = -\frac{1}{2}, h = 0$;
$\begin{bmatrix} \frac{1}{6} & \frac{1}{3} \\ -\frac{1}{2} & 0 \end{bmatrix}$ **b.** $ad - bc = 6$; $\begin{bmatrix} \frac{1}{6} & \frac{2}{6} \\ \frac{-3}{6} & \frac{0}{6} \end{bmatrix} = \begin{bmatrix} \frac{1}{6} & \frac{1}{3} \\ -\frac{1}{2} & 0 \end{bmatrix}$
17. (2, 8) **19.** When at least one of the equations has been or
can easily be solved for one variable, or when the system has
one linear and one non-linear equation, or when there are
more than two variables and equations. **21. See below.**

21.

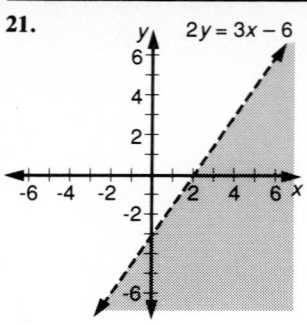

$2y = 3x - 6$

LESSON 5-6 (pp. 275–281)

3. $4 + 3(6) = 22$; $2(4) - 6 = 2$ **5.** one **7.** the 2×2 identity matrix **9.** the 3×3 identity matrix **11.** infinitely many solutions **13.** $n = 14$ **15. a.** (-3, 4, -4, 5)
b. $\begin{matrix} w + 2y = 5 & x + 2z = 6 \\ 3w + 4y = 7 & 3x + 4z = 8 \end{matrix}$ **17.** (-9, 1) **19.** mix A: 75 oz; mix B: 25 oz **21. See below.**

21.

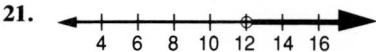

LESSON 5-7 (pp. 282–288)

3. Is $-6 > -2(10) + 6$? Yes. Is $-6 \le \frac{1}{4}(10) - 3$? Yes, so the solution checks. **5.** Is $-2 = -2(4) + 6$? Yes. Is $-2 = \frac{1}{4}(4) - 3$? Yes, so this is a solution for the vertex of the feasible set. **11. a.** (4, 5) **b.** $x \le 6$; $y \ge 0$; $x \ge 0$; $y \le x + 1$; $y \le \frac{1}{2}x + 3$ **13. a. See below. b.** (0, 2), (0, 6), (7, 2) (6, 4) **15. a.** $0 \le x \le 1000$; $0 \le y \le 600$; $20x + 30y \le 24{,}000$ **b. See below. 17. a.** substitution **b.** $x = \frac{1}{2}$, $y = 2$ **19. a.** graphically **b.** $x \approx 1.5$, $y \approx 5$ **21.** a, c, d

13. a.

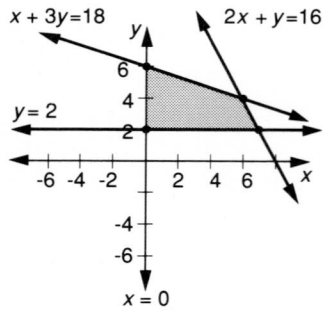

15. b.

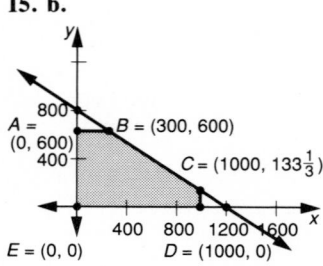

LESSON 5-8 (pp. 288–294)

3. True **5.** $20,965 **9. a. See below. b.** in rounded values, $S = (8, 2)$ **11.** $T = (50, 70)$ **13. See below. 15. a. See below. b.** (8, 0) **17.** $y - 7 = \frac{11}{7}(x - 5)$ **19.** 1400 lb

9. a.

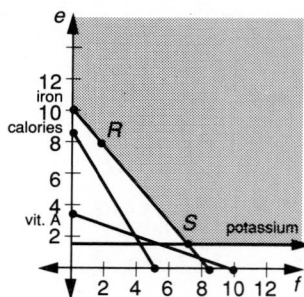

13.

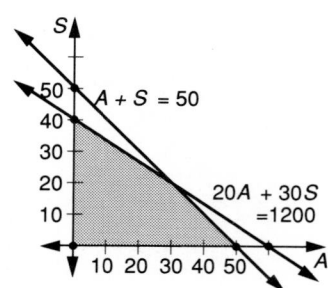

15. a.

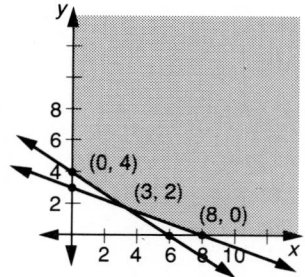

LESSON 5-9 (pp. 295–299)

3. $8.00 **5. a.** $6x + y \le 150$ **b.** $T = (20, 30)$; $U = (25, 0)$ **c.** No; profit is still maximized at Q. **7. a.** h: oz of hamburger; p: potatoes **b. See below.** The inequalities are $h \ge 0$; $p \ge 0$; $.8h + 1.1p \ge 5$; $10h + 0p \ge 30$; $6.5h + 4p \ge 35$ **c. See below. d.** $.11h + 0.5p$ **e.** (3, 4) **f.** 3 oz of hamburger; 4 potatoes **9.** 25% aluminum: 32 kg; 75% aluminum: 128 kg **11. See below.**

7. b.

	Iron (mg)	Vit. A (units)	Protein (g)
hamburger	.8	10	6.5
potato	1.1	0	4
required constraints	5	30	35

7. c.

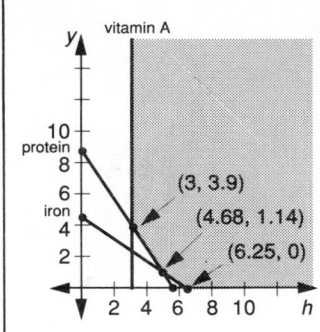

11.

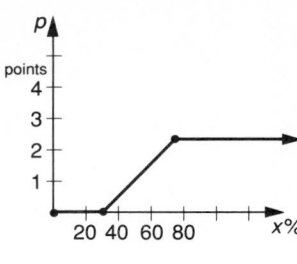

CHAPTER 5 PROGRESS SELF-TEST (p. 301)

1. See below. **2.** From the graph, the solutions are approximately (-1.7, -2.9) and (1.2, -1.4). **3. a.** The system is inconsistent. **b.** The equations represent distinct parallel lines. **4.** Substitute the first two equations into the third: $3(t + 11) - 8(4t) = 4$, $3t + 33 - 32t = 4$, $-29t = -29$, $t = 1$; $s = 4t = 4(1) = 4$; $r = t + 11 = (1) + 11 = 12$. $(r, s, t) = (12, 4, 1)$. **5.** Add twice equation 1 to three times equation 2: $2(-3x + 3y) + 3(-4x - 2y) = 2(2) + 3(3)$, $-6x + 6y - 12x - 6y = 4 + 9$, $-18x = 13$, $x = -\frac{13}{18}$; $-3x + 3y = 2$, $-3(-\frac{13}{18}) + 3y = 2$, $\frac{13}{6} + 3y = 2$, $3y = -\frac{1}{6}$, $y = -\frac{1}{18}$. $(x, y) = \left(-\frac{13}{18}, -\frac{1}{18}\right)$. **6.** If $2e + 2s = 2.78$ and $3e + 4s = 4.99$, multiply the first equation by -2 and add it to the second: $-2(2e + 2s) + (3e + 4s) = -2(2.78) + (4.99)$, $-4e - 4s + 3e + 4s = -5.56 + 4.99$, $-e = -.57$, and $e = .57$.

One egg might be 57 cents. **7.** Det $\begin{bmatrix} 8 & 3 \\ 6 & 5 \end{bmatrix}$ is $(8)(5) - (3)(6) = 40 - 18 = 22$. The inverse of $\begin{bmatrix} 8 & 3 \\ 6 & 5 \end{bmatrix}$ is

$\begin{bmatrix} \frac{5}{22} & \frac{-3}{22} \\ \frac{-6}{22} & \frac{8}{22} \end{bmatrix} = \begin{bmatrix} \frac{5}{22} & \frac{-3}{22} \\ \frac{-3}{11} & \frac{4}{11} \end{bmatrix}$. **8.** Since $\begin{bmatrix} 8 & 3 \\ 6 & 5 \end{bmatrix} \begin{bmatrix} x \\ y \end{bmatrix} =$

$\begin{bmatrix} 41 \\ 39 \end{bmatrix}$, then $\begin{bmatrix} \frac{5}{22} & \frac{-3}{22} \\ \frac{-3}{11} & \frac{4}{11} \end{bmatrix} \begin{bmatrix} 8 & 3 \\ 6 & 5 \end{bmatrix} \begin{bmatrix} x \\ y \end{bmatrix} = \begin{bmatrix} \frac{5}{22} & \frac{-3}{22} \\ \frac{-3}{11} & \frac{4}{11} \end{bmatrix}$

$\begin{bmatrix} 41 \\ 39 \end{bmatrix}$ and $\begin{bmatrix} 1 & 0 \\ 0 & 1 \end{bmatrix} \begin{bmatrix} x \\ y \end{bmatrix} = \begin{bmatrix} \frac{5.41}{22} - \frac{3.39}{22} \\ \frac{-3.41}{11} + \frac{4.39}{11} \end{bmatrix} =$

$\begin{bmatrix} \frac{205}{22} - \frac{137}{22} \\ \frac{-123}{11} + \frac{156}{11} \end{bmatrix} = \begin{bmatrix} \frac{88}{22} \\ \frac{33}{11} \end{bmatrix} = \begin{bmatrix} 4 \\ 3 \end{bmatrix}$. Thus $x = 4$, $y = 3$.

9. The two inequalities are $y \le x$ and $x < z$, which is option c.

10. If c and s represent the numbers of chairs and sofas, respectively, then the system of inequalities is: $7c + 4s \le 133$, $2c + 6s \le 72$, $c \ge 0$, and $s \ge 0$. **11.** See below. There are four vertices: (0, 0), (0, 12), (19, 0), and the intersection of $2c + 6s = 72$ and $7c + 4s = 133$. Add twice equation one to -3 times equation 2: $2(2c + 6s) - 3(7c + 4s) = 2(72) - 3(133)$, $4c + 12s - 21c - 12s = 144 - 399$, $-17c = -255$, $c = 15$; $2c + 6s = 72$ so $2(15) + 6s = 72$, $30 + 6s = 72$, $6s = 42$, $s = 7$. The fourth vertex is (15, 7). **12.** Substitute each of the vertices, (0, 0), (0, 12), (19, 0), and (15, 7), into the profit formula $p = 80c + 70s$. For (0, 0), $p = 80(0) + 70(0) = 0$; for (0, 12), $p = 80(0) + 70(12) = 0 + 840 = 840$; for (19, 0), $p = 80(19) + 70(0) = 1520 + 0 = 1520$; for (15, 7), $p = 80(15) + 70(7) = 1200 + 490 = 1690$. The profit is maximized at \$1690 by making 15 chairs and 7 sofas per day. **13.** $y = 7$

1.

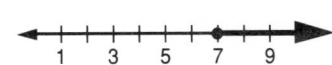

11.

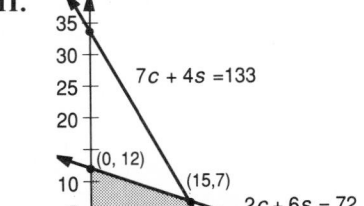

The chart below keys the **Progress Self-Test** questions to the objectives in the **Chapter Review** on pages 302–304 or to the **Vocabulary** (Voc.) on page 300. This will enable you to locate those **Chapter Review** questions that correspond to questions you missed on the **Progress Self-Test.** The lesson where the material is covered is also indicated in the chart.

Question	1	2	3	4	5	6	7	8	9	10	11	12	13
Objective	H	J	D	A	A	F	B	C	E	G	I	G	E
Lesson	5-1	5-2	5-2	5-3	5-4	5-4	5-5	5-6	5-7	5-9	5-9	5-9	5-7

CHAPTER 5 REVIEW (pp. 302–304)

1. a 3. (7, -1) **5.** (-6.5, -10.5) **7.** $\left(\frac{3}{2}, \frac{1}{2}, \frac{1}{5}\right)$ **9. a.** substitution, graphing, linear combination, use of matrices **b.** (-4, -20)

11. a. 2 **b.** $\begin{bmatrix} \frac{1}{2} & 0 \\ 0 & 1 \end{bmatrix}$ **13. a.** 18 **b.** $\begin{bmatrix} \frac{1}{3} & \frac{-2}{9} \\ \frac{1}{6} & \frac{2}{18} \end{bmatrix}$

15. a. $ad - bc$ **b.** $\begin{bmatrix} \dfrac{d}{ad - bc} & \dfrac{-b}{ad - bc} \\ \dfrac{-c}{ad - bc} & \dfrac{a}{ad - bc} \end{bmatrix}$ **17.** (-1, 3)

19. $\left(\frac{4}{7}, \frac{17}{56}\right)$ **21.** $x = 2$ and $y = 8$ **23. a.** inconsistent
b. no solutions **25. a.** consistent **b.** one solution **27.** $t = \frac{21}{4}$
29. a, c **31.** at the vertices **33.** $1.50 **35.** Sugar-O's: $8\frac{1}{3}$ g;
Health-Nut: $16\frac{2}{3}$g **37. a.** Spanish: 90 min; algebra: 15 min
b. Spanish: 3.6 points; algebra: 1.5 points **39. See below.**
41. See below. 43. See below. 45. $x \le$ -3 and $y \le$ -1
47. See below. 49. See below. 51. c

39.

41.
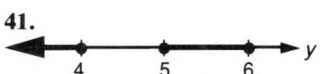

43.
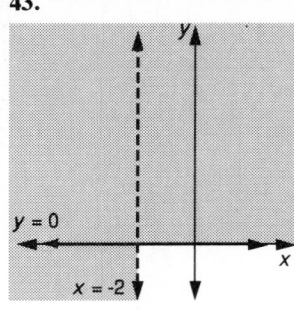

47.
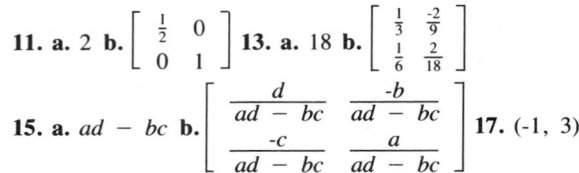

$7c - 3d = $ -1
$7c + 3d = 21$

49.
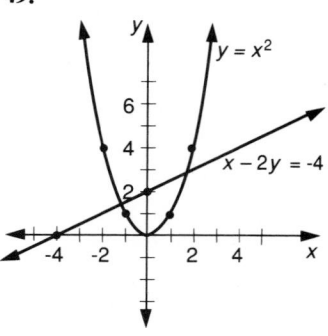

$y = x^2$
$x - 2y = $ -4

LESSON 6-1 (pp. 308–313)

1. d **3.** 20, -20 **5.** 1250 + 150w + 4w² **7.** $x^2 - x - 2$
9. $x^2 + 2xy + y^2$ **11.** 25n² + 80np + 64p² **13.** 4w² − 2w +
$\frac{1}{4}$ **15.** $(x - y)^2 = (x - y)(x - y) = (x - y)x - (x - y)$
$(y) = x^2 - yx - (xy + y^2) = x^2 - yx - xy - y^2 = x^2 -$
$2xy - y^2$ **17.** -x **19.** $\sqrt{(d - b)^2 + (c - a)^2}$ **21.** $\sqrt{104}$
23. x − 3 **25.** $\frac{1}{2}n^2 + \frac{1}{2}n$ **27.** 4xy **29.** $r = \sqrt{\dfrac{140}{\pi}} \approx$

6.7 inches **31. See below. 33.** Use a compass or dividers to
transfer the distance and draw the line with a ruler and
T-square, or use a construction method. **35. a.** $\begin{bmatrix} 1 & 0 \\ 0 & 1 \end{bmatrix}$
b. inverses

31.
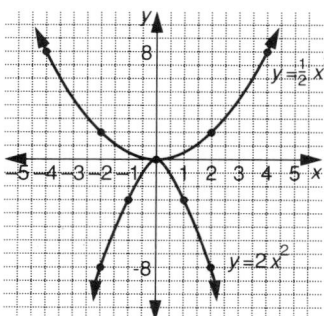

$y = \frac{1}{2}x^2$
$y = 2x^2$

LESSON 6-2 (pp. 314–321)

3. $\dfrac{9.8 \text{ m}}{\text{sec}^2}$ **5.** 15 ft. **7.** $t \approx \frac{1}{4}$ or $t \approx 2.5$ **9.** $h = $ -1.609; therefore ball is below ground. **11. See below. 13. See below.**
15. a. $h = $ -9.8t² + 10t + 1 **b.** 1.2 m **c. See below.**
d. about 1.8 m **17. a.** 96 + 40w + 4w² **b.** 40 + 8w
19. a. $x^2 - 4x + 4$ **b.** 3x² − 12x + 12 **c.** 3x² − 12x
21. (15, 30)

11.
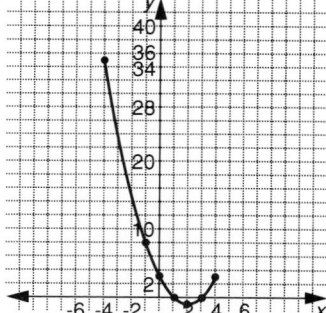

13.

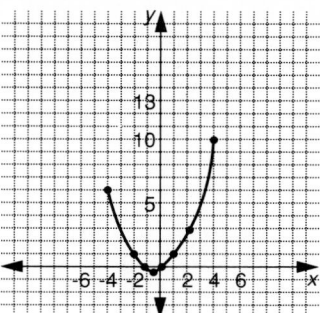

15. c.

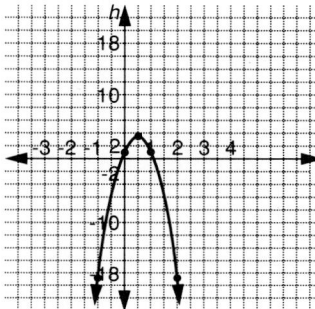

LESSON 6-3 (pp. 322–328)

3. See below. **5.** P_2 **7. a.** See below. **b.** focus = (0, 5); vertex = (0, 0); directrix = $y = -5$ **c.** See below. **9.** up **11.** up **13.** focus = $\left(0, 3\frac{1}{4}\right)$; directrix = $y = \frac{11}{4}$ **15. a.** $y = \frac{x^2}{8}$ **b.** See below. **17. a.** $\pi(r + h)^2 - \pi r^2$ **17 b.** small circumference = $2\pi r$; large circumference = $2\pi(r + h)$ or $2\pi r + 2\pi h$; therefore, larger circle's circumference is $2\pi h$ more than the smaller one. **19. a.** $h = -9.8t^2 + 629$ **b.** 8 seconds **21.** See below. **23.** 31.62

3.

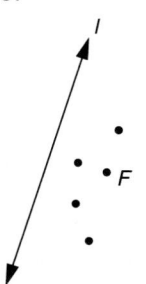

7. a.

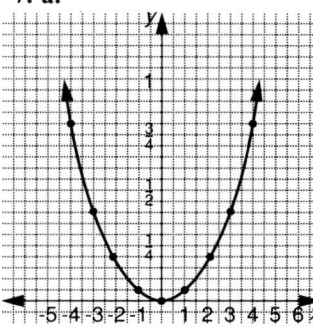

7. c. $\sqrt{(x - 0)^2 + (y - 5)^2} = \sqrt{(x - x)^2 + (y - (-5))^2}$
for (2, 0.2).
$$2^2 + (0.2 - 5)^2 = (0.2 + 5)^2$$
$$2^2 + (4.8)^2 = (5.2)^2$$
$$4 + 23.04 = 27.04$$
$$27.04 = 27.04$$

15. b. $\sqrt{(x - 0)^2 + (y - 2)^2} = \sqrt{(x - x)^2 + (y - (-2))^2}$
$$x^2 + (y - 2)^2 = (y + 2)^2$$
$$x^2 + y^2 - 4y + 4 = y^2 + 4y + 4$$
$$x^2 - 8y = 0$$
$$x^2 = 8y$$
For (4, 2)
$$16 = 16$$

21.

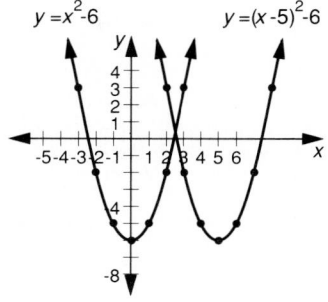

LESSON 6-4 (pp. 329–333)

1. $x = \pm 10$ **b.** $(x - 3)^2 = 100$; $x - 3 = 10$; $x = 13$ **3.** $y = (x - 8)^2$ is the graph of $y = x^2$ moved 8 units to the right. **5. a.** $\left(6, 7\frac{1}{12}\right)$ **b.** $y = 6\frac{11}{12}$ **7. a.** (-7, -2) **b.** $x = -7$ **c.** down **d.** See below. **9.** $x = 11$ **11. a.** ± 34 **b.** 33 or -35. **13.** $y + 5 = -7(x - 2)^2$ **15.** A parabola is a set of all points in a plane whose distance from given point equals its distance from a given line and the point is not on the line. **17. a.** $x^2 + 8x + 16$ **b.** $2x^2 + 16x + 32$ **c.** $2x^2 + 16x + 35$ **19.** $\frac{1}{2}n^2 - \frac{1}{2}n$

7. d.

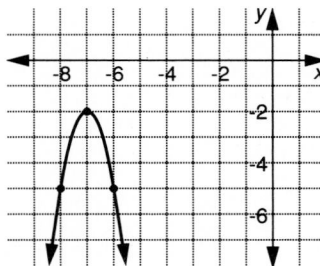

LESSON 6-5 (pp. 334–339)

1. $y = x^2 + 6x + 11$ **3.** $y = 2x^2 - 16x + 31$ **5.** 81 **7.** $\frac{b^2}{4}$ **9.** $\left(\frac{3}{2}, -\frac{5}{4}\right)$ **11.** $\left(-\frac{2}{3}, \frac{11}{3}\right)$ **13. a.** $\left(\frac{11}{8}, \frac{141}{4}\right)$ **b.** 35.25 feet **15.** $(y - 3)^2 = (3 - y)^2$ **17.** $x = -10$ **19.** $z = \sqrt{2} + 5$ **21.** 200 $\frac{ft}{min}$ **23.** True **25.** True

LESSON 6-6 (pp. 340–345)

7. $-1, -\frac{3}{10}$ **9.** h = height; x = distance **11.** 52.2 ft and 343.8 ft **13.** $n + 1, n + 2$ **15. a.** $a = 11; b = -20; c = -4$ **b.** $x = 2$ or $x = -\frac{2}{11}$ **17. a.** $a = 4; b = -12; c = 9$

b. $m = \frac{3}{2}$ **19. a.** $x = 0$ or $x = -\frac{b}{a}$ **b.** $y = 0$ or $y = -\frac{8}{5}$

21. First mistake: one must use $\boxed{+}$ or $\boxed{-}$. Second mistake: one must use two parentheses. $\boxed{\sqrt{x}}\boxed{+}\boxed{(}\,2\,\boxed{\times}\,3\,\boxed{)}$ **23.** $\frac{7}{13}$
25. 0 **27.** The two equations are equivalent.

LESSON 6-7 (pp. 346–352)
7. a 9. a 11. a 13. The square root of a negative number is not real—it's imaginary. **15.** one real root **17.** It does not intercept the x-axis. **19.** 1, rational **21.** False, if discriminant $= 0$, the graph has exactly 1 x-intercept. **23.** $k = 6$ or $k = -6$ **25. a.** error message in line 300 **b.** Add these two statements:

    150 IF A=0, GO TO 650
    650 PRINT "NOT A QUADRATIC EQUATION"

27. 7.63, 2.63 **29.** They have the same roots because the two equations are equivalent. **31.** $\sqrt{7}$ **33.a.** 120 **b.** 127

LESSON 6-8 (pp. 353–356)
3. False **7.** $(i\sqrt{5})(i\sqrt{5}) = i^2 \cdot 5 = -5$ **9.** $x = \pm 4\sqrt{-1}$; $x = \pm 4i$ **11.** $i\sqrt{7}$ **13.** $2i$ **15.** $-3\sqrt{2}$ **19.** $7i$ **21.** $13i$ **23.** 5 **25.** $3i\sqrt{2}$ **27. a.** False: $2i + (-2i) = 0$ **b.** False: $(2i)(3i) = -6$
29. c. $x = \dfrac{-11 \pm \sqrt{41}}{20}$

LESSON 6-9 (pp. 357–361)
3. $a = 14, b = 5$ **5.** $a = 0, b = 1$ **7.** $29 - 7i$ **9.** 5 **11. a.** FOIL **b.** Dist. prop. **c.** $i^2 = -1$ **d.** Comm. prop.
15. $25 - 2i$ **17.** $-4 + 17i$ **19.** $252 + 64i$ **21. a.** $0 + 0i$ **b.** $1 + 0i$ **23. a.** $2a$ **b.** $(a - bi)(a + bi)$; $a^2 - bia + bia - b^2i^2$; $a^2 - b^2(-1)$; $a^2 + b^2$ **25.** $\frac{1}{13} + \frac{5}{13}i$
27. a. $(-8, -4)$ **b.** $-8 \pm \sqrt{2}$ **c. See below. 29.** Girolamo Cardano **31.** $\dfrac{-3 \pm \sqrt{17}}{2}$

27. c.

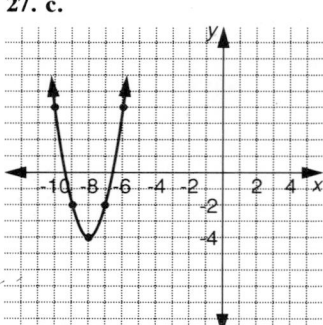

LESSON 6-10 (pp. 362–366)
1. $2 + i, 2 - i$ **3.** $2 + 5i, 2 - 5i$ **5.** $10 + 5\sqrt{6}$
7. $\dfrac{2 - 2\sqrt{2}}{3}$ **9.** $\dfrac{-b}{a}, \dfrac{c}{a}$ **11.** negative **13.** $\dfrac{-5 \pm \sqrt{59}}{6}$
15. a. See below. b. $x = 5$ **c.** $x = 5 \pm i\sqrt{5}$ **d.** Average of roots $= 5$; axis of equation is $x = 5$. **e.** The equation of the axis of symmetry of a parabola is $x = k$, where k is the average of the roots. **17. a.** vertex $(1, 6)$; x-intercepts $(0, 3.45)$, $(0, -1.45)$; axis of symmetry $x = 1$ **b. See below. 19. a.** $AB =$

$$\begin{bmatrix} 0 & 1 \\ 1 & 0 \end{bmatrix}\begin{bmatrix} 0 & -i \\ i & 0 \end{bmatrix} = \begin{bmatrix} i & 0 \\ 0 & -i \end{bmatrix} \begin{bmatrix} -1 & 0 \\ 0 & -1 \end{bmatrix} \cdot BA = \begin{bmatrix} -1 & 0 \\ 0 & -1 \end{bmatrix} \cdot$$

$$\left(\begin{bmatrix} 0 & -i \\ i & 0 \end{bmatrix}\begin{bmatrix} 0 & 1 \\ 1 & 0 \end{bmatrix}\right) = \begin{bmatrix} -1 & 0 \\ 0 & -1 \end{bmatrix}\begin{bmatrix} -i & 0 \\ 0 & i \end{bmatrix} = \begin{bmatrix} i & 0 \\ 0 & -i \end{bmatrix} =$$

AB **b.** $CB = \begin{bmatrix} 1 & 0 \\ 0 & -1 \end{bmatrix}\begin{bmatrix} 0 & -i \\ i & 0 \end{bmatrix} = \begin{bmatrix} 0 & -i \\ -i & 0 \end{bmatrix}\begin{bmatrix} -1 & 0 \\ 0 & -1 \end{bmatrix} \cdot$

$BC = \begin{bmatrix} -1 & 0 \\ 0 & -1 \end{bmatrix} \cdot \left(\begin{bmatrix} 0 & -i \\ i & 0 \end{bmatrix}\begin{bmatrix} 1 & 0 \\ 0 & -1 \end{bmatrix}\right) = \begin{bmatrix} -1 & 0 \\ 0 & -1 \end{bmatrix}$

$\begin{bmatrix} 0 & i \\ -i & 0 \end{bmatrix} = \begin{bmatrix} 0 & -i \\ i & 0 \end{bmatrix} = \begin{bmatrix} 0 & -i \\ -i & 0 \end{bmatrix} = CB$

15. a.

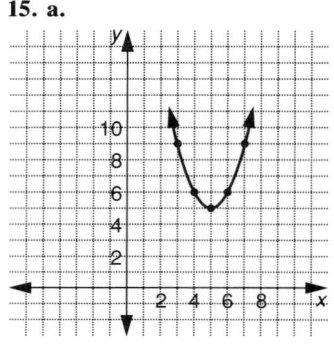

17. b.

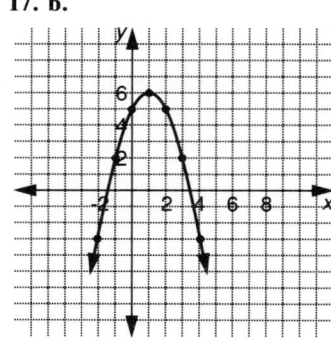

CHAPTER 6 PROGRESS SELF-TEST (p. 369)

1. Rewrite $y = x^2 - 8x + 12$ in the form $y - k = a(x - h)^2$: $y - 12 = x^2 - 8x$, $y - 12 + 16 = x^2 - 8x + 16$, $y + 4 = (x - 4)^2$. The vertex is $(h, k) = (4, -4)$. **2.** The x-intercepts are the value(s) of x for which $y = 0: 0 = x^2 - 8x + 12$, or $(x - 6)(x - 2)$, $x - 6 = 0$ so $x = 6$, or $x - 2 = 0$ so $x = 2$. **3.** $2i - i = 2i^2 = 2(-1) = -2$ **4.** $\sqrt{-8} \cdot \sqrt{-2} = i\sqrt{8} \cdot i\sqrt{2} = i^2\sqrt{16} = (-1)(4) = -4$ **5.** $\dfrac{4 + \sqrt{-8}}{2} = \dfrac{4 + i\sqrt{8}}{2} = \dfrac{4 + 2i\sqrt{2}}{2} = 2 + i\sqrt{2}$

6. $(3i + 2)(6i - 4) = (3i)(6i) + (3i)(-4) + (2)(6i) + (2)(-4) = 18i^2 - 12i + 12i - 8 = 18(-1) - 8 = -18 - 8 = -26$ **7.** $z - w = (2 - 4i) - (1 + 5i) = 2 - 4i - 1 - 5i = 1 - 9i$ **8.** The solution set to $y - 2 = -(x + 1)^2$ is the graph. Since the equation is in the form $y - h = a(x - k)^2$, the vertex is $(-1, 2)$, it opens down, and it is congruent to $y = x^2$. **See below. 9.** Since the directrix, $y = 6$, is one unit from the vertex $(3, 5)$, the focus is also one unit from the vertex, directly below it. The focus is $(3, 4)$. **10.** If $3x^2 + 14x - 5 = 0$, then $(3x - 1)(x + 5) = 0$. If $3x - 1 = 0$, then $3x = 1$ and $x = \frac{1}{3}$; if $x + 5 = 0$,

894

then $x = -5$. The solutions are $x = \frac{1}{3}$, -5. **11.** If $(m + 40)^2 = 2$, then $m + 40 = \pm\sqrt{2}$ and $m = -40 \pm\sqrt{2}$. **12.** If $4x^2 = 2x^2 - 5x + 1$, then $0 = -2x^2 - 5x + 1$ or $0 = 2x^2 + 5x - 1$. Thus

$$x = \frac{-5 \pm \sqrt{5^2 - 4(2)(-1)}}{2(2)} = \frac{-5 \pm \sqrt{25 + 8}}{4} =$$

$\frac{-5 \pm \sqrt{33}}{4}$. **13.** $(m + 40)^2 = 2$; take the square root of both

sides, $m + 40 = \pm\sqrt{2} = m = -40 \pm \sqrt{2}$ **14. a.** The Discriminant Theorem states that if the discriminant is zero, there will be 1 real root, and therefore one x-intercept. **b.** Since the discriminant is positive, there are 2 real roots, and there are 2 x-intercepts. **15. a.** The Discriminant Theorem states that there is 1 real root if the discriminant is 0 and since 0 is a perfect square, the root is rational. **b.** Since the discriminant is negative, there are two complex roots. **16.** $(a - 3)^2 = a^2 - 6a + 9$ (using Binomial-Square Theorem) **17.** $(8v + 1)^2 = 64v^2 + 16v + 1$ (using Binomial-Square Theorem) **18.** General formula is $h = -9.8t^2 + v_0t + h_0$, $v_0 = 10$, $h_0 = 20$; therefore $b = 9.8t^2 + 10t + 20$ **19.** To find the value(s) of t for which $h = 0$, $0 = -16t^2 + 12t + 4$, $0 = -4t^2 + 3t + 1$, $0 = 4t^2 - 3t - 1$,

and $0 = (4t + 1)(t - 1)$. If $4t + 1 = 0$, then $t = -\frac{1}{4}$. If

$t - 1 = 0$, then $t = 1$. The ball hits the ground at $t = 1$, or after 1 second. **21. a.** When the box is folded, the dimensions are $40 - 2s$, $30 - 2s$, and s. The volume is $(40 - 2s)(30 - 2s)(s)$. **b.** If $s = 2$, then $(40 - 2s)(30 - 2s)(s) = (40 - 4)(30 - 4)(2) =$

$(36)(26)(2) = 1872$ cm^3. **22. a.–b. See below. 23.** The coefficient of the squared term (x^2) is what effects the shape of the parabola. Choice **3** has a coefficient of 2 for the x^2 term, all the other parabolas have 1 so they are all the same shape. The choice is **3**.

8.

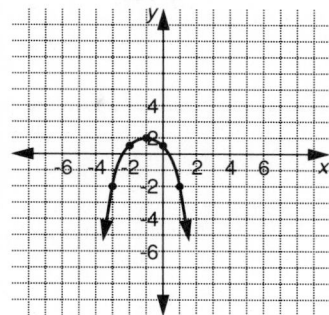

22. a.–b.

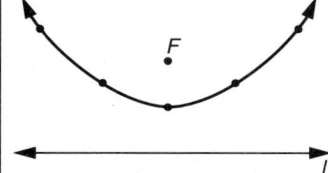

The chart below keys the **Progress Self-Test** questions to the objectives in the **Chapter Review** on pages 370–373 or to the **Vocabulary** (Voc.) on page 367. This will enable you to locate those **Chapter Review** questions that correspond to questions you missed on the **Progress Self-Test.** The lesson where the material is covered is also indicated in the chart.

Question	1	2–3	4–5	6	7–8	9	10	11	12–13	14	15
Objective	B	K	C	C	E	F	K	K	D	D	G & H
Lesson	6-5	6-3	6-8	6-10	6-9	6-4	6-4	6-3	6-6	6-10	6-7, 6-8

Question	16–17	18–20	21	22	23
Objective	A	I	J	A	F
Lesson	6-1	6-2	6-5	6-1	6-4

CHAPTER 6 REVIEW (pp. 370–373)

1. $a^2 + 2ax + x^2$ **3.** $9x^2 + 24x + 16$ **5.** $9t^2 - 90 + 225$ **7.** $y = 3x^2 + 12x + 2$ **9.** $y + 31 = (x + 5)^2$ **11.** b **13.** $6i$ **15.** $2i$ **17.** -3 **19.** $-\frac{1}{2} \pm \frac{1}{2}i$ **21.** $\pm 4\sqrt{3}$ **23.** $\pm 3i$

25. $y = \frac{6}{5}, -\frac{1}{2}$ **27.** $a = \frac{-3 \pm i\sqrt{23}}{8}$ **29.** $x = 1 \pm 2i\sqrt{2}$

31. $x = \frac{-1 \pm 5}{2}$ **33.** $n = \frac{1 \pm i\sqrt{59}}{3}$ **35.** $0 + 2i$

37. $37 + 5i$ **39.** $8 - 6i$ **41.** $6 + 11$ **43.** d **45.** $y - 0.1 = -10(x + 0.3)$ **47.** $k = 7, -5$ **49. a.** $\sqrt{-111} = i\sqrt{111}$ **b.** none **c.** no real solutions **51. a.** $\sqrt{10,400} = 20\sqrt{26}$ **b.** two real roots **c.** irrational **53.** 2 **55.** real, rational **57.** real, irrational **59.** non-real **63.** 4.5 seconds **65.** 150 ft **67.** $5\frac{1}{2}$ by 11 meters **69. See below. 71. See below. 73.** c

75. at $t \approx 0.6$ second and $t \approx 3.4$ seconds **77.** two **79.** one **81. See below.**

69.

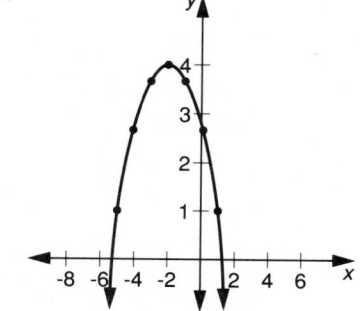

71.

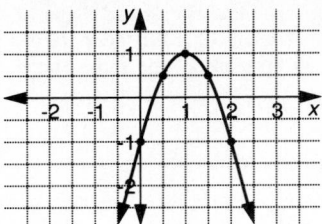

81.

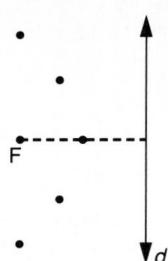

LESSON 7-1 (pp. 376–380)

3. B maps x onto $\frac{x^2}{20}$ **5.** 125 **7.** 10 **9.** 96 feet is not a realistic following distance, since the stopping distance needed is about 240 ft. **11.** independent **13.** 13 **15.** No; the x-values of 16 and 8 are each paired with two different y-values.

17. 2,173,000 **19.** 50% **21. a.** $\frac{9}{16}$ **b.** $\frac{9}{x^2 + 8x + 16}$

c. $\frac{9}{16x^2}$ **d.** $\frac{9x^2}{16}$ **23. a.** inversely, w **b.** $g(w) = \frac{k}{w}$

25. a. $50{,}000 = \frac{1}{8}E$ or $\frac{1}{4}E + \frac{1}{8}E + \frac{1}{2}E + 50{,}000 = E$

b. $400{,}000 **27.** $V = \frac{k}{T}$

LESSON 7-2 (pp. 381–387)

1. the set of allowable substitutions for the independent variable **3.** True **5.** $\{y: 0 \leq y \leq 240\}$ **7.** No: vertical lines for $x > 0$ intersect the graph twice. **9.** yes **11. a. See below.**
b. yes **c.** $D = \{2,3,5\}$, $R = \{4\}$ **13. a. See below. b.** yes
c. $D = \{\text{all real numbers}\}$, $R = \{y: y \geq 0\}$ **15. a. See below. b.** yes **c.** $D = \{x: x \leq 0\}$, $R = \{y: y \geq 0\}$ **17.** 325° F
19. $12 \leq A(t) \leq 138$ **21.** $t \approx 9.8$ and $t \approx 15$ **23. a.** 9

b. -7 **c.** $1 + \frac{x^3}{8}$ **25.** 212 **27.** 36

11. a.

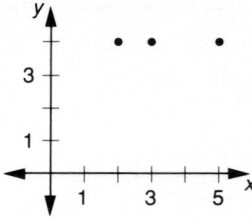

13. a.

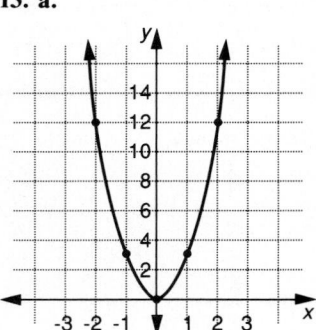

15. a.

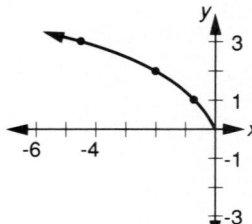

LESSON 7-3 (pp. 388–392)

1. $10,625 **5. a.** 1251 **b.** $7x^2 + 7x - 63$ **c.** $49x^2 + 7x - 9$
d. $49x^2 + 7x - 9$ **9.** $x \neq 3$ and $x \neq -3$ **11.** 1.9 $\boxed{y^x}$ 3
$\boxed{-}\,\boxed{\pi}\,\boxed{=}\,\boxed{\sqrt{x}}$ **13. a.** x **b.** $x = 0$ **15. a.** $(\text{r} \circ \text{s})(x) = 1000 + \sqrt{2(2500 + \sqrt{x})}$ **b.** ≈ 1095 barracuda **17.** K^2 **19. a.** 100 ft
b. $D = \{t: : 0 \leq t \leq 4\}$ **c.** $R = \{h: 0 \leq h \leq 100\}$

LESSON 7-4 (pp. 393–397)
1. $4.25 **5.** 11 **7.** 8 **9.** $6.5 \leq N < 7.5$ **11.** any value of x
13. b **15. a.** 3 **b.** -1 **c.** 6 **d. See below.** **17.** $3x^2 - 4$
19. See below. 21. range = {positive even integers}
23. a. $2\sqrt{5}$ **b.** $7\sqrt{3}$ **c.** 2

15. d.   **19.**

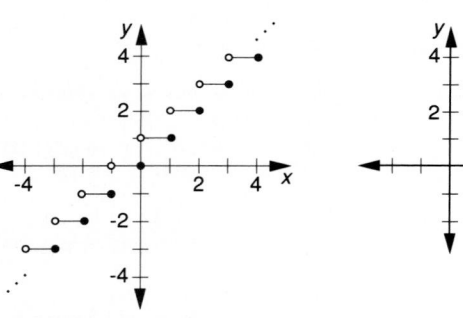

LESSON 7-5 (pp. 398–404)
3. a. $-x$; **b.** x **5. a. See below. b. See below. c. See below.**
d. See below. 9. True **11.** Let $C = $ SQR $(A\,\hat{}\,2 + B\,\hat{}\,2)$
13. $y = x^6$ **15. a. See below. b.** domain = {all real numbers}; range = {all nonpositive numbers} **17. a.** $.015 = |p - 50.015|$ **b.** $50.000 \leq p \leq 50.030$ **19. See below.**

20. iii **23.** $t = \frac{y - m}{x}$ **25.** $\begin{bmatrix} 0 & 1 \\ -1 & 0 \end{bmatrix}$

5. a.   **5. b.**

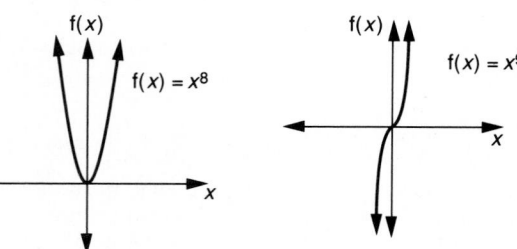

896

5. c.

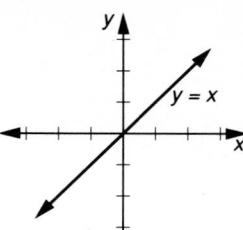

5. d.

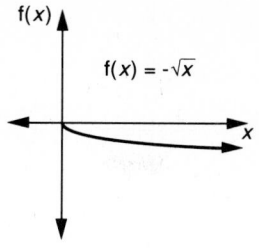

11. c.

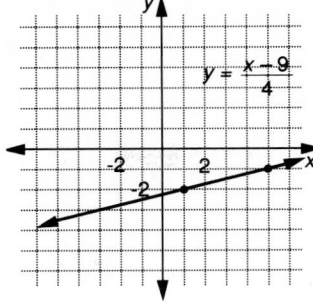

15. a.

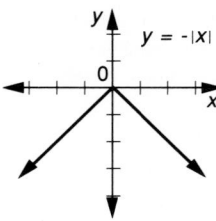

19.

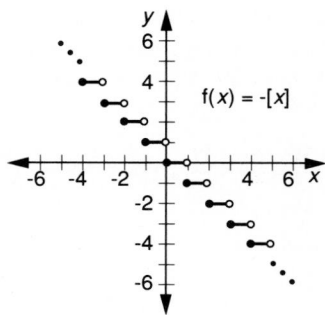

LESSON 7-7 (pp. 411–417)

3. $(h \circ h^{-1})(x) 6\left(\frac{1}{6}x + \frac{5}{6}\right) - 5 = x - 5 - 5 = x$ **5.** $(g \circ f)(x) =$ $x + 4$ **9. a.** domain = {all real numbers}; range = {all real numbers} **b.** See below. **c.** domain = {all real numbers}; range = {all real numbers} **11.** No **13.** No **15. a.** $g^{-1}(x) = \frac{1}{6}x$ **b.** $(g^{-1})^{-1}(x) = 6x$ **c.** f **17.** $x = \pm\frac{2}{17}$ **19.** $x = \pm 2i$ **21.** e **23.** g

9. b.

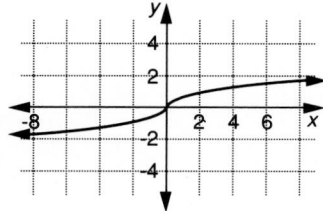

LESSON 7-6 (pp. 405–410)

5. $x = 3y$ **9.** No **11. a.** Yes, it is a function. **b.** $y = \frac{x - 9}{4}$
c. See below. **d.** The slopes are reciprocals. **13. a.** $f(x) =$ 1.3x **b.** $g(y) = .75y$ **15. a.** It is being raised by successive tugs on a rope. **b.** The flag is not always moving due to a re-gripping of the rope. **17. a.** 15 **b.** x **c.** identity function
19. a. $\frac{1}{2}$ **b.** the slope of $y = f(x)$

CHAPTER 7 PROGRESS SELF-TEST (p. 420)

1. $f(3) = 9 \cdot 3^2 - 11 \cdot 3 = 9 \cdot 9 - 33 = 81 - 33 = 48$
2. $T(12) = \frac{12(12 + 1)}{2} = \frac{156}{2} = 78$ **3.** $f(n + 1) =$ $n + 1^2 = n^2 + 2n + 1$ **4.** yes, because for each element in the domain there is associated exactly one range element
5. yes, see answer to Question 4. **6.** $f(g(7)) = f(-8(7)) =$ $f(-56) = (-56)^2 = 3136$ **7.** $g(f(x)) = g(x^2) = -8(x^2) =$ $-8x^2$ **8.** No, because $(g \circ f)(x) \neq x$. **9.** Because x^6 is non-negative for all values of x, the range is {y: y ≥ 0} which im-plies quadrants I and II. **10.** {1, 3, 5} which is the set of first coordinates **11.** {(2, 1), (4, 3), (6, 5)} **12.** Replace $g(x)$ by y. $y = 5x + 10$. Switch x and y coordinates to get $x = 5y +$
10. Solve for y to get $y = \frac{1}{5}(x - 10) = \frac{1}{5}x - 2$. **13.** Apply the vertical-line test to get (b), (c), and (d) **14.** Apply the horizontal-line test to get (b) **15. a. See below. b.** Refer to the graph to get $14.50. **16.** The function is not 1-1 since the horizontal-line test fails **17.** Since the graph of the function is above the x-axis, the range is {y: y > 0}. **18. See below.** Re-flect the original function about the line with equation $y = x$.
19. sample: $x > 0$. Restrict any part of the domain so that the horizontal-line test checks. **20. a.** The domain is the set of all real numbers since there are no undefined values for x.

b. Since x^2 is always any non-negative real number with a minimum value of 0, $x^2 + 2$ has a range {y: y ≥ 2}.
21. $g(x) = -[x + 1]$ so $g(-4.3) = -[-4.3 + 1] = -[-3.3] =$ $-(-4) = 4$ **22. See below.** **23. a.** Substitute the values into $ABS(M - N)$. $ABS(3.2 - 7) = ABS(-3.8) = 3.8$ **b.** The output represents the distance between two numbers on a number line.

15. a.

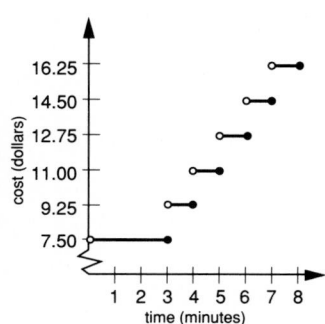

18.

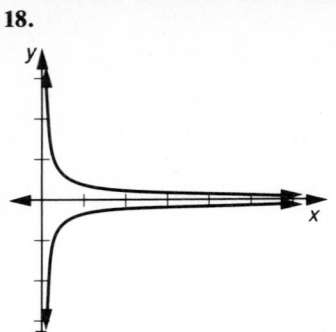

22.

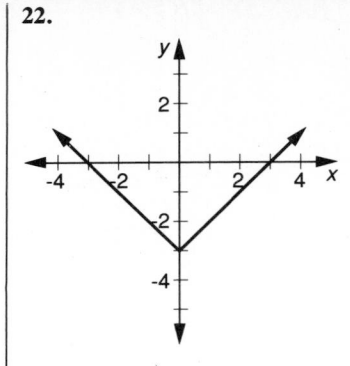

The chart below keys the **Progress Self-Test** questions to the objectives in the **Chapter Review** on pages 421–423 or to the **Vocabulary** (Voc.) on page 419. This will enable you to locate those **Chapter Review** questions that correspond to questions you missed on the **Progress Self-Test.** The lesson where the material is covered is also indicated in the chart.

Question	1–3	4–5	6–7	8	9	10	11	12	13	14	15
Objective	A	E	B	G	I	F	G	D	K	K	H
Lesson	7-1	7-4	7-3	7-7	7-5	7-2	7-6	7-7	7-2	7-6	7-4

Question	16	17	18	19	20	21	22	23
Objective	Voc.	J	L	G	F	A	A	C
Lesson	7-6	7-2	7-6	7-2	7-2	7-4	7-5	7-4

CHAPTER 7 REVIEW (pp. 421–423)

1. 5 **3.** -243 **5.** 40 **7.** -3 **9.** 14 **11.** 9 **13.** $x^2 - 12x + 37$
15. 257 **17. a.** 26,000 **b.** 1000

19. 20 PRINT 100 * INT ((N + 50)/100) **21.** $\frac{1}{2}(x - 7)$

23. $y = \frac{1}{4}x + \frac{1}{2}$ **25.** No, because -1 is mapped to both 1

and -1. **27.** not a function **29.** function **31.** not a function
33. $x = 0$ **35.** $D = \{$all real nos$\}$; $R = \{$all non-negative nos$\}$
37. $D = \{$all real nos$\}$; $R = \{$all integers$\}$ **39.** $D = $
$\{$all real nos$\}$; $R = \{$all reals $\geq$ -5$\}$ **41.** Domain: $\{x: |x| = 6\}$;
Range: $\{y: y \geq 0\}$ **43.** True **45.** B (1950) is the population of
Baltimore in 1950. **47. a.** 15600 **b.** The average yearly
growth in Philadelphia from 1900 to 1950. **49.** c **51.** See
below **53.** See below. **55.** See below. **57.** I and III
59. $D = \{$all real nos$\}$; $R = \{-1 \leq y \leq 1\}$ **61.** $D = $
$\{-4 \leq x \leq 4\}$; $R = \{-4 \leq y \leq 4\}$ **63.** b **65.** See below.
67. They are reflection images over the line $y = x$. **69.** See
below.

51.

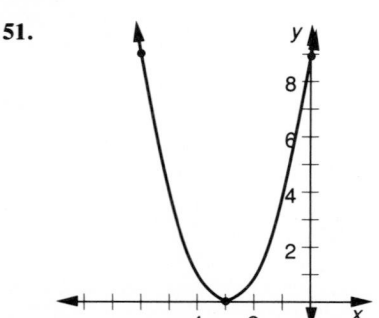

53.

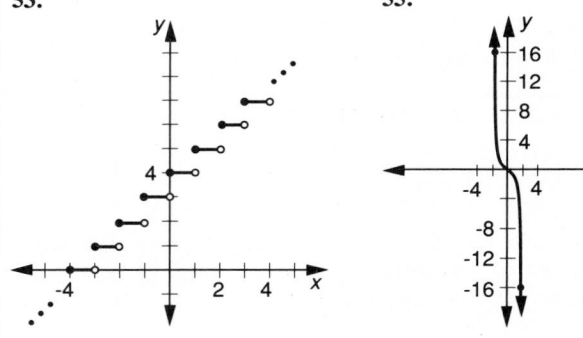

55.

65.

69.

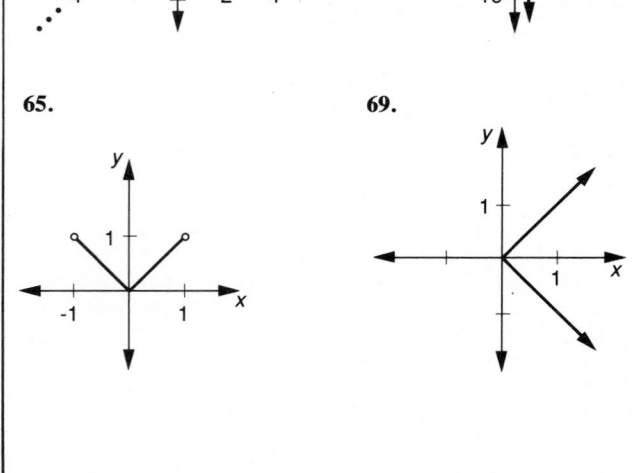

LESSON 8-1 (pp. 426–431)

1. a. 6^5 **b.** $6^2 \cdot 6^3 = (6 \cdot 6) \cdot (6 \cdot 6 \cdot 6)$; $6^5 = 6^5$ **3. a.** 4^{10}
b. $(4^2)^5 = (4 \cdot 4)^5$; $4^{10} = (4 \cdot 4) \cdot (4 \cdot 4) \cdot (4 \cdot 4) \cdot (4 \cdot 4) \cdot (4 \cdot 4)$; $4^{10} = 4^{10}$ **5.** $(2 \cdot 5)^4 = 2^4 \cdot 5^4$; $(10)^4 = 2 \cdot 2 \cdot 2 \cdot 2 \cdot 5 \cdot 5 \cdot 5 \cdot 5$; $10 \cdot 10 \cdot 10 \cdot 10 = 16 \cdot 625$; $10{,}000 = 10{,}000$ **7.** Power of a Product Prop. **9.** Power of a Quotient Prop. **11.** Zero Exponent Theorem **13.** $36x^{14}$ **15.** n^{12}
17. z^{100} **19.** Product of Powers Prop. and Power of a Quotient Property. Zero Exponent Theorem is a third possibility.
21. $x \cdot x^7$, $x^3 \cdot x^5$, $x^4 \cdot x^4$, $x^0 \cdot x^8$ **23.** $y = 0$ **25.** $-256x^2$
27. a. $64\pi \cdot 10^6$ **b.** surface area of the earth in square miles
31. A postulate is a statement in a mathematical system which we assume true without proof. **33.** $A = \frac{1}{6}$; $B = 6\frac{1}{2}$ **35.** $t_1 = 550$; $t_2 = 605$; $t_3 = 665.5$; $t_4 = 732.05$

LESSON 8-2 (pp. 432–437)

1. 1.08 **3.** $2120; $2247.20; $2382.03; $2524.95; $2676.45
5. Solution 1: $(1191.02)(.06) \approx \$71.46$; Solution 2: F(4) = $(1000)(1.06)^4$; $F(3) = (1000)(1406)^3$; $F(4) - F(3) \approx \$71.46$
7. a. True **b.** False **11. a.** $6777.25 **b.** $1386.23
13. a. $300 **b.** $338.23 **c.** $38.23 **15. a.** See below.
b. See below. **17.** $6x^5$ **19.** $1024z^{10}$ **21.** v^{18} **23.** $x = 6$
25. $n = 1, 2, 3, 4, 5, 6$ **27. a.** See below. **b.** $T = ks^2$

15. a.
```
10 PRINT "A PROGRAM TO CALCULATE BANK
     BALANCE"
20 INPUT "PRINCIPAL, ANNUAL RATE,
     NO. OF YEARS", P, R, Y
30 PRINT "YEAR", "AMOUNT"
40 FOR C = 1 TO Y
50 A = P * (1 + R)^C
60 PRINT C, A
70 NEXT C
80 END
```

15. b.

YEAR	AMOUNT
1	265.00
2	280.90
3	297.75
4	315.62
5	334.56
6	354.63
7	375.91
8	398.42
9	422.37
10	447.71

27. a.

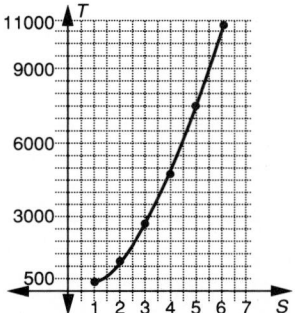

LESSON 8-3 (pp. 438–442)

5. $6; 4; \frac{8}{3}, \frac{16}{9}, \frac{32}{27}$ **7.** ≈ 2.82 ft **9. a.** .16; **b.** $g_n = 100.2^{n-1}$
11. a. 280 **b.** 8.75 **13.** $\approx\$4{,}223.70$ **15. a.** 4; $2\sqrt{2}$; 2
b. yes; $r = \dfrac{1}{\sqrt{2}}$ **c.** 64, 32 **d.** yes; $r = .5$ **17.** G1 = 16;
$R = .25$; $N = 5$ **19.** $1077.28 **21.** $20x^3$ **23.** $\dfrac{z^4}{81}$
25. $m^3(2m^3 + 1)$ **27. a.** See below. **b.** image of graph in
part a, translated 2 to the left **c.** $y = \dfrac{3}{x + 2}$ **29.** 0

27. a.

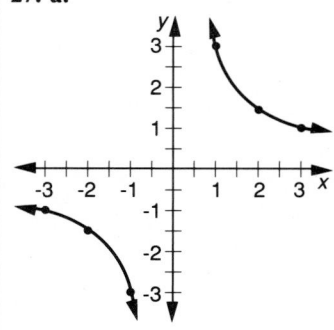

LESSON 8-4 (pp. 443–447)

1. a. b^{x+y} **b.** b^x **c.** 1 **3. a.** 1 **b.** $\frac{1}{8}$ **c.** $\frac{1}{64}$ **5.** d **9.** 10
13. $4y$ **15.** $\frac{1}{5}$ **17.** 6561 **19.** 32 **21.** 32 **23.** $1.5625 \cdot 10^{-5}$
25. $2.5 \cdot 10^{-7}$ cm or $2.5 \cdot 10^{-9}$ m **27. a.** yes **b.** $g_n = 6561\left(\frac{1}{3}\right)^{n-1}$ **c.** ≈ 0.0014 **29. a.** 1st yr = $1100; 2nd yr = $1210; 3rd yr = $1331; 4th yr = $1464.10; 5th yr = $1610.51 **b.** 1st yr = $100; 2nd yr = $110; 3rd yr = $121; 4th yr = $133.10; 5th yr = $146.41 **c.** 1st yr = 100; 2nd yr = 110; 3rd yr = 121; 4th yr = 133.10; 5th yr = $146.41 **d.** increasing **31.** $\dfrac{x - 6}{3}$

LESSON 8-5 (pp. 468–453)

3. 3 **5.** $x = 5$ **9. a.** 80 ⟨y^x⟩ ⟨(⟩ 1 ⟨÷⟩ 3 ⟨)⟩ ⟨=⟩ or 80 ⟨y^x⟩ 3 ⟨1/x⟩ ⟨=⟩
b. 4.31 **13.** 12 **15.** 1.142 **17.** 1.995 **19.** > **21.** < **23.** >
25. = **27.** $2059; yes **29. a.** $F_n = 440(2^{\frac{1}{12}})^{n-1}$ **b.** 831
31. $\dfrac{4}{m}$ **33.** .16 or $\frac{4}{25}$ **35.** 1 **37.** 1.5; $6(.5)^{n-1}$ **39.** $1054.41
41. a. See below. **b.** $z = 3\sqrt{2}$ cm ≈ 4.24 cm **c.** See below.
d. $3\sqrt{3} \approx 5.196$ cm

41. a.

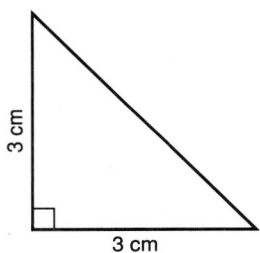

41. c.

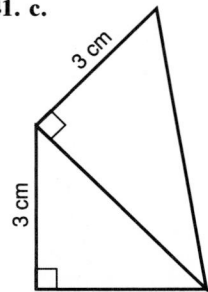

LESSON 8-6 (pp. 454–458)

1. $x^{4/9}$ **3. a.** $\sqrt[5]{100,000^4}$ or $(\sqrt[5]{100,000})^4$, or $(100,000^4)^{\frac{1}{5}}$ or $(100,000^{\frac{1}{5}})^4$ **b.** the second **c.** 10,000 **5.** 8 **7.** 19,683
9. 161,051 **11.** $>$ **13.** ≈ 6.31; $6.31^{\frac{5}{2}} \approx 100.01$
15. 268.0142; $268.0142^{\frac{4}{9}} = 12$ **17.** ≈ 22.5 cm² **19. a.** -2
b. 2 **c.** no **21.** $\frac{10,000}{2401}$ **23.** x^2 **25.** $y^{\frac{13}{6}}$ **27.** ≈ 0.862
29. a; bth; c **31.** $\frac{1}{2}$ **32.** For $a > 0$ and m and n real numbers, or for $a \neq 0$ and m and n integers, $(a^m)^n = a^{mn}$.
33. $2214.84

LESSON 8-7 (pp. 459–462)

1. $\frac{1}{5}$ **3.** $\frac{32}{243}$ **5.** 0.991 **7.** $\frac{1}{81}$ **9.** 4 **11. a.** yes **b.** yes
c. yes **d.** no **e.** yes **f.** yes **13.** positive **15.** $\frac{3}{4}$ **17.** $-3x^{-1}$
19. No, F is directly proportional to $M^{\frac{2}{3}}$ **21. a.** 36 **b.** 338
23. $x = \frac{1}{5}$; $y = \frac{1}{6}$

LESSON 8-8 (pp. 463–467)

1. $\frac{1}{n}$th **3.** 6 **7.** $x^{\frac{3}{2}}$ **11.** 2.15 **13.** 12.58 **15.** 20 **17.** x^2
19. $3\sqrt[3]{2}$ **21.** (b) **23.** $\sqrt[3]{2} + \sqrt[3]{3} > \sqrt[3]{5}$ **25. a.** 13.5, 20.25, 30.375 **b.** $t_n = 4 \cdot \left(\frac{3}{2}\right)^{n-1}$ **27.** 0.000001 or $\frac{1}{1,000,000}$ **29.** 343
31. 2, -3, 4 **33.** $x = \frac{1}{\sqrt[5]{157^3}} \approx \frac{1}{20.77} \approx .048$

LESSON 8-9 (pp. 468–471)

1. -216; 36; -6; 1; $-\frac{1}{6}$; $\frac{1}{36}$; $-\frac{1}{216}$ **3.** 3 **5.** -4 **7.** y **9.** true
11. defined, real, negative **13. a.** $-2x$ **b.** $-2x$ **15.** $x^{\frac{1}{2}}$ or $\sqrt{x}$
b. undefined when $x < 0$ **17.** $-5x^2y^3\sqrt[8]{y^2}$ **19.** $10|a|b^2\sqrt[8]{a^3b2}$
21. a. 7; 5th; x **b.** $x^{\frac{1}{5}} = 7$ **c.** 16,807 **23.** two times
25. a. 6 feet **b.** 42 feet **c.** ≈ 3.12 seconds

LESSON 8-10 (pp. 472–475)

1. zero **3.** two **5.** $w = 64$ **7.** $y = 11$ or -11 **9.** $x = 2$
13. $x = -8\sqrt[3]{9}$ **15.** $s = 175.616$ **17.** 12,558 horsepower
19. a. ≈ 138 mph **b.** ≈ 125 ft **21.** $-5x^2$
23. $20|a|b^2\sqrt{a}$ **25.** ≈ 74.1 years

LESSON 8-11 (pp. 476–479)

1. b. Raise both sides to the $\frac{1}{n^{th}}$ power. **3. a.** $1000 = 500(1 + r)^7$ **b.** 10.4% **5.** $t = 6\frac{1}{2}$ **7.** 8.6% **9.** $r = 288$
11. $x = 1$ **13. a.** 5.07% **b.** yes **15. a.** $\approx 17.45\%$
b. $\approx 17.33\%$ **17.** 128 **19.** 25 **21. a.** $x = -1$ **b.** $x \geq 0$
23. $x \geq 0$; $4x + 30 \geq y$; $4x < y$ **25.** x^{6n} **27.** 5 years $\approx$ 14.9%; 10 years $\approx$ 7.18%; 15 years $\approx$ 4.73%

CHAPTER 8 PROGRESS SELF-TEST (p. 481)

1. $3^{-4} = \left(\frac{1}{3}\right)^4 = \frac{1}{81}$; $-3^4 = -81$; $(-3)^{-4} = \left(-\frac{1}{3}\right)^4 = \frac{1}{81}$;
$(-3)^4 = 81$. From largest to smallest: $(-3)^4$, 3^{-4} and $(-3)^{-4}$, -3^4
2. $625^{\frac{1}{2}} = \sqrt{625} = 25$ **3.** $\sqrt[6]{11,390,625} = 15$. A sequence of keystrokes is $11390625 \boxed{y^x} 6 \boxed{\frac{1}{x}} \boxed{=}$. **4.** $\left(\frac{1}{32}\right)^{-\frac{6}{5}} = (32)^{\frac{6}{5}} = (\sqrt[5]{32})^6 = 2^6 = 64$ **5.** $\sqrt[4]{625x^4y^8} = \sqrt[4]{(5xy^2)^4} = 5y^2 |x|$
6. $\sqrt[5]{-96x^{15}y^3} = \sqrt[5]{(-32x^{15})(3y^3)} = \sqrt[5]{(-2x^3)^5} \cdot \sqrt[5]{3y^3} = -2x^3\sqrt[5]{3y^3}$ **7.** If $9x^4 = 144$, then $x^4 = 16$, $x = \pm 2$. **8.** If $c^{\frac{2}{3}} = 64$, then $\left(c^{\frac{2}{3}}\right)^{\frac{3}{2}} = 64^{\frac{3}{2}}$ so $c = (\sqrt[3]{64})^2 = 4^2 = 16$. **9.** If $5^n \cdot 5^{21} = 5^{29}$, then $5^{n+21} = 5^{29}$ so $n + 21 = 29$ and $n = 8$. **10.** If $T = 2\pi\sqrt{\frac{L}{g}}$, then solving for L: $\frac{T}{2\pi} = \sqrt{\frac{L}{g}}$, $\frac{T^2}{4\pi^2} = \frac{L}{g}$, and
$L = \frac{T^2g}{4\pi^2} = \frac{(1)^2(980)}{4\pi^2} = \frac{980}{4\pi^2} \approx 24.82$ cm. **11.** Using the equation $V = 13,500(1.17)^n$ for $n = 3$, $V \approx 21,621.78$.
12. Using $A = 200\left(1 + \frac{.0575}{365}\right)^{(5)(365)}$, $A = 200(1.000157534)^{1825} \approx 200(1.333) \approx \$266.61$ **13.** For any amount of money to double in n years, $2 = (1 + r)^n$. If $n = 4$, $\sqrt[4]{2} = 1 + r$, and $r = \sqrt[4]{2} - 1 \approx .1892 \approx 19\%$. **14.** If $100(A - 5)^4 = 1600$, then $(A - 5)^4 = 16$, $A - 5 = 16^{\frac{1}{4}} = 2$,

and $A = 7$ or $A = 3$. **15.** If $\frac{1}{6}(20 - P)^{\frac{1}{2}} = 5$, then $(20 - P)^{\frac{1}{2}} = 30$, $20 - P = 30^2 = 900$, $-P = 880$, and $P = -880$. **16.** If $\sqrt[n]{\frac{125}{343}} = \frac{5}{7}$, Then $\left(\frac{125}{343}\right)^{\frac{1}{n}} = \frac{5}{7}$. and $\left(\frac{5^3}{7^3}\right)^{\frac{1}{n}} = \frac{5}{7}$, $\left(\frac{5}{7}\right)^{\frac{3}{n}} = \frac{5}{7}$. Thus $\frac{3}{n} = 1$ and
$n = 3$. **17.** $\frac{2.1 \cdot 10^2}{10^{-3}} = 2.1 \cdot 10^2 \cdot 10^3 = 2.1 \cdot 10^5 = 210,000$ **18.** After 24 hours there are 48 half-hour periods, so there will be $5(2)^{48}$ bacteria. **19.** Each term is 4 times the previous term, and the initial term is 2, so $t_n = t_1 r^{(n-1)} = 2 \cdot 4^{n-1}$. **20.** $a^{-\frac{4}{5}} = \frac{1}{a^{\frac{4}{5}}} = \frac{1}{\sqrt[5]{a^4}}$, which is choice b.
21. $216^{\frac{1}{3}} = \sqrt[3]{216} = \sqrt[3]{6 \cdot 6 \cdot 6} = 6$ **22.** Using $h(x) = 180 \cdot 10^{-.04t}$ with $t = 15$, $h(15) = 180 \cdot 10^{-.04(15)} = 180 \cdot 10^{-.6} \approx 45.2$ hours. **23.** 3, -3
24. False. One could only have -2 if one started with $\pm\sqrt[6]{64}$, otherwise $\sqrt[6]{64}$ means only a positive root. **25.** $x = (40g)(.5)^3 = 5$ grams.

The chart below keys the **Progress Self-Test** questions to the objectives in the **Chapter Review** on pages 482–485 or to the **Vocabulary** (Voc.) on page 480. This will enable you to locate those **Chapter Review** questions that correspond to questions you missed on the **Progress Self-Test.** The lesson where the material is covered is also indicated in the chart.

Question	1	2–3	4	5–6	7	8	9	10	11–12	13	14–15
Objective	A	B	B	C	D	D	F	K	J	J	E
Lesson	8-4, 8-9	8-6	8-7	8-8	8-1	8-7	8-1	8-10	8-2	8-11	8-11

Question	16	17	18	19	20	21	22	23
Objective	D	F	K	G	I	H	K	L
Lesson	8-10	8-4	8-3	8-3	8-5	8-1	8-7	8-3

CHAPTER 8 REVIEW (pp. 482–485)

1. .000064 **3.** .0034 **5.** 625 **7.** 10 **9.** 4.53 **11.** $\frac{1}{4}$ **13.** 512 **15.** 18.566 **17.** False **19.** -2 **21.** 1.41 **23.** 1.79 **25.** $3x\sqrt[3]{2}$ **27.** $-2a^3\sqrt[3]{10}$ **29.** $7x^2\sqrt{2}$ **31.** No real solution **33.** $x = \frac{1}{3}$ or $-\frac{1}{3}$ **35.** $\frac{32}{243}$ **37.** $b = \frac{81}{256}$ **39.** $c = 117,649$ **41.** $x = 15,624$ **43.** $r = 2.8$ **45.** $x = 6$ **47.** $y = 10$ **49.** $-4x^9y$ **51.** $\frac{c}{4}$ **53.** $\frac{1}{2}, \frac{3}{4},$ $\frac{9}{8}, \frac{27}{16}$ **55.** c **57.** $g_n = 2(.5)^{n-1}$ **59.** ≈65.53 **61.** $x^{-2}, x^{\frac{2}{3}},$ $\sqrt{x}, x, x^{\frac{5}{4}}$ **63.** IV, V **65.** II, III **67.** IV **69. a.** -5 **b.** -5 **c.** undefined **71.** -10 has no real 8th roots because they are imaginary numbers. **73.** odd integers $n \geq 3$ **75.** ≈$209.78 **77.** ≈$4202.79 **79.** ≈7.2% **81. a.** $P = k\left(\frac{1}{d}\right)^2$ **b.** $P = kd^{-2}$ **83.** .125 hours **85.** 1.25 mm **87.** ≈6.2 in. × 7.7 in. **88. a.** $P_n = P(.90)^{n-1}$ **b.** ≈14.16 strokes

LESSON 9-1 (pp. 488–493)

1. 4800 **3. a.** 1000 bacteria **b.** after about $2\frac{1}{2}$ hr **5. a.** 3.317 **b.** 3.340 **c.** 3.322 **9.** b; x **11.** c **13. a.** y^{10} **b.** $\sqrt[10]{d}$ **15. a.** 3% **b.** ≈1.095 billion **17. a. See below. b.** 0 **c.** ≈.68 **d.** The domain is all real numbers. The range is all positive real numbers. The graph is an increasing function as x increases. **19. a.** geometric **b.** $a_n = 100(0.9)^{n-1}$ **c.** $a_1 = 100$; $a_n = a_{n-1} \cdot 0.9$ (for $n > 1$) **21.** $H^{-1}(x) = \sqrt[3]{x}$ **23. a.** $y - 100 = \frac{4}{7}(x - 100)$ **b.** 72

17. a.

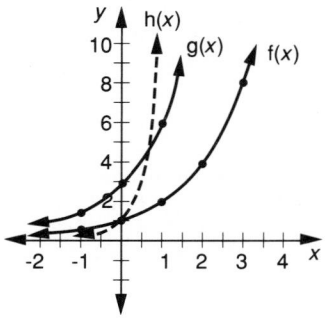

LESSON 9-2 (pp. (494–498)

3. $2035 **7.** 126 g **9.** a **11. a. See below. b. See below. c.** These graphs are the inverses of each other. **13. a.** 2 **b.** iii **c.** all real numbers **d.** all positive numbers **15.** about 270 million **17.** $\sqrt{10}$ is between 3 and 3.5 **19.** $5.54 \leq x \leq 6.80$

11. a.–b.

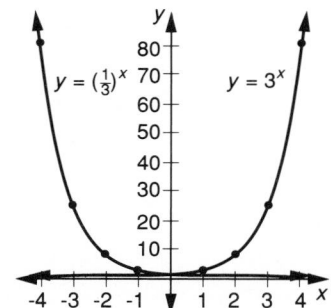

LESSON 9-3 (pp. 499–503)

3. yes **5.** about 40 **9.** 1000 times **13. a.** gastric juice **b.** 10 times **15.** 10,000 times **17. See below. 19.** $(m + 3p)^2$ **21.** 15

17.

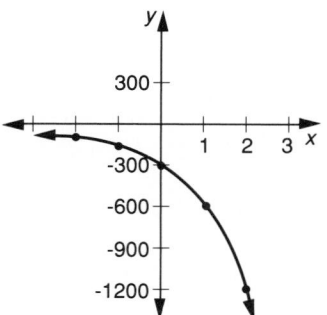

LESSON 9-4 (pp. 504–508)

3. $10^x = y$ **5.** 8 **7.** .5 **9.** undefined **11.** -3.337 **13.** b
15. $x \approx 316.23$ **17.** I2, 3 **19.** b **21.** 200 **23.** See below.

25. 10^4 **27.** 2 **29.** $x^{\frac{13}{12}}$ **31. a.** $x = 0$ and $y = 0$ **b.** $y = x$
and $y = -x$ **c.** $y = 0$ and $x = 0$

23.

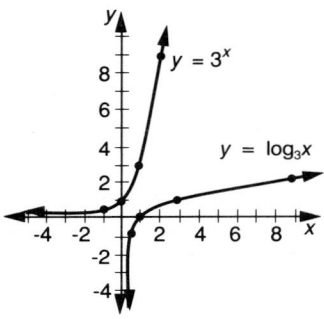

Number of Questions Correct	Money Offered
10	$20,000,000
9	$2,000,000
8	$200,000
7	$20,000
6	$2,000
5	$200
4	$20
3	$2
2	20¢
1	2¢

LESSON 9-5 (pp. 509–512)

1. a. 216, 6 **b.** 1, 6, 3rd **3.** $\log_8 2,097,152 = 7$ **5.** $b^c = a$
7. $\frac{2}{3}$ **9.** 0.5 **13.** $x = 216$ **15.** $x - 729$ **17. a.** See below.

b. True **19. a.** $3, \frac{1}{3}$ **b.** $2, \frac{1}{2}$ **c.** $\log_a b = \dfrac{1}{\log_b a}$ **21.** 5 **23.** 10^9
or 1,000,000,000 **25.** $b^{.85}$ **27.** x^{2rt} **29.** $1118.32

17. a.

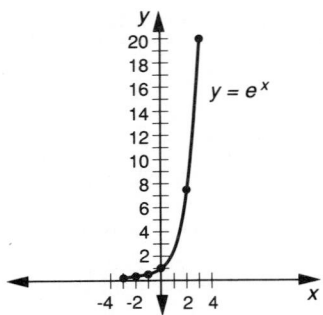

LESSON 9-6 (pp. 513–517)

1. 26.8 **3.** 0 **5.** 1 **7.** $\log 25$ **11.** 4.9069 **13.** 4.6438

15. false; $\log 4 - \log 3 = \log \frac{4}{3}$ **17.** false, $\log_b (3x) =$
$\log_b 3 + \log_b x$ **19. a.** definition of logarithm **b.** Substitution
Property **c.** Power of a Power Property **d.** Commutative Property of Multiplication **e.** Substitution and Logarithm Theorem 2
f. Logarithm Theorem 5 **21.** 5 **23. a.** $pH = 6.1 + \log B -$
$\log C$ **b.** ≈ 1.9055 **25.** $x = 3$ **27.** lemons **29.** ii

LESSON 9-7 (pp. 518–523)

5. $1.11 **7. a.** initial amount **b.** rate of continuous growth or
decay **c.** r is negative. **9. a.** $5466.35 **b.** $5350.43 **11. See
below.** **13. a.** 25% compounded continuously **b.** $25,400
15. 12 **17.** -1 **19.** -0.5 **21.** $x = 75$ **23.** $m = 4$

11.

The graph of $y = e^x$.

LESSON 9-8 (pp. 524–528)

5. $\ln 7.39 \approx 2$ **9.** 5.991 **11.** no **13.** about 13.7 years
15. at about $\left(\frac{1}{2}, -0.693\right)$ **17.** ≈ 13.1 **19.** $\approx 8.5\%$ **b.** $\approx 22\%$
21. $x = \sqrt{7}$ **23.** False **25.** w is any real number.
27. 50,000 mm³

LESSON 9-9 (pp. 529–533)

3. True **5.** $y \approx 2.26$ **7.** the base of the equation is e.
9. a little more than 5.1 cm thick **11.** $y \approx 2.36$
13. $r \approx -0.699$ **15.** about 3.5 days **17.** 30 **19.** a, b, c, e
21. ≈ 2.5 **23.** $f = 8$ **25.** $\begin{bmatrix} 47 & 45 & -26 \\ 18 & 20 & -14 \end{bmatrix}$

CHAPTER 9 PROGRESS SELF-TEST (p. 536)

1. $\log (1,000,000) = \log (10^6) = 6$, since $\log_b b^n = n$.

2. $\log_4 \frac{1}{16} = \log_4 (4^{-2}) = -2$, since $\log_b b^n = n$. **3.** $\ln e^{-6} =$
-6, since $\log_b b^n = n$. **4.** $\log_2 1 = 0$, since $\log_b 1 = 0$
for any non-zero base. **5.** Use a calculator; $\ln (42.7) \approx 3.75$.
6. Use a calculator; $\log 25 \approx 1.40$. **7.** $e^y = 412$, so $\ln(e^y) =$
$\ln(412)$, $y = \ln (412) \approx 6.02$. **8.** $\log_x 8 = \frac{3}{4}$, so $x^{\frac{3}{4}} = 8$,
$x = 8^{\frac{4}{3}} = 16$. **9.** $\log_{m+1} 30 = \log_{12} 30$, so $m + 1 = 12$,
$m = 11$. **10.** $6^x = 32$, $\log 6^x = \log 32$, $x \log 6 = \log 32$,
so $x = \dfrac{\log 32}{\log 6} \approx 1.93$. **11.** $\log 45 \approx 1.65$, so $10^{1.65} \approx 45$,
by the definition of logarithm. **12.** true, by the Powering
Property of Logarithms **13.** true, since $\log \left(\dfrac{M}{N^2}\right) =$

$\log M - \log N^2$ Quotient Property of Logarithms;
$= \log M - 2 \log N$ Powering Property of Logarithms
14. false, $\log_3 7 + \log_3 13 = \log_3 91$, by the Product
Property of Logarithms **15.** 8% per hour **16.** Substitute into
the formula: $x = 8$, $A = 12,000$, so $y = 12,000(.92)^8 \approx$
6159 bacteria. **17.** Substitute $y = 1000$, $x = 2$, and solve
for A in the formula: $1000 = A(.92)^2 \approx 1181$ bacteria.
18. Use the Continuous Compounding Interest Formula:
$N = Pe^{rt}$. Substitute $N = 2P$, $r = 0.07$: $2P = Pe^{0.07t}$,
$2 = e^{0.07t}$, $\ln 2 = 0.07t$, $t \approx 9.90$, so it would take about
10 years. **19.** Since $125 - 105 = 20$, the intensity is $10^{\frac{20}{10}} =$
$10^2 = 100$ times. **20. a. See below. b.** domain is positive
real numbers and range is all real numbers. **c. See below.**
d. The inverse of a logarithmic function is an exponential
function, so the inverse is $y = 3^x$. **e. See below.**

20. a., c., e.

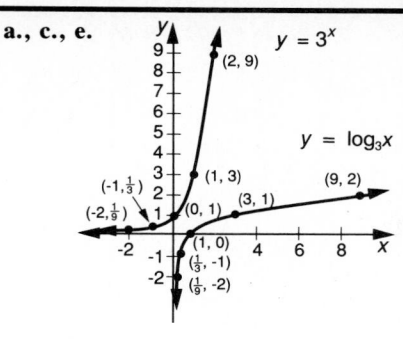

The chart below keys the **Progress Self-Test** questions to the objectives in the **Chapter Review** on pages 537–539 or to the **Vocabulary** (Voc.) on page 535. This will enable you to locate those **Chapter Review** questions that correspond to questions you missed on the **Progress Self-Test**. The lesson where the material is covered is also indicated in the chart.

Question	1	2	3	4	5	6	7	8	9	10	11
Objective	A	A	A	A	A	A	B	C	C	B	D
Lesson	9-4	9-5	9-8	9-5	9-8	9-4	9-9	9-9	9-5	9-9	9-4

Question	12	13–14	15–17	18	19	20a	20b	20c	20d	20e
Objective	E	E	G	G	H	J	F	J	D	I
Lesson	9-8	9-6	9-2	9-1	9-3	9-5	9-5	9-5	9-5	9-1

CHAPTER 9 REVIEW (pp. 537–539)

1. 3 **3.** 9 **5.** 15 **7.** -3 **9.** 4.99 **11.** 4.47 **13.** undefined
15. $x = 3$ **17.** $n \approx 14.21$ **19.** $z \approx 3.09$ **21.** $a \approx 1.78$
23. $x = 11$ **25.** $z = 10,000$ **27.** $x = 225$ **29.** $x = 4$
31. $6^{-3} = \frac{1}{216}$ **35.** $\log 0.0631 \approx -1.2$ **37.** $\log_x z = y$
39. $\log_b xy = \log_b x + \log_b y$ (product property)
41. $\log_b (x^n) = n \log_b x$ (powering property)
43. $\log_b b^n = n$ **45.** all positive real numbers **47.** True
49. True **51.** about $1.68 **53.** about 301 days **55.** about
31.6 times **57.** 100 times **59.** See below. **61.** 60 represents
a decay since the y-values get smaller as the x-values increase. **63. a.** See below. **b.** $x = e^y$

59. **63. a.**

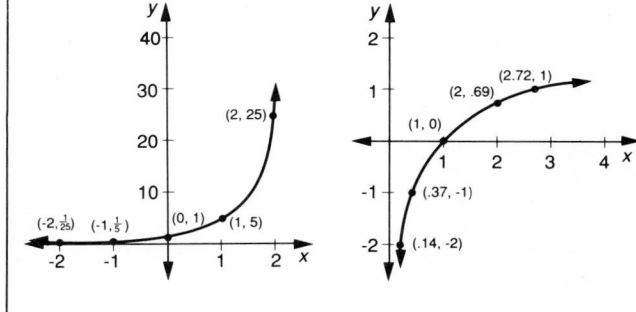

LESSON 10-1 (pp. 542–548)
5. d **7. a.** hypotenuse **b.** $\overline{AC}$ **c.** $\overline{AB}$ **d.** $\angle C$ **e.** the tangent of
f. the sine of **g.** the cosine of **9.** 0.383 **11.** 0.052
13. a. ≈88 km **b.** ≈328 km **15.** ≈12.9 ft **17.** $\frac{180(n-2)}{n}$
19. $(-x, y)$ **21.** False **23.** ≈11,460 years

LESSON 10-2 (pp. 549–554)
1. .866 [INV] [cos] or .866 [2nd] [cos] **3.** 38° **7.** θ **9.** ≈113 ft
11. ≈31° **13.** ≈15° **15.** ≈401 ft **17.** $S = (.2, 0)$; $K =$
$(1, -.6)$; $Y = (.2, -6)$ **19.** ≈37° **21.** SAS—SIDE ANGLE
SIDE; SSS—SIDE SIDE SIDE; ASA—ANGLE SIDE
ANGLE **23.** $x = \frac{3}{2}$

LESSON 10-3 (pp. 555–559)
3. 18° **5.** 1 **7.** $\frac{1}{2}$ **13. a.** $3\sqrt{3}$ inches **b.** $9\sqrt{3}$ sq inches

15. $\sqrt{3}$ **17. a.** $10\sqrt{2}$ m **b.** 14.1 m **19.** ≈9.5° **21.** $a \approx 4.2$
or $a \approx 5.2$ **23. a.** $(1, 0)$ **b.** $(0, -1)$ **c.** $(0, -1)$

LESSON 10-4 (pp. 560–564)
3. $(1, 0)$; 1; 0 **5.** 0 **7.** -1 **9.** 0 **11.** 0 **13.** ≈0.848 **15.** B
17. A **19.** d **21.** d **23.** b **25.** $(\cos θ)^2 + (\sin θ)^2 =$
$(\cos 270°)^2 + (\sin 270°)^2 = 1$; $(0)^2 + (-1)^2 = 1$ **27.** $\frac{1}{2}$
29. about 930 ft **31.** none

LESSON 10-5 (pp. 565–569)
3. a. See below. **b.** negative **5. a.** ≈-0.469; **b.** ≈0.883
7. θ = 65° **9.** -.5 **11.** $\frac{\sqrt{2}}{2}$ **13.** 127° **15.** $\frac{-\sqrt{2}}{2}$ or $\frac{\sqrt{2}}{2}$

17. Sample: 45°, 225° **19.** $\left(\dfrac{-\sqrt{2}}{2}, \dfrac{\sqrt{2}}{2}\right)$ **21.** 6.5°

23. $x \approx 6.35$

3. a.

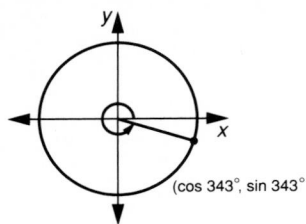

(cos 343°, sin 343°)

LESSON 10-6 (pp. 570–574)

1. True **3.** c **5.** ≈3.3 miles **7.** about $2.52p^2$ units

9. a. ≈49 mm **b.** ≈29° **11.** $\cos C = \dfrac{a^2 + b^2 - c^2}{2ab}$

13. $\dfrac{\sqrt{3}}{2}$ **15.** 0.5 **17.** 20° **19. a.** 2 **b.** ±35 **c. See below.**

d. parabola **21.** 45°

19. c.

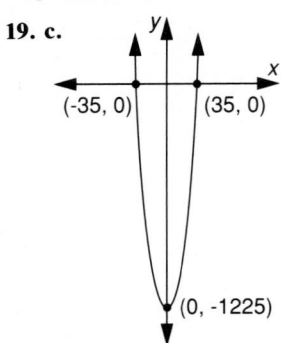

(-35, 0) (35, 0)

(0, -1225)

LESSON 10-7 (pp. 575–580)

5. about 22 miles **7.** 35.9 **9. a.** 42 mm **b.** 55° **c.** ≈55°
d. True **11. a.** m∠ABD = 142° and m∠ADB = 13°
b. ≈282 m **c.** ≈174 m **13.** There is an error somewhere,
since the sine of an angle is always between 1 and -1,

inclusive. **15.** d **17. a.** $\cos \theta = \dfrac{3}{5}$ or $\cos \theta = -\dfrac{3}{5}$

b. See below. 19. False **21. a.** 0 **b.** no **23. a.** $h =$
$-16t^2 + 30t + 12$ **b. See below. c.** ≈26 feet
d. ≈2.2 seconds after being thrown

17. b.

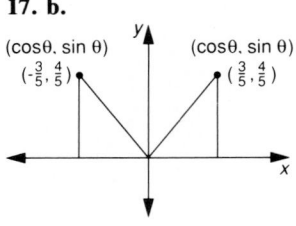

(cosθ, sin θ)
$\left(-\dfrac{3}{5}, \dfrac{4}{5}\right)$ (cosθ, sin θ)
$\left(\dfrac{3}{5}, \dfrac{4}{5}\right)$

23. b.

(height (feet) axis: 24, 16, 8; time (seconds) axis: .6 1.2 1.8 2.4)

LESSON 10-8 (pp. 581–585)

1. a. .515 **b.** 301° **c.** .857 **d.** 121° **3. a.** ≈29° **b.** The
other possible solution, 151°, when added to 42° is greater
than 180°—the sum of 3 angles of a triangle—and this is not

possible. **5.** $x \approx 14.4$ **7.** $x \approx 46.8°$ **9. a.** ≈66.3°, ≈113.7°

b. ≈22.0, ≈5.9 **11.** $\dfrac{\sin B}{AC} = \dfrac{\sin E}{DF}$; $AC = DF$ (given), so

$\sin B = \sin E$; thus $\angle B \cong \angle E$ and $\triangle CAB \cong \triangle FDE$ by AAS

Theorem. **13.** -1 **15.** $\dfrac{1}{2}$ **17. a.–b. See below. c.** No

19. Yes; the vertical-line test holds

17. a.–b.

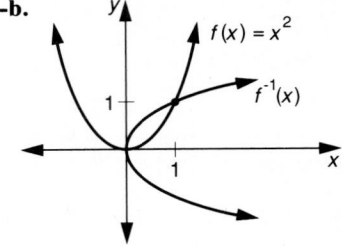

$f(x) = x^2$

$f^{-1}(x)$

LESSON 10-9 (pp. 586–591)

5. 0; 1 **7.** decrease **11.** false **13. a. See below. b.** -315°,
-135°, 45°, 225° **15.** a **17.** No **19. a.** Yes **b.** 3 **21.** cos θ
23. $\angle I \approx 69.5°$ or ≈ 110.5° **25.** area: 64π; circumference: 16π

13. a.

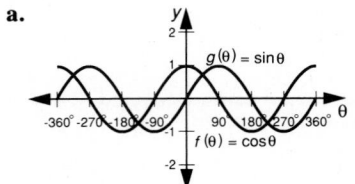

$g(\theta) = \sin\theta$

$f(\theta) = \cos\theta$

(-360° -270° -180° -90°   90° 180° 270° 360°)

LESSON 10-10 (pp. 592–597)

5. $\dfrac{1}{3}\pi$ **9.** -225° **11.** .5 **15. See below. 17.** $\dfrac{\sqrt{2}}{2}$

19. 4π feet **21. a.** all real numbers **b.** all numbers between
-1 and 1, inclusive **23. a.** 20 seconds or $\dfrac{1}{3}$ minute

b. See below. 25. See below.

15.

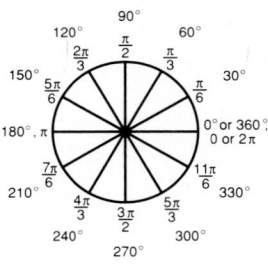

23. b.

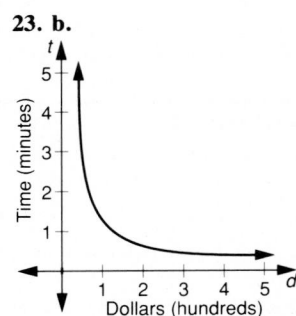

(Time (minutes) axis: 5, 4, 3, 2, 1; Dollars (hundreds) axis: 1 2 3 4 5)

25.

100

-200

CHAPTER 10 PROGRESS SELF-TEST (p. 600)

1. $\cos \theta = \dfrac{\text{adj}}{\text{hyp}} = \dfrac{12}{13} \approx 0.923$ **2.** $\sin \theta = \dfrac{\text{opp}}{\text{hyp}} = \dfrac{5}{13} \approx 0.385$ **3.** $\theta = 45°$ **4.** The coordinates of a point rotated $\theta°$ around the origin are always $(\cos \theta, \sin \theta)$ so (a) represents a correct answer. Furthermore, $\cos 120° = -\dfrac{1}{2} = -0.5$, and $\sin 120° = \dfrac{\sqrt{3}}{2} \approx 0.866$. Thus a., b. and c. are correct.

5. Let θ be the angle of elevation, $\cos \theta = \dfrac{7 \text{ ft}}{14 \text{ ft}} = \dfrac{1}{2}$, so $\theta = 60°$ **6.** $\dfrac{\text{height of ladder}}{\text{length of ladder}} = \dfrac{\text{height}}{14} = \sin 60°$. So the height $= 14\left(\dfrac{\sqrt{3}}{2}\right) = 7\sqrt{3} \approx 12.1$ ft. ≈ 145 in.

7. $\cos 57°$ is positive. Cosine is also positive for Quadrant IV angles. Reflect the point $(\cos 57°, \sin 57°)$ about the x-axis to get the image point. So $x = 360° - 57° = 303°$. **8.** $\cos 210° = -\cos 30° = -\dfrac{\sqrt{3}}{2}$ **9.** If the graph is translated horizontally 360°, the image of the translation coincides with the original graph. Therefore the period is 360°. **10.** 1 to 0, as is seen on the graph (and verified with a calculator) **11.** The greatest y-value on the graph is 1. The lowest y-value is -1. So the range is $-1 \leq g(\theta) \leq 1$. **12.** See below. **13.** Since this is an SAS situation, use the Law of Cosines. $(AB)^2 = (110)^2 + (85)^2 - 2(110)(85)\cos 40°$. Then $(AB)^2 \approx 5000 \Rightarrow AB \approx 71$. So the runners are about 71 m apart. **14.** Since this is an SSS situation, use the Law of Cosines. $8^2 = 11^2 + 5^2 - 2(11)(5)\cos x$. Then $0.745 \approx \cos x$, so $x \approx 42°$. **15.** Since this is an AAS situation, use the Law of Sines. The angle opposite x is $180° - 40° - 83° = 57°$. So $\dfrac{\sin 57°}{x} = \dfrac{\sin 83°}{2.7} \Rightarrow x = \sin 57° \cdot \dfrac{2.7}{\sin 83°} \approx 2$. **16.** Draw $\triangle SLR$: Since this is an SSA situation, use the

Law of Sines. First find $m\angle L$. $\dfrac{\sin L}{421} = \dfrac{\sin 110°}{525} \Rightarrow \sin L \approx 0.754 \Rightarrow m\angle L \approx 49°$. Then $m\angle R = 180° - 110° - 49° = 21°$. So $\dfrac{r}{\sin 21°} = \dfrac{525}{\sin 110°} \Rightarrow r \approx 200$. **17.** Let x be the vertical distance from the eagle. Then $\sin 70° = \dfrac{x}{130} \Rightarrow x = 130(\sin 70°) \approx 122$ feet. Add the 8 feet from the eagle's beak to the ground, and then the nest is about 130 feet off the ground. **18.** $\dfrac{\pi}{3} \cdot \dfrac{180}{\pi} = 60°$

19. $\dfrac{7\pi}{6} = \dfrac{7\pi}{6}\left(\dfrac{180°}{\pi \text{ rad}}\right) = 210°$. So $\sin \dfrac{7\pi}{6} = \sin 210° = -\sin 30 = \dfrac{-1}{2}$. **20.** (a) is true by the Complements Theorem. Since $\cos 690° = \cos(690° - 360°) = \cos 330° = \cos 30° = \dfrac{\sqrt{3}}{2}$; (b) is not true; $\sin\left(\dfrac{-\pi}{2}\right) = \sin\left(\dfrac{\pi}{2}\left(\dfrac{180°}{\pi \text{ rad}}\right)\right) = \sin(-90°) = -1$, so (c) is true; (d) is the Pythagorean Identity and is true for all θ. Thus (b) is the only false statement.

12.

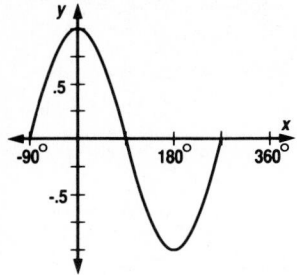

The chart below keys the **Progress Self-Test** questions to the objectives in the **Chapter Review** on pages 601–603 or to the **Vocabulary** (Voc.) on page 599. This will enable you to locate those **Chapter Review** questions that correspond to questions you missed on the **Progress Self-Test.** The lesson where the material is covered is also indicated in the chart.

Question	1–2	3	4	5–6	7	8	9–12	13	14	15	16
Objective	A	C	I	G	F	B	J	H	E	E	E
Lesson	10-1	10-2	10-4	10-2	10-3	10-5	10-9	10-6	10-6	10-8	10-7

Question	17	18	19	20
Objective	G	D	B	F
Lesson	10-2	10-10	10-10	10-3

CHAPTER 10 REVIEW (pp. 601–603)

1. 0.29 **3.** -0.77 **5.** -0.50 **7.** .923 **9.** 2.400 **11.** $\dfrac{\sqrt{2}}{2}$

13. $\dfrac{\sqrt{3}}{2}$ **15.** 1 **17.** $\dfrac{\pi}{4}$, 45° and 135°, $\dfrac{3\pi}{4}$ **19.** ≈ 0.436 rad

21. $\approx 42°$ or $\approx .730$ rad; or $\approx 138°$ or ≈ 2.41 rad **23.** $\dfrac{7\pi}{12}$

25. 3π **27.** 405° **29.** -22.5° **31.** $\approx 139.7°$ **33.** ≈ 25.4
35. $m\angle \approx 39.3°$ or $\approx 140.7°$ **37.** True **39.** True **41.** -.6
43. 41° **45.** ≈ 671 km **47.** $\approx 9.5°$ **49.** about 15 miles

53. $\approx 169°$ **55.** c **57. a.** See below. **b.** 2π **c.** $\dfrac{\pi}{2}, \dfrac{3\pi}{2}$

59. $T_{-90}°, 0$ or $T_{\frac{\pi}{2}}, 0$

57. a.

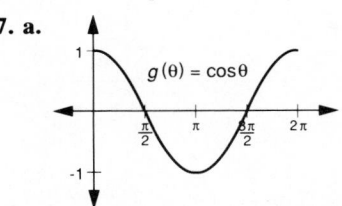

$g(\theta) = \cos\theta$

LESSON 11-1 (pp. 606–610)

1. yes, 1, 4 **3.** no **5.** $a_5y^5 + a_4y^4 + a_3y^3 + a_2y^2 + a_1y + a_0$ **7. a.** $n = 7$; **b.** $a_n = 5$; **c.** $a_{n-1} = 4$; **d.** $a_0 = 0$; **e.** $a_1 = -1$; **f.** $a_2 = 1.3$; **g.** $a_5 = 0$ **9. a.** $P(3) = 196$ (ten thousand) **b.** differs by 101 **11. a.** $25(1.07)^5 + 50(1.07)^4 + 100(1.07)^3 + 200(1.07)^2 + 400(1.07) + 800$ **b.** $25x^5 + 50x^4 + 100x^3 + 200x^2 + 400x + 800$ **c.** 5 **13.** 27.54 ft **15. See below.** **17.** $105x^2 - 5x - 10$ **19.** $\approx 44,500$ increase per year

15.
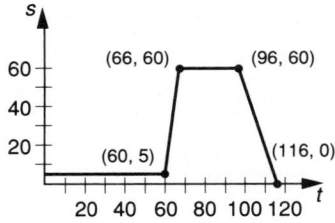

LESSON 11-2 (pp. 611–616)

1. b, degree 9 **3.** b, degree 3 **5.** c, degree 2 **7. a.** $at + bt + ct + ab + b^2 + bc$ **b.** $A = (b + t)(a + b + c) = ba + b^2 + bc + at + bt + ct$ **9.** $8a^3 - 1$ **11. a.** $x \approx 3.6$ **b.** $V \approx 774$ cu. in. **13. a.** $V(x) = 4x^3 - 56x^2 + 180x$ **b.** $V(2) = 168$ **c.** $V(2.01) = 168.03$ **15.** $a^2 - b^2 - c^2 + 2bc$ **17. a.** $V = \frac{\pi}{3}r^2h$ **b.** $r = \sqrt{225 - h^2}$ **c.** $V = -\frac{\pi}{3}h^3 + 75\pi h$ **19.** 4000 **21. a.** 1905 to 1925 **b.** 1925 **23.** 16 times

LESSON 11-3 (pp. 617–622)

1. $3d + e - 2d^2$ **3.** $7x(3x^2 - 4 + 5x^3)$ **5.** $a^2 - b^2$, $a^3 + b^3$ **9. a.** difference of squares **b.** $(x - 16)(x + 16)$ **11. a.** difference of cubes **b.** $(4 - 3c)(16 + 12c + 9c^2)$ **13. a.** perfect square **b.** $(7a - 3b)^2$ **17. a.** factorable **b.** $(5x - 2)(x + 2)$ **19. a.** factorable **b.** $(7z - 8)(z + 1)$ **21. a.** $(4x^2 + 9)(4x^2 - 9)$ **b.** $(4x^2 + 9)(2x + 3)(2x - 3)$ **23.** $8x^3(5 + 3y)(25 - 15y - 9y^2)$ **25.** d **27.** $S(h) = 6h^2 + 28h + 20$ **29. a.** 55 in.² **b.** $A(x) = 4x^2 - 56x + 187$ **31. a.** quadratic; the shape is a parabola **b.** $x = 1, x = 5$

LESSON 11-4 (pp. 623–629)

3. $k = \frac{14}{5}, k = 2,$ or $k = .9$ **5.** $P(4) = 0$ **7.** $k(x) = x(2x - 1) \cdot (x - 8)$; zeros are $x = 0, \frac{1}{2},$ or 8 **9. a. See below.** **b.** $y = (x + 4)(x - 1)(x - 8)$ **11.** $P(x) = k(x + 4)\left(x - \frac{7}{2}\right)\left(x - \frac{5}{3}\right)$ **13.** $P(x) = k(x^3 - .4x^2 - 84.8x + 192)$ **15. a.** $g(x) = x(2x - 5)(4x^2 + 10x + 25)$ **b.** $x = 0, x = \frac{5}{2}$ are zeros **15. c. See below.** **17. a.** $0 \le x \le 9$ **b.** $x = 9, x = 15, x = 0$ **19.** $(3x - 1) \cdot (9x^2 + 3x + 1)$ **21.** $3(x + y)(x - y)$ **23.** 81 $9x^2 + 26x + 24$

9. a.
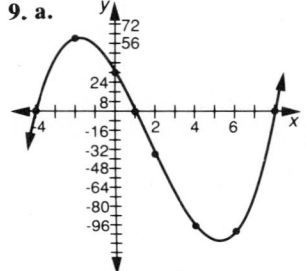

15. c.
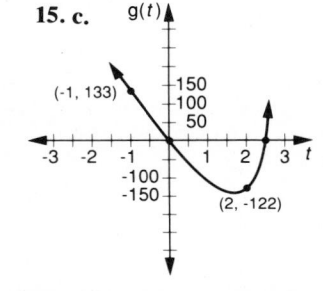

LESSON 11-5 (pp. 630–637)

1. 2 **b.** $x = -2.11, x = 1.13$ **3.** The zero is the x-value where the y-value changes sign. **5. See below.** **7.** 5.3 **9.** $f(x) = -2x^3 + 4x^2 - 1$ **11.** $x \approx -.8$ and $x \approx 2.3$ **13.** $x^4 - y^4$ **15.** $(2x - 3)^2$ **17.** $100(n^2 + 1)(n + 1)(n - 1)$ **19.** slope of $\overline{MT} = -1$, slope of $\overline{AH} = 1$; $(-1)(1) = -1$

5.
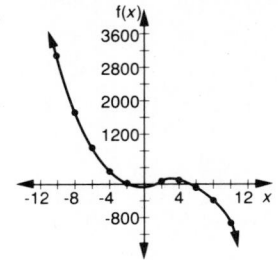

LESSON 11-6 (pp. 638–643)

5. $x = \dfrac{-b \pm \sqrt{b^2 - 4ac}}{2a}$ **7. a.** $x = 0, x = 5; x = -5$ **b.** none **11.** 5 **15.** $x = \frac{7}{3}i$ **17. a.** $1, \dfrac{-1 + i\sqrt{3}}{2}, \dfrac{-1 - i\sqrt{3}}{2}$ **b.** 8 **19.** $(z^2 + 1)(z + 1)(z - 1) = 0; z = i, -i, 1, -1$ **21. a.** $P(n) = n^3 + n^2 - 1$ **b.** $n \approx .75$ **23.** about 275 ft **25.** $x \approx 1.609$ **27.** $x = 25$

LESSON 11-7 (pp. 644–650)

5. The second differences are equal. **7. a.** yes, $y = p(x)$ **b.** 3 **9. a.** no, $y \neq p(x)$ **b.** does not apply **11. a.** 7, 10, 13, 16, 19, 22, 25 **b.** yes **c.** 1 **13. a.** 6, 6, 6, . . . **b.** 1 **c. See below.** **d.** $y = 6x + 5$ **e.** If the 1st differences are equal, that is the slope of the line that models the data. **15.** Consider the following pattern: **a.** $F(5) = 55; F(6) = 91$ **b.** 3 **17.** 3, since the degree is 3 **19. See below.** **21. a.** 4 **b.** $x = 5.0$ or $x = -4.6$ **23. a.** $y = p(x) = -x^3 + 3x^2 - 2$ **b.** 1, $y = -2$ **25.** c

13. c.
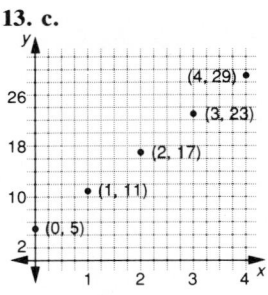

19.
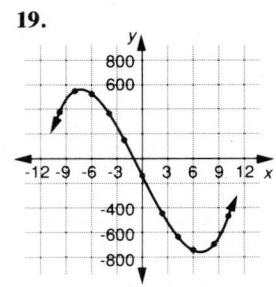

LESSON 11-8 (pp. 651–658)

5. a. $f(6) = \frac{1}{3}(6)^3 + \frac{1}{2}(6)^2 + \frac{1}{6}(6) = 91$ **b.** The six layers contain, respectively, 1, 4, 9, 16, 25, and 36 oranges; the total is 91. **7. a.** 2 **b.** $p(x) = 5x^2 - 2x$ **9.** $(x, y, z) = \left(-\frac{11}{2}, \frac{51}{2}, -22\right)$ **11. a.** $f(1) = 1^2 - 1 + 2 = 2; f(2) = 2^2 - 2 + 2 = 4; f(3) = 3^2 - 3 + 2 = 8$ **b.** $y = 2^n$ **13.** $t_n = f(n) = \frac{1}{2}n^2 + \frac{1}{2}n$ **15. a.** yes **b.** 2 **17. a.** 3 **b.** $x = 0, -\frac{10}{3}, \frac{10}{3}$ **19.** \$334.24 **21.** $4x^2y^2(x + 2y)(x - 2y)$ **23.** $z = 5^{-36}$ **25. a.** $S = kwd^2$ **b.** $d = \sqrt{4 - w^2}$ **c.** $S = -kw^3 + 4kw$ **d.** 3

1. The first money saved earned interest for 5 years. The total is $750x^5 + 600x^4 + 925x^3 + 1075x^2 + 800x$. **2.** If $x = 1.07$, then $750x^5 + 600x^4 + 925x^3 + 1075x^2 + 800x = 750(1.07)^5 + 600(1.07)^4 + 925(1.07)^3 + 1075(1.07)^2 + 800(1.07) \approx 1051.91 + 786.48 + 1133.16 + 1230.77 + 856 = 5058.32$. **3.** $V(x) = x(60 \cdot 2x)(40 - 2x) = x(2400 - 120x - 80x + 4x^2) = x(2400 - 200x + 4x^2) = 4x^3 - 200x^2 + 2400x$ **See below. 4.** The degree is 5. **5.** $P(-2.5) = (-2.5)^4 + 9(-2.5)^2 - 3 - 8(-2.5)^5 = 39.0625 + 56.25 - 3 - 781.25 = -688.9375$ **6.** $(a^2 + 3a - 7)(5a + 2) = a^2(5a + 2) + (3a)(5a + 2) - 7(5a + 2) = 5a^3 + 2a^2 + 15a^2 + 6a - 35a - 14 = 5a^3 + 17a^2 - 29a - 14$ **7.** If $p(x) = 4x^3(5x - 11)(x + \sqrt{7}) = 0$, then $x = 0, x = 0, x = 0, 5x - 11$ so $x = \frac{11}{5}$, and $x + \sqrt{7} = 0$ so $x = -\sqrt{7}$. **8.** If $f(x) = 3x^4 - 12x^3 + 9x^2 = 0$, then $3x^2(x^2 - 4x + 3) = 0$ and $3x^2(x - 3)(x - 1) = 0$. There are 4 zeros: $x = 0, x = 0, x = 3$, and $x = 1$ **9. See below. 10.** Since $y = f(x)$ has degree 3, it has 3 zeros. **11. a.** The zeros are between $x = -2$ and $x = -1$, $x = 1$ and $x = 2$, and $x = 2$ and $x = 3$, because those are the intervals for which the polynomial changes signs. **b.** $x \approx 1.7, x \approx -1.7$ **12.** If $z^3 - 216 = 0$, then $z^3 - 6^3 = 0$, or $(z - 6)(z^2 + 6z + 36) = 0$. If $z^2 + 6z + 36 = 0$, then $z = \dfrac{-6 \pm \sqrt{6^2 - 4(1)(36)}}{2} = \dfrac{-6 \pm \sqrt{36 - 144}}{2} = \dfrac{-6 \pm \sqrt{-108}}{2} = \dfrac{-6 \pm \sqrt{-36 \cdot 3}}{2} = \dfrac{-6 \pm 6i\sqrt{3}}{2} = -3 \pm 3i\sqrt{3}$. The zeros are $z = 6, z = -3 + 3i\sqrt{3}$, and $z = -3 - 3i\sqrt{3}$. **13. c,** Never; a polynomial of degree 11 has 11 complex roots. **14.** If r is a root or zero of a function, then $x - r$ is a factor. Since we know that $f(2) = 0$, then 2 is a root and $(x - 2)$ is a factor of the polynomial. That is option **d**. **15.** Since the zeros are -2, 1, 3, and 5, the factors for the function are $x - (-2), x - 1, x - 3$, and $x - 5$. Thus the function is $f(x) = k(x + 2)(x - 1)(x - 3) \cdot (x - 5) = k(x^2 + x - 2)(x^2 - 2x + 15) = k(x^2(x^2 - 8x + 15) + x(x^2 - 8x + 15) - 2(x^2 - 8x + 15)) = k(x^4 - 8x^3 + 15x^2 + x^3 - 8x^2 + 15x - 2x^2 + 16x - 30) = k(x^4 - 7x^3 + 5x^2 + 31x - 30)$. **16.** $10s^7t^2 + 15s^3t^4 = 5s^3t^2(2s^4 + 3t^2)$ **17.** $9z^2 - 196 = (3z)^2 - (14)^2 = (3z + 14)(3z - 14)$ **18.** $25y^2 + 60y + 36 = (5y + 6)(5y + 6) = (5y + 6)^2$ **19.** Since the second differences are equal, the

data points can be modeled with a polynomial function. **b.** The degree of that function is 2. **See below. 20.** Since the second differences are equal, the general equation is $z = f(x) = ax^2 + bx + c$. Using these data, $f(1) = a(1)^2 + b(1) + c = 0, f(2) = a(2)^2 + b(2) + c = 4, f(3) = a(3)^2 + b(3) + c = 12$. Then:
$$\left. \begin{array}{r} 9a + 3b + c = 12 \\ 4a + 2b + c = 4 \\ a + b + c = 0 \end{array} \right\} \left. \begin{array}{r} 5a + b = 8 \\ 3a + b = 4 \end{array} \right\} 2a = 4; \text{ Thus } a = 2.$$
From $3a + b = 4, 3(2) + b = 4, 6 + b = 4, b = -2$; and from $a + b + c = 0, 2 + (-2) + c = 0, c = 0$. The polynomial function is $z = f(x) = 2x^2 - 2x$. **See below.**

3.

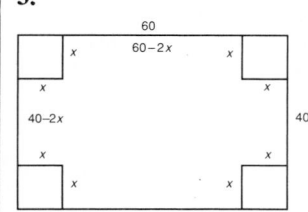

9.

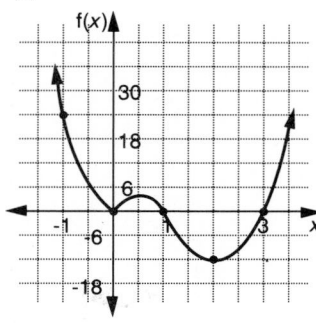

19. b.

n	1	2	3	4	5	6	7	8
t	2	5	9	14	20	27	35	44
1st diff		3	4	5	6	7	8	9
2nd diff			1	1	1	1	1	1

20.

x	-2	-1	0	1	2	3	4
z	12	4	0	0	4	12	24
1st diff		-8	-4	0	4	8	12
2nd diff			4	4	4	4	4

The chart below keys the **Progress Self-Test** questions to the objectives in the **Chapter Review** on pages 662–665 or to the **Vocabulary** (Voc.) on page 659. This will enable you to locate those **Chapter Review** questions that correspond to questions you missed on the **Progress Self-Test.** The lesson where the material is covered is also indicated in the chart.

Question	1–2	3	4–5	6	7–8	9–11	12	13	14	15
Objective	G	G	E	A	C	I	C	F	F	H
Lesson	11-1	11-2	11-1	11-2	11-6	11-5	11-6	11-6	11-4	11-5

Question	16–18	19	20
Objective	B	D	D
Lesson	11-3	11-7	11-7

CHAPTER 11 REVIEW (pp. 662–665)

1. $x^3 + 2x - 3$ **3.** $8y^3 + 60y^2 + 150y + 125$
5. $6x^3 + 2x^2y - 3xy - y^2$ **7.** a^3; $9b^2$ **9.** $(x - 7)^2$
11. $4x(x^2 - 3x - 7)$ **13.** $(r^2s^2 + 9)(rs + 3)(rs - 3)$
15. $(z - 3)(z^2 + 3z + 9)$ **17.** $x = .5, -\frac{1}{3}, 0$ **19.** $x \approx .8$
21. $x = 0, -4, -\frac{7}{9}$; no multiple roots **23.** $n = -4, 2 + 2i\sqrt{3}$,
$2 - 2i\sqrt{3}$; no multiple roots **25.** yes; $a_n = f(n) = -6n +$
11 **27. a.** 2 **b.** i **c.** $f(x) = 5x^2 - x + 1$ **29. a.** 9 **b.** -8

31. a **33.** c **35.** c **37.** True **39.** $p(x) = k(x^2 + 73.5x +$
$310.5)$ **41.** The product is not equal to zero. **43. a.** $150x^7 +$
$150x^6 + 150x^5 + 150x^4 + 150x^3 + 150x^2 + 150x + 150$
b. $\$1484.62$ **c.** $\approx 14\%$ **45.** A reasonable domain for n is
$0 \le n \le 28$ **47.** $S(x) = -4x^2 + 1.5$ **49. a.** #T: 1, 4, 10,
20, 35, 56, 84, . . . **b.** $f(n) = \frac{1}{6}n^3 + \frac{1}{2}n^2 + \frac{1}{3}n$ **51.** False
53. a. $x = 1, 3, 3, 4$ **b.** at least 4 **c.** $f(x) = k(x^4 - 11x^3$
$+ 43x^2 - 69x + 36)$ **55.** 1 **57. a.** $-10 < x < -9, -4 < x <$
-3 **b.** $x \approx -9.20$ or $x \approx -3.39$ **c.** two

LESSON 12-1 (pp. 668–673)
5. The point on the earth's surface above the point where the
earthquake began. **7.** b, c **9. a.** (0, 0) **b.** 5 **c. See below.**
11. a. $y = \pm 8$ **b. See below.** **13.** $(x + 3)^2 + (y + 2)^2 =$
64 **15.** $30\sqrt{3} \approx 52$ mi **17. a.** $x^2 + y^2 - 300x - 200y +$
$15{,}600 = 0$ **b.** $A = 1, B = 0, C = 1, D = -300, E =$
$-200, F = 15{,}600$ **19.** ellipse **21. a. See below.** **b.** y-axis
23. $y = -\frac{4}{5}x$ **25. a.** $y = \pm 10$ **b.** $y = \pm 5\sqrt{3}$
c. $y = \pm\sqrt{100 - x^2}$

1. c.

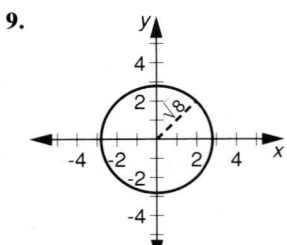

9. c.

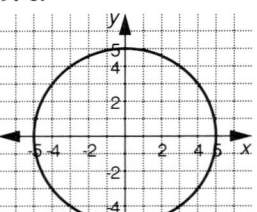

11. b.

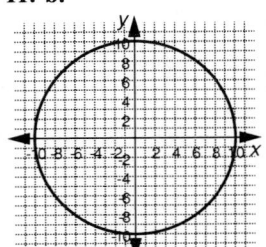

9.

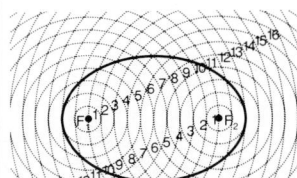

11. a.

21. a.

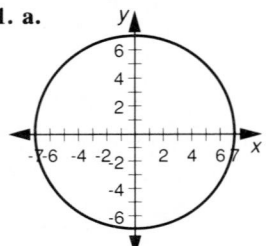

LESSON 12-2 (pp. 674–679)
1. a.–c. See below. **a.** $x^2 + y^2 = 49$ **b.** $y = \sqrt{49 - x^2}$
c. $y = -\sqrt{49 - x^2}$ **5.** $\{(x, y): 9 < x^2 + y^2 < 36\}$ **7.** d
9. See below. **11. a. See below.** **b.** 2 **c.** $x^2 + y^2 = 4$
d. 13 **e.** 30 through 60 **13. a.** $x^2 + y^2 \le r^2$
b. $x^2 + y^2 > r^2$ **15.** $16 < x^2 + y^2 < 36$ **17.** A circle is the
set of all points in a plane at a given distance (radius) from a
fixed point (center). **19. a.** $x^2 + y^2 = 1$ **b.** the unit circle
21. $6T + 3F + 2S + P$

1. a.

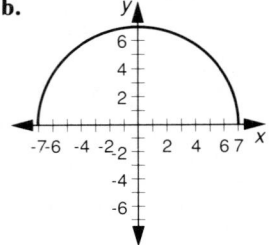

b.

LESSON 12-3 (pp. 680–686)
1. 12 **3.** 20 **5.** vertex **7.** true **9. See below.** **11.** $\frac{12}{20} = \frac{3}{5}$
13. Focal constant $>$ distance between foci **15. a.** $(-10, 0)$,
$(0, -5), (-8, 3), (8, -3), (-8, -3), (-6, 4), (6, -4), (-6, -4)$
b. See below. **c.** ellipse **d.** $x = 0, y = 0$ **17. a. See**
below. **b.** ellipse; F_1 and F; 5 **c. See below.** **19.** $9 < x^2 +$
$y^2 < 49$ **21. a.** $\left(-5, \frac{1}{2}\right)$, **b.** 3 **23.** $\sqrt{(x - c)^2 + y^2}$
25. $x + 3$ **27.** $4a^2 - 4a\sqrt{p} + p$

9.

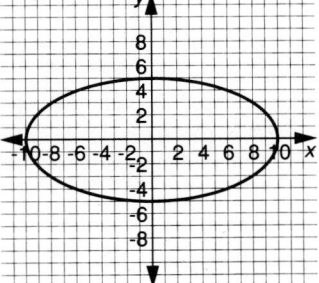

15. b.

17. a. , c.

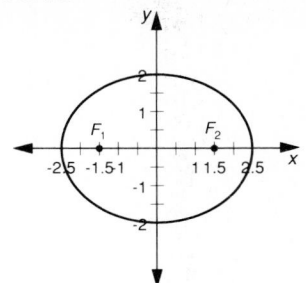

LESSON 12-4 (pp. 687–694)

3. $\overline{AC}$ **5.** E **11.** See below. **13.** $\frac{x^2}{225} + \frac{y^2}{189} \leq 1$ **15.** c

17. a. ≈ 77.4 million mi **b.** 64.2 million mi **19.** See below.

21. $(x - 4)^2 + y^2 < 16$ **23.** 8π **25.** $h = \frac{66}{\pi r} + r$

27. a. ≈ 19.5 **b.** $\angle B \approx 59.7°$; $\angle A \approx 70.3°$

11.

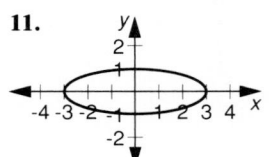

19.

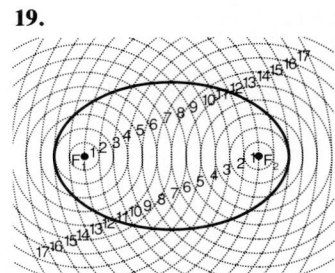

LESSON 12-5 (pp. 695–700)

3. False **5. a.** π **b.** 12π **7.** 50π **9. a.** False **b.** See example 1. **11. a.** See below. **13.** a **15.** b **17.** f

19. $\frac{x^2}{81} + \frac{y^2}{49} = 1$ **21.** a **23.** $y + 1 = 2(x - 3)$

11. a.

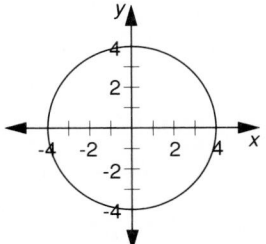

LESSON 12-6 (pp. 701–706)

1. 48 mph **3. a.** (6, 6), (-6, -6) **b.** x-axis, y-axis **c.** 12
5. The equation of the hyperbola is $xy = 8$. Since $8 \cdot 1 = 8$, the point (8, 1) is on the hyperbola. **7.** 3600 **9.** See below.

11. $yx = 64$ **13. a.** 7 **b.** $\frac{x^2}{12.25} + \frac{y^2}{8.25} = 1$ **c.** $\approx 10\pi$

15. See below. **17.** sample: $100i, \frac{1}{i}$ **19.** $x = 0, x = \pm 3$,

$x = \pm 3i$ **21. a.** $L = 100 - \frac{1}{2}N$ **b.** $N = 200$

9.

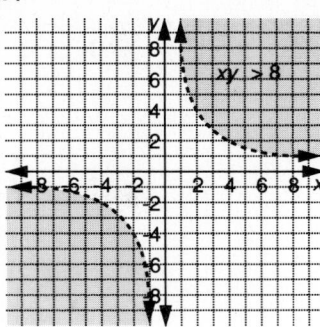

15.

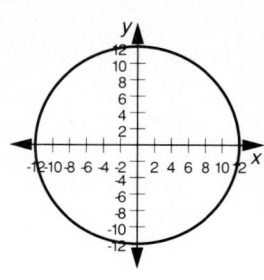

LESSON 12-7 (pp. 707–712)

5. a. (-5, 0), (5, 0) **b.** $\frac{y}{\sqrt{11}} = \pm\frac{x}{5}$ **7.** $\approx$ (6, 3.35),

(6, -3.35) **9.** See below. **11. a.** $\sqrt{160} - \sqrt{20}$

b. $\frac{x^2}{16.716} - \frac{y^2}{8.284} = 1$ **c.** See below. **13. a.** See below.

b. $\frac{\sqrt{29}}{5} \approx 1.1$ **15.** $x^2 - y^2 = 1$ **17.** c **19.** $x^2 +$

$(y - 8)^2 = 64$ **21.** (3, -20)

9.

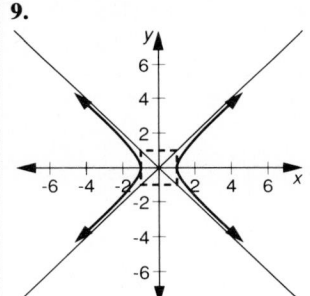

11. c.

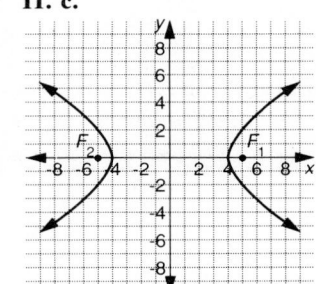

13. a.

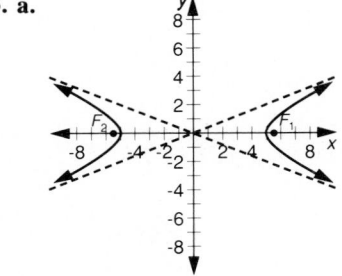

LESSON 12-8 (pp. 713–718)

1. a. no **b.** it has an xy^2 term **3. a.** yes **b.** $1x^2 + 2xy + 3y^2 + 4x + 5y - 6 = 0$ **5.** ellipse **7.** hyperbola
13. (2, 2)$r = \sqrt{6}$ **17.** $3x^2 + 0xy + 0y^2 + 6x - 1y - 5 = 0$; $A = 3, B = 0, C = 0, D = 6, E = -1, F = -5$

19. a. ellipse **b.** $y = \pm\sqrt{64 - \frac{16}{3}x^2}$ **c.** See below.

21. $4\sqrt{74} \approx 34.4$ **23. a.** graphing, substitution or linear combination **b.** (1.5, 6)

909

19. c.

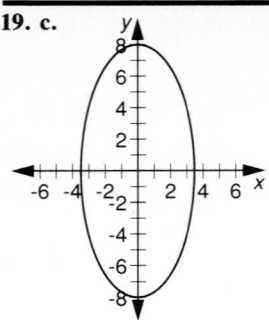

15.

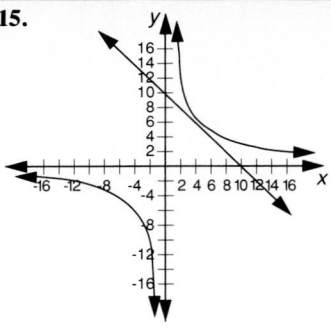

LESSON 12-9 (pp. 719–723)
1. Linear combinations **3. a. See below. b.** $((-2 + \sqrt{10}), (6 + 3\sqrt{10})), ((-2 - \sqrt{10}), (6 - 3\sqrt{10}))$ **5.** (-1, 1), (2, 4)
7. a. inconsistent **b.** Sample: $y = x - 1$ and $y = 2x^2$
9. a. 2 **b.** (-3, 0), (4, -7) **c.** Does $0 = (-3)^2 - 2(-3) - 15$, and $-3 + 0 = -3$? Yes. Does $-7 = 4^2 - 2(4) - 15$, $4 + -7 = -3$? Yes. **11.** $2x - 7 = x^2 - 8x + 18$; $x^2 - 10x + 25 = 0$; $(x - 5)^2 = 0$; $x = 5$, $y = 3$; Does $3 = 5^2 - 8(5) + 18$? Yes. Does $3 = 2(5) -7$? Yes.

13. $\left(\dfrac{4 + \sqrt{41}}{5}, \dfrac{2 - 2\sqrt{41}}{5}\right) \approx (2.08, -2.16)$,

$\left(\dfrac{4 - \sqrt{41}}{5}, \dfrac{2 + 2\sqrt{41}}{5}\right) \approx (-.48, 2.96)$ **15. See below.**

17. $xy = 2$ **19. a.** $5.43 \cdot 10^9$ **b.** $1.387 \cdot 10^9$ km **c.** 75 years
21. $x(x - 2y)(x^2 + 2xy + 4y^2)$ **23. a.** 0°C **b.** True **c.** 1
d. The rate of calories per temperature rise is 1, or it takes 1 calorie to raise the temperature 1 degree C.

3. a.

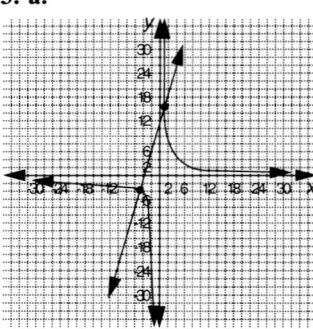

LESSON 12-10 (pp. 724–731)
b. Ex. 1:4; Ex. 2:4; Ex. 3:2; Ex. 4:1 **5.** Both x and y only appear with the exponent 2. **7.** True **9.** $nc = 12,000$ and

$c = \dfrac{12,000}{n}$ **11.** (2.5, 1.9), (2.5, -1.9), (-2.5, 1.9),

(-2.5, -1.9) **13.** (3, 0) **15.** c **17.** If using the real number system, R, the first equation is a circle with center (3, 0) and radius 2, and the second equation is a circle with center at (-3, 0) and radius 2. Therefore, solution set is empty over R, since the circles do not intersect. **19. a.–c. See below.**
21. 0, 1, 2, or infinitely many **23.** 96π **25.** 944 ft

19. a.–c.

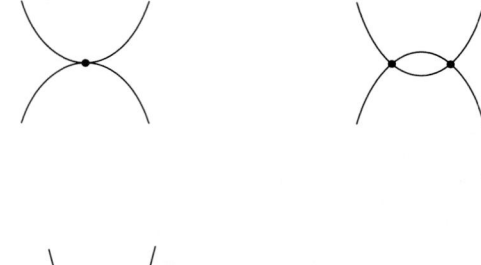

CHAPTER 12 PROGRESS SELF-TEST (p. 734)

1. For $x^2 + 9x + y^2 - 26y - 163 = 0$, $A = 1$, $B = 0$, and $C = 1$. Thus $B^2 - 4AC = 0 - 4 = -4 < 0$, so the equation represents an ellipse. Since $A = C$, the ellipse is a circle. **2.** Complete the square for x and for y: $x^2 + 9x + \frac{81}{4} + y^2 - 26y + 169 - 163 = 0 + \frac{81}{4} + 169$, $\left(x + \frac{9}{2}\right)^2 + (y - 13)^2 = 352.25$. **3.** Since the image of $x^2 + y^2 = 1$ under $S_{a,b}$ is $\left(\frac{x}{a}\right)^2 + \left(\frac{y}{b}\right)^2 = 1$, the image under $S_{3,4}$ is $\left(\frac{x}{3}\right)^2 + \left(\frac{y}{4}\right)^2 = 1$. **4.** The equation represents an ellipse, which is choice b. **5.** The vertices of $\left(\frac{x}{a}\right)^2 + \left(\frac{y}{b}\right)^2 = 1$ are $(-a, 0)$, $(a, 0)$, $(0, b)$, and $(0, -b)$, so the vertices of $\left(\frac{x}{3}\right)^2 +$

$\left(\frac{y}{4}\right)^2 = 1$ are (-3, 0), (3, 0), (0, 4), and (0, -4). **6. See below.** Since $c^2 = 13^2 - 5^2$, $c = 12$ and the foci are at (-12, 0) and (12, 0). Using a vertex on the minor axis as P, $F_1P + F_2P = 13 + 13 = 26$. Since $a = 13$ and $b = 5$, an equation is $\frac{x^2}{169} + \frac{y^2}{25} = 1$. **7.** The area of the ellipse $= \pi ab = (13)(5)\pi = 65\pi \approx 204$. **8. See below.** From the graph, the intersections are about (3.5, 1.5) and (-.5, -2.5). **9.** Since $x - 2 = 4x - x^2$, then $x^2 - 3x - 2 = 0$ and $x = \dfrac{3 \pm \sqrt{3^2 - 4(-2)(1)}}{2} = \dfrac{3 \pm \sqrt{17}}{2}$. The two points of intersection are $\left(\dfrac{3 + \sqrt{17}}{2}, \dfrac{-1 \pm \sqrt{17}}{2}\right)$ and $\left(\dfrac{3 - \sqrt{17}}{2},\right.$

$\left.\dfrac{-1 - \sqrt{17}}{2}\right)$. **10. a. See below.** The length of the major axis is 2.8 + 4.6 = 7.4 billion miles. **b.** $PO = \frac{1}{2}PQ = 3.7$, so $SO = 3.7 - 2.8 = .9$. Since $ST = PO = 3.7$, $TO = \sqrt{3.7^2 - .9^2} = \sqrt{12.88} \approx 3.6$, the length of the minor axis is 7.2 billion miles. **11. See below. 12. See below. 13. a. See below.** The two equations are $x^2 + y^2 = 1600$ and $(x + 25)^2 + (y - 60)^2 = 900$. **14.** Solve the system:

$$x^2 + 50x + 625 \quad + y^2 - 120y + 3600 = 900$$
$$\underline{x^2 \qquad\qquad\quad + y^2 \qquad\qquad = 1600}$$
$$50x + 625 \qquad\quad - 120y + 3600 = -700$$
$$50x = 120y - 4925$$
$$x = 2.4y - 98.5$$

Substitute. $(2.4y - 98.5)^2 + y^2 = 1600$
$5.76y^2 - 472.8y + 9702.25 + y^2 = 1600$
$6.76y^2 - 472.8y + 8102.25 = 0$

$$y = \frac{472.8 \pm \sqrt{(472.8)^2 - 4(6.76)(8102.25)}}{2(6.76)}$$

$$= \frac{472.8 \pm \sqrt{4455}}{13.52}$$

$$\approx \frac{472.8 \pm 66.75}{13.52}$$

The two y-values are 39.9 and 30; the corresponding x-values are -2.74 and -26.5. The two points for the epicenter are about (-2.7, 40) and (-27, 30). **15.** The x-axis and the y-axis

6.

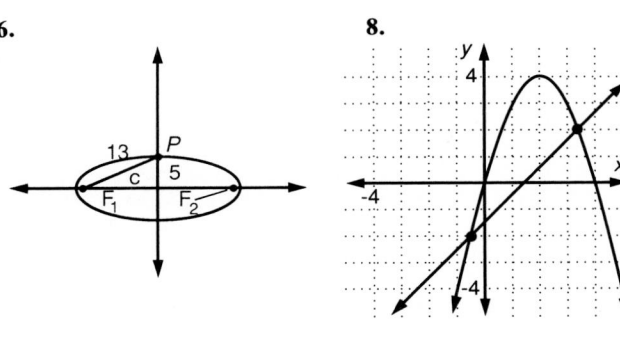

8.

10. a.

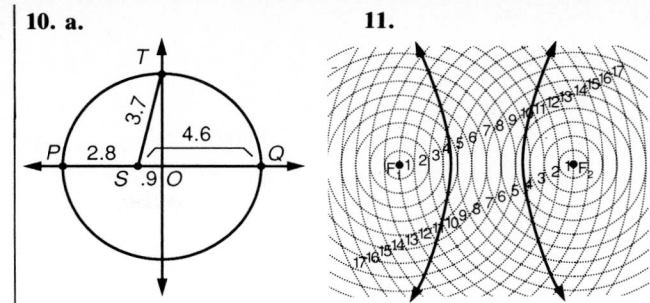

11.

12.

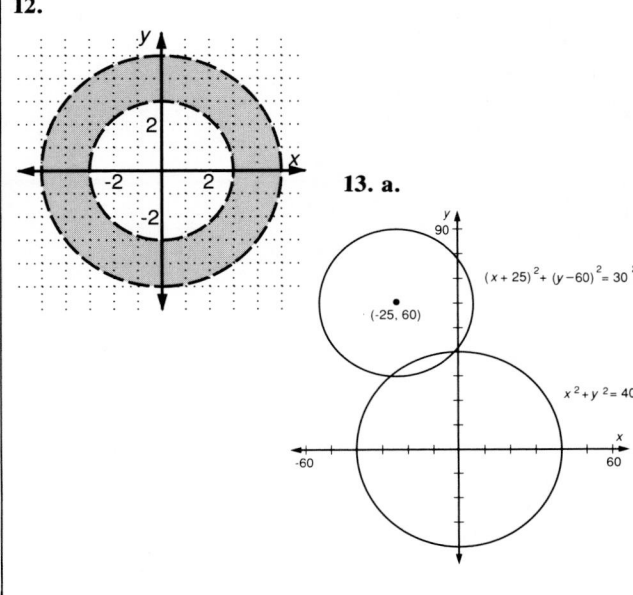

13. a.

The chart below keys the **Progress Self-Test** questions to the objectives in the **Chapter Review** on pages 735–739 or to the **Vocabulary** (Voc.) on page 732. This will enable you to locate those **Chapter Review** questions that correspond to questions you missed on the **Progress Self-Test.** The lesson where the material is covered is also indicated in the chart.

Question	1	2	3	4	5	6	7	8	9	10	11
Objective	F	A	B	G	E	B	C	K	D	H	J
Lesson	12-8	12-8	12-5	12-5	12-4	12-4	12-5	12-9	12-9	12-4	12-3

Question	12	13	14	15	16
Objective	J	H	I	E	J
Lesson	12-2	12-1	12-10	12-6	12-7

CHAPTER 12 REVIEW (pp. 735–739)

1. $x^2 + 0xy + y^2 - 6x + 14y - 42 = 0$ **3.** $\frac{x^2}{6} + \frac{y^2}{2} = 1$

5. $\frac{x^2}{4} - \frac{y^2}{2} = 1$ **7.** $x^2 + y^2 = 6$ **9. a.** Solve the equation $x^2 + y^2 = 20$ for y. $y = \pm \sqrt{20 - x^2}$ **b.** The graph of $x^2 + y^2 = 20$ is the union of the graphs of $y = \sqrt{20 - x^2}$

and $y = -\sqrt{20 - x^2}$. **11.** $\frac{x^2}{144} + \frac{y^2}{169} = 1$ **13.** $\frac{x^2}{16} - \frac{y^2}{33} = 1$
15. $33\pi = 104$ **17.** The circle has an area of 25π, ellipse has an area of 24π; circle has greater area. **19.** (-.5, 5.25), (3, 14) **21.** (-1, -6) **23.** (0, -4), (3, 5)
25. $\left(\frac{1 + \sqrt{17}}{2}, \frac{2 + 3\sqrt{17}}{2}\right), \left(\frac{1 - \sqrt{17}}{2}, \frac{2 - \sqrt{17}}{2}\right)$
27. center (0, 0), radius $\sqrt{5}$ **29.** 26 **31. a.** (-4, 0), (4, 0)

b. $\frac{y}{2} = \pm\frac{x}{4}$ **33.** ellipse **35.** ellipse (circle) **37.** hyperbola

39. *A*: hyperbola; *B*: parabola; *C*: ellipse; *D*: circle **41.** True
43. True **45.** $19.5\pi \approx 61.3$ sq m **47.** $(x - 200)^2 +$
$(y - 100)^2 < 100$ **49.** $(x - 8)^2 + y^2 > 5$ **51.** 12 by 18
53. (10.8, -48.8) **55. a.** \$14 **b.** 420 **57.** See below.

59. See below. **61.** See below. **63.** $\frac{x^2}{49} + \frac{y^2}{16} = 1$ **65.** b

67. See below. **69.** See below.

57.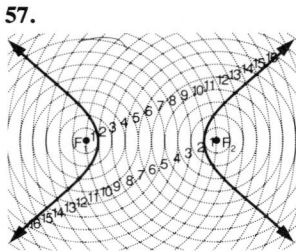

59.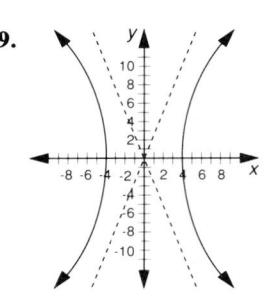

61.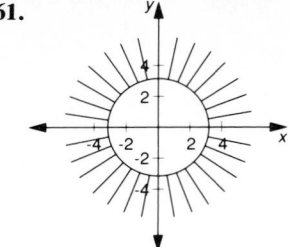

67.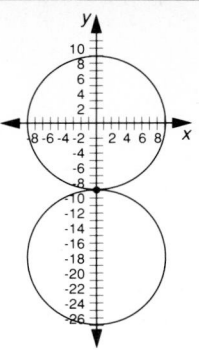

69.

LESSON 13-1 (pp. 742–747)
3. a. 20, 18, 16, 14 **b.** 20 + 18 + 16 + 14 **5.** 500, 500
7. a. 142 **b.** 2520 **9.** The number of terms. **11. a.** 27
b. 57 **c.** 3500 **13. a.** \$24,000; \$32,400 **b.** \$225,600

15. a. 15, 52, 466 **b.** $T = 10 + 3(n - 1)$; $S = \frac{3}{2}n^2 + \frac{17}{2}n$

c. Change lines to following:
    20 LET TERM = 2400
    40 FOR N = 2 TO 8
    50 TERM = TERM + 1200
17. ≈ 173 m **19.** $x(1 - a)$ **21.** 5^{14} **23.** 5^6 **25. a.** -13
b. parabola congruent to $y = 3x^2$, with vertex at (4, -13)

LESSON 13-2 (pp. 748–752)
1. 1, 2 **3.** 62.496 **5.** $\frac{1 - b^{17}}{1 - b}$ **7.** \$1267.19 **9. a.** 6, -4, $\frac{8}{3}$,
$-\frac{16}{9}, \frac{32}{27}, -\frac{64}{81}, \frac{128}{243}, -\frac{256}{729}$ **b.** ≈ 3.46 **11. a.** 56, 28, 14, 7,
3.5, 1.75, .875, .4375, .21875, .109375 **b.** ≈ 111.9
13. 77 **15.** 165,150 **17.** $y = -\frac{3}{2}x + 16$ **19.** ≈ 20.2 sec

LESSON 13-3 (pp. 753–758)
3. b **5.** a **7.** 666 **9.** 2184 **11.** 101 **13. a.** 24 **b.** 720
c. $\approx 5.109 \times 10^{19}$ **15.** $\sum_{i=1}^{7} 2i$ **17.** $\sum_{i=1}^{100} i^2$
19. $\frac{1}{n}\sum_{i=1}^{n} a_i$ **21. b.** 15 **b.** *n* **23.** 5050 **25.** See below.
27. a. ≈ 2.85 in. **b.** 55.46 in. **29.** 100 time as loud

25.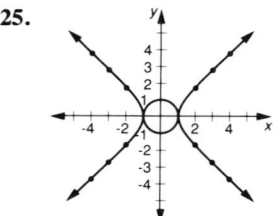

LESSON 13-4 (pp. 759–764)
1. a. No. **b.** This is an infinite geometric series and the
final value cannot be determined. **3. a.** no; **b.** $|r| > 1$

7. a. $\sum_{N=1}^{\infty} 4 \cdot \left(\frac{1}{10}\right)^N = \frac{4}{10} + \frac{4}{100} + \frac{4}{1000} + \ldots$ **b.** $\frac{4}{9}$
9. a. $2.46 + \sum_{N=1}^{\infty} \cdot \frac{8}{1000}\left(\frac{1}{10}\right)^{n-1} = 2.46 + .008 + .0008 +$
$.00008 + \ldots$ **b.** $\frac{1111}{450}$ **11.** They meet when the tortoise has
traveled $1 + .1 + .01 + \ldots = 1.\overline{1}$ m. **13. a.** $\frac{4\sqrt{3}}{12}$
b. $\frac{10\sqrt{3}}{27}$ **c.** $\frac{\sqrt{3}}{4} + \frac{\frac{\sqrt{3}}{12}\left(1 - \frac{4^{n-1}}{9}\right)}{1 - \frac{4}{9}}$ **d.** $\frac{\sqrt{3}}{4} + \frac{\frac{\sqrt{3}}{12}}{\frac{5}{9}}$
15. a. 1 **b.** .5, .4$\overline{9}$ **17. a.** $6 + 11 + 16 + 21 + 26 +$
$31 + 36 + 41 + 46 + 51$ **b.** 285 **19.** $(\pm\sqrt{12}, \pm\sqrt{13})$
21. c **23.** 100^{100} **25.** $8x^3$ **27.** $\frac{1}{9}x^{-4}$

LESSON 13-5 (pp. 765–770)
3. See below. **5.** 28 **7.** 252 **9.** 1 **11.** 15 **13.** 10 **15.** true
17. $x = 11, y = 6$ **19.** the 2nd elements in each row
21. the 4th elements in each row **23. a.** ≈ 35.9 **b.** $\frac{256}{7}$
25. 60 **27. a.** one real root **b.** No real roots **c.** two rational
roots **29.** $6! = 720$

3.
```
   1   8   28   56   70   56   28    8   1
  1   9   36   84  126  126   84   36   9   1
 1  10   47  120  210  252  210  120   47  10   1
```

LESSON 13-6 (pp. 771–775)
5. $(a + b)^n = \sum_{r=0}^{n}\binom{n}{r}a^{n-r}b^r$. **7.** $a^3 - 3a^2b +$
$3ab^2 - b^3$ **9.** $x^6 + 6x^5y + 15x^4y^2 + 20x^3y^3 + 15x^2y^4 +$
$6xy^5 + y^6$ **11.** $a^4 + 8a^3b + 24a^2b^2 + 32ab^3 + 16b^4$
13. $(x + 3)^n$ **15. a.** $a^4 + 4a^3b + 6a^2b^2 + 4ab^3 + b^4$
b. $(a + b)^4$ because $a^2 + 2ab + b^2 = (a + b)^2$
17. 1.010045120210252 **19. a.** 210.4375 **b.** 256 **c.** iv
21. The sixth year **23.** 7 **25.** 3825 lb

LESSON 13-7 (pp. 776–781)
3. { }, {*p*}, {*q*}, {*r*}, {*p, q*}, {*p, r*}, {*q, r*}, {*p, q, r*} **5.** 8
9. 120 **11.** 177,100 **13.** $2^8 = 256$ **15.** *n*! **17. a.** 52
b. 1326 **c.** $\frac{1}{270,725}$ **19.** 1 **21.** $a^8 + 8a^7b + 28a^6b^2 +$

$56a^5b^3 + 70a^4b^4 + 56a^3b^5 + 28a^2b^6 + 8ab^7 + b^8$
23. 54.25 **25.** 165 **27.** c

LESSON 13-8 (pp. 782–787)

1. $\frac{1}{20}$ **3.** $\frac{1}{2}$ **5.** RRRR WRRR RWWR WRWW
RRRW RRWW WWRR WWRW
RRWR RWRW WRWR WWWR
RWRR WRRW RWWW WWWW

7. $\frac{20}{64}$ **9.** $\frac{1}{64}$ **11.** $\frac{1}{256}, \frac{8}{256}, \frac{28}{256}, \frac{56}{256}, \frac{70}{256}, \frac{56}{256}, \frac{28}{256}, \frac{28}{256}, \frac{8}{256}, \frac{1}{256}$
13. a. 1 **b.** 0 **15.** $p^9 + 9p^8q + 36p^7q^2 + 84p^6q^3 + 126p^5q^4 + 126p^4q^5 + 84p^3q^6 + 36p^2q^7 + 9pq^8 + q^9$
17. 3 **19.** 625 **21.** 6.25π in.² **23.** 66.69%

LESSON 13-9 (pp. 788–792)

3. a. mean: -5.14; median: -4; mode: -14 **b.** median or mean
5. a. mean **b.** 156.25 **7.** mean = 30; s.d. ≈ 14.14 **9.** more spread out **11. a.** A few extreme values can affect the mean, but not the median. **b.** The most common income will not reflect the wealth of the community **13.** mean ≈ 9.14; s.d. ≈ 6.96 **15.** Sample: {10, 10, 10, 10} and {0, 0, 0, 40} **17.** $\frac{1}{1140}$ ≈

.000877 **19.** $x^4 - 8x^3y + 24x^2y^2 - 32xy^3 + 16y^4$ **21.** $x = 220$; the total number in the House is about 440

LESSON 13-10 (pp. 793–797)

1. a. $\frac{5}{16}$ It could represent the probability of getting 3 heads in 5 tosses of a fair coin. **b.** a probability function **3.** $\frac{252}{1024}$
7. 2.3% **9.** 68.2% **11.** ≈66% **13.** 15.9% **15.** 769,145
17. 6 **19.** 1 **21.** True **23. a.** $\frac{-3 \pm \sqrt{209}}{10}$ **b.** 1.15 or -1.75

LESSON 13-11 (pp. 798–804)

3. All potential voters; the people who are asked questions **7.** 18.6% of all households with TV are tuned into a particular show. **11.** 500, 15.8 **13. a.** Random number program. Student answers will vary. **b.** The two outputs should be different. **15.** the class; the classmate you called **17.** ≈4.9
19. $\frac{6}{26} = \frac{3}{32}$ **21.** 22.5 **23.** $y - 5 = (x - 6)^2$, $y - 5 = -(x - 6)^2$ **25.** $x = |y|$

CHAPTER 13 PROGRESS SELF-TEST (p. 807)

1. $g_1 = 12$; $g_2 = \frac{1}{2}g_1 = \frac{1}{2}(12) = 6$; $g_3 = \frac{1}{2}g_2 = \frac{1}{2}(6) = 3$; $g_4 = \frac{1}{2}g_3 = \frac{3}{2}$ **b.** The geometric series has first term 12 and constant ratio $\frac{1}{2}$. The sum of the first 12 terms is $S_n = \frac{a(1 - r^n)}{1 - r}$ or $S_{12} = \frac{12\left(1 - \left(\frac{1}{2}\right)^{12}\right)}{1 - \frac{1}{2}} = \frac{12\left(1 + \frac{1}{4096}\right)}{\frac{1}{2}} = \frac{12\left(\frac{4097}{4096}\right)}{\frac{1}{2}} = \frac{12,285}{512} \approx 23.99$ **2.** Using $S_n = \frac{n}{2}[2a_1 + (n - 1)d]$ with $n = 30$, $a_1 = 12$, and $d = 2$, $S_{30} = \frac{30}{2}$

$(2(12) + (29)(2)) = (15)(82) = 1230.$ **3.** $\sum_{i=-2}^{3} 4(10)^i = 4(10)^{-2} + 4(10)^{-1} + 4(10)^0 + 4(10)^1 + 4(10)^2 + 4(10)^3 = .04 + .4 + 4 + 40 + 400 + 4000 = 4444.44$ **4.** Use $(a + b)^4 = a^4 + 4a^3b + 6a^2b^2 + 4ab^3 + b^4$ with $a = x^2$ and $b = -3$: $(x^2 - 3)^4 = (x^2)^4 + 4(x^2)^3(-3) + 6(x^2)^2(-3)^2 + 4(x^2)(-3)^3 + (-3)^4 = x^8 - 12x^6 + 54x^4 - 108x^2 + 81$ **5.** $\binom{15}{3} = \frac{15!}{3! \; 12!} = \frac{15 \cdot 14 \cdot 13 \cdot 12!}{3 \cdot 2 \cdot 1 \cdot 12!} =$

$5 \cdot 7 \cdot 13 = 455$ **6.** $_8C_0 = \frac{8!}{8! \; 0!} = 1$ **7.** $\binom{40}{38} = \frac{40!}{38! \; 2!} =$

$\frac{40 \cdot 39 \cdot 38!}{2 \cdot 1 \cdot 38!} = 20 \cdot 39 = 780$ **8. a.** $2^{10} = 1024$ **b.** $\frac{\binom{10}{5}}{2^{10}} =$

$\frac{252}{1024} \approx .246$ or 25% **9.** The mode is the most frequent score, which is 80. **10.** The mean is the sum of the scores, divided by the number of scores, or $\frac{431}{5} = 86.2$ **11.** To bring her average for 6 scores up to 88, she needs a total of $(6)(88) = 528$ on the 6 scores. Since she already has a total of 431 for the first five scores, she needs $528 - 431 = 97$ on the next quiz. **12.** If $S_n = \frac{n}{2}(1 + n) = 300$, where n is the last integer added, then $\frac{n}{2} + \frac{n^2}{2} = 300$, $n + n^2 = 600$, $n^2 + n - 600 = 0$, $(n + 25)(n - 24) = 0$, and $n = -25$

or $n = 24$. The answer is 24. **13.** $\sum_{i=1}^{20} i^3$ **14.** Since 34.1% of the scores are within one standard deviation of the mean, in each direction, and another 13.6% of the scores are within a second standard deviation, in each direction, the percent within two standard deviations is $2(34.1 + 13.6) = 95\%$. **15.** A score of 24.7 is 5.9 above the mean of 18.8, which is one standard deviation above the mean. The percent of scores at or above one standard deviation above the mean is $13.6 + 2.3$ or about 16%. **16. a.** See below. **b.** See below. **c.** P(n) represents the probability of obtaining exactly n heads when a fair coin is tossed 6 times. **17. a.** $-x$ represents the constant ratio r in a geometric series. The series has a limit if $|r| < 1$ so it has a limit of $|-x| < 1$ or $|x| < 1$. **b.** Since $S = \frac{a}{1 - r}$ with $a = 1$ and $r = -x$, the sum is $\frac{1}{1 - (-x)} = \frac{1}{1 + x}$. **18. a.** See below. **b.** The sum of the numbers in the nth row is $\binom{n}{0} + \binom{n}{1} + \binom{n}{2} + \cdots + \binom{n}{n} = \sum_{i=0}^{n} \binom{n}{i} = \sum_{i=0}^{n} \binom{n}{i} 1^i 1^{n-i} = (1 + 1)^n = 2^n$ **19.** $\binom{n}{n} = 1$, $\binom{n}{1} = n$. So $\binom{n}{n} = \binom{n}{1}$ only if $n = 1$. So the answer is false.

20. The expansion of $(x - y)^7$ begins $\binom{7}{0}x^7 - \binom{7}{1}x^6y + \binom{7}{2}x^5y^2 - \ldots$. The second term is $\binom{7}{1}x^6y$, so the answer is false.

16. a.

n	0	1	2	3	4	5	6
$P(n)$	$\frac{1}{64}$	$\frac{6}{64}$	$\frac{15}{64}$	$\frac{20}{64}$	$\frac{15}{64}$	$\frac{6}{64}$	$\frac{1}{64}$

16. b.

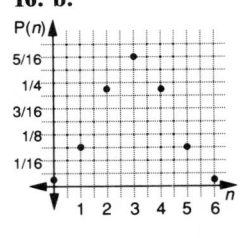

18. a.
```
        1
      1   1
     1  2  1
    1  3  3  1
   1 4  6  4 1
  1 5 10 10 5 1
```

The chart below keys the **Progress Self-Test** questions to the objectives in the **Chapter Review** on pages 808–811 or to the **Vocabulary** (Voc.) on page 805. This will enable you to locate those **Chapter Review** questions that correspond to questions you missed on the **Progress Self-Test.** The lesson where the material is covered is also indicated in the chart.

Question	1	2	3	4	5	6	7	8	9–11	12, 13	14, 15
Objective	A	H	B	D	I	C	C	I	E	A - B	J
Lesson	13-2	13-1	13-3	13-6	13-7	13-7	13-5	13-8	13-9	13-3	13-11

Question	16	17	18 a	18 b	19	20	21	22
Objective	L	F	C	G	G	D	B	K
Lesson	13-10	13-4	13-5	13-7	13-11	13-5	13-3	13-11

CHAPTER 13 REVIEW (pp. 808–811)

1. 990 **3.** 4 **5.** 1830 **7.** .354 + .000354 + .000000354 . . .
b. $\frac{118}{333}$ **9. a.** (-3) + (4) + 1 + 3 + 5 + 7 **b.** 12 **11.** c
13. $\sum_{n=1}^{72} 2n$ **15.** 722 **17.** See below. **19.** 252 **21.** 1 **23.** d
25. 2^{26} = 67,108,864 **27.** $p^7 - 56p^6 + 1344p^5 -$
17,920p^4 + 143,360p^3 − 688,128p^2 + 1,835,008p −
2,097,152 **29.** $\frac{1}{32}a^5 + \frac{5}{8}a^4b + 5a^3b^2 + 20a^2b^3 + 40ab^4 +$
32b^5 **30.** True **31.** False **33.** 82.125; 83.5; 90 or 68
35. ≈10.53 **37.** $|r| < 1$ **39.** $|x| < 3$ **41.** True **43.** $2^5 = 32$
45. $(n − r + 1)$th **47.** 29 mi **49. a.** \$51,257 **b.** \$147,773
51. $\frac{n}{2}(1 + n)$ **53.** 6! = 720 **55.** 316,251 **57.** 45 **59.** $\frac{10}{32}$

61. a. $\frac{120}{1024}$ **b.** $\frac{176}{1024}$ **63.** 13,650,000 **65.** 6'8" **67.** 3.25"

69. seniors **71.** 373 to 595 **73. a.** All households in the town with at least one TV. **b.** It may be difficult or to expensive to poll the entire population. **75. a.** P(0) = $\frac{1}{256}$; P(1) = $\frac{1}{32}$; P(2) = $\frac{7}{64}$; P(3) = $\frac{7}{32}$; P(6) = $\frac{7}{64}$; P(7) = $\frac{1}{32}$; P(8) = $\frac{1}{256}$
b. See below. **c.** binomial probability distribution

17.
```
      1 3 3 1
     1 4 6 4 1
  1 5 10 10 5 1
```

75. b.
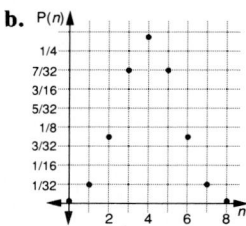

LESSON 14-1 (pp. 814–818)

3. False **5.** The yz-plane **7.** c **9.** See below. **11.** a, b are negative; c is positive. **13.** (6, 8, 10) **15. a.** See below.
b. 80 cubic units **c.** 132 square units **17. a.** A = (13, 0, 5), B = (0, 0, 5), C = (0, 2, 5), E = (13, 0, 0), G = (0, 2, 0), H = (13, 2, 0). **b.** 130 cubic units **c.** 202 square units **19.** y is divided by 3 **21.** y is multiplied by 27 **23.** c
25. e

9.
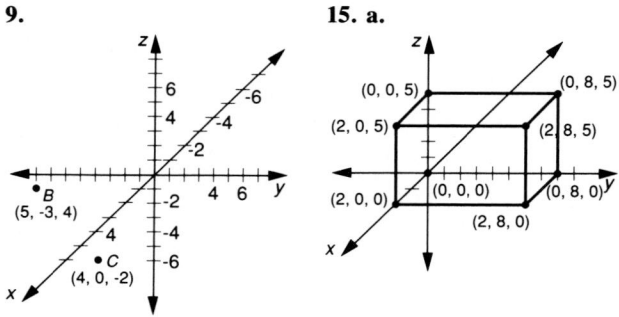

15. a.

LESSON 14-2 (pp. 819–825)
1. True **3.** axis **5.** The z-value of the point where a plane intersects the z-axis. **7.** See below. **9. a.** $\begin{cases} z = 2 \\ x = -3 \\ y = 1 \end{cases}$
b. (-3, 1, 2) **11.** y = 5 **13. a.** 2x + 4y + 5z = 100
b. $0 \le x \le 59, 0 \le y \le 25, 0 \le z \le 20$ **c.** See below.
d. (50, 0, 0), (0, 25, 0), (0, 0, 20); yes

17. 3 − 2i **19.** y = kx, y = mx + b, Ax + By = C
21. $A = P\left(1 + \frac{r}{n}\right)^{nt}$ **23. a.** $\frac{8}{256} = \frac{1}{32}$ **b.** i **c.** $\binom{8}{1}$
d. eighth row

7.
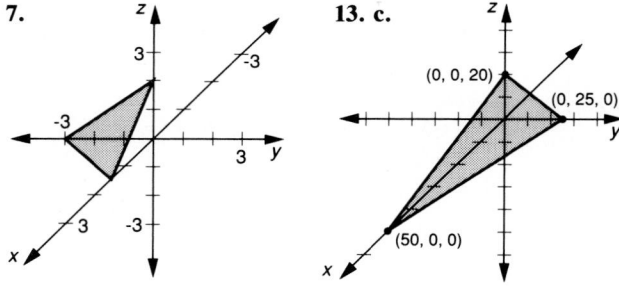

13. c.

LESSON 14-3 (pp. 826–832)
3. 60d + 100w + 200p = 21,200
  30d + 300w + 400p = 46,850
  40d + 80w + 150p = 16,100
b. d = \$45/hr, w = \$85/hr, p = \$50/hr **5. a.** -4; 5
b. $\begin{cases} 4x + 3y + 6z = 132 \\ 3x + 5y + 4z = 130 \end{cases}$ $\begin{cases} -12x - 9y - 18z = -399 \\ 12x + 20y + 16z = 520 \end{cases}$
So 11y − 2z = 124 **c.** x = 18, y = 12, z = 4 **7.** x = 1, y = 2, z = -3 **9.** \$53 **11.** y = -6 **13.** See below.
15. a. 22 m **b.** 39.2 m **c.** 40 m **17. a.** ellipse
b. (-11, 0), (11, 0)

13.

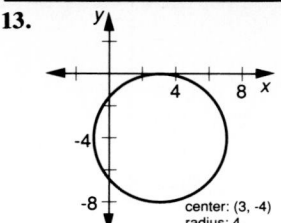

center: (3, -4)
radius: 4

LESSON 14-4 (pp. 833–839)

1. the absolute value of the difference of their x-coordinates
3. Take the absolute value of the difference of the
z-coordinates of the exponents. **5.** 6.3 **7.** 23.2
11. See below. 13. a. $x^2 + y^2 + z^2 = 25$
b. Sample: $(\sqrt{19}, \sqrt{6}, 0)$ **15. a.** (3, 2, -5) **b.** 6
c. Sample (9, 0, 0) and (0, 8, 0) **d.** $(x - a)^2 +$
$(y - b)^2 + (z - c)^2 = r^2$ **17.** $\approx 157\, m$ (must be longer
than $\sqrt{24{,}500}\, m$) **19. a.** 12π cm^2 **b.** $2\sqrt{3}$ cm **c.** $3\sqrt[3]{3}$ cm
d. cylinder

11.

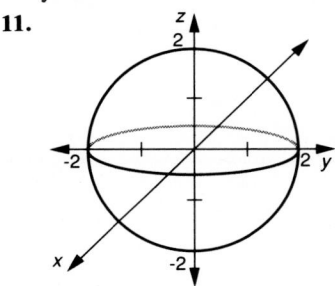

LESSON 14-5 (pp. 840–845)

5. a. a sphere **b.** $x^2 + y^2 + z^2 = 50$ **11. a.** sphere
b. 288π cubic units **c.** 144π square units **13. See below.**
15. See below. 17. a doughnut or torus **19.** True **21.** It
does not intersect the x-axis. **23.** False **25. c**

13.

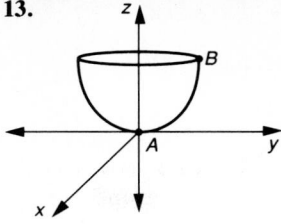

15.

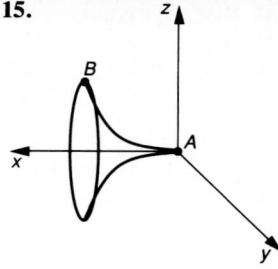

LESSON 14-6 (pp. 846–851)

5. 2 **7.** 4 **9.** True **11.** False; Samples: P_1, P_2, P_3, and P_6
13. $v = 2^n$ **15. a.** a circle in the xy-plane with radius 8 and
center at the origin **b.** $x^2 + y^2 = 64$ **17.** oz of cheese is
32 cal., grape is 6 cal., carrot is 25 cal **19.** SAT scores
21. hyperbola **23.** point **25.** line **27.** Sample: $P(x) =$
$kx(x + 2)(x - 4)$

LESSON 14-7 (pp. 852–856)

1. $w = 1$, $z = 8$, $y = 8.8$, $x = -7.4$ **3.** d, g, h
5. a. $\begin{vmatrix} 1 & -4 & 1 & 1 \\ 3 & -2 & -3 & 15 \\ 2 & 1 & -1 & 8 \end{vmatrix}$ **b.** (3, 0, -2) **7.** $a = \frac{1}{6}$, $b = \frac{1}{2}$,
$c = \frac{1}{3}$, $d = 0$ **9.** $\sqrt{198} \approx 14.1$ **11.** $\sqrt{6900} \approx 83$ cm
13. $x^5 + 10x^4y + 40x^3y^2 + 80x^2y^3 + 80xy^4 + 32y^5$
15. 256 **17.** 100 **19.** $4p^2(p - 3)(p^2 + 3p + 9)$

LESSON 14-8 (pp. 857–864)

5. a. 3 **b.** 9 **c.** 27 **d.** 3^D **9.** 1.5 **11.** $3^D = 9$, $D = 2$
13. $a = 2$, $b = -1$, $c = 0$ **15. a.** $\binom{50}{6} = 15{,}890{,}700$
b. about 1 in 16 million **17.** a parabola **19.** $\theta \approx 104.5°$
21. $t_n = \frac{24}{2^n}$ **23.** $23 \cdot x = 4.5$

CHAPTER 14 PROGRESS SELF-TEST (p. 866)

1. See below. 2. To locate point S, start from R and go 2
units on the x-axis to U, 5 units on the y-axis to I, and 4 units
on the z-axis to S. The coordinates are (2, 5, 4). **3.** The
coordinates of U are (2, 0, 0) and of H are (0, 5, 4). $UH =$
$\sqrt{(x_1 - x_2)^2 + (y_1 - y_2)^2 + (z_1 - z_2)^2} =$
$\sqrt{(2 - 0)^2 + (0 - 5)^2 + (0 - 4)^2} = \sqrt{4 + 25 + 16} =$
$\sqrt{45} \approx 6.7$. **4.** In the upper left front octant, "upper" means
$z > 0$, "left" means $y < 0$, and "front" means $x > 0$.
A sample is (2, -1, 4). **5.** The dimensions of the box are
4, 3, and 2; the volume is (4)(3)(2) = 24. **6. a.** The
set of points 3.5 units from the yz-plane consist of two planes,
each parallel to the yz-plane and 3.5 units from it. An
algebraic description is $x = \pm 3.5$. **b. See below. 7.** An equation for the sphere is $x^2 + y^2 + z^2 = 169$. **8.** For the system
$x + y - z = 2$
$6x + y - z = 4$, the augmented matrix is
$4x - y + 3z = 0$
$\begin{bmatrix} 1 & 1 & -1 & 2 \\ 6 & 1 & 1 & 4 \\ 4 & -1 & 3 & 0 \end{bmatrix}$. **9.** To solve the system, one method is to
find another system without the variable y by adding equations
1 and 3 and then 2 and 3: $\begin{array}{l} 5x + 2z = 2 \\ 10x + 4z = 4 \end{array}$ Since these two

equations are equivalent, this system (and the original system)
has an infinite number of solutions. **10.** If a plane is parallel
to the z-axis, the coefficient of z in its equation is 0. That is
choice d. **11.** The choice is b, a cylinder. Make a sketch with
a line segment parallel to the x-axis, then sketch its path
around the x-axis. **12.** Since the equation of the plane
$4x + y + 2z = 4$ has non-zero coefficients for all three
dimensions, it is false that it is parallel to any coordinate
plane. **13.** Find the intercepts of $4x + y + 2z = 4$ by letting
pairs of coordinate values be zero. **See below. 14.** The equation for the hypersphere is $x^2 + y^2 + z^2 + w^2 = 144$.
15. 0, 1 or infinity, many **16.** The intersection of the sphere
$x^2 + y^2 + z^2 = 49$ with the yz-plane is the circle $y^2 + z^2 =$
49, which has center (0, 0) and radius 7. **17. See below.**
18. When the unit is $\frac{1}{5}$ the size, the boundary is multiplied by

9. Then $5^D = 9$, so $D = \dfrac{\log 9}{\log 5} \approx 1.37$. **19. a.** For the
system the equations are $\begin{array}{r} 4a + 4c + 0s = \$66 \\ 3a + 2c + 1s = \$52.50 \\ 1a + 5c + 1s = \$47 \end{array}$

b. To solve the system using matrices, start with

$$\begin{bmatrix} 4 & 4 & 0 & 66 \\ 3 & 2 & 1 & 52.50 \\ 1 & 5 & 1 & 47 \end{bmatrix}$$ Divide the top row by 4;

$$\begin{bmatrix} 1 & 1 & 0 & 16.50 \\ 3 & 2 & 1 & 52.50 \\ 1 & 5 & 1 & 47 \end{bmatrix}$$; multiply the top row by -3 and add to

row (2), next multiply the top row by -1 and add to row (3);

$$\begin{bmatrix} 1 & 1 & 0 & 16.50 \\ 0 & -1 & 1 & 3 \\ 0 & 4 & 1 & 30.50 \end{bmatrix}$$; multiply row (2) by -4 and add to

row (3), next add row (2) to row (1); $$\begin{bmatrix} 1 & 0 & 1 & 19.50 \\ 0 & -1 & 1 & 3 \\ 0 & 0 & 5 & 42.50 \end{bmatrix}$$;

divide row (3) by 5; $$\begin{bmatrix} 1 & 0 & 1 & 19.50 \\ 0 & -1 & 1 & 3 \\ 0 & 0 & 1 & 8.50 \end{bmatrix}$$; subtract

row (3) from row (2), next subtract row (3) from row (1);

$$\begin{bmatrix} 1 & 0 & 0 & 11.00 \\ 0 & -1 & 0 & -5.50 \\ 0 & 0 & 1 & 8.50 \end{bmatrix}$$; multiply row (2) by -1;

$$\begin{bmatrix} 1 & 0 & 0 & 11.00 \\ 0 & 1 & 0 & 5.50 \\ 0 & 0 & 1 & 8.50 \end{bmatrix}$$; therefore adult: \$11.00; child: \$5.50;

senior: \$8.50.

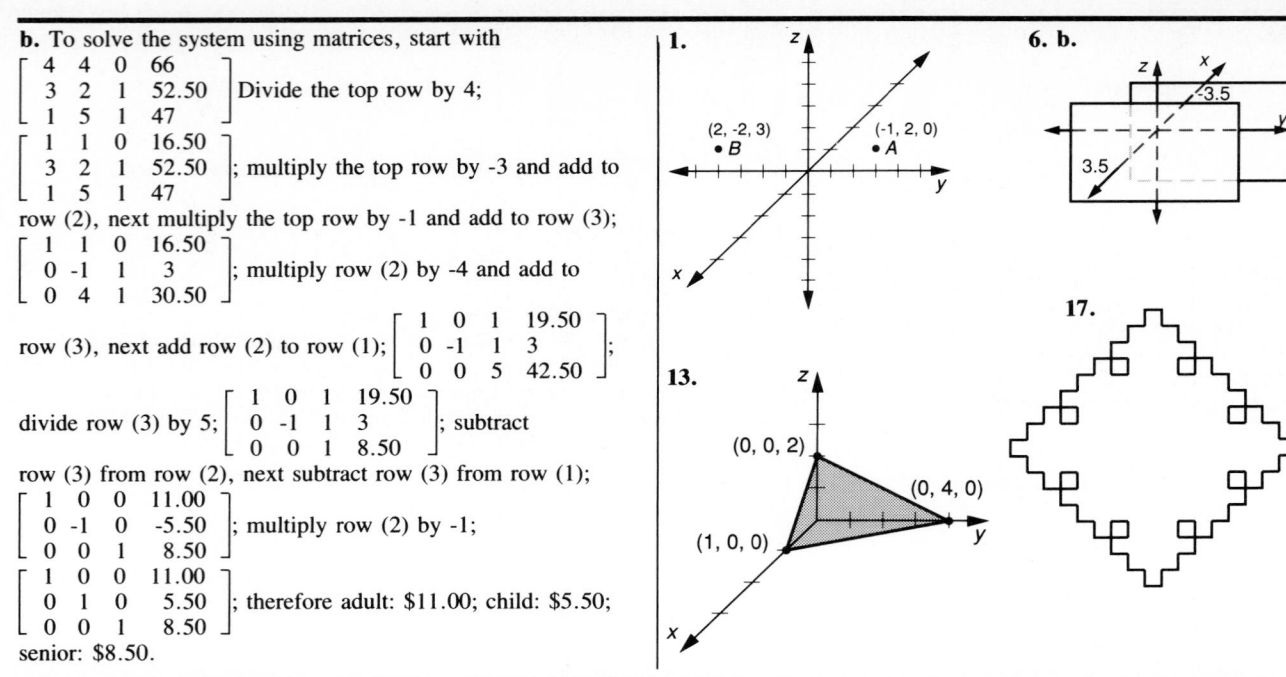

The chart below keys the **Progress Self-Test** questions to the objectives in the **Chapter Review** on pages 867–869 or to the **Vocabulary** (Voc.) on page 865. This will enable you to locate those **Chapter Review** questions that correspond to questions you missed on the **Progress Self-Test.** The lesson where the material is covered is also indicated in the chart.

Question	1, 2	3	4	5	6	7	8	9	10	11	12
Objective	G	B	G	B	D	C	A	A	D	H	D
Lesson	14-1	14-4	14-1	14-1	14-2	14-4	14-7	14-3	14-2	14-5	14-2

Question	13	14	15	16	17	18	19
Objective	G	C	D	H	E	E	F
Lesson	14-2	14-6	14-2	14-2	14-8	14-8	14-3

CHAPTER 14 REVIEW (pp. 867–869)

1. c **3.** $r = 5$, $s = 2$, $t = -4$ **5.** (5,3, 1, -2,) **7.** 4 **9.** 22 **11.** ≈ 10.4 **13.** $x^2 + y^2 + z^2 + w^2 = 49$ **15.** center $(0, 0, 0, 0)$; radius $= 27$ **17.** $z = -7$ **19.** $Ax + By + Cz = D$ where not all of A, B, $C = 0$ **21. a.** infinitely many **b.** The planes for equations 1 and 3 coincide. **23.** $\sqrt{(a - e)^2 + (b - f)^2 + (c - g)^2 + (d - h)^2}$ **25.** A fractal is a set of points that is self-similar. **27. See below.** **29.** m.c. $= 2$; t.i. $= 2$; s.a. $= 9$; es $= 8$ **31.** 1st class: \$395; 2nd class: \$350; 3rd class: \$275 **33. See below.** **35. See below. 37. a. See below. b.** a sphere of radius 3 **39. b.** an infinite double cone with the x-axis as its axis **41. a.** a cone **b.** 21π **43.** a non-circular ellipse **45.** 2 parallel chords, one in each base

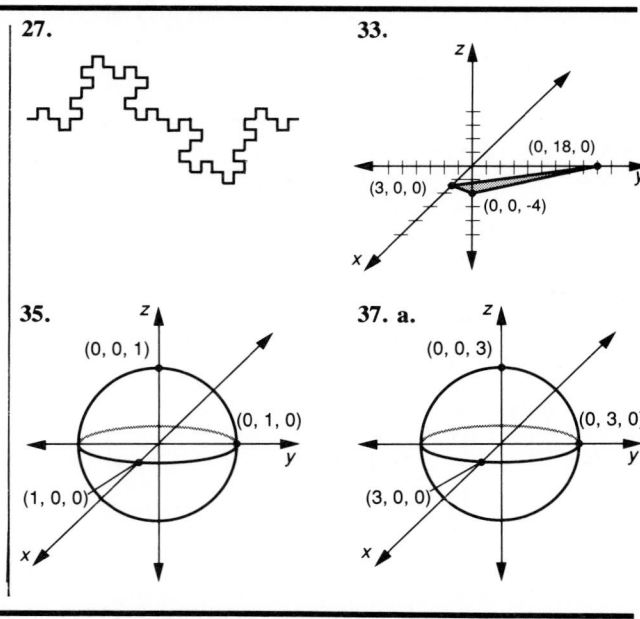

MATHEMATICAL SYMBOLS

$A \cap B$	intersection of sets A and B		$\ln x$	natural logarithm of x
$A \cup B$	union of sets A and B		$\sin \theta$	sine of θ
A'	image of A		$\cos \theta$	cosine of θ
S_k	size change of magnitude k		$\tan \theta$	tangent of θ
$S_{a,b}$	scale change with horizontal magnitude a and vertical magnitude b		rad	radian
			θ	Greek letter theta
r_x	reflection over the x-axis		a_n	''a sub n''; the nth term of a sequence
r_y	reflection over the y-axis			
$r_{y=x}$	reflection over the line $y = x$		$\sum_{i=1}^{n} i$	the sum of the integers from 1 to n.
$T_2 \circ T_1$	composite of transformations T_1 and T_2		S_n	the partial sum of the first n terms of a sequence
R_θ	rotation of magnitude θ counterclockwise			
$T_{h,k}$	translation of h units horizontally and k units vertically		∞	infinity
$\begin{bmatrix} a & b \\ c & d \end{bmatrix}$	2×2 matrix		$\binom{n}{r},\ _nC_r$	the number of ways of choosing r objects from n objects
			(x, y, z)	an ordered triple
M^{-1}	inverse of matrix M		(x, y, z, w)	an ordered 4-tuple
det M	determinant of matrix M		INT (X)	the BASIC equivalent for $[x]$
$\sqrt{}$	radical sign; square root		$\boxed{\sqrt[x]{}}$, $\boxed{\sqrt[x]{y}}$	calculator nth root key
$\sqrt[n]{x}$	the real nth root of x			
i	$\sqrt{-1}$		$\boxed{x!}$	calculator factorial key
$\sqrt{-k}$	a solution of $x^2 = -k, k > 0$		$\boxed{\log}$	calculator common logarithm key
$a + bi$	a complex number, where a and b are real numbers		$\boxed{e^x}$	calculator e^x key
$g \circ f$	composite of functions f and g		$\boxed{\ln}$	calculator natural logarithm key
$|x|$	absolute value of x		$\boxed{\text{DRG}}$	calculator degree key
$[x]$	greatest integer less than or equal to x		$\boxed{\sin}$	calculator sine key
$\lceil x \rceil$	smallest integer greater than or equal to x		$\boxed{\cos}$	calculator cosine key
f^{-1}	inverse of a function f		$\boxed{\tan}$	calculator tangent key
$\log_b m$	logarithm of m to the base b			
e	$2.71828 \ldots$			

GLOSSARY

absolute value function A function whose values are the positive distance between x and 0; $|x| = x$ if $x \geq 0$ and $|x| = -x$ if $x < 0$.

acceleration The rate at which the velocity of a moving object changes.

addition property of equality For all real numbers a, b, and c: if $a = b$, then $a + c = b + c$.

addition property of inequality For all real numbers a, b, and c: if $a < b$, then $a + c < b + c$.

algebraic expression A combination of numbers and variables; sometimes called simply an expression.

analytic description An algebraic description of a situation or object.

angle of depression The angle between the line of sight and the horizontal when the line of sight points down.

angle of elevation The angle between the line of sight and the horizontal when the line of sight points up.

arithmetic sequence A sequence with a constant difference; also called *linear sequence*.

arithmetic series An indicated sum of successive terms of an arithmetic sequence.

arrow notation Function notation used in transformations; also called *mapping notation*.

asymptotes of a hyperbola Two lines which are approached by the points on the branches of a hyperbola as the points get farther from the foci. The asymptotes of the hyperbola with equation $\frac{x^2}{a^2} - \frac{y^2}{b^2} = 1$ are $\frac{y}{b} = \pm \frac{x}{a}$.

augmented matrix A matrix which consists of the coefficients and constants of a system of equations.

automatic graphers Calculators and computer programs that automatically display graphs.

axis of rotation The line about which a point, line, or curve is rotated.

axis of symmetry of a parabola The line perpendicular to the directrix which contains the focus.

base The variable b in the expression b^n.

binomial A polynomial with two terms.

binomial distribution A probability function in which the values of the function are proportional to binomial coefficients.

binomial expansion The result of writing the power of a binomial as a polynomial.

binomial square theorem For all real numbers x and y: $(x + y)^2 = x^2 + 2xy + y^2$ and $(x - y)^2 = x^2 - 2xy + y^2$.

binomial theorem $(a + b)^n = \sum_{r=0}^{n} \binom{n}{r} a^{n-r} b^r$.

boundary A line or curve separating a plane into two regions.

branches of a hyperbola The two separate parts of the graph of a hyperbola.

calculator key sequence A list of keystrokes to be performed on a calculator.

center of a circle The fixed point from which the set of points of the circle are at a given distance.

center of an ellipse The intersection of the axes of the ellipse.

center-radius equation for a circle theorem The circle with center (h, k) and radius r is the set of points (x, y) that satisfies $(x - h)^2 + (y - k)^2 = r^2$.

central limit theorem Suppose random samples of size n are chosen from a population of events in which the probability of an event having certain characteristics is p. Let P(x) equal the number of elements in that sample with the characteristic. Then P is approximated by a normal distribution with mean np and standard deviation $\sqrt{np(1 - p)}$.

circle The set of all points in a plane at a given distance from a fixed point.

coefficient matrix A matrix which represents the coefficients of the variables of a system.

coefficients of a polynomial   The numbers $a_n, a_{n-1}, a_{n-2}, \ldots, a_0$ in the polynomial $a_n x^n + a_{n-1} x^{n-1} + a_{n-2} x^{n-2} + \ldots + a_0$.

combination   Any choice of r objects from n objects.

combined variation   A situation in which direct and inverse variations occur together.

common logarithm   A logarithm to the base 10.

complements theorem   For all θ between $0°$ and $90°$: $\sin \theta = \cos(90° - \theta)$ and $\cos \theta = \sin(90° - \theta)$.

completing the square   A technique used to transform a quadratic from $ax^2 + bx + c$ form to $a(x - h)^2 + k$ form.

complex conjugate   The complex conjugate of $a + bi$ is $a - bi$.

complex number   A number of the form $a + bi$, where a, b are real numbers and $i = \sqrt{-1}$.

composite of f and g $g \circ f$, the result of first applying function f, then applying function g; $(g \circ f)(x) = g(f(x))$.

composite of transformations   Suppose transformation T_1 maps figure F onto figure F', and transformation T_2 maps figure F' onto figure F''. The transformation that maps F onto F'' is called the composite of T_1 and T_2, written $T_2 \circ T_1$.

composition of functions   The operation of first applying one function, then another; denoted by the symbol $\circ$.

compounding   The process of earning interest on the interest of an investment.

compound interest formula $A = P(1 + r)^t$, where P is the amount of money invested at an annual interest rate r compounded annually and A is the total amount after t years.

compound sentence   A sentence in which two clauses are connected by the word ''and'' or by the word ''or.''

conditional statement   If p then q; sometimes written $p \Rightarrow q$.

conic sections   A cross-section of a double cone; also called *conic*.

conjecture   An educated guess.

consistent system   A system that has solutions.

constant-decrease situation   A situation in which a quantity y decreases by a constant amount for every increase in x.

constant-increase situation   A situation in which a quantity y increases by a constant amount for every increase in x.

constant matrix   A matrix which represents the constants in a system of equations.

continuous graph   A graph that can be drawn without picking up a pencil from the paper.

continuously compounded interest formula $A = Pe^{rt}$, where an amount P is invested in an account paying an annual rate r compounded continuously, and A is the amount in the account after t years.

continuous compounding   The limit of the process of earning interest with periods of compounding approaching zero.

converse   The converse of the conditional statement *if p then q* is *if q, then p;* sometimes written $q \Rightarrow p$.

convex regions   A region of the plane in which any two points of the region can be connected by a line segment which is itself entirely within the region.

coordinate plane   A plane determined by two axes in a coordinate system.

cosine function   The correspondence $\theta \to \cos \theta$ that associates θ with the x-coordinate of the image of $(1, 0)$ under R_θ.

cosine of θ (cos θ)   In a right triangle with acute angle θ, $\cos \theta = \dfrac{\text{length of leg adjacent to } \theta}{\text{length of hypotenuse}}$; the first coordinate of $R_\theta(1, 0)$.

counterexample   An instance which proves a conjecture false.

counting numbers   The set $\{1, 2, 3, 4, 5, \ldots\}$; also called the *natural numbers*.

cube root   The cube root x of t is a solution to the equation $x^3 = t$.

cube root function   The function $f(x) = \sqrt[3]{x}$.

cubing function   A powering function defined by $f(x) = x^3$.

data set A set in which an element may be listed more than once.

decibel (dB) A unit of sound intensity; $\frac{1}{10}$ of a bel.

degenerate form of a conic The intersection of a double cone and a plane containing the vertex of the cone. The ellipse degenerates to a single point, the parabola to a single line, and the hyperbola to two lines.

degree of a polynomial The highest exponent of a polynomial in x.

dependent variable In a formula, a variable whose value always depends on the value of the other variable(s).

depreciation A situation described by an exponential function where the growth factor is less than one; also called *exponential decay*.

determinant of a 2x2 matrix The expression $ad - bc$, associated with the matrix

$$M = \begin{bmatrix} a & c \\ b & d \end{bmatrix}.$$

difference of cubes pattern For all a and b: $a^3 - b^3 = (a - b)(a^2 + ab + b^2)$.

difference of squares pattern For all a and b: $a^2 - b^2 = (a + b)(a - b)$.

dimensions $m \times n$ A matrix with m rows and n columns has dimensions $m \times n$.

dimensions of a system A system with m equations and n variables has dimensions $m \times n$.

directly proportional A situation in which as one variable increases in absolute value, so does the other; y is directly proportional to x^n is written as $y = kx^n$, $k \neq 0$, and $n > 0$.

directrix The line whose distance to any point on a parabola is equal to the distance from that point to the focus.

direct variation A situation in which as one variable increases in absolute value, so does the other; y varies directly as x^n or y is directly proportional to x^n is written as $y = kx^n$, $k \neq 0$, and $n > 0$.

discontinuous graph A graph that cannot be drawn without picking up a pencil from the paper.

discrete graph A graph that is made up of unconnected points.

discriminant of a quadratic equation The value of $b^2 - 4ac$, which determines whether $ax^2 + bx + c = 0$ has real solutions.

discriminant theorem If a, b, and c are real and $a \neq 0$, then the equation $ax^2 + bx + c = 0$ has: (a) two real roots, if $b^2 - 4ac > 0$; (b) one real root, if $b^2 - 4ac = 0$; and (c) no real roots, if $b^2 - 4ac < 0$.

discriminant theorem for conics If A, B, C, D, E, and F are real numbers and at least A, B, or C is nonzero, then the graph of $Ax^2 + Bxy + Cy^2 + Dx + Ey + F = 0$ is a hyperbola if $B^2 - 4AC$ is positive, a parabola if $B^2 - 4AC = 0$, and an ellipse if $B^2 - 4AC$ is negative.

disk The union of a circle and its interior.

distance formula in 3-space The distance d between the points (x_1, y_1, z_1) and (x_2, y_2, z_2) is

$$d = \sqrt{(x_1 - x_2)^2 + (y_1 - y_2)^2 + (z_1 - z_2)^2}.$$

distance formula in 4-space The distance d between the points (x_1, y_1, z_1, w_1) and (x_2, y_2, z_2, w_1) is given by $d =$

$$\sqrt{(x_1 - x_2)^2 + (y_1 - y_2)^2 + (z_1 - z_2)^2 + (w_1 - w_2)^2}.$$

domain of a function The set of values which are allowable substitutions for the independent variable.

domain of a variable A set of meaningful numbers or things that can be substituted for a variable.

eccentricity The ratio of the distance between the foci to the focal constant in an ellipse or hyperbola.

element of a matrix The object in a particular row and column of a matrix.

ellipse The ellipse with foci F_1 and F_2 and focal constant d is the set of points P in a plane which satisfy $PF_1 + PF_2 = d$, where F_1 and F_2 are any two points and d is a constant with $d > F_1F_2$.

equal complex numbers Two complex numbers are equal if and only if their real parts are equal and their imaginary parts are equal; $a + bi = c + di$ if and only if $a = c$ and $b = d$.

equal matrices Two matrices which have the same dimensions and in which corresponding elements are equal.

equation   A sentence stating that two expressions are equal.

equation for a hypersphere   In 4-space, an equation for a hypersphere with center at $(0, 0, 0, 0)$ and radius r is $x^2 + y^2 + z^2 + w^2 = r^2$.

equivalent sentences   Sentences that have the same solutions.

equivalent systems   Systems that have the same solutions.

Euler's f(x) notation   Notation that represents functions by naming the function and enclosing the independent variable in parentheses.

evaluating an expression   Substituting for the variables in an expression and calculating a result.

exact value theorem   (a) $\sin 30° = \cos 60° = \frac{1}{2}$;
(b) $\sin 45° = \cos 45° = \frac{\sqrt{2}}{2}$;
(c) $\sin 60° = \cos 30° = \frac{\sqrt{3}}{2}$.

expanded form   The result of using the distributive property to rewrite a product of polynomials.

expanded form of an equation of a circle
$x^2 + y^2 + Dx + Ey + F = 0$.

expanded form of an equation of a parabola   An equation of the form $y = ax^2 + bx + c$, where $a \neq 0$.

explicit formula for nth term   A formula which describes any term in a sequence according to its position.

explicit formula for an arithmetic sequence   The nth term a_n of an arithmetic sequence with first term a_1 and constant difference d is given by the explicit formula $a_n = a_1 + (n - 1)d$.

explicit formula for a geometric sequence   In the geometric sequence with first term g_1 and constant ratio r, $g_n = g_1 r^{n-1}$.

exponent   The number n in the expression b^n.

$\frac{1}{n}$ exponent theorem   When $x \geq 0$ and n is an integer greater than 1, $x^{1/n}$ is an nth root of x.

exponential curve   A graph of an exponential equation.

exponential decay   A situation described by an exponential function where the growth factor is less than one; also called *depreciation*.

exponential function   A function with the independent variable in the exponent; a function with an equation of the form $y = ab^x$.

exponential growth   A situation described by an exponential function where the growth factor is greater than one.

exponential sequence   A sequence with a constant multiplier or constant ratio; also called *geometric sequence*.

exponentiation   An operation by which a variable is raised to a power; also called *powering*.

expression   A combination of numbers and variables.

extended distributive property   To multiply two polynomials, multiply each term in the first polynomial by each term in the second.

exterior of a circle   The region outside a circle; given a circle with center (h, k) and radius r: the exterior of a circle is described by $(x - h)^2 + (y - k)^2 > r^2$.

extraneous solution   A solution that is gained but does not check in the original equation.

factor theorem $x - r$ is a factor of a polynomial $P(x)$ if and only if $P(r) = 0$.

factorial function   The function defined by the equation $f(n) = n! =$ the product of the integers from n to 1.

fair coin   A coin that has an equal probability of landing on either side; also called an *unbiased coin*.

feasible region   The set of solutions to a system of linear inequalities; also called *feasible set*.

Fibonacci sequence   The sequence $1, 1, 2, 3, 5, 8, 13, \ldots$; a recursive definition is
$$\begin{cases} F_1 = 1 \\ F_2 = 1 \\ F_n = F_{n-1} + F_{n-2} \end{cases} \quad \text{for } n \geq 3.$$

field properties   The assumed properties of addition and subtraction of real numbers.

focal constant The sum of the distances from a point on an ellipse to the two foci of the ellipse; the absolute value of the difference of the distances from a point on a hyperbola to the two foci of the hyperbola.

focus (plural *foci*) In a parabola, the point along with the directrix from which a point is equidistant; the two points from which the sum (ellipse) or difference (hyperbola) of distances to a point on the conic section is constant.

formula A sentence stating that a single variable is equal to an expression with one or more different variables on the other side.

4-space The set of ordered 4-tuples (x, y, z, w) of real numbers.

fractal An object that is nearly self-similar; an object of fractional dimension.

function A relation in which for each ordered pair the first coordinate has exactly one second coordinate.

fundamental theorem of algebra Every polynomial equation $P(x) = 0$ of any degree with complex number coefficients has at least one complex number solution.

fundamental theorem of variation If y varies directly as x^n and x is multiplied by a nonzero constant c, then y is multiplied by c^n; if y varies inversely as x^n and x is multiplied by a nonzero constant c, then y is divided by c^n.

general compound interest formula $A = P\left(1 + \dfrac{r}{n}\right)^{nt}$, where P is the amount invested at an annual interest rate r compounded n times per year, and A is the amount after t years.

general form of a quadratic relation An equation of the form $Ax^2 + Bxy + Cy^2 + Dx + Ey + F = 0$, where A, B, C, D, E, and F are real numbers and at least one of A, B, or C is not zero.

geometric sequence A sequence with a constant multiplier or constant ratio; also called *exponential sequence*.

geometric series A indicated sum of successive terms of a geometric sequence.

graph translation theorem In a sentence for a graph, replacing x by $x - h$ and y by $y - k$ causes the graph to undergo the translation $T_{h,k}$.

gravitational constant The acceleration of a moving object due to gravity; near the Earth's surface, it is about 32 ft/sec^2 or 9.8 m/sec^2.

greatest integer function The function denoted by $[x]$, whose values are the greatest integer less than or equal to x; also called the *rounding down function*.

growth factor In the exponential function $y = ab^x$, the amount b by which y is multiplied for every unit increase in x.

half-life The amount of time required for a quantity to decay to half its original value.

half-plane One of the two regions formed by a line dividing a plane.

horizontal line A line whose equation is of the form $y = b$.

horizontal-line test The inverse of a function is itself a function if and only if no horizontal line intersects the graph of the function in more than one point.

horizontal scale change The stretching or shrinking of a figure in only the horizontal direction; a transformation which maps (x, y) onto (kx, y).

hyperbola The set of points P in a plane which satisfy $|PF_1 - PF_2| = d$, where F_1 and F_2 are any two points and d is a constant with $0 < d < F_1F_2$.

hypercube A four-dimensional cube.

hyperplane A plane in 4-space with an equation of the form $Ax + By + Cz + Dw = E$, where not all of A, B, C, and D are zero.

hypersphere The set of points in 4-space at a given distance from a fixed point.

identity function The function defined by $f(x) = x$.

identity transformation A transformation in which each point coincides with its image.

image The object resulting from applying a transformation.

imaginary number A number which is the square root of a negative real number.

imaginary part In a complex number of the form $a + bi$, b is the imaginary part.

inconsistent system A system with no solutions.

independent variable In a formula, a variable upon whose value other variables depend.

index The subscript used for a term in a sequence; the index indicates the position of the term in the sequence.

index variable The variable under the Σ sign in summation notation; also called *index*.

inequality An open sentence containing one of the symbols $<$, $>$, $\leq$, $\geq$, $\neq$, or $\approx$.

infinite geometric series A geometric series with infinitely many terms.

integers The set $\{0, 1, -1, 2, -2, 3, -3, \ldots\}$.

interior of a circle The region inside a circle; for the circle with center (h, k) and radius r: the interior of the circle is described by $(x - h)^2 + (y - k)^2 < r^2$.

intersection of sets The set consisting of those values common to both sets.

interval A solution to an inequality of the form $x \leq a$ or $a \leq x \leq b$, where the $\leq$ can be replaced by $<$, $>$, or $\geq$.

inverse function theorem f and g are inverse functions if and only if $(f \circ g)(x) = (g \circ f)(x) = x$.

inverse-matrix theorem If $ad - bc \neq 0$, the

inverse of $\begin{bmatrix} a & b \\ c & d \end{bmatrix}$ is $\begin{bmatrix} \frac{d}{ad-bc} & \frac{-b}{ad-bc} \\ \frac{-c}{ad-bc} & \frac{a}{ad-bc} \end{bmatrix}$.

inverse of a function The relation obtained by reversing the order of the coordinates of each ordered pair in the function.

inverse of a matrix Matrices M and N are inverse matrices if and only if their product is the identity matrix.

inverse-square graph The graph of $y = \frac{k}{x^2}$.

inverse-square variation An inverse variation described by the equation $y = \frac{k}{x^2}$, with $k \neq 0$.

inverse variation A situation in which as one variable increases in absolute value, the other variable decreases in absolute value; y varies inversely as x^n, or y is inversely proportional to x^n is written as $y = \frac{k}{x^n}$, for $k \neq 0$, $n > 0$.

inversely proportional to In an inverse variation, the same as "varies inversely as".

irrational number A number which cannot be written as a simple fraction; an infinite and nonrepeating decimal.

joint variation A situation in which one quantity varies directly as the product of two or more independent variables, but not inversely as any variable; example: In $y = kxz$, y varies jointly as x and y.

lattice point A point with integer coordinates.

lattice point in 3-space A point (x, y, z) in which x, y, and z are integers.

law of cosines theorem In any triangle ABC, $c^2 = a^2 + b^2 - 2ab \cos C$.

law of sines theorem In any triangle ABC, $\frac{\sin A}{a} = \frac{\sin B}{b} = \frac{\sin C}{c}$.

leading coefficient The coefficient of the variable of highest power in a polynomial in a single variable.

limit A number or figure which the terms of a sequence approach as n gets larger.

linear-combination method A method of solving systems which involves adding multiples of the given equations.

linear-combination situation A situation in which all variables are to the first power and are not multiplied or divided by each other.

linear inequality An inequality in which both sides are linear expressions.

linear polynomial A polynomial of the first degree, such as $mx + b$.

linear-programming problem A problem which leads to systems of linear inequalities whose solution gives a "program" or course of action to follow.

linear-programming theorem The feasible region of a linear-programming problem is convex, and the maximum or minimum quantity is determined at one of the vertices of the region.

linear sequence A sequence with a constant difference; also called *arithmetic sequence*.

line of symmetry A line through a graph such that if the graph were folded along the line, both sides of the graph would coincide.

logarithm of *m* to the base 10 n is the logarithm of m to the base 10, written $n = \log_{10} m$, if and only if $10^n = m$.

logarithm of *m* to the base *b* Let $b > 0$ and $b \neq 1$. Then n is the logarithm of m to the base b, written $n = \log_b m$, if and only if $b^n = m$.

logarithmic curve The graph of a function of the form $y = \log_b x$.

logarithmic scale A scale in which the units are spaced so that the ratio between successive units is the same.

magnitude of a size change The amount by which distances in a preimage are multiplied; also called *scale factor*.

major axis of an ellipse The segment which contains the foci and has two vertices of an ellipse as its endpoints.

mapping notation The notation f: $x \rightarrow y$; also called *arrow notation*.

mathematical model A graph or sentence that describes data or a relation between variables.

matrix A rectangular arrangement of objects.

matrix addition If two matrices A and B have the same dimensions, their sum $A + B$ is the matrix in which each element is the sum of the corresponding elements in A and B.

matrix form of a system A representation of a system using matrices; the matrix form for $\begin{cases} ax + by = e \\ cx + dy = f \end{cases}$ is $\begin{bmatrix} a & b \\ c & d \end{bmatrix}\begin{bmatrix} x \\ y \end{bmatrix} = \begin{bmatrix} e \\ f \end{bmatrix}$.

matrix multiplication Suppose A is an $m \times n$ matrix and B is an $n \times p$ matrix. The product $A \cdot B$ or AB is the $m \times p$ matrix whose element in row i and column j is the product of row i of A and column j of B.

matrix-solution theorem A 2×2 system has exactly one solution if and only if the determinant of the coefficient matrix is not zero.

matrix subtraction Given two matrices A and B having the same dimensions, their difference $A - B$ is the matrix whose element in each position is the difference of the corresponding elements in A and B.

mean The average of all the terms of a data set.

measure of central tendency A number which in some sense is at the "center" of a data set; the mean, mode, or median of a data set.

measure of dispersion A number, like standard deviation, which describes the extent to which elements of a data set are dispersed or spread out.

median The middle term of a data set when the terms are placed in increasing order.

method of finite differences A method of determining whether a sequence can be described by a polynomial formula, using successive differences of terms of the sequence.

midpoint formula The midpoint of the segment with endpoints (x_1, y_1) and (x_2, y_2) is $\left(\dfrac{x_1 + x_2}{2}, \dfrac{y_1 + y_2}{2} \right)$.

minor axis of an ellipse The segment which does not contain the foci and has two vertices of an ellipse as its endpoints.

mode The number which occurs most often in a data set.

model for an operation A pattern that describes many uses of that operation.

monomial A polynomial with one term.

multiplication properties of inequality For all real numbers a, b, and c: if $a < b$ and $c > 0$, then $ac < bc$, and if $a < b$ and $c < 0$, then $ac > bc$.

multiplication property of equality For all real numbers a, b, and c: if $a = b$, then $ac = bc$.

multiplicity of a root In a polynomial equation, the highest power of $x - r$, where r is a root, that appears as a factor of the polynomial.

natural logarithm A logarithm to the base e.

natural numbers The set $\{1, 2, 3, 4, 5, \ldots\}$; also called the *counting numbers*.

negative exponent theorem If $x > 0$, then $x^{-n} = \dfrac{1}{x^n}$.

normal curve The curve of a normal distribution.

normal distribution A function whose graph is the image of the graph of $y = \dfrac{1}{\sqrt{2\pi}}\, e^{-x^2/2}$ under a composite of translations or scale transformations.

normalized scores Scores whose distribution is a normal curve; also called *standardized scores*.

nth power function The function $f(x) = x^n$, where n is a positive integer.

nth root Let n be an integer greater than one. Then b is an nth root of x if and only if $b^n = x$.

nth root of nth power theorem For all real numbers x and integers $n \geq 2$: if n is odd, $\sqrt[n]{x^n} = x$; if n is even, $\sqrt[n]{x^n} = |x|$.

nth term The term occupying the nth position in the listing of a sequence; the general term of a sequence.

number of roots of a polynomial equation theorem Every polynomial equation of degree n has exactly n roots provided that multiple roots are counted as separate roots.

oblique line A line that is neither horizontal or vertical.

octant One of eight regions determined by the intersection of three coordinate planes in 3-space.

one-to-one correspondence A mapping in which each member of one set is mapped to a distinct member of another set, and vice-versa.

open sentence A sentence that may be true or false depending on what values are substituted for the variables.

order of operations Hierarchy used to evaluate expressions worldwide: (1) Perform operations within grouping symbols from inner to outer; (2) Take powers; (3) Do multiplications or divisions from left to right; (4) Do additions or subtractions from left to right.

ordered 4-tuple (x, y, z, w)

ordered triple (x, y, z)

parabola The set consisting of every point in the plane of line l and point F not on l whose distance from F equals its distance from l.

paraboloid A three-dimensional figure created by rotating a parabola in space around its axis of symmetry; the set of points equidistant from a point F (the focus) and a plane P.

partial sum The sum of the first n terms of a sequence.

Pascal's triangle The sequence satisfying

(1) $\dbinom{n}{0} = \dbinom{n}{n} = 1$ and

(2) $\dbinom{n+1}{r+1} = \dbinom{n}{r} + \dbinom{n}{r+1}$,

where n and r are any integers with $0 \leq r \leq n$;

the triangular array
$$
\begin{array}{c}
1 \\
1\ 2\ 1 \\
1\ 3\ 3\ 1 \\
1\ 4\ 6\ 4\ 1 \\
1\ 5\ 10\ 10\ 5\ 1 \\
\vdots
\end{array}
$$
where if x and y are located next to each other on a row, the element just below and directly between them is $x + y$.

perfect square trinomial A trinomial of the form $a^2 + 2ab + b^2$ or $a^2 - 2ab + b^2$.

perfect square trinomial pattern For all a and b: $a^2 + 2ab + b^2 = (a + b)^2$ and $a^2 - 2ab + b^2 = (a - b)^2$.

periodic A relation whose graph can be mapped to itself under a horizontal translation.

permutation An arrangement of n different objects in order.

piecewise linear graph A graph made of segments each of which is a piece of a line.

point matrix A 2×1 matrix.

point-slope form of a linear equation An equation of the form $y - y_1 = m(x - x_1)$, where (x_1, y_1) is a point on the line with slope m.

polynomial difference theorem $y = f(x)$ is a polynomial function of degree n if and only if, for any set of x-values that form an arithmetic sequence, the nth differences of the corresponding y-values are equal.

polynomial in x An expression of the form $a_n x^n + a_{n-1} x^{n-1} + a_{n-2} x^{n-2} + \ldots + a_1 x^1 + a_0$, where n is a positive integer and $a_n \neq 0$.

population The set of all people, events, or items that could be sampled.

postulates Statements assumed to be true in a mathematical system.

power of a power property For any nonnegative bases and real exponents or any nonzero base and integer exponents: $(b^m)^n = b^{mn}$.

power of a product property For any nonnegative bases and real exponents or any nonzero base and integer exponents: $(ab)^m = a^m b^m$.

power of a quotient property For any nonnegative bases and real exponents or any nonzero base and integer exponents: $\left(\dfrac{a}{b}\right)^m = \dfrac{a^m}{b^m}$.

powering An operation by which a variable is raised to a power; also called *exponentiation*.

powering property of logarithms For any positive real number x, $\log_b(x^n) = n \log_b x$.

preimage The object to which a transformation is applied.

principal The original amount of money invested.

probability (of an event) If a situation has a total of t equally likely possibilities and e of these possibilities satisfy conditions for a particular event, then the probability of the event $= \dfrac{e}{t}$.

probability distribution A function which maps a set of events onto their probabilities; also called *probability function*.

product of powers property For any nonnegative bases and real exponents or any nonzero base and integer exponents: $b^m \cdot b^n = b^{m+n}$.

product property of logarithms For any base b and for any positive real numbers x and y: $\log_b(xy) = \log_b x + \log_b y$.

proof An argument showing that a statement is true.

properties Postulates, theorems, or definitions in a mathematical system.

Pythagorean identity For all θ between $0°$ and $90°$: $(\cos \theta)^2 + (\sin \theta)^2 = 1$.

quadratic equation An equation which involves quadratic expressions.

quadratic equation in two variables An equation of the form $Ax^2 + Bxy + Cy^2 + Dx + Ey + F = 0$, where A, B, C, D, E, and F are real numbers and at least one of A, B, or C is not zero.

quadratic expression An expression which contains one or more terms in x^2, y^2, or xy, but no higher powers of x or y.

quadratic form An expression of the form $Ax^2 + Bxy + Cy^2 + Dx + Ey + F$.

quadratic formula If $ax^2 + bx + c = 0$ and $a \neq 0$, then $x = \dfrac{-b \pm \sqrt{b^2 - 4ac}}{2a}$.

quadratic-linear system A system that involves linear and quadratic sentences.

quadratic relation in two variables The sentence $Ax^2 + Bxy + Cy^2 + Dx + Ey + F = 0$ (or the inequality using one of the symbols $>$, $<$, $\geq$, $\leq$) where A, B, C, D, E, and F are real numbers and at least one of A, B, or C is not zero.

quadratic-quadratic system A system that involves two quadratic sentences.

quadratic system A system that involves at least one quadratic sentence.

quartic equation   A fourth degree polynomial equation.

quintic equation   A fifth degree polynomial equation.

quotient of powers property   For any nonnegative bases and real exponents, or any nonzero bases and integer exponents: $\dfrac{b^m}{b^n} = b^{m-n}$.

quotient property of logarithms   For any base b and for any positive real numbers x and y:
$$\log_b\left(\frac{x}{y}\right) = \log_b x - \log_b y.$$

radian   A unit of angle, arc, or rotation measure such that π radians = 180 degrees.

radius   The given distance between a circle and its center.

random numbers   Numbers which have the same probability of being selected.

random sample   A sample in which each element has the same probability as every other element in the population of being selected for the sample.

range of a function   The set of values of the function.

rate of change   Between two points, the quantity $\dfrac{y_2 - y_1}{x_2 - x_1}$; for a line, its slope.

rational exponent theorem   For any positive real number x and positive integers m and n, $x^{m/n} = (x^{1/n})^m$, the mth power of the positive nth root of x, and $x^{m/n} = (x^m)^{1/n}$, the positive nth root of the mth power of x.

rational number   A number which can be written as a simple fraction; a finite or infinitely repeating decimal.

real numbers   Those numbers that can be represented by a decimal.

real part   In a complex number of the form $a + bi$, a is a real part.

rectangular hyperbola   A hyperbola with perpendicular asymptotes.

recursive formula   A set of statements that indicates the first term of a sequence and gives a rule for how the nth term is related to one or more of the previous terms.

recursive formula for an arithmetic sequence   If d is constant, the recursive formula $\begin{cases} a_1 \\ a_n \end{cases} = a_{n-1} + d$ for $n > 1$, generates the arithmetic sequence with first term a_1 and constant difference d.

recursive formula for a geometric sequence   The recursive formula $g_n = r \cdot g_{n-1}$ for $n > 1$ generates the geometric sequence with first term g_1 and constant multiplier $r \neq 0$.

reflection   The reflection image of a point A over a line m is (1) the point A if A is on m, (2) the point A' such that m is the perpendicular bisector of $\overline{AA'}$ if A is not on m.

reflection-symmetric   A figure which coincides with a reflection image of itself.

relation   A set of ordered pairs.

repeated multiplication model for powering   If b is a real number and n is a positive integer, then $b^n = \underbrace{b \cdot b \cdot b \cdot b \cdot \ldots \cdot b}_{n \text{ factors}}$.

replacement set of a variable   A set of meaningful numbers or things that can be substituted for a variable.

Richter scale   A scale based on exponents of 10 used to determine the magnitude of intensity of an earthquake.

root of an equation   A solution to an equation.

root of a power theorem   When $x > 0$, $\sqrt[n]{x^m} = (\sqrt[n]{x})^m = x^{m/n}$.

root of a product theorem   For any positive real numbers x and y and any integer $n > 1$: $\sqrt[n]{xy} = \sqrt[n]{x} \cdot \sqrt[n]{y}$.

rotation   A transformation which turns a figure about a given point or line.

rounding down function   The function, denoted by $[x]$, whose values are the greatest integer less than or equal to x; also called the *greatest integer function*.

rounding up function   The function, denoted by $\lceil x \rceil$, whose values are the smallest integer greater than or equal to x.

row operation Any of the following operations on rows of a matrix: multiplying a row by any nonzero number; adding two rows and replacing one of the rows with the sum; switching two rows.

sample The subset of the population actually studied.

scalar A real number by which a matrix is multiplied.

scalar multiplication The product of a scalar k and a matrix A is the matrix kA in which each element is k times the corresponding element in A.

scale change The stretching or shrinking of a figure in either a horizontal direction only, in a vertical direction only, or in both directions; a horizontal scale change of magnitude a and a vertical scale change of magnitude b maps (x, y) onto (ax, by), and is denoted by $S_{a,b}$.

scale factor In a size change, the amount by which distances are multiplied.

self-similar A property of an object which does not change its appearance significantly when viewed under a microscope of arbitrary magnifying power.

sequence An ordered list.

shrink The contraction of a figure in some direction.

simple interest The amount of money I paid by the bank found by the formula $I = Prt$, where P is the principal, r is the rate, and t is the time.

simulation A procedure used to answer questions about real-world situations by performing experiments that closely model them.

sine function The correspondence $\theta \to \sin\theta$ that associates θ with the y-coordinate of the image of $(1, 0)$ under R_θ.

sine of θ (sin θ) In a right triangle with acute angle θ, $\sin\theta = \dfrac{\text{length of leg opposite } \theta}{\text{length of hypotenuse}}$; the second coordinate of $R_\theta(1, 0)$.

sine wave A graph which can be mapped onto the graph of $g(\theta) = \sin\theta$ by any composite of reflections, translations, and scale changes.

size change The stretching or shrinking of a figure by the same amount in both directions; a special kind of scale change; a size change of magnitude k, denoted by S_k, maps the point (x, y) onto (kx, ky).

slope The slope of a line through two points (x_1, y_1), (x_2, y_2) equals $\dfrac{y_2 - y_1}{x_2 - x_1}$; the same as the rate of change between two points on the line.

slope-intercept form of a linear equation A linear equation of the form $y = mx + b$, where m is the slope and b is the y-intercept.

snowflake curve The limit of a sequence of polygons formed by beginning with F_1 as an equilateral triangle, and forming F_n by drawing an equilateral triangle outward on the middle third of each side of F_{n-1} and then deleting the middle third.

$$F_1 \qquad F_2 \qquad F_3$$

solution set for a system The intersection of the solution sets for individual sentences of a system.

solution to a sentence A value of a variable or values of variables which make a sentence true.

solving a triangle The use of trigonometry to find all the missing measures of sides and angles of a triangle.

sphere The set of points in 3-space at a given distance from a fixed point.

square matrix A matrix with the same number of rows and columns.

square root A square root x of t is a solution to $x^2 = t$.

square root function The function $f(x) = \sqrt{x}$, where x is a nonnegative real number.

squaring function A powering function defined by $f(x) = x^2$.

standard deviation Let S be a data set of n numbers $\{x_1, x_2, \ldots, x_n\}$. Let m be the mean of S. Then the standard deviation s.d. of S is

$$\text{s.d.} = \sqrt{\dfrac{\sum\limits_{i=1}^{n}(x_i - m)^2}{n}}.$$

standard form of an equation for an ellipse The ellipse with foci $(c, 0)$ and $(-c, 0)$ and focal constant $2a$ has equation $\dfrac{x^2}{a^2} + \dfrac{y^2}{b^2} = 1$, where $b^2 = a^2 - c^2$.

standard form of an equation for a hyperbola The hyperbola with foci $(c, 0)$ and $(-c, 0)$ and focal constant $2a$ has equation $\dfrac{x^2}{a^2} - \dfrac{y^2}{b^2} = 1$, where $b^2 = c^2 - a^2$.

standard form of an equation for a plane The equation $Ax + By + Cz = D$ where not all of A, B, and C are zero.

standard form of a linear equation An equation of the form $Ax + By = C$, where A and B are not both zero.

standard form of a quadratic equation An equation of the form $ax^2 + bx + c = 0$, where $a \neq 0$.

standard position for an ellipse A location in which the origin of a coordinate system is midway between the foci with the foci on an axis.

standardized scores Scores whose distribution is a normal curve; also called *normalized scores*.

statistical measure A single number which is used to describe an entire set of numbers.

stratified sample A sample in which the population has first been split into subpopulations and then, from each subpopulation, a sample is selected.

step function A graph that looks like a series of steps; the function $y = [x]$.

stretch The expansion of a figure in some direction.

subscript A number or variable written below and to the right of a variable.

subscripted variable A variable with a subscript.

subset A set whose elements are all chosen from another set.

substitution method A method of solving a system using the Substitution Property.

sum and product of roots theorem r_1 and r_2 are the roots of the equation $ax^2 + bx + c = 0$, with $a \neq$, if and only if $r_1 + r_2 = \dfrac{-b}{a}$ and $r_1 r_2 = \dfrac{c}{a}$.

sum of a series The limit of the partial sums of a series.

sums of cubes pattern For all a and b: $a^3 + b^3 = (a + b)(a^2 - ab + b^2)$.

summation notation A shorthand notation used to restate a series; also called Σ-*notation* or *sigma notation*.

supplements theorem For all θ in degrees: $\sin \theta = \sin(180° - \theta)$.

surface of revolution A surface which is generated by rotating a curve in a plane about a line.

system A set of conditions joined by the word "and"; a special kind of compound sentence.

tangent of θ (tan θ) In a right triangle with acute angle θ, $\tan \theta = \dfrac{\text{length of leg opposite } \theta}{\text{length of leg adjacent to } \theta}$; in general, $\dfrac{\sin \theta}{\cos \theta}$ provided $\cos \theta \neq 0$.

term of a sequence An element of a sequence.

theorems Statements that can be proved in a mathematical system.

3-dimensional coordinate system A coordinate system used to locate all the points in 3-space.

transformation A one-to-one correspondence between sets of points.

trigonometric ratios The ratios of the lengths of the sides in a right triangle.

translation The transformation that maps (x, y) onto $(x + h, y + k)$ is a translation of h units horizontally and k units vertically and is denoted by $T_{h,k}$.

trial One occurence of an experiment.

triangular matrix A matrix which has all zeros below the diagonal from top left to bottom right.

trinomial A polynomial with three terms.

unbiased coin A coin that has an equal probability of landing on either side; also called a *fair coin*.

union of sets The set consisting of those values in either one or both sets.

unit circle The circle with center at the origin and radius 1.

value of a function If $y = f(x)$, the value of y.

variable A symbol that can be replaced by any one of a set of numbers or other objects.

varies directly as In a direct variation, the same as "directly proportional to."

varies inversely as In an inverse variation, the same as "inversely proportional to."

velocity The rate of change of distance with respect to time.

vertex form of an equation of a parabola An equation of the form $y - k = a(x - h)^2$ where (h, k) is the vertex of the parabola.

vertex (vertices) of an ellipse or hyperbola A point (points) of intersection of the ellipse or hyperbola and the line containing its foci.

vertex of a parabola The intersection of a parabola and its axis of symmetry.

vertical line A line with an equation of the form $x = b$; a line with no slope.

vertical-line test for functions No vertical line intersects the graph of a function in more than one point.

vertical scale change The stretching or shrinking of a figure in only the vertical direction.

whole numbers The set $\{0, 1, 2, 3, 4, 5, \ldots\}$.

window The part of the coordinate grid shown on the screen of an automatic grapher.

x-intercept The value of x at a point where a graph crosses the x-axis.

xy-plane The plane in 3-space determined by the x-axis and y-axis.

xz-plane The plane in 3-space determined by the x-axis and z-axis.

y-intercept The value of y at a point where a graph crosses the y-axis.

yz-plane The plane in 3-space determined by the y-axis and z-axis.

z-axis In a 3-dimensional coordinate system, the axis perpendicular to the xy-plane.

z-coordinate The third coordinate in an ordered triple (x, y, z).

zero exponent theorem If b is a nonzero real number, $b^0 = 1$.

zero of a function An x-intercept of the graph of a function.

zero product theorem For all a and b: $ab = 0$ if and only if $a = 0$ or $b = 0$.

zoom A feature on an automatic grapher which enables the window of a graph to be changed without retyping intervals for x and y.

Professional Sourcebook For UCSMP

1 | Overview of UCSMP

The Reasons for UCSMP

■ Recommendations for Change

The mathematics curriculum has undergone changes in every country of the world throughout this century, as a result of an increasing number of students staying in school longer, a greater number of technically competent workers and citizens being needed, and because of major advances in mathematics itself. In the last generation, these developments have been accelerated due to the widespread appearance of computers with their unprecedented abilities to handle and display information.

In the last 100 years, periodically there have been national groups examining the curriculum in light of these changes in society. (A study of these reports can be found in *A History of Mathematics Education in the United States and Canada*, the 30th Yearbook of the National Council of Teachers of Mathematics, 1970.) The most recent era of reports can be said to have begun in the years 1975–1980, with the publication of reports by various national mathematics organizations calling attention to serious problems in the education of our youth.

Beginning in 1980, these reports were joined by governmental and private reports on the state of American education with broad recommendations for school practice. Two of these are notable for their specific remarks about mathematics education.

1983:   National Commission on Excellence in Education. *A Nation At Risk.*

"The teaching of mathematics in high school should equip graduates to: (a) understand geometric and algebraic concepts; (b) understand elementary probability and statistics; (c) apply mathematics in everyday situations; and (d) estimate, approximate, measure, and test the accuracy of their calculations. In addition to the traditional sequence of studies available for college-bound students, new, equally demanding mathematics curricula need to be developed for those who do not plan to continue their formal education immediately." (p. 25)

1983:   College Board (Project EQuality). *Academic Preparation for College: What Students Need to Know and Be Able to Do.*

All students (college-bound or not) should have:
"The ability to apply mathematical techniques in the solution of real-life problems and to recognize when to apply those techniques.
Familiarity with the language, notation, and deductive nature of mathematics and the ability to express quantitative ideas with precision.
The ability to use computers and calculators.
Familiarity with the basic concepts of statistics and statistical reasoning.
Knowledge in considerable depth and detail of algebra, geometry, and functions." (p. 20)

The specific remarks about school mathematics in these documents for the most part mirror what appeared in the earlier reports. Thus, **given what seemed to be a broad consensus on the problems and desirable changes in pre-college mathematics instruction, it was decided at the outset of UCSMP, that UCSMP would not attempt to form its own set of recommendations, but undertake the task of translating the existing recommendations into the reality of classrooms and schools.**

At the secondary (7–12) level, these reports respond to two generally perceived problems pursuant to mathematics education.

GENERAL PROBLEM 1: Students do not learn enough mathematics by the time they leave school.

Specifically:

(A) Many students lack the mathematics background necessary to succeed in college, on the job, or in daily affairs.

(B) Even those students who possess mathematical skills are not introduced to enough applications of the mathematics they know.

(C) Students do not get enough experience with problems and questions that require some thought before answering.

(D) Many students terminate their study of mathematics too soon, not realizing the importance mathematics has in later schooling and in the marketplace.

(E) Students do not read mathematics books and, as a result, do not learn to become independent learners capable of acquiring mathematics outside of school when the need arises.

These situations lead us to want to **upgrade students' achievement.**

GENERAL PROBLEM 2: The school mathematics curriculum has not kept up with changes in mathematics and the ways in which mathematics is used.

Specifically:

(A) Current mathematics curricula have not taken into account today's calculator and computer technology.

(B) Students who do succeed in secondary school mathematics are prepared for calculus, but are not equipped for the other mathematics they will encounter in college.

(C) Statistical ideas are found everywhere, from newspapers to research studies, but are not found in most secondary school mathematics curricula.

(D) The emergence of computer science has increased the importance of a background in discrete mathematics.

(E) Mathematics is now applied to areas outside the realm of the physical sciences, as much as within the field itself, but these applications are rarely taught and even more rarely tested.

(F) Estimation and approximation techniques are important in all of mathematics, from arithmetic on.

These existing situations lead us to a desire to **update the mathematics curriculum.**

Since the inception of UCSMP, reports from national groups of mathematics educators have reiterated the above problems, and research has confirmed their existence. Three reports are of special significance to UCSMP.

Universities have for many years had to recognize that mathematics encompasses far more than algebra, geometry, and analysis. The term **mathematical sciences** is an umbrella designation which includes traditional mathematics as well as a number of other disciplines. The largest of these other disciplines today are statistics, computer science, and applied mathematics. In 1983, the Conference Board of the Mathematical Sciences produced a report, *The Mathematical Sciences Curriculum: What Is Still Fundamental and What Is Not.* THE UCSMP GRADES 7–12 CAN BE CONSIDERED TO BE THE FIRST MATHEMATICAL SCIENCES CURRICULUM.

The Second International Mathematics Study (SIMS) was conducted in 1981–82 and involved 23 populations in 21 countries. At the eighth-grade level, virtually all students attend school in all those countries. At the 12th-grade level, the population tested consisted of those who are in the normal college preparatory courses, which, in the United States, include precalculus and calculus classes.

The UCSMP grades 7–12 can be considered to be the first mathematical sciences curriculum.

At the eighth-grade level, our students scored at or below the international average on all five subtests: arithmetic, measurement, algebra, geometry, and statistics. We are far below the top: Japan looked at the test and decided it was too easy for their 8th-graders, and so gave it at 7th grade. Still, the median Japanese 7th-grader performed at the 95th percentile of United States 8th-graders. These kinds of results have been confirmed in other studies, comparing students at lower-grade levels.

At the twelfth-grade level, about 13% of our population is enrolled in precalculus or calculus; the mean among developed countries is about 16%. Thus, the United States no longer keeps more students in mathematics than other developed countries, yet our advanced placement students do not perform well when compared to their peers in other countries. SIMS found:

1987: Second International Mathematics Study (SIMS). *The Underachieving Curriculum.*

In the U.S., the achievement of the Calculus classes, the nation's **best** mathematics students, was at or near the average achievement of the advanced secondary school mathematics students in other countries. (In most countries, **all** advanced mathematics students take calculus. In the U.S., only about one-fifth do.) The achievement of the U.S. Precalculus students (the majority of twelfth grade college-preparatory students) was substantially below the international average. In some cases the U.S. ranked with the lower one-fourth of all countries in the Study, and was the lowest of the advanced industrialized countries. (*The Underachieving Curriculum, p. vii.*)

The situation is, of course, even worse for those who do not take precalculus mathematics in high school. Such students either have performed poorly in their last mathematics course, a situation which has caused them not to go on in mathematics, or they were performing poorly in junior high school and had to take remedial mathematics as 9th-graders. If these students go to college, they invariably take remedial mathematics, which is taught at a faster pace than in high school, and the failure rates in such courses often exceed 40%. If they do not go to college but join the job market, they lack the mathematics needed to understand today's technology. IT IS NO UNDERSTATEMENT TO SAY THAT UCSMP HAS RECEIVED ITS FUNDING FROM BUSINESS AND INDUSTRY BECAUSE THOSE WHO LEAVE SCHOOLING TO JOIN THE WORK FORCE ARE WOEFULLY WEAK IN THE MATHEMATICS THEY WILL NEED.

SIMS recommended steps to renew school mathematics in the United States. **The UCSMP secondary curriculum implements the curriculum recommendations of the Second International Mathematics Study.**

In 1986, the National Council of Teachers of Mathematics began an ambitious effort to detail the curriculum it would like to see in schools. The "NCTM Standards," as they have come to be called, involve both content and methodology. The *Standards* document is divided into four sections, K–4, 5–8, 9–12, and Evaluation. Space limits our discussion here to just a few quotes from the 5–8 and 9–12 standards.

It is no understatement to say that UCSMP has received its funding from business and industry because those who leave schooling to join the work force are woefully weak in the mathematics they will need.

1989:   National Council of Teachers of Mathematics.
*Curriculum and Evaluation Standards for School
Mathematics*

"The 5–8 curriculum should include the following features:

■ Problem situations that establish the need for new ideas and motivate students should serve as the context for mathematics in grades 5–8. Although a specific idea might be forgotten, the context in which it is learned can be remembered and the idea can be re-created. In developing the problem situations, teachers should emphasize the application to real-world problems as well as to other settings relevant to middle school students.

■ Communication with and about mathematics and mathematical reasoning should permeate the 5–8 curriculum.

■ A broad range of topics should be taught, including number concepts, computation, estimation, functions, algebra, statistics, probability, geometry, and measurement. Although each of these areas is valid mathematics in its own right, they should be taught together as an integrated whole, not as isolated topics; the connections between them should be a prominent feature of the curriculum.

■ Technology, including calculators, computers, and videos, should be used when appropriate. These devices and formats free students from tedious computations and allow them to concentrate on problem solving and other important content. They also give them new means to explore content. As paper-and-pencil computation becomes less important, the skills and understanding required to make proficient use of calculators and computers become more important." (pp. 66–67)

"The standards for grades 9–12 are based on the following assumptions:

■ Students entering grade 9 will have experienced mathematics in the context of the broad, rich curriculum outlined in the K–8 standards.

The UCSMP secondary curriculum is the first full mathematics curriculum that is consistent with the recommendations of the NCTM Standards.

■ The level of computational proficiency suggested in the K–8 standards will be expected of all students; however, no student will be denied access to the study of mathematics in grades 9–12 because of a lack of computational facility.

■ Although arithmetic computation will not be a direct object of study in grades 9–12, conceptual and procedural understandings of number, numeration, and operations, and the ability to make estimations and approximations and to judge the reasonableness of results will be strengthened in the context of applications and problem solving, including those situations dealing with issues of scientific computation.

■ Scientific calculators with graphing capabilities will be available to all students at all times.

■ A computer will be available at all times in every classroom for demonstration purposes, and all students will have access to computers for individual and group work.

■ At least three years of mathematical study will be required of all secondary school students.

■ These three years of mathematical study will revolve around a core curriculum differentiated by the depth and breadth of the treatment of topics and by the nature of applications.

■ Four years of mathematical study will be required of all college-intending students.

■ These four years of mathematical study will revolve around a broadened curriculum that includes extensions of the core topics and for which calculus is no longer viewed as *the* capstone experience.

■ All students will study appropriate mathematics during their senior year." (pp. 124–125)

THE UCSMP SECONDARY CURRICULUM IS THE FIRST FULL MATHEMATICS CURRICULUM THAT IS CONSISTENT WITH THE RECOMMENDATIONS OF THE NCTM STANDARDS.

■ Accomplishing the Goals

We at UCSMP believe that the goals of the various reform groups since 1975 can be accomplished, but not without a substantial reworking of the curriculum. It is not enough simply to insert applications, a bit of statistics, and take students a few times a year to a computer. Currently the greatest amount of time in arithmetic is spent on calculation, in algebra on manipulating polynomials and rational expressions, in geometry on proof, in advanced algebra and later courses on functions. These topics—the core of the curriculum—are the most affected by technology.

It is also not enough to raise graduation requirements, although that is the simplest action to take. Increases in requirements characteristically lead to one of two situations. If the courses are kept the same, the result is typically a greater number of failures and even a greater number of dropouts. If the courses are eased, the result is lower performance for many students as they are brought through a weakened curriculum.

The fundamental problem, as SIMS noted, is the curriculum, and the fundamental problem in the curriculum is **time.** There is not enough time in the current 4-year algebra-geometry-algebra-precalculus curriculum to prepare students for calculus, and the recommendations are asking students to learn even more content.

Fortunately, there is time to be had, because the existing curriculum wastes time. It underestimates what students know when they enter the classroom and needlessly reviews what students have already learned. This needless review has been documented by Jim Flanders, a UCSMP staff member ("How Much of the Content in Mathematics Textbooks is New?" *Arithmetic Teacher,* September, 1987). Examining textbooks of the early 1980s, Flanders reports that at grade 2 there is little new. In grades 3–5, about half the pages have something new on them. But over half the pages in grades 6–8 are totally review.

And then in the 9th grade the axe falls. Flanders found that almost 90% of the pages of first-year algebra texts have content new to the student. The student, having sat for years in mathematics classes where little was new, is overwhelmed. Some people interpret the overwhelming as the student "not being ready" for algebra, but we interpret it as the student being swamped by the pace. When you have been in a classroom in which at most only 1 of 3 days is devoted to anything new, you are not ready for a new idea every day.

This amount of review in grades K–8, coupled with the magnitude of review in previous years, effectively decelerates students at least 1–2 years compared to students in other countries. It explains why almost all industrialized countries of the world, except the U.S. and Canada (and some French-speaking countries who do geometry before algebra), can begin concentrated study of algebra in the 7th or 8th grade.

Thus we believe that ALGEBRA SHOULD BE TAUGHT ONE YEAR EARLIER TO MOST STUDENTS THAN IS CURRENTLY THE CASE.

However, we do not believe students should take calculus one year earlier than they do presently. It seems that most students who take four years of college preparatory mathematics successfully in high schools do not begin college with calculus. As an example, consider the data reported by Bert Waits and Frank Demana in the *Mathematics Teacher* (January, 1988). Of students entering Ohio State University with exactly four years of college preparatory high-school mathematics, only 8% placed into calculus on the Ohio State mathematics placement test. The majority placed into precalculus, with 31% requiring one semester and 42% requiring two semesters of work. The remaining 19% placed into remedial courses below precalculus.

Those students who take algebra in the 8th grade and are successful in calculus at the 12th grade are given quite a bit more than the normal four years of college preparatory mathematics in their "honors" or "advanced" courses. It is not stretching the point too much to say that they take five years of mathematics crammed into four years.

Thus, even with the current curriculum, four years are not enough to take a typical student from algebra to calculus. Given that the latest recommendations ask for students to learn more mathematics, **we believe five years of college preparatory mathematics *beginning with algebra* are necessary to provide the time for students to learn the mathematics they need for college in the 1990s.** The UCSMP secondary curriculum is designed with that in mind.

. . . algebra should be taught one year earlier to most students than is currently the case.

The UCSMP Secondary Curriculum

The UCSMP curriculum for grades 7–12 consists of these six courses:

Transition Mathematics

Algebra

Geometry

Advanced Algebra

Functions, Statistics, and Trigonometry with Computers

Precalculus and Discrete Mathematics

EACH COURSE IS MEANT TO STAND ALONE. Each course has also been tested alone. HOWEVER, TO TAKE BEST ADVANTAGE OF THESE MATERIALS, AND TO HAVE THEM APPROPRIATE FOR THE GREATEST NUMBER OF STUDENTS, IT IS PREFERABLE TO USE THEM IN SEQUENCE.

Each course is meant to stand alone. . . . However, to take best advantage of these materials, and to have them appropriate for the greatest number of students, it is preferable to use them in sequence.

■ Content Features

Transition Mathematics: This text weaves three themes—applied arithmetic, pre-algebra and pre-geometry—by focusing on arithmetic operations in mathematics and the real world. Variables are used as pattern generalizers, abbreviations in formulas, and unknowns in problems, and are represented on the number line and graphed in the coordinate plane. Basic arithmetic and algebraic skills are connected to corresponding geometry topics.

Algebra: This text has a scope far wider than most other algebra texts. It uses statistics and geometry as settings for work with linear expressions and sentences. Probability provides a context for algebraic fractions, functions, and set ideas. There is much work with graphing. Applications motivate all topics, and include exponential growth and compound interest.

Geometry: This text presents coordinates, transformations, measurement formulas, and three-dimensional figures in the first half of the book. Concentrated work with proof-writing is delayed until midyear and later, following a carefully sequenced development of the logical and conceptual precursors to proof.

Advanced Algebra: This course emphasizes facility with algebraic expressions and forms, especially linear and quadratic forms, powers and roots, and functions based on these concepts. Students study logarithmic, trigonometric, polynomial, and other special functions both for their abstract properties and as tools for modeling real-world situations. A geometry course or its equivalent is a prerequisite, for geometric ideas are utilized throughout.

Functions, Statistics, and Trigonometry with Computers (FST): FST integrates statistical and algebraic concepts, and previews calculus in work with functions and intuitive notions of limits. Computers are assumed available for student use in plotting functions, analyzing data, and simulating experiments. Enough trigonometry is available to constitute a standard precalculus course in trigonometry and circular functions.

Precalculus and Discrete Mathematics (PDM): PDM integrates the background students must have, to be successful in calculus, with the discrete mathematics helpful for computer study. The study of number systems, three-dimensional coordinate geometry, and some linear algebra is also included. Mathematical thinking, including specific attention to formal logic and proof, is a theme throughout.

■ General Features

Wider Scope: Geometry and discrete mathematics are present in all courses. Substantial amounts of statistics are integrated into the study of algebra and functions. The history of concepts and recent developments in mathematics and its applications are included as part of the lessons themselves.

Reality Orientation: Each mathematical idea is studied in detail for its applications to the understanding of real-world situations, or the solving of problems like those found in the real world. The reality orientation extends also to the approaches allowed the student in working out problems. Students are expected to use scientific calculators. Calculators are assumed throughout the series (and should be allowed on tests), because virtually all individuals who use mathematics today use calculators.

Problem Solving: Like skills, problem solving must be practiced. When practiced, problem solving becomes far less difficult. All lessons contain a variety of questions so that students do not blindly copy one question to do the next. Explorations are a feature of the first four years, and Projects are offered in the last two years. Some problem-solving techniques are so important that at times they (rather than the problems) are the focus of instruction.

Enhancing Performance: Each book's format is designed to maximize the acquisition of both skills and concepts, with lessons meant to take one day to cover. Within each lesson there is review of material from previous lessons from that chapter or from previous chapters. This gives the student more time to learn the material. The lessons themselves are sequenced into carefully constructed chapters. Progress Self-Test and Chapter Review questions, keyed to objectives in all the dimensions of understanding, are then used to solidify performance of skills and concepts from the chapter, so that they may be applied later with confidence. (See pages T35–T36 for more detail.)

Reading: Reading is emphasized throughout. Students can read; they must learn to read mathematics in order to become able to use mathematics outside of school. Every lesson has reading and contains questions covering that reading. (See page T37 for more detail.)

Understanding: Four dimensions of understanding are emphasized: skill in carrying out various algorithms; developing and using mathematical properties and relationships; applying mathematics in realistic situations; and representing or picturing mathematical concepts. We call this the SPUR approach: **S**kills, **P**roperties, **U**ses, **R**epresentations. On occasion, a fifth dimension of understanding, the historical dimension, is discussed. (See pages T38–T39 for more detail.)

Technology: Scientific calculators are recommended because they use an order of operations closer to that found in algebra and have numerous keys that are helpful in understanding concepts at this level. Work with computers is carefully sequenced within each year and between the years, with gradual gain in sophistication until FST, where computers are an essential element. In all courses, integrated computer exercises show how the computer can be used as a helpful tool in doing mathematics. Students are expected to run and modify programs, but are not taught programming. (See pages T40–T43 for more detail.)

■ Target Populations

We believe that all high-school graduates should take courses through *Advanced Algebra*, that all students planning to go to college should take courses through *Functions, Statistics, and Trigonometry with Computers*, and that students planning majors in technical areas should take all six UCSMP courses.

The fundamental principle in placing students into the first of these courses is that entry should not be based on age, but on mathematical knowledge. Our studies indicate that about 10% of students nationally are ready for *Transition Mathematics* at 6th grade, about another 40% at 7th grade, another 20% at 8th grade, and another 10–15% at 9th grade. We caution that these percentages are national, not local percentages, and the variability in our nation is enormous. We have tested the materials in school districts where few students are at grade level, where *Transition Mathematics* is appropriate for no more than the upper half of 8th-graders. We have tested also in school districts where as many as 90% of the students have successfully used *Transition Mathematics* in 7th grade.

However, the percentages are not automatic. Students who do not reach 7th-grade competence until the 9th-grade level often do not possess the study habits necessary for successful completion of these courses. At the 9th-grade level, *Transition Mathematics* has been substituted successfully either for a traditional pre-algebra course or for the first year of an algebra course spread out over two years. It does not work as a substitute for a general mathematics course in which there is no expectation that students will take algebra the following year.

On page T27 is a description of this curriculum and the populations for which it is intended. The percentiles are national percentiles on a 7th-grade standardized mathematics test using 7th-grade norms, and apply to students entering the program with *Transition Mathematics*. Some school districts have felt that students should also be reading at least at a 7th-grade reading level as well. See page T28 for advice when starting with a later course.

Top 10%: The top 10% nationally reach the 7th-grade level of competence a year early. They are ready for *Transition Mathematics* in 6th grade and take it then. They proceed through the entire curriculum by 11th grade and can take calculus in 12th grade. We recommend that these students be expected to do the Extensions suggested in this Teacher's Edition. Teachers may also wish to enrich courses for these students further with problems from mathematics contests.

50th–90th percentile: These students should be expected to take mathematics at least through the 11th grade, by which time they will have the mathematics needed for all college majors except those in the hard sciences and engineering. For that they need 12th-grade mathematics.

30th–70th percentile: These students begin *Transition Mathematics* one year later, in 8th grade. The college-bound student in this curriculum is more likely to take four years of mathematics because the last course is hands-on with computers and provides the kind of mathematics needed for any major.

15th–50th percentile: Students who do not reach the 7th-grade level in mathematics until 9th grade or later should not be tracked into courses that put them further behind. Rather, they should be put into this curriculum and counseled on study skills. The logic is simple: mathematics is too important to be ignored. If one is behind in one's mathematical knowledge, the need is to work more at it, not less.

Even if a student begins with *Transition Mathematics* at 9th grade, that student can finish *Advanced Algebra* by the time of graduation from high school. That would be enough mathematics to enable the student to get into most colleges.

UCSMP Target Populations in Grades 7–12

Each course is meant to stand alone. However, to take best advantage of these materials, and have them appropriate for the greatest number of students, it is preferable to use them in sequence. Although it is suggested that students begin with *Transition Mathematics,* students may enter the UCSMP curriculum at any point. Below is a brief description of the UCSMP curriculum and the populations for which it is intended.

The top 10% of students are ready for *Transition Mathematics* at 6th grade. These students can proceed through the entire curriculum by 11th grade and take calculus in the 12th grade.

Students in the 50th–90th percentile on a 7th-grade standardized mathematics test should be ready to take *Transition Mathematics* in 7th grade.

Students who do not reach the 7th-grade level in mathematics until the 8th grade **(in the 30th–70th percentile)** begin *Transition Mathematics* in 8th grade.

Students who don't reach the 7th-grade level in mathematics until the 9th grade **(in the 15th–50th percentile)** begin *Transition Mathematics* in the 9th grade.

Grade				
6	Transition Mathematics			
7	Algebra	Transition Mathematics		
8	Geometry	Algebra	Transition Mathematics	
9	Advanced Algebra	Geometry	Algebra	Transition Mathematics
10	Functions, Statistics, and Trigonometry with Computers	Advanced Algebra	Geometry	Algebra
11	Precalculus and Discrete Mathematics	Functions, Statistics, and Trigonometry with Computers	Advanced Algebra	Geometry
12	Calculus (Not part of UCSMP)	Precalculus and Discrete Mathematics	Functions, Statistics, and Trigonometry with Computers	Advanced Algebra

Starting in the Middle of the Series

From the beginning, every UCSMP course has been designed so that it could be used independently of other UCSMP courses. Accordingly, about half of the testing of UCSMP courses after *Transition Mathematics* has been with students who have not had any previous UCSMP courses. We have verified that any of the UCSMP courses can be taken successfully following the typical prerequisite courses in the standard curriculum.

ALGEBRA:
No additional prerequisites other than those needed for success in any algebra course are needed for success in UCSMP *Algebra*. Students who have studied *Transition Mathematics* tend to cover more of UCSMP *Algebra* than other students because they tend to know more algebra, because they are accustomed to the style of the book, and because they have been introduced to more of the applications of algebra.

UCSMP *Algebra* prepares students for any standard geometry course.

GEOMETRY:
No additional prerequisites other than those needed for success in any geometry course are needed for success in UCSMP *Geometry*. UCSMP *Geometry* can be used with faster, average, and slower students who have these prerequisites. Prior study of *Transition Mathematics* and UCSMP *Algebra* insures this background, but this content is also found in virtually all existing middle school or junior high school texts.

Classes of students who have studied UCSMP *Algebra* tend to cover more UCSMP *Geometry* than other classes because they know more geometry and are better at the algebra used in geometry.

Students who have studied UCSMP *Geometry* are ready for any second-year algebra text.

ADVANCED ALGEBRA:
UCSMP *Advanced Algebra* should not be taken before a geometry course but can be used following any standard geometry text. Students who have studied UCSMP *Advanced Algebra* are prepared for courses commonly found at the senior level, including trigonometry or precalculus courses.

FUNCTIONS, STATISTICS, AND TRIGONOMETRY WITH COMPUTERS:
FST assumes that students have completed a second-year algebra course. **No additional prerequisites other than those found in any second-year algebra text are needed for success in *FST*.**

PRECALCULUS AND DISCRETE MATHEMATICS
PDM can be taken successfully by students who have had *FST*, by students who have had typical senior level courses that include study of trigonometry and functions, and by top students who have successfully completed full advanced algebra and trigonometry courses.

PDM provides the background necessary for any typical calculus course, either at the high school or college level, including advanced placement calculus courses.

Development Cycle for UCSMP Texts

The development of each text has been in four stages. First, the overall goals for each course are created by UCSMP in consultation with a national advisory board of distinguished professors, and through discussion with classroom teachers, school administrators, and district and state mathematics supervisors.

The Advisory Board for the Secondary Component at the time of this planning consisted of Arthur F. Coxford, Jr., University of Michigan; David Duncan, University of Northern Iowa; James Fey, University of Maryland; Glenda Lappan, Michigan State University; Anthony Ralston, State University of New York at Buffalo; and James Schultz, Ohio State University.

As part of this stage, UCSMP devoted an annual School Conference, whose participants were mathematics supervisors and teachers, to discuss major issues in a particular area of the curriculum. Past conferences have centered on the following issues:

1984 Changing the Curriculum in Grades 7 and 8

1985 Changing Standards in School Algebra

1986 Functions, Computers, and Statistics in Secondary Mathematics

1987 Pre-College Mathematics

1988 Mathematics Teacher Education for Grades 7–12

At the second stage, UCSMP selects authors who write first drafts of the courses. Half of all UCSMP authors currently teach mathematics in secondary schools, and all authors and editors for the first five courses have secondary school teaching experience. The textbook authors or their surrogates initially teach the first drafts of Secondary Component texts, so that revision may benefit from first-hand classroom experience.

After revision by the authors or editors, materials enter the third stage in the text development. Classes of teachers not connected with the project use the books, and independent evaluators closely study student achievement, attitudes, and issues related to implementation. For the first three years in the series, this stage involved a formative evaluation in six to ten schools, and all teachers who used the materials periodically met at the university to provide feedback to UCSMP staff for a second revision. For the last three years in the series, this stage has involved a second pilot.

The fourth stage consists of a wider comparative evaluation. For the first three books, this evaluation has involved approximately 40 classrooms and thousands of students per book in schools all over the country. For the last three books in the series, this stage has involved a careful formative evaluation. As a result of these studies, the books have been revised for commercial publication by Scott, Foresman and Company, into the edition you are now reading. (See pages T46–T48 for a summary of this research.)

2 UCSMP *Advanced Algebra*

Problems UCSMP *Advanced Algebra* Is Trying to Address

This book is different from many other second-year or advanced algebra books. The differences are due to its attempt to respond to six serious problems which cannot be treated by small changes in content or approach.

PROBLEM 1: Large numbers of students do not know why they need algebra.

Some advanced algebra courses have been motivated almost exclusively by the needs of a minority of their population, those who will take calculus two or three years later. Other advanced algebra courses consist entirely of dozens of problems of one type, followed by dozens of another, or of one skill after another, introduced without motivation, ostensibly designed for the less-gifted student, but actually of ultimate use to few, if any students.

Most word problems in those courses do not constitute applications; problems like them are not encountered outside of school. It is no surprise, then, that many adults—even many of the most educated adults—wonder why they studied algebra for so long. We believe that this is a result of the kind of algebra courses they studied, and the lack of applications in them. The content of advanced algebra has many real-world applications.

The UCSMP *Advanced Algebra* response: Instead of holding off on applications until after skills have been developed, applications are used to motivate virtually all concepts and skills. The ability to apply algebra is made a priority.

Word problems that have little or no use are replaced by more meaningful types of problems. Algebra is continually connected with the arithmetic, algebra, and geometry the student already knows. WE HAVE EVIDENCE FROM OUR STUDIES THAT WE CAN GREATLY REDUCE AND ALMOST ELIMINATE THE "WHY ARE WE STUDYING THIS?" KIND OF QUESTION.

PROBLEM 2: Students do not have enough skill at algebraic manipulation and sentence-solving.

Our response to this problem covers more than just this course. In general, the evidence is that students are rather skillful at simple routine problems, but have a great deal of difficulty with problems involving complicated numbers, different wordings, or new contexts. It is obvious that in order to obtain such skill, students must see problems with all sorts of numbers, a variety of wordings, and many different contexts.

We believe that present courses, which are preoccupied with skill, demonstrate that few students can acquire considerable skill in only two years of algebra study. In UCSMP, we give specific attention to algebraic skills over six years. Simple linear equations, graphing, and simplifications are in *Transition Mathematics*. *Algebra* stresses linear and quadratic sentence-solving, polynomial manipulations, some work with exponents, and more graphing. *Geometry* reviews the work with lines, slopes, radicals, proportions, systems, and formulas. *Advanced Algebra* emphasizes further manipulations with linear and quadratic expressions, powers, roots, logarithms, trigonometric and other functions.

> **We have evidence from our studies that we can greatly reduce and almost eliminate the "Why are we studying this?" kind of question.**

In UCSMP *Advanced Algebra* we employ a four-stage approach to develop skill.

■ **Stage 1** involves a concentrated introduction to the ideas surrounding the skill: why it is needed, how it is done, and the kinds of problems that can be solved with it. Most books are organized to have this stage, because teachers recognize that explanations of an idea require time. At the end of this stage, typically only the best students have the skill. But in UCSMP *Advanced Algebra* this is only the beginning.

■ **Stage 2** takes place during subsequent lessons in the chapter and consists of questions designed to establish some competence in the skill. These are found in the Review questions. By the end of the lessons of the chapter, most students should have some competence in the skills, but some may not have enough.

■ **Stage 3** involves mastery learning. At the end of each chapter is a Progress Self-Test for students to take and judge how they are doing. Worked-out solutions are included to provide feedback and help to the student. This is followed by the Chapter Review to enable students to acquire those skills they didn't have when taking the Progress Self-Test. Teachers are expected to spend 1–3 days on these sections to give students time to reach mastery. By the end of this stage, students should have gained mastery, at least at the level of typical students covering the content.

■ **Stage 4** continues the review through the daily Review sections in *subsequent* chapters. Vital algebra skills receive consistent emphasis throughout the book. Included also are skill sequences consisting of 3 to 4 questions that provide practice on related problems. The evidence (see pages T46–T48) is that this four-stage process enables students to gain competence over a wider range of content than comparable students normally possess.

PROBLEM 3: Even students who succeed in advanced algebra often forget the geometry they learned.

Most advanced algebra texts are written as if the student had never studied geometry. This creates two difficulties: the student forgets the geometry that was learned, and the student does not integrate the important ideas found in geometry with their corresponding applications in algebra.

In UCSMP *Advanced Algebra*, we assume the student has studied geometry, and we are thus able to use geometry in four ways. First, we utilize measurement relationships (formulas for area or volume, ratios in similar figures, and so on) as subject matter to be analyzed from an algebraic point of view. Second, we apply geometric concepts to the study of algebra (such as the use of transformations to study graphs). Third, we emphasize graphing to take advantage of the geometric intuitions students have (such as the sine and cosine graphs are congruent, all parabolas are similar). Fourth, we use the language developed when studying geometry as a mathematical system (such as postulate, theorem, counterexample, and proof) throughout the text.

We do our concentrated work with advanced algebra *after* geometry, because we can so easily take advantage of that geometry. The reverse is not as productive; a student who has taken two years of algebra does not possess much more mathematics to apply in elementary geometry than a student who has taken one. Furthermore, we believe as many students as possible should have concentrated work in geometry. Thus we view the algebra—algebra—geometry sequence used in some schools as not as effective as the algebra—geometry—algebra sequence found in UCSMP.

PROBLEM 4: Students don't read.

Students using traditional texts tell us they don't read because (1) the text is uninteresting, and (2) they don't have to read—the teacher explains it for them. But students *must* learn to read for future success in mathematics. Our response to (1): Every lesson of this book contains reading that we think is informative and interesting. This reading is a resource for information, for examples of how to do problems, for the history of major ideas, for applications of the ideas, for connections between ideas in one place in the book and in another, and for motivation. Questions Covering the Reading in every lesson test student comprehension of the text.

Our response to (2): Because evidence shows that our students can read and understand the text, teachers have the freedom to teach in a variety of ways. It is not necessary for the teacher to explain every day what the text says. In particular, the teacher should not say "You don't have to do problems 20 to 26 because we haven't covered them yet." The teacher can concentrate on developing further examples and explanations specifically tailored to his or her students and the teacher's special strengths.

Some teachers of earlier UCSMP courses were skeptical at first about the amount of reading in the book. As the year progresses, they tend to view the reading as one of the strongest features of this series. Some teachers felt that UCSMP materials were teaching reading comprehension; they all felt that the requirement to read helped develop thinkers who were more critical and aware.

Student comments confirm this. In 1986–1987 one group of eighth-grade students used UCSMP *Algebra* in their home school. They simultaneously studied algebra from a standard text at a nearby high school. Their comments comparing the two texts: ". . . the UCSMP book allows me to figure out things for myself. I feel it makes me more independent in terms of doing my homework." "UCSMP is easier to understand." "The UCSMP homework is much easier to do at home. Applying the Reading (the section of problems now called 'Applying the Mathematics') makes you think."

PROBLEM 5: *The mathematics curriculum has been lagging behind today's widely available and inexpensive technology.*

Despite the nearly universal availability of calculators and widespread availability of computers, most contemporary textbooks still do not integrate this technology into the course scheme. All UCSMP secondary courses assume that students have access to scientific calculators. UCSMP *Advanced Algebra* incorporates the use of an automatic grapher, either through a graphing calculator or a computer. This enables students to acquire a far more accurate view of functions than they would otherwise have.

Many other connections with computers are given in this course. We give templates for programs and talk about computer notation and language. In this we are following current practice in schools. But the influence of computers ranges farther than this. Certain content has been included because of its importance in a computer age, including discrete and continuous domains, iteration, interpretation of algorithms, as well as a great deal of graphing. (See pages T40–T43.)

PROBLEM 6: *Even educated adults sometimes have not been introduced to fundamentally important mathematical ideas.*

Mathematics was created rather recently in human history, and mathematics is a growing subject. These important ideas are often ignored in students' mathematical education, but without this knowledge a person must find it difficult to understand why the mathematics important in one age might not be as important in another. In UCSMP *Advanced Algebra*, we consider the development of mathematics as an important topic.

Trigonometry is often left to later courses taken by far fewer students. Matrices, counting problems, probability, statistics, and 3-dimensional analytic geometry are often never encountered. We believe that every educated adult should be exposed to these topics, at least to the extent covered in UCSMP *Advanced Algebra*.

Goals of UCSMP ADVANCED ALGEBRA

It would be too easy and somewhat misleading to state that the goals of UCSMP *Advanced Algebra* are to remove forever the problems detailed above. Obviously we want to make headway on solving these. A major goal of UCSMP *Advanced Algebra* is for students to develop skills in manipulating linear, quadratic, exponential, logarithmic, and trigonometric expressions and sentences.

The guiding principles for including a topic in UCSMP *Advanced Algebra* were: (1) suitable level of difficulty for average 10th-graders; (2) the importance of the topic for daily living, career development, or future study of mathematics; and (3) the extent to which the topics as a whole provide a balanced view of algebra as preparation not just for calculus, but also for discrete mathematics, statistics, probability, and linear algebra.

We attempt to convey to the student, through historical references and references to recent mathematical work (such as fractals), that algebra continues to develop as an area of human activity. This is to reach for a more lofty goal. WE WANT STUDENTS TO VIEW THEIR STUDY OF MATHEMATICS AS WORTHWHILE, AS FULL OF INTERESTING AND ENTERTAINING INFORMATION, AS RELATED TO ALMOST EVERY ENDEAVOR. We want them to realize that mathematics is still growing and is changing fast. We want them to look for and recognize mathematics in places they haven't before, to use the library, to search through newspapers or almanacs, to get excited by knowledge.

We want students to view their study of mathematics as worthwhile, as full of interesting and entertaining information, as related to almost every endeavor.

Who Should Take UCSMP ADVANCED ALGEBRA?

Virtually all students who expect to graduate from high school should take this course. College-bound students should take advanced algebra because: two years of algebra are required for admission to some colleges and most college majors; algebra is found on all college-entrance examinations; and algebra is necessary to understand science, statistics, computers, economics, medicine, business, and many other disciplines. Without algebra, doors are open to only a few colleges; even at those colleges a student who has no algebra has the choice of only a few majors.

There are just as many reasons for non-college-bound students to take two years of algebra. Technical schools, such as those for the trades, require that students be familiar with formulas, graphs, and trigonometry. Computers abound in the workplace; algebra is the language of programs and it underlies the operation of spreadsheets and many other software packages. Algebra is the language of generalization; without it arithmetic is often seen merely as a collection of unrelated rules and procedures; it is no surprise that study of algebra helps competence in arithmetic.

A prerequisite for this course is a geometry course that includes some transformations and coordinates, such as UCSMP *Geometry*.

Familiarity with a scientific calculator is assumed. Some familiarity with the BASIC computer language is desired. Students who do not have all these prerequisites can succeed in UCSMP *Advanced Algebra;* however, you may need to spend more time on certain chapters than suggested in the Daily Pacing Charts (provided in the Teacher's Edition, preceding each chapter).

3 General Teaching Suggestions

While it is true that most of the content in this book is found in other advanced algebra books, both the content and the approach of UCSMP *Advanced Algebra* represent rather significant departures from standard practice. *A teacher should not expect to use this book to teach exactly the same material in exactly the same way he or she has been accustomed to teaching.*

UCSMP *Advanced Algebra,* like any good mathematics text, can be adapted to a variety of models of teaching from direct instruction through cooperative learning. The suggestions found on this and the following pages provide ideas which lead to success and discourage practices which do not lead to success. These should not be construed as rigid: students, teachers, classes, schools, and school systems vary greatly. But they should not be ignored. These suggestions come from users, from our extensive discussions with teachers of earlier versions of these materials, and from test results.

Optimizing Learning

■ Pace

Students adjust to the pace set by the teacher. There is a natural tendency, when using a new book, to go more slowly, to play it safe should one forget something. Teachers using these materials for the first time have almost invariably said that they would move more quickly the next year. Do not be afraid to move quickly at the outset. **Each lesson is meant to be covered in a day.** We know from our studies that this pace produces the highest performance levels. Students need to be exposed to content in order to learn it. To set a tone of high expectations, it is especially important that Chapter 1 be taught at a one-day-per-lesson pace. At the end of the chapter, spend a few days on the Progress Self-Test and Chapter Review to cinch the major skills.

We recommend that a typical homework assignment be one of the following:

1. Read Lesson *N;* write answers to all questions in Lesson *N;* or

2. Read Lesson *N;* write answers to questions Covering the Reading in Lesson *N,* and Applying the Mathematics, Review, and Exploration in Lesson *N*-1.

Thus, virtually every day students are expected to do the equivalent of a complete set of questions from a lesson. The questions have been designed to cover the key skills, properties, uses, and representations in the lesson. Questions were not written with an odd-even assignment plan in mind. Skipping questions may lead to gaps in student understanding. The Exploration questions may be assigned for all to do, or left as optional work for extra credit.

There are times when it will be difficult to maintain this pace. But be advised: a slow pace can make it difficult to maintain perspective and relate ideas. A student needs to get to later content to realize why he or she was asked to learn earlier content! If you spend too much time in the lessons, you may find that your slowest students may have learned more by having gone through content slowly, but all other students will have learned less. Try to strike a balance, going quickly enough to keep things interesting, but slowly enough to have time for explanations.

Most advanced algebra books contain far more material than can be covered by an average class in a year. This is due to the fact that the definition of advanced algebra varies from state to state and from school to school. For example, in some districts substantial amounts of trigonometry are taught; in others none is studied. Most students should be able to cover 10 or 11 chapters of this text. Your more advanced students should be able to cover 12 or 13 chapters.

■ Review

Every lesson includes Review questions. These questions serve a variety of purposes. First, they develop competence in a topic. Because we do not expect students to master a topic on the day they are introduced to it, these questions, coming *after* the introduction of the topic, help to solidify the ideas. Second, they maintain competence from preceding chapters. This review is particularly effective with topics that have not been studied for some time.

At times we are able to give harder questions in reviews than we could expect students to be able to do on the day they were introduced to the topic. Thus the reviews sometimes serve as questions which integrate ideas from previous lessons.

Finally, we occasionally review an idea that has not been discussed for some time, just before it is to surface again in a lesson. The Notes on Questions usually alert you to this circumstance.

Teachers in classes that perform the best, assign all the Review questions, give students the answers each day, and discuss them when needed. Those who do not assign all reviews tend to get poorer performance. *The Review questions must be assigned to insure optimum performance.*

■ Mastery

The mastery strategy used at the end of each chapter of UCSMP *Advanced Algebra* is one that has been validated by a great deal of research. Its components are a Progress Self-Test (the literature on mastery learning may refer to this as the "formative test"), solutions to that test in the student textbook (the "feedback"), Chapter Review questions tied to the same objectives (the "correctives"), and finally a Chapter Test, again covering the same objectives.

To follow the strategy means assigning the Progress Self-Test as homework to be done *under simulated test conditions.* The next day should be devoted to answering student questions about the problems and doing some problems from the Chapter Review, if there is time. If a particular topic is causing a great deal of trouble, the corresponding Lesson Master (in the Teacher's Resource File) may be of help.

For most classes, as a second night's assignment, we suggest the *even-numbered* Chapter Review questions. Answers to the *even-numbered* questions are not in the student text, so students will have to work on their own. Discuss those Chapter Review questions the next day in class.

A Chapter Test (available in the Teacher's Resource File) should be given on the third day. The *odd-numbered* Chapter Review questions, for which answers are given in the student text, can be useful for studying for that test. In some classes, a third day before the test may be needed. If so, either the odd-numbered Chapter Review questions or selected Lesson Masters can be used as sources of problems.

We strongly recommend that teachers follow this strategy, except for classes of exceptionally talented students (where less review may be needed). THE EVIDENCE IS SUBSTANTIAL THAT USE OF THE CHAPTER END-MATTER MATERIALS PROMOTES HIGHER LEVELS OF PERFORMANCE.

The evidence is substantial that use of the chapter end-matter materials promotes higher levels of performance.

■ Reading

The typical advanced-algebra student who has not used previous UCSMP materials has not been asked to read mathematics. As a result, it is common for students to ask why they have to read.

Our response: You must learn to read because you must read for success in all future courses that use mathematics, not just in mathematics; because you must read for success in life outside of school and on any job; because the reading will help you understand the uses of mathematics; because the reading contains interesting information; because the reading tells you how the material from one lesson is related to other material in the book; because there is not enough time in class to spend doing something that you can do in a study period or at home.

Our suggestion to first-time users is that at the beginning of the school year some class time be spent each day reading the lesson in class. Some days you can have students read out loud; on others have them read silently to themselves. When students read out loud, provide feedback on their ability to read technical symbols correctly. The first few times students read in class, it may help to give them an overview of what they are about to read. After they have read, ask students to summarize the key ideas in the lesson, and encourage them to ask questions about anything that is not clear.

The questions Covering the Reading with each lesson are meant to test comprehension of the material in the text. They can be used as oral exercises during or after oral reading of the text, or as part of a written assignment. Once students are comfortable with the format of the lessons, we suggest you begin to expect that reading be done outside of class on a regular basis.

It is not uncommon for students who are using UCSMP materials for the first time to resist your suggestions to read the text. However, in our trials of earlier versions of this text, teachers have reported that even the most stubborn students have learned to read the text by the end of the first marking period. Student willingness to read regularly carries over into their study of mathematics in following years.

We strongly encourage teachers to present their own explanations and not to rely on the book for everything. We do, however, wish to discourage the practice of always doing these explanations *before* students have had the opportunity to learn on their own.

Students also learn enormous amounts from discussing alternate strategies to problems with you and their classmates, from engaging in well-constructed computer laboratory activities, and from struggling with open-ended Exploration and Extension questions. By teaching students to read outside of class, you are free to use class time more creatively and effectively than if you were compelled to develop all major ideas yourself in class.

Specific reading comprehension tips and strategies are provided in the Teacher's Edition margin notes for appropriate lessons.

■ Understanding— The SPUR Approach

"Understanding" is an easy goal to have, for who can be against it? Yet understanding means different things to different people. In UCSMP texts an approach is taken that we call the SPUR approach. It involves four different aspects, or dimensions, of understanding.

SKILLS: For many people, understanding mathematics means simply knowing *how* to get an answer to a problem with no help from any outside source. But in classrooms, when we speak of understanding how to use a calculator or a computer, we mean using a computer to do something for us. In UCSMP texts, these are both aspects of the same kind of understanding, the understanding of algorithms (procedures) for getting answers. This is the S of SPUR, the Skills dimension, and it ranges from the rote memorization of basic facts to the development of new algorithms for solving problems.

PROPERTIES: During the 1960s, understanding *why* became at least as important as understanding *how*. Mathematicians often view this kind of understanding as the ultimate goal. For instance, mathematics courses for prospective elementary school teachers assume these college students can do arithmetic, and instead teach the properties and principles behind that arithmetic. This is the P of SPUR, the Properties dimension, and it ranges from the rote identification of properties to the discovery of new proofs.

USES: To the person who applies mathematics, neither knowing how to get an answer nor knowing the mathematical reasons behind the process is as important as being able to *use* the answer. For example, a person does not possess full understanding of linear equations until that person can apply them appropriately in real situations. This is the U of SPUR, the Uses dimension. It ranges from the rote application of ideas (for instance, when you encounter a take-away situation, subtract) to the discovery of new applications or models for mathematical ideas. UCSMP texts are notable for their attention to this dimension of understanding.

REPRESENTATIONS: To some people, even having all three dimensions of understanding given above does not comprise full understanding. They require that students *represent* a concept, and deal with the concept in that representation in some way. Ability to use concrete materials and models, or graphs and other pictorial representations, demonstrates this dimension of understanding. This is the R of SPUR, the Representations dimension, and it ranges from the rote manipulation of objects to the invention of new representations of concepts.

The four types of understanding have certain common qualities. For each there are people from whom that type of understanding is preeminent, and who believe that the other types do not convey the *real* understanding of mathematics. Each has aspects that can be memorized and the potential for the highest level of creative thinking. Each can be, and often is, learned in isolation from the others. We know there are students who have S and none of the others; in the 1960s some students learned P and none of the others; there are people on the street who have U and none of the others; and some people believe that children cannot really acquire any of the others without having R. There are continual arguments among educators as to which dimension should come first and which should be emphasized.

Because of this, IN UCSMP TEXTS WE HAVE ADOPTED THE VIEW THAT THE UNDERSTANDING OF MATHEMATICS IS A MULTI-DIMENSIONAL ENTITY. We believe each dimension is important, that each dimension has its easy aspects and its difficult ones. Some skills (for example, long division) take at least as long to learn as geometry proofs; some uses are as easy as putting together beads.

. . . in UCSMP texts we have adopted the view that the understanding of mathematics is a multi-dimensional entity.

Section 3: General Teaching Suggestions

For a specific example of what understanding means in these four dimensions, consider solving $1.06^x = 2$, and what would constitute evidence of that understanding.

Skills understanding means knowing a way to obtain a solution. (Obtain $x \approx 12$ by some means.)

Properties understanding means knowing properties which you can apply. (Identify or justify the steps in obtaining the solution—such as using the definition of logarithm.)

Uses understanding means knowing situations in which you could apply the solving of this equation. (Set up or interpret a solution: If money is invested at a 6% yield a year, in how many years will it double?)

Representations understanding means having a representation of the solving process or a graphical way of interpreting the solution. (Where does the graph of $y = 1.06^x$ intersect the line $y = 2$?)

We believe there are students who prefer one of these dimensions over the others when learning mathematics. Some students prefer applications, some would rather do manipulative skills, some most want to know the theory, and still others like the models and representations best. Thus the most effective teaching allows students opportunities in all these dimensions.

The SPUR approach is not a perfect sorter of knowledge; many ideas and many problems involve more than one dimension. For instance, the mathematics behind an algorithm may involve both S and P. And some understandings do not fit any of these dimensions. In some UCSMP texts, we add a fifth dimension H—the Historical dimension—for it provides still another way of looking at knowledge. (Leonhard Euler, in his most influential book *Algebra,* was the first to use logarithms to solve exponential equations like $1.06^x = 2$, more than a century after logarithms had been invented.)

In this book, you see the SPUR categorization at the end of each chapter in a set of Objectives and corresponding Chapter Review questions. The Progress Self-Test for each chapter and the Lesson Masters (in the Teacher's Resource File) are keyed to these objectives. We never ask students (or teachers) to categorize tasks into the various kinds of understanding; that is not a suitable goal. The categorization is meant only to be a convenient and efficient way to ensure that the book provides the opportunity for teachers to teach and for students to gain a broader and deeper understanding of mathematics than is normally the case.

You may wonder why the Chapter Review Questions and Lesson Masters are organized using the SPUR categorization. It is because we believe that practice is essential for mastery, but that blind practice, in which a student merely copies what was done in a previous problem to do a new one, does not help ultimate performance. The practice must be accompanied by understanding. The properties, uses, and representations enhance understanding and should be covered to obtain mastery, even of the skills.

The Lesson Masters are particularly appropriate for students who wish more practice; for helping students individually with problems they have not seen; after a Chapter Test has been completed, if you feel that students' performance was not high enough; and for in-class work on days when a normal class cannot be conducted. However, they should be used sparingly. *The Lesson Masters should not be part of the normal routine* and should seldom be used when they would delay moving on to the next lesson.

Using Technology

We use calculators and computers in UCSMP because they make important mathematical ideas accessible to students at an early age; they relieve the drudgery of calculation and graphing, particularly with numbers and equations encountered in realistic contexts; and they facilitate exploration and open-ended problem solving by making multiple instances easy to examine. Furthermore, our use of technology has resulted in no loss of paper-and-pencil skill in arithmetic, and has freed up time in the curriculum to spend on other topics that lead to overall better performance by UCSMP students.

Inevitably, calculators will be considered as natural as pencils for doing mathematics.

■ Calculators

Hand-held calculators first appeared in 1971. Not until 1976 did the price of a four-function calculator come below \$50 (equivalent to well over \$100 today). Still, in 1975, a national commission recommended that hand-held calculators be used on all tests starting in eighth grade, and in 1980 the National Council of Teachers of Mathematics recommended that calculators be used in all grades of school from kindergarten on. It is reported that the Achievement section of the College Board exams will allow calculators beginning in 1990, and that the Advanced Placement exam will again allow calculators in the near future. Several standardized test batteries are being developed with calculators. And slowly but surely calculators are being expected on more and more licensing exams outside of school.

The business and mathematics education communities generally believe that paper-and-pencil algorithms are becoming obsolete. (The long division algorithm we use was born only in the late 1400s. Before that time, the abacus was used almost exclusively to get answers to problems. So mechanical means to do problems are really older than paper-and-pencil means.) Increasingly, businesses do not want their employees to use paper-and-pencil algorithms to get answers to arithmetic problems. Banks require that their tellers do all arithmetic using a calculator.

INEVITABLY, CALCULATORS WILL BE CONSIDERED AS NATURAL AS PENCILS FOR DOING MATHEMATICS. A century from now people will be amazed when they learn that some students as recent as the 1980s went to schools where calculators were not used.

In UCSMP *Advanced Algebra* we use calculators in the following ways: to calculate the value of expressions that could be done by hand at this level, but would be tedious, such as $\sqrt{19.4}$; and to generate decimal approximations to quantities which we could not do by hand at this level, such as $\sin 20°$ or $10^{.329}$. We also use calculators to generate patterns or sequences whose properties are then analyzed. We assume that students have access to scientific calculators for work in and out of class. Students will be hampered in their study of UCSMP *Advanced Algebra* if scientific calculators are not permitted.

There are five basic reasons why 4-function nonscientific calculators do not suffice.

1. Applications require the ability to deal with large and small numbers. On many 4-function calculators, a number as large as the population of the U.S. cannot be entered, and on all of them the national debt or the world population could not be entered. The calculator must have the ability to display numbers in scientific notation.

2. 4-function calculators give error messages which do not distinguish between student error and calculator insufficiency. This restricts the kind of problems one can assign.

3. There are keys on scientific calculators that are very useful in this course. The π, power, root, logarithm, trigonometric, factorial, and parentheses keys are all utilized in this book.

4. Order of operations on a scientific calculator is the same as in algebra, so this kind of calculator motivates and reinforces algebra skills. In contrast, order of operations on a 4-function calculator is often different from that used in algebra and could confuse students.

5. A scientific calculator can be used for later courses a student takes; it shows the student there is much more to learn about mathematics.

Students will overuse calculators. Part of learning to use any machine is to make mistakes: using it when you shouldn't, not using it when you should. Anyone who has a word processor has used it for short memos that could much more easily have been handwritten. Anyone who has a microwave has used it for food that could have been cooked either in a conventional oven or on top of the stove.

The overuse dies down, but it takes some months. In the meantime, stress that there are three ways to get answers to arithmetic problems: by paper-and-pencil, mentally, or by using some automatic means (a table, a calculator, a trusty friend, and so on). Some problems require more than one of these means, but the wise applier of arithmetic knows when to use each of these ways.

Good arithmeticians do a lot of calculations mentally, either because they are basic facts (such as 3×5) or because they can be gotten by simple rules (such as $2/3 \times 4/5$, or 100×4.72). They may not use a calculator on these because the likelihood of making an error entering or reading is greater than the likelihood of making a mental error. As a rule, we seldom say, "Do not use calculators here." We want students to learn for themselves when calculator use is appropriate and when not. However, you may feel the need to prod some students to avoid the calculator. An answer of 2.9999999 to $\sqrt{9}$ should be strongly discouraged.

Computers and Graphing Calculators

The computer is a powerful tool for you to use in your classroom to demonstrate the relationships, patterns, properties, and algorithms of algebra. A desirable computer is one with the ability to deal with a good amount of data and to display graphs with accuracy and precision. We recommend that you have access to a microcomputer with BASIC and function graphing software that you can use for classroom demonstrations. Ideally you should have access to a group of microcomputers so that students can work individually or in pairs, occasionally in a laboratory setting.

A classroom set of graphing calculators can serve as an alternative to a computer laboratory equipped with graphing software. A good graphing calculator should display as many as four graphs simultaneously, be able to graph all of the functions in this book, allow the window to be changed with ease, and in general be easy to use.

From the very first chapter of this book, computer programs appear in examples and exercises as contemporary representations of algebra. The BASIC computer language was selected for use in this book because it is packaged for the microcomputers which are most popular in American schools. The programs have been kept short so that they can be typed relatively quickly. It is not necessary for every student to type and run each program. Many programs can be used as classroom demonstrations.

Since this is an advanced algebra course, not a programming course, you should emphasize the *computational* steps of a program. Can the students follow the steps of a program and tell what the output will be? Can the student modify a given program to solve an exercise with different values? Do not ignore the computer questions even if you do not have computers available. THE COMPUTER PROVIDES A CONCRETE ILLUSTRATION OF THE ROLE OF VARIABLES WHICH CAN EASILY BE LEARNED BY STUDENTS AT THIS LEVEL.

The computer provides a concrete illustration of the role of variables which can easily be learned by students at this level.

Section 3: General Teaching Suggestions

Programs in the text follow several conventions.

1. Most programs start with a PRINT statement which serves a dual purpose: it is a title for the program LISTing and a title for the program output.

2. Extended remarks are offset from the body of the program. Brief comments could appear as REM statements (remarks) in longer programs.

3. Indentation in program lines has been used to indicate blocking of lines, particularly in loops. This aid to program readability is not exploited on many computers. You will probably find that these spaces do not appear on your computer screen, and therefore need not be typed.

4. Variable names are kept short, sometimes only one character long. This reduces the amount of typing needed; is implementable on all computer forms of BASIC; and reflects the use of single letters for variables in algebra.

5. Tests for exceptional cases are frequently omitted unless the meaning of the topic is enhanced by the cases. In a program for solving $ax + b = c$, it is not really necessary for a student to write
    IF $a < > 0$ THEN. . .
because he or she should recognize 0 will not work *before* using the computer. However, in a program to compute slope, a zero division is not as obvious to students, so the IF-THEN statement is included.

6. We do not type NEW, which students might have to type if they are not the first user of the day on the computer. We also do not type RUN, which students must do in order to execute their program. And we do not indicate that students must press the RETURN key after each line.

If you have not done much work with BASIC, do not be alarmed. As mentioned before, this is an advanced algebra course, not a programming course. Computer language is explained in the text whenever needed. Appendix C contains an explanation of all BASIC commands and functions that students are expected to know and use in this course. Most programs are either provided in full or are presented in fill-in-the-blank format. Rarely do we expect students to write a program from scratch.

Whether you are a novice or expert in BASIC, we encourage you to try the programs we provide on your own system. Each version of BASIC and each computer has slightly different characteristics, and our generic programs may need to be modified slightly for your system.

Beginning in Chapter 2, some questions ask students to use an *automatic grapher*. By this we mean a computer with a function grapher, or a graphing calculator. If students do not have access to a computer or automatic grapher, exercise caution in your assigning of such questions. It takes time to do a good graph, and many of these questions require comparing two or more graphs.

In addition to the references in the text to BASIC programs and automatic graphers, 30 Computer Masters are provided in the Teacher's Resource File. These blackline masters are keyed to specific lessons in each of Chapters 1–13, with approximately half using BASIC and half using function-graphing software. They are meant for use by a class in a laboratory setting, or by individuals for extra credit work. It is not necessary to do these masters to be successful in UCSMP *Advanced Algebra*. Since each one stands alone, you may do as many or as few as you think appropriate for your class.

Evaluating Learning

■ Grading

No problem seems more difficult than the question of grading. If a teacher has students who perform so well that they all deserve A's and the teacher gives them A's as a result, the teacher will probably not be given plaudits for being successful but will be accused of being too easy. This suggests that the grading scale ought to be based on a fixed level of performance, which is what we recommend.

Never in this book are there ten similar questions in a row. To teach students to be flexible, the wording of questions is varied, and principles are applied in many contexts. Furthermore, in UCSMP *Advanced Algebra* we emphasize the relations between algebra and geometry and between various parts of algebra. Learning to solve problems in a variety of contexts or to discern relationships between properties is more difficult than learning to perform a routine skill. Thus, a natural question that arises is, "How should I grade students in UCSMP courses"?

One way is to increase the number of points on the test to 110 or 120 and use your old scale. (However, do not convert the scores to percents.) A second way is to change the grading scale. One used successfully by many UCSMP pilot teachers is 85–100, A; 72–84, B; 60–71, C; 50–59, D; 0–49, F. Such a low curve may alarm some teachers, but as outlined on pages T46–T48, UCSMP students have performed well on standardized tests compared to students in other classes. STUDENTS IN UCSMP COURSES GENERALLY LEARN MORE MATHEMATICS OVERALL THAN STUDENTS IN COMPARISON CLASSES. We believe that the above grading policies reward students fairly for work well done.

We have also found that a word to your students about why your grading scale is "different" is helpful. They may be so accustomed to another grading scale that they feel they are doing poorly, while you think they are doing well. To encourage students, we often make a basketball analogy. In UCSMP *Advanced Algebra*, almost every question is a different shot (a problem), some close in, some from middle distance, a few from half-court. In a traditional course, most of the shots students try are done over and over again from the same court position close to the basket. ("Do the odd-numbered exercises from 1–49.") Since the variability of the shots in UCSMP *Advanced Algebra* is much greater, it is unrealistic to expect percents of correct shots to be the same.

There are times, however, when you want to practice one specific shot to make it automatic. We suggest focusing in on a few topics for quizzes. The Teacher's Resource File contains at least one quiz for each chapter. If students perform well on quizzes and tests, it has a real effect on interest and motivation. We would like to see grading as a vehicle for breeding success as well as for rating students.

Students in UCSMP courses generally learn more mathematics overall than students in comparison classes.

In the light of all this, here are some general suggestions pertaining to grading:

1. Let students know what they need to know in order to get good grades. All research on the subject indicates that telling students what they are supposed to learn increases the amount of material covered and tends to increase performance.

2. Have confidence in your students. Do not arbitrarily consign some of them to low grades. Let them know that it is possible for all of them to get A's if they learn the material.

3. Some teachers have found that because of the way that the Review questions maintain and improve performance, *cumulative tests* give students an opportunity to do well. For your convenience, the Teacher's Resource File has Chapter Tests in Cumulative Form (in addition to the regular Chapter Tests) for each chapter, beginning with Chapter 2. The Cumulative Tests allow students a chance to show what they have learned about a topic in the intervening weeks.

■ Standardized Tests

At our first conference with school teachers and administators early in the project, we were told in the strongest terms, "Be bold, but remember that you will be judged by old standardized tests."

In UCSMP *Advanced Algebra*, we work in the four dimensions of understanding: Skills, Properties, Uses, and Representations. While it is thought that traditional algebra standardized tests are almost entirely devoted to skills, this is not the case. *School-made placement tests* are most likely to be so distorted, because Properties seem out of favor these days and items for Uses and Representations are felt to be the most difficult to find. Standardized tests are usually more balanced.

We have done an in-depth study of standarized tests. Our conclusions are as follows: Students studying UCSMP courses are likely to do better on the College Board SAT-M than other students. The SAT-M is a problem-solving test, and far more questions on the SAT-M cover content likely to be unfamiliar to other students than to UCSMP students. The ACT exams seem at least as favorable to our students as to students in other books. However, if the UCSMP idea is followed and more students take *Advanced Algebra* in the 10th grade, then there is no question that students in the UCSMP curriculum will far outscore comparable students who are a course behind.

We used items from an algebra standardized test in our studies. It leads us to believe that UCSMP *Advanced Algebra* students will perform at least as well as other advanced algebra students in most schools on such tests.

Finally, a note about curriculum projects. Many people treat books from curriculum projects as "experimental." Few commercial textbooks, however, have been developed on the basis of large-scale testing. Few have been produced as part of a coherent 7–12 curriculum design. This text has gone through extensive prepublication analysis and criticism. It has been revised on the basis of comments and evaluations of the pilot and formative evaluation teachers. It is the intention of UCSMP to provide materials which are successful as well as teachable. SINCE UCSMP ADVANCED ALGEBRA HAS BEEN SUCCESSFULLY TESTED AND REVISED, IT SHOULD BE VIEWED AS A *NEW* TEXT, NOT AS AN EXPERIMENTAL TEXT.

Since UCSMP *Advanced Algebra* has been successfully tested and revised, it should be viewed as a *new* text, not as an experimental text.

4 Research and Development of UCSMP
Advanced Algebra

Selection of Authors

In the spring of 1985, Sharon Senk, Assistant Professor of Mathematics and Education at Syracuse University, was asked to lead the writing team for UCSMP *Advanced Algebra*. Dr. Senk was chosen because of an impressive combination of qualifications. She had been department chair at Newton North H.S., in Newton, Massachusetts, a school which taught geometry and advanced algebra simultaneously; thus she well understood how geometry could affect algebra. While a doctoral student at the University of Chicago, she wrote geometry text materials with Zalman Usiskin, using the van Hiele levels. She is one of the nation's experts in that area. Her dissertation was on the topic of proof-writing, and in particular, she is interested in student problem-solving capabilities and evaluation. She is also interested in the roles computers can play in school mathematics. Thus, she had the broad background and experience necessary for a venture of this type.

The other authors for UCSMP Algebra were chosen by a unique procedure. Announcements that USCMP was looking for authors were placed in several national newsletters, including those of the National Council of Supervisors of Mathematics, the National Council of Teachers of Mathematics, and the Special Interest Group on Research in Mathematics Education of the American Educational Research Association. Those who responded (over 80 in number) were sent a long application form in which they were asked for personal information, their opinions about various issues, asked to edit a lesson enclosed with the application, and to enclose a lesson of their own choosing. Of the 45 individuals who completed applications, 13 were invited to the University to spend a day in a mock planning-writing session. Of these 13, four (Judy Halvorson, Rheta Rubenstein, Denisse Thompson, and Steven Viktora) were chosen to be members of the *Advanced Algebra* writing team.

Pilot Editions and Studies

In the summer of 1985, the authors spent 8 weeks at the University of Chicago writing the first draft of UCSMP *Advanced Algebra*. This draft was edited in Chicago by UCSMP staff (all experienced mathematics teachers) and used in five schools in the year 1985–86. The schools were located in Michigan, Minnesota, New York, Florida, and Illinois. (The teachers in all evaluations are acknowledged on page *iii*.) The teachers that year received loose-leaf materials, a chapter at a time, sometimes only days before they had to teach from them. They gave opinions directly to the authors and to the project continually during the year. Twice they came to the University of Chicago for full-day meetings to discuss the materials.

In the summer of 1986, some of the authors returned to revise the materials. The revision was guided by the comments of the pilot teachers. A second pilot in 1986–87, using the revised materials, took place in six schools. Again the materials were loose-leaf. This time the teachers reported in writing to the project about how each lesson in each chapter fared. Again there were two full-day meetings of all the teachers at which the materials were discussed.

The results of the 1986–87 evaluations showed that students generally performed very well, but there were many places where small improvements could be made. The materials were revised accordingly. Also, by this time, drafts of UCSMP *Geometry* and *Functions, Statistics, and Trigonometry with Computers* existed. To better coordinate with these preceding and following courses in the UCSMP curriculum, some lessons were added, deleted, rewritten, or reordered.

Formative Evaluation and Test Results

In 1985, UCSMP received substantial funding from the Amoco Foundation and the Carnegie Corporation of New York to conduct a large-scale summative evaluation of the first three courses in the UCSMP curriculum. Each of those studies involved over 2000 students in a number of states. No such funding was available for UCSMP *Advanced Algebra*. Thus, although this text went through the same number of revisions and careful scrutiny as those texts, we cannot report data from any study involving large numbers of students.

In 1987–88, a formative evaluation of UCSMP *Advanced Algebra* was conducted with a third version of these materials. The formative evaluation differs from the pilots in four significant ways: (1) All schools in the study were in the Chicago area to enable teachers to be brought in to periodically discuss the materials. (2) Comparison classes were chosen in an attempt to have a controlled study of performance of matched pairs of classes. (3) UCSMP staff visited some classes in the study and interviewed teachers and administrators. (4) Materials for students were provided in three spiral-bound volumes. Comments on the lessons and chapter tests were available to the teachers.

Five teachers in five schools taught nine classes of UCSMP *Advanced Algebra*. Two of the schools were public high schools in Chicago, one was in a suburban working-class community, and the other two were in more affluent suburbs. Typical (not honors) second-year algebra classes were used. In one of the city schools and one of the suburban schools, some students had studied from UCSMP *Geometry*.

A similar number of Comparison classes were selected and tested. However, only 4 pairs matched based on scores at the beginning of the year.

During 1987–88, UCSMP teachers met five times at the University of Chicago to comment on how things were going, what they thought were strong and weak points, how long it took to cover various lessons, which questions were most interesting, which questions might be deleted, and so on. At the end of the school year, fifty multiple-choice and four open-ended questions were given to all classes over two days of testing. The questions were subdivided into the SPUR categories for analysis. The results are quite consistent over those categories. Only results for students who were present for both fall and spring testing in the four well-matched pairs of classes are presented here.

■ **Mean percent correct for all students in the sample of well-matched pairs**

Category	UCSMP (n = 59)	Comparison (n = 57)	Difference (UCSMP − Comparison)
Skills (15 items)	39.7	33.0	+6.7
Properties (9 items)	23.7	21.4	+2.3
Uses (11 items)	35.3	31.1	+4.2
Representations (15 items)	35.9	31.5	+4.5
Total (50 items)	34.7	30.1	+4.7

Overall, UCSMP students scored 15.6 percent higher than the Comparison students.

OVERALL, UCSMP STUDENTS SCORED 15.6 PERCENT HIGHER THAN THE COMPARISON STUDENTS. UCSMP students outperformed Comparison students by more than 20% on the following items:

> solving an exponential equation
> telling when matrices cannot be multiplied
> determining the output of a computer program in BASIC
> giving an equation for a circle with a given center and radius

Teachers felt that particularly strong features of the 1987–88 version of UCSMP *Advanced Algebra* were its clarity and organization, the examples of applications of mathematics, and its suggestions for teaching, particularly for the use of technology. Its major weakness was the lack of high quality supplementary materials. This weakness has been overcome with the huge package of supplementary materials that are now available. (See page T18 for details.)

Overall, both UCSMP and Comparison students found the examples and questions in their texts difficult. Significant positive differences favoring UCSMP students over Comparison students were found in three areas: reading, applications, and technology.

Because of the changes made, we expect results from the formative evaluation to extend to the Scott, Foresman version, further enhancing student performance.

Continuing Research and Development

Our evaluations of UCSMP *Advanced Algebra* have convinced us that the approach is not only sound but quite effective and that no major changes should be made in the materials. However, many minor changes have been made for this edition, based either on careful readings given to the materials by UCSMP and Scott, Foresman editors, on the test results reported above, or on remarks by the teachers in the formative evaluation. In particular, teachers told us where they supplemented and where they felt there was not enough work.

Some material was added to satisfy teachers' requests for certain content. Notable is Chapter 13, Series, Combinations, and Statistics, which did not exist in earlier editions.

The present version of UCSMP *Advanced Algebra* also includes the appearance of four colors, of attractive pictures, and of many more supplements for teachers and students. Teachers, of course, will now have the benefit of having the full text at the beginning of the year. BECAUSE OF THE CHANGES MADE, WE EXPECT RESULTS FROM THE FORMATIVE EVALUATION TO EXTEND TO THE SCOTT, FORESMAN VERSION, FURTHER ENHANCING STUDENT PERFORMANCE.

Since November of 1985, UCSMP has sponsored an annual "Users' Conference" at the University of Chicago, at which users and prospective users of its materials can meet with each other and with authors. This conference now includes all components of the project. It provides a valuable opportunity for reports on UCSMP materials from those not involved in formal studies. We encourage users to attend this conference.

We desire to know of any studies school districts conduct using these materials. UCSMP will be happy to assist school districts by supplying a copy of the noncommercial tests we used in our summative evaluation and other information as needed.

Both Scott, Foresman and Company and UCSMP welcome comments on our books. Please address comments either to Mathematics Product Manager, Scott, Foresman and Company, 1900 East Lake Avenue, Glenview, IL 60025, or to Zalman Usiskin, Director, UCSMP, 5835 S. Kimbark Avenue, Chicago, IL 60637.

5 Bibliography

■ REFERENCES for Sections 1–4 of Professional Sourcebook

College Board. *Academic Preparation for College: What Students Need To Know and Be Able To Do.* New York: College Board, 1983.

Flanders, James. **"How Much of the Content in Mathematics Textbooks Is New?"** *Arithmetic Teacher*, September 1987, pp. 18–23.

Jones, Philip, and Coxford, A. *A History of Mathematics Education in the United States and Canada.* 30th Yearbook of the National Council of Teachers of Mathematics. Reston, VA: NCTM, 1970.

McNight, Curtis, et al. *The Underachieving Curriculum: Assessing U.S. School Mathematics from an International Perspective.* Champaign, IL: Stipes Publishing Company, 1987.

National Commission on Excellence in Education. *A Nation at Risk: The Imperative for Educational Reform.* Washington, DC: U.S. Department of Education, 1983.

National Council of Teachers of Mathematics. *Curriculum and Evaluation Standards for School Mathematics.* Reston, VA: NCTM, 1989.

Senk, Sharon L. **"How Well Do Students Write Geometry Proofs?"** *Mathematics Teacher*, September 1985, pp. 448–456.

Waits, Bert, and Demana, Franklin. **"Is Three Years Enough?"** *Mathematics Teacher*, January 1988, pp. 11–15.

■ REFERENCES from Student Edition or Teaching Notes

Abbott, Edwin Abbott. *Flatland.* New York: Dover Publications, 1952.

Mandelbrot, Benoit B. *The Fractal Geometry of Nature.* San Francisco: W. H. Freeman, 1982.

Peitgen, Hans-Otto, and Richter, P. H. *The Beauty of Fractals.* New York: Springer-Verlag, 1986.

■ ADDITIONAL GENERAL REFERENCES

Hirsch, Christian R., and Zweng, Marilyn J., editors. *The Secondary School Mathematics Curriculum.* Reston, VA: NCTM, 1985. This forward-looking NCTM yearbook gives background for many of the ideas found in UCSMP texts.

Johnson, David R. *Every Minute Counts.* Palo Alto, CA: Dale Seymour Publications, 1982. *Making Minutes Count Even More.* Palo Alto, CA: Dale Seymour Publications, 1986. These booklets provide practical suggestions for using class time effectively. Comments on correcting homework, communicating in the classroom, and opening and closing activities are particularly good.

Kieran, Carolyn, and Wagner, Sigrid, editors. *Research Issues in Learning and Teaching Algebra.* Reston, VA: NCTM, 1989. An overview of recent research and its implications for learning and teaching algebra. See particularly the chapters by Fey and Senk on the impact of computer technology.

The Mathematics Teacher. National Council of Teachers of Mathematics. 1906 Association Drive, Reston, VA 22091. This journal is an excellent source of applications and other teaching suggestions. We believe that every secondary school mathematics teacher should join the NCTM and read this journal regularly.

Section 5: Bibliography

The UMAP Journal, Consortium for Mathematics and Its Applications Project, Inc. 271 Lincoln Street, Suite Number 4, Lexington, MA 02173 This journal is a wonderful source of applications, although many of them are at the college level. COMAP also publishes a quarterly newsletter called *Consortium* that includes "The HiMAP Pull-Out Section." *Consortium* provides information on COMAP modules that are appropriate for high schools.

■ SOURCES for Additional Problems

Coxford, Arthur F., and Shulte, Albert P., editors. ***The Ideas of Algebra, K–12.*** Reston, VA: National Council of Teachers of Mathematics, 1988. This NCTM yearbook contains 34 articles on all aspects of the teaching of algebra.

Eves, Howard. ***An Introduction to the History of Mathematics.*** 5th ed. Philadelphia. Saunders College Publishing, 1983. This comprehensive history includes references to recent 20th-century mathematics, such as the proof of the four-color theorem. There is an outstanding collection of problems.

Garfunkel, Solomon, and Steen, Lynn A., editors. ***For All Practical Purposes: An Introduction to Contemporary Mathematics.*** New York: W. H. Freeman, 1988. Based on the TV series of the same name, this book emphasizes connections between contemporary mathematics and modern society. It is a very good source for linear programming; exponential, logarithmic, and trigonometric functions; geometry; probability; statistics; and computer graphics.

Hanson, Viggo P., and Zweng, Marilyn J., editors. ***Computers in Mathematics Education.*** Reston, VA: NCTM, 1984. This NCTM yearbook provides practical suggestions about some computer activities that can be added to mathematics classes.

Johnson, Otto, executive ed. ***The 1989 Information Please Almanac.*** Boston: Houghton Mifflin Company, 1989. Almanacs are excellent sources of data for problems.

Joint Committee of the Mathematical Association of America and the National Council of Teachers of Mathematics. ***A Sourcebook of Applications of School Mathematics.*** Reston, VA: National Council of Teachers of Mathematics, 1980. This outstanding, comprehensive source of applied problems is organized in sections by mathematical content (advanced arithmetic through combinatorics and probability).

Kastner, Bernice. ***Space Mathematics.*** Washington, D.C.: U.S. Government Printing Office, 1985. This updated version of NASA's 1972 edition of *Space Mathematics, A Resource for Teachers* provides specific data on recent NASA missions and worked problems organized in chapters by mathematical content (algebra, geometry, matrix algebra, conic sections, and so on).

Sharron, Sidney, and Reys, Robert E., editors. ***Applications in School Mathematics.*** Reston, VA: NCTM, 1979. This NCTM yearbook is a collection of essays on applications, ways of including applications in the classroom, mathematical modeling, and other issues related to applications. There is an extensive bibliography on sources of applications.

U.S. Bureau of the Census. ***Statistical Abstract of the United States: 1989.*** 109th ed. Washington, D.C., 1988. This outstanding data source, published annually since 1878, summarizes statistics on the United States and provides reference to other statistical publications.

■ SOFTWARE

Functions. Developed by the North Carolina School of Science and Mathematics. Durham, NC 27705 This is a function plotter for the IBM-PC with 512K memory. It is available for a nominal charge by writing to Helen Compton at NCSSM. NCSSM has also developed software for data analysis and geometric probability.

Green Globs and Graphic Equations. Sunburst Educational Computer Courseware, 39 Washington Ave., Pleasantville, NY 10570-9971. This software, which has function plotting capability, is available for the Apple II family, the IBM-PC and PCjr., and Tandy 1000. It has two games which have students find equations of linear and/or quadratic relations. The game called "Green Globs" enables students to write equations of relations that pass through points on the plane.

Master Grapher. Addison-Wesley Publishing Company, 2725 Sand Hill Road, Menlo Park, CA 94025. This flexible function plotter, developed by Bert Waits and Frank Demana at Ohio State University, is available for the Apple II family, the Macintosh, and the IBM-PC.

True Basic Precalculus. True Basic, Inc., 12 Commerce Ave., West Lebanon, NH 03784. This quality function grapher is available for the IBM-compatible family and the Macintosh.

ADDITIONAL ANSWERS

LESSON 2-6 (pages 86–91)
12.b. different domains for d

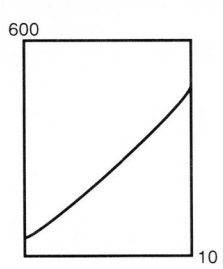

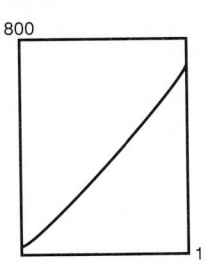

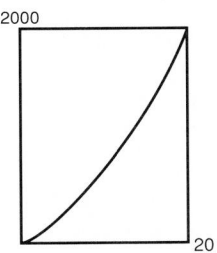

c. about $1590; **d.** $c = 5(18)^2 = \$1620$

13.

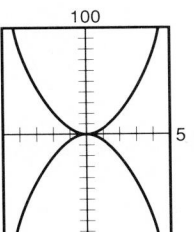

14.

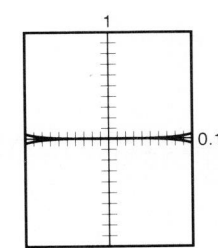

19.a.

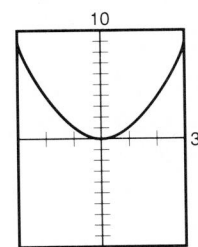

b.

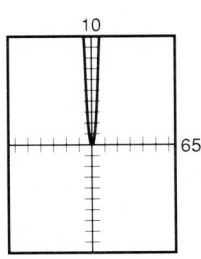

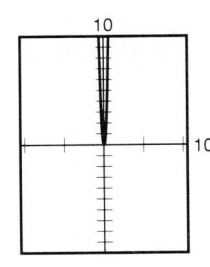

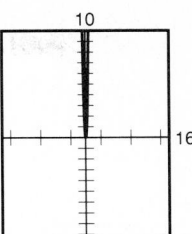

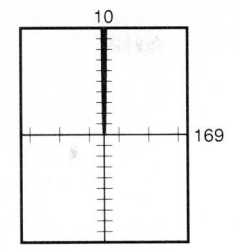

Many answers are possible. The largest value of a on our grapher is $a = 169$.

c.

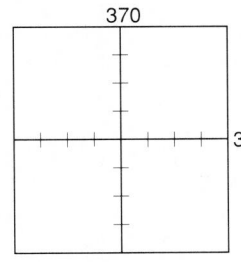

Many answers are possible. The largest value of b on our grapher is 370.

CHAPTER 2 PROGRESS SELF-TEST
(pages 117–118)
13.

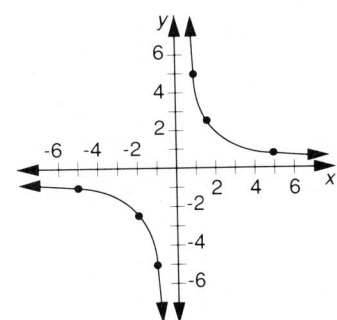

LESSON 3-2 (pages 132–137)
11.

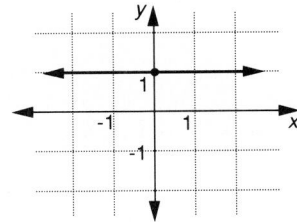

13.a.

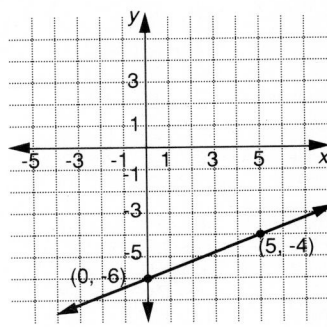

14.

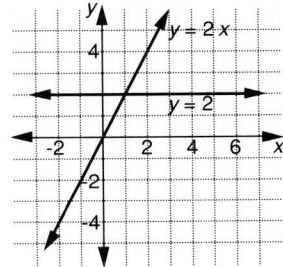

15.c.

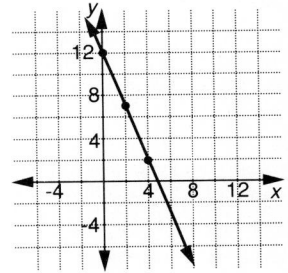

17.a. and b.

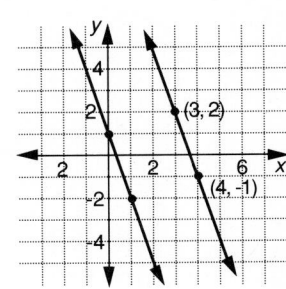

T51

ADDITIONAL ANSWERS

27.a.

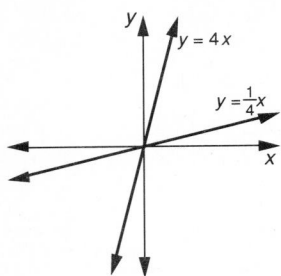

b. $\frac{1}{4}$, 4; **c.** $y = x$; **d.** (a);

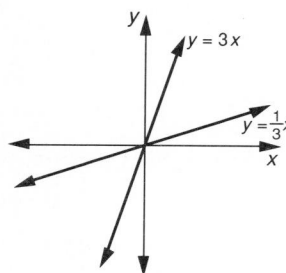

(b) $\frac{1}{3}$, 3   (c) $y = x$

e. If the positive slopes of two lines are reciprocals, then the line $y = x$ bisects the acute angles formed by the lines;
f. If the negative slopes of two lines are reciprocals, then the line $y = -x$ bisects the acute angles formed by the lines.

LESSON 3-4   (pages 143–147)
13.a. horizontal; **b.** x-intercept: none; y-intercept: 4; **c.** See graph below;
14.a. oblique; **b.** x-intercept: -6; y-intercept: -6; **c.** See graph below;
15.a. vertical; **b.** x-intercept: 8; y-intercept: none; **c.** See graph below.

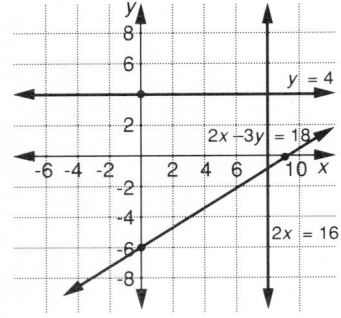

LESSON 3-5   (pages 148–153)
15.a.

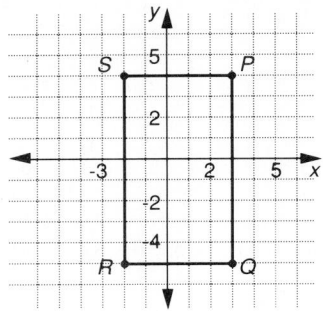

b. $\overline{PQ}$: $x = 3$; $\overline{QR}$: $y = -5$; $\overline{RS}$: $x = -2$; $\overline{SP}$: $y = 4$
20.

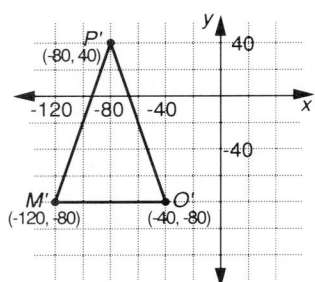

LESSON 3-7   (pages 160–163)
18.

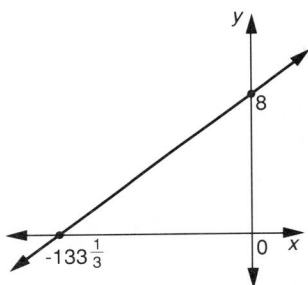

19.a.

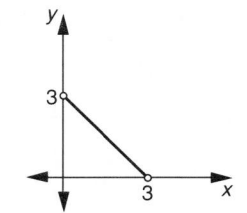

CHAPTER 3 PROGRESS SELF-TEST
(page 175)
2.

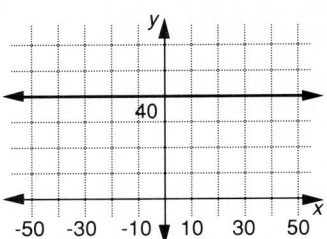

3.

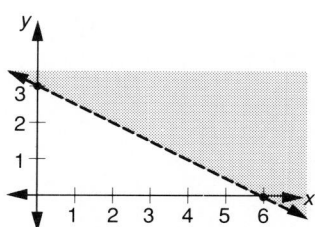

16. $a_n = -7 - 3(n - 1)$;   **17.** $a_1 = -7$; $a_n = a_{n-1} - 3$ for $n > 1$;   **18.a.** Substitute (0,0) into $y > -3x$. Is $0 > -3 \cdot 0$? No, so (0,0) is not in the solution set; **b.** Substitute (2, -1) into $3x - 5y < 8$. Is $3 \cdot 2 - 5(-1) < 8$? No, so (2, -1) is not in the solution set.

CHAPTER 3 REVIEW   (pages 176–179)
73.

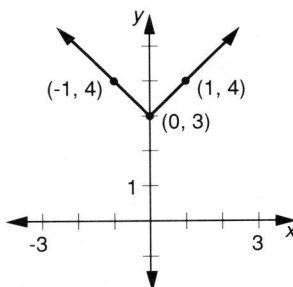

74.

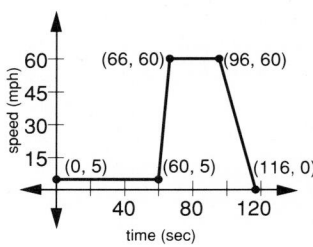

T52

ADDITIONAL ANSWERS

LESSON 4-7 (pages 217–221)

25. Perpendicular lines are lines that meet to form equal adjacent angles; lines that meet to form 90° angles; lines that meet to form right angles; **26.** The lengths of the sides are $\sqrt{34}$, $\sqrt{68}$, and $\sqrt{34}$. Does $(\sqrt{34})^2 + (\sqrt{34})^2 = (\sqrt{68})^2$? Yes, $34 + 34 = 68$, so the matrix represents a right triangle;

27.b. $\begin{bmatrix} -1 & 0 \\ 0 & 1 \end{bmatrix} \begin{bmatrix} 0 & -4 & -6 & -4 & 0 \\ 3 & 3 & 2.5 & 2 & 2 \end{bmatrix} = \begin{bmatrix} 0 & 4 & 6 & 4 & 0 \\ 3 & 3 & 2.5 & 2 & 2 \end{bmatrix}$

28. sample: $R_{60} = \begin{bmatrix} \frac{1}{2} & \frac{-\sqrt{3}}{2} \\ \frac{\sqrt{3}}{2} & \frac{1}{2} \end{bmatrix}$

29.

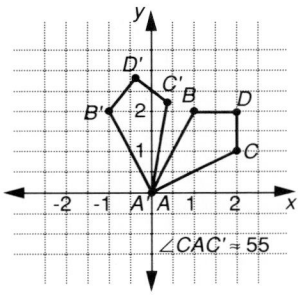

$\angle CAC' \approx 55$

LESSON 4-9 (pages 228–233)

23.b. sample:

```
10   LET A = .67:LET B = .33:
     LET C = .66:LET D = .34
20   LET E = .7:LET F = .3:
     LET G = .6:LET H = .4
30   FOR N = 3 TO 20
40      P1 = A * E + B * G
50      P2 = A * F + B * H
60      P3 = C * E + D * G
70      P4 = C * F + D * H
80      PRINT "M"; N; ":",
        P1, P2
90      PRINT, P3, P4
100     A = P1
110     B = P2
120     C = P3
130     D = P4
140  NEXT N
150 END
```

c. $\begin{bmatrix} \frac{2}{3} & \frac{1}{3} \\ \frac{2}{3} & \frac{1}{3} \end{bmatrix}$

LESSON 4-10 (pages 234–237)

21.a. $\begin{bmatrix} -1 & 0 \\ 0 & -1 \end{bmatrix}$; **b.** $(-a, -b)$;

22.a. $\begin{bmatrix} 0 & 1 \\ 1 & 0 \end{bmatrix}$; **b.** (b, a);

23. The figure is stretched by a factor of 3 in the horizontal dimension only, and raised 2 units in the vertical direction.

CHAPTER 4 PROGRESS SELF-TEST
(page 240)

1.

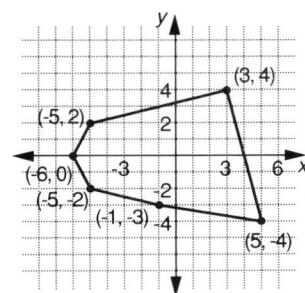

2.

	Peachport	Grapetown	Bananasville	
	14	3	8	first class
	120	190	250	economy class

6. $\begin{bmatrix} -2 & 0 \\ 1 & 5 \end{bmatrix}$; **7.** $\begin{bmatrix} 2 & -2 \\ 8 & 6 \end{bmatrix}$

8. $\begin{bmatrix} 14 & 0 \\ 7 & 35 \end{bmatrix}$; **10.** $y + 2.5 = -\frac{1}{5}(x - 3)$; **11.** $\begin{bmatrix} 0 & 1 \\ 1 & 0 \end{bmatrix}$;

13. $\begin{bmatrix} 23 & 8 & 10 & 5 \\ 11 & 5 & 10 & 15 \\ 2 & 3 & 15 & 15 \end{bmatrix} \begin{bmatrix} 18 \\ 58 \\ 12 \\ 76 \end{bmatrix} = \begin{bmatrix} 1378 \\ 1748 \\ 1530 \end{bmatrix}$

The revenues are:
Los Angeles $1,378,000
Tucson $1,748,000
Santa Fe $1,530,000

14. $\begin{bmatrix} 8 & 11 \\ 5 & 4 \\ 15 & 16 \\ 2 & 0 \end{bmatrix} + \begin{bmatrix} 10 & 14 \\ 11 & 13 \\ 7 & 9 \\ 0 & 3 \end{bmatrix} = \begin{bmatrix} 18 & 25 \\ 16 & 17 \\ 22 & 25 \\ 2 & 3 \end{bmatrix}$;

16. $\begin{bmatrix} 2 & 0 \\ 0 & \frac{1}{2} \end{bmatrix}$; **17.** $\begin{bmatrix} 0 & 1 \\ 1 & 0 \end{bmatrix}$

18. T-4, 12 $(x, y) = (x - 4, y + 12)$;

19. $\triangle ABC = \begin{bmatrix} 7 & -1 & 3 \\ 6 & 2 & -4 \end{bmatrix}$

$\triangle A'B'C' = \begin{bmatrix} -6 & -2 & 4 \\ 7 & -1 & 3 \end{bmatrix}$

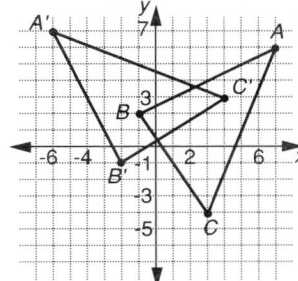

LESSONS 5-1 (pages 246–250)

10. a.

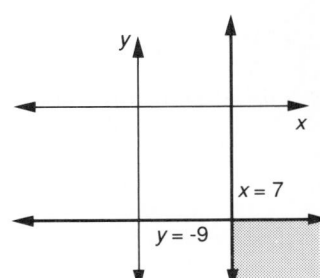

b.

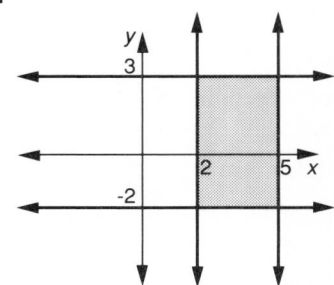

14. b.

17. a.

T53

ADDITIONAL ANSWERS

18.a.

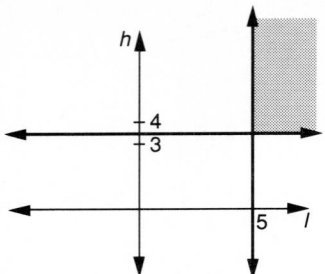

22.

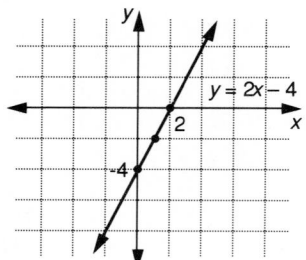

23.

$$\begin{bmatrix} -1 & -4 & 3 \\ 2 & 0 & -3 \end{bmatrix}$$

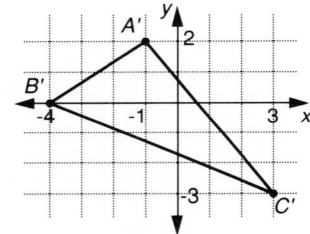

LESSON 5-5 (pages 269–274)
20.b. 55 months, which is the time that the two costs would be the same.
21.

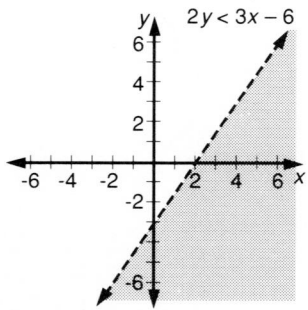

22.e. The area of a triangle with vertices $(0, 0)$, (a, b), and (a, d) is equal to the absolute value of $\frac{1}{2} \det \begin{bmatrix} a & b \\ c & d \end{bmatrix}$; **f.** The area of a triangle defined by $A = (0, 0)$, $B = (12, 0)$, and $C = (0, 5)$ is $\left| \frac{1}{2} \cdot 12 \cdot 5 \right| = 30$ or $\left| \frac{1}{2} \det \begin{bmatrix} 12 & 0 \\ 0 & 5 \end{bmatrix} \right| = 30$.

LESSON 5-7 (pages 282–287)
15.b.

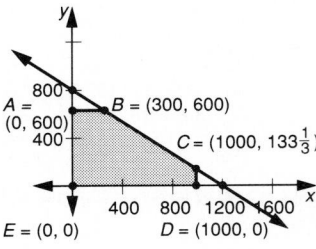

16. graphically, linear combination, substitution, matrix method; **17. a.** substitution; **b.** $x = \frac{1}{2}$, $y = 2$; **18.a.** linear-combination method; **b.** $x = 0$, $y = 3$; **19.a.** graphically; **b.** $x \approx 1.5$, $y \approx 5$

LESSON 5-9 (pages 295–299)
11.

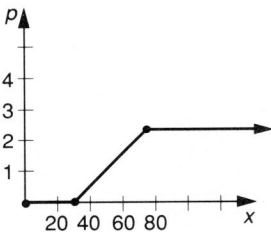

CHAPTER 5 PROGRESS SELF-TEST
(page 301)
10. Let c = the number of chairs built per day, and s = the number of sofas built per day. Then to represent the constraint on the number of hours the carpenters can work per day we write: $7c + 4s \le 133$. For the upholsterers hours: $2c + 6s \le 72$. Since the manufacturer cannot make a negative number of chairs or sofas, we write: $c \ge 0$, and $s \ge 0$. Thus the feasible region is the set of all points satisfying the constraints:
$$\begin{cases} 7c + 4s \le 133 \\ 2c + 6s \le 72 \\ \quad\quad c \ge 0 \\ \quad\quad s \ge 0 \end{cases}$$

11.

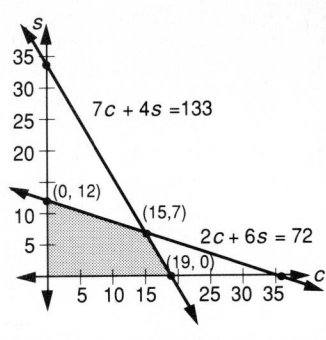

From the graph we can see that the vertices of the feasible region will be solutions to the systems:
$$\begin{cases} s = 0 \\ 7c + 4s = 133 \end{cases} \begin{cases} 7c + 4s = 133 \\ 2c + 6s = 72 \end{cases}$$
$$\begin{cases} 2c + 6s = 72 \\ c = 0 \end{cases} \begin{cases} s = 0 \\ c = 0 \end{cases}$$
The solution to the fourth system is clearly $(0, 0)$. The solution to the first and third are made easy by the substitution method. For
$$\begin{cases} s = 0 \\ 7c + 4s = 133 \end{cases}$$
the solution is $(19, 0)$.
Similarly, for $\begin{cases} 2c + 6s = 72 \\ c = 0 \end{cases}$,
the solution is $(0, 12)$. The second system can be solved by the linear-combination method:
$$\begin{cases} 7c + 4s = 133 \text{ mult. by } -3\text{:} \\ 2c + 6s = 72 \text{ mult. by } 2\text{:} \end{cases}$$
$$\begin{array}{r} -21c - 12s = -399 \\ 4c + 12s = 144 \\ \hline -17c = -255 \\ c = 15 \end{array}$$
Substitute this value for c in the second equation to get $s = 7$. So the solution is $(15, 7)$. Thus, the vertices of the feasible set are the points $(0, 12)$, $(0, 0)$, $(19, 0)$, and $(15, 7)$; **12.** The profit equation is $P = 80c + 70s$. By the Linear-Programming Theorem, we know that this formula is maximized at one of the vertices of the feasible region. So check the vertices to find out which one.
$80(0) + 70(12) = 840$;
$80(0) + 70(0) = 0$;
$80(19) + 70(0) = 1520$;
$80(15) + 70(7) = 1690$. So the profit formula is maximized in the feasible region at the point $(15, 7)$. This means that the manufacturer can maximize profits by producing 15 chairs and 7 sofas per day.

ADDITIONAL ANSWERS

CHAPTER 5 REVIEW   (pages 302–305)

47.

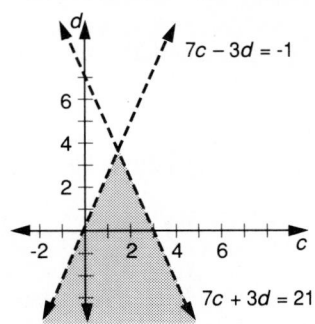

$7c - 3d = -1$

$7c + 3d = 21$

48.

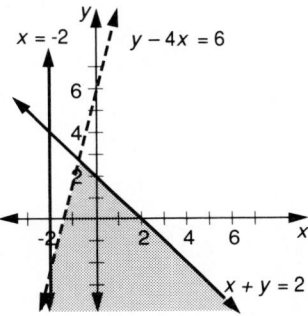

$x = -2$ $y - 4x = 6$

$x + y = 2$

49.

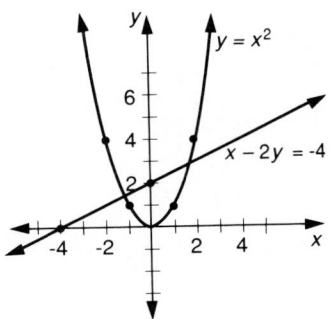

$y = x^2$

$x - 2y = -4$

50.

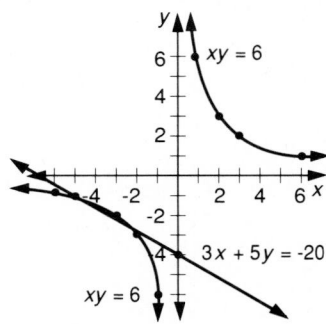

$xy = 6$

$3x + 5y = -20$

$xy = 6$

LESSON 6-3   (pages 322–328)

21.

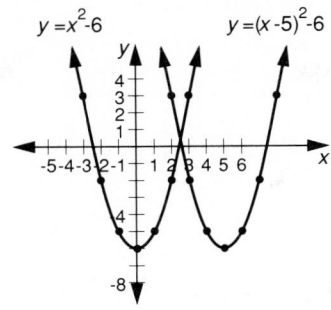

$y = x^2 - 6$ $y = (x - 5)^2 - 6$

LESSON 6-10   (pages 362–366)

19.a.

$$AB = \begin{bmatrix} 0 & 1 \\ 1 & 0 \end{bmatrix}\begin{bmatrix} 0 & -i \\ i & 0 \end{bmatrix} = \begin{bmatrix} i & 0 \\ 0 & -i \end{bmatrix}$$

$$BA = \begin{bmatrix} 0 & -i \\ i & 0 \end{bmatrix}\begin{bmatrix} 0 & 1 \\ 1 & 0 \end{bmatrix} = \begin{bmatrix} -i & 0 \\ 0 & i \end{bmatrix}$$

$$\begin{bmatrix} -1 & 0 \\ 0 & -1 \end{bmatrix} \cdot BA =$$

$$\begin{bmatrix} -1 & 0 \\ 0 & -1 \end{bmatrix}\begin{bmatrix} -i & 0 \\ 0 & i \end{bmatrix} = \begin{bmatrix} i & 0 \\ 0 & -i \end{bmatrix}$$

Thus $AB = \begin{bmatrix} -1 & 0 \\ 0 & -1 \end{bmatrix} \cdot BA$;

b.

$$CB = \begin{bmatrix} 1 & 0 \\ 0 & -1 \end{bmatrix}\begin{bmatrix} 0 & -i \\ i & 0 \end{bmatrix} = \begin{bmatrix} 0 & -i \\ -i & 0 \end{bmatrix}$$

$$BC = \begin{bmatrix} 0 & -i \\ i & 0 \end{bmatrix}\begin{bmatrix} 1 & 0 \\ 0 & -1 \end{bmatrix} = \begin{bmatrix} 0 & i \\ i & 0 \end{bmatrix}$$

$$\begin{bmatrix} -1 & 0 \\ 0 & -1 \end{bmatrix} \cdot BC =$$

$$\begin{bmatrix} -1 & 0 \\ 0 & -1 \end{bmatrix}\begin{bmatrix} 0 & i \\ i & 0 \end{bmatrix} = \begin{bmatrix} 0 & -i \\ -i & 0 \end{bmatrix}$$

Thus $CB = \begin{bmatrix} -1 & 0 \\ 0 & -1 \end{bmatrix} \cdot BC$

LESSON 7-5   (pages 398–404)

16.a.

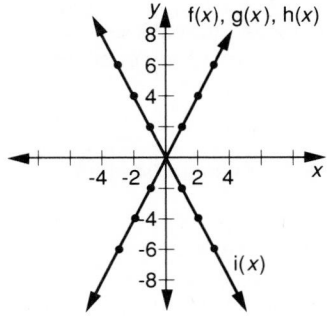

$f(x),\ g(x),\ h(x)$

$i(x)$

b. If $a > 0$, then the graph of $y = a|x|$ is the same as the graph of $y = |ax|$. If $a < 0$, then the graph of $y = a|x|$ is the reflection image of the graph of $y = |ax|$ over the x-axis.

CHAPTER 7 PROGRESS SELF-TEST
(page 420)

15.a.

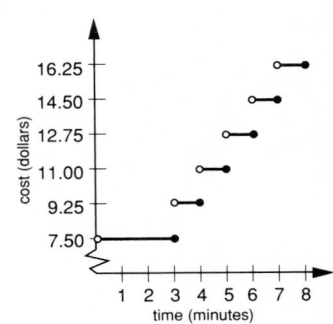

cost (dollars)

time (minutes)

b. $14.50

18.

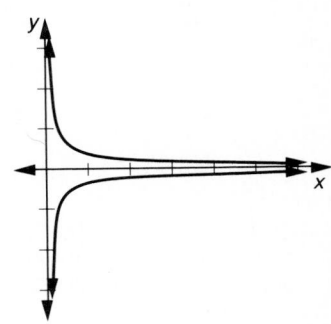

19. sample: $x > 0$. Restrict any part of the domain so that the horizontal-line test checks;   **20.a.** The domain is the set of all real numbers since there are no undefined values of x; **b.** Since x^2 is always any non-negative real number with a minimum value of 0, $f(x) = x^2 + 2$ has a range $\{y: y \geq 2\}$.

22.

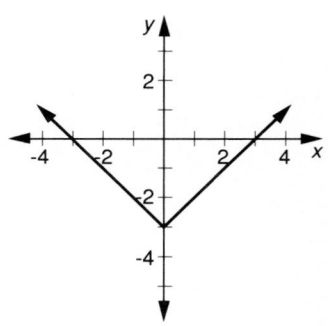

T55

ADDITIONAL ANSWERS

23.b. The absolute value of *M* minus *N*

CHAPTER 7 REVIEW (pages 421–423)
55.

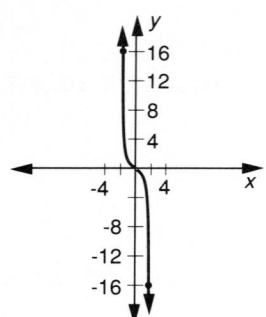

56.

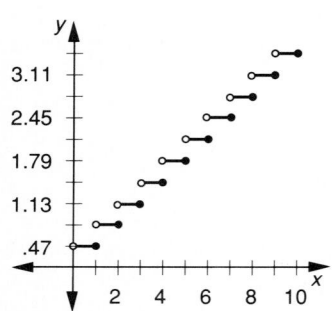

59. Domain = {*x*: -5 ≤ *x* ≤ 5};
Range = {*y*: -1 ≤ *y* ≤ 1}; **60.** Domain =
set of all real numbers except 0; Range =
set of all real numbers except 0; **61.** Domain = {*x*: -4 ≤ *x* ≤ 4}; Range =
{*y*: -4 ≤ *y* ≤ }; **62.** Domain = set of all
real numbers; Range = set of all nonnegative real numbers; **63.** sample:
y = |*x*| {-1 < *x* < 1}

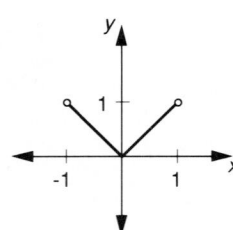

68.

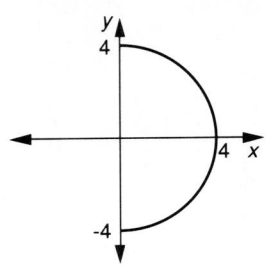

69.

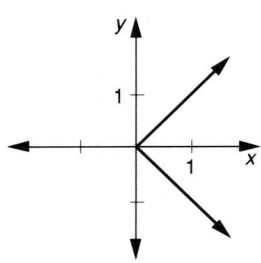

LESSON 8-2 (pages 432–437)
27.a.

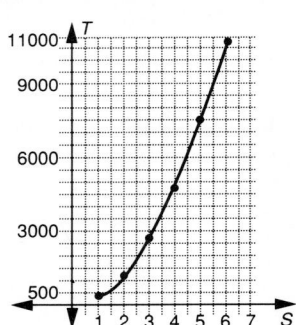

29.a.
$200(1.04)^{18} \approx 405.16$
$200(1.06)^{12} \approx 404.44$
$200(1.08)^9 \approx 399.80$
$200(1.10)^7 \approx 389.74$
b. The rate divided into .72 will give the approximate time needed to double your
money.

LESSON 9-2 (pages 494–498)
11.c. The graphs of $y = 3^x$ and $y = \left(\frac{1}{3}\right)^x$
are reflections of each other over the *y*-axis.
The reason is that a reflection over the *y*-
axis is the same as replacing (*x*, *y*) with
(-*x*, *y*), and 3^{-x} is the same as $\left(\frac{1}{3}\right)^x =$

$(3^{-1})^x$; **12.c.** The car would depreciate
less after 4 years and thus have a greater
dollar value; **d.** Using the model in part
(b) if the car were traded in after 10 years, it
would have no value.

LESSON 9-4 (pages 504–508)
31.c.

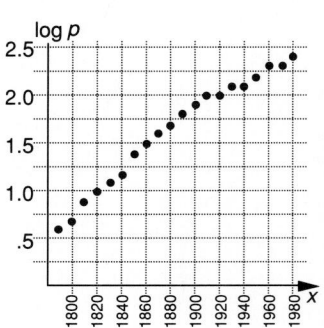

33.a.

x	*P*	log *P*
1790	3.9	0.6
1800	5.3	0.7
1810	7.2	0.9
1820	9.6	1.0
1830	13	1.1
1840	17	1.2
1850	23	1.4
1860	31	1.5
1870	39	1.6
1880	50	1.7
1890	63	1.8
1900	76	1.9
1910	92	2.0
1920	106	2.0
1930	123	2.1
1940	132	2.1
1950	151	2.2
1960	179	2.3
1970	203	2.3
1980	226	2.4

b.

c. The points are approximately collinear.

ADDITIONAL ANSWERS

LESSON 10-2 (pages 549–554)
21. SAS: If, in two triangles, two sides and the included angle of one are congruent respectively to two sides and the included angle of the other, then the triangles are congruent. SSS: If, in two triangles, three sides of one are congruent respectively to three sides of the other, then the triangles are congruent. ASA: If, in two triangles, two angles and the included side of one are congruent respectively to two angles and the included side of the other, then the triangles are congruent.

LESSON 10-4 (pages 560–564)
32.a.–d.

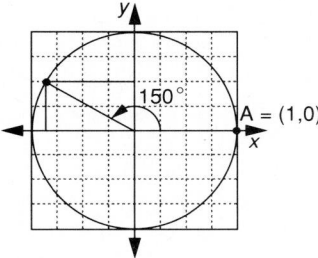

e. cos (150°) ≈ -.85; sin (150°) ≈ .5;
f. cos (150°) ≈ -0.866; sin (150°) = 0.5

LESSON 10-6 (pages 570–574)
12.a. By the Law of Cosines, it should be true that $20^2 = 50^2 + 75^2 - 2(50)(75)$ cos θ. Solving this equation, we get cos θ = 1.03, which is impossible since cos θ is always less than or equal to one; **b.** There does not exist a triangle with sides of 20, 50, and 75 since the sum of any two sides of a triangle must be greater than the third side, yet $20 + 50 < 75$.
19.c.

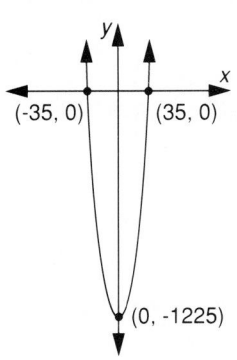

23. The correction term is -2ab cos C, which takes into account how much the included angle varies from 90°.

LESSON 12-2 (pages 674–679)
6.

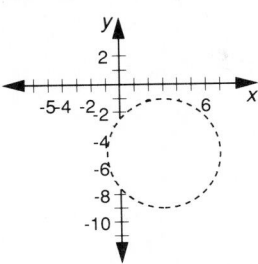

9.

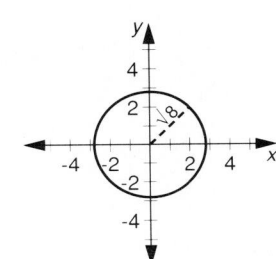

10.

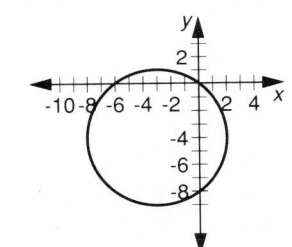

11.a.

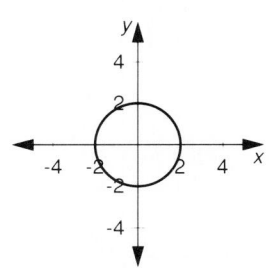

LESSON 12-4 (pages 687–694)
29.a. The graph will be an ellipse with center at (2, -6). Its major axis lies on the line with equation $x = 2$; its vertices are at

(2, -1) and (2, -11). The length of the major axis is 10, and the length of its minor axis is 6; **b.** Answers will vary; **c.** Answers will vary;

d. The graph of $\dfrac{(x - h)^2}{a^2} + \dfrac{(y - k)^2}{b^2} = 1$

is an ellipse with center at (h, k). Equations for its axes of symmetry are $x = h$ and $y = k$. The larger of a and b is the length of the semi-major axis. The smaller of a and b is the length of the semi-minor axis.

LESSON 12-5 (pages 695–700)
25.a.

```
10   INPUT "LENGTH OF HORIZONTAL
     AXIS OF ELLIPSE; A2
20   INPUT "LENGTH OF VERTICAL
     AXIS OF ELLIPSE; B2
30   PRINT "X", "Y"
40   LET A = A2/2
50   LET B = B2/2
60   FOR X = -A TO A STEP 0.5
70   Y1 = SQR(B^2 - (B * X/A)^2)
80   PRINT X, Y1
90   NEXT X
100  FOR X = -A TO A STEP 0.5
110  Y2 = -1 *SQR(B^2 - (B * X/A)^2)
120  PRINT X, Y2
130  NEXT X
140  END
```

b.]RUN
   LENGTH OF HORIZONTAL AXIS OF
     ELLIPSE? 4
   LENGTH OF VERTICAL AXIS OF
     ELLIPSE? 6

X	Y
-2	0
-1.5	1.98431348
-1	2.59807621
-.5	2.90473751
0	3
.5	2.90473751
1	2.59807621
1.5	1.98431348
2	0
-2	0
-1.5	-1.98431348
-1	-2.59807621
-.5	-2.90473751
0	-3
.5	-2.90473751
1	-2.59807621
1.5	-1.98431348
2	0

ADDITIONAL ANSWERS

LESSON 12-7 (pages 707–712)

12.a.

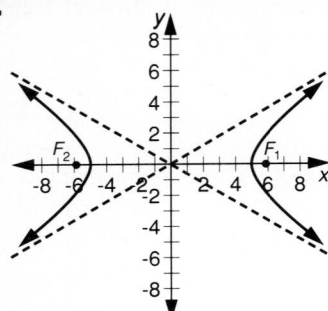

b. $e = \dfrac{\sqrt{34}}{5} \approx 1.2$

13.a.

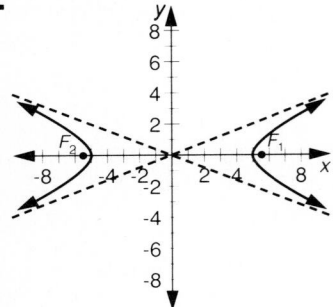

b. $e = \dfrac{\sqrt{29}}{5} \approx 1.1$

LESSON 12-9 (pages 719–723)

12.

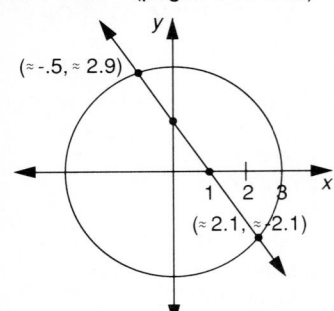

$(\approx -.5, \approx 2.9)$

$(\approx 2.1, \approx 2.1)$

14.b.

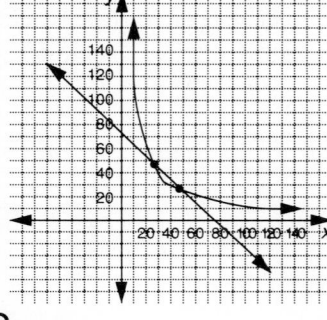

15.

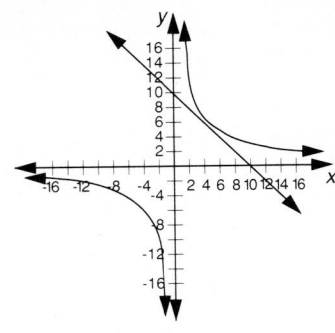

23.

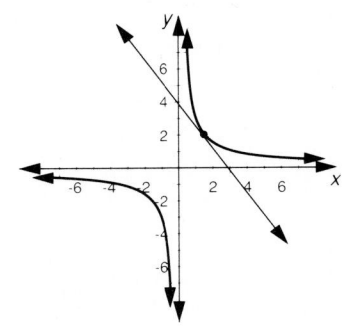

CHAPTER 12 PROGRESS SELF-TEST
(page 734)

12.

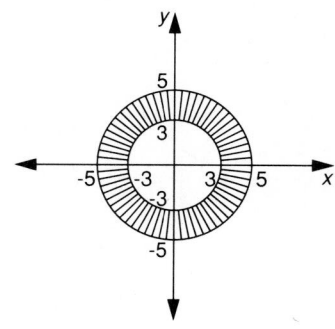

16.

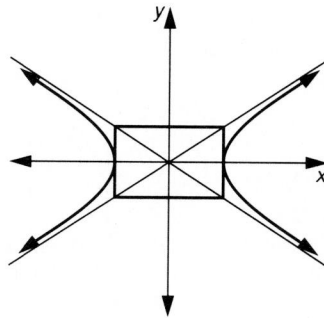

CHAPTER 12 REVIEW (pages 735–739)

67.

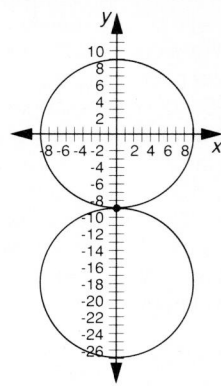

68.

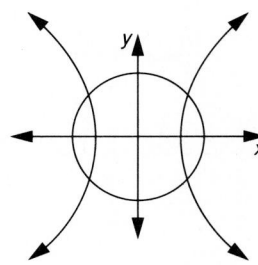

69.

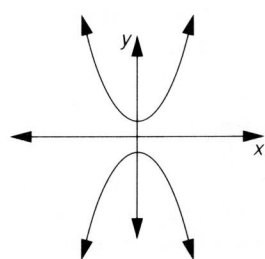

LESSON 13-5 (pages 765–770)

3.

1	8	28	56	70	56	28	8	1
1	9	36	84	126	126	84	36	9	1
1	10	45	120	210	252	210	120	45	10	1

LESSON 14-5 (pages 840–845)

14.

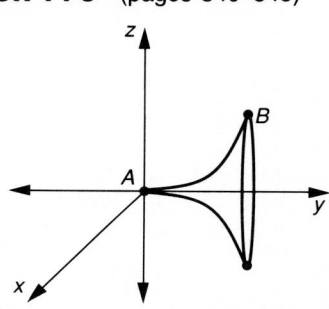

T58

ADDITIONAL ANSWERS

15.

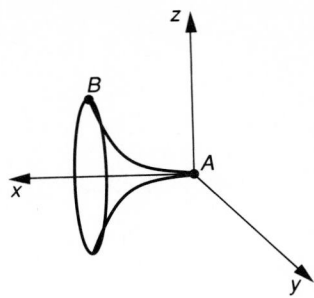

16.a.

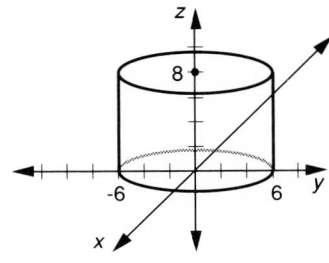

CHAPTER 14 PROGRESS SELF-TEST
(page 866)
6.b. two planes parallel to the *yz*-plane
which intersect the *x*-axis at $x = \pm 3.5$;
8. $\begin{bmatrix} 1 & 1 & -1 & 2 \\ 6 & 1 & 1 & 4 \\ 4 & -1 & 3 & 0 \end{bmatrix}$

13.

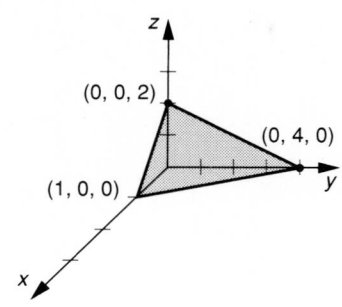

17.

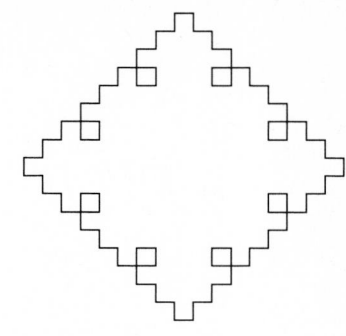

19.a. $\begin{cases} 3a + 2c + s = 52.50 \\ 4a + 4c \qquad\;\; = 66 \\ a + 5c + s = 47 \end{cases}$

INDEX

ACKNOWLEDGMENTS

Unless otherwise acknowledged, all photos are the property of Scott, Foresman and Company. Page positions are as follows: (t)top, (c)center, (b)bottom, (l)left, (r)right, (ins)inset.

2L&R The Bettmann Archive **2C** Art Resource, NY **3** The Bettmann Archive **12** NASA **15** Carolina Biological Supply **19** Nathan Bilow/Stock Imagery **25** David R. Frazier Photolibrary **26** David R. Frazier Photolibrary **31** Carlye Calvin **35** Jim Tuten/FPG **40** Breck P. Kent **42** Eugen Gebhardt/FPG **47** Glennon P. Donahue/Photographic Resources, Inc. **56–57** Stock Imagery **58** Kenneth Garrett/Woodfin Camp & Associates **61** J. C. Stevenson/Earth Scenes **63** Bob Daemmrich/The Image Works **65** NASA **71** D. Brent Justmann/Photographic Resources, Inc. **72** NASA **73** Minordi/Photographic Resources, Inc. **74** David Black **76** John Griffin/The Image Works **78** Mark Antman/The Image Works **79** Milt & Joan Mann/Cameramann International, Ltd. **82** Joe Sohm/The Image Works **84** Frank Oberle/Photographic Resources, Inc. **89** Milt & Joan Mann/Cameramann International, Ltd. **90** Milt & Joan Mann/Cameramann International, Ltd. **99** Ashod Francis/ANIMALS ANIMALS **104** Robert Holland **111** Milt & Joan Mann/Cameramann International, Ltd. **113** Bob Daemmrich/The Image Works **117** Chris Bryant/Photographic Resources, Inc. **118** National Institutes of Health **124–125** Minardi/Photographic Resources, Inc. **128** Vanderschmidt/ANIMALS ANIMALS **131** Milt & Joan Mann/Cameramann International, Ltd. **132** Milt & Joan Mann/Cameramann International, Ltd. **137** David R. Frazier Photolibrary **138** Michael Ponzini/Focus On Sports **141** Focus on Sports **143** Ruth Dixon **145** Tom Ebenhoh/Photographic Resources, Inc. **153** Stock Imagery **156** Sam Fentress/Photographic Resources, Inc. **158** Focus on Sports **161** Dion Ogust/The Image Works **164** J. Purcell/FPG **171** David Falconer/David R. Frazier Photolibrary **172** Focus on Sports **176** Richard Kolar/ANIMALS ANIMALS **179** Terry Murphy/ANIMALS ANIMALS **180–181** Jonathan Daniel/ALLSPORT USA **183** Brent Jones **185** Milt & Joan Mann/Cameramann International, Ltd. **189** Martha Swope **198** Margot Granitsas/The Image Works **202** David R. Frazier Photolibrary **204** Sylvia Johnson/Woodfin Camp & Associates **206** Ron Ruhoff/Stock Imagery **210** Joe Sohm/The Image Works **220** Bob Daemmrich/The Image Works **227** Raymond Stott/The Image Works **228** Milt & Joan Mann/Cameramann International, Ltd. **232** Howard Zryb/FPG **236** David R. Frazier Photolibrary **247** David R. Frazier Photolibrary **250** William Strode/Stock Imagery **256** Ruth Dixon **264** David Lissy/Stock Imagery **269** Vandystadt/ALLSPORT USA **283** Mark Antman/The Image Works **286** Milt & Joan Mann/Cameramann International, Ltd. **293** J. C. Stevenson/ANIMALS ANIMALS **299** Focus on Sports **304** Scott, Foresman **307** ALLSPORT USA **314** Tom Ives **320** Charles Harbutt/Archive Pictures Inc. **328** David Austen/Stock Boston **329** © 1985, Lee Karjala, Karjala's Photo Vision, Fullerton, Ca. All Rights Reserved. **333** John Adams/Stock Imagery **338** John G. Herron/Stock Boston **346** The Bettmann Archive **351** Milt & Joan Mann/Cameramann International, Ltd. **357** Jim Holland/Stock Boston **359** The Bettmann Archive **361** Courtesy DICOMED Corporation **362** Richard Fukukara/West Light **366** Peter Menzel/Stock Boston **372** Frank Siteman/Stock Boston **376** Cary Wolinski/Stock Boston **379** Milt & Joan Mann/Cameramann International, Ltd. **381** Cary Wolinski/Stock Boston **387** Owen Franken/Stock Boston **389** Charles Gupton/Stock Boston **393** Stacy Pick/Stock Boston **397** Signing of the Declaration of Independence by John Trumbull, Courtesy U.S. Capitol Historical Society, National Geographic Society Photographer, George F. Mobley. **403** Tom Ives **405** John Elk III/Stock Boston **410** David Woo/Stock Boston **430** Milt & Joan Mann/Cameramann International, Ltd. **432** Brent Jones **446** John McGrail **448** Adam Woolfitt/Woodfin Camp & Associates **452** Ellis Herwig/Stock Boston **456** Vernon Doucette/Stock Boston **458** Lee Foster/Bruce Coleman Inc. **462** Tom Walker/Stock Boston **467** John Maher/Stock Boston **471** Bohdan Hrynewych/Stock Boston **474** Mickey Pfleger **475** Ellis Herwig/Stock Boston **478** Stacy Pick/Stock Boston **481** John McGrail **484** Charles Fell/Stock Boston **485** Wagstaff/Stock Imagery **486–487** GEOPIC™/Earth Satellite Corp. **488** John Durham/Photo Researchers **491** Michel Tcherevkoff/The Image Bank **497** Michael O'Brian/Archive Pictures Inc. **499** A. Nogues/Sygma **502** David R. Frazier Photolibrary **503** Tom Ives **512** Cary Wolinski/Stock Boston **517** S.I.U./Bruce Coleman Inc. **521** John Coletti/Stock Boston **522** W. Campbell/Sygma **524** NASA **527** Chel Beeson/Stock Imagery **529** Army-Navy Joint Task Force **531** Edith G. Haun/Stock Boston **538** NASA **540–541** David Lissy/Stock Imagery **544** M. & S. Landre/FPG **547** D. C. Lowe/FPG **554** Kenneth Garrett/Woodfin Camp & Associates **559** Mark Antman/The Image Works **561** Bob Daemmrich/Stock Boston **566** Bill Evans/Artistic Photography **573** Milt & Joan Mann/Cameramann International, Ltd. **574** Milt & Joan Mann/Cameramann International, Ltd. **576** Peter Menzel/Stock Boston **585** Elizabeth Crews/Stock Boston **586** Bob Daemmrich/Stock Boston **588** Dr. E. R. Degginger/Bruce Coleman Inc. **591** Bob Ashe/Stock Imagery **604–605** Steve Elmore/The Stock Market **607** David Alan Harvey/Woodfin Camp & Associates **610** Steve Elmore/The Stock Market **616** L. West/FPG **629** John Elk III/Stock Boston **638L** Historical Pictures Service, Chicago **638R** Historical Pictures Service, Chicago **641** Courtesy of International Business Machines Corporation **650** Cezus/FPG **656** Mark Antman/The Image Works **658** Bruce M. Wellman/Stock Boston **668** © 1988 Jeff Schewe, all rights reserved. **672** Eric Kroll/Taurus Photos, Inc. **677** Milt & Joan Mann/Cameramann International, Ltd. **679** M. Berinetti/Photo Researchers **683** NASA **692** A. Pierce Bounds/Uniphoto **699** Bob Martin/ALLSPORT USA **705** Focus on Sports **712** Mike Powell/ALLSPORT USA **717** Marilyn Silverstone/Magnum Photos **724** Mathew Neal McVay/Stock Boston **726** Peter Menzel/Stock Boston **728** Matthew Neal McVay/Stock Boston **731** Vandystadt/ALLSPORT USA **737** Bob Daemmrich/Stock Boston **740–741** Ellis Herwig/Stock Boston **742** Walter Sanders, Courtesy Stadtische Museum, Brunswick, Germany **744** Richard Pasley/Stock Boston **748** Lew Lause/Uniphoto **751** Terry E. Eiler/Stock Boston **763** John Shaw **765** Erich Lessing/Magnum Photos **781** Mark Stephenson/West Light **782** John Running/Stock Boston **791** Harald Sund **798** Richard Hutchings/Photo Researchers **802** Jeffrey W. Myers/Stock Boston **812–813** Milt & Joan Mann/Cameramann International, Ltd. **818** Milt & Joan Mann/Cameramann International, Ltd. **824** M. Timothy O'Keefe/Bruce Coleman Inc. **827** D. P. Hershkowitz/Bruce Coleman inc. **833** NASA **840** Milt & Joan Mann/Cameramann International, Ltd. **856** Peter Beck/Uniphoto **857T** From *THE FRACTAL GEOMETRY OF NATURE* by Benoit B. Mandelbrot. copyright © 1977, 1982, 1983. W. H. Freeman and Company. Reprinted with permission. **857B** From *STUDIES OF GEOMETRY* by Leonard M. Blumenthal and Karl Menger. Copyright © 1970. W. H. Freeman and Company. Reprinted with permission. **859** C. Eric Grace/Phototake **860** Photo Store/Uniphoto **861** From *THE BEAUTY OF FRACTALS,* H.-O. Peitgen, P. H. Richter, © 1986, Springer-Verlag, Berlin, Heidelberg, New York. **862T** Harvey Lloyd/The Stock Market **862B** From *THE SCIENCE OF FRACTAL IMAGES,* H.-O. Peitgen, D. Saupe, Editors, © 1988, Springer-Verlag, Berlin, Heidelberg, New York.